COMPLETE CHINESE HOROSCOPES

COMPLETE CHINESE HOROSCOPES

KWOK MAN-HO
with Martin Palmer and Joanne O'Brien

SUNBURST BOOKS

This edition published 1995 by
Sunburst Books, Deacon House, 65 Old Church Street, Chelsea,
London. SW3 5BS.

ISBN 1 85778 181 3

Printed in Finland

CONTENTS

ACKNOWLEDGEMENTS

The authors wish to express their deep gratitude to the many people, both in the United Kingdom, Hong Kong and other parts of Asia, who gave their time, expertise and encouragement to this work. In particular, we wish to thank our colleagues at the International Consultancy on Religion, Education and Culture (ICOREC) who worked long and hard to prepare the material. To Liz Breuilly, our thanks for devising a computer programme which made it possible to construct the calendar of dates for both Chinese and English days; to Pallavi Mavani and Barbara Cousins who put the material in order and to Kerry Brown who helped make sense of it. To our friends in the Chinese communities around the world who ensured that we remained faithful to the tradition, we owe a debt of gratitude which we can never repay. Finally, to Sue Hogg and Francesca Liversidge, our editors – what can we say that can adequately express our appreciation.

Kwok Man-ho, Joanne O'Brien, Martin Palmer

INTRODUCTION

As you opened this book, you should have bowed slightly, for you are in effect coming into the presence of a traditional Chinese fortune-teller, an astrologer who will share with you secrets and traditions which stretch back thousands of years. Normally you would have to travel to one of the great temples of the Chinese world to find the astrologers in their stalls in order to discover a picture of your life which a full reading can give. Instead, through the use of this book and the assistance of the fortune-tellers and astrologers who have helped to prepare it, we invite you to explore with us the insights and messages of Chinese astrology, its myths and legends, its tales and stories, its revelations and insights.

In this book you will find two very different levels of astrology and fortune-telling. Most people will be familiar with the animal sign of their year of birth. However, the animal sign is only a small part of astrology. At a simple level it can give a brief sketch of your basic personality according to Chinese beliefs. It is in the second level, the Tzu Wei system, that the heart of this book lies. Here, with the help of the charts and calendar, you can act as your own fortune-teller. Through the Tzu Wei system you can explore the world of traditional Chinese astrology as you would do if you had walked through the side streets around a great temple and sat at the feet of a master astrologer. It takes a little time and some patience, but at the end you will be able to discover what one of the most revered systems of astrology the Chinese have ever devised has to say to you – and you alone.

There are three things we would like to stress before you begin. First, do not approach Chinese astrology as you would Western astrology. They are so different that we found any comparison of the two was impossible. There is no correlation between the twelve animals of Chinese astrology and the twelve signs of the Western zodiac, for example. This is quite simply because Western astrology is based upon a system which uses the path of the sun through the heavens, and thus looks to the constellations which lie along this path. The Chinese system focuses upon the Tzu Wei star (the Pole Star of our system – see below) and the constellations which relate to that. Nor is there a correlation between the Chinese interpretations and the assumptions that present-day Westerners bring to astrology. Neither Chinese astrology nor Chinese fortune-telling in general is concerned with psychological insights or nuances. If a Chinese fortune-teller says that you will lose your house by fire or a disaster, that is what he means. You are welcome to read into what he says more than that if you so wish, but you will be doing a disservice to the authentic nature of the reading. Obviously there is much in what a fortune-teller says that is meant to be pondered upon. But there is also much that is meant to be taken at face value because the very sharpness of the fortune-teller's language is intended to make you sit up and take stock.

Secondly, many people think that the animal signs are the most important aspect of Chinese astrology – but this is not so. You will find as you explore this book that the animal signs are only the tip of the Chinese astrological iceberg. Most Western books about Chinese astrology have failed to delve further than the animal signs, usually because they have been written by Westerners, not by practising Chinese astrologers trained in the traditional methods. Through the learning of Kwok Man-ho, we are able to offer you more than just the tip of the iceberg, though it would take us scores if not hundred of volumes to reveal to you the full depths of all the aspects of Chinese astrology.

Finally, it is important to understand that Chinese astrology is not going to give you an absolute, fixed reading. It will tell you what is likely to happen, given your eight characters – your Heavenly Stems and Earthly Branches (see below) – the gods on duty at a particular time, and so on. But your future is to a great extent in your hands. Chinese astrology warns you what may happen. But, within certain parameters, you can alter your fortune. There are many stories of people changing their fortune through acts of kindness and compassion. By understanding the influence of the past in terms of your previous lives on this life, a Chinese fortune-teller can say where this is likely to lead you in the future. A pattern can be, literally, divined. The future can be seen as mapped out if you continue along your present path. What the fortune-teller is not saying is that this is inevitable, even though the stars are involved.

So bow slightly. Be prepared to spend some time working out what Chinese astrology has to say to you through the Tzu Wei system. Then sit and reflect.

The Background to Chinese Astrology

Astrology is one of the most ancient arts of the Chinese; it is supernatural in origin and the most important of the Five Arts of divination. For thousands of years the twin arts of astrology and astronomy were the same. No distinction was made between them. Astronomers observed the stars in order to be able to see what Heaven was planning for earth – and, of course, for humanity. From the earliest days right up to the present century the astronomer-astrologers were officials of the Imperial Court. Their records, stretching back in an unbroken written line for over three thousand years, are some of the most important astronomical documents in the world. To this day, Chinese astrology continues to play a major part in the day-to-day lives of millions of Chinese around the world. Every day they use the Chinese Almanac, the T'ung Shu. The T'ung Shu lists astrological and astronomical data for each day of the Chinese year. On the basis of this certain days will be auspicious and others unlucky. Very few Chinese would dream of starting a new business or setting out on a journey on a day which the T'ung Shu declared to be a bad one.

It is in association with the Almanac, or rather, the calendrical part of the Almanac, that we first come across Chinese astronomy and astrology. If you delve into one of the oldest books of the Chinese, the *Shu Ching* or *Book of Historical Documents*, you will find the story of the Emperor Yao and the brothers Hsis and Ho. The story is traditionally set in the year 2256 BCE. The Emperor Yao wanted to produce a yearly calendar so that the people would know when the seasons began and when to plant and when to reap. So he commanded the brothers Hsis and Ho to observe 'the wide heavens, to calculate and delineate the sun, the moon and the stars' and to produce a calendar based upon their observations (*Shu Ching*, 'The

Canon of Yao', Part 1, Book 2). So legend gives astronomy and astrology a history stretching back over four thousand years, and there seems to be every likelihood that astronomical observations were being undertaken that long ago.

However, there is one very important difference between our present-day expectations of astrology and the expectations of the ancient Chinese. To the ancient Chinese astronomy-astrology revealed what was likely to happen to a state, or to the ruler of that state. It was not a system for personal fortune-telling. This example of a reading can be found in the ancient annals of China for the year 532 BCE: 'In Spring, in the king's first month, a strange star appeared in the constellation of Wu Nu. Pei Tsao of Cheng said to Tzu Ch'an: "In the seventh month, on the cyclical day Wu Tzu, the ruler of Chin, will die."' In Chinese thought the ruler was the state and vice versa.

It is not until the beginning of the Christian era that we find astrology being applied to individuals. The first example occurs *c.* 100 CE. From then on the number of individual astrological readings grew until an entire encyclopedia was constructed around the art (T'ang dynasty, 618–907 CE). Since that time, astrology has been part of everyday life for many Chinese. Echoes of its older role as diviner or forewarner of the fate of nations is still to be found in the modern-day Almanac. For example, in 1986 the Almanac warned that evil forces and armies would be likely to attack from the north. However, it is the personal aspect which now commands the field of Chinese astrology.

So let us now turn to the basic building blocks of Chinese astrology – the animal signs, the Heavenly Stems and the Earthly Branches, the sixty-year cycle and the Pole Star.

The Sixty-Year Cycle

Nowadays everyone seems to know their Chinese animal sign. As Chinese New Year is celebrated ever more widely in the Western world, the newspapers declare this year to be the year of the Tiger or Rabbit and so on. But why are these twelve animals important and what do they mean?

Legend ascribes the creation of the cycle of twelve creatures to the semi-mythological, semi-historical Yellow Emperor, who is supposed to have invented it in 2637 BCE. Certainly the system was in use by the time of Confucius, who lived in the fifth century BCE. It had probably been in use long before his time. Yet, strange to say, that is really all that can be said about the twelve animals. Traditional stories reveal why these particular twelve animals have been chosen; why some are wild and some are domesticated; why the cat does not feature and why the Rat is always put at the top of the list. You can read how the animals were chosen on p. 21 and one version of why the Rat comes first is given in the following legend.

One day the twelve animals of the calendar were arguing as to who should be first in the calendar. The gods, fed up with this bickering, stepped in to settle the argument. They suggested a contest. The first animal to reach the far bank of the river would be the first animal sign. All the creatures assembled on the river bank. The Rat looked up and down the line. He could see that he stood the least chance of swimming swiftly across the river, so he decided to hitch a lift. Looking at his friends, he thought that the Ox, with his great strength and tenacity, was most likely to reach the far bank first. So, as the animals plunged into the river, the Rat jumped nimbly onto the Ox's broad back. Just before the Ox climbed out onto the river bank ahead of all the others, the Rat leaped from his back and landed first. Although the other animals protested strongly that the Rat had cheated, the gods declared him the winner because he had used his head rather than just his strength to win the race. This is why the cycle of twelve yearly animal signs starts with the Rat and is followed by the Ox.

Although the twelve animals are interesting, they are only one part of the Chinese system for counting the years. The ten Heavenly Stems and the twelve Earthly Branches are far more important for time-keeping and astrology.

Chinese time is measured by a cycle of sixty years. Traditionally the Chinese do not celebrate birthdays, but when someone reaches his or her sixtieth birthday, a great feast is held in his or her honour. The sixty-year cycle is used as the main system for giving dates. What we regard as the year of Queen Victoria's death, 1901, is known to the Chinese as the 27th year of the reign of the Emperor Kuang Hsu. Confusion sets in when monarchs reign for more than sixty years – but this has not happened very often.

Sixty is a significant calendrical number because of the combination of Heavenly Stems and Earthly Branches. There are ten Heavenly Stems and twelve Earthly Branches. If you combine these two sets together, then the ten Heavenly Stems have to be repeated six times in order to match the twelve Earthly Branches, which are repeated five times, to bring you back to the start of both the Heavenly Stems and the Earthly Branches, giving you sixty pairs in all. The cycle always begins with the Heavenly Stem Chia and the Earthly Branch Tzu and looks like this:

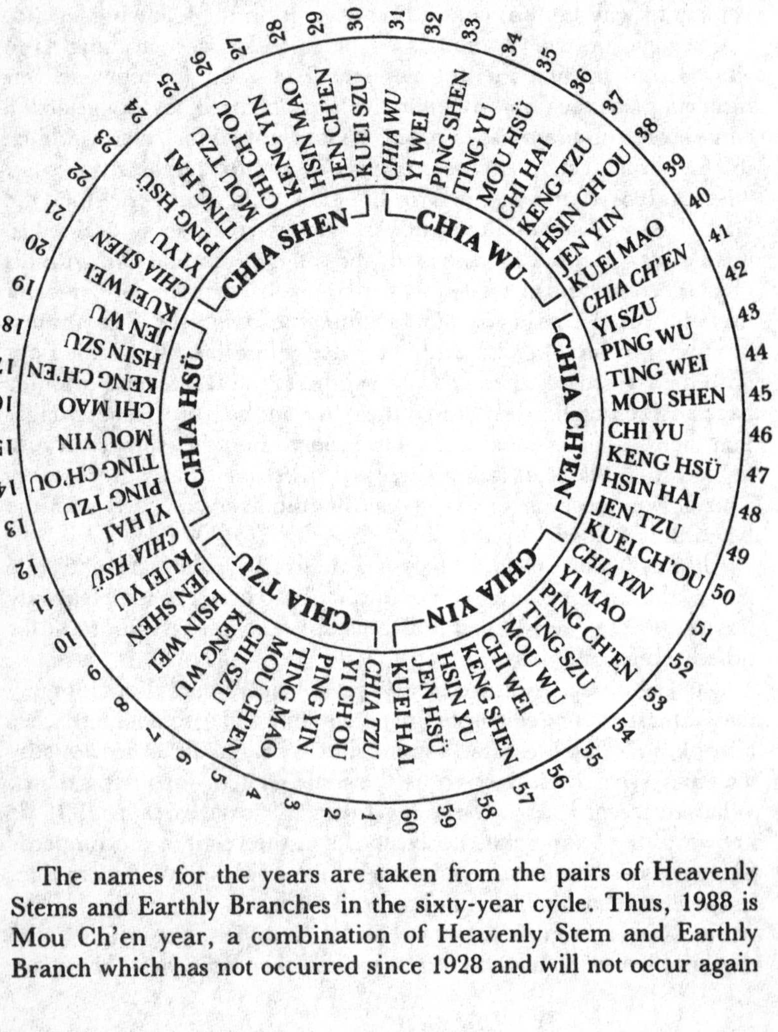

The names for the years are taken from the pairs of Heavenly Stems and Earthly Branches in the sixty-year cycle. Thus, 1988 is Mou Ch'en year, a combination of Heavenly Stem and Earthly Branch which has not occurred since 1928 and will not occur again until 2048. The characters change at the start of each Chinese New Year, which falls somewhere between 21 January and 20 February of the Western calendar.

Where or why the system of Heavenly Stems and Earthly Branches began is unknown. Suffice to say that by the time the *Shu Ching*, the *Book of Historical Documents*, was written the sixty-year cycle of the Heavenly Stems and Earthly Branches was in use. It is difficult to date accurately much of the *Shu Ching*, but by about 1000 BCE, and probably much earlier, the sixty-year cycle was accepted as a dating system.

The link between the animal signs and the sixty-year cycle is made through the Earthly Branches. Each of the twelve Earthly Branches is linked to one of the twelve animal signs, as follows:

Tzu – Rat	Wu – Horse
Ch'ou – Ox	Wei – Ram
Yin – Tiger	Shen – Monkey
Mao – Hare	Yu – Cock
Ch'en – Dragon	Hsü – Dog
Szu – Snake	Hai – Pig

It will become apparent as you work through the horoscope that it is the Earthly Branches rather than the animal signs, and especially their relation to the Heavenly Stems, that carry the key to a full reading.

The sixty-year cycle has been traditionally used to mark the months. The Chinese calendar is based on the lunar year, in contrast to the Western calendar, which is based on the solar year. The lunar and solar years do not correspond exactly: the lunar year consists of twelve moons (months), each of which lasts just over 29½ days. In order to keep the days in each lunar month as full days, each Chinese year is made up of a number of 'small' months of 29 days each and a number of 'big' months of 30 days each. A year with six big months and six small months will have a grand total of 354 days; a year with seven 'big' months and five 'small' months will have 355 days; and one with five 'big' and seven 'small' will have 353 days. Thus the lunar year falls short of the solar year by 10, 11 or 12 days. To bring the Chinese calendar into line with the seasons, and thus with the Western calendar, it is necessary to include an extra month every second or third year. This is called an intercalary month, and it comes immediately after the month it is linked with. In 1982 the extra month was month 4, and it came after the normal month 4. The next extra month came in 1984 and was number 10, following the normal month 10. The next occurrence was in 1987, the extra month being number 6. (The intercalary months are printed in italic in the Calendar Tables at the back of this book.)

Although the lunar months are numbered from 1 to 12 each year, they are also counted according to the sexagenary cycle of Heavenly Stems and Earthly Branches. The sequence is shown in the table opposite. The characters for each lunar month are determined by the Heavenly Stem for the year (column headings) and the number of the month in question (side headings). So in a year whose Heavenly Stem is Ping – 1986, for example – the 6th lunar month had the characters Yi Wei. This cycle repeats every five years, so in 1991, whose Heavenly Stem is Hsin, the 6th lunar month will also have the characters Yi Wei.

As there are twelve lunar months and twelve Earthly Branches, their relationship in the cycle always stays the same, so the 1st lunar month always has Yin as one of its characters, the 2nd Mao, the 3rd Ch'en, and so on, while the Heavenly Stems change according to the cycle.

The same cycle is used for the days as well. The old Chinese week was ten days long, so the first day of every sixth week could return to the beginning of the cycle of sixty, the Heavenly Stem Chia and the Earthly Branch Tzu.

As you can see, each year, each month and each day has its own distinctive combination of Heavenly Stem and Earthly Branch, and we will shortly explain how the system is also used for the hours. By discovering what Heavenly and Earthly characters (that means the Chinese characters) you have for the year, the month, the day and the hour of your birth, you can form an eight-character horoscope and enter properly the world of Chinese astrology. With your eight-character horoscope, the path lies open for you to explore what this ancient art has to tell you.

To find the first six characters of your horoscope – those for the year, the month and the day – you simply need to turn to the Calendar Tables at the back of this book and look up your Western date of birth. There, you will find the Heavenly Stem and Earthly Branch for your Chinese year of birth, and, in the adjacent columns, the numbers and the characters for the lunar month and

The Cycle of Heavenly Stems and Earthly Branches for the Months
(The cycle is shown in relation to the Western years 1984–93)

	Heavenly Stem for the Year					
	Chia (1984)	*Yi (1985)*	*Ping (1986)*	*Ting (1987)*	*Mou (1988)*	*The cycle repeats*
Lunar Month	*Chi (1989)*	*Keng (1990)*	*Hsin (1991)*	*Jen (1992)*	*Kuei (1993)*	
1st	Ping Yin	Mou Yin	Keng Yin	Jen Yin	Chia Yin	
2nd	Ting Mao	Chi Mao	Hsin Mao	Kuei Mao	Yi Mao	
3rd	Mou Ch'en	Keng Ch'en	Jen Ch'en	Chia Ch'en	Ping Ch'en §	
4th	Chi Szu	Hsin Szu	Kuei Szu	Yi Szu	Ting Szu	
5th	Keng Wu	Jen Wu	Chia Wu‡	Ping Wu	Mou Wu	
6th	Hsin Wei	Kuei Wei	Yi Wei	Ting Wei†	Chi Wei	
7th	Jen Shen	Chia Shen	Ping Shen	Mou Shen	Keng Shen	
8th	Kuei Yu	Yi Yu	Ting Yu	Chi Yu	Hsin Yu	
9th	Chia Hsü	Ping Hsü	Mou Hsü	Keng Hsü	Jen Hsü	
10th	Yi Hai*	Ting Hai	Chi Hai	Hsin Hai	Kuei Hai	
11th	Ping Tzu	Mou Tzu	Keng Tzu	Jen Tzu	Chia Tzu	
12th	Ting Ch'ou	Chi Ch'ou	Hsin Ch'ou	Kuei Ch'ou	Yi Ch'ou	

* Extra month in 1984. ‡ Extra month in 1990.
† Extra month in 1987. § Extra month in 1993.

for the day you were born. To simplify the tables we have used a system of codes for the Heavenly Stems and the Earthly Branches, the former being coded from A to K and the latter from 1 to 12. The codes are listed at the front of the Calendar Tables.

Your day of birth also corresponds to one of twenty-eight constellations, each of which is associated with a particular animal and these are also listed in the Calendar Tables. This group is quite separate from the animal signs for the years. The constellations change on a daily basis over twenty-eight days. In four groups of seven they are also linked to and change with the seasons. The spring, summer, autumn and winter groups correspond respectively to the four elements Wood, Fire, Metal and Water. The constellation on duty on the day of your birth will stand with you for your entire life. The characteristics of the constellational animals are as follows:

Crocodile Unstable and slow-witted.
Dragon Clever and quick to understand.
Badger Slow-witted and irreligious.
Hare Literary and impatient.
Fox Loves dressing up; lewd, but not bad at heart.
Tiger Quick to anger, quick to laugh, gluttonous, good-hearted.
Leopard Brave but cruel; disliked.
Griffon Refined and long-lived.
Ox Unstable, with a harsh life.
Bat Cunning; disliked.
Rat Assenting with the lips, dissenting with the heart; spiteful.
Swallow Loves dressing up, straightforward, quick of speech.
Pig A difficult time in spring and summer, a better time in autumn and winter.
Porcupine Trustworthy, kind, easily frightened.
Wolf Knowledgeable; a good planner.
Dog A troublemaker, loquacious, quick to laugh and quick to anger; disliked.
Pheasant Generous.
Cock Trustworthy.
Crow Enjoys leisure and fortune-telling.
Monkey Easily frightened, fond of fruit, long-lived.
Gibbon Clever, quick-thinking, cute in appearance, cowardly.
Tapir Powerful and kind.
Sheep Miserly; a show-off.

Deer Good-natured.
Horse Outstanding; destined to meet the right people at the right time.
Stag Kind; enjoys eating.
Serpent Unskilful.
Earthworm Impatient; enjoys the arts.

The last two characters of your eight-character horoscope – those for the hour of your birth – remain to be discovered. They too are based on the sexagenary cycle, but the Chinese use a different system of calculating the hours to that used in the West. The Chinese 'hour' is equivalent to two Western hours, so there are only twelve 'hours' in the Chinese day. Each one corresponds to an Earthly Branch as follows:

Tzu	11 p.m.–1 a.m.	Wu	11 a.m.–1 p.m.
Ch'ou	1 a.m.–3 a.m.	Wei	1 p.m.–3 p.m.
Yin	3 a.m.–5 a.m.	Shen	3 p.m.–5 p.m.
Mao	5 a.m.–7 a.m.	Yu	5 p.m.–7 p.m.
Ch'en	7 a.m.–9 a.m.	Hsü	7 p.m.–9 p.m.
Szu	9 a.m.–11 a.m.	Hai	9 p.m.–11 p.m.

To find the characters for your 'hour' of birth a special table is used (see p. 18), similar to the one for the months (see above). It works in much the same way, although in this case the coordinates are the Heavenly Stem for the day you were born (column headings) and the 'hour' of your birth (side headings).

Having discovered your own eight-character horoscope, and knowing your animal sign for the year, you can now turn to the fortune-teller captured in this book and begin to discover what secrets Chinese astrology holds for you.

As we mentioned earlier, there are two different systems here for you to use. The first is a quick simple guide to your basic personality according to your animal sign. As you will by now have gathered, although you are a Rat, the Rat appears five times in the sixty-year cycle, each time with a different Heavenly Stem. Thus, you are indeed a Rat, a Tzu, but are you a Chia Tzu (a Rat on the Roof), a Ping Tzu (a Rat in the Field), a Mou Tzu (a Rat in the Warehouse), a Keng Tzu (a Rat on the Beam) or a Jen Tzu (Rat on the Mountain)? Each of these different types will give a slightly different reading in the first part of the book and will be of added significance in the second.

	Heavenly Stem for Day of Birth				
'Hour' of Birth	*Chia Chi*	*Yi Keng*	*Ping Hsin*	*Ting Jen*	*Mou Kuei*
11 p.m. –1 a.m. (Tzu)	Chia Tzu	Ping Tzu	Mou Tzu	Keng Tzu	Jen Tzu
1 a.m. –3 a.m. (Ch'ou)	Yi Ch'ou	Ting Ch'ou	Chi Ch'ou	Hsin Ch'ou	Kuei Ch'ou
3 a.m. –5 a.m. (Yin)	Ping Yin	Mou Yin	Keng Yin	Jen Yin	Chia Yin
5 a.m. –7 a.m. (Mao)	Ting Mao	Chi Mao	Hsin Mao	Kuei Mao	Yi Mao
7 a.m. –9 a.m. (Ch'en)	Mou Ch'en	Keng Ch'en	Jen Ch'en	Chia Ch'en	Ping Ch'en
9 a.m. –11 a.m. (Szu)	Chi Szu	Hsin Szu	Kuei Szu	Yi Szu	Ting Szu
11 a.m. –1 p.m. (Wu)	Keng Wu	Jen Wu	Chia Wu	Ping Wu	Mou Wu
1 p.m. –3 p.m. (Wei)	Hsin Wei	Kuei Wei	Yi Wei	Ting Wei	Chi Wei
3 p.m. –5 p.m. (Shen)	Jen Shen	Chia Shen	Ping Shen	Mou Shen	Keng Shen
5 p.m. –7 p.m. (Yu)	Kuei Yu	Yi Yu	Ting Yu	Chi Yu	Hsin Yu
7 p.m. –9 p.m. (Hsü)	Chia Hsü	Ping Hsü	Mou Hsü	Keng Hsü	Jen Hsü
9 p.m. –11 p.m. (Hai)	Yi Hai	Ting Hai	Chi Hai	Hsin Hai	Kuei Hai

In the busy world of modern Chinese communities, the first system has been developed over the last hundred years or so to give a simple personality reading. Behind it lie the vast resources of the ancient art of astrology and divination. In the second part of the book we give one of the most popular systems, the Tzu Wei (Purple Star). Dating from the T'ang dynasty (618–907 CE), it was first written down by the astrologer Ch'en T'u Nan during the Sung dynasty (960–1280 CE).

The title Tzu Wei is very significant. Tzu Wei is the name of the

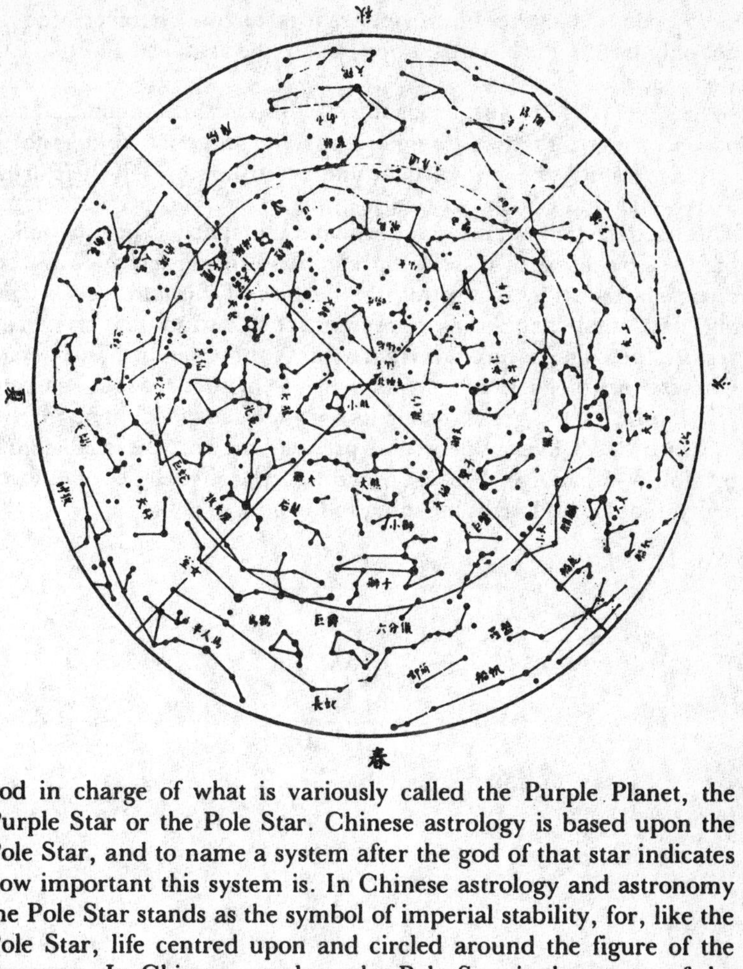

god in charge of what is variously called the Purple Planet, the Purple Star or the Pole Star. Chinese astrology is based upon the Pole Star, and to name a system after the god of that star indicates how important this system is. In Chinese astrology and astronomy the Pole Star stands as the symbol of imperial stability, for, like the Pole Star, life centred upon and circled around the figure of the Emperor. In Chinese astrology the Pole Star is the centre of the astronomical system and the astrological calendar. Its two closest constellations, Ursa Major and Ursa Minor, are seen as the North and South Measures – the measures of each person's lifespan. The god of birth dwells in the Southern Measure and the god of death in the Northern Measure. At the centre of all life, of the entire universe, stands the Pole Star – the Purple Planet or Purple Star. All other stars used in the Tzu Wei system are there because of their relation to the Pole Star. The Heavenly Stems and Earthly Branches of your eight-character horoscope are used to give a detailed reading not only for the Pole Star, but for each of the stars listed in the Tzu Wei system.

Tzu Wei is a very auspicious title for this system of divination and makes us aware that we are entering sacred and powerful territory. But as we study the animal signs and enter the world of the Purple Star, we should remember that in Chinese thought there is a triad. This triad consists of Heaven, Earth and Humanity. The interaction of Heaven and earth is made through us. We can put the universe out of harmony by disturbing the balance of yin and yang – light and dark, male and female, fire and water, and so on – or we can restore the balance through right actions and thoughts. In the end Chinese astrology presents us with a picture of our current relationship to the great cosmic forces which shape all life and give measure to all lives. But it also presents us with the challenging possibility of change, because we are also part of the cosmic force which moulds and gives meaning to life.

THE JADE KING AND THE TWELVE EARTHLY BRANCHES

The Jade King was extremely bored since he had little to do: he was waited on by his aides and servants, and because he lived in Heaven he had no idea what happened on earth. In an effort to amuse himself he summoned his chief adviser.

'I have ruled for many years,' said the King, 'but I have never seen the animals on earth. What do they look like?'

The adviser told him that there were many animals on earth. Did the Jade King wish to see them all?

'Oh no!' replied the King. 'I shall waste too much time if I do that. Instead I want you to select the twelve most interesting animals, and I will grade them according to their peculiarity.'

The adviser thought long and hard as to which animals would please the King. First of all he decided to send an invitation to the rat; he also asked the rat to pass on an invitation to his friend the cat. Further invitations were also sent to the ox, the tiger, the rabbit, the dragon, the snake, the horse, the ram, the monkey, the cock and the dog, telling them to be at the palace at six o'clock the next morning.

The rat was extremely proud to be summoned before the Jade King and set off to tell the cat their good news. The cat was delighted to hear the news, but was afraid that he might oversleep. He therefore made the rat promise to wake him early the next morning. That night the rat pondered on how handsome the cat was and how ugly he would appear in comparison. The only way to prevent the cat taking the limelight was to let him oversleep the next morning.

Early the next day eleven animals were lined up before the Jade King. When the King reached the end of the line he turned to his adviser.

'They are all very interesting, but why are there only eleven?'

The adviser had no answer and, for fear that the King would think he had not performed his task properly, he sent a servant down to earth and ordered him to catch the first animal he found and to bring it up to Heaven. The servant arrived on a road and saw a man carrying a pig, so he took the pig to the parade.

Meanwhile the rat was afraid that the King might not see him because he was so small. The only thing to do was to sit on the ox's back and play a flute. That way the King would be sure to notice him.

The King did indeed notice him, and was so delighted with this unusual animal that he gave him first place. The Jade King gave the ox second place, since he had been so kind as to let the rat sit on his back. Because the tiger looked so courageous he was given third place, and the rabbit, because of his fine white fur, was given fourth place. The King thought the dragon looked like a strong snake on legs, so he gave him fifth place. The snake was given sixth place, the horse seventh, the ram eighth, the monkey ninth, the cock tenth (he was the only bird that the adviser knew his servant could catch), and the dog was given eleventh place. The pig was ugly, but the King had no choice but to give him twelfth place.

After the ceremony had been performed the cat came dashing into the palace and begged the King to give him a chance.

'I'm sorry,' said the King. 'You are too late. I have arranged the twelve Earthly Branches and I cannot go back on my choice.'

When the cat spotted the rat, he chased him with the intention of killing him. That is why, even today, a cat cannot be friends with a rat.

Your Animal Sign Horoscope

THE SIGN OF THE RAT

The Main Attributes of Rat People

Character
You have a good heart but you are occasionally inconsiderate and selfish.

Luck
You will be lucky if you are generous and use your intelligence to the best of your ability.

Wealth
Your energetic and versatile nature will help you achieve financial success. A subsidiary business will prove to be more lucrative than your main business. Do not spend your money as soon as you have earned it.

Occupation
You will be fortunate whatever your job or profession as long as you use your intelligence wisely. You are suited to a managerial job or a career involving buying and selling.

Social life
You are open and generous at the beginning of your friendships, but the critical and petty side of your nature soon surfaces. You will have a successful social life but your friendships will be short-lived.

Business
Nobody will support your large-scale business ventures because you have a petty attitude towards your colleagues. Any small enterprises which you undertake will be successful.

Romance
You are attentive, caring and usually take the initiative. Your love life will be successful because you are not easily upset.

Marriage
You will give your full commitment to your marriage even if your parents and relatives disapprove of the match.

Parents
You are an obedient and cheerful son/daughter. One of your parents will be more sympathetic to you than the other.

Brothers and sisters
Rat people do not forgive easily so it is difficult to heal the frequent rifts between you and your brothers and sisters.

Children
You love your children dearly and encourage their studies at school and at home.

Assets
You will never own many assets because you spend your money so quickly.

Travel
You enjoy travelling more than people born in the other animal years do. You appreciate areas of outstanding natural beauty as opposed to architecture or foreign culture. The Chinese say that you roam the mountains and enjoy the waters.

Health
You will only suffer from minor illnesses during your long life.

Investment
You usually invest sensibly but do not expect large returns.

Skills
Your artistic skills are better than your intellectual skills.

Speculation
You are clever and discriminating, but you will never make great profits because others sometimes distrust you.

Hopes
You have great ambitions, but they are rarely realized because you treat others carelessly and unsympathetically.

Litigation
Your cunning nature helps you win law suits. If there is a possibility of losing a law suit you will try to settle out of court.

Lost property
Do not expect to find lost friends or property immediately; they will appear eventually.

The Character of the Rat

The Rat is first in the cycle of the twelve animals and corresponds to the Earthly Branch Tzu. Tzu is associated with the 11th month and matched to the hours of the day between 11 p.m. and 1 a.m. Wherever humans are found the Rat is also found; rats find their way into every corner of the world and can survive in any conditions.

You are gregarious, sociable, intelligent and polite. You are also strong-willed and humorous. You make friends easily but do not form any deep friendships. When you first meet someone you are open and sincere and expect to be treated in the same way. If you are cheated or deceived you quickly take revenge. You have a vivid imagination, discriminating judgement and the ability to translate your ideas into reality.

Underneath an eloquent, carefree and happy exterior you are calculating and miserly. You refuse to pay more than your fair share of expenses although you are happy to accept others' generosity. The good impression which you initially create is soon destroyed by your criticisms and pettiness. At a superficial level you know how to put others in a good mood and how to maintain a good social atmosphere.

You are impulsive and persistent in business and friendships.

You use your sharp intelligence to assess situations and then take advantage of any available opportunities. You appear to be a patient and forgiving business partner, but you secretly distrust your associates. Try to be more patient and understanding.

You will be a cooperative and loving marriage partner. A man born in this year is passionate from the beginning of a relationship, whereas a woman born in this year is usually passionate and committed after marriage. Someone born in the year of the Dragon will make a good marriage partner because both of you belong to the element Water. Your marriage will be long-lasting in spite of many arguments. You will feel confident and safe if you marry someone born in the year of the Ox. Partnerships between people born in the years of the Rat, the Dragon and the Ox are called a Three Harmony.

You will be happy if you marry someone born in the year of the Monkey provided the Monkey is not too dominant. A marriage with someone born in the year of the Snake, the Dog, the Pig or the Tiger will be happy but not perfect. Avoid marrying someone born in the year of the Horse because the Horse is too independent and honest for the Rat. A woman born in the year of the Horse on the Way (1906, 1966) should be wary of marrying a man born in the year of the Rat: she would be cheated throughout her marriage. You are suited to a marriage with someone born in the year of the Rabbit as long as your relationship is founded on a firm friendship; if your friendship is superficial your marriage will end in disaster.

You are suited to a career as a publisher, writer, commercial trader, critic, accountant, shopkeeper or musician.

Your Luck According to Your Year of Birth

1924, 1984

Born in the year of Chia Tzu, you belong to the Rat on the Roof.

You are impatient and rarely finish a job. You will be plagued by accidents and illnesses when you are young, and throughout life your brothers will be unwilling or unable to support you. If you are an eldest son you will have an unhappy marriage. If you are an eldest daughter you will be clever, active and a capable housewife.

1936, 1996

Born in the year of Ping Tzu, you belong to the Rat in the Field.

You are brave and powerful but you are also impatient. You lack a good education but you are an accomplished planner. You are not very lucky in your youth but by middle age you will be prosperous and well respected. A woman born in either of these years will be garrulous and annoying.

1948, 2008

Born in the year of Mou Tzu, you belong to the Rat in the Warehouse.

You are clever and skilled. You will have problems with your children when they are young but you have a trusting relationship with your husband/wife. A woman born in either of these years will be lucky and amenable.

1900, 1960

Born in the year of Keng Tzu, you belong to the Rat on the Beam.

You will be powerful and well respected. You are a popular and steady friend and your career will be prosperous and successful. A woman born in either of these years will be an efficient housekeeper who keeps a firm control over domestic affairs.

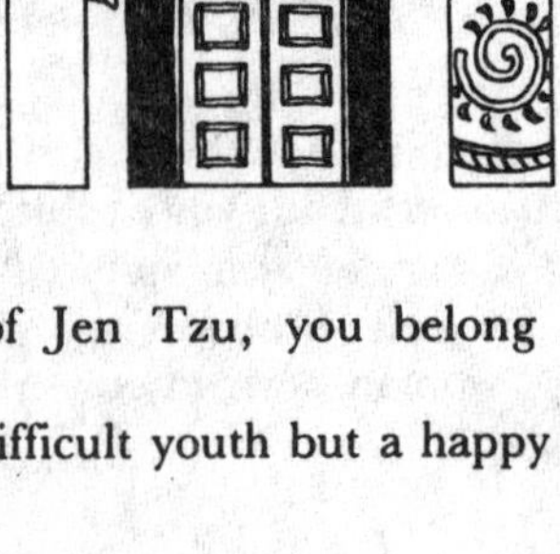

1912, 1972

Born in the year of Jen Tzu, you belong to the Rat on the Mountain.

You will have a difficult youth but a happy middle age. A man

born in these years seems to enjoy life but is secretly preoccupied and worried. His family relationships are unsteady and troubled but he will have the opportunity to marry a good wife. A woman born in either of these years will have an accommodating nature.

Your Luck According to Your Month of Birth

1st month
You have part of the Pig nature because you were born so close to the year of the Pig. You are independent and calm, even in times of crisis. You are popular because you are earnest and straightforward.

2nd month
You are clever, sensitive and intuitive. If you use your talents wisely everything you touch will turn to gold but do not overestimate your own abilities and avoid complacency. You have a busy social life but you upset others easily. A man born in this month likes cleanliness and a woman born in this month takes great care of her appearance. She is straightforward and gentle and enchants unknowingly.

3rd month
You are accessible and popular. Although you appear to run your business affairs with determination and confidence, you are privately concerned and worried. Your friends will recommend you to someone in a position of authority and you can expect to be offered promotion. Your romances may end painfully because you are so shy and emotional.

4th month

You are prosperous and extravagant. You never act without careful forethought but once you have accepted new responsibilities you fulfil your obligations. You never make empty promises and rarely abandon a project in the face of obstacles. A woman born in this month falls in love easily, even if her love is unrequited. She is a good communicator and will prove to be a good friend.

5th month

You are cheerful, approachable and just. You have a natural charm and people of the opposite sex are attracted to you. Your marriage will be successful because you are honest, faithful, loving and level-headed. A man born in this month should not allow himself to be besotted by romance. He should approach work and romance sensibly and positively.

6th month

You are optimistic, open, sympathetic and can adapt to any environment. You are extrovert and extravagant, spending money on yourself and others with little thought for the future. You have many original ideas which will make your fortune. Be satisfied with your earnings; do not be too greedy. You are sensitive and responsive to romance. You will have a happy marriage once you learn to forgive your partner's faults.

7th month

You are gentle and polite in your speech and in your behaviour. You make others happy because you consider each point attentively but you rarely make close friends. You do not use other people but likewise you do not let others use you. You will change your job frequently when you are young because you want to assert your independence. Once you have found a suitable career you will dedicate yourself to it. Approach your work gradually and sensibly. You will never suffer any losses but neither will you be very successful. You are emotionally direct and once you have found the right partner you will be very happy.

8th month

Heaven has given you good fortune. You are attentive and alert and can solve financial difficulties easily. You understand human nature and enjoy cultivating friendships. You quickly adapt to new situations or new jobs. You will enjoy any career that involves an element of risk.

9th month
You are intelligent, sensitive and disciplined. You enjoy working in a stable environment and will work hard to achieve promotion. Others often mistake your forgiving and understanding nature for flattery. You have many friends but none of them are close. You will have an unlucky love life.

10th month
You are quick-witted and perceptive. You are a good planner and never daunted by difficulties or challenges. You may have to work diligently for a long time before the value of your work is finally recognized. The Chinese say, 'One cry will startle people.' Others distrust you because you reveal your emotions easily. A man born in this month has difficulty controlling his physical desires.

11th month
You have an unsociable, moody and inflexible nature. You are quick-tempered and independent. Make an effort to listen to the opinions of others and try to be more open and tolerant. If you can improve these weak points you will be successful in politics or public relations. You have the spirit and drive of a leader, and others will respect you and learn from you. They will recognize your strength – you do not need to push yourself to the forefront. The Chinese say that 'You do not need to reveal your bones'.

12th month
You have a strong will and are adept at putting your ideas into practice but you also change your mind easily. You put all your energy into your work and have the strength to overcome problems. You are more concerned with running an efficient business than with the profits it may yield. Your creativity and intelligence will ensure a prosperous future. The extravagance and independence of women born in this month will cause many marital problems.

Your Luck According to Your Day of Birth

Born on the 1st, 10th, 19th or 28th

You are of noble bearing, independent and trustworthy. Your standards are high and you are always ready to fight for your career. You have a determined character but are overly concerned with yourself and with achieving fame and fortune. You feel the need to complete everything quickly but you frequently fail. Be careful and cautious. You are suited to a career as a civil servant or to a job in the arts. Your fortune fluctuates, and although at times you may receive unexpected money, at others you must control your spending.

Born on the 2nd, 11th, 20th or 29th

You are quiet but honest, open-hearted and extremely popular. Sometimes you like to be alone and at other times you want to be surrounded by friends. Unless you control your temper you will fall into trouble. You are suited to a career as an artistic designer, planner or literary editor. You enjoy life, even if you are in the poorest circumstances. Your fortune does not vary greatly, but your luck will improve after middle age.

Born on the 3rd, 12th, 21st or 30th

You are talented, sensitive and react quickly. You are always ready to fight for what you know is true and just. Others will avoid forming friendships with you if you are too obstinate; they wrongly assume you are too stern and difficult. You have business acumen and are suited to a disciplined job, such as the army, or to any job which has a competitive element, such as politics or the stock exchange. You must learn how to control your spending and think seriously of ways to earn more income.

Born on the 4th, 13th, 22nd or 31st

You are calm, patient and reserved. Your appearance and attitude lead others to think you are unapproachable, although in fact you are warm-hearted. If you change your approach you will be more popular. You are suited to a career as an academic, particularly in the field of theology or philosophy. Because you cannot control your spending you will lose money as easily and as quickly as you make it.

Born on the 5th, 14th or 23rd

Your fiery, obstinate nature makes it difficult for you to accept suggestions or opinions. At times your stubbornness leads to quarrels and problems. You are suited to a career in the arts, as an academic, an administrator or an advertising designer. Your intelligence enables you to work in a highly paid job. You will be lucky with money, often using it to set up new projects.

Born on the 6th, 15th or 24th

Your open, stable and cheerful character provides you with an active social life. You are affectionate and emotional and daydream so often that your mind becomes confused. Your eagerness to help others is often stifled by your indecisiveness. A career in the arts or work as a designer or social worker would be appropriate for you. You will not be very rich but will always have enough to live on.

Born on the 7th, 16th or 25th

You are an exhibitionist but when you show off nobody wants to listen to you or watch you. You enjoy an exciting life, but your head is in the clouds; you must learn to discipline yourself. You are suited to a job which allows you mobility, for example, a reporter, a traveller or an explorer. You do not want to earn a fortune and are quite content with your standard of living.

Born on the 8th, 17th or 26th

You are calm, quiet and a good judge. You have a determined and logical mind but lack social skills. You have a free spirit and are suited to self-employment. Do not buy stocks and shares or put your money in short-term investments. Your fortune is varied – it depends on your approach. There are times of wealth and times of abject poverty.

Born on the 9th, 18th or 27th

You are happy, optimistic and warm-hearted. You have an active life and are not easily troubled by minor matters. On the whole you are magnanimous but occasionally you quarrel unnecessarily with friends. It is important that you learn to control your moods. You should work as sole director or proprietor to avoid disagreements with partners. A job involving buying and selling would be suitable. You have a good income but you are extravagant.

Your Luck According to Your 'Hour' of Birth

Tzu hours: 11 p.m. – 1 a.m.
You are hot-tempered, obstinate, thrifty and shy away from challenges. You are an easy target for gossip. At times you act without sufficient planning but later you regret your actions. You will be able to build a successful business, buy a home and care for your family without a family inheritance. You will achieve fame and success independently of others but if you find yourself in trouble your parents or your marriage partner will always be there to help you out.

Unlucky ages 10, 17, 35, 48, 57.

Age at death 87.

Suitable occupations Artist, politician, architect, electrician or jobs connected with metal or water.

Unsuitable occupations Work connected with earth.

Ch'ou hours: 1 – 3 a.m.
If you want a good career, leave your home town while you are young. Life will be difficult up to the age of twenty but then your fortune will change for the better. You will be wealthy in old age.

Unlucky ages 17, 22, 30, 45.

Age at death 71.

Suitable occupations Commercial trader, teacher, government official, restaurateur, academic, skilled manual worker or jobs connected with the final stages of production.

Unsuitable occupations Work connected with wood.

Yin hours: 3 – 5 a.m.
You are on bad terms with your relatives and your early years will be difficult. You will not be left an inheritance and will leave your home town. After the age of forty everything will work out well. Old age will bring you power and wealth.

Unlucky ages 25, 28, 32, 38, 48.

Age at death 65.

Suitable occupations Doctor, musician, artist, actor, travelling agent/representative.

Unsuitable occupations Work connected with metal.

Mao hours: 5–7 a.m.
You will be very fortunate, with occasional help from your parents but none from your brothers and sisters. You will have a comfortable life and be wealthy if you work away from your home town. Marriage will be unsteady and difficult in the early years, but after middle age you will develop more satisfactory relationships and will have the chance to be wealthy.

Unlucky ages 15, 19, 54.

Age at death 71.

Suitable occupations Mechanical engineer, actor, writer, artist, theologian or work connected with religion.

Unsuitable occupations Work connected with fire.

Ch'en hours: 7–9 a.m.
You are clever, quick-witted and determined. Your warm-hearted nature enables you to form close friendships. Life is busy and varied, but a woman born in the Ch'en hours will be lonely. However, you will have many material possessions and a good salary. Your excessive self-confidence makes working relationships difficult.

Unlucky ages 18, 26, 35, 38.

Age at death 65.

Suitable occupations Entrepreneur, politician, public relations officer, teacher, miner.

Unsuitable occupations Work connected with wood.

Szu hours: 9–11 a.m.
You have outstanding talent and are able to build up your business and care for your family successfully. Family relations are troubled and you would prosper financially if you were to leave your home town. You are kind to your friends and like to help them when they are in trouble. A woman born in the Szu hours is extravagant and may have an unhappy marriage. Men and women born in these hours drink too much.

Unlucky ages 30, 35, 46, 48.

Age at death 88.

Suitable occupations Civil or electrical engineer, architect, wood or wine merchant.

Unsuitable occupations Work connected with water.

Wu hours: 11 a.m.–1 p.m.
You are active, clever, obstinate and extravagant. You prefer travelling to settling down to a job in your local area. A woman born in these hours is likely to have an unusual and fascinating character.

Unlucky ages 5, 11, 23, 32, 44, 53.

Age at death 84.

Suitable occupations Doctor, nurse, politician, film actor, skilled worker, jobs in the service industries or any work connected with oil.

Unsuitable occupations Work connected with gold.

Wei hours: 1–3 p.m.
You have a troubled relationship with your parents, brothers and sisters and marriage partner. You will have serious difficulties in middle age. A woman born in these hours is clever but will always have difficulties with her marriage because she is too active to settle down.

Unlucky ages 18, 25, 55.

Age at death 69.

Suitable occupations Civil engineer, electrical engineer, architect, wood merchant, wine merchant.

Unsuitable occupations Work connected with water.

Shen hours: 3–5 p.m.
You will earn money easily and spend it freely. You will be luckier if you work outside your home town. Your marriage will be harmonious although your parents will not offer you moral support. A woman born in the Shen hours will be married twice. Because you are too active ever to settle down completely it is important that you are seen to behave honourably. Too much time worrying over relationships will cause your business to fail.

Unlucky ages 18, 21, 27, 29, 41, 53.

Age at death 71.

Suitable occupations Finance-related work – e.g. broker, public relations officer, watchmaker, manager – or work connected with metal.

Unsuitable occupations Work connected with wood.

Yu hours: 5–7 p.m.
Your youth is difficult because of troubled family relationships. You will be separated from your brothers and sisters and will leave home when young. You may not be able to have a child but it will be possible to adopt one. A woman born in the Yu hours is warm-hearted, fond of food and can be trusted to keep a secret.

Unlucky ages 18, 24, 31, 48.

Age at death 77.

Suitable occupations Chemist, researcher/writer, teacher, artist, technologist or work connected with the final stages of production.

Unsuitable occupations Work connected with earth.

Hsü hours: 7–9 p.m.
You are brave, capable, hardworking and run your business alone. You are optimistic and will have a successful life and a flourishing career. A woman born in the Hsü hours can be vain and impatient. You are magnanimous but on the other hand money is not important to you. You care little for others but will have a magnificent life.

Unlucky ages 15, 25, 34, 43, 48, 56.

Age at death 77.

Suitable occupations Poet, writer, investor, engineer, rice or cereal merchant, or work connected with metal and agriculture.

Unsuitable occupations Work connected with fire.

Hai hours: 9–11 p.m.
You are manually dextrous and set yourself high standards. Although you are warm-hearted you do not like to make too many friends. A woman born in the Hai hours can be obstinate. Others may be easily upset but you have the ability to forgive and forget. You are hardworking and will be fortunate.

Unlucky ages 10, 25, 35, 38, 48, 55.

Age at death 77.

Suitable occupations Surgeon, monk/nun, hotelier, artist, antiques dealer or work connected with metal.

Unsuitable occupations Work connected with fire.

Practical Advice

Remember to thank anyone who helps you.
Try to establish better relationships with your family.
Be sincere and cheerful, it will help your business prosper.
Help others even if they are not connected with your own affairs.
Do not stay silent if you feel the need to talk.
Be courageous. Accept difficult challenges.
Be careful and calm, particularly when you are driving.
If you fail, do not be afraid to try again.
Be humble. Do not try to attract attention.
Be careful where you go at night-time.
You will be fortunate if you help your friends.
Do not put off till tomorrow what you can do today.

Your Luck Year by Year

Year of the Rat
Three lucky stars, two unlucky stars.

This is a prosperous and successful year for your business, but your unlucky stars will bring sickness or shock.

Year of the Ox
Three lucky stars, two unlucky stars.

Do not initiate any new ventures in your private or public life. Although your three lucky stars are shining, this is not a fortunate year. Do not take any risks.

Year of the Tiger
One travelling star, one lucky star, two unlucky spirits.

This is a good year for travel and emigration. It is also a lonely year and there may be a death in the family.

Year of the Rabbit
One lucky star, one baleful spirit.

Someone in your family may marry during the year. There will be quarrels in your marriage and possibly problems at work. You will be the target of gossip this year.

Year of the Dragon
Three lucky stars, four unlucky stars.

During the year your business will prosper, your income will increase and you will be successful in examinations. Your unlucky stars forecast the death of an older relative or parent and a dangerous threat from one of your friends.

Year of the Snake
One lucky star, two unlucky stars.

You will suffer a serious illness or accident which may leave you scarred. Your lucky star will help you to recover.

Year of the Horse
Two baleful spirits.

This is a year of financial loss, possible imprisonment and general misfortune.

Year of the Ram
Two lucky stars, two unlucky stars.

Your business will prosper, but you will suffer an injustice during the year. You may be burgled or lose something important.

Year of the Monkey
One baleful spirit.

Choose your friends carefully this year. Keep in contact with them; you may need their support.

Year of the Cock
Four lucky stars, one unlucky star.

This is a very fortunate year for you and your family. Your business will prosper and you could marry a wealthy partner. Your bad star is not influential this year. Take care of your hands; you may damage them.

Year of the Dog
One lucky star, four unlucky stars.

This is a year of disaster, loneliness and loss. Do not climb to high places and beware of being bitten by a dog.

Year of the Pig
Four unlucky stars.

This is a fruitless and unfortunate year. You will feel weak and sick during the year, so you must be careful what you eat and drink.

Your Animal Sign Horoscope

THE SIGN OF THE OX

The Main Attributes of Ox People

Character
Your patience and hard work will bring success.

Luck
You are neither lucky or unlucky; your fortune will remain steady throughout your life. You may be threatened occasionally but you will never be in serious danger.

Wealth
You will not earn much in your youth but you will become increasingly wealthy in later life.

Occupation
You are suited to a career in the visual arts.

Social life
You are popular because of your quiet, steady nature.

Business
You approach your work seriously. Try to form a partnership; do not work alone.

Romance
Your gentle, open nature makes you attractive to the opposite sex.

Marriage
You will be very careful about chosing the right marriage partner. You are likely to marry late.

Parents
You will benefit from the strong love and care given you by your parents.

Brothers and sisters
Your differing natures cause tension and arguments between you and your brothers and sisters.

Children
You will love your children deeply; you will feel that no parent could have a greater love than yours.

Assets
You will earn a lot of money from buying, selling or renting your property.

Travel
You are suited to travelling although you suffer occasional mishaps. Be careful when you are travelling.

Health
You will have many recurring illnesses.

Investments
Do not invest money; you will be lucky if you work steadily.

Skills
You are musically talented.

Speculation
Do not speculate; you will not make any losses or profits.

Hopes
Most of your hopes will be realized. You do not hope for material gains.

Litigation
Avoid drawn-out law suits. Sort out legal disputes as quickly as you can.

Lost property
You will not find your lost property easily.

The Character of the Ox

The Ox is the second of the twelve animal signs; it corresponds to the Earthly Branch Ch'ou. Its time spans from the solar term Hsiao Han (the beginning of winter) to Li Ch'un (the beginning of spring).

You stick to your own affairs and follow them through with a dogged persistence even in the most difficult times. Your determination will eventually be rewarded. You are not extravagant and dislike living on credit. All your plans are founded on solid ground. Although your reactions appear to be slow, you have powerful organizational abilities. You are patient and confident, thinking clearly and planning carefully. You appear to be in control of your fate. Although you are stubborn, your projects usually work out successfully because you do not show off and your sincerity encourages respect.

You need a quiet environment to organize your thoughts, and once you have decided to follow a belief, or test a theory, you follow it wholeheartedly. This can make you intolerant and prejudiced. Your plans are thought out carefully and carried out swiftly. You do not doubt our own ideas and cannot accept advice easily. You appear to be calm but underneath you are as hot-tempered and as easily angered as an ox. Others should not provoke you; once you are angry, you will only calm down of your own accord. You are conservative, introvert and wary of any new fashions that might challenge your quiet life. You were probably born into a poor family or a poor area. Your friends will always support you and when you most need aid someone in a position of authority will help you. This help will enable you to establish a stable business, which will be successful because your hard work builds on firm foundations. You are unwilling to undertake business travel and avoid commercial trading or public relations since they cause stress.

The ox has a large stomach, as though it contains all the suffering and bitterness of the world. Like the ox, you mull over life's problems, looking for a solution. But someone born in the year of the Ox has a good heart and is well respected.

A women born in this year lacks social skills but is a good wife and mother, with strong organizational abilities. If her husband is unfaithful she will initially examine her own conduct to see if she is at fault. Wherever the blame lies, she will never forgive or forget her husband's adultery. A man born in this year is stubborn and hard to understand; he seems to have a gloomy outlook on life. Everything will prosper if he learns to be open and accommodating.

You find it difficult to create a romantic atmosphere. Because romance is not important in your life, your romances are short-lived. Learn to respect your partner; treat him/her with sincerity and care. Someone born in the year of the Cock would make an ideal partner because your Earthly Branch Ch'ou (Earth element) corresponds to the Cock's Earthly Branch, Yu (Metal element) The Ox and the Cock are harmonious because the earth produces metal. A marriage with someone born in the year of the Rat would also be auspicious because the Rat is sincere and sensitive. The marriage would be strong, truthful and fortunate. A marriage with someone born in the year of the Monkey would also be fortuitous. You are kind, sincere and honest, and the Monkey person would gently and lovingly tease you. You would always be faithful to this partner. You will be unhappy if you marry someone born in the year of the Ram, the Horse, the Dragon or the Dog. The Horse is too lively, the Dragon and the Dog have too much imagination, and the Ram acts without thinking. There would be discord and possibly tragedy. You would be lonely, your life short, you would not own many possessions and your business would not prosper.

You are suited to a career in medicine, religion or estate management, but your ideal occupation is farming. You could also work as a policeman, a teacher, a philosopher, a soldier or a cook. You are not suited to jobs which require diplomatic skills.

Your Luck According to Your Year of Birth

1925, 1985

Born in the year of Yi Ch'ou, you belong to the Ox in the Sea.

You are a good student, willing to take on new projects. You will be popular with the opposite sex. There will be people beside your parents who are ready to take care of you. You will travel widely. You will have a happy marriage and good relationships with your children but your relatives are not in a position to help you. A woman born in either of these years will be talented but impatient.

1937, 1997

Born in the year of Ting Ch'ou, you belong to the Ox in the Lake.

You are kind and will have a prosperous life. You will have few savings when you are young, but will be wealthy after middle age. Your marriage will be happy and you will have children in later life. A woman born in either of these years will be able and talented.

1949, 2009

Born in the year of Chi Ch'ou, you belong to the Ox inside the Gate.

You are candid and speak without due care and attention. You will never be short of work but you will need money to carry out your plans. You will marry more than once. A woman born in either of these years will be clever and active.

1901, 1961

Born in the year of Hsin Ch'ou, you belong to the Ox on the Way.

You have an accommodating nature. During your youth you will be frightened by an accident. You will never be short of work, but sometimes you will be short of money and at other times financially secure. Your family will not be able to help you during difficult periods, but you will have a long life and a wealthy old age. A woman born in either of these years will live in luxurious surroundings.

1913, 1973
Born in the year of Kuei Ch'ou, you belong to the Ox outside the Gate.

You will have a respected and successful career. You will not be able to save any money when you are young and your family will be unable to help you. Your marriage will be happy and you will have children late in life. A woman born in either of these years will be candid and sincere but will speak without thinking. She will be a good housewife.

Your Luck According to Your Month of Birth

1st month
You are artistic, patient and lucky, and you have good powers of concentration. You have the Ox's obstinate nature, which makes you difficult to approach. Although you have close friends whom you rely upon and trust, you appear not to need anyone, even your marriage partner. You like to be alone and can survive without others. You are not afraid to leave the familiarity of your home town.

2nd month
Your actions are steady and your feelings sensitive. You have a happy nature. You do not worry over small matters and forgive others easily but you are also naive and easily cheated. You have a good *yuanten* – this is the fate which attracts people to one another.

People of the opposite sex are drawn to you and stay with you for a long time. You love literature and prefer books to money; they are your prize possessions. You will never sell them or throw them away. Collecting is a characteristic of people born in the 2nd month of the Ox year. Although you have a good *yuanten*, do not judge others by their appearance. Your relationships will fail if you do not try to understand their inner nature.

3rd month

You are patient, strong-willed and stubborn. You like to work alone; you make your own decisions and persevere with projects to the end. You have an active social life, but you dislike others criticizing your judgement or interrupting your plans so it is difficult for people to feel close to you. You will never admit defeat and insist on solving your own problems. You can determine right from wrong and never cheat others. You cannot relax until you know the truth. You are continually working to achieve your goals, but sometimes you fail to examine the situation carefully and your plans backfire.

4th month

You are intelligent, patient and strong-willed. You have a thorough approach to work and complete every project you undertake. You want to have fame and fortune and work hard to gain authority. Because you are determined to achieve a position of power, you miss out on other opportunities.

5th month

You are kind-hearted and physically strong. You were probably born into a respected and wealthy family. You were spoilt as a child and will be headstrong as an adult; you cannot tolerate losing at work or at play. Your naivety and inexperience make it difficult for you to solve serious problems. You will have a happy marriage even though you marry for looks instead of character. A man born in this month should marry a woman born in the 8th month of the year of the Rat. A woman born in this month should marry a man born in the 8th month of the year of the Cock.

6th month

Your span of attention is very short and your mind is always jumping from one project to the next. You have a dual nature: one side of your character is extrovert, the other side introvert. You like a peaceful life but you also like crowds. You have difficulty discovering what most interests you. Others misunderstand you because you appear to be headstrong when you are often unsure of yourself. Concentrate on your work and take any opportunities that you are offered. Keep working and you will eventually be successful. You approach romance casually; you are sometimes cold and at other times warm towards your partner. It is difficult for you to achieve stability and harmony in your romantic relationships.

7th month

Your calm, gentle and reasonable appearance belies your obstinate character. You overestimate your own abilities; you dislike others interrupting you and often refuse to listen to their advice. You are willing to use devious means to achieve your aims. Your obstinacy hinders your career and unless you change your character your energy will be wasted.

8th month

You have a wide-ranging social life and are attractive to the opposite sex. You have a demonstrative character and are a welcome addition to any social gathering, but nobody truly understands your private character. You enjoy business and will do well in your career. The attraction that people of the opposite sex feel to you causes family trouble. A man born in this month should marry a woman born in the year of the Cock, and a woman born in this month should marry a man born the 4th month of the year of the Snake.

9th month

You are intelligent and well educated. Your intuitive understanding of human nature helps you to prosper in your personal and social life. Your humility, sincerity and kindness draw others to you, but you are often placed in dilemmas because you are too soft-hearted. Try to be more decisive if you want to be successful. Your married life will be fortunate and happy.

10th month

You are honest and open, and rarely quibble over minor matters.

You expect high standards of yourself and of others. You believe in your own ability and will never undertake a project unless you can complete it. You like to talk to people who have similar opinions to yourself; this avoids argument because you believe that your own ideas are right. You manage your financial affairs well and have an active social life. Do not rush romance; your luck will bring you success in love. You will fall in love twice; the first romance will not last but the second will be successful. Your ideal marriage partner will work in the performing arts.

11th month
You are intelligent, strong-willed and obstinate. You are a talented director and a good leader, always ready to defend the weak and the underpriviledged. You enjoy organizational challenges because they give you the opportunity to put your talents to good use. Examine your financial and romantic situations very carefully to avoid mistakes and loss of self-respect.

12th month
You want to be well known and respected and dislike being the subject of gossip or criticism. You set yourself high standards and put your talents to good use whatever you do. You have a good sense of humour and make friends easily. You are sincere in love and willing to sacrifice whatever you have for the sake of your partner.

Your Luck According to Your Day of Birth

Born on the 1st, 10th, 19th or 28th
You are of noble bearing, independent and trustworthy. Your standards are high and you are always ready to fight for your career. You have a determined character but are overly concerned with yourself and with achieving fame and fortune. You feel the need to complete everything quickly but you frequently fail. Be careful and

cautious. You are suited to a career as a civil servant or to a job in the arts. Your fortune fluctuates, and although at times you may receive unexpected money, at others you must control your spending.

Born on the 2nd, 11th, 20th or 29th
You are quiet but honest, open-hearted and extremely popular. Sometimes you like to be alone and at other times you want to be surrounded by friends. Unless you control your temper you will fall into trouble. You are suited to a career as an artistic designer, planner or literary editor. You enjoy life, even if you are in the poorest circumstances. Your fortune will not vary greatly, but your luck will improve after middle age.

Born on the 3rd, 12th, 21st or 30th
You are talented, sensitive and react quickly. You are always ready to fight for what you know is true and just. Others will avoid forming friendships with you if you are too obstinate; they wrongly assume you are too stern and difficult. You have business acumen and are suited to a disciplined job, such as the army, or to any job which has a competitive element, such as politics or the stock exchange. You must learn how to control your spending and think seriously of ways to earn more income.

Born on the 4th, 13th, 22nd or 31st
You are calm, patient and reserved. Your appearance and attitude lead others to think you are unapproachable, although in fact you are warm-hearted. If you change your approach you will be more popular. You are suited to a career as an academic, particularly in the field of theology or philosophy. Because you cannot control your spending you will lose money as easily and as quickly as you make it.

Born on the 5th, 14th or 23rd
Your fiery, obstinate nature makes it difficult for you to accept suggestions or opinions. At times your stubbornness leads to quarrels and problems. You are suited to a career in the arts, as an academic, an administrator or an advertising designer. Your intelligence enables you to work in a highly paid job. You will be lucky with money, often using it to set up new projects.

Born on the 6th, 15th or 24th
Your open, stable and cheerful character provides you with an active social life. You are affectionate and emotional and daydream so often that your mind becomes confused. Your eagerness to help others is often stifled by your indecisiveness. A career in the arts or work as a designer or social worker would be appropriate for you. You will not be very rich but will always have enough to live on.

Born on the 7th, 16th or 25th
You are an exhibitionist but when you show off nobody wants to listen to you or watch you. You enjoy an exciting life, but your head is in the clouds; you must learn to discipline yourself. You are suited to a job which allows you mobility, for example, a reporter, a traveller or an explorer. You do not want to earn a fortune and are quite content with your standard of living.

Born on the 8th, 17th or 26th
You are calm, quiet and a good judge. You have a determined and logical mind but lack social skills. You have a free spirit and are suited to self-employment. Do not buy stocks and shares or put your money in short-term investments. Your fortune is varied – it depends on your approach. There are times of wealth and times of abject poverty.

Born on the 9th, 18th or 27th
You are happy, optimistic and warm-hearted. You have an active life and are not easily troubled by minor matters. On the whole you are magnanimous but occasionally you quarrel unnecessarily with friends. It is important that you learn to control your moods. You should work as sole director or proprietor to avoid disagreements with partners. A job involving buying and selling would be suitable. You have a good income but you are extravagant.

Your Luck According to Your 'Hour' of Birth

Tzu hours: 11 p.m. – 1 a.m.
You are hot-tempered, obstinate, thrifty and shy away from challenges. You are an easy target for gossip. At times you act without sufficient planning but later you regret your actions. You

will be able to build a successful business, buy a home and care for your family without a family inheritance. You will achieve fame and success independently of others but if you find yourself in trouble your parents or your marriage partner will always be there to help you out.

Unlucky ages 10, 17, 35, 48, 57.

Age at death 87.

Suitable occupations Artist, politician, architect, electrician or jobs connected with metal or water.

Unsuitable occupations Work connected with earth.

Ch'ou hours: 1–3 a.m.
If you want a good career, leave your home town while you are young. Life will be difficult up to the age of twenty but then your fortune will change for the better. You will be wealthy in old age.

Unlucky ages 17, 22, 30, 45.

Age at death 71.

Suitable occupations Commercial trader, teacher, government official, restaurateur, academic, skilled manual worker or jobs connected with the final stages of production.

Unsuitable occupations Work connected with wood.

Yin hours: 3–5 a.m.
You are on bad terms with your relatives and your early years will be difficult. You will not be left an inheritance and will leave your home town. After the age of forty everything will work out well. Old age will bring you power and wealth.

Unlucky ages 25, 28, 32, 38, 48.

Age at death 65.

Suitable occupations Doctor, musician, artist, actor, travelling agent/representative.

Unsuitable occupations Work connected with metal.

Mao hours: 5–7 a.m.

You will be very fortunate, with occasional help from your parents but none from your brothers and sisters. You will have a comfortable life and be wealthy if you work away from your home town. Marriage will be unsteady and difficult in the early years, but after middle age you will develop more satisfactory relationships and will have the chance to be wealthy.

Unlucky ages 15, 19, 54.

Age at death 71.

Suitable occupations Mechanical engineer, actor, writer, artist, theologian or work connected with religion.

Unsuitable occupations Work connected with fire.

Ch'en hours: 7–9 a.m.

You are clever, quick-witted and determined. Your warm-hearted nature enables you to form close friendships. Life is busy and varied, but a woman born in the Ch'en hours will be lonely. However, you will have many material possessions and a good salary. Your excessive self-confidence makes working relationships difficult.

Unlucky ages 18, 26, 35, 38.

Age at death 65.

Suitable occupations Entrepreneur, politician, public relations officer, teacher, miner.

Unsuitable occupations Work connected with wood.

Szu hours: 9–11 a.m.
You have outstanding talent and are able to build up your business and care for your family successfully. Family relations are troubled and you would prosper financially if you were to leave your home town. You are kind to your friends and like to help them when they are in trouble. A woman born in the Szu hours is extravagant and may have an unhappy marriage. Men and women born in these hours drink too much.

Unlucky ages 30, 35, 46, 48.

Age at death 88.

Suitable occupations Civil or electrical engineer, architect, wood or wine merchant.

Unsuitable occupations Work connected with water.

Wu hours: 11 a.m.–1 p.m.
You are active, clever, obstinate and extravagant. You prefer travelling to settling down to a job in your local area. A woman born in these hours is likely to have an unusual and fascinating character.

Unlucky ages 5, 11, 23, 32, 44, 53.

Age at death 84.

Suitable occupations Doctor, nurse, politician, film actor, skilled worker, jobs in the service industries or any work connected with oil.

Unsuitable occupations Work connected with gold.

Wei hours: 1–3 p.m.
You have a troubled relationship with your parents, brothers and sisters and marriage partner. You will have serious difficulties in middle age. A woman born in these hours is clever but will always have difficulties with her marriage because she is too active to settle down.

Unlucky ages 18, 25, 55.

Age at death 69.

Suitable occupations Civil engineer, electrical engineer, architect, wood merchant, wine merchant.

Unsuitable occupations Work connected with water.

Shen hours: 3–5 p.m.
You will earn money easily and spend it freely. You will be luckier if you work outside your home town. Your marriage will be harmonious although your parents will not offer you moral support. A woman born in the Shen hours will be married twice. Because you are too active ever to settle down completely it is important that you are seen to behave honourably. Too much time worrying over relationships will cause your business to fail.

Unlucky ages 18, 21, 27, 29, 41, 53.

Age at death 71.

Suitable occupations Finance-related work – e.g. broker, public relations officer, watchmaker, manager – or work connected with metal.

Unsuitable occupations Work connected with wood.

Yu hours: 5–7 p.m.
Your youth is difficult because of troubled family relationships. You will be separated from your brothers and sisters and will leave home when young. You may not be able to have a child but it will be possible to adopt one. A woman born in the Yu hours is warm-hearted, fond of food and can be trusted to keep a secret.

Unlucky ages 18, 24, 31, 48.

Age at death 77.

Suitable occupations Chemist, researcher/writer, teacher, artist, technologist or work connected with the final stages of production.

Unsuitable occupations Work connected with earth.

Hsü hours: 7–9 p.m.
You are brave, capable, hardworking and run your business alone. You are optimistic and will have a successful life and a flourishing career. A woman born in the Hsü hours can be vain and impatient. You are magnanimous but on the other hand money is not important to you. You care little for others but will have a magnificent life.

Unlucky ages 15, 25, 34, 43, 48, 56.

Age at death 77.

Suitable occupations Poet, writer, investor, engineer, rice or cereal merchant, or work connected with metal and agriculture.

Unsuitable occupations Work connected with fire.

Hai hours: 9–11 p.m.
You are manually dextrous and set yourself high standards. Although you are warm-hearted you do not like to make too many friends. A woman born in the Hai hours can be obstinate. Others may be easily upset but you have the ability to forgive and forget. You are hardworking and will be fortunate.

Unlucky ages 10, 25, 35, 38, 48, 55.

Age at death 77.

Suitable occupations Surgeon, monk/nun, hotelier, artist, antiques dealer or work connected with metal.

Unsuitable occupations Work connected with fire.

Practical Advice

You should spend more time visiting temples and monasteries and praying to the gods. In this way you will create better opportunities for yourself in the future.

Be patient, avoid losing your temper and try not to get involved in unreasonable arguments.

Keep your emotions under control.

Sort out any problems as quickly and as efficiently as possible.

Try to give more time to helping other people.

Be single-minded in trying to achieve your goals, but do not let this harm your friendships or yourself.

Try to cultivate peace of mind so that each day passes calmly and safely.

Control your emotions so that you have a clear mind to make plans for the future.

Work hard, but do not expect immediate success. Deal with each problem as it arises.

Do not be flippant or careless.

Give yourself time to think so that you may know yourself better.

Be truthful and honest in both your business and your domestic life.

Your Luck Year by Year

Year of the Rat

Two lucky stars, one unlucky star.

This year your business will prosper, but your unlucky star indicates an illness. However, you will have a quick recovery.

Year of the Ox

One happy god, one unlucky star.

This is not a fortunate year. Your business will not prosper and you will fail an examination.

Year of the Tiger

Two lucky stars, three baleful spirits.

This is a good year for marriages. If you are already married you could have a new baby or a grandchild. Small problems will crop up during the year and you will be bored for long periods of time because of the influence of the three baleful spirits. If you are working in a foreign country this is a good year for visiting relatives at home.

Year of the Rabbit
Four unlucky stars.

This is a year of problems. A member of your family or one of your cousins may die this year. Nothing will work according to plan.

Year of the Dragon
Five unlucky stars.

This is an unlucky year. It is as though you have fallen into thorn bushes and are unable to move; your work and your social activities will be limited throughout the year.

Year of the Snake
Two lucky stars, five unlucky stars, one baleful star.

You will have a good income this year but there will be quarrels and possibly a law suit. During the year the baleful star clouds your vision; you will make wrong decisions or fall into bad company.

Year of the Horse
Two happy stars, three baleful stars.

You will find a suitable marriage partner this year. You may be seriously ill and lose money because you have to pay medical bills. You must be patient and your luck will take a turn for the better. Follow this Chinese saying: 'Be patient; wait until the clouds move away and the bright moon appears again.'

Year of the Ram
Four unlucky stars.

You may lose money this year. Avoid unscrupulous people and be prepared for family disputes. This is an unlucky year.

Year of the Monkey
Five lucky stars, two baleful stars.

This is a prosperous and lucky year for you. You are fortunate in your private life and in business. Everything you touch turns out well. It is a good year for family celebrations. Avoid petty-minded people this year.

Year of the Cock
Two baleful stars.

This is an unlucky year. There may be accidents, illness, financial loss or business failure. Your friends may become your enemies and your hopes may turn to fears. Be careful and cautious this year.

Year of the Dog
Two lucky stars, two baleful stars.

Your business will prosper, but you will not be able to save any money because you will have to make a long journey alone. Avoid quarrels and behave virtuously. Do not worry; there will be more good fortune than bad luck this year.

Year of the Pig
Three unlucky stars.

This is not a lucky year; you will have to deal with financial loss and family quarrels. Nothing will run smoothly this year.

Your Animal Sign Horoscope

THE SIGN OF THE TIGER

The Main Attributes of Tiger People

Character
You have an obstinate character. You never abandon a project. You like to see everything settled and completed.

Luck
You will be lucky because you never argue over minor matters.

Wealth
You will be prosperous because of your determination. The Wealth Stars shine on you.

Occupation
You are a born leader regardless of profession.

Social life
You will lose your reputation or your money if you trust others too much.

Business
Choose business partners who were born in the year of the Pig.

Romance
Your romantic life is unpredictable. Do not be hasty or careless.

Marriage
You will have a stable and happy marriage.

Parents
You are very fortunate; your parents and someone in a position of authority will always take care of you.

Brothers and sisters
You are on good terms with your brothers and sisters. They will support you emotionally and materially.

Children
You will love your children dearly and will take your parental responsibilities seriously.

Assets
Your good fortune helps you to acquire property.

Travel
You will be safe, but take care if you are driving in traffic.

Health
You are sensitive to changes in the weather and will have many minor illnesses.

Investment
Your investments are fruitful but do not take too many risks.

Skills
You will be successful in the field of planning, design, advertising or science.

Speculation
Avoid speculation; you could incur severe financial loss.

Hopes
You will never be very rich, but your hopes for a comfortable life style will be realized.

Litigation
Try to settle any law suits out of court.

Lost property
You seldom lose anything.

The Character of the Tiger

The Tiger is third in the hierarchy of the twelve animals and its character signifies caution. The Tiger corresponds to the Earthly Branch Yin. Yin's hours are between three and five in the morning, the hours when darkness gives way to light, the first month, when yin turns to yang. It is a period when expectations are realized.

You are cautious, optimistic, suspicious, selfish and critical. You reject others' opinions and rarely obey commands. Although you frequently fail, you are always ready to try again. A Chinese proverb says that the tiger lives in the forest, a thousand miles from a town. Likewise someone born in the year of the Tiger likes to be independent and is continually on the move. You are a good organizer with a positive attitude to life. You are also a good leader with a strong will to win, but you are afraid of losing face. In business or in love, your speech does not reflect your emotion and you do not always inspire trust.

You do not enjoy risk, excitement, stimulating ventures or elaborate preparations. You never store things for future use. Others are attracted to your intelligence, your caution and your courage. Many people respect you but they do not always like you. Try to be less obstinate and selfish and more even-tempered.

You approach your business or career seriously; you were given many good opportunities when you were young. You are interested in challenges, not in profit, but you have the intelligence to deal wisely with your finances. The Tiger does not need a good education or a wealthy background because someone born in this year will grasp every auspicious opportunity and challenge.

Although you have an emotional character, you do not approach relationships seriously; you are careless, hasty and inconsiderate. However, some women born in this year are honest and reliable, although most Tiger people are argumentative, excitable and unconventional. You are easily bored and are usually on the move from one partner to the next.

Your ideal marriage partner is someone born in the year of the Horse. The Horse is honest, hardworking and willing to be controlled by the Tiger. This partnership would have a happy and harmonious future. Someone born in the year of the Dragon would also be a good partner since the Dragon gives the Tiger power and energy and instructs him in wordly wisdom. You would also be well matched to someone born in the year of the Dog. You both have honest characters and the Dog is loyal and protective towards the Tiger.

You have a different approach to life from someone born in the year of the Ox. You approach life hastily, whereas the Ox approaches life gradually. You would be happy once you had learned to forgive and forget each other's faults. Avoid a partnership with someone born in the year of the Snake, the Ram or the Monkey. The Snake is too hard and unforgiving for the Tiger, and the Ram is too conservative. The Chinese say that the Ram will be eaten by the Tiger. The Tiger is stern and serious, but the Monkey is cunning, quick-witted, fast-moving, and will easily cheat the Tiger.

You are suited to a career as a soldier, policeman, politician, businessman, explorer or revolutionary, or any other work that involves adventure.

Your Luck According to Your Year of Birth

1926, 1986
Born in the year of Ping Yin, you belong to the Tiger in the Forest.

You are talkative and impatient, but you are also sincere and hard-working. You have not received a good education, but you will be helped by an influential official. You are suited to a disciplined career. A woman born in these years is intelligent and will be a good housewife.

1938, 1998
Born in the year of Mou Yin, you belong to the Tiger Passing through the Mountain.

You are obstinate and easily pleased or easily upset. You will work hard when you are young although you will not be very successful. Your luck will change if you accept a job away from your home town. A woman born in either of these years will be intelligent and active.

1950, 2010

Born in the year of Keng Yin, you belong to the Tiger Going down the Mountain.

You are patient and generous. You are easily pleased and easily upset, and have difficulty hiding your feelings. Although you have a forgiving nature, you argue and complain if someone upsets you. You will have a small income when you are young but a prosperous life after middle age. A woman born in either of these years will be a good housewife and well loved by her family.

1902, 1962

Born in the year of Jen Yin, you belong to the Tiger Passing through the Forest.

You are candid, sincere and thoughtful. You speak quickly and directly, and cannot hide secrets. Your marriage will be stormy and you will have children late in life. There will be many problems in your youth but you will happy and prosperous after middle age. A woman born in either of these years will be fortunate and wealthy.

1914, 1974
Born in the year of Chia Yin, you belong to the Tiger Standing Still.

You are suited to a government or administrative post because most of your life will be spent in the company of officials. Your family is prosperous and you will never be short of money or work. Your relationship with your parents will be troubled. A woman born in either of these years will take charge of the domestic affairs in her marriage.

Your Luck According to Your Month of Birth

1st month
You are honest, open, straightforward and never succumb to flattery. Because this is the first month of the year, you are full of hope, but you must settle down and approach life step by step. Be sincere, polite and patient. Do not rush any business dealings until your business reputation is well established. You will have a busy adult life and much of your time will be spent out of doors. You will have no regrets if you save your money carefully when you are young.

2nd month
You are calm and quiet and approach your work quickly and efficiently. You are well liked and socially popular, but you are late in keeping appointments because you accept so much work. Men born in this month have a wide circle of friends and fantasize about women. A woman born in this month approaches romance

rationally and seriously, and once she has met someone she loves, she becomes deeply committed. She will be an efficient housewife.

3rd month

You have a sensitive nature and are quick to react. You enjoy a good social life and are concerned with the details of social etiquette. You are well liked because you are approachable and friendly and never refuse requests for help. You approach your work intelligently and use your finances wisely. You have a good love life but you must always face the realities of romance for better or worse. You impress the opposite sex and are likely to marry someone with a similar nature to yours.

4th month

You like to work with other people but prefer to have control of your own business. You are liberal, intelligent and hardworking. Your ambitions will be realized and you will be well known. Someone born in the fourth month of the Tiger year is the luckiest of all the animal signs. You will choose your marriage partner with great care because you demand high standards of the opposite sex. Any problems in your career or in your marriage will be sorted out easily. You are protective towards your partner and nurture your marriage as you would nurture a rare flower until it comes into bloom.

5th month

You are gentle, quick-witted, clever and good-natured. But you are also stubborn and determined; you will fail if you do not listen to others' advice. You are too confident, so you disappoint yourself and others. Face facts and reconsider your past mistakes. You will be successful if you are patient and self-effacing. Use your intelligence to develop your business and increase your earnings. You have the potential to be very successful and others will trust you once they see the more positive side to your character.

6th month

You do not have to work very hard to achieve your aims. You are very lucky – you will have a prosperous career and a happy family life. You were probably born of a wealthy family and may never encounter financial difficulties. Spend your money carefully so that you can enjoy it throughout your life. You have an excellent social life; you are well liked and attractive to the opposite sex. You are, however, committed to one person. You are not emotionally close to your friends but you reveal your feelings to your partner. You will have a happy and fortunate married life.

7th month

You understand human needs and difficulties and try to avoid hurting others. You approach your work seriously and positively. You would never admit to being tired. Your dogged perseverance will make you successful.

8th month

You have good social skills and an attractive appearance. You dislike being controlled or depending on others. You will be prosperous, but you must approach your finances seriously. You will have a lucky future if you treat others kindly and generously. One side of your character is talkative and lighthearted, the other side is serious and thoughtful. Your character will change after marriage; you may lose your commitment to your marriage, although your partner cares for you. Do not envy others' wealth and avoid careless talk.

9th month

You are active, hardworking and generous. You have a modern outlook on life and dislike conservative attitudes. You do everything quickly without sufficient forethought. You work quietly and diligently without troubling others. Whatever business you choose, you will be successful. Your marriage will combine spiritual and physical attraction. A man born in this month is attracted to beautiful, confident women. A woman will choose a loyal partner who will lavish attention on her.

10th month

You are easily cheated or involved in trouble because you rarely consider consequences. Even though you do not take life seriously, you will always be lucky. You have strong health and will be offered good career opportunities. You are strong-willed and take immediate action if you discover that you have been cheated. If you work hard your financial success is assured. You will have a happy and fortunate marriage.

11th month
You are suited to active, outdoor jobs. You are impatient: you want everything to happen quickly and finish quickly. Even when you fail in love you dislike wasting time; you expect immediate responses from your partner. You will have a quiet family life but a busy social life. You may feel lonely in your marriage and will look for extramarital emotional attachments.

12th month
You are confident, generous and forgiving. You will be successful in business and will draw on any means to achieve your aims. However, you do not take money seriously – the Chinese say, 'A big chicken never pecks small rice.' You approach your business intelligently and calmly, and there will always be someone to help you build your career. You are a good negotiator and never lose face in your financial dealings but you do not speculate. If you approach romance seriously you will have a good marriage.

Your Luck According to Your Day of Birth

Born on the 1st, 10th, 19th or 28th
You are of noble bearing, independent and trustworthy. Your standards are high and you are always ready to fight for your career. You have a determined character but are overly concerned with yourself and with achieving fame and fortune. You feel the need to complete everything quickly but you frequently fail. Be careful and cautious. You are suited to a career as a civil servant or to a job in the arts. Your fortune fluctuates, and although at times you may receive unexpected money, at others you must control your spending.

Born on the 2nd, 11th, 20th or 29th
You are quiet but honest, open-hearted and extremely popular. Sometimes you like to be alone and at other times you want to be surrounded by friends. Unless you control your temper you will fall into trouble. You are suited to a career as an artistic designer,

planner or literary editor. You enjoy life, even if you are in the poorest circumstances. Your fortune will not vary greatly, but your luck will improve after middle age.

Born on the 3rd, 12th, 21st or 30th

You are talented, sensitive and react quickly. You are always ready to fight for what you know is true and just. Others will avoid forming friendships with you if you are too obstinate; they wrongly assume you are too stern and difficult. You have business acumen and are suited to a disciplined job, such as the army, or to any job which has a competitive element, such as politics or the stock exchange. You must learn how to control your spending and think seriously of ways to earn more income.

Born on the 4th, 13th, 22nd or 31st

You are calm, patient and reserved. Your appearance and attitude lead others to think you are unapproachable, although in fact you are warm-hearted. If you change your approach you will be more popular. You are suited to a career as an academic, particularly in the field of theology or philosophy. Because you cannot control your spending you will lose money as easily and as quickly as you make it.

Born on the 5th, 14th or 23rd

Your fiery, obstinate nature makes it difficult for you to accept suggestions or opinions. At times your stubbornness leads to quarrels and problems. You are suited to a career in the arts, as an academic, an administrator or an advertising designer. Your intelligence enables you to work in a highly paid job. You will be lucky with money, often using it to set up new projects.

Born on the 6th, 15th or 24th

Your open, stable and cheerful character provides you with an active social life. You are affectionate and emotional and daydream so often that your mind becomes confused. Your eagerness to help others is often stifled by your indecisiveness. A career in the arts or work as a designer or social worker would be appropriate for you. You will not be very rich but will always have enough to live on.

Born on the 7th, 16th or 25th

You are an exhibitionist but when you show off nobody wants to listen to you or watch you. You enjoy an exciting life, but your head is in the clouds; you must learn to discipline yourself. You are suited to a job which allows you mobility, for example, a reporter, a traveller or an explorer. You do not want to earn a fortune and are quite content with your standard of living.

Born on the 8th, 17th or 26th

You are calm, quiet and a good judge. You have a determined and logical mind but lack social skills. You have a free spirit and are suited to self-employment. Do not buy stocks and shares or put your money in short-term investments. Your fortune is varied – it depends on your approach. There are times of wealth and times of abject poverty.

Born on the 9th, 18th or 27th

You are happy, optimistic and warm-hearted. You have an active life and are not easily troubled by minor matters. On the whole you are magnanimous but occasionally you quarrel unnecessarily with friends. It is important that you learn to control your moods. You should work as sole director or proprietor to avoid disagreements with partners. A job involving buying and selling would be suitable. You have a good income but you are extravagant.

Your Luck According to Your 'Hour' of Birth

Tzu hours: 11 p.m. – 1 a.m.

You are hot-tempered, obstinate, thrifty and shy away from challenges. You are an easy target for gossip. At times you act without sufficient planning but later you regret your actions. You will be able to build a successful business, buy a home and care for your family without a family inheritance. You will achieve fame and success independently of others but if you find yourself in trouble your parents or your marriage partner will always be there to help you out.

Unlucky ages 10, 17, 35, 48, 57.

Age at death 87.

Suitable occupations Artist, politician, architect, electrician or jobs connected with metal or water.

Unsuitable occupations Work connected with earth.

Ch'ou hours: 1–3 a.m.
If you want a good career, leave your home town while you are young. Life will be difficult up to the age of twenty but then your fortune will change for the better. You will be wealthy in old age.

Unlucky ages 17, 22, 30, 45.

Age at death 71.

Suitable occupations Commercial trader, teacher, government official, restaurateur, academic, skilled manual worker or jobs connected with the final stages of production.

Unsuitable occupations Work connected with wood.

Yin hours: 3–5 a.m.
You are on bad terms with your relatives and your early years will be difficult. You will not be left an inheritance and will leave your home town. After the age of forty everything will work out well. Old age will bring you power and wealth.

Unlucky ages 25, 28, 32, 38, 48.

Age at death 65.

Suitable occupations Doctor, musician, artist, actor, travelling agent/representative.

Unsuitable occupations Work connected with metal.

Mao hours: 5–7 a.m.
You will be very fortunate, with occasional help from your parents but none from your brothers and sisters. You will have a comfortable life and be wealthy if you work away from your home town. Marriage will be unsteady and difficult in the early years, but

after middle age you will develop more satisfactory relationships and will have the chance to be wealthy.

Unlucky ages 15, 19, 54.

Age at death 71.

Suitable occupations Mechanical engineer, actor, writer, artist, theologian or work connected with religion.

Unsuitable occupations Work connected with fire.

Ch'en hours: 7–9 a.m.

You are clever, quick-witted and determined. Your warm-hearted nature enables you to form close friendships. Life is busy and varied, but a woman born in the Ch'en hours will be lonely. However, you will have many material possessions and a good salary. Your excessive self-confidence makes working relationships difficult.

Unlucky ages 18, 26, 35, 38.

Age at death 65.

Suitable occupations Entrepreneur, politician, public relations officer, teacher, miner.

Unsuitable occupations Work connected with wood.

Szu hours: 9–11 a.m.

You have outstanding talent and are able to build up your business and care for your family successfully. Family relations are troubled and you would prosper financially if you were to leave your home town. You are kind to your friends and like to help them when they are in trouble. A woman born in the Szu hours is extravagant and may have an unhappy marriage. Men and women born in these hours drink too much.

Unlucky ages 30, 35, 46, 48.

Age at death 88.

Suitable occupations Civil or electrical engineer, architect, wood or wine merchant.

Unsuitable occupations Work connected with water.

Wu hours: 11 a.m.–1 p.m.
You are active, clever, obstinate and extravagant. You prefer travelling to settling down to a job in your local area. A woman born in these hours is likely to have an unusual and fascinating character.

Unlucky ages 5, 11, 23, 32, 44, 53.

Age at death 84.

Suitable occupations Doctor, nurse, politician, film actor, skilled worker, jobs in the service industries or any work connected with oil.

Unsuitable occupations Work connected with gold.

Wei hours: 1–3 p.m.
You have a troubled relationship with your parents, brothers and sisters and marriage partner. You will have serious difficulties in middle age. A woman born in these hours is clever but will always have difficulties with her marriage because she is too active to settle down.

Unlucky ages 18, 25, 55.

Age at death 69.

Suitable occupations Civil engineer, electrical engineer, architect, wood merchant, wine merchant.

Unsuitable occupations Work connected with water.

Shen hours: 3–5 p.m.
You will earn money easily and spend it freely. You will be luckier if

you work outside your home town. Your marriage will be harmonious although your parents will not offer you moral support. A woman born in the Shen hours will be married twice. Because you are too active ever to settle down completely it is important that you are seen to behave honourably. Too much time worrying over relationships will cause your business to fail.

Unlucky ages 18, 21, 27, 29, 41, 53.

Age at death 71.

Suitable occupations Finance-related work – e.g. broker, public relations officer, watchmaker, manager – or work connected with metal.

Unsuitable occupations Work connected with wood.

Yu hours: 5–7 p.m.

Your youth is difficult because of troubled family relationships. You will be separated from your brothers and sisters and will leave home when young. You may not be able to have a child but it will be possible to adopt one. A woman born in the Yu hours is warm-hearted, fond of food and can be trusted to keep a secret.

Unlucky ages 18, 24, 31, 48.

Age at death 77.

Suitable occupations Chemist, researcher/writer, teacher, artist, technologist or work connected with the final stages of production.

Unsuitable occupations Work connected with earth.

Hsü hours: 7–9 p.m.

You are brave, capable, hardworking and run your business alone. You are optimistic and will have a successful life and a flourishing career. A woman born in the Hsü hours can be vain and impatient. You are magnanimous but on the other hand money is not important to you. You care little for others but will have a magnificent life.

Unlucky ages 15, 25, 34, 43, 48, 56.

Age at death 77.

Suitable occupations Poet, writer, investor, engineer, rice or cereal merchant, or work connected with metal and agriculture.

Unsuitable occupations Work connected with fire.

Hai hours: 9–11 p.m.
You are manually dextrous and set yourself high standards. Although you are warm-hearted you do not like to make too many friends. A woman born in the Hai hours can be obstinate. Others may be easily upset but you have the ability to forgive and forget. You are hardworking and will be fortunate.

Unlucky ages 10, 25, 35, 38, 48, 55.

Age at death 77.

Suitable occupations Surgeon, monk/nun, hotelier, artist, antiques dealer or work connected with metal.

Unsuitable occupations Work connected with fire.

Practical Advice

Take care of your business; do not let it fail because you have fallen in love.
Approach others sincerely and honestly.
Respect superiors and older people. When you go to them for help they will bolster your confidence.
Be kind and warmhearted with friends but cautious towards strangers.
Work diligently if you want to be successful.
Do not rush your life and try not to be too extrovert.
Keep your feet firmly on the ground.
Be strong-willed.

Do not push yourself or others too far – the higher you climb, the farther you fall.
Learn from your mistakes.
Approach your plans seriously; do not give up hope.
Avoid excessive smoking and drinking.

Your Luck Year by Year

Year of the Rat
One baleful spirit, two unlucky stars.

This is an unlucky year. You will be involved in an accident or a disaster and there will be a burial in your family. You will not make any profit, nor will you save any money.

Year of the Ox
Two lucky stars, two unlucky stars.

The lucky stars come to your door this year. You will be fortunate throughout the year. You will suffer minor illnesses, but you will recover quickly.

Year of the Tiger
Four unlucky spirits

This is a year of troubles and financial loss. You will put on mourning clothes and there will be problems in your domestic life.

Year of the Rabbit
Two lucky stars, one unlucky star.

This is a lucky year for your marriage, but you will be involved in an accident. You will recover completely from your injuries.

Year of the Dragon
Three unlucky stars.

This is an unlucky year. There will be more than one burial or serious accident. Your yearly income will be below average and your plans will not run smoothly.

Year of the Snake
One lucky star, three unlucky stars.

You will be given a good opportunity to prove yourself this year. You will be ill and lonely and will face difficulties.

Year of the Horse
Three lucky stars, two unlucky stars.

This is a fortunate and prosperous year; you will be offered good promotion. Beware of revealing your business or family interests to someone who may try to harm you.

Year of the Ram
Two lucky stars, three unlucky stars.

This is a good year to travel or emigrate, but you will lose money and fall ill. You will recover from your illness, but take care of your diet. Wear suitable clothes and be careful at work and at home.

Year of the Monkey
Three lucky stars, one unlucky star, one unlucky spirit.

You have one unlucky star shining on you and one unlucky spirit influencing you. Your life is unsettled. You may be involved in a law suit and threatened with prison, but your lucky stars will save you. This is a good year to emigrate.

Year of the Cock
Two lucky stars, one unlucky star.

Your lucky stars counterbalance the misfortune of the unlucky star. Your bad fortune is transformed into good fortune this year.

Year of the Dog
Two lucky stars, three baleful spirits.

This is a prosperous year. There will be a marriage in the family and there is a possibility that you will marry a relative. It is a good year to start a business. You will travel extensively, there will be quarrels and you will be the subject of malicious gossip. If you work hard this year you will reap financial rewards.

Year of the Pig
One lucky star, two unlucky stars.

This is an unfortunate year. Beware of being bitten by a dog – it may cause serious illness. This is an unsettled year; you will pass through many changes of mood.

Your Animal Sign Horoscope

THE SIGN OF THE RABBIT

The Main Attributes of Rabbit People

Character
You have a winning character; nobody wants to harm you. You can turn your enemies into friends.

Luck
You will have a settled life without any major problems. You never rush into projects without careful forethought.

Wealth
You will never have any financial worries.

Occupation
You are suited to any career. Before you accept a job, examine your motives and your suitability for the work.

Social life
You will have a successful social life because you create a friendly atmosphere.

Business
You are well thought of by your colleagues; you will have a posperous business.

Romance
You are kindhearted and loving. You will never refuse your partner's requests.

Marriage
You will have a successful and happy marriage.

Parents
You have a good relationship with your parents and particularly with your father. He will support you whenever you need help.

Brothers and sisters
You love and respect your brothers and sisters. They will always be ready to help you.

Children
You have an independent character and enjoy a single life. You will be happy if you have children but they will not be the most important part of your life.

Assets
You acquire wealth as easily as you acquire property.

Travel
You do not enjoy long journeys; you like to make short journeys for brief visits.

Health
You will never have any serious illnesses.

Investment
Invest your money or your time in large organizations.

Skills
You have a good imagination and intellect. You can put these to good use in any area of life.

Speculation
You are not a good speculator; avoid taking risks.

Hopes
Most of your hopes will be realized.

Litigation
As long as you are innocent you will win law suits whether you are the defendant or the prosecutor.

Lost property
You will usually find lost property or renew contact with old friends.

The Character of the Rabbit

The Rabbit is the fourth of the twelve animals and corresponds to the Earthly Branch Mao. The Rabbit belongs to the second month, the month of seedlings, and has a lithe and gentle appearance.

You have a youthful and energetic outlook. You create a happy atmosphere and would make a good diplomat. You are elegant, generous, kindhearted and quick-witted. You have a good intellect and attract intelligent and trusting friends. You are a peacemaker with a strong dislike of arguments and quarrels. Sometimes you are patient, other times cautious; sometimes you are obstinate, other times amenable.

You are not interested in politics, competition or finance; you like to leave the troubles of the everyday world behind you. The Chinese say that you are like a lotus growing above dirty ground. You are quick to react and like to execute your plans without delay.

Your immediate environment affects your mood. You care about clothes, food and interior decoration. Whenever your friends come to visit, you like to create a sociable and comfortable atmosphere and you are always attentive to their needs and suggestions. Sometimes you are too concerned and too conservative; try to be more open and tolerant of new ideas.

You have strength and energy and will be fortunate throughout life. Plan your future carefully and calmly. Try not to rush your work even though you have many plans for the future. Your life will be tranquil and stable because you are quiet and forgiving. You have a sympathetic nature and are ready to help others when tragedy strikes. You do not expect others to help you when you are in distress and usually keep your emotions well hidden.

Someone born in the year of the Ram, the Dog or the Pig would be an ideal marriage or business partner. The Ram shares your artistic interests and the Dog or the Pig would help you build a prosperous career. The Chinese say that such a partnership would be as successful as the noonday sun is hot. Someone born in the year of the Rabbit or the Dragon would make a suitable partner, but anyone born in the year of the Rat, the Cock or the Ox would be an unlucky match. Working with them would be as difficult as rowing a boat against the current. Your life would be marked by idleness and disasters.

You are suited to a legal career as a barrister, solicitor or judge, or to a career in diplomacy or public relations. You would also enjoy a literary or artistic career.

Your Luck According to Your Year of Birth

1927, 1987

Born in the year of Ting Mao, you belong to the Rabbit Looking at the Moon.

You are hard-working and competent. You are suited to a job that requires intellect or manual skills and will always have enough work to keep you busy. A woman born in either of these years will be quiet but complaining. She is generous, takes care of her appearance and is suited to a career in a service industry.

1939, 1999

Born in the year of Chi Mao, you belong to the Rabbit Running out of the Forest.

You will be quite successful in your career, but your family will be unable to help you in times of need. Marry someone who is older than you. A woman born in either of these years will have a long and happy marriage.

1951, 2011

Born in the year of Hsin Mao, you belong to the Rabbit in the Burrow.

You are candid and sincere, but speak without thinking first. You are determined and have friends in powerful positions. You appear to enjoy life but are secretly preoccupied and worried. You will be lucky although your relatives will be unable to help you. A woman born in either of these years will be a good housewife.

1903, 1963

Born in the year of Kuei Mao, you belong to the Rabbit Running in the Forest.

You will never be short of money and will be able to transform your misfortune to fortune. You will be poor in your youth, but with the help of an influential acquaintance you will be prosperous from middle age onwards. A woman born in either of these years will be a good housewife.

1915, 1975
Born in the year of Yi Mao, you belong to the Buddha Rabbit.

You have a determined and organized nature and are a skilled writer. You will be wealthy after receiving help from an influential official. A woman born in either of these years will have a long life.

Your Luck According to Your Month of Birth

1st month
You are elegant, well educated and knowledgeable. You are sympathetic and sincere and have a positive attitude to life. Your business will be successful although you will never be wealthy. You handle work cautiously and avoid publicity and fame; you always work quietly and carefully. There is no need to rush your career or your business because you will eventually be successful. Others will be inspired by your approach and will always be ready to help and support you.

2nd month
You are cautious in thought and action, but once you have made a decision you carry out your plans immediately. You have a forgiving and caring character. You like to put people at ease so they can reveal their secrets or their worries. You dislike accepting orders and are unable to take misfortune in your stride. Try not to be too cautious – you may miss good business opportunities. If you think a job is worthwhile, tackle it immediately; do not worry about the rewards you will receive once you have completed it.

3rd month
You have an enthusiastic outlook, an active social life and a kind nature. You concentrate on your own business and never interfere in others' lives. Try to be less single-minded and more patient. Compromise your aims and opinions and develop other interests and hobbies in your life besides work. A woman born in this month is fickle and enjoys being pampered.

4th month
You are ambitious, logical and proud. You are self-centred and always ready to defend your reputation against criticism. You are a perfectionist, but you change your mind so often you are never able to make any firm decisions. Be realistic, learn to accept your capabilities and the capabilities of others. Your selfishness could cause you financial problems.

5th month
Your lucky stars have given you wisdom, courage and energy. You are a generous and caring person and treat others as you would like them to treat you. You have strong sense of morality, but your business will be unsuccessful because you make hasty decisions. Be more patient, learn from your experience and approach life calmly.

6th month
You are honest, energetic, patient and discreet. You will be successful because you approach everything enthusiastically, realistically and openly. You must make your own opportunities – no one else will make them for you. Be strong-willed, particularly in business. Once you have determined the direction of your career you will work diligently. Even if you lack previous experience you will be successful because you listen to the advice of friends and colleagues.

7th month
You are reasonable, dependable and wise, but you are not courageous. You are socially popular because of your open, amenable character. Follow your intuition: it will lead to improved career opportunities. You may inherit property and will be offered many lucky chances. The stars shine favourably on your career,

love life, family and social life. Beware of a corrupt man who may harm you.

8th month

You are resolute, intelligent and courageous, but you make hasty decisions and act without careful thought. Try to plan ahead so that you can do your work more efficiently. You are attracted by new technology and modern ideas. You have a forgiving heart and are a popular and trusted friend. You will never be very successful but you will be able to change your misfortune to fortune.

9th month

You are outwardly perverse and obstinate, but inwardly you are amenable and gentle. You have a deep empathy for other people but you must learn to express your feelings more openly. Like your luck, your mind changes quickly. If you learn to compromise you will be able to cope more efficiently with your problems. Be sensible about your finances and save your money for the future.

10th month

You are active, nostalgic and inquisitive. A woman born in this month is well liked because she creates an easy and comfortable atmosphere. A man born in this month is romantic and intelligent, a skilled writer or artist. He is also too honest, too emotional and too enthusiastic. He overwhelms new acquaintances and is easily won over to sympathetic causes. You must learn to control your spending and then you will discover who your real friends are. You will be very successful if you approach your business honestly and sensibly. Heaven has granted you good fortune, but you will lose it if you are impatient.

11th month

You are introvert, conservative and cautious. You are sensitive towards the worries and needs of others, but you are also an astute judge of character. Everyone who comes to you is treated with dignity, understanding and patience. You are relied upon and trusted. You are very fortunate and, if you use your intelligence wisely, you will always be financially secure. Your future is very promising.

12th month

You have a good memory and an analytical mind. You are wary, proud and independent. You are outwardly cool and collected, but underneath you are emotional and loving. You have a quiet, sensitive nature, but you also have a vicious and prejudiced side to your character. Try to correct these bad characteristics before your friends start to distrust you. Always consider the other side of an argument. Be careful with your finances because your income will be unpredictable.

Your Luck According to Your Day of Birth

Born on the 1st, 10th, 19th or 28th

You are of noble bearing, independent and trustworthy. Your standards are high and you are always ready to fight for your career. You have a determined character but are overly concerned with yourself and with achieving fame and fortune. You feel the need to complete everything quickly but you frequently fail. Be careful and cautious. You are suited to a career as a civil servant or to a job in the arts. Your fortune fluctuates, and although at times you may receive unexpected money, at others you must control your spending.

Born on the 2nd, 11th, 20th or 29th

You are quiet but honest, open-hearted and extremely popular. Sometimes you like to be alone and at other times you want to be surrounded by friends. Unless you control your temper you will fall into trouble. You are suited to a career as an artistic designer, planner or literary editor. You enjoy life, even if you are in the poorest circumstances. Your fortune will not vary greatly, but your luck will improve after middle age.

Born on the 3rd, 12th, 21st or 30th

You are talented, sensitive and react quickly. You are always ready to fight for what you know is true and just. Others will avoid forming friendships with you if you are too obstinate; they wrongly assume you are too stern and difficult. You have business acumen and are suited to a disciplined job, such as the army, or to any job which has a competitive element, such as politics or the stock exchange. You must learn how to control your spending and think seriously of ways to earn more income.

Born on the 4th, 13th, 22nd or 31st

You are calm, patient and reserved. Your appearance and attitude lead others to think you are unapproachable, although in fact you are warm-hearted. If you change your approach you will be more popular. You are suited to a career as an academic, particularly in the field of theology or philosophy. Because you cannot control your spending you will lose money as easily and as quickly as you make it.

Born on the 5th, 14th or 23rd

Your fiery, obstinate nature makes it difficult for you to accept suggestions or opinions. At times your stubbornness leads to quarrels and problems. You are suited to a career in the arts, as an academic, an administrator or an advertising designer. Your intelligence enables you to work in a highly paid job. You will be lucky with money, often using it to set up new projects.

Born on the 6th, 15th or 24th

Your open, stable and cheerful character provides you with an active social life. You are affectionate and emotional and daydream so often that your mind becomes confused. Your eagerness to help others is often stifled by your indecisiveness. A career in the arts or work as a designer or social worker would be appropriate for you. You will not be very rich but will always have enough to live on.

Born on the 7th, 16th or 25th

You are an exhibitionist but when you show off nobody wants to listen to you or watch you. You enjoy an exciting life, but your head is in the clouds; you must learn to discipline yourself. You are suited to a job which allows you mobility, for example, a reporter, a traveller or an explorer. You do not want to earn a fortune and are quite content with your standard of living.

Born on the 8th, 17th or 26th

You are calm, quiet and a good judge. You have a determined and logical mind but lack social skills. You have a free spirit and are suited to self-employment. Do not buy stocks and shares or put your money in short-term investments. Your fortune is varied – it depends on your approach. There are times of wealth and times of abject poverty.

Born on the 9th, 18th or 27th
You are happy, optimistic and warm-hearted. You have an active life and are not easily troubled by minor matters. On the whole you are magnanimous but occasionally you quarrel unnecessarily with friends. It is important that you learn to control your moods. You should work as sole director or proprietor to avoid disagreements with partners. A job involving buying and selling would be suitable. You have a good income but you are extravagant.

Your Luck According to Your 'Hour' of Birth

Tzu hours: 11 p.m. – 1 a.m.
You are hot-tempered, obstinate, thrifty and shy away from challenges. You are an easy target for gossip. At times you act without sufficient planning but later you regret your actions. You will be able to build a successful business, buy a home and care for your family without a family inheritance. You will achieve fame and success independently of others but if you find yourself in trouble your parents or your marriage partner will always be there to help you out.

Unlucky ages 10, 17, 35, 48, 57.

Age at death 87.

Suitable occupations Artist, politician, architect, electrician or jobs connected with metal or water.

Unsuitable occupations Work connected with earth.

Ch'ou hours: 1 – 3 a.m.
If you want a good career, leave your home town while you are young. Life will be difficult up to the age of twenty but then your fortune will change for the better. You will be wealthy in old age.

Unlucky ages 17, 22, 30, 45.

Age at death 71.

Suitable occupations Commercial trader, teacher, government official, restaurateur, academic, skilled manual worker or jobs connected with the final stages of production.

Unsuitable occupations Work connected with wood.

Yin hours: 3–5 a.m.
You are on bad terms with your relatives and your early years will be difficult. You will not be left an inheritance and will leave your home town. After the age of forty everything will work out well. Old age will bring you power and wealth.

Unlucky ages 25, 28, 32, 38, 48.

Age at death 65.

Suitable occupations Doctor, musician, artist, actor, travelling agent/representative.

Unsuitable occupations Work connected with metal.

Mao hours: 5–7 a.m.
You will be very fortunate, with occasional help from your parents but none from your brothers and sisters. You will have a comfortable life and be wealthy if you work away from your home town. Marriage will be unsteady and difficult in the early years, but after middle age you will develop more satisfactory relationships and will have the chance to be wealthy.

Unlucky ages 15, 19, 54.

Age at death 71.

Suitable occupations Mechanical engineer, actor, writer, artist, theologian or work connected with religion.

Unsuitable occupations Work connected with fire.

Ch'en hours: 7–9 a.m.
You are clever, quick-witted and determined. Your warm-hearted nature enables you to form close friendships. Life is busy and varied, but a woman born in the Ch'en hours will be lonely. However, you will have many material possessions and a good salary. Your excessive self-confidence makes working relationships difficult.

Unlucky ages 18, 26, 35, 38.

Age at death 65.

Suitable occupations Entrepreneur, politician, public relations officer, teacher, miner.

Unsuitable occupations Work connected with wood.

Szu hours: 9–11 a.m.
You have outstanding talent and are able to build up your business and care for your family successfully. Family relations are troubled and you would prosper financially if you were to leave your home town. You are kind to your friends and like to help them when they are in trouble. A woman born in the Szu hours is extravagant and may have an unhappy marriage. Men and women born in these hours drink too much.

Unlucky ages 30, 35, 46, 48.

Age at death 88.

Suitable occupations Civil or electrical engineer, architect, wood or wine merchant.

Unsuitable occupations Work connected with water.

Wu hours: 11 a.m.–1 p.m.
You are active, clever, obstinate and extravagant. You prefer travelling to settling down to a job in your local area. A woman born in these hours is likely to have an unusual and fascinating character.

Unlucky ages 5, 11, 23, 32, 44, 53.

Age at death 84.

Suitable occupations Doctor, nurse, politician, film actor, skilled worker, jobs in the service industries or any work connected with oil.

Unsuitable occupations Work connected with gold.

Wei hours: 1–3 p.m.
You have a troubled relationship with your parents, brothers and sisters and marriage partner. You will have serious difficulties in middle age. A woman born in these hours is clever but will always have difficulties with her marriage because she is too active to settle down.

Unlucky ages 18, 25, 55.

Age at death 69.

Suitable occupations Civil engineer, electrical engineer, architect, wood merchant, wine merchant.

Unsuitable occupations Work connected with water.

Shen hours: 3–5 p.m.
You will earn money easily and spend it freely. You will be luckier if you work outside your home town. Your marriage will be harmonious although your parents will not offer you moral support. A woman born in the Shen hours will be married twice. Because you are too active ever to settle down completely it is important that you are seen to behave honourably. Too much time worrying over relationships will cause your business to fail.

Unlucky ages 18, 21, 27, 29, 41, 53.

Age at death 71.

Suitable occupations Finance-related work – e.g. broker, public relations officer, watchmaker, manager – or work connected with metal.

Unsuitable occupations Work connected with wood.

Yu hours: 5–7 p.m.
Your youth is difficult because of troubled family relationships. You will be separated from your brothers and sisters and will leave home when young. You may not be able to have a child but it will be possible to adopt one. A woman born in the Yu hours is warm-hearted, fond of food and can be trusted to keep a secret.

Unlucky ages 18, 24, 31, 48.

Age at death 77.

Suitable occupations Chemist, researcher/writer, teacher, artist, technologist or work connected with the final stages of production.

Unsuitable occupations Work connected with earth.

Hsü hours: 7–9 p.m.
You are brave, capable, hardworking and run your business alone. You are optimistic and will have a successful life and a flourishing career. A woman born in the Hsü hours can be vain and impatient. You are magnanimous but on the other hand money is not important to you. You care little for others but will have a magnificent life.

Unlucky ages 15, 25, 34, 43, 48, 56.

Age at death 77.

Suitable occupations Poet, writer, investor, engineer, rice or cereal merchant, or work connected with metal and agriculture.

Unsuitable occupations Work connected with fire.

Hai hours: 9–11 p.m.
You are manually dextrous and set yourself high standards. Although you are warm-hearted you do not like to make too many friends. A woman born in the Hai hours can be obstinate. Others

may be easily upset but you have the ability to forgive and forget. You are hardworking and will be fortunate.

Unlucky ages 10, 25, 35, 38, 48, 55.

Age at death 77.

Suitable occupations Surgeon, monk/nun, hotelier, artist, antiques dealer or work connected with metal.

Unsuitable occupations Work connected with fire.

Practical Advice

Once you have decided to do something, put it into practice immediately.

Be ready to take responsibility for your actions. Take care before you sign any agreements or contracts.

Consider the long-term effects of your business dealings. The Chinese say: 'Do not kill the chicken, give it time to lay its eggs.'

Be on good terms with your family. They will help you in the future.

Learn to relax; it will be good for your future.

Do not be irritable even if you have just finished a demanding project.

Approach your romantic life sensibly.

Do not be frivolous. Approach your work seriously and gradually.

Do not become involved in any corrupt business dealings or deceitful romantic situations.

Your Luck Year by Year

Year of the Rat

Five lucky stars, two unlucky stars.

This is a fortunate year even though there are minor family quarrels. Your unlucky stars are very weak so they cannot cause too many problems.

Year of the Ox

Seven unlucky stars, seven baleful spirits.

This is a very unlucky year. Your business will collapse or you will be made redundant. Take great care because you may be involved in a serious accident this year.

Year of the Tiger

Three baleful spirits.

This is a year of sickness, law-suits, financial loss and slander. Take care in all your actions.

Year of the Rabbit

Two lucky stars, two unlucky stars.

Your lucky stars are shining strongly. This is a good year to take examinations or accept promotion. Everything will be successful and prosperous. Your income will increase, your business will prosper and your name will become well known. Your unlucky stars will cause minor problems.

Year of the Dragon

One lucky star, one unlucky star.

Take care this year and do not set your expectations too high. Your business or your career will be stable but not successful.

Year of the Snake

One travelling star, two baleful spirits.

There will be many short and busy journeys this year. You may be offered a job away from home. There will be a burial, several accidents and financial loss.

Year of the Horse

One lucky star, two unlucky stars.

This will be a happy and lucky year, although there will be minor problems which you cannot avoid.

Year of the Ram

Three lucky stars, three baleful spirits.

Your fortunes are unsettled this year. Avoid corrupt influences. You will be able to change your misfortune to fortune.

Year of the Monkey

One lucky star, three baleful spirits.

This is an unlucky year, but your lucky star will help you to recover from serious illness.

Year of the Cock

One unlucky star, three baleful spirits.

This is a year of disasters, accidents, law-suits and possible imprisonment. Good fortune evades you throughout the year.

Year of the Dog

Two lucky stars, two unlucky stars.

Heaven will bestow good fortune on you this year, but your unlucky stars indicate a punishment or a law suit.

Year of the Pig

One unlucky star, two baleful spirits.

Take care of your finances and your health. You cannot avoid minor accidents this year.

Your Animal Sign Horoscope

THE SIGN OF THE DRAGON

The Main Attributes of Dragon People

Character
It is difficult to predict the behaviour of someone born in the year of the Dragon. Acquaintances can never guess what you are about to do or what you think. Many people are attracted to your charismatic character. You are quiet, serious and dignified in everything you do.

Luck
You are luckier than most people. You are able, popular and successful in business.

Wealth
You have a natural ability to earn money and this is helped by your upright conduct, good fortune and charismatic character.

Occupation
You are capable, but because you are an exhibitionist you cannot stay in one job for long. Do not be surprised to see a Dragon person hopping from one job to the next – this is an inborn part of the Dragon nature.

Social life
You are willing and able to take on responsibility and fulfil your promises promptly. Your social life is lively and your relationships with others are successful and trusting.

Business

You have a lot of good points, but you are overexcitable and too obstinate. Look for a business partner who is equally able. Choose someone who can use his or her quiet and calm temperament to control you when you become too excited. This combination will be successful.

Romance

If you are a man, you are handsome, attractive, generous and are likely to be surrounded by many women. If you are a woman, you are beautiful and the focus of men's attentions.

Marriage

You have many friends of both sexes so you will have no problem finding a partner. You will have a successful, long-lasting marriage.

Parents

There may be a generation gap between you and your parents and your relationship with them is troubled, especially with your father.

Brothers and sisters

You have a good relationship with your brothers and sisters because your characters are similar. You have the same interests and habits as the brothers and sisters who are closest to you in age. Although your relationship with them is strong, they do not always come to your aid with material help.

Children

Your children are lively and naughty. It is difficult to control them and your impatience and hot temper prevent you from giving them the attention they deserve.

Assets

You own two notable assets. One you have bought with your own money, the other you inherited.

Travel

You enjoy both long and short journeys because you are lively and make friends quickly.

Health
Sometimes you are tired and ill because you have been working and playing too hard. Learn to relax; you do not realize that you have been overworking.

Investment
With your partner's help you must work out a sound investment plan which controls your use of capital. Your investments will then make a profit.

Skills
Your impatience limits your skill. You must work hard for a long time before you are successful.

Speculation
You are a dreamer, constantly thinking of ways to earn money quickly and then impatiently abandoning your plans.

Hopes
Your every hope can be fulfilled because you are fortunate and popular. Heaven and earth are well balanced in your life.

Litigation
You are lucky and will usually win any law suits. However, your good fortune makes a court case unlikely, but beware of pushing your luck too far.

Lost property
Once again this reflects your luck. You normally find lost property without wasting much time.

The Character of the Dragon

From ancient times the Chinese have thought of the Dragon, Unicorn, Phoenix and the Tortoise as four supernatural creatures. They are also lucky creatures and must be respected because they symbolize spirit. According to legend, the Dragon has the face of a horse, the body of a snake and hands like chicken's claws. It can fly, swim underwater, cause rain to fall, spurt forth water and walk through clouds and fog.

The Dragon is the fifth animal of the twelve animal signs and is equal to the Earthly Branch Ch'en. Ch'en can be described as 'skipping about' or 'ready to move'.

The Dragon belongs to the third month and during the day its special time is between 7 a.m. and 9 a.m. At this time the sun and the light are becoming hotter and stronger; it is a sign of hope, the time when the natural world is active.

You have an outstanding character, strong, energetic and authoritative. Your actions are decisive and confident, like a Dragon who puffs out clouds. You will be especially successful in the world of the theatre, politics or commerce.

Your obstinacy and selfishness mask your strong moral code, but you have many good points to counterbalance these faults. You are honest and understanding and would never think of employing devious means to get what you want. You have great curiosity, are self-confident and not afraid to face challenges or difficulties. While you do everything to the best of your ability, you are suspicious of others and do not understand why you should share the fruits of your work.

Most people are influenced and impressed by what appears to be your sensible conversation and advice. You have a warm heart but a quick temper and a proud, sometimes verging on arrogant, nature. Because you consider yourself better than others, you love to give orders but find it difficult to obey the orders of others. You like to have workers under your command. Luckily, people accept your behaviour and you will be successful both socially and in your career. You are charitable and brave and your hard work enables you to fulfil your expectations. Your strong character is like a gift from Heaven.

Like all Dragon people, you are lucky. It is as though you are swimming under a warm sun; your life is comfortable and you will never be short of anything. Whatever career you choose, you will be successful. Even when you give up the idea of fame and fortune to dedicate your life to a worthy cause, you will still fulfil all your expectations. Success is the chief characteristic of the Dragon.

You will never face any romantic difficulties. Members of the opposite sex fall in love with you very easily and throughout your life you will have numerous love affairs. Love is usually treated like a game and you will very rarely be as disappointed or as hurt as your former partners. The Chinese say that this is like drinking bitter wine.

As a Dragon man you are resolute and idealistic. You may be difficult to deal with at a peronal level but are outstanding in company. You are adaptable and comfortable with people from many backgrounds. A woman who loves a Dragon man must consider her relationship very carefully and learn to plan ahead. It is extremely difficult to tie down the Dragon's heart. Men love a Dragon woman more than any other sign and, as long as her nature is understood, she will be a cheerful, warm and understanding partner.

The Dragon is suited to partnerships with the Monkey and the Rat. This combination is called San Ho – a Three Harmony. The mixing of these signs heralds a magnificent future filled with money, honours and good luck. Your family will always be proud of you. The partnership between someone born in the year of the Dragon and someone born in the year of the Snake is also auspicious. The Snake's sense of humour tempers the Dragon's pride. The Snake admires the Dragon's talent and is willing to help whenever possible.

Anyone born in the years of the Ox, the Ram, the Dog or the Pig will be unhappy in partnership with the Dragon. You need constant praise and respect, but the Ox, the Ram, the Dog and the Pig refuse to bow down to you. Your horoscope indicates destruction, separation and sorrow with these partners.

You are able to tackle any kind of job but are particularly suited to a career as a solicitor, managing director, clergyman, doctor, artist or actor.

Your Luck According to Your Year of Birth

1928, 1988

Born in the year Mou Ch'en, you belong to the Yielding Dragon.

You have an accommodating, kind, agile and distinctive character. You are close to, and receive help from, well-disposed officials. You will not be lonely, although your relationship with your children is difficult. A woman born in either of these years is gentle and kind, but usually speaks without thinking carefully beforehand. She will have a good husband.

1940, 2000

Born in the year of Ken Ch'en, you belong to the Angry Dragon.

You are arrogant, always putting yourself before others. Your personal relationships will be difficult, but you will be famous and rich. You are suited to a military career. A woman born in the year of Ken Ch'en is thrifty and hardworking.

1952, 2012

Born in the year of Jen Ch'en, you belong to the Dragon in the Rain.

You will be hardworking. Your early life will be difficult, middle age will bring changing financial luck, but your old age will be prosperous. A woman born in a Jen Ch'en year will be elegant and supportive of her husband.

1904, 1964

Born in the year of Chia Ch'en, you belong to the Cheerful Dragon.

You are handsome and kind and fight to see justice done. You are respected because you can differentiate between private and business matters. Your life will be quiet and peaceful, although your early life will be hard. In old age you will own property and land. A woman born in either of these years will be elegant and supportive of her husband.

1916, 1976

Born in the year of Ping Ch'en, you belong to the Dragon Flying to Heaven.

You are prosperous, clever and active. Your many friends will be

spread throughout the world. You will be financially comfortable in middle age. A woman born in either of these years will be a good mother and wife.

Your Fortune According to Your Month of Birth

1st month

You are patient and talented, quiet, hardworking and honest. If two jobs are required of you, you are capable of doing them both at once. You express your emotions openly whatever they may be. The first month is the strongest month and in this position the Dragon has great influence and power but the inability to form strong friendships is the weak point of someone born in this month.

You are determined and your resolution will eventually reap rewards, just as the continued spring showers nourish the trees and eventually enable the flowers to bloom. Everything you do will succeed and be praised.

2nd month

You are analytical, accommodating, happy and warm-hearted. Although you appear to be shy and weak, you are, in fact, healthy, confident, brave and always willing to take on new challenges. You can be dedicated to your work if you find it interesting, but you are easily dissatisfied when it fails to stimulate you. Although you are very fortunate you must always plan carefully otherwise your business will not be prosperous. Do not take financial risks because you will only lose your money. Be honest in your approach, satisfied with your earnings and learn to cooperate with others. You cannot hope to change the world on your own.

3rd month
You are alert, responsive and intelligent. To outsiders your character appears amenable and gentle, but underneath you are determined and stern. Because you have an appealing manner and kind intentions you make friends very easily. You have the qualities of a good leader because you inspire confidence and trust. Under your reliable leadership business ventures go from strength to strength. The Chinese would say that your fame and influence will spread like the light of the rising sun.

4th month
You are talented, alert and intelligent. You have more energy, determination, confidence and impassioned belief than most people. You are also careful, generous, understanding and occasionally naive. Whatever task you adopt, you have the strength of mind to see it thorough even if it is problematic. You have a high opinion of yourself, but you are also very protective of others and are therefore well liked.

Men and women born in the fourth month will encounter difficulties and must learn to deal with everything gradually and patiently. You will be successful and respected if you follow this advice. The Chinese say that you will shine like the light of a full moon.

5th month
You are intelligent and willing, and ready to fight for a just cause. Others are impressed by your determination and have high expectations of you. When you were young you were well loved and well educated. Your shyness limits your social life but your close relationships are successful because you are considerate. You are full of hope and energy and good opportunities will come your way. Do not be too confident or too greedy, otherwise you will fail.

6th month
You are competitive and will fight for recognition and promotion. In order to protect your fame and fortune you are willing to sacrifice

others. Many people criticize your pride and determination. You are brave, skilled in conversation, adept at planning and smart in appearance. All these factors work to your advantage, but you must avoid arrogance and cultivate humility. You are proud because you know you are talented, but do not be too impatient or intolerant.

7th month

You are clever, talented and elegant. Men born in this month have a gentle and caring side to their nature which is expressed in female company, but in male company a more aggressive and dominant side of their character emerges. Your intelligence, hard work and adaptability inspire confidence and respect. Your horoscope predicts a long life full of wealth and honours. In your youth there may be financial and emotional difficulties, but in later life these problems pass just as night clouds slide away to reveal a full moon.

8th month

You are intelligent and your agile mind is buzzing with new ideas. Whatever your career, you will be more creative than people born in other months of the Dragon year. Whenever possible you use your own intuition and rarely trouble others with trivial questions. You are frequently offered promotion because everyone appreciates your courage, intellect and energy. Although you are successful, do not be too greedy. Ensure that your enthusiasm for new ideas is not undermined by lack of research. Your horoscope is finely balanced between success and failure but your future is bright because the yin and yang in your character are well balanced.

9th month

You are a natural scholar gifted with a sharp intellect, boundless energy and abundant self-confidence. You have good powers of judgement and are full of practical commercial and financial ideas. Money will come easily to you, and when you learn to curb your extravagance you will be even wealthier. Use your good fortune to your own advantage and do not take risks with gambling or short-term investments which promise high yields. The yin and yang in your horoscope are well balanced; your thoughts and actions are in tandem.

10th month

You are talented and honest, and have the determination and stamina to achieve your aims. Your life is filled with projects and schemes which are usually successful. Always think before you act because you are as innocent as a child and often make mistakes. Sometimes you are too proud, at other times too emotional. You are popular and successful in your youth, but will destroy your good fortune if you fail to listen to advice and rely on your own intuition. Your life will be peaceful if you curb your pride and avoid quarrels. People born in this month are welcomed by others because they are truthful and cheerful.

11th month

You are quiet, sensitive and conservative. You shy away from boisterous company and have difficulty establishing close relationships. Others are sometimes hurt by your reticent manner, and unless you learn to share your feelings with others your life will be lonely. The Chinese say that no one wants to sit alone on a hilltop catching the bitter wind. Do not underestimate your capabilities; you must learn to face the public and accept challenges. You are too unassuming ever to achieve fame and fortune, but if you work hard, success is not impossible.

12th month

Your accommodating appearance belies your independence and sharp reactions. Because of your determination and ambition you can be savage in your fight to achieve your goal. You are fortunate because your luck and fate are strong, but you could ruin this through your obstinacy and selfishness. If you are thoughtful and amenable you will be successful. Although your horoscope predicts good fortune, you must be careful. Approach every opportunity thoughtfully and accept help from influential people.

Your Luck According to Your Day of Birth

Born on the 1st, 10th, 19th or 28th

You are of noble bearing, independent and trustworthy. Your standards are high and you are always ready to fight for your career. You have a determined character but are overly concerned with yourself and with achieving fame and fortune. You feel the need to complete everything quickly but you frequently fail. Be careful and cautious. You are suited to a career as a civil servant or to a job in the arts. Your fortune fluctuates, and although at times you may receive unexpected money, at others you must control your spending.

Born on the 2nd, 11th, 20th or 29th

You are quiet but honest, open-hearted and extremely popular. Sometimes you like to be alone and at other times you want to be surrounded by friends. Unless you control your temper you will fall into trouble. You are suited to a career as an artistic designer, planner or literary editor. You enjoy life, even if you are in the poorest circumstances. Your fortune will not vary greatly, but your luck will improve after middle age.

Born on the 3rd, 12th, 21st or 30th

You are talented, sensitive and react quickly. You are always ready to fight for what you know is true and just. Others will avoid forming friendships with you if you are too obstinate; they wrongly assume you are too stern and difficult. You have business acumen and are suited to a disciplined job, such as the army, or to any job which has a competitive element, such as politics or the stock exchange. You must learn how to control your spending and think seriously of ways to earn more income.

Born on the 4th, 13th, 22nd or 31st

You are calm, patient and reserved. Your appearance and attitude lead others to think you are unapproachable, although in fact you are warm-hearted. If you change your approach you will be more popular. You are suited to a career as an academic, particularly in the field of theology or philosophy. Because you cannot control your spending you will lose money as easily and as quickly as you make it.

Born on the 5th, 14th or 23rd
Your fiery, obstinate nature makes it difficult for you to accept suggestions or opinions. At times your stubbornness leads to quarrels and problems. You are suited to a career in the arts, as an academic, an administrator or an advertising designer. Your intelligence enables you to work in a highly paid job. You will be lucky with money, often using it to set up new projects.

Born on the 6th, 15th or 24th
Your open, stable and cheerful character provides you with an active social life. You are affectionate and emotional and daydream so often that your mind becomes confused. Your eagerness to help others is often stifled by your indecisiveness. A career in the arts or work as a designer or social worker would be appropriate for you. You will not be very rich but will always have enough to live on.

Born on the 7th, 16th or 25th
You are an exhibitionist but when you show off nobody wants to listen to you or watch you. You enjoy an exciting life, but your head is in the clouds; you must learn to discipline yourself. You are suited to a job which allows you mobility, for example, a reporter, a traveller or an explorer. You do not want to earn a fortune and are quite content with your standard of living.

Born on the 8th, 17th or 26th
You are calm, quiet and a good judge. You have a determined and logical mind but lack social skills. You have a free spirit and are suited to self-employment. Do not buy stocks and shares or put your money in short-term investments. Your fortune is varied – it depends on your approach. There are times of wealth and times of abject poverty.

Born on the 9th, 18th or 27th
You are happy, optimistic and warm-hearted. You have an active life and are not easily troubled by minor matters. On the whole you are magnanimous but occasionally you quarrel unnecessarily with friends. It is important that you learn to control your moods. You should work as sole director or proprietor to avoid disagreements with partners. A job involving buying and selling would be suitable. You have a good income but you are extravagant.

Your Luck According to Your 'Hour' of Birth

Tzu hours: 11 p.m.–1 a.m.

You are hot-tempered, obstinate, thrifty and shy away from challenges. You are an easy target for gossip. At times you act without sufficient planning but later you regret your actions. You will be able to build a successful business, buy a home and care for your family without a family inheritance. You will achieve fame and success independently of others but if you find yourself in trouble your parents or your marriage partner will always be there to help you out.

Unlucky ages 10, 17, 35, 48, 57.

Age at death 87.

Suitable occupations Artist, politician, architect, electrician or jobs connected with metal or water.

Unsuitable occupations Work connected with earth.

Ch'ou hours: 1–3 a.m.

If you want a good career, leave your home town while you are young. Life will be difficult up to the age of twenty but then your fortune will change for the better. You will be wealthy in old age.

Unlucky ages 17, 22, 30, 45.

Age at death 71.

Suitable occupations Commercial trader, teacher, government official, restaurateur, academic, skilled manual worker or jobs connected with the final stages of production.

Unsuitable occupations Work connected with wood.

Yin hours: 3–5 a.m.

You are on bad terms with your relatives and your early years will be difficult. You will not be left an inheritance and will leave your

home town. After the age of forty everything will work out well. Old age will bring you power and wealth.

Unlucky ages 25, 28, 32, 38, 48.

Age at death 65.

Suitable occupations Doctor, musician, artist, actor, travelling agent/representative.

Unsuitable occupations Work connected with metal.

Mao hours: 5–7 a.m.
You will be very fortunate, with occasional help from your parents but none from your brothers and sisters. You will have a comfortable life and be wealthy if you work away from your home town. Marriage will be unsteady and difficult in the early years, but after middle age you will develop more satisfactory relationships and will have the chance to be wealthy.

Unlucky ages 15, 19, 54.

Age at death 71.

Suitable occupations Mechanical engineer, actor, writer, artist, theologian or work connected with religion.

Unsuitable occupations Work connected with fire.

Ch'en hours: 7–9 a.m.
You are clever, quick-witted and determined. Your warm-hearted nature enables you to form close friendships. Life is busy and varied, but a woman born in the Ch'en hours will be lonely. However, you will have many material possessions and a good salary. Your excessive self-confidence makes working relationships difficult.

Unlucky ages 18, 26, 35, 38.

Age at death 65.

Suitable occupations Entrepreneur, politician, public relations officer, teacher, miner.

Unsuitable occupations Work connected with wood.

Szu hours: 9–11 a.m.
You have outstanding talent and are able to build up your business and care for your family successfully. Family relations are troubled and you would prosper financially if you were to leave your home town. You are kind to your friends and like to help them when they are in trouble. A woman born in the Szu hours is extravagant and may have an unhappy marriage. Men and women born in these hours drink too much.

Unlucky ages 30, 35, 46, 48.

Age at death 88.

Suitable occupations Civil or electrical engineer, architect, wood or wine merchant.

Unsuitable occupations Work connected with water.

Wu hours: 11 a.m.–1 p.m.
You are active, clever, obstinate and extravagant. You prefer travelling to settling down to a job in your local area. A woman born in these hours is likely to have an unusual and fascinating character.

Unlucky ages 5, 11, 23, 32, 44, 53.

Age at death 84.

Suitable occupations Doctor, nurse, politician, film actor, skilled worker, jobs in the service industries or any work connected with oil.

Unsuitable occupations Work connected with gold.

Wei hours: 1–3 p.m.
You have a troubled relationship with your parents, brothers and

sisters and marriage partner. You will have serious difficulties in middle age. A woman born in these hours is clever but will always have difficulties with her marriage because she is too active to settle down.

Unlucky ages 18, 25, 55.

Age at death 69.

Suitable occupations Civil engineer, electrical engineer, architect, wood merchant, wine merchant.

Unsuitable occupations Work connected with water.

Shen hours: 3–5 p.m.

You will earn money easily and spend it freely. You will be luckier if you work outside your home town. Your marriage will be harmonious although your parents will not offer you moral support. A woman born in the Shen hours will be married twice. Because you are too active ever to settle down completely it is important that you are seen to behave honourably. Too much time worrying over relationships will cause your business to fail.

Unlucky ages 18, 21, 27, 29, 41, 53.

Age at death 71.

Suitable occupations Finance-related work – e.g. broker, public relations officer, watchmaker, manager – or work connected with metal.

Unsuitable occupations Work connected with wood.

Yu hours: 5–7 p.m.

Your youth is difficult because of troubled family relationships. You will be separated from your brothers and sisters and will leave home when young. You may not be able to have a child but it will be possible to adopt one. A woman born in the Yu hours is warm-hearted, fond of food and can be trusted to keep a secret.

Unlucky ages 18, 24, 31, 48.

Age at death 77.

Suitable occupations Chemist, researcher/writer, teacher, artist, technologist or work connected with the final stages of production.

Unsuitable occupations Work connected with earth.

Hsü hours: 7–9 p.m.
You are brave, capable, hardworking and run your business alone. You are optimistic and will have a successful life and a flourishing career. A woman born in the Hsü hours can be vain and impatient. You are magnanimous but on the other hand money is not important to you. You care little for others but will have a magnificent life.

Unlucky ages 15, 25, 34, 43, 48, 56.

Age at death 77.

Suitable occupations Poet, writer, investor, engineer, rice or cereal merchant, or work connected with metal and agriculture.

Unsuitable occupations Work connected with fire.

Hai hours: 9–11 p.m.
You are manually dextrous and set yourself high standards. Although you are warm-hearted you do not like to make too many friends. A woman born in the Hai hours can be obstinate. Others may be easily upset but you have the ability to forgive and forget. You are hardworking and will be fortunate.

Unlucky ages 10, 25, 35, 38, 48, 55.

Age at death 77.

Suitable occupations Surgeon, monk/nun, hotelier, artist, antiques dealer or work connected with metal.

Unsuitable occupations Work connected with fire.

Practical Advice

Your work performance is more important to you than your appearance.
Act carefully. Do not let private affairs upset you too much.
Trust your own creativity.
Your bad temper could cause trouble. A calm approach will bring success.
Be decisive about your business plans.
Be patient, otherwise success will turn to failure.
There will be a time of loss and sadness in your life.
Take regular exercise.
Set yourself high goals.
Do not be too obstinate; give others the benefit of the doubt.
Do not procrastinate; start your important jobs today.

Your Luck Year by Year

Year of the Rat
Two lucky stars, two unlucky stars.

This is an excellent financial year; there is one unlucky period but the amount of money you lose will be minimal. You will also be promoted at work.

Year of the Ox
Two lucky stars, one unlucky star.

During the year you will quarrel with petty-minded people, but everything will run smoothly afterwards.

Year of the Tiger
Four unlucky stars.

The Dragon will fight with the Tiger during the year. You will be fortunate but only outside your home country. There may be a period of mourning for one of your relatives.

Year of the Rabbit
Three unlucky stars.

You will be troubled by minor illnesses this year. You will leave your home to travel abroad and bring nothing but illness home.

Year of the Dragon
One lucky star, two unlucky stars.

Your energy is used up on many exciting projects. You will be given the opportunity to further your studies and acquire a skill.

Year of the Snake
Two lucky stars, one baleful spirit.

Under the Pao Chia star everything that you want will be fulfilled. Avoid burial ceremonies; the evil spirits will harm you if you go near graves at night.

Year of the Horse
Four unlucky stars.

This is a year full of disasters and difficulties. A relative will fall ill and you will be unlucky throughout the year.

Year of the Ram
Four unlucky stars.

During the year you will lose money and be injured. Be careful; you will be involved in a law suit and may be sent to prison.

Year of the Monkey
Five unlucky stars.

One of your parents may die. You will quarrel with your friends and be involved in a law suit. Your wife or your husband will be seriously injured.

Year of the Cock
Three lucky stars, one unlucky star.

The Dragon and the Cock are well matched. You will be lucky throughout the year, although there may be a minor illness or a small financial loss.

Year of the Dog
Four unlucky stars.

The Dragon and the Dog are not compatible. It will be a year of quarrels and loss.

Year of the Pig
Three lucky stars.

The Tzu Wei star is shining on you. This is the year in which to marry if you are still single. Everything you touch will turn out well; money, success and fame will come your way.

Your Animal Sign Horoscope

THE SIGN OF THE SNAKE

The Main Attributes of Snake People

Character
Like the Snake, you are cool, quiet and reserved.

Luck
However hard you work in your youth, you will never be able to save money. You will be helped by someone in an influential position and your fortune will improve in middle age. In old age you will be respected and wealthy.

Wealth
You will be fortunate because you have good self-control and can understand situations clearly and logically.

Occupation
You are a quiet person and enjoy thinking and reading. You are suited to work related to astrology.

Social life
You do not want an active social life. You dislike parties and prefer peaceful evenings at home.

Business
Choose a business that suits your qualifications and your environment. You will be slow to start a business and you may lose money at first, but persevere because you will eventually be wealthy and famous.

Romance
You do not take romance seriously. Try to be more constant.

Marriage
You will follow your family's advice when choosing a partner. You are likely to meet your husband or wife through friends or family.

Parents
Because of your reserved nature you rarely discuss your problems with your family and do not want to accept their help.

Brothers and sisters
You find it difficult to discuss your peronal life with your brothers and sisters and they are unable to help you.

Children
You care deeply for your children. You are willing to sacrifice yourself for their needs and take responsibility for their mistakes.

Assets
Your clarity of vision helps you make wise decisions. When you are young you will own property and land.

Travel
You are unable to relax; even when you are on holiday you are making plans for the future.

Health
You have nervous problems because you spend so much time thinking about your life and future.

Investment
Your confidence and good judgement will help you deal successfully with investments.

Skills
You have the necessary patience and power of concentration to acquire new skills.

Speculation
If you are willing to invest your money, you will reap good profits in short-term investment.

Hopes
Your hopes for a wealthy life will be realized.

Litigation
Do not be greedy and you will rarely be involved in law suits. If you are involved in a law suit you will usually win.

Lost property
You have a good memory and will have no difficulty retrieving lost property.

The Character of the Snake

The Snake is the sixth animal in the cycle of the twelve and corresponds to the Earthly Branch Szu. Szu hours are between 9 and 11 o'clock, and belongs to the fourth month, a time of activity, growth and development. The Snake represents kindness, intelligence and wisdom, and those born in this year also have these characteristics.

You are sensitive, amenable, attractive and decisive. You are able to make trusting and long-term friendships. Your ideas are original and well thought out and your actions are planned carefully beforehand. You will be successful because you never abandon your goals until they are achieved or your work until it is finished. You are confident and sensible and a good judge of situations and people. You enjoy debate and investigation and dislike wasting time on idle chatter. Once you have set your mind on something you will complete it no matter how many difficulties you face; at the same time you will rarely lose patience with others.

You will never be short of money or good luck, but your desire for money and property can make you selfish, moody and proud. Although you have a protective and caring side to your character, once you have been offended you will always take revenge.

You jealously guard the things or the people who are close to you.

Even if you have affairs outside marriage, you still cling on to your relationship with your husband/wife and make every effort to keep him/her in your control.

A man born in this year is humorous, romantic and very attractive to women. A woman born in this year is irresistible to men and is usually the centre of attention at a party. Men and women born in this year are drawn to affairs outside married life. If you want a happy marriage, concentrate on domestic affairs; do not let yourself be drawn away by outside interests.

Someone born in the year of the Ox will be a good marriage or business partner. The hard-working Ox person will tolerate your selfishness and will accept family responsibility. A marriage with someone born in the year of the Cock will be successful if you learn to cooperate with each other. Someone born in the year of the Rat, the Rabbit, the Dragon, the Horse or the Ram will make a suitable partner. Avoid choosing someone born in the year of the Tiger, the Monkey or the Pig. The Pig will make a particularly bad partner; the Chinese say that the Pig will fall into the Snake's trap. Your relationship will be full of disagreements over major and minor matters.

You are suited to a career as a philosopher, politician, lawyer, psychologist, teacher, entrepreneur, restaurateur or adviser on public relations or foreign affairs.

Your Luck According to Your Year of Birth

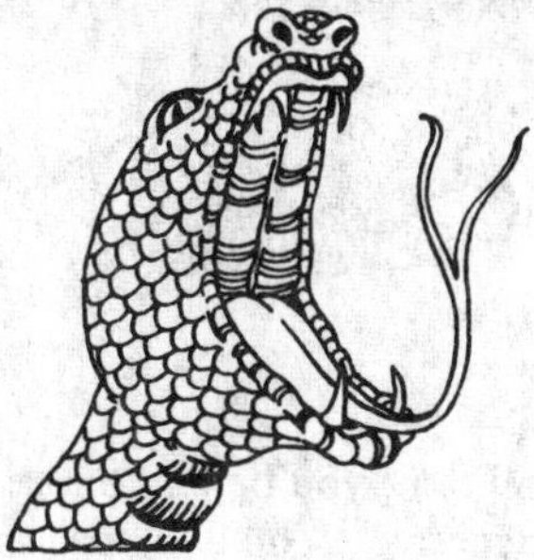

1929, 1989

Born in the year of Chi Szu, you belong to the Prosperous Snake.

You are active and fortunate. You will be well known and wealthy; whatever you do will work out successfully. A woman born in either of these years will be kind and caring, but she will not be as wealthy as a man born in these years.

1941, 2001

Born in the year of Hsin Szu, you belong to the Snake Sleeping in the Winter.

You are thrifty, ambitious and changeable. You will helped by an official in a position of authority and will always be prosperous. A man born in either of these years should marry an older woman.

1953, 2013

Born in the year of Kuei Szu, you belong to the Snake on the Grass.

You are clever and active. You will be unable to accumulate savings in your youth but will be helped by someone in a position of authority. You will be financially secure in your old age. A woman born in either of these years will quarrel with her family in her youth but will be steady and hardworking after marriage.

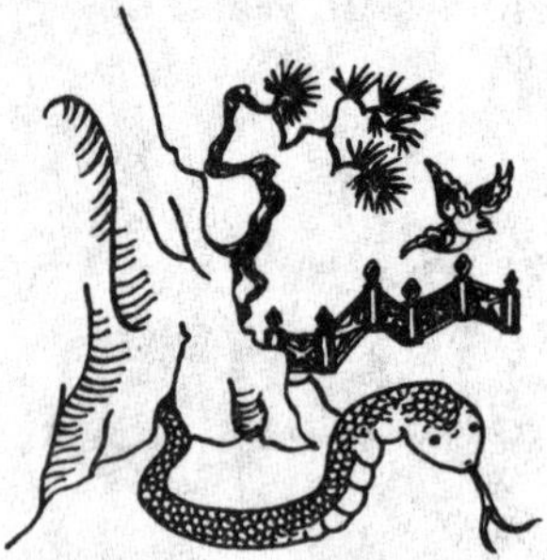

1905, 1965

Born in the year of Yi Szu, you belong to the Snake Coming out the Hole.

You are honest and popular. You will rarely be praised, no matter how kind, generous and heroic you are. Have children late in life; you will argue less with them. A woman born in either of these years will be well known and wealthy.

1917, 1977
Born in the year of Ting Szu, you belong to the Snake in the Fish Pond.

You have an obstinate character, but you will be helped by a wealthy official. An eldest son born in this year will have a lucky life, full of honours and riches.

Your Luck According to Your Month of Birth

1st month
You are content, reserved and active. Your amenable and happy nature makes you a popular friend. You have an open mind and enjoy acquiring new skills or knowledge. Although you work very hard, you miss opportunities because you are too reserved. You will be successful in your career and in married life if you are more confident and relaxed.

2nd month
You have a changeable character: sometimes you are cool and reserved and at other times you are warm and energetic. Your enthusiasm for your friends and career is short-lived due to your impatience. If you learn to relax and concentrate on one project at a time, you will be more successful. You will never be short of wealth or good fortune, but your desires will never be fulfilled if you are dissatisfied with your belongings or your position in life.

3rd month

You have a suspicious, unstable character although you appear to be lively and confident. You respond angrily to orders and disagree with others' ideas. You argue because of lack of confidence, not because you enjoy quarrels. You enjoy study and research and should choose a career which utilizes your skills and interests. Choose work which gives you the freedom to plan and organize your work.

4th month

You are confident, serious and responsible. You are hardworking enough to run your own business but you will only be successful if you are more accommodating and understanding. Do not be too idealistic, do not be jealous of the success of others, and choose a job according to your ability. You will be able to develop your career as soon as you learn to control your finances.

5th month

You are stubborn and excitable. You are considerate on the surface but thoughtless and selfish underneath. You must be more understanding if you want to make and keep friends. Your sense of justice is one of the strongest points of your character; you may criticize your friends but you help them if they are being treated unfairly. Your wishes will be realized late in life. Be patient, act according to the situation and do not let opportunities pass you by.

6th month

You are intelligent and quick in judgement and action. You are carefree and enjoy good food, conversation and clothes. Many people are drawn to your amenable and warm-hearted character. Use your intelligence to your advantage; you have the strength to achieve your goals. You will have an enjoyable life free from financial difficulties, but you will lose money if you become involved in extramarital affairs.

7th month

You are honest, trustworthy and hardworking. You are able to work alongside all types of people. Your success will be affected by your independence and frequent swings of opinion. Try hard to finish your work and to accept the advice of others. Women born in this month enjoy an active social life but are not willing to marry. Men born in this month treat romance as a game and frequently change girlfriends.

8th month
You are active, kind and well respected. You will make a good leader, but will sometimes miss good opportunities because of your inconstancy. You are humble and amenable and have a good sense of humour. Your enthusiasm and adaptability are two of your strongest points and you can enliven any social gathering. You will always have an active social life and your relationships with others will continue to improve as you grow older.

9th month
You are determined to achieve your goals. Once you have put your mind to something, you will see it through to the end regardless of the difficulties along the way. You are a good worker but lack social skills. If you were more understanding you would not be bored and upset by relationships. Be kind and confident and others will help you in return.

10th month
You are active, honest, generous and straightforward. You are trusted by others and can adapt to any career or occupation. You will be successful by middle age because of help from an older friend or colleague when you were younger. This is the month when yang changes to yin; this brings out a weak, complaining and careless side to your character. Try to correct these faults; think carefully before you do anything and listen to others' advice.

11th month
You are intelligent, emotional and peaceful, but you also lack judgement and a strong will. Your luck will improve if you are more responsible and confident. Although you will never have an outstanding career, you will be financially secure if you take life step by step. Do not be too trusting and learn to be patient. Avoid excitment and stress if you want to live a safe and peaceful life.

12th month
You are active, content, just, composed and straightforward. You are unable to hide your feelings or keep a secret. You are generous, work hard to achieve your goals and can adapt to any environment.

If you want to be successful, try to accept others' opinions. A woman born in this month is usually discontented with her marriage partner, regardless of his qualities. Do not betray your husband; be thankful for his good qualities.

Your Luck According to Your Day of Birth

Born on the 1st, 10th, 19th or 28th
You are of noble bearing, independent and trustworthy. Your standards are high and you are always ready to fight for your career. You have a determined character but are overly concerned with yourself and with achieving fame and fortune. You feel the need to complete everything quickly but you frequently fail. Be careful and cautious. You are suited to a career as a civil servant or to a job in the arts. Your fortune fluctuates, and although at times you may receive unexpected money, at others you must control your spending.

Born on the 2nd, 11th, 20th or 29th
You are quiet but honest, open-hearted and extremely popular. Sometimes you like to be alone and at other times you want to be surrounded by friends. Unless you control your temper you will fall into trouble. You are suited to a career as an artistic designer, planner or literary editor. You enjoy life, even if you are in the poorest circumstances. Your fortune will not vary greatly, but your luck will improve after middle age.

Born on the 3rd, 12th, 21st or 30th
You are talented, sensitive and react quickly. You are always ready to fight for what you know is true and just. Others will avoid forming friendships with you if you are too obstinate; they wrongly assume you are too stern and difficult. You have business acumen and are suited to a disciplined job, such as the army, or to any job which has a competitive element, such as politics or the stock exchange. You must learn how to control your spending and think seriously of ways to earn more income.

Born on the 4th, 13th, 22nd or 31st
You are calm, patient and reserved. Your appearance and attitude lead others to think you are unapproachable, although in fact you

are warm-hearted. If you change your approach you will be more popular. You are suited to a career as an academic, particularly in the field of theology or philosophy. Because you cannot control your spending you will lose money as easily and as quickly as you make it.

Born on the 5th, 14th or 23rd

Your fiery, obstinate nature makes it difficult for you to accept suggestions or opinions. At times your stubbornness leads to quarrels and problems. You are suited to a career in the arts, as an academic, an administrator or an advertising designer. Your intelligence enables you to work in a highly paid job. You will be lucky with money, often using it to set up new projects.

Born on the 6th, 15th or 24th

Your open, stable and cheerful character provides you with an active social life. You are affectionate and emotional and daydream so often that your mind becomes confused. Your eagerness to help others is often stifled by your indecisiveness. A career in the arts or work as a designer or social worker would be appropriate for you. You will not be very rich but will always have enough to live on.

Born on the 7th, 16th or 25th

You are an exhibitionist but when you show off nobody wants to listen to you or watch you. You enjoy an exciting life, but your head is in the clouds; you must learn to discipline yourself. You are suited to a job which allows you mobility, for example, a reporter, a traveller or an explorer. You do not want to earn a fortune and are quite content with your standard of living.

Born on the 8th, 17th or 26th

You are calm, quiet and a good judge. You have a determined and logical mind but lack social skills. You have a free spirit and are suited to self-employment. Do not buy stocks and shares or put your money in short-term investments. Your fortune is varied – it depends on your approach. There are times of wealth and times of abject poverty.

Born on the 9th, 18th or 27th

You are happy, optimistic and warm-hearted. You have an active life and are not easily troubled by minor matters. On the whole you are magnanimous but occasionally you quarrel unnecessarily with friends. It is important that you learn to control your moods. You should work as sole director or proprietor to avoid disagreements with partners. A job involving buying and selling would be suitable. You have a good income but you are extravagant.

Your Luck According to Your 'Hour' of Birth

Tzu hours: 11 p.m.–1 a.m.
You are hot-tempered, obstinate, thrifty and shy away from challenges. You are an easy target for gossip. At times you act without sufficient planning but later you regret your actions. You will be able to build a successful business, buy a home and care for your family without a family inheritance. You will achieve fame and success independently of others but if you find yourself in trouble your parents or your marriage partner will always be there to help you out.

Unlucky ages 10, 17, 35, 48, 57.

Age at death 87.

Suitable occupations Artist, politician, architect, electrician or jobs connected with metal or water.

Unsuitable occupations Work connected with earth.

Ch'ou hours: 1–3 a.m.
If you want a good career, leave your home town while you are young. Life will be difficult up to the age of twenty but then your fortune will change for the better. You will be wealthy in old age.

Unlucky ages 17, 22, 30, 45.

Age at death 71.

Suitable occupations Commercial trader, teacher, government official, restaurateur, academic, skilled manual worker or jobs connected with the final stages of production.

Unsuitable occupations Work connected with wood.

Yin hours: 3–5 a.m.
You are on bad terms with your relatives and your early years will be difficult. You will not be left an inheritance and will leave your home town. After the age of forty everything will work out well. Old age will bring you power and wealth.

Unlucky ages 25, 28, 32, 38, 48.

Age at death 65.

Suitable occupations Doctor, musician, artist, actor, travelling agent/representative.

Unsuitable occupations Work connected with metal.

Mao hours: 5–7 a.m.
You will be very fortunate, with occasional help from your parents but none from your brothers and sisters. You will have a comfortable life and be wealthy if you work away from your home town. Marriage will be unsteady and difficult in the early years, but after middle age you will develop more satisfactory relationships and will have the chance to be wealthy.

Unlucky ages 15, 19, 54.

Age at death 71.

Suitable occupations Mechanical engineer, actor, writer, artist, theologian or work connected with religion.

Unsuitable occupations Work connected with fire.

Ch'en hours: 7–9 a.m.
You are clever, quick-witted and determined. Your warm-hearted nature enables you to form close friendships. Life is busy and varied, but a woman born in the Ch'en hours will be lonely. However, you will have many material possessions and a good

salary. Your excessive self-confidence makes working relationships difficult.

Unlucky ages 18, 26, 35, 38.

Age at death 65.

Suitable occupations Entrepreneur, politician, public relations officer, teacher, miner.

Unsuitable occupations Work connected with wood.

Szu hours: 9–11 a.m.
You have outstanding talent and are able to build up your business and care for your family successfully. Family relations are troubled and you would prosper financially if you were to leave your home town. You are kind to your friends and like to help them when they are in trouble. A woman born in the Szu hours is extravagant and may have an unhappy marriage. Men and women born in these hours drink too much.

Unlucky ages 30, 35, 46, 48.

Age at death 88.

Suitable occupations Civil or electrical engineer, architect, wood or wine merchant.

Unsuitable occupations Work connected with water.

Wu hours: 11 a.m.–1 p.m.
You are active, clever, obstinate and extravagant. You prefer travelling to settling down to a job in your local area. A woman born in these hours is likely to have an unusual and fascinating character.

Unlucky ages 5, 11, 23, 32, 44, 53.

Age at death 84.

Suitable occupations Doctor, nurse, politician, film actor, skilled worker, jobs in the service industries or any work connected with oil.

Unsuitable occupations Work connected with gold.

Wei hours: 1–3 p.m.
You have a troubled relationship with your parents, brothers and sisters and marriage partner. You will have serious difficulties in middle age. A woman born in these hours is clever but will always have difficulties with her marriage because she is too active to settle down.

Unlucky ages 18, 25, 55.

Age at death 69.

Suitable occupations Civil engineer, electrical engineer, architect, wood merchant, wine merchant.

Unsuitable occupations Work connected with water.

Shen hours: 3–5 p.m.
You will earn money easily and spend it freely. You will be luckier if you work outside your home town. Your marriage will be harmonious although your parents will not offer you moral support. A woman born in the Shen hours will be married twice. Because you are too active ever to settle down completely it is important that you are seen to behave honourably. Too much time worrying over relationships will cause your business to fail.

Unlucky ages 18, 21, 27, 29, 41, 53.

Age at death 71.

Suitable occupations Finance-related work – e.g. broker, public relations officer, watchmaker, manager – or work connected with metal.

Unsuitable occupations Work connected with wood.

Yu hours: 5–7 p.m.
Your youth is difficult because of troubled family relationships. You will be separated from your brothers and sisters and will leave home when young. You may not be able to have a child but it will be possible to adopt one. A woman born in the Yu hours is warm-hearted, fond of food and can be trusted to keep a secret.

Unlucky ages 18, 24, 31, 48.

Age at death 77.

Suitable occupations Chemist, researcher/writer, teacher, artist, technologist or work connected with the final stages of production.

Unsuitable occupations Work connected with earth.

Hsü hours: 7–9 p.m.
You are brave, capable, hardworking and run your business alone. You are optimistic and will have a successful life and a flourishing career. A woman born in the Hsü hours can be vain and impatient. You are magnanimous but on the other hand money is not important to you. You care little for others but will have a magnificent life.

Unlucky ages 15, 25, 34, 43, 48, 56.

Age at death 77.

Suitable occupations Poet, writer, investor, engineer, rice or cereal merchant, or work connected with metal and agriculture.

Unsuitable occupations Work connected with fire.

Hai hours: 9–11 p.m.
You are manually dextrous and set yourself high standards. Although you are warm-hearted you do not like to make too many friends. A woman born in the Hai hours can be obstinate. Others may be easily upset but you have the ability to forgive and forget. You are hardworking and will be fortunate.

Unlucky ages 10, 25, 35, 38, 48, 55.

Age at death 77.

Suitable occupations Surgeon, monk/nun, hotelier, artist, antiques dealer or work connected with metal.

Unsuitable occupations Work connected with fire.

Practical Advice

Avoid friendships with corrupt or immoral people.
Treat everyone with kindness and respect regardless of their position.
Be thoughtful; even the smallest gift will make your friends and family happy.
Do not be distressed by difficulties. Try your best to overcome them.
Avoid late nights; they are bad for your health.
Be thoughful and obedient to your parents.
Learn to distinguish the good from the bad, the destructive from the constructive.
Face reality; do not harbour impossible dreams.
Make an effort to achieve your goals.
Rest whenever you feel tired because health is the greatest fortune in life.
It is better to have a peaceful mind in a noisy environment than a troubled mind in a peaceful environment.
Use patience and honesty to achieve your goals.

Your Luck Year by Year

Year of the Rat
Three lucky stars.

This is a happy and fortunate year. You will be offered good promotion and if you are single you will meet a suitable marriage partner. You will lose money during the year but your lucky stars will protect you from failure.

Year of the Ox
One lucky star, two unlucky stars.

This is a year of difficulties, disasters and business loss. Be careful and patient. Even though you are intelligent and alert you will be cheated by an unscrupulous acquaintance.

Year of the Tiger
One lucky star, three unlucky stars.

This is a year of quarrels, financial loss and business failure, but your lucky star will help you turn misfortune to fortune.

Year of the Rabbit
Four unlucky stars.

This is a year of disasters and difficulties and most of your time will be spent at home. Be kind, honest and patient. Do not push yourself forward; wait for good fortune to arrive.

Year of the Dragon
Two lucky stars, five unlucky stars.

This is a year when men and woman will be deceitful and adulterous. There will be quarrels, problems and law suits during the year, but your lucky stars will help you fight these misfortunes.

Year of the Snake
Six unlucky stars.

This is a year of financial loss and ill health. Choose your friends wisely and do not place your confidence in little-known acquaintances.

Year of the Horse
Two unlucky stars.

This is a difficult and unfortunate year. For men this is a year of ill health and foreign travel in search of work. Women who have a child this year will suffer a period of ill health after the birth.

Year of the Ram
Three unlucky stars.

There will be problems with your career and your domestic life. You may have to wear mourning clothes during the year.

Year of the Monkey
One lucky star, two unlucky stars.

There will be misfortune and disasters at the beginning of the year, but once these have passed it will be a year of happiness.

Year of the Cock
Three lucky stars, two baleful stars.

This is a good year for business and family life. Your lucky stars are shining on you although there will be some minor problems.

Year of the Dog
Two lucky stars, two unlucky stars.

If you are single you will meet a good marriage partner this year. There will be sickness and financial loss, but your lucky stars will help you. You will have the opportunity to emigrate or to travel abroad.

Year of the Pig
Three unlucky stars.

You will earn a good salary this year but you may put on mourning clothes or be involved in a law suit.

Your Animal Sign Horoscope

THE SIGN OF THE HORSE

The Main Attributes of Horse People

Character
You have the independent and confident nature of the Horse. You are easily flattered by praise, just as a horse is calmed by soft words and gentle stroking.

Luck
You will be successful because you work hard to achieve your goals.

Wealth
Your hard work reaps rewards but you do not find the time to invest your money wisely so you will never be very rich.

Occupation
You are active and alert. You should look for a job that is out of the ordinary.

Social life
You have an average social life but you will be helped by someone in an influential position.

Business
Your business will prosper if you work hard.

Romance
A man born in the year of the Horse does not take romance seriously but romance is the most important thing in life for a woman born in this year.

Marriage
Find a partner who is willing to take care of the house because you are too busy to worry about domestic affairs. Your partner will also have to take care of you as well as the family.

Parents
You are close to your mother but your relationship with your father is unsteady and argumentative.

Brothers and sisters
You are on very bad terms with your brothers and sisters.

Children
You have a good relationship with your children. You never punish them severely and only give them good advice.

Assets
You have to work very hard before you can accumulate any assets. You will be financially stable by the age of forty.

Travel
You travel frequently but you are never satisfied with the results of your journeying.

Health
You have a healthy constitution and rarely suffer any serious illness.

Investment
Think clearly before you invest any money if you want to avoid financial problems.

Skills
Learn a new skill, then perfect it and you will have good fortune.

Speculation
You will make a small profit from short-term investment but avoid taking risks.

Hopes
You are good at work which requires physical and mental effort.

You will be successful in a small family business, but you will never be a millionaire.

Litigation
You will never be lucky in law suits.

Lost property
If you lose property you will rarely find it. If you lose friends or family you are unlikely to make contact with them again.

The Character of the Horse

The Horse is linked to the element Fire and is represented by the Earthly Branch Wu. The Horse's time is one hour before noon and one hour after noon, the brightest time of the day. Wu is matched to the fifth month, a month of flowers and light. Yang's energy is at its strongest during the summer solstice. Wu is a time for creation to show itself in all its natural beauty.

You have an honest, caring character and attract many friends. Although you are popular you cannot keep secrets and sometimes become too involved in your friends' private lives. You have the hardworking, independent and cheerful character of the Horse, but your perseverance is limited; if you fail several times you become impatient and upset.

You care about your appearance and enjoy expensive clothes. Before going out you spend a long time looking at yourself in front of a mirror. You make the most of life; you enjoy music, sport, politics, debating and any other interests which involve people. Your skilled oratory and strong leadership qualities are suited to a political career. You recognize what others are going to say before they have even spoken. You are active, confident and trust your own judgement.

Your impatience and your hot temper are your weakest points. Your ambition also makes you selfish and ready to override those who stand in your way. You always think you will succeed because you have a high opinion of yourself. You are, however, a talented entrepreneur but your impatience sometimes prevents you from achieving your aims. You like to work as part of a team but you always need to be praised and respected. Try to be more tolerant and you will be successful.

You will have a fortunate life. You may not be rich but you will be praised, and you will be the focus of attention because you have an adventurous spirit.

A woman born in the Ping Wu years must take special care because she will usually be on bad terms with her husband. People born in the year of the Horse are usually honest but hesitant in romance. Once they have found a lover they are committed for life.

You are willing to give up everything for the sake of your partner, but this could be your downfall. You are willing to sacrifice yourself for your lover but you neglect everything in your life in order to win his or her heart.

If you are looking for a business or marriage partner, choose someone who was born in the years of the Tiger, the Ram or the Dog. Your ideal partner is someone born in the year of the Ram. Your marriage would be long, fortunate and happy because you would be committed to each other and to your family. You would be reasonably happy if you married someone born in the years of the Dragon, the Snake, the Monkey or the Cock. Your married life would run smoothly because you would respect each other, and this respect would provide a firm basis for husband and wife to achieve their goals. Avoid marrying someone born in the year of the Rat, the Ox, the Rabbit or the Horse. You would always quarrel with your partner because you would never find any common ground. You would be short of money and your career would flounder. Your partner might leave you or suffer a serious injury.

You are suited to a career as an explorer, geographer, actor, advertising executive, artist, builder, entrepreneur, skilled worker, doctor, soldier, politician or chemist.

Your Luck According to Your Year of Birth

1930, 1990

Born in the year of Keng Wu, you belong to the Horse in the Hall.

You are candid and sincere but speak without sufficient forethought. You will never be short of work and will be helped by an influential official. A man born in these years has a powerful character and is a devoted father and husband. A woman born in these years will make a good wife and mother.

1942, 2002

Born in the year of Jen Wu, you belong to the Horse in the Army.

You are hardworking, thrifty and have a troubled relationship with your family. You will be poor in your youth but wealthy and famous in old age. A woman born in these years will earn or receive a great fortune.

1954, 2014

Born in the year of Chia Wu, you belong to the Horse in the Clouds.

You are accommodating, kind and quick to act. You will be wealthy, and when in need you will be helped by an influential official. You are able to turn suffering and hardship into happiness and health. You enjoy a wide circle of friends. You will have few children but your old age will be prosperous. A woman born in either of these years will be a good housewife, but she speaks without thinking first.

1906, 1966

Born in the year of Ping Wu, you belong to the Horse on the Way.

You will not earn much money when you are young so you must work diligently. You are suited to a career in sales, trade or craft. You will have a prosperous old age. A woman born in either of these years will have a quiet nature and be a good housewife, but she will usually be on bad terms with her husband.

1918, 1978
Born in the year of Mou Wu, you belong to the Horse within the Gate.

You are accommodating and kind. When you are young you will meet accidents and disasters and will often quarrel with your brothers. You will have a prosperous old age.

Your Luck According to Your Month of Birth

1st month
You are obstinate, proud, romantic and powerful. Your intelligence, independence and patience give you the strength to persevere, regardless of problems and failures. You have a regal presence and will be respected by others.

You will have a relaxed attitude towards money in the first thirty years of your life; you spend it as easily as you earn it. From the age of thirty you will be very wealthy, particularly if you own your own business. You will also receive unexpected money.

You never accept other people's advice. You are too self-centred and concerned with fortune and fame. You will be happier and more successful if you correct these faults.

2nd month
You are active, generous, honourable, impassioned and masculine. You are likely to come from a respectable and wealthy background. You have an innocent character and fail to understand the ways of the world, but you are socially popular and attractive to the opposite

sex. Your pride is your weak point because you know you are attractive and expect others to flatter you. Once you have learned to curb your pride you can expect a long and happy marriage. You will be prosperous, but do not risk your savings in short-term investment.

3rd month

You are kind and generous, but you are also a daydreamer. You enjoy an active social life. You are easily disappointed because you aim too high for your abilities. Most of the time you sink into a dream world where you can find satisfaction. Your bravery and generosity are respected, but you will encounter difficulties and disasters. You are constantly tired and nervous because you try too hard to be successful. You will be prosperous when you are young, but will save very little because of your extravagance. Try to plan your finances carefully.

4th month

You are careful, stylish, proud, obstinate, active and vain. You respect your parents, family and relatives, but you upset others by your conversation. Be more polite, accept criticism and listen to others' opinions. You will have many duties and responsibilities and will travel extensively. Your life will be busy and difficult. Your salary is spent as soon as it is earned.

5th month

You are talented but slow to react. You are a gifted writer and good at interpreting others' motives and feelings. You are seldom wrong in your judgements. You can improve your weak points by studying the conversation and behaviour of others. Before marriage you will be passionate and dedicated to your partner, but this will disappear after marriage. A man born in this month puts his energy into work; a woman born in this month puts her energy into housework.

6th month

You are straightforward, clever, brave, passionate and socially popular. You like to demonstrate your abilities by working as a entrepreneur, artist, politician or diplomat. Everything you do when you are young will work out successfully, but after middle age you will have to find a suitable business partner if you want to be wealthy and famous. Someone born in the year of the Tiger, the Ram or the Ox would make a suitable partner.

7th month
You are kind, honourable, careful and understanding. You approach work and play seriously. You are willing to sacrifice yourself to help others, but sometimes miss good opportunities because you fail to see things clearly. You are not lucky, but if you are patient you will have a peaceful life. Everything may seem hopeless at first, but take life step by step. Be patient; you will be successful in the end. You have few savings because you are extravagant, but you will be helped by someone in an influential position.

8th month
You fail to see the practical side of life and judge everything emotionally. You are an exhibitionist: you consider yourself to be the first and the best. Try to empathize with others instead of charging ahead with your plans. Concentrate on one thing at a time to avoid swift changes of mood. It will be easier to find a partner if you try to understand other people's hobbies and interests.

9th month
You are kind, straightforward, clever, frank and warm-hearted. You never refuse requests for help, but you never ask for help when you are in trouble. Your relationship with your family and friends is strong and trusting. You appear dull, but you are intelligent. If you want to be successful do not let any opportunities pass you by. There will be difficulties after middle age, so be careful not to undertake any new projects without careful consideration. Accept the advice of older, more experienced people.

10th month
You are brave, confident, patient and very intelligent. You are inspired by the simplest of conversations and will be successful in whatever you do. You are a self-reliant worker, a talented inventor and a skilled student and researcher. Try not to show off because this weakness will isolate you from others as you grow older. There will be times when you may need others' advice. Once you have

found a good working partner, you will be helped by someone in an influential position.

11th month
People born in this month are usually lonely; they have few if any relatives. You are independent, confident and seldom affected by the opinions of others. Whatever you deal with, you use your own ideas and imagination. You enjoy investigating suspicious incidents and secret matters. You are easily satisfied so you do not always put the necessary effort into your work; as a result your promotion or development is limited. You enjoy making friends, but if you wish to be happier, try to be more generous and do not force yourself on others.

12th month
You are sensitive, intelligent and kind; your family are proud of you. Your weak points are pride, selfishness and swift changes of mood. You sometimes like to be alone and at other times you want a busy social life. There are two sides to your character: one side is lazy and cruel, the other is hardworking and generous. You are usually a good judge of character, but you do not always want to face reality, particulary if you are a woman. You will be lucky if you correct this weak point.

Your Luck According to Your Day of Birth

Born on the 1st, 10th, 19th or 28th
You are of noble bearing, independent and trustworthy. Your standards are high and you are always ready to fight for your career. You have a determined character but are overly concerned with yourself and with achieving fame and fortune. You feel the need to complete everything quickly but you frequently fail. Be careful and cautious. You are suited to a career as a civil servant or to a job in the arts. Your fortune fluctuates, and although at times you may receive unexpected money, at others you must control your spending.

Born on the 2nd, 11th, 20th or 29th
You are quiet but honest, open-hearted and extremely popular. Sometimes you like to be alone and at other times you want to be

surrounded by friends. Unless you control your temper you will fall into trouble. You are suited to a career as an artistic designer, planner or literary editor. You enjoy life, even if you are in the poorest circumstances. Your fortune will not vary greatly, but your luck will improve after middle age.

Born on the 3rd, 12th, 21st or 30th

You are talented, sensitive and react quickly. You are always ready to fight for what you know is true and just. Others will avoid forming friendships with you if you are too obstinate; they wrongly assume you are too stern and difficult. You have business acumen and are suited to a disciplined job, such as the army, or to any job which has a competitive element, such as politics or the stock exchange. You must learn how to control your spending and think seriously of ways to earn more income.

Born on the 4th, 13th, 22nd or 31st

You are calm, patient and reserved. Your appearance and attitude lead others to think you are unapproachable, although in fact you are warm-hearted. If you change your approach you will be more popular. You are suited to a career as an academic, particularly in the field of theology or philosophy. Because you cannot control your spending you will lose money as easily and as quickly as you make it.

Born on the 5th, 14th or 23rd

Your fiery, obstinate nature makes it difficult for you to accept suggestions or opinions. At times your stubbornness leads to quarrels and problems. You are suited to a career in the arts, as an academic, an administrator or an advertising designer. Your intelligence enables you to work in a highly paid job. You will be lucky with money, often using it to set up new projects.

Born on the 6th, 15th or 24th

Your open, stable and cheerful character provides you with an active social life. You are affectionate and emotional and daydream so often that your mind becomes confused. Your eagerness to help others is often stifled by your indecisiveness. A career in the arts or work as a designer or social worker would be appropriate for you. You will not be very rich but will always have enough to live on.

Born on the 7th, 16th or 25th

You are an exhibitionist but when you show off nobody wants to listen to you or watch you. You enjoy an exciting life, but your head is in the clouds; you must learn to discipline yourself. You are suited to a job which allows you mobility, for example, a reporter, a traveller or an explorer. You do not want to earn a fortune and are quite content with your standard of living.

Born on the 8th, 17th or 26th

You are calm, quiet and a good judge. You have a determined and logical mind but lack social skills. You have a free spirit and are suited to self-employment. Do not buy stocks and shares or put your money in short-term investments. Your fortune is varied – it depends on your approach. There are times of wealth and times of abject poverty.

Born on the 9th, 18th or 27th

You are happy, optimistic and warm-hearted. You have an active life and are not easily troubled by minor matters. On the whole you are magnanimous but occasionally you quarrel unnecessarily with friends. It is important that you learn to control your moods. You should work as sole director or proprietor to avoid disagreements with partners. A job involving buying and selling would be suitable. You have a good income but you are extravagant.

Your Luck According to Your 'Hour' of Birth

Tzu hours: 11 p.m. – 1 a.m.

You are hot-tempered, obstinate, thrifty and shy away from challenges. You are an easy target for gossip. At times you act without sufficient planning but later you regret your actions. You will be able to build a successful business, buy a home and care for your family without a family inheritance. You will achieve fame and success independently of others but if you find yourself in trouble your parents or your marriage partner will always be there to help you out.

Unlucky ages 10, 17, 35, 48, 57.

Age at death 87.

Suitable occupations Artist, politician, architect, electrician or jobs connected with metal or water.

Unsuitable occupations Work connected with earth.

Ch'ou hours: 1–3 a.m.
If you want a good career, leave your home town while you are young. Life will be difficult up to the age of twenty but then your fortune will change for the better. You will be wealthy in old age.

Unlucky ages 17, 22, 30, 45.

Age at death 71.

Suitable occupations Commercial trader, teacher, government official, restaurateur, academic, skilled manual worker or jobs connected with the final stages of production.

Unsuitable occupations Work connected with wood.

Yin hours: 3–5 a.m.
You are on bad terms with your relatives and your early years will be difficult. You will not be left an inheritance and will leave your home town. After the age of forty everything will work out well. Old age will bring you power and wealth.

Unlucky ages 25, 28, 32, 38, 48.

Age at death 65.

Suitable occupations Doctor, musician, artist, actor, travelling agent/representative.

Unsuitable occupations Work connected with metal.

Mao hours: 5–7 a.m.
You will be very fortunate, with occasional help from your parents but none from your brothers and sisters. You will have a comfortable life and be wealthy if you work away from your home town. Marriage will be unsteady and difficult in the early years, but

after middle age you will develop more satisfactory relationships and will have the chance to be wealthy.

Unlucky ages 15, 19, 54.

Age at death 71.

Suitable occupations Mechanical engineer, actor, writer, artist, theologian or work connected with religion.

Unsuitable occupations Work connected with fire.

Ch'en hours: 7–9 a.m.
You are clever, quick-witted and determined. Your warm-hearted nature enables you to form close friendships. Life is busy and varied, but a woman born in the Ch'en hours will be lonely. However, you will have many material possessions and a good salary. Your excessive self-confidence makes working relationships difficult.

Unlucky ages 18, 26, 35, 38.

Age at death 65.

Suitable occupations Entrepreneur, politician, public relations officer, teacher, miner.

Unsuitable occupations Work connected with wood.

Szu hours: 9–11 a.m.
You have outstanding talent and are able to build up your business and care for your family successfully. Family relations are troubled and you would prosper financially if you were to leave your home town. You are kind to your friends and like to help them when they are in trouble. A woman born in the Szu hours is extravagant and may have an unhappy marriage. Men and women born in these hours drink too much.

Unlucky ages 30, 35, 46, 48.

Age at death 88.

Suitable occupations Civil or electrical engineer, architect, wood or wine merchant.

Unsuitable occupations Work connected with water.

Wu hours: 11 a.m.–1 p.m.
You are active, clever, obstinate and extravagant. You prefer travelling to settling down to a job in your local area. A woman born in these hours is likely to have an unusual and fascinating character.

Unlucky ages 5, 11, 23, 32, 44, 53.

Age at death 84.

Suitable occupations Doctor, nurse, politician, film actor, skilled worker, jobs in the service industries or any work connected with oil.

Unsuitable occupations Work connected with gold.

Wei hours: 1–3 p.m.
You have a troubled relationship with your parents, brothers and sisters and marriage partner. You will have serious difficulties in middle age. A woman born in these hours is clever but will always have difficulties with her marriage because she is too active to settle down.

Unlucky ages 18, 25, 55.

Age at death 69.

Suitable occupations Civil engineer, electrical engineer, architect, wood merchant, wine merchant.

Unsuitable occupations Work connected with water.

Shen hours: 3–5 p.m.
You will earn money easily and spend it freely. You will be luckier if

you work outside your home town. Your marriage will be harmonious although your parents will not offer you moral support. A woman born in the Shen hours will be married twice. Because you are too active ever to settle down completely it is important that you are seen to behave honourably. Too much time worrying over relationships will cause your business to fail.

Unlucky ages 18, 21, 27, 29, 41, 53.

Age at death 71.

Suitable occupations Finance-related work – e.g. broker, public relations officer, watchmaker, manager – or work connected with metal.

Unsuitable occupations Work connected with wood.

Yu hours: 5–7 p.m.

Your youth is difficult because of troubled family relationships. You will be separated from your brothers and sisters and will leave home when young. You may not be able to have a child but it will be possible to adopt one. A woman born in the Yu hours is warm-hearted, fond of food and can be trusted to keep a secret.

Unlucky ages 18, 24, 31, 48.

Age at death 77.

Suitable occupations Chemist, researcher/writer, teacher, artist, technologist or work connected with the final stages of production.

Unsuitable occupations Work connected with earth.

Hsü hours: 7–9 p.m.

You are brave, capable, hardworking and run your business alone. You are optimistic and will have a successful life and a flourishing career. A woman born in the Hsü hours can be vain and impatient. You are magnanimous but on the other hand money is not important to you. You care little for others but will have a magnificent life.

Unlucky ages 15, 25, 34, 43, 48, 56.

Age at death 77.

Suitable occupations Poet, writer, investor, engineer, rice or cereal merchant, or work connected with metal and agriculture.

Unsuitable occupations Work connected with fire.

Hai hours: 9–11 p.m.
You are manually dextrous and set yourself high standards. Although you are warm-hearted you do not like to make too many friends. A woman born in the Hai hours can be obstinate. Others may be easily upset but you have the ability to forgive and forget. You are hardworking and will be fortunate.

Unlucky ages 10, 25, 35, 38, 48, 55.

Age at death 77.

Suitable occupations Surgeon, monk/nun, hotelier, artist, antiques dealer or work connected with metal.

Unsuitable occupations Work connected with fire.

Practical Advice

You will achieve your goals if you work hard.
Think carefully before you say or do anything.
Be concerned about other people and they will repay you in kind.
Try to examine your own shortcomings before others criticize you.
Make a detailed plan before you undertake any new project.
Do not expect 100 per cent success. As long as you are satisfied that you have done something to the best of your ability, good luck will stay by your side.
Approach life easily; do not let problems weigh you down.
Be honest with others and give them a helping hand when they need it.

Have a cheerful outlook. This will draw others to you.
Be patient; accept the peaceful moments in life.

Your Luck Year by Year

Year of the Rat
Four unlucky stars.

This is an unlucky year, full of difficulties and disasters. You will quarrel with your family or your friends and be involved in law suits.

Year of the Ox
Two lucky stars, four unlucky stars.

Your lucky stars are shining on you this year; all your misfortune will turn to fortune. This is not a lucky year for your family. Be careful, do not be too proud, and everything will work out well.

Year of the Tiger
Four unlucky stars.

This is a difficult year, a year of financial and business problems. Choose your friends carefully because some may try to trick you.

Year of the Rabbit
Four lucky stars, one unlucky star.

This is a fortunate year. You will earn a good salary and your problems will be ironed out because your lucky stars are at their brightest. Be careful to avoid quarrels and do not become involved in projects which might tarnish your good name. This is a peaceful and successful year.

Year of the Dragon
Four unlucky stars.

Bad luck dominates your life this year. You will leave your family to travel abroad. You will be alone and lonely this year.

Year of the Snake
Six baleful spirits.

This is a year of illness and extensive foreign travel. Think carefully before you choose friends or partners or lend money. Do not make any important decisions – wait for another year.

Year of the Horse
Two lucky stars, three unlucky stars.

This is a lucky year, a year of excellent opportunities for promotion. You will also be financially successful if you are self-employed. You are likely to suffer from ill health this year.

Year of the Ram
One lucky star, three baleful spirits.

Everything proves to be difficult this year. You will leave your family and travel abroad.

Year of the Monkey
One strong travelling star, one lonely star.

This year you have the freedom of a tiger who has escaped from its cage. You will be very lucky and financially successful, but you will also be lonely and lose one of your relatives.

Year of the Cock
Two lucky stars, three baleful spirits.

There will be many lucky times this year, but you will also be surrounded by corrupt men. Whatever you do, you must take care.

Year of the Dog
One lucky star, two unlucky stars.

You will be successful in your examinations, but you will be involved in law suits and wear mourning clothes for one of your relatives.

Year of the Pig
One lucky star, three unlucky stars.

This is an unlucky year. You will suffer from ill health, but your lucky star will help you solve your problems.

Your Animal Sign Horoscope

THE SIGN OF THE RAM

The Main Attributes of Ram People

Character
Your considerate and capable nature helps you deal efficiently with life's problems. You will work hard to achieve success in your career.

Luck
You will never be very lucky but you are able to turn misfortune to fortune.

Wealth
Although you have a good salary you do not have many savings because you spend freely on your active social life.

Occupation
You are not suited to an office job because you dislike sedentary work. If you choose an active job that takes you beyond the confines of an office you will be offered a good income and promotional opportunities.

Social life
You are socially successful and treat your friends with sincerity and honesty.

Business
If you work very hard you will be successful in business, but you will face many difficulties because of keen competition.

Romance
You have a very emotional nature, but when you meet someone you love you do not have the confidence to show your feelings. You will miss many good opportunities.

Marriage
You rarely take the initiative in a relationship and are likely to be introduced to your marriage partner by friends.

Parents
You have a difficult relationship with your parents and will leave home once you have your own income.

Brothers and sisters
You have a troubled relationship with your brothers and sisters and when you need help they are unlikely to give it.

Children
You will love your children very much and will often spoil them.

Assets
You will earn a good income and will own land and property, particularly after middle age.

Travel
You are a good traveller and enjoy travelling at home and abroad.

Health
You will never suffer serious illness, but you should take care of your liver and your eyes.

Investment
If you plan your investments wisely you will reap rich rewards.

Skills
You are skilled in art and design.

Speculation
You will never receive unexpected money. Avoid gambling and short-term investments.

Hopes
You will never achieve all your aims because your fortune varies.

Litigation
Try to avoid law suits because there is a 50 per cent chance that you will lose.

Lost property
You will recover lost property or find lost friends easily.

The Character of the Ram

The Ram is the eighth animal in the cycle of twelve and corresponds to the Earthly Branch Wei. The Ram is matched to the sixth month of the year and its favourable hours are between 1 and 3 p.m. Wei represents the silence before action begins. The Ram controls the time of harvest, when the yang is at its strongest and is ready for its move to yin.

You have a mild and amenable character and a sensitive nature that appreciates the simple things in life. You are the most peaceful and gentle of the twelve animals, but you are also hesitant and nervous. You worry over minor matters and prefer to leave your decisions to fate. You dislike making rules as much as you dislike living according to rules. Your bad time-keeping often embarrasses your friends, and your lack of confidence makes you unsuitable for positions of responsibilty. Others are hurt and annoyed by your obstinacy, hesitancy and dissatisfaction with your life and your belongings. But your kindness and care for the sick and the poor are redeeming points of your character.

You can adapt to any career or life style as long as you are comfortable. You are interested in spiritual matters and are likely to hold strong religious beliefs. Although your inventiveness and adaptability are suited to most types of occupation, you avoid menial or dirty jobs. If you are wealthy and well provided for, you are content and will try to maintain that standard, but you are quickly dissatisfied as soon as problems arise or work becomes difficult. You like to give orders but are too hesitant to give them efficiently. Try to accept orders rather than give them. Your luck will improve gradually and you will be successful if you work for an efficient leader and in pleasant conditions. You are a daydreamer and need someone to guide and protect you through life. As long as you are offered educational opportunities you will be a good artist or scholar. Avoid disciplined jobs or a career that requires leadership qualities.

Women born in this year are attractive and beautiful but they are also shy and easily embarrassed. They are frightened to speak or attract attention in public places and blush when complimented. Men born in this year are confident, attractive and emotionally controlled. They are careful not to reveal their feelings until they are sure that they will be reciprocated. Avoid marrying someone born in the Year of the Ram; he/she would be a good lover but not a reliable marriage partner, though he/she would not quarrel or argue. Someone born in the year of the Rabbit, the Horse or the Pig would make a good marriage or business partner. The Chinese call this combination a San Ho or Three Harmony. Someone born in the year of the Rabbit holds passionate beliefs and can be a good financial and social organizer. A Rabbit person would provide you with a safe, happy home. Someone born in the year of the Horse is selfish and independent but would nevertheless take care of you because you are so dependent on others. Someone born in the year of the Pig is a hard worker and capable of earning a good living. You would be able to share his/her fortune and fame.

You are not well matched to any of the remaining animal signs. Avoid marrying someone born in the year of the Ox. Your dependent, hesitant nature is unsuited to the Ox's earnest, hardworking character. You are not suited to someone born in the year of the Dog, who lacks confidence, or to someone born in the year of the Rat, who will never reveal his/her thoughts or feelings. A partnership or marriage with a Dog or a Rat person would be fraught with disasters and unhappiness.

You are suited to a job as an artist, scholar, dancer, philosopher, actor, singer, poet, author or work related to advertising.

Your Luck According to Your Year of Birth

1931, 1991

Born in the year of Hsi Wei, you belong to the Prosperous Ram.

You are idealistic and forgiving. There will be many problems in your youth but these will lessen as you grow older. You will have a happy, peaceful marriage. A woman born in either of these years will be lucky and prosperous, but an eldest son born in either of these years will have an unhappy relationship with his parents.

1943, 2003

Born in the year of Kuei Wei, you belong to the Ram in a Flock of Sheep.

You are candid and sincere but speak without thinking. You are kind but seldom receive praise or thanks. There will be many problems in your youth and middle age, but your old age will be prosperous and happy. A woman born in either of these years will be elegant and well dressed.

1955, 2015

Born in the year of Yi Wei, you belong to the Ram Respected by Others.

In your youth and middle age you will be thrifty, hard-working and honest and your old age will be fortunate and prosperous. You will have many children but your brothers and sisters will be unable to help you in times of need. If you start your own business you will have to provide the necessary funding.

1907, 1967

Born in the year of Ting Wei, you belong to the Lonely Ram.

You enjoy debate and are a good judge of the truth. Your moods swing easily between happiness and sadness. You will never be short of money and will always live in comfortable surroundings. You will be on bad terms with your brothers and will have children late in life.

1919, 1979

Born in the year of Chi Wei, you belong to the Ram Running on the Mountain.

You have a straightforward character and are a talented debater. You have an elegant bearing, a happy nature and are respected by your friends. You will be helped by someone in a position of authority and will have a prosperous and lucky life.

Your Luck According to Your Month of Birth

1st month
You are active, independent and truthful. You will be lucky in your youth and your fortune will continue to improve as you grow older. You have a strong sense of justice and are ready to fight for the truth. You are a skilled speaker and a popular character, but do not be too confident of your own ability. Learn to trust others. You will have a steady career and are likely to work in a position of authority, but you should avoid extravangance because you will never be wealthy.

2nd month
You are amenable, honest, kind and well liked by friends and relatives. You do not want to struggle for fame or fortune and are content to lead a peaceful life. You will, however, achieve a prominent position in society and will be fortunate throughout your life. Handle your business carefully and develop it according to your finances and your ability.

3rd month

You are honest, reserved and hardworking but never take the initiative. Although you like to follow others' ideas you become angry if you are given orders. Others will put their confidence in you when you learn to be humble and considerate. You are suited to a career as a researcher but you will never be wealthy. There will be periods of failure during your life and you will lose money through trickery. You will never be lucky but you will receive a sum of unexpected money.

4th month

You are a thoughtful, solitary person and dislike anyone disturbing your quiet life. You are obstinate and single-minded and will never be lucky until you learn to finish the work you are given. You receive a good income but you are an extravagant spender. Although you have a warm heart you are too shy to express your feelings. This is why offers of friendship and requests for help are usually met with a cool response. Try to be more concerned for and positive towards others. You are suited to a post as an assistant administrator which involves detailed examination of issues but does not involve delegation or responsibility for others.

5th month

You are talkative, careful, sensitive and elegant. You are suited to any environment but dislike making decisions or accepting responsibility. Try to be more patient and do not abandon your work when you are faced with difficulties. You will miss many good opportunities because of your impatience but in times of need you will usually receive unexpected money. You will have few savings because your money is spent on your interests and hobbies. A man born in this month should try to marry a gentle and accommodating woman.

6th month

You are kind, honest, warm-hearted and popular. You can deal easily with many types of people. You will have a peaceful, lucky and happy life because the sixth month of the year of the Ram is a fortunate month. You will have few problems with your family, friends, finances or career. If you are not satisfied with your peaceful life your good fortune will turn to misfortune. Try to be patient, constant and open to advice. Remember to work hard even though your lucky star is always shining on you.

7th month

You are kind, honest, quick to act and rarely worry over minor problems. You have a just nature and will never use your influence or authority to oppress or humiliate others. Once you have made a promise you will try hard to keep your word. Your kindness and openness are appreciated by others and you are a popular friend.

8th month

You are amenable, kind and quick in thought and action. You are hardworking and thorough, and although you are agreeable to work with, you are stubborn if things are not working to your advantage. There will be problems establishing your career when you are young, but you should not abandon hope as things will improve as you grow older. Learn to accept the advice of others and you will be successful and content. You will never be wealthy.

9th month

You are capable and sensible but you take life too seriously. You want to complete everything to perfection and make the same demands on your friends and family, but you are easily upset if you fail or if your friends do not meet your exacting standards. Try to relax and concentrate on your immediate work not on its future success or failure. You are a good financial manager and will inherit property from your family. You are suited to a job in the arts.

10th month

You are calm, reserved and intelligent. You are jealous of the success of others and like to repeat gossip that may hurt them; you are ready to use any means available to achieve your goals. You are suited to a research job that is related to your interests. You will have a lucky life and will be well known in the arts. Your relationships will improve if you avoid gossip and jealousy.

11th month

You are intelligent, alert and honest. You are a good judge, a competent worker and an eloquent speaker. Although you have good friends and an active social life your impatience and frequent changes of mind make it difficult to establish long-term friendships. Your good fortune will be destroyed unless you learn to thank the people who help you. Avoid short-term investment.

12th month
You are kind, just, idealistic and hardworking. Try to temper your straightforward, brusque manner because it hurts and offends others. One side of your character is sensitive to the needs of the poor and the other side of your character is vain and ambitious. Whenever you fail you put the blame on others and rarely recognize your own faults. You are also sensitive and frightened to be alone. You will never be wealthy and should make an effort to save money when you are young.

Your Luck According to Your Day of Birth

Born on the 1st, 10th, 19th or 28th
You are of noble bearing, independent and trustworthy. Your standards are high and you are always ready to fight for your career. You have a determined character but are overly concerned with yourself and with achieving fame and fortune. You feel the need to complete everything quickly but you frequently fail. Be careful and cautious. You are suited to a career as a civil servant or to a job in the arts. Your fortune fluctuates, and although at times you may receive unexpected money, at others you must control your spending.

Born on the 2nd, 11th, 20th or 29th
You are quiet but honest, open-hearted and extremely popular. Sometimes you like to be alone and at other times you want to be surrounded by friends. Unless you control your temper you will fall into trouble. You are suited to a career as an artistic designer, planner or literary editor. You enjoy life, even if you are in the poorest circumstances. Your fortune will not vary greatly, but your luck will improve after middle age.

Born on the 3rd, 12th, 21st or 30th
You are talented, sensitive and react quickly. You are always ready to fight for what you know is true and just. Others will avoid forming friendships with you if you are too obstinate; they wrongly

assume you are too stern and difficult. You have business acumen and are suited to a disciplined job, such as the army, or to any job which has a competitive element, such as politics or the stock exchange. You must learn how to control your spending and think seriously of ways to earn more income.

Born on the 4th, 13th, 22nd or 31st

You are calm, patient and reserved. Your appearance and attitude lead others to think you are unapproachable, although in fact you are warm-hearted. If you change your approach you will be more popular. You are suited to a career as an academic, particularly in the field of theology or philosophy. Because you cannot control your spending you will lose money as easily and as quickly as you make it.

Born on the 5th, 14th or 23rd

Your fiery, obstinate nature makes it difficult for you to accept suggestions or opinions. At times your stubbornness leads to quarrels and problems. You are suited to a career in the arts, as an academic, an administrator or an advertising designer. Your intelligence enables you to work in a highly paid job. You will be lucky with money, often using it to set up new projects.

Born on the 6th, 15th or 24th

Your open, stable and cheerful character provides you with an active social life. You are affectionate and emotional and daydream so often that your mind becomes confused. Your eagerness to help others is often stifled by your indecisiveness. A career in the arts or work as a designer or social worker would be appropriate for you. You will not be very rich but will always have enough to live on.

Born on the 7th, 16th or 25th

You are an exhibitionist but when you show off nobody wants to listen to you or watch you. You enjoy an exciting life, but your head is in the clouds; you must learn to discipline yourself. You are suited to a job which allows you mobility, for example, a reporter, a traveller or an explorer. You do not want to earn a fortune and are quite content with your standard of living.

Born on the 8th, 17th or 26th
You are calm, quiet and a good judge. You have a determined and logical mind but lack social skills. You have a free spirit and are suited to self-employment. Do not buy stocks and shares or put your money in short-term investments. Your fortune is varied – it depends on your approach. There are times of wealth and times of abject poverty.

Born on the 9th, 18th or 27th
You are happy, optimistic and warm-hearted. You have an active life and are not easily troubled by minor matters. On the whole you are magnanimous but occasionally you quarrel unnecessarily with friends. It is important that you learn to control your moods. You should work as sole director or proprietor to avoid disagreements with partners. A job involving buying and selling would be suitable. You have a good income but you are extravagant.

Your Luck According to Your 'Hour' of Birth

Tzu hours: 11 p.m.–1 a.m.
You are hot-tempered, obstinate, thrifty and shy away from challenges. You are an easy target for gossip. At times you act without sufficient planning but later you regret your actions. You will be able to build a successful business, buy a home and care for your family without a family inheritance. You will achieve fame and success independently of others but if you find yourself in trouble your parents or your marriage partner will always be there to help you out.

Unlucky ages 10, 17, 35, 48, 57.

Age at death 87.

Suitable occupations Artist, politician, architect, electrician or jobs connected with metal or water.

Unsuitable occupations Work connected with earth.

Ch'ou hours: 1–3 a.m.
If you want a good career, leave your home town while you are

young. Life will be difficult up to the age of twenty but then your fortune will change for the better. You will be wealthy in old age.

Unlucky ages 17, 22, 30, 45.

Age at death 71.

Suitable occupations Commercial trader, teacher, government official, restaurateur, academic, skilled manual worker or jobs connected with the final stages of production.

Unsuitable occupations Work connected with wood.

Yin hours: 3–5 a.m.
You are on bad terms with your relatives and your early years will be difficult. You will not be left an inheritance and will leave your home town. After the age of forty everything will work out well. Old age will bring you power and wealth.

Unlucky ages 25, 28, 32, 38, 48.

Age at death 65.

Suitable occupations Doctor, musician, artist, actor, travelling agent/representative.

Unsuitable occupations Work connected with metal.

Mao hours: 5–7 a.m.
You will be very fortunate, with occasional help from your parents but none from your brothers and sisters. You will have a comfortable life and be wealthy if you work away from your home town. Marriage will be unsteady and difficult in the early years, but after middle age you will develop more satisfactory relationships and will have the chance to be wealthy.

Unlucky ages 15, 19, 54.

Age at death 71.

Suitable occupations Mechanical engineer, actor, writer, artist, theologian or work connected with religion.

Unsuitable occupations Work connected with fire.

Ch'en hours: 7–9 a.m.
You are clever, quick-witted and determined. Your warm-hearted nature enables you to form close friendships. Life is busy and varied, but a woman born in the Ch'en hours will be lonely. However, you will have many material possessions and a good salary. Your excessive self-confidence makes working relationships difficult.

Unlucky ages 18, 26, 35, 38.

Age at death 65.

Suitable occupations Entrepreneur, politician, public relations officer, teacher, miner.

Unsuitable occupations Work connected with wood.

Szu hours: 9–11 a.m.
You have outstanding talent and are able to build up your business and care for your family successfully. Family relations are troubled and you would prosper financially if you were to leave your home town. You are kind to your friends and like to help them when they are in trouble. A woman born in the Szu hours is extravagant and may have an unhappy marriage. Men and women born in these hours drink too much.

Unlucky ages 30, 35, 46, 48.

Age at death 88.

Suitable occupations Civil or electrical engineer, architect, wood or wine merchant.

Unsuitable occupations Work connected with water.

Wu hours: 11 a.m.–1 p.m.
You are active, clever, obstinate and extravagant. You prefer travelling to settling down to a job in your local area. A woman born in these hours is likely to have an unusual and fascinating character.

Unlucky ages 5, 11, 23, 32, 44, 53.

Age at death 84.

Suitable occupations Doctor, nurse, politician, film actor, skilled worker, jobs in the service industries or any work connected with oil.

Unsuitable occupations Work connected with gold.

Wei hours: 1–3 p.m.
You have a troubled relationship with your parents, brothers and sisters and marriage partner. You will have serious difficulties in middle age. A woman born in these hours is clever but will always have difficulties with her marriage because she is too active to settle down.

Unlucky ages 18, 25, 55.

Age at death 69.

Suitable occupations Civil engineer, electrical engineer, architect, wood merchant, wine merchant.

Unsuitable occupations Work connected with water.

Shen hours: 3–5 p.m.
You will earn money easily and spend it freely. You will be luckier if you work outside your home town. Your marriage will be harmonious although your parents will not offer you moral support. A woman born in the Shen hours will be married twice. Because you are too active ever to settle down completely it is important that you are seen to behave honourably. Too much time worrying over relationships will cause your business to fail.

Unlucky ages 18, 21, 27, 29, 41, 53.

Age at death 71.

Suitable occupations Finance-related work – e.g. broker, public relations officer, watchmaker, manager – or work connected with metal.

Unsuitable occupations Work connected with wood.

Yu hours: 5–7 p.m.
Your youth is difficult because of troubled family relationships. You will be separated from your brothers and sisters and will leave home when young. You may not be able to have a child but it will be possible to adopt one. A woman born in the Yu hours is warm-hearted, fond of food and can be trusted to keep a secret.

Unlucky ages 18, 24, 31, 48.

Age at death 77.

Suitable occupations Chemist, researcher/writer, teacher, artist, technologist or work connected with the final stages of production.

Unsuitable occupations Work connected with earth.

Hsü hours: 7–9 p.m.
You are brave, capable, hardworking and run your business alone. You are optimistic and will have a successful life and a flourishing career. A woman born in the Hsü hours can be vain and impatient. You are magnanimous but on the other hand money is not important to you. You care little for others but will have a magnificent life.

Unlucky ages 15, 25, 34, 43, 48, 56.

Age at death 77.

Suitable occupations Poet, writer, investor, engineer, rice or cereal merchant, or work connected with metal and agriculture.

Unsuitable occupations Work connected with fire.

Hai hours: 9–11 p.m.
You are manually dextrous and set yourself high standards. Although you are warm-hearted you do not like to make too many friends. A woman born in the Hai hours can be obstinate. Others may be easily upset but you have the ability to forgive and forget. You are hardworking and will be fortunate.

Unlucky ages 10, 25, 35, 38, 48, 55.

Age at death 77.

Suitable occupations Surgeon, monk/nun, hotelier, artist, antiques dealer or work connected with metal.

Unsuitable occupations Work connected with fire.

Practical Advice

Plan carefully before doing anything.
Do not be greedy.
Concentrate on your work because even a small mistake can lead to failure.
Rest when you feel tired.
Accept the advice of your superiors.
Do not argue over minor matters.
Lead an active life.
Do not judge people by appearance. Be polite and humble.
Avoid listening to or repeating gossip.
Always try to be on good terms with your family and friends.
Do not try to copy the views and opinions of others.
Be honest and virtuous so that you are always prepared for new challenges.

Your Luck Year by Year

Year of the Rat
Two lucky stars, one unlucky star.

Your business will prosper during the year and you will receive an unexpected sum of money. This is a good year to fall in love if you are single. You may suffer minor illnesses such as headaches and colds.

Year of the Ox
Three unlucky stars.

There is misfortune when the Ox meets the Ram. This is a year of quarrels, disruption and financial loss. Be careful because you may be involved in a law suit.

Year of the Tiger
Three lucky stars, two unlucky stars.

You will be promoted to a position of authority during the year and your relationship with your family will be happy and stable. Be on your guard because this is also a year of accidents and disasters.

Year of the Rabbit
Two lucky stars, four unlucky stars.

Your investments will yield good profits this year and you will receive an unexpected sum of money. You may suffer loss or be accidentally injured this year.

Year of the Dragon
Three lucky stars, three unlucky stars.

All your efforts this year are wasted, no matter how hard you work or how extensively you travel. There will be quarrels and arguments but your lucky stars will protect you from accidents.

Year of the Snake
Two lucky stars, two unlucky stars.

During this lucky year you will be offered a position of authority. This is also a year of mourning because one of your relatives will die.

Year of the Horse
Two lucky stars, three unlucky stars.

The Horse and the Ram are well matched so this is a lucky year. Although you are not in a position of high authority your career will be successful. There will be many happy moments during the year but you will suffer from ill health.

Year of the Ram
One lucky star, three unlucky stars.

This is a good year for study and improving your literary skills. Your health will deteriorate if you work too hard.

Year of the Monkey
Two lucky stars.

This is an excellent year for your career and your finances. Everything will run smoothly during the year.

Year of the Cock
Four unlucky spirits.

This is an unfortunate year of quarrels, mourning and law suits. You are unable to earn a good salary and will spend most of your savings.

Year of the Dog
One lucky star, two unlucky stars.

You will be plagued by difficulties throughout the year. There will be problems with your business, finance and family.

Year of the Pig
One lucky star, four unlucky stars.

This is an unstable year. Choose your friends carefully. Someone who is a friend today may be an enemy tomorrow.

Your energy is used up on many exciting projects. You will be given the opportunity to further your studies and acquire a skill.

Year of the Snake
Two lucky stars, one baleful spirit.

Under the Pao Chia star everything that you want will be fulfilled. Avoid burial ceremonies; the evil spirits will harm you if you go near graves at night.

Year of the Horse
Four unlucky stars.

This is a year full of disasters and difficulties. A relative will fall ill and you will be unlucky throughout the year.

Year of the Ram
Four unlucky stars.

During the year you will lose money and be injured. Be careful; you will be involved in a law suit and may be sent to prison.

Year of the Monkey
Five unlucky stars.

One of your parents may die. You will quarrel with your friends and be involved in a law suit. Your wife or your husband will be seriously injured.

Year of the Cock
Three lucky stars, one unlucky star.

The Dragon and the Cock are well matched. You will be lucky throughout the year, although there may be a minor illness or a small financial loss.

Year of the Dog
Four unlucky stars.

The Dragon and the Dog are not compatible. It will be a year of quarrels and loss.

Year of the Pig
Three lucky stars.

The Tzu Wei star is shining on you. This is the year in which to marry if you are still single. Everything you touch will turn out well; money, success and fame will come your way.

Your Animal Sign Horoscope

THE SIGN OF THE MONKEY

The Main Attributes of Monkey People

Character
You are intelligent and intellectual.

Luck
You are fortunate, and at some time in your life you will receive an unexpected sum of money.

Wealth
You will always earn a good income because your versatility and quick thinking are suited to many different jobs. If you have a part-time job in addition to your main employment, the part-time job will give you the better income. However, you usually spend your money as quickly as you earn it.

Occupation
You are suited to a career as a journalist or to any work connected with newspapers.

Social life
You will have many friends and an active social life.

Business
You are a good organizer and will be as successful in your career as you are in your social life.

Romance
You are too active to settle down with one partner.

Marriage
Although you have difficulties making a commitment to one person, once you do marry you will be loyal to your partner. You will not need introductions because you will be able to find a suitable partner on your own.

Parents
You have a good relationship with your parents and they will always be able to help you.

Brothers and sisters
You have a happy and caring relationship with your brothers and sisters.

Children
You will have a loving and obedient children who will take good care of you in your old age.

Assets
You will own fixed assets by the age of forty and land and property in your old age.

Travel
You travel well and benefit from your holidays. You will enjoy short and long trips.

Health
You have good health, but do not be overconfident. Do not push yourself but give your body time to rest.

Investment
You will be successful as long as you check the risks involved before you invest.

Skills
Do not force yourself to learn skills you are not suited to. There are certain skills that you will acquire easily, regardless of your education.

Speculation
Avoid speculation, particularly gambling.

Hopes
If you use your intelligence your hopes will realized.

Litigation
Try to settle legal matters out of court.

Lost property
When you find lost property it is usually damaged.

The Character of the Monkey

The Monkey is the most active of the twelve animals and the closest in appearance to humans. The Monkey is the ninth animal chosen by the Jade Emperor and corresponds to the Earthly Branch Shen.

Autumn is the ideal time for Shen because it is the season of maturity and fruitfulness. Shen represents a time of hard work and completion. The Monkey belongs to the seventh month of the year and its special time is between 3 and 5 p.m., the hours of sunset.

The Monkey is a cunning and wily animal, and although people born in these years can be cunning and wily there are some who are trustworthy and honest. A man born in the year of the Monkey is handsome, while a woman born in these years is attractive. Monkey people are active, intellectual, wise and warm-hearted. They are talented, inventive and creative, always ready to solve new problems. A Monkey person may appear accommodating but is obstinate at heart.

You are socially adept and make friends easily; others are attracted by your intelligence and kindness. You are ready to fight and sacrifice yourself for a just cause, but you often fight for the truth because you want to be popular and respected. You have a double-sided character; one side is kind and amenable and the other is cunning, vain and manipulative. You usually put yourself first, but your arrogance could jeopardize your friendships.

You are well read and have an excellent memory. Your creative powers and intellectual ability will help you achieve financial success. Every problem is a new challenge for you and you cannot rest until you have found a solution. You have the ability to make bad situations look promising and are ready to tell lies to achieve your aims. You will dedicate yourself to any task or cause as long as you have something to gain. Others dislike this aspect of your character, but they are willing to forgive you because of your friendly and alluring nature. You set yourself difficult goals and work hard to achieve them. A combination of fortune and determination will help you win success. From middle age onwards you will be famous and wealthy; your life will be peaceful and enjoyable.

Your relationships are easily ruined by your unpredictable and childish behaviour. You quickly forget old partners in favour of new relationships. A woman born in the year of the Monkey will begin to have relationships with men when she is very young. You have an alluring character and once you fall in love you will be committed to your partner. You are well liked because you are continually smiling and you can adapt to any situation. Your marriage will be successful because you will respect and support your husband and care for your children, and they will love and respect you in return.

A man born in the year of the Monkey is energetic, cheerful and healthy. You understand women and are able to win their favour easily because of your charming and accommodating character. Do not marry your first love – there will be many women in your life. When you do eventually marry, pay attention to your wife and children to prove that you are committed to your marriage.

People born in the year of the Rat, the Dragon and the Monkey would make ideal marriage or business partners. Your most unsuitable marriage or business partner is someone born in the year of the Tiger or the Pig. Monkey people treat romance as a game, and anyone born in a Tiger or Pig year will be tricked and dominated by someone born in the year of the Monkey. This combination will result in misfortune and illness throughout the marriage.

A marriage to someone born in the year of the Ox, the Rabbit, the Snake, the Horse, the Ram, the Cock, the Dog or the Monkey will be fortunate if you are attentive and understanding.

Your Luck According to Your Year of Birth

1932, 1992

Born in the year of Jen Shen, you belong to the Elegant Monkey.

You are intelligent and kind but you are also over-thrifty and prone to unpredictable changes of mood. You will be famous and marry a devoted wife/husband. Your children will be attractive and well liked.

1944, 2004

Born in the year of Chia Shen, you belong to the Monkey Climbing a Tree.

You have an exceptional character. You may have had a difficult time in your youth, but your old age will be lucky and prosperous. Your marriage will be happy and you will have children late in life. A woman born in either of these years will be talented and make a good housewife.

1956, 2016

Born in the year of Ping Shen, you belong to the Monkey Climbing up the Mountain.

You will be fortunate if you make a career of trade; you will be wealthy enough to buy a farm or a plot of land. In your old age you will be well respected and live in luxury.

1908, 1968

Born in the year of Mou Shen, you belong to the Lonely Monkey.

You are impatient and have swift changes of mood. You are hardworking and thrifty and will be helped by someone in an influential position. You will not have a happy relationship with your children. A woman born in either of these years will be understanding, good at handicrafts, fond of children and an efficient housewife.

1920, 1980

Born in the year of Keng Shen, you belong to the Monkey in a Fruit Tree.

You are very active, elegant and fortunate. You will be helped by an influential official. You will rarely be praised, even if you have saved someone's life. A woman born in either of these years will never be helped by her family.

Your Luck According to Your Month of Birth

1st month
You are accommodating, kind and humble. You are a good planner and willing to take up a challenge, but you often override others' actions and opinions. Good human relationships are essential if you want to achieve success. You are healthy and active, but will be more fortunate if you work outside your home town. At some time in your life you will lose a small amount of money. Do not jump headlong into romance because you will lose your good reputation.

2nd month
You are intelligent, kind and hardworking, and fight to achieve your goals. You enjoy gossip and have an active social life, but you must try not to be oversensitive to comment or criticism. Although you are true to your opinions, you are not a good judge of situations or character. If you want to be fortunate and well liked, work hard and keep your promises. If you fulfil your duty towards others you will rarely be dissappointed. Do not place too much hope on romance.

3rd month

You are active, straightforward, careful and magnanimous. You will be fortunate throughout life. You give more time to your hobbies than to work and thoroughly enjoy life's pleasures and luxuries. Curb your flippant attitude if you want to be successful. You have an honourable nature and were probably born into a rich family; even if your family is poor, you will be well known one day. You have great talents and will eventually be wealthy. Your prospects are good and you will have a happy, peaceful and enjoyable marriage. The Chinese say that you are like the sun rising in the east; you are welcomed and respected by all people. You are able to change unhappy situations into joyful occasions.

4th month

You have a vivid imagination and a strong sense of morality. Although you will be well known and wealthy, you will never cease to work diligently to improve yourself. Anyone born in this month will be a successful entrepreneur. Your hard work is recognized and praised by many people and there will always be someone in a position of authority to help you. You have good health and a winning character; your good fortune will be with you throughout life.

5th month

You are intelligent, quick to react and approach life seriously. You have a warm heart and will fight for justice. Men and women born in this month are complimented on their elegance and style. Your progress is hindered by your idleness and you have difficulty facing or understanding reality. Work hard if you want to be successful. You are an exhibitionist, but be careful not to hurt others' feelings or lose friends in your eagerness to entertain. Always be careful how you treat other people.

6th month

You have an alluring and attractive character and are more talented, observant and charismatic than most people. You are prone to swift changes of mood; one moment you are happy, the next sad; one moment angry, the next frightened or lonely. You like to be in the company of many people. As long as you use your powers of observation, you will be successful. Do not linger over trivial everyday problems; concentrate on the more important issues in the world around you and you will be much happier. You will have a lucky life and in times of need will be helped by someone in power.

7th month
You are a confident, just and straightforward character. You will never be overcome by difficulties or poor living conditions. Your speech is elegant and your movements careful. You are drawn to new challenges and new experiences and are always ready to fight for a just cause. Be patient and work diligently when you are young and by middle age you will be wealthy and lucky. Women born in this month are attracted to handsome men; they do not care if they have money or power because they believe that good looks are all-important.

8th month
You are stubborn, abide by the law and take life seriously. Some people born in this month are accommodating but also have a stern character. You are suited to a career as an artist and never miss an opportunity to work creatively. Your relationships with others will improve if you are more malleable and open in your reactions and attitudes. Try not to hurt others or arouse jealousies with your clever, artful conversation. You will have a good career but will change jobs frequently.

9th month
You are physically and mentally sensitive, always afraid that you will catch an infectious disease. Even when you see knives in a butcher's shop, you are afraid that someone will kill you. You are sensitive because you lack self-confidence and fear competition. You lack good judgement, courage and strength. Your greatest wish is to live peacefully in a quiet place. Try not to be so sensitive – it hinders your good fortune. Your life will improve once you stop pushing yourself so hard.

10th month
You are elegant, clever and active. You have a busy social life and are happiest in a noisy environment. You cannot tolerate confined spaces or regular hours; even if you have to stay at home on a rainy day you become impatient. You are suited to self-employment or a

career in foreign affairs. Regardless of your background, you will be loved and respected by many people because you have an attractive appearance and character. You will be a devoted marriage partner.

11th month

You are passionate, accommodating and kind, but you are also a daydreamer. You have an unconventional character and like to do things your own way. Instead of approaching life step by step, you take life in leaps and bounds. Once you have established a career or business you will soon become well known. A man born in this month is attractive to women and will be helped by friends whenever he has difficulties. A woman born in this month is well liked by men and is treated with the same respect as a wife or mother. You do not like to argue and have excellent relationships with others. You enjoy talking to others but you should try to control your tongue because you like to gossip.

12th month

You are intelligent and can establish a good balance between work and play. You will always be praised by others because you never waste time or abandon a job before it is finished. You are generous and charitable; you inspire confidence in others and are likely to be chosen as a public representative. You are healthy, even-tempered and kind, and do not need to worry about the day-to-day affairs of life. There are two sides to your character; one is kind, the other is harsh and selfish. Cultivate the generous side of your nature.

Your Luck According to Your Day of Birth

Born on the 1st, 10th, 19th or 28th

You are of noble bearing, independent and trustworthy. Your standards are high and you are always ready to fight for your career. You have a determined character but are overly concerned with yourself and with achieving fame and fortune. You feel the need to complete everything quickly but you frequently fail. Be careful and cautious. You are suited to a career as a civil servant or to a job in the arts. Your fortune fluctuates, and although at times you may receive unexpected money, at others you must control your spending.

Born on the 2nd, 11th, 20th or 29th
You are quiet but honest, open-hearted and extremely popular. Sometimes you like to be alone and at other times you want to be surrounded by friends. Unless you control your temper you will fall into trouble. You are suited to a career as an artistic designer, planner or literary editor. You enjoy life, even if you are in the poorest circumstances. Your fortune will not vary greatly, but your luck will improve after middle age.

Born on the 3rd, 12th, 21st or 30th
You are talented, sensitive and react quickly. You are always ready to fight for what you know is true and just. Others will avoid forming friendships with you if you are too obstinate; they wrongly assume you are too stern and difficult. You have business acumen and are suited to a disciplined job, such as the army, or to any job which has a competitive element, such as politics or the stock exchange. You must learn how to control your spending and think seriously of ways to earn more income.

Born on the 4th, 13th, 22nd or 31st
You are calm, patient and reserved. Your appearance and attitude lead others to think you are unapproachable, although in fact you are warm-hearted. If you change your approach you will be more popular. You are suited to a career as an academic, particularly in the field of theology or philosophy. Because you cannot control your spending you will lose money as easily and as quickly as you make it.

Born on the 5th, 14th or 23rd
Your fiery, obstinate nature makes it difficult for you to accept suggestions or opinions. At times your stubbornness leads to quarrels and problems. You are suited to a career in the arts, as an academic, an administrator or an advertising designer. Your intelligence enables you to work in a highly paid job. You will be lucky with money, often using it to set up new projects.

Born on the 6th, 15th or 24th
Your open, stable and cheerful character provides you with an active social life. You are affectionate and emotional and daydream so often that your mind becomes confused. Your eagerness to help

others is often stifled by your indecisiveness. A career in the arts or work as a designer or social worker would be appropriate for you. You will not be very rich but will always have enough to live on.

Born on the 7th, 16th or 25th
You are an exhibitionist but when you show off nobody wants to listen to you or watch you. You enjoy an exciting life, but your head is in the clouds; you must learn to discipline yourself. You are suited to a job which allows you mobility, for example, a reporter, a traveller or an explorer. You do not want to earn a fortune and are quite content with your standard of living.

Born on the 8th, 17th or 26th
You are calm, quiet and a good judge. You have a determined and logical mind but lack social skills. You have a free spirit and are suited to self-employment. Do not buy stocks and shares or put your money in short-term investments. Your fortune is varied – it depends on your approach. There are times of wealth and times of abject poverty.

Born on the 9th, 18th or 27th
You are happy, optimistic and warm-hearted. You have an active life and are not easily troubled by minor matters. On the whole you are magnanimous but occasionally you quarrel unnecessarily with friends. It is important that you learn to control your moods. You should work as sole director or proprietor to avoid disagreements with partners. A job involving buying and selling would be suitable. You have a good income but you are extravagant.

Your Luck According to Your 'Hour' of Birth

Tzu hours: 11 p.m. – 1 a.m.
You are hot-tempered, obstinate, thrifty and shy away from challenges. You are an easy target for gossip. At times you act without sufficient planning but later you regret your actions. You will be able to build a successful business, buy a home and care for your family without a family inheritance.. You will achieve fame and success independently of others but if you find yourself in trouble your parents or your marriage partner will always be there to help you out.

Unlucky ages 10, 17, 35, 48, 57.

Age at death 87.

Suitable occupations Artist, politician, architect, electrician or jobs connected with metal or water.

Unsuitable occupations Work connected with earth.

Ch'ou hours: 1–3 a.m.
If you want a good career, leave your home town while you are young. Life will be difficult up to the age of twenty but then your fortune will change for the better. You will be wealthy in old age.

Unlucky ages 17, 22, 30, 45.

Age at death 71.

Suitable occupations Commercial trader, teacher, government official, restaurateur, academic, skilled manual worker or jobs connected with the final stages of production.

Unsuitable occupations Work connected with wood.

Yin hours: 3–5 a.m.
You are on bad terms with your relatives and your early years will be difficult. You will not be left an inheritance and will leave your home town. After the age of forty everything will work out well. Old age will bring you power and wealth.

Unlucky ages 25, 28, 32, 38, 48.

Age at death 65.

Suitable occupations Doctor, musician, artist, actor, travelling agent/representative.

Unsuitable occupations Work connected with metal.

Mao hours: 5–7 a.m.
You will be very fortunate, with occasional help from your parents but none from your brothers and sisters. You will have a comfortable life and be wealthy if you work away from your home town. Marriage will be unsteady and difficult in the early years, but after middle age you will develop more satisfactory relationships and will have the chance to be wealthy.

Unlucky ages 15, 19, 54.

Age at death 71.

Suitable occupations Mechanical engineer, actor, writer, artist, theologian or work connected with religion.

Unsuitable occupations Work connected with fire.

Ch'en hours: 7–9 a.m.
You are clever, quick-witted and determined. Your warm-hearted nature enables you to form close friendships. Life is busy and varied, but a woman born in the Ch'en hours will be lonely. However, you will have many material possessions and a good salary. Your excessive self-confidence makes working relationships difficult.

Unlucky ages 18, 26, 35, 38.

Age at death 65.

Suitable occupations Entrepreneur, politician, public relations officer, teacher, miner.

Unsuitable occupations Work connected with wood.

Szu hours: 9–11 a.m.
You have outstanding talent and are able to build up your business and care for your family successfully. Family relations are troubled and you would prosper financially if you were to leave your home town. You are kind to your friends and like to help them when they are in trouble. A woman born in the Szu hours is extravagant and

may have an unhappy marriage. Men and women born in these hours drink too much.

Unlucky ages 30, 35, 46, 48.

Age at death 88.

Suitable occupations Civil or electrical engineer, architect, wood or wine merchant.

Unsuitable occupations Work connected with water.

Wu hours: 11 a.m.–1 p.m.
You are active, clever, obstinate and extravagant. You prefer travelling to settling down to a job in your local area. A woman born in these hours is likely to have an unusual and fascinating character.

Unlucky ages 5, 11, 23, 32, 44, 53.

Age at death 84.

Suitable occupations Doctor, nurse, politician, film actor, skilled worker, jobs in the service industries or any work connected with oil.

Unsuitable occupations Work connected with gold.

Wei hours: 1–3 p.m.
You have a troubled relationship with your parents, brothers and sisters and marriage partner. You will have serious difficulties in middle age. A woman born in these hours is clever but will always have difficulties with her marriage because she is too active to settle down.

Unlucky ages 18, 25, 55.

Age at death 69.

Suitable occupations Civil engineer, electrical engineer, architect, wood merchant, wine merchant.

Unsuitable occupations Work connected with water.

Shen hours: 3–5 p.m.
You will earn money easily and spend it freely. You will be luckier if you work outside your home town. Your marriage will be harmonious although your parents will not offer you moral support. A woman born in the Shen hours will be married twice. Because you are too active ever to settle down completely it is important that you are seen to behave honourably. Too much time worrying over relationships will cause your business to fail.

Unlucky ages 18, 21, 27, 29, 41, 53.

Age at death 71.

Suitable occupations Finance-related work – e.g. broker, public relations officer, watchmaker, manager – or work connected with metal.

Unsuitable occupations Work connected with wood.

Yu hours: 5–7 p.m.
Your youth is difficult because of troubled family relationships. You will be separated from your brothers and sisters and will leave home when young. You may not be able to have a child but it will be possible to adopt one. A woman born in the Yu hours is warm-hearted, fond of food and can be trusted to keep a secret.

Unlucky ages 18, 24, 31, 48.

Age at death 77.

Suitable occupations Chemist, researcher/writer, teacher, artist, technologist or work connected with the final stages of production.

Unsuitable occupations Work connected with earth.

Hsü hours: 7–9 p.m.
You are brave, capable, hardworking and run your business alone. You are optimistic and will have a successful life and a flourishing career. A woman born in the Hsü hours can be vain and impatient.

You are magnanimous but on the other hand money is not important to you. You care little for others but will have a magnificent life.

Unlucky ages 15, 25, 34, 43, 48, 56.

Age at death 77.

Suitable occupations Poet, writer, investor, engineer, rice or cereal merchant, or work connected with metal and agriculture.

Unsuitable occupations Work connected with fire.

Hai hours: 9–11 p.m.
You are manually dextrous and set yourself high standards. Although you are warm-hearted you do not like to make too many friends. A woman born in the Hai hours can be obstinate. Others may be easily upset but you have the ability to forgive and forget. You are hardworking and will be fortunate.

Unlucky ages 10, 25, 35, 38, 48, 55.

Age at death 77.

Suitable occupations Surgeon, monk/nun, hotelier, artist, antiques dealer or work connected with metal.

Unsuitable occupations Work connected with fire.

Practical Advice

Set yourself regular goals, but be content with the things you receive.
Work hard to achieve your goals, but at the same time take the feelings of others into account.
Judge fairly and wisely so that you do not antagonize others.
Try to avoid smoking and drinking.
You will fail unless you think of the future.
Be generous and charitable towards others.

Always be sincere.
Be grateful to anyone who helps you; try not to bear grudges.
You will have a peaceful life if you accept the advice of elders.
If you are asked to do something, think carefully before you accept.
Do not take on a job unless you are sure you can complete it.
Be humble and help those who are in difficulty.

Your Luck Year by Year

Year of the Rat
Three lucky stars, three unlucky stars.

This is a profitable year for business, but there will be something from your past which troubles you. Beware of law suits. If you are in trouble this year, the happiness god Chiang Hsing will help you by turning misfortune to fortune.

Year of the Ox
One lucky star, two unlucky stars.

This is a year of luck and good health. A baby will be born and most of your efforts will be successful. You may lose some money and suffer a minor illness.

Year of the Tiger
One weak lucky star, one travelling star.

This is a year of loss and extensive travelling. Avoid quarrels with your marriage partner.

Year of the Rabbit
Three lucky stars, two unlucky stars.

This is a good year for you – all your wishes will come true. Your lucky stars will help you to fight any bad luck this year.

Year of the Dragon
One lucky star, four unlucky stars.

This is an unsettled year. You will lose money but your good-luck star helps you to achieve literary fame. Be alert, there may be unexpected accidents.

Year of the Snake
Three lucky stars, one baleful spirit.

You will be helped by someone in an influential position, but this is a year of disagreements. You will have to wear mourning clothes this year.

Year of the Horse
Four unlucky stars.

Take care because you may be involved in law suits. This is an unlucky year, a year of difficulties and disasters. Some of this misfortune can be avoided if you are kind and thoughtful towards others.

Year of the Ram
Five unlucky stars.

This is a year of ill health and loneliness. You will leave your family after disagreements.

Year of the Monkey
One lucky star, five unlucky stars.

There will be many happy events this year. Be patient and avoid quarrelling with your friends. You may wear mourning clothes or suffer illness.

Year of the Cock
One lucky star, two baleful spirits.

This is an unlucky year. Your careless, thoughtless life style will bring misfortune.

Year of the Dog
Three baleful spirits.

This is an unlucky year. You may have to wear mourning clothes for one of your relatives.

Year of the Pig
One lucky star, two unlucky stars.

This is a year of trouble, sickness, loneliness and financial loss. You will travel extensively during the year.

Your Animal Sign Horoscope

THE SIGN OF THE COCK

The Main Attributes of Cock People

Character
You have a steady character and a modern outlook. Your ideas and aims match the changing world.

Luck
You will be neither lucky nor unlucky. In times of need you will be helped by your relatives or by a colleague.

Wealth
You will be in financial trouble unless you learn to manage your affairs. Although you will earn a good salary, you will spend it quickly and carelessly.

Occupation
You are suited to self-employment, but you will not be fortunate in your work.

Social life
You have an active social life. It is unusual for you to have quiet nights at home.

Business
Your business will be successful because you think clearly, imaginatively and logically.

Romance
You will have many opportunities to meet a suitable partner and will deal seriously with romance once you have fallen in love.

Marriage
You will have a happy and fruitful marriage.

Parents
Your parents love you deeply, but your relationship with them is sometimes fraught and argumentative.

Brothers and sisters
Although you quarrel, you will always be on good terms with your brothers and sisters.

Children
You do not believe in punishing your children. You let them follow their own ideas and feelings.

Assets
Because your aims are sensible and your character stable you will easily obtain fixed assets. There may be periods of severe loss.

Travel
You will always travel safely, but you will rarely benefit from your journeys.

Health
You catch cold easily. Take care of your kidneys.

Investment
You use your intelligence to invest wisely.

Skills
Your skills will never be fully recognized. Even if you work hard you will be criticized; this is part of your fate.

Speculation
Avoid short-term investment; you are not interested in it and you will never be lucky.

Hopes
Your hopes will never be fulfilled because you lack perseverance.

Litigation
You will not be lucky in court; try to settle any law suits out of court.

Lost property
You will always have difficulty finding lost property or regaining contact with friends or relatives.

The Character of the Cock

The Cock is tenth in the cycle of the twelve animals and corresponds to the Earthly Branch Yu. The character for Yu is shaped like a vine, and it is matched to the eighth month, the time when the grape has had a chance to ferment.

The Cock is a popular animal in Chinese legend and traditionally is one of the animals who passes on advice from Heaven. Someone born in the year of the Cock is intuitive, honest and intelligent. Your decisions are respected and your business or career will always be successful. You accept challenges and are rarely defeated by obstacles.

You are sometimes impatient and rude, particularly if you do not understand others' actions or aims. You are so straightforward you are often hurtful; others take this as a sign of selfishness. You like to be the centre of attention; you distrust others and rarely accept friendly advice. You have an independent spirit. People like you but fail to understand your spirit. They are disappointed when they discover that you are an exhibitionist who prefers talking to acting. However, you are wise and courageous when faced by difficult circumstances. You are particularly astute in business and financial negotiations, but you waste more money than you save.

You enjoy well-dressed, polite company and like to create a romantic atmosphere. Men born in this year like to impress women with their appearance and intelligent conversation. Once they have committed themselves to marriage they are responsible and dedicated partners. Women born in the year of the Cock are attractive and loving, but they are bad financial managers and should try to marry someone who will take responsibility for the household finances.

You are suited to a partnership with someone born in the year of the Ox because your conservative characters are well matched. Someone born in the year of the Dragon would bring good fortune and success to your marriage or business partnership. A business partnership with someone born in the year of the Snake would be fortunate and harmonious. Avoid marrying someone born in the year of the Rabbit, the Cock, the Rat or the Dog because you would experience bad luck, misfortune and accidents. A partnership with any of the other twelve animals would be comfortable but not prosperous or fortunate.

You are suited to a career as a tailor or fashion designer, entertainer, beautician, politician, author or member of the armed forces. You are also suited to a job in a service industry or in foreign affairs.

Your Luck According to Your Year of Birth

1933, 1993

Born in the year of Kuei Yu, you belong to the Cock in the Hen Roost.

You are straightforward and just. You like to gossip and are unable to keep secrets. Your family will not be able to support you financially but you will never be short of money. You will have a prosperous old age. A woman born in one of these years will have a happy family and be successful in business.

1945, 2005
Born in the year of Yi Yu, you belong to the Singing Cock.

You are straightforward, idealistic and speak without sufficient forethought. You will have a long and prosperous life. You will be on good terms with your relatives but your brothers will never support you. A woman born in either of these years will be a good housewife.

1957, 2017
Born in the year of Ting Yu, you belong to the Lonely Cock.

You are sentimental and sociable. You will make friends with wealthy and influential people. Your youth will be difficult, but your old age will be prosperous. A woman born in either of these years will be talented, elegant and lucky.

1909, 1969
Born in the year of Chi Yu, you belong to the Cock Announcing the Dawn.

You will have a prosperous life, but your family relationships will be troubled. You are clever and understanding. You will have children late in life. A woman born in either of these years will be thrifty and erratic.

1921, 1981
Born in the year of Hsin Yu, you belong to the Cock in a Cage.

You are clever, active, prosperous and healthy. You are a good debater and well respected. Your relatives will be unable to help you in times of trouble. A woman born in either of these years will be talented and fortunate.

Your Luck According to Your Month of Birth

1st month
You are quiet, brave and resolute. You would make an excellent diplomat or politician because you have an amenable character and

can handle delicate issues efficiently. You have a healthy constitution, but you should avoid eating excessively. Take more exercise in the open air and reduce your nicotine and alcohol intake.

2nd month
You like a comfortable and independent life style; you do not like to be controlled or advised by other people. You will only hurt yourself if you fail to listen to advice. If you continue to be headstrong, your friends will abandon you. Try to be humble and tolerant. Others respect you in spite of your obstinacy, and with the help of an influential friend you will one day be very successful.

3rd month
You have a good sense of direction; you know when to stop and when to continue. You have a just and courageous nature, and although you are sensitive, others see the cool, confident side of your character. You can be selfish, suspicious and proud, but you are dutiful and obedient to your parents and older relatives. A man born in this month has a jealous nature but is also open and amenable. He will be successful if he works in literature or the arts.

4th month
You are active, open and tolerant. You are also generous, helpful and well loved by your friends and your family. Your future is prosperous and fortunate because you have an inquiring mind, a good intellect and excellent managerial skills. You will be a loving partner and husband. Heaven has given you the gift of good health.

5th month
You are energetic, kind, straightforward and understanding. You are hardworking and quick in your thoughts and actions. Although you are popular and will make a good leader, you are also self-centred and proud. Your success will last longer if you are more forgiving. You approach life cautiously and are a good judge of character. If you have been born into a wealthy family, do not take your parents' money and support for granted. You will be successful if you work away from your home town.

6th month

You have a sensitive and unsettled nature and are easily upset by the smallest disturbances. You lack the patience to complete your projects and so waste time and energy. You need someone who is willing to pick up the pieces and finish the work for you. Although you appear to be gentle and quiet, you will use any means at your disposal to achieve your aims. This is the hidden side of your character. Concentrate on the present; do not worry whether you will win or lose. Take life gradually if you hope to achieve your aims.

7th month

You have a concise and orderly mind. Whenever you have a new plan you carry it out methodically and successfully. You make firm friendships because you are a good judge of character. You are attracted to new ideas and new developments. You will be successful if you organize your work efficiently. Your luck will change for the better as you grow older. Do not abandon hope when you fail – you will always recover. In times of need you will be helped by someone in an influential position. Avoid corrupting influences.

8th month

You are generous, elegant and popular. Your motto is 'Enjoy life'. You are also vain, rarely fulfil your promises and easily fall into temptation. These are the weak points of your character, the points that others usually criticize, so try to correct them. You have a natural flair for the arts and you are suited to a literary, musical or artistic career. The path ahead of you is not always smooth, so try to avoid quarrels. If you do face trouble you will always find a solution. You will always have a comfortable standard of living.

9th month

You are emotional, obstinate and brave. You like to express your individuality in your ideas and actions. Others are naturally drawn to your charismatic nature, but you must learn to control your anger and your impatience. Try to find a job that involves personal contact. Build your career gradually and avoid entering into partnerships.

10th month

You are amenable, kind and honest. You are sometimes obstinate and proud, but you have a gentle and understanding heart. Those who recognize this trust and love you. You are a good leader and a determined fighter. The Chinese say that your luck is like the sun rising in the east. You pretend to be healthy and energetic, but you have a sensitive body and are plagued by minor illnesses that respond to the changing seasons. Take care of your respiratory system. There will be difficulties in your youth, but your hopes will be realized after middle age. Your family will be stable and respected.

11th month

Regardless of your age, your mind is as innocent as that of a new born baby. You are a good debater and enjoy investigating mysteries. You set yourself difficult goals but always work hard to achieve them. You will have a happy and contented old age. Make the most of lucky opportunities because they will arrive at irregular intervals. Your misfortune will turn to fortune as long as you control your temper. You are lucky because your natural innocence will carry you safely through life.

12th month

You have a generous nature, a masculine appearance and are impassioned in your beliefs. You are very emotional, although you appear to manage romantic situations calmly. You are just, honest, confident and persuasive. Although your goals may seem impossible, you nevertheless approach them fearlessly and steadily until you have achieved your aim. You like to work alone and enjoy privacy. You are not very lucky, but when good fortune arrives you know how to make the most of it. You will be fortunate if you handle your finances sensibly.

Your Luck According to Your Day of Birth

Born on the 1st, 10th, 19th or 28th

You are of noble bearing, independent and trustworthy. Your standards are high and you are always ready to fight for your career. You have a determined character but are overly concerned with yourself and with achieving fame and fortune. You feel the need to complete everything quickly but you frequently fail. Be careful and cautious. You are suited to a career as a civil servant or to a job in the arts. Your fortune fluctuates, and although at times you may receive unexpected money, at others you must control your spending.

Born on the 2nd, 11th, 20th or 29th

You are quiet but honest, open-hearted and extremely popular. Sometimes you like to be alone and at other times you want to be surrounded by friends. Unless you control your temper you will fall into trouble. You are suited to a career as an artistic designer, planner or literary editor. You enjoy life, even if you are in the poorest circumstances. Your fortune will not vary greatly, but your luck will improve after middle age.

Born on the 3rd, 12th, 21st or 30th

You are talented, sensitive and react quickly. You are always ready to fight for what you know is true and just. Others will avoid forming friendships with you if you are too obstinate; they wrongly assume you are too stern and difficult. You have business acumen and are suited to a disciplined job, such as the army, or to any job which has a competitive element, such as politics or the stock exchange. You must learn how to control your spending and think seriously of ways to earn more income.

Born on the 4th, 13th, 22nd or 31st

You are calm, patient and reserved. Your appearance and attitude lead others to think you are unapproachable, although in fact you are warm-hearted. If you change your approach you will be more popular. You are suited to a career as an academic, particularly in the field of theology or philosophy. Because you cannot control your spending you will lose money as easily and as quickly as you make it.

Born on the 5th, 14th or 23rd
Your fiery, obstinate nature makes it difficult for you to accept suggestions or opinions. At times your stubbornness leads to quarrels and problems. You are suited to a career in the arts, as an academic, an administrator or an advertising designer. Your intelligence enables you to work in a highly paid job. You will be lucky with money, often using it to set up new projects.

Born on the 6th, 15th or 24th
Your open, stable and cheerful character provides you with an active social life. You are affectionate and emotional and daydream so often that your mind becomes confused. Your eagerness to help others is often stifled by your indecisiveness. A career in the arts or work as a designer or social worker would be appropriate for you. You will not be very rich but will always have enough to live on.

Born on the 7th, 16th or 25th
You are an exhibitionist but when you show off nobody wants to listen to you or watch you. You enjoy an exciting life, but your head is in the clouds; you must learn to discipline yourself. You are suited to a job which allows you mobility, for example, a reporter, a traveller or an explorer. You do not want to earn a fortune and are quite content with your standard of living.

Born on the 8th, 17th or 26th
You are calm, quiet and a good judge. You have a determined and logical mind but lack social skills. You have a free spirit and are suited to self-employment. Do not buy stocks and shares or put your money in short-term investments. Your fortune is varied – it depends on your approach. There are times of wealth and times of abject poverty.

Born on the 9th, 18th or 27th
You are happy, optimistic and warm-hearted. You have an active life and are not easily troubled by minor matters. On the whole you are magnanimous but occasionally you quarrel unnecessarily with friends. It is important that you learn to control your moods. You should work as sole director or proprietor to avoid disagreements with partners. A job involving buying and selling would be suitable. You have a good income but you are extravagant.

Your Luck According to Your 'Hour' of Birth

Tzu hours: 11 p.m.–1 a.m.
You are hot-tempered, obstinate, thrifty and shy away from challenges. You are an easy target for gossip. At times you act without sufficient planning but later you regret your actions. You will be able to build a successful business, buy a home and care for your family without a family inheritance. You will achieve fame and success independently of others but if you find yourself in trouble your parents or your marriage partner will always be there to help you out.

Unlucky ages 10, 17, 35, 48, 57.

Age at death 87.

Suitable occupations Artist, politician, architect, electrician or jobs connected with metal or water.

Unsuitable occupations Work connected with earth.

Ch'ou hours: 1–3 a.m.
If you want a good career, leave your home town while you are young. Life will be difficult up to the age of twenty but then your fortune will change for the better. You will be wealthy in old age.

Unlucky ages 17, 22, 30, 45.

Age at death 71.

Suitable occupations Commercial trader, teacher, government official, restaurateur, academic, skilled manual worker or jobs connected with the final stages of production.

Unsuitable occupations Work connected with wood.

Yin hours: 3–5 a.m.
You are on bad terms with your relatives and your early years will be difficult. You will not be left an inheritance and will leave your

home town. After the age of forty everything will work out well. Old age will bring you power and wealth.

Unlucky ages 25, 28, 32, 38, 48.

Age at death 65.

Suitable occupations Doctor, musician, artist, actor, travelling agent/representative.

Unsuitable occupations Work connected with metal.

Mao hours: 5–7 a.m.
You will be very fortunate, with occasional help from your parents but none from your brothers and sisters. You will have a comfortable life and be wealthy if you work away from your home town. Marriage will be unsteady and difficult in the early years, but after middle age you will develop more satisfactory relationships and will have the chance to be wealthy.

Unlucky ages 15, 19, 54.

Age at death 71.

Suitable occupations Mechanical engineer, actor, writer, artist, theologian or work connected with religion.

Unsuitable occupations Work connected with fire.

Ch'en hours: 7–9 a.m.
You are clever, quick-witted and determined. Your warm-hearted nature enables you to form close friendships. Life is busy and varied, but a woman born in the Ch'en hours will be lonely. However, you will have many material possessions and a good salary. Your excessive self-confidence makes working relationships difficult.

Unlucky ages 18, 26, 35, 38.

Age at death 65.

Suitable occupations Entrepreneur, politician, public relations officer, teacher, miner.

Unsuitable occupations Work connected with wood.

Szu hours: 9–11 a.m.

You have outstanding talent and are able to build up your business and care for your family successfully. Family relations are troubled and you would prosper financially if you were to leave your home town. You are kind to your friends and like to help them when they are in trouble. A woman born in the Szu hours is extravagant and may have an unhappy marriage. Men and women born in these hours drink too much.

Unlucky ages 30, 35, 46, 48.

Age at death 88.

Suitable occupations Civil or electrical engineer, architect, wood or wine merchant.

Unsuitable occupations Work connected with water.

Wu hours: 11 a.m.–1 p.m.

You are active, clever, obstinate and extravagant. You prefer travelling to settling down to a job in your local area. A woman born in these hours is likely to have an unusual and fascinating character.

Unlucky ages 5, 11, 23, 32, 44, 53.

Age at death 84.

Suitable occupations Doctor, nurse, politician, film actor, skilled worker, jobs in the service industries or any work connected with oil.

Unsuitable occupations Work connected with gold.

Wei hours: 1–3 p.m.

You have a troubled relationship with your parents, brothers and

sisters and marriage partner. You will have serious difficulties in middle age. A woman born in these hours is clever but will always have difficulties with her marriage because she is too active to settle down.

Unlucky ages 18, 25, 55.

Age at death 69.

Suitable occupations Civil engineer, electrical engineer, architect, wood merchant, wine merchant.

Unsuitable occupations Work connected with water.

Shen hours: 3–5 p.m.
You will earn money easily and spend it freely. You will be luckier if you work outside your home town. Your marriage will be harmonious although your parents will not offer you moral support. A woman born in the Shen hours will be married twice. Because you are too active ever to settle down completely it is important that you are seen to behave honourably. Too much time worrying over relationships will cause your business to fail.

Unlucky ages 18, 21, 27, 29, 41, 53.

Age at death 71.

Suitable occupations Finance-related work – e.g. broker, public relations officer, watchmaker, manager – or work connected with metal.

Unsuitable occupations Work connected with wood.

Yu hours: 5–7 p.m.
Your youth is difficult because of troubled family relationships. You will be separated from your brothers and sisters and will leave home when young. You may not be able to have a child but it will be possible to adopt one. A woman born in the Yu hours is warm-hearted, fond of food and can be trusted to keep a secret.

Unlucky ages 18, 24, 31, 48.

Age at death 77.

Suitable occupations Chemist, researcher/writer, teacher, artist, technologist or work connected with the final stages of production.

Unsuitable occupations Work connected with earth.

Hsü hours: 7–9 p.m.
You are brave, capable, hardworking and run your business alone. You are optimistic and will have a successful life and a flourishing career. A woman born in the Hsü hours can be vain and impatient. You are magnanimous but on the other hand money is not important to you. You care little for others but will have a magnificent life.

Unlucky ages 15, 25, 34, 43, 48, 56.

Age at death 77.

Suitable occupations Poet, writer, investor, engineer, rice or cereal merchant, or work connected with metal and agriculture.

Unsuitable occupations Work connected with fire.

Hai hours: 9–11 p.m.
You are manually dextrous and set yourself high standards. Although you are warm-hearted you do not like to make too many friends. A woman born in the Hai hours can be obstinate. Others may be easily upset but you have the ability to forgive and forget. You are hardworking and will be fortunate.

Unlucky ages 10, 25, 35, 38, 48, 55.

Age at death 77.

Suitable occupations Surgeon, monk/nun, hotelier, artist, antiques dealer or work connected with metal.

Unsuitable occupations Work connected with fire.

Practical Advice

Your good luck will be destroyed by careless action and behaviour.
Clarify all misunderstandings as soon as possible.
Never abandon hope even though you are faced by difficulties.
Investigate fixed assets carefully before you invest your money.
Your work will run smoothly if you listen to the advice of your elders.
Do not overwork; it will ruin your concentration.
Be confident in yourself.
Be polite and kind; do not discriminate.
Do not bring career problems home with you.
Do not take competition too seriously.
Do not boast about your wealth in front of your friends; you will only spoil your friendships.
Do not expect too much; just be glad that each day has passed peacefully.

Your Luck Year by Year

Year of the Rat
One lucky star, two unlucky stars, two baleful spirits.

You will spend money celebrating weddings, birthdays and other happy events. You will lose a small sum of money.

Year of the Ox
One lucky star, four unlucky stars, one baleful spirit.

Your career will be fortunate, but you will be involved in an accident and a law suit.

Year of the Tiger
One lucky star, one baleful spirit.

This is a good year for promotion. If you own your own business you will make incredible profits this year. Your lucky star will help you turn misfortune into fortune.

Year of the Rabbit
No lucky or unlucky stars this year.

You will receive unexpected money as well as earning a good salary, whatever work you do. However, you will spend it as fast as you receive it. You will be involved in a law suit.

Year of the Dragon
Three lucky stars.

This is a lucky year. You will become well known and will be offered a position of authority.

Year of the Snake
One unlucky star.

You will be promoted to a position of authority, but your income will still be low. You will lose money and be involved in many accidents.

Year of the Horse
One lucky star, one baleful spirit.

This is a year of loss and quarrels if you lose your patience. Your lucky star gives you the opportunity to marry and to celebrate happy family events.

Year of the Ram
One lucky star, three unlucky stars.

This is a good year for your career or your business, but you may have to wear mourning clothes.

Year of the Monkey
Four unlucky stars.

This is an unlucky year of law suits and ill health.

Year of the Cock
Two lucky stars, one unlucky star, three baleful spirits.

Although this is a year of loss and misfortune, your lucky stars will give you the opportunity for promotion to a position of authority. Your lucky stars will also help you to avoid accidents and law suits.

Year of the Dog.
One lucky star, one unlucky star.

This is a year of improvements in your career and family life. You will travel extensively. There will be unhappy periods during the year.

Year of the Pig

Four unlucky stars.

This is an unlucky year of accidents and disasters. You will have problems with your career.

Your Animal Sign Horoscope

THE SIGN OF THE DOG

The Main Attributes of Dog People

Character
You are kind and honest. You are always ready to help others because you want to be popular.

Luck
You are always lucky because people trust you.

Wealth
Your hard work will reap rewards. You usually invest wisely.

Occupation
You are suited to any kind of work. Before you accept a job make sure that you can fulfil the responsibilities it entails.

Social life
You are well liked and have an active social life. You will be helped by your friends when you are in trouble.

Business
You will have a very busy and prosperous business life.

Romance
You have difficulty creating romantic situations. You approach your relationships honestly, but you are overemotional and sensitive.

Parents
Your parents love you very much, but you will be away from them for long periods of time.

Brothers and sisters
Your many brothers and sisters do not offer you much support.

Children
You love your children deeply and work hard to support them.

Assets
You have few assets. Do not try to accumulate many because you will only lose them.

Travel
You enjoy travel and all your journeys will be fortunate.

Health
You have good health, a strong physique and will live a long life.

Investment
Do not expect to earn money quickly. Work steadily and gradually if you want to make a substantial profit.

Skills
You are very good at scientific work but avoid work that involves studying.

Speculation
You will never earn much money from speculation. You will lose a lot of money if you take risks.

Hopes
Most of your hopes will be realized, but do not be too greedy.

Litigation
You are likely to win law suits, but it is better to avoid them if you can.

Lost property
You will always find lost property and regain contact with lost friends or relatives.

The Character of the Dog

The Dog is eleventh in the cycle of the twelve animals and corresponds to the Earthly Branch Hsü. Its appropriate time of day is between 7 and 9 p.m. The Dog belongs to the ninth month of the year, the season when the leaves wither and the flowers die.

The Dog is a trusting and loyal companion and the same can be said of those born in the year of the Dog. You are alert, responsible and just. You are willing to sacrifice yourself for anyone you respect and you will never betray a friend. Once you have made a promise you will fulfil it regardless of the difficulties it involves. You are observant and sensitive and keep a cool head in times of distress. Others think you are too obstinate and too critical, but you cannot help noticing and commenting on others' weaknesses. Try to be more tolerant.

You are active, energetic and clever, and if you discover an injustice you will try to correct it immediately. There is also a pessimistic side to your nature. You dislike crowded places and traditional customs; you are emotional, but have difficulty expressing your emotions; you appear to be cool, but are often moody and unsettled. Try to improve your weak points.

Although you lack elegance, you inspire confidence in others. You are a good listener who knows how to absorb information and use it efficiently. You will never be famous or wealthy, but will be popular and financially secure. You are content with a peaceful life and will never yearn for riches or luxuries.

Your lack of confidence causes romantic problems, but you will make a loyal and honest partner. You hesitate in making decisions because you are afraid that you will lose your lover. You are likely to marry a colleague or a friend because you are already comfortable in his/her presence and have already established a trusting relationship.

A man born in the year of the Dog is kind, determined and popular. Even when you fall in love you have difficulty expressing your emotions. Your partner will have to be patient and encouraging. A woman born in this year is honest, liberal and sensitive. You have an attractive, gentle and winning character. You will be fortunate if you marry early.

You are suited to marriage or partnership with someone born in the year of the Tiger. You can rely on the Tiger's bravery and romance and a Tiger person would be a supportive partner. People born in the years of the Tiger and the Dog are usually attracted at first sight. You are also suited to a partnership with someone born in the year of the Rabbit; the Rabbit's amenable and loyal character would suit your loyal nature. Someone born in the year of the Horse would make you confident and happy provided you give him/her freedom in return.

Tiger, Horse and Rabbit people are called a Three Harmony since a marriage between them would be long, happy and prosperous. Avoid a marriage or business partnership with someone born in the year of the Dragon, the Ram, the Ox or the Cock. Your partnership would result in disasters, financial loss and misfortune. A marriage with someone born in the year of the Rat, the Snake, the Monkey or the Dog would be comfortable and peaceful as long as you established a mutual respect.

You are suited to a career as a politician, philosopher, educationalist, entrepreneur, clergyman, doctor, judge, policeman, actor, writer or secret agent.

Your Luck According to Your Year of Birth

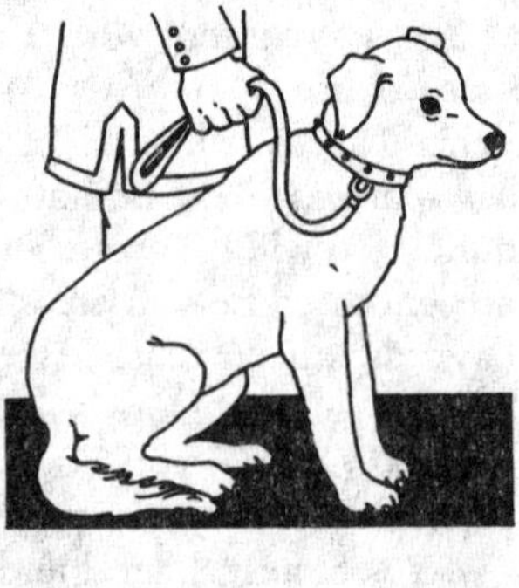

1934, 1994

Born in the year of Chia Hsü, you belong to the Dog on Guard.

You are good at arguments but often speak without sufficient forethought. Although you enjoy a busy life, you have a reflective nature. Your talent will bring you fame, wealth and power.

1946, 2006

Born in the year of Ping Hsü, you belong to the Sleepy Dog.

You will have a lucky, fortunate life. In times of need you will be helped by an influential official. You will be a good parent. A woman born in either of these years will be respected and properous.

1958, 2018

Born in the year of Mou Hsü, you belong to the Dog Going into the Mountain.

You are kind and independent. You will be poor in your early years but prosperous in your old age. You would make a good astrologer.

1910, 1970

Born in the year of Keng Hsü, you belong to the Temple Dog.

On the whole you will have a happy life, but your early years will

be marred by disasters. Your prosperity will be threatened by a retiring, quiet man. A woman born in either of these years will be prosperous.

1922, 1982

Born in the year of Jen Hsü, you belong to the Family Dog.

As long as you are kind towards others you will have enough money to live on. You can never keep hold of money for long so you will always have to work hard. You will be prosperous if you are offered help from someone in a position of power. You will have a peaceful youth and a happy old age. A woman born in either of these years will be a good housewife.

Your Luck According to Your Month of Birth

1st month
You are peaceful, honest, caring and refined. You work steadily and quietly until all your tasks are finished. You like the best of everything and enjoy eating good food. People born in this month put on weight easily. You are adept at clarifying difficult matters and have a good intellect. Try not to be too obstinate; it hinders your success.

2nd month
You are careful, honest, brave and hardworking. As soon as you have established your aim in life you will accept every challenge. Your generous and liberal attitude inspires respect in others. You are a good judge of character and always ready to sacrifice yourself for others. You will be fortunate in your business and career and will be helped by someone in an influential position. You will be wealthy if you are not too avaricious.

3rd month
You are energetic, sensitive, talented and quick to react. You have good judgement and are willing to fight for justice. Although you are always ready to help others, you are often misunderstood because of your lack of eloquence and your moody character. Your dignity, sensitivity and good taste are suited to a cultural or artistic career. If you use these points to your advantage you will be well known after middle age.

4th month
You are determined, honest, accommodating and sensible. You care what other people think of you and are usually suspicious of their ideas and their behaviour. You have a sly character and try to win others with flattery or deceit. You are hardworking, emotional and full of energy; you finish every task regardless of its complexity. You will never be wealthy, but you will be financially secure. You will lead a quiet, peaceful life; your future luck will depend on your behaviour.

5th month
Most people born in this month come from happy, peaceful families. You are quick-witted, kind, honest, straightforward and accommodating. You are well liked because of your vivid imagination and attractive character. You could never be a leader because you empathize too much with others. You are very sensitive to the sufferings of others. You are suited to a job as a secretary or an assistant. You will be fortunate once you have learned to cope with life's difficulties and hardships. Do not be an exhibitionist; try to make more friends and learn to cooperate with others.

6th month
You are brave, intelligent, eloquent and quick to act. You are ready to help others but unwilling to take orders. You will have a lucky life, your problems will be easily solved, and others will help you when you are in need. Your health is strong, your education is thorough, and you will never be short of food or clothes. You will have a happy marriage and a prosperous future. Most of your wishes will be fulfilled. Work diligently and do not be greedy.

7th month
You are kind, liberal, emotional, artistic and intelligent. You are well liked by everyone because you are ready to help others at any time. Your weak points are your pride, your moodiness and your determination to achieve your aims regardless of the methods you use. You are never defeated by the obstacles in your path. You will be fortunate in your youth but unlucky in later life. You will be promoted but will eventually lose your job. You will also be disappointed by an offer of help. Be careful before you accept help from someone in a prominent position.

8th month
You have an excellent memory and can adapt to any environment. You are clever and responsible but must learn to control your temper. You may seem weak but you have a persevering character. You are never overcome by difficulties. You have the courage to accept mistakes and to correct them. If you want to be successful try to communicate more with the people you work with and live with. You will always be able to solve the small difficulties that crop up in your life. Do not be greedy; there will be disasters if you aspire to great wealth.

9th month

You are calm, critical and inactive. You think quicker than you act and are unsuited to physical work or hobbies. You are suited to office work or to work connected with the natural sciences or journalism. Do not overestimate your own abilities but approach your work step by step. Avoid running your own business. The Chinese say that your luck is never ending like the rising of the sun and moon. You will destroy your luck if you are too ambitious or become involved in scandal.

10th month

You are honest, kind, active, clever and socially popular. You will have a very lucky and successful old age. You often avoid reality and sink into an imaginary world; you must learn to concentrate on your work. You will be famous and wealthy, but there will be many difficulties in your life. Always check your plans carefully if you want to avoid loss or disaster.

11th month

You are talented and have good powers of concentration. You are a born leader. You are very confident but also reserved; there is a side to your character that is hidden from most people. Others criticize your point of view or your attitude; you appear to be hard but you have a kind heart. You must be very careful because you will have many enemies in business, in your career and in your social life. You need not worry if you are honest and straightforward.

12th month

You are independent and hardworking, but unwilling to accept orders from others. You are socially competitive, concerned with your self-image and bored by any issue that does not relate to you. You have a wilful character and will quarrel or fight unless you are the centre of conversation. Amend your weak points if you want to be trusted. Once you have learned to be patient and considerate others will help you. Instead of destroying your fortune, you will be successful.

Your Luck According to Your Day of Birth

Born on the 1st, 10th, 19th or 28th

You are of noble bearing, independent and trustworthy. Your standards are high and you are always ready to fight for your career. You have a determined character but are overly concerned with yourself and with achieving fame and fortune. You feel the need to complete everything quickly but you frequently fail. Be careful and cautious. You are suited to a career as a civil servant or to a job in the arts. Your fortune fluctuates, and although at times you may receive unexpected money, at others you must control your spending.

Born on the 2nd, 11th, 20th or 29th

You are quiet but honest, open-hearted and extremely popular. Sometimes you like to be alone and at other times you want to be surrounded by friends. Unless you control your temper you will fall into trouble. You are suited to a career as an artistic designer, planner or literary editor. You enjoy life, even if you are in the poorest circumstances. Your fortune will not vary greatly, but your luck will improve after middle age.

Born on the 3rd, 12th, 21st or 30th

You are talented, sensitive and react quickly. You are always ready to fight for what you know is true and just. Others will avoid forming friendships with you if you are too obstinate; they wrongly assume you are too stern and difficult. You have business acumen and are suited to a disciplined job, such as the army, or to any job which has a competitive element, such as politics or the stock exchange. You must learn how to control your spending and think seriously of ways to earn more income.

Born on the 4th, 13th, 22nd or 31st

You are calm, patient and reserved. Your appearance and attitude lead others to think you are unapproachable, although in fact you are warm-hearted. If you change your approach you will be more popular. You are suited to a career as an academic, particularly in the field of theology or philosophy. Because you cannot control your spending you will lose money as easily and as quickly as you make it.

Born on the 5th, 14th or 23rd

Your fiery, obstinate nature makes it difficult for you to accept suggestions or opinions. At times your stubbornness leads to quarrels and problems. You are suited to a career in the arts, as an academic, an administrator or an advertising designer. Your intelligence enables you to work in a highly paid job. You will be lucky with money, often using it to set up new projects.

Born on the 6th, 15th or 24th

Your open, stable and cheerful character provides you with an active social life. You are affectionate and emotional and daydream so often that your mind becomes confused. Your eagerness to help others is often stifled by your indecisiveness. A career in the arts or work as a designer or social worker would be appropriate for you. You will not be very rich but will always have enough to live on.

Born on the 7th, 16th or 25th

You are an exhibitionist but when you show off nobody wants to listen to you or watch you. You enjoy an exciting life, but your head is in the clouds; you must learn to discipline yourself. You are suited to a job which allows you mobility, for example, a reporter, a traveller or an explorer. You do not want to earn a fortune and are quite content with your standard of living.

Born on the 8th, 17th or 26th

You are calm, quiet and a good judge. You have a determined and logical mind but lack social skills. You have a free spirit and are suited to self-employment. Do not buy stocks and shares or put your money in short-term investments. Your fortune is varied – it depends on your approach. There are times of wealth and times of abject poverty.

Born on the 9th, 18th or 27th

You are happy, optimistic and warm-hearted. You have an active life and are not easily troubled by minor matters. On the whole you are magnanimous but occasionally you quarrel unnecessarily with friends. It is important that you learn to control your moods. You should work as sole director or proprietor to avoid disagreements with partners. A job involving buying and selling would be suitable. You have a good income but you are extravagant.

Your Luck According to Your 'Hour' of Birth

Tzu hours: 11 p.m.–1 a.m.

You are hot-tempered, obstinate, thrifty and shy away from challenges. You are an easy target for gossip. At times you act without sufficient planning but later you regret your actions. You will be able to build a successful business, buy a home and care for your family without a family inheritance. You will achieve fame and success independently of others but if you find yourself in trouble your parents or your marriage partner will always be there to help you out.

Unlucky ages 10, 17, 35, 48, 57.

Age at death 87.

Suitable occupations Artist, politician, architect, electrician or jobs connected with metal or water.

Unsuitable occupations Work connected with earth.

Ch'ou hours: 1–3 a.m.

If you want a good career, leave your home town while you are young. Life will be difficult up to the age of twenty but then your fortune will change for the better. You will be wealthy in old age.

Unlucky ages 17, 22, 30, 45.

Age at death 71.

Suitable occupations Commercial trader, teacher, government official, restaurateur, academic, skilled manual worker or jobs connected with the final stages of production.

Unsuitable occupations Work connected with wood.

Yin hours: 3–5 a.m.

You are on bad terms with your relatives and your early years will be difficult. You will not be left an inheritance and will leave your

home town. After the age of forty everything will work out well. Old age will bring you power and wealth.

Unlucky ages 25, 28, 32, 38, 48.

Age at death 65.

Suitable occupations Doctor, musician, artist, actor, travelling agent/representative.

Unsuitable occupations Work connected with metal.

Mao hours: 5–7 a.m.
You will be very fortunate, with occasional help from your parents but none from your brothers and sisters. You will have a comfortable life and be wealthy if you work away from your home town. Marriage will be unsteady and difficult in the early years, but after middle age you will develop more satisfactory relationships and will have the chance to be wealthy.

Unlucky ages 15, 19, 54.

Age at death 71.

Suitable occupations Mechanical engineer, actor, writer, artist, theologian or work connected with religion.

Unsuitable occupations Work connected with fire.

Ch'en hours: 7–9 a.m.
You are clever, quick-witted and determined. Your warm-hearted nature enables you to form close friendships. Life is busy and varied, but a woman born in the Ch'en hours will be lonely. However, you will have many material possessions and a good salary. Your excessive self-confidence makes working relationships difficult.

Unlucky ages 18, 26, 35, 38.

Age at death 65.

Suitable occupations Entrepreneur, politician, public relations officer, teacher, miner.

Unsuitable occupations Work connected with wood.

Szu hours: 9–11 a.m.
You have outstanding talent and are able to build up your business and care for your family successfully. Family relations are troubled and you would prosper financially if you were to leave your home town. You are kind to your friends and like to help them when they are in trouble. A woman born in the Szu hours is extravagant and may have an unhappy marriage. Men and women born in these hours drink too much.

Unlucky ages 30, 35, 46, 48.

Age at death 88.

Suitable occupations Civil or electrical engineer, architect, wood or wine merchant.

Unsuitable occupations Work connected with water.

Wu hours: 11 a.m.–1 p.m.
You are active, clever, obstinate and extravagant. You prefer travelling to settling down to a job in your local area. A woman born in these hours is likely to have an unusual and fascinating character.

Unlucky ages 5, 11, 23, 32, 44, 53.

Age at death 84.

Suitable occupations Doctor, nurse, politician, film actor, skilled worker, jobs in the service industries or any work connected with oil.

Unsuitable occupations Work connected with gold.

Wei hours: 1–3 p.m.
You have a troubled relationship with your parents, brothers and

sisters and marriage partner. You will have serious difficulties in middle age. A woman born in these hours is clever but will always have difficulties with her marriage because she is too active to settle down.

Unlucky ages 18, 25, 55.

Age at death 69.

Suitable occupations Civil engineer, electrical engineer, architect, wood merchant, wine merchant.

Unsuitable occupations Work connected with water.

Shen hours: 3–5 p.m.
You will earn money easily and spend it freely. You will be luckier if you work outside your home town. Your marriage will be harmonious although your parents will not offer you moral support. A woman born in the Shen hours will be married twice. Because you are too active ever to settle down completely it is important that you are seen to behave honourably. Too much time worrying over relationships will cause your business to fail.

Unlucky ages 18, 21, 27, 29, 41, 53.

Age at death 71.

Suitable occupations Finance-related work – e.g. broker, public relations officer, watchmaker, manager – or work connected with metal.

Unsuitable occupations Work connected with wood.

Yu hours: 5–7 p.m.
Your youth is difficult because of troubled family relationships. You will be separated from your brothers and sisters and will leave home when young. You may not be able to have a child but it will be possible to adopt one. A woman born in the Yu hours is warm-hearted, fond of food and can be trusted to keep a secret.

Unlucky ages 18, 24, 31, 48.

Age at death 77.

Suitable occupations Chemist, researcher/writer, teacher, artist, technologist or work connected with the final stages of production.

Unsuitable occupations Work connected with earth.

Hsü hours: 7–9 p.m.
You are brave, capable, hardworking and run your business alone. You are optimistic and will have a successful life and a flourishing career. A woman born in the Hsü hours can be vain and impatient. You are magnanimous but on the other hand money is not important to you. You care little for others but will have a magnificent life.

Unlucky ages 15, 25, 34, 43, 48, 56.

Age at death 77.

Suitable occupations Poet, writer, investor, engineer, rice or cereal merchant, or work connected with metal and agriculture.

Unsuitable occupations Work connected with fire.

Hai hours: 9–11 p.m.
You are manually dextrous and set yourself high standards. Although you are warm-hearted you do not like to make too many friends. A woman born in the Hai hours can be obstinate. Others may be easily upset but you have the ability to forgive and forget. You are hardworking and will be fortunate.

Unlucky ages 10, 25, 35, 38, 48, 55.

Age at death 77.

Suitable occupations Surgeon, monk/nun, hotelier, artist, antiques dealer or work connected with metal.

Unsuitable occupations Work connected with fire.

Practical Advice

Give yourself time to consider your situation; decide on the best approach before acting.
Do not try to trick others with your eloquent speech.
Push yourself; do not spoil opportunities with your bad moods.
Be patient when younger relatives or less experienced people come to you for help.
Abide by your decisions.
Clarify misunderstandings immediately.
You will be successful if you are honest and loyal to others.
Be respectful and polite to your superiors and older relatives.
You will achieve greater success if you cooperate with others.
Correct minor mistakes because they may be the mistakes that ruin your plans.
If you are greedy you will suffer a great loss.

Your Luck Year by Year

Year of the Rat
Two lucky stars, two baleful spirits.

This is a lucky and prosperous year, but there will be periods of loss and accidents.

Year of the Ox
Four baleful spirits.

This is an unlucky year. Beware of accidents and take care of your health. You are unable to make any important decisions and will have to listen to the complaints of others.

Year of the Tiger
Six unlucky stars.

Unlucky stars are shining on you this year. It is a year of failure and financial loss. You will be hurt or deceived by a close friend. Beware of corrupt influences.

Year of the Rabbit
Three lucky stars.

This is a year of promotion and profit. It is a lucky and happy year for you.

Year of the Dragon
Three baleful spirits.

This is an unlucky year of quarrels, loss and disasters.

Year of the Snake
Three lucky stars, three unlucky stars.

You will be offered good promotion this year, but try not to get involved in any corrupt dealings. Your lucky stars are shining on you; problems will be sorted out and you will win a law suit.

Year of the Horse
Two lucky stars, one unlucky star.

You will be offered promotion this year, your salary will be increased and you will be given a position of authority. There may be a small loss and a period of mourning.

Year of the Ram
Two lucky stars, four unlucky stars.

This is a year of loss and business decline, but you will pull through these difficulties because a lucky star is shining on you.

Year of the Monkey
Three unlucky stars.

This is a year of social gatherings and parties. You will be financially stable, travel extensively and eat good food.

Year of the Cock
Two unlucky stars.

You are confronted with bad luck whichever direction you go. You will lose your job, be involved in a law suit and suffer from ill health.

Year of the Dog
One lucky star, three unlucky stars.

Attend as many social gatherings as possible this year. This is the best way to avert the disasters that the year holds in store.

Year of the Pig

Two lucky stars.

You will receive unexpected money. You will be untouched by difficulties this year. If you start your own business you will make a large profit.

Your Animal Sign Horoscope

THE SIGN OF THE PIG

The Main Attributes of Pig People

Character
You have an honest and virtuous character. You approach every task seriously and complete it efficiently.

Luck
You will be neither lucky nor unlucky, but will succeed through hard work.

Wealth
You cannot achieve a balance between spending and saving, so although you may have a good salary you will not have many savings.

Occupation
You are suited to quiet, reflective jobs such as a writer, potter, artist, researcher or craft worker.

Social life
You feel uncomfortable in the company of other people. You are withdrawn at parties and other large gatherings.

Business
Do not push your career or your business too far. Take it step by step, so it can progress smoothly and naturally. This is your safest way to success.

Romance

It is difficult to find the right partner, but once you meet the right person, you will fall deeply in love.

Marriage

In spite of falling so deeply in love, your love may dwindle after marriage. You and your partner may have one or more affairs.

Parents

Your parents may not give you any money, but they love you and offer you moral support.

Brothers and sisters

Your relationship with your brothers and sisters is good, but they cannot help you financially.

Children

A pig is extremely fond of its piglets. If you tried to take a piglet away from its mother, she would attack you. In the same way, you are extremely fond of your family and children and you are willing to work hard for them.

Assets

You own property, but will sell it at a loss.

Travel

The pig cannot walk long distances and you are not suited to long journeys. You may have an accident if you travel long distances.

Health

You have a healthy constitution, although you occasionally suffer from minor illnesses.

Investment

Be patient, avoid arguments, and so long as you are patient your investments will yield good profits.

Skills

You are suited to quiet, studious jobs. You will be successful and famous if you work hard in your chosen profession.

Speculation
Do not expect a great profit if you gamble or speculate.

Hopes
Very few of your hopes will be fulfilled.

Litigation
Do your best to settle any dispute out of court; in court you will probably lose.

Lost property
After waiting a long time you will find what you have lost and re-establish contact with old friends.

The Character of the Pig

The Pig is represented by the Earthly Branch Hai. It is the last animal of the twelve animal signs. The Pig belongs to the tenth month, a cold month when all creatures are desolate. The time corresponding to Hai is between 9 and 11 p.m. Hai can also be written as 'Hut', which means the edible kernel inside a nut; alternatively it can mean 'central' or 'blossom'.

You have lofty ideas but may be a selfish and overconfident leader. You are reserved, hard-working and warm-hearted, but you can also be impatient and waste time on aimless pursuits. Take no notice of the Pig's ugly face; Pig people are brave, careful, affectionate and cooperative. They represent kindness and innocence and are willing to serve others. You will rarely find a Pig person who is deceitful or betrays his or her friends. Pig people are true, frank and generous. Of all the twelve animal signs, the Pig suffers most and will probably be treated badly.

You tolerate being the butt of others' jokes. You concentrate on your own work and have no desire to compete with others. You seldom tell lies, and others appreciate your attitude and your kindness. Once you decide to accept someone as a friend, your relationship with him or her will be sincere and trustworthy. If you are taken advantage of or persecuted, you protect yourself without harming others.

Pig people are like Monkey people: they are talented and clever. You are a keen learner and an avid reader. Your self-respect and self-confidence made you unpopular when you were young, but these characteristics are more acceptable to others as you grow older.

Your social life is limited but your few close friends are firm friends; you are ready to sacrifice yourself for them. Someone born in the year of the Pig makes an excellent marriage partner. He/she is devoted and protective. A woman born in this year is a good housewife. Although your reactions are slow, you are not stupid. No matter what career you pursue, you can cope with responsibility. You are a skilled writer and have a sensible approach to most things but are inept at financial management. You carry out your work skilfully and thoroughly.

Many Pig people are famous, but they are easily frightened and angered if someone threatens their fame. You can suffer pain and difficulty, but cannot bear being given a bad reputation. You sometimes upset others by your sarcasm. You do not need to work very hard to obtain your daily living as others will bring you jobs and money. The Chinese say that pigs are wary of the hand that feeds them because they know that they will eventually be killed for market. Likewise the Pig person understands his or her situation clearly. You find it difficult to trust others and are wary if they offer support. Others abuse your weak points in business and romance. You will pass through several unhappy relationships before you find an ideal partner, but once you do, you will look after your partner in sickness and in health.

A man who is born in the year of the pig loves his family deeply. He is attracted to women of small physical build and to women born in the year of the Rabbit or the Ram. A woman born in the year of the Pig is active and careful. She will not show her feelings until she knows her partner's emotions. As long as her husband gives her confidence and looks after her, she will be a caring, loyal wife, a loving mother and a good housewife.

To have a happy, prosperous marriage, marry someone born in the year of the Ram or the Rabbit because your good luck will benefit your children. Avoid marrying someone born in the year of the Snake, the Monkey or the Pig because he/she will bring misfortune. If there is mutual respect you will have a peaceful life with someone born in the year of the Rat, the Ox, the Tiger, the Dragon, the Horse, the Cock or the Dog.

You are suited to a career as a scientist, writer, painter, musician, engineer, skilled worker, technician, doctor or actor.

Your Luck According to Your Year of Birth

1935, 1995

Born in the year of Yi Hai, you belong to the Pig Passing By.

Your youth will be problematic, but your later life will be happy and peaceful. Family relationships are difficult, but you may be close to older people outside your family circle. Your marriage will be happy and prosperous, and you will have two sons and two daughters-in-law. You are impatient and speak without due consideration.

1947, 2007

Born in the year of Ting Hai, you belong to the Pig Passing the Mountain.

You are clever and talented. Your relationship with your children will be difficult and it would be advisable to have them early in life. Be kind and your life will be long, lucky and prosperous.

1959, 2019

Born in the year of Chi Hai, you belong to the Monastery Pig.

You are intelligent and financially comfortable, but you will not be helped by your mother or other relations.

1911, 1971

Born in the year of Hsin Hai, you belong to the Pig in the Garden.

You do not worry about matters which do not concern you. Your youth is poor and unhappy, but in the later years you will be wealthy and honoured. A woman born in either of these years will be a good housewife.

1923, 1983
Born in the year of Kuei Hai, you belong to the Pig in the Forest.

You have an obstinate nature and will not be supported by your relatives. You will have a fortunate life and a prosperous old age.

Your Luck According to Your Month of Birth

1st month
Your character is affected by the character of the previous year, the Dog year. You are sincere, intelligent and determined to see each task through to its end. Although you are ambitious, you sometimes react slowly and carelessly. Your marriage partner will have similar interests and hobbies and you will meet each other through social activities. The Chinese say that your love will be as durable and strong as the rising sun and moon. Every task you approach will be successful, your career will run smoothly and your marriage will be happy. Do not be avaricious; greed will bring loss and misfortune.

2nd month
Your honesty, determination and financial acumen enable your business to prosper. You form strong relationships with others and must use this talent to further your career. People in influential positions are willing to help you. Do not be obsessed with the idea of fame and fortune. Your plans initially run smoothly but then difficulties arise. Do not abandon projects halfway through; persevere and in the end everything will work out successfully. You will be tempted by affairs outside your marriage, but try to be faithful to your partner.

3rd month
You are brave and straightforward, but you are a daydreamer; instead of working towards your goals, you pass your time thinking about them. You seldom consider the people around you and recklessly rush into new projects. Learn to accept others' advice and do not be overconfident. Avoid quarrelling; if you want to be successful be on good terms with older relatives or influential people. Your luck seems to be against you, but in fact it is in your favour. You will be successful if you approach your work gradually, concentrate on your strong points and put in sufficient groundwork.

4th month
You are elegant, quick-witted and therefore popular at social gatherings. You are determined and ambitious and have the confidence to carry out your goals. Your social life is active because you are kind, accommodating and open, but you are sometimes held back by nervousness and worry. You earn money easily, but your earnings are soon spent because of your busy social life. You will marry at about the age of twenty. A woman born in this month will be a good wife because she has the four characteristics: the Chinese say that a good wife is virtuous, skilled in conversation, beautiful in appearance and talented at needlework.

5th month
You are stubborn, although you seem to follow in others' footsteps. You are trustworthy and straightforward, but you take your work too seriously and find it difficult to deal with others. Fortunately your patience and fortitude enable you to achieve your goals. Once you learn to treat people leniently, they will help you with your career. Everybody is talented in some way, but they must learn to put this talent to good use; you must nurture your confidence and you too will one day be successful. Because you are easily frightened you could never cope with a position of power, but you will always have an adequate income. Do not expect any sudden windfalls or inheritances. You can expect a satisfying profit if you run your own business, but do not speculate. After middle age your future looks happy and prosperous.

6th month

You are pessimistic and slow to react, but once you have made a decision you carry out your work competently and quickly. Although you are talented, you are unsure of your capabilities and easily upset by small matters. People sometimes ignore you because you fail to use your talents to the best of your ability. You are too emotional, lack judgement and abandon projects hastily. Everything will work out well if you acknowledge your weak points and try to correct them. You seem to be lucky, but more often than not your efforts are misplaced and your energy wasted. The Chinese say that you aim for the moon on the water or the flowers in the mirror. Do not try to expand your business: you will lose money or meet misfortune. Do not act as a guarantor, do not quarrel, avoid gossip and then your business should be safe.

7th month

You make friends easily but lose them just as quickly through arguments. You are unsure of your future and are easily distracted, often regretting words said in haste. You abandon projects when they are half completed because you are easily bored. Learn to be humble if you want to be successful, but do not expect rapid promotion opportunities. Persevere with your work; do not expect sudden windfalls or inheritances. Be patient; you will never be extremely wealthy, but one day you may be able to afford property outside your own country. There may be unavoidable financial losses during your life so choose your friends carefully and approach them warily.

8th month

You are elegant, charitable, hardworking and socially popular. People want to make friends with you wherever you go. Once you decide to take on a project, you will see it through to a successful end no matter how tired you are. You are a responsible, respected and active leader. You will always be financially comfortable and will one day receive an unexpected sum of money. Do not be greedy, otherwise you will court arguments. If you run your own business you will be helped by an influential person. Remember to cultivate your kindness, understanding and virtue.

9th month
You are sensitive, kind and socially active. You approach everything seriously, no matter how large or small, and try your best to make it succeed. You tire easily because you spend too much time thinking and working. You have many hobbies and are socially popular. Your strong self-respect and resolute attitude enable you to complete your work efficiently and without complaint. You enjoy eating and have difficulty keeping slim. Heaven has bestowed good fortune on you throughout your life. No matter what business you run or career you practise, you will be financially secure, particularly after middle age.

10th month
You have an outstanding character: you are honest, trustworthy, open and warm. Your friendships are firm and long-standing. Because you are moderately opinioned, active and considerate, you are loved and respected by everyone. You are strong and resolute but never stubborn. Control your finances, otherwise you will run into debt; you have a good income, but you are an extravagant spender.

11th month
You are sensitive, alert and courageous, but your confidence and outspoken manner sometimes cause difficulties. You have a keen interest in new fashions and ideas, but you do not alter your opinions easily. Although you are fond of your friends and family you do not involve yourself in many social activities. Throughout life you will be lucky and free from worry. Your career and business will prosper, but you must always be alert and active, otherwise your luck will disappear.

12th month
You have a cheerful, open character. As long as you feel confident in your own ability you will be successful in your work. You have a frank and honest character and are ready to fight for your beliefs. Try to curb your outspoken manner because you sometimes hurt other people. Be patient and try not to exaggerate. You will not fail if you approach people and plans with an open mind. Your luck is good but you will never attain a position of authority. There will be career and

business difficulties and you must learn not to trust others implicitly. Your problems can be solved if you work hard and avoid quarrels. You will damage your family relationships and lose money if you are too obstinate.

Your Luck According to Your Day of Birth

Born on the 1st, 10th, 19th or 28th

You are of noble bearing, independent and trustworthy. Your standards are high and you are always ready to fight for your career. You have a determined character but are overly concerned with yourself and with achieving fame and fortune. You feel the need to complete everything quickly but you frequently fail. Be careful and cautious. You are suited to a career as a civil servant or to a job in the arts. Your fortune fluctuates, and although at times you may receive unexpected money, at others you must control your spending.

Born on the 2nd, 11th, 20th or 29th

You are quiet but honest, open-hearted and extremely popular. Sometimes you like to be alone and at other times you want to be surrounded by friends. Unless you control your temper you will fall into trouble. You are suited to a career as an artistic designer, planner or literary editor. You enjoy life, even if you are in the poorest circumstances. Your fortune will not vary greatly, but your luck will improve after middle age.

Born on the 3rd, 12th, 21st or 30th

You are talented, sensitive and react quickly. You are always ready to fight for what you know is true and just. Others will avoid forming friendships with you if you are too obstinate; they wrongly assume you are too stern and difficult. You have business acumen and are suited to a disciplined job, such as the army, or to any job which has a competitive element, such as politics or the stock exchange. You must learn how to control your spending and think seriously of ways to earn more income.

Born on the 4th, 13th, 22nd or 31st

You are calm, patient and reserved. Your appearance and attitude lead others to think you are unapproachable, although in fact you are warm-hearted. If you change your approach you will be more popular. You are suited to a career as an academic, particularly in the field of theology or philosophy. Because you cannot control your spending you will lose money as easily and as quickly as you make it.

Born on the 5th, 14th or 23rd

Your fiery, obstinate nature makes it difficult for you to accept suggestions or opinions. At times your stubbornness leads to quarrels and problems. You are suited to a career in the arts, as an academic, an administrator or an advertising designer. Your intelligence enables you to work in a highly paid job. You will be lucky with money, often using it to set up new projects.

Born on the 6th, 15th or 24th

Your open, stable and cheerful character provides you with an active social life. You are affectionate and emotional and daydream so often that your mind becomes confused. Your eagerness to help others is often stifled by your indecisiveness. A career in the arts or work as a designer or social worker would be appropriate for you. You will not be very rich but will always have enough to live on.

Born on the 7th, 16th or 25th

You are an exhibitionist but when you show off nobody wants to listen to you or watch you. You enjoy an exciting life, but your head is in the clouds; you must learn to discipline yourself. You are suited to a job which allows you mobility, for example, a reporter, a traveller or an explorer. You do not want to earn a fortune and are quite content with your standard of living.

Born on the 8th, 17th or 26th

You are calm, quiet and a good judge. You have a determined and logical mind but lack social skills. You have a free spirit and are suited to self-employment. Do not buy stocks and shares or put your money in short-term investments. Your fortune is varied – it depends on your approach. There are times of wealth and times of abject poverty.

Born on the 9th, 18th or 27th

You are happy, optimistic and warm-hearted. You have an active life and are not easily troubled by minor matters. On the whole you are magnanimous but occasionally you quarrel unnecessarily with friends. It is important that you learn to control your moods. You should work as sole director or proprietor to avoid disagreements with partners. A job involving buying and selling would be suitable. You have a good income but you are extravagant.

Your Luck According to Your 'Hour' of Birth

Tzu hours: 11 p.m. – 1 a.m.
You are hot-tempered, obstinate, thrifty and shy away from challenges. You are an easy target for gossip. At times you act without sufficient planning but later you regret your actions. You will be able to build a successful business, buy a home and care for your family without a family inheritance. You will achieve fame and success independently of others but if you find yourself in trouble your parents or your marriage partner will always be there to help you out.

Unlucky ages 10, 17, 35, 48, 57.

Age at death 87.

Suitable occupations Artist, politician, architect, electrician or jobs connected with metal or water.

Unsuitable occupations Work connected with earth.

Ch'ou hours: 1–3 a.m.
If you want a good career, leave your home town while you are young. Life will be difficult up to the age of twenty but then your fortune will change for the better. You will be wealthy in old age.

Unlucky ages 17, 22, 30, 45.

Age at death 71.

Suitable occupations Commercial trader, teacher, government official, restaurateur, academic, skilled manual worker or jobs connected with the final stages of production.

Unsuitable occupations Work connected with wood.

Yin hours: 3–5 a.m.
You are on bad terms with your relatives and your early years will be difficult. You will not be left an inheritance and will leave your home town. After the age of forty everything will work out well. Old age will bring you power and wealth.

Unlucky ages 25, 28, 32, 38, 48.

Age at death 65.

Suitable occupations Doctor, musician, artist, actor, travelling agent/representative.

Unsuitable occupations Work connected with metal.

Mao hours: 5–7 a.m.
You will be very fortunate, with occasional help from your parents but none from your brothers and sisters. You will have a comfortable life and be wealthy if you work away from your home town. Marriage will be unsteady and difficult in the early years, but after middle age you will develop more satisfactory relationships and will have the chance to be wealthy.

Unlucky ages 15, 19, 54.

Age at death 71.

Suitable occupations Mechanical engineer, actor, writer, artist, theologian or work connected with religion.

Unsuitable occupations Work connected with fire.

Ch'en hours: 7–9 a.m.
You are clever, quick-witted and determined. Your warm-hearted nature enables you to form close friendships. Life is busy and varied, but a woman born in the Ch'en hours will be lonely. However, you will have many material possessions and a good

salary. Your excessive self-confidence makes working relationships difficult.

Unlucky ages 18, 26, 35, 38.

Age at death 65.

Suitable occupations Entrepreneur, politician, public relations officer, teacher, miner.

Unsuitable occupations Work connected with wood.

Szu hours: 9–11 a.m.
You have outstanding talent and are able to build up your business and care for your family successfully. Family relations are troubled and you would prosper financially if you were to leave your home town. You are kind to your friends and like to help them when they are in trouble. A woman born in the Szu hours is extravagant and may have an unhappy marriage. Men and women born in these hours drink too much.

Unlucky ages 30, 35, 46, 48.

Age at death 88.

Suitable occupations Civil or electrical engineer, architect, wood or wine merchant.

Unsuitable occupations Work connected with water.

Wu hours: 11 a.m.–1 p.m.
You are active, clever, obstinate and extravagant. You prefer travelling to settling down to a job in your local area. A woman born in these hours is likely to have an unusual and fascinating character.

Unlucky ages 5, 11, 23, 32, 44, 53.

Age at death 84.

Suitable occupations Doctor, nurse, politician, film actor, skilled worker, jobs in the service industries or any work connected with oil.

Unsuitable occupations Work connected with gold.

Wei hours: 1–3 p.m.
You have a troubled relationship with your parents, brothers and sisters and marriage partner. You will have serious difficulties in middle age. A woman born in these hours is clever but will always have difficulties with her marriage because she is too active to settle down.

Unlucky ages 18, 25, 55.

Age at death 69.

Suitable occupations Civil engineer, electrical engineer, architect, wood merchant, wine merchant.

Unsuitable occupations Work connected with water.

Shen hours: 3–5 p.m.
You will earn money easily and spend it freely. You will be luckier if you work outside your home town. Your marriage will be harmonious although your parents will not offer you moral support. A woman born in the Shen hours will be married twice. Because you are too active ever to settle down completely it is important that you are seen to behave honourably. Too much time worrying over relationships will cause your business to fail.

Unlucky ages 18, 21, 27, 29, 41, 53.

Age at death 71.

Suitable occupations Finance-related work – e.g. broker, public relations officer, watchmaker, manager – or work connected with metal.

Unsuitable occupations Work connected with wood.

Yu hours: 5–7 p.m.
Your youth is difficult because of troubled family relationships. You will be separated from your brothers and sisters and will leave home when young. You may not be able to have a child but it will be possible to adopt one. A woman born in the Yu hours is warm-hearted, fond of food and can be trusted to keep a secret.

Unlucky ages 18, 24, 31, 48.

Age at death 77.

Suitable occupations Chemist, researcher/writer, teacher, artist, technologist or work connected with the final stages of production.

Unsuitable occupations Work connected with earth.

Hsü hours: 7–9 p.m.
You are brave, capable, hardworking and run your business alone. You are optimistic and will have a successful life and a flourishing career. A woman born in the Hsü hours can be vain and impatient. You are magnanimous but on the other hand money is not important to you. You care little for others but will have a magnificent life.

Unlucky ages 15, 25, 34, 43, 48, 56.

Age at death 77.

Suitable occupations Poet, writer, investor, engineer, rice or cereal merchant, or work connected with metal and agriculture.

Unsuitable occupations Work connected with fire.

Hai hours: 9–11 p.m.
You are manually dextrous and set yourself high standards. Although you are warm-hearted you do not like to make too many friends. A woman born in the Hai hours can be obstinate. Others may be easily upset but you have the ability to forgive and forget. You are hardworking and will be fortunate.

Unlucky ages 10, 25, 35, 38, 48, 55.

Age at death 77.

Suitable occupations Surgeon, monk/nun, hotelier, artist, antiques dealer or work connected with metal.

Unsuitable occupations Work connected with fire.

Practical Advice

Do not be afraid to take up a challenge, but do not hurt other people's pride.

Try your best to avoid arguments.

There will be problems if you borrow or lend money.

You will be successful if you concentrate on your work.

Be kind to others. Once you decide to do something, do it immediately and you will be successful.

Work hard and listen to advice.

Kindness wins love and respect. As soon as others have confidence in you, your business will flourish.

You will be fortunate if you are cheerful and friendly towards others.

Work on new ideas; do not limit yourself to traditional ways.

You will have a peaceful life if you keep healthy and approach life carefully.

Your Luck Year by Year

Year of the Rat

One lucky star, two baleful spirits.

Your business will suffer this year. You will have accidents but will be saved by the happiness god, T'ai Yang, who is shining this year.

Year of the Ox
One baleful star, two unlucky stars.

This is a year of parties and good food. Your savings will be low this year and you will have many quarrels and accidents. It is an unlucky year. You will travel long distances.

Year of the Tiger
Three lucky stars.

This is a year of parties and good food. You will save money and the happiness gods will be with you. You will be promoted during this happy year.

Year of the Rabbit
Three lucky stars.

The happiness gods are with you throughout this enjoyable and prosperous year. You will accumulate savings, be promoted to a position of authority and receive many invitations to social occasions.

Year of the Dragon
Two lucky stars.

You will be promoted to a position of authority this year. You will lead a group of people working outside your home town. You will have a happy and successful year.

Year of the Snake
One lucky travelling star, three unlucky stars, one baleful spirit.

Like a tiger escaping its cage, you will earn money from a partnership or from speculation, but you will also lose a large sum of money. You will wear mourning clothes during the year.

Year of the Horse
One lucky star, two unlucky stars.

There will be accidents and disasters this year.

Year of the Ram
One lucky star, two unlucky stars.

You will be promoted to a position of authority, but you will also be involved in an accident or disaster.

Year of the Monkey

Two lucky stars, three unlucky stars.

You will receive unexpected money. You will wear mourning clothes. This is a year of quarrels and business loss.

Year of the Cock

One lucky star, five unlucky stars.

You will be promoted from the position of assistant to group leader, but there will be no rewards for your hard work. You will be involved in a law suit, lose money and suffer an accident.

Year of the Dog

One lucky star, five unlucky stars.

This is an unlucky, uncomfortable year. Nothing seems to go well, but things will get better because the happiness god T'ien Hsi is with you.

Year of the Pig

Seven unlucky stars.

Your career is unstable and it is a year of accident and injury. Your business will go into decline and nothing will go according to plan.

Tzu Wei (Purple Star) Astrological System

INTRODUCTION

Tzu Wei (Purple Star) astrology was written down in the Sung dynasty (960–1280 AD). It was drawn together and elaborated on by the master astrologer Ch'en T'u Nan, who is also known as Ch'en Hsi I (this was an additional name taken at the age of twenty in ancient China). However, elements of the Tzu Wei system were already being practised during the T'ang dynasty (618–907 AD). It is an accurate method of fortune-telling yet has the advantage of being simple to use.

The Tzu Wei method centres on the Chinese concept of *ming* (life or fate). It attempts to explain why one person's *ming* is so different from another's. Why do some people have good fortune, social position, riches or long life, when others are unlucky, suffer tragedies, are poor or die young? How is it that some never have to work but are well off, while others have to work as labourers for a pittance?

In Tzu Wei astrology your *ming* is believed to be controlled by your horoscope. Your horoscope comes with you at birth, and is based on your year of birth, your month of birth, your day of birth and your hour of birth. This means that to understand your *ming* – to discover if your fate is good or bad – you need to examine your horoscope. The Tzu Wei method provides a means of doing this in detail.

In China the Tzu Wei method is very well known. It remains pure and distinct from the other main ancient Chinese astrological system, the Szu Chu (Four-Pole astrology). In Japan the two have been fused. If you want to study Chinese astrology, you should start with the Tzu Wei method.

In Chinese, Tzu Wei is the name of the god of the Pole Star and

Tzu Wei astrology is called *Tzu Wei Tou Shu*, which literally means 'Purple Star Calculation'. This reflects the many stages of calculation required to arrive at your horoscope.

Many stars are used to calculate your horoscope. These include the Tzu Wei stars, real and imaginary, and other real or imaginary stars. These stars are plotted on the Tzu Wei chart, which is a visual representation of your horoscope.

Drawing up the Tzu Wei chart may be time-consuming, but once complete it is easy to use. It has two particular advantages. The first is that you can read it yourself, without the help of a professional astrologer. The second is that the chart can be used to obtain readings for any time in your life. This means that you can keep it to hand and consult it to find out when, for example, it would be a good time for you to embark on a particular venture.

In the following chapters you will come across many different star names. Opposite is a list of all the stars used in the Tzu Wei system with a literal English translation of their names. The English names do not reflect to any great extent the complex nature of the stars.

The Stars in the Tzu Wei System

1	Tzu Wei	Purple Star	
2	Lien Chen	Pure Virtue Star	
3	T'ien K'uei	Heavenly Leader Star	
4	Tso Fu and Yu Pi	Left and Right Assistant Stars	
5	Hua Ch'üan	Transforming Authority Star	
6	T'ien Chi	Heavenly Secret Star	
7	T'ien T'ung	Heavenly Unity Star	
8	T'ai-yang	The Sun	
9	T'ai-yin	The Moon	
10	T'ien Hsiang	Heavenly Minister Star	
11	T'ien Ts'un	Heavenly Store Star	
12	T'ien Yüeh	Heavenly Halberd Star	
13	Chü Men	Great Door Star	
14	Ch'i Sha	Seven Killings Star	
15	Hua Lu	Transforming Salary Star	
16	Wu Ch'ü	Military Music Star	
17	T'ien Fu	Southern Star	
18	T'an Lang	Greedy Wolf Star	
19	T'ien Liang	Heavenly Roof-Beam Star	
20	P'o Chün	Broken Army Star	
21	Hua K'o	Transforming Examination Class Star	
22	Fire Star		
23	Ringing Star		
24	Yang Jen	Sheep-Blade Star	
25	T'o Lo	Hump-Back Star	
26	Hua Chi	Transforming Jealousy Star	
27	T'ien K'ung	Heavenly Void Star	
28	Ti Chieh	Earthly Robbery Star	
29	Wen Ch'ü	Literary Music Star	Literary Stars
30	Wen Ch'ang	Literary Prosperity Star	
31	I-ma	Travelling Star	
32	T'ien Yao	Heavenly Beauty Star	
33	T'ien Hao	Heavenly Destroyer Star	
34	Hung Luan	Red Phoenix Star	
35	T'ien Hsi	Heavenly Happiness Star	
36	T'ien Hsing	Heavenly Punishment Star	

HOW TO COMPILE YOUR TZU WEI CHART

You will find that this first section requires a lot of looking up of tables and filling in of squares. Don't give up! Once you have followed through the twenty-one stages described below you will have unlocked the door to one of the most detailed horoscopes you will ever receive.

The Tzu Wei Chart

The Tzu Wei chart is a visual representation of your horoscope. On A4 paper first draw up the grid or *ching* (well) on which the chart is based. This consists of twelve boxes around a central square (see Figure 1). Then label each box with one of the twelve Earthly Branches as follows: the first of the Earthly Branches, Tzu, appears in the box second from the right on the bottom row. The following eleven, Ch'ou, Yin, Mao, Ch'en, Szu, Wu, Wei, Shen, Yu, Hsü and Hai appear in consecutive boxes running clockwise from the box containing Tzu (see Figure 2).

Your Lunar Birthday and Your Pa Tzu (Eight Characters)

The Pa Tzu are the eight characters on which your horoscope is based. They are arranged in four pairs. The first pair corresponds to the year of birth, the second pair to the month, the third pair to the day and the fourth to the time. Each pair consists of a Heavenly Stem and an Earthly Branch.

Figure 1 *The grid or* ching *(well)*

Figure 2 *The boxes labelled with the twelve Earthly Branches*

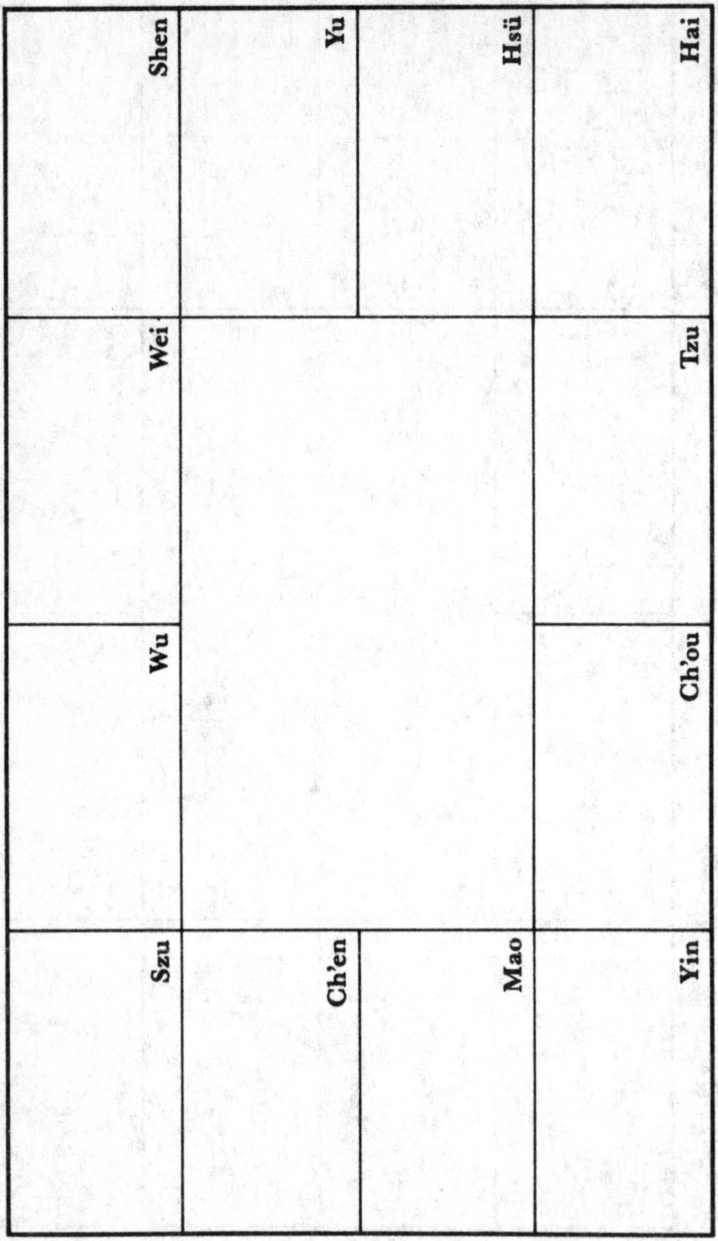

To find your eight characters you first need to convert your date and time of birth to the lunar (Chinese) calendar. The three steps of the conversion (your solar birthday, your lunar birthday and your eight characters) appear in the central square of the Tzu Wei chart.

First, at the top of the central square enter your year, month, date and hour of birth according to the solar (Western) calendar. Next, convert this to the lunar (Chinese) calendar. Look up your date of birth (solar) in the Calendar Tables which appear at the back of this book.

The Heavenly Stem and Earthly Branch for the year are shown at the start of the lunar (Chinese) year in which your birthday falls. In the case of 1 September 1986 the Chinese name for the year is Ping Yin. Thus the first pair of characters in our example of the eight-character horoscope are the Heavenly Stem Ping and the Earthly Branch Yin.

The lunar month and date are shown in the second column of the Calendar Tables. Using the same example, in 1986, 1 September is equivalent to the 27th day of the 7th lunar month.

The Chinese system of hours is shown in the table on p. 17 of the Introduction. In our example someone born at 8 p.m. would have the Earthly Branch Hsü as the character for his or her 'hour' of birth.

You are now in a position to enter the details of the year, month, date and 'hour' of birth according to the lunar calendar on the Tzu Wei chart. They go in the central square, immediately below the solar entry.

Next you need to find the characters for your eight-character horoscope. You already have the pair for the year – in our example these are Ping Yin. The characters for the month are shown in code in the third column of the Calendar Tables. Staying with our example, in 1986 the 7th month has the code C9. At the start of the Calendar Tables you will find the list of codes for the Heavenly Stems and the Earthly Branches. The Heavenly Stems are coded from A to K and the Earthly Branches from 1 to 12. The code C9 is equivalent to the Heavenly Stem Ping and the Earthly Branch Shen and these thus form the second pair of characters of the eight-character horoscope in our example and are entered in the central square of the Tzu Wei chart.

The code corresponding to the day is given in the fourth column of the Calendar Tables. Still using the same example, the 27th day of the 7th month in Ping Yin year (1 September 1986) has the code E9. Looking up the codes at the start of the tables, we find that this corresponds to the Heavenly Stem Mou and the Earthly Branch Shen, and these too are entered in the central square of the Tzu Wei chart.

By now you should have found the first six characters for your eight-character horoscope. The last two characters are those for your 'hour' of birth. We have already found the Earthly Branch for the 'hour' in our example – it is Hsü. So all that remains is to find the Heavenly Stem for the 'hour' and this can be done using Table 1. This table is based on the Earthly Branch for your 'hour' of birth and the Heavenly Stem for your day of birth. So if the Earthly Branch for the 'hour' is Hsü and the Heavenly Stem for the day is Mou, then the Heavenly Stem for the 'hour' is Jen. You can now enter the last pair of characters of your Pa Tzu – your eight characters – in the central square of the Tzu Wei chart, which should look like Figure 3.

Table 1 *The Heavenly Stem for the 'Hour' of Birth*

Earthly Branch for 'Hour' of Birth	*Heavenly Stem for Day of Birth*				
	Chia Chi	*Yi Keng*	*Ping Hsin*	*Ting Jen*	*Mou Kuei*
Tzu	Chia	Ping	Mou	Keng	Jen
Ch'ou	Yi	Ting	Chi	Hsin	Kuei
Yin	Ping	Mou	Keng	Jen	Chia
Mao	Ting	Chi	Hsin	Kuei	Yi
Ch'en	Mou	Keng	Jen	Chia	Ping
Szu	Chi	Hsin	Kuei	Yi	Ting
Wu	Keng	Jen	Chia	Ping	Mou
Wei	Hsin	Kuei	Yi	Ting	Chi
Shen	Jen	Chia	Ping	Mou	Keng
Yu	Kuei	Yi	Ting	Chi	Hsin
Hsü	Chia	Ping	Mou	Keng	Jen
Hai	Yi	Ting	Chi	Hsin	Kuei

Finally, immediately below the eight-character entry, write the word 'Element'. This will be filled in later. Then write your name and today's date at the bottom of the central square.

Figure 3 *Information entered in the central square: example for 1 September 1986, 8 p.m.*

<table>
<tr><td>Szu</td><td>Wu</td><td>Wei</td><td>Shen</td></tr>
<tr><td>Ch'en</td><td colspan="2" rowspan="2">Date and time of birth (solar):
1986 September 1st 8 p.m.
Date and time of birth (lunar):
Ping Yin 7th 27th Hsü
Eight characters:
Ping Yin Ping Shen Mou Shen Jen Hsü
Element:
Name:
Today's date:</td><td>Yu</td></tr>
<tr><td>Mao</td><td>Hsü</td></tr>
<tr><td>Yin</td><td>Ch'ou</td><td>Tzu</td><td>Hai</td></tr>
</table>

The Ming Palace

Locating your Ming (Life/Fate) Palace on the Tzu Wei chart is the first step in the calculation of your horoscope.

The Ming Palace may appear in any one of the twelve boxes labelled with the Twelve Earthly Branches. To locate your Ming Palace use Table 2. Find the Earthly Branch for the month you were born in the column headings and the Earthly Branch for your 'hour' of birth in the side headings. The entry in the main body of the table is the Earthly Branch of the box in which your Ming Palace is located. For example, if you were born on 1 September 1986 at 8 p.m., the branch for the month is Shen and the branch for the 'hour' is Hsü. The Ming Palace is located in the box labelled with the Earthly Branch Hsü. The box in which the Ming Palace appears becomes the key box on the chart.

The Twelve Palaces

The Ming Palace is one of twelve palaces concerned with different aspects of your life. The other eleven palaces are the Brothers' and Sisters' Palace, the Marital Palace, the Man and Woman Palace, the Wealth Palace, the Sickness Palace, the Moving Palace, the Servants' Palace, the Officials' Palace, the Property Palace, the Fortune and Virtue Palace and the Parents' Palace. The aspects of your life with which each palace is associated are as follows:

Ming Palace

Your physical appearance, natural abilities and business success or failure are included under this palace. In short, it is concerned with good and bad luck as it affects your whole life.

Brothers' and Sisters' Palace

Your relationships with your brothers, sisters, friends and colleagues are all dealt with under this palace.

Marital Palace

This palace is concerned with your *yuanten* – the appointed fate by which you and your partner are brought together, your affinity. Is this strong or weak? After marriage will you be happy or not?

Table 2 *Locating the Ming (Life/Fate) Palace*

Earthly Branch for 'Hour' of Birth	*Earthly Branch for Month of Birth*											
	Tzu	*Ch'ou*	*Yin*	*Mao*	*Ch'en*	*Szu*	*Wu*	*Wei*	*Shen*	*Yu*	*Hsü*	*Hai*
Tzu	Tzu	Ch'ou	Yin	Mao	Ch'en	Szu	Wu	Wei	Shen	Yu	Hsü	Hai
Ch'ou	Hai	Tzu	Ch'ou	Yin	Mao	Ch'en	Szu	Wu	Wei	Shen	Yu	Hsü
Yin	Hsü	Hai	Tzu	Ch'ou	Yin	Mao	Ch'en	Szu	Wu	Wei	Shen	Yu
Mao	Yu	Hsü	Hai	Tzu	Ch'ou	Yin	Mao	Ch'en	Szu	Wu	Wei	Shen
Ch'en	Shen	Yu	Hsü	Hai	Tzu	Ch'ou	Yin	Mao	Ch'en	Szu	Wu	Wei
Szu	Wei	Shen	Yu	Hsü	Hai	Tzu	Ch'ou	Yin	Mao	Ch'en	Szu	Wu
Wu	Wu	Wei	Shen	Yu	Hsü	Hai	Tzu	Ch'ou	Yin	Mao	Ch'en	Szu
Wei	Szu	Wu	Wei	Shen	Yu	Hsü	Hai	Tzu	Ch'ou	Yin	Mao	Ch'en
Shen	Ch'en	Szu	Wu	Wei	Shen	Yu	Hsü	Hai	Tzu	Ch'ou	Yin	Mao
Yu	Mao	Ch'en	Szu	Wu	Wei	Shen	Yu	Hsü	Hai	Tzu	Ch'ou	Yin
Hsü	Yin	Mao	Ch'en	Szu	Wu	Wei	Shen	Yu	Hsü	Hai	Tzu	Ch'ou
Hai	Ch'ou	Yin	Mao	Ch'en	Szu	Wu	Wei	Shen	Yu	Hsü	Hai	Tzu

Man and Woman Palace
This palace covers two aspects. The first is sexual happiness and fertility. The second is your relationship with your children: are they well behaved and obedient?

Wealth Palace
This palace is concerned with your level of income and overall wealth.

Sickness Palace
This palace deals with physical health including illness and accident.

Moving Palace
There are two aspects included under this palace. The first is your success at work: do you develop and expand into new areas? The second is travel: is it auspicious or not for you to travel?

Servants' Palace
Your relationships with your inferiors, for example, staff working under you, are covered by this palace. Are they honest or do they harm you?

Officials' Palace
This palace is concerned with your relationship with your superiors: is this harmonious? A second aspect covered by this palace is whether you are suited to your job.

Property Palace
Is your family life favoured by good luck? Are you likely to own much property? This palace deals with both questions.

Fortune and Virtue Palace
This palace deals with your longevity and your physical and psychological condition. It also includes leisure activities.

Parents' Palace
This palace concerns your parents' good and bad luck, their longevity and mutual harmony. Your relationship with your parents, whether they love you and support you, is also included.

Once the Ming Palace has been located in a box, then the other eleven palaces can be assigned to the remaining eleven boxes. In Table 3 the Earthly Branch on which the Ming Palace appears is given on the side headings and the other eleven palaces in the column headings. The entry in the main body of the table is the Earthly Branch of the box in which the palace is located. For example if the Ming Palace appears in the box labelled Hsü, then the Brothers' and Sisters' Palace appears in the box labelled Yu, the Marital Palace in the box labelled Shen, the Man and Woman Palace in the box labelled Wei, and so on. Figure 4 shows how the palaces are entered on the Tzu Wei chart for our example of 1 September 1986, 8 p.m., in which the Ming Palace appears in the box labelled Hsü.

The palaces become new labels for the boxes they appear in. A palace is a place or a space. Stars which appear in a particular box affect that aspect of your life governed by the palace associated with that box.

The Five Elements

Each individual's horoscope is associated with one of the five elements: Water, Fire, Earth, Wood or Metal.

This element can be calculated from the Earthly Branch of the box in which the Ming Palace is located and the Heavenly Stem for the year of your birth. In Table 4 these Earthly Branches appear in the side headings and the Heavenly Stems in the column headings; the elements are shown in the main body of the table. For the example of 1 September 1986, 8 p.m., the Ming Palace is located in the box labelled with the Earthly Branch Hsü and the Heavenly Stem for the year of birth is Ping. This gives the element Wood.

You can now enter your element in the central square of the Tzu Wei chart under the eight-character entry.

The Tzu Wei Star

Tzu Wei (Purple Star) is the leading star of the Tzu Wei star group. It is equated with the Pole Star and is a symbol of the Pei Tou stars (the Great Bear constellation, Ursa Major).

Figure 4 *Locating the Twelve Palaces: example for 1 September 1986, 8 p.m.*

<table>
<tr><td>Sickness Szu</td><td>Wealth Wu</td><td>Man and Woman Wei</td><td>Marital Shen</td></tr>
<tr><td>Moving Ch'en</td><td colspan="2" rowspan="2">Date and time of birth (solar):
1986 September 1st 8 p.m.
Date and time of birth (lunar):
Ping Yin 7th 27th Hsü
Eight characters:
Ping Yin Ping Shen Mou Shen Jen Hsü
Element:
Name:
Today's date:</td><td>Brothers' and Sisters' Yu</td></tr>
<tr><td>Servants' Mao</td><td>Ming Hsü</td></tr>
<tr><td>Officials' Yin</td><td>Property Ch'ou</td><td>Fortune and Virtue Tzu</td><td>Parents' Hai</td></tr>
</table>

Table 3 *Locating the Twelve Palaces*

Location of the Ming Palace	*Palaces* *Brothers' and Sisters' Palace*	*Marital Palace*	*Man and Woman Palace*	*Wealth Palace*	*Sickness Palace*	*Moving Palace*	*Servants' Palace*	*Officials' Palace*	*Property Palace*	*Fortune and Virtue Palace*	*Parents' Palace*
Tzu	Hai	Hsü	Yu	Shen	Wei	Wu	Szu	Ch'en	Mao	Yin	Ch'ou
Ch'ou	Tzu	Hai	Hsü	Yu	Shen	Wei	Wu	Szu	Ch'en	Mao	Yin
Yin	Ch'ou	Tzu	Hai	Hsü	Yu	Shen	Wei	Wu	Szu	Ch'en	Mao
Mao	Yin	Ch'ou	Tzu	Hai	Hsü	Yu	Shen	Wei	Wu	Szu	Ch'en
Ch'en	Mao	Yin	Ch'ou	Tzu	Hai	Hsü	Yu	Shen	Wei	Wu	Szu
Szu	Ch'en	Mao	Yin	Ch'ou	Tzu	Hai	Hsü	Yu	Shen	Wei	Wu
Wu	Szu	Ch'en	Mao	Yin	Ch'ou	Tzu	Hai	Hsü	Yu	Shen	Wei
Wei	Wu	Szu	Ch'en	Mao	Yin	Ch'ou	Tzu	Hai	Hsü	Yu	Shen
Shen	Wei	Wu	Szu	Ch'en	Mao	Yin	Ch'ou	Tzu	Hai	Hsü	Yu
Yu	Shen	Wei	Wu	Szu	Ch'en	Mao	Yin	Ch'ou	Tzu	Hai	Hsü
Hsü	Yu	Shen	Wei	Wu	Szu	Ch'en	Mao	Yin	Ch'ou	Tzu	Hai
Hai	Hsü	Yu	Shen	Wei	Wu	Szu	Ch'en	Mao	Yin	Ch'ou	Tzu

Table 4 *The Five Elements*

Location of the Ming Palace	*Heavenly Stem for the Year of Birth*									
	Chia	*Yi*	*Ping*	*Ting*	*Mou*	*Chi*	*Keng*	*Hsin*	*Jen*	*Kuei*
Tzu *Ch'ou*	Water	Fire	Earth	Wood	Metal	Water	Fire	Earth	Wood	Metal
Yin *Mao*	Fire	Earth	Wood	Metal	Water	Fire	Earth	Wood	Metal	Water
Ch'en *Szu*	Wood	Metal	Water	Fire	Earth	Wood	Metal	Water	Fire	Earth
Wu *Wei*	Earth	Wood	Metal	Water	Fire	Earth	Wood	Metal	Water	Fire
Shen *Yu*	Metal	Water	Fire	Earth	Wood	Metal	Water	Fire	Earth	Wood
Hsü *Hai*	Fire	Earth	Wood	Metal	Water	Fire	Earth	Wood	Metal	Water

The location of the Tzu Wei star on the Tzu Wei chart is calculated from the number of the day on which you were born and the element of your horoscope. In Table 5 the day appears in the side headings and element in the column headings. The main body of the table gives the Earthly Branch of the box in which the Tzu Wei star should be located. In our example, 1 September 1986, 8 p.m., is equivalent to the 27th day of the 7th lunar month and the element is Wood. This means that the Tzu Wei star is located in the box labelled Hsü. In the case of this horoscope this is a particularly lucky location as both the Ming Palace and the Tzu Wei star appear in the same box.

The Tzu Wei Star Group

The Tzu Wei star group consists of five stars which form a group around the Tzu Wei star. Although the Tzu Wei star itself can be equated with the Pole Star, the other stars in the group do not correspond to other stars in the Great Bear constellation. T'ai-yang (literally, 'extreme yang') is in fact the Sun. The other stars – T'ien Chi (Heavenly Secret), Wu Ch'ü (Military Music), T'ien T'ung (Heavenly Unity) and Lien Chen (Pure Virtue) – are all imaginary.

On the Tzu Wei chart each of these stars is located in a different box, and this depends on the location of the Tzu Wei star. Table 6 gives the Earthly Branch of the box containing the Tzu Wei star in the side headings and the names of the other stars in the Tzu Wei group in the column headings. The Earthly Branch for the box in which each star is located is given in the main body of the table. For the example 1 September 1986, 8 p.m., we have already established that the Tzu Wei star appears in the box labelled Hsü. Using Table 6 we find that T'ien Chi appears in the box labelled Yu, Tai-yang is in the box labelled Wei, Wu Ch'ü in the box labelled Wu, T'ien T'ung in the box labelled Szu and Lien Chen in the box labelled Yin (see Figure 5).

T'ien Fu (Southern Star)

In Tzu Wei astrology T'ien Fu is the Southern Star. In the sky it appears opposite the Tzu Wei star. Its position on the chart depends

Figure 5 *Locating the T'zu Wei star group*

T'ien T'ung Sickness Szu	**Wu Ch'ü** Wealth Wu	**T'ai-yang** Man and Woman Wei	 Marital Shen
  Moving Ch'en	Date and time of birth (solar): 1986 September 1st 8 p.m. Date and time of birth (lunar): Ping Yin 7th 27th Hsü Eight characters: Ping Yin Ping Shen Mou Shen Jen Hsü Element: **Wood** Name: Today's date:		**T'ien Chi** Brothers' and Sisters' Yu
  Servants' Mao			**Tzu Wei** Ming Hsü
Lien Chen Officials' Yin	 Property Ch'ou	 Fortune and Virtue Tzu	 Parents' Hai

Table 5 *Locating the Tzu Wei Star*

	Element				
Day of Birth	*Wood*	*Fire*	*Earth*	*Metal*	*Water*
1st	Ch'en	Yu	Wu	Hai	Ch'ou
2nd	Ch'ou	Wu	Hai	Ch'en	Yin
3rd	Yin	Hai	Ch'en	Ch'ou	Yin
4th	Szu	Ch'en	Ch'ou	Yin	Mao
5th	Yin	Ch'ou	Yin	Tzu	Mao
6th	Mao	Yin	Wei	Szu	Ch'en
7th	Wu	Hsü	Tzu	Yin	Ch'en
8th	Mao	Wei	Szu	Mao	Szu
9th	Ch'en	Tzu	Yin	Ch'ou	Szu
10th	Wei	Szu	Mao	Wu	Wu
11th	Ch'en	Yin	Shen	Mao	Wu
12th	Szu	Mao	Ch'ou	Ch'en	Wei
13th	Shen	Hai	Wu	Yin	Wei
14th	Szu	Shen	Mao	Wei	Shen
15th	Wu	Ch'ou	Ch'en	Ch'en	Shen
16th	Yu	Wu	Yu	Szu	Yu
17th	Wu	Mao	Yin	Mao	Yu
18th	Wei	Ch'en	Wei	Shen	Hsü
19th	Hsü	Tzu	Ch'en	Szu	Hsü
20th	Wei	Yu	Szu	Wu	Hai
21st	Shen	Yin	Hsü	Ch'en	Hai
22nd	Hai	Wei	Mao	Yu	Tzu
23rd	Shen	Ch'en	Shen	Wu	Tzu
24th	Yu	Szu	Szu	Wei	Ch'ou
25th	Tzu	Ch'ou	Wu	Szu	Ch'ou
26th	Yu	Hsü	Hai	Hsü	Yin
27th	Hsü	Mao	Ch'en	Wei	Yin
28th	Ch'ou	Shen	Yu	Shen	Mao
29th	Hsü	Szu	Wu	Wu	Mao
30th	Hai	Wu	Wei	Hai	Ch'en

on the position of the Tzu Wei star. Table 7 gives the location of the Tzu Wei star in the left-hand column and the location of T'ien Fu in the right-hand column. For the example 1 September 1986, 8 p.m., the Tzu Wei star is in the box labelled Hsü. This means that T'ien Fu appears in the box labelled Wu.

Figure 6 *Locating the T'ien Fu star group*

<table>
<tr>
<td>T'ien T'ung

Sickness Szu</td>
<td>Wu Ch'ü
T'ien Fu

Wealth Wu</td>
<td>T'ai-yang
T'ai-yin

Man and Woman Wei</td>
<td>T'an Lang

Marital Shen</td>
</tr>
<tr>
<td>P'o Chün

Moving Ch'en</td>
<td colspan="2" rowspan="2">Date and time of birth (solar):
1986 September 1st 8 p.m.
Date and time of birth (lunar):
Ping Yin 7th 27th Hsü
Eight characters:
Ping Yin Ping Shen Mou Shen Jen Hsü
Element: Wood
Name:
Today's date:</td>
<td>T'ien Chi
Chü Men

Brothers' and Sisters' Yu</td>
</tr>
<tr>
<td>

Servants' Mao</td>
<td>Tzu Wei
T'ien Hsiang

Ming Hsü</td>
</tr>
<tr>
<td>Lien Chen

Officials' Yin</td>
<td>

Property Ch'ou</td>
<td>Ch'i Sha

Fortune and Virtue Tzu</td>
<td>T'ien Liang

Parents' Hai</td>
</tr>
</table>

Table 6 *Locating the Tzu Wei Star Group*

Location of Tzu Wei Star	*T'ien Chi*	*T'ai-yang*	*Wu Ch'ü*	*T'ien T'ung*	*Lien Chen*
Tzu	Hai	Yu	Shen	Wei	Ch'en
Ch'ou	Tzu	Hsü	Yu	Shen	Szu
Yin	Ch'ou	Hai	Hsü	Yu	Wu
Mao	Yin	Tzu	Hai	Hsü	Wei
Ch'en	Mao	Ch'ou	Tzu	Hai	Shen
Szu	Ch'en	Yin	Ch'ou	Tzu	Yu
Wu	Szu	Mao	Yin	Ch'ou	Hsü
Wei	Wu	Ch'en	Mao	Yin	Hai
Shen	Wei	Szu	Ch'en	Mao	Tzu
Yu	Shen	Wu	Szu	Ch'en	Ch'ou
Hsü	Yu	Wei	Wu	Szu	Yin
Hai	Hsü	Shen	Wei	Wu	Mao

Table 7 *Locating T'ien Fu (Southern Star)*

Location of Tzu Wei Star	*T'ien Fu*
Tzu	Ch'en
Ch'ou	Mao
Yin	Yin
Mao	Ch'ou
Ch'en	Tzu
Szu	Hai
Wu	Hsü
Wei	Yu
Shen	Shen
Yu	Wei
Hsü	Wu
Hai	Szu

The T'ien Fu Star Group

Like the Tzu Wei star, T'ien Fu is accompanied by a group of seven stars. Of these, T'ai-yin (the Moon) is real and the others – T'an Lang (Greedy Wolf), Chü Men (Great Door), T'ien Hsiang (Heavenly Minister), T'ien Liang (Heavenly Roof-beam), Ch'i Sha (Seven Killings) and P'o Chün (Broken Army) – are imaginary. The location of these stars depends on the location of T'ien Fu itself. Table 8 gives the Earthly Branch of the box containing T'ien Fu in the side headings and the names of the other stars in the group in the column headings. The Earthly Branches of the boxes in which these stars are to be located are given in the main body of the table. For the example 1 September 1986, 8 p.m., we already know that T'ien Fu appears in the box labelled Wu. This means that T'ai-yin appears in the box labelled Wei, T'an Lang in the box labelled Shen, Chü Men in the box labelled Yu, T'ien Hsiang in the box labelled Hsü, T'ien Liang in the box labelled Hai, Ch'i Sha in the box labelled Tzu and P'o Chün in the box labelled Ch'en.

Table 8 *Locating the T'ien Fu Star Group*

Location of T'ien Fu	*T'ai-yin*	*T'an Lang*	*Chü Men*	*T'ien Hsiang*	*T'ien Liang*	*Ch'i Sha*	*P'o Chün*
Tzu	Ch'ou	Yin	Mao	Ch'en	Szu	Wu	Hsü
Ch'ou	Yin	Mao	Ch'en	Szu	Wu	Wei	Hai
Yin	Mao	Ch'en	Szu	Wu	Wei	Shen	Tzu
Mao	Ch'en	Szu	Wu	Wei	Shen	Yu	Ch'ou
Ch'en	Szu	Wu	Wei	Shen	Yu	Hsü	Yin
Szu	Wu	Wei	Shen	Yu	Hsü	Hai	Mao
Wu	Wei	Shen	Yu	Hsü	Hai	Tzu	Ch'en
Wei	Shen	Yu	Hsü	Hai	Tzu	Ch'ou	Szu
Shen	Yu	Hsü	Hai	Tzu	Ch'ou	Yin	Wu
Yu	Hsü	Hai	Tzu	Ch'ou	Yin	Mao	Wei
Hsü	Hai	Tzu	Ch'ou	Yin	Mao	Ch'en	Shen
Hai	Tzu	Ch'ou	Yin	Mao	Ch'en	Szu	Yu

The Fire Star and the Ringing Star

The Fire Star is the Chinese name for Mars. The location of the Fire Star on the Tzu Wei chart is dependent on your 'hour' and year of birth. Table 9 gives the Earthly Branch for the 'hour' of birth in the side headings and the Earthly Branch for the year of birth in the column headings. The location of the Fire Star is given in the body of the table. For 1 September 1986, 8 p.m., the Earthly Branch for the 'hour' is Hsü and the Earthly Branch for the year is Yin. This means that the Fire Star is located in the box labelled Hai.

Table 9 *Locating the Fire Star*

Earthly Branch for 'Hour' of Birth	*Earthly Branch for Year of Birth*: *Tzu*	*Ch'ou*	*Yin*	*Mao*	*Ch'en*	*Szu*	*Wu*	*Wei*	*Shen*	*Yu*	*Hsü*	*Hai*
Tzu	Yin	Mao	Ch'ou	Yu	Yin	Mao	Ch'ou	Yu	Yin	Mao	Ch'ou	Yu
Ch'ou	Mao	Ch'en	Yin	Hsü	Mao	Ch'en	Yin	Hsü	Mao	Ch'en	Yin	Hsü
Yin	Ch'en	Szu	Mao	Hai	Ch'en	Szu	Mao	Hai	Ch'en	Szu	Mao	Hai
Mao	Szu	Wu	Ch'en	Tzu	Szu	Wu	Ch'en	Tzu	Szu	Wu	Ch'en	Tzu
Ch'en	Wu	Wei	Szu	Ch'ou	Wu	Wei	Szu	Ch'ou	Wu	Wei	Szu	Ch'ou
Szu	Wei	Shen	Wu	Yin	Wei	Shen	Wu	Yin	Wei	Shen	Wu	Yin
Wu	Shen	Yu	Wei	Mao	Shen	Yu	Wei	Mao	Shen	Yu	Wei	Mao
Wei	Yu	Hsü	Shen	Ch'en	Yu	Hsü	Shen	Ch'en	Yu	Hsü	Shen	Ch'en
Shen	Hsü	Hai	Yu	Szu	Hsü	Hai	Yu	Szu	Hsü	Hai	Yu	Szu
Yu	Hai	Tzu	Hsü	Wu	Hai	Tzu	Hsü	Wu	Hai	Tzu	Hsü	Wu
Hsü	Tzu	Ch'ou	Hai	Wei	Tzu	Ch'ou	Hai	Wei	Tzu	Ch'ou	Hai	Wei
Hai	Ch'ou	Yin	Tzu	Shen	Ch'ou	Yin	Tzu	Shen	Ch'ou	Yin	Tzu	Shen

Table 10 *Locating the Ringing Star*

Earthly Branch for 'Hour' of Birth	*Earthly Branch for Year of Birth*											
	Tzu	*Ch'ou*	*Yin*	*Mao*	*Ch'en*	*Szu*	*Wu*	*Wei*	*Shen*	*Yu*	*Hsü*	*Hai*
Tzu	Hsü	Hsü	Mao	Hsü	Hsü	Hsü	Mao	Hsü	Hsü	Hsü	Mao	Hsü
Ch'ou	Hai	Hai	Ch'en	Hai	Hai	Hai	Ch'en	Hai	Hai	Hai	Ch'en	Hai
Yin	Tzu	Tzu	Szu	Tzu	Tzu	Tzu	Szu	Tzu	Tzu	Tzu	Szu	Tzu
Mao	Ch'ou	Ch'ou	Wu	Ch'ou	Ch'ou	Ch'ou	Wu	Ch'ou	Ch'ou	Ch'ou	Wu	Ch'ou
Ch'en	Yin	Yin	Wei	Yin	Yin	Yin	Wei	Yin	Yin	Yin	Wei	Yin
Szu	Mao	Mao	Shen	Mao	Mao	Mao	Shen	Mao	Mao	Mao	Shen	Mao
Wu	Ch'en	Ch'en	Yu	Ch'en	Ch'en	Ch'en	Yu	Ch'en	Ch'en	Ch'en	Yu	Ch'en
Wei	Szu	Szu	Hsü	Szu	Szu	Szu	Hsü	Szu	Szu	Szu	Hsü	Szu
Shen	Wu	Wu	Hai	Wu	Wu	Wu	Hai	Wu	Wu	Wu	Hai	Wu
Yu	Wei	Wei	Tzu	Wei	Wei	Wei	Tzu	Wei	Wei	Wei	Tzu	Wei
Hsü	Shen	Shen	Ch'ou	Shen	Shen	Shen	Ch'ou	Shen	Shen	Shen	Ch'ou	Shen
Hai	Yu	Yu	Yin	Yu	Yu	Yu	Yin	Yu	Yu	Yu	Yin	Yu

The Ringing Star is an imaginary star. Its location on the Tzu Wei chart is also dependent on your 'hour' and year of birth. Use Table 10 in the same way as Table 9 to locate your Ringing Star. For the example 1 September 1986, 8 p.m., the Ringing Star is located in the box labelled Ch'ou.

The Literary Stars

There are two imaginary Literary stars – Wen Ch'ü (Literary Music) and Wen Ch'ang (Literary Prosperity). Wen Ch'u guards literature and painting and Wen Ch'ang blesses examinations. The position of these two stars on the Tzu Wei chart is dependent on your 'hour' of birth. Table 11 gives the Earthly Branch for the 'hour' in the side headings. The Earthly Branch for the location of Wen Ch'ü is given in the left-hand column and the Earthly Branch for the location of Wen Ch'ang in the right-hand column. For the example 1 September 1986, 8 p.m., the Earthly Branch for the 'hour' is Hsü. This means that Wen Ch'ü is located in the box labelled Yin and Wen Ch'ang in the box labelled Tzu.

Table 11 *Locating the Literary Stars: Wen Chü and Wen Ch'ang*

Earthly Branch for 'Hour' of Birth	*Wen Ch'ü*	*Wen Ch'ang*
Tzu	Ch'en	Hsü
Ch'ou	Szu	Yu
Yin	Wu	Shen
Mao	Wei	Wei
Ch'en	Shen	Wu
Szu	Yu	Szu
Wu	Hsü	Ch'en
Wei	Hai	Mao
Shen	Tzu	Yin
Yu	Ch'ou	Ch'ou
Hsü	Yin	Tzu
Hai	Mao	Hai

Yang Jen (Sheep-Blade Star) and T'o Lo (Hump-Back Star)

Yang Jen (Sheep-Blade Star) and T'o Lo (Hump-Back Star) are usually inauspicious. Their location on the Tzu Wei chart depends on your year of birth. In Table 12 the Heavenly Stem for the year is given in the side headings. The Earthly Branch of the box in which Yang Jen is to be located appears in the left-hand column, and the Earthly Branch of the box in which T'o Lo is to be located appears in the right-hand column.

For the example 1 September 1986, 8 p.m., the Heavenly Stem for the year is Ping. This means that Yang Jen is located in the box labelled Wu and T'o Lo in the box labelled Ch'en (see Figure 7).

Table 12 *Locating Yang Jen and T'o Lo*

Heavenly Stem for Year of Birth	*Yang Jen*	*T'o Lo*
Chia	Mao	Ch'ou
Yi	Ch'en	Yin
Ping	Wu	Ch'en
Ting	Wei	Szu
Mou	Wu	Ch'en
Chi	Wei	Szu
Keng	Yu	Wei
Hsin	Hsü	Shen
Jen	Tzu	Hsü
Kuei	Ch'ou	Hai

By now you should have twenty different stars on your Tzu Wei chart. These are the main stars of your horoscope. The following are minor stars.

The Yearly Stars

There are three Yearly stars – T'ien Ts'un (Heavenly Store), T'ien K'uei (Heavenly Leader) and T'ien Yüeh (Heavenly Halberd).

Their position on the Tzu Wei chart depends on the Heavenly Stem for the year you were born. Table 13 shows how to locate them. For the example 1 September 1986, 8 p.m. the Heavenly

Figure 7 *Locating the Fire Star, Ringing Star, Literary Stars and Yang Jen (Sheep-Blade) and T'o Lo (Hump-Back)*

<table>
<tr>
<td>T'ien T'ung

Sickness Szu</td>
<td>Wu Ch'ü
T'ien Fu
Yang Jen

Wealth Wu</td>
<td>T'ai-yang
T'ai-yin

Man and Woman Wei</td>
<td>T'an Lang

Marital Shen</td>
</tr>
<tr>
<td>P'o Chün
T'o Lo

Moving Ch'en</td>
<td colspan="2" rowspan="2">Date and time of birth (solar):
1986 September 1st 8 p.m.
Date and time of birth (lunar):
Ping Yin 7th 27th Hsü
Eight characters:
Ping Yin Ping Shen Mou Shen Jen Hsü
Element: Wood
Name:
Today's date:</td>
<td>T'ien Chi
Chü Men

Brothers' and Sisters' Yu</td>
</tr>
<tr>
<td>

Servants' Mao</td>
<td>Tzu Wei
T'ien Hsiang

Ming Hsü</td>
</tr>
<tr>
<td>Lien Chen
Wen Ch'ü

Officials' Yin</td>
<td>Ringing Star

Property Ch'ou</td>
<td>Ch'i Sha
Wen Ch'ang

Fortune and Virtue Tzu</td>
<td>T'ien Liang
Fire Star

Parents' Hai</td>
</tr>
</table>

Table 13 *Locating the Yearly Stars*

Heavenly Stem for Year of Birth	*T'ien Ts'un*	*T'ien K'uei*	*T'ien Yüeh*
Chia	Yin	Ch'ou	Wei
Yi	Mao	Tzu	Shen
Ping	Szu	Hai	Yu
Ting	Wu	Yu	Hai
Mou	Szu	Wei	Ch'ou
Chi	Wu	Shen	Tzu
Keng	Shen	Wei	Ch'ou
Hsin	Yu	Wu	Yin
Jen	Hai	Szu	Mao
Kuei	Tzu	Mao	Szu

Stem for the year is Ping. This means that T'ien Ts'un is located in the box labelled with the Earthly Branch Szu, T'ien K'uei in the box labelled Hai and T'ien Yüeh in the box labelled Yu.

The Monthly Stars

There are three Monthly stars – Tso Fu (Right Assistant), Yu Pi (Left Assistant) and I-ma (Travelling Star). The position of these stars on the Tzu Wei chart depends on the Earthly Branch of the month in which you were born. Table 14 shows how to locate the monthly stars. For the example 1 September 1986, 8 p.m., the Earthly Branch for the month is Shen. This means that Tso Fu is located in the box labelled with the Earthly Branch Hsü, Yu Pi is located in the box labelled Ch'en and I-ma is located in the box labelled Yin.

The Hourly Stars

There are two Hourly stars – T'ien K'ung (Heavenly Void) and Ti Chieh (Earthly Robbery). Their positions on the Tzu Wei chart depend on the Earthly Branch for the 'hour' you were born. Table 15 shows how to locate them. For the example 1 September 1986, 8 p.m., the Earthly Branch for the 'hour' is Hsü. This means that T'ien K'ung is located in the box labelled Ch'ou and Ti Chieh in the box labelled Yu (see Figure 8).

Table 14 *Locating the Monthly Stars*

Earthly Branch for Month of Birth	*Tso Fu*	*Yu Pi*	*I-ma*
Tzu	Yin	Tzu	Yin
Ch'ou	Mao	Hai	Hai
Yin	Ch'en	Hsü	Shen
Mao	Szu	Yu	Szu
Ch'en	Wu	Shen	Yin
Szu	Wei	Wei	Hai
Wu	Shen	Wu	Shen
Wei	Yu	Szu	Szu
Shen	Hsü	Ch'en	Yin
Yu	Hai	Mao	Hai
Hsü	Tzu	Yin	Shen
Hai	Ch'ou	Ch'ou	Szu

Table 15 *Locating the Hourly Stars*

Earthly Branch for 'Hour' of Birth	*T'ien K'ung*	*Ti Chieh*
Tzu	Hai	Hai
Ch'ou	Hsü	Tzu
Yin	Yu	Ch'ou
Mao	Shen	Yin
Ch'en	Wei	Mao
Szu	Wu	Ch'en
Wu	Szu	Szu
Wei	Ch'en	Wu
Shen	Mao	Wei
Yu	Yin	Shen
Hsü	Ch'ou	Yu
Hai	Tzu	Hsü

The Miscellaneous Yearly Stars

There are three Miscellaneous stars whose position on the Tzu Wei chart depends on your year of birth. These are T'ien Hao (Heavenly Destroyer), Hung Luan (Red Phoenix) and T'ien Hsi

Figure 8 *Locating the Yearly, Monthly and Hourly stars*

T'ien T'ung **T'ien Ts'un** Sickness Szu	Wu Ch'ü T'ien Fu Yang Jen Wealth Wu	T'ai-yang T'ai-yin Man and Woman Wei	T'an Lang Marital Shen
P'o Chün **Yu Pi** T'o Lo Moving Ch'en	Date and time of birth (solar): 1986 September 1st 8 p.m. Date and time of birth (lunar): Ping Yin 7th 27th Hsü Eight characters: Ping Yin Ping Shen Mou Shen Jen Hsü Element: Wood Name: Today's date:		T'ien Chi **T'ien Yüeh** Chü Men **Ti Chieh** Brothers' and Sisters' Yu
  Servants' Mao			Tzu Wei **Tso Fu** T'ien Hsiang Ming Hsü
Lien Chen **I-ma** Wen Ch'ü Officials' Yin	Ringing **T'ien K'ung** Star Property Ch'ou	Ch'i Sha Wen Ch'ang Fortune and Virtue Tzu	T'ien Liang **T'ien K'uei** Fire Star Parents' Hai

Table 16 *Locating the Miscellaneous Yearly Stars*

Earthly Branch for Year of Birth	*T'ien Hao*	*Hung Luan*	*T'ien Hsi*
Tzu	Ch'ou	Mao	Yu
Ch'ou	Yin	Yin	Shen
Yin	Mao	Ch'ou	Wei
Mao	Ch'en	Tzu	Wu
Ch'en	Szu	Hai	Szu
Szu	Wu	Hsü	Ch'en
Wu	Wei	Yu	Mao
Wei	Shen	Shen	Yin
Shen	Yu	Wei	Ch'ou
Yu	Hsü	Wu	Tzu
Hsü	Hai	Szu	Hai
Hai	Tzu	Ch'en	Hsü

(Heavenly Happiness). Table 16 shows how to locate these. For the example 1 September 1986, 8 p.m., the Earthly Branch for the year is Yin. This means that T'ien Hao is located in the box labelled Mao, Hung Luan in the box labelled Ch'ou and T'ien Hsi in the box labelled Wei.

The Miscellaneous Monthly Stars

There are two Miscellaneous stars whose position on the Tzu Wei chart depends on your month of birth. These are T'ien Yao (Heavenly Beauty) and T'ien Hsing (Heavenly Punishment). Table 17 shows how to locate these. For the example 1 September 1986, 8 p.m., the Earthly Branch for the month is Shen. This means that in this case T'ien Yao is located in the box labelled Wei and T'ien Hsing in the box labelled Mao.

The Transforming Stars

There are four Transforming stars – Hua Lu (Transforming Salary), Hua Ch'üan (Transforming Authority), Hua K'o (Transforming Examination Class) and Hua Chi (Transforming Jealousy).

Table 17 *Locating the Miscellaneous Monthly Stars*

Earthly Branch for Month of Birth	*T'ien Yao*	*T'ien Hsing*
Tzu	Hai	Wei
Ch'ou	Tzu	Shen
Yin	Ch'ou	Yu
Mao	Yin	Hsü
Ch'en	Mao	Hai
Szu	Ch'en	Tzu
Wu	Szu	Ch'ou
Wei	Wu	Yin
Shen	Wei	Mao
Yu	Shen	Ch'en
Hsü	Yu	Szu
Hai	Hsü	Wu

Table 18 shows how to locate them on the Tzu Wei chart. For the example 1 September 1986, 8 p.m., the Heavenly Stem for the month is Ping. This means that Hua Lu appears in the same box as T'ien T'ung (Heavenly Unity), Hua Ch'üan appears in the same box as T'ien Chi (Heavenly Secret), Hua K'o appears in the same box as Wen Ch'ang (Literary Prosperity) and Hua Chi in the same box as Lien Chen (Pure Virtue) (see Figure 9).

You should now have thirty-seven stars on your Tzu Wei chart: twenty major stars and seventeen minor stars. The major stars are strong and stable, and their degree of influence is rarely affected by the minor stars. The minor stars are unstable, and whether they are good or bad depends on the Earthly Branch of the box in which they appear. The individual readings will tell you whether a minor star is good or bad in a particular box.

The Degrees of Influence

Each of the twenty main stars has a degree of influence attached to it, depending on where it is located in the Tzu Wei chart. There are four different symbols used in this chart: * corresponds to excellent,

Table 18 *Locating the Transforming Stars*

Heavenly Stem for Month of Birth	*Hua Lu*	*Hua Ch'üan*	*Hua K'o*	*Hua Chi*
Chia	Lien Chen	P'o Chün	Wu Ch'ü	T'ai-yang
Yi	T'ien Chi	T'ien Liang	Tzu Wei	T'ai-yin
Ping	T'ien T'ung	T'ien Chi	Wen Ch'ang	Lien Chen
Ting	T'ai-yin	T'ien T'ung	T'ien Chi	Chü Men
Mou	T'an Lang	T'ai-yin	T'ai-yang	T'ien Chi
Chi	Wu Ch'ü	T'an Lang	T'ien Liang	Wen Ch'ü
Keng	T'ai-yang	Wu Ch'ü	T'ien Fu	T'ien T'ung
Hsin	Chü Men	T'ai-yang	Wen Ch'ü	Wen Ch'ang
Jen	T'ien Liang	Tzu Wei	Tien Fu	Wu Ch'ü
Kuei	P'o Chün	Chü Men	T'ai-yin	T'an Lang

☆ to good, + to poor and – to bad. The degree depends on the Earthly Branch of the box in which the star appears and can be found in Table 19. Figure 10 shows the degree of influence for each star marked on the Tzu Wei chart for the example 1 September 1986, 8 p.m.

Figure 9 *Locating the Miscellaneous and Transforming stars*

<table>
<tr>
<td>T'ien T'ung
T'ien Ts'un
Hua Lu

Sickness Szu</td>
<td>Wu Ch'ü
T'ien Fu
Yang Jen

Wealth Wu</td>
<td>T'ai-yang
T'ai-yin
T'ien Hsi
T'ien Yao

Man and Woman Wei</td>
<td>T'an Lang

Marital Shen</td>
</tr>
<tr>
<td>P'o Chün
T'o Lo
Yu Pi

Moving Ch'en</td>
<td colspan="2" rowspan="2">Date and time of birth (solar):
1986 September 1st 8 p.m.
Date and time of birth (lunar):
Ping Yin 7th 27th Hsü
Eight characters:
Ping Yin Ping Shen Mou Shen Jen Hsü
Element: Wood
Name:
Today's date:</td>
<td>T'ien Chi
Chü Men
T'ien Yüeh
Ti Chieh
Hua Ch'üan

Brothers' and Sisters' Yu</td>
</tr>
<tr>
<td>**T'ien Hao**
T'ien Hsing

Servants' Mao</td>
<td>Tzu Wei
T'ien Hsiang
Tso Fu

Ming Hsü</td>
</tr>
<tr>
<td>Lien Chen
Wen Ch'ü
I-ma
Hua Chi

Officials' Yin</td>
<td>Ringing Star
T'ien K'ung
Hung Luan

Property Ch'ou</td>
<td>Ch'i Sha
Wen Ch'ang
Hua K'o

Fortune and Virtue Tzu</td>
<td>T'ien Liang
Fire Star
T'ien K'uei

Parents' Hai</td>
</tr>
</table>

Figure 10 *The degrees of influence of the main and secondary stars*

<table>
<tr><td>T'ien T'ung* T'ien Ts'un
Hua Lu

Sickness Szu</td><td>Wu Ch'ü*
T'ien Fu*
Yang Jen–

Wealth Wu</td><td>T'ai-yang* T'ien Hsi
T'ai-yin* T'ien Yao

Man and Woman Wei</td><td>T'an Lang+

Marital Shen</td></tr>
<tr><td>P'o Chün* Yu Pi
T'o Lo*

Moving Ch'en</td><td colspan="2" rowspan="2">Date and time of birth (solar):
1986 September 1st 8 p.m.
Date and time of birth (lunar):
Ping Yin 7th 27th Hsü
Eight characters:
Ping Yin Ping Shen Mou Shen Jen Hsü
Element: Wood
Name:
Today's date:</td><td>T'ien Chi* T'ien Yüeh
Chü Men* Ti Chieh
Hua Ch'üan

Brothers' and Sisters' Yu</td></tr>
<tr><td>T'ien Hao
T'ien Hsing

Servants' Mao</td><td>Tzu Wei* Tso Fu
T'ien Hsiang*

Ming Hsü</td></tr>
<tr><td>Lien Chen* I-ma
Wen Ch'ü+ Hua Chi

Officials' Yin</td><td>Ringing T'ien K'ung
Star+ Hung Luan

Property Ch'ou</td><td>Ch'i Sha* Hua K'o
Wen Ch'ang☆

Fortune and Virtue Tzu</td><td>T'ien Liang+ T'ien K'uei
Fire Star+

Parents' Hai</td></tr>
</table>

Table 19 *The Degrees of Influence for the Main Stars*

Location	*Tzu Wei*	*T'ien Chi*	*T'ai-yang*	*Wu Ch'ü*	*T'ien T'ung*	*Lien Chen*	*T'ien Fu*	*T'ai-yin*	*T'an Lang*	*Chü Men*	*T'ien Hsiang*	*T'ien Liang*	*Ch'i Sha*	*P'o Chün*	*Fire and Ringing Stars*	*Literary Stars*	*Yang Jen and T'o Lo*
Tzu	☆	*	+	☆	*	+	☆	*	☆	☆	+	*	☆	☆	−	☆	−
Ch'ou	+	+	☆	☆	+	☆	*	☆	☆	+	*	☆	☆	+	+	☆	☆
Yin	☆	+	☆	☆	☆	☆	☆	+	+	☆	☆	☆	☆	−	☆	+	−
Mao	+	☆	*	☆	☆	−	☆	+	+	☆	+	*	☆	−	+	☆	−
Ch'en	☆	☆	*	☆	☆	☆	☆	+	☆	+	☆	☆	☆	☆	−	*	☆
Szu	☆	+	*	+	☆	−	☆	+	−	+	☆	+	☆	+	+	☆	−
Wu	*	*	*	☆	+	+	☆	+	☆	☆	+	*	☆	☆	☆	+	−
Wei	+	+	☆	☆	+	☆	*	☆	☆	+	☆	☆	☆	+	+	☆	☆
Shen	☆	☆	+	☆	+	☆	☆	☆	+	+	☆	+	☆	−	−	*	−
Yu	+	☆	+	☆	☆	−	☆	*	+	☆	+	+	☆	−	+	☆	−
Hsü	☆	☆	+	☆	☆	☆	☆	*	☆	+	☆	☆	☆	☆	☆	+	☆
Hai	☆	+	+	+	☆	−	☆	*	−	+	☆	+	☆	+	+	☆	−

The Great and Small Limits

The Great Limits are periods of ten years and the Small Limits periods of one year in your life. On the Tzu Wei chart each box is also labelled with Great and Small Limits. This means each box on the chart will have three different main labels, the Earthly Branch, the Palace and now the Great and Small Limits. The stars in a given box affect the period of your life shown by the limits labelling that box.

The Great Limits

To fill in the Great Limits on the Tzu Wei chart, follow these instructions.

To find out what your Great Limits (ten-year periods) are:

(a) Write down your element.

(b) Find the number corresponding to this element.

Wood = 3
Fire = 6
Metal = 4
Water = 2
Earth = 5

(c) Write down your first Great Limit. This ten-year period runs from the age corresponding to the number of your element:

for Wood: 3–12 years of age
for Fire: 6–15 years of age
for Metal: 4–13 years of age
for Water: 2–11 years of age
for Earth: 5–14 years of age

(d) Calculate the series based on your first Great Limit:

for Wood: 3–12, 13–22, 23–32, 33–42, 43–52, etc.
for Fire: 6–15, 16–25, 26–35, 36–45, 46–55, etc.
for Metal: 4–13, 14–23, 24–33, 34–43, 44–53, etc.
for Water: 2–11, 12–21, 22–31, 32–41, 42–51, etc.
for Earth: 5–14, 15–24, 25–34, 35–44, 45–54, etc.

The first Great Limit is entered in the box in which your Ming Palace appears. The others are entered in order running round the boxes on the edge of the chart.

To find out whether your Great Limits run clockwise or anticlockwise around the Tzu Wei chart:

(e) Write down whether you are a yin person (woman) or a yang person (man).

(f) Write down whether the Heavenly Stem for the year you were born is yin or yang.

Yang Heavenly Stems: Chia, Ping, Mou, Keng, Jen
Yin Heavenly Stems: Yi, Ting, Chi, Hsin, Kuei

(g) You work out whether your Great Limits run clockwise or anticlockwise around the chart as follows:

A yin person born in a year with a yin Heavenly Stem runs clockwise (yin + yin→CW).

A yang person born in a year with a yang Heavenly Stem runs clockwise (yang + yang→CW).

A yin person born in a year with a yang Heavenly Stem runs anticlockwise (yin + yang→ACW).

A yang person born in a year with a yin Heavenly Stem runs anticlockwise (yang + yin→ACW).

For the example 1 September 1986, 8 p.m., the element is Wood and the number corresponding to this element is 3. This means that the Great Limits series is 3–12, 13–22, 23–32, 33–42, 43–52, etc.

The Ming Palace is located in the box Hsü. This means that the first Great Limit labels this box. Let us suppose that the person born on this date is female (a yin person). The Heavenly Stem for the year is Ping. This is a yang Heavenly Stem.

A yin person born in a year with a yang Heavenly Stem runs anticlockwise (yin + yang→ACW).

This means that the second Great Limit appears in the box labelled Yu, the third in the box labelled Shen, and so on (Figure 11).

The Small Limits

The Small Limits are simpler to fill in on the chart. If you were born in a year with Earthly Branch:

Yin, Wu or Hsü – start from the box labelled Ch'en
Shen, Tzu or Ch'en – start from the box labelled Hsü
Szu, Yu or Ch'ou – start from the box labelled Wei

Hai, Mao or Wei – start from the box labelled Ch'ou

The first Small Limit is year 1, the second year 2, the third year 3, and so on up to year 12. Then the cycle repeats itself, so that year 13 falls in the same box as year 1, year 14 in the same box as year 2, year 15 in the same box as year 3, and so on.

The sequence is as follows:

Year	*Year*	*Year*	*Year*	*Year*	*Year*	*Year*	*Year*
1	13	25	37	49	61	73	85
2	14	26	38	50	62	74	86
3	15	27	39	51	63	75	87
4	16	28	40	52	64	76	88
5	17	29	41	53	65	77	89
6	18	30	42	54	66	78	90
7	19	31	43	55	67	79	91
8	20	32	44	56	68	80	92
9	21	33	45	57	69	81	93
10	22	34	46	58	70	82	94
11	23	35	47	59	71	83	95
12	24	36	48	60	72	84	96

Thus, if the Small Limit for year 1 falls in the box labelled Ch'en, so will the Small Limits for the years 13, 25, 37, 49, 61, 73 and 85.

If you are a yin person (woman) the Small Limits run anticlockwise around the chart and if you are a yang person (man) they run clockwise.

For the example 1 September 1986, 8 p.m., the Earthly Branch for the year is Yin. This means that the first Small Limit goes in the box labelled Ch'en. As the person born on this date is female, the Small Limits run anticlockwise. This means the second Small Limit goes in the box labelled Mao, the third in the box labelled Yin, and so on (see Figure 11).

The ten-year period covered by a Great Limit will also be affected by the Small Limits for each of those years. This means that although a particular ten-year period has a poor prospect, this can be modified from year to year according to the Small Limits readings.

Figure 11 *Filling in the Great and Small Limits, and borrowed stars*

T'ien T'ung* T'ien Ts'un Hua Lu 53-62 12 Sickness Szu	Wu Ch'ü* T'ien Fu* Yang Jen– 43-52 11 Wealth Wu	T'ai-yang* T'ien Hsi T'ai-yin* T'ien Yao 33-42 10 Man and Woman Wei	T'an Lang+ 23-32 9 Marital Shen
P'o Chün* Yu Pi T'o Lo* 63-72 1 Moving Ch'en	Date and time of birth (solar): 1986 September 1st 8 p.m. Date and time of birth (lunar): Ping Yin 7th 27th Hsü Eight characters: Ping Yin Ping Shen Mou Shen Jen Hsü Element: Wood Name: Today's date:		T'ien Chi* T'ien Yüeh Chü Men* Ti Chieh Hua Ch'üan 13-22 8 Brothers' and Sisters' Yu
T'ien Chi T'ien Hao **Chü Men** T'ien Hsing 73-82 2 Servants' Mao			Tzu Wei* Tso Fu T'ien Hsiang* 3-12 7 Ming Hsü
Lien Chen* I-ma Wen Ch'ü+ Hua Chi 83-92 3 Officials' Yin	Ringing T'ien K'ung Star+ Hung Luan 93-102 4 Property Ch'ou	Ch'i Sha* Hua K'o Wen Ch'ang☆ 103-112 5 Fortune and Virtue Tzu	T'ien Liang+ T'ien K'uei Fire Star+ 113-122 6 Parents' Hai

Borrowing

On the Tzu Wei chart there is likely to be a concentration of stars in some palaces and very few or even no stars in others. If there are no stars in a palace this does not spell bad luck. It simply means that you have no particular fate, lucky or unlucky, for that palace.

If there are no main stars in a palace, then you can borrow the main stars from another palace according to the following rules:

The Ming Palace borrows from the Moving Palace (and vice versa)

The Brothers' and Sisters' Palace borrows from the Servants' Palace (and vice versa)

The Marital Palace borrows from the Officials' Palace (and vice versa)

The Man and Woman Palace borrows from the Property Palace (and vice versa)

The Wealth Palace borrows from the Fortune and Virtue Palace (and vice versa)

The Sickness Palace borrows from the Parents' Palace (and vice versa)

In the example 1 September 1986, 8 p.m., the Servants' Palace (in the box labelled Mao) has no main stars (see Figure 10). Using the rules outlined above, the main stars from Brothers' and Sisters' Palace can be borrowed for the Servants' Palace. These are T'ien Chi and Chü Men.

Borrowed stars influence the palace they have moved to. They also influence the ten-year period of your life covered by the Great Limit for that box and the one-year periods covered by the Small Limits.

HOW TO READ YOUR TZU WEI CHART

The first way of reading the Tzu Wei chart is based on the palaces and these give you readings for different aspects of your life, for example, your relationship with your parents, wealth, illness. The second way of reading the Tzu Wei chart is based on the Great and Small Limits, and this can predict whether a certain ten-year period or a one-year period is auspicious or not. The following are descriptions of how to make both types of reading.

The Palaces Reading

In the following chapters the tables used to read the Tzu Wei chart are arranged by palace. At the start of each chapter is a description of the aspects of your life covered by that particular palace. There is also a list of the stars divided into four groups, according to whether a star brings good or bad luck when it appears in that particular palace. The groups are: stars which bring extremely good luck, stars which bring moderately good luck, stars which bring bad luck and stars which bring extremely bad luck.

The table for each palace gives a detailed description of the significance a star exerts in that particular palace. It also shows how its significance alters if other stars also appear in the same palace, and what degree of influence the major stars have.

The tables are arranged as follows: the star of primary concern appears in the first column. If it is a major star, its degree of influence (see p. 70/83) is specified in the second column. Other stars which may also appear in that particular palace are listed in the third column. These stars may be referred to by name – e.g. 'Either of the Literary stars', 'Yang Jen *or* T'o Lu' – or the entry may simply say 'Any' (meaning 'Any star'), 'Any lucky star' or 'No unlucky stars'. In the latter two cases you should turn to the groups of lucky and unlucky stars listed at the front of the table to identify which stars are lucky and which unlucky. Very rarely the degree of influence of these other stars may be specified in the fourth column. The reading appears in the fifth column.

Not all stars appear in all palaces. If a certain star appears in a particular palace and is not listed in the table for that palace, this means that it is an 'interrupting star' and exerts only a minor influence. You can find out whether it brings good or bad luck by looking at the list of good-luck and bad-luck stars at the start of each table. However, not all interrupting stars are important enough to be listed.

You must distinguish between 'or' and 'and' in the table. 'T'ien K'uei *or* T'o Lo appears in the Ming Palace' is a different statement to 'T'ien K'uei *and* T'o Lo appear in the Ming Palace'.

In using the chart make sure you look at the readings for all possible combinations of stars in your horoscope. In the example for 1 September 1986, 8 p.m., there are six different readings for the three stars which appear in the Ming Palace, as follows:

Example of a reading for the Ming Palace for someone born on 1 September 1986, 8 p.m. (see Figure 11)

Tzu Wei*	You are reflective and refined. Your living conditions will improve in later life. You may be wealthy and famous.
Tzu Wei* with T'ien Hsiang*	You will have good clothes and enjoy dressing well.
Tzu Wei* with Tso Fu	Your social position will be elevated.
T'ien Hsiang*	You will have a successful social life and will enjoy helping people. You will enjoy involvement on a committee or an association. People respect and support you and this will bring you promotion and a good income.

T'ien Hsiang* with Tso Fu	You will have a position of authority and be wealthy. If you work in politics you will gain a high position.
Tso Fu	You are sedate and gentle.

The Great and Small Limits Readings

The Great and Small Limits readings predict whether a particular ten-year or a one-year period in your life is lucky or unlucky. This depends on whether the stars which appear in the box are lucky or unlucky.

Let us look at the example of someone born on 1 September 1986, 8 p.m., and obtain a reading for the ten-year period of this person's life between the ages of three and twelve. There are three stars which appear in the box labelled by this Great Limit: Tzu Wei (Purple Star), T'ien Hsiang (Heavenly Minister) and Tso Fu (Left Assistant). To find out if these stars, when they appear in this particular box, are lucky or unlucky we need to look at its palace labelling. In this case the box is labelled Ming Palace. Then turn to the start of the tables for the Ming Palace and find the list of stars divided into four groups depending on whether they bring good or bad luck in the Ming Palace. Tzu Wei, T'ien Hsiang and Tso Fu all bring extremely good luck in the Ming Palace. This means that this ten-year period from ages three to twelve is extremely auspicious.

If we wish to narrow down further and obtain a reading for the year in which this person is three, we look at the Small Limits. In this case the stars which appear in the box labelled with the Small Limit 3 are Lien Chen (Pure Virtue), Wen Ch'ü (Literary Music), I-ma (Travelling Star) and Hua Chi (Heavenly Secret). This box is labelled Officials' Palace. In the Officials' Palace Lien Chen and Wen Ch'ü bring extremely good luck. I-ma brings moderately good luck. Hua Chi brings bad luck. This means that on average this third year will be fairly lucky. This will also apply to the ages of 15, 27, 39, 51, 63, 75 and 87.

The following tables, therefore, give detailed readings for each palace of each of the stars in all possible combinations. By drawing up your own individual grid of stars, palaces, and so on, you can obtain a full Tzu Wei reading for yourself.

THE MING (LIFE/FATE) PALACE

The Ming Palace is concerned with your physical appearance, your character, abilities and the likelihood of you making progress, and developments at work.

The stars which bring great good luck in the Ming Palace are:

Tzu Wei (Purple Star)
T'ien Chi (Heavenly Secret)
T'ai-yang (Sun)
T'ien Fu (Southern Star)
T'ai-yin (Moon)
T'ien T'ung (Heavenly Unity)
T'ien Hsiang (Heavenly Minister)
T'ien Liang (Heavenly Roof-Beam)
Wen Ch'ü (Literary Music)
Wen Ch'ang (Literary Prosperity)
T'ien Ts'un (Heavenly Store)
T'ien K'uei (Heavenly Leader)
T'ien Yüeh (Heavenly Halberd)
Tso Fu (Left Assistant)
Yu Pi (Right Assistant)
Hua Lu (Transforming Salary)
Hua Ch'üan (Transforming Authority)

The stars which bring moderately good luck in this palace are:

Wu Ch'ü (Military Music)
Ch'i Sha (Seven Killings)
I-ma (Travelling Star)
Hung Luan (Red Phoenix)
T'ien Hsi (Heavenly Happiness)

The stars which bring bad luck in this palace are:

Lien Chen (Pure Virtue)
T'an Lang (Greedy Wolf)

Chü Men (Great Door)
P'o Chün (Broken Army)
Fire Star
Ringing Star
Yang Jen (Sheep-Blade)
T'o Lo (Hump-Back)
T'ien Yao (Heavenly Beauty)
T'ien Hsing (Heavenly Punishment)
T'ien Hao (Heavenly Destroyer

The stars which bring extremely bad luck in this palace are:

T'ien K'ung (Heavenly Void)
Ti Chieh (Earthly Robbery)
Hua Chi (Transforming Jealousy

Star	*Degree of influence*	*Other stars which appear in the Ming Palace*	*Degree of influence*	*Reading*
Tzu Wei	Any	Any		You are reflective and refined. Your living conditions will improve in later life. You may be wealthy and famous.
	Any	T'ien Fu		You will enjoy material well-being and good fortune.
	Any	T'an Lang		The opposite sex will bring you financial ruin or personal disaster.
	Any	T'ien Hsiang		You will have good clothes and enjoy dressing well.
	Any	Ch'i Sha		Whatever your line of work you will be in a position of authority.
	Any	Fire Star Ringing Star Yang Jen T'o Lo T'ien K'ung Ti Chieh		There will be a rift between you and your relatives. You will bring each other harm. You will live alone.
	Any	Either of the Literary stars T'ien Ts'un T'ien K'uei T'ien Yüeh Tso Fo *or* Yu Pi		Your social position will be elevated.

Star	*Degree of influence*	*Other stars*	*Degree of influence*	*Reading*
T'ien Chi	Any	Any		Your eyebrows are thick, your eyes alert, your forehead wide but your chin narrow. Although you have a hot temper, your heart is kind and charitable. You are intelligent, but you are always imagining things. The Chinese say: 'Clever but hindered by that cleverness.'
	* ☆	Any		You are wise and you will be successful and make great progress.
	+ –	Any		You are impatient and have a hot temper. Your imagination is too wild and you are unlikely to realize your aims.
	Any	T'ia-yin		You will be favoured by fortune in respect of social position and money.
	Any	Chü Men		You will either have a long life and little money, or you

Star	*Degree of influence*	*Other stars*	*Degree of influence*	*Reading*
				will have a lot of money and die young.
	Any	T'ien Liang		You have an aptitude for organization at work.
	Any	Fire Star, Ringing Star *or* either of the Literary stars		Your life will be like a wave fluctating between fortune and bad luck.
	Any	Yang Jen T'o Lo T'ien K'ung *or* Ti Chieh		You will be lonely and poor throughout your life.
		T'ien Ts'un T'ien K'uei T'ien Yüeh Tso Fu *or* Yu Pi		Your social position will be good and you will be rich.
T'ai-yang	Any	Any		Your physical appearance is round and full. You are stern and clever. You will treat people kindly and are full of energy. You have a tendency to show off. You are extravagant and will be a spendthrift.
	* ☆	Any		You will be successful in politics or finance.

Star	Degree of influence	Other stars	Degree of influence	Reading
	+ –	Any		You will become lazy even if you work hard when young.
	Any	T'ai-yin		You will be promoted to a high position. You will enjoy the authority and the renown it brings you. However, this promotion will bring you no concrete benefits. There will be no respite in the work required to build up your reputation.
	* ☆	Chü Men		You will be well known and hold a responsible position.
	+ –	Chü Men		When young, you will work hard and have success, but after middle age you will grow inattentive and lazy and start to make losses.
	* ☆	T'ien Liang		You will live in splendour and hold a high rank.
	+ –	T'ien Liang		You will be poor and unemployed, like a beggar.

Star	*Degree of influence*	*Other stars*	*Degree of influence*	*Reading*
	* ☆	Fire Star, Ringing Star *or* either of the Literary stars		Your work will run smoothly and you will be prosperous.
	+ –	Fire Star, Ringing Star *or* either of the Literary stars		Your luck will fluctuate.
	Any	Yang Jen T'o Lo T'ien K'ung *or* Ti Chieh		You are too extravagant. This will be your downfall.
	* ☆	T'ien Ts'un T'ien K'uei T'ien Yüeh Tso Fu *or* Yu Pi		You will be promoted to a high position and become rich.
	+ –	T'ien Ts'un T'ien K'uei T'ien Yüeh Tso Fu *or* Yu Pi		You will neither be wealthy nor poor.
Wu Ch'ü	Any	Any		You are physically short and slim and your voice is high and piercing. You have a strong will and are good at making decisions. You are quick-witted but sometimes impatient and hot-tempered. You rush at things and lack foresight.

Star	*Degree of influence*	*Other stars*	*Degree of influence*	*Reading*
	Any	No other unlucky stars		You will have financial success.
	Any	T'ien Fu		You will be successful in business and politics.
	Any	T'an Lang		You will be rich but miserly.
	Any	T'ien Hsiang		You will have broad knowledge. If you study subjects in more detail you will be successful.
	Any	Ch'i Sha		You are honest and discriminating. You are not prejudiced towards your friends.
	Any	P'o Chün		You will lose money and property and have a harsh life.
	Any	T'ien Ts'un		You will expand your business and make your family prosperous. You will become rich.
	Any	I-ma		You will leave your home town to expand your business. If you do not, it will go into decline and your future will be gloomy.

Star	*Degree of influence*	*Other stars*	*Degree of influence*	*Reading*
	Any	Fire Star *or* Ringing Star	☆	Your life will be average.
	Any	Fire Star *or* Ringing Star	+ –	You may have the opportunity to become wealthy and well known.
	Any	Tso Fu Yu Pi T'ien K'uei *or* T'ien Yüeh		You will leave your home town and your family to expand your business.
	Any	T'ien K'ung *or* Ti Chieh		If you try to make a lot of money, legally or illegally, you will not succeed or may die. You will have disagreements with your colleagues.
T'ien T'ung	Any	Any		Your manner is gentle, modest and warm.
	Any	No unlucky stars		You will be well known and wealthy.
	*	T'ai-yin		You will be a well-known doctor or will be given a special scholarship. You will be successful.
	+ –	T'ai-yin		Your whole life will be harsh. You will have no success.

Star	*Degree of influence*	*Other stars*	*Degree of influence*	*Reading*
	*	T'ien Liang		You will be promoted to a high position and make great profits.
	+ –	T'ien Liang		Your life will be harsh.
	Any	Chü Men		You will be plagued with troubles and arguments. The opposite sex will bring harm to your name.
	Any	T'ien Ts'un		You will be rich and noble all your life. You will be materially well off.
	Any	Fire Star Ringing Star Yang Jen T'o Lo		You will be pursued to repay your debts. If you cannot repay them you may be forced to do something illegal which will bring you trouble.
	Any	Literary stars T'ien K'uei T'ien Yüeh Tso Fu *or* Yu Pi		You will have a title and be well known. You will enjoy a good reputation and a peaceful and prosperous life.
Lien Chen	Any	Any		You have thick eyebrows and large eyes. You are clever and like to display your authority.

Star	*Degree of influence*	*Other stars*	*Degree of influence*	*Reading*
	Any	No unlucky stars		You will be rich and powerful.
	Any	T'ien Fu		You are likely to have a high position and be well known. You will live in splendour.
	Any	T'an Lang		You will have little money and a harsh life.
	Any	T'ien Hsiang		You are suited to business enterprise. You are not suited to work in politics or studying. Select your job carefully.
	Any	Ch'i Sha		Unless you leave your home town you will be unable to make progress at work.
	Any	P'o Chün		You will either be disabled or die young.
	Any	T'ien Ts'un		You will have social standing and be wealthy.
	Any	Fire Star Ringing Star Yang Jen T'o Lo		You are likely to break the law.
	Any	Literary stars T'ien K'uei *or* T'ien Yüeh		You will be rich and noble all your life.

Star	*Degree of influence*	*Other stars*	*Degree of influence*	*Reading*
	Any	Tso Fu *or* Yu Pi		Your social life will be excellent and your business prosperous.
	Any	T'ien K'ung *or* Ti Chieh		You will have accidents and unexpected expenses. This means you will be unable to save and will not be rich.
T'ien Fu	Any	Any		You treat people gently and politely. You know how to work hard and how to make progress. You are clever and if you use your abilities you will have a peaceful life.
	Any	Literary stars T'ien K'uei T'ien Yüeh		You are intelligent and will pass many examinations.
	Any	Fire Star Ringing Star Yang Jen T'o Lo		You start a project with enthusiasm but this peters out. The Chinese say you have a lion's head but a snake's tail. When you reach old age you will have an increasingly harsh life.

Star	*Degree of influence*	*Other stars*	*Degree of influence*	*Reading*
	Any	Tso Fu *or* Yu Pi		You will have a successful social life. This will provide you with opportunities to expand your business.
	Any	T'ien Ts'un		You will be able to save money and will be offered promotion.
	Any	T'ien K'ung *or* Ti Chieh		You will have a harsh life and lack material things.
T'ai-yin	Any	Any		You are good-looking.
	* ☆	Any		You will have a good education. You will be well known and have a good social position.
	+ –	Any		You will separate from your marriage partner and will die young.
	* ☆	Fire Star Ringing Star Yang Jen T'o Lo T'ien K'ung *or* Ti Chieh		You have abilities but you do not work hard. You do not make as much progress at work as you might.
	* ☆	T'ien Ts'un Literary stars T'ien K'uei T'ien Yüeh		Your polite and gentle character is well respected. You approach your work

Star	*Degree of influence*	*Other stars*	*Degree of influence*	*Reading*
		I-ma Tso Fu *or* Yu Pi		sensibly and gradually and will be promoted to a high position. You will have a prosperous life.
	+ –	Fire Star Ringing Star Yang Jen T'o Lo T'ien K'ung *and* Ti Chieh		You will succumb to overindulgence in drink and sex.
	+ –	Either of the Literary stars		You will work in the area of religion or astrology or as a medium in contact with the supernatural.
T'an Lang	Any	Any		You have protruding bones over your eyes. You are realistic and firm when making plans.
	* ☆	Any		You are not only fortunate but will also have a long life.
	+ –	Any		You like to show off your authority and intelligence. In the end you will be lost.
	Any	Fire Star Ringing Star T'ien K'uei *or* T'ien Yüeh		You will have more than enough money and material possessions.

Star	*Degree of influence*	*Other stars*	*Degree of influence*	*Reading*
	Any	Either of the Literary stars* Yang Jen *or* T'o Lo		You have just enough material possessions. You are greedy for sex. If more than one of these subordinate stars appear, you should take special care.
	Any	Tso Fu *or* Yu Pi		You will make a profit.
	Any	T'ien K'ung *or* Ti Chieh		You are over-indulgent in your desire for fame and money. This will bring disaster.
	* ☆	T'ien Ts'un		You will have great wealth.
Chü Men	Any	Any		You appear to be unfriendly but in fact you make a good friend. You are obstinate but give up easily when you have to do anything. This means that you are unlikely to succeed.
	* ☆	Any		You are a careful manager and have an aptitude for business.

*This is an exception to the general rule that the Literary stars bring good luck in the Ming Palace.

Star	*Degree of influence*	*Other stars*	*Degree of influence*	*Reading*
	+ –	Any		You are over-attentive and this means that you will suffer from nervous complaints. You have no patience to finish your work.
	Any	Fire Star Ringing Star Literary stars Yang Jen T'o Lo T'ien K'ung Ti Chieh		You are clever but you may have a short life. Sometimes your intelligence will be a drawback. You may commit suicide.
	* ☆	T'ien K'uei T'ien Yüeh Tso Fu *or* Yu Pi T'ien Ts'un		You will be promoted to a high position and be successful.
	+ –	T'ien K'uei T'ien Yüeh Tso Fu *or* Yu Pi T'ien Ts'un		You will have an average life.
T'ien Hsiang	Any	Any		You will have a successful social life and will always help others. You will enjoy working on a committee or with an association. People respect and support you and this will bring you promotion and a good income.

Star	*Degree of influence*	*Other stars*	*Degree of influence*	*Reading*
	+ –	Any		You will have a small business, e.g. street vendor.
	Any	Fire Star Ringing Star Yang Jen T'o Lo T'ien K'ung Ti Chieh		You should not expect to be rich or noble. You will have an average life.
	* ☆	Literary stars T'ien K'uei T'ien Yüeh Tso Fu *or* Yu Pi T'ien Ts'un		You will attain a position of authority and be wealthy. If you work in politics you will gain a high position.
	+ –	Literary stars T'ien K'uei T'ien Yüeh Tso Fu *or* Yu Pi T'ien Ts'un		(The same reading as above.)
T'ien Liang	Any	Any		You enjoy peaceful surroundings and you have leadership qualities. You are clever but your nature is gentle and sincere. You never display your talents.
	+ –	Any		You will have trouble in relation to the opposite sex. This will bring you into disrepute.

Star	*Degree of influence*	*Other stars*	*Degree of influence*	*Reading*
	Any	Fire Star Ringing Star Yang Jen To Lo T'ien K'ung Ti Chieh		You are likely to separate from or divorce your marriage partner. You may have other lovers.
	Any	Literary stars T'ien K'uei T'ien Yüeh Tso Fu *or* Yu Pi		You will have good luck.
	Any	T'ien Ts'un		You will have the opportunity to save vast amounts of money.
Ch'i Sha	Any	Any		Your eyes have a distinctive characteristic (perhaps a mark). Your appearance is stern and serious. You dislike compromise. You have a hot temper and never hide your feelings. You are quick to express happiness or anger.
	Any	No unlucky stars		You will be successful.
	Any	Fire Star *or* Ringing Star	☆	You may be promoted to a higher position.
	Any	Fire Star *or* Ringing Star	+ –	Your position will be average.

Star	*Degree of influence*	*Other stars*	*Degree of influence*	*Reading*
	Any	T'ien Ts'un I-ma		You will not only be rich but also noble.
	Any	T'ien K'uei T'ien Yüeh		You will be famous throughout the country or you will be a very important official.
	Any	Yang Jen T'o Lo T'ien K'ung Ti Chieh		Even if you are healthy, you may die young. You are likely to die from an accident or sudden illness.
P'o Chün	* ☆	Any		You will build up great wealth.
	+ –	Any		You will create a large business but it will destroy you.
	Any	Literary stars T'ien Ts'un T'ien K'uei T'ien Yüeh Tso Fu *or* Yu Pi		You will have authority and wealth.
	Any	Fire Star Ringing Star Yang Jen T'o Lo T'ien K'ung Ti Chieh		You will have a harsh and difficult life.

Star	*Degree of influence*	*Other stars*	*Degree of influence*	*Reading*
Fire Star *and* **Ringing Star**	Any	Any		You are taciturn. Your work is rushed and careless and you never make detailed or considered plans. You would like to run a large business but are unlikely to succeed; you have no interest in a small business.
	* ☆	Any		You will have authority and the chance of a high position.
	+ –	Any		Your life will fluctuate between good and bad luck. You are likely to die young.
Fire Star *or* **Ringing Star**	Any	Either of the Literary stars		You are suited to work as a labourer. You are not suited to politics or business.
	Any	Yang Jen T'o Lo		You may be deformed, disabled or have the scars of a major operation.
	* ☆	T'ien K'uei T'ien Yüeh		You will have authority and wealth.
	+ –	T'ien K'uei T'ien Yüeh		You will suffer from a long illness.

Star	*Degree of influence*	*Other stars*	*Degree of influence*	*Reading*
	* ☆	Tso Fu *or* Yu Pi		Your social life will be successful.
	+ –	Tso Fu *or* Yu Pi		You will have lasting authority and financial power.
	* ☆	T'ien K'ung Ti Chieh		You give the impression of having great authority when you really have none.
	+ –	T'ien K'ung Ti Chieh		You will not have lasting authority or financial power.
	* ☆	T'ien Ts'un I-ma		You will not be short of material goods.
	+ –	T'ien Ts'un I-ma		Travel to distant places will result in an accident or a disaster. You may lose money or your life.
Wen Ch'ü *or* **Wen Ch'ang**	Any	Any		You have fine facial features and are intelligent. You like study. Your conduct is refined and you take care of your appearance.
	* ☆	Any		You will be successful in your occupation.
	+ –	Any		You will never have any money.

Star	*Degree of influence*	*Other stars*	*Degree of influence*	*Reading*
	Any	Yang Jen *or* T'o Lo		You are likely to be disabled and may die young. If you have a high position or are well known this will bring you no genuine benefit.
	Any	T'ien Ts'un T'ien K'uei T'ien Yüeh Tso Fu *or* Yu Pi		You will be an important person in your country.
T'ien Ts'un		Any		You will have a long life and be wealthy.
		Tso Fu *or* Yu Pi		You will be well known in business or in politics.
		T'ien K'ung Ti Chieh		You will work hard but with little success.
Yang Jen *or* **T'o Lo**	Any	Any		You are courageous and good at decision making.
	* ☆	Any		Your decision-making ability is excellent and you will make great progress in your work.
	+ –	Any		Your life will be full of disasters and you may be disabled.
	+ –	T'ien K'uei *or* T'ien Yüeh		Your life will be fortunate and long.

Star	*Degree of influence*	*Other stars*	*Degree of influence*	*Reading*
	Any	Tso Fu *or* Yu Pi		You will suffer from robbery. Your property may be harmed or you will lose your life.
	☆	Tso Fu *or* Yu Pi		You will have great wealth and long life.
	Any	T'ien K'ung Ti Chieh		You will either have financial difficulties or a short life.
T'ien K'uei *or* **T'ien Yüeh**		Any		Your character and exterior are stern. Your conduct is refined.
		Tso Fu *or* Yu Pi		You will have extremely good fortune. You will stay healthy and live long.
		T'ien K'ung Ti Chieh		You will suffer from recurrent illness.
Tso Fu *or* **Yu Pi**		Any		You are sedate and gentle.
		T'ien K'ung *or* Ti Chieh		You will make no progress in your work. Your standard of living will be below average.
T'ien K'ung *or* **Ti Chieh**		Any		You will waste time and money. You will fluctuate between success and loss.

Star	*Degree of influence*	*Other stars*	*Degree of influence*	*Reading*
		I-ma		You will die far away from home, perhaps in a foreign country.
I-ma		Any		You like travelling or your work will involve travelling.
T'ien Hao		Any		You spend money like water and fluctuate between success and loss.
Hung Luan		Any		The opposite sex likes you. You may take advantage of this.
T'ien Hsi		Any		You take nothing seriously and are always happy.
T'ien Yao		Any		You will drown in drink and sex.
T'ien Hsing		Any		You will be lonely and will easily fall into legal difficulties.
Hua Lu		Any		You will have many chances of promotion.
Hua Ch'üan		Any		You will obtain power and authority.
Hua K'o		Any		You will be lucky in examinations.

Star	*Degree of influence*	*Other stars*	*Degree of influence*	*Reading*
Hua Chi		Any		You will easily miss opportunities and are unlikely to have success.

THE BROTHERS' AND SISTERS' PALACE

The Brothers' and Sisters' Palace is concerned with the relationship between you and your brothers and sisters. This relationship is controlled by the *yuanten* (predestined attachment) between you. *Yuanten* covers a broad range of meanings. If the *yuanten* between you is strong, you love one another and will stay together. If weak, you have little feeling for one another and may separate.

The Brothers' and Sisters' Palace is also concerned with how much help, material or otherwise, you and your brothers and sisters can give each other.

The following stars bring extremely good luck in the Brothers' and Sisters' Palace:

- T'ien Chi (Heavenly Secret)
- T'ien T'ung (Heavenly Unity)
- T'ien Fu (Southern Star)
- T'ien Hsiang (Heavenly Minister)
- T'ien Liang (Heavenly Roof-Beam)
- T'ien K'uei (Heavenly Leader)
- T'ien Yüeh (Heavenly Halberd)
- Tso Fu (Left Assistant)
- Yu Pi (Right Assistant)

These stars bring moderately good luck:

- Tzu Wei (Purple Star)
- T'ai-yang (Sun)
- T'ai-yin (Moon)
- Wen Ch'ü (Literary Music)
- Wen Ch'ang (Literary Prosperity)
- T'ien Ts'un (Heavenly Store)

These stars bring bad luck:

Wu Ch'ü (Military Music)
Fire Star
Ringing Star

These stars bring extremely bad luck:

Lien Chen (Pure Virtue)
T'an Lang (Greedy Wolf)
Chü Men (Great Door)
Ch'i Sha (Seven Killings)
P'o Chün (Broken Army)
Yang Jen (Sheep-Blade)
T'o Lo (Hump-Back)
T'ien K'ung (Heavenly Void)
Ti Chieh (Earthly Robbery)
Hua Chi (Transforming Jealousy)

Star	*Degree of influence*	*Other stars which appear in the Brothers' and Sisters' Palace*	*Degree of influence*	*Reading*
Tzu Wei	Any	Any		You and your brothers and sisters will support one another.
	Any	T'ien Fu T'ien Hsiang		You will receive help from your brothers and sisters.
	Any	T'an Lang		One brother or sister will marry late or not at all.
	Any	Ch'i Sha		There will be a rift between you and one of your brothers and sisters. You may harm them.
	Any	P'o Chün		There will be a rift between you and your brothers and sisters, but this will not be as serious as the situation above.
	Any	T'ien Ts'un		You will receive material support from your brothers and sisters.
	Any	Fire Star Ringing Star Yang Jen T'o Lo T'ien K'ung Ti Chieh		You will not be in harmony with your brothers and sisters.

Star	*Degree of influence*	*Other stars*	*Degree of influence*	*Reading*
	Any	Literary stars T'ien K'uei T'ien Yüeh Tso Fu *or* Yu Pi		You are in harmony with your brothers and sisters. You will stay together.
T'ien Chi	Any	Any		You will not have many brothers and sisters, but they will be a great support to you.
	+ –	Any		You will not be in harmony with your brothers and sisters.
	Any	T'ai-yin T'ien Liang		Your brothers and sisters will give you moral support.
	Any	T'ien Ts'un *or* Chü Men		You will receive material support from your brothers and sisters.
	Any	Fire Star Ringing Star Yang Jen T'o Lo T'ien K'ung *or* Ti Chieh		There will not be any harmony between you and your brothers and sisters. You will not help one another.
	Any	Literary stars T'ien K'uei T'ien Yüeh Tso Fu *or* Yu Pi		There will be great harmony between you and your brothers and sisters. Your eldest brother or sister will care for you as a parent.

Star	*Degree of influence*	*Other stars*	*Degree of influence*	*Reading*
T'ai-yang	* ☆	Any		Your brothers and sisters will help one another.
	–	Any		Not only will there be lack of harmony between your brothers and sisters, but they will actively quarrel with one another.
	Any	T'ai-yin T'ien Liang T'ien Ts'un		Your *yuanten* (predestined attachment) with your brothers and sisters will be strong. You will have a deep love for one another, will help one another and are likely to stay together.
	Any	Chü Men		Your *yuanten* (predestined attachment) with your brothers and sisters is fairly weak.
	Any	Fire Star Ringing Star Yang Jen T'o Lo T'ien K'ung Ti Chieh		You and your brothers and sisters all have differing opinions. There will be no feeling between you.
Wu Ch'ü	Any	Any		You come from a small family.

Star	*Degree of influence*	*Other stars*	*Degree of influence*	*Reading*
	Any	T'ien Fu T'ien Hsiang T'ien Ts'un		You will receive substantial material help from your brothers and sisters.
	Any	T'an Lang Ch'i Sha P'o Chün		There will be no harmony between you and your brothers and sisters and you will quarrel easily.
	Any	Fire Star Ringing Star Yang Jen T'o Lo T'ien K'ung Ti Chieh		Your *yuanten* (predestined attachment) with your brothers and sisters is weak. There will be no harmony between you, and you will be lonely.
	Any	Literary stars T'ien K'uei T'ien Yüeh Tso Fu *or* Yu Pi	Any	Although you will receive material support from your brothers and sisters you are likely to separate.
T'ien T'ung	Any	Any	Any	You will have many brothers and sisters and will be in harmony with all of them.
	Any	Chü Men		(The above reading does not hold.)

Star	*Degree of influence*	*Other stars*	*Degree of influence*	*Reading*
	Any	Fire Star Ringing Star Yang Jen T'o Lo T'ien T'ung Ti Chieh		Your brothers and sisters will be scattered in different places. You will lack harmony.
	Any	Literary stars T'ien K'uei T'ien Yüeh Tso Fu *or* Yu Pi		You will be in harmony with your brothers and sisters and help one another.
Lien Chen	Any	Any		You will have few brothers and sisters and lack harmony.
	Any	T'ien Fu T'ien Hsiang T'ien Ts'un Literary stars T'ien K'uei T'ien Yüeh Tso Fu *or* Yu Pi		You and your brothers and sisters do not help one another but you are in harmony.
	Any	T'an Lang Ch'i Sha P'o Chün Ringing Star Fire Star Yang Jen T'o Lo T'ien K'ung Ti Chieh		You will not be in harmony with your brothers and sisters and you will quarrel frequently.
T'ien Fu	Any	Any		You will have many brothers and sisters and you all will live in harmony.

Star	*Degree of influence*	*Other stars*	*Degree of influence*	*Reading*
		T'ien Ts'un		You will receive material support from your brothers and sisters.
	Any	Fire Star Ringing Star Yang Jen T'o Lo		You will have few brothers and sisters. You will be unable to help each other.
	Any	Literary stars T'ien K'uei T'ien Yüeh		You will live in harmony and help each other.
	Any	Tso Fu *or* Yu Pi		You and your brothers and sisters will help one another greatly and this will bring you business success.
	Any	T'ien K'ung Ti Chieh		You will be out of harmony with your brothers and sisters. You may fight and harm one another.
T'ai-yin	* ☆	Any		You will have many brothers and sisters and will help each other.
	–	Any		You will have few brothers and sisters and will not help one another.

Star	*Degree of influence*	*Other stars*	*Degree of influence*	*Reading*
	Any	Fire Star Ringing Star Yang Jen T'o Lo T'ien K'ung Ti Chieh		You will be in harmony even though your brothers and sisters will be scattered in many different places.
	Any	Literary stars T'ien K'uei T'ien Yüeh Tso Fu *or* Yu Pi		You and your brothers and sisters will be in harmony and will help each other.
	Any	T'ien Ts'un		You will receive material help from your brothers and sisters.
T'an Lang	☆	Any		You will have few brothers or sisters and they will not help each other.
	–	Any		Your brothers and sisters will cause you harm. You may suffer financial loss.
	Any	Any		You will be cold towards your brothers and sisters, even those born of the same parents. However, the devious nature of your brothers and sisters appeals to you.

Star	Degree of influence	Other stars	Degree of influence	Reading
	Any	Fire Star Ringing Star Yang Jen T'o Lo T'ien K'ung Ti Chieh		You will suffer a disaster caused by your brothers and sisters. In the course of doing something for them you may have an accident.
	Any	Either of the Literary stars T'ien K'uei T'ien Yüeh Tso Fu *or* Yu Pi		You and your brothers and sisters will not help one another, but you will live in harmony.
	Any	T'ien Ts'un		You will live happily with your brothers and sisters.
Chü Men	Any	Any		You will have few brothers and sisters.
	Any	T'ien Ts'un		(As above.)
	Any	Fire Star Ringing Star Yang Jen T'o Lo T'ien K'ung Ti Chieh		You and your brothers and sisters will distrust and loathe one another. You will speak ill of one another.
	Any	Either of the Literary stars Tso Fu *or* Yu Pi		Although you and your brothers and sisters will not help one another you all get on well.
T'ien Hsiang	Any	Any		You will have two or three brothers or sisters and will help one another.

Star	*Degree of influence*	*Other stars*	*Degree of influence*	*Reading*
	Any	T'ien Ts'un		You will receive material support from your brothers and sisters.
	Any	Fire Star Ringing Star Yang Jen T'o Lo T'ien K'ung Ti Chieh		Your *yuanten* (predestined attachment) for your brothers and sisters is weak so you will either be separated by circumstances or will stay together but not live in harmony.
	Any	Either of the Literary stars T'ien K'uei T'ien Yüeh Tso Fu *and* Yu Pi		You and your brothers and sisters will live in harmony and help one another. You will be close and supportive.
T'ien Liang	Any	Any		Although you will have few brothers and sisters you will all assist one another.
	Any	T'ien Ts'un		You will receive material support from your brothers and sisters.

Star	*Degree of influence*	*Other stars*	*Degree of influence*	*Reading*
	Any	Fire Star Ringing Star Yang Jen T'o Lo T'ien Kung Ti Chieh		Your *yuanten* (predestined attachment) is weak and you will not be in harmony. It is unlikely and inadvisable for you to stay together.
	Any	Literary Stars T'ien K'uei T'ien Yüeh Tso Fu *and* Yu Pi		Your feelings for your brothers and sisters will be harmonious and you will help one another.
Ch'i Sha	Any	Any		You will have three brothers or sisters.
	Any	T'ien Ts'un		You will receive material help from your brothers and sisters.
	Any	Fire Star Ringing Star Yang Jen T'o Lo T'ien K'ung Ti Chieh		You and your brothers and sisters will bring harm to one another and will quarrel constantly.
	Any	Literary stars T'ien K'uei T'ien Yüeh Tso Fu *or* Yu Pi		You will be in harmony with your brothers and sisters and you will all help each other.
P'o Chün	Any	Any		You will have many brothers and sisters but they will not help you.

Star	*Degree of influence*	*Other stars*	*Degree of influence*	*Reading*
	Any	T'ien Ts'un		You will receive material help from your brothers and sisters.
		Fire Star Ringing Star Yang Jen T'o Lo T'ien K'ung Ti Chieh		You will either have no brothers or sisters or you will live separately and not see one another.
	Any	Either of the Literary stars T'ien K'uei T'ien Yüeh Tso Fu *or* Yu Pi		You will live in harmony with your brothers and sisters and will help one another.
Fire Star *or* **Ringing Star**	Any	Any		You and your brothers and sisters will not be in harmony and your feelings for one another will be cold.
	Any	Either of the Literary stars *or* T'ien Ts'un		(These stars make the above reading weaker.)
	Any	T'ien K'uei T'ien Yüeh Tso Fu *or* Yu Pi		You will receive help from your brothers and sisters.
	Any	Yang Jen T'o Lo T'ien K'ung Ti Chieh		Your brothers and sisters will cause you worry and you will suffer a loss.

Star	*Degree of influence*	*Other stars*	*Degree of influence*	*Reading*
Wen Chü *or* **Wen Ch'ang**	Any	Any		You will be in harmony and receive moral support from your brothers and sisters. Your business will prosper.
	Any	T'ien Ts'un		As well as moral support, you will also receive material support from your brothers and sisters.
	Any	T'ien K'uei T'ien Yüeh Tso Fu *or* Yu Pi		Your brothers and sisters will help you to achieve a comfortable life.
	Any	Yang Jen T'o Lo		Your *yuanten* (predestined attachment) with your brothers and sisters is weak. You may live apart or a brother or sister may die unexpectedly.
T'ien Ts'un	Any	Any		Your brothers and sisters will receive material support from one another.
	Any	Tso Fu *or* Yu Pi		Your brothers and sisters will live in harmony and will help one another.

Star	*Degree of influence*	*Other stars*	*Degree of influence*	*Reading*
	Any	T'ien K'ung Ti Chieh		Your brothers and sisters will be cold towards one another. They may cause you loss.
Yang Jen *or* **T'o Lo**	Any	Any		Your brothers and sisters will be few in number.
	Any	T'ien K'uei *or* T'ien Yüeh Tso Fu *or* Yu Pi		You will have even fewer brothers and sisters than in the above case.
	Any	T'ien K'ung Ti Chieh		There will be enmity and suspicion between you and your brothers and sisters.
T'ien K'uei *or* **T'ien Yüeh**		Any		You will receive great benefit from your brothers and sisters.
		Tso Fu *or* Yu Pi		Your brothers and sisters will live in harmony and help one another.
		T'ien K'ung Ti Chieh		You will be in reasonable harmony with your brothers and sisters.
Tso Fu *or* **Yu Pi**		Any		Your brothers and sisters will live in harmony and help one another.

Star	*Degree of influence*	*Other stars*	*Degree of influence*	*Reading*
		T'ien K'ung Ti Chieh		There will be a lack of harmony between you and your brothers and sisters and you will not help one another.
T'ien K'ung *or* **Ti Chieh**		Any		You will care deeply for your brothers and sisters and work hard for them. They will cause you worry.
Hua Chi		Any		You will make sacrifices for your brothers and sisters.

THE MARITAL PALACE

The Marital Palace concerns the appearance, nature and character of your marriage partner and describes your relationship and love life.

These stars bring extremely good luck in the Marital Palace:

- T'ai-yang (Sun)
- T'ien T'ung (Heavenly Unity)
- T'ien Fu (Southern Star)
- T'ien Liang (Heavenly Roof-Beam)
- T'ien Ts'un (Heavenly Store)
- T'ien K'uei (Heavenly Leader)
- T'ien Yüeh (Heavenly Halberd)

These stars bring moderately good luck:

- Tzu Wei (Purple Star)
- T'ien Chi (Heavenly Secret)
- T'ai-yin (Moon)
- T'ien Hsiang (Heavenly Minister)
- Wen Ch'ü (Literary Music)
- Wen Ch'ang (Literary Prosperity)

These stars bring bad luck in the Marital Palace:

- Wu Ch'ü (Military Music)
- Chü Men (Great Door)
- Fire Star
- Ringing Star
- Tso Fu (Left Assistant)*
- Yu Pi (Right Assistant)*
- T'ien Yao (Heavenly Beauty)

*These are generally good-luck stars.

These stars bring extremely bad luck in the Marital Palace:

- Lien Chen (Pure Virtue)
- T'an Lang (Greedy Wolf)
- Ch'i Sha (Seven Killings)
- P'o Chün (Broken Army)
- Yang Jen (Sheep-Blade)
- T'o Lo (Hump-Back)
- T'ien K'ung (Heavenly Void)
- Ti Chieh (Earthly Robbery)
- Hua Chi (Transforming Jealousy)

Star	*Degree of influence*	*Other stars which appear in the Marital Palace*	*Degree of influence*	*Reading*
Tzu Wei	Any	Any		Your partner's well-bred background causes marital problems. However, if you marry late (over the age of twenty-eight), even if your partner is well-bred, he/she will be attractive to you and you will live in harmony.
	Any	T'ien Fu		Your feelings for each other will be strong and you will love one another until the end.
	Any	T'an Lang		You will either separate or one of you will die before old age.
	Any	T'an Lang *and* any other lucky star		Your marriage will be long and fortunate.
		T'ien Hsiang		There will be a big discrepancy in your ages.
	Any	Ch'i Sha		You will quarrel easily and may separate or one of you may die.

Star	*Degree of influence*	*Other stars*	*Degree of influence*	*Reading*
	Any	P'o Chün		There will be a rift between you which sours your feelings for each other. You will cause each other harm. However, if the woman is older than the man, this trouble can be avoided.
	Any	T'ien Ts'un		You will receive substantial material support from your partner.
	Any	Fire Star Ringing Star Yang Jen T'o Lo T'ien K'ung Ti Chieh		There will be a rift between you and you are likely to harm your partner.
	Any	Either of Literary stars T'ien K'uei T'ien Yüeh Tso Fu *or* Yu Pi		Your partner will bring you great happiness in your love life.
T'ien Chi	Any	Any		If you are a man your wife will be young but impatient. If you are a woman there will be a great discrepancy between your ages.

Star	*Degree of influence*	*Other stars*	*Degree of influence*	*Reading*
	Any	T'ai-yin		If you are a man your wife will be pretty. If you are a woman your husband will be handsome.
	Any	Chü Men		Your partner will be good-looking.
	Any	T'ien Liang		Your partner will be good-looking but the difference in your ages will be great.
	Any	T'ien Ts'un		Your partner will be virtuous.
T'ai-yang	Any	Any		Your partner will help you gain promotion, but if you marry too early (e.g. at sixteen years of age) there will be a rift between you and your partner.
	Any	T'ai-yin		You will benefit greatly from your partner.
	Any	Chü Men		Your life will be average unless other unlucky stars also appear under this palace.
	Any	T'ien Liang		Your partner will be extremely virtuous and clever.

Star	*Degree of influence*	*Other stars*	*Degree of influence*	*Reading*
	Any	T'ien Ts'un		Your partner will offer you material support.
	Any	Fire Star Ringing Star Yang Jen T'o Lo T'ien K'ung Ti Chieh		There will be a rift between you and your partner and you may harm each other. If you marry late you will avoid this problem.
Wu Chü	Any	Any		You may separate from your partner or your partner may die. If you marry late you will avoid this trouble.
	Any	T'ien Ts'un		Your partner will bring you great wealth.
	Any	T'an Lang		Unless you marry late there will be a rift between you, and you will harm your partner.
	Any	T'ien Hsiang		You will not be in harmony with your partner.
	Any	Ch'i Sha		You will separate or your partner may die.

Star	*Degree of influence*	*Other stars*	*Degree of influence*	*Reading*
	Any	Fire Star Ringing Star Yang Jen T'o Lo T'ien K'ung Ti Chieh		You will quarrel and may separate or one of you may die.
	Any	Either of the Literary stars T'ien K'uei T'ien Yüeh Tso Fu *or* Yu Pi		Your partner will bring you great wealth.
T'ien T'ung	Any	Any		Your partner will be yielding and kind.
	Any	T'ai-yin		Your partner will be good-looking.
	Any	Chü Men		Your partner will be clever but is likely to die young.
	Any	T'ien Liang		You will love each other dearly and will live in harmony. Your family will have good fortune.
	Any	T'ien Ts'un		You will be united in your love for each other, and your partner will ensure that you are financially secure.

Star	*Degree of influence*	*Other stars*	*Degree of influence*	*Reading*
	Any	Fire Star Ringing Star Yang Jen T'o Lo T'ien K'ung Ti Chieh		You will not be in harmony. You may separate or one of you may die.
	Any	Literary stars T'ien K'uei T'ien Yüeh Tso Fu *or* Yu Pi		You will be in harmony. Your love life will be excellent.
Lien Chen	Any	Any		You will either separate or one partner may die.
	Any	T'ien Fu T'ien Hsiang T'ien Ts'un Literary stars T'ien K'uei T'ien Yüeh Tso Fu *or* Yu Pi		You will marry someone with a hot temper. You must be patient to avoid quarrels.
	Any	T'an Lang Ch'i Sha P'o Chün Fire Star Ringing Star Yang Jen T'o Lo T'ien K'ung Ti Chieh		There will be a rift between you which will not be easily reconciled. At times in your marriage you will separate.

Star	*Degree of influence*	*Other stars*	*Degree of influence*	*Reading*
T'ien Fu	Any	Any		Your partner will be very capable and will show great ability. You will receive substantial material support from him/her.
	Any	Fire Star Ringing Star Yang Jen T'o Lo T'ien K'ung Ti Chieh		Your partner will be too intelligent for you and your ideas will differ greatly. You are likely to suffer.
	Any	Either of the Literary stars T'ien K'uei T'ien Yüeh Tso Fu *or* Yu Pi		Your partner will be brilliantly capable. You will have enough material possessions and your love life will be happy.
T'ai-yin	Any	Any		Your partner will be good-looking and will have a high-class air.
	Any	Fire Star Ringing Star Yang Jen T'o Lo T'ien K'ung Ti Chieh		You will separate because your partner will be too good-looking and will attract others.
	Any	Literary stars T'ien K'uei T'ien Yüeh Tso Fu *or* Yu Pi		You will be a happy couple.

Star	*Degree of influence*	*Other stars*	*Degree of influence*	*Reading*
T'an Lang	Any	Any		You will change partner many times.
		T'ien Ts'un Fire Star Ringing Star Yang Jen T'o Lo T'ien K'ung Ti Chieh		You will divorce.
	Any	Either of the Literary stars T'ien K'uei T'ien Yüeh Tso Fu *or* Yu Pi		If you marry late you will avoid separation or the untimely death of one partner.
Chü Men	Any	Any		You will have no feeling for each other and will quarrel constantly.
	Any	T'ien Ts'un		There will be discord and you will argue constantly.
	Any	Fire Star Ringing Star Yang Jen T'o Lo T'ien K'ung Ti Chieh		You will either separate or one partner will die early.
	Any	Literary stars T'ien K'uei T'ien Yüeh Tso Fu *or* Yu Pi		You will appear to be in love and live in harmony, but this will not be the case.

Star	*Degree of influence*	*Other stars*	*Degree of influence*	*Reading*
T'ien Hsiang	Any	Any		The husband will be younger than the wife. You will be distant relatives.
	Any	T'ien Ts'un		You will both have the same aspirations and will help each other to build a strong foundation for achieving them.
	Any	Fire Star Ringing Star Yang Jen T'o Lo T'ien K'ung Ti Chieh		Your feelings for each other will not be good.
	Any	Literary stars T'ien K'uei T'ien Yüeh Tso Fu *or* Yu Pi		You will be cooperative and will forgive each other's faults.
T'ien Liang	Any	Any		Your partner will be good-looking. If you are a woman your husband will be younger than you.
	Any	T'ien Ts'un		You will respect each other. Your love life will be good.
	Any	Fire Star Ringing Star Yang Jen T'o Lo T'ien K'ung Ti Chieh		There will be discord in your marriage; you will quarrel constantly.

Star	*Degree of influence*	*Other stars*	*Degree of influence*	*Reading*
	Any	Literary stars T'ien K'uei T'ien Yüeh Tso Fu *and* Yu Pi		You will respect and love each other dearly.
Ch'i Sha	Any	Any		Early on in your marriage you will cause your partner harm.
	Any	Any lucky star		(The above reading is still true but may be delayed.)
	Any	Fire Star Ringing Star Yang Jen T'o Lo T'ien K'ung Ti Chieh		You will change your marriage partner many times.
P'o Chün	Any	Any		There will be a rift between you and your partner early on. You will cause your partner harm.
	Any	Any lucky star		(The above reading is delayed, not avoided.)
	Any	Fire Star Ringing Star Yang Jen T'o Lo T'ien K'ung Ti Chieh		You will change your partner many times. You are likely to live with your boyfriend or girlfriend rather than marry.

Star	*Degree of influence*	*Other stars*	*Degree of influence*	*Reading*
Fire Star *or* **Ringing Star**	* ☆	Any lucky star		You can avoid misfortune.
	+ –	Any unlucky star		You will lack harmony. You will separate or one of you may die.
Wen Ch'ü *or* **Wen Ch'ang**	Any	Any		Your partner will be virtuous.
Wen Ch'ü *and* **Wen Ch'ang**	Any	Any		You will commit adultery.
Yang Jen *or* **T'o Lo**	Any	Any		There will be a rift between you and your partner and you will harm each other.
Tso Fu *or* **Yu Pi**		Any		You will be co-operative and will progress well at work.
T'ien K'ung *or* **Ti Chieh**		Any		Your partner will cause you distress.
T'ien Ts'un		Any		You will receive material support from your partner. This will help you to make progress at work.

Star	*Degree of influence*	*Other stars*	*Degree of influence*	*Reading*
T'ien Yao		Any		Your partner succumbs to drink and sex.
Hua Chi		Any		There will be a rift between you and your partner.

THE MAN AND WOMAN PALACE

The Man and Woman Palace is concerned with your children. How many children will you have? What will your relationship with them be like?

The stars which bring extremely good luck in the Man and Woman Palace are:

T'ai-yang (Sun)
T'ien T'ung (Heavenly Unity)
T'ien Fu (Southern Star)
T'ai-yin (Moon)
T'ien K'uei (Heavenly Leader)
T'ien Yüeh (Heavenly Halberd)

The stars which bring moderately good luck are:

Tzu Wei (Purple Star)
T'ien Chi (Heavenly Secret)
T'ien Hsiang (Heavenly Minister)
T'ien Liang (Heavenly Roof-Beam)
Wen Ch'ü (Literary Music)
Wen Ch'ang (Literary Prosperity)
T'ien Ts'un (Heavenly Store)
Tso Fu (Left Assistant)
Yu Pi (Right Assistant)

The stars which bring bad luck are:

Wu Ch'ü (Military Music)
P'o Chün (Broken Army)

The stars which bring extremely bad luck are:

Lien Chen (Pure Virtue)
T'an Lang (Greedy Wolf)
Chü Men (Great Door)
T'o Lo (Hump-Back)
T'ien T'ung (Heavenly Unity)

Ch'i Sha (Seven Killings)
Fire Star
Ringing Star
Yang Jen (Sheep-Blade)
Ti Chieh (Earthly Robbery)
Hua Chi (Transforming Jealousy)

Star	*Degree of influence*	*Other stars appearing in in the Man and Woman Palace*	*Degree of influence*	*Reading*
Tzu Wei	Any	Any		Your children will have a successful business.
	Any	T'ien Fu		Your children will be prosperous in their work.
	Any	T'an Lang		Your children will be successful but their relationships with the opposite sex will not be good.
	Any	T'ien Hsiang		Your children will be successful in politics.
	Any	Ch'i Sha		Your children will be few. You may have only one or two boys.
	Any	P'o Chün		There will be a rift between you and your children. You will live apart.
	Any	T'ien Ts'un		Your children will save money and be rich. They will have a comfortable old age.
	Any	T'ien Ts'un *and* T'ien K'ung *or* Ti Chieh		Your children will not always be able to offer you financial support.

Star	*Degree of influence*	*Other stars*	*Degree of influence*	*Reading*
	Any	Fire Star Ringing Star Yang Jen T'o Lo T'ien K'ung T'i Chieh		There will be a rift and discord between you and your children.
	Any	Literary stars T'ien K'uei T'ien Yüeh Tso Fu *or* Yu Pi		Your children will be successful in business. They will be clever and obedient.
T'ien Chi	Any	Any		Your children will be particularly clever or even outstanding.
	Any	T'ai-yin T'ien Liang		You will have pleasant, attractive children.
	Any	Chü Men T'ien Ts'un		You will have creative children. They will be adept socially in later life.
	Any	Fire Star Ringing Star Yang Jen T'o Lo T'ien K'ung Ti Chieh		When your children are young, a parent or child may die.
	Any	Literary stars T'ien K'uei T'ien Yüeh Tso Fu *or* Yu Pi		Your children will already be outstanding in some way when they are young.

Star	*Degree of influence*	*Other stars*	*Degree of influence*	*Reading*
T'ai-yang	Any	Any		Your son will bring you renown and a high social position.
	Any	T'ai-yin Chü Men		Your *yuanten* (predestined attachment) with your children will be weak. You are likely to live apart.
	Any	T'ien Liang T'ien Fu		Your *yuanten* (predestined attachment) is strong. In old age your children will care for you. You need not worry about money or material things.
	Any	Fire Star Ringing Star Yang Jen T'o Lo T'ien K'ung Ti Chieh		You will argue with your children and will suffer as a result.
	Any	Literary Stars T'ien K'uei T'ien Yüeh Tso Fu *or* Yu Pi		Your children will have good brains and bring you renown.
Wu Ch'ü	Any	Any		There will be a rift between you and your children.

Star	*Degree of influence*	*Other stars*	*Degree of influence*	*Reading*
	Any	T'ien Fu T'ien Hsiang Either of the Literary stars T'ien Ts'un T'ien K'uei T'ien Yüeh Tso Fu *or* Yu Pi		Your children will make great progress in their work.
	Any	T'an Lang Ch'i Sha P'o Chün Fire Star Ringing Star Yang Jen T'o Lo T'ien K'ung Ti Chieh		When your children are very young there will be a lack of harmony or a parent or child may die.
T'ien T'ung	Any	Any		You will have more daughters than sons. They will all be good-looking.
	Any	T'ai-yin		You will have more daughters than sons. Their good looks will cause you many problems.
	Any	Chü Men		You will not be in harmony with your children. You will be suspicious of one another.

Star	*Degree of influence*	*Other stars*	*Degree of influence*	*Reading*
	Any	T'ien Liang		Your *yuanten* (predestined attachment) with your daughters is stronger than that with your sons. As a result you and your daughters love each other and are likely to stay together.
	Any	T'ien Ts'un		You will have substantial material help from your children.
	Any	Fire Star Ringing Star Yang Jen T'o Lo T'ien K'ung Ti Chieh		There will be no harmony between you and your children.
	Any	Either of the Literary stars T'ien K'uei Tien Yüeh Tso Fu *or* Yu Pi		Your *yuanten* (predestined attachment) is strong. You will be in harmony with your children.
Lien Chen	Any	Any		There will be a great rift between you and your children. A child or parent may die.

Star	*Degree of influence*	*Other stars*	*Degree of influence*	*Reading*
	Any	T'ien Fu T'ien Hsiang T'ien Ts'un Either of the Literary stars T'ien K'uei T'ien Yüeh Tso Fu *or* Yu Pi		Your children will be few in number. There will be no great rift between you but neither will you be in harmony.
	Any	T'an Lang Ch'i Sha P'o Chün Fire Star Ringing Star Yang Jen T'o Lo T'ien K'ung Ti Chieh		Your *yuanten* (predestined attachment) with your sons will be weak. You may separate, or a parent or son may die when the son is young.
T'ien Fu	Any	Any		You will have many children. One of them will be very wealthy.
	Any	T'ien Ts'un		(The above reading is almost certain to be true.)
	Any	Either of the Literary stars T'ien K'uei T'ien Yüeh		Your children will be intelligent. In old age you will be comfortable.
	Any	Tso Fu *or* Yu Pi		Your children will be helpful assistants to you. They will develop your family business.

Star	*Degree of influence*	*Other stars*	*Degree of influence*	*Reading*
	Any	Fire Star Ringing Star Yang Jen T'o Lo		You will have more daughters than sons.
	Any	T'ien K'ung Ti Chieh		Your children will suffer loss or a son may die.
T'ai-yin	Any	Any		You are more likely to have daughters than sons. Only a daughter will develop your business; if you have a son he will be unable to help you.
	* ☆	Any		Your children will give you happiness and moral support.
	Any	Any lucky star		(The above reading applies.)
	+ –	Any		Your children will cause you suffering.
	Any	Any unlucky star		(The above reading applies.)
T'an Lang	Any	Any		You will be full of energy and physically strong. However, it will be difficult for you to offer your children material support.

Star	*Degree of influence*	*Other stars*	*Degree of influence*	*Reading*
	Any	T'ien Ts'un		It will be easier for you to support your children than in the above case.
	Any	Fire Star Ringing Star Yang Jen T'o Lo T'ien K'ung Ti Chieh		You will lose contact with your children.
	Any	Either of the Literary stars T'ien K'uei T'ien Yüeh Tso Fu *or* Yu Pi		You and your children's fate is average.
Chü Men	Any	Any		Your sons will not be in harmony with you. You will all have different ideas, aspirations and interests.
	Any	T'ien Ts'un		You will quarrel constantly about money and hide your money from each other.
	Any	Fire Star Ringing Star Yang Jen T'o Lo T'ien K'ung Ti Chieh		Your relationship with your sons will deteriorate and you will quarrel constantly.

Star	*Degree of influence*	*Other stars*	*Degree of influence*	*Reading*
	Any	Either of the Literary stars T'ien K'uei T'ien Yüeh Tso Fu *or* Yu Pi		Although you will not be in harmony with your sons this will not present any great problem.
T'ien Hsiang	Any	Any		Your children will work in literary, cultural or political areas. Their careers will prosper.
	Any	T'ien Ts'un		Your children will not only flourish in the above areas, but also in finance. They will be materially well off.
	Any	Fire Star Ringing Star Yang Jen T'o Lo T'ien K'ung Ti Chieh		When your children are young they will cause many problems.
	Any	Either of the Literary stars T'ien K'uei Tien Yüeh Tso Fu *or* Yu Pi		Your children will be obedient.
T'ien Liang	Any	Any		A daughter may be outstanding.

Star	*Degree of Influence*	*Other stars*	*Degree of Influence*	*Reading*
	Any	T'ien Ts'un		Your children will make great developments in financial affairs: e.g. investment, buying and selling, lending money.
	Any	Fire Star Ringing Star Yang Jen T'o Lo T'ien K'ung Ti Chieh		Your sons will not share your ideas and you will quarrel constantly.
	Any	Either of the Literary stars T'ien K'uei T'ien Yüeh Tso Fu *or* Yu Pi		You will be in harmony and will give each other moral support.
Ch'i Sha	Any	Any		You will have few children (especially sons). If you do have a son it will be difficult for you to live happily together.
	Any	T'ien Ts'un		(The above unlucky reading is improved.)
	Any	Fire Star Ringing Star Yang Jen T'o Lo T'ien Kung Ti Chieh		There will be a rift between you which will never be resolved – you will argue until death.

Star	*Degree of Influence*	*Other stars*	*Degree of Influence*	*Reading*
		Literary stars T'ien K'uei T'ien Yüeh Tso Fu *or* Yu Pi		Your ideas will differ and there will be a lack of harmony. Your children will not follow your advice.
P'o Chün	Any	Any		Your sons will not be in harmony with you and you will live apart.
	Any	Any lucky star		(The above unlucky reading is improved.)
	Any	Any unlucky star		(The above unlucky reading is made worse.)
	Any	T'ien Ts'un		You will have many children. They will use their wealth to develop their businesses and will have success.
	Any	T'ien Ts'un *and* no unlucky stars		Your children will care for you in your old age.
Fire Star *or* **Ringing Star**	Any	Any		You will not be in harmony with your sons.
	☆	Any		Your children will be bad-tempered, but they will be successful.

Star	*Degree of influence*	*Other stars*	*Degree of influence*	*Reading*
	Any	Any lucky star		(As above.)
	+ –	Any		Your children will always be quarrelling with you or one child may die.
	Any	Any unlucky star		(As above.)
Wen Ch'ü *or* **Wen Ch'ang**	Any	Any		Your children will be clever and will do well at school. They will also be physically healthy.
	* ☆	Any		Your children will make successful progress at work.
Yang Jen *or* **T'o Lo**	Any	Any		Your children will frequently be ill and prone to accidents, or they may die.
T'ien K'uei *or* **T'ien Yüeh**		Any		Your children will be gentle, clever and quick.
Tso Fu *or* **Yu Pi**		Any		Your children will be very obedient.
T'ien K'ung *or* **Ti Chieh**		Any		Your children could cause you heartache. One of your children may disappear.

Star	*Degree of Influence*	*Other stars*	*Degree of Influence*	*Reading*
T'ien Ts'un		Any		You will have very few children – possibly just one child.
Hua Chi		Any		There will be a rift between you and you may bring harm to your children.

THE WEALTH PALACE

The Wealth Palace is concerned with your personal wealth and also your capacity for earning money.

The stars which bring extremely good luck in the Wealth Palace are:

- Tzu Wei (Purple Star)
- T'ai-yang (Sun)
- Wu Ch'ü (Military Music)
- T'ien Fu (Southern Star)
- T'ai-yin (Moon)
- T'ien Ts'un (Heavenly Store)
- Hua Lu (Transforming Salary)

The stars which bring moderately good luck in this palace are:

- T'ien Chi (Heavenly Secret)
- T'ien T'ung (Heavenly Unity)
- Lien Chen (Pure Virtue)
- Chü Men (Great Door)
- T'ien Hsiang (Heavenly Minister)
- T'ien Liang (Heavenly Roof-Beam)
- Ch'i Sha (Seven Killings)
- P'o Chün (Broken Army)
- Wen Chü (Literary Music)
- Wen Ch'ang (Literary Prosperity)
- T'ien K'uei (Heavenly Leader)
- T'ien Yüeh (Heavenly Halberd)
- Tso Fu (Left Assistant)
- Yu Pi (Right Assistant)
- Hua Ch'üan (Transforming Authority)
- Hua K'o (Transforming Examination Class)

The stars which bring bad luck in this palace are:

T'an Lang (Greedy Wolf)
Yang Jen (Sheep-Blade)
T'o Lo (Hump-Back)
Fire Star
Ringing Star
Hua Chi (Transforming Jealousy)

The stars which bring extremely bad luck in this palace are:

T'ien K'ung (Heavenly Void)
Ti Chieh (Earthly Robbery)

Star	*Degree of Influence*	*Other stars appearing in the Wealth Palace*	*Degree of Influence*	*Reading*
Tzu Wei	Any	Any		You will work either with gold or on commission. You will gain a steady income and have many business interests. You have influential connections which will also bring you wealth.
	Any	T'ien Fu T'ien Hsiang T'ien Ts'un		You will use your renown, your position in society or your title to create a business and earn a lot of money.
	Any	T'an Lang Ch'i Sha P'o Chün		Although you know how to organize financial accounts, your income will not be quite satisfactory.
	Any	Fire Star Ringing Star Yang Jen T'o Lo T'ien K'ung Ti Chieh		You will spend a lot of money to live up to your position. You will spend too much and suffer the consequences.
	Any	Either of the Literary stars T'ien K'uei T'ien Yüeh Tso Fu *or* Yu Pi		You will be successful in three different areas: you will be well known, have a high social position and wealth.

Star	*Degree of influence*	*Other stars*	*Degree of influence*	*Reading*
T'ien Chi	Any	Any		You will make much money in religious matters or in the art of fortune-telling.
	–	Any		Your income will be small.
	Any	T'ai-yang Chü Men		You will earn a good income from a sideline. This will be related to your own interests.
	Any	T'ien Liang T'ien Ts'un		Your fame in religious affairs will bring you wealth.
	Any	Fire Star Ringing Star Yang Jen T'o Lo T'ien K'ung Ti Chieh		You will work hard but earn little income from it.
	Any	Either of the Literary stars T'ien K'uei T'ien Yüeh Tso Fu *or* Yu Pi		You will work hard, which will bring you a good position and increase your income.
T'ai-yang	* ☆	Any		You will gain a large income from a business enterprise or writing.
	–	Any		You will overspend and have very few savings.

Star	*Degree of influence*	*Other stars*	*Degree of influence*	*Reading*
	Any	T'ai-yin Chü Men		You will miss opportunities to earn money.
	Any	T'ien Liang T'ien Ts'un		You will be lucky in acquiring money; you will have an endless supply of it.
	Any	Fire Star Ringing Star Yang Jen T'o Lo T'ien K'ung Ti Chieh		You will spend too much and waste lots of money.
	Any	Either of the Literary stars T'ien K'uei T'ien Yüeh Tso Fu *or* Yu Pi		Your income and expenditure will be balanced. You will not waste money and will therefore save a reasonable amount.
Wu Chü	Any	Any		You will earn a lot of money quite unexpectedly.
	Any	Any unlucky star		You will have a large income but will be in danger of losing it.
	Any	T'ien Fu T'ien Ts'un		You will be involved in speculation. You will earn money steadily.

Star	*Degree of influence*	*Other stars*	*Degree of influence*	*Reading*
	Any	T'an Lang Ch'i Sha		Your business is likely to be in speculation.
	Any	T'an Lang Ch'i Sha *and* no other unlucky stars		You will make much money.
	Any	T'an Lang Ch'i Sha *and* any unlucky star.		You will suffer disaster.
	Any	T'ien Hsiang	Any	You will work in politics. You will work steadily and your income will increase – you will step on solid ground.
	Any	P'o Chün	Any	You will participate in speculation and are likely to lose money.
	Any	Fire Star Ringing Star Yang Jen T'o Lo	*	You will make a lot of money.
	Any	Fire Star Ringing Star Yang Jen T'o Lo	+ –	You will lose money.
	Any	T'ien K'ung Ti Chieh		Your speculation will fail due to your bad judgement. This will cause you suffering.

Star	*Degree of influence*	*Other stars*	*Degree of influence*	*Reading*
	Any	T'ien K'uei T'ien Yüeh Tso Fu *or* Yu Pi		You will receive help from your relatives and friends.
	Any	Either of the Literary stars		You will use your intelligence in business and earn a large income.
T'ien T'ung	Any	Any		You will work in a service industry. You will move from poverty to wealth. After middle age your income will be steady.
	Any	T'ai-yin T'ien Liang T'ien Ts'un T'ien K'uei T'ien Yüeh Tso Fu *or* Yu Pi		You will earn a lot of money.
	Any	Chü Men Fire Star Ringing Star Yang Jen T'o Lo T'ien K'ung Ti Chieh		You will spend money as soon as you receive it; you will never be wealthy.

Star	*Degree of influence*	*Other stars*	*Degree of influence*	*Reading*
	Any	Either of the Literary stars		You will use your creativity and intelligence to bring you success. You will save money and your wealth will grow.
Lien Chen	Any	Any		You will earn money unexpectedly.
	Any	T'ien Fu T'ien Ts'un T'ien Hsiang		You will gain great wealth from an industrial, commercial or electrical business. You will enjoy this wealth to the end of your life.
	Any	T'an Lang Ch'i Sha P'o Chün		You will earn large amounts of money unexpectedly but will spend them quickly. You will be unable to save.
	Any	Fire Star Ringing Star Yang Jen T'o Lo T'ien K'ung Ti Chieh		You are likely to earn money by illegal means.
	Any	Either of the Literary stars T'ien K'uei T'ien Yüeh Tso Fu *or* Yu Pi		You will have a good salary and a comfortable life.

Star	*Degree of influence*	*Other stars*	*Degree of influence*	*Reading*
T'ien Fu	Any	Any		You will be extremely rich.
	Any	Fire Star Ringing Star Yang Jen T'o Lo		Your luck in wealth will be unsteady. At times you will be rich and at times poor.
	Any	T'ien K'ung Ti Chieh		Even if you become a billionaire you will spend all your money. In old age you will be poor.
	Any	Either of the Literary stars T'ien K'uei T'ien Yüeh		Your luck in wealth will be steady. By old age you will have many savings.
	Any	Tso Fu *or* Yu Pi		You will earn a lot of money and will use this to raise yourself in politics.
T'ai-yin	* ☆	Any		You will have a steady occupation and earn a lot of money.
	Any	Any lucky star		(As above.)
	–	Any		Your occupation will be unsteady. You will have to work hard to make money.
	Any	Any unlucky star		(As above.)

Star	*Degree of influence*	*Other stars*	*Degree of influence*	*Reading*
T'an Lang	☆	Any		Although you will not be rich in your youth, in middle age your income will increase.
	Any	Fire Star Ringing Star *or* any lucky star	Any	(As above.)
	Any	Fire Star Ringing Star	+ –	You will have a harsh life.
	Any	Any unlucky star		You will have a harsh life.
Chü Men	Any	Any		Your income will not come through trade or exchange, it will come through advising others, e.g. as a solicitor or fortune-teller.
	☆	Any		You will save money and make it grow.
	Any	Any lucky star		(As above.)
	+ –	Any		The Chinese say: 'Your hand holds water', i.e. you will spend money like water.
	Any	Any unlucky star		(As above.)

Star	*Degree of influence*	*Other stars*	*Degree of influence*	*Reading*
T'ien Liang	Any	Any		You will earn a good income from religious work, medical work and research into unusual topics.
	* ☆	Any		Money will pour in. You will be prosperous and there is no need to worry.
	–	Any		You will have a harsh life. You will work hard for nothing.
	Any	Fire Star Ringing Star Yang Jen T'o Lo T'ien K'ung Ti Chieh		When young you will suffer from poverty. In middle age you will earn more, but you will never be rich.
	Any	Literary stars T'ien K'uei T'ien Yüeh Tso Fu *or* Yu Pi		You have no need to work hard for you will always have money. Your style of living will be comfortable.
T'ien Hsiang	Any	Any		You will have a wealthy style of living.

Star	*Degree of influence*	*Other stars*	*Degree of influence*	*Reading*
	Any	Fire Star Ringing Star Yang Jen T'o Lo T'ien K'ung Ti Chieh		You need not worry about having enough to live on, but you will not be able to save money.
	Any	Either of the Literary stars T'ien K'uei T'ien Yüeh Tso Fu *or* Yu Pi		You will earn a good income by working in the service industry.
Ch'i Sha	Any	Any		You will gain money unexpectedly.
	Any	T'ien K'ung Ti Chieh		You will always be poor.
P'o Chün	Any	Any		You will be very rich as a result of financial speculation.
	+	Any		You will go bankrupt.
	Any	Fire Star Ringing Star Yang Jen T'o Lo T'ien K'ung *or* Ti Chieh		Your financial success will be insecure. You will sometimes keep your head above water and sometimes go under. You will be on the edge of bankruptcy.

Star	*Degree of influence*	*Other stars*	*Degree of influence*	*Reading*
	Any	Literary stars T'ien K'uei T'ien Yüeh Tso Fu *or* Yu Pi		Your finances will fluctuate substantially throughout your life.
	*	Literary stars T'ien K'uei T'ien Yüeh Tso Fu *or* Yu Pi		Despite the above reading, eventually you will be successful.
	+ −	Literary stars T'ien K'uei T'ien Yüeh Tso Fu *or* Yu Pi		After all the fluctuations mentioned above, you will go bankrupt.
T'ien Ts'un	Any	Any		You will be very rich, but your wealth will not come of its own accord. You must save it little by little.
	Any	T'ien K'ung Ti Chieh		You will earn money quickly but eventually lose it.
Fire Star *or* **Ringing Star**	Any	Any		Your fortunes will be unstable, both in property and money. Today you are rich and tomorrow you will be poor.

Star	*Degree of influence*	*Other stars*	*Degree of influence*	*Reading*
	Any	Either of the Literary stars		You will have good qualifications but will be unable to get a suitable job. This will bring you worry and poverty.
	Any	Yang Jen T'o Lo		You will suffer from a lack of money throughout your life.
	Any	T'ien K'uei T'ien Yüeh		Your income will be irregular – sometimes great, sometimes small.
	Any	Tso Fu *or* Yu Pi		You will earn a good income with the help of friends.
	Any	T'ien K'ung Ti Chieh		Because of rushing to produce results, you will suffer great loss.
Wen Ch'ü *or* **Wen Ch'ang**	Any	Any		Your finances and property will be stable and your income regular.
	Any	Yang Jen T'o Lo		Your income will be low and you will have to budget carefully.
	Any	T'ien K'uei T'ien Yüeh		You will have a good income without having to work very hard.

Star	*Degree of influence*	*Other stars*	*Degree of influence*	*Reading*
	Any	Tso Fu *or* Yu Pi		You will need assistance to find out how to earn a good income.
	Any	T'ien K'ung Ti Chieh		You will be cheated and will lose money. You will not have material wealth although you have the capacity for work. You will have a poor and harsh life.
Yang Jen *or* **T'o Lo**	Any	Any		You will have no reward for your hard work throughout your life. You will have a poor and harsh life.
	*	Any		You may have a regular income plus income from a sideline.
	Any	T'ien K'uei *or* T'ien Yüeh		Although you work hard your standard of living will only be moderately comfortable.
	Any	Tso Fu *or* Yu Pi		Your entire life will be harsh but there will be someone to advise you. This will help to improve your standard of living.

Star	*Degree of influence*	*Other stars*	*Degree of influence*	*Reading*
	Any	T'ien K'ung Ti Chieh		You will have a poor and harsh life.
T'ien K'uei *or* **T'ien Yüeh**		Any		Money will flow in regularly and you will have a comfortable life.
		Tso Fu *or* Yu Pi		You will be rich and comfortable throughout your life.
		T'ien K'ung Ti Chieh		Although you will not have great wealth you will never need to worry about your livelihood.
Tso Fu *or* **Yu Pi**		Any		With your friends' or elders' help you will be prosperous in middle age. In old age you will be comfortable, happy and rich.
		T'ien K'ung Ti Chieh		You will have just enough to live on. You will be unable to make any more money.
T'ien K'ung *or* **Ti Chieh**		Any		Out of every ten attempts nine will fail. In old age you will not have enough money.

Star	*Degree of influence*	*Other stars*	*Degree of influence*	*Reading*
Hua Lu		Any		You will have two or three opportunities to make money. Your life style will be wealthy.
Hua Chi		Any		You have no *yuanten* (predestined) attachment) with money.
Hua Ch'üan		Any		You will have a great amount of money.
Hua K'o		Any		You will have no need to worry about your livelihood. You will always be prosperous.

THE SICKNESS PALACE

The Sickness Palace is concerned with your physical health – your condition and your strength. It is also concerned with illness.

The stars which bring extremely good luck in the Sickness Palace are:

- T'ien T'ung (Heavenly Unity)
- T'ien Liang (Heavenly Roof-Beam)
- T'ien Yüeh (Heavenly Halberd)
- T'ien Fu (Southern Star)
- T'ien Hsiang (Heavenly Minister)
- T'ien K'uei (Heavenly Leader)

The stars which bring fairly good luck are:

- Tzu Wei (Purple Star)
- T'ai-yang (Sun)
- T'ai-yin (Moon)
- Fire Star
- Ringing Star
- T'ien Ts'un (Heavenly Store)
- Tso Fu (Left Assistant)
- Yu Pi (Right Assistant)

The stars which bring bad luck are:

- T'ien Chi (Heavenly Secret)
- Wen Ch'ü (Literary Music)
- Wen Ch'ang (Literary Prosperity)
- Wu Ch'ü (Military Music)

The stars which bring extremely bad luck are:

- Lien Chen (Pure Virtue)
- Chü Men (Great Door)
- P'o Chün (Broken Army)
- T'o Lo (Hump-Back)
- Ti Chieh (Earthly Robbery)
- T'an Lang (Greedy Wolf)
- Ch'i Sha (Seven Killings)
- Yang Jen (Sheep-Blade)
- T'ien K'ung (Heavenly Void)
- Hua Chi (Transforming Jealousy)

Star	*Degree of influence*	*Other stars which appear in the Sickness Palace*	*Degree of influence*	*Reading*
Tzu Wei	Any	Any		You will never suffer serious illness.
	Any	Any unlucky star		You may have nervous complaints.
T'ien Chi	Any	Any		As a child you tended to be sickly, but you will have very few serious illnesses.
	Any	T'ai-yin		You are prone to purulent boils. Your skin bruises easily.
	Any	Chü Men		You are likely to be anaemic.
	Any	T'ien Liang		You are likely to have bladder and lower abdominal problems.
	Any	Fire Star Ringing Star Yang Jen T'o Lo T'ien K'ung Ti Chieh		You will suffer from eye problems.
	Any	Either of the Literary stars T'ien K'uei T'ien Yüeh Tso Fu *or* Yu Pi		Your legs, arms and trunk are weak.
T'ai-yang	Any	Any		You are likely to have eye problems.
	* ☆ Any	Any Any lucky star }		The above illness will not afflict you.

Star	*Degree of influence*	*Other stars*	*Degree of influence*	*Reading*
Wu Ch'ü	Any	Any		You are likely to have nasal problems. When young you are easily hurt. You may have a scar on your hand, leg or head.
T'ien T'ung	Any	Any		You are likely to have ear problems.
	Any	T'ai-yin Chü Men		You have a weak heart.
	Any	T'ien Liang T'ien Ts'un		You have bad circulation.
		Fire Star Ringing Star Yang Jen T'o Lo T'ien K'ung Ti Chieh		You are physically weak and will suffer from minor illnesses.
	Any	Either of the Literary stars T'ien K'uei T'ien Yüeh Tso Fu *or* Yu Pi		You are physically strong and unlikely to become ill.

Star	*Degree of influence*	*Other stars*	*Degree of influence*	*Reading*
Lien Chen	Any	Any		You will suffer from ill health all your life.
	Any	T'ien Fu T'ien Hsiang T'ien Ts'un Either of the Literary stars T'ien K'uei T'ien Yüeh Tso Fu *or* Yu Pi		You are strong and seldom ill.
	Any	T'an Lang Ch'i Sha P'o Chün Fire Star Ringing Star Yang Jen T'o Lo T'ien K'ung Ti Chieh		You are weak and often ill.
T'ien Fu	Any	Any		You are seldom ill; even if you are unwell you recover easily.
	Any	Any unlucky star		You are likely to have gall-bladder problems or mental problems.

Star	*Degree of influence*	*Other stars*	*Degree of influence*	*Reading*
T'ai-yin	* ☆	Any		You are unlikely to suffer from illness.
	Any	Any unlucky star		
	–	Any		You will suffer from eye and liver problems and other illness. If you are a woman you are likely to suffer from gynaecological problems.
	Any	Any unlucky star		
T'an Lang	Any	Any		You are likely to suffer from venereal disease or other sexual illnesses.
Chü Men	Any	Any		When young you will have skin problems. When an adult you will have stomach problems.
T'ien Hsiang	Any	Any		You are physically strong and unlikely to be ill.
T'ien Liang	* ☆	Any		You are seldom ill and will have a long life.
	Any	Any lucky star		
	–	Any		You are likely to have a heart attack.
	Any	Any unlucky star		

Star	*Degree of influence*	*Other stars*	*Degree of influence*	*Reading*
Ch'i Sha	Any	Any		When young you are susceptible to illness, particularly intestinal problems. In middle age you are likely to suffer from piles.
P'o Chün	Any	Any		When young you are likely to get boils. Your lungs are weak.
T'ien Ts'un	Any	Any		You are physically strong and unlikely to become ill.
Fire Star *or* **Ringing Star**	Any	Any		Your bodily functions will deteriorate. You also suffer from allergies and if you have a transplant your body may reject the organ.
	Any	Either of the Literary stars		Your bodily functions are disturbed: e.g. when it is cold you sweat.
	Any	Yang Jen T'o Lo		You are unlikely to live long.
	Any	T'ien K'uei T'ien Yüeh		You will never suffer from illness.
	Any	T'ien K'ung Ti Chieh		You will suffer from many illnesses, disasters and injuries.

Star	*Degree of influence*	*Other stars*	*Degree of influence*	*Reading*
Wen Ch'ü *or* **Wen Ch'ang**	Any	Any		Your natural bodily functions will deteriorate.
Yang Jen *or* **T'o Lo**	Any	Any		You are likely to suffer injuries, such as broken bones.
T'ien K'uei *or* **T'ien Yüeh**		Any		You will be physically strong all your life and will seldom be ill.
Tso Fu *or* **Yu Pi**		Any		You will be physically strong and seldom ill.
T'ien K'ung *or* **Ti Chieh**		Any		You will have many illnesses which will make you unhappy and miserable.
Hua Chi		Any		You are physically weak and easily fall ill. You are likely to die young.

THE MOVING PALACE

The Moving Palace is concerned with your social life – how you relate to people and how best to develop your business.

The stars which bring extremely good luck in the Moving Palace are:

- Tzu Wei (Purple Star)
- Wu Ch'ü (Military Music)
- T'ien Fu (Southern Star)
- T'ien Hsiang (Heavenly Minister)
- Wen Ch'ü (Literary Music)
- Wen Ch'ang (Literary Prosperity)
- T'ien K'uei (Heavenly Leader)
- T'ien Yüeh (Heavenly Halberd)
- T'ai-yang (Sun)
- Lien Chen (Pure Virtue)
- T'ai-yin (Moon)
- T'ien Liang (Heavenly Roof-Beam)
- T'ien Ts'un (Heavenly Store)
- Tso Fu (Left Assistant)
- Yu Pi (Right Assistant)
- Hau K'o (Transforming Examination Class)

The stars which bring moderately good luck are:

- T'ien Chi (Heavenly Secret)
- I-ma (Travelling Star)
- Hua Ch'üan (Transforming Authority)
- T'ien T'ung (Heavenly Unity)
- Hua Lu (Transforming Salary)

The stars which bring bad luck are:

- T'an Lang (Greedy Wolf)
- Ch'i Sha (Seven Killings)
- Chü Men (Great Door)
- T'o Lo (Hump-Back)

- Fire Star
- Ringing Star
- Yang Jen (Sheep-Blade)

The stars which bring extremely bad luck are:

- T'ien K'ung (Heavenly Void)
- Hua Chi (Transforming Jealousy)
- Ti Chieh (Earthly Robbery)

Star	*Degree of influence*	*Other stars which appear in the Moving Palace*	*Degree of influence*	*Reading*
Tzu Wei	Any	Any		You will have friends to help you in a foreign place.
	Any	T'ien Fu T'ien Hsiang T'ien Ts'un		You will have great success abroad. The Chinese say: 'Wear brocade and return home with honour.'
	Any	T'an Lang Ch'i Sha P'o Chün		You will have support from older people. Take care that the opposite sex does not ruin your name.
	Any	Fire Star Ringing Star T'ien K'ung Ti Chieh		When you put a plan into practice, you will often achieve the reverse of what you intended.
	Any	Either of the Literary stars T'ien K'uei T'ien Yüeh Tso Fu *or* Yu Pi		You have position, renown and money.

Star	*Degree of influence*	*Other stars*	*Degree of influence*	*Reading*
T'ien Chi	Any	Any		You should leave your home and work in a foreign country. If you stay at home you will work extremely hard for little reward. Your social connections will bring you great fortune.
	Any	T'ai-yin T'ien Ts'un Literary stars T'ien K'uei T'ien Yüeh Tso Fu *or* Yu Pi		You will always be busy and will have good fortune. You treat people well when you are abroad.
	Any	Chü Men T'ien Liang Fire Star Ringing Star Yang Jen T'o Lo T'ien K'ung Ti Chieh		Because you will not work hard it is difficult for you to save money. If you work as an artist you will be successful.
T'ai-yang	Any	Any		You are suited to living and working abroad. You should have a job in which you are physically active.

Star	*Degree of influence*	*Other stars*	*Degree of influence*	*Reading*
	Any	T'ai-yin T'ien Ts'un Literary stars T'ien Fu T'ien Yüeh Tso Fu *or* Yu Pi		You will work hard for many years and be prosperous.
	Any	Chü Men T'ien K'ung Fire Star Ringing Star Yang Jen T'o Lo Ti Chieh		You will work for a pittance.
Wu Ch'ü	Any	Any		You will always be busy but will make no money.
	Any	T'ien Fu T'an Lang T'ien Hsiang Ch'i Sha T'ien Ts'un		You will earn great sums of money unexpectedly.
	Any	P'o Chün Yang Jen T'o Lo Fire Star Ringing Star		If you leave home you will suffer or meet disasters unless you work as an artist.
	Any	Either of the Literary stars T'ien K'uei T'ien Yüeh Hua K'o		You will make progress in a foreign country. Your name will be known in distant places.

Star	*Degree of influence*	*Other stars*	*Degree of influence*	*Reading*
	Any	Tso Fu *or* Yu Pi		You will be supported by strong and powerful people and will become rich.
	Any	T'ien K'ung Ti Chieh		You will be cheated in a foreign country. You may lose money or your life may be in danger.
T'ien T'ung	Any	Any		The help that you receive from older people in foreign countries will bring business success and an introduction to a marriage partner.
	Any	T'ai-yin Chü Men		You will work extremely hard but will suffer and be miserable.
	Any	T'ien Liang T'ien Ts'un		Older people will recommend you and help you. This means you will be able to make progress.
	Any	Fire Star Ringing Star Yang Jen T'o Lo T'ien K'ung Ti Chieh		You will have many difficult times. Your plans will not work out and you will make no progress.

Star	*Degree of influence*	*Other stars*	*Degree of influence*	*Reading*
	Any	Either of the Literary stars T'ien K'uei T'ien Yüeh Tso Fu *or* Yu Pi		Your life will be prosperous. Your relations with people will be good and your work will go well.
Lien Chen	Any	Any		You are likely to leave home as you dislike living there.
	Any	T'ien Fu T'ien Ts'un		You will work in an unusual job. You will gain a great fortune in a foreign country.
	Any	T'an Lang Ch'i Sha		Although you will gain money unexpectedly, you will not be able to keep it for long.
	Any	T'ien Hsiang Either of the Literary stars T'ien K'uei T'ien Yüeh Tso Fu *or* Yu Pi		You should live away from home if you want your business to prosper. If you remain in your home town you will not succeed.
	Any	P'o Chün Fire Star Ringing Star Yang Jen T'o Lo T'ien K'ung *or* Ti Chieh		You are not suited to living in distant places. If you do your life or your money will be in danger.

Star	*Degree of influence*	*Other stars*	*Degree of influence*	*Reading*
T'ien Fu	Any	Any		You will get support and help from someone to increase your income.
	Any	Any unlucky star		(The unlucky star has no effect on the above reading.)
	Any	T'ien K'ung Ti Chieh		Your life and property are safe.
T'ai-yin	Any	Any		You will have a high position, renown and wealth.
	–	Any		You will suffer a disaster in a foreign country.
T'an Lang	Any	Any		You will work hard but you will lose your determination in later life.
	Any	Any lucky star		You have unusual features to your character which, when they express themselves, will bring you great wealth.
	Any	Any unlucky star		You will suffer from a robbery or a disaster which will leave you penniless.
Chü Men	Any	Any		You will have a difficult, unstable life.

Star	*Degree of influence*	*Other stars*	*Degree of influence*	*Reading*
	Any	Any lucky star		(The above reading applies.)
	Any	Any unlucky star		(The unlucky star increases your suffering.)
T'ien Hsiang	Any	Any		You will develop a successful business in a foreign country.
	Any	T'ien Ts'un		You will enjoy material stability.
	Any	Fire Star Ringing Star Yang Jen T'o Lo T'ien K'ung Ti Chieh		Your livelihood is unstable. You will easily cause others to dislike you. Your inferiors will bring you trouble.
	Any	Literary stars T'ien K'uei T'ien Yüeh Tso Fu *or* Yu Pi		You will have a high position, a good name and make great progress in business.
T'ien Liang	Any	Any		Someone will support you and bring you success.
Ch'i Sha	Any	Any		You will not work in one place but will have to travel a great deal.
	Any	T'ien Ts'un		You will have the opportunity to make progress in business and attain success.

Star	*Degree of influence*	*Other stars*	*Degree of influence*	*Reading*
	Any	Fire Star Ringing Star Yang Jen T'o Lo T'ien K'ung Ti Chieh		You will be forced to travel to make a living.
	Any	Either of the Literary stars T'ien Ts'un T'ien K'uei T'ien Yüeh Tso Fo *or* Yu Pi		You will be promoted to a high position, and be well known and successful in business.
P'o Chün	Any	Any		You will have a harsh life in a foreign country. Your life will be unstable.
	Any	T'ien Ts'un		You will be successful in earning money but you will have to work hard.
	Any	Fire Star Ringing Star Yang Jen T'o Lo T'ien K'ung Ti Chieh		Work where your interest lies – as an artist – then you will be prosperous. Otherwise you will not be successful.
	Any	Either of the Literary stars T'ien K'uei T'ien Yüeh Tso Fu *or* Yu Pi		You will live abroad and have a stable life.

Star	*Degree of influence*	*Other stars*	*Degree of influence*	*Reading*
Fire Star *or* **Ringing Star**	Any	Any		You will have an unstable and harsh life.
	Any	Literary stars Yang Jen T'o Lo T'ien K'ung Ti Chieh		You will have a difficult life. You will work for a pittance.
	*	T'ien Ts'un T'ien K'uei T'ien Yüeh Tso Fu *or* Yu Pi		You may make successful progress in business. If not your life will be harsh.
Wen Ch'ü *or* **Wen Ch'ang**	Any	Any		You will gain renown in a foreign country.
	Any	Any unlucky star		You will be notorious and no one will trust you.
Yang Jen *or* **T'o Lo**	*	Any		You will be successful in your work.
	–	Any		You are easily cheated – you will have a harsh and unrewarding life. Everything will be lost.
Hua Lu *or* **T'ien Ts'un**		Any		You will be successful one day.

Star	*Degree of influence*	*Other stars*	*Degree of influence*	*Reading*
T'ien K'uei *or* **T'ien Yüeh**		Any		You will have a comfortable and stable life.
Tso Fu *or* **Yu Pi**		Any		You have a competitive spirit. In business you will be successful and hold a high position.
T'ien K'ung *or* **Ti Chieh**		Any		You will suffer a great loss in a foreign country. You will be unable to recover from this.
Hua K'o		Any		Other people will admire your skills and your work. This will bring you success.
Hua Chi		Any		You work for a pittance. Your standard of living will be average.
I-ma		Any		You have to travel widely in a foreign country.
Hua Ch'üan		Any		You will be offered promotion and make good progress in your work.

THE SERVANTS' PALACE

The Servants' Palace is concerned with how your inferiors and colleagues relate to you.

The stars which bring extremely good luck in the Servants' Palace are:

T'ai-yang (Sun)
T'ai-yin (Moon)
T'ien Liang (Heavenly Roof-Beam)
T'ien Yüeh (Heavenly Halberd)
Tso Fu (Left Assistant)
Yu Pi (Right Assistant)
T'ien Fu (Southern Star)
T'ien Hsiang (Heavenly Minister)
Wen Ch'ü (Literary Music)
Wen Ch'ang (Literary Prosperity)
T'ien Ts'un (Heavenly Store)
T'ien K'uei (Heavenly Leader)

The stars which bring moderately good luck are:

Tzu Wei (Purple Star)
T'ien T'ung (Heavenly Unity)
Wu Ch'ü (Military Music)
Lien Chen (Pure Virtue)

The stars which bring bad luck are:

T'ien Chi (Heavenly Secret)
P'o Chün (Broken Army)
Fire Star
Ringing Star
T'an Lang (Greedy Wolf)
Hua Chi (Transforming Jealousy)

The stars which bring extremely bad luck are:

Chü Men (Great Door)
Yang Jen (Sheep Blade)
T'ien K'ung (Heavenly Void)
Ch'i Sha (Seven Killings)
T'o Lo (Hump-Back)
Ti Chieh (Earthly Robbery)

Star	*Degree of influence*	*Other stars which appear in the Servants' Palace*	*Degree of influence*	*Reading*
Tzu Wei	Any	Any		Your inferiors will be helpful or you will have many good friends who will assist you in business and help you to make money.
	Any	T'ien Fu T'ien Hsiang T'ien Ts'un Either of the Literary stars T'ien K'uei T'ien Yüeh Tso Fu *or* Yu Pi		You will be given a lot of help by your inferiors or servants.
	Any	T'an Lang Ch'i Sha P'o Chün Fire Star Ringing Star Yang Jen T'o Lo T'ien K'ung *or* Ti Chieh		Your inferiors will not help you, however many people there are under you.
T'ien Chi	Any	Any		Your inferiors will be cooperative.
	–	Any		You will not be liked by your inferiors or by older people.

Star	*Degree of influence*	*Other stars*	*Degree of influence*	*Reading*
	Any	T'ien Liang T'ien Ts'un Either of the Literary stars T'ien K'uei T'ien Yüeh Tso Fu *or* Yu Pi		During the first half of your life you will not be helped by your inferiors. In the second half you will always be helped by them.
	Any	T'ai-yin Chü Men Fire Star Ringing Star Yang Jen T'o Lo T'ien K'ung Ti Chieh		Not only will your inferiors not help you but they will also be jealous and suspicious.
T'ai-yang	* ☆	Any		Your inferiors and friends will be good to you. They will help you develop your work.
	+ –	Any		Your inferiors will be unable to help you. They will also be jealous and suspicious of you and of one another. They may betray you and cause you loss.
	Any	T'ai-yin T'ien Liang T'ien Ts'un		Your colleagues will help you to achieve success in your career.

Star	*Degree of influence*	*Other stars*	*Degree of influence*	*Reading*
	Any	Chü Men		You will always be on bad terms with your inferiors.
	Any	Fire Star Ringing Star Yang Jen T'o Lo T'ien K'ung Ti Chieh		Your inferiors will refuse to obey you.
	Any	Either of the Literary stars T'ien K'uei T'ien Yüeh Tso Fu *or* Yu Pi		You will be supported by inferiors and elders. This will bring you promotion to a high position.
Wu Ch'ü *or* **Wen Ch'ang**	Any	Any		Your inferiors will be supportive and help your career.
	Any	T'ien Fu T'ien Hsiang T'ien Ts'un T'ien K'uei T'ien Yüeh Tso Fu *or* Yu Pi		Your inferiors will be helpful, especially those of the opposite sex.
	Any	T'an Lang Ch'i Sha P'o Chün Fire Star Ringing Star Yang Jen T'o Lo T'ien K'ung Ti Chieh		You will not be helped by the opposite sex. This will make you suspicious and jealous.

Star	*Degree of influence*	*Other stars*	*Degree of influence*	*Reading*
T'ien T'ung	Any	Any		The help of your friends and inferiors will bring you great success.
	Any	T'ai-yin T'ien Liang		You will be in harmony with your inferiors. You will be respected.
	Any	Chü Men T'ien Ts'un		You will be an incompetent leader because you fail to see others' aims and ideas. Your relationship with others improves after middle age.
	Any	Fire Star Ringing Star Yang Jen T'o Lo T'ien K'ung Ti Chieh		You will be too considerate towards your inferiors. You will be cheated and suffer loss.
	Any	Either of the Literary stars T'ien K'uei T'ien Yüeh Tso Fu *or* Yu Pi		You will be very kind to your inferiors and they will respect you, cooperate with you and help you. You will be successful at work.

Star	*Degree of influence*	*Other stars*	*Degree of influence*	*Reading*
Lien Chen	Any	Any		You will be too stern with your inferiors. They will be unhappy and may take revenge.
	Any	T'ien Fu T'ien Hsiang T'ien Ts'un		(The unlucky reading above will be improved.)
	Any	T'an Lang Ch'i Sha P'o Chün		(The unlucky reading above will deteriorate.)
	Any	Fire Star Ringing Star Yang Jen T'o Lo T'ien K'ung Ti Chieh		Your inferiors will be rebellious.
		Either of the Literary stars T'ien K'uei T'ien Yüeh Tso Fu *or* Yu Pi		You will treat your inferiors too sternly. This will make them unhappy but they will not cause you harm.
T'ien Fu	Any	Any		Your inferiors and elders will respect you. Your work will be successful and you will be happy in your job. You will get on well with people.

Star	*Degree of influence*	*Other stars*	*Degree of influence*	*Reading*
	Any	T'ien Ts'un		Your inferiors will be able to help and support you. They will bring you success.
	Any	Fire Star Ringing Star Yang Jen T'o Lo		Your inferiors will disobey you. As a result your business will never make much money.
	Any	Either of the Literary stars T'ien K'uei *or* T'ien Yüeh		Your inferiors will bring you success at work.
	Any	Tso Fu *or* Yu Pi		Your inferiors will be intelligent and capable. This will bring you promotion and renown.
	Any	T'ien K'ung Ti Chieh		You will be unable to recover from the loss caused by arguments with your inferiors.
T'ai-yin	Any	Any		The reliability of your inferiors will help you achieve a successful career.
	Any	T'ien Ts'un		You will receive material help from your inferiors.

Star	*Degree of influence*	*Other stars*	*Degree of influence*	*Reading*
	Any	Fire Star Ringing Star Yang Jen T'o Lo T'ien K'ung Ti Chieh		You will not be welcomed by inferiors or elders. Your relationship with them will limit your career.
	Any	T'ien K'uei T'ien Yüeh Tso Fu *or* Yu Pi		Your inferiors and elders will respect you.
T'an Lang	Any	Any		You will have a great disaster as a result of your inferiors. Their dependence on you will be a burden.
	Any	Any lucky star		(The above reading remains the same.)
	Any	Any unlucky star		(The above reading will deteriorate.)
Chü Men	Any	Any		Your inferiors will cause you disaster and loss.
	Any	Any unlucky star		(The above reading deteriorates even further.)
T'ien Hsiang	Any	Any		You will have helpful and reliable inferiors. This means that your work will be successful.

Star	*Degree of influence*	*Other stars*	*Degree of influence*	*Reading*
	Any	T'ien Ts'un		Your inferiors will be reliable and will give you material help.
	Any	Fire Star Ringing Star Yang Jen T'o Lo T'ien K'ung Ti Chieh		Your inferiors will cause you loss.
	Any	Either of the Literary stars T'ien K'uei T'ien Yüeh Tso Fu *or* Yu Pi		Your inferiors will be strong. They will help you to achieve promotion.
T'ien Liang	Any	Any		Your inferiors will be reliable and helpful.
	Any	Any unlucky star		(The above reading turns bad.)
Ch'i Sha	Any	Any		Your inferiors will be unreliable. They will be arrogant and rebel against your instructions.
	Any	Any lucky star		(The above reading is still unavoidable.)

Star	*Degree of influence*	*Other stars*	*Degree of influence*	*Reading*
	Any	Fire Star Ringing Star Yang Jen T'o Lo T'ien K'ung Ti Chieh		Your inferiors will cause you disaster and loss.
P'o Chün	Any	Any		Your inferiors will rebel against you. You will easily make enemies.
	*	Any		You will be supported by your colleagues.
Fire Star *or* **Ringing Star**	Any	Any		You will be very kind to your inferiors but they will treat you as an enemy. This will bring you misfortune.
	Any	Either of the Literary stars		You will lose a lot of money.
	Any	Yang Jen T'o Lo		You are likely to quarrel with your inferiors, which will cause you loss.
	Any	T'ien K'uei T'ien Yüeh		Your relationship with your inferiors is quarrelsome and suspicious.
	Any	Tso Fu *or* Yu Pi		You will have no good inferiors to help you.

Star	*Degree of influence*	*Other stars*	*Degree of influence*	*Reading*
	Any	T'ien K'ung Ti Chieh		Your inferiors will cause you trouble.
Wen Ch'ü *or* **Wen Ch'ang**	Any	Any		Your inferiors and elders will be reliable and helpful.
	–	Any		(The lucky reading above deteriorates.)
Yang Jen *or* **T'o Lo**	Any	Any		Lack of support from inferiors leads to tension and failure.
T'ien K'uei *or* **T'ien Yüeh**		Any		Your inferiors will support you and help you to gain promotion.
Tso Fu *or* **Yu Pi**		Any		Your inferiors and elders will have the same aims – to maintain your good position and renown.
		T'ien K'ung Ti Chieh		Although your elders and inferiors will support you they will bring you no real benefit.
T'ien K'ung *or* **Ti Chieh**		Any		Your inferiors will rebel against you. They will bring you disaster and harm you.

Star	*Degree of influence*	*Other stars*	*Degree of influence*	*Reading*
T'ien Ts'un		Any		Your inferiors will give you financial support.
		T'ien K'ung Ti Chieh		Your inferiors will not give you financial support.
Hua Chi		Any		Because your inferiors rebel, you will suffer great loss.

THE OFFICIALS' PALACE

The Officials' Palace is concerned with how you relate to older people. It is also concerned with your career – is it fortunate or not?

The stars which bring extremely good luck in the Officials' Palace are:

Tzu Wei (Purple Star)
Lien Chen (Pure Virtue)
T'ien Ts'un (Heavenly Store)
T'ien K'uei (Heavenly Leader)
Tso Fu (Left Assistant)
Yu Pi (Right Assistant)
T'ai-yang (Sun)
T'ien Hsiang (Heavenly Minister)
Wen Ch'ü (Literary Music)
Wen Ch'ang (Literary Prosperity)
T'ien Yüeh (Heavenly Halberd)
Hua Ch'üan (Transforming Authority)

The stars which bring moderately good luck are:

T'ien Chi (Heavenly Secret)
T'ien T'ung (Heavenly Unity)
T'ai-yin (Moon)
Chü Men (Great Door)
Ch'i Sha (Seven Killings)
Hua K'o (Transforming Examination Class)
P'o Chün (Broken Army)
Wu Ch'ü (Military Music)
T'ien Fu (Southern Star)
T'an Lang (Greedy Wolf)
T'ien Liang (Heavenly Roof-Beam)
Hua Lu (Transforming Salary)

The stars which bring bad luck are:

Fire Star
Ringing Star
Yang Jen (Sheep-Blade)
T'o Lo (Hump-Back)

The stars which bring extremely bad luck are:

T'ien K'ung (Heavenly Void)
Ti Chieh (Earthly Robbery)

Star	*Degree of influence*	*Other stars which appear in the Officials' Palace*	*Degree of influence*	*Reading*
Tzu Wei	Any	Any		You will be a skilled and expert chairman, director, government official or administrator. Your work will be successful.
	Any	T'ien Fu T'ien Hsiang		Your authority will be great and your position high. You will work in financial affairs or politics. You will become well known and receive a good income.
	Any	Ch'i Sha P'o Chün		You will have unexpected success.
	Any	T'an Lang		You may use the opposite sex to gain promotion.
	Any	T'ien Ts'un		You will be promoted to a high position and acquire great wealth.
	Any	Fire Star Ringing Star Yang Jen T'o Lo T'ien K'ung Ti Chieh		Your standard of living will be average.

Star	*Degree of influence*	*Other stars*	*Degree of influence*	*Reading*
	Any	Literary stars T'ien K'uei T'ien Yüeh Tso Fu *or* Yu Pi		Your business will be favoured with good luck. You will progress smoothly to success.
T'ien Chi	Any	Any		You will have success in religious, educational, academic or cultural work.
	Any	T'ai-yin *or* Chü Men	☆	You will be well known in a distant place.
	Any	T'ai-yin *or* Chü Men	+	Although you will be well known in a distant place, your renown will not last long.
	Any	T'ien Liang T'ien Ts'un		You will have a good position and authority. You will make progress in politics or financial affairs.
	Any	Fire Star Ringing Star Yang Jen T'o Lo T'ien K'ung Ti Chieh		You will work extremely hard but will have difficult times. You will not be able to develop your work.

Star	*Degree of influence*	*Other stars*	*Degree of influence*	*Reading*
	Any	Literary stars T'ien Kuei T'ien Yüeh Tso Fu *or* Yu Pi		Although your business appears to be successful you will have no real authority and you will not reap any benefit.
T'ai-yang	Any	Any		You will have a high position and will have success in business or politics.
	Any	T'ai-yin T'ien Ts'un		You will have both a high position in life and a good income.
	*	Chü Men T'ien Liang		You will maintain a good position in life.
	–	Chü Men T'ien Liang		You will lose your position of authority.
	Any	Fire Star Ringing Star Yang Jen T'o Lo T'ien K'ung Ti Chieh		You will have an unstable and changeable life – like a boat bobbing up and down in the water without an anchor.
	Any	Literary stars T'ien K'uei T'ien Yüeh Tso Fu *or* Yu Pi		You will have a stable livelihood, not floating about without an anchor. You will work methodically and will be successful.

Star	*Degree of influence*	*Other stars*	*Degree of influence*	*Reading*
Wu Ch'ü	Any	Any		You will be successful in finance, industry and the transport business.
	Any	T'ien Fu T'ien Ts'un		You will be promoted and your life will be prosperous.
	Any	Ch'i Sha T'ien Hsiang		If you want to maintain your authority and be successful, you should leave your home town.
	Any	T'an Lang P'o Chün		Because you become involved in corruption you will lose your job if it is connected with politics. However, if you work in finance in a foreign country, you will be successful.
	Any	Fire Star Ringing Star Yang Jen T'o Lo		You will not have an outstanding life or be able to develop your business interests very far.

Star	*Degree of influence*	*Other stars*	*Degree of influence*	*Reading*
	Any	Either of the Literary stars T'o Fu *or* Yu Pi		You will be very lucky. You will be particularly successful if you work in an occupation related to finance.
		T'ien K'uei T'ien Yüeh		All aspects of your life will be stable and without any untoward events.
		T'ien K'ung Ti Chieh		You will work very hard but without reward and will have a harsh life.
T'ien T'ung	Any	Any		You will be successful in your career if you choose to work in a service industry or a career involving handicrafts.
	*	T'ai-yin Ch'u Men		As you grow older your business will improve by leaps and bounds.
	–	T'ai-yin Chü Men		You will have an uneventful life with no particular successes or failures.
	Any	T'ien Liang T'ien Ts'un		You will have authority and wealth.

Star	*Degree of influence*	*Other stars*	*Degree of influence*	*Reading*
	Any	Fire Star Ringing Star Yang Jen T'o Lo T'ien K'ung Ti Chieh		There will be many unexpected events in your life and a lot of bad luck.
	Any	Either of the Literary stars T'ien K'uei T'ien Yüeh Tso Fu *or* Yu Pi		You will achieve fame and have a good position.
Lien Chen	Any	Any		If you work in a large corporation you will have a senior position but, like the flower that opens only for the shortest time at night and then dies, so your position will be short-lived.
	Any	T'ien Ts'un		You will be rich and have good health, but you will not be well known.
	Any	P'o Chün		In your livelihood you will experience ups and downs and be generally unstable.

Star	*Degree of influence*	*Other stars*	*Degree of influence*	*Reading*
	Any	T'ien Fu T'ien Hsiang		You will have a good position in your job and eventually you will achieve fame and wealth.
	Any	T'an Lang Ch'i Sha		You will be very successful in an unusual form of business or trade and receive a large income from it. However, you will be unsuccessful if you go into politics.
	Any	Fire Star Ringing Star Yang Jen T'o Lo T'ien K'ung Ti Chieh		You will have an unsteady career and experience fluctuating luck.
		Literary stars T'ien K'uei T'ien Yüeh Tso Fu *or* Yu Pi		You will be promoted to a senior position in your job.
T'ien Fu	Any	Any		You will be successful in politics and business.
	Any	Any lucky star		Your success will be greater than the above case and will come to you earlier in life.
	Any	Any unlucky star		Your success will be late in coming.

Star	*Degree of influence*	*Other stars*	*Degree of influence*	*Reading*
	Any	T'ien K'ung Ti Chieh		You will have an uneventful life.
T'ai-yin	Any	Any		You will be successful in the building industry or government service.
	Any * ☆	Any lucky star Any	}	You will have the chance of promotion.
	Any + –	Any unlucky star Any	}	You will swing between success and failure.
T'an Lang	Any	Any		You will have success in entertainment or cultural work.
	Any	T'ien Ts'un		You will become wealthy from entertainment or cultural work.
	Any	Fire Star Ringing Star Tso Fu *or* Yu Pi		You will have a managerial role in a financial business.
	Any	Either of the Literary stars T'ien K'uei T'ien Yüeh		You will have an influential role in politics.
	Any	Yang Jen T'o Lo T'ien K'ung Ti Chieh		Your life will be average.

Star	*Degree of influence*	*Other stars*	*Degree of influence*	*Reading*
Chü Men	Any	Any		If you use your intellience, and work either as a judge, in specialized study or in a business enterprise, you will have great success.
	Any	T'ien Ts'un		You will be successful in business and earn a lot of money.
	Any	Fire Star Ringing Star Yang Jen T'o Lo T'ien K'ung Ti Chieh		You will change jobs many times.
	Any	Either of the Literary stars T'ien K'uei T'ien Yüeh Tso Fu *or* Yu Pi		Whatever your job, you will be successful.
T'ien Hsiang	Any	Any		You will be successful in medicine, finance, or politics.
		Fire Star Ringing Star Yang Jen T'o Lo T'ien K'ung Ti Chieh		Whatever your job, there will be no harmony between you and your workmates. You may be cheated or lose money.

Star	*Degree of influence*	*Other stars*	*Degree of influence*	*Reading*
	Any	Literary stars T'ien K'uei T'ien Yüeh Tso Fu *or* Yu Pi		You will make great strides in politics.
T'ien Liang	Any	Any		You will go far in religion, academia, public sanitation, business, the civil service or the military.
	Any	T'ien Ts'un		You will earn a lot of money.
	Any	Fire Star Ringing Star Yang Jen T'o Lo T'ien K'ung Ti Chieh		Your life and fortune will be average.
	Any	Either of the Literary stars T'ien K'uei T'ien Yüeh Tso Fu *or* Yu Pi		You will have success in politics.
Ch'i Sha	Any	Any		You will have great success in heavy industry, the police force or the army. This star remains unaffected by other lucky or unlucky stars.

Star	*Degree of influence*	*Other stars*	*Degree of influence*	*Reading*
P'o Chün	Any	Any		You will be successful in transport, the army or the police force.
	Any	Fire Star Ringing Star Yang Jen T'o Lo T'ien K'ung Ti Chieh		You will make little progress at work.
	Any	Literary stars T'ien K'uei T'ien Yüeh		You will be promoted to a high position at work.
Fire Star *or* **Ringing Star**	Any	Any		When young your job will be unstable. In middle age it will become stable.
	+ –	Any		Your fortune fluctuates between success and failure.
	Any	Either of the Literary stars T'ien K'ung Ti Chieh		Your life will be average.
	Any	T'ien K'uei T'ien Yüeh Tso Fu *or* Yu Pi		You will have success in commerce or finance.

Star	*Degree of influence*	*Other stars*	*Degree of influence*	*Reading*
Wen Ch'ü *or* **Wen Ch'ang**	Any	Any		You will have great success in skilled academic or cultural work.
	–	Any		You have no success in the above types of work.
Yang Jen *or* **T'o Lo**	Any	Any		You will have success in the army or police force.
	–	Any		You will have no success in these types of work.
	Any	T'ien K'ung Ti Chieh		You will die while at work.
T'ien Ts'un		Any		You will have success in finance.
		T'ien K'ung Ti Chieh		You will have no success in finance.
T'ien K'uei *or* **T'ien Yüeh**		Any		Your superiors will be happy with your work. This will lead to promotion earlier than usual. You will be successful in politics.
Tso Fu *or* **Yu Pi**		Any		You will have success in politics. Your inferiors will respect you. Your colleagues will give you good recommendations.

Star	*Degree of influence*	*Other stars*	*Degree of influence*	*Reading*
T'ien K'ung *or* **Ti Chieh**		Any		Whatever your career, you will have a managerial role.
Hua Ch'üan		Any		Whatever your career, you will have a managerial role.
Hua Chi		Any		Your fortunes will fluctuate. At times you will keep your head above water and at times go under.

THE PROPERTY PALACE

The Property Palace is concerned with your surroundings and situation at home and how much property you own.

The stars which bring extremely good luck in the Property Palace are:

- Wu Ch'ü (Military Music)
- T'ai-yin (Moon)
- T'ien Fu (Southern Star)
- T'ien Ts'un (Heavenly Store)

The stars which bring moderately good luck are:

- Tzu Wei (Purple Star)
- T'ien T'ung (Heavenly Unity)
- T'ien Hsiang (Heavenly Minister)
- Tso Fu (Left Assistant)
- Yu Pi (Right Assistant)
- T'ien Liang (Heavenly Roof-Beam)
- T'ai-yang (Sun)
- Ch'i Sha (Seven Killings)
- Wen Ch'ü (Literary Music)
- Wen Ch'ang (Literary Prosperity)
- T'ien K'uei (Heavenly Leader)
- T'ien Yüeh (Heavenly Halberd)

The stars which bring bad luck are:

- T'ien Chi (Heavenly Secret)
- Chü Men (Great Door)
- Fire Star
- Ringing Star
- Lien Chen (Pure Virtue)
- P'o Chün (Broken Army)
- Yang Jen (Sheep-Blade)
- T'o Lo (Hump-Back)

The stars which bring extremely bad luck are:

- T'an Lang (Greedy Wolf)
- Ti Chieh (Earthly Robbery)
- T'ien K'ung (Heavenly Void)
- Hua Chi (Transforming Jealousy)

Star	*Degree of influence*	*Other stars which appear in the Property Palace*	*Degree of influence*	*Reading*
Tzu Wei	Any	Any		You will own a lot of property.
	Any	T'ien Fu T'ien Ts'un		You will own many properties. The number will increase every year.
	Any	T'an Lang P'o Chün		You will have few properties; even if you do have several properties you will eventually lose some.
	Any	T'ien Hsiang Ch'i Sha		You will own a moderate amount of property.
	Any	Literary stars T'ien K'uei T'ien Yüeh Tso Fu *or* Yu Pi		You will gain more property and its value will increase greatly.
T'ien Chi	Any	Any		Although at first you sell all your property, as time goes on you will acquire more.
	*	Chü Men T'ai-yin		You will be able to keep the property that you inherit in the family.
	–	Chü Men T'ai-yin		You will need to sell the property that you inherit.

Star	*Degree of influence*	*Other stars*	*Degree of influence*	*Reading*
	Any	T'ien Liang T'ien Ts'un		You will start buying property when you are young and will increase your holding annually.
	Any	Fire Star Ringing Star Yang Jen T'o Lo T'ien K'ung Ti Chieh		You will not own any property.
	Any	T'ien K'uei T'ien Yüeh Tso Fu *or* Yu Pi		You will possess a lot of property.
T'ai-yang	Any	Any		You will inherit some property and will increase the amount during your lifetime.
	–	Any		In middle age your property holdings will decrease.
	*	T'ien Liang Chü Men		You will be able to keep the property that you inherit and increase its value.
	–	T'ien Liang Chü Men		You will need to sell all your inherited property.

Star	*Degree of influence*	*Other stars*	*Degree of influence*	*Reading*
	Any	T'ai-yin T'ien Ts'un		From your early years you will buy houses and land, so that by your middle years you will have amassed a large amount of property.
	Any	Fire Star Ringing Star Yang Jen T'o Lo T'ien K'ung Ti Chieh		You will never have property.
	Any	Either of the Literary stars Tso Fu *or* Yu Pi		You will own a lot of property.
Wu Ch'ü	Any	Any		You will own a lot of property.
	Any	T'ien Fu T'ien Ts'un Fire Star Ringing Star Either of the Literary stars		You will buy a lot of property.
	Any	T'an Lang T'ien Hsiang T'ien K'uei T'ien Yüeh Tso Fu *or* Yu Pi		By the time you reach old age you will possess a lot of property.
	Any	Ch'i Sha Yang Jen T'o Lo		Because you have no interest in acquiring property, you will own none.

Star	*Degree of influence*	*Other stars*	*Degree of influence*	*Reading*
	Any	P'o Chün T'ien K'ung Ti Chieh		You will sell all the property that you inherit.
T'ien T'ung	* ☆	Any		You will not own any property until you are middle-aged.
	* ☆	Any lucky star		You will own property when you are young.
	–	Any		You will not own any property.
Lien Chen	Any	Any		You will probably not inherit any property. If you do inherit property, you will have to sell it quickly.
	Any	T'ien Fu Ch'i Sha Either of the Literary stars T'ien K'uei T'ien Yüeh Tso Fu *or* Yu Pi T'ien Ts'un		You will not only inherit property, but will be able to buy more throughout your life.
	Any	T'an Lang T'ien Hsiang P'o Chün Fire Star Ringing Star Yang Jen T'o Lo T'ien K'ung Ti Chieh		You will not be able to keep the property that you inherit. You will have to sell it.

Star	*Degree of influence*	*Other stars*	*Degree of influence*	*Reading*
T'ien Fu	Any	Any		You will become wealthy through buying property and increasing your stock each year.
	Any	T'ien Ts'un		You will start to buy property at an early age. By the time you reach middle age you will have a large holding.
	Any	Fire Star Ringing Star Yang Jen T'o Lo		You will buy and sell property frequently.
		Either of the Literary stars T'ien K'uei T'ien Yüeh		By old age you will have acquired a lot of property.
		Tso Fu *or* Yu Pi		You will own a lot of property and will live in a particularly splendid house.
		T'ien K'ung Ti Chieh		You will not have any property. Should you inherit any, you will have to sell it.
T'ai-yin	* ☆	Any lucky star		You will not only own a house but land too.

Star	*Degree of influence*	*Other stars*	*Degree of influence*	*Reading*
	–	Any unlucky star		You will not own any property, or you will have to sell what property you do own.
T'an Lang	Any	Any		You will not own any property.
	Any	T'ien Ts'un		By the time you reach old age you will own some property.
	Any	Fire Star Ringing Star		You will own a lot of property but will need to take care of it because there is a danger of fire.
	Any	Either of the Literary stars Tso Fu *or* Yu Pi		By the time you reach old age you will have acquired some property.
	Any	Yang Jen T'o Lo T'ien K'ung Ti Chieh		You will never own property.
Chü Men	*	Any lucky star		You will be able to earn money easily and buy property.
	–	Any unlucky star		You will never own property.
T'ien Hsiang	Any	Any lucky star		You will own property throughout your life and will greatly benefit from it.

Star	*Degree of influence*	*Other stars*	*Degree of influence*	*Reading*
	Any	Any unlucky star		You will own nothing.
T'ien Liang	Any	Any		You will own some property.
	Any	Any lucky star		(The above reading is improved.)
	Any	Any unlucky star		You will own very little property.
Ch'i Sha *or* **P'o Chün**	Any	Any		You will be able to keep the property that you have inherited, but will not inherit any more.
	+ –	Any unlucky star		You will have to sell the property that you have.
Fire Star *or* **Ringing Star**	Any	Any		You will either give away most of your inherited property or have to sell much of it.
	Any	Either of the Literary stars Yang Jen T'o Lo T'ien K'ung Ti Chieh		You will not be able to buy any property.
	Any	T'ien Ts'un T'ien K'uei T'ien Yüeh Tso Fu *or* Yu Pi		You will increase your stock of property.

Star	*Degree of influence*	*Other stars*	*Degree of influence*	*Reading*
Wen Ch'ü *or* **Wen Ch'ang**	Any	Any		You will be able to maintain your inherited property and will acquire a little more.
	–	Yang Jen T'o Lo T'ien K'ung Ti Chieh		Your stock of property will decrease.
Yang Jen *or* **T'o Lo**	Any	Any		You will lose your property.
	☆	Any		You will gain more property.
T'ien Ts'un		Any		You will not only possess a lot of property but will benefit financially from it.
T'ien K'uei *or* **T'ien Yüeh**		Any		You will be able to maintain your inherited property: a farm and farmhouse.
Tso Fu *or* **Yu Pi**		Any		You will be able to keep your inherited property.
T'ien K'ung *or* **Ti Chieh**		Any		You will lose your inherited property.
Hua Chi		Any		You will not be able to buy any property.

THE FORTUNE AND VIRTUE PALACE

The Fortune and Virtue Palace is concerned with what generally interest you – your hobbies and how you enjoy yourself.

The stars which bring extremely good luck in the Fortune and Virtue Palace are:

- T'ien T'ung (Heavenly Unity)
- T'ai-yin (Moon)
- T'ien Liang (Heavenly Roof-Beam)
- Wen Ch'ü (Literary Music)
- Wen Ch'ang (Literary Prosperity)
- T'ien Fu (Southern Star)
- T'ien Hsiang (Heavenly Minister)
- T'ien K'uei (Heavenly Leader)
- T'ien Yüeh (Heavenly Halberd)
- Tso Fu (Left Assistant)
- Yu Pi (Right Assistant)

The stars which bring moderately good luck are:

- Tzu Wei (Purple Star)
- T'ien Ts'un (Heavenly Store)
- T'ai-yang (Sun)
- I-ma (Travelling Star)

The stars which bring bad luck are:

- T'ien Chi (Heavenly Secret)
- Lien Chen (Pure Virtue)
- Fire Star
- Ringing Star
- T'ien Yao (Heavenly Beauty)
- Wu Ch'ü (Military Music)
- Ch'i Sha (Seven Killings)
- Yang Jen (Sheep-Blade)
- T'o Lo (Hump-Back)

The stars which bring extremely bad luck are:

T'an Lang (Greedy Wolf)	Chü Men (Great Door)
P'o Chün (Brokent Army)	T'ien K'ung (Heavenly Void)
Ti Chieh (Earthly Robbery)	Hua Chi (Transforming Jealousy)

Star	*Degree of influence*	*Other stars which appear in the Fortune and Virtue Palace*	*Degree of influence*	*Reading*
Tzu Wei	Any	Any		You want to work on projects connected with charity or community work without regard to personal financial rewards. You like to make friends with famous people and those in important positions.
	Any	T'ien Fu T'ien Hsiang T'ien Ts'un Either of the Literary stars T'ien K'uei T'ien Yüeh Tso Fu *or* Yu Pi		You will be comfortably off and will have no need to worry about your living expenses.
	Any	T'an Lang Ch'i Sha P'o Chün Fire Star Ringing Star Yang Jen T'o Lo T'ien K'ung Ti Chieh		You will have a hard life with little enjoyment.

Star	*Degree of influence*	*Other stars*	*Degree of influence*	*Reading*
T'ien Chi	Any	Any		You are very interested in religious, literary and cultural studies. When you are young you will have to work very hard but you will be comfortably off from your middle years onwards.
	Any	Any lucky star		It will not be material pleasures that interest you but those of the spirit. Relationships with people and ideas will form the main source of your enjoyment. You will be happy throughout your life.
	Any	Any unlucky star		Your spirit will suffer and you will have a hard life. You will not be interested in enjoying yourself.
T'ai-yang	Any	Any		You are very fond of politics and like to make friends with people in high positions.

Star	*Degree of influence*	*Other stars*	*Degree of influence*	*Reading*
Wu Ch'ü	Any	Any		You will have such a busy life that you will not have any time to enjoy yourself.
T'ien T'ung	Any	Any		You enjoy making lots of friends, especially members of the opposite sex.
Lien Chen	Any	Any		You are particularly fond of running and enjoy training hard. You will work in an active job.
T'ien Fu	Any	Any		You prefer to live in the countryside rather than the town. You enjoy eating and drinking.
	Any	T'ien K'ung Ti Chieh		You will not have much money and will suffer from stomach or digestive troubles. This means that you will not be interested in enjoying yourself.
T'ai-yin	Any	Any		You enjoy living in the countryside and will be involved in religious affairs.
T'an Lang	Any	Any		You will have a hard life with little enjoyment.

Star	*Degree of influence*	*Other stars*	*Degree of influence*	*Reading*
Chü Men	Any	Any		You will be so busy that you will not have time to enjoy yourself.
T'ien Liang	Any	Any		You will be interested in education and cultural affairs. You enjoy writing and will want to publish your work.
Ch'i Sha	Any	Any		You will have a hard life without enjoyment.
P'o Chün	Any	Any		You will work very hard and be very busy all your life. You will experience little enjoyment.
Fire Star *or* **Ringing Star** **Yang Jen** *or* **T'o Lo** **T'ien K'ung** **Ti Chieh** *or* **Hua Chi**	Any	Any		You will always be hardworking, so much so that you will not know how to enjoy yourself.
Wen Ch'ü *or* **Wen Ch'ang**	* ☆	Any		You will be very interested in cultural and artistic affairs. You will enjoy yourself very much.

Star	*Degree of influence*	*Other stars*	*Degree of influence*	*Reading*
	–	Any unlucky star		Although you have the above interests, you will be unable to follow them up.
T'ien Ts'un		Any		You will have a long and happy life and be very interested in material pleasures, such as clothes, food and drink.
T'ien K'uei *or* **T'ien Yüeh**		Any		You like working on community or charity projects.
Tso Fu *or* **Yu Pi**		Any		You greatly enjoy your social life, especially meeting the opposite sex.
I-ma		Any		You enjoy travelling and admiring beautiful views.
T'ien Yao		Any		You enjoy making friends with members of the opposite sex.

THE PARENTS' PALACE

The Parents' Palace is concerned with the relationship between you and your parents. This relationship is controlled by your *yuanten* (the predestined attachment between your parents and yourself). If your *yuanten* is strong, you will love one another and stay together. If weak, you will have little feeling for each other and may move away.

This palace is also concerned with how much material benefit and moral support your parents can give you.

The stars which bring extremely good luck in the Parents' Palace are:

- T'ai-yang (Sun)
- T'ai-yin (Moon)
- T'ien Liang (Heavenly Roof-Beam)
- T'ien Yüeh (Heavenly Halberd)
- T'ien Fu (Southern Star)
- T'ien Hsiang (Heavenly Minister)
- T'ien K'uei (Heavenly Leader)

The stars which bring moderately good luck are:

- Tzu Wei (Purple Star)
- T'ien T'ung (Heavenly Unity)
- T'ien Ts'un (Heavenly Store)
- T'ien Chi (Heavenly Secret)
- Wen Ch'ü (Literary Music)
- Wen Ch'ang (Literary Prosperity)
- Tso Fu (Left Assistant)
- Yu Pi (Right Assistant)

The star which brings bad luck is:

- Wu Ch'ü (Military Music)*

* This is generally a lucky star.

The stars which bring extremely bad luck are:

- Lien Chen (Pure Virtue)
- Chü Men (Great Door)
- P'o Chün (Broken Army)
- Fire Star
- Ringing Star
- Ti Chieh (Earthly Robbery)
- T'an Lang (Greedy Wolf)
- Ch'i Sha (Seven Killings)
- Yang Jen (Sheep-Blade)
- T'o Lo (Hump-Back)
- T'ien K'ung (Heavenly Void)
- Hua Chi (Transforming Jealousy)

Star	*Degree of influence*	*Other stars which appear in the Parents' Palace*	*Degree of influence*	*Reading*
Tzu Wei	Any	Any		You will receive many benefits from your parents.
	Any	T'ien Fu T'ien Hsiang Either of the Literary stars T'ien Ts'un T'ien K'uei T'ien Yüeh Tso Fu *or* Yu Pi		You will receive great moral and material support from your parents.
	Any	T'an Lang		Although you live with your parents, in spirit and feeling you are not in harmony with them.
	Any	Ch'i Sha P'o Chün		There will be a rift between you and one of your parents.
	Any	Fire Star Ringing Star Yang Jen T'o Lo T'ien K'ung Ti Chieh		Your *yuanten* (predestined attachment) with your parents is weak. You may live apart from your parents or one of them may die.
T'ien Chi	Any	Any		Your parents will give you a good education but they will not spoil you.

Star	*Degree of influence*	*Other stars*	*Degree of influence*	*Reading*
	Any	T'ai-yin T'ien Liang T'ien Ts'un		You will receive long-term benefits from your parents. This will last until your middle years.
	Any	Chü Men		You will only receive short-term benefits from your parents, or when you are young you may lose your father or mother.
	Any	Fire Star Ringing Star Yang Jen T'o Lo T'ien K'ung Ti Chieh		You may lose one of your parents while you are young.
		Either of the Literary stars T'ien K'uei T'ien Yüeh Tso Fu *or* Yu Pi		Your parents are well educated. They have taught you well and this means that your business will expand and be successful.
T'ai-yang	Any	Any		You will receive many benefits from your father.
	–	Any		Your father will die or you will live apart from him when you are young.

Star	*Degree of influence*	*Other stars*	*Degree of influence*	*Reading*
	Any	T'ai-yin T'ien Liang T'ien Ts'un		Your parents will help and support you.
	Any	Chü Men		Your relationship with your father is tense and argumentative.
	Any	Fire Star Ringing Star Yang Jen T'o Lo T'ien K'ung Ti Chieh		When young you will have no *yuanten* (predestined attachment) with your father. You may live apart from him or he may not take care of you.
	Any	Either of the Literary stars T'ien K'uei T'ien Yüeh Tso Fu *or* Yu Pi		Your father will be a great help to you and will bring you social advantages.
Wu Ch'ü	Any	Any		Your *yuanten* (predestined attachment) is weak and your relationship with your parents is troubled.
	Any	T'ien Fu T'ien Hsiang T'ien Ts'un		Your *yuanten* is very strong and you are in harmony with your parents.

Star	*Degree of influence*	*Other stars*	*Degree of influence*	*Reading*
	Any	T'an Lang Ch'i Sha P'o Chün		You are not close to your parents and and will either live apart from them or one of them may die.
	Any	Fire Star Ringing Star Yang Jen T'o Lo T'ien K'ung Ti Chieh		When you are young there will be a rift between you and your parents.
	Any	Either of the Literary stars T'ien K'uei T'ien Yüeh Tso Fu *and* Yu Pi		Your parents will not only support you materially but will give you a good education and moral support.
T'ien T'ung	Any	Any		Your mother loves you dearly.
	Any	T'ai-yin T'ien Liang		Both your parents love you dearly.
	Any	Chü Men Fire Star Ringing Star Yang Jen T'o Lo T'ien K'ung Ti Chieh		Your parents do not love you. You are forever arguing. Sometimes you are very rude or cruel to one of your parents.
	Any	Literary stars T'ien Ts'un T'ien K'uei T'ien Yüeh Tso Fu *or* Yu Pi		You will be supported by your parents. They love you and give you material things.

Star	*Degree of influence*	*Other stars*	*Degree of influence*	*Reading*
Lien Chen	Any	Any		There will be a rift between you and one of your parents.
	Any	T'ien Fu T'ien Hsiang Wen Ch'ü T'ien Ts'un T'ien K'uei T'ien Yüeh Tso Fu *or* Yu Pi		When you are young you will cause your parents to worry. However, there will be no serious rift between you.
	Any	T'an Lang Ch'i Sha P'o Chün Fire Star Ringing Star Yang Jen T'o Lo T'ien K'ung Ti Chieh		When you are young there will be a rift between you and one parent. In middle age you will move away from your parents or one of them will die.
T'ien Fu	Any	Any		You will have great material support from your parents.
	Any	T'ien Ts'un		(As above.)
	Any	Fire Star Ringing Star Yang Jen T'o Lo T'ien K'ung Ti Chieh		You are likely to move away from one or other of your parents or one of them may die.

Star	*Degree of influence*	*Other stars*	*Degree of influence*	*Reading*
	Any	Either of the Literary stars T'ien K'uei T'ien Yüeh Tso Fu *or* Yu Pi		Your parents will give you many benefits which will enable you to have a comfortable and wealthy life.
T'ai-yin	Any	Any		Your *yuanten* (predestined attachment) with your mother is greater than that with your father.
	+ –	Any		Your *yuanten* with your mother is weak.
	Any	T'ien Ts'un		You will receive substantial material support from your mother.
	Any	Fire Star Ringing Star Yang Jen T'o Lo T'ien K'ung Ti Chieh		When you are young there will be a rift between you and your mother.
	Any	Literary stars T'ien K'uei T'ien Yüeh Tso Fu *or* Yu Pi		Your mother will give you great support. Your business will be prosperous.
T'an Lang	Any	Any		There will be a rift between you and both or one of your parents.

Star	*Degree of influence*	*Other stars*	*Degree of influence*	*Reading*
	+ –	Any		You have no *yuanten* (predestined attachment) with your parents.
	Any	Literary stars T'ien Ts'un Tso Fu *or* Yu Pi		In later life there will be a rift between you and your parents.
	Any	T'ien K'uei *or* T'ien Yüeh		Your *yuanten* with your parents is strong.
	Any	Fire Star Ringing Star Yang Jen T'o Lo T'ien K'ung *or* Ti Chieh		When young you will be in conflict with your parents.
Chü Men	Any	Any		Your relationship with your parents is unstable and unhappy.
	+ –	Any		There will be a rift between you and your parents and you may harm one of them.
	Any	T'ien Ts'un		(The above reading is improved.)

Star	*Degree of influence*	*Other stars*	*Degree of influence*	*Reading*
	Any	Fire Star Ringing Star Yang Jen T'o Lo T'ien K'ung *or* Ti Chieh		Your brothers' and sisters' relationship with your parents and yourself will be unstable and argumentative.
	Any	Either of the Literary stars T'ien K'uei T'ien Yüeh Tso Fu *or* Yu Pi		In later life your brothers' and sisters' relationship with you and your parents will be troubled and unhappy.
T'ien Hsiang	Any	Any		Your parents will give you material and moral support. Your *yuanten* (predestined attachment) with your parents is deep.
	Any	T'ien Ts'un		You will receive great benefits from your parents.
	Any	Fire Star Ringing Star Yang Jen T'o Lo T'ien K'ung Ti Chieh		There will be a rift between you and your parents. You may live apart or you may cause your parents to die.

Star	*Degree of influence*	*Other stars*	*Degree of influence*	*Reading*
		Either of the Literary stars T'ien K'uei T'ien Yüeh Tso Fu *or* Yu Pi		Your parents' support and encouragement helps you to achieve social success.
T'ien Liang	Any	Any		Your parents will be long-lived.
	+ –	Any		In later life there will be a rift between you and your parents.
	Any	T'ien Ts'un		Your parents will offer you substantial material support.
	Any	Fire Star Ringing Star Yang Jen T'o Lo T'ien K'ung *or* Ti Chieh		There will be a rift between you and one parent.
	Any	Literary stars T'ien K'uei T'ien Yüeh Tso Fu *or* Yu Pi		Your parents will be long-lived.
Ch'i Sha	Any	Any		Your parents will be short-lived. There will be a rift between you and one parent.

Star	*Degree of influence*	*Other stars*	*Degree of influence*	*Reading*
	Any	Any lucky star		(The above reading is unchanged, but may be delayed until later life.)
	Any	Any unlucky star		(The above unlucky reading deteriorates.)
P'o Chün	Any	Any		When young there will be a rift between you and one parent. You may harm them.
	Any	Any unlucky star		(The above reading deteriorates).
Fire Star *or* **Ringing Star**	Any	Any		You have *yuanten* (predestined attachment) with only one parent.
	Any	T'ien K'uei T'ien Yüeh		(The above reading is improved.)
	Any	Any stars other than T'ien K'uei *and* T'ien Yüeh		(The above reading deteriorates.)
Wen Ch'ü *or* **Wen Ch'ang**	Any	Any		You have *yuanten* (predestined attachment) with both parents.
	Any	T'ien K'uei T'ien Yüeh T'ien Ts'un		You will receive many benefits from your parents.

Star	*Degree of influence*	*Other stars*	*Degree of influence*	*Reading*
	Any	Yang Jen T'o Lo		There will be a rift between you and one parent.
Yang Jen *or* **T'o Lo**	Any	Any		There will be a rift between you and one parent. You may harm them.
	Any	T'ien K'ung Ti Chieh		There will be a rift between you and your parents.
	Any	T'ien K'ung Ti Chieh *and* any other lucky star		(The above reading may be delayed.)
T'ien Ts'un		Any		You will receive many benefits from your parents.
		Tso Fu *or* Yu Pi		Your parents will give you moral rather than material support.
		T'ien K'ung Ti Chieh		When you are young there will be a rift between you and your parents.
T'ien K'uei *or* **T'ien Yüeh**		Any		Your *yuanten* (predestined attachment) with your parents is strong. You will stay together.
		Tso Fu *or* Yu Pi		You will receive many benefits from your parents.

Star	*Degree of influence*	*Other stars*	*Degree of influence*	*Reading*
		T'ien K'ung Ti Chieh		Although T'ien K'ung and Ti Chieh are generally unlucky, they will not harm your parents because T'ien K'uei and T'ien Yüeh are strong lucky stars in this palace.
Tso Fu *or* **Yu Pi**		Any		You have *yuanten* (predestined attachment) with your parents.
T'ien K'ung *or* **Ti Chieh**		Any		Your *yuanten* (predestined attachment) with one parent is weak.
Hua Chi		Any		There will be a rift between you and one of your parents.

The Calendar Tables

Much of the material covered below has appeared earlier in the book; it is repeated here in this form to assist the reader to use the Calendar Tables as easily as possible.

The Chinese calendar uses the sexagenary cycle of Heavenly Stems and Earthly Branches for numbering the years, the months and the days (see pp. 10–17). In the pages that follow we have listed the Chinese equivalents for the Western calendar dates from 5 February 1924 to 23 January 2001. To simplify matters, in the main body of the tables we have used codes for the Heavenly Stems and Earthly Branches, and these are shown below.

The tables are divided into years according to the Chinese calendar, and each year is named by a Heavenly Stem and an Earthly Branch from the sexagenary cycle. Thus the first year, which runs from the Western date of 5 February 1924 to 23 January 1925, is Chia Tzu; the next year, from 24 January 1925 to 12 February 1926, is Yi Ch'ou; the next, from 13 February 1926 to 1 February 1927, is Ping Yin; and so on. To find the characters for your year of birth, simply turn to your Western birthday in the tables and look for the heading to the Chinese year in which it appears. For example, someone born on 10 January 1925 comes under the year Chia Tzu.

In the left-hand column of the tables are listed the days and months according to the Western calendar, 10.1 meaning 10 January. The next column gives the corresponding days and months for the Chinese calendar. Thus, in 1925, 10 January becomes 16.12 in the Chinese calendar, that is, the 16th day of the 12th month. Therefore someone born on 10 January 1925 was born on the 16th day of the 12th month in Chia Tzu year.

Note that the relationship between the Western and the Chinese calendars varies from year to year. The 10th of January will not invariably be the 16th day of the 12th month. This is because in the Chinese system the number of days in a year fluctuates between 353 and 355, with an additional intercalary month every two to three years to keep the calendars in line (see p. 13). Thus in the tables you will see every so often a year with two months which have the same number, the second of which is set in italic – this is the extra month.

The variable number of days in the year is also the reason why the Chinese New Year changes from year to year in relation to the Western calendar, falling anywhere between 21 January and 20 February.

The third column of the tables lists the codes (see below) for the Heavenly Stems and Earthly Branches for the months. In the example already given, 10 January 1925 has the code D2, which gives the Heavenly Stem Ting and the Earthly Branch Ch'ou. These are the characters for the 12th month in Chia Tzu year.

In the fourth column are the codes for the Heavenly Stems and Earthly Branches for the days. For 10 January 1925 the code is A7, which gives the Heavenly Stem Chia and the Earthly Branch Wu. These are the characters for the 16th day of the 12th month in Chia Tzu year.

The characters for the 'hours' are not listed in the Calendar – to do so would have meant including twelve separate entries for each day. The characters for the 'hours' can be found on p. 18.

Finally, in the right-hand column are listed the constellations. There are twenty-eight in all and they change from day to day. For 10 January 1925 the constellation is Pheasant.

Codes for the Heavenly Stems and Earthly Branches

Heavenly Stems		*Earthly Branches*	
Code	*Character*	*Code*	*Character*
A	Chia	1	Tzu
B	Yi	2	Ch'ou
C	Ping	3	Yin
D	Ting	4	Mao
E	Mou	5	Ch'en
F	Chi	6	Szu
G	Keng	7	Wu
H	Hsin	8	Wei
J*	Jen	9	Shen
K	Kuei	10	Yu
		11	Hsü
		12	Hai

*To avoid possible confusion with the number 1, we have not used the letter I.

CHIA TZU YEAR

Solar date	*Lunar date*	*Month HS/EB*	*Day HS/EB*	*Constellation*
1924				
5 2	1. 1	C3	A3	Pig
6 2	2. 1	C3	B4	Porcupine
7 2	3. 1	C3	C5	Wolf
8 2	4. 1	C3	D6	Dog
9 2	5. 1	C3	E7	Pheasant
10. 2	6. 1	C3	F8	Cock
11. 2	7. 1	C3	G9	Crow
12. 2	8. 1	C3	H10	Monkey
13. 2	9. 1	C3	J11	Gibbon
14. 2	10. 1	C3	K12	Tapir
15. 2	11. 1	C3	A1	Sheep
16. 2	12. 1	C3	B2	Deer
17. 2	13. 1	C3	C3	Horse
18. 2	14. 1	C3	D4	Stag
19. 2	15. 1	C3	E5	Serpent
20. 2	16. 1	C3	F6	Earthworm
21. 2	17. 1	C3	G7	Crocodile
22. 2	18. 1	C3	H8	Dragon
23. 2	19. 1	C3	J9	Badger
24. 2	20. 1	C3	K10	Hare
25. 2	21. 1	C3	A11	Fox
26. 2	22. 1	C3	B12	Tiger
27. 2	23. 1	C3	C1	Leopard
28. 2	24. 1	C3	D2	Griffon
29. 2	25. 1	C3	E3	Ox
1. 3	26. 1	C3	F4	Bat
2. 3	27. 1	C3	G5	Rat
3. 3	28. 1	C3	H6	Swallow
4. 3	29. 1	C3	J7	Pig
5. 3	1. 2	D4	K8	Porcupine
6. 3	2. 2	D4	A9	Wolf
7. 3	3. 2	D4	B10	Dog
8. 3	4. 2	D4	C11	Pheasant
9. 3	5. 2	D4	D12	Cock
10. 3	6. 2	D4	E1	Crow
11. 3	7. 2	D4	F2	Monkey
12. 3	8. 2	D4	G3	Gibbon
13. 3	9. 2	D4	H4	Tapir
14. 3	10. 2	D4	J5	Sheep
15. 3	11. 2	D4	K6	Deer
16. 3	12. 2	D4	A7	Horse
17. 3	13. 2	D4	B8	Stag
18. 3	14. 2	D4	C9	Serpent
19. 3	15. 2	D4	D10	Earthworm
20. 3	16. 2	D4	E11	Crocodile
21. 3	17. 2	D4	F12	Dragon
22. 3	18. 2	D4	G1	Badger
23. 3	19. 2	D4	H2	Hare
24. 3	20. 2	D4	J3	Fox
25. 3	21. 2	D4	K4	Tiger
26. 3	22. 2	D4	A5	Leopard
27. 3	23. 2	D4	B6	Griffon
28. 3	24. 2	D4	C7	Ox
29. 3	25. 2	D4	D8	Bat
30. 3	26. 2	D4	E9	Rat
31. 3	27. 2	D4	F10	Swallow
1. 4	28. 2	D4	G11	Pig
2. 4	29. 2	D4	H12	Porcupine
3. 4	30. 2	D4	J1	Wolf
4. 4	1. 3	E5	K2	Dog
5. 4	2. 3	E5	A3	Pheasant
6. 4	3. 3	E5	B4	Cock
7. 4	4. 3	E5	C5	Crow
8. 4	5. 3	E5	D6	Monkey
9. 4	6. 3	E5	E7	Gibbon
10. 4	7. 3	E5	F8	Tapir
11. 4	8. 3	E5	G9	Sheep
12. 4	9. 3	E5	H10	Deer
13. 4	10. 3	E5	J11	Horse
14. 4	11. 3	E5	K12	Stag
15. 4	12. 3	E5	A1	Serpent
16. 4	13. 3	E5	B2	Earthworm
17. 4	14. 3	E5	C3	Crocodile
18. 4	15. 3	E5	D4	Dragon
19. 4	16. 3	E5	E5	Badger
20. 4	17. 3	E5	F6	Hare
21. 4	18. 3	E5	G7	Fox
22. 4	19. 3	E5	H8	Tiger
23. 4	20. 3	E5	J9	Leopard
24. 4	21. 3	E5	K10	Griffon
25. 4	22. 3	E5	A11	Ox
26. 4	23. 3	E5	B12	Bat
27. 4	24. 3	E5	C1	Rat
28. 4	25. 3	E5	D2	Swallow
29. 4	26. 3	E5	E3	Pig
30. 4	27. 3	E5	F4	Porcupine
1. 5	28. 3	E5	G5	Wolf
2. 5	29. 3	E5	H6	Dog
3. 5	30. 3	E5	J7	Pheasant
4. 5	1. 4	F6	K8	Cock
5. 5	2. 4	F6	A9	Crow
6. 5	3. 4	F6	B10	Monkey
7. 5	4. 4	F6	C11	Gibbon
8. 5	5. 4	F6	D12	Tapir
9. 5	6. 4	F6	E1	Sheep
10. 5	7. 4	F6	F2	Deer
11. 5	8. 4	F6	G3	Horse
12. 5	9. 4	F6	H4	Stag
13. 5	10. 4	F6	J5	Serpent
14. 5	11. 4	F6	K6	Earthworm
15. 5	12. 4	F6	A7	Crocodile
16. 5	13. 4	F6	B8	Dragon
17. 5	14. 4	F6	C9	Badger
18. 5	15. 4	F6	D10	Hare
19. 5	16. 4	F6	E11	Fox
20. 5	17. 4	F6	F12	Tiger
21. 5	18. 4	F6	G1	Leopard
22. 5	19. 4	F6	H2	Griffon
23. 5	20. 4	F6	J3	Ox
24. 5	21. 4	F6	K4	Bat
25. 5	22. 4	F6	A5	Rat
26. 5	23. 4	F6	B6	Swallow
27. 5	24. 4	F6	C7	Pig
28. 5	25. 4	F6	D8	Porcupine
29. 5	26. 4	F6	E9	Wolf
30. 5	27. 4	F6	F10	Dog
31. 5	28. 4	F6	G11	Pheasant
1. 6	29. 4	F6	H12	Cock
2. 6	1. 5	G7	J1	Crow
3. 6	2. 5	G7	K2	Monkey
4. 6	3. 5	G7	A3	Gibbon
5. 6	4. 5	G7	B4	Tapir
6. 6	5. 5	G7	C5	Sheep
7. 6	6. 5	G7	D6	Deer
8. 6	7. 5	G7	E7	Horse
9. 6	8. 5	G7	F8	Stag
10. 6	9. 5	G7	G9	Serpent
11. 6	10. 5	G7	H10	Earthworm
12. 6	11. 5	G7	J11	Crocodile
13. 6	12. 5	G7	K12	Dragon
14. 6	13. 5	G7	A1	Badger
15. 6	14. 5	G7	B2	Hare
16. 6	15. 5	G7	C3	Fox
17. 6	16. 5	G7	D4	Tiger
18. 6	17. 5	G7	E5	Leopard
19. 6	18. 5	G7	F6	Griffon
20. 6	19. 5	G7	G7	Ox
21. 6	20. 5	G7	H8	Bat
22. 6	21. 5	G7	J9	Rat
23. 6	22. 5	G7	K10	Swallow
24. 6	23. 5	G7	A11	Pig

Solar date	Lunar date	Month HS/EB	Day HS/EB	Constellation
25. 6	24. 5	G7	B12	Porcupine
26. 6	25. 5	G7	C1	Wolf
27. 6	26. 5	G7	D2	Dog
28. 6	27. 5	G7	E3	Pheasant
29. 6	28. 5	G7	F4	Cock
30. 6	29. 5	G7	G5	Crow
1. 7	30. 5	G7	H6	Monkey
2. 7	1. 6	H8	J7	Gibbon
3. 7	2. 6	H8	K8	Tapir
4. 7	3. 6	H8	A9	Sheep
5. 7	4. 6	H8	B10	Deer
6. 7	5. 6	H8	C11	Horse
7. 7	6. 6	H8	D12	Stag
8. 7	7. 6	H8	E1	Serpent
9. 7	8. 6	H8	F2	Earthworm
10. 7	9. 6	H8	G3	Crocodile
11. 7	10. 6	H8	H4	Dragon
12. 7	11. 6	H8	J5	Badger
13. 7	12. 6	H8	K6	Hare
14. 7	13. 6	H8	A7	Fox
15. 7	14. 6	H8	B8	Tiger
16. 7	15. 6	H8	C9	Leopard
17. 7	16. 6	H8	D10	Griffon
18. 7	17. 6	H8	E11	Ox
19. 7	18. 6	H8	F12	Bat
20. 7	19. 6	H8	G1	Rat
21. 7	20. 6	H8	H2	Swallow
22. 7	21. 6	H8	J3	Pig
23. 7	22. 6	H8	K4	Porcupine
24. 7	23. 6	H8	A5	Wolf
25. 7	24. 6	H8	B6	Dog
26. 7	25. 6	H8	C7	Pheasant
27. 7	26. 6	H8	D8	Cock
28. 7	27. 6	H8	E9	Crow
29. 7	28. 6	H8	F10	Monkey
30. 7	29. 6	H8	G11	Gibbon
31. 7	30. 6	H8	H12	Tapir
1. 8	1. 7	J9	J1	Sheep
2. 8	2. 7	J9	K2	Deer
3. 8	3. 7	J9	A3	Horse
4. 8	4. 7	J9	B4	Stag
5. 8	5. 7	J9	C5	Serpent
6. 8	6. 7	J9	D6	Earthworm
7. 8	7. 7	J9	E7	Crocodile
8. 8	8. 7	J9	F8	Dragon
9. 8	9. 7	J9	G9	Badger
10. 8	10. 7	J9	H10	Hare
11. 8	11. 7	J9	J11	Fox
12. 8	12. 7	J9	K12	Tiger
13. 8	13. 7	J9	A1	Leopard
14. 8	14. 7	J9	B2	Griffon
15. 8	15. 7	J9	C3	Ox
16. 8	16. 7	J9	D4	Bat
17. 8	17. 7	J9	E5	Rat
18. 8	18. 7	J9	F6	Swallow
19. 8	19. 7	J9	G7	Pig
20. 8	20. 7	J9	H8	Porcupine
21. 8	21. 7	J9	J9	Wolf
22. 8	22. 7	J9	K10	Dog
23. 8	23. 7	J9	A11	Pheasant
24. 8	24. 7	J9	B12	Cock
25. 8	25. 7	J9	C1	Crow
26. 8	26. 7	J9	D2	Monkey
27. 8	27. 7	J9	E3	Gibbon
28. 8	28. 7	J9	F4	Tapir
29. 8	29. 7	J9	G5	Sheep
30. 8	1. 8	K10	H6	Deer
31. 8	2. 8	K10	J7	Horse
1. 9	3. 8	K10	K8	Stag
2. 9	4. 8	K10	A9	Serpent
3. 9	5. 8	K10	B10	Earthworm
4. 9	6. 8	K10	C11	Crocodile
5. 9	7. 8	K10	D12	Dragon
6. 9	8. 8	K10	E1	Badger
7. 9	9. 8	K10	F2	Hare
8. 9	10. 8	K10	G3	Fox
9. 9	11. 8	K10	H4	Tiger
10. 9	12. 8	K10	J5	Leopard
11. 9	13. 8	K10	K6	Griffon
12. 9	14. 8	K10	A7	Ox
13. 9	15. 8	K10	B8	Bat
14. 9	16. 8	K10	C9	Rat
15. 9	17. 8	K10	D10	Swallow
16. 9	18. 8	K10	E11	Pig
17. 9	19. 8	K10	F12	Porcupine
18. 9	20. 8	K10	G1	Wolf
19. 9	21. 8	K10	H2	Dog
20. 9	22. 8	K10	J3	Pheasant
21. 9	23. 8	K10	K4	Cock
22. 9	24. 8	K10	A5	Crow
23. 9	25. 8	K10	B6	Monkey
24. 9	26. 8	K10	C7	Gibbon
25. 9	27. 8	K10	D8	Tapir
26. 9	28. 8	K10	E9	Sheep
27. 9	29. 8	K10	F10	Deer
28. 9	30. 8	K10	G11	Horse
29. 9	1. 9	A11	H12	Stag
30. 9	2. 9	A11	J1	Serpent
1.10	3. 9	A11	K2	Earthworm
2.10	4. 9	A11	A3	Crocodile
3.10	5. 9	A11	B4	Dragon
4.10	6. 9	A11	C5	Badger
5.10	7. 9	A11	D6	Hare
6.10	8. 9	A11	E7	Fox
7.10	9. 9	A11	F8	Tiger
8.10	10. 9	A11	G9	Leopard
9.10	11. 9	A11	H10	Griffon
10.10	12. 9	A11	J11	Ox
11.10	13. 9	A11	K12	Bat
12.10	14. 9	A11	A1	Rat
13.10	15. 9	A11	B2	Swallow
14.10	16. 9	A11	C3	Pig
15.10	17. 9	A11	D4	Porcupine
16.10	18. 9	A11	E5	Wolf
17.10	19. 9	A11	F6	Dog
18.10	20. 9	A11	G7	Pheasant
19.10	21. 9	A11	H8	Cock
20.10	22. 9	A11	J9	Crow
21.10	23. 9	A11	K10	Monkey
22.10	24. 9	A11	A11	Gibbon
23.10	25. 9	A11	B12	Tapir
24.10	26. 9	A11	C1	Sheep
25.10	27. 9	A11	D2	Deer
26.10	28. 9	A11	E3	Horse
27.10	29. 9	A11	F4	Stag
28.10	1.10	B12	G5	Serpent
29.10	2.10	B12	H6	Earthworm
30.10	3.10	B12	J7	Crocodile
31.10	4.10	B12	K8	Dragon
1.11	5.10	B12	A9	Badger
2.11	6.10	B12	B10	Hare
3.11	7.10	B12	C11	Fox
4.11	8.10	B12	D12	Tiger
5.11	9.10	B12	E1	Leopard
6.11	10.10	B12	F2	Griffon
7.11	11.10	B12	G3	Ox
8.11	12.10	B12	H4	Bat
9.11	13.10	B12	J5	Rat
10.11	14.10	B12	K6	Swallow
11.11	15.10	B12	A7	Pig
12.11	16.10	B12	B8	Porcupine
13.11	17.10	B12	C9	Wolf
14.11	18.10	B12	D10	Dog
15.11	19.10	B12	E11	Pheasant
16.11	20.10	B12	F12	Cock
17.11	21.10	B12	G1	Crow

Solar date	Lunar date	Month HS/EB	Day HS/EB	Constellation	Solar date	Lunar date	Month HS/EB	Day HS/EB	Constellation
18.11	22.10	B12	H2	Monkey	23.12	27.11	C1	C1	Serpent
19.11	23.10	B12	J3	Gibbon	24.12	28.11	C1	D2	Earthworm
20.11	24.10	B12	K4	Tapir	25.12	29.11	C1	E3	Crocodile
21.11	25.10	B12	A5	Sheep	26.12	1.12	D2	F4	Dragon
22.11	26.10	B12	B6	Deer	27.12	2.12	D2	G5	Badger
23.11	27.10	B12	C7	Horse	28.12	3.12	D2	H6	Hare
24.11	28.10	B12	D8	Stag	29.12	4.12	D2	J7	Fox
25.11	29.10	B12	E9	Serpent	30.12	5.12	D2	K8	Tiger
26.11	30.10	B12	F10	Earthworm	31.12	6.12	D2	A9	Leopard
27.11	1.11	C1	G11	Crocodile					
28.11	2.11	C1	H12	Dragon	**1925**				
29.11	3.11	C1	J1	Badger	1. 1	7.12	D2	B10	Griffon
30.11	4.11	C1	K2	Hare	2. 1	8.12	D2	C11	Ox
1.12	5.11	C1	A3	Fox	3. 1	9.12	D2	D12	Bat
2.12	6.11	C1	B4	Tiger	4. 1	10.12	D2	E1	Rat
3.12	7.11	C1	C5	Leopard	5. 1	11.12	D2	F2	Swallow
4.12	8.11	C1	D6	Griffon	6. 1	12.12	D2	G3	Pig
5.12	9.11	C1	E7	Ox	7. 1	13.12	D2	H4	Porcupine
6.12	10.11	C1	F8	Bat	8. 1	14.12	D2	J5	Wolf
7.12	11.11	C1	G9	Rat	9. 1	15.12	D2	K6	Dog
8.12	12.11	C1	H10	Swallow	10. 1	16.12	D2	A7	Pheasant
9.12	13.11	C1	J11	Pig	11. 1	17.12	D2	B8	Cock
10.12	14.11	C1	K12	Porcupine	12. 1	18.12	D2	C9	Crow
11.12	15.11	C1	A1	Wolf	13. 1	19.12	D2	D10	Monkey
12.12	16.11	C1	B2	Dog	14. 1	20.12	D2	E11	Gibbon
13.12	17.11	C1	C3	Pheasant	15. 1	21.12	D2	F12	Tapir
14.12	18.11	C1	D4	Cock	16. 1	22.12	D2	G1	Sheep
15.12	19.11	C1	E5	Crow	17. 1	23.12	D2	H2	Deer
16.12	20.11	C1	F6	Monkey	18. 1	24.12	D2	J3	Horse
17.12	21.11	C1	G7	Gibbon	19. 1	25.12	D2	K4	Stag
18.12	22.11	C1	H8	Tapir	20. 1	26.12	D2	A5	Serpent
19.12	23.11	C1	J9	Sheep	21. 1	27.12	D2	B6	Earthworm
20.12	24.11	C1	K10	Deer	22. 1	28.12	D2	C7	Crocodile
21.12	25.11	C1	A11	Horse	23. 1	29.12	D2	D8	Dragon
22.12	26.11	C1	B12	Stag					

YI CH'OU YEAR

24. 1	1. 1	E3	E9	Badger	26. 2	4. 2	F4	H6	Griffon
25. 1	2. 1	E3	F10	Hare	27. 2	5. 2	F4	J7	Ox
26. 1	3. 1	E3	G11	Fox	28. 2	6. 2	F4	K8	Bat
27. 1	4. 1	E3	H12	Tiger	1. 3	7. 2	F4	A9	Rat
28. 1	5. 1	E3	J1	Leopard	2. 3	8. 2	F4	B10	Swallow
29. 1	6. 1	E3	K2	Griffon	3. 3	9. 2	F4	C11	Pig
30. 1	7. 1	E3	A3	Ox	4. 3	10. 2	F4	D12	Porcupine
31. 1	8. 1	E3	B4	Bat	5. 3	11. 2	F4	E1	Wolf
1. 2	9. 1	E3	C5	Rat	6. 3	12. 2	F4	F2	Dog
2. 2	10. 1	E3	D6	Swallow	7. 3	13. 2	F4	G3	Pheasant
3. 2	11. 1	E3	E7	Pig	8. 3	14. 2	F4	H4	Cock
4. 2	12. 1	E3	F8	Porcupine	9. 3	15. 2	F4	J5	Crow
5. 2	13. 1	E3	G9	Wolf	10. 3	16. 2	F4	K6	Monkey
6. 2	14. 1	E3	H10	Dog	11. 3	17. 2	F4	A7	Gibbon
7. 2	15. 1	E3	J11	Pheasant	12. 3	18. 2	F4	B8	Tapir
8. 2	16. 1	E3	K12	Cock	13. 3	19. 2	F4	C9	Sheep
9. 2	17. 1	E3	A1	Crow	14. 3	20. 2	F4	D10	Deer
10. 2	18. 1	E3	B2	Monkey	15. 3	21. 2	F4	E11	Horse
11. 2	19. 1	E3	C3	Gibbon	16. 3	22. 2	F4	F12	Stag
12. 2	20. 1	E3	D4	Tapir	17. 3	23. 2	F4	G1	Serpent
13. 2	21. 1	E3	E5	Sheep	18. 3	24. 2	F4	H2	Earthworm
14. 2	22. 1	E3	F6	Deer	19. 3	25. 2	F4	J3	Crocodile
15. 2	23. 1	E3	G7	Horse	20. 3	26. 2	F4	K4	Dragon
16. 2	24. 1	E3	H8	Stag	21. 3	27. 2	F4	A5	Badger
17. 2	25. 1	E3	J9	Serpent	22. 3	28. 2	F4	B6	Hare
18. 2	26. 1	E3	K10	Earthworm	23. 3	29. 2	F4	C7	Fox
19. 2	27. 1	E3	A11	Crocodile	24. 3	1. 3	G5	D8	Tiger
20. 2	28. 1	E3	B12	Dragon	25. 3	2. 3	G5	E9	Leopard
21. 2	29. 1	E3	C1	Badger	26. 3	3. 3	G5	F10	Griffon
22. 2	30. 1	E3	D2	Hare	27. 3	4. 3	G5	G11	Ox
23. 2	1. 2	F4	E3	Fox	28. 3	5. 3	G5	H12	Bat
24. 2	2. 2	F4	F4	Tiger	29. 3	6. 3	G5	J1	Rat
25. 2	3. 2	F4	G5	Leopard	30. 3	7. 3	G5	K2	Swallow

Solar date	*Lunar date*	*Month HS/EB*	*Day HS/EB*	*Constellation*
31. 3	8. 3	G5	A3	Pig
1. 4	9. 3	G5	B4	Porcupine
2. 4	10. 3	G5	C5	Wolf
3. 4	11. 3	G5	D6	Dog
4. 4	12. 3	G5	E7	Pheasant
5. 4	13. 3	G5	F8	Cock
6. 4	14. 3	G5	G9	Crow
7. 4	15. 3	G5	H10	Monkey
8. 4	16. 3	G5	J11	Gibbon
9. 4	17. 3	G5	K12	Tapir
10. 4	18. 3	G5	A1	Sheep
11. 4	19. 3	G5	B2	Deer
12. 4	20. 3	G5	C3	Horse
13. 4	21. 3	G5	D4	Stag
14. 4	22. 3	G5	E5	Serpent
15. 4	23. 3	G5	F6	Earthworm
16. 4	24. 3	G5	G7	Crocodile
17. 4	25. 3	G5	H8	Dragon
18. 4	26. 3	G5	J9	Badger
19. 4	27. 3	G5	K10	Hare
20. 4	28. 3	G5	A11	Fox
21. 4	29. 3	G5	B12	Tiger
22. 4	30. 3	G5	C1	Leopard
23. 4	1. 4	H6	D2	Griffon
24. 4	2. 4	H6	E3	Ox
25. 4	3. 4	H6	F4	Bat
26. 4	4. 4	H6	G5	Rat
27. 4	5. 4	H6	H6	Swallow
28. 4	6. 4	H6	J7	Pig
29. 4	7. 4	H6	K8	Porcupine
30. 4	8. 4	H6	A9	Wolf
1. 5	9. 4	H6	B10	Dog
2. 5	10. 4	H6	C11	Pheasant
3. 5	11. 4	H6	D12	Cock
4. 5	12. 4	H6	E1	Crow
5. 5	13. 4	H6	F2	Monkey
6. 5	14. 4	H6	G3	Gibbon
7. 5	15. 4	H6	H4	Tapir
8. 5	16. 4	H6	J5	Sheep
9. 5	17. 4	H6	K6	Deer
10. 5	18. 4	H6	A7	Horse
11. 5	19. 4	H6	B8	Stag
12. 5	20. 4	H6	C9	Serpent
13. 5	21. 4	H6	D10	Earthworm
14. 5	22. 4	H6	E11	Crocodile
15. 5	23. 4	H6	F12	Dragon
16. 5	24. 4	H6	G1	Badger
17. 5	25. 4	H6	H2	Hare
18. 5	26. 4	H6	J3	Fox
19. 5	27. 4	H6	K4	Tiger
20. 5	28. 4	H6	A5	Leopard
21. 5	29. 4	H6	B6	Griffon
22. 5	*1. 4*	*H6*	C7	Ox
23. 5	*2. 4*	*H6*	D8	Bat
24. 5	*3. 4*	*H6*	E9	Rat
25. 5	*4. 4*	*H6*	F10	Swallow
26. 5	*5. 4*	*H6*	G11	Pig
27. 5	*6. 4*	*H6*	H12	Porcupine
28. 5	*7. 4*	*H6*	J1	Wolf
29. 5	*8. 4*	*H6*	K2	Dog
30. 5	*9. 4*	*H6*	A3	Pheasant
31. 5	*10. 4*	*H6*	B4	Cock
1. 6	*11. 4*	*H6*	C5	Crow
2. 6	*12. 4*	*H6*	D6	Monkey
3. 6	*13. 4*	*H6*	E7	Gibbon
4. 6	*14. 4*	*H6*	F8	Tapir
5. 6	*15. 4*	*H6*	G9	Sheep
6. 6	*16. 4*	*H6*	H10	Deer
7. 6	*17. 4*	*H6*	J11	Horse
8. 6	*18. 4*	*H6*	K12	Stag
9. 6	*19. 4*	*H6*	A1	Serpent
10. 6	*20. 4*	*H6*	B2	Earthworm
11. 6	*21. 4*	*H6*	C3	Crocodile
12. 6	*22. 4*	*H6*	D4	Dragon
13. 6	*23. 4*	*H6*	E5	Badger
14. 6	*24. 4*	*H6*	F6	Hare
15. 6	*25. 4*	*H6*	G7	Fox
16. 6	*26. 4*	*H6*	H8	Tiger
17. 6	*27. 4*	*H6*	J9	Leopard
18. 6	*28. 4*	*H6*	K10	Griffon
19. 6	*29. 4*	*H6*	A11	Ox
20. 6	*30. 4*	*H6*	B12	Bat
21. 6	1. 5	J7	C1	Rat
22. 6	2. 5	J7	D2	Swallow
23. 6	3. 5	J7	E3	Pig
24. 6	4. 5	J7	F4	Porcupine
25. 6	5. 5	J7	G5	Wolf
26. 6	6. 5	J7	H6	Dog
27. 6	7. 5	J7	J7	Pheasant
28. 6	8. 5	J7	K8	Cock
29. 6	9. 5	J7	A9	Crow
30. 6	10. 5	J7	B10	Monkey
1. 7	11. 5	J7	C11	Gibbon
2. 7	12. 5	J7	D12	Tapir
3. 7	13. 5	J7	E1	Sheep
4. 7	14. 5	J7	F2	Deer
5. 7	15. 5	J7	G3	Horse
6. 7	16. 5	J7	H4	Stag
7. 7	17. 5	J7	J5	Serpent
8. 7	18. 5	J7	K6	Earthworm
9. 7	19. 5	J7	A7	Crocodile
10. 7	20. 5	J7	B8	Dragon
11. 7	21. 5	J7	C9	Badger
12. 7	22. 5	J7	D10	Hare
13. 7	23. 5	J7	E11	Fox
14. 7	24. 5	J7	F12	Tiger
15. 7	25. 5	J7	G1	Leopard
16. 7	26. 5	J7	H2	Griffon
17. 7	27. 5	J7	J3	Ox
18. 7	28. 5	J7	K4	Bat
19. 7	29. 5	J7	A5	Rat
20. 7	30. 5	J7	B6	Swallow
21. 7	1. 6	K8	C7	Pig
22. 7	2. 6	K8	D8	Porcupine
23. 7	3. 6	K8	E9	Wolf
24. 7	4. 6	K8	F10	Dog
25. 7	5. 6	K8	G11	Pheasant
26. 7	6. 6	K8	H12	Cock
27. 7	7. 6	K8	J1	Crow
28. 7	8. 6	K8	K2	Monkey
29. 7	9. 6	K8	A3	Gibbon
30. 7	10. 6	K8	B4	Tapir
31. 7	11. 6	K8	C5	Sheep
1. 8	12. 6	K8	D6	Deer
2. 8	13. 6	K8	E7	Horse
3. 8	14. 6	K8	F8	Stag
4. 8	15. 6	K8	G9	Serpent
5. 8	16. 6	K8	H10	Earthworm
6. 8	17. 6	K8	J11	Crocodile
7. 8	18. 6	K8	K12	Dragon
8. 8	19. 6	K8	A1	Badger
9. 8	20. 6	K8	B2	Hare
10. 8	21. 6	K8	C3	Fox
11. 8	22. 6	K8	D4	Tiger
12. 8	23. 6	K8	E5	Leopard
13. 8	24. 6	K8	F6	Griffon
14. 8	25. 6	K8	G7	Ox
15. 8	26. 6	K8	H8	Bat
16. 8	27. 6	K8	J9	Rat
17. 8	28. 7	K8	K10	Swallow
18. 8	29. 7	K8	A11	Pig
19. 8	1. 7	A9	B12	Porcupine
20. 8	2. 7	A9	C1	Wolf
21. 8	3. 7	A9	D2	Dog
22. 8	4. 7	A9	E3	Pheasant
23. 8	5. 7	A9	F4	Cock

Solar date	Lunar date	Month HS/EB	Day HS/EB	Constellation
24. 8	6. 7	A9	G5	Crow
25. 8	7. 7	A9	H6	Monkey
26. 8	8. 7	A9	J7	Gibbon
27. 8	9. 7	A9	K8	Tapir
28. 8	10. 7	A9	A9	Sheep
29. 8	11. 7	A9	B10	Deer
30. 8	12. 7	A9	C11	Horse
31. 8	13. 7	A9	D12	Stag
1. 9	14. 7	A9	E1	Serpent
2. 9	15. 7	A9	F2	Earthworm
3. 9	16. 7	A9	G3	Crocodile
4. 9	17. 7	A9	H4	Dragon
5. 9	18. 7	A9	J5	Badger
6. 9	19. 7	A9	K6	Hare
7. 9	20. 7	A9	A7	Fox
8. 9	21. 7	A9	B8	Tiger
9. 9	22. 7	A9	C9	Leopard
10. 9	23. 7	A9	D10	Griffon
11. 9	24. 7	A9	E11	Ox
12. 9	25. 7	A9	F12	Bat
13. 9	26. 7	A9	G1	Rat
14. 9	27. 7	A9	H2	Swallow
15. 9	28. 7	A9	J3	Pig
16. 9	29. 7	A9	K4	Porcupine
17. 9	30. 7	A9	A5	Wolf
18. 9	1. 8	B10	B6	Dog
19. 9	2. 8	B10	C7	Pheasant
20. 9	3. 8	B10	D8	Cock
21. 9	4. 8	B10	E9	Crow
22. 9	5. 8	B10	F10	Monkey
23. 9	6. 8	B10	G11	Gibbon
24. 9	7. 8	B10	H12	Tapir
25. 9	8. 8	B10	J1	Sheep
26. 9	9. 8	B10	K2	Deer
27. 9	10. 8	B10	A3	Horse
28. 9	11. 8	B10	B4	Stag
29. 9	12. 8	B10	C5	Serpent
30. 9	13. 8	B10	D6	Earthworm
1.10	14. 8	B10	E7	Crocodile
2.10	15. 8	B10	F8	Dragon
3.10	16. 8	B10	G9	Badger
4.10	17. 8	B10	H10	Hare
5.10	18. 8	B10	J11	Fox
6.10	19. 8	B10	K12	Tiger
7.10	20. 8	B10	A1	Leopard
8.10	21. 8	B10	B2	Griffon
9.10	22. 8	B10	C3	Ox
10.10	23. 8	B10	D4	Bat
11.10	24. 8	B10	E5	Rat
12.10	25. 8	B10	F6	Swallow
13.10	26. 8	B10	G7	Pig
14.10	27. 8	B10	H8	Porcupine
15.10	28. 8	B10	J9	Wolf
16.10	29. 8	B10	K10	Dog
17.10	30. 8	B10	A11	Pheasant
18.10	1. 9	C11	B12	Cock
19.10	2. 9	C11	C1	Crow
20.10	3. 9	C11	D2	Monkey
21.10	4. 9	C11	E3	Gibbon
22.10	5. 9	C11	F4	Tapir
23.10	6. 9	C11	G5	Sheep
24.10	7. 9	C11	H6	Deer
25.10	8. 9	C11	J7	Horse
26.10	9. 9	C11	K8	Stag
27.10	10. 9	C11	A9	Serpent
28.10	11. 9	C11	B10	Earthworm
29.10	12. 9	C11	C11	Crocodile
30.10	13. 9	C11	D12	Dragon
31.10	14. 9	C11	E1	Badger
1.11	15. 9	C11	F2	Hare
2.11	16. 9	C11	G3	Fox
3.11	17. 9	C11	H4	Tiger
4.11	18. 9	C11	J5	Leopard
5.11	19. 9	C11	K6	Griffon
6.11	20. 9	C11	A7	Ox
7.11	21. 9	C11	B8	Bat
8.11	22. 9	C11	C9	Rat
9.11	23. 9	C11	D10	Swallow
10.11	24. 9	C11	E11	Pig
11.11	25. 9	C11	F12	Porcupine
12.11	26. 9	C11	G1	Wolf
13.11	27. 9	C11	H2	Dog
14.11	28. 9	C11	J3	Pheasant
15.11	29. 9	C11	K4	Cock
16.11	1.10	D12	A5	Crow
17.11	2.10	D12	B6	Monkey
18.11	3.10	D12	C7	Gibbon
19.11	4.10	D12	D8	Tapir
20.11	5.10	D12	E9	Sheep
21.11	6.10	D12	F10	Deer
22.11	7.10	D12	G11	Horse
23.11	8.10	D12	H12	Stag
24.11	9.10	D12	J1	Serpent
25.11	10.10	D12	K2	Earthworm
26.11	11.10	D12	A3	Crocodile
27.11	12.10	D12	B4	Dragon
28.11	13.10	D12	C5	Badger
29.11	14.10	D12	D6	Hare
30.11	15.10	D12	E7	Fox
1.12	16.10	D12	F8	Tiger
2.12	17.10	D12	G9	Leopard
3.12	18.10	D12	H10	Griffon
4.12	19.10	D12	J11	Ox
5.12	20.10	D12	K12	Bat
6.12	21.10	D12	A1	Rat
7.12	22.10	D12	B2	Swallow
8.12	23.10	D12	C3	Pig
9.12	24.10	D12	D4	Porcupine
10.12	25.10	D12	E5	Wolf
11.12	26.10	D12	F6	Dog
12.12	27.10	D12	G7	Pheasant
13.12	28.10	D12	H8	Cock
14.12	29.10	D12	J9	Crow
15.12	30.10	D12	K10	Monkey
16.12	1.11	E1	A11	Gibbon
17.12	2.11	E1	B12	Tapir
18.12	3.11	E1	C1	Sheep
19.12	4.11	E1	D2	Deer
20.12	5.11	E1	E3	Horse
21.12	6.11	E1	F4	Stag
22.12	7.11	E1	G5	Serpent
23.12	8.11	E1	H6	Earthworm
24.12	9.11	E1	J7	Crocodile
25.12	10.11	E1	K8	Dragon
26.12	11.11	E1	A9	Badger
27.12	12.11	E1	B10	Hare
28.12	13.11	E1	C11	Fox
29.12	14.11	E1	D12	Tiger
30.12	15.11	E1	E1	Leopard
31.12	16.11	E1	F2	Griffon
1926				
1. 1	17.11	E1	G3	Ox
2. 1	18.11	E1	H4	Bat
3. 1	19.11	E1	J5	Rat
4. 1	20.11	E1	K6	Swallow
5. 1	21.11	E1	A7	Pig
6. 1	22.11	E1	B8	Porcupine
7. 1	23.11	E1	C9	Wolf
8. 1	24.11	E1	D10	Dog
9. 1	25.11	E1	E11	Pheasant
10. 1	26.11	E1	F12	Cock
11. 1	27.11	E1	G1	Crow
12. 1	28.11	E1	H2	Monkey
13. 1	29.11	E1	J3	Gibbon
14. 1	1.12	F2	K4	Tapir

Solar date	*Lunar date*	*Month HS/EB*	*Day HS/EB*	*Constellation*
15. 1	2.12	F2	A5	Sheep
16. 1	3.12	F2	B6	Deer
17. 1	4.12	F2	C7	Horse
18. 1	5.12	F2	D8	Stag
19. 1	6.12	F2	E9	Serpent
20. 1	7.12	F2	F10	Earthworm
21. 1	8.12	F2	G11	Crocodile
22. 1	9.12	F2	H12	Dragon
23. 1	10.12	F2	J1	Badger
24. 1	11.12	F2	K2	Hare
25. 1	12.12	F2	A3	Fox
26. 1	13.12	F2	B4	Tiger
27. 1	14.12	F2	C5	Leopard
28. 1	15.12	F2	D6	Griffon
29. 1	16.12	F2	E7	Ox
30. 1	17.12	F2	F8	Bat
31. 1	18.12	F2	G9	Rat
1. 2	19.12	F2	H10	Swallow
2. 2	20.12	F2	J11	Pig
3. 2	21.12	F2	K12	Porcupine
4. 2	22.12	F2	A1	Wolf
5. 2	23.12	F2	B2	Dog
6. 2	24.12	F2	C3	Pheasant
7. 2	25.12	F2	D4	Cock
8. 2	26.12	F2	E5	Crow
9. 2	27.12	F2	F6	Monkey
10. 2	28.12	F2	G7	Gibbon
11. 2	29.12	F2	H8	Tapir
12. 2	30.12	F2	J9	Sheep

PING YIN YEAR

13. 2	1. 1	G3	K10	Deer
14. 2	2. 1	G3	A11	Horse
15. 2	3. 1	G3	B12	Stag
16. 2	4. 1	G3	C1	Serpent
17. 2	5. 1	G3	D2	Earthworm
18. 2	6. 1	G3	E3	Crocodile
19. 2	7. 1	G3	F4	Dragon
20. 2	8. 1	G3	G5	Badger
21. 2	9. 1	G3	H6	Hare
22. 2	10. 1	G3	J7	Fox
23. 2	11. 1	G3	K8	Tiger
24. 2	12. 1	G3	A9	Leopard
25. 2	13. 1	G3	B10	Griffon
26. 2	14. 1	G3	C11	Ox
27. 2	15. 1	G3	D12	Bat
28. 2	16. 1	G3	E1	Rat
1. 3	17. 1	G3	F2	Swallow
2. 3	18. 1	G3	G3	Pig
3. 3	19. 1	G3	H4	Porcupine
4. 3	20. 1	G3	J5	Wolf
5. 3	21. 1	G3	K6	Dog
6. 3	22. 1	G3	A7	Pheasant
7. 3	23. 1	G3	B8	Cock
8. 3	24. 1	G3	C9	Crow
9. 3	25. 1	G3	D10	Monkey
10. 3	26. 1	G3	E11	Gibbon
11. 3	27. 1	G3	F12	Tapir
12. 3	28. 1	G3	G1	Sheep
13. 3	29. 1	G3	H2	Deer
14. 3	1. 2	H4	J3	Horse
15. 3	2. 2	H4	K4	Stag
16. 3	3. 2	H4	A5	Serpent
17. 3	4. 2	H4	B6	Earthworm
18. 3	5. 2	H4	C7	Crocodile
19. 3	6. 2	H4	D8	Dragon
20. 3	7. 2	H4	E9	Badger
21. 3	8. 2	H4	F10	Hare
22. 3	9. 2	H4	G11	Fox
23. 3	10. 2	H4	H12	Tiger
24. 3	11. 2	H4	J1	Leopard
25. 3	12. 2	H4	K2	Griffon
26. 3	13. 2	H4	A3	Ox
27. 3	14. 2	H4	B4	Bat
28. 3	15. 2	H4	C5	Rat
29. 3	16. 2	H4	D6	Swallow
30. 3	17. 2	H4	E7	Pig
31. 3	18. 2	H4	F8	Porcupine
1. 4	19. 2	H4	G9	Wolf
2. 4	20. 2	H4	H10	Dog
3. 4	21. 2	H4	J11	Pheasant
4. 4	22. 2	H4	K12	Cock
5. 4	23. 2	H4	A1	Crow
6. 4	24. 2	H4	B2	Monkey
7. 4	25. 2	H4	C3	Gibbon
8. 4	26. 2	H4	D4	Tapir
9. 4	27. 2	H4	E5	Sheep
10. 4	28. 2	H4	F6	Deer
11. 4	29. 2	H4	G7	Horse
12. 4	1. 3	J5	H8	Stag
13. 4	2. 3	J5	J9	Serpent
14. 4	3. 3	J5	K10	Earthworm
15. 4	4. 3	J5	A11	Crocodile
16. 4	5. 3	J5	B12	Dragon
17. 4	6. 3	J5	C1	Badger
18. 4	7. 3	J5	D2	Hare
19. 4	8. 3	J5	E3	Fox
20. 4	9. 3	J5	F4	Tiger
21. 4	10. 3	J5	G5	Leopard
22. 4	11. 3	J5	H6	Griffon
23. 4	12. 3	J5	J7	Ox
24. 4	13. 3	J5	K8	Bat
25. 4	14. 3	J5	A9	Rat
26. 4	15. 3	J5	B10	Swallow
27. 4	16. 3	J5	C11	Pig
28. 4	17. 3	J5	D12	Porcupine
29. 4	18. 3	J5	E1	Wolf
30. 4	19. 3	J5	F2	Dog
1. 5	20. 3	J5	G3	Pheasant
2. 5	21. 3	J5	H4	Cock
3. 5	22. 3	J5	J5	Crow
4. 5	23. 3	J5	K6	Monkey
5. 5	24. 3	J5	A7	Gibbon
6. 5	25. 3	J5	B8	Tapir
7. 5	26. 3	J5	C9	Sheep
8. 5	27. 3	J5	D10	Deer
9. 5	28. 3	J5	E11	Horse
10. 5	29. 3	J5	F12	Stag
11. 5	30. 3	J5	G1	Serpent
12. 5	1. 4	K6	H2	Earthworm
13. 5	2. 4	K6	J3	Crocodile
14. 5	3. 4	K6	K4	Dragon
15. 5	4. 4	K6	A5	Badger
16. 5	5. 4	K6	B6	Hare
17. 5	6. 4	K6	C7	Fox
18. 5	7. 4	K6	D8	Tiger
19. 5	8. 4	K6	E9	Leopard
20. 5	9. 4	K6	F10	Griffon
21. 5	10. 4	K6	G11	Ox
22. 5	11. 4	K6	H12	Bat
23. 5	12. 4	K6	J1	Rat
24. 5	13. 4	K6	K2	Swallow
25. 5	14. 4	K6	A3	Pig
26. 5	15. 4	K6	B4	Porcupine
27. 5	16. 4	K6	C5	Wolf
28. 5	17. 4	K6	D6	Dog
29. 5	18. 4	K6	E7	Pheasant

Solar date	*Lunar date*	*Month HS/EB*	*Day HS/EB*	*Constellation*
30. 5	19. 4	K6	F8	Cock
31. 5	20. 4	K6	G9	Crow
1. 6	21. 4	K6	H10	Monkey
2. 6	22. 4	K6	J11	Gibbon
3. 6	23. 4	K6	K12	Tapir
4. 6	24. 4	K6	A1	Sheep
5. 6	25. 4	K6	B2	Deer
6. 6	26. 4	K6	C3	Horse
7. 6	27. 4	K6	D4	Stag
8. 6	28. 4	K6	E5	Serpent
9. 6	29. 4	K6	F6	Earthworm
10. 6	1. 5	A7	G7	Crocodile
11. 6	2. 5	A7	H8	Dragon
12. 6	3. 5	A7	J9	Badger
13. 6	4. 5	A7	K10	Hare
14. 6	5. 5	A7	A11	Fox
15. 6	6. 5	A7	B12	Tiger
16. 6	7. 5	A7	C1	Leopard
17. 6	8. 5	A7	D2	Griffon
18. 6	9. 5	A7	E3	Ox
19. 6	10. 5	A7	F4	Bat
20. 6	11. 5	A7	G5	Rat
21. 6	12. 5	A7	H6	Swallow
22. 6	13. 5	A7	J7	Pig
23. 6	14. 5	A7	K8	Porcupine
24. 6	15. 5	A7	A9	Wolf
25. 6	16. 5	A7	B10	Dog
26. 6	17. 5	A7	C11	Pheasant
27. 6	18. 5	A7	D12	Cock
28. 6	19. 5	A7	E1	Crow
29. 6	20. 5	A7	F2	Monkey
30. 6	21. 5	A7	G3	Gibbon
1. 7	22. 5	A7	H4	Tapir
2. 7	23. 5	A7	J5	Sheep
3. 7	24. 5	A7	K6	Deer
4. 7	25. 5	A7	A7	Horse
5. 7	26. 5	A7	B8	Stag
6. 7	27. 5	A7	C9	Serpent
7. 7	28. 5	A7	D10	Earthworm
8. 7	29. 5	A7	E11	Crocodile
9. 7	30. 5	A7	F12	Dragon
10. 7	1. 6	B8	G1	Badger
11. 7	2. 6	B8	H2	Hare
12. 7	3. 6	B8	J3	Fox
13. 7	4. 6	B8	K4	Tiger
14. 7	5. 6	B8	A5	Leopard
15. 7	6. 6	B8	B6	Griffon
16. 7	7. 6	B8	C7	Ox
17. 7	8. 6	B8	D8	Bat
18. 7	9. 6	B8	E9	Rat
19. 7	10. 6	B8	F10	Swallow
20. 7	11. 6	B8	G11	Pig
21. 7	12. 6	B8	H12	Porcupine
22. 7	13. 6	B8	J1	Wolf
23. 7	14. 6	B8	K2	Dog
24. 7	15. 6	B8	A3	Pheasant
25. 7	16. 6	B8	B4	Cock
26. 7	17. 6	B8	C5	Crow
27. 7	18. 6	B8	D6	Monkey
28. 7	19. 6	B8	E7	Gibbon
29. 7	20. 6	B8	F8	Tapir
30. 7	21. 6	B8	G9	Sheep
31. 7	22. 6	B8	H10	Deer
1. 8	23. 6	B8	J11	Horse
2. 8	24. 6	B8	K12	Stag
3. 8	25. 6	B8	A1	Serpent
4. 8	26. 6	B8	B2	Earthworm
5. 8	27. 6	B8	C3	Crocodile
6. 8	28. 6	B8	D4	Dragon
7. 8	29. 6	B8	E5	Badger
8. 8	1. 7	C9	F6	Hare
9. 8	2. 7	C9	G7	Fox
10. 8	3. 7	C9	H8	Tiger

Solar date	*Lunar date*	*Month HS/EB*	*Day HS/EB*	*Constellation*
11. 8	4. 7	C9	J9	Leopard
12. 8	5. 7	C9	K10	Griffon
13. 8	6. 7	C9	A11	Ox
14. 8	7. 7	C9	B12	Bat
15. 8	8. 7	C9	C1	Rat
16. 8	9. 7	C9	D2	Swallow
17. 8	10. 7	C9	E3	Pig
18. 8	11. 7	C9	F4	Porcupine
19. 8	12. 7	C9	G5	Wolf
20. 8	13. 7	C9	H6	Dog
21. 8	14. 7	C9	J7	Pheasant
22. 8	15. 7	C9	K8	Cock
23. 8	16. 7	C9	A9	Crow
24. 8	17. 7	C9	B10	Monkey
25. 8	18. 7	C9	C11	Gibbon
26. 8	19. 7	C9	D12	Tapir
27. 8	20. 7	C9	E1	Sheep
28. 8	21. 7	C9	F2	Deer
29. 8	22. 7	C9	G3	Horse
30. 8	23. 7	C9	H4	Stag
31. 8	24. 7	C9	J5	Serpent
1. 9	25. 7	C9	K6	Earthworm
2. 9	26. 7	C9	A7	Crocodile
3. 9	27. 7	C9	B8	Dragon
4. 9	28. 7	C9	C9	Badger
5. 9	29. 7	C9	D10	Hare
6. 9	30. 7	C9	E11	Fox
7. 9	1. 8	D10	F12	Tiger
8. 9	2. 8	D10	G1	Leopard
9. 9	3. 8	D10	H2	Griffon
10. 9	4. 8	D10	J3	Ox
11. 9	5. 8	D10	K4	Bat
12. 9	6. 8	D10	A5	Rat
13. 9	7. 8	D10	B6	Swallow
14. 9	8. 8	D10	C7	Pig
15. 9	9. 8	D10	D8	Porcupine
16. 9	10. 8	D10	E9	Wolf
17. 9	11. 8	D10	F10	Dog
18. 9	12. 8	D10	G11	Pheasant
19. 9	13. 8	D10	H12	Cock
20. 9	14. 8	D10	J1	Crow
21. 9	15. 8	D10	K2	Monkey
22. 9	16. 8	D10	A3	Gibbon
23. 9	17. 8	D10	B4	Tapir
24. 9	18. 8	D10	C5	Sheep
25. 9	19. 8	D10	D6	Deer
26. 9	20. 8	D10	E7	Horse
27. 9	21. 8	D10	F8	Stag
28. 9	22. 8	D10	G9	Serpent
29. 9	23. 8	D10	H10	Earthworm
30. 9	24. 8	D10	J11	Crocodile
1.10	25. 8	D10	K12	Dragon
2.10	26. 8	D10	A1	Badger
3.10	27. 8	D10	B2	Hare
4.10	28. 8	D10	C3	Fox
5.10	29. 8	D10	D4	Tiger
6.10	30. 8	D10	E5	Leopard
7.10	1. 9	E11	F6	Griffon
8.10	2. 9	E11	G7	Ox
9.10	3. 9	E11	H8	Bat
10.10	4. 9	E11	J9	Rat
11.10	5. 9	E11	K10	Swallow
12.10	6. 9	E11	A11	Pig
13.10	7. 9	E11	B12	Porcupine
14.10	8. 9	E11	C1	Wolf
15.10	9. 9	E11	D2	Dog
16.10	10. 9	E11	E3	Pheasant
17.10	11. 9	E11	F4	Cock
18.10	12. 9	E11	G5	Crow
19.10	13. 9	E11	H6	Monkey
20.10	14. 9	E11	J7	Gibbon
21.10	15. 9	E11	K8	Tapir
22.10	16. 9	E11	A9	Sheep

Solar date	Lunar date	Month HS/EB	Day HS/EB	Constellation
23.10	17. 9	E11	B10	Deer
24.10	18. 9	E11	C11	Horse
25.10	19. 9	E11	D12	Stag
26.10	20. 9	E11	E1	Serpent
27.10	21. 9	E11	F2	Earthworm
28.10	22. 9	E11	G3	Crocodile
29.10	23. 9	E11	H4	Dragon
30.10	24. 9	E11	J5	Badger
31.10	25. 9	E11	K6	Hare
1.11	26. 9	E11	A7	Fox
2.11	27. 9	E11	B8	Tiger
3.11	28. 9	E11	C9	Leopard
4.11	29. 9	E11	D10	Griffon
5.11	1.10	F12	E11	Ox
6.11	2.10	F12	F12	Bat
7.11	3.10	F12	G1	Rat
8.11	4.10	F12	H2	Swallow
9.11	5.10	F12	J3	Pig
10.11	6.10	F12	K4	Porcupine
11.11	7.10	F12	A5	Wolf
12.11	8.10	F12	B6	Dog
13.11	9.10	F12	C7	Pheasant
14.11	10.10	F12	D8	Cock
15.11	11.10	F12	E9	Crow
16.11	12.10	F12	F10	Monkey
17.11	13.10	F12	G11	Gibbon
18.11	14.10	F12	H12	Tapir
19.11	15.10	F12	J1	Sheep
20.11	16.10	F12	K2	Deer
21.11	17.10	F12	A3	Horse
22.11	18.10	F12	B4	Stag
23.11	19.10	F12	C5	Serpent
24.11	20.10	F12	D6	Earthworm
25.11	21.10	F12	E7	Crocdile
26.11	22.10	F12	F8	Dragon
27.11	23.10	F12	G9	Badger
28.11	24.10	F12	H10	Hare
29.11	25.10	F12	J11	Fox
30.11	26.10	F12	K12	Tiger
1.12	27.10	F12	A1	Leopard
2.12	28.10	F12	B2	Griffon
3.12	29.10	F12	C3	Ox
4.12	30.10	F12	D4	Bat
5.12	1.11	G1	E5	Rat
6.12	2.11	G1	F6	Swallow
7.12	3.11	G1	G7	Pig
8.12	4.11	G1	H8	Porcupine
9.12	5.11	G1	J9	Wolf
10.12	6.11	G1	K10	Dog
11.12	7.11	G1	A11	Pheasant
12.12	8.11	G1	B12	Cock
13.12	9.11	G1	C1	Crow

Solar date	Lunar date	Month HS/EB	Day HS/EB	Constellation
14.12	10.11	G1	D2	Monkey
15.12	11.11	G1	E3	Gibbon
16.12	12.11	G1	F4	Tapir
17.12	13.11	G1	G5	Sheep
18.12	14.11	G1	H6	Deer
19.12	15.11	G1	J7	Horse
20.12	16.11	G1	K8	Stag
21.12	17.11	G1	A9	Serpent
22.12	18.11	G1	B10	Earthworm
23.12	19.11	G1	C11	Crocodile
24.12	20.11	G1	D12	Dragon
25.12	21.11	G1	E1	Badger
26.12	22.11	G1	F2	Hare
27.12	23.11	G1	G3	Fox
28.12	24.11	G1	H4	Tiger
29.12	25.11	G1	J5	Leopard
30.12	26.11	G1	K6	Griffon
31.12	27.11	G1	A7	Ox
1927				
1. 1	28.11	G1	B8	Bat
2. 1	29.11	G1	C9	Rat
3. 1	30.11	G1	D10	Swallow
4. 1	1.12	H2	E11	Pig
5. 1	2.12	H2	F12	Porcupine
6. 1	3.12	H2	G1	Wolf
7. 1	4.12	H2	H2	Dog
8. 1	5.12	H2	J3	Pheasant
9. 1	6.12	H2	K4	Cock
10. 1	7.12	H2	A5	Crow
11. 1	8.12	H2	B6	Monkey
12. 1	9.12	H2	C7	Gibbon
13. 1	10.12	H2	D8	Tapir
14. 1	11.12	H2	E9	Sheep
15. 1	12.12	H2	F10	Deer
16. 1	13.12	H2	G11	Horse
17. 1	14.12	H2	H12	Stag
18. 1	15.12	H2	J1	Serpent
19. 1	16.12	H2	K2	Earthworm
20. 1	17.12	H2	A3	Crocodile
21. 1	18.12	H2	B4	Dragon
22. 1	19.12	H2	C5	Badger
23. 1	20.12	H2	D6	Hare
24. 1	21.12	H2	E7	Fox
25. 1	22.12	H2	F8	Tiger
26. 1	23.12	H2	G9	Leopard
27. 1	24.12	H2	H10	Griffon
28. 1	25.12	H2	J11	Ox
29. 1	26.12	H2	K12	Bat
30. 1	27.12	H2	A1	Rat
31. 1	28.12	H2	B2	Swallow
1. 2	29.12	H2	C3	Pig

TING MAO YEAR

2. 2	1. 1	J3	D4	Porcupine
3. 2	2. 1	J3	E5	Wolf
4. 2	3. 1	J3	F6	Dog
5. 2	4. 1	J3	G7	Pheasant
6. 2	5. 1	J3	H8	Cock
7. 2	6. 1	J3	J9	Crow
8. 2	7. 1	J3	K10	Monkey
9. 2	8. 1	J3	A11	Gibbon
10. 2	9. 1	J3	B12	Tapir
11. 2	10. 1	J3	C1	Sheep
12. 2	11. 1	J3	D2	Deer
13. 2	12. 1	J3	E3	Horse
14. 2	13. 1	J3	F4	Stag
15. 2	14. 1	J3	G5	Serpent
16. 2	15. 1	J3	H6	Earthworm
17. 2	16. 1	J3	J7	Crocodile
18. 2	17. 1	J3	K8	Dragon
19. 2	18. 1	J3	A9	Badger
20. 2	19. 1	J3	B10	Hare
21. 2	20. 1	J3	C11	Fox
22. 2	21. 1	J3	D12	Tiger
23. 2	22. 1	J3	E1	Leopard
24. 2	23. 1	J3	F2	Griffon
25. 2	24. 1	J3	G3	Ox
26. 2	25. 1	J3	H4	Bat
27. 2	26. 1	J3	J5	Rat
28. 2	27. 1	J3	K6	Swallow
1. 3	28. 1	J3	A7	Pig
2. 3	29. 1	J3	B8	Porcupine
3. 3	30. 1	J3	C9	Wolf
4. 3	1. 2	K4	D10	Dog
5. 3	2. 2	K4	E11	Pheasant

Solar date	*Lunar date*	*Month HS/EB*	*Day HS/EB*	*Constellation*
6. 3	3. 2	K4	F12	Cock
7. 3	4. 2	K4	G1	Crow
8. 3	5. 2	K4	H2	Monkey
9. 3	6. 2	K4	J3	Gibbon
10. 3	7. 2	K4	K4	Tapir
11. 3	8. 2	K4	A5	Sheep
12. 3	9. 2	K4	B6	Deer
13. 3	10. 2	K4	C7	Horse
14. 3	11. 2	K4	D8	Stag
15. 3	12. 2	K4	E9	Serpent
16. 3	13. 2	K4	F10	Earthworm
17. 3	14. 2	K4	G11	Crocodile
18. 3	15. 2	K4	H12	Dragon
19. 3	16. 2	K4	J1	Badger
20. 3	17. 2	K4	K2	Hare
21. 3	18. 2	K4	A3	Fox
22. 3	19. 2	K4	B4	Tiger
23. 3	20. 2	K4	C5	Leopard
24. 3	21. 2	K4	D6	Griffon
25. 3	22. 2	K4	E7	Ox
26. 3	23. 2	K4	F8	Bat
27. 3	24. 2	K4	G9	Rat
28. 3	25. 2	K4	H10	Swallow
29. 3	26. 2	K4	J11	Pig
30. 3	27. 2	K4	K12	Porcupine
31. 3	28. 2	K4	A1	Wolf
1. 4	29. 2	K4	B2	Dog
2. 4	1. 3	A5	C3	Pheasant
3. 4	2. 3	A5	D4	Cock
4. 4	3. 3	A5	E5	Crow
5. 4	4. 3	A5	F6	Monkey
6. 4	5. 3	A5	G7	Gibbon
7. 4	6. 3	A5	H8	Tapir
8. 4	7. 3	A5	J9	Sheep
9. 4	8. 3	A5	K10	Deer
10. 4	9. 3	A5	A11	Horse
11. 4	10. 3	A5	B12	Stag
12. 4	11. 3	A5	C1	Serpent
13. 4	12. 3	A5	D2	Earthworm
14. 4	13. 3	A5	E3	Crocodile
15. 4	14. 3	A5	F4	Dragon
16. 4	15. 3	A5	G5	Badger
17. 4	16. 3	A5	H6	Hare
18. 4	17. 3	A5	J7	Fox
19. 4	18. 3	A5	K8	Tiger
20. 4	19. 3	A5	A9	Leopard
21. 4	20. 3	A5	B10	Griffon
22. 4	21. 3	A5	C11	Ox
23. 4	22. 3	A5	D12	Bat
24. 4	23. 3	A5	E1	Rat
25. 4	24. 3	A5	F2	Swallow
26. 4	25. 3	A5	G3	Pig
27. 4	26. 3	A5	H4	Porcupine
28. 4	27. 3	A5	J5	Wolf
29. 4	28. 3	A5	K6	Dog
30. 4	29. 3	A5	A7	Pheasant
1. 5	1. 4	B6	B8	Cock
2. 5	2. 4	B6	C9	Crow
3. 5	3. 4	B6	D10	Monkey
4. 5	4. 4	B6	E11	Gibbon
5. 5	5. 4	B6	F12	Tapir
6. 5	6. 4	B6	G1	Sheep
7. 5	7. 4	B6	H2	Deer
8. 5	8. 4	B6	J3	Horse
9. 5	9. 4	B6	K4	Stag
10. 5	10. 4	B6	A5	Serpent
11. 5	11. 4	B6	B6	Earthworm
12. 5	12. 4	B6	C7	Crocodile
13. 5	13. 4	B6	D8	Dragon
14. 5	14. 4	B6	E9	Badger
15. 5	15. 4	B6	F10	Hare
16. 5	16. 4	B6	G11	Fox
17. 5	17. 4	B6	H12	Tiger
18. 5	18. 4	B6	J1	Leopard
19. 5	19. 4	B6	K2	Griffon
20. 5	20. 4	B6	A3	Ox
21. 5	21. 4	B6	B4	Bat
22. 5	22. 4	B6	C5	Rat
23. 5	23. 4	B6	D6	Swallow
24. 5	24. 4	B6	E7	Pig
25. 5	25. 4	B6	F8	Porcupine
26. 5	26. 4	B6	G9	Wolf
27. 5	27. 4	B6	H10	Dog
28. 5	28. 4	B6	J11	Pheasant
29. 5	29. 4	B6	K12	Cock
30. 5	30. 4	B6	A1	Crow
31. 5	1. 5	C7	B2	Monkey
1. 6	2. 5	C7	C3	Gibbon
2. 6	3. 5	C7	D4	Tapir
3. 6	4. 5	C7	E5	Sheep
4. 6	5. 5	C7	F6	Deer
5. 6	6. 5	C7	G7	Horse
6. 6	7. 5	C7	H8	Stag
7. 6	8. 5	C7	J9	Serpent
8. 6	9. 5	C7	K10	Earthworm
9. 6	10. 5	C7	A11	Crocodile
10. 6	11. 5	C7	B12	Dragon
11. 6	12. 5	C7	C1	Badger
12. 6	13. 5	C7	D2	Hare
13. 6	14. 5	C7	E3	Fox
14. 6	15. 5	C7	F4	Tiger
15. 6	16. 5	C7	G5	Leopard
16. 6	17. 5	C7	H6	Griffon
17. 6	18. 5	C7	J7	Ox
18. 6	19. 5	C7	K8	Bat
19. 6	20. 5	C7	A9	Rat
20. 6	21. 5	C7	B10	Swallow
21. 6	22. 5	C7	C11	Pig
22. 6	23. 5	C7	D12	Porcupine
23. 6	24. 5	C7	E1	Wolf
24. 6	25. 5	C7	F2	Dog
25. 6	26. 5	C7	G3	Pheasant
26. 6	27. 5	C7	H4	Cock
27 6	28. 5	C7	J5	Crow
28. 6	29. 5	C7	K6	Monkey
29. 6	1. 6	D8	A7	Gibbon
30. 6	2. 6	D8	B8	Tapir
1. 7	3. 6	D8	C9	Sheep
2. 7	4. 6	D8	D10	Deer
3. 7	5. 6	D8	E11	Horse
4. 7	6. 6	D8	F12	Stag
5. 7	7. 6	D8	G1	Serpent
6. 7	8. 6	D8	H2	Earthworm
7. 7	9. 6	D8	J3	Crocodile
8. 7	10. 6	D8	K4	Dragon
9. 7	11. 6	D8	A5	Badger
10. 7	12. 6	D8	B6	Hare
11. 7	13. 6	D8	C7	Fox
12. 7	14. 6	D8	D8	Tiger
13. 7	15. 6	D8	E9	Leopard
14. 7	16. 6	D8	F10	Griffon
15. 7	17. 6	D8	G11	Ox
16. 7	18. 6	D8	H12	Bat
17. 7	19. 6	D8	J1	Rat
18. 7	20. 6	D8	K2	Swallow
19. 7	21. 6	D8	A3	Pig
20. 7	22. 6	D8	B4	Porcupine
21. 7	23. 6	D8	C5	Wolf
22. 7	24. 6	D8	D6	Dog
23. 7	25. 6	D8	E7	Pheasant
24. 7	26. 6	D8	F8	Cock
25. 7	27. 6	D8	G9	Crow
26. 7	28. 6	D8	H10	Monkey
27. 7	29. 6	D8	J11	Gibbon
28. 7	30. 6	D8	K12	Tapir
29. 7	1. 7	E9	A1	Sheep

Solar date	*Lunar date*	*Month HS/EB*	*Day HS/EB*	*Constellation*
30. 7	2. 7	E9	B2	Deer
31. 7	3. 7	E9	C3	Horse
1. 8	4. 7	E9	D4	Stag
2. 8	5. 7	E9	E5	Serpent
3. 8	6. 7	E9	F6	Earthworm
4. 8	7. 7	E9	G7	Crocodile
5. 8	8. 7	E9	H8	Dragon
6. 8	9. 7	E9	J9	Badger
7. 8	10. 7	E9	K10	Hare
8. 8	11. 7	E9	A11	Fox
9. 8	12. 7	E9	B12	Tiger
10. 8	13. 7	E9	C1	Leopard
11. 8	14. 7	E9	D2	Griffon
12. 8	15. 7	E9	E3	Ox
13. 8	16. 7	E9	F4	Bat
14. 8	17. 7	E9	G5	Rat
15. 8	18. 7	E9	H6	Swallow
16. 8	19. 7	E9	J7	Pig
17. 8	20. 7	E9	K8	Porcupine
18. 8	21. 7	E9	A9	Wolf
19. 8	22. 7	E9	B10	Dog
20. 8	23. 7	E9	C11	Pheasant
21. 8	24. 7	E9	D12	Cock
22. 8	25. 7	E9	E1	Crow
23. 8	26. 7	E9	F2	Monkey
24. 8	27. 7	E9	G3	Gibbon
25. 8	28. 7	E9	H4	Tapir
26. 8	29. 7	E9	J5	Sheep
27. 8	1. 8	F10	K6	Deer
28. 8	2. 8	F10	A7	Horse
29. 8	3. 8	F10	B8	Stag
30. 8	4. 8	F10	C9	Serpent
31. 8	5. 8	F10	D10	Earthworm
1. 9	6. 8	F10	E11	Crocodile
2. 9	7. 8	F10	F12	Dragon
3. 9	8. 8	F10	G1	Badger
4. 9	9. 8	F10	H2	Hare
5. 9	10. 8	F10	J3	Fox
6. 9	11. 8	F10	K4	Tiger
7. 9	12. 8	F10	A5	Leopard
8. 9	13. 8	F10	B6	Griffon
9. 9	14. 8	F10	C7	Ox
10. 9	15. 8	F10	D8	Bat
11. 9	16. 8	F10	E9	Rat
12. 9	17. 8	F10	F10	Swallow
13. 9	18. 8	F10	G11	Pig
14. 9	19. 8	F10	H12	Porcupine
15. 9	20. 8	F10	J1	Wolf
16. 9	21. 8	F10	K2	Dog
17. 9	22. 8	F10	A3	Pheasant
18. 9	23. 8	F10	B4	Cock
19. 9	24. 8	F10	C5	Crow
20. 9	25. 8	F10	D6	Monkey
21. 9	26. 8	F10	E7	Gibbon
22. 9	27. 8	F10	F8	Tapir
23. 9	28. 8	F10	G9	Sheep
24. 9	29. 8	F10	H10	Deer
25. 9	30. 8	F10	J11	Horse
26. 9	1. 9	G11	K12	Stag
27. 9	2. 9	G11	A1	Serpent
28. 9	3. 9	G11	B2	Earthworm
29. 9	4. 9	G11	C3	Crocodile
30. 9	5. 9	G11	D4	Dragon
1.10	6. 9	G11	E5	Badger
2.10	7. 9	G11	F6	Hare
3.10	8. 9	G11	G7	Fox
4.10	9. 9	G11	H8	Tiger
5.10	10. 9	G11	J9	Leopard
6.10	11. 9	G11	K10	Griffon
7.10	12. 9	G11	A11	Ox
8.10	13. 9	G11	B12	Bat
9.10	14. 9	G11	C1	Rat
10.10	15. 9	G11	D2	Swallow
11.10	16. 9	G11	E3	Pig
12.10	17. 9	G11	F4	Porcupine
13.10	18. 9	G11	G5	Wolf
14.10	19. 9	G11	H6	Dog
15.10	20. 9	G11	J7	Pheasant
16.10	21. 9	G11	K8	Cock
17.10	22. 9	G11	A9	Crow
18.10	23. 9	G11	B10	Monkey
19.10	24. 9	G11	C11	Gibbon
20.10	25. 9	G11	D12	Tapir
21.10	26. 9	G11	E1	Sheep
22.10	27. 9	G11	F2	Deer
23.10	28. 9	G11	G3	Horse
24.10	29. 9	G11	H4	Stag
25.10	1.10	H12	J5	Serpent
26.10	2.10	H12	K6	Earthworm
27.10	3.10	H12	A7	Crocodile
28.10	4.10	H12	B8	Dragon
29.10	5.10	H12	C9	Badger
30.10	6.10	H12	D10	Hare
31.10	7.10	H12	E11	Fox
1.11	8.10	H12	F12	Tiger
2.11	9.10	H12	G1	Leopard
3.11	10.10	H12	H2	Griffon
4.11	11.10	H12	J3	Ox
5.11	12.10	H12	K4	Bat
6.11	13.10	H12	A5	Rat
7.11	14.10	H12	B6	Swallow
8.11	15.10	H12	C7	Pig
9.11	16.10	H12	D8	Porcupine
10.11	17.10	H12	E9	Wolf
11.11	18.10	H12	F10	Dog
12.11	19.10	H12	G11	Pheasant
13.11	20.10	H12	H12	Cock
14.11	21.10	H12	J1	Crow
15.11	22.10	H12	K2	Monkey
16.11	23.10	H12	A3	Gibbon
17.11	24.10	H12	B4	Tapir
18.11	25.10	H12	C5	Sheep
19.11	26.10	H12	D6	Deer
20.11	27.10	H12	E7	Horse
21.11	28.10	H12	F8	Stag
22.11	29.10	H12	G9	Serpent
23.11	30.10	H12	H10	Earthworm
24.11	1.11	J1	J11	Crocodile
25.11	2.11	J1	K12	Dragon
26.11	3.11	J1	A1	Badger
27.11	4.11	J1	B2	Hare
28.11	5.11	J1	C3	Fox
29.11	6.11	J1	D4	Tiger
30.11	7.11	J1	E5	Leopard
1.12	8.11	J1	F6	Griffon
2.12	9.11	J1	G7	Ox
3.12	10.11	J1	H8	Bat
4.12	11.11	J1	J9	Rat
5.12	12.11	J1	K10	Swallow
6.12	13.11	J1	A11	Pig
7.12	14.11	J1	B12	Porcupine
8.12	15.11	J1	C1	Wolf
9.12	16.11	J1	D2	Dog
10.12	17.11	J1	E3	Pheasant
11.12	18.11	J1	F4	Cock
12.12	19.11	J1	G5	Crow
13.12	20.11	J1	H6	Monkey
14.12	21.11	J1	J7	Gibbon
15.12	22.11	J1	K8	Tapir
16.12	23.11	J1	A9	Sheep
17.12	24.11	J1	B10	Deer
18.12	25.11	J1	C11	Horse
19.12	26.11	J1	D12	Stag
20.12	27.11	J1	E1	Serpent
21.12	28.11	J1	F2	Earthworm
22.12	29.11	J1	G3	Crocodile

Solar date	*Lunar date*	*Month HS/EB*	*Day HS/EB*	*Constellation*
23.12	30.11	J1	H4	Dragon
24.12	1.12	K2	J5	Badger
25.12	2.12	K2	K6	Hare
26.12	3.12	K2	A7	Fox
27.12	4.12	K2	B8	Tiger
28.12	5.12	K2	C9	Leopard
29.12	6.12	K2	D10	Griffon
30.12	7.12	K2	E11	Ox
31.12	8.12	K2	F12	Bat
1928				
1. 1	9.12	K2	G1	Rat
2. 1	10.12	K2	H2	Swallow
3. 1	11.12	K2	J3	Pig
4. 1	12.12	K2	K4	Porcupine
5. 1	13.12	K2	A5	Wolf
6. 1	14.12	K2	B6	Dog
7. 1	15.12	K2	C7	Pheasant
8. 1	16.12	K2	D8	Cock
9. 1	17.12	K2	E9	Crow
10. 1	18.12	K2	F10	Monkey
11. 1	19.12	K2	G11	Gibbon
12. 1	20.12	K2	H12	Tapir
13. 1	21.12	K2	J1	Sheep
14. 1	22.12	K2	K2	Deer
15. 1	23.12	K2	A3	Horse
16. 1	24.12	K2	B4	Stag
17. 1	25.12	K2	C5	Serpent
18. 1	26.12	K2	D6	Earthworm
19. 1	27.12	K2	E7	Crocodile
20. 1	28.12	K2	F8	Dragon
21. 1	29.12	K2	G9	Badger
22. 1	30.12	K2	H10	Hare

MOU CH'EN YEAR

Solar date	*Lunar date*	*Month HS/EB*	*Day HS/EB*	*Constellation*
23. 1	1. 1	A3	J11	Fox
24. 1	2. 1	A3	K12	Tiger
25. 1	3. 1	A3	A1	Leopard
26. 1	4. 1	A3	B2	Griffon
27. 1	5. 1	A3	C3	Ox
28. 1	6. 1	A3	D4	Bat
29. 1	7. 1	A3	E5	Rat
30. 1	8. 1	A3	F6	Swallow
31. 1	9. 1	A3	G7	Pig
1. 2	10. 1	A3	H8	Porcupine
2. 2	11. 1	A3	J9	Wolf
3. 2	12. 1	A3	K10	Dog
4. 2	13. 1	A3	A11	Pheasant
5. 2	14. 1	A3	B12	Cock
6. 2	15. 1	A3	C1	Crow
7. 2	16. 1	A3	D2	Monkey
8. 2	17. 1	A3	E3	Gibbon
9. 2	18. 1	A3	F4	Tapir
10. 2	19. 1	A3	G5	Sheep
11. 2	20. 1	A3	H6	Deer
12. 2	21. 1	A3	J7	Horse
13. 2	22. 1	A3	K8	Stag
14. 2	23. 1	A3	A9	Serpent
15. 2	24. 1	A3	B10	Earthworm
16. 2	25. 1	A3	C11	Crocodile
17. 2	26. 1	A3	D12	Dragon
18. 2	27. 1	A3	E1	Badger
19. 2	28. 1	A3	F2	Hare
20. 2	29. 1	A3	G3	Fox
21. 2	1. 2	B4	H4	Tiger
22. 2	2. 2	B4	J5	Leopard
23. 2	3. 2	B4	K6	Griffon
24. 2	4. 2	B4	A7	Ox
25. 2	5. 2	B4	B8	Bat
26. 2	6. 2	B4	C9	Rat
27. 2	7. 2	B4	D10	Swallow
28. 2	8. 2	B4	E11	Pig
29. 2	9. 2	B4	F12	Porcupine
1. 3	10. 2	B4	G1	Wolf
2. 3	11. 2	B4	H2	Dog
3. 3	12. 2	B4	J3	Pheasant
4. 3	13. 2	B4	K4	Cock
5. 3	14. 2	B4	A5	Crow
6. 3	15. 2	B4	B6	Monkey
7. 3	16. 2	B4	C7	Gibbon
8. 3	17. 2	B4	D8	Tapir
9. 3	18. 2	B4	E9	Sheep
10. 3	19. 2	B4	F10	Deer
11. 3	20. 2	B4	G11	Horse
12. 3	21. 2	B4	H12	Stag
13. 3	22. 2	B4	J1	Serpent
14. 3	23. 2	B4	K2	Earthworm
15. 3	24. 2	B4	A3	Crocodile
16. 3	25. 2	B4	B4	Dragon
17. 3	26. 2	B4	C5	Badger
18. 3	27. 2	B4	D6	Hare
19. 3	28. 2	B4	E7	Fox
20. 3	29. 2	B4	F8	Tiger
21. 3	30. 2	B4	G9	Leopard
22. 3	*1. 2*	*B4*	H10	Griffon
23. 3	*2. 2*	*B4*	J11	Ox
24. 3	*3. 2*	*B4*	K12	Bat
25. 3	*4. 2*	*B4*	A1	Rat
26. 3	*5. 2*	*B4*	B2	Swallow
27. 3	*6. 2*	*B4*	C3	Pig
28. 3	*7. 2*	*B4*	D4	Porcupine
29. 3	*8. 2*	*B4*	E5	Wolf
30. 3	*9. 2*	*B4*	F6	Dog
31. 3	*10. 2*	*B4*	G7	Pheasant
1. 4	*11. 2*	*B4*	H8	Cock
2. 4	*12. 2*	*B4*	J9	Crow
3. 4	*13. 2*	*B4*	K10	Monkey
4. 4	*14. 2*	*B4*	A11	Gibbon
5. 4	*15. 2*	*B4*	B12	Tapir
6. 4	*16. 2*	*B4*	C1	Sheep
7. 4	*17. 2*	*B4*	D2	Deer
8. 4	*18. 2*	*B4*	E3	Horse
9. 4	*19. 2*	*B4*	F4	Stag
10. 4	*20. 2*	*B4*	G5	Serpent
11. 4	*21. 2*	*B4*	H6	Earthworm
12. 4	*22. 2*	*B4*	J7	Crocodile
13. 4	*23. 2*	*B4*	K8	Dragon
14. 4	*24. 2*	*B4*	A9	Badger
15. 4	*25. 2*	*B4*	B10	Hare
16. 4	*26. 2*	*B4*	C11	Fox
17. 4	*27. 2*	*B4*	D12	Tiger
18. 4	*28. 2*	*B4*	E1	Leopard
19. 4	*29. 2*	*B4*	F2	Griffon
20. 4	1. 3	C5	G3	Ox
21. 4	2. 3	C5	H4	Bat
22. 4	3. 3	C5	J5	Rat
23. 4	4. 3	C5	K6	Swallow
24. 4	5. 3	C5	A7	Pig
25. 4	6. 3	C5	B8	Porcupine
26. 4	7. 3	C5	C9	Wolf
27. 4	8. 3	C5	D10	Dog
28. 4	9. 3	C5	E11	Pheasant
29. 4	10. 3	C5	F12	Cock
30. 4	11. 3	C5	G1	Crow
1. 5	12. 3	C5	H2	Monkey
2. 5	13. 3	C5	J3	Gibbon
3. 5	14. 3	C5	K4	Tapir

Solar date	*Lunar date*	*Month HS/EB*	*Day HS/EB*	*Constellation*
4. 5	15. 3	C5	A5	Sheep
5. 5	16. 3	C5	B6	Deer
6. 5	17. 3	C5	C7	Horse
7. 5	18. 3	C5	D8	Stag
8. 5	19. 3	C5	E9	Serpent
9. 5	20. 3	C5	F10	Earthworm
10. 5	21. 3	C5	G11	Crocodile
11. 5	22. 3	C5	H12	Dragon
12. 5	23. 3	C5	J1	Badger
13. 5	24. 3	C5	K2	Hare
14. 5	25. 3	C5	A3	Fox
15. 5	26. 3	C5	B4	Tiger
16. 5	27. 3	C5	C5	Leopard
17. 5	28. 3	C5	D6	Griffon
18. 5	29. 3	C5	E7	Ox
19. 5	1. 4	D6	F8	Bat
20. 5	2. 4	D6	G9	Rat
21. 5	3. 4	D6	H10	Swallow
22. 5	4. 4	D6	J11	Pig
23. 5	5. 4	D6	K12	Porcupine
24. 5	6. 4	D6	A1	Wolf
25. 5	7. 4	D6	B2	Dog
26. 5	8. 4	D6	C3	Pheasant
27. 5	9. 4	D6	D4	Cock
28. 5	10. 4	D6	E5	Crow
29. 5	11. 4	D6	F6	Monkey
30. 5	12. 4	D6	G7	Gibbon
31. 5	13. 4	D6	H8	Tapir
1. 6	14. 4	D6	J9	Sheep
2. 6	15. 4	D6	K10	Deer
3. 6	16. 4	D6	A11	Horse
4. 6	17. 4	D6	B12	Stag
5. 6	18. 4	D6	C1	Serpent
6. 6	19. 4	D6	D2	Earthworm
7. 6	20. 4	D6	E3	Crocodile
8. 6	21. 4	D6	F4	Dragon
9. 6	22. 4	D6	G5	Badger
10. 6	23. 4	D6	H6	Hare
11. 6	24. 4	D6	J7	Fox
12. 6	25. 4	D6	K8	Tiger
13. 6	26. 4	D6	A9	Leopard
14. 6	27. 4	D6	B10	Griffon
15. 6	28. 4	D6	C11	Ox
16. 6	29. 4	D6	D12	Bat
17. 6	30. 4	D6	E1	Rat
18. 6	1. 5	E7	F2	Swallow
19. 6	2. 5	E7	G3	Pig
20. 6	3. 5	E7	H4	Porcupine
21. 6	4. 5	E7	J5	Wolf
22. 6	5. 5	E7	K6	Dog
23. 6	6. 5	E7	A7	Pheasant
24. 6	7. 5	E7	B8	Cock
25. 6	8. 5	E7	C9	Crow
26. 6	9. 5	E7	D10	Monkey
27. 6	10. 5	E7	E11	Gibbon
28. 6	11. 5	E7	F12	Tapir
29. 6	12. 5	E7	G1	Sheep
30. 6	13. 5	E7	H2	Deer
1. 7	14. 5	E7	J3	Horse
2. 7	15. 5	E7	K4	Stag
3. 7	16. 5	E7	A5	Serpent
4. 7	17. 5	E7	B6	Earthworm
5. 7	18. 5	E7	C7	Crocodile
6. 7	19. 5	E7	D8	Dragon
7. 7	20. 5	E7	E9	Badger
8. 7	21. 5	E7	F10	Hare
9. 7	22. 5	E7	G11	Fox
10. 7	23. 5	E7	H12	Tiger
11. 7	24. 5	E7	J1	Leopard
12. 7	25. 5	E7	K2	Griffon
13. 7	26. 5	E7	A3	Ox
14. 7	27. 5	E7	B4	Bat
15. 7	28. 5	E7	C5	Rat
16. 7	29. 5	E7	D6	Swallow
17. 7	1. 6	F8	E7	Pig
18. 7	2. 6	F8	F8	Porcupine
19. 7	3. 6	F8	G9	Wolf
20. 7	4. 6	F8	H10	Dog
21. 7	5. 6	F8	J11	Pheasant
22. 7	6. 6	F8	K12	Cock
23. 7	7. 6	F8	A1	Crow
24. 7	8. 6	F8	B2	Monkey
25. 7	9. 6	F8	C3	Gibbon
26. 7	10. 6	F8	D4	Tapir
27. 7	11. 6	F8	E5	Sheep
28. 7	12. 6	F8	F6	Deer
29. 7	13. 6	F8	G7	Horse
30. 7	14. 6	F8	H8	Stag
31. 7	15. 6	F8	J9	Serpent
1. 8	16. 6	F8	K10	Earthworm
2. 8	17. 6	F8	A11	Crocodile
3. 8	18. 6	F8	B12	Dragon
4. 8	19. 6	F8	C1	Badger
5. 8	20. 6	F8	D2	Hare
6. 8	21. 6	F8	E3	Fox
7. 8	22. 6	F8	F4	Tiger
8. 8	23. 6	F8	G5	Leopard
9. 8	24. 6	F8	H6	Griffon
10. 8	25. 6	F8	J7	Ox
11. 8	26. 6	F8	K8	Bat
12. 8	27. 6	F8	A9	Rat
13. 8	28. 6	F8	B10	Swallow
14. 8	29. 6	F8	C11	Pig
15. 8	1. 7	G9	D12	Porcupine
16. 8	2. 7	G9	E1	Wolf
17. 8	3. 7	G9	F2	Dog
18. 8	4. 7	G9	G3	Pheasant
19. 8	5. 7	G9	H4	Cock
20. 8	6. 7	G9	J5	Crow
21. 8	7. 7	G9	K6	Monkey
22. 8	8. 7	G9	A7	Gibbon
23. 8	9. 7	G9	B8	Tapir
24. 8	10. 7	G9	C9	Sheep
25. 8	11. 7	G9	D10	Deer
26. 8	12. 7	G9	E11	Horse
27. 8	13. 7	G9	F12	Stag
28. 8	14. 7	G9	G1	Serpent
29. 8	15. 7	G9	H2	Earthworm
30. 8	16. 7	G9	J3	Crocodile
31. 8	17. 7	G9	K4	Dragon
1. 9	18. 7	G9	A5	Badger
2. 9	19. 7	G9	B6	Hare
3. 9	20. 7	G9	C7	Fox
4. 9	21. 7	G9	D8	Tiger
5. 9	22. 7	G9	E9	Leopard
6. 9	23. 7	G9	F10	Griffon
7. 9	24. 7	G9	G11	Ox
8. 9	25. 7	G9	H12	Bat
9. 9	26. 7	G9	J1	Rat
10. 9	27. 7	G9	K2	Swallow
11. 9	28. 7	G9	A3	Pig
12. 9	29. 7	G9	B4	Porcupine
13. 9	30. 7	G9	C5	Wolf
14. 9	1. 8	H10	D6	Dog
15. 9	2. 8	H10	E7	Pheasant
16. 9	3. 8	H10	F8	Cock
17. 9	4. 8	H10	G9	Crow
18. 9	5. 8	H10	H10	Monkey
19. 9	6. 8	H10	J11	Gibbon
20. 9	7. 8	H10	K12	Tapir
21. 9	8. 8	H10	A1	Sheep
22. 9	9. 8	H10	B2	Deer
23. 9	10. 8	H10	C3	Horse
24. 9	11. 8	H10	D4	Stag
25. 9	12. 8	H10	E5	Serpent
26. 9	13. 8	H10	F6	Earthworm

Solar date	*Lunar date*	*Month HS/EB*	*Day HS/EB*	*Constellation*
27. 9	14. 8	H10	G7	Crocodile
28. 9	15. 8	H10	H8	Dragon
29. 9	16. 8	H10	J9	Badger
30. 9	17. 8	H10	K10	Hare
1.10	18. 8	G10	A11	Fox
2.10	19. 8	G10	B12	Tiger
3.10	20. 8	G10	C1	Leopard
4.10	21. 8	G10	D2	Griffon
5.10	22. 8	G10	E3	Ox
6.10	23. 8	G10	F4	Bat
7.10	24. 8	G10	G5	Rat
8.10	25. 8	G10	H6	Swallow
9.10	26. 8	G10	J7	Pig
10.10	27. 8	G10	K8	Porcupine
11.10	28. 8	G10	A9	Wolf
12.10	29. 8	G10	B10	Dog
13.10	1. 9	J11	C11	Pheasant
14.10	2. 9	J11	D12	Cock
15.10	3. 9	J11	E1	Crow
16.10	4. 9	J11	F2	Monkey
17.10	5. 9	J11	G3	Gibbon
18.10	6. 9	J11	H4	Tapir
19.10	7. 9	J11	J5	Sheep
20.10	8. 9	J11	K6	Deer
21.10	9. 9	J11	A7	Horse
22.10	10. 9	J11	B8	Stag
23.10	11. 9	J11	C9	Serpent
24.10	12. 9	J11	D10	Earthworm
25.10	13. 9	J11	E11	Crocodile
26.10	14. 9	J11	F12	Dragon
27.10	15. 9	J11	G1	Badger
28.10	16. 9	J11	H2	Hare
29.10	17. 9	J11	J3	Fox
30.10	18. 9	J11	K4	Tiger
31.10	19. 9	J11	A5	Leopard
1.11	20. 9	J11	B6	Griffon
2.11	21. 9	J11	C7	Ox
3.11	22. 9	J11	D8	Bat
4.11	23. 9	J11	E9	Rat
5.11	24. 9	J11	F10	Swallow
6.11	25. 9	J11	G11	Pig
7.11	26. 9	J11	H12	Porcupine
8.11	27. 9	J11	J1	Wolf
9.11	28. 9	J11	K2	Dog
10.11	29. 9	J11	A3	Pheasant
11.11	30. 9	J11	B4	Cock
12.11	1.10	K12	C5	Crow
13.11	2.10	K12	D6	Monkey
14.11	3.10	K12	E7	Gibbon
15.11	4.10	K12	F8	Tapir
16.11	5.10	K12	G9	Sheep
17.11	6.10	K12	H10	Deer
18.11	7.10	K12	J11	Horse
19.11	8.10	K12	K12	Stag
20.11	9.10	K12	A1	Serpent
21.11	10.10	K12	B2	Earthworm
22.11	11.10	K12	C3	Crocodile
23.11	12.10	K12	D4	Dragon
24.11	13.10	K12	E5	Badger
25.11	14.10	K12	F6	Hare
26.11	15.10	K12	G7	Fox
27.11	16.10	K12	H8	Tiger
28.11	17.10	K12	J9	Leopard
29.11	18.10	K12	K10	Griffon
30.11	19.10	K12	A11	Ox
1.12	20.10	K12	B12	Bat
2.12	21.10	K12	C1	Rat
3.12	22.10	K12	D2	Swallow
4.12	23.10	K12	E3	Pig

Solar date	*Lunar date*	*Month HS/EB*	*Day HS/EB*	*Constellation*
5.12	24.10	K12	F4	Porcupine
6.12	25.10	K12	G5	Wolf
7.12	26.10	K12	H6	Dog
8.12	27.10	K12	J7	Pheasant
9.12	28.10	K12	K8	Cock
10.12	29.10	K12	A9	Crow
11.12	30.10	K12	B10	Monkey
12.12	1.11	A1	C11	Gibbon
13.12	2.11	A1	D12	Tapir
14.12	3.11	A1	E1	Sheep
15.12	4.11	A1	F2	Deer
16.12	5.11	A1	G3	Horse
17.12	6.11	A1	H4	Stag
18.12	7.11	A1	J5	Serpent
19.12	8.11	A1	K6	Earthworm
20.12	9.11	A1	A7	Crocodile
21.12	10.11	A1	B8	Dragon
22.12	11.11	A1	C9	Badger
23.12	12.11	A1	D10	Hare
24.12	13.11	A1	E11	Fox
25.12	14.11	A1	F12	Tiger
26.12	15.11	A1	G1	Leopard
27.12	16.11	A1	H2	Griffon
28.12	17.11	A1	J3	Ox
29.12	18.11	A1	K4	Bat
30.12	19.11	A1	A5	Rat
31.12	20.11	A1	B6	Swallow
1929				
1. 1	21.11	A1	C7	Pig
2. 1	22.11	A1	D8	Porcupine
3. 1	23.11	A1	E9	Wolf
4. 1	24.11	A1	F10	Dog
5. 1	25.11	A1	G11	Pheasant
6. 1	26.11	A1	H12	Cock
7. 1	27.11	A1	J1	Crow
8. 1	28.11	A1	K2	Monkey
9. 1	29.11	A1	A3	Gibbon
10. 1	30.11	A1	B4	Tapir
11. 1	1.12	B2	C5	Sheep
12. 1	2.12	B2	D6	Deer
13. 1	3.12	B2	E7	Horse
14. 1	4.12	B2	F8	Stag
15. 1	5.12	B2	G9	Serpent
16. 1	6.12	B2	H10	Earthworm
17. 1	7.12	B2	J11	Crocodile
18. 1	8.12	B2	K12	Dragon
19. 1	9.12	B2	A1	Badger
20. 1	10.12	B2	B2	Hare
21. 1	11.12	B2	C3	Fox
22. 1	12.12	B2	D4	Tiger
23. 1	13.12	B2	E5	Leopard
24. 1	14.12	B2	F6	Griffon
25. 1	15.12	B2	G7	Ox
26. 1	16.12	B2	H8	Bat
27. 1	17.12	B2	J9	Rat
28. 1	18.12	B2	K10	Swallow
29. 1	19.12	B2	A11	Pig
30. 1	20.12	B2	B12	Porcupine
31. 1	21.12	B2	C1	Wolf
1. 2	22.12	B2	D2	Dog
2. 2	23.12	B2	E3	Pheasant
3. 2	24.12	B2	F4	Cock
4. 2	25.12	B2	G5	Crow
5. 2	26.12	B2	H6	Monkey
6. 2	27.12	B2	J7	Gibbon
7. 2	28.12	B2	K8	Tapir
8. 2	29.12	B2	A9	Sheep
9. 2	30.12	B2	B10	Deer

CHI SZU YEAR

Solar date	*Lunar date*	*Month HS/EB*	*Day HS/EB*	*Constellation*
10. 2	1. 1	C3	C11	Horse
11. 2	2. 1	C3	D12	Stag
12. 2	3. 1	C3	E1	Serpent
13. 2	4. 1	C3	F2	Earthworm
14. 2	5. 1	C3	G3	Crocodile
15. 2	6. 1	C3	H4	Dragon
16. 2	7. 1	C3	J5	Badger
17. 2	8. 1	C3	K6	Hare
18. 2	9. 1	C3	A7	Fox
19. 2	10. 1	C3	B8	Tiger
20. 2	11. 1	C3	C9	Leopard
21. 2	12. 1	C3	D10	Griffon
22. 2	13. 1	C3	E11	Ox
23. 2	14. 1	C3	F12	Bat
24. 2	15. 1	C3	G1	Rat
25. 2	16. 1	C3	H2	Swallow
26. 2	17. 1	C3	J3	Pig
27. 2	18. 1	C3	K4	Porcupine
28. 2	19. 1	C3	A5	Wolf
1. 3	20. 1	C3	B6	Dog
2. 3	21. 1	C3	C7	Pheasant
3. 3	22. 1	C3	D8	Cock
4. 3	23. 1	C3	E9	Crow
5. 3	24. 1	C3	F10	Monkey
6. 3	25. 1	C3	G11	Gibbon
7. 3	26. 1	C3	H12	Tapir
8. 3	27. 1	C3	J1	Sheep
9. 3	28. 1	C3	K2	Deer
10. 3	29. 1	C3	A3	Horse
11. 3	1. 2	D4	B4	Stag
12. 3	2. 2	D4	C5	Serpent
13. 3	3. 2	D4	D6	Earthworm
14. 3	4. 2	D4	E7	Crocodile
15. 3	5. 2	D4	F8	Dragon
16. 3	6. 2	D4	G9	Badger
17. 3	7. 2	D4	H10	Hare
18. 3	8. 2	D4	J11	Fox
19. 3	9. 2	D4	K12	Tiger
20. 3	10. 2	D4	A1	Leopard
21. 3	11. 2	D4	B2	Griffon
22. 3	12. 2	D4	C3	Ox
23. 3	13. 2	D4	D4	Bat
24. 3	14. 2	D4	E5	Rat
25. 3	15. 2	D4	F6	Swallow
26. 3	16. 2	D4	G7	Pig
27. 3	17. 2	D4	H8	Porcupine
28. 3	18. 2	D4	J9	Wolf
29. 3	19. 2	D4	K10	Dog
30. 3	20. 2	D4	A11	Pheasant
31. 3	21. 2	D4	B12	Cock
1. 4	22. 2	D4	C1	Crow
2. 4	23. 2	D4	D2	Monkey
3. 4	24. 2	D4	E3	Gibbon
4. 4	25. 2	D4	F4	Tapi
5. 4	26. 2	D4	G5	Sheep
6. 4	27. 2	D4	H6	Deer
7. 4	28. 2	D4	J7	Horse
8. 4	29. 2	D4	K8	Stag
9. 4	30. 2	D4	A9	Serpent
10. 4	1. 3	E5	B10	Earthworm
11. 4	2. 3	E5	C11	Crocodile
12. 4	3. 3	E5	D12	Dragon
13. 4	4. 3	E5	E1	Badger
14. 4	5. 3	E5	F2	Hare
15. 4	6. 3	E5	G3	Fox
16. 4	7. 3	E5	H4	Tiger
17. 4	8. 3	E5	J5	Leopard
18. 4	9. 3	E5	K6	Griffon
19. 4	10. 3	E5	A7	Ox
20. 4	11. 3	E5	B8	Bat
21. 4	12. 3	E5	C9	Rat
22. 4	13. 3	E5	D10	Swallow
23. 4	14. 3	E5	E11	Pig
24. 4	15. 3	E5	F12	Porcupine
25. 4	16. 3	E5	G1	Wolf
26. 4	17. 3	E5	H2	Dog
27. 4	18. 3	E5	J3	Pheasant
28. 4	19. 3	E5	K4	Cock
29. 4	20. 3	E5	A5	Crow
30. 4	21. 3	E5	B6	Monkey
1. 5	22. 3	E5	C7	Gibbon
2. 5	23. 3	E5	D8	Tapir
3. 5	24. 3	E5	E9	Sheep
4. 5	25. 3	E5	F10	Deer
5. 5	26. 3	E5	G11	Horse
6. 5	27. 3	E5	H12	Stag
7. 5	28. 3	E5	J1	Serpent
8. 5	29. 3	E5	K2	Earthworm
9. 5	1. 4	F6	A3	Crocodile
10. 5	2. 4	F6	B4	Dragon
11. 5	3. 4	F6	C5	Badger
12. 5	4. 4	F6	D6	Hare
13. 5	5. 4	F6	E7	Fox
14. 5	6. 4	F6	F8	Tiger
15. 5	7. 4	F6	G9	Leopard
16. 5	8. 4	F6	H10	Griffon
17. 5	9. 4	F6	J11	Ox
18. 5	10. 4	F6	K12	Bat
19. 5	11. 4	F6	A1	Rat
20. 5	12. 4	F6	B2	Swallow
21. 5	13. 4	F6	C3	Pig
22. 5	14. 4	F6	D4	Porcupine
23. 5	15. 4	F6	E5	Wolf
24. 5	16. 4	F6	F6	Dog
25. 5	17. 4	F6	G7	Pheasant
26. 5	18. 4	F6	H8	Cock
27. 5	19. 4	F6	J9	Crow
28. 5	20. 4	F6	K10	Monkey
29. 5	21. 4	F6	A11	Gibbon
30. 5	22. 4	F6	B12	Tapir
31. 5	23. 4	F6	C1	Sheep
1. 6	24. 4	F6	D2	Deer
2. 6	25. 4	F6	E3	Horse
3. 6	26. 4	F6	F4	Stag
4. 6	27. 4	F6	G5	Serpent
5. 6	28. 4	F6	H6	Earthworm
6. 6	29. 4	F6	J7	Crocodile
7. 6	1. 5	G7	K8	Dragon
8. 6	2. 5	G7	A9	Badger
9. 6	3. 5	G7	B10	Hare
10. 6	4. 5	G7	C11	Fox
11. 6	5. 5	G7	D12	Tiger
12. 6	6. 5	G7	E1	Leopard
13. 6	7. 5	G7	F2	Griffon
14. 6	8. 5	G7	G3	Ox
15. 6	9. 5	G7	H4	Bat
16. 6	10. 5	G7	J5	Rat
17. 6	11. 5	G7	K6	Swallow
18. 6	12. 5	G7	A7	Pig
19. 6	13. 5	G7	B8	Porcupine
20. 6	14. 5	G7	C9	Wolf
21. 6	15. 5	G7	D10	Dog
22. 6	16. 5	G7	E11	Pheasant
23. 6	17. 5	G7	F12	Cock
24. 6	18. 5	G7	G1	Crow
25. 6	19. 5	G7	H2	Monkey
26. 6	20. 5	G7	J3	Gibbon
27. 6	21. 5	G7	K4	Tapir
28. 6	22. 5	G7	A5	Sheep
29. 6	23. 5	G7	B6	Deer
30. 6	24. 5	G7	C7	Horse
1. 7	25. 5	G7	D8	Stag

Solar date	Lunar date	Month HS/EB	Day HS/EB	Constellation
2. 7	26. 5	G7	E9	Serpent
3. 7	27. 5	G7	F10	Earthworm
4. 7	28. 5	G7	G11	Crocodile
5. 7	29. 5	G7	H12	Dragon
6. 7	30. 5	G7	J1	Badger
7. 7	1. 6	H8	K2	Hare
8. 7	2. 6	H8	A3	Fox
9. 7	3. 6	H8	B4	Tiger
10. 7	4. 6	H8	C5	Leopard
11. 7	5. 6	H8	D6	Griffon
12. 7	6. 6	H8	E7	Ox
13. 7	7. 6	H8	F8	Bat
14 7	8. 6	H8	G9	Rat
15. 7	9. 6	H8	H10	Swallow
16. 7	10. 6	H8	J11	Pig
17. 7	11. 6	H8	K12	Porcupine
18. 7	12. 6	H8	A1	Wolf
19. 7	13 6	H8	B2	Dog
20. 7	14. 6	H8	C3	Pheasant
21. 7	15. 6	H8	D4	Cock
22. 7	16. 6	H8	E5	Crow
23. 7	17. 6	H8	F6	Monkey
24. 7	18. 6	H8	G7	Gibbon
25. 7	19. 6	H8	H8	Tapir
26. 7	20. 6	H8	J9	Sheep
27. 7	21. 6	H8	K10	Deer
28. 7	22. 6	H8	A11	Horse
29. 7	23. 6	H8	B12	Stag
30. 7	24. 6	H8	C1	Serpent
31. 7	25. 6	H8	D2	Earthworm
1. 8	26. 6	H8	E3	Crocodile
2. 8	27. 6	H8	F4	Dragon
3. 8	28. 6	H8	G5	Badger
4. 8	29. 6	H8	H6	Hare
5. 8	1. 7	J9	J7	Fox
6. 8	2. 7	J9	K8	Tiger
7. 8	3. 7	J9	A9	Leopard
8. 8	4. 7	J9	B10	Griffon
9. 8	5. 7	J9	C11	Ox
10. 8	6. 7	J9	D12	Bat
11. 8	7. 7	J9	E1	Rat
12. 8	8. 7	J9	F2	Swallow
13. 8	9. 7	J9	G3	Pig
14. 8	10. 7	J9	H4	Porcupine
15. 8	11. 7	J9	J5	Wolf
16. 8	12. 7	J9	K6	Dog
17. 8	13. 7	J9	A7	Pheasant
18. 8	14. 7	J9	B8	Cock
19. 8	15. 7	J9	C9	Crow
20. 8	16. 7	J9	D10	Monkey
21. 8	17. 7	J9	E11	Gibbon
22. 8	18. 7	J9	F12	Tapir
23. 8	19. 7	J9	G1	Sheep
24. 8	20. 7	J9	H2	Deer
25. 8	21. 7	J9	J3	Horse
26. 8	22. 7	J9	K4	Stag
27. 8	23. 7	J9	A5	Serpent
28. 8	24. 7	J9	B6	Earthworm
29. 8	25. 7	J9	C7	Crocodile
30. 8	26. 7	J9	D8	Dragon
31. 8	27. 7	J9	E9	Badger
1. 9	28. 7	J9	F10	Hare
2. 9	29. 7	J9	G11	Fox
3. 9	1. 8	K10	H12	Tiger
4. 9	2. 8	K10	J1	Leopard
5. 9	3. 8	K10	K2	Griffon
6. 9	4. 8	K10	A3	Ox
7. 9	5. 8	K10	B4	Bat
8. 9	6. 8	K10	C5	Rat
9. 9	7. 8	K10	D6	Swallow
10. 9	8. 8	K10	E7	Pig
11. 9	9. 8	K10	F8	Porcupine
12. 9	10. 8	K10	G9	Wolf
13. 9	11. 8	K10	H10	Dog
14. 9	12. 8	K10	J11	Pheasant
15. 9	13. 8	K10	K12	Cock
16. 9	14. 8	K10	A1	Crow
17. 9	15. 8	K10	B2	Monkey
18. 9	16. 8	K10	C3	Gibbon
19. 9	17. 8	K10	D4	Tapir
20. 9	18. 8	K10	E5	Sheep
21. 9	19. 8	K10	F6	Deer
22. 9	20. 8	K10	G7	Horse
23. 9	21. 8	K10	H8	Stag
24. 9	22. 8	K10	J9	Serpent
25. 9	23. 8	K10	K10	Earthworm
26. 9	24. 8	K10	A11	Crocodile
27. 9	25. 8	K10	B12	Dragon
28. 9	26. 8	K10	C1	Badger
29. 9	27. 8	K10	D2	Hare
30. 9	28. 8	K10	E3	Fox
1.10	29. 8	K10	F4	Tiger
2.10	30. 8	K10	G5	Leopard
3.10	1. 9	A11	H6	Griffon
4.10	2. 9	A11	J7	Ox
5.10	3. 9	A11	K8	Bat
6.10	4. 9	A11	A9	Rat
7.10	5. 9	A11	B10	Swallow
8.10	6. 9	A11	C11	Pig
9.10	7. 9	A11	D12	Porcupine
10.10	8. 9	A11	E1	Wolf
11.10	9. 9	A11	F2	Dog
12.10	10. 9	A11	G3	Pheasant
13.10	11. 9	A11	H4	Cock
14.10	12. 9	A11	J5	Crow
15.10	13. 9	A11	K6	Monkey
16.10	14. 9	A11	A7	Gibbon
17.10	15. 9	A11	B8	Tapir
18.10	16. 9	A11	C9	Sheep
19.10	17. 9	A11	D10	Deer
20.10	18. 9	A11	E11	Horse
21.10	19. 9	A11	F12	Stag
22.10	20. 9	A11	G1	Serpent
23.10	21. 9	A11	H2	Earthworm
24.10	22. 9	A11	J3	Crocodile
25.10	23. 9	A11	K4	Dragon
26.10	24. 9	A11	A5	Badger
27.10	25. 9	A11	B6	Hare
28.10	26. 9	A11	C7	Fox
29.10	27. 9	A11	D8	Tiger
30.10	28. 9	A11	E9	Leopard
31.10	29. 9	A11	F10	Griffon
1.11	1.10	B12	G11	Ox
2.11	2.10	B12	H12	Bat
3.11	3.10	B12	J1	Rat
4.11	4.10	B12	K2	Swallow
5.11	5.10	B12	A3	Pig
6.11	6.10	B12	B4	Porcupine
7.11	7.10	B12	C5	Wolf
8.11	8.10	B12	D6	Dog
9.11	9.10	B12	E7	Pheasant
10.11	10.10	B12	F8	Cock
11.11	11.10	B12	G9	Crow
12.11	12.10	B12	H10	Monkey
13.11	13.10	B12	J11	Gibbon
14.11	14.10	B12	K12	Tapir
15.11	15.10	B12	A1	Sheep
16.11	16.10	B12	B2	Deer
17.11	17.10	B12	C3	Horse
18.11	18.10	B12	D4	Stag
19.11	19.10	B12	E5	Serpent
20 11	20.10	B12	F6	Earthworm
21.11	21.10	B12	G7	Crocodile
22.11	22.10	B12	H8	Dragon
23.11	23.10	B12	J9	Badger
24.11	24.10	B12	K10	Hare

Solar date	*Lunar date*	*Month HS/EB*	*Day HS/EB*	*Constellation*
25.11	25.10	B12	A11	Fox
26.11	26.10	B12	B12	Tiger
27.11	27.10	B12	C1	Leopard
28.11	28.10	B12	D2	Griffon
29.11	29.10	B12	E3	Ox
30.11	30.10	B12	F4	Bat
1.12	1.11	C1	G5	Rat
2.12	2.11	C1	H6	Swallow
3.12	3.11	C1	J7	Pig
4.12	4.11	C1	K8	Porcupine
5.12	5.11	C1	A9	Wolf
6.12	6.11	C1	B10	Dog
7.12	7.11	C1	C11	Pheasant
8.12	8.11	C1	D12	Cock
9.12	9.11	C1	E1	Crow
10.12	10.11	C1	F2	Monkey
11.12	11.11	C1	G3	Gibbon
12.12	12.11	C1	H4	Tapir
13.12	13.11	C1	J5	Sheep
14.12	14.11	C1	K6	Deer
15.12	15.11	C1	A7	Horse
16.12	16.11	C1	B8	Stag
17.12	17.11	C1	C9	Serpent
18.12	18.11	C1	D10	Earthworm
19.12	19.11	C1	E11	Crocodile
20.12	20.11	C1	F12	Dragon
21.12	21.11	C1	G1	Badger
22.12	22.11	C1	H2	Hare
23.12	23.11	C1	J3	Fox
24.12	24.11	C1	K4	Tiger
25.12	25.11	C1	A5	Leopard
26.12	26.11	C1	B6	Griffon
27.12	27.11	C1	C7	Ox
28.12	28.11	C1	D8	Bat

Solar date	*Lunar date*	*Month HS/EB*	*Day HS/EB*	*Constellation*
29.12	29.11	C1	E9	Rat
30.12	30.11	C1	F10	Swallow
31.12	1.12	D2	G11	Pig
1930				
1. 1	2.12	D2	H12	Porcupine
2. 1	3.12	D2	J1	Wolf
3. 1	4.12	D2	K2	Dog
4. 1	5.12	D2	A3	Pheasant
5. 1	6.12	D2	B4	Cock
6. 1	7.12	D2	C5	Crow
7. 1	8.12	D2	D6	Monkey
8. 1	9.12	D2	E7	Gibbon
9. 1	10.12	D2	F8	Tapir
10. 1	11.12	D2	G9	Sheep
11. 1	12.12	D2	H10	Deer
12. 1	13.12	D2	J11	Horse
13. 1	14.12	D2	K12	Stag
14. 1	15.12	D2	A1	Serpent
15. 1	16.12	D2	B2	Earthworm
16. 1	17.12	D2	C3	Crocodile
17. 1	18.12	D2	D4	Dragon
18. 1	19.12	D2	E5	Badger
19. 1	20.12	D2	F6	Hare
20. 1	21.12	D2	G7	Fox
21. 1	22.12	D2	H8	Tiger
22. 1	23.12	D2	J9	Leopard
23. 1	24.12	D2	K10	Griffon
24. 1	25.12	D2	A11	Ox
25. 1	26.12	D2	B12	Bat
26. 1	27.12	D2	C1	Rat
27. 1	28.12	D2	D2	Swallow
28. 1	29.12	D2	E3	Pig
29. 1	30.12	D2	F4	Porcupine

KENG WU YEAR

30. 1	1. 1	E3	G5	Wolf
31. 1	2. 1	E3	H6	Dog
1. 2	3. 1	E3	J7	Pheasant
2. 2	4. 1	E3	K8	Cock
3. 2	5. 1	E3	A9	Crow
4. 2	6. 1	E3	B10	Monkey
5. 2	7. 1	E3	C11	Gibbon
6. 2	8. 1	E3	D12	Tapir
7. 2	9. 1	E3	E1	Sheep
8. 2	10. 1	E3	F2	Deer
9. 2	11. 1	E3	G3	Horse
10. 2	12. 1	E3	H4	Stag
11. 2	13. 1	E3	J5	Serpent
12. 2	14. 1	E3	K6	Earthworm
13. 2	15. 1	E3	A7	Crocodile
14. 2	16. 1	E3	B8	Dragon
15. 2	17. 1	E3	C9	Badger
16. 2	18. 1	E3	D10	Hare
17. 2	19. 1	E3	E11	Fox
18. 2	20. 1	E3	F12	Tiger
19. 2	21. 1	E3	G1	Leopard
20. 2	22. 1	E3	H2	Griffon
21. 2	23. 1	E3	J3	Ox
22. 2	24. 1	E3	K4	Bat
23. 2	25. 1	E3	A5	Rat
24. 2	26. 1	E3	B6	Swallow
25. 2	27. 1	E3	C7	Pig
26. 2	28. 1	E3	D8	Porcupine
27. 2	29. 1	E3	E9	Wolf
28. 2	1. 2	F4	F10	Dog
1. 3	2. 2	F4	G11	Pheasant
2. 3	3. 2	F4	H12	Cock
3. 3	4. 2	F4	J1	Crow
4. 3	5. 2	F4	K2	Monkey

5. 3	6. 2	F4	A3	Gibbon
6. 3	7. 2	F4	B4	Tapir
7. 3	8. 2	F4	C5	Sheep
8. 3	9. 2	F4	D6	Deer
9. 3	10. 2	F4	E7	Horse
10. 3	11. 2	F4	F8	Stag
11. 3	12. 2	F4	G9	Serpent
12. 3	13. 2	F4	H10	Earthworm
13. 3	14. 2	F4	J11	Crocodile
14. 3	15. 2	F4	K12	Dragon
15. 3	16. 2	F4	A1	Badger
16. 3	17. 2	F4	B2	Hare
17. 3	18. 2	F4	C3	Fox
18. 3	19. 2	F4	D4	Tiger
19. 3	20. 2	F4	E5	Leopard
20. 3	21. 2	F4	F6	Griffon
21. 3	22. 2	F4	G7	Ox
22. 3	23. 2	F4	H8	Bat
23. 3	24. 2	F4	J9	Rat
24. 3	25. 2	F4	K10	Swallow
25. 3	26. 2	F4	A11	Pig
26. 3	27. 2	F4	B12	Porcupine
27. 3	28. 2	F4	C1	Wolf
28. 3	29. 2	F4	D2	Dog
29. 3	30. 2	F4	E3	Pheasant
30. 3	1. 3	G5	F4	Cock
31. 3	2. 3	G5	G5	Crow
1. 4	3. 3	G5	H6	Monkey
2. 4	4. 3	G5	J7	Gibbon
3. 4	5. 3	G5	K8	Tapir
4. 4	6. 3	G5	A9	Sheep
5. 4	7. 3	G5	B10	Deer
6. 4	8. 3	G5	C11	Horse
7. 4	9. 3	G5	D12	Stag

Solar date	*Lunar date*	*Month HS/EB*	*Day HS/EB*	*Constellation*
8. 4	10. 3	G5	E1	Serpent
9. 4	11. 3	G5	F2	Earthworm
10. 4	12. 3	G5	G3	Crocodile
11. 4	13. 3	G5	H4	Dragon
12. 4	14. 3	G5	J5	Badger
13. 4	15. 3	G5	K6	Hare
14. 4	16. 3	G5	A7	Fox
15. 4	17. 3	G5	B8	Tiger
16. 4	18. 3	G5	C9	Leopard
17. 4	19. 3	G5	D10	Griffon
18. 4	20. 3	G5	E11	Ox
19. 4	21. 3	G5	F12	Bat
20. 4	22. 3	G5	G1	Rat
21. 4	23. 3	G5	H2	Swallow
22. 4	24. 3	G5	J3	Pig
23. 4	25. 3	G5	K4	Porcupine
24. 4	26. 3	G5	A5	Wolf
25. 4	27. 3	G5	B6	Dog
26. 4	28. 3	G5	C7	Pheasant
27. 4	29. 3	G5	D8	Cock
28. 4	30. 3	G5	E9	Crow
29. 4	1. 4	H6	F10	Monkey
30. 4	2. 4	H6	G11	Gibbon
1. 5	3. 4	H6	H12	Tapir
2. 5	4. 4	H6	J1	Sheep
3. 5	5. 4	H6	K2	Deer
4. 5	6. 4	H6	A3	Horse
5. 5	7. 4	H6	B4	Stag
6. 5	8. 4	H6	C5	Serpent
7. 5	9. 4	H6	D6	Earthworm
8. 5	10. 4	H6	E7	Crocodile
9. 5	11. 4	H6	F8	Dragon
10. 5	12. 4	H6	G9	Badger
11. 5	13. 4	H6	H10	Hare
12. 5	14. 4	H6	J11	Fox
13. 5	15. 4	H6	K12	Tiger
14. 5	16. 4	H6	A1	Leopard
15. 5	17. 4	H6	B2	Griffon
16. 5	18. 4	H6	C3	Ox
17. 5	19. 4	H6	D4	Bat
18. 5	20. 4	H6	E5	Rat
19. 5	21. 4	H6	F6	Swallow
20. 5	22. 4	H6	G7	Pig
21. 5	23. 4	H6	H8	Porcupine
22. 5	24. 4	H6	J9	Wolf
23. 5	25. 4	H6	K10	Dog
24. 5	26. 4	H6	A11	Pheasant
25. 5	27. 4	H6	B12	Cock
26. 5	28. 4	H6	C1	Crow
27. 5	29. 4	H6	D2	Monkey
28. 5	1. 5	J7	E3	Gibbon
29. 5	2. 5	J7	F4	Tapir
30. 5	3. 5	J7	G5	Sheep
31. 5	4. 5	J7	H6	Deer
1. 6	5. 5	J7	J7	Horse
2. 6	6. 5	J7	K8	Stag
3. 6	7. 5	J7	A9	Serpent
4. 6	8. 5	J7	B10	Earthworm
5. 6	9. 5	J7	C11	Crocodile
6. 6	10. 5	J7	D12	Dragon
7. 6	11. 5	J7	E1	Badger
8. 6	12. 5	J7	F2	Hare
9. 6	13. 5	J7	G3	Fox
10. 6	14. 5	J7	H4	Tiger
11. 6	15. 5	J7	J5	Leopard
12. 6	16. 5	J7	K6	Griffon
13. 6	17. 5	J7	A7	Ox
14. 6	18. 5	J7	B8	Bat
15. 6	19. 5	J7	C9	Rat
16. 6	20. 5	J7	D10	Swallow
17. 6	21. 5	J7	E11	Pig
18. 6	22. 5	J7	F12	Porcupine
19. 6	23. 5	J7	G1	Wolf
20. 6	24. 5	J7	H2	Dog
21. 6	25. 5	J7	J3	Pheasant
22. 6	26. 5	J7	K4	Cock
23. 6	27. 5	J7	A5	Crow
24. 6	28. 5	J7	B6	Monkey
25. 6	29. 5	J7	C7	Gibbon
26. 6	1. 6	K8	D8	Tapir
27. 6	2. 6	K8	E9	Sheep
28. 6	3. 6	K8	F10	Deer
29. 6	4. 6	K8	G11	Horse
30. 6	5. 6	K8	H12	Stag
1. 7	6. 6	K8	J1	Serpent
2. 7	7. 6	K8	K2	Earthworm
3. 7	8. 6	K8	A3	Crocodile
4. 7	9. 6	K8	B4	Dragon
5. 7	10. 6	K8	C5	Badger
6. 7	11. 6	K8	D6	Hare
7. 7	12. 6	K8	E7	Fox
8. 7	13. 6	K8	F8	Tiger
9. 7	14. 6	K8	G9	Leopard
10. 7	15. 6	K8	H10	Griffon
11. 7	16. 6	K8	J11	Ox
12. 7	17. 6	K8	K12	Bat
13. 7	18. 6	K8	A1	Rat
14. 7	19. 6	K8	B2	Swallow
15. 7	20. 6	K8	C3	Pig
16. 7	21. 6	K8	D4	Porcupine
17. 7	22. 6	K8	E5	Wolf
18. 7	23. 6	K8	F6	Dog
19. 7	24. 6	K8	G7	Pheasant
20. 7	25. 6	K8	H8	Cock
21. 7	26. 6	K8	J9	Crow
22. 7	27. 6	K8	K10	Monkey
23. 7	28. 6	K8	A11	Gibbon
24. 7	29. 6	K8	B12	Tapir
25. 7	30. 6	K8	C1	Sheep
26. 7	*1. 6*	*K8*	D2	Deer
27. 7	*2. 6*	*K8*	E3	Horse
28. 7	*3. 6*	*K8*	F4	Stag
29. 7	*4. 6*	*K8*	G5	Serpent
30. 7	*5. 6*	*K8*	H6	Earthworm
31. 7	*6. 6*	*K8*	J7	Crocodile
1. 8	*7. 6*	*K8*	K8	Dragon
2. 8	*8. 6*	*K8*	A9	Badger
3. 8	*9. 6*	*K8*	B10	Hare
4. 8	*10. 6*	*K8*	C11	Fox
5. 8	*11. 6*	*K8*	D12	Tiger
6. 8	*12. 6*	*K8*	E1	Leopard
7. 8	*13. 6*	*K8*	F2	Griffon
8. 8	*14. 6*	*K8*	G3	Ox
9. 8	*15. 6*	*K8*	H4	Bat
10. 8	*16. 6*	*K8*	J5	Rat
11. 8	*17. 6*	*K8*	K6	Swallow
12. 8	*18. 6*	*K8*	A7	Pig
13. 8	*19. 6*	*K8*	B8	Porcupine
14. 8	*20. 6*	*K8*	C9	Wolf
15. 8	*21. 6*	*K8*	D10	Dog
16. 8	*22. 6*	*K8*	E11	Pheasant
17. 8	*23. 6*	*K8*	F12	Cock
18. 8	*24. 6*	*K8*	G1	Crow
19. 8	*25. 6*	*K8*	H2	Monkey
20. 8	*26. 6*	*K8*	J3	Gibbon
21. 8	*27. 6*	*K8*	K4	Tapir
22. 8	*28. 6*	*K8*	A5	Sheep
23. 8	*29. 6*	*K8*	B6	Deer
24. 8	1. 7	A9	C7	Horse
25. 8	2. 7	A9	D8	Stag
26. 8	3. 7	A9	E9	Serpent
27. 8	4. 7	A9	F10	Earthworm
28. 8	5. 7	A9	G11	Crocodile
29. 8	6. 7	A9	H12	Dragon
30. 8	7. 7	A9	J1	Badger
31. 8	8. 7	A9	K2	Hare

Solar date	Lunar date	Month HS/EB	Day HS/EB	Constellation
1. 9	9. 7	A9	A3	Fox
2. 9	10. 7	A9	B4	Tiger
3. 9	11. 7	A9	C5	Leopard
4. 9	12. 7	A9	D6	Griffon
5. 9	13. 7	A9	E7	Ox
6. 9	14. 7	A9	F8	Bat
7. 9	15. 7	A9	G9	Rat
8. 9	16. 7	A9	H10	Swallow
9. 9	17. 7	A9	J11	Pig
10. 9	18. 7	A9	K12	Porcupine
11. 9	19. 7	A9	A1	Wolf
12. 9	20. 7	A9	B2	Dog
13. 9	21. 7	A9	C3	Pheasant
14. 9	22. 7	A9	D4	Cock
15. 9	23. 7	A9	E5	Crow
16. 9	24. 7	A9	F6	Monkey
17. 9	25. 7	A9	G7	Gibbon
18. 9	26. 7	A9	H8	Tapir
19. 9	27. 7	A9	J9	Sheep
20. 9	28. 7	A9	K10	Deer
21. 9	29. 7	A9	A11	Horse
22. 9	1. 8	B10	B12	Stag
23. 9	2. 8	B10	C1	Serpent
24. 9	3. 8	B10	D2	Earthworm
25. 9	4. 8	B10	E3	Crocodile
26. 9	5. 8	B10	F4	Dragon
27. 9	6. 8	B10	G5	Badger
28. 9	7. 8	B10	H6	Hare
29. 9	8. 8	B10	J7	Fox
30. 9	9. 8	B10	K8	Tiger
1.10	10. 8	B10	A9	Leopard
2.10	11. 8	B10	B10	Griffon
3.10	12. 8	B10	C11	Ox
4.10	13. 8	B10	D12	Bat
5.10	14. 8	B10	E1	Rat
6.10	15. 8	B10	F2	Swallow
7.10	16. 8	B10	G3	Pig
8.10	17. 8	B10	H4	Porcupine
9.10	18. 8	B10	J5	Wolf
10.10	19. 8	B10	K6	Dog
11.10	20. 8	B10	A7	Pheasant
12.10	21. 8	B10	B8	Cock
13.10	22. 8	B10	C9	Crow
14.10	23. 8	B10	D10	Monkey
15.10	24. 8	B10	E11	Gibbon
16.10	25. 8	B10	F12	Tapir
17.10	26. 8	B10	G1	Sheep
18.10	27. 8	B10	H2	Deer
19.10	28. 8	B10	J3	Horse
20.10	29. 8	B10	K4	Stag
21.10	30. 8	B10	A5	Serpent
22.10	1. 9	C11	B6	Earthworm
23.10	2. 9	C11	C7	Crocodile
24.10	3. 9	C11	D8	Dragon
25.10	4. 9	C11	E9	Badger
26.10	5. 9	C11	F10	Hare
27.10	6. 9	C11	G11	Fox
28.10	7. 9	C11	H12	Tiger
29.10	8. 9	C11	J1	Leopard
30.10	9. 9	C11	K2	Griffon
31.10	10. 9	C11	A3	Ox
1.11	11. 9	C11	B4	Bat
2.11	12. 9	C11	C5	Rat
3.11	13. 9	C11	D6	Swallow
4.11	14. 9	C11	E7	Pig
5.11	15. 9	C11	F8	Porcupine
6.11	16. 9	C11	G9	Wolf
7.11	17. 9	C11	H10	Dog
8.11	18. 9	C11	J11	Pheasant
9.11	19. 9	C11	K12	Cock
10.11	20. 9	C11	A1	Crow
11.11	21. 9	C11	B2	Monkey
12.11	22. 9	C11	C3	Gibbon

Solar date	Lunar date	Month HS/EB	Day HS/EB	Constellation
13.11	23. 9	C11	D4	Tapir
14.11	24. 9	C11	E5	Sheep
15.11	25. 9	C11	F6	Deer
16.11	26. 9	C11	G7	Horse
17.11	27. 9	C11	H8	Stag
18.11	28. 9	C11	J9	Serpent
19.11	29. 9	C11	K10	Earthworm
20.11	1.10	D12	A11	Crocodile
21.11	2.10	D12	B12	Dragon
22.11	3.10	D12	C1	Badger
23.11	4.10	D12	D2	Hare
24.11	5.10	D12	E3	Fox
25.11	6.10	D12	F4	Tiger
26.11	7.10	D12	G5	Leopard
27.11	8.10	D12	H6	Griffon
28.11	9.10	D12	J7	Ox
29.11	10.10	D12	K8	Bat
30.11	11.10	D12	A9	Rat
1.12	12.10	D12	B10	Swallow
2.12	13.10	D12	C11	Pig
3.12	14.10	D12	D12	Porcupine
4.12	15.10	D12	E1	Wolf
5.12	16.10	D12	F2	Dog
6.12	17.10	D12	G3	Pheasant
7.12	18.10	D12	H4	Cock
8.12	19.10	D12	J5	Crow
9.12	20.10	D12	K6	Monkey
10.12	21.10	D12	A7	Gibbon
11.12	22.10	D12	B8	Tapir
12.12	23.10	D12	C9	Sheep
13.12	24.10	D12	D10	Deer
14.12	25.10	D12	E11	Horse
15.12	26.10	D12	F12	Stag
16.12	27.10	D12	G1	Serpent
17.12	28.10	D12	H2	Earthworm
18.12	29.10	D12	J3	Crocodile
19.12	30.10	D12	K4	Dragon
20.12	1.11	E1	A5	Badger
21.12	2.11	E1	B6	Hare
22.12	3.11	E1	C7	Fox
23.12	4.11	E1	D8	Tiger
24.12	5.11	E1	E9	Leopard
25.12	6.11	E1	F10	Griffon
26.12	7.11	E1	G11	Ox
27.12	8.11	E1	H12	Bat
28.12	9.11	E1	J1	Rat
29.12	10.11	E1	K2	Swallow
30.12	11.11	E1	A3	Pig
31.12	12.11	E1	B4	Porcupine
1931				
1. 1	13.11	E1	C5	Wolf
2. 1	14.11	E1	D6	Dog
3. 1	15.11	E1	E7	Pheasant
4. 1	16.11	E1	F8	Cock
5. 1	17.11	E1	G9	Crow
6. 1	18.11	E1	H10	Monkey
7. 1	19.11	E1	J11	Gibbon
8. 1	20.11	E1	K12	Tapir
9. 1	21.11	E1	A1	Sheep
10. 1	22.11	E1	B2	Deer
11. 1	23.11	E1	C3	Horse
12. 1	24.11	E1	D4	Stag
13. 1	25.11	E1	E5	Serpent
14. 1	26.11	E1	F6	Earthworm
15. 1	27.11	E1	G7	Crocodile
16. 1	28.11	E1	H8	Dragon
17. 1	29.11	E1	J9	Badger
18. 1	30.11	E1	K10	Hare
19. 1	1.12	F2	A11	Fox
20. 1	2.12	F2	B12	Tiger
21. 1	3.12	F2	C1	Leopard
22. 1	4.12	F2	D2	Griffon

Solar date	*Lunar date*	*Month HS/EB*	*Day HS/EB*	*Constellation*	*Solar date*	*Lunar date*	*Month HS/EB*	*Day HS/EB*	*Constellation*
23. 1	5.12	F2	E3	Ox	5. 2	18.12	F2	H4	Tapir
24. 1	6.12	F2	F4	Bat	6. 2	19.12	F2	J5	Sheep
25. 1	7.12	F2	G5	Rat	7. 2	20.12	F2	K6	Deer
26. 1	8.12	F2	H6	Swallow	8. 2	21.12	F2	A7	Horse
27. 1	9.12	F2	J7	Pig	9. 2	22.12	F2	B8	Stag
28. 1	10.12	F2	K8	Porcupine	10. 2	23.12	F2	C9	Serpent
29. 1	11.12	F2	A9	Wolf	11. 2	24.12	F2	D10	Earthworm
30. 1	12.12	F2	B10	Dog	12. 2	25.12	F2	E11	Crocodile
31. 1	13.12	F2	C11	Pheasant	13. 2	26.12	F2	F12	Dragon
1. 2	14.12	F2	D12	Cock	14. 2	27.12	F2	G1	Badger
2. 2	15.12	F2	E1	Crow	15. 2	28.12	F2	H2	Hare
3. 2	16.12	F2	F2	Monkey	16. 2	29.12	F2	J3	Fox
4. 2	17.12	F2	G3	Gibbon					

HSIN WEI YEAR

17. 2	1. 1	G3	K4	Tiger	13. 4	26. 2	H4	E11	Fox
18. 2	2. 1	G3	A5	Leopard	14. 4	27. 2	H4	F12	Tiger
19. 2	3. 1	G3	B6	Griffon	15. 4	28. 2	H4	G1	Leopard
20. 2	4. 1	G3	C7	Ox	16. 4	29. 2	H4	H2	Griffon
21. 2	5. 1	G3	D8	Bat	17. 4	30. 2	H4	J3	Ox
22. 2	6. 1	G3	E9	Rat	18. 4	1. 3	J5	K4	Bat
23. 2	7. 1	G3	F10	Swallow	19. 4	2. 3	J5	A5	Rat
24. 2	8. 1	G3	G11	Pig	20. 4	3. 3	J5	B6	Swallow
25. 2	9. 1	G3	H12	Porcupine	21. 4	4. 3	J5	C7	Pig
26. 2	10. 1	G3	J1	Wolf	22. 4	5. 3	J5	D8	Porcupine
27. 2	11. 1	G3	K2	Dog	23. 4	6. 3	J5	E9	Wolf
28. 2	12. 1	G3	A3	Pheasant	24. 4	7. 3	J5	F10	Dog
1. 3	13. 1	G3	B4	Cock	25. 4	8. 3	J5	G11	Pheasant
2. 3	14. 1	G3	C5	Crow	26. 4	9. 3	J5	H12	Cock
3. 3	15. 1	G3	D6	Monkey	27. 4	10. 3	J5	J1	Crow
4. 3	16. 1	G3	E7	Gibbon	28. 4	11. 3	J5	K2	Monkey
5. 3	17. 1	G3	F8	Tapir	29. 4	12. 3	J5	A3	Gibbon
6. 3	18. 1	G3	G9	Sheep	30. 4	13. 3	J5	B4	Tapir
7. 3	19. 1	G3	H10	Deer	1. 5	14. 3	J5	C5	Sheep
8. 3	20. 1	G3	J11	Horse	2. 5	15. 3	J5	D6	Deer
9. 3	21. 1	G3	K12	Stag	3. 5	16. 3	J5	E7	Horse
10. 3	22. 1	G3	A1	Serpent	4. 5	17. 3	J5	F8	Stag
11. 3	23. 1	G3	B2	Earthworm	5. 5	18. 3	J5	G9	Serpent
12. 3	24. 1	G3	C3	Crocodile	6. 5	19. 3	J5	H10	Earthworm
13. 3	25. 1	G3	D4	Dragon	7. 5	20. 3	J5	J11	Crocodile
14. 3	26. 1	G3	E5	Badger	8. 5	21. 3	J5	K12	Dragon
15. 3	27. 1	G3	F6	Hare	9. 5	22. 3	J5	A1	Badger
16. 3	28. 1	G3	G7	Fox	10. 5	23. 3	J5	B2	Hare
17. 3	29. 1	G3	H8	Tiger	11. 5	24. 3	J5	C3	Fox
18. 3	30. 1	G3	J9	Leopard	12. 5	25. 3	J5	D4	Tiger
19. 3	1. 2	H4	K10	Griffon	13. 5	26. 3	J5	E5	Leopard
20. 3	2. 2	H4	A11	Ox	14. 5	27. 3	J5	F6	Griffon
21. 3	3. 2	H4	B12	Bat	15. 5	28. 3	J5	G7	Ox
22. 3	4. 2	H4	C1	Rat	16. 5	29. 3	J5	H8	Bat
23. 3	5. 2	H4	D2	Swallow	17. 5	1. 4	K6	J9	Rat
24. 3	6. 2	H4	E3	Pig	18. 5	2. 4	K6	K10	Swallow
25. 3	7. 2	H4	F4	Porcupine	19. 5	3. 4	K6	A11	Pig
26. 3	8. 2	H4	G5	Wolf	20. 5	4. 4	K6	B12	Porcupine
27. 3	9. 2	H4	H6	Dog	21. 5	5. 4	K6	C1	Wolf
28. 3	10. 2	H4	J7	Pheasant	22. 5	6. 4	K6	D2	Dog
29. 3	11. 2	H4	K8	Cock	23. 5	7. 4	K6	E3	Pheasant
30. 3	12. 2	H4	A9	Crow	24. 5	8. 4	K6	F4	Cock
31. 3	13. 2	H4	B10	Monkey	25. 5	9. 4	K6	G5	Crow
1. 4	14. 2	H4	C11	Gibbon	26. 5	10. 4	K6	H6	Monkey
2. 4	15. 2	H4	D12	Tapir	27. 5	11. 4	K6	J7	Gibbon
3. 4	16. 2	H4	E1	Sheep	28. 5	12. 4	K6	K8	Tapir
4. 4	17. 2	H4	F2	Deer	29. 5	13. 4	K6	A9	Sheep
5. 4	18. 2	H4	G3	Horse	30. 5	14. 4	K6	B10	Deer
6. 4	19. 2	H4	H4	Stag	31. 5	15. 4	K6	C11	Horse
7. 4	20. 2	H4	J5	Serpent	1. 6	16. 4	K6	D12	Stag
8. 4	21. 2	H4	K6	Earthworm	2. 6	17. 4	K6	E1	Serpent
9. 4	22. 2	H4	A7	Crocodile	3. 6	18. 4	K6	F2	Earthworm
10. 4	23. 2	H4	B8	Dragon	4. 6	19. 4	K6	G3	Crocodile
11. 4	24. 2	H4	C9	Badger	5. 6	20. 4	K6	H4	Dragon
12. 4	25. 2	H4	D10	Hare	6. 6	21. 4	K6	J5	Badger

Solar date	*Lunar date*	*Month HS/EB*	*Day HS/EB*	*Constellation*
7. 6	22. 4	K6	K6	Hare
8. 6	23. 4	K6	A7	Fox
9. 6	24. 4	K6	B8	Tiger
10. 6	25. 4	K6	C9	Leopard
11. 6	26. 4	K6	D10	Griffon
12. 6	27. 4	K6	E11	Ox
13. 6	28. 4	K6	F12	Bat
14. 6	29. 4	K6	G1	Rat
15. 6	30. 4	K6	H2	Swallow
16. 6	1. 5	A7	J3	Pig
17. 6	2. 5	A7	K4	Porcupine
18. 6	3. 5	A7	A5	Wolf
19. 6	4. 5	A7	B6	Dog
20. 6	5. 5	A7	C7	Pheasant
21. 6	6. 5	A7	D8	Cock
22. 6	7. 5	A7	E9	Crow
23. 6	8. 5	A7	F10	Monkey
24. 6	9. 5	A7	G11	Gibbon
25. 6	10. 5	A7	H12	Tapir
26. 6	11. 5	A7	J1	Sheep
27. 6	12. 5	A7	K2	Deer
28. 6	13. 5	A7	A3	Horse
29. 6	14. 5	A7	B4	Stag
30. 6	15. 5	A7	C5	Serpent
1. 7	16. 5	A7	D6	Earthworm
2. 7	17. 5	A7	E7	Crocodile
3. 7	18. 5	A7	F8	Dragon
4. 7	19. 5	A7	G9	Badger
5. 7	20. 5	A7	H10	Hare
6. 7	21. 5	A7	J11	Fox
7. 7	22. 5	A7	K12	Tiger
8. 7	23. 5	A7	A1	Leopard
9. 7	24. 5	A7	B2	Griffon
10. 7	25. 5	A7	C3	Ox
11. 7	26. 5	A7	D4	Bat
12. 7	27. 5	A7	E5	Rat
13. 7	28. 5	A7	F6	Swallow
14. 7	29. 5	A7	G7	Pig
15. 7	1. 6	B8	H8	Porcupine
16. 7	2. 6	B8	J9	Wolf
17. 7	3. 6	B8	K10	Dog
18. 7	4. 6	B8	A11	Pheasant
19. 7	5. 6	B8	B12	Cock
20. 7	6. 6	B8	C1	Crow
21. 7	7. 6	B8	D2	Monkey
22. 7	8. 6	B8	E3	Gibbon
23. 7	9. 6	B8	F4	Tapir
24. 7	10. 6	B8	G5	Sheep
25. 7	11. 6	B8	H6	Deer
26. 7	12. 6	B8	J7	Horse
27. 7	13. 6	B8	K8	Stag
28. 7	14. 6	B8	A9	Serpent
29. 7	15. 6	B8	B10	Earthworm
30. 7	16. 6	B8	C11	Crocodile
31. 7	17. 6	B8	D12	Dragon
1. 8	18. 6	B8	E1	Badger
2. 8	19. 6	B8	F2	Hare
3. 8	20. 6	B8	G3	Fox
4. 8	21. 6	B8	H4	Tiger
5. 8	22. 6	B8	J5	Leopard
6. 8	23. 6	B8	K6	Griffon
7. 8	24. 6	B8	A7	Ox
8. 8	25. 6	B8	B8	Bat
9. 8	26. 6	B8	C9	Rat
10. 8	27. 6	B8	D10	Swallow
11. 8	28. 6	B8	E11	Pig
12. 8	29. 6	B8	F12	Porcupine
13. 8	30. 6	B8	G1	Wolf
14. 8	1. 7	C9	H2	Dog
15. 8	2. 7	C9	J3	Pheasant
16. 8	3. 7	C9	K4	Cock
17. 8	4. 7	C9	A5	Crow
18. 8	5. 7	C9	B6	Monkey

Solar date	*Lunar date*	*Month HS/EB*	*Day HS/EB*	*Constellation*
19. 8	6. 7	C9	C7	Gibbon
20. 8	7. 7	C9	D8	Tapir
21. 8	8. 7	C9	E9	Sheep
22. 8	9. 7	C9	F10	Deer
23. 8	10. 7	C9	G11	Horse
24. 8	11. 7	C9	H12	Stag
25. 8	12. 7	C9	J1	Serpent
26. 8	13. 7	C9	K2	Earthworm
27. 8	14. 7	C9	A3	Crocodile
28. 8	15. 7	C9	B4	Dragon
29. 8	16. 7	C9	C5	Badger
30. 8	17. 7	C9	D6	Hare
31. 8	18. 7	C9	E7	Fox
1. 9	19. 7	C9	F8	Tiger
2. 9	20. 7	C9	G9	Leopard
3. 9	21. 7	C9	H10	Griffon
4. 9	22. 7	C9	J11	Ox
5. 9	23. 7	C9	K12	Bat
6. 9	24. 7	C9	A1	Rat
7. 9	25. 7	C9	B2	Swallow
8. 9	26. 7	C9	C3	Pig
9. 9	27. 7	C9	D4	Porcupine
10. 9	28. 7	C9	E5	Wolf
11. 9	29. 7	C9	F6	Dog
12. 9	1. 8	D10	G7	Pheasant
13. 9	2. 8	D10	H8	Cock
14. 9	3. 8	D10	J9	Crow
15. 9	4. 8	D10	K10	Monkey
16. 9	5. 8	D10	A11	Gibbon
17. 9	6. 8	D10	B12	Tapir
18. 9	7. 8	D10	C1	Sheep
19. 9	8. 8	D10	D2	Deer
20. 9	9. 8	D10	E3	Horse
21. 9	10. 8	D10	F4	Stag
22. 9	11. 8	D10	G5	Serpent
23. 9	12. 8	D10	H6	Earthworm
24. 9	13. 8	D10	J7	Crocodile
25. 9	14. 8	D10	K8	Dragon
26. 9	15. 8	D10	A9	Badger
27. 9	16. 8	D10	B10	Hare
28. 9	17. 8	D10	C11	Fox
29. 9	18. 8	D10	D12	Tiger
30. 9	19. 8	D10	E1	Leopard
1.10	20. 8	D10	F2	Griffon
2.10	21. 8	D10	G3	Ox
3.10	22. 8	D10	H4	Bat
4.10	23. 8	D10	J5	Rat
5.10	24. 8	D10	K6	Swallow
6.10	25. 8	D10	A7	Pig
7.10	26. 8	D10	B8	Porcupine
8.10	27. 8	D10	C9	Wolf
9.10	28. 8	D10	D10	Dog
10.10	29. 8	D10	E11	Pheasant
11.10	1. 9	E11	F12	Cock
12.10	2. 9	E11	G1	Crow
13.10	3. 9	E11	H2	Monkey
14.10	4. 9	E11	J3	Gibbon
15.10	5. 9	E11	K4	Tapir
16.10	6. 9	E11	A5	Sheep
17.10	7. 9	E11	B6	Deer
18.10	8. 9	E11	C7	Horse
19.10	9. 9	E11	D8	Stag
20.10	10. 9	E11	E9	Serpent
21.10	11. 9	E11	F10	Earthworm
22.10	12. 9	E11	G11	Crocodile
23.10	13. 9	E11	H12	Dragon
24.10	14. 9	E11	J1	Badger
25.10	15. 9	E11	K2	Hare
26.10	16. 9	E11	A3	Fox
27.10	17. 9	E11	B4	Tiger
28.10	18. 9	E11	C5	Leopard
29.10	19. 9	E11	D6	Griffon
30.10	20. 9	E11	E7	Ox

Solar date	*Lunar date*	*Month HS/EB*	*Day HS/EB*	*Constellation*
31.10	21. 9	E11	F8	Bat
1.11	22. 9	E11	G9	Rat
2.11	23. 9	E11	H10	Swallow
3.11	24. 9	E11	J11	Pig
4.11	25. 9	E11	K12	Porcupine
5.11	26. 9	E11	A1	Wolf
6.11	27. 9	E11	B2	Dog
7.11	28. 9	E11	C3	Pheasant
8.11	29. 9	E11	D4	Cock
9.11	30. 9	E11	E5	Crow
10.11	1.10	F12	F6	Monkey
11.11	2.10	F12	G7	Gibbon
12.11	3.10	F12	H8	Tapir
13.11	4.10	F12	J9	Sheep
14.11	5.10	F12	K10	Deer
15.11	6.10	F12	A11	Horse
16.11	7.10	F12	B12	Stag
17.11	8.10	F12	C1	Serpent
18.11	9.10	F12	D2	Earthworm
19.11	10.10	F12	E3	Crocodile
20.11	11.10	F12	F4	Dragon
21.11	12.10	F12	G5	Badger
22.11	13.10	F12	H6	Hare
23.11	14.10	F12	J7	Fox
24.11	15.10	F12	K8	Tiger
25.11	16.10	F12	A9	Leopard
26.11	17.10	F12	B10	Griffon
27.11	18.10	F12	C11	Ox
28.11	19.10	F12	D12	Bat
29.11	20.10	F12	E1	Rat
30.11	21.10	F12	F2	Swallow
1.12	22.10	F12	G3	Pig
2.12	23.10	F12	H4	Porcupine
3.12	24.10	F12	J5	Wolf
4.12	25.10	F12	K6	Dog
5.12	26.10	F12	A7	Pheasant
6.12	27.10	F12	B8	Cock
7.12	28.10	F12	C9	Crow
8.12	29.10	F12	D10	Monkey
9.12	1.11	G1	E11	Gibbon
10.12	2.11	G1	F12	Tapir
11.12	3.11	G1	G1	Sheep
12.12	4.11	G1	H2	Deer
13.12	5.11	G1	J3	Horse
14.12	6.11	G1	K4	Stag
15.12	7.11	G1	A5	Serpent
16.12	8.11	G1	B6	Earthworm
17.12	9.11	G1	C7	Crocodile
18.12	10.11	G1	D8	Dragon
19.12	11.11	G1	E9	Badger

Solar date	*Lunar date*	*Month HS/EB*	*Day HS/EB*	*Constellation*
20.12	12.11	G1	F10	Hare
21.12	13.11	G1	G11	Fox
22.12	14.11	G1	H12	Tiger
23.12	15.11	G1	J1	Leopard
24.12	16.11	G1	K2	Griffon
25.12	17.11	G1	A3	Ox
26.12	18.11	G1	B4	Bat
27.12	19.11	G1	C5	Rat
28.12	20.11	G1	D6	Swallow
29.12	21.11	G1	E7	Pig
30.12	22.11	G1	F8	Porcupine
31.12	23.11	G1	G9	Wolf
1932				
1. 1	24.11	G1	H10	Dog
2. 1	25.11	G1	J11	Pheasant
3. 1	26.11	G1	K12	Cock
4. 1	27.11	G1	A1	Crow
5. 1	28.11	G1	B2	Monkey
6. 1	29.11	G1	C3	Gibbon
7. 1	30.11	G1	D4	Tapir
8. 1	1.12	H2	E5	Sheep
9. 1	2.12	H2	F6	Deer
10. 1	3.12	H2	G7	Horse
11. 1	4.12	H2	H8	Stag
12. 1	5.12	H2	J9	Serpent
13. 1	6.12	H2	K10	Earthworm
14. 1	7.12	H2	A11	Crocodile
15. 1	8.12	H2	B12	Dragon
16. 1	9.12	H2	C1	Badger
17. 1	10.12	H2	D2	Hare
18. 1	11.12	H2	E3	Fox
19. 1	12.12	H2	F4	Tiger
20. 1	13.12	H2	G5	Leopard
21. 1	14.12	H2	H6	Griffon
22. 1	15.12	H2	J7	Ox
23. 1	16.12	H2	K8	Bat
24. 1	17.12	H2	A9	Rat
25. 1	18.12	H2	B10	Swallow
26. 1	19.12	H2	C11	Pig
27. 1	20.12	H2	D12	Porcupine
28. 1	21.12	H2	E1	Wolf
29. 1	22.12	H2	F2	Dog
30. 1	23.12	H2	G3	Pheasant
31. 1	24.12	H2	H4	Cock
1. 2	25.12	H2	J5	Crow
2. 2	26.12	H2	K6	Monkey
3. 2	27.12	H2	A7	Gibbon
4. 2	28.12	H2	B8	Tapir
5. 2	29.12	H2	C9	Sheep

JEN SHEN YEAR

6. 2	1. 1	J3	D10	Deer
7. 2	2. 1	J3	E11	Horse
8. 2	3. 1	J3	F12	Stag
9. 2	4. 1	J3	G1	Serpent
10. 2	5. 1	J3	H2	Earthworm
11. 2	6. 1	J3	J3	Crocodile
12. 2	7. 1	J3	K4	Dragon
13. 2	8. 1	J3	A5	Badger
14. 2	9. 1	J3	B6	Hare
15. 2	10. 1	J3	C7	Fox
16. 2	11. 1	J3	D8	Tiger
17. 2	12. 1	J3	E9	Leopard
18. 2	13. 1	J3	F10	Griffon
19. 2	14. 1	J3	G11	Ox
20. 2	15. 1	J3	H12	Bat
21. 2	16. 1	J3	J1	Rat
22. 2	17. 1	J3	K2	Swallow
23. 2	18. 1	J3	A3	Pig

24. 2	19. 1	J3	B4	Porcupine
25. 2	20. 1	J3	C5	Wolf
26. 2	21. 1	J3	D6	Dog
27. 2	22. 1	J3	E7	Pheasant
28. 2	23. 1	J3	F8	Cock
29. 2	24. 1	J3	G9	Crow
1. 3	25. 1	J3	H10	Monkey
2. 3	26. 1	J3	J11	Gibbon
3. 3	27. 1	J3	K12	Tapir
4. 3	28. 1	J3	A1	Sheep
5. 3	29. 1	J3	B2	Deer
6. 3	30. 1	J3	C3	Horse
7. 3	1. 2	K4	D4	Stag
8. 3	2. 2	K4	E5	Serpent
9. 3	3. 2	K4	F6	Earthworm
10. 3	4. 2	K4	G7	Crocodile
11. 3	5. 2	K4	H8	Dragon
12. 3	6. 2	K4	J9	Badger

Solar date	Lunar date	Month HS/EB	Day HS/EB	Constellation
13. 3	7. 2	K4	K10	Hare
14. 3	8. 2	K4	A11	Fox
15. 3	9. 2	K4	B12	Tiger
16. 3	10. 2	K4	C1	Leopard
17. 3	11. 2	K4	D2	Griffon
18. 3	12. 2	K4	E3	Ox
19. 3	13. 2	K4	F4	Bat
20. 3	14. 2	K4	G5	Rat
21. 3	15. 2	K4	H6	Swallow
22. 3	16. 2	K4	J7	Pig
23. 3	17. 2	K4	K8	Porcupine
24. 3	18. 2	K4	A9	Wolf
25. 3	19. 2	K4	B10	Dog
26. 3	20. 2	K4	C11	Pheasant
27. 3	21. 2	K4	D12	Cock
28. 3	22. 2	K4	E1	Crow
29. 3	23. 2	K4	F2	Monkey
30. 3	24. 2	K4	G3	Gibbon
31. 3	25. 2	K4	H4	Tapir
1. 4	26. 2	K4	J5	Sheep
2. 4	27. 2	K4	K6	Deer
3. 4	28. 2	K4	A7	Horse
4. 4	29. 2	K4	B8	Stag
5. 4	30. 2	K4	C9	Serpent
6. 4	1. 3	A5	D10	Earthworm
7. 4	2. 3	A5	E11	Crocodile
8. 4	3. 3	A5	F12	Dragon
9. 4	4. 3	A5	G1	Badger
10. 4	5. 3	A5	H2	Hare
11. 4	6. 3	A5	J3	Fox
12. 4	7. 3	A5	K4	Tiger
13. 4	8. 3	A5	A5	Leopard
14. 4	9. 3	A5	B6	Griffon
15. 4	10. 3	A5	C7	Ox
16. 4	11. 3	A5	D8	Bat
17. 4	12. 3	A5	E9	Rat
18. 4	13. 3	A5	F10	Swallow
19. 4	14. 3	A5	G11	Pig
20. 4	15. 3	A5	H12	Porcupine
21. 4	16. 3	A5	J1	Wolf
22. 4	17. 3	A5	K2	Dog
23. 4	18. 3	A5	A3	Pheasant
24. 4	19. 3	A5	B4	Cock
25. 4	20. 3	A5	C5	Crow
26. 4	21. 3	A5	D6	Monkey
27. 4	22. 3	A5	E7	Gibbon
28. 4	23. 3	A5	F8	Tapir
29. 4	24. 3	A5	G9	Sheep
30. 4	25. 3	A5	H10	Deer
1. 5	26. 3	A5	J11	Horse
2. 5	27. 3	A5	K12	Stag
3. 5	28. 3	A5	A1	Serpent
4. 5	29. 3	A5	B2	Earthworm
5. 5	30. 3	A5	C3	Crocodile
6. 5	1. 4	B6	D4	Dragon
7. 5	2. 4	B6	E5	Badger
8. 5	3. 4	B6	F6	Hare
9. 5	4. 4	B6	G7	Fox
10. 5	5. 4	B6	H8	Tiger
11. 5	6. 4	B6	J9	Leopard
12. 5	7. 4	B6	K10	Griffon
13. 5	8. 4	B6	A11	Ox
14. 5	9. 4	B6	B12	Bat
15. 5	10. 4	B6	C1	Rat
16. 5	11. 4	B6	D2	Swallow
17. 5	12. 4	B6	E3	Pig
18. 5	13. 4	B6	F4	Porcupine
19. 5	14. 4	B6	G5	Wolf
20. 5	15. 4	B6	H6	Dog
21. 5	16. 4	B6	J7	Pheasant
22. 5	17. 4	B6	K8	Cock
23. 5	18. 4	B6	A9	Crow
24. 5	19. 4	B6	B10	Monkey
25. 5	20. 4	B6	C11	Gibbon
26. 5	21. 4	B6	D12	Tapir
27. 5	22. 4	B6	E1	Sheep
28. 5	23. 4	B6	F2	Deer
29. 5	24. 4	B6	G3	Horse
30. 5	25. 4	B6	H4	Stag
31. 5	26. 4	B6	J5	Serpent
1. 6	27. 4	B6	K6	Earthworm
2. 6	28. 4	B6	A7	Crocodile
3. 6	29. 4	B6	B8	Dragon
4. 6	1. 5	C7	C9	Badger
5. 6	2. 5	C7	D10	Hare
6. 6	3. 5	C7	E11	Fox
7. 6	4. 5	C7	F12	Tiger
8. 6	5. 5	C7	G1	Leopard
9. 6	6. 5	C7	H2	Griffon
10. 6	7. 5	C7	J3	Ox
11. 6	8. 5	C7	K4	Bat
12. 6	9. 5	C7	A5	Rat
13. 6	10. 5	C7	B6	Swallow
14. 6	11. 5	C7	C7	Pig
15. 6	12. 5	C7	D8	Porcupine
16. 6	13. 5	C7	E9	Wolf
17. 6	14. 5	C7	F10	Dog
18. 6	15. 5	C7	G11	Pheasant
19. 6	16. 5	C7	H12	Cock
20. 6	17. 5	C7	J1	Crow
21. 6	18. 5	C7	K2	Monkey
22. 6	19. 5	C7	A3	Gibbon
23. 6	20. 5	C7	B4	Tapir
24. 6	21. 5	C7	C5	Sheep
25. 6	22. 5	C7	D6	Deer
26. 6	23. 5	C7	E7	Horse
27. 6	24. 5	C7	F8	Stag
28. 6	25. 5	C7	G9	Serpent
29. 6	26. 5	C7	H10	Earthworm
30. 6	27. 5	C7	J11	Crocodile
1. 7	28. 5	C7	K12	Dragon
2. 7	29. 5	C7	A1	Badger
3. 7	30. 5	C7	B2	Hare
4. 7	1. 6	D8	C3	Fox
5. 7	2. 6	D8	D4	Tiger
6. 7	3. 6	D8	E5	Leopard
7. 7	4. 6	D8	F6	Griffon
8. 7	5. 6	D8	G7	Ox
9. 7	6. 6	D8	H8	Bat
10. 7	7. 6	D8	J9	Rat
11. 7	8. 6	D8	K10	Swallow
12. 7	9. 6	D8	A11	Pig
13. 7	10. 6	D8	B12	Porcupine
14. 7	11. 6	D8	C1	Wolf
15. 7	12. 6	D8	D2	Dog
16. 7	13. 6	D8	E3	Pheasant
17. 7	14. 6	D8	F4	Cock
18. 7	15. 6	D8	G5	Crow
19. 7	16. 6	D8	H6	Monkey
20. 7	17. 6	D8	J7	Gibbon
21. 7	18. 6	D8	K8	Tapir
22. 7	19. 6	D8	A9	Sheep
23. 7	20. 6	D8	B10	Deer
24. 7	21. 6	D8	C11	Horse
25. 7	22. 6	D8	D12	Stag
26. 7	23. 6	D8	E1	Serpent
27. 7	24. 6	D8	F2	Earthworm
28. 7	25. 6	D8	G3	Crocodile
29. 7	26. 6	D8	H4	Dragon
30. 7	27. 6	D8	J5	Badger
31. 7	28. 6	D8	K6	Hare
1. 8	29. 6	D8	A7	Fox
2. 8	1. 7	E9	B8	Tiger
3. 8	2. 7	E9	C9	Leopard
4. 8	3. 7	E9	D10	Griffon
5. 8	4. 7	E9	E11	Ox

Solar date	*Lunar date*	*Month HS/EB*	*Day HS/EB*	*Constellation*
6. 8	5. 7	E9	F12	Bat
7. 8	6. 7	E9	G1	Rat
8. 8	7. 7	E9	H2	Swallow
9. 8	8. 7	E9	J3	Pig
10. 8	9. 7	E9	K4	Porcupine
11. 8	10. 7	E9	A5	Wolf
12. 8	11. 7	E9	B6	Dog
13. 8	12. 7	E9	C7	Pheasant
14. 8	13. 7	E9	D8	Cock
15. 8	14. 7	E9	E9	Crow
16. 8	15. 7	E9	F10	Monkey
17. 8	16. 7	E9	G11	Gibbon
18. 8	17. 7	E9	H12	Tapir
19. 8	18. 7	E9	J1	Sheep
20. 8	19. 7	E9	K2	Deer
21. 8	20. 7	E9	A3	Horse
22. 8	21. 7	E9	B4	Stag
23. 8	22. 7	E9	C5	Serpent
24. 8	23. 7	E9	D6	Earthworm
25. 8	24. 7	E9	E7	Crocodile
26. 8	25. 7	E9	F8	Dragon
27. 8	26. 7	E9	G9	Badger
28. 8	27. 7	E9	H10	Hare
29. 8	28. 7	E9	J11	Fox
30. 8	29. 7	E9	K12	Tiger
31. 8	30. 7	E9	A1	Leopard
1. 9	1. 8	F10	B2	Griffon
2. 9	2. 8	F10	C3	Ox
3. 9	3. 8	F10	D4	Bat
4. 9	4. 8	F10	E5	Rat
5. 9	5. 8	F10	F6	Swallow
6. 9	6. 8	F10	G7	Pig
7. 9	7. 8	F10	H8	Porcupine
8. 9	8. 8	F10	J9	Wolf
9. 9	9. 8	F10	K10	Dog
10. 9	10. 8	F10	A11	Pheasant
11. 9	11. 8	F10	B12	Cock
12. 9	12. 8	F10	C1	Crow
13. 9	13. 8	F10	D2	Monkey
14. 9	14. 8	F10	E3	Gibbon
15. 9	15. 8	F10	F4	Tapir
16. 9	16. 8	F10	G5	Sheep
17. 9	17. 8	F10	H6	Deer
18. 9	18. 8	F10	J7	Horse
19. 9	19. 8	F10	K8	Stag
20. 9	20. 8	F10	A9	Serpent
21. 9	21. 8	F10	B10	Earthworm
22. 9	22. 8	F10	C11	Crocodile
23. 9	23. 8	F10	D12	Dragon
24. 9	24. 8	F10	E1	Badger
25. 9	25. 8	F10	F2	Hare
26. 9	26. 8	F10	G3	Fox
27. 9	27. 8	F10	H4	Tiger
28. 9	28. 8	F10	J5	Leopard
29. 9	29. 8	F10	K6	Griffon
30. 9	1. 9	G11	A7	Ox
1.10	2. 9	G11	B8	Bat
2.10	3. 9	G11	C9	Rat
3.10	4. 9	G11	D10	Swallow
4.10	5. 9	G11	E11	Pig
5.10	6. 9	G11	F12	Porcupine
6.10	7. 9	G11	G1	Wolf
7.10	8. 9	G11	H2	Dog
8.10	9. 9	G11	J3	Pheasant
9.10	10. 9	G11	K4	Cock
10.10	11. 9	G11	A5	Crow
11.10	12. 9	G11	B6	Monkey
12.10	13. 9	G11	C7	Gibbon
13.10	14. 9	G11	D8	Tapir
14.10	15. 9	G11	E9	Sheep
15.10	16. 9	G11	F10	Deer
16.10	17. 9	G11	G11	Horse
17.10	18. 9	G11	H12	Stag
18.10	19. 9	G11	J1	Serpent
19.10	20. 9	G11	K2	Earthworm
20.10	21. 9	G11	A3	Crocodile
21.10	22. 9	G11	B4	Dragon
22.10	23. 9	G11	C5	Badger
23.10	24. 9	G11	D6	Hare
24.10	25. 9	G11	E7	Fox
25.10	26. 9	G11	F8	Tiger
26.10	27. 9	G11	G9	Leopard
27.10	28. 9	G11	H10	Griffon
28.10	29. 9	G11	J11	Ox
29.10	1.10	H12	K12	Bat
30.10	2.10	H12	A1	Rat
31.10	3.10	H12	B2	Swallow
1.11	4.10	H12	C3	Pig
2.11	5.10	H12	D4	Porcupine
3.11	6.10	H12	E5	Wolf
4.11	7.10	H12	F6	Dog
5.11	8.10	H12	G7	Pheasant
6.11	9.10	H12	H8	Cock
7.11	10.10	H12	J9	Crow
8.11	11.10	H12	K10	Monkey
9.11	12.10	H12	A11	Gibbon
10.11	13.10	H12	B12	Tapir
11.11	14.10	H12	C1	Sheep
12.11	15.10	H12	D2	Deer
13.11	16.10	H12	E3	Horse
14.11	17.10	H12	F4	Stag
15.11	18.10	H12	G5	Serpent
16.11	19.10	H12	H6	Earthworm
17.11	20.10	H12	J7	Crocodile
18.11	21.10	H12	K8	Dragon
19.11	22.10	H12	A9	Badger
20.11	23.10	H12	B10	Hare
21.11	24.10	H12	C11	Fox
22.11	25.10	H12	D12	Tiger
23.11	26.10	H12	E1	Leopard
24.11	27.10	H12	F2	Griffon
25.11	28.10	H12	G3	Ox
26.11	29.10	H12	H4	Bat
27.11	30.10	H12	J5	Rat
28.11	1.11	J1	K6	Swallow
29.11	2.11	J1	A7	Pig
30.11	3.11	J1	B8	Porcupine
1.12	4.11	J1	C9	Wolf
2.12	5.11	J1	D10	Dog
3.12	6.11	J1	E11	Pheasant
4.12	7.11	J1	F12	Cock
5.12	8.11	J1	G1	Crow
6.12	9.11	J1	H2	Monkey
7.12	10.11	J1	J3	Gibbon
8.12	11.11	J1	K4	Tapir
9.12	12.11	J1	A5	Sheep
10.12	13.11	J1	B6	Deer
11.12	14.11	J1	C7	Horse
12 12	15.11	J1	D8	Stag
13.12	16.11	J1	E9	Serpent
14.12	17.11	J1	F10	Earthworm
15.12	18.11	J1	G11	Crocodile
16.12	19.11	J1	H12	Dragon
17.12	20.11	J1	J1	Badger
18.12	21.11	J1	K2	Hare
19.12	22.11	J1	A3	Fox
20.12	23.11	J1	B4	Tiger
21.12	24.11	J1	C5	Leopard
22.12	25.11	J1	D6	Griffon
23.12	26.11	J1	E7	Ox
24.12	27.11	J1	F8	Bat
25.12	28.11	J1	G9	Rat
26.12	29.11	J1	H10	Swallow
27.12	1.12	K2	J11	Pig
28.12	2.12	K2	K12	Porcupine
29.12	3.12	K2	A1	Wolf

Solar date	*Lunar date*	*Month HS/EB*	*Day HS/EB*	*Constellation*
30.12	4.12	K2	B2	Dog
31.12	5.12	K2	C3	Pheasant
1933				
1. 1	6.12	K2	D4	Cock
2. 1	7.12	K2	E5	Crow
3. 1	8.12	K2	F6	Monkey
4. 1	9.12	K2	G7	Gibbon
5. 1	10.12	K2	H8	Tapir
6. 1	11.12	K2	J9	Sheep
7. 1	12.12	K2	K10	Deer
8. 1	13.12	K2	A11	Horse
9. 1	14.12	K2	B12	Stag
10. 1	15.12	K2	C1	Serpent
11. 1	16.12	K2	D2	Earthworm
12. 1	17.12	K2	E3	Crocodile
13. 1	18.12	K2	F4	Dragon
14. 1	19.12	K2	G5	Badger
15. 1	20.12	K2	H6	Hare
16. 1	21.12	K2	J7	Fox
17. 1	22.12	K2	K8	Tiger
18. 1	23.12	K2	A9	Leopard
19. 1	24.12	K2	B10	Griffon
20. 1	25.12	K2	C11	Ox
21. 1	26.12	K2	D12	Bat
22. 1	27.12	K2	E1	Rat
23. 1	28.12	K2	F2	Swallow
24. 1	29.12	K2	G3	Pig
25. 1	30.12	K2	H4	Porcupine

KUEI YU YEAR

26. 1	1. 1	A3	J5	Wolf
27. 1	2. 1	A3	K6	Dog
28. 1	3. 1	A3	A7	Pheasant
29. 1	4. 1	A3	B8	Cock
30. 1	5. 1	A3	C9	Crow
31. 1	6. 1	A3	D10	Monkey
1. 2	7. 1	A3	E11	Gibbon
2. 2	8. 1	A3	F12	Tapir
3. 2	9. 1	A3	G1	Sheep
4. 2	10. 1	A3	H2	Deer
5. 2	11. 1	A3	J3	Horse
6. 2	12. 1	A3	K4	Stag
7. 2	13. 1	A3	A5	Serpent
8. 2	14. 1	A3	B6	Earthworm
9. 2	15. 1	A3	C7	Crocodile
10. 2	16. 1	A3	D8	Dragon
11. 2	17. 1	A3	E9	Badger
12. 2	18. 1	A3	F10	Hare
13. 2	19. 1	A3	G11	Fox
14. 2	20. 1	A3	H12	Tiger
15. 2	21. 1	A3	J1	Leopard
16. 2	22. 1	A3	K2	Griffon
17. 2	23. 1	A3	A3	Ox
18. 2	24. 1	A3	B4	Bat
19. 2	25. 1	A3	C5	Rat
20. 2	26. 1	A3	D6	Swallow
21. 2	27. 1	A3	E7	Pig
22. 2	28. 1	A3	F8	Porcupine
23. 2	29. 1	A3	G9	Wolf
24. 2	1. 2	B4	H10	Dog
25. 2	2. 2	B4	J11	Pheasant
26. 2	3. 2	B4	K12	Cock
27. 2	4. 2	B4	A1	Crow
28. 2	5. 2	B4	B2	Monkey
1. 3	6. 2	B4	C3	Gibbon
2. 3	7. 2	B4	D4	Tapir
3. 3	8. 2	B4	E5	Sheep
4. 3	9. 2	B4	F6	Deer
5. 3	10. 2	B4	G7	Horse
6. 3	11. 2	B4	H8	Stag
7. 3	12. 2	B4	J9	Serpent
8. 3	13. 2	B4	K10	Earthworm
9. 3	14. 2	B4	A11	Crocodile
10. 3	15. 2	B4	B12	Dragon
11. 3	16. 2	B4	C1	Badger
12. 3	17. 2	B4	D2	Hare
13. 3	18. 2	B4	E3	Fox
14. 3	19. 2	B4	F4	Tiger
15. 3	20. 2	B4	G5	Leopard
16. 3	21. 2	B4	H6	Griffon
17. 3	22. 2	B4	J7	Ox
18. 3	23. 2	B4	K8	Bat
19. 3	24. 2	B4	A9	Rat
20. 3	25. 2	B4	B10	Swallow
21. 3	26. 2	B4	C11	Pig
22. 3	27. 2	B4	D12	Porcupine
23. 3	28. 2	B4	E1	Wolf
24. 3	29. 2	B4	F2	Dog
25. 3	30. 2	B4	G3	Pheasant
26. 3	1. 3	C5	H4	Cock
27. 3	2. 3	C5	J5	Crow
28. 3	3. 3	C5	K6	Monkey
29. 3	4. 3	C5	A7	Gibbon
30. 3	5. 3	C5	B8	Tapir
31. 3	6. 3	C5	C9	Sheep
1. 4	7. 3	C5	D10	Deer
2. 4	8. 3	C5	E11	Horse
3. 4	9. 3	C5	F12	Stag
4. 4	10. 3	C5	G1	Serpent
5. 4	11. 3	C5	H2	Earthworm
6. 4	12. 3	C5	J3	Crocodile
7. 4	13. 3	C5	K4	Dragon
8. 4	14. 3	C5	A5	Badger
9. 4	15. 3	C5	B6	Hare
10. 4	16. 3	C5	C7	Fox
11. 4	17. 3	C5	D8	Tiger
12. 4	18. 3	C5	E9	Leopard
13. 4	19. 3	C5	F10	Griffon
14. 4	20. 3	C5	G11	Ox
15. 4	21. 3	C5	H12	Bat
16. 4	22. 3	C5	J1	Rat
17. 4	23. 3	C5	K2	Swallow
18. 4	24. 3	C5	A3	Pig
19. 4	25. 3	C5	B4	Porcupine
20. 4	26. 3	C5	C5	Wolf
21. 4	27. 3	C5	D6	Dog
22. 4	28. 3	C5	E7	Pheasant
23. 4	29. 3	C5	F8	Cock
24. 4	30. 3	C5	G9	Crow
25. 4	1. 4	D6	H10	Monkey
26. 4	2. 4	D6	J11	Gibbon
27. 4	3. 4	D6	K12	Tapir
28. 4	4. 4	D6	A1	Sheep
29. 4	5. 4	D6	B2	Deer
30. 4	6. 4	D6	C3	Horse
1. 5	7. 4	D6	D4	Stag
2. 5	8. 4	D6	E5	Serpent
3. 5	9. 4	D6	F6	Earthworm
4. 5	10. 4	D6	G7	Crocodile
5. 5	11. 4	D6	H8	Dragon
6. 5	12. 4	D6	J9	Badger
7. 5	13. 4	D6	K10	Hare
8. 5	14. 4	D6	A11	Fox
9. 5	15. 4	D6	B12	Tiger
10. 5	16. 4	D6	C1	Leopard
11. 5	17. 4	D6	D2	Griffon

Solar date	Lunar date	Month HS/EB	Day HS/EB	Constellation
12. 5	18. 4	D6	E3	Ox
13. 5	19. 4	D6	F4	Bat
14. 5	20. 4	D6	G5	Rat
15. 5	21. 4	D6	H6	Swallow
16. 5	22. 4	D6	J7	Pig
17. 5	23. 4	D6	K8	Porcupine
18. 5	24. 4	D6	A9	Wolf
19. 5	25. 4	D6	B10	Dog
20. 5	26. 4	D6	C11	Pheasant
21. 5	27. 4	D6	D12	Cock
22. 5	28. 4	D6	E1	Crow
23. 5	29. 4	D6	F2	Monkey
24. 5	1. 5	E7	G3	Gibbon
25. 5	2. 5	E7	H4	Tapir
26. 5	3. 5	E7	J5	Sheep
27. 5	4. 5	E7	K6	Deer
28. 5	5. 5	E7	A7	Horse
29. 5	6. 5	E7	B8	Stag
30. 5	7. 5	E7	C9	Serpent
31. 5	8. 5	E7	D10	Earthworm
1. 6	9. 5	E7	E11	Crocodile
2. 6	10. 5	E7	F12	Dragon
3. 5	11. 5	E7	G1	Badger
4. 5	12. 5	E7	H2	Hare
5. 6	13. 5	E7	J3	Fox
6. 6	14. 5	E7	K4	Tiger
7. 6	15. 5	E7	A5	Leopard
8. 6	16. 5	E7	B6	Griffon
9. 6	17. 5	E7	C7	Ox
10. 6	18. 5	E7	D8	Bat
11. 6	19. 5	E7	E9	Rat
12. 6	20. 5	E7	F10	Swallow
13. 6	21. 5	E7	G11	Pig
14. 6	22. 5	E7	H12	Porcupine
15. 6	23. 5	E7	J1	Wolf
16. 6	24. 5	E7	K2	Dog
17. 6	25. 5	E7	A3	Pheasant
18. 6	26. 5	E7	B4	Cock
19. 6	27. 5	E7	C5	Crow
20. 6	28. 5	E7	D6	Monkey
21. 6	29. 5	E7	E7	Gibbon
22. 6	30. 5	E7	F8	Tapir
23. 6	*1. 5*	*E7*	G9	Sheep
24. 6	*2. 5*	*E7*	H10	Deer
25. 6	*3 5*	*E7*	J11	Horse
26. 6	*4. 5*	*E7*	K12	Stag
27. 6	*5. 5*	*E7*	A1	Serpent
28. 6	*6. 5*	*E7*	B2	Earthworm
29. 6	*7. 5*	*E7*	C3	Crocodile
30. 6	*8. 5*	*E7*	D4	Dragon
1. 7	*9. 5*	*E7*	E5	Badger
2. 7	*10. 5*	*E7*	F6	Hare
3. 7	*11. 5*	*E7*	G7	Fox
4. 7	*12. 5*	*E7*	H8	Tiger
5. 7	*13. 5*	*E7*	J9	Leopard
6. 7	*14. 5*	*E7*	K10	Griffon
7. 7	*15. 5*	*E7*	A11	Ox
8. 7	*16. 5*	*E7*	B12	Bat
9. 7	*17. 5*	*E7*	C1	Rat
10. 7	*18. 5*	*E7*	D2	Swallow
11. 7	*19. 5*	*E7*	E3	Pig
12. 7	*20. 5*	*E7*	F4	Porcupine
13. 7	*21. 5*	*E7*	G5	Wolf
14. 7	*22. 5*	*E7*	H6	Dog
15. 7	*23. 5*	*E7*	J7	Pheasant
16. 7	*24. 5*	*E7*	K8	Cock
17. 7	*25. 5*	*E7*	A9	Crow
18. 7	*26. 5*	*E7*	B10	Monkey
19. 7	*27. 5*	*E7*	C11	Gibbon
20. 7	*28. 5*	*E7*	D12	Tapir
21. 7	*29. 5*	*E7*	E1	Sheep
22. 7	*30. 5*	*E7*	F2	Deer
23. 7	1. 6	F8	G3	Horse

Solar date	Lunar date	Month HS/EB	Day HS/EB	Constellation
24. 7	2. 6	F8	H4	Stag
25. 7	3. 6	F8	J5	Serpent
26. 7	4. 6	F8	K6	Earthworm
27. 7	5. 6	F8	A7	Crocodile
28. 7	6. 6	F8	B8	Dragon
29. 7	7. 6	F8	C9	Badger
30. 7	8. 6	F8	D10	Hare
31. 7	9. 6	F8	E11	Fox
1. 8	10. 6	F8	F12	Tiger
2. 8	11. 6	F8	G1	Leopard
3. 8	12. 6	F8	H2	Griffon
4. 8	13. 6	F8	J3	Ox
5. 8	14. 6	F8	K4	Bat
6. 8	15. 6	F8	A5	Rat
7. 8	16. 6	F8	B6	Swallow
8. 8	17. 6	F8	C7	Pig
9. 8	18. 6	F8	D8	Porcupine
10. 8	19. 6	F8	E9	Wolf
11. 8	20. 6	F8	F10	Dog
12. 8	21. 6	F8	G11	Pheasant
13. 8	22. 6	F8	H12	Cock
14. 8	23. 6	F8	J1	Crow
15. 8	24. 6	F8	K2	Monkey
16. 8	25. 6	F8	A3	Gibbon
17. 8	26. 6	F8	B4	Tapir
18. 8	27. 6	F8	C5	Sheep
19. 8	28. 6	F8	D6	Deer
20. 8	29. 6	F8	E7	Horse
21. 8	1. 7	G9	F8	Stag
22. 8	2. 7	G9	G9	Serpent
23. 8	3. 7	G9	H10	Earthworm
24. 8	4. 7	G9	J11	Crocodile
25. 8	5. 7	G9	K12	Dragon
26. 8	6. 7	G9	A1	Badger
27. 8	7. 7	G9	B2	Hare
28. 8	8. 7	G9	C3	Fox
29. 8	9. 7	G9	D4	Tiger
30. 8	10. 7	G9	E5	Leopard
31. 8	11. 7	G9	F6	Griffon
1. 9	12. 7	G9	G7	Ox
2. 9	13. 7	G9	H8	Bat
3. 9	14. 7	G9	J9	Rat
4. 9	15. 7	G9	K10	Swallow
5. 9	16. 7	G9	A11	Pig
6. 9	17. 7	G9	B12	Porcupine
7. 9	18. 7	G9	C1	Wolf
8. 9	19. 7	G9	D2	Dog
9. 9	20. 7	G9	E3	Pheasant
10. 9	21. 7	G9	F4	Cock
11. 9	22. 7	G9	G5	Crow
12. 9	23. 7	G9	H6	Monkey
13. 9	24. 7	G9	J7	Gibbon
14. 9	25. 7	G9	K8	Tapir
15. 9	26. 7	G9	A9	Sheep
16. 9	27. 7	G9	B10	Deer
17. 9	28. 7	G9	C11	Horse
18. 9	29. 7	G9	D12	Stag
19. 9	30. 7	G9	E1	Serpent
20. 9	1. 8	H10	F2	Earthworm
21. 9	2. 8	H10	G3	Crocodile
22. 9	3. 8	H10	H4	Dragon
23. 9	4. 8	H10	J5	Badger
24. 9	5. 8	H10	K6	Hare
25. 9	6. 8	H10	A7	Fox
26. 9	7. 8	H10	B8	Tiger
27. 9	8. 8	H10	C9	Leopard
28. 9	9. 8	H10	D10	Griffon
29. 9	10. 8	H10	E11	Ox
30. 9	11. 8	H10	F12	Bat
1.10	12. 8	H10	G1	Rat
2.10	13. 8	H10	H2	Swallow
3.10	14. 8	H10	J3	Pig
4.10	15. 8	H10	K4	Porcupine

Solar date	*Lunar date*	*Month HS/EB*	*Day HS/EB*	*Constellation*
5.10	16. 8	H10	A5	Wolf
6.10	17. 8	H10	B6	Dog
7.10	18. 8	H10	C7	Pheasant
8.10	19. 8	H10	D8	Cock
9.10	20. 8	H10	E9	Crow
10.10	21. 8	H10	F10	Monkey
11.10	22. 8	H10	G11	Gibbon
12.10	23. 8	H10	H12	Tapir
13.10	24. 8	H10	J1	Sheep
14.10	25. 8	H10	K2	Deer
15.10	26. 8	H10	A3	Horse
16.10	27. 8	H10	B4	Stag
17.10	28. 8	H10	C5	Serpent
18.10	29. 8	H10	D6	Earthworm
19.10	1. 9	J11	E7	Crocodile
20.10	2. 9	J11	F8	Dragon
21.10	3. 9	J11	G9	Badger
22.10	4. 9	J11	H10	Hare
23.10	5. 9	J11	J11	Fox
24.10	6. 9	J11	K12	Tiger
25.10	7. 9	J11	A1	Leopard
26.10	8. 9	J11	B2	Griffon
27.10	9. 9	J11	C3	Ox
28.10	10. 9	J11	D4	Bat
29.10	11. 9	J11	E5	Rat
30.10	12. 9	J11	F6	Swallow
31.10	13. 9	J11	G7	Pig
1.11	14. 9	J11	H8	Porcupine
2.11	15. 9	J11	J9	Wolf
3.11	16. 9	J11	K10	Dog
4.11	17. 9	J11	A11	Pheasant
5.11	18. 9	J11	B12	Cock
6.11	19. 9	J11	C1	Crow
7.11	20. 9	J11	D2	Monkey
8.11	21. 9	J11	E3	Gibbon
9.11	22. 9	J11	F4	Tapir
10.11	23. 9	J11	G5	Sheep
11.11	24. 9	J11	H6	Deer
12.11	25. 9	J11	J7	Horse
13.11	26. 9	J11	K8	Stag
14.11	27. 9	J11	A9	Serpent
15.11	28. 9	J11	B10	Earthworm
16.11	29. 9	J11	C11	Crocodile
17.11	30. 9	J11	D12	Dragon
18.11	1.10	K12	E1	Badger
19.11	2.10	K12	F2	Hare
20.11	3.10	K12	G3	Fox
21.11	4.10	K12	H4	Tiger
22.11	5.10	K12	J5	Leopard
23.11	6.10	K12	K6	Griffon
24.11	7.10	K12	A7	Ox
25.11	8.10	K12	B8	Bat
26.11	9.10	K12	C9	Rat
27.11	10.10	K12	D10	Swallow
28.11	11.10	K12	E11	Pig
29.11	12.10	K12	F12	Porcupine
30.11	13.10	K12	G1	Wolf
1.12	14.10	K12	H2	Dog
2.12	15.10	K12	J3	Pheasant
3.12	16.10	K12	K4	Cock
4.12	17.10	K12	A5	Crow
5.12	18.10	K12	B6	Monkey
6.12	19.10	K12	C7	Gibbon
7.12	20.10	K12	D8	Tapir
8.12	21.10	K12	E9	Sheep
9.12	22.10	K12	F10	Deer
10.12	23.10	K12	G11	Horse
11.12	24.10	K12	H12	Stag
12.12	25.10	K12	J1	Serpent
13.12	26.10	K12	K2	Earthworm
14.12	27.10	K12	A3	Crocodile
15.12	28.10	K12	B4	Dragon
16.12	29.10	K12	C5	Badger
17.12	1.11	A1	D6	Hare
18.12	2.11	A1	E7	Fox
19.12	3.11	A1	F8	Tiger
20.12	4.11	A1	G9	Leopard
21.12	5.11	A1	H10	Griffon
22.12	6.11	A1	J11	Ox
23.12	7.11	A1	K12	Bat
24.12	8.11	A1	A1	Rat
25.12	9.11	A1	B2	Swallow
26.12	10.11	A1	C3	Pig
27.12	11.11	A1	D4	Porcupine
28.12	12.11	A1	E5	Wolf
29.12	13.11	A1	F6	Dog
30.12	14.11	A1	G7	Pheasant
31.12	15.11	A1	H8	Cock
1934				
1. 1	16.11	A1	J9	Crow
2. 1	17.11	A1	K10	Monkey
3. 1	18.11	A1	A11	Gibbon
4. 1	19.11	A1	B12	Tapir
5. 1	20.11	A1	C1	Sheep
6. 1	21.11	A1	D2	Deer
7. 1	22.11	A1	E3	Horse
8. 1	23.11	A1	F4	Stag
9. 1	24.11	A1	G5	Serpent
10. 1	25.11	A1	H6	Earthworm
11. 1	26.11	A1	J7	Crocodile
12. 1	27.11	A1	K8	Dragon
13. 1	28.11	A1	A9	Badger
14. 1	29.11	A1	B10	Hare
15. 1	1.12	B2	C11	Fox
16. 1	2.12	B2	D12	Tiger
17. 1	3.12	B2	E1	Leopard
18. 1	4.12	B2	F2	Griffon
19. 1	5.12	B2	G3	Ox
20. 1	6.12	B2	H4	Bat
21. 1	7.12	B2	J5	Rat
22. 1	8.12	B2	K6	Swallow
23. 1	9.12	B2	A7	Pig
24. 1	10.12	B2	B8	Porcupine
25. 1	11.12	B2	C9	Wolf
26. 1	12.12	B2	D10	Dog
27. 1	13.12	B2	E11	Pheasant
28. 1	14.12	B2	F12	Cock
29. 1	15.12	B2	G1	Crow
30. 1	16.12	B2	H2	Monkey
31. 1	17.12	B2	J3	Gibbon
1. 2	18.12	B2	K4	Tapir
2. 2	19.12	B2	A5	Sheep
3. 2	20.12	B2	B6	Deer
4. 2	21.12	B2	C7	Horse
5. 2	22.12	B2	D8	Stag
6. 2	23.12	B2	E9	Serpent
7. 2	24.12	B2	F10	Earthworm
8. 2	25.12	B2	G11	Crocodile
9. 2	26.12	B2	H12	Dragon
10. 2	27.12	B2	J1	Badger
11. 2	28.12	B2	K2	Hare
12. 2	29.12	B2	A3	Fox
13. 2	30.12	B2	B4	Tiger

CHIA HSÜ YEAR

Solar date	*Lunar date*	*Month HS/EB*	*Day HS/EB*	*Constellation*
14. 2	1. 1	C3	C5	Leopard
15. 2	2. 1	C3	D6	Griffon
16. 2	3. 1	C3	E7	Ox
17. 2	4. 1	C3	F8	Bat
18. 2	5. 1	C3	G9	Rat
19. 2	6. 1	C3	H10	Swallow
20. 2	7. 1	C3	J11	Pig
21. 2	8. 1	C3	K12	Porcupine
22. 2	9. 1	C3	A1	Wolf
23. 2	10. 1	C3	B2	Dog
24. 2	11. 1	C3	C3	Pheasant
25. 2	12. 1	C3	D4	Cock
26. 2	13. 1	C3	E5	Crow
27. 2	14. 1	C3	F6	Monkey
28. 2	15. 1	C3	G7	Gibbon
1. 3	16. 1	C3	H8	Tapir
2. 3	17. 1	C3	J9	Sheep
3. 3	18. 1	C3	K10	Deer
4. 3	19. 1	C3	A11	Horse
5. 3	20. 1	C3	B12	Stag
6. 3	21. 1	C3	C1	Serpent
7. 3	22. 1	C3	D2	Earthworm
8. 3	23. 1	C3	E3	Crocodile
9. 3	24. 1	C3	F4	Dragon
10. 3	25. 1	C3	G5	Badger
11. 3	26. 1	C3	H6	Hare
12. 3	27. 1	C3	J7	Fox
13. 3	28. 1	C3	K8	Tiger
14. 3	29. 1	C3	A9	Leopard
15. 3	1. 2	D4	B10	Griffon
16. 3	2. 2	D4	C11	Ox
17. 3	3. 2	D4	D12	Bat
18. 3	4. 2	D4	E1	Rat
19. 3	5. 2	D4	F2	Swallow
20. 3	6. 2	D4	G3	Pig
21. 3	7. 2	D4	H4	Porcupine
22. 3	8. 2	D4	J5	Wolf
23. 3	9. 2	D4	K6	Dog
24. 3	10. 2	D4	A7	Pheasant
25. 3	11. 2	D4	B8	Cock
26. 3	12. 2	D4	C9	Crow
27. 3	13. 2	D4	D10	Monkey
28. 3	14. 2	D4	E11	Gibbon
29. 3	15. 2	D4	F12	Tapir
30. 3	16. 2	D4	G1	Sheep
31. 3	17. 2	D4	H2	Deer
1. 4	18. 2	D4	J3	Horse
2. 4	19. 2	D4	K4	Stag
3. 4	20. 2	D4	A5	Serpent
4. 4	21. 2	D4	B6	Earthworm
5. 4	22. 2	D4	C7	Crocodile
6. 4	23. 2	D4	D8	Dragon
7. 4	24. 2	D4	E9	Badger
8. 4	25. 2	D4	F10	Hare
9. 4	26. 2	D4	G11	Fox
10. 4	27. 2	D4	H12	Tiger
11. 4	28. 2	D4	J1	Leopard
12. 4	29. 2	D4	K2	Griffon
13. 4	30. 2	D4	A3	Ox
14. 4	1. 3	E5	B4	Bat
15. 4	2. 3	E5	C5	Rat
16. 4	3. 3	E5	D6	Swallow
17. 4	4. 3	E5	E7	Pig
18. 4	5. 3	E5	F8	Porcupine
19. 4	6. 3	E5	G9	Wolf
20. 4	7. 3	E5	H10	Dog
21. 4	8. 3	E5	J11	Pheasant
22. 4	9. 3	E5	K12	Cock
23. 4	10. 3	E5	A1	Crow
24. 4	11. 3	E5	B2	Monkey
25. 4	12. 3	E5	C3	Gibbon
26. 4	13. 3	E5	D4	Tapir
27. 4	14. 3	E5	E5	Sheep
28. 4	15. 3	E5	F6	Deer
29. 4	16. 3	E5	G7	Horse
30. 4	17. 3	E5	H8	Stag
1. 5	18. 3	E5	J9	Serpent
2. 5	19. 3	E5	K10	Earthworm
3. 5	20. 3	E5	A11	Crocodile
4. 5	21. 3	E5	B12	Dragon
5. 5	22. 3	E5	C1	Badger
6. 5	23. 3	E5	D2	Hare
7. 5	24. 3	E5	E3	Fox
8. 5	25. 3	E5	F4	Tiger
9. 5	26. 3	E5	G5	Leopard
10. 5	27. 3	E5	H6	Griffon
11. 5	28. 3	E5	J7	Ox
12. 5	29 3	E5	K8	Bat
13. 5	1. 4	F6	A9	Rat
14. 5	2. 4	F6	B10	Swallow
15. 5	3. 4	F6	C11	Pig
16. 5	4. 4	F6	D12	Porcupine
17. 5	5. 4	F6	E1	Wolf
18. 5	6. 4	F6	F2	Dog
19. 5	7. 4	F6	G3	Pheasant
20. 5	8. 4	F6	H4	Cock
21. 5	9. 4	F6	J5	Crow
22. 5	10. 4	F6	K6	Monkey
23. 5	11. 4	F6	A7	Gibbon
24. 5	12. 4	F6	B8	Tapir
25. 5	13. 4	F6	C9	Sheep
26. 5	14. 4	F6	D10	Deer
27. 5	15. 4	F6	E11	Horse
28. 5	16. 4	F6	F12	Stag
29. 5	17. 4	F6	G1	Serpent
30. 5	18. 4	F6	H2	Earthworm
31. 5	19. 4	F6	J3	Crocodile
1. 6	20. 4	F6	K4	Dragon
2. 6	21. 4	F6	A5	Badger
3. 6	22. 4	F6	B6	Hare
4. 6	23. 4	F6	C7	Fox
5. 6	24. 4	F6	D8	Tiger
6. 6	25. 4	F6	E9	Leopard
7. 6	26. 4	F6	F10	Griffon
8. 6	27. 4	F6	G11	Ox
9. 6	28. 4	F6	H12	Bat
10. 6	29. 4	F6	J1	Rat
11. 6	30. 4	F6	K2	Swallow
12. 6	1. 5	G7	A3	Pig
13. 6	2. 5	G7	B4	Porcupine
14. 6	3. 5	G7	C5	Wolf
15. 6	4. 5	G7	D6	Dog
16. 6	5. 5	G7	E7	Pheasant
17. 6	6. 5	G7	F8	Cock
18. 6	7. 5	G7	G9	Crow
19. 6	8. 5	G7	H10	Monkey
20. 6	9. 5	G7	J11	Gibbon
21. 6	10. 5	G7	K12	Tapir
22. 6	11. 5	G7	A1	Sheep
23. 6	12. 5	G7	B2	Deer
24. 6	13. 5	G7	C3	Horse
25. 6	14. 5	G7	D4	Stag
26. 6	15. 5	G7	E5	Serpent
27. 6	16. 5	G7	F6	Earthworm
28. 6	17. 5	G7	G7	Crocodile
29. 6	18. 5	G7	H8	Dragon
30. 6	19. 5	G7	J9	Badger
1. 7	20. 5	G7	K10	Hare
2. 7	21. 5	G7	A11	Fox
3. 7	22. 5	G7	B12	Tiger
4. 7	23. 5	G7	C1	Leopard
5. 7	24. 5	G7	D2	Griffon

Solar date	Lunar date	Month HS/EB	Day HS/EB	Constellation
6. 7	25. 5	G7	E3	Ox
7. 7	26. 5	G7	F4	Bat
8. 7	27. 5	G7	G5	Rat
9. 7	28. 5	G7	H6	Swallow
10. 7	29. 5	G7	J7	Pig
11. 7	30. 5	G7	K8	Porcupine
12. 7	1. 6	H8	A9	Wolf
13. 7	2. 6	H8	B10	Dog
14. 7	3. 6	H8	C11	Pheasant
15. 7	4. 6	H8	D12	Cock
16. 7	5. 6	H8	E1	Crow
17. 7	6. 6	H8	F2	Monkey
18. 7	7. 6	H8	G3	Gibbon
19. 7	8. 6	H8	H4	Tapir
20. 7	9. 6	H8	J5	Sheep
21. 7	10. 6	H8	K6	Deer
22. 7	11. 6	H8	A7	Horse
23. 7	12. 6	H8	B8	Stag
24. 7	13. 6	H8	C9	Serpent
25. 7	14. 6	H8	D10	Earthworm
26. 7	15. 6	H8	E11	Crocodile
27. 7	16. 6	H8	F12	Dragon
28. 7	17. 6	H8	G1	Badger
29. 7	18. 6	H8	H2	Hare
30. 7	19. 6	H8	J3	Fox
31. 7	20. 6	H8	K4	Tiger
1. 8	21. 6	H8	A5	Leopard
2. 8	22. 6	H8	B6	Griffon
3. 8	23. 6	H8	C7	Ox
4. 8	24. 6	H8	D8	Bat
5. 8	25. 6	H8	E9	Rat
6. 8	26. 6	H8	F10	Swallow
7. 8	27. 6	H8	G11	Pig
8. 8	28. 6	H8	H12	Porcupine
9. 8	29. 6	H8	J1	Wolf
10. 8	1. 7	J9	K2	Dog
11. 8	2. 7	J9	A3	Pheasant
12. 8	3. 7	J9	B4	Cock
13. 8	4. 7	J9	C5	Crow
14. 8	5. 7	J9	D6	Monkey
15. 8	6. 7	J9	E7	Gibbon
16. 8	7. 7	J9	F8	Tapir
17. 8	8. 7	J9	G9	Sheep
18. 8	9. 7	J9	H10	Deer
19. 8	10. 7	J9	J11	Horse
20. 8	11. 7	J9	K12	Stag
21. 8	12. 7	J9	A1	Serpent
22. 8	13. 7	J9	B2	Earthworm
23. 8	14. 7	J9	C3	Crocodile
24. 8	15. 7	J9	D4	Dragon
25. 8	16. 7	J9	E5	Badger
26. 8	17. 7	J9	F6	Hare
27. 8	18. 7	J9	G7	Fox
28. 8	19. 7	J9	H8	Tiger
29. 8	20. 7	J9	J9	Leopard
30. 8	21. 7	J9	K10	Griffon
31. 8	22. 7	J9	A11	Ox
1. 9	23. 7	J9	B12	Bat
2. 9	24. 7	J9	C1	Rat
3. 9	25. 7	J9	D2	Swallow
4. 9	26. 7	J9	E3	Pig
5. 9	27. 7	J9	F4	Porcupine
6. 9	28. 7	J9	G5	Wolf
7. 9	29. 7	J9	H6	Dog
8. 9	30. 7	J9	J7	Pheasant
9. 9	1. 8	K10	K8	Cock
10. 9	2. 8	K10	A9	Crow
11. 9	3. 8	K10	B10	Monkey
12. 9	4. 8	K10	C11	Gibbon
13. 9	5. 8	K10	D12	Tapir
14. 9	6. 8	K10	E1	Sheep
15. 9	7. 8	K10	F2	Deer
16. 9	8. 8	K10	G3	Horse

Solar date	Lunar date	Month HS/EB	Day HS/EB	Constellation
17. 9	9. 8	K10	H4	Stag
18. 9	10. 8	K10	J5	Serpent
19. 9	11. 8	K10	K6	Earthworm
20. 9	12. 8	K10	A7	Crocodile
21. 9	13. 8	K10	B8	Dragon
22. 9	14. 8	K10	C9	Badger
23. 9	15. 8	K10	D10	Hare
24. 9	16. 8	K10	E11	Fox
25. 9	17. 8	K10	F12	Tiger
26. 9	18. 8	K10	G1	Leopard
27. 9	19. 8	K10	H2	Griffon
28. 9	20. 8	K10	J3	Ox
29. 9	21. 8	K10	K4	Bat
30. 9	22. 8	K10	A5	Rat
1.10	23. 8	K10	B6	Swallow
2.10	24. 8	K10	C7	Pig
3.10	25. 8	K10	D8	Porcupine
4.10	26. 8	K10	E9	Wolf
5.10	27. 8	K10	F10	Dog
6.10	28. 8	K10	G11	Pheasant
7.10	29. 8	K10	H12	Cock
8.10	1. 9	A11	J1	Crow
9.10	2. 9	A11	K2	Monkey
10.10	3. 9	A11	A3	Gibbon
11.10	4. 9	A11	B4	Tapir
12.10	5. 9	A11	C5	Sheep
13.10	6. 9	A11	D6	Deer
14.10	7. 9	A11	E7	Horse
15.10	8. 9	A11	F8	Stag
16.10	9. 9	A11	G9	Serpent
17.10	10. 9	A11	H10	Earthworm
18.10	11. 9	A11	J11	Crocodile
19.10	12. 9	A11	K12	Dragon
20.10	13. 9	A11	A1	Badger
21.10	14. 9	A11	B2	Hare
22.10	15. 9	A11	C3	Fox
23.10	16. 9	A11	D4	Tiger
24.10	17. 9	A11	E5	Leopard
25.10	18. 9	A11	F6	Griffon
26.10	19. 9	A11	G7	Ox
27.10	20. 9	A11	H8	Bat
28.10	21. 9	A11	J9	Rat
29.10	22. 9	A11	K10	Swallow
30.10	23. 9	A11	A11	Pig
31.10	24. 9	A11	B12	Porcupine
1.11	25. 9	A11	C1	Wolf
2.11	26. 9	A11	D2	Dog
3.11	27. 9	A11	E3	Pheasant
4.11	28. 9	A11	F4	Cock
5.11	29. 9	A11	G5	Crow
6.11	30. 9	A11	H6	Monkey
7.11	1.10	B12	J7	Gibbon
8.11	2.10	B12	K8	Tapir
9.11	3.10	B12	A9	Sheep
10.11	4.10	B12	B10	Deer
11.11	5.10	B12	C11	Horse
12.11	6.10	B12	D12	Stag
13.11	7.10	B12	E1	Serpent
14.11	8.10	B12	F2	Earthworm
15.11	9.10	B12	G3	Crocodile
16.11	10.10	B12	H4	Dragon
17.11	11.10	B12	J5	Badger
18.11	12.10	B12	K6	Hare
19.11	13.10	B12	A7	Fox
20.11	14.10	B12	B8	Tiger
21.11	15.10	B12	C9	Leopard
22.11	16.10	B12	D10	Griffon
23.11	17.10	B12	E11	Ox
24.11	18.10	B12	F12	Bat
25.11	19.10	B12	G1	Rat
26.11	20.10	B12	H2	Swallow
27.11	21.10	B12	J3	Pig
28.11	22.10	B12	K4	Porcupine

Solar date	*Lunar date*	*Month HS/EB*	*Day HS/EB*	*Constellation*
29.11	23.10	B12	A5	Wolf
30.11	24.10	B12	B6	Dog
1.12	25.10	B12	C7	Pheasant
2.12	26.10	B12	D8	Cock
3.12	27.10	B12	E9	Crow
4.12	28.10	B12	F10	Monkey
5.12	29.10	B12	G11	Gibbon
6.12	30.10	B12	H12	Tapir
7.12	1.11	C1	J1	Sheep
8.12	2.11	C1	K2	Deer
9.12	3.11	C1	A3	Horse
10.12	4.11	C1	B4	Stag
11.12	5.11	C1	C5	Serpent
12.12	6.11	C1	D6	Earthworm
13.12	7.11	C1	E7	Crocodile
14.12	8.11	C1	F8	Dragon
15.12	9.11	C1	G9	Badger
16.12	10.11	C1	H10	Hare
17.12	11.11	C1	J11	Fox
18.12	12.11	C1	K12	Tiger
19.12	13.11	C1	A1	Leopard
20.12	14.11	C1	B2	Griffon
21.12	15.11	C1	C3	Ox
22.12	16.11	C1	D4	Bat
23.12	17.11	C1	E5	Rat
24.12	18.11	C1	F6	Swallow
25.12	19.11	C1	G7	Pig
26.12	20.11	C1	H8	Porcupine
27.12	21.11	C1	J9	Wolf
28.12	22.11	C1	K10	Dog
29.12	23.11	C1	A11	Pheasant
30.12	24.11	C1	B12	Cock
31.12	25.11	C1	C1	Crow
1935				
1. 1	26.11	C1	D2	Monkey
2. 1	27.11	C1	E3	Gibbon
3. 1	28.11	C1	F4	Tapir
4. 1	29.11	C1	G5	Sheep
5. 1	1.12	D2	H6	Deer
6. 1	2.12	D2	J7	Horse
7. 1	3.12	D2	K8	Stag
8. 1	4.12	D2	A9	Serpent
9. 1	5.12	D2	B10	Earthworm
10. 1	6.12	D2	C11	Crocodile
11. 1	7.12	D2	D12	Dragon
12. 1	8.12	D2	E1	Badger
13. 1	9.12	D2	F2	Hare
14. 1	10.12	D2	G3	Fox
15. 1	11.12	D2	H4	Tiger
16. 1	12.12	D2	J5	Leopard
17. 1	13.12	D2	K6	Griffon
18. 1	14.12	D2	A7	Ox
19. 1	15.12	D2	B8	Bat
20. 1	16.12	D2	C9	Rat
21. 1	17.12	D2	D10	Swallow
22. 1	18.12	D2	E11	Pig
23. 1	19.12	D2	F12	Porcupine
24. 1	20.12	D2	G1	Wolf
25. 1	21.12	D2	H2	Dog
26. 1	22.12	D2	J3	Pheasant
27. 1	23.12	D2	K4	Cock
28. 1	24.12	D2	A5	Crow
29. 1	25.12	D2	B6	Monkey
30. 1	26.12	D2	C7	Gibbon
31. 1	27.12	D2	D8	Tapir
1. 2	28.12	D2	E9	Sheep
2. 2	29.12	D2	F10	Deer
3. 2	30.12	D2	G11	Horse

YI HAI YEAR

4. 2	1. 1	E3	H12	Stag
5. 2	2. 1	E3	J1	Serpent
6. 2	3. 1	E3	K2	Earthworm
7. 2	4. 1	E3	A3	Crocodile
8. 2	5. 1	E3	B4	Dragon
9. 2	6. 1	E3	C5	Badger
10. 2	7. 1	E3	D6	Hare
11. 2	8. 1	E3	E7	Fox
12. 2	9. 1	E3	F8	Tiger
13. 2	10. 1	E3	G9	Leopard
14. 2	11. 1	E3	H10	Griffon
15. 2	12. 1	E3	J11	Ox
16. 2	13. 1	E3	K12	Bat
17. 2	14. 1	E3	A1	Rat
18. 2	15. 1	E3	B2	Swallow
19. 2	16. 1	E3	C3	Pig
20. 2	17. 1	E3	D4	Porcupine
21. 2	18. 1	E3	E5	Wolf
22. 2	19. 1	E3	F6	Dog
23. 2	20. 1	E3	G7	Pheasant
24. 2	21. 1	E3	H8	Cock
25. 2	22. 1	E3	J9	Crow
26. 2	23. 1	E3	K10	Monkey
27. 2	24. 1	E3	A11	Gibbon
28. 2	25. 1	E3	B12	Tapir
1. 3	26. 1	E3	C1	Sheep
2. 3	27. 1	E3	D2	Deer
3. 3	28. 1	E3	E3	Horse
4. 3	29. 1	E3	F4	Stag
5. 3	1. 2	F4	G5	Serpent
6. 3	2. 2	F4	H6	Earthworm
7. 3	3. 2	F4	J7	Crocodile
8. 3	4. 2	F4	K8	Dragon
9. 3	5. 2	F4	A9	Badger
10. 3	6. 2	F4	B10	Hare
11. 3	7. 2	F4	C11	Fox
12. 3	8. 2	F4	D12	Tiger
13. 3	9. 2	F4	E1	Leopard
14. 3	10. 2	F4	F2	Griffon
15. 3	11. 2	F4	G3	Ox
16. 3	12. 2	F4	H4	Bat
17. 3	13. 2	F4	J5	Rat
18. 3	14. 2	F4	K6	Swallow
19. 3	15. 2	F4	A7	Pig
20. 3	16. 2	F4	B8	Porcupine
21. 3	17. 2	F4	C9	Wolf
22. 3	18. 2	F4	D10	Dog
23. 3	19. 2	F4	E11	Pheasant
24. 3	20. 2	F4	F12	Cock
25. 3	21. 2	F4	G1	Crow
26. 3	22. 2	F4	H2	Monkey
27. 3	23. 2	F4	J3	Gibbon
28. 3	24. 2	F4	K4	Tapir
29. 3	25. 2	F4	A5	Sheep
30. 3	26. 2	F4	B6	Deer
31. 3	27. 2	F4	C7	Horse
1. 4	28. 2	F4	D8	Stag
2. 4	29. 2	F4	E9	Serpent
3. 4	1. 3	G5	F10	Earthworm
4. 4	2. 3	G5	G11	Crocodile
5. 4	3. 3	G5	H12	Dragon
6. 4	4. 3	G5	J1	Badger
7. 4	5. 3	G5	K2	Hare
8. 4	6. 3	G5	A3	Fox

Solar date	Lunar date	Month HS/EB	Day HS/EB	Constellation
9. 4	7. 3	G5	B4	Tiger
10. 4	8. 3	G5	C5	Leopard
11. 4	9. 3	G5	D6	Griffon
12. 4	10. 3	G5	E7	Ox
13. 4	11. 3	G5	F8	Bat
14. 4	12. 3	G5	G9	Rat
15. 4	13. 3	G5	H10	Swallow
16. 4	14. 3	G5	J11	Pig
17. 4	15. 3	G5	K12	Porcupine
18. 4	16. 3	G5	A1	Wolf
19. 4	17. 3	G5	B2	Dog
20. 4	18. 3	G5	C3	Pheasant
21. 4	19. 3	G5	D4	Cock
22. 4	20. 3	G5	E5	Crow
23. 4	21. 3	G5	F6	Monkey
24. 4	22. 3	G5	G7	Gibbon
25. 4	23. 3	G5	H8	Tapir
26. 4	24. 3	G5	J9	Sheep
27. 4	25. 3	G5	K10	Deer
28. 4	26. 3	G5	A11	Horse
29. 4	27. 3	G5	B12	Stag
30. 4	28. 3	G5	C1	Serpent
1. 5	29. 3	G5	D2	Earthworm
2. 5	30. 3	G5	E3	Crocodile
3. 5	1. 4	H6	F4	Dragon
4. 5	2. 4	H6	G5	Badger
5. 5	3. 4	H6	H6	Hare
6. 5	4. 4	H6	J7	Fox
7. 5	5. 4	H6	K8	Tiger
8. 5	6. 4	H6	A9	Leopard
9. 5	7. 4	H6	B10	Griffon
10. 5	8. 4	H6	C11	Ox
11. 5	9. 4	H6	D12	Bat
12. 5	10. 4	H6	E1	Rat
13. 5	11. 4	H6	F2	Swallow
14. 5	12. 4	H6	G3	Pig
15. 5	13. 4	H6	H4	Porcupine
16. 5	14. 4	H6	J5	Wolf
17. 5	15. 4	H6	K6	Dog
18. 5	16. 4	H6	A7	Pheasant
19. 5	17. 4	H6	B8	Cock
20. 5	18. 4	H6	C9	Crow
21. 5	19. 4	H6	D10	Monkey
22. 5	20. 4	H6	E11	Gibbon
23. 5	21. 4	H6	F12	Tapir
24. 5	22. 4	H6	G1	Sheep
25. 5	23. 4	H6	H2	Deer
26. 5	24. 4	H6	J3	Horse
27. 5	25. 4	H6	K4	Stag
28. 5	26. 4	H6	A5	Serpent
29. 5	27. 4	H6	B6	Earthworm
30. 5	28. 4	H6	C7	Crocodile
31. 5	29. 4	H6	D8	Dragon
1. 6	1. 5	J7	E9	Badger
2. 6	2. 5	J7	F10	Hare
3. 6	3. 5	J7	G11	Fox
4. 6	4. 5	J7	H12	Tiger
5. 6	5. 5	J7	J1	Leopard
6. 6	6. 5	J7	K2	Griffon
7. 6	7. 5	J7	A3	Ox
8. 6	8. 5	J7	B4	Bat
9. 6	9. 5	J7	C5	Rat
10. 6	10. 5	J7	D6	Swallow
11. 6	11. 5	J7	E7	Pig
12. 6	12. 5	J7	F8	Porcupine
13. 6	13. 5	J7	G9	Wolf
14. 6	14. 5	J7	H10	Dog
15. 6	15. 5	J7	J11	Pheasant
16. 6	16. 5	J7	K12	Cock
17. 6	17. 5	J7	A1	Crow
18. 6	18. 5	J7	B2	Monkey
19. 6	19. 5	J7	C3	Gibbon
20. 6	20. 5	J7	D4	Tapir
21. 6	21. 5	J7	E5	Sheep
22. 6	22. 5	J7	F6	Deer
23. 6	23. 5	J7	G7	Horse
24. 6	24. 5	J7	H8	Stag
25. 6	25. 5	J7	J9	Serpent
26. 6	26. 5	J7	K10	Earthworm
27. 6	27. 5	J7	A11	Crocodile
28. 6	28. 5	J7	B12	Dragon
29. 6	29. 5	J7	C1	Badger
30. 6	30. 5	J7	D2	Hare
1. 7	1. 6	K8	E3	Fox
2. 7	2. 6	K8	F4	Tiger
3. 7	3. 6	K8	G5	Leopard
4. 7	4. 6	K8	H6	Griffon
5. 7	5. 6	K8	J7	Ox
6. 7	6. 6	K8	K8	Bat
7. 7	7. 6	K8	A9	Rat
8. 7	8. 6	K8	B10	Swallow
9. 7	9. 6	K8	C11	Pig
10. 7	10. 6	K8	D12	Porcupine
11. 7	11. 6	K8	E1	Wolf
12. 7	12. 6	K8	F2	Dog
13. 7	13. 6	K8	G3	Pheasant
14. 7	14. 6	K8	H4	Cock
15. 7	15. 6	K8	J5	Crow
16. 7	16. 6	K8	K6	Monkey
17. 7	17. 6	K8	A7	Gibbon
18. 7	18. 6	K8	B8	Tapir
19. 7	19. 6	K8	C9	Sheep
20. 7	20. 6	K8	D10	Deer
21. 7	21. 6	K8	E11	Horse
22. 7	22. 6	K8	F12	Stag
23. 7	23. 6	K8	G1	Serpent
24. 7	24. 6	K8	H2	Earthworm
25. 7	25. 6	K8	J3	Crocodile
26. 7	26. 6	K8	K4	Dragon
27. 7	27. 6	K8	A5	Badger
28. 7	28. 6	K8	B6	Hare
29. 7	29. 6	K8	C7	Fox
30. 7	1. 7	A9	D8	Tiger
31. 7	2. 7	A9	E9	Leopard
1. 8	3. 7	A9	F10	Griffon
2. 8	4. 7	A9	G11	Ox
3. 8	5. 7	A9	H12	Bat
4. 8	6. 7	A9	J1	Rat
5. 8	7. 7	A9	K2	Swallow
6. 8	8. 7	A9	A3	Pig
7. 8	9. 7	A9	B4	Porcupine
8. 8	10. 7	A9	C5	Wolf
9. 8	11. 7	A9	D6	Dog
10. 8	12. 7	A9	E7	Pheasant
11. 8	13. 7	A9	F8	Cock
12. 8	14. 7	A9	G9	Crow
13. 8	15. 7	A9	H10	Monkey
14. 8	16. 7	A9	J11	Gibbon
15. 8	17. 7	A9	K12	Tapir
16. 8	18. 7	A9	A1	Sheep
17. 8	19. 7	A9	B2	Deer
18. 8	20. 7	A9	C3	Horse
19. 8	21. 7	A9	D4	Stag
20. 8	22. 7	A9	E5	Serpent
21. 8	23. 7	A9	F6	Earthworm
22. 8	24. 7	A9	G7	Crocodile
23. 8	25. 7	A9	H8	Dragon
24. 8	26. 7	A9	J9	Badger
25. 8	27. 7	A9	K10	Hare
26. 8	28. 7	A9	A11	Fox
27. 8	29. 7	A9	B12	Tiger
28. 8	30. 7	A9	C1	Leopard
29. 8	1. 8	B10	D2	Griffon
30. 8	2. 8	B10	E3	Ox
31. 8	3. 8	B10	F4	Bat
1. 9	4. 8	B10	G5	Rat

Solar date	*Lunar date*	*Month HS/EB*	*Day HS/EB*	*Constellation*
2. 9	5. 8	B10	H6	Swallow
3. 9	6. 8	B10	J7	Pig
4. 9	7. 8	B10	K8	Porcupine
5. 9	8. 8	B10	A9	Wolf
6. 9	9. 8	B10	B10	Dog
7. 9	10. 8	B10	C11	Pheasant
8. 9	11. 8	B10	D12	Cock
9. 9	12. 8	B10	E1	Crow
10. 9	13. 3	B10	F2	Monkey
11. 9	14. 8	B10	G3	Gibbon
12. 9	15. 8	B10	H4	Tapir
13. 9	16. 8	B10	J5	Sheep
14. 9	17. 8	B10	K6	Deer
15. 9	18. 8	B10	A7	Horse
16. 9	19. 8	B10	B8	Stag
17. 9	20. 8	B10	C9	Serpent
18. 9	21. 8	B10	D10	Earthworm
19. 9	22. 8	B10	E11	Crocodile
20. 9	23. 8	B10	F12	Dragon
21. 9	24. 8	B10	G1	Badger
22. 9	25. 8	B10	H2	Hare
23. 9	26. 8	B10	J3	Fox
24. 9	27. 8	B10	K4	Tiger
25. 9	28. 8	B10	A5	Leopard
26. 9	29. 8	B10	B6	Griffon
27. 9	30. 8	B10	C7	Ox
28. 9	1. 9	C11	D8	Bat
29. 9	2. 9	C11	E9	Rat
30. 9	3. 9	C11	F10	Swallow
1.10	4. 9	C11	G11	Pig
2.10	5. 9	C11	H12	Porcupine
3.10	6. 9	C11	J1	Wolf
4.10	7. 9	C11	K2	Dog
5.10	8. 9	C11	A3	Pheasant
6.10	9. 9	C11	B4	Cock
7.10	10. 9	C11	C5	Crow
8.10	11. 9	C11	D6	Monkey
9.10	12. 9	C11	E7	Gibbon
10.10	13. 9	C11	F8	Tapir
11.10	14. 9	C11	G9	Sheep
12.10	15. 9	C11	H10	Deer
13.10	16. 9	C11	J11	Horse
14.10	17. 9	C11	K12	Stag
15.10	18. 9	C11	A1	Serpent
16.10	19. 9	C11	B2	Earthworm
17.10	20. 9	C11	C3	Crocodile
18.10	21. 9	C11	D4	Dragon
19.10	22. 9	C11	E5	Badger
20.10	23. 9	C11	F6	Hare
21.10	24. 9	C11	G7	Fox
22.10	25. 9	C11	H8	Tiger
23.10	26. 9	C11	J9	Leopard
24.10	27. 9	C11	K10	Griffon
25.10	28. 9	C11	A11	Ox
26.10	29. 9	C11	B12	Bat
27.10	1.10	D12	C1	Rat
28.10	2.10	D12	D2	Swallow
29.10	3.10	D12	E3	Pig
30.10	4.10	D12	F4	Porcupine
31.10	5.10	D12	G5	Wolf
1.11	6.10	D12	H6	Dog
2.11	7.10	D12	J7	Pheasant
3.11	8.10	D12	K8	Cock
4.11	9.10	D12	A9	Crow
5.11	10.10	D12	B10	Monkey
6.11	11.10	D12	C11	Gibbon
7.11	12.10	D12	D12	Tapir
8.11	13.10	D12	E1	Sheep
9.11	14.10	D12	F2	Deer
10.11	15.10	D12	G3	Horse
11.11	16.10	D12	H4	Stag
12.11	17.10	D12	J5	Serpent
13.11	18.10	D12	K6	Earthworm

Solar date	*Lunar date*	*Month HS/EB*	*Day HS/EB*	*Constellation*
14.11	19.10	D12	A7	Crocodile
15.11	20.10	D12	B8	Dragon
16.11	21.10	D12	C9	Badger
17.11	22.10	D12	D10	Hare
18.11	23.10	D12	E11	Fox
19.11	24.10	D12	F12	Tiger
20.11	25.10	D12	G1	Leopard
21.11	26.10	D12	H2	Griffon
22.11	27.10	D12	J3	Ox
23.11	28.10	D12	K4	Bat
24.11	29.10	D12	A5	Rat
25.11	30.10	D12	B6	Swallow
26.11	1.11	E1	C7	Pig
27.11	2.11	E1	D8	Porcupine
28.11	3.11	E1	E9	Wolf
29.11	4.11	E1	F10	Dog
30.11	5.11	E1	G11	Pheasant
1.12	6.11	E1	H12	Cock
2.12	7.11	E1	J1	Crow
3.12	8.11	E1	K2	Monkey
4.12	9.11	E1	A3	Gibbon
5.12	10.11	E1	B4	Tapir
6.12	11.11	E1	C5	Sheep
7.12	12.11	E1	D6	Deer
8.12	13.11	E1	E7	Horse
9.12	14.11	E1	F8	Stag
10.12	15.11	E1	G9	Serpent
11.12	16.11	E1	H10	Earthworm
12.12	17.11	E1	J11	Crocodile
13.12	18.11	E1	K12	Dragon
14.12	19.11	E1	A1	Badger
15.12	20.11	E1	B2	Hare
16.12	21.11	E1	C3	Fox
17.12	22.11	E1	D4	Tiger
18.12	23.11	E1	E5	Leopard
19.12	24.11	E1	F6	Griffon
20.12	25.11	E1	G7	Ox
21.12	26.11	E1	H8	Bat
22.12	27.11	E1	J9	Rat
23.12	28.11	E1	K10	Swallow
24.12	29.11	E1	A11	Pig
25.12	30.11	E1	B12	Porcupine
26.12	1.12	F2	C1	Wolf
27.12	2.12	F2	D2	Dog
28.12	3.12	F2	E3	Pheasant
29.12	4.12	F2	F4	Cock
30.12	5.12	F2	G5	Crow
31.12	6.12	F2	H6	Monkey
1936				
1. 1	7.12	F2	J7	Gibbon
2. 1	8.12	F2	K8	Tapir
3. 1	9.12	F2	A9	Sheep
4. 1	10.12	F2	B10	Deer
5. 1	11.12	F2	C11	Horse
6. 1	12.12	F2	D12	Stag
7. 1	13.12	F2	E1	Serpent
8. 1	14.12	F2	F2	Earthworm
9. 1	15.12	F2	G3	Crocodile
10. 1	16.12	F2	H4	Dragon
11. 1	17.12	F2	J5	Badger
12. 1	18.12	F2	K6	Hare
13. 1	19.12	F2	A7	Fox
14. 1	20.12	F2	B8	Tiger
15. 1	21.12	F2	C9	Leopard
16. 1	22.12	F2	D10	Griffon
17. 1	23.12	F2	E11	Ox
18. 1	24.12	F2	F12	Bat
19. 1	25.12	F2	G1	Rat
20. 1	26.12	F2	H2	Swallow
21. 1	27.12	F2	J3	Pig
22. 1	28.12	F2	K4	Porcupine
23. 1	29.12	F2	A5	Wolf

PING TZU YEAR

Solar date	*Lunar date*	*Month HS/EB*	*Day HS/EB*	*Constellation*
24. 1	1. 1	G3	B6	Dog
25. 1	2. 1	G3	C7	Pheasant
26. 1	3. 1	G3	D8	Cock
27. 1	4. 1	G3	E9	Crow
28. 1	5. 1	G3	F10	Monkey
29. 1	6. 1	G3	G11	Gibbon
30. 1	7. 1	G3	H12	Tapir
31. 1	8. 1	G3	J1	Sheep
1. 2	9. 1	G3	K2	Deer
2. 2	10. 1	G3	A3	Horse
3. 2	11. 1	G3	B4	Stag
4. 2	12. 1	G3	C5	Serpent
5. 2	13. 1	G3	D6	Earthworm
6. 2	14. 1	G3	E7	Crocodile
7. 2	15. 1	G3	F8	Dragon
8. 2	16. 1	G3	G9	Badger
9. 2	17. 1	G3	H10	Hare
10. 2	18. 1	G3	J11	Fox
11. 2	19. 1	G3	K12	Tiger
12. 2	20. 1	G3	A1	Leopard
13. 2	21. 1	G3	B2	Griffon
14. 2	22. 1	G3	C3	Ox
15. 2	23. 1	G3	D4	Bat
16. 2	24. 1	G3	E5	Rat
17. 2	25. 1	G3	F6	Swallow
18. 2	26. 1	G3	G7	Pig
19. 2	27. 1	G3	H8	Porcupine
20. 2	28. 1	G3	J9	Wolf
21. 2	29. 1	G3	K10	Dog
22. 2	30. 1	G3	A11	Pheasant
23. 2	1. 2	H4	B12	Cock
24. 2	2. 2	H4	C1	Crow
25. 2	3. 2	H4	D2	Monkey
26. 2	3. 2	H4	E3	Griffon
27. 2	4. 2	H4	F4	Tapir
28. 2	6. 2	H4	G5	Sheep
29. 2	7. 2	H4	H6	Deer
1. 3	8. 2	H4	J7	Horse
2. 3	9. 2	H4	K8	Stag
3. 3	10. 2	H4	A9	Serpent
4. 3	11. 2	H4	B10	Earthworm
5. 3	12. 2	H4	C11	Crocodile
6. 3	13. 2	H4	D12	Dragon
7. 3	14. 2	H4	E1	Badger
8. 3	15. 2	H4	F2	Hare
9. 3	16. 2	H4	G3	Fox
10. 3	17. 2	H4	H4	Tiger
11. 3	18. 2	H4	J5	Leopard
12. 3	19. 2	H4	K6	Griffon
13. 3	20. 2	H4	A7	Ox
14. 3	21. 2	H4	B8	Bat
15. 3	22. 2	H4	C9	Rat
16. 3	23. 2	H4	D10	Swallow
17. 3	24. 2	H4	E11	Pig
18. 3	25. 2	H4	F12	Porcupine
19. 3	26. 2	H4	G1	Wolf
20. 3	27. 2	H4	H2	Dog
21. 3	28. 2	H4	J3	Pheasant
22. 3	29. 2	H4	K4	Cock
23. 3	1. 3	J5	A5	Crow
24. 3	2. 3	J5	B6	Monkey
25. 3	3. 3	J5	C7	Gibbon
26. 3	4. 3	J5	D8	Tapir
27. 3	5. 3	J5	E9	Sheep
28. 3	6. 3	J5	F10	Deer
29. 3	7. 3	J5	G11	Horse
30. 3	8. 3	J5	H12	Stag
31. 3	9. 3	J5	J1	Serpent
1. 4	10. 3	J5	K2	Earthworm
2. 4	11. 3	J5	A3	Crocodile
3. 4	12. 3	J5	B4	Dragon

Solar date	*Lunar date*	*Month HS/EB*	*Day HS/EB*	*Constellation*
4. 4	13. 3	J5	C5	Badger
5. 4	14. 3	J5	D6	Hare
6. 4	15. 3	J5	E7	Fox
7. 4	16. 3	J5	F8	Tiger
8. 4	17. 3	J5	G9	Leopard
9. 4	18. 3	J5	H10	Griffon
10. 4	19. 3	J5	J11	Ox
11. 4	20. 3	J5	K12	Bat
12. 4	21. 3	J5	A1	Rat
13. 4	22. 3	J5	B2	Swallow
14. 4	23. 3	J5	C3	Pig
15. 4	24. 3	J5	D4	Porcupine
16. 4	25. 3	J5	E5	Wolf
17. 4	26. 3	J5	F6	Dog
18. 4	27. 3	J5	G7	Pheasant
19. 4	28. 3	J5	H8	Cock
20. 4	29. 3	J5	J9	Crow
21. 4	*1. 3*	*J5*	K10	Monkey
22. 4	*2. 3*	*J5*	A11	Gibbon
23. 4	*3. 3*	*J5*	B12	Tapir
24. 4	*4. 3*	*J5*	C1	Sheep
25. 4	*5. 3*	*J5*	D2	Deer
26. 4	*6. 3*	*J5*	E3	Horse
27. 4	*7. 3*	*J5*	F4	Stag
28. 4	*8. 3*	*J5*	G5	Serpent
29. 4	*9. 3*	*J5*	H6	Earthworm
30. 4	*10. 3*	*J5*	J7	Crocodile
1. 5	*11. 3*	*J5*	K8	Dragon
2. 5	*12. 3*	*J5*	A9	Badger
3. 5	*13. 3*	*J5*	B10	Hare
4. 5	*14. 3*	*J5*	C11	Fox
5. 5	*15. 3*	*J5*	D12	Tiger
6. 5	*16. 3*	*J5*	E1	Leopard
7. 5	*17. 3*	*J5*	F2	Griffon
8. 5	*18. 3*	*J5*	G3	Ox
9. 5	*19. 3*	*J5*	H4	Bat
10. 5	*20. 3*	*J5*	J5	Rat
11. 5	*21. 3*	*J5*	K6	Swallow
12. 5	*22. 3*	*J5*	A7	Pig
13. 5	*23. 3*	*J5*	B8	Porcupine
14. 5	*24. 3*	*J5*	C9	Wolf
15. 5	*25. 3*	*J5*	D10	Dog
16. 5	*26. 3*	*J5*	E11	Pheasant
17. 5	*27. 3*	*J5*	F12	Cock
18. 5	*28. 3*	*J5*	G1	Crow
19. 5	*29. 3*	*J5*	H2	Monkey
20. 5	*30. 3*	*J5*	J3	Gibbon
21. 5	1. 4	K6	K4	Tapir
22. 5	2. 4	K6	A5	Sheep
23. 5	3. 4	K6	B6	Deer
24. 5	4. 4	K6	C7	Horse
25. 5	5. 4	K6	D8	Stag
26. 5	6. 4	K6	E9	Serpent
27. 5	7. 4	K6	F10	Earthworm
28. 5	8. 4	K6	G11	Crocodile
29. 5	9. 4	K6	H12	Dragon
30. 5	10. 4	K6	J1	Badger
31. 5	11. 4	K6	K2	Hare
1. 6	12. 4	K6	A3	Fox
2. 6	13. 4	K6	B4	Tiger
3. 6	14. 4	K6	C5	Leopard
4. 6	15. 4	K6	D6	Griffon
5. 6	16. 4	K6	E7	Ox
6. 6	17. 4	K6	F8	Bat
7. 6	18. 4	K6	G9	Rat
8. 6	19. 4	K6	H10	Swallow
9. 6	20. 4	K6	J11	Pig
10. 6	21. 4	K6	K12	Porcupine
11. 6	22. 4	K6	A1	Wolf
12. 6	23. 4	K6	B2	Dog
13. 6	24. 4	K6	C3	Pheasant

Solar date	*Lunar date*	*Month HS/EB*	*Day HS/EB*	*Constellation*
14. 6	25. 4	K6	D4	Cock
15. 6	26. 4	K6	E5	Crow
16. 6	27. 4	K6	F6	Monkey
17. 6	28. 4	K6	C7	Gibbon
18. 6	29. 4	K6	H8	Tapir
19. 6	1. 5	A7	J9	Sheep
20. 6	2. 5	A7	K10	Deer
21. 6	3. 5	A7	A11	Horse
22. 6	4. 5	A7	B12	Stag
23. 6	5. 5	A7	C1	Serpent
24. 6	6. 5	A7	D2	Earthworm
25. 6	7. 5	A7	E3	Crocodile
26. 6	8. 5	A7	F4	Dragon
27. 6	9. 5	A7	G5	Badger
28. 6	10. 5	A7	H6	Hare
29. 6	11. 5	A7	J7	Fox
30. 6	12. 5	A7	K8	Tiger
1. 7	13. 5	A7	A9	Leopard
2. 7	14. 5	A7	B10	Griffon
3. 7	15. 5	A7	C11	Ox
4. 7	16. 5	A7	D12	Bat
5. 7	17. 5	A7	E1	Rat
6. 7	18. 5	A7	F2	Swallow
7. 7	19. 5	A7	G3	Pig
8. 7	20. 5	A7	H4	Porcupine
9. 7	21. 5	A7	J5	Wolf
10. 7	22. 5	A7	K6	Dog
11. 7	23. 5	A7	A7	Pheasant
12. 7	24. 5	A7	B8	Cock
13. 7	25. 5	A7	C9	Crow
14. 7	26. 5	A7	D10	Monkey
15. 7	27. 5	A7	E11	Gibbon
16. 7	28. 5	A7	F12	Tapir
17. 7	29. 5	A7	G1	Sheep
18. 7	1. 6	B8	H2	Deer
19. 7	2. 6	B8	J3	Horse
20. 7	3. 6	B8	K4	Stag
21. 7	4. 6	B8	A5	Serpent
22. 7	5. 6	B8	B6	Earthworm
23. 7	6. 6	B8	C7	Crocodile
24. 7	7. 6	B8	D8	Dragon
25. 7	8. 6	B8	E9	Badger
26. 7	9. 6	B8	F10	Hare
27. 7	10. 6	B8	G11	Fox
28. 7	11. 6	B8	H12	Tiger
29. 7	12. 6	B8	J1	Leopard
30. 7	13. 6	B8	K2	Griffon
31. 7	14. 6	B8	A3	Ox
1. 8	15. 6	B8	B4	Bat
2. 8	16. 6	B8	C5	Rat
3. 8	17. 6	B8	D6	Swallow
4. 8	18. 6	B8	E7	Pig
5. 8	19. 6	B8	F8	Porcupine
6. 8	20. 6	B8	G9	Wolf
7. 8	21. 6	B8	H10	Dog
8. 8	22. 6	B8	J11	Pheasant
9. 8	23. 6	B8	K12	Cock
10. 8	24. 6	B8	A1	Crow
11. 8	25. 6	B8	B2	Monkey
12. 8	26. 6	B8	C3	Gibbon
13. 8	27. 6	B8	D4	Tapir
14. 8	28. 6	B8	E5	Sheep
15. 8	29. 6	B8	F6	Deer
16. 8	30. 6	B8	G7	Horse
17. 8	1. 7	C9	H8	Stag
18. 8	2. 7	C9	J9	Serpent
19. 8	3. 7	C9	K10	Earthworm
20. 8	4. 7	C9	A11	Crocodile
21. 8	5. 7	C9	B12	Dragon
22. 8	6. 7	C9	C1	Badger
23. 8	7. 7	C9	D2	Hare
24. 8	8. 7	C9	E3	Fox
25. 8	9. 7	C9	F4	Tiger

Solar date	*Lunar date*	*Month HS/EB*	*Day HS/EB*	*Constellation*
26. 8	10. 7	C9	G5	Leopard
27. 8	11. 7	C9	H6	Griffon
28. 8	12. 7	C9	J7	Ox
29. 8	13. 7	C9	K8	Bat
30. 8	14. 7	C9	A9	Rat
31. 8	15. 7	C9	B10	Swallow
1. 9	16. 7	C9	C11	Pig
2. 9	17. 7	C9	D12	Porcupine
3. 9	18. 7	C9	E1	Wolf
4. 9	19. 7	C9	F2	Dog
5. 9	20. 7	C9	G3	Pheasant
6. 9	21. 7	C9	H4	Cock
7. 9	22. 7	C9	J5	Crow
8. 9	23. 7	C9	K6	Monkey
9. 9	24. 7	C9	A7	Gibbon
10. 9	25. 7	C9	B8	Tapir
11. 9	26. 7	C9	C9	Sheep
12. 9	27. 7	C9	D10	Deer
13. 9	28. 7	C9	E11	Horse
14. 9	29. 7	C9	F12	Stag
15. 9	30. 7	C9	G1	Serpent
16. 9	1. 8	D10	H2	Earthworm
17. 9	2. 8	D10	J3	Crocodile
18. 9	3. 8	D10	K4	Dragon
19. 9	4. 8	D10	A5	Badger
20. 9	5. 8	D10	B6	Hare
21. 9	6. 8	D10	C7	Fox
22. 9	7. 8	D10	D8	Tiger
23. 9	8. 8	D10	E9	Leopard
24. 9	9. 8	D10	F10	Griffon
25. 9	10. 8	D10	G11	Ox
26. 9	11. 8	D10	H12	Bat
27. 9	12. 8	D10	J1	Rat
28. 9	13. 8	D10	K2	Swallow
29. 9	14. 8	D10	A3	Pig
30. 9	15. 8	D10	B4	Porcupine
1.10	16. 8	D10	C5	Wolf
2.10	17. 8	D10	D6	Dog
3.10	18. 8	D10	E7	Pheasant
4.10	19. 8	D10	F8	Cock
5.10	20. 8	D10	G9	Crow
6.10	21. 8	D10	H10	Monkey
7.10	22. 8	D10	J11	Gibbon
8.10	23. 8	D10	K12	Tapir
9.10	24. 8	D10	A1	Sheep
10.10	25. 8	D10	B2	Deer
11.10	26. 8	D10	C3	Horse
12.10	27. 8	D10	D4	Stag
13.10	28. 8	D10	E5	Serpent
14.10	29. 8	D10	F6	Earthworm
15.10	1. 9	E11	G7	Crocodile
16.10	2. 9	E11	H8	Dragon
17.10	3. 9	E11	J9	Badger
18.10	4. 9	E11	K10	Hare
19.10	5. 9	E11	A11	Fox
20.10	6. 9	E11	B12	Tiger
21.10	7. 9	E11	C1	Leopard
22.10	8. 9	E11	D2	Griffon
23.10	9. 9	E11	E3	Ox
24.10	10. 9	E11	F4	Bat
25.10	11. 9	E11	G5	Rat
26.10	12. 9	E11	H6	Swallow
27.10	13. 9	E11	J7	Pig
28.10	14. 9	E11	K8	Porcupine
29.10	15. 9	E11	A9	Wolf
30.10	16. 9	E11	B10	Dog
31.10	17. 9	E11	C11	Pheasant
1.11	18. 9	E11	D12	Cock
2.11	19. 9	E11	E1	Crow
3.11	20. 9	E11	F2	Monkey
4.11	21. 9	E11	G3	Gibbon
5.11	22. 9	E11	H4	Tapir
6.11	23. 9	E11	J5	Sheep

Solar date	Lunar date	Month HS/EB	Day HS/EB	Constellation
7.11	24. 9	E11	K6	Deer
8.11	25. 9	E11	A7	Horse
9.11	26. 9	E11	B8	Stag
10.11	27. 9	E11	C9	Serpent
11.11	28. 9	E11	D10	Earthworm
12.11	29. 9	E11	E11	Crocodile
13.11	30. 9	E11	F12	Dragon
14.11	1.10	F12	G1	Badger
15.11	2.10	F12	H2	Hare
16.11	3.10	F12	J3	Fox
17.11	4.10	F12	K4	Tiger
18.11	5.10	F12	A5	Leopard
19.11	6.10	F12	B6	Griffon
20.11	7.10	F12	C7	Ox
21.11	8.10	F12	D8	Bat
22.11	9.10	F12	E9	Rat
23.11	10.10	F12	F10	Swallow
24.11	11.10	F12	G11	Pig
25.11	12.10	F12	H12	Porcupine
26.11	13.10	F12	J1	Wolf
27.11	14.10	F12	K2	Dog
28.11	15.10	F12	A3	Pheasant
29.11	16.10	F12	B4	Cock
30.11	17.10	F12	C5	Crow
1.12	18.10	F12	D6	Monkey
2.12	19.10	F12	E7	Gibbon
3.12	20.10	F12	F8	Tapir
4.12	21.10	F12	G9	Sheep
5.12	22.10	F12	H10	Deer
6.12	23.10	F12	J11	Horse
7.12	24.10	F12	K12	Stag
8.12	25.10	F12	A1	Serpent
9.12	26.10	F12	B2	Earthworm
10.12	27.10	F12	C3	Crocodile
11.12	28.10	F12	D4	Dragon
12.12	29.10	F12	E5	Badger
13.12	30.10	F12	F6	Hare
14.12	1.11	G1	G7	Fox
15.12	2.11	G1	H8	Tiger
16.12	3.11	G1	J9	Leopard
17.12	4.11	G1	K10	Griffon
18.12	5.11	G1	A11	Ox
19.12	6.11	G1	B12	Bat
20.12	7.11	G1	C1	Rat
21.12	8.11	G1	D2	Swallow
22.12	9.11	G1	E3	Pig
23.12	10.11	G1	F4	Porcupine
24.12	11.11	G1	G5	Wolf
25.12	12.11	G1	H6	Dog
26.12	13.11	G1	J7	Pheasant
27.12	14.11	G1	K8	Cock
28.12	15.11	G1	A9	Crow
29.12	16.11	G1	B10	Monkey
30.12	17.11	G1	C11	Gibbon
31.12	18.11	G1	D12	Tapir
1937				
1. 1	19.11	G1	E1	Sheep
2. 1	20.11	G1	F2	Deer
3. 1	21.11	G1	G3	Horse
4. 1	22.11	G1	H4	Stag
5. 1	23.11	G1	J5	Serpent
6. 1	24.11	G1	K6	Earthworm
7. 1	25.11	G1	A7	Crocodile
8. 1	26.11	G1	B8	Dragon
9. 1	27.11	G1	C9	Badger
10. 1	28.11	G1	D10	Hare
11. 1	29.11	G1	E11	Fox
12. 1	30.11	G1	F12	Tiger
13. 1	1.12	H2	G1	Leopard
14. 1	2.12	H2	H2	Griffon
15. 1	3.12	H2	J3	Ox
16. 1	4.12	H2	K4	Bat
17. 1	5.12	H2	A5	Rat
18. 1	6.12	H2	B6	Swallow
19. 1	7.12	H2	C7	Pig
20. 1	8.12	H2	D8	Porcupine
21. 1	9.12	H2	E9	Wolf
22. 1	10.12	H2	F10	Dog
23. 1	11.12	H2	G11	Pheasant
24. 1	12.12	H2	H12	Cock
25. 1	13.12	H2	J1	Crow
26. 1	14.12	H2	K2	Monkey
27. 1	15.12	H2	A3	Gibbon
28. 1	16.12	H2	B4	Tapir
29. 1	17.12	H2	C5	Sheep
30. 1	18.12	H2	D6	Deer
31. 1	19.12	H2	E7	Horse
1. 2	20.12	H2	F8	Stag
2. 2	21.12	H2	G9	Serpent
3. 2	22.12	H2	H10	Earthworm
4. 2	23.12	H2	J11	Crocodile
5. 2	24.12	H2	K12	Dragon
6. 2	25.12	H2	A1	Badger
7. 2	26.12	H2	B2	Hare
8. 2	27.12	H2	C3	Fox
9. 2	28.12	H2	D4	Tiger
10. 2	29.12	H2	E5	Leopard

TING CH'OU YEAR

11. 2	1. 1	J3	F6	Griffon
12. 2	2. 1	J3	G7	Ox
13. 2	3. 1	J3	H8	Bat
14. 2	4. 1	J3	J9	Rat
15. 2	5. 1	J3	K10	Swallow
16. 2	6. 1	J3	A11	Pig
17. 2	7. 1	J3	B12	Porcupine
18. 2	8. 1	J3	C1	Wolf
19. 2	9. 1	J3	D2	Dog
20. 2	10. 1	J3	E3	Pheasant
21. 2	11. 1	J3	F4	Cock
22. 2	12. 1	J3	G5	Crow
23. 2	13. 1	J3	H6	Monkey
24. 2	14. 1	J3	J7	Gibbon
25. 2	15. 1	J3	K8	Tapir
26. 2	16. 1	J3	A9	Sheep
27. 2	17. 1	J3	B10	Deer
28. 2	18. 1	J3	C11	Horse
1. 3	19. 1	J3	D12	Stag
2. 3	20. 1	J3	E1	Serpent
3. 3	21. 1	J3	F2	Earthworm
4. 3	22. 1	J3	G3	Crocodile
5. 3	23. 1	J3	H4	Dragon
6. 3	24. 1	J3	J5	Badger
7. 3	25. 1	J3	K6	Hare
8. 3	26. 1	J3	A7	Fox
9. 3	27. 1	J3	B8	Tiger
10. 3	28. 1	J3	C9	Leopard
11. 3	29. 1	J3	D10	Griffon
12. 3	30. 1	J3	E11	Ox
13. 3	1. 2	K4	F12	Bat
14. 3	2. 2	K4	G1	Rat
15. 3	3. 2	K4	H2	Swallow
16. 3	4. 2	K4	J3	Pig
17. 3	5. 2	K4	K4	Porcupine
18. 3	6. 2	K4	A5	Wolf
19. 3	7. 2	K4	B6	Dog
20. 3	8. 2	K4	C7	Pheasant

Solar date	*Lunar date*	*Month HS/EB*	*Day HS/EB*	*Constellation*
21. 3	9. 2	K4	D8	Cock
22. 3	10. 2	K4	E9	Crow
23. 3	11. 2	K4	F10	Monkey
24. 3	12. 2	K4	G11	Gibbon
25. 3	13. 2	K4	H12	Tapir
26. 3	14. 2	K4	J1	Sheep
27. 3	15. 2	K4	K2	Deer
28. 3	16. 2	K4	A3	Horse
29. 3	17. 2	K4	B4	Stag
30. 3	18. 2	K4	C5	Serpent
31. 3	19. 2	K4	D6	Earthworm
1. 4	20. 2	K4	E7	Crocodile
2. 4	21. 2	K4	F8	Dragon
3. 4	22. 2	K4	G9	Badger
4. 4	23. 2	K4	H10	Hare
5. 4	24. 2	K4	J11	Fox
6. 4	25. 2	K4	K12	Tiger
7. 4	26. 2	K4	A1	Leopard
8. 4	27. 2	K4	B2	Griffon
9. 4	28. 2	K4	C3	Ox
10. 4	29. 2	K4	D4	Bat
11. 4	1. 3	A5	E5	Rat
12. 4	2. 3	A5	F6	Swallow
13. 4	3. 3	A5	G7	Pig
14. 4	4. 3	A5	H8	Porcupine
15. 4	5. 3	A5	J9	Wolf
16. 4	6. 3	A5	K10	Dog
17. 4	7. 3	A5	A11	Pheasant
18. 4	8. 3	A5	B12	Cock
19. 4	9. 3	A5	C1	Crow
20. 4	10. 3	A5	D2	Monkey
21. 4	11. 3	A5	E3	Gibbon
22. 4	12. 3	A5	F4	Tapir
23. 4	13. 3	A5	G5	Sheep
24. 4	14. 3	A5	H6	Deer
25. 4	15. 3	A5	J7	Horse
26. 4	16. 3	A5	K8	Stag
27. 4	17. 3	A5	A9	Serpent
28. 4	18. 3	A5	B10	Earthworm
29. 4	19. 3	A5	C11	Crocodile
30. 4	20. 3	A5	D12	Dragon
1. 5	21. 3	A5	E1	Badger
2. 5	22. 3	A5	F2	Hare
3. 5	23. 3	A5	G3	Fox
4. 5	24. 3	A5	H4	Tiger
5. 5	25. 3	A5	J5	Leopard
6. 5	26. 3	A5	K6	Griffon
7. 5	27. 3	A5	A7	Ox
8. 5	28. 3	A5	B8	Bat
9. 5	29. 3	A5	C9	Rat
10. 5	1. 4	B6	D10	Swallow
11. 5	2. 4	B6	E11	Pig
12. 5	3. 4	B6	F12	Porcupine
13. 5	4. 4	B6	G1	Wolf
14. 5	5. 4	B6	H2	Dog
15. 5	6. 4	B6	J3	Pheasant
16. 5	7. 4	B6	K4	Cock
17. 5	8. 4	B6	A5	Crow
18. 5	9. 4	B6	B6	Monkey
19. 5	10. 4	B6	C7	Gibbon
20. 5	11. 4	B6	D8	Tapir
21. 5	12. 4	B6	E9	Sheep
22. 5	13. 4	B6	F10	Deer
23. 5	14. 4	B6	G11	Horse
24. 5	15. 4	B6	H12	Stag
25. 5	16. 4	B6	J1	Serpent
26. 5	17. 4	B6	K2	Earthworm
27. 5	18. 4	B6	A3	Crocodile
28. 5	19. 4	B6	B4	Dragon
29. 5	20. 4	B6	C5	Badger
30. 5	21. 4	B6	D6	Hare
31. 5	22. 4	B6	E7	Fox
1. 6	23. 4	B6	F8	Tiger

Solar date	*Lunar date*	*Month HS/EB*	*Day HS/EB*	*Constellation*
2. 6	24. 4	B6	G9	Leopard
3. 6	25. 4	B6	H10	Griffon
4. 6	26. 4	B6	J11	Ox
5. 6	27. 4	B6	K12	Bat
6. 6	28. 4	B6	A1	Rat
7. 6	29. 4	B6	B2	Swallow
8. 6	30. 4	B6	C3	Pig
9. 6	1. 5	C7	D4	Porcupine
10. 6	2. 5	C7	E5	Wolf
11. 6	3. 5	C7	F6	Dog
12. 6	4. 5	C7	G7	Pheasant
13. 6	5. 5	C7	H8	Cock
14. 6	6. 5	C7	J9	Crow
15. 6	7. 5	C7	K10	Monkey
16. 6	8. 5	C7	A11	Gibbon
17. 6	9. 5	C7	B12	Tapir
18. 6	10. 5	C7	C1	Sheep
19. 6	11. 5	C7	D2	Deer
20. 6	12. 5	C7	E3	Horse
21. 6	13. 5	C7	F4	Stag
22. 6	14. 5	C7	G5	Serpent
23. 6	15. 5	C7	H6	Earthworm
24. 6	16. 5	C7	J7	Crocodile
25. 6	17. 5	C7	K8	Dragon
26. 6	18. 5	C7	A9	Badger
27. 6	19. 5	C7	B10	Hare
28. 6	20. 5	C7	C11	Fox
29. 6	21. 5	C7	D12	Tiger
30. 6	22. 5	C7	E1	Leopard
1. 7	23. 5	C7	F2	Griffon
2. 7	24. 5	C7	G3	Ox
3. 7	25. 5	C7	H4	Bat
4. 7	26. 5	C7	J5	Rat
5. 7	27. 5	C7	K6	Swallow
6. 7	28. 5	C7	A7	Pig
7. 7	29. 5	C7	B8	Porcupine
8. 7	1. 6	D8	C9	Wolf
9. 7	2. 6	D8	D10	Dog
10. 7	3. 6	D8	E11	Pheasant
11. 7	4. 6	D8	F12	Cock
12. 7	5. 6	D8	G1	Crow
13. 7	6. 6	D8	H2	Monkey
14. 7	7. 6	D8	J3	Gibbon
15. 7	8. 6	D8	K4	Tapir
16. 7	9. 6	D8	A5	Sheep
17. 7	10. 6	D8	B6	Deer
18. 7	11. 6	D8	C7	Horse
19. 7	12. 6	D8	D8	Stag
20. 7	13. 6	D8	E9	Serpent
21. 7	14. 6	D8	F10	Earthworm
22. 7	15. 6	D8	G11	Crocodile
23. 7	16. 6	D8	H12	Dragon
24. 7	17. 6	D8	J1	Badger
25. 7	18. 6	D8	K2	Hare
26. 7	19. 6	D8	A3	Fox
27. 7	20. 6	D8	B4	Tiger
28. 7	21. 6	D8	C5	Leopard
29. 7	22. 6	D8	D6	Griffon
30. 7	23. 6	D8	E7	Ox
31. 7	24. 6	D8	F8	Bat
1. 8	25. 6	D8	G9	Rat
2. 8	26. 6	D8	H10	Swallow
3. 8	27. 6	D8	J11	Pig
4. 8	28. 6	D8	K12	Porcupine
5. 8	29. 6	D8	A1	Wolf
6. 8	1. 7	E9	B2	Dog
7. 8	2. 7	E9	C3	Pheasant
8. 8	3. 7	E9	D4	Cock
9. 8	4. 7	E9	E5	Crow
10. 8	5. 7	E9	F6	Monkey
11. 8	6. 7	E9	G7	Gibbon
12. 8	7. 7	E9	H8	Tapir
13. 8	8. 7	E9	J9	Sheep

Solar date	*Lunar date*	*Month HS/EB*	*Day HS/EB*	*Constellation*
14. 8	9. 7	E9	K10	Deer
15. 8	10. 7	E9	A11	Horse
16. 8	11. 7	E9	B12	Stag
17. 8	12. 7	E9	C1	Serpent
18. 8	13. 7	E9	D2	Earthworm
19. 8	14. 7	E9	E3	Crocodile
20. 8	15. 7	E9	F4	Dragon
21. 8	16. 7	E9	G5	Badger
22. 8	17. 7	E9	H6	Hare
23. 8	18. 7	E9	J7	Fox
24. 8	19. 7	E9	K8	Tiger
25. 8	20. 7	E9	A9	Leopard
26. 8	21. 7	E9	B10	Griffon
27. 8	22. 7	E9	C11	Ox
28. 8	23. 7	E9	D12	Bat
29. 8	24. 7	E9	E1	Rat
30. 8	25. 7	E9	F2	Swallow
31. 8	26. 7	E9	G3	Pig
1. 9	27. 7	E9	H4	Porcupine
2. 9	28. 7	E9	J5	Wolf
3. 9	29. 7	E9	K6	Dog
4. 9	30. 7	E9	A7	Pheasant
5. 9	1. 8	F10	B8	Cock
6. 9	2. 8	F10	C9	Crow
7. 9	3. 8	F10	D10	Monkey
8. 9	4. 8	F10	E11	Gibbon
9. 9	5. 8	F10	F12	Tapir
10. 9	6. 8	F10	G1	Sheep
11. 9	7. 8	F10	H2	Deer
12. 9	8. 8	F10	J3	Horse
13. 9	9. 8	F10	K4	Stag
14. 9	10. 8	F10	A5	Serpent
15. 9	11. 8	F10	B6	Earthworm
16. 9	12. 8	F10	C7	Crocodile
17. 9	13. 8	F10	D8	Dragon
18. 9	14. 8	F10	E9	Badger
19. 9	15. 8	F10	F10	Hare
20. 9	16. 8	F10	G11	Fox
21. 9	17. 8	F10	H12	Tiger
22. 9	18. 8	F10	J1	Leopard
23. 9	19. 8	F10	K2	Griffon
24. 9	20. 8	F10	A3	Ox
25. 9	21. 8	F10	B4	Bat
26. 9	22. 8	F10	C5	Rat
27. 9	23. 8	F10	D6	Swallow
28. 9	24. 8	F10	E7	Pig
29. 9	25. 8	F10	F8	Porcupine
30. 9	26. 8	F10	G9	Wolf
1.10	27. 8	F10	H10	Dog
2.10	28. 8	F10	J11	Pheasant
3.10	29. 8	F10	K12	Cock
4.10	1. 9	G11	A1	Crow
5.10	2. 9	G11	B2	Monkey
6.10	3. 9	G11	C3	Gibbon
7.10	4. 9	G11	D4	Tapir
8.10	5. 9	G11	E5	Sheep
9.10	6. 9	G11	F6	Deer
10.10	7. 9	G11	G7	Horse
11.10	8. 9	G11	H8	Stag
12.10	9. 9	G11	J9	Serpent
13.10	10. 9	G11	K10	Earthworm
14.10	11. 9	G11	A11	Crocodile
15.10	12. 9	G11	B12	Dragon
16.10	13. 9	G11	C1	Badger
17.10	14. 9	G11	D2	Hare
18.10	15. 9	G11	E3	Fox
19.10	16. 9	G11	F4	Tiger
20.10	17. 9	G11	G5	Leopard
21.10	18. 9	G11	H6	Griffon
22.10	19. 9	G11	J7	Ox
23.10	20. 9	G11	K8	Bat
24.10	21. 9	G11	A9	Rat
25.10	22. 9	G11	B10	Swallow
26.10	23. 9	G11	C11	Pig
27.10	24. 9	G11	D12	Porcupine
28.10	25. 9	G11	E1	Wolf
29.10	26. 9	G11	F2	Dog
30.10	27. 9	G11	G3	Pheasant
31.10	28. 9	G11	H4	Cock
1.11	29. 9	G11	J5	Crow
2.11	30. 9	G11	K6	Monkey
3.11	1.10	H12	A7	Gibbon
4.11	2.10	H12	B8	Tapir
5.11	3.10	H12	C9	Sheep
6.11	4.10	H12	D10	Deer
7.11	5.10	H12	E11	Horse
8.11	6.10	H12	F12	Stag
9.11	7.10	H12	G1	Serpent
10.11	8.10	H12	H2	Earthworm
11.11	9.10	H12	J3	Crocodile
12.11	10.10	H12	K4	Dragon
13.11	11.10	H12	A5	Badger
14.11	12.10	H12	B6	Hare
15.11	13.10	H12	C7	Fox
16.11	14.10	H12	D8	Tiger
17.11	15.10	H12	E9	Leopard
18.11	16.10	H12	F10	Griffon
19.11	17.10	H12	G11	Ox
20.11	18.10	H12	H12	Bat
21.11	19.10	H12	J1	Rat
22.11	20.10	H12	K2	Swallow
23.11	21.10	H12	A3	Pig
24.11	22.10	H12	B4	Porcupine
25.11	23.10	H12	C5	Wolf
26.11	24.10	H12	D6	Dog
27.11	25.10	H12	E7	Pheasant
28.11	26.10	H12	F8	Cock
29.11	27.10	H12	G9	Crow
30.11	28.10	H12	H10	Monkey
1.12	29.10	H12	J11	Gibbon
2.12	30.10	H12	K12	Tapir
3.12	1.11	J1	A1	Sheep
4.12	2.11	J1	B2	Deer
5.12	3.11	J1	C3	Horse
6.12	4.11	J1	D4	Stag
7.12	5.11	J1	E5	Serpent
8.12	6.11	J1	F6	Earthworm
9.12	7.11	J1	G7	Crocodile
10.12	8.11	J1	H8	Dragon
11.12	9.11	J1	J9	Badger
12.12	10.11	J1	K10	Hare
13.12	11.11	J1	A11	Fox
14.12	12.11	J1	B12	Tiger
15.12	13.11	J1	C1	Leopard
16.12	14.11	J1	D2	Griffon
17.12	15.11	J1	E3	Ox
18.12	16.11	J1	F4	Bat
19.12	17.11	J1	G5	Rat
20.12	18.11	J1	H6	Swallow
21.12	19.11	J1	J7	Pig
22.12	20.11	J1	K8	Porcupine
23.12	21.11	J1	A9	Wolf
24.12	22.11	J1	B10	Dog
25.12	23.11	J1	C11	Pheasant
26.12	24.11	J1	D12	Cock
27.12	25.11	J1	E1	Crow
28.12	26.11	J1	F2	Monkey
29.12	27.11	J1	G3	Gibbon
30.12	28.11	J1	H4	Tapir
31.12	29.11	J1	J5	Sheep
1938				
1. 1	30.11	J1	K6	Deer
2. 1	1.12	K2	A7	Horse
3. 1	2.12	K2	B8	Stag
4. 1	3.12	K2	C9	Serpent

Solar date	*Lunar date*	*Month HS/EB*	*Day HS/EB*	*Constellation*
5. 1	4.12	K2	D10	Earthworm
6. 1	5.12	K2	E11	Crocodile
7. 1	6.12	K2	F12	Dragon
8. 1	7.12	K2	G1	Badger
9. 1	8.12	K2	H2	Hare
10. 1	9.12	K2	J3	Fox
11. 1	10.12	K2	K4	Tiger
12. 1	11.12	K2	A5	Leopard
13. 1	12.12	K2	B6	Griffon
14. 1	13.12	K2	C7	Ox
15. 1	14.12	K2	D8	Bat
16. 1	15.12	K2	E9	Rat
17. 1	16.12	K2	F10	Swallow
18. 1	17.12	K2	G11	Pig
19. 1	18.12	K2	H12	Porcupine
20. 1	19.12	K2	J1	Wolf
21. 1	20.12	K2	K2	Dog
22. 1	21.12	K2	A3	Pheasant
23. 1	22.12	K2	B4	Cock
24. 1	23.12	K2	C5	Crow
25. 1	24.12	K2	D6	Monkey
26. 1	25.12	K2	E7	Gibbon
27. 1	26.12	K2	F8	Tapir
28. 1	27.12	K2	G9	Sheep
29. 1	28.12	K2	H10	Deer
30. 1	29.12	K2	J11	Horse

MOU YIN YEAR

31. 1	1. 1	A3	K12	Stag
1. 2	2. 1	A3	A1	Serpent
2. 2	3. 1	A3	B2	Earthworm
3. 2	4. 1	A3	C3	Crocodile
4. 2	5. 1	A3	D4	Dragon
5. 2	6. 1	A3	E5	Badger
6. 2	7. 1	A3	F6	Hare
7. 2	8. 1	A3	G7	Fox
8. 2	9. 1	A3	H8	Tiger
9. 2	10. 1	A3	J9	Leopard
10. 2	11. 1	A3	K10	Griffon
11. 2	12. 1	A3	A11	Ox
12. 2	13. 1	A3	B12	Bat
13. 2	14. 1	A3	C1	Rat
14. 2	15. 1	A3	D2	Swallow
15. 2	16. 1	A3	E3	Pig
16. 2	17. 1	A3	F4	Porcupine
17. 2	18. 1	A3	G5	Wolf
18. 2	19. 1	A3	H6	Dog
19. 2	20. 1	A3	J7	Pheasant
20. 2	21. 1	A3	K8	Cock
21. 2	22. 1	A3	A9	Crow
22. 2	23. 1	A3	B10	Monkey
23. 2	24. 1	A3	C11	Gibbon
24. 2	25. 1	A3	D12	Tapir
25. 2	26. 1	A3	E1	Sheep
26. 2	27. 1	A3	F2	Deer
27. 2	28. 1	A3	G3	Horse
28. 2	29. 1	A3	H4	Stag
1. 3	30. 1	A3	J5	Serpent
2. 3	1. 2	B4	K6	Earthworm
3. 3	2. 2	B4	A7	Crocodile
4. 3	3. 2	B4	B8	Dragon
5. 3	4. 2	B4	C9	Badger
6. 3	5. 2	B4	D10	Hare
7. 3	6. 2	B4	E11	Fox
8. 3	7. 2	B4	F12	Tiger
9. 3	8. 2	B4	G1	Leopard
10. 3	9. 2	B4	H2	Griffon
11. 3	10. 2	B4	J3	Ox
12. 3	11. 2	B4	K4	Bat
13. 3	12. 2	B4	A5	Rat
14. 3	13. 2	B4	B6	Swallow
15. 3	14. 2	B4	C7	Pig
16. 3	15. 2	B4	D8	Porcupine
17. 3	16. 2	B4	E9	Wolf
18. 3	17. 2	B4	F10	Dog
19. 3	18. 2	B4	G11	Pheasant
20. 3	19. 2	B4	H12	Cock
21. 3	20. 2	B4	J1	Crow
22. 3	21. 2	B4	K2	Monkey
23. 3	22. 2	B4	A3	Gibbon
24. 3	23. 2	B4	B4	Tapir
25. 3	24. 2	B4	C5	Sheep
26. 3	25. 2	B4	D6	Deer
27. 3	26. 2	B4	E7	Horse
28. 3	27. 2	B4	F8	Stag
29. 3	28. 2	B4	G9	Serpent
30. 3	29. 2	B4	H10	Earthworm
31. 3	30. 2	B4	J11	Crocodile
1. 4	1. 3	C5	K12	Dragon
2. 4	2. 3	C5	A1	Badger
3. 4	3. 3	C5	B2	Hare
4. 4	4. 3	C5	C3	Fox
5. 4	5. 3	C5	D4	Tiger
6. 4	6. 3	C5	E5	Leopard
7. 4	7. 3	C5	F6	Griffon
8. 4	8. 3	C5	G7	Ox
9. 4	9. 3	C5	H8	Bat
10. 4	10. 3	C5	J9	Rat
11. 4	11. 3	C5	K10	Swallow
12. 4	12. 3	C5	A11	Pig
13. 4	13. 3	C5	B12	Porcupine
14. 4	14. 3	C5	C1	Wolf
15. 4	15. 3	C5	D2	Dog
16. 4	16. 3	C5	E3	Pheasant
17. 4	17. 3	C5	F4	Cock
18. 4	18. 3	C5	G5	Crow
19. 4	19. 3	C5	H6	Monkey
20. 4	20. 3	C5	J7	Gibbon
21. 4	21. 3	C5	K8	Tapir
22. 4	22. 3	C5	A9	Sheep
23. 4	23. 3	C5	B10	Deer
24. 4	24. 3	C5	C11	Horse
25. 4	25. 3	C5	D12	Stag
26. 4	26. 3	C5	E1	Serpent
27. 4	27. 3	C5	F2	Earthworm
28. 4	28. 3	C5	G3	Crocodile
29. 4	29. 3	C5	H4	Dragon
30. 4	1. 4	D6	J5	Badger
1. 5	2. 4	D6	K6	Hare
2. 5	3. 4	D6	A7	Fox
3. 5	4. 4	D6	B8	Tiger
4. 5	5. 4	D6	C9	Leopard
5. 5	6. 4	D6	D10	Griffon
6. 5	7. 4	D6	E11	Ox
7. 5	8. 4	D6	F12	Bat
8. 5	9. 4	D6	G1	Rat
9. 5	10. 4	D6	H2	Swallow
10. 5	11. 4	D6	J3	Pig
11. 5	12. 4	D6	K4	Porcupine
12. 5	13. 4	D6	A5	Wolf
13. 5	14. 4	D6	B6	Dog
14. 5	15. 4	D6	C7	Pheasant
15. 5	16. 4	D6	D8	Cock
16. 5	17. 4	D6	E9	Crow
17. 5	18. 4	D6	F10	Monkey
18. 5	19. 4	D6	G11	Gibbon

Solar date	*Lunar date*	*Month HS/EB*	*Day HS/EB*	*Constellation*
19. 5	20. 4	D6	H12	Tapir
20. 5	21. 4	D6	J1	Sheep
21. 5	22. 4	D6	K2	Deer
22. 5	23. 4	D6	A3	Horse
23. 5	24. 4	D6	B4	Stag
24. 5	25. 4	D6	C5	Serpent
25. 5	26. 4	D6	D6	Earthworm
26. 5	27. 4	D6	E7	Crocodile
27. 5	28. 4	D6	F8	Dragon
28. 5	29. 4	D6	G9	Badger
29. 5	1. 5	E7	H10	Hare
30. 5	2. 5	E7	J11	Fox
31. 5	3. 5	E7	K12	Tiger
1. 6	4. 5	E7	A1	Leopard
2. 6	5. 5	E7	B2	Griffon
3. 6	6. 5	E7	C3	Ox
4. 6	7. 5	E7	D4	Bat
5. 6	8. 5	E7	E5	Rat
6. 6	9. 5	E7	F6	Swallow
7. 6	10. 5	E7	G7	Pig
8. 6	11. 5	E7	H8	Porcupine
9. 6	12. 5	E7	J9	Wolf
10. 6	13. 5	E7	K10	Dog
11. 6	14. 5	E7	A11	Pheasant
12. 6	15. 5	E7	B12	Cock
13. 6	16. 5	E7	C1	Crow
14. 6	17. 5	E7	D2	Monkey
15. 6	18. 5	E7	E3	Gibbon
16. 6	19. 5	E7	F4	Tapir
17. 6	20. 5	E7	G5	Sheep
18. 6	21. 5	E7	H6	Deer
19. 6	22. 5	E7	J7	Horse
20. 6	23. 5	E7	K8	Stag
21. 6	24. 5	E7	A9	Serpent
22. 6	25. 5	E7	B10	Earthworm
23. 6	26. 5	E7	C11	Crocodile
24. 6	27. 5	E7	D12	Dragon
25. 6	28. 5	E7	E1	Badger
26. 6	29. 5	E7	F2	Hare
27. 6	30. 5	E7	G3	Fox
28. 6	1. 6	F8	H4	Tiger
29. 6	2. 6	F8	J5	Leopard
30. 6	3. 6	F8	K6	Griffon
1. 7	4. 6	F8	A7	Ox
2. 7	5. 6	F8	B8	Bat
3. 7	6. 6	F8	C9	Rat
4. 7	7. 6	F8	D10	Swallow
5. 7	8. 6	F8	E11	Pig
6. 7	9. 6	F8	F12	Porcupine
7. 7	10. 6	F8	G1	Wolf
8. 7	11. 6	F8	H2	Dog
9. 7	12. 6	F8	J3	Pheasant
10. 7	13. 6	F8	K4	Cock
11. 7	14. 6	F8	A5	Crow
12. 7	15. 6	F8	B6	Monkey
13. 7	16. 6	F8	C7	Gibbon
14. 7	17. 6	F8	D8	Tapir
15. 7	18. 6	F8	E9	Sheep
16. 7	19. 6	F8	F10	Deer
17. 7	20. 6	F8	G11	Horse
18. 7	21. 6	F8	H12	Stag
19. 7	22. 6	F8	J1	Serpent
20. 7	23. 6	F8	K2	Earthworm
21. 7	24. 6	F8	A3	Crocodile
22. 7	25. 6	F8	B4	Dragon
23. 7	26. 6	F8	C5	Badger
24. 7	27. 6	F8	D6	Hare
25. 7	28. 6	F8	E7	Fox
26. 7	29. 6	F8	F8	Tiger
27. 7	1. 7	G9	G9	Leopard
28. 7	2. 7	G9	H10	Griffon
29. 7	3. 7	G9	J11	Ox
30. 7	4. 7	G9	K12	Bat
31. 7	5. 7	G9	A1	Rat
1. 8	6. 7	G9	B2	Swallow
2. 8	7. 7	G9	C3	Pig
3. 8	8. 7	G9	D4	Porcupine
4. 8	9. 7	G9	E5	Wolf
5. 8	10. 7	G9	F6	Dog
6. 8	11. 7	G9	G7	Pheasant
7. 8	12. 7	G9	H8	Cock
8. 8	13. 7	G9	J9	Crow
9. 8	14. 7	G9	K10	Monkey
10. 8	15. 7	G9	A11	Gibbon
11. 8	16. 7	G9	B12	Tapir
12. 8	17. 7	G9	C1	Sheep
13. 8	18. 7	G9	D2	Deer
14. 8	19. 7	G9	E3	Horse
15. 8	20. 7	G9	F4	Stag
16. 8	21. 7	G9	G5	Serpent
17. 8	22. 7	G9	H6	Earthworm
18. 8	23. 7	G9	J7	Crocodile
19. 8	24. 7	G9	K8	Dragon
20. 8	25. 7	G9	A9	Badger
21. 8	26. 7	G9	B10	Hare
22. 8	27. 7	G9	C11	Fox
23. 8	28. 7	G9	D12	Tiger
24. 8	29. 7	G9	E1	Leopard
25. 8	*1. 7*	*G9*	F2	Griffon
26. 8	*2. 7*	*G9*	G3	Ox
27. 8	*3. 7*	*G9*	H4	Bat
28. 8	*4. 7*	*G9*	J5	Rat
29. 8	*5. 7*	*G9*	K6	Swallow
30. 8	*6. 7*	*G9*	A7	Pig
31. 8	*7. 7*	*G9*	B8	Porcupine
1. 9	*8. 7*	*G9*	C9	Wolf
2. 9	*9. 7*	*G9*	D10	Dog
3. 9	*10. 7*	*G9*	E11	Pheasant
4. 9	*11. 7*	*G9*	F12	Cock
5. 9	*12. 7*	*G9*	G1	Crow
6. 9	*13. 7*	*G9*	H2	Monkey
7. 9	*14. 7*	*G9*	J3	Gibbon
8. 9	*15. 7*	*G9*	K4	Tapir
9. 9	*16. 7*	*G9*	A5	Sheep
10. 9	*17. 7*	*G9*	B6	Deer
11. 9	*18. 7*	*G9*	C7	Horse
12. 9	*19. 7*	*G9*	D8	Stag
13. 9	*20. 7*	*G9*	E9	Serpent
14. 9	*21. 7*	*G9*	F10	Earthworm
15. 9	*22. 7*	*G9*	G11	Crocodile
16. 9	*23. 7*	*G9*	H12	Dragon
17. 9	*24. 7*	*G9*	J1	Badger
18. 9	*25. 7*	*G9*	K2	Hare
19. 9	*26. 7*	*G9*	A3	Fox
20. 9	*27. 7*	*G9*	B4	Tiger
21. 9	*28. 7*	*G9*	C5	Leopard
22. 9	*29. 7*	*G9*	D6	Griffon
23. 9	*30. 7*	*G9*	E7	Ox
24. 9	1. 8	H10	F8	Bat
25. 9	2. 8	H10	G9	Rat
26. 9	3. 8	H10	H10	Swallow
27. 9	4. 8	H10	J11	Pig
28. 9	5. 8	H10	K12	Porcupine
29. 9	6. 8	H10	A1	Wolf
30. 9	7. 8	H10	B2	Dog
1.10	8. 8	H10	C3	Pheasant
2.10	9. 8	H10	D4	Cock
3.10	10. 8	H10	E5	Crow
4.10	11. 8	H10	F6	Monkey
5.10	12. 8	H10	G7	Gibbon
6.10	13. 8	H10	H8	Tapir
7.10	14. 8	H10	J9	Sheep
8.10	15. 8	H10	K10	Deer
9.10	16. 8	H10	A11	Horse
10.10	17. 8	H10	B12	Stag
11.10	18. 8	H10	C1	Serpent

Solar date	Lunar date	Month HS/EB	Day HS/EB	Constellation
12.10	19. 8	H10	D2	Earthworm
13.10	20. 8	H10	E3	Crocodile
14.10	21. 8	H10	F4	Dragon
15.10	22. 8	H10	G5	Badger
16.10	23. 8	H10	H6	Hare
17.10	24. 8	H10	J7	Fox
18.10	25. 8	H10	K8	Tiger
19.10	26. 8	H10	A9	Leopard
20.10	27. 8	H10	B10	Griffon
21.10	28. 8	H10	C11	Ox
22.10	29. 8	H10	D12	Bat
23.10	1. 9	J11	E1	Rat
24.10	2. 9	J11	F2	Swallow
25.10	3. 9	J11	G3	Pig
26.10	4. 9	J11	H4	Porcupine
27.10	5. 9	J11	J5	Wolf
28.10	6. 9	J11	K6	Dog
29.10	7. 9	J11	A7	Pheasant
30.10	8. 9	J11	B8	Cock
31.10	9. 9	J11	C9	Crow
1.11	10. 9	J11	D10	Monkey
2.11	11. 9	J11	E11	Gibbon
3.11	12. 9	J11	F12	Tapir
4.11	13. 9	J11	G1	Sheep
5.11	14. 9	J11	H2	Deer
6.11	15. 9	J11	J3	Horse
7.11	16. 9	J11	K4	Stag
8.11	17. 9	J11	A5	Serpent
9.11	18. 9	J11	B6	Earthworm
10.11	19. 9	J11	C7	Crocodile
11.11	20. 9	J11	D8	Dragon
12.11	21. 9	J11	E9	Badger
13.11	22. 9	J11	F10	Hare
14.11	23. 9	J11	G11	Fox
15.11	24. 9	J11	H12	Tiger
16.11	25. 9	J11	J1	Leopard
17.11	26. 9	J11	K2	Griffon
18.11	27. 9	J11	A3	Ox
19.11	28. 9	J11	B4	Bat
20.11	29. 9	J11	C5	Rat
21.11	30. 9	J11	D6	Swallow
22.11	1.10	K12	E7	Pig
23.11	2.10	K12	F8	Porcupine
24.11	3.10	K12	G9	Wolf
25.11	4.10	K12	H10	Dog
26.11	5.10	K12	J11	Pheasant
27.11	6.10	K12	K12	Cock
28.11	7.10	K12	A1	Crow
29.11	8.10	K12	B2	Monkey
30.11	9.10	K12	C3	Gibbon
1.12	10.10	K12	D4	Tapir
2.12	11.10	K12	E5	Sheep
3.12	12.10	K12	F6	Deer
4.12	13.10	K12	G7	Horse
5.12	14.10	K12	H8	Stag
6.12	15.10	K12	J9	Serpent
7.12	16.10	K12	K10	Earthworm
8.12	17.10	K12	A11	Crocodile
9.12	18.10	K12	B12	Dragon
10.12	19.10	K12	C1	Badger
11.12	20.10	K12	D2	Hare
12.12	21.10	K12	E3	Fox
13.12	22.10	K12	F4	Tiger
14.12	23.10	K12	G5	Leopard
15.12	24.10	K12	H6	Griffon
16.12	25.10	K12	J7	Ox

Solar date	Lunar date	Month HS/EB	Day HS/EB	Constellation
17.12	26.10	K12	K8	Bat
18.12	27.10	K12	A9	Rat
19.12	28.10	K12	B10	Swallow
20.12	29.10	K12	C11	Pig
21.12	30.10	K12	D12	Porcupine
22.12	1.11	A1	E1	Wolf
23.12	2.11	A1	F2	Dog
24.12	3.11	A1	G3	Pheasant
25.12	4.11	A1	H4	Cock
26.12	5.11	A1	J5	Crow
27.12	6.11	A1	K6	Monkey
28.12	7.11	A1	A7	Gibbon
29.12	8.11	A1	B8	Tapir
30.12	9.11	A1	C9	Sheep
31.12	10.11	A1	D10	Deer
1939				
1. 1	11.11	A1	E11	Horse
2. 1	12.11	A1	F12	Stag
3. 1	13.11	A1	G1	Serpent
4. 1	14.11	A1	H2	Earthworm
5. 1	15.11	A1	J3	Crocodile
6. 1	16.11	A1	K4	Dragon
7. 1	17.11	A1	A5	Badger
8. 1	18.11	A1	B6	Hare
9. 1	19.11	A1	C7	Fox
10. 1	20.11	A1	D8	Tiger
11. 1	21.11	A1	E9	Leopard
12. 1	22.11	A1	F10	Griffon
13. 1	23.11	A1	G11	Ox
14. 1	24.11	A1	H12	Bat
15. 1	25.11	A1	J1	Rat
16. 1	26.11	A1	K2	Swallow
17. 1	27.11	A1	A3	Pig
18. 1	28.11	A1	B4	Porcupine
19. 1	29.11	A1	C5	Wolf
20. 1	1.12	B2	D6	Dog
21. 1	2.12	B2	E7	Pheasant
22. 1	3.12	B2	F8	Cock
23. 1	4.12	B2	G9	Crow
24. 1	5.12	B2	H10	Monkey
25. 1	6.12	B2	J11	Gibbon
26. 1	7.12	B2	K12	Tapir
27. 1	8.12	B2	A1	Sheep
28. 1	9.12	B2	B2	Deer
29. 1	10.12	B2	C3	Horse
30. 1	11.12	B2	D4	Stag
31. 1	12.12	B2	E5	Serpent
1. 2	13.12	B2	F6	Earthworm
2. 2	14.12	B2	G7	Crocodile
3. 2	15.12	B2	H8	Dragon
4. 2	16.12	B2	J9	Badger
5. 2	17.12	B2	K10	Hare
6. 2	18.12	B2	A11	Fox
7. 2	19.12	B2	B12	Tiger
8. 2	20.12	B2	C1	Leopard
9. 2	21.12	B2	D2	Griffon
10. 2	22.12	B2	E3	Ox
11. 2	23.12	B2	F4	Bat
12. 2	24.12	B2	G5	Rat
13. 2	25.12	B2	H6	Swallow
14. 2	26.12	B2	J7	Pig
15. 2	27.12	B2	K8	Porcupine
16. 2	28.12	B2	A9	Wolf
17. 2	29.12	B2	B10	Dog
18. 2	30.12	B2	C11	Pheasant

CHI MAO YEAR

Solar date	*Lunar date*	*Month HS/EB*	*Day HS/EB*	*Constellation*
19. 2	1. 1	C3	D12	Cock
20. 2	2. 1	C3	E1	Crow
21. 2	3. 1	C3	F2	Monkey
22. 2	4. 1	C3	G3	Gibbon
23. 2	5. 1	C3	H4	Tapir
24. 2	6. 1	C3	J5	Sheep
25. 2	7. 1	C3	K6	Deer
26. 2	8. 1	C3	A7	Horse
27. 2	9. 1	C3	B8	Stag
28. 2	10. 1	C3	C9	Serpent
1. 3	11. 1	C3	D10	Earthworm
2. 3	12. 1	C3	E11	Crocodile
3. 3	13. 1	C3	F12	Dragon
4. 3	14. 1	C3	G1	Badger
5. 3	15. 1	C3	H2	Hare
6. 3	16. 1	C3	J3	Fox
7. 3	17. 1	C3	K4	Tiger
8. 3	18. 1	C3	A5	Leopard
9. 3	19. 1	C3	B6	Griffon
10. 3	20. 1	C3	C7	Ox
11. 3	21. 1	C3	D8	Bat
12. 3	22. 1	C3	E9	Rat
13. 3	23. 1	C3	F10	Swallow
14. 3	24. 1	C3	G11	Pig
15. 3	25. 1	C3	H12	Porcupine
16. 3	26. 1	C3	J1	Wolf
17. 3	27. 1	C3	K2	Dog
18. 3	28. 1	C3	A3	Pheasant
19. 3	29. 1	C3	B4	Cock
20. 3	30. 1	C3	C5	Crow
21. 3	1. 2	D4	D6	Monkey
22. 3	2. 2	D4	E7	Gibbon
23. 3	3. 2	D4	F8	Tapir
24. 3	4. 2	D4	G9	Sheep
25. 3	5. 2	D4	H10	Deer
26. 3	6. 2	D4	J11	Horse
27. 3	7. 2	D4	K12	Stag
28. 3	8. 2	D4	A1	Serpent
29. 3	9. 2	D4	B2	Earthworm
30. 3	10. 2	D4	C3	Crocodile
31. 3	11. 2	D4	D4	Dragon
1. 4	12. 2	D4	E5	Badger
2. 4	13. 2	D4	F6	Hare
3. 4	14. 2	D4	G7	Fox
4. 4	15. 2	D4	H8	Tiger
5. 4	16. 2	D4	J9	Leopard
6. 4	17. 2	D4	K10	Griffon
7. 4	18. 2	D4	A11	Ox
8. 4	19. 2	D4	B12	Bat
9. 4	20. 2	D4	C1	Rat
10. 4	21. 2	D4	D2	Swallow
11. 4	22. 2	D4	E3	Pig
12. 4	23. 2	D4	F4	Porcupine
13. 4	24. 2	D4	G5	Wolf
14. 4	25. 2	D4	H6	Dog
15. 4	26. 2	D4	J7	Pheasant
16. 4	27. 2	D4	K8	Cock
17. 4	28. 2	D4	A9	Crow
18. 4	29. 2	D4	B10	Monkey
19. 4	30. 2	D4	C11	Gibbon
20. 4	1. 3	E5	D12	Tapir
21. 4	2. 3	E5	E1	Sheep
22. 4	3. 3	E5	F2	Deer
23. 4	4. 3	E5	G3	Horse
24. 4	5. 3	E5	H4	Stag
25. 4	6. 3	E5	J5	Serpent
26. 4	7. 3	E5	K6	Earthworm
27. 4	8. 3	E5	A7	Crocodile
28. 4	9. 3	E5	B8	Dragon
29. 4	10. 3	E5	C9	Badger
30. 4	11. 3	E5	D10	Hare
1. 5	12. 3	E5	E11	Fox
2. 5	13. 3	E5	F12	Tiger
3. 5	14. 3	E5	G1	Leopard
4. 5	15. 3	E5	H2	Griffon
5. 5	16. 3	E5	J3	Ox
6. 5	17. 3	E5	K4	Bat
7. 5	18. 3	E5	A5	Rat
8. 5	19. 3	E5	B6	Swallow
9. 5	20. 3	E5	C7	Pig
10. 5	21. 3	E5	D8	Porcupine
11. 5	22. 3	E5	E9	Wolf
12. 5	23. 3	E5	F10	Dog
13. 5	24. 3	E5	G11	Pheasant
14. 5	25. 3	E5	H12	Cock
15. 5	26. 3	E5	J1	Crow
16. 5	27. 3	E5	K2	Monkey
17. 5	28. 3	E5	A3	Gibbon
18. 5	29. 3	E5	B4	Tapir
19. 5	1. 4	F6	C5	Sheep
20. 5	2. 4	F6	D6	Deer
21. 5	3. 4	F6	E7	Horse
22. 5	4. 4	F6	F8	Stag
23. 5	5. 4	F6	G9	Serpent
24. 5	6. 4	F6	H10	Earthworm
25. 5	7. 4	F6	J11	Crocodile
26. 5	8. 4	F6	K12	Dragon
27. 5	9. 4	F6	A1	Badger
28. 5	10. 4	F6	B2	Hare
29. 5	11. 4	F6	C3	Fox
30 5	12. 4	F6	D4	Tiger
31. 5	13. 4	F6	E5	Leopard
1. 6	14. 4	F6	F6	Griffon
2. 6	15. 4	F6	G7	Ox
3. 6	16. 4	F6	H8	Bat
4. 6	17. 4	F6	J9	Rat
5. 6	18. 4	F6	K10	Swallow
6. 6	19. 4	F6	A11	Pig
7. 6	20. 4	F6	B12	Porcupine
8. 6	21. 4	F6	C1	Wolf
9. 6	22. 4	F6	D2	Dog
10. 6	23. 4	F6	E3	Pheasant
11. 6	24. 4	F6	F4	Cock
12. 6	25. 4	F6	G5	Crow
13. 6	26. 4	F6	H6	Monkey
14. 6	27. 4	F6	J7	Gibbon
15. 6	28. 4	F6	K8	Tapir
16. 6	29. 4	F6	A9	Sheep
17. 6	1. 5	G7	B10	Deer
18. 6	2. 5	G7	C11	Horse
19. 6	3. 5	G7	D12	Stag
20. 6	4. 5	G7	E1	Serpent
21. 6	5. 5	G7	F2	Earthworm
22. 6	6. 5	G7	G3	Crocodile
23. 6	7. 5	G7	H4	Dragon
24. 6	8. 5	G7	J5	Badger
25. 6	9. 5	G7	K6	Hare
26. 6	10. 5	G7	A7	Fox
27. 6	11. 5	G7	B8	Tiger
28. 6	12. 5	G7	C9	Leopard
29. 6	13. 5	G7	D10	Griffon
30 6	14. 5	G7	E11	Ox
1. 7	15. 5	G7	F12	Bat
2. 7	16. 5	G7	G1	Rat
3. 7	17. 5	G7	H2	Swallow
4. 7	18. 5	G7	J3	Pig
5. 7	19. 5	G7	K4	Porcupine
6. 7	20. 5	G7	A5	Wolf
7. 7	21. 5	G7	B6	Dog
8. 7	22. 5	G7	C7	Pheasant
9. 7	23. 5	G7	D8	Cock
10. 7	24. 5	G7	E9	Crow

Solar date	Lunar date	Month HS/EB	Day HS/EB	Constellation	Solar date	Lunar date	Month HS/EB	Day HS/EB	Constellation
11. 7	25. 5	G7	F10	Monkey	22. 9	10. 8	K10	J11	Ox
12. 7	26. 5	G7	G11	Gibbon	23. 9	11. 8	K10	K12	Bat
13. 7	27. 5	G7	H12	Tapir	24. 9	12. 8	K10	A1	Rat
14. 7	28. 5	G7	J1	Sheep	25. 9	13. 8	K10	B2	Swallow
15. 7	29. 5	G7	K2	Deer	26. 9	14. 8	K10	C3	Pig
16. 7	30. 5	G7	A3	Horse	27. 9	15. 8	K10	D4	Porcupine
17. 7	1. 6	H8	B4	Stag	28. 9	16. 8	K10	E5	Wolf
18. 7	2. 6	H8	C5	Serpent	29. 9	17. 8	K10	F6	Dog
19. 7	3. 6	H8	D6	Earthworm	30. 9	18. 8	K10	G7	Pheasant
20. 7	4. 6	H8	E7	Crocodile	1.10	19. 8	K10	H8	Cock
21. 7	5. 6	H8	F8	Dragon	2.10	20. 8	K10	J9	Crow
22. 7	6. 6	H8	G9	Badger	3.10	21. 8	K10	K10	Monkey
23. 7	7. 6	H8	H10	Hare	4.10	22. 8	K10	A11	Gibbon
24. 7	8. 6	H8	J11	Fox	5.10	23. 8	K10	B12	Tapir
25. 7	9. 6	H8	K12	Tiger	6.10	24. 8	K10	C1	Sheep
26. 7	10. 6	H8	A1	Leopard	7.10	25. 8	K10	D2	Deer
27. 7	11. 6	H8	B2	Griffon	8.10	26. 8	K10	E3	Horse
28. 7	12. 6	H8	C3	Ox	9.10	27. 8	K10	F4	Stag
29. 7	13. 6	H8	D4	Bat	10.10	28. 8	K10	G5	Serpent
30. 7	14. 6	H8	E5	Rat	11.10	29. 8	K10	H6	Earthworm
31. 7	15. 6	H8	F6	Swallow	12.10	30. 8	K10	J7	Crocodile
1. 8	16. 6	H8	G7	Pig	13.10	1. 9	A11	K8	Dragon
2. 8	17. 6	H8	H8	Porcupine	14.10	2. 9	A11	A9	Badger
3. 8	18. 6	H8	J9	Wolf	15.10	3. 9	A11	B10	Hare
4. 8	19. 6	H8	K10	Dog	16.10	4. 9	A11	C11	Fox
5. 8	20. 6	H8	A11	Pheasant	17.10	5. 9	A11	D12	Tiger
6. 8	21. 6	H8	B12	Cock	18.10	6. 9	A11	E1	Leopard
7. 8	22. 6	H8	C1	Crow	19.10	7. 9	A11	F2	Griffon
8. 8	23. 6	H8	D2	Monkey	20.10	8. 9	A11	G3	Ox
9. 8	24. 6	H8	E3	Gibbon	21.10	9. 9	A11	H4	Bat
10. 8	25. 6	H8	F4	Tapir	22.10	10. 9	A11	J5	Rat
11. 8	26. 6	H8	G5	Sheep	23.10	11. 9	A11	K6	Swallow
12. 8	27. 6	H8	H6	Deer	24.10	12. 9	A11	A7	Pig
13. 8	28. 6	H8	J7	Horse	25.10	13. 9	A11	B8	Porcupine
14. 8	29. 6	H8	K8	Stag	26.10	14. 9	A11	C9	Wolf
15. 8	1. 7	J9	A9	Serpent	27.10	15. 9	A11	D10	Dog
16. 8	2. 7	J9	B10	Earthworm	28.10	16. 9	A11	E11	Pheasant
17. 8	3. 7	J9	C11	Crocodile	29.10	17. 9	A11	F12	Cock
18. 8	4. 7	J9	D12	Dragon	30.10	18. 9	A11	G1	Crow
19. 8	5. 7	J9	E1	Badger	31.10	19. 9	A11	H2	Monkey
20. 8	6. 7	J9	F2	Hare	1.11	20. 9	A11	J3	Gibbon
21. 8	7. 7	J9	G3	Fox	2.11	21. 9	A11	K4	Tapir
22. 8	8. 7	J9	H4	Tiger	3.11	22. 9	A11	A5	Sheep
23. 8	9. 7	J9	J5	Leopard	4.11	23. 9	A11	B6	Deer
24. 8	10. 7	J9	K6	Griffon	5.11	24. 9	A11	C7	Horse
25. 8	11. 7	J9	A7	Ox	6.11	25. 9	A11	D8	Stag
26. 8	12. 7	J9	B8	Bat	7.11	26. 9	A11	E9	Serpent
27. 8	13. 7	J9	C9	Rat	8.11	27. 9	A11	F10	Earthworm
28. 8	14. 7	J9	D10	Swallow	9.11	28. 9	A11	G11	Crocodile
29. 8	15. 7	J9	E11	Pig	10.11	29. 9	A11	H12	Dragon
30. 8	16. 7	J9	F12	Porcupine	11.11	1.10	B12	J1	Badger
31. 8	17. 7	J9	G1	Wolf	12.11	2.10	B12	K2	Hare
1. 9	18. 7	J9	H2	Dog	13.11	3.10	B12	A3	Fox
2. 9	19. 7	J9	J3	Pheasant	14.11	4.10	B12	B4	Tiger
3. 9	20. 7	J9	K4	Cock	15.11	5.10	B12	C5	Leopard
4. 9	21. 7	J9	A5	Crow	16.11	6.10	B12	D6	Griffon
5. 9	22. 7	J9	B6	Monkey	17.11	7.10	B12	E7	Ox
6. 9	23. 7	J9	C7	Gibbon	18.11	8.10	B12	F8	Bat
7. 9	24. 7	J9	D8	Tapir	19.11	9.10	B12	G9	Rat
8. 9	25. 7	J9	E9	Sheep	20.11	10.10	B12	H10	Swallow
9. 9	26. 7	J9	F10	Deer	21.11	11.10	B12	J11	Pig
10. 9	27. 7	J9	G11	Horse	22.11	12.10	B12	K12	Porcupine
11. 9	28. 7	J9	H12	Stag	23.11	13.10	B12	A1	Wolf
12. 9	29. 7	J9	J1	Serpent	24.11	14.10	B12	B2	Dog
13. 9	1. 8	K10	K2	Earthworm	25.11	15.10	B12	C3	Pheasant
14. 9	2. 8	K10	A3	Crocodile	26.11	16.10	B12	D4	Cock
15. 9	3. 8	K10	B4	Dragon	27.11	17.10	B12	E5	Crow
16. 9	4. 8	K10	C5	Badger	28.11	18.10	B12	F6	Monkey
17. 9	5. 8	K10	D6	Hare	29.11	19.10	B12	G7	Gibbon
18. 9	6. 8	K10	E7	Fox	30.11	20.10	B12	H8	Tapir
19. 9	7. 8	K10	F8	Tiger	1.12	21.10	B12	J9	Sheep
20. 9	8. 8	K10	G9	Leopard	2.12	22.10	B12	K10	Deer
21. 9	9. 8	K10	H10	Griffon	3.12	23.10	B12	A11	Horse

Solar date	*Lunar date*	*Month HS/EB*	*Day HS/EB*	*Constellation*
4.12	24.10	B12	B12	Stag
5.12	25.10	B12	C1	Serpent
6.12	26.10	B12	D2	Earthworm
7.12	27.10	B12	E3	Crocodile
8.12	28.10	B12	F4	Dragon
9.12	29.10	B12	G5	Badger
10.12	30.10	B12	H6	Hare
11.12	1.11	C1	J7	Fox
12.12	2.11	C1	K8	Tiger
13.12	3.11	C1	A9	Leopard
14.12	4.11	C1	B10	Griffon
15.12	5.11	C1	C11	Ox
16.12	6.11	C1	D12	Bat
17.12	7.11	C1	E1	Rat
18.12	8.11	C1	F2	Swallow
19.12	9.11	C1	G3	Pig
20.12	10.11	C1	H4	Porcupine
21.12	11.11	C1	J5	Wolf
22.12	12.11	C1	K6	Dog
23.12	13.11	C1	A7	Pheasant
24.12	14.11	C1	B8	Cock
25.12	15.11	C1	C9	Crow
26.12	16.11	C1	D10	Monkey
27.12	17.11	C1	E11	Gibbon
28.12	18.11	C1	F12	Tapir
29.12	19.11	C1	G1	Sheep
30.12	20.11	C1	H2	Deer
31.12	21.11	C1	J3	Horse
1940				
1. 1	22.11	C1	K4	Stag
2. 1	23.11	C1	A5	Serpent
3. 1	24.11	C1	B6	Earthworm
4. 1	25.11	C1	C7	Crocodile

Solar date	*Lunar date*	*Month HS/EB*	*Day HS/EB*	*Constellation*
5. 1	26.11	C1	D8	Dragon
6. 1	27.11	C1	E9	Badger
7. 1	28.11	C1	F10	Hare
8. 1	29.11	C1	G11	Fox
9. 1	1.12	D2	H12	Tiger
10. 1	2.12	D2	J1	Leopard
11. 1	3.12	D2	K2	Griffon
12. 1	4.12	D2	A3	Ox
13. 1	5.12	D2	B4	Bat
14. 1	6.12	D2	C5	Rat
15. 1	7.12	D2	D6	Swallow
16. 1	8.12	D2	E7	Pig
17. 1	9.12	D2	F8	Porcupine
18. 1	10.12	D2	G9	Wolf
19. 1	11.12	D2	H10	Dog
20. 1	12.12	D2	J11	Pheasant
21. 1	13.12	D2	K12	Cock
22. 1	14.12	D2	A1	Crow
23. 1	15.12	D2	B2	Monkey
24. 1	16.12	D2	C3	Gibbon
25. 1	17.12	D2	D4	Tapir
26. 1	18.12	D2	E5	Sheep
27. 1	19.12	D2	F6	Deer
28. 1	20.12	D2	G7	Horse
29. 1	21.12	D2	H8	Stag
30. 1	22.12	D2	J9	Serpent
31. 1	23.12	D2	K10	Earthworm
1. 2	24.12	D2	A11	Crocodile
2. 2	25.12	D2	B12	Dragon
3. 2	26.12	D2	C1	Badger
4. 2	27.12	D2	D2	Hare
5. 2	28.12	D2	E3	Fox
6. 2	29.12	D2	F4	Tiger
7. 2	30.12	D2	G5	Leopard

KENG CH'EN YEAR

8. 2	1. 1	E3	H6	Griffon
9. 2	2. 1	E3	J7	Ox
10. 2	3. 1	E3	K8	Bat
11. 2	4. 1	E3	A9	Rat
12. 2	5. 1	E3	B10	Swallow
13. 2	6. 1	E3	C11	Pig
14. 2	7. 1	E3	D12	Porcupine
15. 2	8. 1	E3	E1	Wolf
16. 2	9. 1	E3	F2	Dog
17. 2	10. 1	E3	G3	Pheasant
18. 2	11. 1	E3	H4	Cock
19. 2	12. 1	E3	J5	Crow
20. 2	13. 1	E3	K6	Monkey
21. 2	14. 1	E3	A7	Gibbon
22. 2	15. 1	E3	B8	Tapir
23. 2	16. 1	E3	C9	Sheep
24. 2	17. 1	E3	D10	Deer
25. 2	18. 1	E3	E11	Horse
26. 2	19. 1	E3	F12	Stag
27. 2	20. 1	E3	G1	Serpent
28. 2	21. 1	E3	H2	Earthworm
29. 2	22. 1	E3	J3	Crocodile
1. 3	23. 1	E3	K4	Dragon
2. 3	24. 1	E3	A5	Badger
3. 3	25. 1	E3	B6	Hare
4. 3	26. 1	E3	C7	Fox
5. 3	27. 1	E3	D8	Tiger
6. 3	28. 1	E3	E9	Leopard
7. 3	29. 1	E3	F10	Griffon
8. 3	30. 1	E3	G11	Ox
9. 3	1. 2	F4	H12	Bat
10. 3	2. 2	F4	J1	Rat
11. 3	3. 2	F4	K2	Swallow
12. 3	4. 2	F4	A3	Pig

13. 3	5. 2	F4	B4	Porcupine
14. 3	6. 2	F4	C5	Wolf
15. 3	7. 2	F4	D6	Dog
16. 3	8. 2	F4	E7	Pheasant
17. 3	9. 2	F4	F8	Cock
18. 3	10. 2	F4	G9	Crow
19. 3	11. 2	F4	H10	Monkey
20. 3	12. 2	F4	J11	Gibbon
21. 3	13. 2	F4	K12	Tapir
22. 3	14. 2	F4	A1	Sheep
23. 3	15. 2	F4	B2	Deer
24. 3	16. 2	F4	C3	Horse
25. 3	17. 2	F4	D4	Stag
26. 3	18. 2	F4	E5	Serpent
27. 3	19. 2	F4	F6	Earthworm
28. 3	20. 2	F4	G7	Crocodile
29. 3	21. 2	F4	H8	Dragon
30. 3	22. 2	F4	J9	Badger
31. 3	23. 2	F4	K10	Hare
1. 4	24. 2	F4	A11	Fox
2. 4	25. 2	F4	B12	Tiger
3. 4	26. 2	F4	C1	Leopard
4. 4	27. 2	F4	D2	Griffon
5. 4	28. 2	F4	E3	Ox
6. 4	29. 2	F4	F4	Bat
7. 4	30. 2	F4	G5	Rat
8. 4	1. 3	G5	H6	Swallow
9. 4	2. 3	G5	J7	Pig
10. 4	3. 3	G5	K8	Porcupine
11. 4	4. 3	G5	A9	Wolf
12. 4	5. 3	G5	B10	Dog
13. 4	6. 3	G5	C11	Pheasant
14. 4	7. 3	G5	D12	Cock
15. 4	8. 3	G5	E1	Crow

Solar date	Lunar date	Month HS/EB	Day HS/EB	Constellation
16. 4	9. 3	G5	F2	Monkey
17. 4	10. 3	G5	G3	Gibbon
18. 4	11. 3	G5	H4	Tapir
19. 4	12. 3	G5	J5	Sheep
20. 4	13. 3	G5	K6	Deer
21. 4	14. 3	G5	A7	Horse
22. 4	15. 3	G5	B8	Stag
23. 4	16. 3	G5	C9	Serpent
24. 4	17. 3	G5	D10	Earthworm
25. 4	18. 3	G5	E11	Crocodile
26. 4	19. 3	G5	F12	Dragon
27. 4	20. 3	G5	G1	Badger
28. 4	21. 3	G5	H2	Hare
29. 4	22. 3	G5	J3	Fox
30. 4	23. 3	G5	K4	Tiger
1. 5	24. 3	G5	A5	Leopard
2. 5	25. 3	G5	B6	Griffon
3. 5	26. 3	G5	C7	Ox
4. 5	27. 3	G5	D8	Bat
5. 5	28. 3	G5	E9	Rat
6. 5	29. 3	G5	F10	Swallow
7. 5	1. 4	H6	G11	Pig
8. 5	2. 4	H6	H12	Porcupine
9. 5	3. 4	H6	J1	Wolf
10. 5	4. 4	H6	K2	Dog
11. 5	5. 4	H6	A3	Pheasant
12. 5	6. 4	H6	B4	Cock
13. 5	7. 4	H6	C5	Crow
14. 5	8. 4	H6	D6	Monkey
15. 5	9. 4	H6	E7	Gibbon
16. 5	10. 4	H6	F8	Tapir
17. 5	11. 4	H6	G9	Sheep
18. 5	12. 4	H6	H10	Deer
19. 5	13. 4	H6	J11	Horse
20. 5	14. 4	H6	K12	Stag
21. 5	15. 4	H6	A1	Serpent
22. 5	16. 4	H6	B2	Earthworm
23. 5	17. 4	H6	C3	Crocodile
24. 5	18. 4	H6	D4	Dragon
25. 5	19. 4	H6	E5	Badger
26. 5	20. 4	H6	F6	Hare
27. 5	21. 4	H6	G7	Fox
28. 5	22. 4	H6	H8	Tiger
29. 5	23. 4	H6	J9	Leopard
30. 5	24. 4	H6	K10	Griffon
31. 5	25. 4	H6	A11	Ox
1. 6	26. 4	H6	B12	Bat
2. 6	27. 4	H6	C1	Rat
3. 6	28. 4	H6	D2	Swallow
4. 6	29. 4	H6	E3	Pig
5. 6	30. 4	H6	F4	Porcupine
6. 6	1. 5	J7	G5	Wolf
7. 6	2. 5	J7	H6	Dog
8. 6	3. 5	J7	J7	Pheasant
9. 6	4. 5	J7	K8	Cock
10. 6	5. 5	J7	A9	Crow
11. 6	6. 5	J7	B10	Monkey
12. 6	7. 5	J7	C11	Gibbon
13. 6	8. 5	J7	D12	Tapir
14. 6	9. 5	J7	E1	Sheep
15. 6	10. 5	J7	F2	Deer
16. 6	11. 5	J7	G3	Horse
17. 6	12. 5	J7	H4	Stag
18. 6	13. 5	J7	J5	Serpent
19. 6	14. 5	J7	K6	Earthworm
20. 6	15. 5	J7	A7	Crocodile
21. 6	16. 5	J7	B8	Dragon
22. 6	17. 5	J7	C9	Badger
23. 6	18. 5	J7	D10	Hare
24. 6	19. 5	J7	E11	Fox
25. 6	20. 5	J7	F12	Tiger
26. 6	21. 5	J7	G1	Leopard
27. 6	22. 5	J7	H2	Griffon

Solar date	Lunar date	Month HS/EB	Day HS/EB	Constellation
28. 6	23. 5	J7	J3	Ox
29. 6	24. 5	J7	K4	Bat
30. 6	25. 5	J7	A5	Rat
1. 7	26. 5	J7	B6	Swallow
2. 7	27. 5	J7	C7	Pig
3. 7	28. 5	J7	D8	Porcupine
4. 7	29. 5	J7	E9	Wolf
5. 7	1. 6	K8	F10	Dog
6. 7	2. 6	K8	G11	Pheasant
7. 7	3. 6	K8	H12	Cock
8. 7	4. 6	K8	J1	Crow
9. 7	5. 6	K8	K2	Monkey
10. 7	6. 6	K8	A3	Gibbon
11. 7	7. 6	K8	B4	Tapir
12. 7	8. 6	K8	C5	Sheep
13. 7	9. 6	K8	D6	Deer
14. 7	10. 6	K8	E7	Horse
15. 7	11. 6	K8	F8	Stag
16. 7	12. 6	K8	G9	Serpent
17. 7	13. 6	K8	H10	Earthworm
18. 7	14. 6	K8	J11	Crocodile
19. 7	15. 6	K8	K12	Dragon
20. 7	16. 6	K8	A1	Badger
21. 7	17. 6	K8	B2	Hare
22. 7	18. 6	K8	C3	Fox
23. 7	19. 6	K8	D4	Tiger
24. 7	20. 6	K8	E5	Leopard
25. 7	21. 6	K8	F6	Griffon
26. 7	22. 6	K8	G7	Ox
27. 7	23. 6	K8	H8	Bat
28. 7	24. 6	K8	J9	Rat
29. 7	25. 6	K8	K10	Swallow
30. 7	26. 6	K8	A11	Pig
31. 7	27. 6	K8	B12	Porcupine
1. 8	28. 6	K8	C1	Wolf
2. 8	29. 6	K8	D2	Dog
3. 8	30. 6	K8	E3	Pheasant
4. 8	1. 7	A9	F4	Cock
5. 8	2. 7	A9	G5	Crow
6. 8	3. 7	A9	H6	Monkey
7. 8	4. 7	A9	J7	Gibbon
8. 8	5. 7	A9	K8	Tapir
9. 8	6. 7	A9	A9	Sheep
10. 8	7. 7	A9	B10	Deer
11. 8	8. 7	A9	C11	Horse
12. 8	9. 7	A9	D12	Stag
13. 8	10. 7	A9	E1	Serpent
14. 8	11. 7	A9	F2	Earthworm
15. 8	12. 7	A9	G3	Crocodile
16. 8	13. 7	A9	H4	Dragon
17. 8	14. 7	A9	J5	Badger
18. 8	15. 7	A9	K6	Hare
19. 8	16. 7	A9	A7	Fox
20. 8	17. 7	A9	B8	Tiger
21. 8	18. 7	A9	C9	Leopard
22. 8	19. 7	A9	D10	Griffon
23. 8	20. 7	A9	E11	Ox
24. 8	21. 7	A9	F12	Bat
25. 8	22. 7	A9	G1	Rat
26. 8	23. 7	A9	H2	Swallow
27. 8	24. 7	A9	J3	Pig
28. 8	25. 7	A9	K4	Porcupine
29. 8	26. 7	A9	A5	Wolf
30. 8	27. 7	A9	B6	Dog
31. 8	28. 7	A9	C7	Pheasant
1. 9	29. 7	A9	D8	Cock
2. 9	1. 8	B10	E9	Crow
3. 9	2. 8	B10	F10	Monkey
4. 9	3. 8	B10	G11	Gibbon
5. 9	4. 8	B10	H12	Tapir
6. 9	5. 8	B10	J1	Sheep
7. 9	6. 8	B10	K2	Deer
8. 9	7. 8	B10	A3	Horse

Solar date	Lunar date	Month HS/EB	Day HS/EB	Constellation
9. 9	8. 8	B10	B4	Stag
10. 9	9. 8	B10	C5	Serpent
11. 9	10. 8	B10	D6	Earthworm
12. 9	11. 8	B10	E7	Crocodile
13. 9	12. 8	B10	F8	Dragon
14. 9	13. 8	B10	G9	Badger
15. 9	14. 8	B10	H10	Hare
16. 9	15. 8	B10	J11	Fox
17. 9	16. 8	B10	K12	Tiger
18. 9	17. 8	B10	A1	Leopard
19. 9	18. 8	B10	B2	Griffon
20. 9	19. 8	B10	C3	Ox
21. 9	20. 8	B10	D4	Bat
22. 9	21. 8	B10	E5	Rat
23. 9	22. 8	B10	F6	Swallow
24. 9	23. 8	B10	G7	Pig
25. 9	24. 8	B10	H8	Porcupine
26. 9	25. 8	B10	J9	Wolf
27. 9	26. 8	B10	K10	Dog
28. 9	27. 8	B10	A11	Pheasant
29. 9	28. 8	B10	B12	Cock
30. 9	29. 8	B10	C1	Crow
1.10	1. 9	C11	D2	Monkey
2.10	2. 9	C11	E3	Gibbon
3.10	3. 9	C11	F4	Tapir
4.10	4. 9	C11	G5	Sheep
5.10	5. 9	C11	H6	Deer
6.10	6. 9	C11	J7	Horse
7.10	7. 9	C11	K8	Stag
8.10	8. 9	C11	A9	Serpent
9.10	9. 9	C11	B10	Earthworm
10.10	10. 9	C11	C11	Crocodile
11.10	11. 9	C11	D12	Dragon
12.10	12. 9	C11	E1	Badger
13.10	13. 9	C11	F2	Hare
14.10	14. 9	C11	G3	Fox
15.10	15. 9	C11	H4	Tiger
16.10	16. 9	C11	J5	Leopard
17.10	17. 9	C11	K6	Griffon
18.10	18. 9	C11	A7	Ox
19.10	19. 9	C11	B8	Bat
20.10	20. 9	C11	C9	Rat
21.10	21. 9	C11	D10	Swallow
22.10	22. 9	C11	E11	Pig
23.10	23. 9	C11	F12	Porcupine
24.10	24. 9	C11	G1	Wolf
25.10	25. 9	C11	H2	Dog
26.10	26. 9	C11	J3	Pheasant
27.10	27. 9	C11	K4	Cock
28.10	28. 9	C11	A5	Crow
29.10	29. 9	C11	B6	Monkey
30.10	30. 9	C11	C7	Gibbon
31.10	1.10	D12	D8	Tapir
1.11	2.10	D12	E9	Sheep
2.11	3.10	D12	F10	Deer
3.11	4.10	D12	G11	Horse
4.11	5.10	D12	H12	Stag
5.11	6.10	D12	J1	Serpent
6.11	7.10	D12	K2	Earthworm
7.11	8.10	D12	A3	Crocodile
8.11	9.10	D12	B4	Dragon
9.11	10.10	D12	C5	Badger
10.11	11.10	D12	D6	Hare
11.11	12.10	D12	E7	Fox
12.11	13.10	D12	F8	Tiger
13.11	14.10	D12	G9	Leopard
14.11	15.10	D12	H10	Griffon
15.11	16.10	D12	J11	Ox
16.11	17.10	D12	K12	Bat
17.11	18.10	D12	A1	Rat
18.11	19.10	D12	B2	Swallow
19.11	20.10	D12	C3	Pig
20.11	21.10	D12	D4	Porcupine
21.11	22.10	D12	E5	Wolf
22.11	23.10	D12	F6	Dog
23.11	24.10	D12	G7	Pheasant
24.11	25.10	D12	H8	Cock
25.11	26.10	D12	J9	Crow
26.11	27.10	D12	K10	Monkey
27.11	28.10	D12	A11	Gibbon
28.11	29.10	D12	B12	Tapir
29.11	1.11	E1	C1	Sheep
30.11	2.11	E1	D2	Deer
1.12	3.11	E1	E3	Horse
2.12	4.11	E1	F4	Stag
3.12	5.11	E1	G5	Serpent
4.12	6.11	E1	H6	Earthworm
5.12	7.11	E1	J7	Crocodile
6.12	8.11	E1	K8	Dragon
7.12	9.11	E1	A9	Badger
8.12	10.11	E1	B10	Hare
9.12	11.11	E1	C11	Fox
10.12	12.11	E1	D12	Tiger
11.12	13.11	E1	E1	Leopard
12.12	14.11	E1	F2	Griffon
13.12	15.11	E1	G3	Ox
14.12	16.11	E1	H4	Bat
15.12	17.11	E1	J5	Rat
16.12	18.11	E1	K6	Swallow
17.12	19.11	E1	A7	Pig
18.12	20.11	E1	B8	Porcupine
19.12	21.11	E1	C9	Wolf
20.12	22.11	E1	D10	Dog
21.12	23.11	E1	E11	Pheasant
22.12	24.11	E1	F12	Cock
23.12	25.11	E1	G1	Crow
24.12	26.11	E1	H2	Monkey
25.12	27.11	E1	J3	Gibbon
26.12	28.11	E1	K4	Tapir
27.12	29.11	E1	A5	Sheep
28.12	30.11	E1	B6	Deer
29.12	1.12	F2	C7	Horse
30.12	2.12	F2	D8	Stag
31.12	3.12	F2	E9	Serpent
1941				
1. 1	4.12	F2	F10	Earthworm
2. 1	5.12	F2	G11	Crocodile
3. 1	6.12	F2	H12	Dragon
4. 1	7.12	F2	J1	Badger
5. 1	8.12	F2	K2	Hare
6. 1	9.12	F2	A3	Fox
7. 1	10.12	F2	B4	Tiger
8. 1	11.12	F2	C5	Leopard
9. 1	12.12	F2	D6	Griffon
10. 1	13.12	F2	E7	Ox
11. 1	14.12	F2	F8	Bat
12. 1	15.12	F2	G9	Rat
13. 1	16.12	F2	H10	Swallow
14. 1	17.12	F2	J11	Pig
15. 1	18.12	F2	K12	Porcupine
16. 1	19.12	F2	A1	Wolf
17. 1	20.12	F2	B2	Dog
18. 1	21.12	F2	C3	Pheasant
19. 1	22.12	F2	D4	Cock
20. 1	23.12	F2	E5	Crow
21. 1	24.12	F2	F6	Monkey
22. 1	25.12	F2	G7	Gibbon
23. 1	26.12	F2	H8	Tapir
24. 1	27.12	F2	J9	Sheep
25. 1	28.12	F2	K10	Deer
26. 1	29.12	F2	A11	Horse

HSIN SZU YEAR

Solar date	Lunar date	Month HS/EB	Day HS/EB	Constellation
27. 1	1. 1	G3	B12	Stag
28. 1	2. 1	G3	C1	Serpent
29. 1	3. 1	G3	D2	Earthworm
30. 1	4. 1	G3	E3	Crocodile
31. 1	5. 1	G3	F4	Dragon
1. 2	6. 1	G3	G5	Badger
2. 2	7. 1	G3	H6	Hare
3. 2	8. 1	G3	J7	Fox
4. 2	9. 1	G3	K8	Tiger
5. 2	10. 1	G3	A9	Leopard
6. 2	11. 1	G3	B10	Griffon
7. 2	12. 1	G3	C11	Ox
8. 2	13. 1	G3	D12	Bat
9. 2	14. 1	G3	E1	Rat
10. 2	15. 1	G3	F2	Swallow
11. 2	16. 1	G3	G3	Pig
12. 2	17. 1	G3	H4	Porcupine
13. 2	18. 1	G3	J5	Wolf
14. 2	19. 1	G3	K6	Dog
15. 2	20. 1	G3	A7	Pheasant
16. 2	21. 1	G3	B8	Cock
17. 2	22. 1	G3	C9	Crow
18. 2	23. 1	G3	D10	Monkey
19. 2	24. 1	G3	E11	Gibbon
20. 2	25. 1	G3	F12	Tapir
21. 2	26. 1	G3	G1	Sheep
22. 2	27. 1	G3	H2	Deer
23. 2	28. 1	G3	J3	Horse
24. 2	29. 1	G3	K4	Stag
25. 2	30. 1	G3	A5	Serpent
26. 2	1. 2	H4	B6	Earthworm
27. 2	2. 2	H4	C7	Crocodile
28. 2	3. 2	H4	D8	Dragon
1. 3	4. 2	H4	E9	Badger
2. 3	5. 2	H4	F10	Hare
3. 3	6. 2	H4	G11	Fox
4. 3	7. 2	H4	H12	Tiger
5. 3	8. 2	H4	J1	Leopard
6. 3	9. 2	H4	K2	Griffon
7. 3	10. 2	H4	A3	Ox
8. 3	11. 2	H4	B4	Bat
9. 3	12. 2	H4	C5	Rat
10. 3	13. 2	H4	D6	Swallow
11. 3	14. 2	H4	E7	Pig
12. 3	15. 2	H4	F8	Porcupine
13. 3	16. 2	H4	G9	Wolf
14. 3	17. 2	H4	H10	Dog
15. 3	18. 2	H4	J11	Pheasant
16. 3	19. 2	H4	K12	Cock
17. 3	20. 2	H4	A1	Crow
18. 3	21. 2	H4	B2	Monkey
19. 3	22. 2	H4	C3	Gibbon
20. 3	23. 2	H4	D4	Tapir
21. 3	24. 2	H4	E5	Sheep
22. 3	25. 2	H4	F6	Deer
23. 3	26. 2	H4	G7	Horse
24. 3	27. 2	H4	H8	Stag
25. 3	28. 2	H4	J9	Serpent
26. 3	29. 2	H4	K10	Earthworm
27. 3	30. 2	H4	A11	Crocodile
28. 3	1. 3	J5	B12	Dragon
29. 3	2. 3	J5	C1	Badger
30. 3	3. 3	J5	D2	Hare
31. 3	4. 3	J5	E3	Fox
1. 4	5. 3	J5	F4	Tiger
2. 4	6. 3	J5	G5	Leopard
3. 4	7. 3	J5	H6	Griffon
4. 4	8. 3	J5	J7	Ox
5. 4	9. 3	J5	K8	Bat
6. 4	10. 3	J5	A9	Rat
7. 4	11. 3	J5	B10	Swallow

Solar date	Lunar date	Month HS/EB	Day HS/EB	Constellation
8. 4	12. 3	J5	C11	Pig
9. 4	13. 3	J5	D12	Porcupine
10. 4	14. 3	J5	E1	Wolf
11. 4	15. 3	J5	F2	Dog
12. 4	16. 3	J5	G3	Pheasant
13. 4	17. 3	J5	H4	Cock
14. 4	18. 3	J5	J5	Crow
15. 4	19. 3	J5	K6	Monkey
16. 4	20. 3	J5	A7	Gibbon
17. 4	21. 3	J5	B8	Tapir
18. 4	22. 3	J5	C9	Sheep
19. 4	23. 3	J5	D10	Deer
20. 4	24. 3	J5	E11	Horse
21. 4	25. 3	J5	F12	Stag
22. 4	26. 3	J5	G1	Serpent
23. 4	27. 3	J5	H2	Earthworm
24. 4	28. 3	J5	J3	Crocodile
25. 4	29. 3	J5	K4	Dragon
26. 4	1. 4	K6	A5	Badger
27. 4	2. 4	K6	B6	Hare
28. 4	3. 4	K6	C7	Fox
29. 4	4. 4	K6	D8	Tiger
30. 4	5. 4	K6	E9	Leopard
1. 5	6. 4	K6	F10	Griffon
2. 5	7. 4	K6	G11	Ox
3. 5	8. 4	K6	H12	Bat
4. 5	9. 4	K6	J1	Rat
5. 5	10. 4	K6	K2	Swallow
6. 5	11. 4	K6	A3	Pig
7. 5	12. 4	K6	B4	Porcupine
8. 5	13. 4	K6	C5	Wolf
9. 5	14. 4	K6	D6	Dog
10. 5	15. 4	K6	E7	Pheasant
11. 5	16. 4	K6	F8	Cock
12. 5	17. 4	K6	G9	Crow
13. 5	18. 4	K6	H10	Monkey
14. 5	19. 4	K6	J11	Gibbon
15. 5	20. 4	K6	K12	Tapir
16. 5	21. 4	K6	A1	Sheep
17. 5	22. 4	K6	B2	Deer
18. 5	23. 4	K6	C3	Horse
19. 5	24. 4	K6	D4	Stag
20. 5	25. 4	K6	E5	Serpent
21. 5	26. 4	K6	F6	Earthworm
22. 5	27. 4	K6	G7	Crocodile
23. 5	28. 4	K6	H8	Dragon
24. 5	29. 4	K6	J9	Badger
25. 5	30. 4	K6	K10	Hare
26. 5	1. 5	A7	A11	Fox
27. 5	2. 5	A7	B12	Tiger
28. 5	3. 5	A7	C1	Leopard
29. 5	4. 5	A7	D2	Griffon
30. 5	5. 5	A7	E3	Ox
31. 5	6. 5	A7	F4	Bat
1. 6	7. 5	A7	G5	Rat
2. 6	8. 5	A7	H6	Swallow
3. 6	9. 5	A7	J7	Pig
4. 6	10. 5	A7	K8	Porcupine
5. 6	11. 5	A7	A9	Wolf
6. 6	12. 5	A7	B10	Dog
7. 6	13. 5	A7	C11	Pheasant
8. 6	14. 5	A7	D12	Cock
9. 6	15. 5	A7	E1	Crow
10. 6	16. 5	A7	F2	Monkey
11. 6	17. 5	A7	G3	Gibbon
12. 6	18. 5	A7	H4	Tapir
13. 6	19. 5	A7	J5	Sheep
14. 6	20. 5	A7	K6	Deer
15. 6	21. 5	A7	A7	Horse
16. 6	22. 5	A7	B8	Stag
17. 6	23. 5	A7	C9	Serpent

Solar date	*Lunar date*	*Month HS/EB*	*Day HS/EB*	*Constellation*
18. 6	24. 5	A7	D10	Earthworm
19. 6	25. 5	A7	E11	Crocodile
20. 6	26. 5	A7	F12	Dragon
21. 6	27. 5	A7	G1	Badger
22. 6	28. 5	A7	H2	Hare
23. 6	29. 5	A7	J3	Fox
24. 6	30. 5	A7	K4	Tiger
25. 6	1. 6	B8	A5	Leopard
26. 6	2. 6	B8	B6	Griffon
27. 6	3. 6	B8	C7	Ox
28. 6	4. 6	B8	D8	Bat
29. 6	5. 6	B8	E9	Rat
30. 6	6. 6	B8	F10	Swallow
1. 7	7. 6	B8	G11	Pig
2. 7	8. 6	B8	H12	Porcupine
3. 7	9. 6	B8	J1	Wolf
4. 7	10. 6	B8	K2	Dog
5. 7	11. 6	B8	A3	Pheasant
6. 7	12. 6	B8	B4	Cock
7. 7	13. 6	B8	C5	Crow
8. 7	14. 6	B8	D6	Monkey
9. 7	15. 6	B8	E7	Gibbon
10. 7	16. 6	B8	F8	Tapir
11. 7	17. 6	B8	G9	Sheep
12. 7	18. 6	B8	H10	Deer
13. 7	19. 6	B8	J11	Horse
14. 7	20. 6	B8	K12	Stag
15. 7	21. 6	B8	A1	Serpent
16. 7	22. 6	B8	B2	Earthworm
17. 7	23. 6	B8	C3	Crocodile
18. 7	24. 6	B8	D4	Dragon
19. 7	25. 6	B8	E5	Badger
20. 7	26. 6	B8	F6	Hare
21. 7	27. 6	B8	G7	Fox
22. 7	28. 6	B8	H8	Tiger
23. 7	29. 6	B8	J9	Leopard
24. 7	*1. 6*	*B8*	K10	Griffon
25. 7	*2. 6*	*B8*	A11	Ox
26. 7	*3. 6*	*B8*	B12	Bat
27. 7	*4. 6*	*B8*	C1	Rat
28. 7	*5. 6*	*B8*	D2	Swallow
29. 7	*6. 6*	*B8*	E3	Pig
30. 7	*7. 6*	*B8*	F4	Porcupine
31. 7	*8. 6*	*B8*	G5	Wolf
1. 8	*9. 6*	*B8*	H6	Dog
2. 8	*10. 6*	*B8*	J7	Pheasant
3. 8	*11. 6*	*B8*	K8	Cock
4. 8	*12. 6*	*B8*	A9	Crow
5. 8	*13. 6*	*B8*	B10	Monkey
6. 8	*14. 6*	*B8*	C11	Gibbon
7. 8	*15. 6*	*B8*	D12	Tapir
8. 8	*16. 6*	*B8*	E1	Sheep
9. 8	*17. 6*	*B8*	F2	Deer
10. 8	*18. 6*	*B8*	G3	Horse
11. 8	*19. 6*	*B8*	H4	Stag
12. 8	*20. 6*	*B8*	J5	Serpent
13. 8	*21. 6*	*B8*	K6	Earthworm
14. 8	*22. 6*	*B8*	A7	Crocodile
15. 8	*23. 6*	*B8*	B8	Dragon
16. 8	*24. 6*	*B8*	C9	Badger
17. 8	*25. 6*	*B8*	D10	Hare
18. 8	*26. 6*	*B8*	E11	Fox
19. 8	*27. 6*	*B8*	F12	Tiger
20. 8	*28. 6*	*B8*	G1	Leopard
21. 8	*29. 6*	*B8*	H2	Griffon
22. 8	*30. 6*	*B8*	J3	Ox
23. 8	1. 7	C9	K4	Bat
24. 8	2. 7	C9	A5	Rat
25. 8	3. 7	C9	B6	Swallow
26. 8	4. 7	C9	C7	Pig
27. 8	5. 7	C9	D8	Porcupine
28. 8	6. 7	C9	E9	Wolf
29. 8	7. 7	C9	F10	Dog
30. 8	8. 7	C9	G11	Pheasant
31. 8	9. 7	C9	H12	Cock
1. 9	10. 7	C9	J1	Crow
2. 9	11. 7	C9	K2	Monkey
3. 9	12. 7	C9	A3	Gibbon
4. 9	13. 7	C9	B4	Tapir
5. 9	14. 7	C9	C5	Sheep
6. 9	15. 7	C9	D6	Deer
7. 9	16. 7	C9	E7	Horse
8. 9	17. 7	C9	F8	Stag
9. 9	18. 7	C9	G9	Serpent
10. 9	19. 7	C9	H10	Earthworm
11. 9	20. 7	C9	J11	Crocodile
12. 9	21. 7	C9	K12	Dragon
13. 9	22. 7	C9	A1	Badger
14. 9	23. 7	C9	B2	Hare
15. 9	24. 7	C9	C3	Fox
16. 9	25. 7	C9	D4	Tiger
17. 9	26. 7	C9	E5	Leopard
18. 9	27. 7	C9	F6	Griffon
19. 9	28. 7	C9	G7	Ox
20. 9	29. 7	C9	H8	Bat
21. 9	1. 8	D10	J9	Rat
22. 9	2. 8	D10	K10	Swallow
23. 9	3. 8	D10	A11	Pig
24. 9	4. 8	D10	B12	Porcupine
25. 9	5. 8	D10	C1	Wolf
26. 9	6. 8	D10	D2	Dog
27. 9	7. 8	D10	E3	Pheasant
28. 9	8. 8	D10	F4	Cock
29. 9	9. 8	D10	G5	Crow
30. 9	10. 8	D10	H6	Monkey
1.10	11. 8	D10	J7	Gibbon
2.10	12. 8	D10	K8	Tapir
3.10	13. 8	D10	A9	Sheep
4.10	14. 8	D10	B10	Deer
5.10	15. 8	D10	C11	Horse
6.10	16. 8	D10	D12	Stag
7.10	17. 8	D10	E1	Serpent
8.10	18. 8	D10	F2	Earthworm
9.10	19. 8	D10	G3	Crocodile
10.10	20. 8	D10	H4	Dragon
11.10	21. 8	D10	J5	Badger
12.10	22. 8	D10	K6	Hare
13.10	23. 8	D10	A7	Fox
14.10	24. 8	D10	B8	Tiger
15.10	25. 8	D10	C9	Leopard
16.10	26. 8	D10	D10	Griffon
17.10	27. 8	D10	E11	Ox
18.10	28. 8	D10	F12	Bat
19.10	29. 8	D10	G1	Rat
20.10	1. 9	E11	H2	Swallow
21.10	2. 9	E11	J3	Pig
22.10	3. 9	E11	K4	Porcupine
23.10	4. 9	E11	A5	Wolf
24.10	5. 9	E11	B6	Dog
25.10	6. 9	E11	C7	Pheasant
26.10	7. 9	E11	D8	Cock
27.10	8. 9	E11	E9	Crow
28.10	9. 9	E11	F10	Monkey
29.10	10. 9	E11	G11	Gibbon
30.10	11. 9	E11	H12	Tapir
31.10	12. 9	E11	J1	Sheep
1.11	13. 9	E11	K2	Deer
2.11	14. 9	E11	A3	Horse
3.11	15. 9	E11	B4	Stag
4.11	16. 9	E11	C5	Serpent
5.11	17. 9	E11	D6	Earthworm
6.11	18. 9	E11	E7	Crocodile
7.11	19. 9	E11	F8	Dragon
8.11	20. 9	E11	G9	Badger
9.11	21. 9	E11	H10	Hare
10.11	22. 9	E11	J11	Fox

Solar date	Lunar date	Month HS/EB	Day HS/EB	Constellation
11.11	23. 9	E11	K12	Tiger
12.11	24. 9	E11	A1	Leopard
13.11	25. 9	E11	B2	Griffon
14.11	26. 9	E11	C3	Ox
15.11	27. 9	E11	D4	Bat
16.11	28. 9	E11	E5	Rat
17.11	29. 9	E11	F6	Swallow
18.11	30. 9	E11	G7	Pig
19.11	1.10	F12	H8	Porcupine
20.11	2.10	F12	J9	Wolf
21.11	3.10	F12	K10	Dog
22.11	4.10	F12	A11	Pheasant
23.11	5.10	F12	B12	Cock
24.11	6.10	F12	C1	Crow
25.11	7.10	F12	D2	Monkey
26.11	8.10	F12	E3	Gibbon
27.11	9.10	F12	F4	Tapir
28.11	10.10	F12	G5	Sheep
29.11	11.10	F12	H6	Deer
30.11	12.10	F12	J7	Horse
1.12	13.10	F12	K8	Stag
2.12	14.10	F12	A9	Serpent
3.12	15.10	F12	B10	Earthworm
4.12	16.10	F12	C11	Crocodile
5.12	17.10	F12	D12	Dragon
6.12	18.10	F12	E1	Badger
7.12	19.10	F12	F2	Hare
8.12	20.10	F12	G3	Fox
9.12	21.10	F12	H4	Tiger
10.12	22.10	F12	J5	Leopard
11.12	23.10	F12	K6	Griffon
12.12	24.10	F12	A7	Ox
13.12	25.10	F12	B8	Bat
14.12	26.10	F12	C9	Rat
15.12	27.10	F12	D10	Swallow
16.12	28.10	F12	E11	Pig
17.12	29.10	F12	F12	Porcupine
18.12	1.11	G1	G1	Wolf
19.12	2.11	G1	H2	Dog
20.12	3.11	G1	J3	Pheasant
21.12	4.11	G1	K4	Cock
22.12	5.11	G1	A5	Crow
23.12	6.11	G1	B6	Monkey
24.12	7.11	G1	C7	Gibbon
25.12	8.11	G1	D8	Tapir
26.12	9.11	G1	E9	Sheep
27.12	10.11	G1	F10	Deer
28.12	11.11	G1	G11	Horse
29.12	12.11	G1	H12	Stag
30.12	13.11	G1	J1	Serpent
31.12	14.11	G1	K2	Earthworm
1942				
1. 1	15.11	G1	A3	Crocodile
2. 1	16.11	G1	B4	Dragon
3. 1	17.11	G1	C5	Badger
4. 1	18.11	G1	D6	Hare
5. 1	19.11	G1	E7	Fox
6. 1	20.11	G1	F8	Tiger
7. 1	21.11	G1	G9	Leopard
8. 1	22.11	G1	H10	Griffon
9. 1	23.11	G1	J11	Ox
10. 1	24.11	G1	K12	Bat
11. 1	25.11	G1	A1	Rat
12. 1	26.11	G1	B2	Swallow
13. 1	27.11	G1	C3	Pig
14. 1	28.11	G1	D4	Porcupine
15. 1	29.11	G1	E5	Wolf
16. 1	30.11	G1	F6	Dog
17. 1	1.12	H2	G7	Pheasant
18. 1	2.12	H2	H8	Cock
19. 1	3.12	H2	J9	Crow
20. 1	4.12	H2	K10	Monkey
21. 1	5.12	H2	A11	Gibbon
22. 1	6.12	H2	B12	Tapir
23. 1	7.12	H2	C1	Sheep
24. 1	8.12	H2	D2	Deer
25. 1	9.12	H2	E3	Horse
26. 1	10.12	H2	F4	Stag
27. 1	11.12	H2	G5	Serpent
28. 1	12.12	H2	H6	Earthworm
29. 1	13.12	H2	J7	Crocodile
30. 1	14.12	H2	K8	Dragon
31. 1	15.12	H2	A9	Badger
1. 2	16.12	H2	B10	Hare
2. 2	17.12	H2	C11	Fox
3. 2	18.12	H2	D12	Tiger
4. 2	19.12	H2	E1	Leopard
5. 2	20.12	H2	F2	Griffon
6. 2	21.12	H2	G3	Ox
7. 2	22.12	H2	H4	Bat
8. 2	23.12	H2	J5	Rat
9. 2	24.12	H2	K6	Swallow
10. 2	25.12	H2	A7	Pig
11. 2	26.12	H2	B8	Porcupine
12. 2	27.12	H2	C9	Wolf
13. 2	28.12	H2	D10	Dog
14. 2	29.12	H2	E11	Pheasant

JEN WU YEAR

Solar date	Lunar date	Month HS/EB	Day HS/EB	Constellation
15. 2	1. 1	J3	F12	Cock
16. 2	2. 1	J3	G1	Crow
17. 2	3. 1	J3	H2	Monkey
18. 2	4. 1	J3	J3	Gibbon
19. 2	5. 1	J3	K4	Tapir
20. 2	6. 1	J3	A5	Sheep
21. 2	7. 1	J3	B6	Deer
22. 2	8. 1	J3	C7	Horse
23. 2	9. 1	J3	D8	Stag
24. 2	10. 1	J3	E9	Serpent
25. 2	11. 1	J3	F10	Earthworm
26. 2	12. 1	J3	G11	Crocodile
27. 2	13. 1	J3	H12	Dragon
28. 2	14. 1	J3	J1	Badger
1. 3	15. 1	J3	K2	Hare
2. 3	16. 1	J3	A3	Fox
3. 3	17. 1	J3	B4	Tiger
4. 3	18. 1	J3	C5	Leopard
5. 3	19. 1	J3	D6	Griffon
6. 3	20. 1	J3	E7	Ox
7. 3	21. 1	J3	F8	Bat
8. 3	22. 1	J3	G9	Rat
9. 3	23. 1	J3	H10	Swallow
10. 3	24. 1	J3	J11	Pig
11. 3	25. 1	J3	K12	Porcupine
12. 3	26. 1	J3	A1	Wolf
13. 3	27. 1	J3	B2	Dog
14. 3	28. 1	J3	C3	Pheasant
15. 3	29. 1	J3	D4	Cock
16. 3	30. 1	J3	E5	Crow
17. 3	1. 2	K4	F6	Monkey
18. 3	2. 2	K4	G7	Gibbon
19. 3	3. 2	K4	H8	Tapir
20. 3	4. 2	K4	J9	Sheep
21. 3	5. 2	K4	K10	Deer
22. 3	6. 2	K4	A11	Horse
23. 3	7. 2	K4	B12	Stag
24. 3	8. 2	K4	C1	Serpent

Solar date	*Lunar date*	*Month HS/EB*	*Day HS/EB*	*Constellation*
25. 3	9. 2	K4	D2	Earthworm
26. 3	10. 2	K4	E3	Crocodile
27. 3	11. 2	K4	F4	Dragon
28. 3	12. 2	K4	G5	Badger
29. 3	13. 2	K4	H6	Hare
30. 3	14. 2	K4	J7	Fox
31. 3	15. 2	K4	K8	Tiger
1. 4	16. 2	K4	A9	Leopard
2. 4	17. 2	K4	B10	Griffon
3. 4	18. 2	K4	C11	Ox
4. 4	19. 2	K4	D12	Bat
5. 4	20. 2	K4	E1	Rat
6. 4	21. 2	K4	F2	Swallow
7. 4	22. 2	K4	G3	Pig
8. 4	23. 2	K4	H4	Porcupine
9. 4	24. 2	K4	J5	Wolf
10. 4	25. 2	K4	K6	Dog
11. 4	26. 2	K4	A7	Pheasant
12. 4	27. 2	K4	B8	Cock
13. 4	28. 2	K4	C9	Crow
14. 4	29. 2	K4	D10	Monkey
15. 4	1. 3	A5	E11	Gibbon
16. 4	2. 3	A5	F12	Tapir
17. 4	3. 3	A5	G1	Sheep
18. 4	4. 3	A5	H2	Deer
19. 4	5. 3	A5	J3	Horse
20. 4	6. 3	A5	K4	Stag
21. 4	7. 3	A5	A5	Serpent
22. 4	8. 3	A5	B6	Earthworm
23. 4	9. 3	A5	C7	Crocodile
24. 4	10. 3	A5	D8	Dragon
25. 4	11. 3	A5	E9	Badger
26. 4	12. 3	A5	F10	Hare
27. 4	13. 3	A5	G11	Fox
28. 4	14. 3	A5	H12	Tiger
29. 4	15. 3	A5	J1	Leopard
30. 4	16. 3	A5	K2	Griffon
1. 5	17. 3	A5	A3	Ox
2. 5	18. 3	A5	B4	Bat
3. 5	19. 3	A5	C5	Rat
4. 5	20. 3	A5	D6	Swallow
5. 5	21. 3	A5	E7	Pig
6. 5	22. 3	A5	F8	Porcupine
7. 5	23. 3	A5	G9	Wolf
8. 5	24. 3	A5	H10	Dog
9. 5	25. 3	A5	J11	Pheasant
10. 5	26. 3	A5	K12	Cock
11. 5	27. 3	A5	A1	Crow
12. 5	28. 3	A5	B2	Monkey
13. 5	29. 3	A5	C3	Gibbon
14. 5	30. 3	A5	D4	Tapir
15. 5	1. 4	B6	E5	Sheep
16. 5	2. 4	B6	F6	Deer
17. 5	3. 4	B6	G7	Horse
18. 5	4. 4	B6	H8	Stag
19. 5	5. 4	B6	J9	Serpent
20. 5	6. 4	B6	K10	Earthworm
21. 5	7. 4	B6	A11	Crocodile
22. 5	8. 4	B6	B12	Dragon
23. 5	9. 4	B6	C1	Badger
24. 5	10. 4	B6	D2	Hare
25. 5	11. 4	B6	E3	Fox
26. 5	12. 4	B6	F4	Tiger
27. 5	13. 4	B6	G5	Leopard
28. 5	14. 4	B6	H6	Griffon
29. 5	15. 4	B6	J7	Ox
30. 5	16. 4	B6	K8	Bat
31. 5	17. 4	B6	A9	Rat
1. 6	18. 4	B6	B10	Swallow
2. 6	19. 4	B6	C11	Pig
3. 6	20. 4	B6	D12	Porcupine
4. 6	21. 4	B6	E1	Wolf
5. 6	22. 4	B6	F2	Dog
6. 6	23. 4	B6	G3	Pheasant
7. 6	24. 4	B6	H4	Cock
8. 6	25. 4	B6	J5	Crow
9. 6	26. 4	B6	K6	Monkey
10. 6	27. 4	B6	A7	Gibbon
11. 6	28. 4	B6	B8	Tapir
12. 6	29. 4	B6	C9	Sheep
13. 6	30. 4	B6	D10	Deer
14. 6	1. 5	C7	E11	Horse
15. 6	2. 5	C7	F12	Stag
16. 6	3. 5	C7	G1	Serpent
17. 6	4. 5	C7	H2	Earthworm
18. 6	5. 5	C7	J3	Crocodile
19. 6	6. 5	C7	K4	Dragon
20. 6	7. 5	C7	A5	Badger
21. 6	8. 5	C7	B6	Hare
22. 6	9. 5	C7	C7	Fox
23. 6	10. 5	C7	D8	Tiger
24. 6	11. 5	C7	E9	Leopard
25. 6	12. 5	C7	F10	Griffon
26. 6	13. 5	C7	G11	Ox
27. 6	14. 5	C7	H12	Bat
28. 6	15. 5	C7	J1	Rat
29. 6	16. 5	C7	K2	Swallow
30. 6	17. 5	C7	A3	Pig
1. 7	18. 5	C7	B4	Porcupine
2. 7	19. 5	C7	C5	Wolf
3. 7	20. 5	C7	D6	Dog
4. 7	21. 5	C7	E7	Pheasant
5. 7	22. 5	C7	F8	Cock
6. 7	23. 5	C7	G9	Crow
7. 7	24. 5	C7	H10	Monkey
8. 7	25. 5	C7	J11	Gibbon
9. 7	26. 5	C7	K12	Tapir
10. 7	27. 5	C7	A1	Sheep
11. 7	28. 5	C7	B2	Deer
12. 7	29. 5	C7	C3	Horse
13. 7	1. 6	D8	D4	Stag
14. 7	2. 6	D8	E5	Serpent
15. 7	3. 6	D8	F6	Earthworm
16. 7	4. 6	D8	G7	Crocodile
17. 7	5. 6	D8	H8	Dragon
18. 7	6. 6	D8	J9	Badger
19. 7	7. 6	D8	K10	Hare
20. 7	8. 6	D8	A11	Fox
21. 7	9. 6	D8	B12	Tiger
22. 7	10. 6	D8	C1	Leopard
23. 7	11. 6	D8	D2	Griffon
24. 7	12. 6	D8	E3	Ox
25. 7	13. 6	D8	F4	Bat
26. 7	14. 6	D8	G5	Rat
27. 7	15. 6	D8	H6	Swallow
28. 7	16. 6	D8	J7	Pig
29. 7	17. 6	D8	K8	Porcupine
30. 7	18. 6	D8	A9	Wolf
31. 7	19. 6	D8	B10	Dog
1. 8	20. 6	D8	C11	Pheasant
2. 8	21. 6	D8	D12	Cock
3. 8	22. 6	D8	E1	Crow
4. 8	23. 6	D8	F2	Monkey
5. 8	24. 6	D8	G3	Gibbon
6. 8	25. 6	D8	H4	Tapir
7. 8	26. 6	D8	J5	Sheep
8. 8	27. 6	D8	K6	Deer
9. 8	28. 6	D8	A7	Horse
10. 8	29. 6	D8	B8	Stag
11. 8	30. 6	D8	C9	Serpent
12. 8	1. 7	E9	D10	Earthworm
13. 8	2. 7	E9	E11	Crocodile
14. 8	3. 7	E9	F12	Dragon
15. 8	4. 7	E9	G1	Badger
16. 8	5. 7	E9	H2	Hare
17. 8	6. 7	E9	J3	Fox

Solar date	*Lunar date*	*Month HS/EB*	*Day HS/EB*	*Constellation*
18. 8	7. 7	E9	K4	Tiger
19. 8	8. 7	E9	A5	Leopard
20. 8	9. 7	E9	B6	Griffon
21. 8	10. 7	E9	C7	Ox
22. 8	11. 7	E9	D8	Bat
23. 8	12. 7	E9	E9	Rat
24. 8	13. 7	E9	F10	Swallow
25. 8	14. 7	E9	G11	Pig
26. 8	15. 7	E9	H12	Porcupine
27. 8	16. 7	E9	J1	Wolf
28. 8	17. 7	E9	K2	Dog
29. 8	18. 7	E9	A3	Pheasant
30. 8	19. 7	E9	B4	Cock
31. 8	20. 7	E9	C5	Crow
1. 9	21. 7	E9	D6	Monkey
2. 9	22. 7	E9	E7	Gibbon
3. 9	23. 7	E9	F8	Tapir
4. 9	24. 7	E9	G9	Sheep
5. 9	25. 7	E9	H10	Deer
6. 9	26. 7	E9	J11	Horse
7. 9	27. 7	E9	K12	Stag
8. 9	28. 7	E9	A1	Serpent
9. 9	29. 7	E9	B2	Earthworm
10. 9	1. 8	F10	C3	Crocodile
11. 9	2. 8	F10	D4	Dragon
12. 9	3. 8	F10	E5	Badger
13. 9	4. 8	F10	F6	Hare
14. 9	5. 8	F10	G7	Fox
15. 9	6. 8	F10	H8	Tiger
16. 9	7. 8	F10	J9	Leopard
17. 9	8. 8	F10	K10	Griffon
18. 9	9. 8	F10	A11	Ox
19. 9	10. 8	F10	B12	Bat
20. 9	11. 8	F10	C1	Rat
21. 9	12. 8	F10	D2	Swallow
22. 9	13. 8	F10	E3	Pig
23. 9	14. 8	F10	F4	Porcupine
24. 9	15. 8	F10	G5	Wolf
25. 9	16. 8	F10	H6	Dog
26. 9	17. 8	F10	J7	Pheasant
27. 9	18. 8	F10	K8	Cock
28. 9	19. 8	F10	A9	Crow
29. 9	20. 8	F10	B10	Monkey
30. 9	21. 8	F10	C11	Gibbon
1.10	22. 8	F10	D12	Tapir
2.10	23. 8	F10	E1	Sheep
3.10	24. 8	F10	F2	Deer
4.10	25. 8	F10	G3	Horse
5.10	26. 8	F10	H4	Stag
6.10	27. 8	F10	J5	Serpent
7.10	28. 8	F10	K6	Earthworm
8.10	29. 8	F10	A7	Crocodile
9.10	30. 8	F10	B8	Dragon
10.10	1. 9	G11	C9	Badger
11.10	2. 9	G11	D10	Hare
12.10	3. 9	G11	E11	Fox
13.10	4. 9	G11	F12	Tiger
14.10	5. 9	G11	G1	Leopard
15.10	6. 9	G11	H2	Griffon
16.10	7. 9	G11	J3	Ox
17.10	8. 9	G11	K4	Bat
18.10	9. 9	G11	A5	Rat
19.10	10. 9	G11	B6	Swallow
20.10	11. 9	G11	C7	Pig
21.10	12. 9	G11	D8	Porcupine
22.10	13. 9	G11	E9	Wolf
23.10	14. 9	G11	F10	Dog
24.10	15. 9	G11	G11	Pheasant
25.10	16. 9	G11	H12	Cock
26.10	17. 9	G11	J1	Crow
27.10	18. 9	G11	K2	Monkey
28.10	19. 9	G11	A3	Gibbon
29.10	20. 9	G11	B4	Tapir

Solar date	*Lunar date*	*Month HS/EB*	*Day HS/EB*	*Constellation*
30.10	21. 9	G11	C5	Sheep
31.10	22. 9	G11	D6	Deer
1.11	23. 9	G11	E7	Horse
2.11	24. 9	G11	F8	Stag
3.11	25. 9	G11	G9	Serpent
4.11	26. 9	G11	H10	Earthworm
5.11	27. 9	G11	J11	Crocodile
6.11	28. 9	G11	K12	Dragon
7.11	29. 9	G11	A1	Badger
8.11	1.10	H12	B2	Hare
9.11	2.10	H12	C3	Fox
10.11	3.10	H12	D4	Tiger
11.11	4.10	H12	E5	Leopard
12.11	5.10	H12	F6	Griffon
13.11	6.10	H12	G7	Ox
14.11	7.10	H12	H8	Bat
15.11	8.10	H12	J9	Rat
16.11	9.10	H12	K10	Swallow
17.11	10.10	H12	A11	Pig
18.11	11.10	H12	B12	Porcupine
19.11	12.10	H12	C1	Wolf
20.11	13.10	H12	D2	Dog
21.11	14.10	H12	E3	Pheasant
22.11	15.10	H12	F4	Cock
23.11	16.10	H12	G5	Crow
24.11	17.10	H12	H6	Monkey
25.11	18.10	H12	J7	Gibbon
26.11	19.10	H12	K8	Tapir
27.11	20.10	H12	A9	Sheep
28.11	21.10	H12	B10	Deer
29.11	22.10	H12	C11	Horse
30.11	23.10	H12	D12	Stag
1.12	24.10	H12	E1	Serpent
2.12	25.10	H12	F2	Earthworm
3.12	26.10	H12	G3	Crocodile
4.12	27.10	H12	H4	Dragon
5.12	28.10	H12	J5	Badger
6.12	29.10	H12	K6	Hare
7.12	30.10	H12	A7	Fox
8.12	1.11	J1	B8	Tiger
9.12	2.11	J1	C9	Leopard
10.12	3.11	J1	D10	Griffon
11.12	4.11	J1	E11	Ox
12.12	5.11	J1	F12	Bat
13.12	6.11	J1	G1	Rat
14.12	7.11	J1	H2	Swallow
15.12	8.11	J1	J3	Pig
16.12	9.11	J1	K4	Porcupine
17.12	10.11	J1	A5	Wolf
18.12	11.11	J1	B6	Dog
19.12	12.11	J1	C7	Pheasant
20.12	13.11	J1	D8	Cock
21.12	14.11	J1	E9	Crow
22.12	15.11	J1	F10	Monkey
23.12	16.11	J1	G11	Gibbon
24.12	17.11	J1	H12	Tapir
25.12	18.11	J1	J1	Sheep
26.12	19.11	J1	K2	Deer
27.12	20.11	J1	A3	Horse
28.12	21.11	J1	B4	Stag
29.12	22.11	J1	C5	Serpent
30.12	23.11	J1	D6	Earthworm
31.12	24.11	J1	E7	Crocodile
1943				
1. 1	25.11	J1	F8	Dragon
2. 1	26.11	J1	G9	Badger
3. 1	27.11	J1	H10	Hare
4. 1	28.11	J1	J11	Fox
5. 1	29.11	J1	K12	Tiger
6. 1	1.12	K2	A1	Leopard
7. 1	2.12	K2	B2	Griffon
8. 1	3.12	K2	C3	Ox

Solar date	*Lunar date*	*Month HS/EB*	*Day HS/EB*	*Constellation*
9. 1	4.12	K2	D4	Bat
10. 1	5.12	K2	E5	Rat
11. 1	6.12	K2	F6	Swallow
12. 1	7.12	K2	G7	Pig
13. 1	8.12	K2	H8	Porcupine
14. 1	9.12	K2	J9	Wolf
15. 1	10.12	K2	K10	Dog
16. 1	11.12	K2	A11	Pheasant
17. 1	12.12	K2	B12	Cock
18. 1	13.12	K2	C1	Crow
19. 1	14.12	K2	D2	Monkey
20. 1	15.12	K2	E3	Gibbon
21. 1	16.12	K2	F4	Tapir
22. 1	17.12	K2	G5	Sheep

Solar date	*Lunar date*	*Month HS/EB*	*Day HS/EB*	*Constellation*
23. 1	18.12	K2	H6	Deer
24. 1	19.12	K2	J7	Horse
25. 1	20.12	K2	K8	Stag
26. 1	21.12	K2	A9	Serpent
27. 1	22.12	K2	B10	Earthworm
28. 1	23.12	K2	C11	Crocodile
29. 1	24.12	K2	D12	Dragon
30. 1	25.12	K2	E1	Badger
31. 1	26.12	K2	F2	Hare
1. 2	27.12	K2	G3	Fox
2. 2	28.12	K2	H4	Tiger
3. 2	29.12	K2	J5	Leopard
4. 2	30.12	K2	K6	Griffon

KUEI WEI YEAR

5. 2	1. 1	A3	A7	Ox
6. 2	2. 1	A3	B8	Bat
7. 2	3. 1	A3	C9	Rat
8. 2	4. 1	A3	D10	Swallow
9. 2	5. 1	A3	E11	Pig
10. 2	6. 1	A3	F12	Porcupine
11. 2	7. 1	A3	G1	Wolf
12. 2	8. 1	A3	H2	Dog
13. 2	9. 1	A3	J3	Pheasant
14. 2	10. 1	A3	K4	Cock
15. 2	11. 1	A3	A5	Crow
16. 2	12. 1	A3	B6	Monkey
17. 2	13. 1	A3	C7	Gibbon
18. 2	14. 1	A3	D8	Tapir
19. 2	15. 1	A3	E9	Sheep
20. 2	16. 1	A3	F10	Deer
21. 2	17. 1	A3	G11	Horse
22. 2	18. 1	A3	H12	Stag
23. 2	19. 1	A3	J1	Serpent
24. 2	20. 1	A3	K2	Earthworm
25. 2	21. 1	A3	A3	Crocodile
26. 2	22. 1	A3	B4	Dragon
27. 2	23. 1	A3	C5	Badger
28. 2	24. 1	A3	D6	Hare
1. 3	25. 1	A3	E7	Fox
2. 3	26. 1	A3	F8	Tiger
3. 3	27. 1	A3	G9	Leopard
4. 3	28. 1	A3	H10	Griffon
5. 3	29. 1	A3	J11	Ox
6. 3	1. 2	B4	K12	Bat
7. 3	2. 2	B4	A1	Rat
8. 3	3. 2	B4	B2	Swallow
9. 3	4. 2	B4	C3	Pig
10. 3	5. 2	B4	D4	Porcupine
11. 3	6. 2	B4	E5	Wolf
12. 3	7. 2	B4	F6	Dog
13. 3	8. 2	B4	G7	Pheasant
14. 3	9. 2	B4	H8	Cock
15. 3	10. 2	B4	J9	Crow
16. 3	11. 2	B4	K10	Monkey
17. 3	12. 2	B4	A11	Gibbon
18. 3	13. 2	B4	B12	Tapir
19. 3	14. 2	B4	C1	Sheep
20. 3	15. 2	B4	D2	Deer
21. 3	16. 2	B4	E3	Horse
22. 3	17. 2	B4	F4	Stag
23. 3	18. 2	B4	G5	Serpent
24. 3	19. 2	B4	H6	Earthworm
25. 3	20. 2	B4	J7	Crocodile
26. 3	21. 2	B4	K8	Dragon
27. 3	22. 2	B4	A9	Badger
28. 3	23. 2	B4	B10	Hare
29. 3	24. 2	B4	C11	Fox
30. 3	25. 2	B4	D12	Tiger

31. 3	26. 2	B4	E1	Leopard
1. 4	27. 2	B4	F2	Griffon
2. 4	28. 2	B4	G3	Ox
3. 4	29. 2	B4	H4	Bat
4. 4	30. 2	B4	J5	Rat
5. 4	1. 3	C5	K6	Swallow
6. 4	2. 3	C5	A7	Pig
7. 4	3. 3	C5	B8	Porcupine
8. 4	4. 3	C5	C9	Wolf
9. 4	5. 3	C5	D10	Dog
10. 4	6. 3	C5	E11	Pheasant
11. 4	7. 3	C5	F12	Cock
12. 4	8. 3	C5	G1	Crow
13. 4	9. 3	C5	H2	Monkey
14. 4	10. 3	C5	J3	Gibbon
15. 4	11. 3	C5	K4	Tapir
16. 4	12. 3	C5	A5	Sheep
17. 4	13. 3	C5	B6	Deer
18. 4	14. 3	C5	C7	Horse
19. 4	15. 3	C5	D8	Stag
20. 4	16. 3	C5	E9	Serpent
21. 4	17. 3	C5	F10	Earthworm
22. 4	18. 3	C5	G11	Crocodile
23. 4	19. 3	C5	H12	Dragon
24. 4	20. 3	C5	J1	Badger
25. 4	21. 3	C5	K2	Hare
26. 4	22. 3	C5	A3	Fox
27. 4	23. 3	C5	B4	Tiger
28. 4	24. 3	C5	C5	Leopard
29. 4	25. 3	C5	D6	Griffon
30. 4	26. 3	C5	E7	Ox
1. 5	27. 3	C5	F8	Bat
2. 5	28. 3	C5	G9	Rat
3. 5	29. 3	C5	H10	Swallow
4. 5	1. 4	D6	J11	Pig
5. 5	2. 4	D6	K12	Porcupine
6. 5	3. 4	D6	A1	Wolf
7. 5	4. 4	D6	B2	Dog
8. 5	5. 4	D6	C3	Pheasant
9. 5	6. 4	D6	D4	Cock
10. 5	7. 4	D6	E5	Crow
11. 5	8. 4	D6	F6	Monkey
12. 5	9. 4	D6	G7	Gibbon
13. 5	10. 4	D6	H8	Tapir
14. 5	11. 4	D6	J9	Sheep
15. 5	12. 4	D6	K10	Deer
16. 5	13. 4	D6	A11	Horse
17. 5	14. 4	D6	B12	Stag
18. 5	15. 4	D6	C1	Serpent
19. 5	16. 4	D6	D2	Earthworm
20. 5	17. 4	D6	E3	Crocodile
21. 5	18. 4	D6	F4	Dragon
22. 5	19. 4	D6	G5	Badger
23. 5	20. 4	D6	H6	Hare

Solar date	Lunar date	Month HS/EB	Day HS/EB	Constellation
24. 5	21. 4	D6	J7	Fox
25. 5	22. 4	D6	K8	Tiger
26. 5	23. 4	D6	A9	Leopard
27. 5	24. 4	D6	B10	Griffon
28. 5	25. 4	D6	C11	Ox
29. 5	26. 4	D6	D12	Bat
30. 5	27. 4	D6	E1	Rat
31. 5	28. 4	D6	F2	Swallow
1. 6	29. 4	D6	G3	Pig
2. 6	30. 4	D6	H4	Porcupine
3. 6	1. 5	E7	J5	Wolf
4. 6	2. 5	E7	K6	Dog
5. 6	3. 5	E7	A7	Pheasant
6. 6	4. 5	E7	B8	Cock
7. 6	5. 5	E7	C9	Crow
8. 6	6. 5	E7	D10	Monkey
9. 6	7. 5	E7	E11	Gibbon
10. 6	8. 5	E7	F12	Tapir
11. 6	9. 5	E7	G1	Sheep
12. 6	10. 5	E7	H2	Deer
13. 6	11. 5	E7	J3	Horse
14. 6	12. 5	E7	K4	Stag
15. 6	13. 5	E7	A5	Serpent
16. 6	14. 5	E7	B6	Earthworm
17. 6	15. 5	E7	C7	Crocodile
18. 6	16. 5	E7	D8	Dragon
19. 6	17. 5	E7	E9	Badger
20. 6	18. 5	E7	F10	Hare
21. 6	19. 5	E7	G11	Fox
22. 6	20. 5	E7	H12	Tiger
23. 6	21. 5	E7	J1	Leopard
24. 6	22. 5	E7	K2	Griffon
25. 6	23. 5	E7	A3	Ox
26. 6	24. 5	E7	B4	Bat
27. 6	25. 5	E7	C5	Rat
28. 6	26. 5	E7	D6	Swallow
29. 6	27. 5	E7	E7	Pig
30. 6	28. 5	E7	F8	Porcupine
1. 7	29. 5	E7	G9	Wolf
2. 7	1. 6	F8	H10	Dog
3. 7	2. 6	F8	J11	Pheasant
4. 7	3. 6	F8	K12	Cock
5. 7	4. 6	F8	A1	Crow
6. 7	5. 6	F8	B2	Monkey
7. 7	6. 6	F8	C3	Gibbon
8. 7	7. 6	F8	D4	Tapir
9. 7	8. 6	F8	E5	Sheep
10. 7	9. 6	F8	F6	Deer
11. 7	10. 6	F8	G7	Horse
12. 7	11. 6	F8	H8	Stag
13. 7	12. 6	F8	J9	Serpent
14. 7	13. 6	F8	K10	Earthworm
15. 7	14. 6	F8	A11	Crocodile
16. 7	15. 6	F8	B12	Dragon
17. 7	16. 6	F8	C1	Badger
18. 7	17. 6	F8	D2	Hare
19. 7	18. 6	F8	E3	Fox
20. 7	19. 6	F8	F4	Tiger
21. 7	20. 6	F8	G5	Leopard
22. 7	21. 6	F8	H6	Griffon
23. 7	22. 6	F8	J7	Ox
24. 7	23. 6	F8	K8	Bat
25. 7	24. 6	F8	A9	Rat
26. 7	25. 6	F8	B10	Swallow
27. 7	26. 6	F8	C11	Pig
28. 7	27. 6	F8	D12	Porcupine
29. 7	28. 6	F8	E1	Wolf
30. 7	29. 6	F8	F2	Dog
31. 7	30. 6	F8	G3	Pheasant
1. 8	1. 7	G9	H4	Cock
2. 8	2. 7	G9	J5	Crow
3. 8	3. 7	G9	K6	Monkey
4. 8	4. 7	G9	A7	Gibbon

Solar date	Lunar date	Month HS/EB	Day HS/EB	Constellation
5. 8	5. 7	G9	B8	Tapir
6. 8	6. 7	G9	C9	Sheep
7. 8	7. 7	G9	D10	Deer
8. 8	8. 7	G9	E11	Horse
9. 8	9. 7	G9	F12	Stag
10. 8	10. 7	G9	G1	Serpent
11. 8	11. 7	G9	H2	Earthworm
12. 8	12. 7	G9	J3	Crocodile
13. 8	13. 7	G9	K4	Dragon
14. 8	14. 7	G9	A5	Badger
15. 8	15. 7	G9	B6	Hare
16. 8	16. 7	G9	C7	Fox
17. 8	17. 7	G9	D8	Tiger
18. 8	18. 7	G9	E9	Leopard
19. 8	19. 7	G9	F10	Griffon
20. 8	20. 7	G9	G11	Ox
21. 8	21. 7	G9	H12	Bat
22. 8	22. 7	G9	J1	Rat
23. 8	23. 7	G9	K2	Swallow
24. 8	24. 7	G9	A3	Pig
25. 8	25. 7	G9	B4	Porcupine
26. 8	26. 7	G9	C5	Wolf
27. 8	27. 7	G9	D6	Dog
28. 8	28. 7	G9	E7	Pheasant
29. 8	29. 7	G9	F8	Cock
30. 8	30. 7	G9	G9	Crow
31. 8	1. 8	H10	H10	Monkey
1. 9	2. 8	H10	J11	Gibbon
2. 9	3. 8	H10	K12	Tapir
3. 9	4. 8	H10	A1	Sheep
4. 9	5. 8	H10	B2	Deer
5. 9	6. 8	H10	C3	Horse
6. 9	7. 8	H10	D4	Stag
7. 9	8. 8	H10	E5	Serpent
8. 9	9. 8	H10	F6	Earthworm
9. 9	10. 8	H10	G7	Crocodile
10. 9	11. 8	H10	H8	Dragon
11. 9	12. 8	H10	J9	Badger
12. 9	13. 8	H10	K10	Hare
13. 9	14. 8	H10	A11	Fox
14. 9	15. 8	H10	B12	Tiger
15. 9	16. 8	H10	C1	Leopard
16. 9	17. 8	H10	D2	Griffon
17. 9	18. 8	H10	E3	Ox
18. 9	19. 8	H10	F4	Bat
19. 9	20. 8	H10	G5	Rat
20. 9	21. 8	H10	H6	Swallow
21. 9	22. 8	H10	J7	Pig
22. 9	23. 8	H10	K8	Porcupine
23. 9	24. 8	H10	A9	Wolf
24. 9	25. 8	H10	B10	Dog
25. 9	26. 8	H10	C11	Pheasant
26. 9	27. 8	H10	D12	Cock
27. 9	28. 8	H10	E1	Crow
28. 9	29. 8	H10	F2	Monkey
29. 9	1. 9	J11	G3	Gibbon
30. 9	2. 9	J11	H4	Tapir
1.10	3. 9	J11	J5	Sheep
2.10	4. 9	J11	K6	Deer
3.10	5. 9	J11	A7	Horse
4.10	6. 9	J11	B8	Stag
5.10	7. 9	J11	C9	Serpent
6.10	8. 9	J11	D10	Earthworm
7.10	9. 9	J11	E11	Crocodile
8.10	10. 9	J11	F12	Dragon
9.10	11. 9	J11	G1	Badger
10.10	12. 9	J11	H2	Hare
11.10	13. 9	J11	J3	Fox
12.10	14. 9	J11	K4	Tiger
13.10	15. 9	J11	A5	Leopard
14.10	16. 9	J11	B6	Griffon
15.10	17. 9	J11	C7	Ox
16.10	18. 9	J11	D8	Bat

Solar date	Lunar date	Month HS/EB	Day HS/EB	Constellation
17.10	19. 9	J11	E9	Rat
18.10	20. 9	J11	F10	Swallow
19.10	21. 9	J11	G11	Pig
20.10	22. 9	J11	H12	Porcupine
21.10	23. 9	J11	J1	Wolf
22.10	24. 9	J11	K2	Dog
23.10	25. 9	J11	A3	Pheasant
24.10	26. 9	J11	B4	Cock
25.10	27. 9	J11	C5	Crow
26.10	28. 9	J11	D6	Monkey
27.10	29. 9	J11	E7	Gibbon
28.10	30. 9	J11	F8	Tapir
29.10	1.10	K12	G9	Sheep
30.10	2.10	K12	H10	Deer
31.10	3.10	K12	J11	Horse
1.11	4.10	K12	K12	Stag
2.11	5.10	K12	A1	Serpent
3.11	6.10	K12	B2	Earthworm
4.11	7.10	K12	C3	Crocodile
5.11	8.10	K12	D4	Dragon
6.11	9.10	K12	E5	Badger
7.11	10.10	K12	F6	Hare
8.11	11.10	K12	G7	Fox
9.11	12.10	K12	H8	Tiger
10.11	13.10	K12	J9	Leopard
11.11	14.10	K12	K10	Griffon
12.11	15.10	K12	A11	Ox
13.11	16.10	K12	B12	Bat
14.11	17.10	K12	C1	Rat
15.11	18.10	K12	D2	Swallow
16.11	19.10	K12	E3	Pig
17.11	20.10	K12	F4	Porcupine
18.11	21.10	K12	G5	Wolf
19.11	22.10	K12	H6	Dog
20.11	23.10	K12	J7	Pheasant
21.11	24.10	K12	K8	Cock
22.11	25.10	K12	A9	Crow
23.11	26.10	K12	B10	Monkey
24.11	27.10	K12	C11	Gibbon
25.11	28.10	K12	D12	Tapir
26.11	29.10	K12	E1	Sheep
27.11	1.11	A1	F2	Deer
28.11	2.11	A1	G3	Horse
29.11	3.11	A1	H4	Stag
30.11	4.11	A1	J5	Serpent
1.12	5.11	A1	K6	Earthworm
2.12	6.11	A1	A7	Crocodile
3.12	7.11	A1	B8	Dragon
4.12	8.11	A1	C9	Badger
5.12	9.11	A1	D10	Hare
6.12	10.11	A1	E11	Fox
7.12	11.11	A1	F12	Tiger
8.12	12.11	A1	G1	Leopard
9.12	13.11	A1	H2	Griffon
10.12	14.11	A1	J3	Ox
11.12	15.11	A1	K4	Bat
12.12	16.11	A1	A5	Rat
13.12	17.11	A1	B6	Swallow
14.12	18.11	A1	C7	Pig
15.12	19.11	A1	D8	Porcupine
16.12	20.11	A1	E9	Wolf
17.12	21.11	A1	F10	Dog
18.12	22.11	A1	G11	Pheasant
19.12	23.11	A1	H12	Cock
20.12	24.11	A1	J1	Crow
21.12	25.11	A1	K2	Monkey
22.12	26.11	A1	A3	Gibbon
23.12	27.11	A1	B4	Tapir
24.12	28.11	A1	C5	Sheep
25.12	29.11	A1	D6	Deer
26.12	30.11	A1	E7	Horse
27.12	1.12	B2	F8	Stag
28.12	2.12	B2	G9	Serpent
29.12	3.12	B2	H10	Earthworm
30.12	4.12	B2	J11	Crocodile
31.12	5.12	B2	K12	Dragon
1944				
1. 1	6.12	B2	A1	Badger
2. 1	7.12	B2	B2	Hare
3. 1	8.12	B2	C3	Fox
4. 1	9.12	B2	D4	Tiger
5. 1	10.12	B2	E5	Leopard
6. 1	11.12	B2	F6	Griffon
7. 1	12.12	B2	G7	Ox
8. 1	13.12	B2	H8	Bat
9. 1	14.12	B2	J9	Rat
10. 1	15.12	B2	K10	Swallow
11. 1	16.12	B2	A11	Pig
12. 1	17.12	B2	B12	Porcupine
13. 1	18.12	B2	C1	Wolf
14. 1	19.12	B2	D2	Dog
15. 1	20.12	B2	E3	Pheasant
16. 1	21.12	B2	F4	Cock
17. 1	22.12	B2	G5	Crow
18. 1	23.12	B2	H6	Monkey
19. 1	24.12	B2	J7	Gibbon
20. 1	25.12	B2	K8	Tapir
21. 1	26.12	B2	A9	Sheep
22. 1	27.12	B2	B10	Deer
23. 1	28.12	B2	C11	Horse
24. 1	29.12	B2	D12	Stag

CHIA SHEN YEAR

25. 1	1. 1	C3	E1	Serpent
26. 1	2. 1	C3	F2	Earthworm
27. 1	3. 1	C3	G3	Crocodile
28. 1	4. 1	C3	H4	Dragon
29. 1	5. 1	C3	J5	Badger
30. 1	6. 1	C3	K6	Hare
31. 1	7. 1	C3	A7	Fox
1. 2	8. 1	C3	B8	Tiger
2. 2	9. 1	C3	C9	Leopard
3. 2	10. 1	C3	D10	Griffon
4. 2	11. 1	C3	E11	Ox
5. 2	12. 1	C3	F12	Bat
6. 2	13. 1	C3	G1	Rat
7. 2	14. 1	C3	H2	Swallow
8. 2	15. 1	C3	J3	Pig
9. 2	16. 1	C3	K4	Porcupine
10 2	17. 1	C3	A5	Wolf
11. 2	18. 1	C3	B6	Dog
12. 2	19. 1	C3	C7	Pheasant
13. 2	20. 1	C3	D8	Cock
14. 2	21. 1	C3	E9	Crow
15. 2	22. 1	C3	F10	Monkey
16. 2	23. 1	C3	G11	Gibbon
17. 2	24. 1	C3	H12	Tapir
18. 2	25. 1	C3	J1	Sheep
19. 2	26. 1	C3	K2	Deer
20. 2	27. 1	C3	A3	Horse
21. 2	28. 1	C3	B4	Stag
22. 2	29. 1	C3	C5	Serpent
23. 2	30. 1	C3	D6	Earthworm
24. 2	1. 2	D4	E7	Crocodile
25. 2	2. 2	D4	F8	Dragon
26. 2	3. 2	D4	G9	Badger
27. 2	4. 2	D4	H10	Hare

Solar date	*Lunar date*	*Month HS/EB*	*Day HS/EB*	*Constellation*
28. 2	5. 2	D4	J11	Fox
29. 2	6. 2	D4	K12	Tiger
1. 3	7. 2	D4	A1	Leopard
2. 3	8. 2	D4	B2	Griffon
3. 3	9. 2	D4	C3	Ox
4. 3	10. 2	D4	D4	Bat
5. 3	11. 2	D4	E5	Rat
6. 3	12. 2	D4	F6	Swallow
7. 3	13. 2	D4	G7	Pig
8. 3	14. 2	D4	H8	Porcupine
9. 3	15. 2	D4	J9	Wolf
10. 3	16. 2	D4	K10	Dog
11. 3	17. 2	D4	A11	Pheasant
12. 3	18. 2	D4	B12	Cock
13. 3	19. 2	D4	C1	Crow
14. 3	20. 2	D4	D2	Monkey
15. 3	21. 2	D4	E3	Gibbon
16. 3	22. 2	D4	F4	Tapir
17. 3	23. 2	D4	G5	Sheep
18. 3	24. 2	D4	H6	Deer
19. 3	25. 2	D4	J7	Horse
20. 3	26. 2	D4	K8	Stag
21. 3	27. 2	D4	A9	Serpent
22. 3	28. 2	D4	B10	Earthworm
23. 3	29. 2	D4	C11	Crocodile
24. 3	1. 3	E5	D12	Dragon
25. 3	2. 3	E5	E1	Badger
26. 3	3. 3	E5	F2	Hare
27. 3	4. 3	E5	G3	Fox
28. 3	5. 3	E5	H4	Tiger
29. 3	6. 3	E5	J5	Leopard
30. 3	7. 3	E5	K6	Griffon
31. 3	8. 3	E5	A7	Ox
1. 4	9. 3	E5	B8	Bat
2. 4	10. 3	E5	C9	Rat
3. 4	11. 3	E5	D10	Swallow
4. 4	12. 3	E5	E11	Pig
5. 4	13. 3	E5	F12	Porcupine
6. 4	14. 3	E5	G1	Wolf
7. 4	15. 3	E5	H2	Dog
8. 4	16. 3	E5	J3	Pheasant
9. 4	17. 3	E5	K4	Cock
10. 4	18. 3	E5	A5	Crow
11. 4	19. 3	E5	B6	Monkey
12. 4	20. 3	E5	C7	Gibbon
13. 4	21. 3	E5	D8	Tapir
14. 4	22. 3	E5	E9	Sheep
15. 4	23. 3	E5	F10	Deer
16. 4	24. 3	E5	G11	Horse
17. 4	25. 3	E5	H12	Stag
18. 4	26. 3	E5	J1	Serpent
19. 4	27. 3	E5	K2	Earthworm
20. 4	28. 3	E5	A3	Crocodile
21. 4	29. 3	E5	B4	Dragon
22. 4	30. 3	E5	C5	Badger
23. 4	1. 4	F6	D6	Hare
24. 4	2. 4	F6	E7	Fox
25. 4	3. 4	F6	F8	Tiger
26. 4	4. 4	F6	G9	Leopard
27. 4	5. 4	F6	H10	Griffon
28. 4	6. 4	F6	J11	Ox
29. 4	7. 4	F6	K12	Bat
30. 4	8. 4	F6	A1	Rat
1. 5	9. 4	F6	B2	Swallow
2. 5	10. 4	F6	C3	Pig
3. 5	11. 4	F6	D4	Porcupine
4. 5	12. 4	F6	E5	Wolf
5. 5	13. 4	F6	F6	Dog
6. 5	14. 4	F6	G7	Pheasant
7. 5	15. 4	F6	H8	Cock
8. 5	16. 4	F6	J9	Crow
9. 5	17. 4	F6	K10	Monkey
10. 5	18. 4	F6	A11	Gibbon
11. 5	19. 4	F6	B12	Tapir
12. 5	20. 4	F6	C1	Sheep
13. 5	21. 4	F6	D2	Deer
14. 5	22. 4	F6	E3	Horse
15. 5	23. 4	F6	F4	Stag
16. 5	24. 4	F6	G5	Serpent
17. 5	25. 4	F6	H6	Earthworm
18. 5	26. 4	F6	J7	Crocodile
19. 5	27. 4	F6	K8	Dragon
20. 5	28. 4	F6	A9	Badger
21. 5	29. 4	F6	B10	Hare
22. 5	*1. 4*	*F6*	C11	Fox
23. 5	*2. 4*	*F6*	D12	Tiger
24. 5	*3. 4*	*F6*	E1	Leopard
25. 5	*4. 4*	*F6*	F2	Griffon
26. 5	*5. 4*	*F6*	G3	Ox
27. 5	*6. 4*	*F6*	H4	Bat
28. 5	*7. 4*	*F6*	J5	Rat
29. 5	*8. 4*	*F6*	K6	Swallow
30. 5	*9. 4*	*F6*	A7	Pig
31. 5	*10. 4*	*F6*	B8	Porcupine
1. 6	*11. 4*	*F6*	C9	Wolf
2. 6	*12. 4*	*F6*	D10	Dog
3. 6	*13. 4*	*F6*	E11	Pheasant
4. 6	*14. 4*	*F6*	F12	Cock
5. 6	*15. 4*	*F6*	G1	Crow
6. 6	*16. 4*	*F6*	H2	Monkey
7. 6	*17. 4*	*F6*	J3	Gibbon
8. 6	*18. 4*	*F6*	K4	Tapir
9. 6	*19. 4*	*F6*	A5	Sheep
10. 6	*20. 4*	*F6*	B6	Deer
11. 6	*21. 4*	*F6*	C7	Horse
12. 6	*22. 4*	*F6*	D8	Stag
13. 6	*23. 4*	*F6*	E9	Serpent
14. 6	*24. 4*	*F6*	F10	Earthworm
15. 6	*25. 4*	*F6*	G11	Crocodile
16. 6	*26. 4*	*F6*	H12	Dragon
17. 6	*27. 4*	*F6*	J1	Badger
18. 6	*28. 4*	*F6*	K2	Hare
19. 6	*29. 4*	*F6*	A3	Fox
20. 6	*30. 4*	*F6*	B4	Tiger
21. 6	1. 5	G7	C5	Leopard
22. 6	2. 5	G7	D6	Griffon
23. 6	3. 5	G7	E7	Ox
24. 6	4. 5	G7	F8	Bat
25. 6	5. 5	G7	G9	Rat
26. 6	6. 5	G7	H10	Swallow
27. 6	7. 5	G7	J11	Pig
28. 6	8. 5	G7	K12	Porcupine
29. 6	9. 5	G7	A1	Wolf
30. 6	10. 5	G7	B2	Dog
1. 7	11. 5	G7	C3	Pheasant
2. 7	12. 5	G7	D4	Cock
3. 7	13. 5	G7	E5	Crow
4. 7	14. 5	G7	F6	Monkey
5. 7	15. 5	G7	G7	Gibbon
6. 7	16. 5	G7	H8	Tapir
7. 7	17. 5	G7	J9	Sheep
8. 7	18. 5	G7	K10	Deer
9. 7	19. 5	G7	A11	Horse
10. 7	20. 5	G7	B12	Stag
11. 7	21. 5	G7	C1	Serpent
12. 7	22. 5	G7	D2	Earthworm
13. 7	23. 5	G7	E3	Crocodile
14. 7	24. 5	G7	F4	Dragon
15. 7	25. 5	G7	G5	Badger
16. 7	26. 5	G7	H6	Hare
17. 7	27. 5	G7	J7	Fox
18. 7	28. 5	G7	K8	Tiger
19. 7	29. 5	G7	A9	Leopard
20. 7	1. 6	H8	B10	Griffon
21. 7	2. 6	H8	C11	Ox
22. 7	3. 6	H8	D12	Bat

Solar date	Lunar date	Month HS/EB	Day HS/EB	Constellation	Solar date	Lunar date	Month HS/EB	Day HS/EB	Constellation
23. 7	4. 6	H8	E1	Rat	4.10	18. 8	K10	H2	Earthworm
24. 7	5. 6	H8	F2	Swallow	5.10	19. 8	K10	J3	Crocodile
25. 7	6. 6	H8	G3	Pig	6.10	20. 8	K10	K4	Dragon
26. 7	7. 6	H8	H4	Porcupine	7.10	21. 8	K10	A5	Badger
27. 7	8. 6	H8	J5	Wolf	8.10	22. 8	K10	B6	Hare
28. 7	9. 6	H8	K6	Dog	9.10	23. 8	K10	C7	Fox
29. 7	10. 6	H8	A7	Pheasant	10.10	24. 8	K10	D8	Tiger
30. 7	11. 6	H8	B8	Cock	11.10	25. 8	K10	E9	Leopard
31. 7	12. 6	H8	C9	Crow	12.10	26. 8	K10	F10	Griffon
1. 8	13. 6	H8	D10	Monkey	13.10	27. 8	K10	G11	Ox
2. 8	14. 6	H8	E11	Gibbon	14.10	28. 8	K10	H12	Bat
3. 8	15. 6	H8	F12	Tapir	15.10	29. 8	K10	J1	Rat
4. 8	16. 6	H8	G1	Sheep	16.10	30. 8	K10	K2	Swallow
5. 8	17. 6	H8	H2	Deer	17.10	1. 9	A11	A3	Pig
6. 8	18. 6	H8	J3	Horse	18.10	2. 9	A11	B4	Porcupine
7. 8	19. 6	H8	K4	Stag	19.10	3. 9	A11	C5	Wolf
8. 8	20. 6	H8	A5	Serpent	20.10	4. 9	A11	D6	Dog
9. 8	21. 6	H8	B6	Earthworm	21.10	5. 9	A11	E7	Pheasant
10. 8	22. 6	H8	C7	Crocodile	22.10	6. 9	A11	F8	Cock
11. 8	23. 6	H8	D8	Dragon	23.10	7. 9	A11	G9	Crow
12. 8	24. 6	H8	E9	Badger	24.10	8. 9	A11	H10	Monkey
13. 8	25. 6	H8	F10	Hare	25.10	9. 9	A11	J11	Gibbon
14. 8	26. 6	H8	G11	Fox	26.10	10. 9	A11	K12	Tapir
15. 8	27. 6	H8	H12	Tiger	27.10	11. 9	A11	A1	Sheep
16. 8	28. 6	H8	J1	Leopard	28.10	12. 9	A11	B2	Deer
17. 8	29. 6	H8	K2	Griffon	29.10	13. 9	A11	C3	Horse
18. 8	30. 6	H8	A3	Ox	30.10	14. 9	A11	D4	Stag
19. 8	1. 7	J9	B4	Bat	31.10	15. 9	A11	E5	Serpent
20. 8	2. 7	J9	C5	Rat	1.11	16. 9	A11	F6	Earthworm
21. 8	3. 7	J9	D6	Swallow	2.11	17. 9	A11	G7	Crocodile
22. 8	4. 7	J9	E7	Pig	3.11	18. 9	A11	H8	Dragon
23. 8	5. 7	J9	F8	Porcupine	4.11	19. 9	A11	J9	Badger
24. 8	6. 7	J9	G9	Wolf	5.11	20. 9	A11	K10	Hare
25. 8	7. 7	J9	H10	Dog	6.11	21. 9	A11	A11	Fox
26. 8	8. 7	J9	J11	Pheasant	7.11	22. 9	A11	B12	Tiger
27. 8	9. 7	J9	K12	Cock	8.11	23. 9	A11	C1	Leopard
28. 8	10. 7	J9	A1	Crow	9.11	24. 9	A11	D2	Griffon
29. 8	11. 7	J9	B2	Monkey	10.11	25. 9	A11	E3	Ox
30. 8	12. 7	J9	C3	Gibbon	11.11	26. 9	A11	F4	Bat
31. 8	13. 7	J9	D4	Tapir	12.11	27. 9	A11	G5	Rat
1. 9	14. 7	J9	E5	Sheep	13.11	28. 9	A11	H6	Swallow
2. 9	15. 7	J9	F6	Deer	14.11	29. 9	A11	J7	Pig
3. 9	16. 7	J9	G7	Horse	15.11	30. 9	A11	K8	Porcupine
4. 9	17. 7	J9	H8	Stag	16.11	1.10	B12	A9	Wolf
5. 9	18. 7	J9	J9	Serpent	17.11	2.10	B12	B10	Dog
6. 9	19. 7	J9	K10	Earthworm	18.11	3.10	B12	C11	Pheasant
7. 9	20. 7	J9	A11	Crocodile	19.11	4.10	B12	D12	Cock
8. 9	21. 7	J9	B12	Dragon	20.11	5.10	B12	E1	Crow
9. 9	22. 7	J9	C1	Badger	21.11	6.10	B12	F2	Monkey
10. 9	23. 7	J9	D2	Hare	22.11	7.10	B12	G3	Gibbon
11. 9	24. 7	J9	E3	Fox	23.11	8.10	B12	H4	Tapir
12. 9	25. 7	J9	F4	Tiger	24.11	9.10	B12	J5	Sheep
13. 9	26. 7	J9	G5	Leopard	25.11	10.10	B12	K6	Deer
14. 9	27. 7	J9	H6	Griffon	26.11	11.10	B12	A7	Horse
15. 9	28. 7	J9	J7	Ox	27.11	12.10	B12	B8	Stag
16. 9	29. 7	J9	K8	Bat	28.11	13.10	B12	C9	Serpent
17. 9	1. 8	K10	A9	Rat	29.11	14.10	B12	D10	Earthworm
18. 9	2. 8	K10	B10	Swallow	30.11	15.10	B12	E11	Crocodile
19. 9	3. 8	K10	C11	Pig	1.12	16.10	B12	F12	Dragon
20. 9	4. 8	K10	D12	Porcupine	2.12	17.10	B12	G1	Badger
21. 9	5. 8	K10	E1	Wolf	3.12	18.10	B12	H2	Hare
22. 9	6. 8	K10	F2	Dog	4.12	19.10	B12	J3	Fox
23. 9	7. 8	K10	G3	Pheasant	5.12	20.10	B12	K4	Tiger
24. 9	8. 8	K10	H4	Cock	6.12	21.10	B12	A5	Leopard
25. 9	9. 8	K10	J5	Crow	7.12	22.10	B12	B6	Griffon
26. 9	10. 8	K10	K6	Monkey	8.12	23.10	B12	C7	Ox
27. 9	11. 8	K10	A7	Gibbon	9.12	24.10	B12	D8	Bat
28. 9	12. 8	K10	B8	Tapir	10.12	25.10	B12	E9	Rat
29. 9	13. 8	K10	C9	Sheep	11.12	26.10	B12	F10	Swallow
30. 9	14. 8	K10	D10	Deer	12.12	27.10	B12	G11	Pig
1.10	15. 8	K10	E11	Horse	13.12	28.10	B12	H12	Porcupine
2.10	16. 8	K10	F12	Stag	14.12	29.10	B12	J1	Wolf
3.10	17. 8	K10	G1	Serpent	15.12	1.11	C1	K2	Dog

Solar date	*Lunar date*	*Month HS/EB*	*Day HS/EB*	*Constellation*
16.12	2.11	C1	A3	Pheasant
17.12	3.11	C1	B4	Cock
18.12	4.11	C1	C5	Crow
19.12	5.11	C1	D6	Monkey
20.12	6.11	C1	E7	Gibbon
21.12	7.11	C1	F8	Tapir
22.12	8.11	C1	G9	Sheep
23.12	9.11	C1	H10	Deer
24.12	10.11	C1	J11	Horse
25.12	11.11	C1	K12	Stag
26.12	12.11	C1	A1	Serpent
27.12	13.11	C1	B2	Earthworm
28.12	14.11	C1	C3	Crocodile
29.12	15.11	C1	D4	Dragon
30.12	16.11	C1	E5	Badger
31.12	17.11	C1	F6	Hare
1945				
1. 1	18.11	C1	G7	Fox
2. 1	19.11	C1	H8	Tiger
3. 1	20.11	C1	J9	Leopard
4. 1	21.11	C1	K10	Griffon
5. 1	22.11	C1	A11	Ox
6. 1	23.11	C1	B12	Bat
7. 1	24.11	C1	C1	Rat
8. 1	25.11	C1	D2	Swallow
9. 1	26.11	C1	E3	Pig
10. 1	27.11	C1	F4	Porcupine
11. 1	28.11	C1	G5	Wolf
12. 1	29.11	C1	H6	Dog
13. 1	30.11	C1	J7	Pheasant
14. 1	1.12	D2	K8	Cock
15. 1	2.12	D2	A9	Crow
16. 1	3.12	D2	B10	Monkey
17. 1	4.12	D2	C11	Gibbon
18. 1	5.12	D2	D12	Tapir
19. 1	6.12	D2	E1	Sheep
20. 1	7.12	D2	F2	Deer
21. 1	8.12	D2	G3	Horse
22. 1	9.12	D2	H4	Stag
23. 1	10.12	D2	J5	Serpent
24. 1	11.12	D2	K6	Earthworm
25. 1	12.12	D2	A7	Crocodile
26. 1	13.12	D2	B8	Dragon
27. 1	14.12	D2	C9	Badger
28. 1	15.12	D2	D10	Hare
29. 1	16.12	D2	E11	Fox
30. 1	17.12	D2	F12	Tiger
31. 1	18.12	D2	G1	Leopard
1. 2	19.12	D2	H2	Griffon
2. 2	20.12	D2	J3	Ox
3. 2	21.12	D2	K4	Bat
4. 2	22.12	D2	A5	Rat
5. 2	23.12	D2	B6	Swallow
6. 2	24.12	D2	C7	Pig
7. 2	25.12	D2	D8	Porcupine
8. 2	26.12	D2	E9	Wolf
9. 2	27.12	D2	F10	Dog
10. 2	28.12	D2	G11	Pheasant
11. 2	29.12	D2	H12	Cock
12. 2	30.12	D2	J1	Crow

YI YU YEAR

13. 2	1. 1	E3	K2	Monkey
14. 2	2. 1	E3	A3	Gibbon
15. 2	3. 1	E3	B4	Tapir
16. 2	4. 1	E3	C5	Sheep
17. 2	5. 1	E3	D6	Deer
18. 2	6. 1	E3	E7	Horse
19. 2	7. 1	E3	F8	Stag
20. 2	8. 1	E3	G9	Serpent
21. 2	9. 1	E3	H10	Earthworm
22. 2	10. 1	E3	J11	Crocodile
23. 2	11. 1	E3	K12	Dragon
24. 2	12. 1	E3	A1	Badger
25. 2	13. 1	E3	B2	Hare
26. 2	14. 1	E3	C3	Fox
27. 2	15. 1	E3	D4	Tiger
28. 2	16. 1	E3	E5	Leopard
1. 3	17. 1	E3	F6	Griffon
2. 3	18. 1	E3	G7	Ox
3. 3	19. 1	E3	H8	Bat
4. 3	20. 1	E3	J9	Rat
5. 3	21. 1	E3	K10	Swallow
6. 3	22. 1	E3	A11	Pig
7. 3	23. 1	E3	B12	Porcupine
8. 3	24. 1	E3	C1	Wolf
9. 3	25. 1	E3	D2	Dog
10. 3	26. 1	E3	E3	Pheasant
11. 3	27. 1	E3	F4	Cock
12. 3	28. 1	E3	G5	Crow
13. 3	29. 1	E3	H6	Monkey
14. 3	1. 2	F4	J7	Gibbon
15. 3	2. 2	F4	K8	Tapir
16. 3	3. 2	F4	A9	Sheep
17. 3	4. 2	F4	B10	Deer
18. 3	5. 2	F4	C11	Horse
19. 3	6. 2	F4	D12	Stag
20. 3	7. 2	F4	E1	Serpent
21. 3	8. 2	F4	F2	Earthworm
22. 3	9. 2	F4	G3	Crocodile
23. 3	10. 2	F4	H4	Dragon
24. 3	11. 2	F4	J5	Badger
25. 3	12. 2	F4	K6	Hare
26. 3	13. 2	F4	A7	Fox
27. 3	14. 2	F4	B8	Tiger
28. 3	15. 2	F4	C9	Leopard
29. 3	16. 2	F4	D10	Griffon
30. 3	17. 2	F4	E11	Ox
31. 3	18. 2	F4	F12	Bat
1. 4	19. 2	F4	G1	Rat
2. 4	20. 2	F4	H2	Swallow
3. 4	21. 2	F4	J3	Pig
4. 4	22. 2	F4	K4	Porcupine
5. 4	23. 2	F4	A5	Wolf
6. 4	24. 2	F4	B6	Dog
7. 4	25. 2	F4	C7	Pheasant
8. 4	26. 2	F4	D8	Cock
9. 4	27. 2	F4	E9	Crow
10. 4	28. 2	F4	F10	Monkey
11. 4	29. 2	F4	G11	Gibbon
12. 4	1. 3	G5	H12	Tapir
13. 4	2. 3	G5	J1	Sheep
14. 4	3. 3	G5	K2	Deer
15. 4	4. 3	G5	A3	Horse
16. 4	5. 3	G5	B4	Stag
17. 4	6. 3	G5	C5	Serpent
18. 4	7. 3	G5	D6	Earthworm
19. 4	8. 3	G5	E7	Crocodile
20. 4	9. 3	G5	F8	Dragon
21. 4	10. 3	G5	G9	Badger
22. 4	11. 3	G5	H10	Hare
23. 4	12. 3	G5	J11	Fox
24. 4	13. 3	G5	K12	Tiger
25. 4	14. 3	G5	A1	Leopard
26. 4	15. 3	G5	B2	Griffon
27. 4	16. 3	G5	C3	Ox

Solar date	Lunar date	Month HS/EB	Day HS/EB	Constellation
28. 4	17. 3	G5	D4	Bat
29. 4	18. 3	G5	E5	Rat
30. 4	19. 3	G5	F6	Swallow
1. 5	20. 3	G5	G7	Pig
2. 5	21. 3	G5	H8	Porcupine
3. 5	22. 3	G5	J9	Wolf
4. 5	23. 3	G5	K10	Dog
5. 5	24. 3	G5	A11	Pheasant
6. 5	25. 3	G5	B12	Cock
7. 5	26. 3	G5	C1	Crow
8. 5	27. 3	G5	D2	Monkey
9. 5	28. 3	G5	E3	Gibbon
10. 5	29. 3	G5	F4	Tapir
11. 5	30. 3	G5	G5	Sheep
12. 5	1. 4	H6	H6	Deer
13. 5	2. 4	H6	J7	Horse
14. 5	3. 4	H6	K8	Stag
15. 5	4. 4	H6	A9	Serpent
16. 5	5. 4	H6	B10	Earthworm
17. 5	6. 4	H6	C11	Crocodile
18. 5	7. 4	H6	D12	Dragon
19. 5	8. 4	H6	E1	Badger
20. 5	9. 4	H6	F2	Hare
21. 5	10. 4	H6	G3	Fox
22. 5	11. 4	H6	H4	Tiger
23. 5	12. 4	H6	J5	Leopard
24. 5	13. 4	H6	K6	Griffon
25. 5	14. 4	H6	A7	Ox
26. 5	15. 4	H6	B8	Bat
27. 5	16. 4	H6	C9	Rat
28. 5	17. 4	H6	D10	Swallow
29. 5	18. 4	H6	E11	Pig
30. 5	19. 4	H6	F12	Porcupine
31. 5	20. 4	H6	G1	Wolf
1. 6	21. 4	H6	H2	Dog
2. 6	22. 4	H6	J3	Pheasant
3. 6	23. 4	H6	K4	Cock
4. 6	24. 4	H6	A5	Crow
5. 6	25. 4	H6	B6	Monkey
6. 6	26. 4	H6	C7	Gibbon
7. 6	27. 4	H6	D8	Tapir
8. 6	28. 4	H6	E9	Sheep
9. 6	29. 4	H6	F10	Deer
10. 6	1. 5	J7	G11	Horse
11. 6	2. 5	J7	H12	Stag
12. 6	3. 5	J7	J1	Serpent
13. 6	4. 5	J7	K2	Earthworm
14. 6	5. 5	J7	A3	Crocodile
15. 6	6. 5	J7	B4	Dragon
16. 6	7. 5	J7	C5	Badger
17. 6	8. 5	J7	D6	Hare
18. 6	9. 5	J7	E7	Fox
19. 6	10. 5	J7	F8	Tiger
20. 6	11. 5	J7	G9	Leopard
21. 6	12. 5	J7	H10	Griffon
22. 6	13. 5	J7	J11	Ox
23. 6	14. 5	J7	K12	Bat
24. 6	15. 5	J7	A1	Rat
25. 6	16. 5	J7	B2	Swallow
26. 6	17. 5	J7	C3	Pig
27. 6	18. 5	J7	D4	Porcupine
28. 6	19. 5	J7	E5	Wolf
29. 6	20. 5	J7	F6	Dog
30. 6	21. 5	J7	G7	Pheasant
1. 7	22. 5	J7	H8	Cock
2. 7	23. 5	J7	J9	Crow
3. 7	24. 5	J7	K10	Monkey
4. 7	25. 5	J7	A11	Gibbon
5. 7	26. 5	J7	B12	Tapir
6. 7	27. 5	J7	C1	Sheep
7. 7	28. 5	J7	D2	Deer
8. 7	29. 5	J7	E3	Horse
9. 7	1. 6	K8	F4	Stag
10. 7	2. 6	K8	G5	Serpent
11. 7	3. 6	K8	H6	Earthworm
12. 7	4. 6	K8	J7	Crocodile
13. 7	5. 6	K8	K8	Dragon
14. 7	6. 6	K8	A9	Badger
15. 7	7. 6	K8	B10	Hare
16. 7	8. 6	K8	C11	Fox
17. 7	9. 6	K8	D12	Tiger
18. 7	10. 6	K8	E1	Leopard
19. 7	11. 6	K8	F2	Griffon
20. 7	12. 6	K8	G3	Ox
21. 7	13. 6	K8	H4	Bat
22. 7	14. 6	K8	J5	Rat
23. 7	15. 6	K8	K6	Swallow
24. 7	16. 6	K8	A7	Pig
25. 7	17. 6	K8	B8	Porcupine
26. 7	18. 6	K8	C9	Wolf
27. 7	19. 6	K8	D10	Dog
28. 7	20. 6	K8	E11	Pheasant
29. 7	21. 6	K8	F12	Cock
30. 7	22. 6	K8	G1	Crow
31. 7	23. 6	K8	H2	Monkey
1. 8	24. 6	K8	J3	Gibbon
2. 8	25. 6	K8	K4	Tapir
3. 8	26. 6	K8	A5	Sheep
4. 8	27. 6	K8	B6	Deer
5. 8	28. 6	K8	C7	Horse
6. 8	29. 6	K8	D8	Stag
7. 8	30. 6	K8	E9	Serpent
8. 8	1. 7	A9	F10	Earthworm
9. 8	2. 7	A9	G11	Crocodile
10. 8	3. 7	A9	H12	Dragon
11. 8	4. 7	A9	J1	Badger
12. 8	5. 7	A9	K2	Hare
13. 8	6. 7	A9	A3	Fox
14. 8	7. 7	A9	B4	Tiger
15. 8	8. 7	A9	C5	Leopard
16. 8	9. 7	A9	D6	Griffon
17. 8	10. 7	A9	E7	Ox
18. 8	11. 7	A9	F8	Bat
19. 8	12. 7	A9	G9	Rat
20. 8	13. 7	A9	H10	Swallow
21. 8	14. 7	A9	J11	Pig
22. 8	15. 7	A9	K12	Porcupine
23. 8	16. 7	A9	A1	Wolf
24. 8	17. 7	A9	B2	Dog
25. 8	18. 7	A9	C3	Pheasant
26. 8	19. 7	A9	D4	Cock
27. 8	20. 7	A9	E5	Crow
28. 8	21. 7	A9	F6	Monkey
29. 8	22. 7	A9	G7	Gibbon
30. 8	23. 7	A9	H8	Tapir
31. 8	24. 7	A9	J9	Sheep
1. 9	25. 7	A9	K10	Deer
2. 9	26. 7	A9	A11	Horse
3. 9	27. 7	A9	B12	Stag
4. 9	28. 7	A9	C1	Serpent
5. 9	29. 7	A9	D2	Earthworm
6. 9	1. 8	B10	E3	Crocodile
7. 9	2. 8	B10	F4	Dragon
8. 9	3. 8	B10	G5	Badger
9. 9	4. 8	B10	H6	Hare
10. 9	5. 8	B10	J7	Fox
11. 9	6. 8	B10	K8	Tiger
12. 9	7. 8	B10	A9	Leopard
13. 9	8. 8	B10	B10	Griffon
14. 9	9. 8	B10	C11	Ox
15. 9	10. 8	B10	D12	Bat
16. 9	11. 8	B10	E1	Rat
17. 9	12. 8	B10	F2	Swallow
18. 9	13. 8	B10	G3	Pig
19. 9	14. 8	B10	H4	Porcupine
20. 9	15. 8	B10	J5	Wolf

Solar date	*Lunar date*	*Month HS/EB*	*Day HS/EB*	*Constellation*
21. 9	16. 8	B10	K6	Dog
22. 9	17. 8	B10	A7	Pheasant
23. 9	18. 8	B10	B8	Cock
24. 9	19. 8	B10	C9	Crow
25. 9	20. 8	B10	D10	Monkey
26. 9	21. 8	B10	E11	Gibbon
27. 9	22. 8	B10	F12	Tapir
28. 9	23. 8	B10	G1	Sheep
29. 9	24. 8	B10	H2	Deer
30. 9	25. 8	B10	J3	Horse
1.10	26. 8	B10	K4	Stag
2.10	27. 8	B10	A5	Serpent
3.10	28. 8	B10	B6	Earthworm
4.10	29. 8	B10	C7	Crocodile
5.10	30. 8	B10	D8	Dragon
6.10	1. 9	C11	E9	Badger
7.10	2. 9	C11	F10	Hare
8.10	3. 9	C11	G11	Fox
9.10	4. 9	C11	H12	Tiger
10.10	5. 9	C11	J1	Leopard
11.10	6. 9	C11	K2	Griffon
12.10	7. 9	C11	A3	Ox
13.10	8. 9	C11	B4	Bat
14.10	9. 9	C11	C5	Rat
15.10	10. 9	C11	D6	Swallow
16.10	11. 9	C11	E7	Pig
17.10	12. 9	C11	F8	Porcupine
18.10	13. 9	C11	G9	Wolf
19.10	14. 9	C11	H10	Dog
20.10	15. 9	C11	J11	Pheasant
21.10	16. 9	C11	K12	Cock
22.10	17. 9	C11	A1	Crow
23.10	18. 9	C11	B2	Monkey
24.10	19. 9	C11	C3	Gibbon
25.10	20. 9	C11	D4	Tapir
26.10	21. 9	C11	E5	Sheep
27.10	22. 9	C11	F6	Deer
28.10	23. 9	C11	G7	Horse
29.10	24. 9	C11	H8	Stag
30.10	25. 9	C11	J9	Serpent
31.10	26. 9	C11	K10	Earthworm
1.11	27. 9	C11	A11	Crocodile
2.11	28. 9	C11	B12	Dragon
3.11	29. 9	C11	C1	Badger
4.11	30. 9	C11	D2	Hare
5.11	1.10	D12	E3	Fox
6.11	2.10	D12	F4	Tiger
7.11	3.10	D12	G5	Leopard
8.11	4.10	D12	H6	Griffon
9.11	5.10	D12	J7	Ox
10.11	6.10	D12	K8	Bat
11.11	7.10	D12	A9	Rat
12.11	8.10	D12	B10	Swallow
13.11	9.10	D12	C11	Pig
14.11	10.10	D12	D12	Porcupine
15.11	11.10	D12	E1	Wolf
16.11	12.10	D12	F2	Dog
17.11	13.10	D12	G3	Pheasant
18.11	14.10	D12	H4	Cock
19.11	15.10	D12	J5	Crow
20.11	16.10	D12	K6	Monkey
21.11	17.10	D12	A7	Gibbon
22.11	18.10	D12	B8	Tapir
23.11	19.10	D12	C9	Sheep
24.11	20.10	D12	D10	Deer
25.11	21.10	D12	E11	Horse
26.11	22.10	D12	F12	Stag
27.11	23.10	D12	G1	Serpent

Solar date	*Lunar date*	*Month HS/EB*	*Day HS/EB*	*Constellation*
28.11	24.10	D12	H2	Earthworm
29.11	25.10	D12	J3	Crocodile
30.11	26.10	D12	K4	Dragon
1.12	27.10	D12	A5	Badger
2.12	28.10	D12	B6	Hare
3.12	29.10	D12	C7	Fox
4.12	30.10	D12	D8	Tiger
5.12	1.11	E1	E9	Leopard
6.12	2.11	E1	F10	Griffon
7.12	3.11	E1	G11	Ox
8.12	4.11	E1	H12	Bat
9.12	5.11	E1	J1	Rat
10.12	6.11	E1	K2	Swallow
11.12	7.11	E1	A3	Pig
12.12	8.11	E1	B4	Porcupine
13.12	9.11	E1	C5	Wolf
14.12	10.11	E1	D6	Dog
15.12	11.11	E1	E7	Pheasant
16.12	12.11	E1	F8	Cock
17.12	13.11	E1	G9	Crow
18.12	14.11	E1	H10	Monkey
19.12	15.11	E1	J11	Gibbon
20.12	16.11	E1	K12	Tapir
21.12	17.11	E1	A1	Sheep
22.12	18.11	E1	B2	Deer
23.12	19.11	E1	C3	Horse
24.12	20.11	E1	D4	Stag
25.12	21.11	E1	E5	Serpent
26.12	22.11	E1	F6	Earthworm
27.12	23.11	E1	G7	Crocodile
28.12	24.11	E1	H8	Dragon
29.12	25.11	E1	J9	Badger
30.12	26.11	E1	K10	Hare
31.12	27.11	E1	A11	Fox
1946				
1. 1	28.11	E1	B12	Tiger
2. 1	29.11	E1	C1	Leopard
3. 1	1.12	F2	D2	Griffon
4. 1	2.12	F2	E3	Ox
5. 1	3.12	F2	F4	Bat
6. 1	4.12	F2	G5	Rat
7. 1	5.12	F2	H6	Swallow
8. 1	6.12	F2	J7	Pig
9. 1	7.12	F2	K8	Porcupine
10. 1	8.12	F2	A9	Wolf
11. 1	9.12	F2	B10	Dog
12. 1	10.12	F2	C11	Pheasant
13. 1	11.12	F2	D12	Cock
14. 1	12.12	F2	E1	Crow
15. 1	13.12	F2	F2	Monkey
16. 1	14.12	F2	G3	Gibbon
17. 1	15.12	F2	H4	Tapir
18. 1	16.12	F2	J5	Sheep
19. 1	17.12	F2	K6	Deer
20. 1	18.12	F2	A7	Horse
21. 1	19.12	F2	B8	Stag
22. 1	20.12	F2	C9	Serpent
23. 1	21.12	F2	D10	Earthworm
24. 1	22.12	F2	E11	Crocodile
25. 1	23.12	F2	F12	Dragon
26. 1	24.12	F2	G1	Badger
27. 1	25.12	F2	H2	Hare
28. 1	26.12	F2	J3	Fox
29. 1	27.12	F2	K4	Tiger
30. 1	28.12	F2	A5	Leopard
31. 1	29.12	F2	B6	Griffon
1. 2	30.12	F2	C7	Ox

PING HSÜ YEAR

Solar date	*Lunar date*	*Month HS/EB*	*Day HS/EB*	*Constellation*
2. 2	1. 1	G3	D8	Bat
3. 2	2. 1	G3	E9	Rat
4. 2	3. 1	G3	F10	Swallow
5. 2	4. 1	G3	G11	Pig
6. 2	5. 1	G3	H12	Porcupine
7. 2	6. 1	G3	J1	Wolf
8. 2	7. 1	G3	K2	Dog
9. 2	8. 1	G3	A3	Pheasant
10. 2	9. 1	G3	B4	Cock
11. 2	10. 1	G3	C5	Crow
12. 2	11. 1	G3	D6	Monkey
13. 2	12. 1	G3	E7	Gibbon
14. 2	13. 1	G3	F8	Tapir
15. 2	14. 1	G3	G9	Sheep
16. 2	15. 1	G3	H10	Deer
17. 2	16. 1	G3	J11	Horse
18. 2	17. 1	G3	K12	Stag
19. 2	18. 1	G3	A1	Serpent
20. 2	19. 1	G3	B2	Earthworm
21. 2	20. 1	G3	C3	Crocodile
22. 2	21. 1	G3	D4	Dragon
23. 2	22. 1	G3	E5	Badger
24. 2	23. 1	G3	F6	Hare
25. 2	24. 1	G3	G7	Fox
26. 2	25. 1	G3	H8	Tiger
27. 2	26. 1	G3	J9	Leopard
28. 2	27. 1	G3	K10	Griffon
1. 3	28. 1	G3	A11	Ox
2. 3	29. 1	G3	B12	Bat
3. 3	30. 1	G3	C1	Rat
4. 3	1. 2	H4	D2	Swallow
5. 3	2. 2	H4	E3	Pig
6. 3	3. 2	H4	F4	Porcupine
7. 3	4. 2	H4	G5	Wolf
8. 3	5. 2	H4	H6	Dog
9. 3	6. 2	H4	J7	Pheasant
10. 3	7. 2	H4	K8	Cock
11. 3	8. 2	H4	A9	Crow
12. 3	9. 2	H4	B10	Monkey
13. 3	10. 2	H4	C11	Gibbon
14. 3	11. 2	H4	D12	Tapir
15. 3	12. 2	H4	E1	Sheep
16. 3	13. 2	H4	F2	Deer
17. 3	14. 2	H4	G3	Horse
18. 3	15. 2	H4	H4	Stag
19. 3	16. 2	H4	J5	Serpent
20. 3	17. 2	H4	K6	Earthworm
21. 3	18. 2	H4	A7	Crocodile
22. 3	19. 2	H4	B8	Dragon
23. 3	20. 2	H4	C9	Badger
24. 3	21. 2	H4	D10	Hare
25. 3	22. 2	H4	E11	Fox
26. 3	23. 2	H4	F12	Tiger
27. 3	24. 2	H4	G1	Leopard
28. 3	25. 2	H4	H2	Griffon
29. 3	26. 2	H4	J3	Ox
30. 3	27. 2	H4	K4	Bat
31. 3	28. 2	H4	A5	Rat
1. 4	29. 2	H4	B6	Swallow
2. 4	1. 3	J5	C7	Pig
3. 4	2. 3	J5	D8	Porcupine
4. 4	3. 3	J5	E9	Wolf
5. 4	4. 3	J5	F10	Dog
6. 4	5. 3	J5	G11	Pheasant
7. 4	6. 3	J5	H12	Cock
8. 4	7. 3	J5	J1	Crow
9. 4	8. 3	J5	K2	Monkey
10. 4	9. 3	J5	A3	Gibbon
11. 4	10. 3	J5	B4	Tapir
12. 4	11. 3	J5	C5	Sheep
13. 4	12. 3	J5	D6	Deer
14. 4	13. 3	J5	E7	Horse
15. 4	14. 3	J5	F8	Stag
16. 4	15. 3	J5	G9	Serpent
17. 4	16. 3	J5	H10	Earthworm
18. 4	17. 3	J5	J11	Crocodile
19. 4	18. 3	J5	K12	Dragon
20. 4	19. 3	J5	A1	Badger
21. 4	20. 3	J5	B2	Hare
22. 4	21. 3	J5	C3	Fox
23. 4	22. 3	J5	D4	Tiger
24. 4	23. 3	J5	E5	Leopard
25. 4	24. 3	J5	F6	Griffon
26. 4	25. 3	J5	G7	Ox
27. 4	26. 3	J5	H8	Bat
28. 4	27. 3	J5	J9	Rat
29. 4	28. 3	J5	K10	Swallow
30. 4	29. 3	J5	A11	Pig
1. 5	1. 4	K6	B12	Porcupine
2. 5	2. 4	K6	C1	Wolf
3. 5	3. 4	K6	D2	Dog
4. 5	4. 4	K6	E3	Pheasant
5. 5	5. 4	K6	F4	Cock
6. 5	6. 4	K6	G5	Crow
7. 5	7. 4	K6	H6	Monkey
8. 5	8. 4	K6	J7	Gibbon
9. 5	9. 4	K6	K8	Tapir
10. 5	10. 4	K6	A9	Sheep
11. 5	11. 4	K6	B10	Deer
12. 5	12. 4	K6	C11	Horse
13. 5	13. 4	K6	D12	Stag
14. 5	14. 4	K6	E1	Serpent
15. 5	15. 4	K6	F2	Earthworm
16. 5	16. 4	K6	G3	Crocodile
17. 5	17. 4	K6	H4	Dragon
18. 5	18. 4	K6	J5	Badger
19. 5	19. 4	K6	K6	Hare
20. 5	20. 4	K6	A7	Fox
21. 5	21. 4	K6	B8	Tiger
22. 5	22. 4	K6	C9	Leopard
23. 5	23. 4	K6	D10	Griffon
24. 5	24. 4	K6	E11	Ox
25. 5	25. 4	K6	F12	Bat
26. 5	26. 4	K6	G1	Rat
27. 5	27. 4	K6	H2	Swallow
28. 5	28. 4	K6	J3	Pig
29. 5	29. 4	K6	K4	Porcupine
30. 5	30. 4	K6	A5	Wolf
31. 5	1. 5	A7	B6	Dog
1. 6	2. 5	A7	C7	Pheasant
2. 6	3. 5	A7	D8	Cock
3. 6	4. 5	A7	E9	Crow
4. 6	5. 5	A7	F10	Monkey
5. 6	6. 5	A7	G11	Gibbon
6. 6	7. 5	A7	H12	Tapir
7. 6	8. 5	A7	J1	Sheep
8. 6	9. 5	A7	K2	Deer
9. 6	10. 5	A7	A3	Horse
10. 6	11. 5	A7	B4	Stag
11. 6	12. 5	A7	C5	Serpent
12. 6	13. 5	A7	D6	Earthworm
13. 6	14. 5	A7	E7	Crocodile
14. 6	15. 5	A7	F8	Dragon
15. 6	16. 5	A7	G9	Badger
16. 6	17. 5	A7	H10	Hare
17. 6	18. 5	A7	J11	Fox
18. 6	19. 5	A7	K12	Tiger
19. 6	20. 5	A7	A1	Leopard
20. 6	21. 5	A7	B2	Griffon
21. 6	22. 5	A7	C3	Ox
22. 6	23. 5	A7	D4	Bat
23. 6	24. 5	A7	E5	Rat

Solar date	*Lunar date*	*Month HS/EB*	*Day HS/EB*	*Constellation*
24. 6	25. 5	A7	F6	Swallow
25. 6	26. 5	A7	G7	Pig
26. 6	27. 5	A7	H8	Porcupine
27. 6	28. 5	A7	J9	Wolf
28. 6	29. 5	A7	K10	Dog
29. 6	1. 6	B8	A11	Pheasant
30. 6	2. 6	B8	B12	Cock
1. 7	3. 6	B8	C1	Crow
2. 7	4. 6	B8	D2	Monkey
3. 7	5. 6	B8	E3	Gibbon
4. 7	6. 6	B8	F4	Tapir
5. 7	7. 6	B8	G5	Sheep
6. 7	8. 6	B8	H6	Deer
7. 7	9. 6	B8	J7	Horse
8. 7	10. 6	B8	K8	Stag
9. 7	11. 6	B8	A9	Serpent
10. 7	12. 6	B8	B10	Earthworm
11. 7	13. 6	B8	C11	Crocodile
12. 7	14. 6	B8	D12	Dragon
13. 7	15. 6	B8	E1	Badger
14. 7	16. 6	B8	F2	Hare
15. 7	17. 6	B8	G3	Fox
16. 7	18. 6	B8	H4	Tiger
17. 7	19. 6	B8	J5	Leopard
18. 7	20. 6	B8	K6	Griffon
19. 7	21. 6	B8	A7	Ox
20. 7	22. 6	B8	B8	Bat
21. 7	23. 6	B8	C9	Rat
22. 7	24. 6	B8	D10	Swallow
23. 7	25. 6	B8	E11	Pig
24. 7	26. 6	B8	F12	Porcupine
25. 7	27. 6	B8	G1	Wolf
26. 7	28. 6	B8	H2	Dog
27. 7	29. 6	B8	J3	Pheasant
28. 7	1. 7	C9	K4	Cock
29. 7	2. 7	C9	A5	Crow
30. 7	3. 7	C9	B6	Monkey
31. 7	4. 7	C9	C7	Gibbon
1. 8	5. 7	C9	D8	Tapir
2. 8	6. 7	C9	E9	Sheep
3. 8	7. 7	C9	F10	Deer
4. 8	8. 7	C9	G11	Horse
5. 8	9. 7	C9	H12	Stag
6. 8	10. 7	C9	J1	Serpent
7. 8	11. 7	C9	K2	Earthworm
8. 8	12. 7	C9	A3	Crocodile
9. 8	13. 7	C9	B4	Dragon
10. 8	14. 7	C9	C5	Badger
11. 8	15. 7	C9	D6	Hare
12. 8	16. 7	C9	E7	Fox
13. 8	17. 7	C9	F8	Tiger
14. 8	18. 7	C9	G9	Leopard
15. 8	19. 7	C9	H10	Griffon
16. 8	20. 7	C9	J11	Ox
17. 8	21. 7	C9	K12	Bat
18. 8	22. 7	C9	A1	Rat
19. 8	23. 7	C9	B2	Swallow
20. 8	24. 7	C9	C3	Pig
21. 8	25. 7	C9	D4	Porcupine
22. 8	26. 7	C9	E5	Wolf
23. 8	27. 7	C9	F6	Dog
24. 8	28. 7	C9	G7	Pheasant
25. 8	29. 7	C9	H8	Cock
26. 8	30. 7	C9	J9	Crow
27. 8	1. 8	D10	K10	Monkey
28. 8	2. 8	D10	A11	Gibbon
29. 8	3. 8	D10	B12	Tapir
30. 8	4. 8	D10	C1	Sheep
31. 8	5. 8	D10	D2	Deer
1. 9	6. 8	D10	E3	Horse
2. 9	7. 8	D10	F4	Stag
3. 9	8. 8	D10	G5	Serpent
4. 9	9. 8	D10	H6	Earthworm
5. 9	10. 8	D10	J7	Crocodile
6. 9	11. 8	D10	K8	Dragon
7. 9	12. 8	D10	A9	Badger
8. 9	13. 8	D10	B10	Hare
9. 9	14. 8	D10	C11	Fox
10. 9	15. 8	D10	D12	Tiger
11. 9	16. 8	D10	E1	Leopard
12. 9	17. 8	D10	F2	Griffon
13. 9	18. 8	D10	G3	Ox
14. 9	19. 8	D10	H4	Bat
15. 9	20. 8	D10	J5	Rat
16. 9	21. 8	D10	K6	Swallow
17. 9	22. 8	D10	A7	Pig
18. 9	23. 8	D10	B8	Porcupine
19. 9	24. 8	D10	C9	Wolf
20. 9	25. 8	D10	D10	Dog
21. 9	26. 8	D10	E11	Pheasant
22. 9	27. 8	D10	F12	Cock
23. 9	28. 8	D10	G1	Crow
24. 9	29. 8	D10	H2	Monkey
25. 9	1. 9	E11	J3	Gibbon
26. 9	2. 9	E11	K4	Tapir
27. 9	3. 9	E11	A5	Sheep
28. 9	4. 9	E11	B6	Deer
29. 9	5. 9	E11	C7	Horse
30. 9	6. 9	E11	D8	Stag
1.10	7. 9	E11	E9	Serpent
2.10	8. 9	E11	F10	Earthworm
3.10	9. 9	E11	G11	Crocodile
4.10	10. 9	E11	H12	Dragon
5.10	11. 9	E11	J1	Badger
6.10	12. 9	E11	K2	Hare
7.10	13. 9	E11	A3	Fox
8.10	14. 9	E11	B4	Tiger
9.10	15. 9	E11	C5	Leopard
10.10	16. 9	E11	D6	Griffon
11.10	17. 9	E11	E7	Ox
12.10	18. 9	E11	F8	Bat
13.10	19. 9	E11	G9	Rat
14.10	20. 9	E11	H10	Swallow
15.10	21. 9	E11	J11	Pig
16.10	22. 9	E11	K12	Porcupine
17.10	23. 9	E11	A1	Wolf
18.10	24. 9	E11	B2	Dog
19.10	25. 9	E11	C3	Pheasant
20.10	26. 9	E11	D4	Cock
21.10	27. 9	E11	E5	Crow
22.10	28. 9	E11	F6	Monkey
23.10	29. 9	E11	G7	Gibbon
24.10	30. 9	E11	H8	Tapir
25.10	1.10	F12	J9	Sheep
26.10	2.10	F12	K10	Deer
27.10	3.10	F12	A11	Horse
28.10	4.10	F12	B12	Stag
29.10	5.10	F12	C1	Serpent
30.10	6.10	F12	D2	Earthworm
31.10	7.10	F12	E3	Crocodile
1.11	8.10	F12	F4	Dragon
2.11	9.10	F12	G5	Badger
3.11	10.10	F12	H6	Hare
4.11	11.10	F12	J7	Fox
5.11	12.10	F12	K8	Tiger
6.11	13.10	F12	A9	Leopard
7.11	14.10	F12	B10	Griffon
8.11	15.10	F12	C11	Ox
9.11	16.10	F12	D12	Bat
10.11	17.10	F12	E1	Rat
11.11	18.10	F12	F2	Swallow
12.11	19.10	F12	G3	Pig
13.11	20.10	F12	H4	Porcupine
14.11	21.10	F12	J5	Wolf
15.11	22.10	F12	K6	Dog
16.11	23.10	F12	A7	Pheasant

Solar date	*Lunar date*	*Month HS/EB*	*Day HS/EB*	*Constellation*
17.11	24.10	F12	B8	Cock
18.11	25.10	F12	C9	Crow
19.11	26.10	F12	D10	Monkey
20.11	27.10	F12	E11	Gibbon
21.11	28.10	F12	F12	Tapir
22.11	29.10	F12	G1	Sheep
23.11	30.10	F12	H2	Deer
24.11	1.11	G1	J3	Horse
25.11	2.11	G1	K4	Stag
26.11	3.11	G1	A5	Serpent
27.11	4.11	G1	B6	Earthworm
28.11	5.11	G1	C7	Crocodile
29.11	6.11	G1	D8	Dragon
30.11	7.11	G1	E9	Badger
1.12	8.11	G1	F10	Hare
2.12	9.11	G1	G11	Fox
3.12	10.11	G1	H12	Tiger
4.12	11.11	G1	J1	Leopard
5.12	12.11	G1	K2	Griffon
6.12	13.11	G1	A3	Ox
7.12	14.11	G1	B4	Bat
8.12	15.11	G1	C5	Rat
9.12	16.11	G1	D6	Swallow
10.12	17.11	G1	E7	Pig
11.12	18.11	G1	F8	Porcupine
12.12	19.11	G1	G9	Wolf
13.12	20.11	G1	H10	Dog
14.12	21.11	G1	J11	Pheasant
15.12	22.11	G1	K12	Cock
16.12	23.11	G1	A1	Crow
17.12	24.11	G1	B2	Monkey
18.12	25.11	G1	C3	Gibbon
19.12	26.11	G1	D4	Tapir
20.12	27.11	G1	E5	Sheep
21.12	28.11	G1	F6	Deer
22.12	29.11	G1	G7	Horse
23.12	1.12	H2	H8	Stag
24.12	2.12	H2	J9	Serpent
25.12	3.12	H2	K10	Earthworm
26.12	4.12	H2	A11	Crocodile
27.12	5.12	H2	B12	Dragon
28.12	6.12	H2	C1	Badger
29.12	7.12	H2	D2	Hare
30.12	8.12	H2	E3	Fox
31.12	9.12	H2	F4	Tiger
1947				
1. 1	10.12	H2	G5	Leopard
2. 1	11.12	H2	H6	Griffon
3. 1	12.12	H2	J7	Ox
4. 1	13.12	H2	K8	Bat
5. 1	14.12	H2	A9	Rat
6. 1	15.12	H2	B10	Swallow
7. 1	16.12	H2	C11	Pig
8. 1	17.12	H2	D12	Porcupine
9. 1	18.12	H2	E1	Wolf
10. 1	19.12	H2	F2	Dog
11. 1	20.12	H2	G3	Pheasant
12. 1	21.12	H2	H4	Cock
13. 1	22.12	H2	J5	Crow
14. 1	23.12	H2	K6	Monkey
15. 1	24.12	H2	A7	Gibbon
16. 1	25.12	H2	B8	Tapir
17. 1	26.12	H2	C9	Sheep
18. 1	27.12	H2	D10	Deer
19. 1	28.12	H2	E11	Horse
20. 1	29.12	H2	F12	Stag
21. 1	30.12	H2	G1	Serpent

TING HAI YEAR

22. 1	1. 1	J3	H2	Earthworm
23. 1	2. 1	J3	J3	Crocodile
24. 1	3. 1	J3	K4	Dragon
25. 1	4. 1	J3	A5	Badger
26. 1	5. 1	J3	B6	Hare
27. 1	6. 1	J3	C7	Fox
28. 1	7. 1	J3	D8	Tiger
29. 1	8. 1	J3	E9	Leopard
30. 1	9. 1	J3	F10	Griffon
31. 1	10. 1	J3	G11	Ox
1. 2	11. 1	J3	H12	Bat
2. 2	12. 1	J3	J1	Rat
3. 2	13. 1	J3	K2	Swallow
4. 2	14. 1	J3	A3	Pig
5. 2	15. 1	J3	B4	Porcupine
6. 2	16. 1	J3	C5	Wolf
7. 2	17. 1	J3	D6	Dog
8. 2	18. 1	J3	E7	Pheasant
9. 2	19. 1	J3	F8	Cock
10. 2	20. 1	J3	G9	Crow
11. 2	21. 1	J3	H10	Monkey
12. 2	22. 1	J3	J11	Gibbon
13. 2	23. 1	J3	K12	Tapir
14. 2	24. 1	J3	A1	Sheep
15. 2	25. 1	J3	B2	Deer
16. 2	26. 1	J3	C3	Horse
17. 2	27. 1	J3	D4	Stag
18. 2	28. 1	J3	E5	Serpent
19. 2	29. 1	J3	F6	Earthworm
20. 2	30. 1	J3	G7	Crocodile
21. 2	1. 2	K4	H8	Dragon
22. 2	2. 2	K4	J9	Badger
23. 2	3. 2	K4	K10	Hare
24. 2	4. 2	K4	A11	Fox
25. 2	5. 2	K4	B12	Tiger
26. 2	6. 2	K4	C1	Leopard
27. 2	7. 2	K4	D2	Griffon
28. 2	8. 2	K4	E3	Ox
1. 3	9. 2	K4	F4	Bat
2. 3	10. 2	K4	G5	Rat
3. 3	11. 2	K4	H6	Swallow
4. 3	12. 2	K4	J7	Pig
5. 3	13. 2	K4	K8	Porcupine
6. 3	14. 2	K4	A9	Wolf
7. 3	15. 2	K4	B10	Dog
8. 3	16. 2	K4	C11	Pheasant
9. 3	17. 2	K4	D12	Cock
10. 3	18. 2	K4	E1	Crow
11. 3	19. 2	K4	F2	Monkey
12. 3	20. 2	K4	G3	Gibbon
13. 3	21. 2	K4	H4	Tapir
14. 3	22. 2	K4	J5	Sheep
15. 3	23. 2	K4	K6	Deer
16. 3	24. 2	K4	A7	Horse
17. 3	25. 2	K4	B8	Stag
18. 3	26. 2	K4	C9	Serpent
19. 3	27. 2	K4	D10	Earthworm
20. 3	28. 2	K4	E11	Crocodile
21. 3	29. 2	K4	F12	Dragon
22. 3	30. 2	K4	G1	Badger
23. 3	*1. 2*	*K4*	H2	Hare
24. 3	*2. 2*	*K4*	J3	Fox
25. 3	*3. 2*	*K4*	K4	Tiger
26. 3	*4. 2*	*K4*	A5	Leopard
27. 3	*5. 2*	*K4*	B6	Griffon
28. 3	*6. 2*	*K4*	C7	Ox
29. 3	*7. 2*	*K4*	D8	Bat
30. 3	*8. 2*	*K4*	E9	Rat

Solar date	Lunar date	Month HS/EB	Day HS/EB	Constellation
31. 3	*9. 2*	*K4*	F10	Swallow
1. 4	*10. 2*	*K4*	G11	Pig
2. 4	*11. 2*	*K4*	H12	Porcupine
3. 4	*12. 2*	*K4*	J1	Wolf
4. 4	*13. 2*	*K4*	K2	Dog
5. 4	*14. 2*	*K4*	A3	Pheasant
6. 4	*15. 2*	*K4*	B4	Cock
7. 4	*16. 2*	*K4*	C5	Crow
8. 4	*17. 2*	*K4*	D6	Monkey
9. 4	*18. 2*	*K4*	E7	Gibbon
10. 4	*19. 2*	*K4*	F8	Tapir
11. 4	*20. 2*	*K4*	G9	Sheep
12. 4	*21. 2*	*K4*	H10	Deer
13. 4	*22. 2*	*K4*	J11	Horse
14. 4	*23. 2*	*K4*	K12	Stag
15. 4	*24. 2*	*K4*	A1	Serpent
16. 4	*25. 2*	*K4*	B2	Earthworm
17. 4	*26. 2*	*K4*	C3	Crocodile
18. 4	*27. 2*	*K4*	D4	Dragon
19. 4	*28. 2*	*K4*	E5	Badger
20. 4	*29. 2*	*K4*	F6	Hare
21. 4	1. 3	A5	G7	Fox
22. 4	2. 3	A5	H8	Tiger
23. 4	3. 3	A5	J9	Leopard
24. 4	4. 3	A5	K10	Griffon
25. 4	5. 3	A5	A11	Ox
26. 4	6. 3	A5	B12	Bat
27. 4	7. 3	A5	C1	Rat
28. 4	8. 3	A5	D2	Swallow
29. 4	9. 3	A5	E3	Pig
30. 4	10. 3	A5	F4	Porcupine
1. 5	11. 3	A5	G5	Wolf
2. 5	12. 3	A5	H6	Dog
3. 5	13. 3	A5	J7	Pheasant
4. 5	14. 3	A5	K8	Cock
5. 5	15. 3	A5	A9	Crow
6. 5	16. 3	A5	B10	Monkey
7. 5	17. 3	A5	C11	Gibbon
8. 5	18. 3	A5	D12	Tapir
9. 5	19. 3	A5	E1	Sheep
10. 5	20. 3	A5	F2	Deer
11. 5	21. 3	A5	G3	Horse
12. 5	22. 3	A5	H4	Stag
13. 5	23. 3	A5	J5	Serpent
14. 5	24. 3	A5	K6	Earthworm
15. 5	25. 3	A5	A7	Crocodile
16. 5	26. 3	A5	B8	Dragon
17. 5	27. 3	A5	C9	Badger
18. 5	28. 3	A5	D10	Hare
19. 5	29. 3	A5	E11	Fox
20. 5	1. 4	B6	F12	Tiger
21. 5	2. 4	B6	G1	Leopard
22. 5	3. 4	B6	H2	Griffon
23. 5	4. 4	B6	J3	Ox
24. 5	5. 4	B6	K4	Bat
25. 5	6. 4	B6	A5	Rat
26. 5	7. 4	B6	B6	Swallow
27. 5	8. 4	B6	C7	Pig
28. 5	9. 4	B6	D8	Porcupine
29. 5	10. 4	B6	E9	Wolf
30. 5	11. 4	B6	F10	Dog
31. 5	12. 4	B6	G11	Pheasant
1. 6	13. 4	B6	H12	Cock
2. 6	14. 4	B6	J1	Crow
3. 6	15. 4	B6	K2	Monkey
4. 6	16. 4	B6	A3	Gibbon
5. 6	17. 4	B6	B4	Tapir
6. 6	18. 4	B6	C5	Sheep
7. 6	19. 4	B6	D6	Deer
8. 6	20. 4	B6	E7	Horse
9. 6	21. 4	B6	F8	Stag
10. 6	22. 4	B6	G9	Serpent
11. 6	23. 4	B6	H10	Earthworm

Solar date	Lunar date	Month HS/EB	Day HS/EB	Constellation
12. 6	24. 4	B6	J11	Crocodile
13. 6	25. 4	B6	K12	Dragon
14. 6	26. 4	B6	A1	Badger
15. 6	27. 4	B6	B2	Hare
16. 6	28. 4	B6	C3	Fox
17. 6	29. 4	B6	D4	Tiger
18. 6	30. 4	B6	E5	Leopard
19. 6	1. 5	C7	F6	Griffon
20. 6	2. 5	C7	G7	Ox
21. 6	3. 5	C7	H8	Bat
22. 6	4. 5	C7	J9	Rat
23. 6	5. 5	C7	K10	Swallow
24. 6	6. 5	C7	A11	Pig
25. 6	7. 5	C7	B12	Porcupine
26. 6	8. 5	C7	C1	Wolf
27. 6	9. 5	C7	D2	Dog
28. 6	10. 5	C7	E3	Pheasant
29. 6	11. 5	C7	F4	Cock
30. 6	12. 5	C7	G5	Crow
1. 7	13. 5	C7	H6	Monkey
2. 7	14. 5	C7	J7	Gibbon
3. 7	15. 5	C7	K8	Tapir
4. 7	16. 5	C7	A9	Sheep
5. 7	17. 5	C7	B10	Deer
6. 7	18. 5	C7	C11	Horse
7. 7	19. 5	C7	D12	Stag
8. 7	20. 5	C7	E1	Serpent
9. 7	21. 5	C7	F2	Earthworm
10. 7	22. 5	C7	G3	Crocodile
11. 7	23. 5	C7	H4	Dragon
12. 7	24. 5	C7	J5	Badger
13. 7	25. 5	C7	K6	Hare
14. 7	26. 5	C7	A7	Fox
15. 7	27. 5	C7	B8	Tiger
16. 7	28. 5	C7	C9	Leopard
17. 7	29. 5	C7	D10	Griffon
18. 7	1. 6	D8	E11	Ox
19. 7	2. 6	D8	F12	Bat
20. 7	3. 6	D8	G1	Rat
21. 7	4. 6	D8	H2	Swallow
22. 7	5. 6	D8	J3	Pig
23. 7	6. 6	D8	K4	Porcupine
24. 7	7. 6	D8	A5	Wolf
25. 7	8. 6	D8	B6	Dog
26. 7	9. 6	D8	C7	Pheasant
27. 7	10. 6	D8	D8	Cock
28. 7	11. 6	D8	E9	Crow
29. 7	12. 6	D8	F10	Monkey
30. 7	13. 6	D8	G11	Gibbon
31. 7	14. 6	D8	H12	Tapir
1. 8	15. 6	D8	J1	Sheep
2. 8	16. 6	D8	K2	Deer
3. 8	17. 6	D8	A3	Horse
4. 8	18. 6	D8	B4	Stag
5. 8	19. 6	D8	C5	Serpent
6. 8	20. 6	D8	D6	Earthworm
7. 8	21. 6	D8	E7	Crocodile
8. 8	22. 6	D8	F8	Dragon
9. 8	23. 6	D8	G9	Badger
10. 8	24. 6	D8	H10	Hare
11. 8	25. 6	D8	J11	Fox
12. 8	26. 6	D8	K12	Tiger
13. 8	27. 6	D8	A1	Leopard
14. 8	28. 6	D8	B2	Griffon
15. 8	29. 6	D8	C3	Ox
16. 8	1. 7	E9	D4	Bat
17. 8	2. 7	E9	E5	Rat
18. 8	3. 7	E9	F6	Swallow
19. 8	4. 7	E9	G7	Pig
20. 8	5. 7	E9	H8	Porcupine
21. 8	6. 7	E9	J9	Wolf
22. 8	7. 7	E9	K10	Dog
23. 8	8. 7	E9	A11	Pheasant

Solar date	*Lunar date*	*Month HS/EB*	*Day HS/EB*	*Constellation*
24. 8	9. 7	E9	B12	Cock
25. 8	10. 7	E9	C1	Crow
26. 8	11. 7	E9	D2	Monkey
27. 8	12. 7	E9	E3	Gibbon
28. 8	13. 7	E9	F4	Tapir
29. 8	14. 7	E9	G5	Sheep
30. 8	15. 7	E9	H6	Deer
31. 8	16. 7	E9	J7	Horse
1. 9	17. 7	E9	K8	Stag
2. 9	18. 7	E9	A9	Serpent
3. 9	19. 7	E9	B10	Earthworm
4. 9	20. 7	E9	C11	Crocodile
5. 9	21. 7	E9	D12	Dragon
6. 9	22. 7	E9	E1	Badger
7. 9	23. 7	E9	F2	Hare
8. 9	24. 7	E9	G3	Fox
9. 9	25. 7	E9	H4	Tiger
10. 9	26. 7	E9	J5	Leopard
11. 9	27. 7	E9	K6	Griffon
12. 9	28. 7	E9	A7	Ox
13. 9	29. 7	E9	B8	Bat
14. 9	30. 7	E9	C9	Rat
15. 9	1. 8	F10	D10	Swallow
16. 9	2. 8	F10	E11	Pig
17. 9	3. 8	F10	F12	Porcupine
18. 9	4. 8	F10	G1	Wolf
19. 9	5. 8	F10	H2	Dog
20. 9	6. 8	F10	J3	Pheasant
21. 9	7. 8	F10	K4	Cock
22. 9	8. 8	F10	A5	Crow
23. 9	9. 8	F10	B6	Monkey
24. 9	10. 8	F10	C7	Gibbon
25. 9	11. 8	F10	D8	Tapir
26. 9	12. 8	F10	E9	Sheep
27. 9	13. 8	F10	F10	Deer
28. 9	14. 8	F10	G11	Horse
29. 9	15. 8	F10	H12	Stag
30. 9	16. 8	F10	J1	Serpent
1.10	17. 8	F10	K2	Earthworm
2.10	18. 8	F10	A3	Crocodile
3.10	19. 8	F10	B4	Dragon
4.10	20. 8	F10	C5	Badger
5.10	21. 8	F10	D6	Hare
6.10	22. 8	F10	E7	Fox
7.10	23. 8	F10	F8	Tiger
8.10	24. 8	F10	G9	Leopard
9.10	25. 8	F10	H10	Griffon
10.10	26. 8	F10	J11	Ox
11.10	27. 8	F10	K12	Bat
12.10	28. 8	F10	A1	Rat
13.10	29. 8	F10	B2	Swallow
14.10	1. 9	G11	C3	Pig
15.10	2. 9	G11	D4	Porcupine
16.10	3. 9	G11	E5	Wolf
17.10	4. 9	G11	F6	Dog
18.10	5. 9	G11	G7	Pheasant
19.10	6. 9	G11	H8	Cock
20.10	7. 9	G11	J9	Crow
21.10	8. 9	G11	K10	Monkey
22.10	9. 9	G11	A11	Gibbon
23.10	10. 9	G11	B12	Tapir
24.10	11. 9	G11	C1	Sheep
25.10	12. 9	G11	D2	Deer
26.10	13. 9	G11	E3	Horse
27.10	14. 9	G11	F4	Stag
28.10	15. 9	G11	G5	Serpent
29.10	16. 9	G11	H6	Earthworm
30.10	17. 9	G11	J7	Crocodile
31.10	18. 9	G11	K8	Dragon
1.11	19. 9	G11	A9	Badger
2.11	20. 9	G11	B10	Hare
3.11	21. 9	G11	C11	Fox
4.11	22. 9	G11	D12	Tiger
5.11	23. 9	G11	E1	Leopard
6.11	24. 9	G11	F2	Griffon
7.11	25. 9	G11	G3	Ox
8.11	26. 9	G11	H4	Bat
9.11	27. 9	G11	J5	Rat
10.11	28. 9	G11	K6	Swallow
11.11	29. 9	G11	A7	Pig
12.11	30. 9	G11	B8	Porcupine
13.11	1.10	H12	C9	Wolf
14.11	2.10	H12	D10	Dog
15.11	3.10	H12	E11	Pheasant
16.11	4.10	H12	F12	Cock
17.11	5.10	H12	G1	Crow
18.11	6.10	H12	H2	Monkey
19.11	7.10	H12	J3	Gibbon
20.11	8.10	H12	K4	Tapir
21.11	9.10	H12	A5	Sheep
22.11	10.10	H12	B6	Deer
23.11	11.10	H12	C7	Horse
24.11	12.10	H12	D8	Stag
25.11	13.10	H12	E9	Serpent
26.11	14.10	H12	F10	Earthworm
27.11	15.10	H12	G11	Crocodile
28.11	16.10	H12	H12	Dragon
29.11	17.10	H12	J1	Badger
30.11	18.10	H12	K2	Hare
1.12	19.10	H12	A3	Fox
2.12	20.10	H12	B4	Tiger
3.12	21.10	H12	C5	Leopard
4.12	22.10	H12	D6	Griffon
5.12	23.10	H12	E7	Ox
6.12	24.10	H12	F8	Bat
7.12	25.10	H12	G9	Rat
8.12	26.10	H12	H10	Swallow
9.12	27.10	H12	J11	Pig
10.12	28.10	H12	K12	Porcupine
11.12	29.10	H12	A1	Wolf
12.12	1.11	J1	B2	Dog
13.12	2.11	J1	C3	Pheasant
14.12	3.11	J1	D4	Cock
15.12	4.11	J1	E5	Crow
16.12	5.11	J1	F6	Monkey
17.12	6.11	J1	G7	Gibbon
18.12	7.11	J1	H8	Tapir
19.12	8.11	J1	J9	Sheep
20.12	9.11	J1	K10	Deer
21.12	10.11	J1	A11	Horse
22.12	11.11	J1	B12	Stag
23.12	12.11	J1	C1	Serpent
24.12	13.11	J1	D2	Earthworm
25.12	14.11	J1	E3	Crocodile
26.12	15.11	J1	F4	Dragon
27.12	16.11	J1	G5	Badger
28.12	17.11	J1	H6	Hare
29.12	18.11	J1	J7	Fox
30.12	19.11	J1	K8	Tiger
31.12	20.11	J1	A9	Leopard
1948				
1. 1	21.11	J1	B10	Griffon
2. 1	22.11	J1	C11	Ox
3. 1	23.11	J1	D12	Bat
4. 1	24.11	J1	E1	Rat
5. 1	25.11	J1	F2	Swallow
6. 1	26.11	J1	G3	Pig
7. 1	27.11	J1	H4	Porcupine
8. 1	28.11	J1	J5	Wolf
9. 1	29.11	J1	K6	Dog
10. 1	30.11	J1	A7	Pheasant
11. 1	1.12	K2	B8	Cock
12. 1	2.12	K2	C9	Crow
13. 1	3.12	K2	D10	Monkey
14. 1	4.12	K2	E11	Gibbon

Solar date	*Lunar date*	*Month HS/EB*	*Day HS/EB*	*Constellation*
15. 1	5.12	K2	F12	Tapir
16. 1	6.12	K2	G1	Sheep
17. 1	7.12	K2	H2	Deer
18. 1	8.12	K2	J3	Horse
19. 1	9.12	K2	K4	Stag
20. 1	10.12	K2	A5	Serpent
21. 1	11.12	K2	B6	Earthworm
22. 1	12.12	K2	C7	Crocodile
23. 1	13.12	K2	D8	Dragon
24. 1	14.12	K2	E9	Badger
25. 1	15.12	K2	F10	Hare
26. 1	16.12	K2	G11	Fox
27. 1	17.12	K2	H12	Tiger
28. 1	18.12	K2	J1	Leopard
29. 1	19.12	K2	K2	Griffon
30. 1	20.12	K2	A3	Ox
31. 1	21.12	K2	B4	Bat
1. 2	22.12	K2	C5	Rat
2. 2	23.12	K2	D6	Swallow
3. 2	24.12	K2	E7	Pig
4. 2	25.12	K2	F8	Porcupine
5. 2	26.12	K2	G9	Wolf
6. 2	27.12	K2	H10	Dog
7. 2	28.12	K2	J11	Pheasant
8. 2	29.12	K2	K12	Cock
9. 2	30.12	K2	A1	Crow

MOU TZU YEAR

10. 2	1. 1	A3	B2	Monkey
11. 2	2. 1	A3	C3	Gibbon
12. 2	3. 1	A3	D4	Tapir
13. 2	4. 1	A3	E5	Sheep
14. 2	5. 1	A3	F6	Deer
15. 2	6. 1	A3	G7	Horse
16. 2	7. 1	A3	H8	Stag
17. 2	8. 1	A3	J9	Serpent
18. 2	9. 1	A3	K10	Earthworm
19. 2	10. 1	A3	A11	Crocodile
20. 2	11. 1	A3	B12	Dragon
21. 2	12. 1	A3	C1	Badger
22. 2	13. 1	A3	D2	Hare
23. 2	14. 1	A3	E3	Fox
24. 2	15. 1	A3	F4	Tiger
25. 2	16. 1	A3	G5	Leopard
26. 2	17. 1	A3	H6	Griffon
27. 2	18. 1	A3	J7	Ox
28. 2	19. 1	A3	K8	Bat
29. 2	20. 1	A3	A9	Rat
1. 3	21. 1	A3	B10	Swallow
2. 3	22. 1	A3	C11	Pig
3. 3	23. 1	A3	D12	Porcupine
4. 3	24. 1	A3	E1	Wolf
5. 3	25. 1	A3	F2	Dog
6. 3	26. 1	A3	G3	Pheasant
7. 3	27. 1	A3	H4	Cock
8. 3	28. 1	A3	J5	Crow
9. 3	29. 1	A3	K6	Monkey
10. 3	30. 1	A3	A7	Gibbon
11. 3	1. 2	B4	B8	Tapir
12. 3	2. 2	B4	C9	Sheep
13. 3	3. 2	B4	D10	Deer
14. 3	4. 2	B4	E11	Horse
15. 3	5. 2	B4	F12	Stag
16. 3	6. 2	B4	G1	Serpent
17. 3	7. 2	B4	H2	Earthworm
18. 3	8. 2	B4	J3	Crocodile
19. 3	9. 2	B4	K4	Dragon
20. 3	10. 2	B4	A5	Badger
21. 3	11. 2	B4	B6	Hare
22. 3	12. 2	B4	C7	Fox
23. 3	13. 2	B4	D8	Tiger
24. 3	14. 2	B4	E9	Leopard
25. 3	15. 2	B4	F10	Griffon
26. 3	16. 2	B4	G11	Ox
27. 3	17. 2	B4	H12	Bat
28. 3	18. 2	B4	J1	Rat
29. 3	19. 2	B4	K2	Swallow
30. 3	20. 2	B4	A3	Pig
31. 3	21. 2	B4	B4	Porcupine
1. 4	22. 2	B4	C5	Wolf
2. 4	23. 2	B4	D6	Dog
3. 4	24. 2	B4	E7	Pheasant
4. 4	25. 2	B4	F8	Cock

5. 4	26. 2	B4	G9	Crow
6. 4	27. 2	B4	H10	Monkey
7. 4	28. 2	B4	J11	Gibbon
8. 4	29. 2	B4	K12	Tapir
9. 4	1. 3	C5	A1	Sheep
10. 4	2. 3	C5	B2	Deer
11. 4	3. 3	C5	C3	Horse
12. 4	4. 3	C5	D4	Stag
13. 4	5. 3	C5	E5	Serpent
14. 4	6. 3	C5	F6	Earthworm
15. 4	7. 3	C5	G7	Crocodile
16. 4	8. 3	C5	H8	Dragon
17. 4	9. 3	C5	J9	Badger
18. 4	10. 3	C5	K10	Hare
19. 4	11. 3	C5	A11	Fox
20. 4	12. 3	C5	B12	Tiger
21. 4	13. 3	C5	C1	Leopard
22. 4	14. 3	C5	D2	Griffon
23. 4	15. 3	C5	E3	Ox
24. 4	16. 3	C5	F4	Bat
25. 4	17. 3	C5	G5	Rat
26. 4	18. 3	C5	H6	Swallow
27. 4	19. 3	C5	J7	Pig
28. 4	20. 3	C5	K8	Porcupine
29. 4	21. 3	C5	A9	Wolf
30. 4	22. 3	C5	B10	Dog
1. 5	23. 3	C5	C11	Pheasant
2. 5	24. 3	C5	D12	Cock
3. 5	25. 3	C5	E1	Crow
4. 5	26. 3	C5	F2	Monkey
5. 5	27. 3	C5	G3	Gibbon
6. 5	28. 3	C5	H4	Tapir
7. 5	29. 3	C5	J5	Sheep
8. 5	30. 3	C5	K6	Deer
9. 5	1. 4	D6	A7	Horse
10. 5	2. 4	D6	B8	Stag
11. 5	3. 4	D6	C9	Serpent
12. 5	4. 4	D6	D10	Earthworm
13. 5	5. 4	D6	E11	Crocodile
14. 5	6. 4	D6	F12	Dragon
15. 5	7. 4	D6	G1	Badger
16. 5	8. 4	D6	H2	Hare
17. 5	9. 4	D6	J3	Fox
18. 5	10. 4	D6	K4	Tiger
19. 5	11. 4	D6	A5	Leopard
20. 5	12. 4	D6	B6	Griffon
21. 5	13. 4	D6	C7	Ox
22. 5	14. 4	D6	D8	Bat
23. 5	15. 4	D6	E9	Rat
24. 5	16. 4	D6	F10	Swallow
25. 5	17. 4	D6	G11	Pig
26. 5	18. 4	D6	H12	Porcupine
27. 5	19. 4	D5	J1	Wolf
28. 5	20. 4	D6	K2	Dog
29. 5	21. 4	D6	A3	Pheasant

Solar date	*Lunar date*	*Month HS/EB*	*Day HS/EB*	*Constellation*
30. 5	22. 4	D6	B4	Cock
31. 5	23. 4	D6	C5	Crow
1. 6	24. 4	D6	D6	Monkey
2. 6	25. 4	D6	E7	Gibbon
3. 6	26. 4	D6	F8	Tapir
4. 6	27. 4	D6	G9	Sheep
5. 6	28. 4	D6	H10	Deer
6. 6	29. 4	D6	J11	Horse
7. 6	1. 5	E7	K12	Stag
8. 6	2. 5	E7	A1	Serpent
9. 6	3. 5	E7	B2	Earthworm
10. 6	4. 5	E7	C3	Crocodile
11. 6	5. 5	E7	D4	Dragon
12. 6	6. 5	E7	E5	Badger
13. 6	7. 5	E7	F6	Hare
14. 6	8. 5	E7	G7	Fox
15. 6	9. 5	E7	H8	Tiger
16. 6	10. 5	E7	J9	Leopard
17. 6	11. 5	E7	K10	Griffon
18. 6	12. 5	E7	A11	Ox
19. 6	13. 5	E7	B12	Bat
20. 6	14. 5	E7	C1	Rat
21. 6	15. 5	E7	D2	Swallow
22. 6	16. 5	E7	E3	Pig
23. 6	17. 5	E7	F4	Porcupine
24. 6	18. 5	E7	G5	Wolf
25. 6	19. 5	E7	H6	Dog
26. 6	20. 5	E7	J7	Pheasant
27. 6	21. 5	E7	K8	Cock
28. 6	22. 5	E7	A9	Crow
29. 6	23. 5	E7	B10	Monkey
30. 6	24. 5	E7	C11	Gibbon
1. 7	25. 5	E7	D12	Tapir
2. 7	26. 5	E7	E1	Sheep
3. 7	27. 5	E7	F2	Deer
4. 7	28. 5	E7	G3	Horse
5. 7	29. 5	E7	H4	Stag
6. 7	30. 5	E7	J5	Serpent
7. 7	1. 6	F8	K6	Earthworm
8. 7	2. 6	F8	A7	Crocodile
9. 7	3. 6	F8	B8	Dragon
10. 7	4. 6	F8	C9	Badger
11. 7	5. 6	F8	D10	Hare
12. 7	6. 6	F8	E11	Fox
13. 7	7. 6	F8	F12	Tiger
14. 7	8. 6	F8	G1	Leopard
15. 7	9. 6	F8	H2	Griffon
16. 7	10. 6	F8	J3	Ox
17. 7	11. 6	F8	K4	Bat
18. 7	12. 6	F8	A5	Rat
19. 7	13. 6	F8	B6	Swallow
20. 7	14. 6	F8	C7	Pig
21. 7	15. 6	F8	D8	Porcupine
22. 7	16. 6	F8	E9	Wolf
23. 7	17. 6	F8	F10	Dog
24. 7	18. 6	F8	G11	Pheasant
25. 7	19. 6	F8	H12	Cock
26. 7	20. 6	F8	J1	Crow
27. 7	21. 6	F8	K2	Monkey
28. 7	22. 6	F8	A3	Gibbon
29. 7	23. 6	F8	B4	Tapir
30. 7	24. 6	F8	C5	Sheep
31. 7	25. 6	F8	D6	Deer
1. 8	26. 6	F8	E7	Horse
2. 8	27. 6	F8	F8	Stag
3. 8	28. 6	F8	G9	Serpent
4. 8	29. 6	F8	H10	Earthworm
5. 8	1. 7	G9	J11	Crocodile
6. 8	2. 7	G9	K12	Dragon
7. 8	3. 7	G9	A1	Badger
8. 8	4. 7	G9	B2	Hare
9. 8	5. 7	G9	C3	Fox
10. 8	6. 7	G9	D4	Tiger
11. 8	7. 7	G9	E5	Leopard
12. 8	8. 7	G9	F6	Griffon
13. 8	9. 7	G9	G7	Ox
14. 8	10. 7	G9	H8	Bat
15. 8	11. 7	G9	J9	Rat
16. 8	12. 7	G9	K10	Swallow
17. 8	13. 7	G9	A11	Pig
18. 8	14. 7	G9	B12	Porcupine
19. 8	15. 7	G9	C1	Wolf
20. 8	16. 7	G9	D2	Dog
21. 8	17. 7	G9	E3	Pheasant
22. 8	18. 7	G9	F4	Cock
23. 8	19. 7	G9	G5	Crow
24. 8	20. 7	G9	H6	Monkey
25. 8	21. 7	G9	J7	Gibbon
26. 8	22. 7	G9	K8	Tapir
27. 8	23. 7	G9	A9	Sheep
28. 8	24. 7	G9	B10	Deer
29. 8	25. 7	G9	C11	Horse
30. 8	26. 7	G9	D12	Stag
31. 8	27. 7	G9	E1	Serpent
1. 9	28. 7	G9	F2	Earthworm
2. 9	29. 7	G9	G3	Crocodile
3. 9	1. 8	H10	H4	Dragon
4. 9	2. 8	H10	J5	Badger
5. 9	3. 8	H10	K6	Hare
6. 9	4. 8	H10	A7	Fox
7. 9	5. 8	H10	B8	Tiger
8. 9	6. 8	H10	C9	Leopard
9. 9	7. 8	H10	D10	Griffon
10. 9	8. 8	H10	E11	Ox
11. 9	9. 8	H10	F12	Bat
12. 9	10. 8	H10	G1	Rat
13. 9	11. 8	H10	H2	Swallow
14. 9	12. 8	H10	J3	Pig
15. 9	13. 8	H10	K4	Porcupine
16. 9	14. 8	H10	A5	Wolf
17. 9	15. 8	H10	B6	Dog
18. 9	16. 8	H10	C7	Pheasant
19. 9	17. 8	H10	D8	Cock
20. 9	18. 8	H10	E9	Crow
21. 9	19. 8	H10	F10	Monkey
22. 9	20. 8	H10	G11	Gibbon
23. 9	21. 8	H10	H12	Tapir
24. 9	22. 8	H10	J1	Sheep
25. 9	23. 8	H10	K2	Deer
26. 9	24. 8	H10	A3	Horse
27. 9	25. 8	H10	B4	Stag
28. 9	26. 8	H10	C5	Serpent
29. 9	27. 8	H10	D6	Earthworm
30. 9	28. 8	H10	E7	Crocodile
1.10	29. 8	H10	F8	Dragon
2.10	30. 8	H10	G9	Badger
3.10	1. 9	J11	H10	Hare
4.10	2. 9	J11	J11	Fox
5.10	3. 9	J11	K12	Tiger
6.10	4. 9	J11	A1	Leopard
7.10	5. 9	J11	B2	Griffon
8.10	6. 9	J11	C3	Ox
9.10	7. 9	J11	D4	Bat
10.10	8. 9	J11	E5	Rat
11.10	9. 9	J11	F6	Swallow
12.10	10. 9	J11	G7	Pig
13.10	11. 9	J11	H8	Porcupine
14.10	12. 9	J11	J9	Wolf
15.10	13. 9	J11	K10	Dog
16.10	14. 9	J11	A11	Pheasant
17.10	15. 9	J11	B12	Cock
18.10	16. 9	J11	C1	Crow
19.10	17. 9	J11	D2	Monkey
20.10	18. 9	J11	E3	Gibbon
21.10	19. 9	J11	F4	Tapir
22.10	20. 9	J11	G5	Sheep

Solar date	Lunar date	Month HS/EB	Day HS/EB	Constellation
23.10	21. 9	J11	H6	Deer
24.10	22. 9	J11	J7	Horse
25.10	23. 9	J11	K8	Stag
26.10	24. 9	J11	A9	Serpent
27.10	25. 9	J11	B10	Earthworm
28.10	26. 9	J11	C11	Crocodile
29.10	27. 9	J11	D12	Dragon
30.10	28. 9	J11	E1	Badger
31.10	29. 9	J11	F2	Hare
1.11	1.10	K12	G3	Fox
2.11	2.10	K12	H4	Tiger
3.11	3.10	K12	J5	Leopard
4.11	4.10	K12	K6	Griffon
5.11	5.10	K12	A7	Ox
6.11	6.10	K12	B8	Bat
7.11	7.10	K12	C9	Rat
8.11	8.10	K12	D10	Swallow
9.11	9.10	K12	E11	Pig
10.11	10.10	K12	F12	Porcupine
11.11	11.10	K12	G1	Wolf
12.11	12.10	K12	H2	Dog
13.11	13.10	K12	J3	Pheasant
14.11	14.10	K12	K4	Cock
15.11	15.10	K12	A5	Crow
16.11	16.10	K12	B6	Monkey
17.11	17.10	K12	C7	Gibbon
18.11	18.10	K12	D8	Tapir
19.11	19.10	K12	E9	Sheep
20.11	20.10	K12	F10	Deer
21.11	21.10	K12	G11	Horse
22.11	22.10	K12	H12	Stag
23.11	23.10	K12	J1	Serpent
24.11	24.10	K12	K2	Earthworm
25.11	25.10	K12	A3	Crocodile
26.11	26.10	K12	B4	Dragon
27.11	27.10	K12	C5	Badger
28.11	28.10	K12	D6	Hare
29.11	29.10	K12	E7	Fox
30.11	30.10	K12	F8	Tiger
1.12	1.11	A1	G9	Leopard
2.12	2.11	A1	H10	Griffon
3.12	3.11	A1	J11	Ox
4.12	4.11	A1	K12	Bat
5.12	5.11	A1	A1	Rat
6.12	6.11	A1	B2	Swallow
7.12	7.11	A1	C3	Pig
8.12	8.11	A1	D4	Porcupine
9.12	9.11	A1	E5	Wolf
10.12	10.11	A1	F6	Dog
11.12	11.11	A1	G7	Pheasant
12.12	12.11	A1	H8	Cock
13.12	13.11	A1	J9	Crow
14.12	14.11	A1	K10	Monkey
15.12	15.11	A1	A11	Gibbon
16.12	16.11	A1	B12	Tapir
17.12	17.11	A1	C1	Sheep
18.12	18.11	A1	D2	Deer
19.12	19.11	A1	E3	Horse
20.12	20.11	A1	F4	Stag
21.12	21.11	A1	G5	Serpent
22.12	22.11	A1	H6	Earthworm
23.12	23.11	A1	J7	Crocodile
24.12	24.11	A1	K8	Dragon
25.12	25.11	A1	A9	Badger
26.12	26.11	A1	B10	Hare
27.12	27.11	A1	C11	Fox
28.12	28.11	A1	D12	Tiger
29.12	29.11	A1	E1	Leopard
30.12	1.12	B2	F2	Griffon
31.12	2.12	B2	G3	Ox
1949				
1. 1	3.12	B2	H4	Bat
2. 1	4.12	B2	J5	Rat
3. 1	5.12	B2	K6	Swallow
4. 1	6.12	B2	A7	Pig
5. 1	7.12	B2	B8	Porcupine
6. 1	8.12	B2	C9	Wolf
7. 1	9.12	B2	D10	Dog
8. 1	10.12	B2	E11	Pheasant
9. 1	11.12	B2	F12	Cock
10. 1	12.12	B2	G1	Crow
11. 1	13.12	B2	H2	Monkey
12. 1	14.12	B2	J3	Gibbon
13. 1	15.12	B2	K4	Tapir
14. 1	16.12	B2	A5	Sheep
15. 1	17.12	B2	B6	Deer
16. 1	18.12	B2	C7	Horse
17. 1	19.12	B2	D8	Stag
18. 1	20.12	B2	E9	Serpent
19. 1	21.12	B2	F10	Earthworm
20. 1	22.12	B2	G11	Crocodile
21. 1	23.12	B2	H12	Dragon
22. 1	24.12	B2	J1	Badger
23. 1	25.12	B2	K2	Hare
24. 1	26.12	B2	A3	Fox
25. 1	27.12	B2	B4	Tiger
26. 1	28.12	B2	C5	Leopard
27. 1	29.12	B2	D6	Griffon
28. 1	30.12	B2	E7	Ox

CHI CH'OU YEAR

Solar date	Lunar date	Month HS/EB	Day HS/EB	Constellation
29. 1	1. 1	C3	F8	Bat
30. 1	2. 1	C3	G9	Rat
31. 1	3. 1	C3	H10	Swallow
1. 2	4. 1	C3	J11	Pig
2. 2	5. 1	C3	K12	Porcupine
3. 2	6. 1	C3	A1	Wolf
4. 2	7. 1	C3	B2	Dog
5. 2	8. 1	C3	C3	Pheasant
6. 2	9. 1	C3	D4	Cock
7. 2	10. 1	C3	E5	Crow
8. 2	11. 1	C3	F6	Monkey
9. 2	12. 1	C3	G7	Gibbon
10. 2	13. 1	C3	H8	Tapir
11. 2	14. 1	C3	J9	Sheep
12. 2	15. 1	C3	K10	Deer
13. 2	16. 1	C3	A11	Horse
14. 2	17. 1	C3	B12	Stag
15. 2	18. 1	C3	C1	Serpent
16. 2	19. 1	C3	D2	Earthworm
17. 2	20. 1	C3	E3	Crocodile
18. 2	21. 1	C3	F4	Dragon
19. 2	22. 1	C3	G5	Badger
20. 2	23. 1	C3	H6	Hare
21. 2	24. 1	C3	J7	Fox
22. 2	25. 1	C3	K8	Tiger
23. 2	26. 1	C3	A9	Leopard
24. 2	27. 1	C3	B10	Griffon
25. 2	28. 1	C3	C11	Ox
26. 2	29. 1	C3	D12	Bat
27. 2	30. 1	C3	E1	Rat
28. 2	1. 2	D4	F2	Swallow
1. 3	2. 2	D4	G3	Pig
2. 3	3. 2	D4	H4	Porcupine
3. 3	4. 2	D4	J5	Wolf
4. 3	5. 2	D4	K6	Dog
5. 3	6. 2	D4	A7	Pheasant

Solar date	*Lunar date*	*Month HS/EB*	*Day HS/EB*	*Constellation*
6. 3	7. 2	D4	B8	Cock
7. 3	8. 2	D4	C9	Crow
8. 3	9. 2	D4	D10	Monkey
9. 3	10. 2	D4	E11	Gibbon
10. 3	11. 2	D4	F12	Tapir
11. 3	12. 2	D4	G1	Sheep
12. 3	13. 2	D4	H2	Deer
13. 3	14. 2	D4	J3	Horse
14. 3	15. 2	D4	K4	Stag
15. 3	16. 2	D4	A5	Serpent
16. 3	17. 2	D4	B6	Earthworm
17. 3	18. 2	D4	C7	Crocodile
18. 3	19. 2	D4	D8	Dragon
19. 3	20. 2	D4	E9	Badger
20. 3	21. 2	D4	F10	Hare
21. 3	22. 2	D4	G11	Fox
22. 3	23. 2	D4	H12	Tiger
23. 3	24. 2	D4	J1	Leopard
24. 3	25. 2	D4	K2	Griffon
25. 3	26. 2	D4	A3	Ox
26. 3	27. 2	D4	B4	Bat
27. 3	28. 2	D4	C5	Rat
28. 3	29. 2	D4	D6	Swallow
29. 3	1. 3	E5	E7	Pig
30. 3	2. 3	E5	F8	Porcupine
31. 3	3. 3	E5	G9	Wolf
1. 4	4. 3	E5	H10	Dog
2. 4	5. 3	E5	J11	Pheasant
3. 4	6. 3	E5	K12	Cock
4. 4	7. 3	E5	A1	Crow
5. 4	8. 3	E5	B2	Monkey
6. 4	9. 3	E5	C3	Gibbon
7. 4	10. 3	E5	D4	Tapir
8. 4	11. 3	E5	E5	Sheep
9. 4	12. 3	E5	F6	Deer
10. 4	13. 3	E5	G7	Horse
11. 4	14. 3	E5	H8	Stag
12. 4	15. 3	E5	J9	Serpent
13. 4	16. 3	E5	K10	Earthworm
14. 4	17. 3	E5	A11	Crocodile
15. 4	18. 3	E5	B12	Dragon
16. 4	19. 3	E5	C1	Badger
17. 4	20. 3	E5	D2	Hare
18. 4	21. 3	E5	E3	Fox
19. 4	22. 3	E5	F4	Tiger
20. 4	23. 3	E5	G5	Leopard
21. 4	24. 3	E5	H6	Griffon
22. 4	25. 3	E5	J7	Ox
23. 4	26. 3	E5	K8	Bat
24. 4	27. 3	E5	A9	Rat
25. 4	28. 3	E5	B10	Swallow
26. 4	29. 3	E5	C11	Pig
27. 4	30. 3	E5	D12	Porcupine
28. 4	1. 4	F6	E1	Wolf
29. 4	2. 4	F6	F2	Dog
30. 4	3. 4	F6	G3	Pheasant
1. 5	4. 4	F6	H4	Cock
2. 5	5. 4	F6	J5	Crow
3. 5	6. 4	F6	K6	Monkey
4. 5	7. 4	F6	A7	Gibbon
5. 5	8. 4	F6	B8	Tapir
6. 5	9. 4	F6	C9	Sheep
7. 5	10. 4	F6	D10	Deer
8. 5	11. 4	F6	E11	Horse
9. 5	12. 4	F6	F12	Stag
10. 5	13. 4	F6	G1	Serpent
11. 5	14. 4	F6	H2	Earthworm
12. 5	15. 4	F6	J3	Crocodile
13. 5	16. 4	F6	K4	Dragon
14. 5	17. 4	F6	A5	Badger
15. 5	18. 4	F6	B6	Hare
16. 5	19. 4	F6	C7	Fox
17. 5	20. 4	F6	D8	Tiger

Solar date	*Lunar date*	*Month HS/EB*	*Day HS/EB*	*Constellation*
18. 5	21. 4	F6	E9	Leopard
19. 5	22. 4	F6	F10	Griffon
20. 5	23. 4	F6	G11	Ox
21. 5	24. 4	F6	H12	Bat
22. 5	25. 4	F6	J1	Rat
23. 5	26. 4	F6	K2	Swallow
24. 5	27. 4	F6	A3	Pig
25. 5	28. 4	F6	B4	Porcupine
26. 5	29. 4	F6	C5	Wolf
27. 5	30. 4	F6	D6	Dog
28. 5	1. 5	G7	E7	Pheasant
29. 5	2. 5	G7	F8	Cock
30. 5	3. 5	G7	G9	Crow
31. 5	4. 5	G7	H10	Monkey
1. 6	5. 5	G7	J11	Gibbon
2. 6	6. 5	G7	K12	Tapir
3. 6	7. 5	G7	A1	Sheep
4. 6	8. 5	G7	B2	Deer
5. 6	9. 5	G7	C3	Horse
6. 6	10. 5	G7	D4	Stag
7. 6	11. 5	G7	E5	Serpent
8. 6	12. 5	G7	F6	Earthworm
9. 6	13. 5	G7	G7	Crocodile
10. 6	14. 5	G7	H8	Dragon
11. 6	15. 5	G7	J9	Badger
12. 6	16. 5	G7	K10	Hare
13. 6	17. 5	G7	A11	Fox
14. 6	18. 5	G7	B12	Tiger
15. 6	19. 5	G7	C1	Leopard
16. 6	20. 5	G7	D2	Griffon
17. 6	21. 5	G7	E3	Ox
18. 6	22. 5	G7	F4	Bat
19. 6	23. 5	G7	G5	Rat
20. 6	24. 5	G7	H6	Swallow
21. 6	25. 5	G7	J7	Pig
22. 6	26. 5	G7	K8	Porcupine
23. 6	27. 5	G7	A9	Wolf
24. 6	28. 5	G7	B10	Dog
25. 6	29. 5	G7	C11	Pheasant
26. 6	1. 6	H8	D12	Cock
27. 6	2. 6	H8	E1	Crow
28. 6	3. 6	H8	F2	Monkey
29. 6	4. 6	H8	G3	Gibbon
30. 6	5. 6	H8	H4	Tapir
1. 7	6. 6	H8	J5	Sheep
2. 7	7. 6	H8	K6	Deer
3. 7	8. 6	H8	A7	Horse
4. 7	9. 6	H8	B8	Stag
5. 7	10. 6	H8	C9	Serpent
6. 7	11. 6	H8	D10	Earthworm
7. 7	12. 6	H8	E11	Crocodile
8. 7	13. 6	H8	F12	Dragon
9. 7	14. 6	H8	G1	Badger
10. 7	15. 6	H8	H2	Hare
11. 7	16. 6	H8	J3	Fox
12. 7	17. 6	H8	K4	Tiger
13. 7	18. 6	H8	A5	Leopard
14. 7	19. 6	H8	B6	Griffon
15. 7	20. 6	H8	C7	Ox
16. 7	21. 6	H8	D8	Bat
17. 7	22. 6	H8	E9	Rat
18. 7	23. 6	H8	F10	Swallow
19. 7	24. 6	H8	G11	Pig
20. 7	25. 6	H8	H12	Porcupine
21. 7	26. 6	H8	J1	Wolf
22. 7	27. 6	H8	K2	Dog
23. 7	28. 6	H8	A3	Pheasant
24. 7	29. 6	H8	B4	Cock
25. 7	30. 6	H8	C5	Crow
26. 7	1. 7	J9	D6	Monkey
27. 7	2. 7	J9	E7	Gibbon
28. 7	3. 7	J9	F8	Tapir
29. 7	4. 7	J9	G9	Sheep

Solar date	*Lunar date*	*Month HS/EB*	*Day HS/EB*	*Constellation*
30. 7	5. 7	J9	H10	Deer
31. 7	6. 7	J9	J11	Horse
1. 8	7. 7	J9	K12	Stag
2. 8	8. 7	J9	A1	Serpent
3. 8	9. 7	J9	B2	Earthworm
4. 8	10. 7	J9	C3	Crocodile
5. 8	11. 7	J9	D4	Dragon
6. 8	12. 7	J9	E5	Badger
7. 8	13. 7	J9	F6	Hare
8. 8	14. 7	J9	G7	Fox
9. 8	15. 7	J9	H8	Tiger
10. 8	16. 7	J9	J9	Leopard
11. 8	17. 7	J9	K10	Griffon
12. 8	18. 7	J9	A11	Ox
13. 8	19. 7	J9	B12	Bat
14. 8	20. 7	J9	C1	Rat
15. 8	21. 7	J9	D2	Swallow
16. 8	22. 7	J9	E3	Pig
17. 8	23. 7	J9	F4	Porcupine
18. 8	24. 7	J9	G5	Wolf
19. 8	25. 7	J9	H6	Dog
20. 8	26. 7	J9	J7	Pheasant
21. 8	27. 7	J9	K8	Cock
22. 8	28. 7	J9	A9	Crow
23. 8	29. 7	J9	B10	Monkey
24. 8	*1. 7*	*J9*	C11	Gibbon
25. 8	*2. 7*	*J9*	D12	Tapir
26. 8	*3. 7*	*J9*	E1	Sheep
27. 8	*4. 7*	*J9*	F2	Deer
28. 8	*5. 7*	*J9*	G3	Horse
29. 8	*6. 7*	*J9*	H4	Stag
30. 8	*7. 7*	*J9*	J5	Serpent
31. 8	*8. 7*	*J9*	K6	Earthworm
1. 9	*9. 7*	*J9*	A7	Crocodile
2. 9	*10. 7*	*J9*	B8	Dragon
3. 9	*11. 7*	*J9*	C9	Badger
4. 9	*12. 7*	*J9*	D10	Hare
5. 9	*13. 7*	*J9*	E11	Fox
6. 9	*14. 7*	*J9*	F12	Tiger
7. 9	*15. 7*	*J9*	G1	Leopard
8. 9	*16. 7*	*J9*	H2	Griffon
9. 9	*17. 7*	*J9*	J3	Ox
10. 9	*18. 7*	*J9*	K4	Bat
11. 9	*19. 7*	*J9*	A5	Rat
12. 9	*20. 7*	*J9*	B6	Swallow
13. 9	*21. 7*	*J9*	C7	Pig
14. 9	*22. 7*	*J9*	D8	Porcupine
15. 9	*23. 7*	*J9*	E9	Wolf
16. 9	*24. 7*	*J9*	F10	Dog
17. 9	*25. 7*	*J9*	G11	Pheasant
18. 9	*26. 7*	*J9*	H12	Cock
19. 9	*27. 7*	*J9*	J1	Crow
20. 9	*28. 7*	*J9*	K2	Monkey
21. 9	*29. 7*	*J9*	A3	Gibbon
22. 9	1. 8	K10	B4	Tapir
23. 9	2. 8	K10	C5	Sheep
24. 9	3. 8	K10	D6	Deer
25. 9	4. 8	K10	E7	Horse
26. 9	5. 8	K10	F8	Stag
27. 9	6. 8	K10	G9	Serpent
28. 9	7. 8	K10	H10	Earthworm
29. 9	8. 8	K10	J11	Crocodile
30. 9	9. 8	K10	K12	Dragon
1.10	10. 8	K10	A1	Badger
2.10	11. 8	K10	B2	Hare
3.10	12. 8	K10	C3	Fox
4.10	13. 8	K10	D4	Tiger
5.10	14. 8	K10	E5	Leopard
6.10	15. 8	K10	F6	Griffon
7.10	16. 8	K10	G7	Ox
8.10	17. 8	K10	H8	Bat
9.10	18. 8	K10	J9	Rat
10.10	19. 8	K10	K10	Swallow
11.10	20. 8	K10	A11	Pig
12.10	21. 8	K10	B12	Porcupine
13.10	22. 8	K10	C1	Wolf
14.10	23. 8	K10	D2	Dog
15.10	24. 8	K10	E3	Pheasant
16.10	25. 8	K10	F4	Cock
17.10	26. 8	K10	G5	Crow
18.10	27. 8	K10	H6	Monkey
19.10	28. 8	K10	J7	Gibbon
20.10	29. 8	K10	K8	Tapir
21.10	30. 8	K10	A9	Sheep
22.10	1. 9	A11	B10	Deer
23.10	2. 9	A11	C11	Horse
24.10	3. 9	A11	D12	Stag
25.10	4. 9	A11	E1	Serpent
26.10	5. 9	A11	F2	Earthworm
27.10	6. 9	A11	G3	Crocodile
28.10	7. 9	A11	H4	Dragon
29.10	8. 9	A11	J5	Badger
30.10	9. 9	A11	K6	Hare
31.10	10. 9	A11	A7	Fox
1.11	11. 9	A11	B8	Tiger
2.11	12. 9	A11	C9	Leopard
3.11	13. 9	A11	D10	Griffon
4.11	14. 9	A11	E11	Ox
5.11	15. 9	A11	F12	Bat
6.11	16. 9	A11	G1	Rat
7.11	17. 9	A11	H2	Swallow
8.11	18. 9	A11	J3	Pig
9.11	19. 9	A11	K4	Porcupine
10.11	20. 9	A11	A5	Wolf
11.11	21. 9	A11	B6	Dog
12.11	22. 9	A11	C7	Pheasant
13.11	23. 9	A11	D8	Cock
14.11	24. 9	A11	E9	Crow
15.11	25. 9	A11	F10	Monkey
16.11	26. 9	A11	G11	Gibbon
17.11	27. 9	A11	H12	Tapir
18.11	28. 9	A11	J1	Sheep
19.11	29. 9	A11	K2	Deer
20.11	1.10	B12	A3	Horse
21.11	2.10	B12	B4	Stag
22.11	3.10	B12	C5	Serpent
23.11	4.10	B12	D6	Earthworm
24.11	5.10	B12	E7	Crocodile
25.11	6.10	B12	F8	Dragon
26.11	7.10	B12	G9	Badger
27.11	8.10	B12	H10	Hare
28.11	9.10	B12	J11	Fox
29.11	10.10	B12	K12	Tiger
30.11	11.10	B12	A1	Leopard
1.12	12.10	B12	B2	Griffon
2.12	13.10	B12	C3	Ox
3.12	14.10	B12	D4	Bat
4.12	15.10	B12	E5	Rat
5.12	16.10	B12	F6	Swallow
6.12	17.10	B12	G7	Pig
7.12	18.10	B12	H8	Porcupine
8.12	19.10	B12	J9	Wolf
9.12	20.10	B12	K10	Dog
10.12	21.10	B12	A11	Pheasant
11.12	22.10	B12	B12	Cock
12.12	23.10	B12	C1	Crow
13.12	24.10	B12	D2	Monkey
14.12	25.10	B12	E3	Gibbon
15.12	26.10	B12	F4	Tapir
16.12	27.10	B12	G5	Sheep
17.12	28.10	B12	H6	Deer
18.12	29.10	B12	J7	Horse
19.12	30.10	B12	K8	Stag
20.12	1.11	C1	A9	Serpent
21.12	2.11	C1	B12	Earthworm
22.12	3.11	C1	C11	Crocodile

Solar date	*Lunar date*	*Month HS/EB*	*Day HS/EB*	*Constellation*
23.12	4.11	C1	D12	Dragon
24.12	5.11	C1	E1	Badger
25.12	6.11	C1	F2	Hare
26.12	7.11	C1	G3	Fox
27.12	8.11	C1	H4	Tiger
28.12	9.11	C1	J5	Leopard
29.12	10.11	C1	K6	Griffon
30.12	11.11	C1	A7	Ox
31.12	12.11	C1	B8	Bat
1950				
1. 1	13.11	C1	C9	Rat
2. 1	14.11	C1	D10	Swallow
3. 1	15.11	C1	E11	Pig
4. 1	16.11	C1	F12	Porcupine
5. 1	17.11	C1	G1	Wolf
6. 1	18.11	C1	H2	Dog
7. 1	19.11	C1	J3	Pheasant
8. 1	20.11	C1	K4	Cock
9. 1	21.11	C1	A5	Crow
10. 1	22.11	C1	B6	Monkey
11. 1	23.11	C1	C7	Gibbon
12. 1	24.11	C1	D8	Tapir
13. 1	25.11	C1	E9	Sheep
14. 1	26.11	C1	F10	Deer
15. 1	27.11	C1	G11	Horse
16. 1	28.11	C1	H12	Stag
17. 1	29.11	C1	J1	Serpent
18. 1	1.12	D2	K2	Earthworm
19. 1	2.12	D2	A3	Crocodile
20. 1	3.12	D2	B4	Dragon
21. 1	4.12	D2	C5	Badger
22. 1	5.12	D2	D6	Hare
23. 1	6.12	D2	E7	Fox
24. 1	7.12	D2	F8	Tiger
25. 1	8.12	D2	G9	Leopard
26. 1	9.12	D2	H10	Griffon
27. 1	10.12	D2	J11	Ox
28. 1	11.12	D2	K12	Bat
29. 1	12.12	D2	A1	Rat
30. 1	13.12	D2	B2	Swallow
31. 1	14.12	D2	C3	Pig
1. 2	15.12	D2	D4	Porcupine
2. 2	16.12	D2	E5	Wolf
3. 2	17.12	D2	F6	Dog
4. 2	18.12	D2	G7	Pheasant
5. 2	19.12	D2	H8	Cock
6. 2	20.12	D2	J9	Crow
7. 2	21.12	D2	K10	Monkey
8. 2	22.12	D2	A11	Gibbon
9. 2	23.12	D2	B12	Tapir
10. 2	24.12	D2	C1	Sheep
11. 2	25.12	D2	D2	Deer
12. 2	26.12	D2	E3	Horse
13. 2	27.12	D2	F4	Stag
14. 2	28.12	D2	G5	Serpent
15. 2	29.12	D2	H6	Earthworm
16. 2	30.12	D2	J7	Crocodile

KENG YIN YEAR

Solar date	*Lunar date*	*Month HS/EB*	*Day HS/EB*	*Constellation*
17. 2	1. 1	E3	K8	Dragon
18. 2	2. 1	E3	A9	Badger
19. 2	3. 1	E3	B10	Hare
20. 2	4. 1	E3	C11	Fox
21. 2	5. 1	E3	D12	Tiger
22. 2	6. 1	E3	E1	Leopard
23. 2	7. 1	E3	F2	Griffon
24. 2	8. 1	E3	G3	Ox
25. 2	9. 1	E3	H4	Bat
26. 2	10. 1	E3	J5	Rat
27. 2	11. 1	E3	K6	Swallow
28. 2	12. 1	E3	A7	Pig
1. 3	13. 1	E3	B8	Porcupine
2. 3	14. 1	E3	C9	Wolf
3. 3	15. 1	E3	D10	Dog
4. 3	16. 1	E3	E11	Pheasant
5. 3	17. 1	E3	F12	Cock
6. 3	18. 1	E3	G1	Crow
7. 3	19. 1	E3	H2	Monkey
8. 3	20. 1	E3	J3	Gibbon
9. 3	21. 1	E3	K4	Tapir
10. 3	22. 1	E3	A5	Sheep
11. 3	23. 1	E3	B6	Deer
12. 3	24. 1	E3	C7	Horse
13. 3	25. 1	E3	D8	Stag
14. 3	26. 1	E3	E9	Serpent
15. 3	27. 1	E3	F10	Earthworm
16. 3	28. 1	E3	G11	Crocodile
17. 3	29. 1	E3	H12	Dragon
18. 3	1. 2	F4	J1	Badger
19. 3	2. 2	F4	K2	Hare
20. 3	3. 2	F4	A3	Fox
21. 3	4. 2	F4	B4	Tiger
22. 3	5. 2	F4	C5	Leopard
23. 3	6. 2	F4	D6	Griffon
24. 3	7. 2	F4	E7	Ox
25. 3	8. 2	F4	F8	Bat
26. 3	9. 2	F4	G9	Rat
27. 3	10. 2	F4	H10	Swallow
28. 3	11. 2	F4	J11	Pig
29. 3	12. 2	F4	K12	Porcupine
30. 3	13. 2	F4	A1	Wolf
31. 3	14. 2	F4	B2	Dog
1. 4	15. 2	F4	C3	Pheasant
2. 4	16. 2	F4	D4	Cock
3. 4	17. 2	F4	E5	Crow
4. 4	18. 2	F4	F6	Monkey
5. 4	19. 2	F4	G7	Gibbon
6. 4	20. 2	F4	H8	Tapir
7. 4	21. 2	F4	J9	Sheep
8. 4	22. 2	F4	K10	Deer
9. 4	23. 2	F4	A11	Horse
10. 4	24. 2	F4	B12	Stag
11. 4	25. 2	F4	C1	Serpent
12. 4	26. 2	F4	D2	Earthworm
13. 4	27. 2	F4	E3	Crocodile
14. 4	28. 2	F4	F4	Dragon
15. 4	29. 2	F4	G5	Badger
16. 4	30. 2	F4	H6	Hare
17. 4	1. 3	G5	J7	Fox
18. 4	2. 3	G5	K8	Tiger
19. 4	3. 3	G5	A9	Leopard
20. 4	4. 3	G5	B10	Griffon
21. 4	5. 3	G5	C11	Ox
22. 4	6. 3	G5	D12	Bat
23. 4	7. 3	G5	E1	Rat
24. 4	8. 3	G5	F2	Swallow
25. 4	9. 3	G5	G3	Pig
26. 4	10. 3	G5	H4	Porcupine
27. 4	11. 3	G5	J5	Wolf
28. 4	12. 3	G5	K6	Dog
29. 4	13. 3	G5	A7	Pheasant
30. 4	14. 3	G5	B8	Cock
1. 5	15. 3	G5	C9	Crow
2. 5	16. 3	G5	D10	Monkey
3. 5	17. 3	G5	E11	Gibbon
4. 5	18. 3	G5	F12	Tapir
5. 5	19. 3	G5	G1	Sheep

Solar date	*Lunar date*	*Month HS/EB*	*Day HS/EB*	*Constellation*
6. 5	20. 3	G5	H2	Deer
7. 5	21. 3	G5	J3	Horse
8. 5	22. 3	G5	K4	Stag
9. 5	23. 3	G5	A5	Serpent
10. 5	24. 3	G5	B6	Earthworm
11. 5	25. 3	G5	C7	Crocodile
12. 5	26. 3	G5	D8	Dragon
13. 5	27. 3	G5	E9	Badger
14. 5	28. 3	G5	F10	Hare
15. 5	29. 3	G5	G11	Fox
16. 5	30. 3	G5	H12	Tiger
17. 5	1. 4	H6	J1	Leopard
18. 5	2. 4	H6	K2	Griffon
19. 5	3. 4	H6	A3	Ox
20. 5	4. 4	H6	B4	Bat
21. 5	5. 4	H6	C5	Rat
22. 5	6. 4	H6	D6	Swallow
23. 5	7. 4	H6	E7	Pig
24. 5	8. 4	H6	F8	Porcupine
25. 5	9. 4	H6	G9	Wolf
26. 5	10. 4	H6	H10	Dog
27. 5	11. 4	H6	J11	Pheasant
28. 5	12. 4	H6	K12	Cock
29. 5	13. 4	H6	A1	Crow
30. 5	14. 4	H6	B2	Monkey
31. 5	15. 4	H6	C3	Gibbon
1. 6	16. 4	H6	D4	Tapir
2. 6	17. 4	H6	E5	Sheep
3. 6	18. 4	H6	F6	Deer
4. 6	19. 4	H6	G7	Horse
5. 6	20. 4	H6	H8	Stag
6. 6	21. 4	H6	J9	Serpent
7. 6	22. 4	H6	K10	Earthworm
8. 6	23. 4	H6	A11	Crocodile
9. 6	24. 4	H6	B12	Dragon
10. 6	25. 4	H6	C1	Badger
11. 6	26. 4	H6	D2	Hare
12. 6	27. 4	H6	E3	Fox
13. 6	28. 4	H6	F4	Tiger
14. 6	29. 4	H6	G5	Leopard
15. 6	1. 5	J7	H6	Griffon
16. 6	2. 5	J7	J7	Ox
17. 6	3. 5	J7	K8	Bat
18. 6	4. 5	J7	A9	Rat
19. 6	5. 5	J7	B10	Swallow
20. 6	6. 5	J7	C11	Pig
21. 6	7. 5	J7	D12	Porcupine
22. 6	8. 5	J7	E1	Wolf
23. 6	9. 5	J7	F2	Dog
24. 6	10. 5	J7	G3	Pheasant
25. 6	11. 5	J7	H4	Cock
26. 6	12. 5	J7	J5	Crow
27. 6	13. 5	J7	K6	Monkey
28. 6	14. 5	J7	A7	Gibbon
29. 6	15. 5	J7	B8	Tapir
30. 6	16. 5	J7	C9	Sheep
1. 7	17. 5	J7	D10	Deer
2. 7	18. 5	J7	E11	Horse
3. 7	19. 5	J7	F12	Stag
4. 7	20. 5	J7	G1	Serpent
5. 7	21. 5	J7	H2	Earthworm
6. 7	22. 5	J7	J3	Crocodile
7. 7	23. 5	J7	K4	Dragon
8. 7	24. 5	J7	A5	Badger
9. 7	25. 5	J7	B6	Hare
10. 7	26. 5	J7	C7	Fox
11. 7	27. 5	J7	D8	Tiger
12. 7	28. 5	J7	E9	Leopard
13. 7	29. 5	J7	F10	Griffon
14. 7	30. 5	J7	G11	Ox
15. 7	1. 6	K8	H12	Bat
16. 7	2. 6	K8	J1	Rat
17. 7	3. 6	K8	K2	Swallow
18. 7	4. 6	K8	A3	Pig
19. 7	5. 6	K8	B4	Porcupine
20. 7	6. 6	K8	C5	Wolf
21. 7	7. 6	K8	D6	Dog
22. 7	8. 6	K8	E7	Pheasant
23. 7	9. 6	K8	F8	Cock
24. 7	10. 6	K8	G9	Crow
25. 7	11. 6	K8	H10	Monkey
26. 7	12. 6	K8	J11	Gibbon
27. 7	13. 6	K8	K12	Tapir
28. 7	14. 6	K8	A1	Sheep
29. 7	15. 6	K8	B2	Deer
30. 7	16. 6	K8	C3	Horse
31. 7	17. 6	K8	D4	Stag
1. 8	18. 6	K8	E5	Serpent
2. 8	19. 6	K8	F6	Earthworm
3. 8	20. 6	K8	G7	Crocodile
4. 8	21. 6	K8	H8	Dragon
5. 8	22. 6	K8	J9	Badger
6. 8	23. 6	K8	K10	Hare
7. 8	24. 6	K8	A11	Fox
8. 8	25. 6	K8	B12	Tiger
9. 8	26. 6	K8	C1	Leopard
10. 8	27. 6	K8	D2	Griffon
11. 8	28. 6	K8	E3	Ox
12. 8	29. 6	K8	F4	Bat
13. 8	30. 6	K8	G5	Rat
14. 8	1. 7	A9	H6	Swallow
15. 8	2. 7	A9	J7	Pig
16. 8	3. 7	A9	K8	Porcupine
17. 8	4. 7	A9	A9	Wolf
18. 8	5. 7	A9	B10	Dog
19. 8	6. 7	A9	C11	Pheasant
20. 8	7. 7	A9	D12	Cock
21. 8	8. 7	A9	E1	Crow
22. 8	9. 7	A9	F2	Monkey
23. 8	10. 7	A9	G3	Gibbon
24. 8	11. 7	A9	H4	Tapir
25. 8	12. 7	A9	J5	Sheep
26. 8	13. 7	A9	K6	Deer
27. 8	14. 7	A9	A7	Horse
28. 8	15. 7	A9	B8	Stag
29. 8	16. 7	A9	C9	Serpent
30. 8	17. 7	A9	D10	Earthworm
31. 8	18. 7	A9	E11	Crocodile
1. 9	19. 7	A9	F12	Dragon
2. 9	20. 7	A9	G1	Badger
3. 9	21. 7	A9	H2	Hare
4. 9	22. 7	A9	J3	Fox
5. 9	23. 7	A9	K4	Tiger
6. 9	24. 7	A9	A5	Leopard
7. 9	25. 7	A9	B6	Griffon
8. 9	26. 7	A9	C7	Ox
9. 9	27. 7	A9	D8	Bat
10. 9	28. 7	A9	E9	Rat
11. 9	29. 7	A9	F10	Swallow
12. 9	1. 8	B10	G11	Pig
13. 9	2. 8	B10	H12	Porcupine
14. 9	3. 8	B10	J1	Wolf
15. 9	4. 8	B10	K2	Dog
16. 9	5. 8	B10	A3	Pheasant
17. 9	6. 8	B10	B4	Cock
18. 9	7. 8	B10	C5	Crow
19. 9	8. 8	B10	D6	Monkey
20. 9	9. 8	B10	E7	Gibbon
21. 9	10. 8	B10	F8	Tapir
22. 9	11. 8	B10	G9	Sheep
23. 9	12. 8	B10	H10	Deer
24. 9	13. 8	B10	J11	Horse
25. 9	14. 8	B10	K12	Stag
26. 9	15. 8	B10	A1	Serpent
27. 9	16. 8	B10	B2	Earthworm
28. 9	17. 8	B10	C3	Crocodile

Solar date	*Lunar date*	*Month HS/EB*	*Day HS/EB*	*Constellation*
29. 9	18. 8	B10	D4	Dragon
30. 9	19. 8	B10	E5	Badger
1.10	20. 8	B10	F6	Hare
2.10	21. 8	B10	G7	Fox
3.10	22. 8	B10	H8	Tiger
4.10	23. 8	B10	J9	Leopard
5.10	24. 8	B10	K10	Griffon
6.10	25. 8	B10	A11	Ox
7.10	26. 8	B10	B12	Batr
8.10	27. 8	B10	C1	Rat
9.10	28. 8	B10	D2	Swallow
10.10	29. 8	B10	E3	Pig
11.10	1. 9	C11	F4	Porcupine
12.10	2. 9	C11	G5	Wolf
13.10	3. 9	C11	H6	Dog
14.10	4. 9	C11	J7	Pheasant
15.10	5. 9	C11	K8	Cock
16.10	6. 9	C11	A9	Crow
17.10	7. 9	C11	B10	Monkey
18.10	8. 9	C11	C11	Gibbon
19.10	9. 9	C11	D12	Tapir
20.10	10. 9	C11	E1	Sheep
21.10	11. 9	C11	F2	Deer
22.10	12. 9	C11	G3	Horse
23.10	13. 9	C11	H4	Stag
24.10	14. 9	C11	J5	Serpent
25.10	15. 9	C11	K6	Earthworm
26.10	16. 9	C11	A7	Crocodile
27.10	17. 9	C11	B8	Dragon
28.10	18. 9	C11	C9	Badger
29.10	19. 9	C11	D10	Hare
30.10	20. 9	C11	E11	Fox
31.10	21. 9	C11	F12	Tiger
1.11	22. 9	C11	G1	Leopard
2.11	23. 9	C11	H2	Griffon
3.11	24. 9	C11	J3	Ox
4.11	25. 9	C11	K4	Bat
5.11	26. 9	C11	A5	Rat
6.11	27. 9	C11	B6	Swallow
7.11	28. 9	C11	C7	Pig
8.11	29. 9	C11	D8	Porcupine
9.11	30. 9	C11	E9	Wolf
10.11	1.10	D12	F10	Dog
11.11	2.10	D12	G11	Pheasant
12.11	3.10	D12	H12	Cock
13.11	4.10	D12	J1	Crow
14.11	5.10	D12	K2	Monkey
15.11	6.10	D12	A3	Gibbon
16.11	7.10	D12	B4	Tapir
17.11	8.10	D12	C5	Sheep
18.11	9.10	D12	D6	Deer
19.11	10.10	D12	E7	Horse
20.11	11.10	D12	F8	Stag
21.11	12.10	D12	G9	Serpent
22.11	13.10	D12	H10	Earthworm
23.11	14.10	D12	J11	Crocodile
24.11	15.10	D12	K12	Dragon
25.11	16.10	D12	A1	Badger
26.11	17.10	D12	B2	Hare
27.11	18.10	D12	C3	Fox
28.11	19.10	D12	D4	Tiger
29.11	20.10	D12	E5	Leopard
30.11	21.10	D12	F6	Griffon
1.12	22.10	D12	G7	Ox
2.12	23.10	D12	H8	Bat
3.12	24.10	D12	J9	Rat
4.12	25.10	D12	K10	Swallow
5.12	26.10	D12	A11	Pig
6.12	27.10	D12	B12	Porcupine
7.12	28.10	D12	C1	Wolf
8.12	29.10	D12	D2	Dog
9.12	1.11	E1	E3	Pheasant
10.12	2.11	E1	F4	Cock
11.12	3.11	E1	G5	Crow
12.12	4.11	E1	H6	Monkey
13.12	5.11	E1	J7	Gibbon
14.12	6.11	E1	K8	Tapir
15.12	7.11	E1	A9	Sheep
16.12	8.11	E1	B10	Deer
17.12	9.11	E1	C11	Horse
18.12	10.11	E1	D12	Stag
19.12	11.11	E1	E1	Serpent
20.12	12.11	E1	F2	Earthworm
21.12	13.11	E1	G3	Crocodile
22.12	14.11	E1	H4	Dragon
23.12	15.11	E1	J5	Badger
24.12	16.11	E1	K6	Hare
25.12	17.11	E1	A7	Fox
26.12	18.11	E1	B8	Tiger
27.12	19.11	E1	C9	Leopard
28.12	20.11	E1	D10	Griffon
29.12	21.11	E1	E11	Ox
30.12	22.11	E1	F12	Bat
31.12	23.11	E1	G1	Rat
1951				
1. 1	23.11	E1	H2	Swallow
2. 1	25.11	E1	J3	Pig
3. 1	26.11	E1	K4	Porcupine
4. 1	27.11	E1	A5	Wolf
5. 1	28.11	E1	B6	Dog
6. 1	29.11	E1	C7	Pheasant
7. 1	30.11	E1	D8	Cock
8. 1	1.12	F2	E9	Crow
9. 1	2.12	F2	F10	Monkey
10. 1	3.12	F2	G11	Gibbon
11. 1	4.12	F2	H12	Tapir
12. 1	5.12	F2	J1	Sheep
13. 1	6.12	F2	K2	Deer
14. 1	7.12	F2	A3	Horse
15. 1	8.12	F2	B4	Stag
16. 1	9.12	F2	C5	Serpent
17. 1	10.12	F2	D6	Earthworm
18. 1	11.12	F2	E7	Crocodile
19. 1	12.12	F2	F8	Dragon
20. 1	13.12	F2	G9	Badger
21. 1	14.12	F2	H10	Hare
22. 1	15.12	F2	J11	Fox
23. 1	16.12	F2	K12	Tiger
24. 1	17.12	F2	A1	Leopard
25. 1	18.12	F2	B2	Griffon
26. 1	19.12	F2	C3	Ox
27. 1	20.12	F2	D4	Bat
28. 1	21.12	F2	E5	Rat
29. 1	22.12	F2	F6	Swallow
30. 1	23.12	F2	G7	Pig
31. 1	24.12	F2	H8	Porcupine
1. 2	25.12	F2	J9	Wolf
2. 2	26.12	F2	K10	Dog
3. 2	27.12	F2	A11	Pheasant
4. 2	28.12	F2	B12	Cock
5. 2	29.12	F2	C1	Crow

HSIN MAO YEAR

Solar date	Lunar date	Month HS/EB	Day HS/EB	Constellation
6. 2	1. 1	G3	D2	Monkey
7. 2	2. 1	G3	E3	Gibbon
8. 2	3. 1	G3	F4	Tapir
9. 2	4. 1	G3	G5	Sheep
10. 2	5. 1	G3	H6	Deer
11. 2	6. 1	G3	J7	Horse
12. 2	7. 1	G3	K8	Stag
13. 2	8. 1	G3	A9	Serpent
14. 2	9. 1	G3	B10	Earthworm
15. 2	10. 1	G3	C11	Crocodile
16. 2	11. 1	G3	D12	Dragon
17. 2	12. 1	G3	E1	Badger
18. 2	13. 1	G3	F2	Hare
19. 2	14. 1	G3	G3	Fox
20. 2	15. 1	G3	H4	Tiger
21. 2	16. 1	G3	J5	Leopard
22. 2	17. 1	G3	K6	Griffon
23. 2	18. 1	G3	A7	Ox
24. 2	19. 1	G3	B8	Bat
25. 2	20. 1	G3	C9	Rat
26. 2	21. 1	G3	D10	Swallow
27. 2	22. 1	G3	E11	Pig
28. 2	23. 1	G3	F12	Porcupine
1. 3	24. 1	G3	G1	Wolf
2. 3	25. 1	G3	H2	Dog
3. 3	26. 1	G3	J3	Pheasant
4. 3	27. 1	G3	K4	Cock
5. 3	28. 1	G3	A5	Crow
6. 3	29. 1	G3	B6	Monkey
7. 3	30. 1	G3	C7	Gibbon
8. 3	1. 2	H4	D8	Tapir
9. 3	2. 2	H4	E9	Sheep
10. 3	3. 2	H4	F10	Deer
11. 3	4. 2	H4	G11	Horse
12. 3	5. 2	H4	H12	Stag
13. 3	6. 2	H4	J1	Serpent
14. 3	7. 2	H4	K2	Earthworm
15. 3	8. 2	H4	A3	Crocodile
16. 3	9. 2	H4	B4	Dragon
17. 3	10. 2	H4	C5	Badger
18. 3	11. 2	H4	D6	Hare
19. 3	12. 2	H4	E7	Fox
20. 3	13. 2	H4	F8	Tiger
21. 3	14. 2	H4	G9	Leopard
22. 3	15. 2	H4	H10	Griffon
23. 3	16. 2	H4	J11	Ox
24. 3	17. 2	H4	K12	Bat
25. 3	18. 2	H4	A1	Rat
26. 3	19. 2	H4	B2	Swallow
27. 3	20. 2	H4	C3	Pig
28. 3	21. 2	H4	D4	Porcupine
29. 3	22. 2	H4	E5	Wolf
30. 3	23. 2	H4	F6	Dog
31. 3	24. 2	H4	G7	Pheasant
1. 4	25. 2	H4	H8	Cock
2. 4	26. 2	H4	J9	Crow
3. 4	27. 2	H4	K10	Monkey
4. 4	28. 2	H4	A11	Gibbon
5. 4	29. 2	H4	B12	Tapir
6. 4	1. 3	J5	C1	Sheep
7. 4	2. 3	J5	D2	Deer
8. 4	3. 3	J5	E3	Horse
9. 4	4. 3	J5	F4	Stag
10. 4	5. 3	J5	G5	Serpent
11. 4	6. 3	J5	H6	Earthworm
12. 4	7. 3	J5	J7	Crocodile
13. 4	8. 3	J5	K8	Dragon
14. 4	9. 3	J5	A9	Badger
15. 4	10. 3	J5	B10	Hare
16. 4	11. 3	J5	C11	Fox
17. 4	12. 3	J5	D12	Tiger
18. 4	13. 3	J5	E1	Leopard
19. 4	14. 3	J5	F2	Griffon
20. 4	15. 3	J5	G3	Ox
21. 4	16. 3	J5	H4	Bat
22. 4	17. 3	J5	J5	Rat
23. 4	18. 3	J5	K6	Swallow
24. 4	19. 3	J5	A7	Pig
25. 4	20. 3	J5	B8	Porcupine
26. 4	21. 3	J5	C9	Wolf
27. 4	22. 3	J5	D10	Dog
28. 4	23. 3	J5	E11	Pheasant
29. 4	24. 3	J5	F12	Cock
30. 4	25. 3	J5	G1	Crow
1. 5	26. 3	J5	H2	Monkey
2. 5	27. 3	J5	J3	Gibbon
3. 5	28. 3	J5	K4	Tapir
4. 5	29. 3	J5	A5	Sheep
5. 5	30. 3	J5	B6	Deer
6. 5	1. 4	K6	C7	Horse
7. 5	2. 4	K6	D8	Stag
8. 5	3. 4	K6	E9	Serpent
9. 5	4. 4	K6	F10	Earthworm
10. 5	5. 4	K6	G11	Crocodile
11. 5	6. 4	K6	H12	Dragon
12. 5	7. 4	K6	J1	Badger
13. 5	8. 4	K6	K2	Hare
14. 5	9. 4	K6	A3	Fox
15. 5	10. 4	K6	B4	Tiger
16. 5	11. 4	K6	C5	Leopard
17. 5	12. 4	K6	D6	Griffon
18. 5	13. 4	K6	E7	Ox
19. 5	14. 4	K6	F8	Bat
20. 5	15. 4	K6	G9	Rat
21. 5	16. 4	K6	H10	Swallow
22. 5	17. 4	K6	J11	Pig
23. 5	18. 4	K6	K12	Porcupine
24. 5	19. 4	K6	A1	Wolf
25. 5	20. 4	K6	B2	Dog
26. 5	21. 4	K6	C3	Pheasant
27. 5	22. 4	K6	D4	Cock
28. 5	23. 4	K6	E5	Crow
29. 5	24. 4	K6	F6	Monkey
30. 5	25. 4	K6	G7	Gibbon
31. 5	26. 4	K6	H8	Tapir
1. 6	27. 4	K6	J9	Sheep
2. 6	28. 4	K6	K10	Deer
3. 6	29. 4	K6	A11	Horse
4. 6	30. 4	K6	B12	Stag
5. 6	1. 5	A2	C1	Serpent
6. 6	2. 5	A7	D2	Earthworm
7. 6	3. 5	A7	E3	Crocodile
8. 6	4. 5	A7	F4	Dragon
9. 6	5. 5	A7	G5	Badger
10. 6	6. 5	A7	H6	Hare
11. 6	7. 5	A7	J7	Fox
12. 6	8. 5	A7	K8	Tiger
13. 6	9. 5	A7	A9	Leopard
14. 6	10. 5	A7	B10	Griffon
15. 6	11. 5	A7	C11	Ox
16. 6	12. 5	A7	D12	Bat
17. 6	13. 5	A7	E1	Rat
18. 6	14. 5	A7	F2	Swallow
19. 6	15. 5	A7	G3	Pig
20. 6	16. 5	A7	H4	Porcupine
21. 6	17. 5	A7	J5	Wolf
22. 6	18. 5	A7	K6	Dog
23. 6	19. 5	A7	A7	Pheasant
24. 6	20. 5	A7	B8	Cock
25. 6	21. 5	A7	C9	Crow
26. 6	22. 5	A7	D10	Monkey
27. 6	23. 5	A7	E11	Gibbon

Solar date	*Lunar date*	*Month HS/EB*	*Day HS/EB*	*Constellation*
28. 6	24. 5	A7	F12	Tapir
29. 6	25. 5	A7	G1	Sheep
30. 6	26. 5	A7	H2	Deer
1. 7	27. 5	A7	J3	Horse
2. 7	28. 5	A7	K4	Stag
3. 7	29. 5	A7	A5	Serpent
4. 7	1. 6	B8	B6	Earthworm
5. 7	2. 6	B8	C7	Crocodile
6. 7	3. 6	B8	D8	Dragon
7. 7	4. 6	B8	E9	Badger
8. 7	5. 6	B8	F10	Hare
9. 7	6. 6	B8	G11	Fox
10. 7	7. 6	B8	H12	Tiger
11. 7	8. 6	B8	J1	Leopard
12. 7	9. 6	B8	K2	Griffon
13. 7	10. 6	B8	A3	Ox
14. 7	11. 6	B8	B4	Bat
15. 7	12. 6	B8	C5	Rat
16. 7	13. 6	B8	D6	Swallow
17. 7	14. 6	B8	E7	Pig
18. 7	15. 6	B8	F8	Porcupine
19. 7	16. 6	B8	G9	Wolf
20. 7	17. 6	B8	H10	Dog
21. 7	18. 6	B8	J11	Pheasant
22. 7	19. 6	B8	K12	Cock
23. 7	20. 6	B8	A1	Crow
24. 7	21. 6	B8	B2	Monkey
25. 7	22. 6	B8	C3	Gibbon
26. 7	23. 6	B8	D4	Tapir
27. 7	24. 6	B8	E5	Sheep
28. 7	25. 6	B8	F6	Deer
29. 7	26. 6	B8	G7	Horse
30. 7	27. 6	B8	H8	Stag
31. 7	28. 6	B8	J9	Serpent
1. 8	29. 6	B8	K10	Earthworm
2. 8	30. 6	B8	A11	Crocodile
3. 8	1. 7	C9	B12	Dragon
4. 8	2. 7	C9	C1	Badger
5. 8	3. 7	C9	D2	Hare
6. 8	4. 7	C9	E3	Fox
7. 8	5. 7	C9	F4	Tiger
8. 8	6. 7	C9	G5	Leopard
9. 8	7. 7	C9	H6	Griffon
10. 8	8. 7	C9	J7	Ox
11. 8	9. 7	C9	K8	Bat
12. 8	10. 7	C9	A9	Rat
13. 8	11. 7	C9	B10	Swallow
14. 8	12. 7	C9	C11	Pig
15. 8	13. 7	C9	D12	Porcupine
16. 8	14. 7	C9	E1	Wolf
17. 8	15. 7	C9	F2	Dog
18. 8	16. 7	C9	G3	Pheasant
19. 8	17. 7	C9	H4	Cock
20. 8	18. 7	C9	J5	Crow
21. 8	19. 7	C9	K6	Monkey
22. 8	20. 7	C9	A7	Gibbon
23. 8	21. 7	C9	B8	Tapir
24. 8	22. 7	C9	C9	Sheep
25. 8	23. 7	C9	D10	Deer
26. 8	24. 7	C9	E11	Horse
27. 8	25. 7	C9	F12	Stag
28. 8	26. 7	C9	G1	Serpent
29. 8	27. 7	C9	H2	Earthworm
30. 8	28. 7	C9	J3	Crocodile
31. 8	29. 7	C9	K4	Dragon
1. 9	1. 8	D10	A5	Badger
2. 9	2. 8	D10	B6	Hare
3. 9	3. 8	D10	C7	Fox
4. 9	4. 8	D10	D8	Tiger
5. 9	5. 8	D10	E9	Leopard
6. 9	6. 8	D10	F10	Griffon
7. 9	7. 8	D10	G11	Ox
8. 9	8. 8	D10	H12	Bat
9. 9	9. 8	D10	J1	Rat
10. 9	10. 8	D10	K2	Swallow
11. 9	11. 8	D10	A3	Pig
12. 9	12. 8	D10	B4	Porcupine
13. 9	13. 8	D10	C5	Wolf
14. 9	14. 8	D10	D6	Dog
15. 9	15. 8	D10	E7	Pheasant
16. 9	16. 8	D10	F8	Cock
17. 9	17. 8	D10	G9	Crow
18. 9	18. 8	D10	H10	Monkey
19. 9	19. 8	D10	J11	Gibbon
20. 9	20. 8	D10	K12	Tapir
21. 9	21. 8	D10	A1	Sheep
22. 9	22. 8	D10	B2	Deer
23. 9	23. 8	D10	C3	Horse
24. 9	24. 8	D10	D4	Stag
25. 9	25. 8	D10	E5	Serpent
26. 9	26. 8	D10	F6	Earthworm
27. 9	27. 8	D10	G7	Crocodile
28. 9	28. 8	D10	H8	Dragon
29. 9	29. 8	D10	J9	Badger
30. 9	30. 8	D10	K10	Hare
1.10	1. 9	E11	A11	Fox
2.10	2. 9	E11	B12	Tiger
3.10	3. 9	E11	C1	Leopard
4.10	4. 9	E11	D2	Griffon
5.10	5. 9	E11	E3	Ox
6.10	6. 9	E11	F4	Bat
7.10	7. 9	E11	G5	Rat
8.10	8. 9	E11	H6	Swallow
9.10	9. 9	E11	J7	Pig
10.10	10. 9	E11	K8	Porcupine
11.10	11. 9	E11	A9	Wolf
12.10	12. 9	E11	B10	Dog
13.10	13. 9	E11	C11	Pheasant
14.10	14. 9	E11	D12	Cock
15.10	15. 9	E11	E1	Crow
16.10	16. 9	E11	F2	Monkey
17.10	17. 9	E11	G3	Gibbon
18.10	18. 9	E11	H4	Tapir
19.10	19. 9	E11	J5	Sheep
20.10	20. 9	E11	K6	Deer
21.10	21. 9	E11	A7	Horse
22.10	22. 9	E11	B8	Stag
23.10	23. 9	E11	C9	Serpent
24.10	24. 9	E11	D10	Earthworm
25.10	25. 9	E11	E11	Crocodile
26.10	26. 9	E11	F12	Dragon
27.10	27. 9	E11	G1	Badger
28.10	28. 9	E11	H2	Hare
29.10	29. 9	E11	J3	Fox
30.10	1.10	F12	K4	Tiger
31.10	2.10	F12	A5	Leopard
1.11	3.10	F12	B6	Griffon
2.11	4.10	F12	C7	Ox
3.11	5.10	F12	D8	Bat
4.11	6.10	F12	E9	Rat
5.11	7.10	F12	F10	Swallow
6.11	8.10	F12	G11	Pig
7.11	9.10	F12	H12	Porcupine
8.11	10.10	F12	J1	Wolf
9.11	11.10	F12	K2	Dog
10.11	12.10	F12	A3	Pheasant
11.11	13.10	F12	B4	Cock
12.11	14.10	F12	C5	Crow
13.11	15.10	F12	D6	Monkey
14.11	16.10	F12	E7	Gibbon
15.11	17.10	F12	F8	Tapir
16.11	18.10	F12	G9	Sheep
17.11	19.10	F12	H10	Deer
18.11	20.10	F12	J11	Horse
19.11	21.10	F12	K12	Stag
20.11	22.10	F12	A1	Serpent

Solar date	Lunar date	Month HS/EB	Day HS/EB	Constellation
21.11	23.10	F12	B2	Earthworm
22.11	24.10	F12	C3	Crocodile
23.11	25.10	F12	D4	Dragon
24.11	26.10	F12	E5	Badger
25.11	27.10	F12	F6	Hare
26.11	28.10	F12	G7	Fox
27.11	29.10	F12	H8	Tiger
28.11	30.10	F12	J9	Leopard
29.11	1.11	G1	K10	Griffon
30.11	2.11	G1	A11	Ox
1.12	3.11	G1	B12	Bat
2.12	4.11	G1	C1	Rat
3.12	5.11	G1	D2	Swallow
4.12	6.11	G1	E3	Pig
5.12	7.11	G1	F4	Porcupine
6.12	8.11	G1	G5	Wolf
7.12	9.11	G1	H6	Dog
8.12	10.11	G1	J7	Pheasant
9.12	11.11	G1	K8	Cock
10.12	12.11	G1	A9	Crow
11.12	13.11	G1	B10	Monkey
12.12	14.11	G1	C11	Gibbon
13.12	15.11	G1	D12	Tapir
14.12	16.11	G1	E1	Sheep
15.12	17.11	G1	F2	Deer
16.12	18.11	G1	G3	Horse
17.12	19.11	G1	H4	Stag
18.12	20.11	G1	J5	Serpent
19.12	21.11	G1	K6	Earthworm
20.12	22.11	G1	A7	Crocodile
21.12	23.11	G1	B8	Dragon
22.12	24.11	G1	C9	Badger
23.12	25.11	G1	D10	Hare
24.12	26.11	G1	E11	Fox
25.12	27.11	G1	F12	Tiger

Solar date	Lunar date	Month HS/EB	Day HS/EB	Constellation
26.12	28.11	G1	G1	Leopard
27.12	29.11	G1	H2	Griffon
28.12	1.12	H2	J3	Ox
29.12	2.12	H2	K4	Bat
30.12	3.12	H2	A5	Rat
31.12	4.12	H2	B6	Swallow
1952				
1. 1	5.12	H2	C7	Pig
2. 1	6.12	H2	D8	Porcupine
3. 1	7.12	H2	E9	Wolf
4. 1	8.12	H2	F10	Dog
5. 1	9.12	H2	G11	Pheasant
6. 1	10.12	H2	H12	Cock
7. 1	11.12	H2	J1	Crow
8. 1	12.12	H2	K2	Monkey
9. 1	13.12	H2	A3	Gibbon
10. 1	14.12	H2	B4	Tapir
11. 1	15.12	H2	C5	Sheep
12. 1	16.12	H2	D6	Deer
13. 1	17.12	H2	E7	Horse
14. 1	18.12	H2	F8	Stag
15. 1	19.12	H2	G9	Serpent
16. 1	20.12	H2	H10	Earthworm
17. 1	21.12	H2	J11	Crocodile
18. 1	22.12	H2	K12	Dragon
19. 1	23.12	H2	A1	Badger
20. 1	24.12	H2	B2	Hare
21. 1	25.12	H2	C3	Fox
22. 1	26.12	H2	D4	Tiger
23. 1	27.12	H2	E5	Leopard
24. 1	28.12	H2	F6	Griffon
25. 2	29.12	H2	G7	Ox
26. 1	30.12	H2	H8	Bat

JEN CH'EN YEAR

27. 1	1. 1	J3	J9	Rat
28. 1	2. 1	J3	K10	Swallow
29. 1	3. 1	J3	A11	Pig
30. 1	4. 1	J3	B12	Porcupine
31. 1	5. 1	J3	C1	Wolf
1. 2	6. 1	J3	D2	Dog
2. 2	7. 1	J3	E3	Pheasant
3. 2	8. 1	J3	F4	Cock
4. 2	9. 1	J3	G5	Crow
5. 2	10. 1	J3	H6	Monkey
6. 2	11. 1	J3	J7	Gibbon
7. 2	12. 1	J3	K8	Tapir
8. 2	13. 1	J3	A9	Sheep
9. 2	14. 1	J3	B10	Deer
10. 2	15. 1	J3	C11	Horse
11. 2	16. 1	J3	D12	Stag
12. 2	17. 1	J3	E1	Serpent
13. 2	18. 1	J3	F2	Earthworm
14. 2	19. 1	J3	G3	Crocodile
15. 2	20. 1	J3	H4	Dragon
16. 2	21. 1	J3	J5	Badger
17. 2	22. 1	J3	K6	Hare
18. 2	23. 1	J3	A7	Fox
19. 2	24. 1	J3	B8	Tiger
20. 2	25. 1	J3	D9	Leopard
21. 2	26. 1	J3	D10	Griffon
22. 2	27. 1	J3	E11	Ox
23. 2	28. 1	J3	F12	Bat
24. 2	29. 1	J3	G1	Rat
25. 2	1. 2	K4	H2	Swallow
26. 2	2. 2	K4	J3	Pig
27. 2	3. 2	K4	K4	Porcupine
28. 2	4. 2	K4	A5	Wolf

29. 2	5. 2	K4	B6	Dog
1. 3	6. 2	K4	C7	Pheasant
2. 3	7. 2	K4	D8	Cock
3. 3	8. 2	K4	E9	Crow
4. 3	9. 2	K4	F10	Monkey
5. 3	10. 2	K4	G11	Gibbon
6. 3	11. 2	K4	H12	Tapir
7. 3	12. 2	K4	J1	Sheep
8. 3	13. 2	K4	K2	Deer
9. 3	14. 2	K4	A3	Horse
10. 3	15. 2	K4	B4	Stag
11. 3	16. 2	K4	C5	Serpent
12. 3	17. 2	K4	D6	Earthworm
13. 3	18. 2	K4	E7	Crocodile
14. 3	19. 2	K4	F8	Dragon
15. 3	20. 2	K4	G9	Badger
16. 3	21. 2	K4	H10	Hare
17. 3	22. 2	K4	J11	Fox
18. 3	23. 2	K4	K12	Tiger
19. 3	24. 2	K4	A1	Leopard
20. 3	25. 2	K4	B2	Griffon
21. 3	26. 2	K4	C3	Ox
22. 3	27. 2	K4	D4	Bat
23. 3	28. 2	K4	E5	Rat
24. 3	29. 2	K4	F6	Swallow
25. 3	30. 2	K4	G7	Pig
26. 3	1. 3	A5	H8	Porcupine
27. 3	2. 3	A5	J9	Wolf
28. 3	3. 3	A5	K10	Dog
29. 3	4. 3	A5	A11	Pheasant
30. 3	5. 3	A5	B12	Cock
31. 3	6. 3	A5	C1	Crow
1. 4	7. 3	A5	D2	Monkey

Solar date	*Lunar date*	*Month HS/EB*	*Day HS/EB*	*Constellation*
2. 4	8. 3	A5	E3	Gibbon
3. 4	9. 3	A5	F4	Tapir
4. 4	10. 3	A5	G5	Sheep
5. 4	11. 3	A5	H6	Deer
6. 4	12. 3	A5	J7	Horse
7. 4	13. 3	A5	K8	Stag
8. 4	14. 3	A5	A9	Serpent
9. 4	15. 3	A5	B10	Earthworm
10. 4	16. 3	A5	C11	Crocodile
11. 4	17. 3	A5	D12	Dragon
12. 4	18. 3	A5	E1	Badger
13. 4	19. 3	A5	F2	Hare
14. 4	20. 3	A5	G3	Fox
15. 4	21. 3	A5	H4	Tiger
16. 4	22. 3	A5	J5	Leopard
17. 4	23. 3	A5	K6	Griffon
18. 4	24. 3	A5	A7	Ox
19. 4	25. 3	A5	B8	Bat
20. 4	26. 3	A5	C9	Rat
21. 4	27. 3	A5	D10	Swallow
22. 4	28. 3	A5	E11	Pig
23. 4	29. 3	A5	F12	Porcupine
24. 4	1. 4	B6	G1	Wolf
25. 4	2. 4	B6	H2	Dog
26. 4	3. 4	B6	J3	Pheasant
27. 4	4. 4	B6	K4	Cock
28. 4	5. 4	B6	A5	Crow
29. 4	6. 4	B6	B6	Monkey
30. 4	7. 4	B6	C7	Gibbon
1. 5	8. 4	B6	D8	Tapir
2. 5	9. 4	B6	E9	Sheep
3. 5	10. 4	B6	F10	Deer
4. 5	11. 4	B6	G11	Horse
5. 5	12. 4	B6	H12	Stag
6. 5	13. 4	B6	J1	Serpent
7. 5	14. 4	B6	K2	Earthworm
8. 5	15. 4	B6	A3	Crocodile
9. 5	16. 4	B6	B4	Dragon
10. 5	17. 4	B6	C5	Badger
11. 5	18. 4	B6	D6	Hare
12. 5	19. 4	B6	E7	Fox
13. 5	20. 4	B6	F8	Tiger
14. 5	21. 4	B6	G9	Leopard
15. 5	22. 4	B6	H10	Griffon
16. 5	23. 4	B6	J11	Ox
17. 5	24. 4	B6	K12	Bat
18. 5	25. 4	B6	A1	Rat
19. 5	26. 4	B6	B2	Swallow
20. 5	27. 4	B6	C3	Pig
21. 5	28. 4	B6	D4	Porcupine
22. 5	29. 4	B6	E5	Wolf
23. 5	30. 4	B6	F6	Dog
24. 5	1. 5	C7	G7	Pheasant
25. 5	2. 5	C7	H8	Cock
26. 5	3. 5	C7	J9	Crow
27. 5	4. 5	C7	K10	Monkey
28. 5	5. 5	C7	A11	Gibbon
29. 5	6. 5	C7	B12	Tapir
30. 5	7. 5	C7	C1	Sheep
31. 5	8. 5	C7	D2	Deer
1. 6	9. 5	C7	E3	Horse
2. 6	10. 5	C7	F4	Stag
3. 6	11. 5	C7	G5	Serpent
4. 6	12. 5	C7	H6	Earthworm
5. 6	13. 5	C7	J7	Crocodile
6. 6	14. 5	C7	K8	Dragon
7. 6	15. 5	C7	A9	Badger
8. 6	16. 5	C7	B10	Hare
9. 6	17. 5	C7	C11	Fox
10. 6	18. 5	C7	D12	Tiger
11. 6	19. 5	C7	E1	Leopard
12. 6	20. 5	C7	F2	Griffon
13. 6	21. 5	C7	G3	Ox

Solar date	*Lunar date*	*Month HS/EB*	*Day HS/EB*	*Constellation*
14. 6	22. 5	C7	H4	Bat
15. 6	23. 5	C7	J5	Rat
16. 6	24. 5	C7	K6	Swallow
17. 6	25. 5	C7	A7	Pig
18. 6	26. 5	C7	B8	Porcupine
19. 6	27. 5	C7	C9	Wolf
20. 6	28. 5	C7	D10	Dog
21. 6	29. 5	C7	E11	Pheasant
22. 6	*1. 5*	*C7*	F12	Cock
23. 6	*2. 5*	*C7*	G1	Crow.
24. 6	*3. 5*	*C7*	H2	Monkey
25. 6	*4. 5*	*C7*	J3	Gibbon
26. 6	*5. 5*	*C7*	K4	Tapir
27. 6	*6. 5*	*C7*	A5	Sheep
28. 6	*7. 5*	*C7*	B6	Deer
29. 6	*8. 5*	*C7*	C7	Horse
30. 6	*9. 5*	*C7*	D8	Stag
1. 7	*10. 5*	*C7*	E9	Serpent
2. 7	*11. 5*	*C7*	F10	Earthworm
3. 7	*12. 5*	*C7*	G11	Crocodile
4. 7	*13. 5*	*C7*	H12	Dragon
5. 7	*14. 5*	*C7*	J1	Badger
6. 7	*15. 5*	*C7*	K2	Hare
7. 7	*16. 5*	*C7*	A3	Fox
8. 7	*17. 5*	*C7*	B4	Tiger
9. 7	*18. 5*	*C7*	C5	Leopard
10. 7	*19. 5*	*C7*	D6	Griffon
11. 7	*20. 5*	*C7*	E7	Ox
12. 7	*21. 5*	*C7*	F8	Bat
13. 7	*22. 5*	*C7*	G9	Rat
14. 7	*23. 5*	*C7*	H10	Swallow
15. 7	*24. 5*	*C7*	J11	Pig
16. 7	*25. 5*	*C7*	K12	Porcupine
17. 7	*26. 5*	*C7*	A1	Wolf
18. 7	*27. 5*	*C7*	B2	Dog
19. 7	*28. 5*	*C7*	C3	Pheasant
20. 7	*29. 5*	*C7*	D4	Cock
21. 7	*30. 5*	*C7*	E5	Crow
22. 7	1. 6	D8	F6	Monkey
23. 7	2. 6	D8	G7	Gibbon
24. 7	3. 6	D8	H8	Tapir
25. 7	4. 6	D8	J9	Sheep
26. 7	5. 6	D8	K10	Deer
27. 7	6. 6	D8	A11	Horse
28. 7	7. 6	D8	B12	Stag
29. 7	8. 6	D8	C1	Serpent
30. 7	9. 6	D8	D2	Earthworm
31. 7	10. 6	D8	E3	Crocodile
1. 8	11. 6	D8	F4	Dragon
2. 8	12. 6	D8	G5	Badger
3. 8	13. 6	D8	H6	Hare
4. 8	14. 6	D8	J7	Fox
5. 8	15. 6	D8	K8	Tiger
6. 8	16. 6	D8	A9	Leopard
7. 8	17. 6	D8	B10	Griffon
8. 8	18. 6	D8	C11	Ox
9. 8	19. 6	D8	D12	Bat
10. 8	20. 6	D8	E1	Rat
11. 8	21. 6	D8	F2	Swallow
12. 8	22. 6	D8	G3	Pig
13. 8	23. 6	D8	H4	Porcupine
14. 8	24. 6	D8	J5	Wolf
15. 8	25. 6	D8	K6	Dog
16. 8	26. 6	D8	A7	Pheasant
17. 8	27. 6	D8	B8	Cock
18. 8	28. 6	D8	C9	Crow
19. 8	29. 6	D8	D10	Monkey
20. 8	1. 7	E9	E11	Gibbon
21. 8	2. 7	E9	F12	Tapir
22. 8	3. 7	E9	G1	Sheep
23. 8	4. 7	E9	H2	Deer
24. 8	5. 7	E9	J3	Horse
25. 8	6. 7	E9	K4	Stag

Solar date	*Lunar date*	*Month HS/EB*	*Day HS/EB*	*Constellation*
26. 8	7. 7	E9	A5	Serpent
27. 8	8. 7	E9	B6	Earthworm
28. 8	9. 7	E9	C7	Crocodile
29. 8	10. 7	E9	D8	Dragon
30. 8	11. 7	E9	E9	Badger
31. 8	12. 7	E9	F10	Hare
1. 9	13. 7	E9	G11	Fox
2. 9	14. 7	E9	H12	Tiger
3. 9	15. 7	E9	J1	Leopard
4. 9	16. 7	E9	K2	Griffon
5. 9	17. 7	E9	A3	Ox
6. 9	18. 7	E9	B4	Bat
7. 9	19. 7	E9	C5	Rat
8. 9	20. 7	E9	D6	Swallow
9. 9	21. 7	E9	E7	Pig
10. 9	22. 7	E9	F8	Porcupine
11. 9	23. 7	E9	G9	Wolf
12. 9	24. 7	E9	H10	Dog
13. 9	25. 7	E9	J11	Pheasant
14. 9	26. 7	E9	K12	Cock
15. 9	27. 7	E9	A1	Crow
16. 9	28. 7	E9	B2	Monkey
17. 9	29. 7	E9	C3	Gibbon
18. 9	30. 7	E9	D4	Tapir
19. 9	1. 8	F10	E5	Sheep
20. 9	2. 8	F10	F6	Deer
21. 9	3. 8	F10	G7	Horse
22. 9	4. 8	F10	H8	Stag
23. 9	5. 8	F10	J9	Serpent
24. 9	6. 8	F10	K10	Earthworm
25. 9	7. 8	F10	A11	Crocodile
26. 9	8. 8	F10	B12	Dragon
27. 9	9. 8	F10	C1	Badger
28. 9	10. 8	F10	D2	Hare
29. 9	11. 8	F10	E3	Fox
30. 9	12. 8	F10	F4	Tiger
1.10	13. 8	F10	G5	Leopard
2.10	14. 8	F10	H6	Griffon
3.10	15. 8	F10	J7	Ox
4.10	16. 8	F10	K8	Bat
5.10	17. 8	F10	A9	Rat
6.10	18. 8	F10	B10	Swallow
7.10	19. 8	F10	C11	Pig
8.10	20. 8	F10	D12	Porcupine
9.10	21. 8	F10	E1	Wolf
10.10	22. 8	F10	F2	Dog
11.10	23. 8	F10	G3	Pheasant
12.10	24. 8	F10	H4	Cock
13.10	25. 8	F10	J5	Crow
14.10	26. 8	F10	K6	Monkey
15.10	27. 8	F10	A7	Gibbon
16.10	28. 8	F10	B8	Tapir
17.10	29. 8	F10	C9	Sheep
18.10	30. 8	F10	D10	Deer
19.10	1. 9	G11	E11	Horse
20.10	2. 9	G11	F12	Stag
21.10	3. 9	G11	G1	Serpent
22.10	4. 9	G11	H2	Earthworm
23.10	5. 9	G11	J3	Crocodile
24.10	6. 9	G11	K4	Dragon
25.10	7. 9	G11	A5	Badger
26.10	8. 9	G11	B6	Hare
27.10	9. 9	G11	C7	Fox
28.10	10. 9	G11	D8	Tiger
29.10	11. 9	G11	E9	Leopard
30.10	12. 9	G11	F10	Griffon
31.10	13. 9	G11	G11	Ox
1.11	14. 9	G11	H12	Bat
2.11	15. 9	G11	J1	Rat
3.11	16. 9	G11	K2	Swallow
4.11	17.19	G11	A3	Pig
5.11	18. 9	G11	B4	Porcupine
6.11	19. 9	G11	C5	Wolf

Solar date	*Lunar date*	*Month HS/EB*	*Day HS/EB*	*Constellation*
7.11	20. 9	G11	D6	Dog
8.11	21. 9	G11	E7	Pheasant
9.11	22. 9	G11	F8	Cock
10.11	23. 9	G11	G9	Crow
11.11	24. 9	G11	H10	Monkey
12.11	25. 9	G11	J11	Gibbon
13.11	26. 9	G11	K12	Tapir
14.11	27. 9	G11	A1	Sheep
15.11	28. 9	G11	B2	Deer
16.11	29. 9	G11	C3	Horse
17.11	1.10	H12	D4	Stag
18.11	2.10	H12	E5	Serpent
19.11	3.10	H12	F6	Earthworm
20.11	4.10	H12	G7	Crocodile
21.11	5.10	H12	H8	Dragon
22.11	6.10	H12	J9	Badger
23.11	7.10	H12	K10	Hare
24.11	8.10	H12	A11	Fox
25.11	9.10	H12	B12	Tiger
26.11	10.10	H12	C1	Leopard
27.11	11.10	H12	D2	Griffon
28.11	12.10	H12	E3	Ox
29.11	13.10	H12	F4	Bat
30.11	14.10	H12	G5	Rat
1.12	15.10	H12	H6	Swallow
2.12	16.10	H12	J7	Pig
3.12	17.10	H12	K8	Porcupine
4.12	18.10	H12	A9	Wolf
5.12	19.10	H12	B10	Dog
6.12	20.10	H12	C11	Pheasant
7.12	21.10	H12	D12	Cock
8.12	22.10	H12	E1	Crow
9.12	23.10	H12	F2	Monkey
10.12	24.10	H12	G3	Gibbon
11.12	25.10	H12	H4	Tapir
12.12	26.10	H12	J5	Sheep
13.12	27.10	H12	K6	Deer
14.12	28.10	H12	A7	Horse
15.12	29.10	H12	B8	Stag
16.12	30.10	H12	C9	Serpent
17.12	1.11	J1	D10	Earthworm
18.12	2.11	J1	E11	Crocodile
19.12	3.11	J1	F12	Dragon
20.12	4.11	J1	G1	Badger
21.12	5.11	J1	H2	Hare
22.12	6.11	J1	J3	Fox
23.12	7.11	J1	K4	Tiger
24.12	8.11	J1	A5	Leopard
25.12	9.11	J1	B6	Griffon
26.12	10.11	J1	C7	Ox
27.12	11.11	J1	D8	Bat
28.12	12.11	J1	E9	Rat
29.12	13.11	J1	F10	Swallow
30.12	14.11	J1	G11	Pig
31.12	15.11	J1	H12	Porcupine
1953				
1. 1	16.11	J1	J1	Wolf
2. 1	17.11	J1	K2	Dog
3. 1	18.11	J1	A3	Pheasant
4. 1	19.11	J1	B4	Cock
5. 1	20.11	J1	C5	Crow
6. 1	21.11	J1	D6	Monkey
7. 1	22.11	J1	E7	Gibbon
8. 1	23.11	J1	F8	Tapir
9. 1	24.11	J1	G9	Sheep
10. 1	25.11	J1	H10	Deer
11. 1	26.11	J1	J11	Horse
12. 1	27.11	J1	K12	Stag
13. 1	28.11	J1	A1	Serpent
14. 1	29.11	J1	B2	Earthworm
15. 1	1.12	K2	C3	Crocodile
16. 1	2.12	K2	D4	Dragon

Solar date	*Lunar date*	*Month HS/EB*	*Day HS/EB*	*Constellation*
17. 1	3.12	K2	E5	Badger
18. 1	4.12	K2	F6	Hare
19. 1	5.12	K2	G7	Fox
20. 1	6.12	K2	H8	Tiger
21. 1	7.12	K2	J9	Leopard
22. 1	8.12	K2	K10	Griffon
23. 1	9.12	K2	A11	Ox
24. 1	10.12	K2	B12	Batr
25. 1	11.12	K2	C1	Rat
26. 1	12.12	K2	D2	Swallow
27. 1	13.12	K2	E3	Pig
28. 1	14.12	K2	F4	Porcupine
29. 1	15.12	K2	G5	Wolf
30. 1	16.12	K2	H6	Dog
31. 1	17.12	K2	J7	Pheasant
1. 2	18.12	K2	K8	Cock
2. 2	19.12	K2	A9	Crow
3. 2	20.12	K2	B10	Monkey
4. 2	21.12	K2	C11	Gibbon
5. 2	22.12	K2	D12	Tapir
6. 2	23.12	K2	E1	Sheep
7. 2	24.12	K2	F2	Deer
8. 2	25.12	K2	G3	Horse
9. 2	26.12	K2	H4	Stag
10. 2	27.12	K2	J5	Serpent
11. 2	28.12	K2	K6	Earthworm
12. 2	29.12	K2	A7	Crocodile
13. 2	30.12	K2	B8	Dragon

KUEI SZU YEAR

14. 2	1. 1	A3	C9	Badger
15. 2	2. 1	A3	D10	Hare
16. 2	3. 1	A3	E11	Fox
17. 2	4. 1	A3	F12	Tiger
18. 2	5. 1	A3	G1	Leopard
19. 2	6. 1	A3	H2	Griffon
20. 2	7. 1	A3	J3	Ox
21. 2	8. 1	A3	K4	Bat
22. 2	9. 1	A3	A5	Rat
23. 2	10. 1	A3	B6	Swallow
24. 2	11. 1	A3	C7	Pig
25. 2	12. 1	A3	D8	Porcupine
26. 2	13. 1	A3	E9	Wolf
27. 2	14. 1	A3	F10	Dog
28. 2	15. 1	A3	G11	Pheasant
1. 3	16. 1	A3	H12	Cock
2. 3	17. 1	A3	J1	Crow
3. 3	18. 1	A3	K2	Monkey
4. 3	19. 1	A3	A3	Gibbon
5. 3	20. 1	A3	B4	Tapir
6. 3	21. 1	A3	C5	Sheep
7. 3	22. 1	A3	D6	Deer
8. 3	23. 1	A3	E7	Horse
9. 3	24. 1	A3	F8	Stag
10. 3	25. 1	A3	G9	Serpent
11. 3	26. 1	A3	H10	Earthworm
12. 3	27. 1	A3	J11	Crocodile
13. 3	28. 1	A3	K12	Dragon
14. 3	29. 1	A3	A1	Badger
15. 3	1. 2	B4	B2	Hare
16. 3	2. 2	B4	C3	Fox
17. 3	3. 2	B4	D4	Tiger
18. 3	4. 2	B4	E5	Leopard
19. 3	5. 2	B4	F6	Griffon
20. 3	6. 2	B4	G7	Ox
21. 3	7. 2	B4	H8	Bat
22. 3	8. 2	B4	J9	Rat
23. 3	9. 2	B4	K10	Swallow
24. 3	10. 2	B4	A11	Pig
25. 3	11. 2	B4	B12	Porcupine
26. 3	12. 2	B4	C1	Wolf
27. 3	13. 2	B4	D2	Dog
28. 3	14. 2	B4	E3	Pheasant
29. 3	15. 2	B4	F4	Cock
30. 3	16. 2	B4	G5	Crow
31. 3	17. 2	B4	H6	Monkey
1. 4	18. 2	B4	J7	Gibbon
2. 4	19. 2	B4	K8	Tapir
3. 4	20. 2	B4	A9	Sheep
4. 4	21. 2	B4	B10	Deer
5. 4	22. 2	B4	C11	Horse
6. 4	23. 2	B4	D12	Stag
7. 4	24. 2	B4	E1	Serpent
8. 4	25. 2	B4	F2	Earthworm
9. 4	26. 2	B4	G3	Crocodile
10. 4	27. 2	B4	H4	Dragon
11. 4	28. 2	B4	J5	Badger
12. 4	29. 2	B4	K6	Hare
13. 4	30. 2	B4	A7	Fox
14. 4	1. 3	C5	B8	Tiger
15. 4	2. 3	C5	C9	Leopard
16. 4	3. 3	C5	D10	Griffon
17. 4	4. 3	C5	E11	Ox
18. 4	5. 3	C5	F12	Bat
19. 4	6. 3	C5	G1	Rat
20. 4	7. 3	C5	H2	Swallow
21. 4	8. 3	C5	J3	Pig
22. 4	9. 3	C5	K4	Porcupine
23. 4	10. 3	C5	A5	Wolf
24. 4	11. 3	C5	B6	Dog
25. 4	12. 3	C5	C7	Pheasant
26. 4	13. 3	C5	D8	Cock
27. 4	14. 3	C5	E9	Crow
28. 4	15. 3	C5	F10	Monkey
29. 4	16. 3	C5	G11	Gibbon
30. 4	17. 3	C5	H12	Tapir
1. 5	18. 3	C5	J1	Sheep
2. 5	19. 3	C5	K2	Deer
3. 5	20. 3	C5	A3	Horse
4. 5	21. 3	C5	B4	Stag
5. 5	22. 3	C5	C5	Serpent
6. 5	23. 3	C5	D6	Earthworm
7. 5	24. 3	C5	E7	Crocodile
8. 5	25. 3	C5	F8	Dragon
9. 5	26. 3	C5	G9	Badger
10. 5	27. 3	C5	H10	Hare
11. 5	28. 3	C5	J11	Fox
12. 5	29. 3	C5	K12	Tiger
13. 5	1. 4	D6	A1	Leopard
14. 5	2. 4	D6	B2	Griffon
15. 5	3. 4	D6	C3	Ox
16. 5	4. 4	D6	D4	Bat
17. 5	5. 4	D6	E5	Rat
18. 5	6. 4	D6	F6	Swallow
19. 5	7. 4	D6	G7	Pig
20. 5	8. 4	D6	H8	Porcupine
21. 5	9. 4	D6	J9	Wolf
22. 5	10. 4	D6	K10	Dog
23. 5	11. 4	D6	A11	Pheasant
24. 5	12. 4	D6	B12	Cock
25. 5	13. 4	D6	C1	Crow
26. 5	14. 4	D6	D2	Monkey
27. 5	15. 4	D6	E3	Gibbon
28. 5	16. 4	D6	F4	Tapir
29. 5	17. 4	D6	G5	Sheep
30. 5	18. 4	D6	H6	Deer
31. 5	19. 4	D6	J7	Horse
1. 6	20. 4	D6	K8	Stag

Solar date	Lunar date	Month HS/EB	Day HS/EB	Constellation
2. 6	21. 4	D6	A9	Serpent
3. 6	22. 4	D6	B10	Earthworm
4. 6	23. 4	D6	C11	Crocodile
5. 6	24. 4	D6	D12	Drgon
6. 6	25. 4	D6	E1	Badger
7. 6	26. 4	D6	F2	Hare
8. 6	27. 4	D6	G3	Fox
9. 6	28. 4	D6	H4	Tiger
10. 6	29. 4	D6	J5	Leopard
11. 6	1. 5	E7	K6	Griffon
12. 6	2. 5	E7	A7	Ox
13. 6	3. 5	E7	B8	Bat
14. 6	4. 5	E7	C9	Rat
15. 6	5. 5	E7	D10	Swallow
16. 6	6. 5	E7	E11	Pig
17. 6	7. 5	E7	F12	Porcupine
18. 6	8. 5	E7	G1	Wolf
19. 6	9. 5	E7	H2	Dog
20. 6	10. 5	E7	J3	Pheasant
21. 6	11. 5	E7	K4	Cock
22. 6	12. 5	E7	A5	Crow
23. 6	13. 5	E7	B6	Monkey
24. 6	14. 5	E7	C7	Gibbon
25. 6	15. 5	E7	D8	Tapir
26. 6	16. 5	E7	E9	Sheep
27. 6	17. 5	E7	F10	Deer
28. 6	18. 5	E7	G11	Horse
29. 6	19. 5	E7	H12	Stag
30. 6	20. 5	E7	J1	Serpent
1. 7	21. 5	E7	K2	Earthworm
2. 7	22. 5	E7	A3	Crocodile
3. 7	23. 5	E7	B4	Dragon
4. 7	24. 5	E7	C5	Badger
5. 7	25. 5	E7	D6	Hare
6. 7	26. 5	E7	E7	Fox
7. 7	27. 5	E7	F8	Tiger
8. 7	28. 5	E7	G9	Leopard
9. 7	29. 5	E7	H10	Griffon
10. 7	30. 5	E7	J11	Ox
11. 7	1. 6	F8	K12	Bat
12. 7	2. 6	F8	A1	Rat
13. 7	3. 6	F8	B2	Swallow
14. 7	4. 6	F8	C3	Pig
15. 7	5. 6	F8	D4	Porcupine
16. 7	6. 6	F8	E5	Wolf
17. 7	7. 6	F8	F6	Dog
18. 7	8. 6	F8	G7	Pheasant
19. 7	9. 6	F8	H8	Cock
20. 7	10. 6	F8	J9	Crow
21. 7	11. 6	F8	K10	Monkey
22. 7	12. 6	F8	A11	Gibbon
23. 7	13. 6	F8	B12	Tapir
24. 7	14. 6	F8	C1	Sheep
25. 7	15. 6	F8	D2	Deer
26. 7	16. 6	F8	E3	Horse
27. 7	17. 6	F8	F4	Stag
28. 7	18. 6	F8	G5	Serpent
29. 7	19. 6	F8	H6	Earthworm
30. 7	20. 6	F8	J7	Crocodile
31. 7	21. 6	F8	K8	Dragon
1. 8	22. 6	F8	A9	Badger
2. 8	23. 6	F8	B10	Hare
3. 8	24. 6	F8	C11	Fox
4. 8	25. 6	F8	D12	Tiger
5. 8	26. 6	F8	E1	Leopard
6. 8	27. 6	F8	F2	Griffon
7. 8	28. 6	F8	G3	Ox
8. 8	29. 6	F8	H4	Bat
9. 8	30. 6	F8	J5	Rat
10. 8	1. 7	G9	K6	Swallow
11. 8	2. 7	G9	A7	Pig
12. 8	3. 7	G9	B8	Porcupine
13. 8	4. 7	G9	C9	Wolf
14. 8	5. 7	G9	D10	Dog
15. 8	6. 7	G9	E11	Pheasant
16. 8	7. 7	G9	F12	Cock
17. 8	8. 7	G9	G1	Crow
18. 8	9. 7	G9	H2	Monkey
19. 8	10. 7	G9	J3	Gibbon
20. 8	11. 7	G9	K4	Tapir
21. 8	12. 7	G9	A5	Sheep
22. 8	13. 7	G9	B6	Deer
23. 8	14. 7	G9	C7	Horse
24. 8	15. 7	G9	D8	Stag
25. 8	16. 7	G9	E9	Serpent
26. 8	17. 7	G9	F10	Earthworm
27. 8	18. 7	G9	G11	Crocodile
28. 8	19. 7	G9	H12	Dragon
29. 8	20. 7	G9	J1	Badger
30. 8	21. 7	G9	K2	Hare
31. 8	22. 7	G9	A3	Fox
1. 9	23. 7	G9	B4	Tiger
2. 9	24. 7	G9	C5	Leopard
3. 9	25. 7	G9	D6	Griffon
4. 9	26. 7	G9	E7	Ox
5. 9	27. 7	G9	F8	Bat
6. 9	28. 7	G9	G9	Rat
7. 9	29. 7	G9	H10	Swallow
8. 9	1. 8	H10	J11	Pig
9. 9	2. 8	H10	K12	Porcupine
10. 9	3. 8	H10	A1	Wolf
11. 9	4. 8	H10	B2	Dog
12. 9	5. 8	H10	C3	Pheasant
13. 9	6. 8	H10	D4	Cock
14. 9	7. 8	H10	E5	Crow
15. 9	8. 8	H10	F6	Monkey
16. 9	9. 8	H10	G7	Gibbon
17. 9	10. 8	H10	H8	Tapir
18. 9	11. 8	H10	J9	Sheep
19. 9	12. 8	H10	K10	Deer
20. 9	13. 8	H10	A11	Horse
21. 9	14. 8	H10	B12	Stag
22. 9	15. 8	H10	C1	Serpent
23. 9	16. 8	H10	D2	Earthworm
24. 9	17. 8	H10	E3	Crocodile
25. 9	18. 8	H10	F4	Dragon
26. 9	19. 8	H10	G5	Badger
27. 9	20. 8	H10	H6	Hare
28. 9	21. 8	H10	J7	Fox
29. 9	22. 8	H10	K8	Tiger
30. 9	23. 8	H10	A9	Leopard
1.10	24. 8	H10	B10	Griffon
2.10	25. 8	H10	C11	Ox
3.10	26. 8	H10	D12	Bat
4.10	27. 8	H10	E1	Rat
5.10	28. 8	H10	F2	Swallow
6.10	29. 8	H10	G3	Pig
7.10	30. 8	H10	H4	Porcupine
8.10	1. 9	J11	J5	Wolf
9.10	2. 9	J11	K6	Dog
10.10	3. 9	J11	A7	Pheasant
11.10	4. 9	J11	B8	Cock
12.10	5. 9	J11	C9	Crow
13.10	6. 9	J11	D10	Monkey
14.10	7. 9	J11	E11	Gibbon
15.10	8. 9	J11	F12	Tapir
16.10	9. 9	J11	G1	Sheep
17.10	10. 9	J11	H2	Deer
18.10	11. 9	J11	J3	Horse
19.10	12. 9	J11	K4	Stag
20.10	13. 9	J11	A5	Serpent
21.10	14. 9	J11	B6	Earthworm
22.10	15. 9	J11	C7	Crocodile
23.10	16. 9	J11	D8	Dragon
24.10	17. 9	J11	E9	Badger
25.10	18. 9	J11	F10	Hare

Solar date	Lunar date	Month HS/EB	Day HS/EB	Constellation
26.10	19. 9	J11	G11	Fox
27.10	20. 9	J11	H12	Tiger
28.10	21. 9	J11	J1	Leopard
29.10	22. 9	J11	K2	Griffon
30.10	23. 9	J11	A3	Ox
31.10	24. 9	J11	B4	Bat
1.11	25. 9	J11	C5	Rat
2.11	26. 9	J11	D6	Swallow
3.11	27. 9	J11	E7	Pig
4.11	28. 9	J11	F8	Porcupine
5.11	29. 9	J11	G9	Wolf
6.11	30. 9	J11	H10	Dog
7.11	1.10	K12	J11	Pheasant
8.11	2.10	K12	K12	Cock
9.11	3.10	K12	A1	Crow
10.11	4.10	K12	B2	Monkey
11.11	5.10	K12	C3	Gibbon
12.11	6.10	K12	D4	Tapir
13.11	7.10	K12	E5	Sheep
14.11	8.10	K12	F6	Deer
15.11	9.10	K12	G7	Horse
16.11	10.10	K12	H8	Stag
17.11	11.10	K12	J9	Serpent
18.11	12.10	K12	K10	Earthworm
19.11	13.10	K12	A11	Crocodile
20.11	14.10	K12	B12	Dragon
21.11	15.10	K12	C1	Badger
22.11	16.10	K12	D2	Hare
23.11	17.10	K12	E3	Fox
24.11	18.10	K12	F4	Tiger
25.11	19.10	K12	G5	Leopard
26.11	20.10	K12	H6	Griffon
27.11	21.10	K12	J7	Ox
28.11	22.10	K12	K8	Bat
29.11	23.10	K12	A9	Rat
30.11	24.10	K12	B10	Swallow
1.12	25.10	K12	C11	Pig
2.12	26.10	K12	D12	Porcupine
3.12	27.10	K12	E1	Wolf
4.12	28.10	K12	F2	Dog
5.12	29.10	K12	G3	Pheasant
6.12	1.11	A1	H4	Cock
7.12	2.11	A1	J5	Crow
8.12	3.11	A1	K6	Monkey
9.12	4.11	A1	A7	Gibbon
10.12	5.11	A1	B8	Tapir
11.12	6.11	A1	C9	Sheep
12.12	7.11	A1	D10	Deer
13.12	8.11	A1	E11	Horse
14.12	9.11	A1	F12	Stag
15.12	10.11	A1	G1	Serpent
16.12	11.11	A1	H2	Earthworm
17.12	12.11	A1	J3	Crocodile
18.12	13.11	A1	K4	Dragon
19.12	14.11	A1	A5	Badger
20.12	15.11	A1	B6	Hare
21.12	16.11	A1	C7	Fox
22.12	17.11	A1	D8	Tiger
23.12	18.11	A1	E9	Leopard
24.12	19.11	A1	F10	Griffon
25.12	20.11	A1	G11	Ox
26.12	21.11	A1	H12	Bat
27.12	22.11	A1	J1	Rat
28.12	23.11	A1	K2	Swallow
29.12	24.11	A1	A3	Pig
30.12	25.11	A1	B4	Porcupine
31.12	26.11	A1	C5	Wolf
1954				
1. 1	27.11	A1	D6	Dog
2. 1	28.11	A1	E7	Pheasant
3. 1	29.11	A1	F8	Cock
4. 1	30.11	A1	G9	Crow
5. 1	1.12	B2	H10	Monkey
6. 1	2.12	B2	J11	Gibbon
7. 1	3.12	B2	K12	Tapir
8. 1	4.12	B2	A1	Sheep
9. 1	5.12	B2	B2	Deer
10. 1	6.12	B2	C3	Horse
11. 1	7.12	B2	D4	Stag
12. 1	8.12	B2	E5	Serpent
13. 1	9.12	B2	F6	Earthworm
14. 1	10.12	B2	G7	Crocodile
15. 1	11.12	B2	H8	Dragon
16. 1	12.12	B2	J9	Badger
17. 1	13.12	B2	K10	Hare
18. 1	14.12	B2	A11	Fox
19. 1	15.12	B2	B12	Tiger
20. 1	16.12	B2	C1	Leopard
21. 1	17.12	B2	D2	Griffon
22. 1	18.12	B2	E3	Ox
23. 1	19.12	B2	F4	Bat
24. 1	20.12	B2	G5	Rat
25. 1	21.12	B2	H6	Swallow
26. 1	22.12	B2	J7	Pig
27. 1	23.12	B2	K8	Porcupine
28. 1	24.12	B2	A9	Wolf
29. 1	25.12	B2	B10	Dog
30. 1	26.12	B2	C11	Pheasant
31. 1	27.12	B2	D12	Cock
1. 2	28.12	B2	E1	Crow
2. 2	29.12	B2	F2	Monkey

CHIA WU YEAR

3. 2	1. 1	C3	G3	Gibbon
4. 2	2. 1	C3	H4	Tapir
5. 2	3. 1	C3	J5	Sheep
6. 2	4. 1	C3	K6	Deer
7. 2	5. 1	C3	A7	Horse
8. 2	6. 1	C3	B8	Stag
9. 2	7. 1	C3	C9	Serpent
10. 2	8. 1	C3	D10	Earthworm
11. 2	9. 1	C3	E11	Crocodile
12. 2	10. 1	C3	F12	Dragon
13. 2	11. 1	C3	G1	Badger
14. 2	12. 1	C3	H2	Hare
15. 2	13. 1	C3	J3	Fox
16. 2	14. 1	C3	K4	Tiger
17. 2	15. 1	C3	A5	Leopard
18. 2	16. 1	C3	B6	Griffon
19. 2	17. 1	C3	C7	Ox
20. 2	18. 1	C3	D8	Bat
21. 2	19. 1	C3	E9	Rat
22. 2	20. 1	C3	F10	Swallow
23. 2	21. 1	C3	G11	Pig
24. 2	22. 1	C3	H12	Porcupine
25. 2	23. 1	C3	J1	Wolf
26. 2	24. 1	C3	K2	Dog
27. 2	25. 1	C3	A3	Pheasant
28. 2	26. 1	C3	B4	Cock
1. 3	27. 1	C3	C5	Crow
2. 3	28. 1	C3	D6	Monkey
3. 3	29. 1	C3	E7	Gibbon
4. 3	30. 1	C3	F8	Tapir
5. 3	1. 2	D4	G9	Sheep
6. 3	2. 2	D4	H10	Deer
7. 3	3. 2	D4	J11	Horse
8. 3	4. 2	D4	K12	Stag

Solar date	Lunar date	Month HS/EB	Day HS/EB	Constellation	Solar date	Lunar date	Month HS/EB	Day HS/EB	Constellation
9. 3	5. 2	D4	A1	Serpent	21. 5	19. 4	F6	D2	Dog
10. 3	6. 2	D4	B2	Earthworm	22. 5	20. 4	F6	E3	Pheasant
11. 3	7. 2	D4	C3	Crocodile	23. 5	21. 4	F6	F4	Cock
12. 3	8. 2	D4	D4	Dragon	24. 5	22. 4	F6	G5	Crow
13. 3	9. 2	D4	E5	Badger	25. 5	23. 4	F6	H6	Monkey
14. 3	10. 2	D4	F6	Hare	26. 5	24. 4	F6	J7	Gibbon
15. 3	11. 2	D4	G7	Fox	27. 5	25. 4	F6	K8	Tapir
16. 3	12. 2	D4	H8	Tiger	28. 5	26. 4	F6	A9	Sheep
17. 3	13. 2	D4	J9	Leopard	29. 5	27. 4	F6	B10	Deer
18. 3	14. 2	D4	K10	Griffon	30. 5	28. 4	F6	C11	Horse
19. 3	15. 2	D4	A11	Ox	31. 5	29. 4	F6	D12	Stag
20. 3	16. 2	D4	B12	Bat	1. 6	1. 5	G7	E1	Serpent
21. 3	17. 2	D4	C1	Rat	2. 6	2. 5	G7	F2	Earthworm
22. 3	18. 2	D4	D2	Swallow	3. 6	3. 5	G7	G3	Crocodile
23. 3	19. 2	D4	E3	Pig	4. 6	4. 5	G7	H4	Dragon
24. 3	20. 2	D4	F4	Porcupine	5. 6	5. 5	G7	J5	Badger
25. 3	21. 2	D4	G5	Wolf	6. 6	6. 5	G7	K6	Hare
26. 3	22, 2	D4	H6	Dog	7. 6	7. 5	G7	A7	Fox
27. 3	23. 2	D4	J7	Pheasant	8. 6	8. 5	G7	B8	Tiger
28. 3	24. 2	D4	K8	Cock	9. 6	9. 5	G7	C9	Leopard
29. 3	25. 2	D4	A9	Crow	10. 6	10. 5	G7	D10	Griffon
30. 3	26. 2	D4	B10	Monkey	11. 6	11. 5	G7	E11	Ox
31. 3	27. 2	D4	C11	Gibbon	12. 6	12. 5	G7	F12	Bat
1. 4	28. 2	D4	D12	Tapir	13. 6	13. 5	G7	G1	Rat
2. 4	29. 2	D4	E1	Sheep	14. 6	14. 5	G7	H2	Swallow
3. 4	1. 3	E5	F2	Deer	15. 6	15. 5	G7	J3	Pig
4. 4	2. 3	E5	G3	Horse	16. 6	16. 5	G7	K4	Porcupine
5. 4	3. 3	E5	H4	Stag	17. 6	17. 5	G7	A5	Wolf
6. 4	4. 3	E5	J5	Serpent	18. 6	18. 5	G7	B6	Dog
7. 4	5. 3	E5	K6	Earthworm	19. 6	19. 5	G7	C7	Pheasant
8. 4	6. 3	E5	A7	Crocodile	20. 6	20. 5	G7	D8	Cock
9. 4	7. 3	E5	B8	Dragon	21. 6	21. 5	G7	E9	Crow
10. 4	8. 3	E5	C9	Badger	22. 6	22. 5	G7	F10	Monkey
11. 4	9. 3	E5	D10	Hare	23. 6	23. 5	G7	G11	Gibbon
12. 4	10. 3	E5	E11	Fox	24. 6	24. 5	G7	H12	Tapir
13. 4	11. 3	E5	F12	Tiger	25. 6	25. 5	G7	J1	Sheep
14. 4	12. 3	E5	G1	Leopard	26. 6	26. 5	G7	K2	Deer
15. 4	13. 3	E5	H2	Griffon	27. 6	27. 5	G7	A3	Horse
16. 4	14. 3	E5	J3	Ox	28. 6	28. 5	G7	B4	Stag
17. 4	15. 3	E5	K4	Bat	29. 6	29. 5	G7	C5	Serpent
18. 4	16. 3	E5	A5	Rat	30. 6	1. 6	H8	D6	Earthworm
19. 4	17. 3	E5	B6	Swallow	1. 7	2. 6	H8	E7	Crocodile
20. 4	18. 3	E5	C7	Pig	2. 7	3. 6	H8	F8	Dragon
21. 4	19. 3	E5	D8	Porcupine	3. 7	4. 6	H8	G9	Badger
22. 4	20. 3	E5	E9	Wolf	4. 7	5. 6	H8	H10	Hare
23. 4	21. 3	E5	F10	Dog	5. 7	6. 6	H8	J11	Fox
24. 4	22. 3	E5	G11	Pheasant	6. 7	7. 6	H8	K12	Tiger
25. 4	23. 3	E5	H12	Cock	7. 7	8. 6	H8	A1	Leopard
26. 4	24. 3	E5	J1	Crow	8. 7	9. 6	H8	B2	Griffon
27. 4	25. 3	E5	K2	Monkey	9. 7	10. 6	H8	C3	Ox
28. 4	26. 3	E5	A3	Gibbon	10. 7	11. 6	H8	D4	Bat
29. 4	27. 3	E5	B4	Tapir	11. 7	12. 6	H8	E5	Rat
30. 4	28. 3	E5	C5	Sheep	12. 7	13. 6	H8	F6	Swallow
1. 5	29. 3	E5	D6	Deer	13. 7	14. 6	H8	G7	Pig
2. 5	30. 3	E5	E7	Horse	14. 7	15. 6	H8	H8	Porcupine
3. 5	1. 4	F6	F8	Stag	15. 7	16. 6	H8	J9	Wolf
4. 4	2. 4	F6	G9	Serpent	16. 7	17. 6	H8	K10	Dog
5. 5	3. 4	F6	H10	Earthworm	17. 7	18. 6	H8	A11	Pheasant
6. 5	4. 4	F6	J11	Crocodile	18. 7	19. 6	H8	B12	Cock
7. 5	5. 4	F6	K12	Dragon	19. 7	20. 6	H8	C1	Crow
8. 5	6. 4	F6	A1	Badger	20. 7	21. 6	H8	D2	Monkey
9. 5	7. 4	F6	B2	Hare	21. 7	22. 6	H8	E3	Gibbon
10. 5	8. 4	F6	C3	Fox	22. 7	23. 6	H8	F4	Tapir
11. 5	9. 4	F6	D4	Tiger	23. 7	24. 6	H8	G5	Sheep
12. 5	10. 4	F6	E5	Leopard	24. 7	25. 6	H8	H6	Deer
13. 5	11. 4	F6	F6	Griffon	25. 7	26. 6	H8	J7	Horse
14. 5	12. 4	F6	G7	Ox	26. 7	27. 6	H8	K8	Stag
15. 5	13. 4	F6	H8	Bat	27. 7	28. 6	H8	A9	Serpent
16. 5	14. 4	F6	J9	Rat	28. 7	29. 6	H8	B10	Earthworm
17. 5	15. 4	F6	K10	Swallow	29. 7	30. 6	H8	C11	Crocodile
18. 5	16. 4	F6	A11	Pig	30. 7	1. 7	J9	D12	Dragon
19. 5	17. 4	F6	B12	Porcupine	31. 7	2. 7	J9	E1	Badger
20. 5	18. 4	F6	C1	Wolf	1. 8	3. 7	J9	F2	Hare

Solar date	*Lunar date*	*Month HS/EB*	*Day HS/EB*	*Constellation*
2. 8	4. 7	J9	G3	Fox
3. 8	5. 7	J9	H4	Tiger
4. 8	6. 7	J9	J5	Leopard
5. 8	7. 7	J9	K6	Griffon
6. 8	8. 7	J9	A7	Ox
7. 8	9. 7	J9	B8	Bat
8. 8	10. 7	J9	C9	Rat
9. 8	11. 7	J9	D10	Swallow
10. 8	12. 7	J9	E11	Pig
11. 8	13. 7	J9	F12	Porcupine
12. 8	14. 7	J9	G1	Wolf
13. 8	15. 7	J9	H2	Dog
14. 8	16. 7	J9	J3	Pheasant
15. 8	17. 7	J9	K4	Cock
16. 8	18. 7	J9	A5	Crow
17. 8	19. 7	J9	B6	Monkey
18. 8	20. 7	J9	C7	Gibbon
19. 8	21. 7	J9	D8	Tapir
20. 8	22. 7	J9	E9	Sheep
21. 8	23. 7	J9	F10	Deer
22. 8	24. 7	J9	G11	Horse
23. 8	25. 7	J9	H12	Stag
24. 8	26. 7	J9	J1	Serpent
25. 8	27. 7	J9	K2	Earthworm
26. 8	28. 7	J9	A3	Crocodile
27. 8	29. 7	J9	B4	Dragon
28. 8	1. 8	K10	C5	Badger
29. 8	2. 8	K10	D6	Hare
30. 8	3. 8	K10	E7	Fox
31. 8	4. 8	K10	F8	Tiger
1. 9	5. 8	K10	G9	Leopard
2. 9	6. 8	K10	H10	Griffon
3. 9	7. 8	K10	J11	Ox
4. 9	8. 8	K10	K12	Bat
5. 9	9. 8	K10	A1	Rat
6. 9	10. 8	K10	B2	Swallow
7. 9	11. 8	K10	C3	Pig
8. 9	12. 8	K10	D4	Porcupine
9. 9	13. 8	K10	E5	Wolf
10. 9	14. 8	K10	F6	Dog
11. 9	15. 8	K10	G7	Pheasant
12. 9	16. 8	K10	H8	Cock
13. 9	17. 8	K10	J9	Crow
14. 9	18. 8	K10	K10	Monkey
15. 9	19. 8	K10	A11	Gibbon
16. 9	20. 8	K10	B12	Tapir
17. 9	21. 8	K10	C1	Sheep
18. 9	22. 8	K10	D2	Deer
19. 9	23. 8	K10	E3	Horse
20. 9	24. 8	K10	F4	Stag
21. 9	25. 8	K10	G5	Serpent
22. 9	26. 8	K10	H6	Earthworm
23. 9	27. 8	K10	J7	Crocodile
24. 9	28. 8	K10	K8	Dragon
25. 9	29. 8	K10	A9	Badger
26. 9	30. 8	K10	B10	Hare
27. 9	1. 9	A11	C11	Fox
28. 9	2. 9	A11	D12	Tiger
29. 9	3. 9	A11	E1	Leopard
30. 9	4. 9	A11	F2	Griffon
1.10	5. 9	A11	G3	Ox
2.10	6. 9	A11	H4	Bat
3.10	7. 9	A11	J5	Rat
4.10	8. 9	A11	K6	Swallow
5.10	9. 9	A11	A7	Pig
6.10	10. 9	A11	B8	Porcupine
7.10	11. 9	A11	C9	Wolf
8.10	12. 9	A11	D10	Dog
9.10	13. 9	A11	E11	Pheasant
10.10	14. 9	A11	F12	Cock
11.10	15. 9	A11	G1	Crow
12.10	16. 9	A11	H2	Monkey
13.10	17. 9	A11	J3	Gibbon

Solar date	*Lunar date*	*Month HS/EB*	*Day HS/EB*	*Constellation*
14.10	18. 9	A11	K4	Tapir
15.10	19. 9	A11	A5	Sheep
16.10	20. 9	A11	B6	Deer
17.10	21. 9	A11	C7	Horse
18.10	22. 9	A11	D8	Stag
19.10	23. 9	A11	E9	Serpent
20.10	24. 9	A11	F10	Earthworm
21.10	25. 9	A11	G11	Crocodile
22.10	26. 9	A11	H12	Dragon
23.10	27. 9	A11	J1	Badger
24.10	28. 9	A11	K2	Hare
25.10	29. 9	A11	A3	Fox
26.10	30. 9	A11	B4	Tiger
27.10	1.10	B12	C5	Leopard
28.10	2.10	B12	D6	Griffon
29.10	3.10	B12	E7	Ox
30.10	4.10	B12	F8	Bat
31.10	5.10	B12	G9	Rat
1.11	6.10	B12	H10	Swallow
2.11	7.10	B12	J11	Pig
3.11	8.10	B12	K12	Porcupine
4.11	9.10	B12	A1	Wolf
5.11	10.10	B12	B2	Dog
6.11	11.10	B12	C3	Pheasant
7.11	12.10	B12	D4	Cock
8.11	13.10	B12	E5	Crow
9.11	14.10	B12	F6	Monkey
10.11	15.10	B12	G7	Gibbon
11.11	16.10	B12	H8	Tapir
12.11	17.10	B12	J9	Sheep
13.11	18.10	B12	K10	Deer
14.11	19.10	B12	A11	Horse
15.11	20.10	B12	B12	Stag
16.11	21.10	B12	C1	Serpent
17.11	22.10	B12	D2	Earthworm
18.11	23.10	B12	E3	Crocodile
19.11	24.10	B12	F4	Dragon
20.11	25.10	B12	G5	Badger
21.11	26.10	B12	H6	Hare
22.11	27.10	B12	J7	Fox
23.11	28.10	B12	K8	Tiger
24.11	29.10	B12	A9	Leopard
25.11	1.11	C1	B10	Griffon
26.11	2.11	C1	C11	Ox
27.11	3.11	C1	D12	Bat
28.11	4.11	C1	E1	Rat
29.11	5.11	C1	F2	Swallow
30.11	6.11	C1	G3	Pig
1.12	7.11	C1	H4	Porcupine
2.12	8.11	C1	J5	Wolf
3.12	9.11	C1	K6	Dog
4.12	10.11	C1	A7	Pheasant
5.12	11.11	C1	B8	Cock
6.12	12.11	C1	C9	Crow
7.12	13.11	C1	D10	Monkey
8.12	14.11	C1	E11	Gibbon
9.12	15.11	C1	F12	Tapir
10.12	16.11	C1	G1	Sheep
11.12	17.11	C1	H2	Deer
12.12	18.11	C1	J3	Horse
13.12	19.11	C1	K4	Stag
14.12	20.11	C1	A5	Serpent
15.12	21.11	C1	B6	Earthworm
16.12	22.11	C1	C7	Crocodile
17.12	23.11	C1	D8	Dragon
18.12	24.11	C1	E9	Badger
19.12	25.11	C1	F10	Hare
20.12	26.11	C1	G11	Fox
21.12	27.11	C1	H12	Tiger
22.12	28.11	C1	J1	Leopard
23.12	29.11	C1	K2	Griffon
24.12	30.11	C1	A3	Ox
25.12	1.12	D2	B4	Bat

Solar date	*Lunar date*	*Month HS/EB*	*Day HS/EB*	*Constellation*
26.12	2.12	D2	C5	Rat
27.12	3.12	D2	D6	Swallow
28.12	4.12	D2	E7	Pig
29.12	5.12	D2	F8	Porcupine
30.12	6.12	D2	G9	Wolf
31.12	7.12	D2	H10	Dog
1955				
1. 1	8.12	D2	J11	Pheasant
2. 1	9.12	D2	K12	Cock
3. 1	10.12	D2	A1	Crow
4. 1	11.12	D2	B2	Monkey
5. 1	12.12	D2	C3	Gibbon
6. 1	13.12	D2	D4	Tapir
7. 1	14.12	D2	E5	Sheep

Solar date	*Lunar date*	*Month HS/EB*	*Day HS/EB*	*Constellation*
8. 1	15.12	D2	F6	Deer
9. 1	16.12	D2	G7	Horse
10. 1	17.12	D2	H8	Stag
11. 1	18.12	D2	J9	Serpent
12. 1	19.12	D2	K10	Earthworm
13. 1	20.12	D2	A11	Crocodile
14. 1	21.12	D2	B12	Dragon
15. 1	22.12	D2	C1	Badger
16. 1	23.12	D2	D2	Hare
17. 1	24.12	D2	E3	Fox
18. 1	25.12	D2	F4	Tiger
19. 1	26.12	D2	G5	Leopard
20. 1	27.12	D2	H6	Griffon
21. 1	28.12	D2	J7	Ox
22. 1	29.12	D2	K8	Bat
23. 1	30.12	D2	A9	Rat

YI WEI YEAR

24. 1	1. 1	E3	B10	Swallow
25. 1	2. 1	E3	C11	Pig
26. 1	3. 1	E3	D12	Porcupine
27. 1	4. 1	E3	E1	Wolf
28. 1	5. 1	E3	F2	Dog
29. 1	6. 1	E3	G3	Pheasant
30. 1	7. 1	E3	H4	Cock
31. 1	8. 1	E3	J5	Crow
1. 2	9. 1	E3	K6	Monkey
2. 2	10. 1	E3	A7	Gibbon
3. 2	11. 1	E3	B8	Tapir
4. 2	12. 1	E3	C9	Sheep
5. 2	13. 1	E3	D10	Deer
6. 2	14. 1	E3	E11	Horse
7. 2	15. 1	E3	F12	Stag
8. 2	16. 1	E3	G1	Serpent
9. 2	17. 1	E3	H2	Earthworm
10. 2	18. 1	E3	J3	Crocodile
11. 2	19. 1	E3	K4	Dragon
12. 2	20. 1	E3	A5	Badger
13. 2	21. 1	E3	B6	Hare
14. 2	22. 1	E3	C7	Fox
15. 2	23. 1	E3	D8	Tiger
16. 2	24. 1	E3	E9	Leopard
17. 2	25. 1	E3	F10	Griffon
18. 2	26. 1	E3	G11	Ox
19. 2	27. 1	E3	H12	Bat
20. 2	28. 1	E3	J1	Rat
21. 2	29. 1	E3	K2	Swallow
22. 2	1. 2	F4	A3	Pig
23. 2	2. 2	F4	B4	Porcupine
24. 2	3. 2	F4	C5	Wolf
25. 2	4. 2	F4	D6	Dog
26. 2	5. 2	F4	E7	Pheasant
27. 2	6. 2	F4	F8	Cock
28. 2	7. 2	F4	G9	Crow
1. 3	8. 2	F4	H10	Monkey
2. 3	9. 2	F4	J11	Gibbon
3. 3	10. 2	F4	K12	Tapir
4. 3	11. 2	F4	A1	Sheep
5. 3	12. 2	F4	B2	Deer
6. 3	13. 2	F4	C3	Horse
7. 3	14. 2	F4	D4	Stag
8. 3	15. 2	F4	E5	Serpent
9. 3	16. 2	F4	F6	Earthworm
10. 3	17. 2	F4	G7	Crocodile
11. 3	18. 2	F4	H8	Dragon
12. 3	19. 2	F4	H8	Badger
13. 3	20. 2	F4	K10	Hare
14. 3	21. 2	F4	A11	Fox
15. 3	22. 2	F4	B12	Tiger
16. 3	23. 2	F4	C1	Leopard

17. 3	24. 2	F4	D2	Griffon
18. 3	25. 2	F4	E3	Ox
19. 3	26. 2	F4	F4	Bat
20. 3	27. 2	F4	G5	Rat
21. 3	28. 2	F4	H6	Swallow
22. 3	29. 2	F4	J7	Pig
23. 3	30. 2	F4	K8	Porcupine
24. 3	1. 3	G5	A9	Wolf
25. 3	2. 3	G5	B10	Dog
26. 3	3. 3	G5	C11	Pheasant
27. 3	4. 3	G5	D12	Cock
28. 3	5. 3	G5	E1	Crow
29. 3	6. 3	G5	F2	Monkey
30. 3	7. 3	G5	G3	Gibbon
31. 3	8. 3	G5	H4	Tapir
1. 4	9. 3	G5	J5	Sheep
2. 4	10. 3	G5	K6	Deer
3. 4	11. 3	G5	A7	Horse
4. 4	12. 3	G5	B8	Stag
5. 4	13. 3	G5	C9	Serpent
6. 4	14. 3	G5	D10	Earthworm
7. 4	15. 3	G5	E11	Crocodile
8. 4	16. 3	G5	F12	Dragon
9. 4	17. 3	G5	G1	Badger
10. 4	18. 3	G5	H2	Hare
11. 4	19. 3	G5	J3	Fox
12. 4	20. 3	G5	K4	Tiger
13. 4	21. 3	G5	A5	Leopard
14. 4	22. 3	G5	B6	Griffon
15. 4	23. 3	G5	C7	Ox
16. 4	24. 3	G5	D8	Bat
17. 4	15. 3	G5	E9	Rat
18. 4	26. 3	G5	F10	Swallow
19. 4	27. 3	G5	G11	Pig
20. 4	28. 3	G5	H12	Porcupine
21. 4	29. 3	G5	J1	Wolf
22. 4	*1. 3*	*G5*	K2	Dog
23. 4	*2. 3*	*G5*	A3	Pheasant
24. 4	*3. 3*	*G5*	B4	Cock
25. 4	*4. 3*	*G5*	C5	Crow
26. 4	*5. 3*	*G5*	D6	Monkey
27. 4	*6. 3*	*G5*	E7	Gibbon
28. 4	*7. 3*	*G5*	F8	Tapir
29. 4	*8. 3*	*G5*	G9	Sheep
30. 4	*9. 3*	*G5*	H10	Deer
1. 5	*10. 3*	*G5*	J11	Horse
2. 5	*11. 3*	*G5*	K12	Stag
3. 5	*12. 3*	*G5*	A1	Serpent
4. 5	*13. 3*	*G5*	B2	Earthworm
5. 5	*14. 3*	*G5*	C3	Crocodile
6. 5	*15. 3*	*G5*	D4	Dragon
7. 5	*16. 3*	*G5*	E5	Badger

Solar date	*Lunar date*	*Month HS/EB*	*Day HS/EB*	*Constellation*
8. 5	*17. 3*	*G5*	F6	Hare
9. 5	*18. 3*	*G5*	G7	Fox
10. 5	*19. 3*	*G5*	H8	Tiger
11. 5	*20. 3*	*G5*	J9	Leopard
12. 5	*21. 3*	*G5*	K10	Griffon
13. 5	*22. 3*	*G5*	A11	Ox
14. 5	*23. 3*	*G5*	B12	Bat
15. 5	*24. 3*	*G5*	C1	Rat
16. 5	*25. 3*	*G5*	D2	Swallow
17. 5	*26. 3*	*G5*	E3	Pig
18. 5	*27. 3*	*G5*	F4	Porcupine
19. 5	*28. 3*	*G5*	G5	Wolf
20. 5	*29. 3*	*G5*	H6	Dog
21. 5	*30. 3*	*G5*	J7	Pheasant
22. 5	1. 4	H6	K8	Cock
23. 5	2. 4	H6	A9	Crow
24. 5	3. 4	H6	B10	Monkey
25. 5	4. 4	H6	C11	Gibbon
26. 5	5. 4	H6	D12	Tapir
27. 5	6. 4	H6	E1	Sheep
28. 5	7. 4	H6	F2	Deer
29. 5	8. 4	H6	G3	Horse
30. 5	9. 4	H6	H4	Stag
31. 5	10. 4	H6	J5	Serpent
1. 6	11. 4	H6	K6	Earthworm
2. 6	12. 4	H6	A7	Crocodile
3. 6	13. 4	H6	B8	Dragon
4. 6	14. 4	H6	C9	Badger
5. 6	15. 4	H6	D10	Hare
6. 6	16. 4	H6	E11	Fox
7. 6	17. 4	H6	F12	Tiger
8. 6	18. 4	H6	G1	Leopard
9. 6	19. 4	H6	H2	Griffon
10. 6	20. 4	H6	J3	Ox
11. 6	21. 4	H6	K4	Bat
12. 6	22. 4	H6	A5	Rat
13. 6	23. 4	H6	B6	Swallow
14. 6	24. 4	H6	C7	Pig
15. 6	25. 4	H6	D8	Porcupine
16. 6	26. 4	H6	E9	Wolf
17. 6	27. 4	H6	F10	Dog
18. 6	28. 4	H6	G11	Pheasant
19. 6	29. 4	H6	H12	Cock
20. 6	1. 5	J7	J1	Crow
21. 6	2. 5	J7	K2	Monkey
22. 6	3. 5	J7	A3	Gibbon
23. 6	4. 5	J7	B4	Tapir
24. 6	5. 5	J7	C5	Sheep
25. 6	6. 5	J7	D6	Deer
26. 6	7. 5	J7	E7	Horse
27. 6	8. 5	J7	F8	Stag
28. 6	9. 5	J7	G9	Serpent
29. 6	10. 5	J7	H10	Earthworm
30. 6	11. 5	J7	J11	Crocodile
1. 7	12. 5	J7	K12	Dragon
2. 7	13. 5	J7	A1	Badger
3. 7	14. 5	J7	B2	Hare
4. 7	15. 5	J7	C3	Fox
5. 7	16. 5	J7	D4	Tiger
6. 7	17. 5	J7	E5	Leopard
7. 7	18. 5	J7	F6	Griffon
8. 7	19. 5	J7	G7	Ox
9. 7	20. 5	J7	H8	Bat
10. 7	21. 5	J7	J9	Rat
11. 7	22. 5	J7	K10	Swallow
12. 7	23. 5	J7	A11	Pig
13. 7	24. 5	J7	B12	Porcupine
14. 7	25. 5	J7	C1	Wolf
15. 7	26. 5	J7	D2	Dog
16. 7	27. 5	J7	E3	Pheasant
17. 7	28. 5	J7	F4	Cock
18. 7	29. 5	J7	G5	Crow
19. 7	1. 6	K8	H6	Monkey

Solar date	*Lunar date*	*Month HS/EB*	*Day HS/EB*	*Constellation*
20. 7	2. 6	K8	J7	Gibbon
21. 7	3. 6	K8	K8	Tapir
22. 7	4. 6	K8	A9	Sheep
23. 7	5. 6	K8	B10	Deer
24. 7	6. 6	K8	C11	Horse
25. 7	7. 6	K8	D12	Stag
26. 7	8. 6	K8	E1	Serpent
27. 7	9. 6	K8	F2	Earthworm
28. 7	10. 6	K8	G3	Crocodile
29. 7	11. 6	K8	H4	Dragon
30. 7	12. 6	K8	J5	Badger
31. 7	13. 6	K8	K6	Hare
1. 8	14. 6	K8	A7	Fox
2. 8	15. 6	K8	B8	Tiger
3. 8	16. 6	K8	C9	Leopard
4. 8	17. 6	K8	D10	Griffon
5. 8	18. 6	K8	E11	Ox
6. 8	19. 6	K8	F12	Bat
7. 8	20. 6	K8	G1	Rat
8. 8	21. 6	K8	H2	Swallow
9. 8	22. 6	K8	J3	Pig
10. 8	23. 6	K8	K4	Porcupine
11. 8	24. 6	K8	A5	Wolf
12. 8	25. 6	K8	B6	Dog
13. 8	26. 6	K8	C7	Pheasant
14. 8	27. 6	K8	D8	Cock
15. 8	28. 6	K8	E9	Crow
16. 8	29. 6	K8	F10	Monkey
17. 8	30. 6	K8	G11	Gibbon
18. 8	1. 7	A9	H12	Tapir
19. 8	2. 7	A9	J1	Sheep
20. 8	3. 7	A9	K2	Deer
21. 8	4. 7	A9	A3	Horse
22. 8	5. 7	A9	B4	Stag
23. 8	6. 7	A9	C5	Serpent
24. 8	7. 7	A9	D6	Earthworm
25. 8	8. 7	A9	E7	Crocodile
26. 8	9. 7	A9	F8	Dragon
27. 8	10. 7	A9	G9	Badger
28. 8	11. 7	A9	H10	Hare
29. 8	12. 7	A9	J11	Fox
30. 8	13. 7	A9	K12	Tiger
31. 8	14. 7	A9	A1	Leopard
1. 9	15. 7	A9	B2	Griffon
2. 9	16. 7	A9	C3	Ox
3. 9	17. 7	A9	D4	Bat
4. 9	18. 7	A9	E5	Rat
5. 9	19. 7	A9	F6	Swallow
6. 9	20. 7	A9	G7	Pig
7. 9	21. 7	A9	H8	Porcupine
8. 9	22. 7	A9	J9	Wolf
9. 9	23. 7	A9	K10	Dog
10. 9	24. 7	A9	A11	Pheasant
11. 9	25. 7	A9	B12	Cock
12. 9	26. 7	A9	C1	Crow
13. 9	27. 7	A9	D2	Monkey
14. 9	28. 7	A9	E3	Gibbon
15. 9	29. 7	A9	F4	Tapir
16. 9	1. 8	B10	G5	Sheep
17. 9	2. 8	B10	H6	Deer
18. 9	3. 8	B10	J7	Horse
19. 9	4. 8	B10	K8	Stag
20. 9	5. 8	B10	A9	Serpent
21. 9	6. 8	B10	B10	Earthworm
22. 9	7. 8	B10	C11	Crocodile
23. 9	8. 8	B10	D12	Dragon
24. 9	9. 8	B10	E1	Badger
25. 9	10. 8	B10	F2	Hare
26. 9	11. 8	B10	G3	Fox
27. 9	12. 8	B10	H4	Tiger
28. 9	13. 8	B10	J5	Leopard
29. 9	14. 8	B10	K6	Griffon
30. 9	15. 8	B10	A7	Ox

Solar date	Lunar date	Month HS/EB	Day HS/EB	Constellation
1.10	16. 8	B10	B8	Bat
2.10	17. 8	B10	C9	Rat
3.10	18. 8	B10	D10	Swallow
4.10	19. 8	B10	E11	Pig
5.10	20. 8	B10	F12	Porcupine
6.10	21. 8	B10	G1	Wolf
7.10	22. 8	B10	H2	Dog
8.10	23. 8	B10	J3	Pheasant
9.10	24. 8	B10	K4	Cock
10.10	25. 8	B10	A5	Crow
11.10	26. 8	B10	B6	Monkey
12.10	27. 8	B10	C7	Gibbon
13.10	28. 8	B10	D8	Tapir
14.10	29. 8	B10	E9	Sheep
15.10	30. 8	B10	F10	Deer
16.10	1. 9	C11	G11	Horse
17.10	2. 9	C11	H12	Stag
18.10	3. 9	C11	J1	Serpent
19.10	4. 9	C11	K2	Earthworm
20.10	5. 9	C11	A3	Crocodile
21.10	6. 9	C11	B4	Dragon
22.10	7. 9	C11	C5	Badger
23.10	8. 9	C11	D6	Hare
24.10	9. 9	C11	E7	Fox
25.10	10. 9	C11	F8	Tiger
26.10	11. 9	C11	G9	Leopard
27.10	12. 9	C11	H10	Griffon
28.10	13. 9	C11	J11	Ox
29.10	14. 9	C11	K12	Bat
30.10	15. 9	C11	A1	Rat
31.10	16. 9	C11	B2	Swallow
1.11	17. 9	C11	C3	Pig
2.11	18. 9	C11	D4	Porcupine
3.11	19. 9	C11	E5	Wolf
4.11	20. 9	C11	F6	Dog
5.11	21. 9	C11	G7	Pheasant
6.11	22. 9	C11	H8	Cock
7.11	23. 9	C11	J9	Crow
8.11	24. 9	C11	K10	Monkey
9.11	25. 9	C11	A11	Gibbon
10.11	26. 9	C11	B12	Tapir
11.11	27. 9	C11	C1	Sheep
12.11	28. 9	C11	D2	Deer
13.11	29. 9	C11	E3	Horse
14.11	1.10	D12	F4	Stag
15.11	2.10	D12	G5	Serpent
16.11	3.10	D12	H6	Earthworm
17.11	4.10	D12	J7	Crocodile
18.11	5.10	D12	K8	Dragon
19.11	6.10	D12	A9	Badger
20.11	7.10	D12	B10	Hare
21.11	8.10	D12	C11	Fox
22.11	9.10	D12	D12	Tiger
23.11	10.10	D12	E1	Leopard
24.11	11.10	D12	F2	Griffon
25.11	12.10	D12	G3	Ox
26.11	13.10	D12	H4	Bat
27.11	14.10	D12	J5	Rat
28.11	15.10	D12	K6	Swallow
29.11	16.10	D12	A7	Pig
30.11	17.10	D12	B8	Porcupine
1.12	18.10	D12	C9	Wolf
2.12	19.10	D12	D10	Dog
3.12	20.10	D12	E11	Pheasant
4.12	21.10	D12	F12	Cock
5.12	22.10	D12	G1	Crow
6.12	23.10	D12	H2	Monkey
7.12	24.10	D12	J3	Gibbon

Solar date	Lunar date	Month HS/EB	Day HS/EB	Constellation
8.12	25.10	D12	K4	Tapir
9.12	26.10	D12	A5	Sheep
10.12	27.10	D12	B6	Deer
11.12	28.10	D12	C7	Horse
12.12	29.10	D12	D8	Stag
13.12	30.10	D12	E9	Serpent
14.12	1.11	E1	F10	Earthworm
15.12	2.11	E1	G11	Crocodile
16.12	3.11	E1	H12	Dragon
17.12	4.11	E1	J1	Badger
18.12	5.11	E1	K2	Hare
19.12	6.11	E1	A3	Fox
20.12	7.11	E1	B4	Tiger
21.12	8.11	E1	C5	Leopard
22.12	9.11	E1	D6	Griffon
23.12	10.11	E1	E7	Ox
24.12	11.11	E1	F8	Bat
25.12	12.11	E1	G9	Rat
26.12	13.11	E1	H10	Swallow
27.12	14.11	E1	J11	Pig
28.12	15.11	E1	K12	Porcupine
29.12	16.11	E1	A1	Wolf
30.12	17.11	E1	B2	Dog
31.12	18.11	E1	C3	Pheasant
1956				
1. 1	19.11	E1	D4	Cock
2. 1	20.11	E1	E5	Crow
3. 1	21.11	E1	F6	Monkey
4. 1	22.11	E1	G7	Gibbon
5. 1	23.11	E1	H8	Tapir
6. 1	24.11	E1	J9	Sheep
7. 1	25.11	E1	K10	Deer
8. 1	26.11	E1	A11	Horse
9. 1	27.11	E1	B12	Stag
10. 1	28.11	E1	C1	Serpent
11. 1	29.11	E1	D2	Earthworm
12. 1	30.11	E1	E3	Crocodile
13. 1	1.12	F2	F4	Dragon
14. 1	2.12	F2	G5	Badger
15. 1	3.12	F2	H6	Hare
16. 1	4.12	F2	J7	Fox
17. 1	5.12	F2	K8	Tiger
18. 1	6.12	F2	A9	Leopard
19. 1	7.12	F2	B10	Griffon
20. 1	8.12	F2	C11	Ox
21. 1	9.12	F2	D12	Bat
22. 1	10.12	F2	E1	Rat
23. 1	11.12	F2	F2	Swallow
24. 1	12.12	F2	G3	Pig
25. 1	13.12	F2	H4	Porcupine
26. 1	14.12	F2	J5	Wolf
27. 1	15.12	F2	K6	Dog
28. 1	16.12	F2	A7	Pheasant
29. 1	17.12	F2	B8	Cock
30. 1	18.12	F2	C9	Crow
31. 1	19.12	F2	D10	Monkey
1. 2	20.12	F2	E11	Gibbon
2. 2	21.12	F2	F12	Tapir
3. 2	22.12	F2	G1	Sheep
4. 2	23.12	F2	H2	Deer
5. 2	24.12	F2	J3	Horse
6. 2	25.12	F2	K4	Stag
7. 2	26.12	F2	A5	Serpent
8. 2	27.12	F2	B6	Earthworm
9. 2	28.12	F2	C7	Crocodile
10. 2	29.12	F2	D8	Dragon
11. 2	30.12	F2	E9	Badger

PING SHEN YEAR

Solar date	*Lunar date*	*Month HS/EB*	*Day HS/EB*	*Constellation*
12. 2	1. 1	G3	F10	Hare
13. 2	2. 1	G3	G11	Fox
14. 2	3. 1	G3	H12	Tiger
15. 2	4. 1	G3	J1	Leopard
16. 2	5. 1	G3	K2	Griffon
17. 2	6. 1	G3	A3	Ox
18. 2	7. 1	G3	B4	Bat
19. 2	8. 1	G3	C5	Rat
20. 2	9. 1	G3	D6	Swallow
21. 2	10. 1	G3	E7	Pig
22. 2	11. 1	G3	F8	Porcupine
23. 2	12. 1	G3	G9	Wolf
24. 2	13. 1	G3	H10	Dog
25. 2	14. 1	G3	J11	Pheasant
26. 2	15. 1	G3	K12	Cock
27. 2	16. 1	G3	A1	Crow
28. 2	17. 1	G3	B2	Monkey
29. 2	18. 1	G3	C3	Gibbon
1. 3	19. 1	G3	D4	Tapir
2. 3	20. 1	G3	E5	Sheep
3. 3	21. 1	G3	F6	Deer
4. 3	22. 1	G3	G7	Horse
5. 3	23. 1	G3	H8	Stag
6. 3	24. 1	G3	J9	Serpent
7. 3	25. 1	G3	K10	Earthworm
8. 3	26. 1	G3	A11	Crocodile
9. 3	27. 1	G3	B12	Dragon
10. 3	28. 1	G3	C1	Badger
11. 3	29. 1	G3	D2	Hare
12. 3	1. 2	H4	E3	Fox
13. 3	2. 2	H4	F4	Tiger
14. 3	3. 2	H4	G5	Leopard
15. 3	4. 2	H4	H6	Griffon
16. 3	5. 2	H4	J7	Ox
17. 3	6. 2	H4	K8	Bat
18. 3	7. 2	H4	A9	Rat
19. 3	8. 2	H4	B10	Swallow
20. 3	9. 2	H4	C11	Pig
21. 3	10. 2	H4	D12	Porcupine
22. 3	11. 2	H4	E1	Wolf
23. 3	12. 2	H4	F2	Dog
24. 3	13. 2	H4	G3	Pheasant
25. 3	14. 2	H4	H4	Cock
26. 3	15. 2	H4	J5	Crow
27. 3	16. 2	H4	K6	Monkey
28. 3	18. 2	H4	A7	Gibbon
29. 3	18. 2	H4	B8	Tapir
30. 3	19. 2	H4	C9	Sheep
31. 3	20. 2	H4	D10	Deer
1. 4	21. 2	H4	E11	Horse
2. 4	22. 2	H4	F12	Stag
3. 4	23. 2	H4	G1	Serpent
4. 4	24. 2	H4	H2	Earthworm
5. 4	25. 2	H4	J3	Crocodile
6. 4	26. 2	H4	K4	Dragon
7. 4	27. 2	H4	A5	Badger
8. 4	28. 2	H4	B6	Hare
9. 4	29. 2	H4	C7	Fox
10. 4	30. 2	H4	D8	Tiger
11. 4	1. 3	J5	E9	Leopard
12. 4	2. 3	J5	F10	Griffon
13. 4	3. 3	J5	G11	Ox
14. 4	4. 3	J5	H12	Bat
15. 4	5. 3	J5	J1	Rat
16. 4	6. 3	J5	K2	Swallow
17. 4	7. 3	J5	A3	Pig
18. 4	8. 3	J5	B4	Porcupine
19. 4	9. 3	J5	C5	Wolf
20. 4	10. 3	J5	D6	Dog
21. 4	11. 3	J5	E7	Pheasant
22. 4	12. 3	J5	F8	Cock
23. 4	13. 3	J5	G9	Crow
24. 4	14. 3	J5	H10	Monkey
25. 4	15. 3	J5	J11	Gibbon
26. 4	16. 3	J5	K12	Tapir
27. 4	17. 3	J5	A1	Sheep
28. 4	18. 3	J5	B2	Deer
29. 4	19. 3	J5	C3	Horse
30. 4	20. 3	J5	D4	Stag
1. 5	21. 3	J5	E5	Serpent
2. 5	22. 3	J5	F6	Earthworm
3. 5	23. 3	J5	G7	Crocodile
4. 5	24. 3	J5	H8	Dragon
5. 5	25. 3	J5	J9	Badger
6. 5	26. 3	J5	K10	Hare
7. 5	27. 3	J5	A11	Fox
8. 5	28. 3	J5	B12	Tiger
9. 5	29. 3	J5	C1	Leopard
10. 5	1. 4	K6	D2	Griffon
11. 5	2. 4	K6	E3	Ox
12. 5	3. 4	K6	F4	Bat
13. 5	4. 4	K6	G5	Rat
14. 5	5. 4	K6	H6	Swallow
15. 5	6. 4	K6	J7	Pig
16. 5	7. 4	K6	K8	Porcupine
17. 5	8. 4	K6	A9	Wolf
18. 5	9. 4	K6	B10	Dog
19. 5	10. 4	K6	C11	Pheasant
20. 5	11. 4	K6	D12	Cock
21. 5	12. 4	K6	E1	Crow
22. 5	13. 4	K6	F2	Monkey
23. 5	14. 4	K6	G3	Gibbon
24. 5	15. 4	K6	H4	Tapir
25. 5	16. 4	K6	J5	Sheep
26. 5	17. 4	K6	K6	Deer
27. 5	18. 4	K6	A7	Horse
28. 5	19. 4	K6	B8	Stag
29. 5	20. 4	K6	C9	Serpent
30. 5	21. 4	K6	D10	Earthworm
31. 5	22. 4	K6	E11	Crocodile
1. 6	23. 4	K6	F12	Dragon
2. 6	24. 4	K6	G1	Badger
3. 6	25. 4	K6	H2	Hare
4. 6	26. 4	K6	J3	Fox
5. 6	27. 4	K6	K4	Tiger
6. 6	28. 4	K6	A5	Leopard
7. 6	29. 4	K6	B6	Griffon
8. 6	30. 4	K6	C7	Ox
9. 6	1. 5	A7	D8	Bat
10. 6	2. 5	A7	E9	Rat
11. 6	3. 5	A7	F10	Swallow
12. 6	4. 5	A7	G11	Pig
13. 6	5. 5	A7	H12	Porcupine
14. 6	6. 5	A7	J1	Wolf
15. 6	7. 5	A7	K2	Dog
16. 6	8. 5	A7	A3	Pheasant
17. 6	9. 5	A7	B4	Cock
18. 6	10. 5	A7	C5	Crow
19. 6	11. 5	A7	D6	Monkey
20. 6	12. 5	A7	E7	Gibbon
21. 6	13. 5	A7	F8	Tapir
22. 6	14. 5	A7	G9	Sheep
23. 6	15. 5	A7	H10	Deer
24. 6	16. 5	A7	J11	Horse
25. 6	17. 5	A7	K12	Stag
26. 6	18. 5	A7	A1	Serpent
27. 6	19. 5	A7	B2	Earthworm
28. 6	20. 5	A7	C3	Crocodile
29. 6	21. 5	A7	D4	Dragon
30. 6	22. 5	A7	E5	Badger
1. 7	23. 5	A7	F6	Hare
2. 7	24. 5	A7	G7	Fox

Solar date	Lunar date	Month HS/EB	Day HS/EB	Constellation
3. 7	25. 5	A7	H8	Tiger
4. 7	26. 5	A7	J9	Leopard
5. 7	27. 5	A7	K10	Griffon
6. 7	28. 5	A7	A11	Ox
7. 7	29. 5	A7	B12	Bat
8. 7	1. 6	B8	C1	Rat
9. 7	2. 6	B8	D2	Swallow
10. 7	3. 6	B8	E3	Pig
11. 7	4. 6	B8	F4	Porcupine
12. 7	5. 6	B8	G5	Wolf
13. 7	6. 6	B8	H6	Dog
14. 7	7. 6	B8	J7	Pheasant
15. 7	8. 6	B8	K8	Cock
16. 7	9. 6	B8	A9	Crow
17. 7	10. 6	B8	B10	Monkey
18. 7	11. 6	B8	C11	Gibbon
19. 7	12. 6	B8	D12	Tapir
20. 7	13. 6	B8	E1	Sheep
21. 7	14. 6	B8	F2	Deer
22. 7	15. 6	B8	G3	Horse
23. 7	16. 6	B8	H4	Stag
24. 7	17. 6	B8	J5	Serpent
25. 7	18. 6	B8	K6	Earthworm
26. 7	19. 6	B8	A7	Crocodile
27. 7	20. 6	B8	B8	Dragon
28. 7	21. 6	B8	C9	Badger
29. 7	22. 6	B8	D10	Hare
30. 7	23. 6	B8	E11	Fox
31. 7	24. 6	B8	F12	Tiger
1. 8	25. 6	B8	G1	Leopard
2. 8	26. 6	B8	H2	Griffon
3. 8	27. 6	B8	J3	Ox
4. 8	28. 6	B8	K4	Bat
5. 8	29. 6	B8	A5	Rat
6. 8	1. 7	C9	B6	Swallow
7. 8	2. 7	C9	C7	Pig
8. 8	3. 7	C9	D8	Porcupine
9. 8	4. 7	C9	E9	Wolf
10. 8	5. 7	C9	F10	Dog
11. 8	6. 7	C9	G11	Pheasant
12. 8	7. 7	C9	H12	Cock
13. 8	8. 7	C9	J1	Crow
14. 8	9. 7	C9	K2	Monkey
15. 8	10. 7	C9	A3	Gibbon
16. 8	11. 7	C9	B4	Tapir
17. 8	12. 7	C9	C5	Sheep
18. 8	13. 7	C9	D6	Deer
19. 8	14. 7	C9	E7	Horse
20. 8	15. 7	C9	F8	Stag
21. 8	16. 7	C9	G9	Serpent
22. 8	17. 7	C9	H10	Earthworm
23. 8	18. 7	C9	J11	Crocodile
24. 8	19. 7	C9	K12	Dragon
25. 8	20. 7	C9	A1	Badger
26. 8	21. 7	C9	B2	Hare
27. 8	22. 7	C9	C3	Fox
28. 8	23. 7	C9	D4	Tiger
29. 8	24. 7	C9	E5	Leopard
30. 8	25. 7	C9	F6	Griffon
31. 8	26. 7	C9	G7	Ox
1. 9	27. 7	C9	H8	Bat
2. 9	28. 7	C9	J9	Rat
3. 9	29. 7	C9	K10	Swallow
4. 9	30. 7	C9	A11	Pig
5. 9	1. 8	D10	B12	Porcupine
6. 9	2. 8	D10	C1	Wolf
7. 9	3. 8	D10	D2	Dog
8. 9	4. 8	D10	E3	Pheasant
9. 9	5. 8	D10	F4	Cock
10. 9	6. 8	D10	G5	Crow
11. 9	7. 8	D10	H6	Monkey
12. 9	8. 8	D10	J7	Gibbon
13. 9	9. 8	D10	K8	Tapir
14. 9	10. 8	D10	A9	Sheep
15. 9	11. 8	D10	B10	Deer
16. 9	12. 8	D10	C11	Horse
17. 9	13. 8	D10	D12	Stag
18. 9	14. 8	D10	E1	Serpent
19. 9	15. 8	D10	F2	Earthworm
20. 9	16. 8	D10	G3	Crocodile
21. 9	17. 8	D10	H4	Dragon
22. 9	18. 8	D10	J5	Badger
23. 9	19. 8	D10	K6	Hare
24. 9	20. 8	D10	A7	Fox
25. 9	21. 8	D10	B8	Tiger
26. 9	22. 8	D10	C9	Leopard
27. 9	23. 8	D10	D10	Griffon
28. 9	24. 8	D10	E11	Ox
29. 9	25. 8	D10	F12	Bat
30. 9	26. 8	D10	G1	Rat
1.10	27. 8	D10	H2	Swallow
2.10	28. 8	D10	J3	Pig
3.10	29. 8	D10	K4	Porcupine
4.10	1. 9	E11	A5	Wolf
5.10	2. 9	E11	B6	Dog
6.10	3. 9	E11	C7	Pheasant
7.10	4. 9	E11	D8	Cock
8.10	5. 9	E11	E9	Crow
9.10	6. 9	E11	F10	Monkey
10.10	7. 9	E11	G11	Gibbon
11.10	8. 9	E11	H12	Tapir
12.10	9. 9	E11	J1	Sheep
13.10	10. 9	E11	K2	Deer
14.10	11. 9	E11	A3	Horse
15.10	12. 9	E11	B4	Stag
16.10	13. 9	E11	C5	Serpent
17.10	14. 9	E11	D6	Earthworm
18.10	15. 9	E11	E7	Crocodile
19.10	16. 9	E11	F8	Dragon
20.10	17. 9	E11	G9	Badger
21.10	18. 9	E11	H10	Hare
22.10	19. 9	E11	J11	Fox
23.10	20. 9	E11	K12	Tiger
24.10	21. 9	E11	A1	Leopard
25.10	22. 9	E11	B2	Griffon
26.10	23. 9	E11	C3	Ox
27.10	24. 9	E11	D4	Bat
28.10	25. 9	E11	E5	Rat
29.10	26. 9	E11	F6	Swallow
30.10	27. 9	E11	G7	Pig
31.10	28. 9	E11	H8	Porcupine
1.11	29. 9	E11	J9	Wolf
2.11	30. 9	E11	K10	Dog
3.11	1.10	F12	A11	Pheasant
4.11	2.10	F12	B12	Cock
5.11	3.10	F12	C1	Crow
6.11	4.10	F12	D2	Monkey
7.11	5.10	F12	E3	Gibbon
8.11	6.10	F12	F4	Tapir
9.11	7.10	F12	G5	Sheep
10.11	8.10	F12	H6	Deer
11.11	9.10	F12	J7	Horse
12.11	10.10	F12	K8	Stag
13.11	11.10	F12	A9	Serpent
14.11	12.10	F12	B10	Earthworm
15.11	13.10	F12	C11	Crocodile
16.11	14.10	F12	D12	Dragon
17.11	15.10	F12	E1	Badger
18.11	16.10	F12	F2	Hare
19.11	17.10	F12	G3	Fox
20.11	18.10	F12	H4	Tiger
21.11	19.10	F12	J5	Leopard
22.11	20.10	F12	K6	Griffon
23.11	21.10	F12	A7	Ox
24.11	22.10	F12	B8	Bat
25.11	23.10	F12	C9	Rat

Solar date	Lunar date	Month HS/EB	Day HS/EB	Constellation
26.11	24.10	F12	D10	Swallow
27.11	25.10	F12	E11	Pig
28.11	26.10	F12	F12	Porcupine
29.11	27.10	F12	G1	Wolf
30.11	28.10	F12	H2	Dog
1.12	29.10	F12	J3	Pheasant
2.12	1.11	G1	K4	Cock
3.12	2.11	G1	A5	Crow
4.12	3.11	G1	B6	Monkey
5.12	4.11	G1	C7	Gibbon
6.12	5.11	G1	D8	Tapir
7.12	6.11	G1	E9	Sheep
8.12	7.11	G1	F10	Deer
9.12	8.11	G1	G11	Horse
10.12	9.11	G1	H12	Stag
11.12	10.11	G1	J1	Serpent
12.12	11.11	G1	K2	Earthworm
13.12	12.11	G1	A3	Crocodile
14.12	13.11	G1	B4	Dragon
15.12	14.11	G1	C5	Badger
16.12	15.11	G1	D6	Hare
17.12	16.11	G1	E7	Fox
18.12	17.11	G1	F8	Tiger
19.12	18.11	G1	G9	Leopard
20.12	19.11	G1	H10	Griffon
21.12	20.11	G1	J11	Ox
22.12	21.11	G1	K12	Bat
23.12	22.11	G1	A1	Rat
24.12	23.11	G1	B2	Swallow
25.12	24.11	G1	C3	Pig
26.12	25.11	G1	D4	Porcupine
27.12	26.11	G1	E5	Wolf
28.12	27.11	G1	F6	Dog
29.12	28.11	G1	G7	Pheasant
30.12	29.11	G1	H8	Cock
31.12	30.11	G1	J9	Crow
1957				
1. 1	1.12	H2	K10	Monkey
2. 1	2.12	H2	A11	Gibbon
3. 1	3.12	H2	B12	Tapir
4. 1	4.12	H2	C1	Sheep
5. 1	5.12	H2	D2	Deer
6. 1	6.12	H2	E3	Horse
7. 1	7.12	H2	F4	Stag
8. 1	8.12	H2	G5	Serpent
9. 1	9.12	H2	H6	Earthworm
10. 1	10.12	H2	J7	Crocodile
11. 1	11.12	H2	K8	Dragon
12. 1	12.12	H2	A9	Badger
13. 1	13.12	H2	B10	Hare
14. 1	14.12	H2	C11	Fox
15. 1	15.12	H2	D12	Tiger
16. 1	16.12	H2	E1	Leopard
17. 1	17.12	H2	F2	Griffon
18. 1	18.12	H2	G3	Ox
19. 1	19.12	H2	H4	Bat
20. 1	20.12	H2	J5	Rat
21. 1	21.12	H2	K6	Swallow
22. 1	22.12	H2	A7	Pig
23. 1	23.12	H2	B8	Porcupine
24. 1	24.12	H2	C9	Wolf
25. 1	25.12	H2	D10	Dog
26. 1	26.12	H2	E11	Pheasant
27. 1	27.12	H2	F12	Cock
28. 1	28.12	H2	G1	Crow
29. 1	29.12	H2	H2	Monkey
30. 1	30.12	H2	J3	Gibbon

TING YU YEAR

31. 1	1. 1	J3	K4	Tapir
1. 2	2. 1	J3	A5	Sheep
2. 2	3. 1	J3	B6	Deer
3. 2	4. 1	J3	C7	Horse
4. 2	5. 1	J3	D8	Stag
5. 2	6. 1	J3	E9	Serpent
6. 2	7. 1	J3	F10	Earthworm
7. 2	8. 1	J3	G11	Crocodile
8. 2	9. 1	J3	H12	Dragon
9. 2	10. 1	J3	J1	Badger
10. 2	11. 1	J3	K2	Hare
11. 2	12. 1	J3	A3	Fox
12. 2	13. 1	J3	B4	Tiger
13. 2	14. 1	J3	C5	Leopard
14. 2	15. 1	J3	D6	Griffon
15. 2	16. 1	J3	E7	Ox
16. 2	17. 1	J3	F8	Bat
17. 2	18. 1	J3	G9	Rat
18. 2	19. 1	J3	H10	Swallow
19. 2	20. 1	J3	J11	Pig
20. 2	21. 1	J3	K12	Porcupine
21. 2	22. 1	J3	A1	Wolf
22. 2	23. 1	J3	B2	Dog
23. 2	24. 1	J3	C3	Pheasant
24. 2	25. 1	J3	D4	Cock
25. 2	26. 1	J3	E5	Crow
26. 2	27. 1	J3	F6	Monkey
27. 2	28. 1	J3	G7	Gibbon
28. 2	29. 1	J3	H8	Tapir
1. 3	30. 1	J3	J9	Sheep
2. 3	1. 2	K4	K10	Deer
3. 3	2. 2	K4	A11	Horse
4. 3	3. 2	K4	B12	Stag
5. 3	4. 2	K4	C1	Serpent
6. 3	5. 2	K4	D2	Earthworm
7. 3	6. 2	K4	E3	Crocodile
8. 3	7. 2	K4	F4	Dragon
9. 3	8. 2	K4	G5	Badger
10. 3	9. 2	K4	H6	Hare
11. 3	10. 2	K4	J7	Fox
12. 3	11. 2	K4	K8	Tiger
13. 3	12. 2	K4	A9	Leopard
14. 3	13. 2	K4	B10	Griffon
15. 3	14. 2	K4	C11	Ox
16. 3	15. 2	K4	D12	Bat
17. 3	16. 2	K4	E1	Rat
18. 3	17. 2	K4	F2	Swallow
19. 3	18. 2	K4	G3	Pig
20. 3	19. 2	K4	H4	Porcupine
21. 3	20. 2	K4	J5	Wolf
22. 3	21. 2	K4	K6	Dog
13. 3	22. 2	K4	A7	Pheasant
24. 3	23. 2	K4	B8	Cock
25. 3	24. 2	K4	C9	Crow
26. 3	25. 2	K4	D10	Monkey
27. 3	26. 2	K4	E11	Gibbon
28. 3	27. 2	K4	F12	Tapir
29. 3	28. 2	K4	G1	Sheep
30. 3	29. 2	K4	H2	Deer
31. 3	1. 3	A5	J3	Horse
1. 4	2. 3	A5	K4	Stag
2. 4	3. 3	A5	A5	Serpent
3. 4	4. 3	A5	B6	Earthworm
4. 4	5. 3	A5	C7	Crocodile
5. 4	6. 3	A5	D8	Dragon
6. 4	7. 3	A5	E9	Badger
7. 4	8. 3	A5	F10	Hare
8. 4	9. 3	A5	G11	Fox

Solar date	Lunar date	Month HS/EB	Day HS/EB	Constellation
9. 4	10. 3	A5	H12	Tiger
10. 4	11. 3	A5	J1	Leopard
11. 4	12. 3	A5	K2	Griffon
12. 4	13. 3	A5	A3	Ox
13. 4	14. 3	A5	B4	Bat
14. 4	15. 3	A5	C5	Rat
15. 4	16. 3	A5	D6	Swallow
16. 4	17. 3	A5	E7	Pig
17. 4	18. 3	A5	F8	Porcupine
18. 4	19. 3	A5	G9	Wolf
19. 4	20. 3	A5	H10	Dog
20. 4	21. 3	A5	J11	Pheasant
21. 4	22. 3	A5	K12	Cock
22. 4	23. 3	A5	A1	Crow
23. 4	24. 3	A5	B2	Monkey
24. 4	25. 3	A5	C3	Gibbon
25. 4	26. 3	A5	D4	Tapir
26. 4	27. 3	A5	E5	Sheep
27. 4	28. 3	A5	F6	Deer
28. 4	29. 3	A5	G7	Horse
29. 4	30. 3	A5	H8	Stag
30. 4	1. 4	B6	J9	Serpent
1. 5	2. 4	B6	K10	Earthworm
2. 5	3. 4	B6	A11	Crocodile
3. 5	4. 4	B6	B12	Dragon
4. 5	5. 4	B6	C1	Badger
5. 5	6. 4	B6	D2	Hare
6. 5	7. 4	B6	E3	Fox
7. 5	8. 4	B6	F4	Tiger
8. 5	9. 4	B6	G5	Leopard
9. 5	10. 4	B6	H6	Griffon
10. 5	11. 4	B6	J7	Ox
11. 5	12. 4	B6	K8	Bat
12. 5	13. 4	B6	A9	Rat
13. 5	14. 4	B6	B10	Swallow
14. 5	15. 4	B6	C11	Pig
15. 5	16. 4	B6	D12	Porcupine
16. 5	17. 4	B6	E1	Wolf
17. 5	18. 4	B6	F2	Dog
18. 5	19. 4	B6	G3	Pheasant
19. 5	20. 4	B6	H4	Cock
20. 5	21. 4	B6	J5	Crow
21. 5	22. 4	B6	K6	Monkey
22. 5	23. 4	B6	A7	Gibbon
23. 5	24. 4	B6	B8	Tapir
24. 5	25. 4	B6	C9	Sheep
25. 5	26. 4	B6	D10	Deer
26. 5	27. 4	B6	E11	Horse
27. 5	28. 4	B6	F12	Stag
28. 5	29. 4	B6	G1	Serpent
19. 5	1. 5	C7	H2	Earthworm
30. 5	2. 5	C7	J3	Crocodile
31. 5	3. 5	C7	K4	Dragon
1. 6	4. 5	C7	A5	Badger
2. 6	5. 5	C7	B6	Hare
3. 6	6. 5	C7	C7	Fox
4. 6	7. 5	C7	D8	Tiger
5. 6	8. 5	C7	E9	Leopard
6. 6	9. 5	C7	F10	Griffon
7. 6	10. 5	C7	G11	Ox
8. 6	11. 5	C7	H12	Bat
9. 6	12. 5	C7	J1	Rat
10. 6	13. 5	C7	K2	Swallow
11. 6	14. 5	C7	A3	Pig
12. 6	15. 5	C7	B4	Porcupine
13. 6	16. 5	C7	C5	Wolf
14. 6	17. 5	C7	D6	Dog
15. 6	18. 5	C7	E7	Pheasant
16. 6	19. 5	C7	F8	Cock
17. 6	20. 5	C7	G9	Crow
18. 6	21. 5	C7	H10	Monkey
19. 6	22. 5	C7	J11	Gibbon
20. 6	23. 5	C7	K12	Tapir

Solar date	Lunar date	Month HS/EB	Day HS/EB	Constellation
21. 6	24. 5	C7	A1	Sheep
22. 6	25. 5	C7	B2	Deer
23. 6	26. 5	C7	C3	Horse
24. 6	27. 5	C7	D4	Stag
25. 6	28. 5	C7	E5	Serpent
26. 6	29. 5	C7	F6	Earthworm
27. 6	30. 5	C7	G7	Crocodile
28. 6	1. 6	D8	H8	Dragon
29. 6	2. 6	D8	J9	Badger
30. 6	3. 6	D8	K10	Hare
1. 7	4. 6	D8	A11	Fox
2. 7	5. 6	D8	B12	Tiger
3. 7	6. 6	D8	C1	Leopard
4. 7	7. 6	D8	D2	Griffon
5. 7	8. 6	D8	E3	Ox
6. 7	9. 6	D8	F4	Bat
7. 7	10. 6	D8	G5	Rat
8. 7	11. 6	D8	H6	Swallow
9. 7	12. 6	D8	J7	Pig
10. 7	13. 6	D8	K8	Porcupine
11. 7	14. 6	D8	A9	Wolf
12. 7	15. 6	D8	B10	Dog
13. 7	16. 6	D8	C11	Pheasant
14. 7	17. 6	D8	D12	Cock
15. 7	18. 6	D8	E1	Crow
16. 7	19. 6	D8	F2	Monkey
17. 7	20. 6	D8	G3	Gibbon
18. 7	21. 6	D8	H4	Tapir
19. 7	22. 6	D8	J5	Sheep
20. 7	23. 6	D8	K6	Deer
21. 7	24. 6	D8	A7	Horse
22. 7	25. 6	D8	B8	Stag
23. 7	26. 6	D8	C9	Serpent
24. 7	27. 6	D8	D10	Earthworm
25. 7	28. 6	D8	E11	Crocodile
26. 7	29. 6	D8	F12	Dragon
27. 7	1. 7	E9	G1	Badger
28. 7	2. 7	E9	H2	Hare
29. 7	3. 7	E9	J3	Fox
30. 7	4. 7	E9	K4	Tiger
31. 7	5. 7	E9	A5	Leopard
1. 8	6. 7	E9	B6	Griffon
2. 8	7. 7	E9	C7	Ox
3. 8	8. 7	E9	D8	Bat
4. 8	9. 7	E9	E9	Rat
5. 8	10. 7	E9	F10	Swallow
6. 8	11. 7	E9	G11	Pig
7. 8	12. 7	E9	H12	Porcupine
8. 8	13. 7	E9	J1	Wolf
9. 8	14. 7	E9	K2	Dog
10. 8	15. 7	E9	A3	Pheasant
11. 8	16. 7	E9	B4	Cock
12. 8	17. 7	E9	C5	Crow
13. 8	18. 7	E9	D6	Monkey
14. 8	19. 7	E9	E7	Gibbon
15. 8	20. 7	E9	F8	Tapir
16. 8	21. 7	E9	G9	Sheep
17. 8	22. 7	E9	H10	Deer
18. 8	23. 7	E9	J11	Horse
19. 8	24. 7	E9	K12	Stag
20. 8	25. 7	E9	A1	Serpent
21. 8	26. 7	E9	B2	Earthworm
22. 8	27. 7	E9	C3	Crocodile
23. 8	28. 7	E9	D4	Dragon
24. 8	29. 7	E9	E5	Badger
25. 8	1. 8	F10	F6	Hare
26. 8	2. 8	F10	G7	Fox
27. 8	3. 8	F10	H8	Tiger
28. 8	4. 8	F10	J9	Leopard
29. 8	5. 8	F10	K10	Griffon
30. 8	6. 8	F10	A11	Ox
31. 8	7. 8	F10	B12	Bat
1. 9	8. 8	F10	C1	Rat

Solar date	*Lunar date*	*Month HS/EB*	*Day HS/EB*	*Constellation*
2. 9	9. 8	F10	D2	Swallow
3. 9	10. 8	F10	E3	Pig
4. 9	11. 8	F10	F4	Porcupine
5. 9	12. 8	F10	G5	Wolf
6. 9	13. 8	F10	H6	Dog
7. 9	14. 8	F10	J7	Pheasant
8. 9	15. 8	F10	K8	Cock
9. 9	16. 8	F10	A9	Crow
10. 9	17. 8	F10	B10	Monkey
11. 9	18. 8	F10	C11	Gibbon
12. 9	19. 8	F10	D12	Tapir
13. 9	20. 8	F10	E1	Sheep
14. 9	21. 8	F10	F2	Deer
15. 9	22. 8	F10	G3	Horse
16. 9	23. 8	F10	H4	Stag
17. 9	24. 8	F10	J5	Serpent
18. 9	25. 8	F10	K6	Earthworm
19. 9	26. 8	F10	A7	Crocodile
20. 9	27. 8	F10	B8	Dragon
21. 9	28. 8	F10	C9	Badger
22. 9	29. 8	F10	D10	Hare
23. 9	30. 8	F10	E11	Fox
24. 9	*1. 8*	*F10*	F12	Tiger
25. 9	*2. 8*	*F10*	G1	Leopard
26. 9	*3. 8*	*F10*	H2	Griffon
27. 9	*4. 8*	*F10*	J3	Ox
28. 9	*5. 8*	*F10*	K4	Bat
29. 9	*6. 8*	*F10*	A5	Rat
30. 9	*7. 8*	*F10*	B6	Swallow
1.10	*8. 8*	*F10*	C7	Pig
2.10	*9. 8*	*F10*	D8	Porcupine
3.10	*10. 8*	*F10*	E9	Wolf
4.10	*11. 8*	*F10*	F10	Dog
5.10	*12. 8*	*F10*	G11	Pheasant
6.10	*13. 8*	*F10*	H12	Cock
7.10	*14. 8*	*F10*	J1	Crow
8.10	*15. 8*	*F10*	K2	Monkey
9.10	*16. 8*	*F10*	A3	Gibbon
10.10	*17. 8*	*F10*	B4	Tapir
11.10	*18. 8*	*F10*	C5	Sheep
12.10	*19. 8*	*F10*	D6	Deer
13.10	*20. 8*	*F10*	E7	Horse
14.10	*21. 8*	*F10*	F8	Stag
15.10	*22. 8*	*F10*	G9	Serpent
16.10	*23. 8*	*F10*	H10	Earthworm
17.10	*24. 8*	*F10*	J11	Crocodile
18.10	*25. 8*	*F10*	K12	Dragon
19.10	*26. 8*	*F10*	A1	Badger
20.10	*27. 8*	*F10*	B2	Hare
21.10	*28. 8*	*F10*	C3	Fox
22.10	*29. 8*	*F10*	D4	Tiger
23.10	1. 9	G11	E5	Leopard
24.10	2. 9	G11	F6	Griffon
25.10	3. 9	G11	G7	Ox
26.10	4. 9	G11	H8	Bat
27.10	5. 9	G11	J9	Rat
28.10	6. 9	G11	K10	Swallow
29.10	7. 9	G11	A11	Pig
30.10	8. 9	G11	B12	Porcupine
31.10	9. 9	G11	C1	Wolf
1.11	10. 9	G11	D2	Dog
2.11	11. 9	G11	E3	Pheasant
3.11	12. 9	G11	F4	Cock
4.11	13. 9	G11	G5	Crow
5.11	14. 9	G11	H6	Monkey
6.11	15. 9	G11	J7	Gibbon
7.11	16. 9	G11	K8	Tapir
8.11	17. 9	G11	A9	Sheep
9.11	18. 9	G11	B10	Deer
10.11	19. 9	G11	C11	Horse
11.11	20. 9	G11	D12	Stag
12.11	21. 9	G11	E1	Serpent
13.11	22. 9	G11	F2	Earthworm
14.11	23. 9	G11	G3	Crocodile
15.11	24. 9	G11	H4	Dragon
16.11	25. 9	G11	J5	Badger
17.11	26. 9	G11	K6	Hare
18.11	27. 9	G11	A7	Fox
19.11	28. 9	G11	B8	Tiger
20.11	29. 9	G11	C9	Leopard
21.11	30. 9	G11	D10	Griffon
22.11	1.10	H12	E11	Ox
23.11	2.10	H12	F12	Bat
24.11	3.10	H12	G1	Rat
25.11	4.10	H12	H2	Swallow
26.11	5.10	H12	J3	Pig
27.11	6.10	H12	K4	Porcupine
28.11	7.10	H12	A5	Wolf
29.11	8.10	H12	B6	Dog
30.11	9.10	H12	C7	Pheasant
1.12	10.10	H12	D8	Cock
2.12	11.10	H12	E9	Crow
3.12	12.10	H12	F10	Monkey
4.12	13.10	H12	G11	Gibbon
5.12	14.10	H12	H12	Tapir
6.12	15.10	H12	J1	Sheep
7.12	16.10	H12	K2	Deer
8.12	17.10	H12	A3	Horse
9.12	18.10	H12	B4	Stag
10.12	19.10	H12	C5	Serpent
11.12	20.10	H12	D6	Earthworm
12.12	21.10	H12	E7	Crocodile
13.12	22.10	H12	F8	Dragon
14.12	23.10	H12	G9	Badger
15.12	24.10	H12	H10	Hare
16.12	25.10	H12	J11	Fox
17.12	26.10	H12	K12	Tiger
18.12	27.10	H12	A1	Leopard
19.12	28.10	H12	B2	Griffon
20.12	29.10	H12	C3	Ox
21.12	1.11	J1	D4	Bat
22.12	2.11	J1	E5	Rat
23.12	3.11	J1	F6	Swallow
24.12	4.11	J1	G7	Pig
25.12	5.11	J1	H8	Porcupine
26.12	6.11	J1	J9	Wolf
27.12	7.11	J1	K10	Dog
28.12	8.11	J1	A11	Pheasant
29.12	9.11	J1	B12	Cock
30.12	10.11	J1	C1	Crow
31.12	11.11	J1	D2	Monkey
1958				
1. 1	12.11	J1	E3	Gibbon
2. 1	13.11	J1	F4	Tapir
3. 1	14.11	J1	G5	Sheep
4. 1	15.11	J1	H6	Deer
5. 1	16.11	J1	J7	Horse
6. 1	17.11	J1	K8	Stag
7. 1	18.11	J1	A9	Serpent
8. 1	19.11	J1	B10	Earthworm
9. 1	20.11	J1	C11	Crocodile
10. 1	21.11	J1	D12	Dragon
11. 1	22.11	J1	E1	Badger
12. 1	23.11	J1	F2	Hare
13. 1	24.11	J1	G3	Fox
14. 1	25.11	J1	H4	Tiger
15. 1	26.11	J1	J5	Leopard
16. 1	27.11	J1	K6	Griffon
17. 1	28.11	J1	A7	Ox
18. 1	29.11	J1	B8	Bat
19. 1	30.11	J1	C9	Rat
20. 1	1.12	K2	D10	Swallow
21. 1	2.12	K2	E11	Pig
22. 1	3.12	K2	F12	Porcupine
23. 1	4.12	K2	G1	Wolf

Solar date	*Lunar date*	*Month HS/EB*	*Day HS/EB*	*Constellation*	*Solar date*	*Lunar date*	*Month HS/EB*	*Day HS/EB*	*Constellation*
24. 1	5.12	K2	H2	Dog	6. 2	18.12	K2	A3	Crocodile
25. 1	6.12	K2	J3	Pheasant	7. 2	19.12	K2	B4	Dragon
26. 1	7.12	K2	K4	Cock	8. 2	20.12	K2	C5	Badger
27. 1	8.12	K2	A5	Crow	9. 2	21.12	K2	D6	Hare
28. 1	9.12	K2	B6	Monkey	10. 2	22.12	K2	E7	Fox
29. 1	10.12	K2	C7	Gibbon	11. 2	23.12	K2	F8	Tiger
30. 1	11.12	K2	D8	Tapir	12. 2	24.12	K2	G9	Leopard
31. 1	12.12	K2	E9	Sheep	13. 2	25.12	K2	H10	Griffon
1. 2	13.12	K2	F10	Deer	14. 2	26.12	K2	J11	Ox
2. 2	14.12	K2	G11	Horse	15. 2	27.12	K2	K12	Bat
3. 2	15.12	K2	H12	Stag	16. 2	28.12	K2	A1	Rat
4. 2	16.12	K2	J1	Serpent	17. 2	29.12	K2	B2	Swallow
5. 2	17.12	K2	K2	Earthworm					

MOU HSÜ YEAR

18. 2	1. 1	A3	C3	Pig	14. 4	26. 2	B4	H10	Swallow
19. 2	2. 1	A3	D4	Porcupine	15. 4	27. 2	B4	J11	Pig
20. 2	3. 1	A3	E5	Wolf	16. 4	28. 2	B4	K12	Porcupine
21. 2	4. 1	A3	F6	Dog	17. 4	29. 2	B4	A1	Wolf
22. 2	5. 1	A3	G7	Pheasant	18. 4	30. 2	B4	B2	Dog
23. 2	6. 1	A3	H8	Cock	19. 4	1. 3	C5	C3	Pheasant
24. 2	7. 1	A3	J9	Crow	20. 4	2. 3	C5	D4	Cock
25. 2	8. 1	A3	K10	Monkey	21. 4	3. 3	C5	E5	Crow
26. 2	9. 1	A3	A11	Gibbon	22. 4	4. 3	C5	F6	Monkey
27. 2	10. 1	A3	B12	Tapir	23. 4	5. 3	C5	G7	Gibbon
28. 2	11. 1	A3	C1	Sheep	24. 4	6. 3	C5	H8	Tapir
1. 3	12. 1	A3	D2	Deer	25. 4	7. 3	C5	J9	Sheep
2. 3	13. 1	A3	E3	Horse	26. 4	8. 3	C5	K10	Deer
3. 3	14. 1	A3	F4	Stag	27. 4	9. 3	C5	A11	Horse
4. 3	15. 1	A3	G5	Serpent	28. 4	10. 3	C5	B12	Stag
5. 3	16. 1	A3	H6	Earthworm	29. 4	11. 3	C5	C1	Serpent
6. 3	17. 1	A3	J7	Crocodile	30. 4	12. 3	C5	D2	Earthworm
7. 3	18. 1	A3	K8	Dragon	1. 5	13. 3	C5	E3	Crocodile
8. 3	19. 1	A3	A9	Badger	2. 5	14. 3	C5	F4	Dragon
9. 3	20. 1	A3	B10	Hare	3. 5	15. 3	C5	G5	Badger
10. 3	21. 1	A3	C11	Fox	4. 5	16. 3	C5	H6	Hare
11. 3	22. 1	A3	D12	Tiger	5. 5	17. 3	C5	J7	Fox
12. 3	23. 1	A3	E1	Leopard	6. 5	18. 3	C5	K8	Tiger
13. 3	24. 1	A3	F2	Griffon	7. 5	19. 3	C5	A9	Leopard
14. 3	25. 1	A3	G3	Ox	8. 5	20. 3	C5	B10	Griffon
15. 3	26. 1	A3	H4	Bat	9. 5	21. 3	C5	C11	Ox
16. 3	27. 1	A3	J5	Rat	10. 5	22. 3	C5	D12	Bat
17. 3	28. 1	A3	K6	Swallow	11. 5	23. 3	C5	E1	Rat
18. 3	29. 1	A3	A7	Pig	12. 5	24. 3	C5	F2	Swallow
19. 3	30. 1	A3	B8	Porcupine	13. 5	25. 3	C5	G3	Pig
20. 3	1. 2	B4	C9	Wolf	14. 5	26. 3	C5	H4	Porcupine
21. 3	2. 2	B4	D10	Dog	15. 5	27. 3	C5	J5	Wolf
22. 3	3. 2	B4	E11	Pheasant	16. 5	28. 3	C5	K6	Dog
23. 3	4. 2	B4	F12	Cock	17. 5	29. 3	C5	A7	Pheasant
24. 3	5. 2	B4	G1	Crow	18. 5	30. 3	C5	B8	Cock
25. 3	6. 2	B4	H2	Monkey	19. 5	1. 4	D6	C9	Crow
26. 3	7. 2	B4	J3	Gibbon	20. 5	2. 4	D6	D10	Monkey
27. 3	8. 2	B4	K4	Tapir	21. 5	3. 4	D6	E11	Gibbon
28. 3	9. 2	B4	A5	Sheep	22. 5	4. 4	D6	F12	Tapir
29. 3	10. 2	B4	B6	Deer	23. 5	5. 4	D6	G1	Sheep
30. 3	11. 2	B4	C7	Horse	24. 5	6. 4	D6	H2	Deer
31. 3	12. 2	B4	D8	Stag	25. 5	7. 4	D6	J3	Horse
1. 4	13. 2	B4	E9	Serpent	26. 5	8. 4	D6	K4	Stag
2. 4	14. 2	B4	F10	Earthworm	27. 5	9. 4	D6	A5	Serpent
3. 4	15. 2	B4	G11	Crocodile	28. 5	10. 4	D6	B6	Earthworm
4. 4	16. 2	B4	H12	Dragon	29. 5	11. 4	D6	C7	Crocodile
5. 4	17. 2	B4	J1	Badger	30. 5	12. 4	D6	D8	Dragon
6. 4	18. 2	B4	K2	Hare	31. 5	13. 4	D6	E9	Badger
7. 4	19. 2	B4	A3	Fox	1. 6	14. 4	D6	F10	Hare
8. 4	20. 2	B4	B4	Tiger	2. 6	15. 4	D6	G11	Fox
9. 4	21. 2	B4	C5	Leopard	3. 6	16. 4	D6	H12	Tiger
10. 4	22. 2	B4	D6	Griffon	4. 6	17. 4	D6	J1	Leopard
11. 4	23. 2	B4	E7	Ox	5. 6	18. 4	D6	K2	Griffon
12. 4	24. 2	B4	F8	Bat	6. 6	19. 4	D6	A3	Ox
13. 4	25. 2	B4	G9	Rat	7. 6	20. 4	D6	B4	Bat

Solar date	*Lunar date*	*Month HS/EB*	*Day HS/EB*	*Constellation*
8. 6	21. 4	D6	C5	Rat
9. 6	22. 4	D6	D6	Swallow
10. 6	23. 4	D6	E7	Pig
11. 6	24. 4	D6	F8	Porcupine
12. 6	25. 4	D6	G9	Wolf
13. 6	26. 4	D6	H10	Dog
14. 6	27. 4	D6	J11	Pheasant
15. 6	28. 4	D6	K12	Cock
16. 6	29. 4	D6	A1	Crow
17. 6	1. 5	E7	B2	Monkey
18. 6	2. 5	E7	C3	Gibbon
19. 6	3. 5	E7	D4	Tapir
20. 6	4. 5	E7	E5	Sheep
21. 6	5. 5	E7	F6	Deer
22. 6	6. 5	E7	G7	Horse
23. 6	7. 5	E7	H8	Stag
24. 6	8. 5	E7	J9	Serpent
25. 6	9. 5	E7	K10	Earthworm
26. 6	10. 5	E7	A11	Crocodile
27. 6	11. 5	E7	B12	Dragon
28. 6	12. 5	E7	C1	Badger
29. 6	13. 5	E7	D2	Hare
30. 6	14. 5	E7	E3	Fox
1. 7	15. 5	E7	F4	Tiger
2. 7	16. 5	E7	G5	Leopard
3. 7	17. 5	E7	H6	Griffon
4. 7	18. 5	E7	J7	Ox
5. 7	19. 5	E7	K8	Bat
6. 7	20. 5	E7	A9	Rat
7. 7	21. 5	E7	B10	Swallow
8. 7	22. 5	E7	C11	Pig
9. 7	23. 5	E7	D12	Porcupine
10. 7	24. 5	E7	E1	Wolf
11. 7	25. 5	E7	F2	Dog
12. 7	26. 5	E7	G3	Pheasant
13. 7	27. 5	E7	H4	Cock
14. 7	28. 5	E7	J5	Crow
15. 7	29. 5	E7	K6	Monkey
16. 7	30. 5	E7	A7	Gibbon
17. 7	1. 6	F8	B8	Tapir
18. 7	2. 6	F8	C9	Sheep
19. 7	3. 6	F8	D10	Deer
20. 7	4. 6	F8	E11	Horse
21. 7	5. 6	F8	F12	Stag
22. 7	6. 6	F8	G1	Serpent
23. 7	7. 6	F8	H2	Earthworm
24. 7	8. 6	F8	J3	Crocodile
25. 7	9. 6	F8	K4	Dragon
26. 7	10. 6	F8	A5	Badger
27. 7	11. 6	F8	B6	Hare
28. 7	12. 6	F8	C7	Fox
29. 7	13. 6	F8	D8	Tiger
30. 7	14. 6	F8	E9	Leopard
31. 7	15. 6	F8	F10	Griffon
1. 8	16. 6	F8	G11	Ox
2. 8	17. 6	F8	H12	Bat
3. 8	18. 6	F8	J1	Rat
4. 8	19. 6	F8	K2	Swallow
5. 8	20. 6	F8	A3	Pig
6. 8	21. 6	F8	B4	Porcupine
7. 8	22. 6	F8	C5	Wolf
8. 8	23. 6	F8	D6	Dog
9. 8	24. 6	F8	E7	Pheasant
10. 8	25. 6	F8	F8	Cock
11. 8	26. 6	F8	G9	Crow
12. 8	27. 6	F8	H10	Monkey
13. 8	28. 6	F8	J11	Gibbon
14. 8	29. 6	F8	K12	Tapir
15. 8	1. 7	G9	A1	Sheep
16. 8	2. 7	G9	B2	Deer
17. 8	3. 7	G9	C3	Horse
18. 8	4. 7	G9	D4	Stag
19. 8	5. 7	G9	E5	Serpent
20. 8	6. 7	G9	F6	Earthworm
21. 8	7. 7	G9	G7	Crocodile
22. 8	8. 7	G9	H8	Dragon
23. 8	9. 7	G9	J9	Badger
24. 8	10. 7	G9	K10	Hare
25. 8	11. 7	G9	A11	Fox
26. 8	12. 7	G9	B12	Tiger
27. 8	13. 7	G9	C1	Leopard
28. 8	14. 7	G9	D2	Griffon
29. 8	15. 7	G9	E3	Ox
30. 8	16. 7	G9	F4	Bat
31. 8	17. 7	G9	G5	Rat
1. 9	18. 7	G9	H6	Swallow
2. 9	19. 7	G9	J7	Pig
3. 9	20. 7	G9	K8	Porcupine
4. 9	21. 7	G9	A9	Wolf
5. 9	22. 7	G9	B10	Dog
6. 9	23. 7	G9	C11	Pheasant
7. 9	24. 7	G9	D12	Cock
8. 9	25. 7	G9	E1	Crow
9. 9	26. 7	G9	F2	Monkey
10. 9	27. 7	G9	G3	Gibbon
11. 9	28. 7	G9	H4	Tapir
12. 9	29. 7	G9	J5	Sheep
13. 9	1. 8	H10	K6	Deer
14. 9	2. 8	H10	A7	Horse
15. 9	3. 8	H10	B8	Stag
16. 9	4. 8	H10	C9	Serpent
17. 9	5. 8	H10	D10	Earthworm
18. 9	6. 8	H10	E11	Crocodile
19. 9	7. 8	H10	F12	Dragon
20. 9	8. 8	H10	G1	Badger
21. 9	9. 8	H10	H2	Hare
22. 9	10. 8	H10	J3	Fox
23. 9	11. 8	H10	K4	Tiger
24. 9	12. 8	H10	A5	Leopard
25. 9	13. 8	H10	B6	Griffon
26. 9	14. 8	H10	C7	Ox
27. 9	15. 8	H10	D8	Bat
28. 9	16. 8	H10	E9	Rat
29. 9	17. 8	H10	F10	Swallow
30. 9	18. 8	H10	G11	Pig
1.10	19. 8	H10	H12	Porcupine
2.10	20. 8	H10	J1	Wolf
3.10	21. 8	H10	K2	Dog
4.10	22. 8	H10	A3	Pheasant
5.10	23. 8	H10	B4	Cock
6.10	24. 8	H10	C5	Crow
7.10	25. 8	H10	D6	Monkey
8.10	26. 8	H10	E7	Gibbon
9.10	27. 8	H10	F8	Tapir
10.10	28. 8	H10	G9	Sheep
11.10	29. 8	H10	H10	Deer
12.10	30. 8	H10	J11	Horse
13.10	1. 9	J11	K12	Stag
14.10	2. 9	J11	A1	Serpent
15.10	3. 9	J11	B2	Earthworm
16.10	4. 9	J11	C3	Crocodile
17.10	5. 9	J11	D4	Dragon
18.10	6. 9	J11	E5	Badger
19.10	7. 9	J11	F6	Hare
20.10	8. 9	J11	G7	Fox
21.10	9. 9	J11	H8	Tiger
22.10	10. 9	J11	J9	Leopard
23.10	11. 9	J11	K10	Griffon
24.10	12. 9	J11	A11	Ox
25.10	13. 9	J11	B12	Bat
26.10	14. 9	J11	C1	Rat
27.10	15. 9	J11	D2	Swallow
28.10	16. 9	J11	E3	Pig
29.10	17. 9	J11	F4	Porcupine
30.10	18. 9	J11	G5	Wolf
31.10	19. 9	J11	H6	Dog

Solar date	*Lunar date*	*Month HS/EB*	*Day HS/EB*	*Constellation*
1.11	20. 9	J11	J7	Pheasant
2.11	21. 9	J11	K8	Cock
3.11	22. 9	J11	A9	Crow
4.11	23. 9	J11	B10	Monkey
5.11	24. 9	J11	C11	Gibbon
6.11	25. 9	J11	D12	Tapir
7.11	26. 9	J11	E1	Sheep
8.11	27. 9	J11	F2	Deer
9.11	28. 9	J11	G3	Horse
10.11	29. 9	J11	H4	Stag
11.11	1.10	K12	J5	Serpent
12.11	2.10	K12	K6	Earthworm
13.11	3.10	K12	A7	Crocodile
14.11	4.10	K12	B8	Dragon
15.11	5.10	K12	C9	Badger
16.11	6.10	K12	D10	Hare
17.11	7.10	K12	E11	Fox
18.11	8.10	K12	F12	Tiger
19.11	9.10	K12	G1	Leopard
20.11	10.10	K12	H2	Griffon
21.11	11.10	K12	J3	Ox
22.11	12.10	K12	K4	Bat
23.11	13.10	K12	A5	Rat
24.11	14.10	K12	B6	Swallow
25.11	15.10	K12	C7	Pig
26.11	16.10	K12	D8	Porcupine
27.11	17.10	K12	E9	Wolf
28.11	18.10	K12	F10	Dog
29.11	19.10	K12	G11	Pheasant
30.11	20.10	K12	H12	Cock
1.12	21.10	K12	J1	Crow
2.12	22.10	K12	K2	Monkey
3.12	23.10	K12	A3	Gibbon
4.12	24.10	K12	B4	Tapir
5.12	25.10	K12	C5	Sheep
6.12	26.10	K12	D6	Deer
7.12	27.10	K12	E7	Horse
8.12	28.10	K12	F8	Stag
9.12	29.10	K12	G9	Serpent
10.12	30.10	K12	H10	Earthworm
11.12	1.11	A1	J11	Crocodile
12.12	2.11	A1	K12	Dragon
13.12	3.11	A1	A1	Badger
14.12	4.11	A1	B2	Hare
15.12	5.11	A1	C3	Fox
16.12	6.11	A1	D4	Tiger
17.12	7.11	A1	E5	Leopard
18.12	8.11	A1	F6	Griffon
19.12	9.11	A1	G7	Ox
20.12	10.11	A1	H8	Bat
21.12	11.11	A1	J9	Rat
22.12	12.11	A1	K10	Swallow
23.12	13.11	A1	A11	Pig
24.12	14.11	A1	B12	Porcupine
25.12	15.11	A1	C1	Wolf
26.12	16.11	A1	D2	Dog
27.12	17.11	A1	E3	Pheasant
28.12	18.11	A1	F4	Cock
29.12	19.11	A1	G5	Crow
30.12	20.11	A1	H6	Monkey
31.12	21.11	A1	J7	Gibbon
1959				
1. 1	22.11	A1	K8	Tapir
2. 1	23.11	A1	A9	Sheep
3. 1	24.11	A1	B10	Deer
4. 1	25.11	A1	C11	Horse
5. 1	26.11	A1	D12	Stag
6. 1	27.11	A1	E1	Serpent
7. 1	28.11	A1	F2	Earthworm
8. 1	29.11	A1	G3	Crocodile
9. 1	1.12	B2	H4	Dragon
10. 1	2.12	B2	J5	Badger
11. 1	3.12	B2	K6	Hare
12. 1	4.12	B2	A7	Fox
13. 1	5.12	B2	B8	Tiger
14. 1	6.12	B2	C9	Leopard
15. 1	7.12	B2	D10	Griffon
16. 1	8.12	B2	E11	Ox
17. 1	9.12	B2	F12	Bat
18. 1	10.12	B2	G1	Rat
19. 1	11.12	B2	H2	Swallow
20. 1	12.12	B2	J3	Pig
21. 1	13.12	B2	K4	Porcupine
22. 1	14.12	B2	A5	Wolf
23. 1	15.12	B2	B6	Dog
24. 1	16.12	B2	C7	Pheasant
25. 1	17.12	B2	D8	Cock
26. 1	18.12	B2	E9	Crow
27. 1	19.12	B2	F10	Monkey
28. 1	20.12	B2	G11	Gibbon
29. 1	21.12	B2	H12	Tapir
30. 1	22.12	B2	J1	Sheep
31. 1	23.12	B2	K2	Deer
1. 2	24.12	B2	A3	Horse
2. 2	25.12	B2	B4	Stag
3. 2	26.12	B2	C5	Serpent
4. 2	27.12	B2	D6	Earthworm
5. 2	28.12	B2	E7	Crocodile
6. 2	29.12	B2	F8	Dragon
7. 2	30.12	B2	G9	Badger

CHI HAI YEAR

8. 2	1. 1	C3	H10	Hare
9. 2	2. 1	C3	J11	Fox
10. 2	3. 1	C3	K12	Tiger
11. 2	4. 1	C3	A1	Leopard
12. 2	5. 1	C3	B2	Griffon
13. 2	6. 1	C3	C3	Ox
14. 2	7. 1	C3	D4	Bat
15. 2	8. 1	C3	E5	Rat
16. 2	9. 1	C3	F6	Swallow
17. 2	10. 1	C3	G7	Pig
18. 2	11. 1	C3	H8	Porcupine
19. 2	12. 1	C3	J9	Wolf
20. 2	13. 1	C3	K10	Dog
21. 2	14. 1	C3	A11	Pheasant
22. 2	15. 1	C3	B12	Cock
23. 2	16. 1	C3	C1	Crow
24. 2	17. 1	C3	D2	Monkey
25. 2	18. 1	C3	E3	Gibbon
26. 2	19. 1	C3	F4	Tapir
27. 2	20. 1	C3	G5	Sheep
28. 2	21. 1	C3	H6	Deer
1. 3	22. 1	C3	J7	Horse
2. 3	23. 1	C3	K8	Stag
3. 3	24. 1	C3	A9	Serpent
4. 3	25. 1	C3	B10	Earthworm
5. 3	26. 1	C3	C11	Crocodile
6. 3	27. 1	C3	D12	Dragon
7. 3	28. 1	C3	E1	Badger
8. 3	29. 1	C3	F2	Hare
9. 3	1. 2	D4	G3	Fox
10. 3	2. 2	D4	H4	Tiger
11. 3	3. 2	D4	J5	Leopard
12. 3	4. 2	D4	K6	Griffon
13. 3	5. 2	D4	A7	Ox

Solar date	*Lunar date*	*Month HS/EB*	*Day HS/EB*	*Constellation*
14. 3	6. 2	D4	B8	Bat
15. 3	7. 2	D4	C9	Rat
16. 3	8. 2	D4	D10	Swallow
17. 3	9. 2	D4	E11	Pig
18. 3	10. 2	D4	F12	Porcupine
19. 3	11. 2	D4	G1	Wolf
20. 3	12. 2	D4	H4	Dog
21. 3	13. 2	D4	J3	Pheasant
22. 3	14. 2	D4	K4	Cock
23. 3	15. 2	D4	A5	Crow
24. 3	16. 2	D4	B6	Monkey
25. 3	17. 2	D4	C7	Gibbon
26. 3	18. 2	D4	D8	Tapir
27. 3	19. 2	D4	E9	Sheep
28. 3	20. 2	D4	F10	Deer
29. 3	21. 1	D4	G11	Horse
30. 3	22. 2	D4	H12	Stag
31. 3	23. 2	D4	J1	Serpent
1. 4	24. 2	D4	K2	Earthworm
2. 4	25. 2	D4	A3	Crocodile
3. 4	26. 2	D4	B4	Dragon
4. 4	27. 2	D4	C5	Badger
5. 4	28. 2	D4	D6	Hare
6. 4	29. 2	D4	E7	Fox
7. 4	30. 2	D4	F8	Tiger
8. 4	1. 3	E5	G9	Leopard
9. 4	2. 3	E5	H10	Griffon
10. 4	3. 3	E5	J11	Ox
11. 4	4. 3	E5	K12	Bat
12. 4	5. 3	E5	A1	Rat
13. 4	6. 3	E5	B2	Swallow
14. 4	7. 3	E5	C3	Pig
15. 4	8. 3	E5	D4	Porcupine
16. 4	9. 3	E5	E5	Wolf
17. 4	10. 3	E5	F6	Dog
18. 4	11. 3	E5	G7	Pheasant
19. 4	12. 3	E5	H8	Cock
20. 4	13. 3	E5	J9	Crow
21. 4	14. 3	E5	K10	Monkey
22. 4	15. 3	E5	A11	Gibbon
23. 4	16. 3	E5	B12	Tapir
24. 4	17. 3	E5	C1	Sheep
25. 4	18. 3	E5	D2	Deer
26. 4	19. 3	E5	E3	Horse
27. 4	20. 3	E5	F4	Stag
28. 4	21. 3	E5	G5	Serpent
29. 4	22. 3	E5	H6	Earthworm
30. 4	23. 3	E5	J7	Crocodile
1. 5	24. 3	E5	K8	Dragon
2. 5	25. 3	E5	A9	Badger
3. 5	26. 3	E5	B10	Hare
4. 5	27. 3	E5	C11	Fox
5. 5	28. 3	E5	D12	Tiger
6. 5	29. 3	E5	E1	Leopard
7. 5	30. 3	E5	F2	Griffon
8. 5	1. 4	F6	G3	Ox
9. 5	2. 4	F6	H4	Bat
10. 5	3. 4	F6	J5	Rat
11. 5	4. 4	F6	K6	Swallow
12. 5	5. 4	F6	A7	Pig
13. 5	6. 4	F6	B8	Porcupine
14. 5	7. 4	F6	C9	Wolf
15. 5	8. 4	F6	D10	Dog
16. 5	9. 4	F6	E11	Pheasant
17. 5	10. 4	F6	F12	Cock
18. 5	11. 4	F6	G1	Crow
19. 5	12. 4	F6	H2	Monkey
20. 5	13. 4	F6	J3	Gibbon
21. 5	14. 4	F6	K4	Tapir
22. 5	15. 4	F6	A5	Sheep
23. 5	16. 4	F6	B6	Deer
24. 5	17. 4	F6	C7	Horse
25. 5	18. 4	F6	D8	Stag
26. 5	19. 4	F6	E9	Serpent
27. 5	20. 4	F6	F10	Earthworm
28. 5	21. 4	F6	G11	Crocodile
29. 5	22. 4	F6	H12	Dragon
30. 5	23. 4	F6	J1	Badger
31. 5	24. 4	F6	K2	Hare
1. 6	25. 4	F6	A3	Fox
2. 6	26. 4	F6	B4	Tiger
3. 6	27. 4	F6	C5	Leopard
4. 6	28. 4	F6	D6	Griffon
5. 6	29. 4	F6	E7	Ox
6. 6	1. 5	G7	F8	Bat
7. 6	2. 5	G7	G9	Rat
8. 6	3. 5	G7	H10	Swallow
9. 6	4. 5	G7	J11	Pig
10. 6	5. 5	G7	K12	Porcupine
11. 6	6. 5	G7	A1	Wolf
12. 6	7. 5	G7	B2	Dog
13. 6	8. 5	G7	C3	Pheasant
14. 6	9. 5	G7	D4	Cock
15. 6	10. 5	G7	E5	Crow
16. 6	11. 5	G7	F6	Monkey
17. 6	12. 5	G7	G7	Gibbon
18. 6	13. 5	G7	H8	Tapir
19. 6	14. 5	G7	J9	Sheep
20. 6	15. 5	G7	K10	Deer
21. 6	16. 5	G7	A11	Horse
22. 6	17. 5	G7	B12	Stag
23. 6	18. 5	G7	C1	Serpent
24. 6	19. 5	G7	D2	Earthworm
25. 6	20. 5	G7	E3	Crocodile
26. 6	21. 5	G7	F4	Dragon
27. 6	22. 5	G7	G5	Badger
28. 6	23. 5	G7	H6	Hare
29. 6	24. 5	G7	J7	Fox
30. 6	25. 5	G7	K8	Tiger
1. 7	26. 5	G7	A9	Leopard
2. 7	27. 5	G7	B10	Griffon
3. 7	28. 5	G7	C11	Ox
4. 7	29. 5	G7	D12	Bat
5. 7	30. 5	G7	E1	Rat
6. 7	1. 6	H8	F2	Swallow
7. 7	2. 6	H8	G3	Pig
8. 7	3. 6	H8	H4	Porcupine
9. 7	4. 6	H8	J5	Wolf
10. 7	5. 6	H8	K6	Dog
11. 7	6. 6	H8	A7	Pheasant
12. 7	7. 6	H8	B8	Cock
13. 7	8. 6	H8	C9	Crow
14. 7	9. 6	H8	D10	Monkey
15. 7	10. 6	H8	E11	Gibbon
16. 7	11. 6	H8	F12	Tapir
17. 7	12. 6	H8	G1	Sheep
18. 7	13. 6	H8	H2	Deer
19. 7	14. 6	H8	J3	Horse
20. 7	15. 6	H8	K4	Stag
21. 7	16. 6	H8	A5	Serpent
22. 7	17. 6	H8	B6	Earthworm
23. 7	18. 6	H8	C7	Crocodile
24. 7	19. 6	H8	D8	Dragon
25. 7	20. 6	H8	E9	Badger
26. 7	21. 6	H8	F10	Hare
27. 7	22. 6	H8	G11	Fox
28. 7	23. 6	H8	H12	Tiger
29. 7	24. 6	H8	J1	Leopard
30. 7	25. 6	H8	K2	Griffon
31. 7	26. 6	H8	A3	Ox
1. 8	27. 6	H8	B4	Bat
2. 8	28. 6	H8	C5	Rat
3. 8	29. 6	H8	D6	Swallow
4. 8	1. 7	J9	E7	Pig
5. 8	2. 7	J9	F8	Porcupine
6. 8	3. 7	J9	G9	Wolf

Solar date	*Lunar date*	*Month HS/EB*	*Day HS/EB*	*Constellation*
7. 8	4. 7	J9	H10	Dog
8. 8	5. 7	J9	J11	Pheasant
9. 8	6. 7	J9	K12	Cock
10. 8	7. 7	J9	A1	Crow
11. 8	8. 7	J9	B2	Monkey
12. 8	9. 7	J9	C3	Gibbon
13. 8	10. 7	J9	D4	Tapir
14. 8	11. 7	J9	E5	Sheep
15. 8	12. 7	J9	F6	Deer
16. 8	13. 7	J9	G7	Horse
17. 8	14. 7	J9	H8	Stag
18. 8	15. 7	J9	J9	Serpent
19. 8	16. 7	J9	K10	Earthworm
20. 8	17. 7	J9	A11	Crocodile
21. 8	18. 7	J9	B12	Dragon
22. 8	19. 7	J9	C1	Badger
23. 8	20. 7	J9	D2	Hare
24. 8	21. 7	J9	E3	Fox
25. 8	22. 7	J9	F4	Tiger
26. 8	23. 7	J9	G4	Leopard
27. 8	24. 7	J9	H6	Griffon
28. 8	25. 7	J9	J7	Ox
29. 8	26. 7	J9	K8	Bat
30. 8	27. 7	J9	A9	Rat
31. 8	28. 7	J9	B10	Swallow
1. 9	29. 7	J9	C11	Pig
2. 9	30. 7	J9	D12	Porcupine
3. 9	1. 8	K10	E1	Wolf
4. 9	2. 8	K10	F2	Dog
5. 9	3. 8	K10	G3	Pheasant
6. 9	4. 8	K10	H4	Cock
7. 9	5. 8	K10	J5	Crow
8. 9	6. 8	K10	K6	Monkey
9. 9	7. 8	K10	A7	Gibbon
10. 9	8. 8	K10	B8	Tapir
11. 9	9. 8	K10	C9	Sheep
12. 9	10. 8	K10	D10	Deer
13. 9	11. 8	K10	E11	Horse
14. 9	12. 8	K10	F12	Stag
15. 9	13. 8	K10	G1	Serpent
16. 9	14. 8	K10	H2	Earthworm
17. 9	15. 8	K10	J3	Crocodile
18. 9	16. 8	K10	K4	Dragon
19. 9	17. 8	K10	A5	Badger
20. 9	18. 8	K10	B6	Hare
21. 9	19. 8	K10	C7	Fox
22. 9	20. 8	K10	D8	Tiger
23. 9	21. 8	K10	E9	Leopard
24. 9	22. 8	K10	F10	Griffon
25. 9	23. 8	K10	G11	Ox
26. 9	24. 8	K10	H12	Bat
27. 9	25. 8	K10	J1	Rat
28. 9	26. 8	K10	K2	Swallow
29. 9	27. 8	K10	A3	Pig
30. 9	28. 8	K10	B4	Porcupine
1.10	29. 8	K10	C5	Wolf
2.10	1. 9	A11	D6	Dog
3.10	2. 9	A11	E7	Pheasant
4.10	3. 9	A11	F8	Cock
5.10	4. 9	A11	G9	Crow
6.10	5. 9	A11	H10	Monkey
7.10	6. 9	A11	J11	Gibbon
8.10	7. 9	A11	K12	Tapir
9.10	8. 9	A11	A1	Sheep
10.10	9. 9	A11	B2	Deer
11.10	10. 9	A11	C3	Horse
12.10	11. 9	A11	D4	Stag
13.10	12. 9	A11	E5	Serpent
14.10	13. 9	A11	F6	Earthworm
15.10	14. 9	A11	G7	Crocodile
16.10	15. 9	A11	H8	Dragon
17.10	16. 9	A11	J9	Badger
18.10	17. 9	A11	K10	Hare
19.10	18. 9	A11	A11	Fox
20.10	19. 9	A11	B12	Tiger
21.10	20. 9	A11	C1	Leopard
22.10	21. 9	A11	D2	Griffon
23.10	22. 9	A11	E3	Ox
24.10	23. 9	A11	F4	Bat
25.10	24. 9	A11	G5	Rat
26.10	25. 9	A11	H6	Swallow
27.10	26. 9	A11	J7	Pig
28.10	27. 9	A11	K8	Porcupine
29.10	28. 9	A11	A9	Wolf
30.10	29. 9	A11	B10	Dog
31.10	30. 9	A11	C11	Pheasant
1.11	1.10	B12	D12	Cock
2.11	2.10	B12	E1	Crow
3.11	3.10	B12	F2	Monkey
4.11	4.10	B12	G3	Gibbon
5.11	5.10	B12	H4	Tapir
6.11	6.10	B12	J5	Sheep
7.11	7.10	B12	K6	Deer
8.11	8.10	B12	A7	Horse
9.11	9.10	B12	B8	Stag
10.11	10.10	B12	C9	Serpent
11.11	11.10	B12	D10	Earthworm
12.11	12.10	B12	E11	Crocodile
13.11	13.10	B12	F12	Dragon
14.11	14.10	B12	G1	Badger
15.11	15.10	B12	H2	Hare
16.11	16.10	B12	J3	Fox
17.11	17.10	B12	K4	Tiger
18.11	18.10	B12	A5	Leopard
19.11	19.10	B12	B6	Griffon
20.11	20.10	B12	C7	Ox
21.11	21.10	B12	D8	Bat
22.11	22.10	B12	E9	Rat
23.11	23.10	B12	F10	Swallow
24.11	24.10	B12	G11	Pig
25.11	25.10	B12	H12	Porcupine
26.11	26.10	B12	J1	Wolf
27.11	27.10	B12	K2	Dog
28.11	28.10	B12	A3	Pheasant
29.11	29.10	B12	B4	Cock
30.11	1.11	C1	C5	Crow
1.12	2.11	C1	D6	Monkey
2.12	3.11	C1	E7	Gibbon
3.12	4.11	C1	F8	Tapir
4.12	5.11	C1	G9	Sheep
5.12	6.11	C1	H10	Deer
6.12	7.11	C1	J11	Horse
7.12	8.11	C1	K12	Stag
8.12	9.11	C1	A1	Serpent
9.12	10.11	C1	B2	Earthworm
10.12	11.11	C1	C3	Crocodile
11.12	12.11	C1	D4	Dragon
12.12	13.11	C1	E5	Badger
13.12	14.11	C1	F6	Hare
14.12	15.11	C1	G7	Fox
15.12	16.11	C1	H8	Tiger
16.12	17.11	C1	J9	Leopard
17.12	18.11	C1	K10	Griffon
18.12	19.11	C1	A11	Ox
19.12	20.11	C1	B12	Bat
20.12	21.11	C1	C1	Rat
21.12	22.11	C1	D2	Swallow
22.12	23.11	C1	E3	Pig
23.12	24.11	C1	F4	Porcupine
24.12	25.11	C1	G5	Wolf
25.12	26.11	C1	H6	Dog
26.12	27.11	C1	J7	Pheasant
27.12	28.11	C1	K8	Cock
28.12	29.11	C1	A9	Crow
29.12	30.11	C1	B10	Monkey
30.12	1.12	D2	C11	Gibbon

Solar date	*Lunar date*	*Month HS/EB*	*Day HS/EB*	*Constellation*
31.12	2.12	D2	D12	Tapir
1960				
1. 1	3.12	D2	E1	Sheep
2. 1	4.12	D2	F2	Deer
3. 1	5.12	D2	G3	Horse
4. 1	6.12	D2	H4	Stag
5. 1	7.12	D2	J5	Serpent
6. 1	8.12	D2	K6	Earthworm
7. 1	9.12	D2	A7	Crocodile
8. 1	10.12	D2	B8	Dragon
9. 1	11.12	D2	C9	Badger
10. 1	12.12	D2	D10	Hare
11. 1	13.12	D2	E11	Fox
12. 1	14.12	D2	F12	Tiger

Solar date	*Lunar date*	*Month HS/EB*	*Day HS/EB*	*Constellation*
13. 1	15.12	D2	G1	Leopard
14. 1	16.12	D2	H2	Griffon
15. 1	17.12	D2	J3	Ox
16. 1	18.12	D2	K4	Bat
17. 1	19.12	D2	A5	Rat
18. 1	20.12	D2	B6	Swallow
19. 1	21.12	D2	C7	Pig
20. 1	22.12	D2	D8	Porcupine
21. 1	23.12	D2	E9	Wolf
22. 1	24.12	D2	F10	Dog
23. 1	25.12	D2	G11	Pheasant
24. 1	26.12	D2	H12	Cock
25. 1	27.12	D2	J1	Crow
26. 1	28.12	D2	K2	Monkey
27. 1	29.12	D2	A3	Gibbon

KENG TZU YEAR

28. 1	1. 1	E3	B4	Tapir
29. 1	2. 1	E3	C5	Sheep
30. 1	3. 1	E3	D6	Deer
31. 1	4. 1	E3	E7	Horse
1. 2	5. 1	E3	F8	Stag
2. 2	6. 1	E3	G9	Serpent
3. 2	7. 1	E3	H10	Earthworm
4. 2	8. 1	E3	J11	Crocodile
5. 2	9. 1	E3	K12	Dragon
6. 2	10. 1	E3	A1	Badger
7. 2	11. 1	E3	B2	Hare
8. 2	12. 1	E3	C3	Fox
9. 2	13. 1	E3	D4	Tiger
10. 2	14. 1	E3	E5	Laopard
11. 2	15. 1	E3	F6	Griffon
12. 2	16. 1	E3	G7	Ox
13. 1	17. 1	E3	H8	Bat
14. 1	18. 1	E3	J9	Rat
15. 2	19. 1	E3	K10	Swallow
16. 2	20. 1	E3	A11	Pig
17. 2	21. 1	E3	B12	Porcupine
18. 2	22. 1	E3	C1	Wolf
19. 2	23. 1	E3	D2	Dog
20. 2	24. 1	E3	E3	Pheasant
21. 2	25. 1	E3	F4	Cock
22. 2	26. 1	E3	G5	Crow
23. 2	27. 1	E3	H6	Monkey
24. 2	28. 1	E3	J7	Gibbon
25. 2	29. 1	E3	K8	Tapir
26. 2	30. 1	E3	A9	Sheep
27. 2	1. 2	F4	B10	Deer
28. 2	2. 2	F4	C11	Horse
29. 2	3. 2	F4	D12	Stag
1. 3	4. 2	F4	E1	Serpent
2. 3	5. 2	F4	F2	Earthworm
3. 3	6. 2	F4	G3	Crocodile
4. 3	7. 2	F4	H4	Dragon
5. 3	8. 2	F4	J5	Badger
6. 3	9. 2	F4	K6	Hare
7. 3	10. 2	F4	A7	Fox
8. 3	11. 2	F4	B8	Tiger
9. 3	12. 2	F4	C9	Leopard
10. 3	13. 2	F4	D10	Griffon
11. 3	14. 2	F4	E11	Ox
12. 3	15. 2	F4	F12	Bat
13. 3	16. 2	F4	G1	Rat
14. 3	17. 2	F4	H2	Swallow
15. 3	18. 2	F4	J3	Pig
16. 3	19. 2	F4	K4	Porcupine
17. 3	20. 2	F4	A5	Wolf
18. 3	21. 2	F4	B6	Dog
19. 3	22. 2	F4	C7	Pheasant
20. 3	23. 2	F4	D8	Cock

21. 3	24. 2	F4	E9	Crow
22. 3	25. 2	F4	F10	Monkey
23. 3	26. 2	F4	G11	Gibbon
24. 3	27. 2	F4	H12	Tapir
25. 3	28. 2	F4	J1	Sheep
26. 3	29. 2	F4	K2	Deer
27. 3	1. 3	G5	A3	Horse
28. 3	2. 3	G5	B4	Stag
29. 3	3. 3	G5	C5	Serpent
30. 3	4. 3	G5	D6	Earthworm
31. 3	5. 3	G5	E7	Crocodile
1. 4	6. 3	G5	F8	Dragon
2. 4	7. 3	G5	G9	Badger
3. 4	8. 3	G5	H10	Hare
4. 4	9. 3	G5	J11	Fox
5. 4	10. 3	G5	K12	Tiger
6. 4	11. 3	G5	A1	Leopard
7. 4	12. 3	G5	B2	Griffon
8. 4	13. 3	G5	C3	Ox
9. 4	14. 3	G5	D4	Bat
10. 4	15. 3	G5	E5	Rat
11. 4	16. 3	G5	F6	Swallow
12. 4	17. 3	G5	G7	Pig
13. 4	18. 3	G5	H8	Porcupine
14. 4	19. 3	G5	J9	Wolf
15. 4	20. 3	G5	K10	Dog
16. 4	21. 3	G5	A11	Pheasant
17. 4	22. 3	G5	B12	Cock
18. 4	23. 3	G5	C1	Crow
19. 4	24. 3	G5	D2	Monkey
20. 4	25. 3	G5	E3	Gibbon
21. 4	26. 3	G5	F4	Tapir
22. 4	27. 3	G5	G5	Sheep
23. 4	28. 3	G5	H6	Deer
24. 4	29. 3	G5	J7	Horse
25. 4	30. 3	G5	K8	Stag
26. 4	1. 4	H6	A9	Serpent
27. 4	2. 4	H6	B10	Earthworm
28. 4	3. 4	H6	C11	Crocodile
29. 4	4. 4	H6	D12	Dragon
30. 4	5. 4	H6	E1	Badger
1. 5	6. 4	H6	F2	Hare
2. 5	7. 4	H6	G3	Fox
3. 5	8. 4	H6	H4	Tiger
4. 5	9. 4	H6	J5	Leopard
5. 5	10. 4	H6	K6	Griffon
6. 5	11. 4	H6	A7	Ox
7. 5	12. 4	H6	B8	Bat
8. 5	13. 4	H6	C9	Rat
9. 5	14. 4	H6	D10	Swallow
10. 5	15. 4	H6	E11	Pig
11. 5	16. 4	H6	F12	Porcupine
12. 5	17. 4	H6	G1	Wolf

Solar date	*Lunar date*	*Month HS/EB*	*Day HS/EB*	*Constellation*
13. 5	18. 4	H6	H2	Dog
14. 5	19. 4	H6	J3	Pheasant
15. 5	20. 4	H6	K4	Cock
16. 5	21. 4	H6	A5	Crow
17. 5	22. 4	H6	B6	Monkey
18. 5	23. 4	H6	C7	Gibbon
19. 5	24. 4	H6	D8	Tapir
20. 5	25. 4	H6	E9	Sheep
21. 5	26. 4	H6	F10	Deer
22. 5	27. 4	H6	G11	Horse
23. 5	28. 4	H6	H12	Stag
24. 5	29. 4	H6	J1	Serpent
25. 5	1. 5	J7	K2	Earthworm
26. 5	2. 5	J7	A3	Crocodile
27. 5	3. 5	J7	B4	Dragon
28. 5	4. 5	J7	C5	Badger
29. 5	5. 5	J7	D6	Hare
30. 5	6. 5	J7	E7	Fox
31. 5	7. 5	J7	F8	Tiger
1. 6	8. 5	J7	G9	Leopard
2. 6	9. 5	J7	H10	Griffon
3. 6	10. 5	J7	J11	Ox
4. 6	11. 5	J7	K12	Bat
5. 6	12. 5	J7	A1	Rat
6. 6	13. 5	J7	B2	Swallow
7. 6	14. 5	J7	C3	Pig
8. 6	15. 5	J7	D4	Porcupine
9. 6	16. 5	J7	E5	Wolf
10. 6	17. 5	J7	F6	Dog
11. 6	18. 5	J7	G7	Pheasant
12. 6	19. 5	J7	H8	Cock
13. 6	20. 5	J7	J9	Crow
14. 6	21. 5	J7	K10	Monkey
15. 6	22. 5	J7	A11	Gibbon
16. 6	23. 5	J7	B12	Tapir
17. 6	24. 5	J7	C1	Sheep
18. 6	25. 5	J7	D2	Deer
19. 6	26. 5	J7	E3	Horse
20. 6	27. 5	J7	F4	Stag
21. 6	28. 5	J7	G5	Serpent
22. 6	29. 5	J7	H6	Earthworm
23. 6	30. 5	J7	J7	Crocodile
24. 6	1. 6	K8	K8	Dragon
25. 6	2. 6	K8	A9	Badger
26. 6	3. 6	K8	B10	Hare
27. 6	4. 6	K8	C11	Fox
28. 6	5. 6	K8	D12	Tiger
29. 6	6. 6	K8	E1	Leopard
30. 6	7. 6	K8	F2	Griffon
1. 7	8. 6	K8	G3	Ox
2. 7	9. 6	K8	H4	Bat
3. 7	10. 6	K8	J5	Rat
4. 7	11. 6	K8	K6	Swallow
5. 7	12. 6	K8	A7	Pig
6. 7	13. 6	K8	B8	Porcupine
7. 7	14. 6	K8	C9	Wolf
8. 7	15. 6	K8	D10	Dog
9. 7	16. 6	K8	E11	Pheasant
10. 7	17. 6	K8	F12	Cock
11. 7	18. 6	K8	G1	Crow
12. 7	19. 6	K8	H2	Monkey
13. 7	20. 6	K8	J3	Gibbon
14. 7	21. 6	K8	K4	Tapir
15. 7	22. 6	K8	A5	Sheep
16. 7	23. 6	K8	B6	Deer
17. 7	24. 6	K8	C7	Horse
18. 7	25. 6	K8	D8	Stag
19. 7	26. 6	K8	E9	Serpent
20. 7	27. 6	K8	F10	Earthworm
21. 7	28. 6	K8	G11	Crocodile
22. 7	29. 6	K8	H12	Dragon
23. 7	30. 6	K8	J1	Badger
24. 7	*1. 6*	*K8*	K2	Hare

Solar date	*Lunar date*	*Month HS/EB*	*Day HS/EB*	*Constellation*
25. 7	*2. 6*	*K8*	A3	Fox
26. 7	*3. 6*	*K8*	B4	Tiger
27. 7	*4. 6*	*K8*	C5	Leopard
28. 7	*5. 6*	*K8*	D6	Griffon
29. 7	*6. 6*	*K8*	E7	Ox
30. 7	*7. 6*	*K8*	F8	Bat
31. 7	*8. 6*	*K8*	G9	Rat
1. 8	*9. 6*	*K8*	H10	Swallow
2. 8	*10. 6*	*K8*	J11	Pig
3. 8	*11. 6*	*K8*	K12	Porcupine
4. 8	*12. 6*	*K8*	A1	Wolf
5. 8	*13. 6*	*K8*	B2	Dog
6. 8	*14. 6*	*K8*	C3	Pheasant
7. 8	*15. 6*	*K8*	D4	Cock
8. 8	*16. 6*	*K8*	E5	Crow
9. 8	*17. 6*	*K8*	F6	Monkey
10. 8	*18. 6*	*K8*	G7	Gibbon
11. 8	*19. 6*	*K8*	H8	Tapir
12. 8	*20. 6*	*K8*	J9	Sheep
13. 8	*21. 6*	*K8*	K10	Deer
14. 8	*22. 6*	*K8*	A11	Horse
15. 8	*23. 6*	*K8*	B12	Stag
16. 8	*24. 6*	*K8*	C1	Serpent
17. 8	*25. 6*	*K8*	D2	Earthworm
18. 8	*26. 6*	*K8*	E3	Crocodile
19. 8	*27. 6*	*K8*	F4	Dragon
20. 8	*28. 6*	*K8*	G5	Badger
21. 8	*29. 6*	*K8*	H6	Hare
22. 8	1. 7	A9	J7	Fox
23. 8	2. 7	A9	K8	Tiger
24. 8	3. 7	A9	A9	Leopard
25. 8	4. 7	A9	B10	Griffon
26. 8	5. 7	A9	C11	Ox
27. 8	6. 7	A9	D12	Bat
28. 8	7. 7	A9	E1	Rat
29. 8	8. 7	A9	F2	Swallow
30. 8	9. 7	A9	G3	Pig
31. 8	10. 7	A9	H4	Porcupine
1. 9	11. 7	A9	J5	Wolf
2. 9	12. 7	A9	K6	Dog
3. 9	13. 7	A9	A7	Pheasant
4. 9	14. 7	A9	B8	Cock
5. 9	15. 7	A9	C9	Crow
6. 9	16. 7	A9	D10	Monkey
7. 9	17. 7	A9	E11	Gibbon
8. 9	18. 7	A9	F12	Tapir
9. 9	19. 7	A9	G1	Sheep
10. 9	20. 7	A9	H2	Deer
11. 9	21. 7	A9	J3	Horse
12. 9	22. 7	A9	K4	Stag
13. 9	23. 7	A9	A5	Serpent
14. 9	24. 7	A9	B6	Earthworm
15. 9	25. 7	A9	C7	Crocodile
16. 9	26. 7	A9	D8	Dragon
17. 9	27. 7	A9	E9	Badger
18. 9	29. 7	A9	F10	Hare
19. 9	29. 7	A9	G11	Fox
20. 9	30. 7	A9	H12	Tiger
21. 9	1. 8	B10	J1	Leopard
22. 9	2. 8	B10	K2	Griffon
23. 9	3. 8	B10	A3	Ox
24. 9	4. 8	B10	B4	Bat
25. 9	5. 8	B10	C5	Rat
26. 9	6. 8	B10	D6	Swallow
27. 9	7. 8	B10	E7	Pig
28. 9	8. 8	B10	F8	Porcupine
29. 9	9. 8	B10	G9	Wolf
30. 9	10. 8	B10	H10	Dog
1.10	11. 8	B10	J11	Pheasant
2.10	12. 8	B10	K12	Cock
3.10	13. 8	B10	A1	Crow
4.10	14. 8	B10	B2	Monkey
5.10	15. 8	B10	C3	Gibbon

Solar date	*Lunar date*	*Month HS/EB*	*Day HS/EB*	*Constellation*
6.10	16. 8	B10	D4	Tapir
7.10	17. 8	B10	E5	Sheep
8.10	18. 8	B10	F6	Deer
9.10	19. 8	B10	G7	Horse
10.10	20. 8	B10	H8	Stag
11.10	21. 8	B10	J9	Serpent
12.10	22. 8	B10	K10	Earthworm
13.10	23. 8	B10	A11	Crocodile
14.10	24. 8	B10	B12	Dragon
15.10	25. 8	B10	C1	Badger
16.10	26. 8	B10	D2	Hare
17.10	27. 8	B10	E3	Fox
18.10	28. 8	B10	F4	Tiger
19.10	29. 8	B10	G5	Leopard
20.10	1. 9	C11	H6	Griffon
21.10	2. 9	C11	J7	Ox
22.10	3. 9	C11	K8	Bat
23.10	4. 9	C11	A9	Rat
24.10	5. 9	C11	B10	Swallow
25.10	6. 9	C11	C11	Pig
26.10	7. 9	C11	D12	Porcupine
27.10	8. 9	C11	E1	Wolf
28.10	9. 9	C11	F2	Dog
29.10	10. 9	C11	G3	Pheasant
30.10	11. 9	C11	H4	Cock
31.10	12. 9	C11	J5	Crow
1.11	13. 9	C11	K6	Monkey
2.11	14. 9	C11	A7	Gibbon
3.11	15. 9	C11	B8	Tapir
4.11	16. 9	C11	C9	Sheep
5.11	17. 9	C11	D10	Deer
6.11	18. 9	C11	E11	Horse
7.11	19. 9	C11	F12	Stag
8.11	20. 9	C11	G1	Serpent
9.11	21. 9	C11	H2	Earthworm
10.11	22. 9	C11	J3	Crocodile
11.11	23. 9	C11	K4	Dragon
12.11	24. 9	C11	A5	Badger
13.11	25. 9	C11	B6	Hare
14.11	26. 9	C11	C7	Fox
15.11	27. 9	C11	D8	Tiger
16.11	28. 9	C11	E9	Leopard
17.11	29. 9	C11	F10	Griffon
18.11	30. 9	C11	G11	Ox
19.11	1.10	D12	H12	Bat
20.11	2.10	D12	J1	Rat
21.11	3.10	D12	K2	Swallow
22.11	4.10	D12	A3	Pig
23.11	5.10	D12	B4	Porcupine
24.11	6.10	D12	C5	Wolf
25.11	7.10	D12	D6	Dog
26.11	8.10	D12	E7	Pheasant
27.11	9.10	D12	F8	Cock
28.11	10.10	D12	G9	Crow
29.11	11.10	D12	H10	Monkey
30.11	12.10	D12	J11	Gibbon
1.12	13.10	D12	K12	Tapir
2.12	14.10	D12	A1	Sheep
3.12	15.10	D12	B2	Deer
4.12	16.10	D12	C3	Horse
5.12	17.10	D12	D4	Stag
6.12	18.10	D12	E5	Serpent
7.12	19.10	D12	F6	Earthworm
8.12	20.10	D12	G7	Crocodile
9.12	21.10	D12	H8	Dragon
10.12	22.10	D12	J9	Badger
11.12	23.10	D12	K10	Hare

Solar date	*Lunar date*	*Month HS/EB*	*Day HS/EB*	*Constellation*
12.12	24.10	D12	A11	Fox
13.12	25.10	D12	B12	Tiger
14.12	26.10	D12	C1	Leopard
15.12	27.10	D12	D2	Griffon
16.12	28.10	D12	E3	Ox
17.12	29.10	D12	F4	Bat
18.12	1.11	E1	G5	Rat
19.12	2.11	E1	H6	Swallow
20.12	3.11	E1	J7	Pig
21.12	4.11	E1	K8	Porcupine
22.12	5.11	E1	A9	Wolf
23.12	6.11	E1	B10	Dog
24.12	7.11	E1	C11	Pheasant
25.12	8.11	E1	D12	Cock
26.12	9.11	E1	E1	Crow
27.12	10.11	E1	F2	Monkey
28.12	11.11	E1	G3	Gibbon
29.12	12.11	E1	H4	Tapir
30.12	13.11	E1	J5	Sheep
31.12	14.11	E1	K6	Deer
1961				
1. 1	15.11	E1	A7	Horse
2. 1	16.11	E1	B8	Stag
3. 1	17.11	E1	C9	Serpent
4. 1	18.11	E1	D10	Earthworm
5. 1	19.11	E1	E11	Crocodile
6. 1	20.11	E1	F12	Dragon
7. 1	21.11	E1	G1	Badger
8. 1	22.11	E1	H2	Hare
9. 1	23.11	E1	J3	Fox
10. 1	24.11	E1	K4	Tiger
11. 1	25.11	E1	A5	Leopard
12. 1	26.11	E1	B6	Griffon
13. 1	27.11	E1	C7	Ox
14. 1	28.11	E1	D8	Bat
15. 1	29.11	E1	E9	Rat
16. 1	30.11	E1	F10	Swallow
17. 1	1.12	F2	G11	Pig
18. 1	2.12	F2	H12	Porcupine
19. 1	3.12	F2	J1	Wolf
20. 1	4.12	F2	K2	Dog
21. 1	5.12	F2	A3	Pheasant
22. 1	6.12	F2	B4	Cock
23. 1	7.12	F2	C5	Crow
24. 1	8.12	F2	D6	Monkey
25. 1	9.12	F2	E7	Gibbon
26. 1	10.12	F2	F8	Tapir
27. 1	11.12	F2	G9	Sheep
28. 1	12.12	F2	H10	Deer
29. 1	13.12	F2	J11	Horse
30. 1	14.12	F2	K12	Stag
31. 1	15.12	F2	A1	Serpent
1. 2	16.12	F2	B2	Earthworm
2. 2	17.12	F2	C3	Crocodile
3. 2	18.12	F2	D4	Dragon
4. 2	19.12	F2	E5	Badger
5. 2	20.12	F2	F6	Hare
6. 2	21.12	F2	G7	Fox
7. 2	22.12	F2	H8	Tiger
8. 2	23.12	F2	J9	Leopard
9. 2	24.12	F2	K10	Griffon
10. 2	25.12	F2	A11	Ox
11. 2	26.12	F2	B12	Bat
12. 2	27.12	F2	C1	Rat
13. 2	28.12	F2	D2	Swallow
14. 2	29.12	F2	E3	Pig

HSIN CH'OU YEAR

Solar date	Lunar date	Month HS/EB	Day HS/EB	Constellation
15. 2	1. 1	G3	F4	Porcupine
16. 2	2. 1	G3	G5	Wolf
17. 2	3. 1	G3	H6	Dog
18. 2	4. 1	G3	J7	Pheasant
19. 2	5. 1	G3	K8	Cock
20. 2	6. 1	G3	A9	Crow
21. 2	7. 1	G3	B10	Monkey
22. 2	8. 1	G3	C11	Gibbon
23. 2	9. 1	G3	D12	Tapir
24. 2	10. 1	G3	E1	Sheep
25. 2	11. 1	G3	F2	Deer
26. 2	12. 1	G3	G3	Horse
27. 2	13. 1	G3	H4	Stag
28. 2	14. 1	G3	J5	Serpent
1. 3	15. 1	G3	K6	Earthworm
2. 3	16. 1	G3	A7	Crocodile
3. 3	17. 1	G3	B8	Dragon
4. 3	18. 1	G3	C9	Badger
5. 3	19. 1	G3	D10	Hare
6. 3	20. 1	G3	E11	Fox
7. 3	21. 1	G3	F12	Tiger
8. 3	22. 1	G3	G1	Leopard
9. 3	23. 1	G3	H2	Griffon
10. 3	24. 1	G3	J3	Ox
11. 3	25. 1	G3	K4	Bat
12. 3	26. 1	G3	A5	Rat
13. 3	27. 1	G3	B6	Swallow
14. 3	28. 1	G3	C7	Pig
15. 3	29. 1	G3	D8	Porcupine
16. 3	30. 1	G3	E9	Wolf
17. 3	1. 2	H4	F10	Dog
18. 3	2. 2	H4	G11	Pheasant
19. 3	3. 2	H4	H12	Cock
20. 3	4. 2	H4	J1	Crow
21. 3	5. 2	H4	K2	Monkey
22. 3	6. 2	H4	A3	Gibbon
23. 3	7. 2	H4	B4	Tapir
24. 3	8. 2	H4	C5	Sheep
25. 3	9. 2	H4	D6	Deer
26. 3	10. 2	H4	E7	Horse
27. 3	11. 2	H4	F8	Stag
28. 3	12. 2	H4	G9	Serpent
29. 3	13. 2	H4	H10	Earthworm
30. 3	14. 2	H4	J11	Crocodile
31. 3	15. 2	H4	K12	Dragon
1. 4	16. 2	H4	A1	Badger
2. 4	17. 2	H4	B2	Hare
3. 4	18. 2	H4	C3	Fox
4. 4	19. 2	H4	D4	Tiger
5. 4	20. 2	H4	E5	Leopard
6. 4	21. 2	H4	F6	Griffon
7. 4	22. 2	H4	G7	Ox
8. 4	23. 2	H4	H8	Bat
9. 4	24. 2	H4	J9	Rat
10. 4	25. 2	H4	K10	Swallow
11. 4	26. 2	H4	A11	Pig
12. 4	27. 2	H4	B12	Porcupine
13. 4	28. 2	H4	C1	Wolf
14. 4	29. 2	H4	D2	Dog
15. 4	1. 3	J5	E3	Pheasant
16. 4	2. 3	J5	F4	Cock
17. 4	3. 3	J5	G5	Crow
18. 4	4. 3	J5	H6	Monkey
19. 4	5. 3	J5	J7	Gibbon
20. 4	6. 3	J5	K8	Tapir
21. 4	7. 3	J5	A9	Sheep
22. 4	8. 3	J5	B10	Deer
23. 4	9. 3	J5	C11	Horse
24. 4	10. 3	J5	D12	Stag
25. 4	11. 3	J5	E1	Serpent
26. 4	12. 3	J5	F2	Earthworm
27. 4	13. 3	J5	G3	Crocodile
28. 4	14. 3	J5	H4	Dragon
29. 4	15. 3	J5	J5	Badger
30. 4	16. 3	J5	K6	Hare
1. 5	17. 3	J5	A7	Fox
2. 5	18. 3	J5	B8	Tiger
3. 5	19. 3	J5	C9	Leopard
4. 5	20. 3	J5	D10	Griffon
5. 5	21. 3	J5	E11	Ox
6. 5	22. 3	J5	F12	Bat
7. 5	23. 3	J5	G1	Rat
8. 5	24. 3	J5	H2	Swallow
9. 5	25. 3	J5	J3	Pig
10. 5	26. 3	J5	K4	Porcupine
11. 5	27. 3	J5	A5	Wolf
12. 5	28. 3	J5	B6	Dog
13. 5	29. 3	J5	C7	Pheasant
14. 5	30. 3	J5	D8	Cock
15. 5	1. 4	K6	E9	Crow
16. 5	2. 4	K6	F10	Monkey
17. 5	3. 4	K6	G11	Gibbon
18. 5	4. 4	K6	H12	Tapir
19. 5	5. 4	K6	J1	Sheep
20. 5	6. 4	K6	K2	Deer
21. 5	7. 4	K6	A3	Horse
22. 5	8. 4	K6	B4	Stag
23. 5	9. 4	K6	C5	Serpent
24. 5	10. 4	K6	D6	Earthworm
25. 5	11. 4	K6	E7	Crocodile
26. 5	12. 4	K6	F8	Dragon
27. 5	13. 4	K6	G9	Badger
28. 5	14. 4	K6	H10	Hare
29. 5	15. 4	K6	J11	Fox
30. 5	16. 4	K6	K12	Tiger
31. 5	17. 4	K6	A1	Leopard
1. 6	18. 4	K6	B2	Griffon
2. 6	19. 4	K6	C3	Ox
3. 6	20. 4	K6	D4	Bat
4. 6	21. 4	K6	E5	Rat
5. 6	22. 4	K6	F6	Swallow
6. 6	23. 4	K6	G7	Pig
7. 6	24. 4	K6	H8	Porcupine
8. 6	25. 4	K6	J9	Wolf
9. 6	26. 4	K6	K10	Dog
10. 6	27. 4	K6	A11	Pheasant
11. 6	28. 4	K6	B12	Cock
12. 6	29. 4	K6	C1	Crow
13. 6	1. 5	A7	D2	Monkey
14. 6	2. 5	A7	E3	Gibbon
15. 6	3. 5	A7	F4	Tapir
16. 6	4. 5	A7	G5	Sheep
17. 6	5. 5	A7	H6	Deer
18. 6	6. 5	A7	J7	Horse
19. 6	7. 5	A7	K8	Stag
20. 6	8. 5	A7	A9	Serpent
21. 6	9. 5	A7	B10	Earthworm
22. 6	10. 5	A7	C11	Crocodile
23. 6	11. 5	A7	D12	Dragon
24. 6	12. 5	A7	E1	Badger
25. 6	13. 5	A7	F2	Hare
26. 6	14. 5	A7	G3	Fox
27. 6	15. 5	A7	H4	Tiger
28. 6	16. 5	A7	J5	Leopard
29. 6	17. 5	A7	K6	Griffon
30. 6	18. 5	A7	A7	Ox
1. 7	19. 5	A7	B8	Bat
2. 7	20. 5	A7	C9	Rat
3. 7	21. 5	A7	D10	Swallow
4. 7	22. 5	A7	E11	Pig
5. 7	23. 5	A7	F12	Porcupine
6. 7	24. 5	A7	G1	Wolf

Solar date	Lunar date	Month HS/EB	Day HS/EB	Constellation
7. 7	25. 5	A7	H2	Dog
8. 7	26. 5	A7	J3	Pheasant
9. 7	27. 5	A7	K4	Cock
10. 7	28. 5	A7	A5	Crow
11. 7	29. 5	A7	B6	Monkey
12. 7	30. 5	A7	C7	Gibbon
13. 7	1. 6	B8	D8	Tapir
14. 7	2. 6	B8	E9	Sheep
15. 7	3. 6	B8	F10	Deer
16. 7	4. 6	B8	G11	Horse
17. 7	5. 6	B8	H12	Stag
18. 7	6. 6	B8	J1	Serpent
19. 7	7. 6	B8	K2	Earthworm
20. 7	8. 6	B8	A3	Crocodile
21. 7	9. 6	B8	B4	Dragon
22. 7	10. 6	B8	C5	Badger
23. 7	11. 6	B8	D6	Hare
24. 7	12. 6	B8	E7	Fox
25. 7	13. 6	B8	F8	Tiger
26. 7	14. 6	B8	G9	Leopard
27. 7	15. 6	B8	H10	Griffon
28. 7	16. 6	B8	J11	Ox
29. 7	17. 6	B8	K12	Bat
30. 7	18. 6	B8	A1	Rat
31. 7	19. 6	B8	B2	Swallow
1. 8	20. 6	B8	C3	Pig
2. 8	21. 6	B8	D4	Porcupine
3. 8	22. 6	B8	E5	Wolf
4. 8	23. 6	B8	F6	Dog
5. 8	24. 6	B8	G7	Pheasant
6. 8	25. 6	B8	H8	Cock
7. 8	26. 6	B8	J9	Crow
8. 8	27. 6	B8	K10	Monkey
9. 8	28. 6	B8	A11	Gibbon
10. 8	29. 6	B8	B12	Tapir
11. 8	1. 7	C9	C1	Sheep
12. 8	2. 7	C9	D2	Deer
13. 8	3. 7	C9	E3	Horse
14. 8	4. 7	C9	F4	Stag
15. 8	5. 7	C9	G5	Serpent
16. 8	6. 7	C9	H6	Earthworm
17. 8	7. 7	C9	J7	Crocodile
18. 8	8. 7	C9	K8	Dragon
19. 8	9. 7	C9	A9	Badger
20. 8	10. 7	C9	B10	Hare
21. 8	11. 7	C9	C11	Fox
22. 8	12. 7	C9	D12	Tiger
23. 8	13. 7	C9	E1	Leopard
24. 8	14. 7	C9	F2	Griffon
25. 8	15. 7	C9	G3	Ox
26. 8	16. 7	C9	H4	Bat
27. 8	17. 7	C9	J5	Rat
28. 8	18. 7	C9	K6	Swallow
29. 8	19. 7	C9	A7	Pig
30. 8	20. 7	C9	B8	Porcupine
31. 8	21. 7	C9	C9	Wolf
1. 9	22. 7	C9	D10	Dog
2. 9	23. 7	C9	E11	Pheasant
3. 9	24. 7	C9	F12	Cock
4. 9	25. 7	C9	G1	Crow
5. 9	26. 7	C9	H2	Monkey
6. 9	27. 7	C9	J3	Gibbon
7. 9	28. 7	C9	K4	Tapir
8. 9	29. 7	C9	A5	Sheep
9. 9	30. 7	C9	B6	Deer
10. 9	1. 8	D10	C7	Horse
11. 9	2. 8	D10	D8	Stag
12. 9	3. 8	D10	E9	Serpent
13. 9	4. 8	D10	F10	Earthworm
14. 9	5. 8	D10	G11	Crocodile
15. 9	6. 8	D10	H12	Dragon
16. 9	7. 8	D10	J1	Badger
17. 9	8. 8	D10	K2	Hare
18. 9	9. 8	D10	A3	Fox
19. 9	10. 8	D10	B4	Tiger
20. 9	11. 8	D10	C5	Leopard
21. 9	12. 8	D10	D6	Griffon
22. 9	13. 8	D10	E7	Ox
23. 9	14. 8	D10	F8	Bat
24. 9	15. 8	D10	G9	Rat
25. 9	16. 8	D10	H10	Swallow
26. 9	17. 8	D10	J11	Pig
27. 9	18. 8	D10	K12	Porcupine
28. 9	19. 8	D10	A1	Wolf
29. 9	20. 8	D10	B2	Dog
30. 9	21. 8	D10	C3	Pheasant
1.10	22. 8	D10	D4	Cock
2.10	23. 8	D10	E5	Crow
3.10	24. 8	D10	F6	Monkey
4.10	25. 8	D10	G7	Gibbon
5.10	26. 8	D10	H8	Tapir
6.10	27. 8	D10	J9	Sheep
7.10	28. 8	D10	K10	Deer
8.10	29. 8	D10	A11	Horse
9.10	30. 8	D10	B12	Stag
10.10	1. 9	E11	C1	Serpent
11.10	2. 9	E11	D2	Earthworm
12.10	3. 9	E11	E3	Crocodile
13.10	4. 9	E11	F4	Dragon
14.10	5. 9	E11	G5	Badger
15.10	6. 9	E11	H6	Hare
16.10	7. 9	E11	J7	Fox
17.10	8. 9	E11	K8	Tiger
18.10	9. 9	E11	A9	Leopard
19.10	10. 9	E11	B10	Griffon
20.10	11. 9	E11	C11	Ox
21.10	12. 9	E11	D12	Bat
22.10	13. 9	E11	E1	Rat
23.10	14. 9	E11	F2	Swallow
24.10	15. 9	E11	G3	Pig
25.10	16. 9	E11	H4	Porcupine
26.10	17. 9	E11	J5	Wolf
27.10	18. 9	E11	K6	Dog
28.10	19. 9	E11	A7	Pheasant
29.10	20. 9	E11	B8	Cock
30.10	21. 9	E11	C9	Crow
31.10	22. 9	E11	D10	Monkey
1.11	23. 9	E11	E11	Gibbon
2.11	24. 9	E11	F12	Tapir
3.11	25. 9	E11	G1	Sheep
4.11	26. 9	E11	H2	Deer
5.11	27. 9	E11	J3	Horse
6.11	28. 9	E11	K4	Stag
7.11	29. 9	E11	A5	Serpent
8.11	1.10	F12	B6	Earthworm
9.11	2.10	F12	C7	Crocodile
10.11	3.10	F12	D8	Dragon
11.11	4.10	F12	E9	Badger
12.11	5.10	F12	F10	Hare
13.11	6.10	F12	G11	Fox
14.11	7.10	F12	H12	Tiger
15.11	8.10	F12	J1	Leopard
16.11	9.10	F12	K2	Griffon
17.11	10.10	F12	A3	Ox
18.11	11.10	F12	B4	Bat
19.11	12.10	F12	C5	Rat
20.11	13.10	F12	D6	Swallow
21.11	14.10	F12	E7	Pig
22.11	15.10	F12	F8	Porcupine
23.11	16.10	F12	G9	Wolf
24.11	17.10	F12	H10	Dog
25.11	18.10	F12	J11	Pheasant
26.11	19.10	F12	K12	Cock
27.11	20.10	F12	A1	Crow
28.11	21.10	F12	B2	Monkey
29.11	22.10	F12	C3	Gibbon

Solar date	*Lunar date*	*Month HS/EB*	*Day HS/EB*	*Constellation*
30.11	23.10	F12	D4	Tapir
1.12	24.10	F12	E5	Sheep
2.12	25.10	F12	F6	Deer
3.12	26.10	F12	G7	Horse
4.12	27.10	F12	H8	Stag
5.12	28.10	F12	J9	Serpent
6.12	29.10	F12	K10	Earthworm
7.12	30.10	F12	A11	Crocodile
8.12	1.11	G1	B12	Dragon
9.12	2.11	G1	C1	Badger
10.12	3.11	G1	D2	Hare
11.12	4.11	G1	E3	Fox
12.12	5.11	G1	F4	Tiger
13.12	6.11	G1	G5	Leopard
14.12	7.11	G1	H6	Griffon
15.12	8.11	G1	J7	Ox
16.12	9.11	G1	K8	Bat
17.12	10.11	G1	A9	Rat
18.12	11.11	G1	B10	Swallow
19.12	12.11	G1	C11	Pig
20.12	13.11	G1	D12	Porcupine
21.12	14.11	G1	E1	Wolf
22.12	15.11	G1	F2	Dog
23.12	16.11	G1	G3	Pheasant
24.12	17.11	G1	H4	Cock
25.12	18.11	G1	J5	Crow
26.12	19.11	G1	K6	Monkey
27.12	20.11	G1	A7	Gibbon
28.12	21.11	G1	B8	Tapir
29.12	22.11	G1	C9	Sheep
30.12	23.11	G1	D10	Deer
31.12	24.11	G1	E11	Horse
1962				
1. 1	25.11	G1	F12	Stag
2. 1	26.11	G1	G1	Serpent
3. 1	27.11	G1	H2	Earthworm
4. 1	28.11	G1	J3	Crocodile
5. 1	29.11	G1	K4	Dragon
6. 1	1.12	H2	A5	Badger
7. 1	2.12	H2	B6	Hare
8. 1	3.12	H2	C7	Fox
9. 1	4.12	H2	D8	Tiger
10. 1	5.12	H2	E9	Leopard
11. 1	5.12	H2	F10	Griffon
12. 1	7.12	H2	G11	Ox
13. 1	8.12	H2	H12	Bat
14. 1	9.12	H2	J1	Rat
15. 1	10.12	H2	K2	Swallow
16. 1	11.12	H2	A3	Pig
17. 1	12.12	H2	B4	Porcupine
18. 1	13.12	H2	C5	Wolf
19. 1	14.12	H2	D6	Dog
20. 1	15.12	H2	E7	Pheasant
21. 1	16.12	H2	F8	Cock
22. 1	17.12	H2	G9	Crow
23. 1	18.12	H2	H10	Monkey
24. 1	19.12	H2	J11	Gibbon
25. 1	20.12	H2	K12	Tapir
26. 1	21.12	H2	A1	Sheep
27. 1	22.12	H2	B2	Deer
28. 1	23.12	H2	C3	Horse
29. 1	24.12	H2	D4	Stag
30. 1	25.12	H2	E5	Serpent
31. 1	26.12	H2	F6	Earthworm
1. 2	27.12	H2	G7	Crocodile
2. 2	28.12	H2	H8	Dragon
3. 2	29.12	H2	J9	Badger
4. 2	30.12	H2	K10	Hare

JEN YIN YEAR

5. 2	1. 1	J3	A11	Fox
6. 2	2. 1	J3	B12	Tiger
7. 2	3. 1	J3	C1	Leopard
8. 2	4. 1	J3	D2	Griffon
9. 2	5. 1	J3	E3	Ox
10. 2	6. 1	J3	F4	Bat
11. 2	7. 1	J3	G5	Rat
12. 2	8. 1	J3	H6	Swallow
13. 2	9. 1	J3	J7	Pig
14. 2	10. 1	J3	K8	Porcupine
15. 2	11. 1	J3	A9	Wolf
16. 2	12. 1	J3	B10	Dog
17. 2	13. 1	J3	C11	Pheasant
18. 2	14. 1	J3	D12	Cock
19. 2	15. 1	J3	E1	Crow
20. 2	16. 1	J3	F2	Monkey
21. 2	17. 1	J3	G3	Gibbon
22. 2	18. 1	J3	H4	Tapir
23. 2	19. 1	J3	J5	Sheep
24. 2	20. 1	J3	K6	Deer
25. 2	21. 1	J3	A7	Horse
26. 2	22. 1	J3	B8	Stag
27. 2	23. 1	J3	C9	Serpent
28. 2	24. 1	J3	D10	Earthworm
1. 3	25. 1	J3	E11	Crocodile
2. 3	26. 1	J3	F12	Dragon
3. 3	27. 1	J3	G1	Badger
4. 3	28. 1	J3	H2	Hare
5. 3	29. 1	J3	J3	Fox
6. 3	1. 2	K4	K4	Tiger
7. 3	2. 2	K4	A5	Leopard
8. 3	3. 2	K4	B6	Griffon
9. 3	4. 2	K4	C7	Ox
10. 3	5. 2	K4	D8	Bat
11. 3	6. 2	K4	E9	Rat
12. 3	7. 2	K4	F10	Swallow
13. 3	8. 2	K4	G11	Pig
14. 3	9. 2	K4	H12	Porcupine
15. 3	10. 2	K4	J1	Wolf
16. 3	11. 2	K4	K2	Dog
17. 3	12. 2	K4	A3	Pheasant
18. 3	13. 2	K4	B4	Cock
19. 3	14. 2	K4	C5	Crow
20. 3	15. 2	K4	D6	Monkey
21. 3	16. 2	K4	E7	Gibbon
22. 3	17. 2	K4	F8	Tapir
23. 3	18. 2	K4	G9	Sheep
24. 3	19. 2	K4	H10	Deer
25. 3	20. 2	K4	J11	Horse
26. 3	21. 2	K4	K12	Stag
27. 3	22. 2	K4	A1	Serpent
28. 3	23. 2	K4	B2	Earthworm
29. 3	24. 2	K4	C3	Crocodile
30. 3	25. 2	K4	D4	Dragon
31. 3	26. 2	K4	E5	Badger
1. 4	27. 2	K4	F6	Hare
2. 4	28. 2	K4	G7	Fox
3. 4	29. 2	K4	H8	Tiger
4. 4	30. 2	K4	J9	Leopard
5. 4	1. 3	A5	K10	Griffon
6. 4	2. 3	A5	A11	Ox
7. 4	3. 3	A5	B12	Bat
8. 4	4. 3	A5	C1	Rat
9. 4	5. 3	A5	D2	Swallow
10. 4	6. 3	A5	E3	Pig
11. 4	7. 3	A5	F4	Porcupine

Solar date	*Lunar date*	*Month HS/EB*	*Day HS/EB*	*Constellation*
12. 4	8. 3	A5	G5	Wolf
13. 4	9. 3	A5	H6	Dog
14. 4	10. 3	A5	J7	Pheasant
15. 4	11. 3	A5	K8	Cock
16. 4	12. 3	A5	A9	Crow
17. 4	13. 3	A5	B10	Monkey
18. 4	14. 3	A5	C11	Gibbon
19. 4	15. 3	A5	D12	Tapir
20. 4	16. 3	A5	E1	Sheep
21. 4	17. 3	A5	F2	Deer
22. 4	18. 3	A5	G3	Horse
23. 4	19. 3	A5	H4	Stag
24. 4	20. 3	A5	J5	Serpent
25. 4	21. 3	A5	K6	Earthworm
26. 4	22. 3	A5	A7	Crocodile
27. 4	23. 3	A5	B8	Dragon
28. 4	24. 3	A5	C9	Badger
29. 4	25. 3	A5	D10	Hare
30. 4	26. 3	A5	E11	Fox
1. 5	27. 3	A5	F12	Tiger
2. 5	28. 3	A5	G1	Leopard
3. 5	29. 3	A5	H2	Griffon
4. 5	1. 4	B6	J3	Ox
5. 5	2. 4	B6	K4	Bat
6. 5	3. 4	B6	A5	Rat
7. 5	4. 4	B6	B6	Swallow
8. 5	5. 4	B6	C7	Pig
9. 5	6. 4	B6	D8	Porcupine
10. 5	7. 4	B6	E9	Wolf
11. 5	8. 4	B6	F10	Dog
12. 5	9. 4	B6	G11	Pheasant
13. 5	10. 4	B6	H12	Cock
14. 5	11. 4	B6	J1	Crow
15. 5	12. 4	B6	K2	Monkey
16. 5	13. 4	B6	A3	Gibbon
17. 5	14. 4	B6	B4	Tapir
18. 5	15. 4	B6	C5	Sheep
19. 5	16. 4	B6	D6	Deer
20. 5	17. 4	B6	E7	Horse
21. 5	18. 4	B6	F8	Stag
22. 5	19. 4	B6	G9	Serpent
23. 5	20. 4	B6	H10	Earthworm
24. 5	21. 4	B6	J11	Crocodile
25. 5	22. 4	B6	K12	Dragon
26. 5	23. 4	B6	A1	Badger
27. 5	24. 4	B6	B2	Hare
28. 5	25. 4	B6	C3	Fox
29. 5	26. 4	B6	D4	Tiger
30. 5	27. 4	B6	E5	Leopard
31. 5	28. 4	B6	F6	Griffon
1. 6	29. 4	B6	G7	Ox
2. 6	1. 5	C7	H8	Bat
3. 6	2. 5	C7	J9	Rat
4. 6	3. 5	C7	K10	Swallow
5. 6	4. 5	C7	A11	Pig
6. 6	5. 5	C7	B12	Porcupine
7. 6	6. 5	C7	C1	Wolf
8. 6	7. 5	C7	D2	Dog
9. 6	8. 5	C7	E3	Pheasant
10. 6	9. 5	C7	F4	Cock
11. 6	10. 5	C7	G5	Crow
12. 6	11. 5	C7	H6	Monkey
13. 6	12. 5	C7	J7	Gibbon
14. 6	13. 5	C7	K8	Tapir
15. 6	14. 5	C7	A9	Sheep
16. 6	15. 5	C7	B10	Deer
17. 6	16. 5	C7	C11	Horse
18. 6	17. 5	C7	D12	Stag
19. 6	18. 5	C7	E1	Serpent
20. 6	19. 5	C7	F2	Earthworm
21. 6	20. 5	C7	G3	Crocodile
22. 6	21. 5	C7	H4	Dragon
23. 6	22. 5	C7	J5	Badger
24. 6	23. 5	C7	K6	Hare
25. 6	24. 5	C7	A7	Fox
26. 6	25. 5	C7	B8	Tiger
27. 6	26. 5	C7	C9	Leopard
28. 6	27. 5	C7	D10	Griffon
29. 6	28. 5	C7	E11	Ox
30. 6	29. 5	C7	F12	Bat
1. 7	30. 5	C7	G1	Rat
2. 7	1. 6	D8	H2	Swallow
3. 7	2. 6	D8	J3	Pig
4. 7	3. 6	D8	K4	Porcupine
5. 7	4. 6	D8	A5	Wolf
6. 7	5. 6	D8	B6	Dog
7. 7	6. 6	D8	C7	Pheasant
8. 7	7. 6	D8	D8	Cock
9. 7	8. 6	D8	E9	Crow
10. 7	9. 6	D8	F10	Monkey
11. 7	10. 6	D8	G11	Gibbon
12. 7	11. 6	D8	H12	Tapir
13. 7	12. 6	D8	J1	Sheep
14. 7	13. 6	D8	K2	Deer
15. 7	14. 6	D8	A3	Horse
16. 7	15. 6	D8	B4	Stag
17. 7	16. 6	D8	C5	Serpent
18. 7	17. 6	D8	D6	Earthworm
19. 7	18. 6	D8	E7	Crocodile
20. 7	19. 6	D8	F8	Dragon
21. 7	20. 6	D8	G9	Badger
22. 7	21. 6	D8	H10	Hare
23. 7	22. 6	D8	J11	Fox
24. 7	23. 6	D8	K12	Tiger
25. 7	24. 6	D8	A1	Leopard
26. 7	25. 6	D8	B2	Griffon
27. 7	26. 6	D8	C3	Ox
28. 7	27. 6	D8	D4	Bat
29. 7	28. 6	D8	E5	Rat
30. 7	29. 6	D8	F6	Swallow
31. 7	1. 7	E9	G7	Pig
1. 8	2. 7	E9	H8	Porcupine
2. 8	3. 7	E9	J9	Wolf
3. 8	4. 7	E9	K10	Dog
4. 8	5. 7	E9	A11	Pheasant
5. 8	6: 7	E9	B12	Cock
6. 8	7. 7	E9	C1	Crow
7. 8	8. 7	E9	D2	Monkey
8. 8	9. 7	E9	E3	Gibbon
9. 8	10. 7	E9	F4	Tapir
10. 8	11. 7	E9	G5	Sheep
11. 8	12. 7	E9	H6	Deer
12. 8	13. 7	E9	J7	Horse
13. 8	14. 7	E9	K8	Stag
14. 8	15. 7	E9	A9	Serpent
15. 8	16. 7	E9	B10	Earthworm
16. 8	17. 7	E9	C11	Crocodile
17. 8	18. 7	E9	D12	Dragon
18. 8	19. 7	E9	E1	Badger
19. 8	20. 7	E9	F2	Hare
20. 8	21. 7	E9	G3	Fox
21. 8	22. 7	E9	H4	Tiger
22. 8	23. 7	E9	J5	Leopard
23. 8	24. 7	E9	K6	Griffon
24. 8	25. 7	E9	A7	Ox
25. 8	26. 7	E9	B8	Bat
26. 8	27. 7	E9	C9	Rat
27. 8	28. 7	E9	D10	Swallow
28. 8	29. 7	E9	E11	Pig
29. 8	30. 7	E9	F12	Porcupine
30. 8	1. 8	F10	G1	Wolf
31. 8	2. 8	F10	H2	Dog
1. 9	3. 8	F10	J3	Pheasant
2. 9	4. 8	F10	K4	Cock
3. 9	5. 8	F10	A5	Crow
4. 9	6. 8	F10	B6	Monkey

Solar date	Lunar date	Month HS/EB	Day HS/EB	Constellation
5. 9	7. 8	F10	C7	Gibbon
6. 9	8. 8	F10	D8	Tapir
7. 9	9. 8	F10	E9	Sheep
8. 9	10. 8	F10	F10	Deer
9. 9	11. 8	F10	G11	Horse
10. 9	12. 8	F10	H12	Stag
11. 9	13. 8	F10	J1	Serpent
12. 9	14. 8	F10	K2	Earthworm
13. 9	15. 8	F10	A3	Crocodile
14. 9	16. 8	F10	B4	Dragon
15. 9	17. 8	F10	C5	Badger
16. 9	18. 8	F10	D6	Hare
17. 9	19. 8	F10	E7	Fox
18. 9	20. 8	F10	F8	Tiger
19. 9	21. 8	F10	G9	Leopard
20. 9	22. 8	F10	H10	Griffon
21. 9	23. 8	F10	J11	Ox
22. 9	24. 8	F10	K12	Bat
23. 9	25. 8	F10	A1	Rat
24. 9	26. 8	F10	B2	Swallow
25. 9	27. 8	F10	C3	Pig
26. 9	28. 8	F10	D4	Porcupine
27. 9	29. 8	F10	E5	Wolf
28. 9	30. 8	F10	F6	Dog
29. 9	1. 9	G11	G7	Pheasant
30. 9	2. 9	G11	H8	Cock
1.10	3. 9	G11	J9	Crow
2.10	4. 9	G11	K10	Monkey
3.10	5. 9	G11	A11	Gibbon
4.10	6. 9	G11	B12	Tapir
5.10	7. 9	G11	C1	Sheep
6.10	8. 9	G11	D2	Deer
7.10	9. 9	G11	E3	Horse
8.10	10. 9	G11	F4	Stag
9.10	11. 9	G11	G5	Serpent
10.10	12. 9	G11	H6	Earthworm
11.10	13. 9	G11	J7	Crocodile
12.10	14. 9	G11	K8	Dragon
13.10	15. 9	G11	A9	Badger
14.10	16. 9	G11	B10	Hare
15.10	17. 9	G11	C11	Fox
16.10	18. 9	G11	D12	Tiger
17.10	19. 9	G11	E1	Leopard
18.10	20. 9	G11	F2	Griffon
19.10	21. 9	G11	G3	Ox
20.10	22. 9	G11	H4	Bat
21.10	23. 9	G11	J5	Rat
22.10	24. 9	G11	K6	Swallow
23.10	25. 9	G11	A7	Pig
24.10	26. 9	G11	B8	Porcupine
25.10	27. 9	G11	C9	Wolf
26.10	28. 9	G11	D10	Dog
27.10	29. 9	G11	E11	Pheasant
28.10	1.10	H12	F12	Cock
29.10	2.10	H12	G1	Crow
30.10	3.10	H12	H2	Monkey
31.10	4.10	H12	J3	Gibbon
1.11	5.10	H12	K4	Tapir
2.11	6.10	H12	A5	Sheep
3.11	7.10	H12	B6	Deer
4.11	8.10	H12	C7	Horse
5.11	9.10	H12	D8	Stag
6.11	10.10	H12	E9	Serpent
7.11	11.10	H12	F10	Earthworm
8.11	12.10	H12	G11	Crocodile
9.11	13.10	H12	H12	Dragon
10.11	14.10	H12	J1	Badger
11.11	15.10	H12	K2	Hare
12.11	16.10	H12	A3	Fox
13.11	17.10	H12	B4	Tiger
14.11	18.10	H12	C5	Leopard
15.11	19.10	H12	D6	Griffon
16.11	20.10	H12	E7	Ox
17.11	21.10	H12	F8	Bat
18.11	22.10	H12	G9	Rat
19.11	23.10	H12	H10	Swallow
20.11	24.10	H12	J11	Pig
21.11	25.10	H12	K12	Porcupine
22.11	26.10	H12	A1	Wolf
23.11	27.10	H12	B2	Dog
24.11	28.10	H12	C3	Pheasant
25.11	29.10	H12	D4	Cock
26.11	30.10	H12	E5	Crow
27.11	1.11	J1	F6	Monkey
28.11	2.11	J1	G7	Gibbon
29.11	3.11	J1	H8	Tapir
30.11	4.11	J1	J9	Sheep
1.12	5.11	J1	K10	Deer
2.12	6.11	J1	A11	Horse
3.12	7.11	J1	B12	Stag
4.12	8.11	J1	C1	Serpent
5.12	9.11	J1	D2	Earthworm
6.12	10.11	J1	E3	Crocodile
7.12	11.11	J1	F4	Dragon
8.12	12.11	J1	G5	Badger
9.12	13.11	J1	H6	Hare
10.12	14.11	J1	J7	Fox
11.12	15.11	J1	K8	Tiger
12.12	16.11	J1	A9	Leopard
13.12	17.11	J1	B10	Griffon
14.12	18.11	J1	C11	Ox
15.12	19.11	J1	D12	Bat
16.12	20.11	J1	E1	Rat
17.12	21.11	J1	F2	Swallow
18.12	22.11	J1	G3	Pig
19.12	23.11	J1	H4	Porcupine
20.12	24.11	J1	J5	Wolf
21.12	25.11	J1	K6	Dog
22.12	26.11	J1	A7	Pheasant
23.12	27.11	J1	B8	Cock
24.12	28.11	J1	C9	Crow
25.12	29.11	J1	D10	Monkey
26.12	30.11	J1	E11	Gibbon
27.12	1.12	K2	F12	Tapir
28.12	2.12	K2	G1	Sheep
29.12	3.12	K2	H2	Deer
30.12	4.12	K2	J3	Horse
31.12	5.12	K2	K4	Stag
1963				
1. 1	6.12	K2	A5	Serpent
2. 1	7.12	K2	B6	Earthworm
3. 1	8.12	K2	C7	Crocodile
4. 1	9.12	K2	D8	Dragon
5. 1	10.12	K2	E9	Badger
6. 1	11.12	K2	F10	Hare
7. 1	12.12	K2	G11	Fox
8. 1	13.12	K2	H12	Tiger
9. 1	14.12	K2	J1	Leopard
10. 1	15.12	K2	K2	Griffon
11. 1	16.12	K2	A3	Ox
12. 1	17.12	K2	B4	Bat
13. 1	18.12	K2	C5	Rat
14. 1	19.12	K2	D6	Swallow
15. 1	20.12	K2	E7	Pig
16. 1	21.12	K2	F8	Porcupine
17. 1	22.12	K2	G9	Wolf
18. 1	23.12	K2	H10	Dog
19. 1	24.12	K2	J11	Pheasant
20. 1	25.12	K2	K12	Cock
21. 1	26.12	K2	A1	Crow
22. 1	27.12	K2	B2	Monkey
23. 1	28.12	K2	C3	Gibbon
24. 1	29.12	K2	D4	Tapir

KUEI MAO YEAR

Solar date	*Lunar date*	*Month HS/EB*	*Day HS/EB*	*Constellation*
25. 1	1. 1	A3	E5	Sheep
26. 1	2. 1	A3	F6	Deer
27. 1	3. 1	A3	G7	Horse
28. 1	4. 1	A3	H8	Stag
29. 1	5. 1	A3	J9	Serpent
30. 1	6. 1	A3	K10	Earthworm
31. 1	7. 1	A3	A11	Crocodile
1. 2	8. 1	A3	B12	Dragon
2. 2	9. 1	A3	C1	Badger
3. 2	10. 1	A3	D2	Hare
4. 2	11. 1	A3	E3	Fox
5. 2	12. 1	A3	F4	Tiger
6. 2	13. 1	A3	G5	Leopard
7. 2	14. 1	A3	H6	Griffon
8. 2	15. 1	A3	J7	Ox
9. 2	16. 1	A3	K8	Bat
10. 2	17. 1	A3	A9	Rat
11. 2	18. 1	A3	B10	Swallow
12. 2	19. 1	A3	C1	Pig
13. 2	20. 1	A3	D12	Porcupine
14. 2	21. 1	A3	E1	Wolf
15. 2	22. 1	A3	F2	Dog
16. 2	23. 1	A3	G3	Pheasant
17. 2	24. 1	A3	H4	Cock
18. 2	25. 1	A3	J5	Crow
19. 2	26. 1	A3	K6	Monkey
20. 2	27. 1	A3	A7	Gibbon
21. 2	28. 1	A3	B8	Tapir
22. 2	29. 1	A3	C9	Sheep
23. 2	30. 1	A3	D10	Deer
24. 2	1. 2	B4	E11	Horse
25. 2	2. 2	B4	F12	Stag
26. 2	3. 2	B4	G1	Serpent
27. 2	4. 2	B4	H2	Earthworm
28. 2	5. 2	B4	J3	Crocodile
1. 3	6. 2	B4	K4	Dragon
2. 3	7. 2	B4	A5	Badger
3. 3	8. 2	B4	B6	Hare
4. 3	9. 2	B4	C7	Fox
5. 3	10. 2	B4	D8	Tiger
6. 3	11. 2	B4	E9	Leopard
7. 3	12. 2	B4	F10	Griffon
8. 3	13. 2	B4	G11	Ox
9. 3	14. 2	B4	H12	Bat
10. 3	15. 2	B4	J1	Rat
11. 3	16. 2	B4	K2	Swallow
12. 3	17. 2	B4	A3	Pig
13. 3	18. 2	B4	B4	Porcupine
14. 3	19. 2	B4	C5	Wolf
15. 3	20. 2	B4	D6	Dog
16. 3	21. 2	B4	E7	Pheasant
17. 3	22. 2	B4	F8	Cock
18. 3	23. 2	B4	G9	Crow
19. 3	24. 2	B4	H10	Monkey
20. 3	25. 2	B4	J11	Gibbon
21. 3	26. 2	B4	K12	Tapir
22. 3	27. 2	B4	A1	Sheep
23. 3	28. 2	B4	B2	Deer
24. 3	29. 2	B4	C3	Horse
25. 3	1. 3	C5	D4	Stag
26. 3	2. 3	C5	E5	Serpent
27. 3	3. 3	C5	F6	Earthworm
28. 3	4. 3	C5	G7	Crocodile
29. 3	5. 3	C5	H8	Dragon
30. 3	6. 3	C5	J9	Badger
31. 3	7. 3	C5	K10	Hare
1. 4	8. 3	C5	A11	Fox
2. 4	9. 3	C5	B12	Tiger
3. 4	10. 3	C5	C1	Leopard
4. 4	11. 3	C5	D2	Griffon
5. 4	12. 3	C5	E3	Ox
6. 4	13. 3	C5	F4	Bat
7. 4	14. 3	C5	G5	Rat
8. 4	15. 3	C5	H6	Swallow
9. 4	16. 3	C5	J7	Pig
10. 4	17. 3	C5	K8	Porcupine
11. 4	18. 3	C5	A9	Wolf
12. 4	19. 3	C5	B10	Dog
13. 4	20. 3	C5	C11	Pheasant
14. 4	21. 3	C5	D12	Cock
15. 4	22. 3	C5	E1	Crow
16. 4	23. 3	C5	F2	Monkey
17. 4	24. 3	C5	G3	Gibbon
18. 4	25. 3	C5	H4	Tapir
19. 4	26. 3	C5	J5	Sheep
20. 4	27. 3	C5	K6	Deer
21. 4	28. 3	C5	A7	Horse
22. 4	29. 3	C5	B8	Stag
23. 4	30. 3	C5	C9	Serpent
24. 4	1. 4	D6	D10	Earthworm
25. 4	2. 4	D6	E11	Crocodile
26. 4	3. 4	D6	F12	Dragon
27. 4	4. 4	D6	G1	Badger
28. 4	5. 4	D6	H2	Hare
29. 4	6. 4	D6	J3	Fox
30. 4	7. 4	D6	K4	Tiger
1. 5	8. 4	D6	A5	Leopard
2. 5	9. 4	D6	B6	Griffon
3. 5	10. 4	D6	C7	Ox
4. 5	11. 4	D6	D8	Bat
5. 5	12. 4	D6	E9	Rat
6. 5	13. 4	D6	F10	Swallow
7. 5	14. 4	D6	G11	Pig
8. 5	15. 4	D6	H12	Porcupine
9. 5	16. 4	D6	J1	Wolf
10. 5	17. 4	D6	K2	Dog
11. 5	18. 4	D6	A3	Pheasant
12. 5	19. 4	D6	B4	Cock
13. 5	20. 4	D6	C5	Crow
14. 5	21. 4	D6	D6	Monkey
15. 5	22. 4	D6	E7	Gibbon
16. 5	23. 4	D6	F8	Tapir
17. 5	24. 4	D6	G9	Sheep
18. 5	25. 4	D6	H10	Deer
19. 5	26. 4	D6	J11	Horse
20. 5	27. 4	D6	K12	Stag
21. 5	28. 4	D6	A1	Serpent
22. 5	29. 4	D6	B2	Earthworm
23. 5	*1. 4*	*D6*	C3	Crocodile
24. 5	*2. 4*	*D6*	D4	Dragon
25. 5	*3. 4*	*D6*	E5	Badger
26. 5	*4. 4*	*D6*	F6	Hare
27. 5	*5. 4*	*D6*	G7	Fox
28. 5	*6. 4*	*D6*	H8	Tiger
29. 5	*7. 4*	*D6*	J9	Leopard
30. 5	*8. 4*	*D6*	K10	Griffon
31. 5	*9. 4*	*D6*	A11	Ox
1. 6	*10. 4*	*D6*	B12	Bat
2. 6	*11. 4*	*D6*	C1	Rat
3. 6	*12. 4*	*D6*	D2	Swallow
4. 6	*13. 4*	*D6*	E3	Pig
5. 6	*14. 4*	*D6*	F4	Porcupine
6. 6	*15. 4*	*D6*	G5	Wolf
7. 6	*16. 4*	*D6*	H6	Dog
8. 6	*17. 4*	*D6*	J7	Pheasant
9. 6	*18. 4*	*D6*	K8	Cock
10. 6	*19. 4*	*D6*	A9	Crow
11. 6	*20. 4*	*D6*	B10	Monkey
12. 6	*21. 4*	*D6*	C11	Gibbon
13. 6	*22. 4*	*D6*	D12	Tapir
14. 6	*23. 4*	*D6*	E1	Sheep
15. 6	*24. 4*	*D6*	F2	Deer

Solar date	*Lunar date*	*Month HS/EB*	*Day HS/EB*	*Constellation*
16. 6	*25. 4*	*D6*	G3	Horse
17. 6	*26. 4*	*D6*	H4	Stag
18. 6	*27. 4*	*D6*	J5	Serpent
19. 6	*28. 4*	*D6*	K6	Earthworm
20. 6	*29. 4*	*D6*	A7	Crocodile
21. 6	1. 5	E7	B8	Dragon
22. 6	2. 5	E7	C9	Badger
23. 6	3. 5	E7	D10	Hare
24. 6	4. 5	E7	E11	Fox
25. 6	5. 5	E7	F12	Tiger
26. 6	6. 5	E7	G1	Leopard
27. 6	7. 5	E7	H2	Griffon
28. 6	8. 5	E7	J3	Ox
29. 6	9. 5	E7	K4	Bat
30. 6	10. 5	E7	A5	Rat
1. 7	11. 5	E7	B6	Swallow
2. 7	12. 5	E7	C7	Pig
3. 7	13. 5	E7	D8	Porcupine
4. 7	14. 5	E7	E9	Wolf
5. 7	15. 5	E7	F10	Dog
6. 7	16. 5	E7	G11	Pheasant
7. 7	17. 5	E7	H12	Cock
8. 7	18. 5	E7	J1	Crow
9. 7	19. 5	E7	K2	Monkey
10. 7	20. 5	E7	A3	Gibbon
11. 7	21. 5	E7	B4	Tapir
12. 7	22. 5	E7	C5	Sheep
13. 7	23. 5	E7	D6	Deer
14. 7	24. 5	E7	E7	Horse
15. 7	25. 5	E7	F8	Stag
16. 7	26. 5	E7	G9	Serpent
17. 7	27. 5	E7	H10	Earthworm
18. 7	28. 5	E7	J11	Crocodile
19. 7	29. 5	E7	K12	Dragon
20. 7	30. 5	E7	A1	Badger
21. 7	1. 6	F8	B2	Hare
22. 7	2. 6	F8	C3	Fox
23. 7	3. 6	F8	D4	Tiger
24. 7	4. 6	F8	E5	Leopard
25. 7	5. 6	F8	F6	Griffon
26. 7	6. 6	F8	G7	Ox
27. 7	7. 6	F8	H8	Bat
28. 7	8. 6	F8	J9	Rat
29. 7	9. 6	F8	K10	Swallow
30. 7	10. 6	F8	A11	Pig
31. 7	11. 6	F8	B12	Porcupine
1. 8	12. 6	F8	C1	Wolf
2. 8	13. 6	F8	D2	Dog
3. 8	14. 6	F8	E3	Pheasant
4. 8	15. 6	F8	F4	Cock
5. 8	16. 6	F8	G5	Crow
6. 8	17. 6	F8	H6	Monkey
7. 8	18. 6	F8	J7	Gibbon
8. 8	19. 6	F8	K8	Tapir
9. 8	20. 6	F8	A9	Sheep
10. 8	21. 6	F8	B10	Deer
11. 8	22. 6	F8	C11	Horse
12. 8	23. 6	F8	D12	Stag
13. 8	24. 6	F8	E1	Serpent
14. 8	25. 6	F8	F2	Earthworm
15. 8	26. 6	F8	G3	Crocodile
16. 8	27. 6	F8	H4	Dragon
17. 8	28. 6	F8	J5	Badger
18. 8	29. 6	F8	K6	Hare
19. 8	1. 7	G9	A7	Fox
20. 8	2. 7	G9	B8	Tiger
21. 8	3. 7	G9	C9	Leopard
22. 8	4. 7	G9	D10	Griffon
23. 8	5. 7	G9	E11	Ox
24. 8	6. 7	G9	F12	Bat
25. 8	7. 7	G9	G1	Rat
26. 8	8. 7	G9	H2	Swallow
27. 8	9. 7	G9	J3	Pig
28. 8	10. 7	G9	K4	Porcupine
29. 8	11. 7	G9	A5	Wolf
30. 8	12. 7	G9	B6	Dog
31. 8	13. 7	G9	C7	Pheasant
1. 9	14. 7	G9	D8	Cock
2. 9	15. 7	G9	E9	Crow
3. 9	16. 7	G9	F10	Monkey
4. 9	17. 7	G9	G11	Gibbon
5. 9	18. 7	G9	H12	Tapir
6. 9	19. 7	G9	J1	Sheep
7. 9	20. 7	G9	K2	Deer
8. 9	21. 7	G9	A3	Horse
9. 9	22. 7	G9	B4	Stag
10. 9	23. 7	G9	C5	Serpent
11. 9	24. 7	G9	D6	Earthworm
12. 9	25. 7	G9	E7	Crocodile
13. 9	26. 7	G9	F8	Dragon
14. 9	27. 7	G9	G9	Badger
15. 9	28. 7	G9	H10	Hare
16. 9	29. 7	G9	J11	Fox
17. 9	30. 7	G9	K12	Tiger
18. 9	1. 8	H10	A1	Leopard
19. 9	2. 8	H10	B2	Griffon
20. 9	3. 8	H10	C3	Ox
21. 9	4. 8	H10	D4	Bat
22. 9	5. 8	H10	E5	Rat
23. 9	6. 8	H10	F6	Swallow
24. 9	7. 8	H10	G7	Pig
25. 9	8. 8	H10	H8	Porcupine
26. 9	9. 8	H10	J9	Wolf
27. 9	10. 8	H10	K10	Dog
28. 9	11. 8	H10	A11	Pheasant
29. 9	12. 8	H10	B12	Cock
30. 9	13. 8	H10	C1	Crow
1.10	14. 8	H10	D2	Monkey
2.10	15. 8	H10	E3	Gibbon
3.10	16. 8	H10	F4	Tapir
4.10	17. 8	H10	G5	Sheep
5.10	18. 8	H10	H6	Deer
6.10	19. 8	H10	J7	Horse
7.10	20. 8	H10	K8	Stag
8.10	21. 8	H10	A9	Serpent
9.10	22. 8	H10	B10	Earthworm
10.10	23. 8	H10	C11	Crocodile
11.10	24. 8	H10	D12	Dragon
12.10	25. 8	H10	E1	Badger
13.10	26. 8	H10	F2	Hare
14.10	27. 8	H10	G3	Fox
15.10	28. 8	H10	H4	Tiger
16.10	29. 8	H10	J5	Leopard
17.10	1. 9	J11	K6	Griffon
18.10	2. 9	J11	A7	Ox
19.10	3. 9	J11	B8	Bat
20.20	4. 9	J11	C9	Rat
21.10	5. 9	J11	D10	Swallow
22.10	6. 9	J11	E11	Pig
23.10	7. 9	J11	F12	Porcupine
24.10	8. 9	J11	G1	Wolf
25.10	9. 9	J11	H2	Dog
26.10	10. 9	J11	J3	Pheasant
27.10	11. 9	J11	K4	Cock
28.10	12. 9	J11	A5	Crow
29.10	13. 9	J11	B6	Monkey
30.10	14. 9	J11	C7	Gibbon
31.10	15. 9	J11	D8	Tapir
1.11	16. 9	J11	E9	Sheep
2.11	17. 9	J11	F10	Deer
3.11	18. 9	J11	G11	Horse
4.11	19. 9	J11	H12	Stag
5.11	20. 9	J11	J1	Serpent
6.11	21. 9	J11	K2	Earthworm
7.11	22. 9	J11	A3	Crocodile
8.11	23. 9	J11	B4	Dragon

Solar date	*Lunar date*	*Month HS/EB*	*Day HS/EB*	*Constellation*	*Solar date*	*Lunar date*	*Month HS/EB*	*Day HS/EB*	*Constellation*
9.11	24. 9	J11	C5	Badger	28.12	13.11	A1	B6	Deer
10.11	25. 9	J11	D6	Hare	29.12	14.11	A1	C7	Horse
11.11	26. 9	J11	E7	Fox	30.12	15.11	A1	D8	Stag
12.11	27. 9	J11	F8	Tiger	31.12	16.11	A1	E9	Serpent
13.11	28. 9	J11	G9	Leopard					
14.11	29. 9	J11	H10	Griffon	**1964**				
15.11	30. 9	J11	J11	Ox	1. 1	17.11	A1	F10	Earthworm
16.11	1.10	K12	K12	Bat	2. 1	18.11	A1	G11	Crocodile
17.11	2.10	K12	A1	Rat	3. 1	19.11	A1	H12	Dragon
18.11	3.10	K12	B2	Swallow	4. 1	20.11	A1	J1	Badger
19.11	4.10	K12	C3	Pig	5. 1	21.11	A1	K2	Hare
20.11	5.10	K12	D4	Porcupine	6. 1	22.11	A1	A3	Fox
21.11	6.10	K12	E5	Wolf	7. 1	23.11	A1	B4	Tiger
22.11	7.10	K12	F6	Dog	8. 1	24.11	A1	C5	Leopard
23.11	8.10	K12	G7	Pheasant	9. 1	25.11	A1	D6	Griffon
24.11	9.10	K12	H8	Cock	10. 1	26.11	A1	E7	Ox
25.11	10.10	K12	J9	Crow	11. 1	27.11	A1	F8	Bat
26.11	11.10	K12	K10	Monkey	12. 1	28.11	A1	G9	Rat
27.11	12.10	K12	A11	Gibbon	13. 1	29.11	A1	H10	Swallow
28.11	13.10	K12	B12	Tapir	14. 1	30.11	A1	J11	Pig
29.11	14.10	K12	C1	Sheep	15. 1	1.12	B2	K12	Porcupine
30.11	15.10	K12	D2	Deer	16. 1	2.12	B2	A1	Wolf
1.12	16.10	K12	E3	Horse	17. 1	3.12	B2	B2	Dog
2.12	17.10	K12	F4	Stag	18. 1	4.12	B2	C3	Pheasant
3.12	18.10	K12	G5	Serpent	19. 1	5.12	B2	D4	Cock
4.12	19.10	K12	H6	Earthworm	20. 1	6.12	B2	E5	Crow
5.12	20.20	K12	J7	Crocodile	21. 1	7.12	B2	F6	Monkey
6.12	21.10	K12	K8	Dragon	22. 1	8.12	B2	G7	Gibbon
7.12	22.10	K12	A9	Badger	23. 1	9.12	B2	H8	Tapir
8.12	23.10	K12	B10	Hare	24. 1	10.12	B2	J9	Sheep
9.12	24.10	K12	C11	Fox	25. 1	11.12	B2	K10	Deer
10.12	25.10	K12	D12	Tiger	26. 1	12.12	B2	A11	Horse
11.12	26.10	K12	E1	Leopard	27. 1	13.12	B2	B12	Stag
12.12	27.10	K12	F2	Griffon	28. 1	14.12	B2	C1	Serpent
13.12	28.10	K12	G3	Ox	29. 1	15.12	B2	D2	Earthworm
14.12	29.10	K12	H4	Bat	30. 1	16.12	B2	E3	Crocodile
15.12	30.10	K12	J5	Rat	31. 1	17.12	B2	F4	Dragon
16.12	1.11	A1	K6	Swallow	1. 2	18.12	B2	G5	Badger
17.12	2.11	A1	A7	Pig	2. 2	19.12	B2	H6	Hare
18.12	3.11	A1	B8	Porcupine	3. 2	20.12	B2	J7	Fox
19.12	4.11	A1	C9	Wolf	4. 2	21.12	B2	K8	Tiger
20.12	5.11	A1	D10	Dog	5. 2	22.12	B2	A9	Leopard
21.12	6.11	A1	E11	Pheasant	6. 2	23.12	B2	B10	Griffon
22.12	7.11	A1	F12	Cock	7. 2	24.12	B2	C11	Ox
23.12	8.11	A1	G1	Crow	8. 2	25.12	B2	D12	Bat
24.12	9.11	A1	H2	Monkey	9. 2	26.12	B2	E1	Rat
25.12	10.11	A1	J3	Gibbon	10. 2	27.12	B2	F2	Swallow
26.12	11.11	A1	K4	Tapir	11. 2	28.12	B2	G3	Pig
27.12	12.11	A1	A5	Sheep	12. 2	29.12	B2	H4	Porcupine

CHIA CH'EN YEAR

13. 2	1. 1	C3	J5	Wolf	3. 3	20. 1	C3	H12	Tiger
14. 2	2. 1	C3	K6	Dog	4. 3	21. 1	C3	J1	Leopard
15. 2	3. 1	C3	A7	Pheasant	5. 3	22. 1	C3	K2	Griffon
16. 2	4. 1	C3	B8	Cock	6. 3	23. 1	C3	A3	Ox
17. 2	5. 1	C3	C9	Crow	7. 3	24. 1	C3	B4	Bat
18. 2	6. 1	C3	D10	Monkey	8. 3	25. 1	C3	C5	Rat
19. 2	7. 1	C3	E11	Gibbon	9. 3	26. 1	C3	D6	Swallow
20. 2	8. 1	C3	F12	Tapir	10. 3	27. 1	C3	E7	Pig
21. 2	9. 1	C3	G1	Sheep	11. 3	28. 1	C3	F8	Porcupine
22. 2	10. 1	C3	H2	Deer	12. 3	29. 1	C3	G9	Wolf
23. 2	11. 1	C3	J3	Horse	13. 3	30. 1	C3	H10	Dog
24. 2	12. 1	C3	K4	Stag	14. 3	1. 2	D4	J11	Pheasant
25. 2	13. 1	C3	A5	Serpent	15. 3	2. 2	D4	K12	Cock
26. 2	14. 1	C3	B6	Earthworm	16. 3	3. 2	D4	A1	Crow
27. 2	15. 1	C3	C7	Crocodile	17. 3	4. 2	D4	B2	Monkey
28. 2	16. 1	C3	D8	Dragon	18. 3	5. 2	D4	C3	Gibbon
29. 2	17. 1	C3	E9	Badger	19. 3	6. 2	D4	D4	Tapir
1. 3	18. 1	C3	F10	Hare	20. 3	7. 2	D4	E5	Sheep
2. 3	19. 1	C3	G11	Fox	21. 3	8. 2	D4	F6	Deer

Solar date	*Lunar date*	*Month HS/EB*	*Day HS/EB*	*Constellation*
22. 3	9. 2	D4	G7	Horse
23. 3	10. 2	D4	H8	Stag
24. 3	11. 2	D4	J9	Serpent
25. 3	12. 2	D4	K10	Earthworm
26. 3	13. 2	D4	A11	Crocodile
27. 3	14. 2	D4	B12	Dragon
28. 3	15. 2	D4	C1	Badger
29. 3	16. 2	D4	D2	Hare
30. 3	17. 2	D4	E3	Fox
31. 3	18. 2	D4	F4	Tiger
1. 4	19. 2	D4	G5	Leopard
2. 4	20. 2	D4	H6	Griffon
3. 4	21. 2	D4	J7	Ox
4. 4	22. 2	D4	K8	Bat
5. 4	23. 2	D4	A9	Rat
6. 4	24. 2	D4	B10	Swallow
7. 4	25. 2	D4	C11	Pig
8. 4	26. 2	D4	D12	Porcupine
9. 4	27. 2	D4	E1	Wolf
10. 4	28. 2	D4	F2	Dog
11. 4	29. 2	D4	G3	Pheasant
12. 4	1. 3	E5	H4	Cock
13. 4	2. 3	E5	J5	Crow
14. 4	3. 3	E5	K6	Monkey
15. 4	4. 3	E5	A7	Gibbon
16. 4	5. 3	E5	B8	Tapir
17. 4	6. 3	E5	C9	Sheep
18. 4	7. 3	E5	D10	Deer
19. 4	8. 3	E5	E11	Horse
20. 4	9. 3	E5	F12	Stag
21. 4	10. 3	E5	G1	Serpent
22. 4	11. 3	E5	H2	Earthworm
23. 4	12. 3	E5	J3	Crocodile
24. 4	13. 3	E5	K4	Dragon
25. 4	14. 3	E5	A5	Badger
26. 4	15. 3	E5	B6	Hare
27. 4	16. 3	E5	C7	Fox
28. 4	17. 3	E5	D8	Tiger
29. 4	18. 3	E5	E9	Leopard
30. 4	19. 3	E5	F10	Griffon
1. 5	20. 3	E5	G11	Ox
2. 5	21. 3	E5	H12	Bat
3. 5	22. 3	E5	J1	Rat
4. 5	23. 3	E5	K2	Swallow
5. 5	24. 3	E5	A3	Pig
6. 4	25. 3	E5	B4	Porcupine
7. 5	26. 3	E5	C5	Wolf
8. 5	27. 3	E5	D6	Dog
9. 5	28. 3	E5	E7	Pheasant
10. 5	29. 3	E5	F8	Cock
11. 5	30. 3	E5	G9	Crow
12. 5	1. 4	F6	H10	Monkey
13. 5	2. 4	F6	J11	Gibbon
14. 5	3. 4	F6	K12	Tapir
15. 5	4. 4	F6	A1	Sheep
16. 5	5. 4	F6	B2	Deer
17. 5	6. 4	F6	C3	Horse
18. 5	7. 4	F6	D4	Stag
19. 5	8. 4	F6	E5	Serpent
20. 5	9. 4	F6	F6	Earthworm
21. 5	10. 4	F6	G7	Crocodile
22. 5	11. 4	F6	H8	Dragon
23. 5	12. 4	F6	J9	Badger
24. 5	13. 4	F6	K10	Hare
25. 5	14. 4	F6	A11	Fox
26. 5	15. 4	F6	B12	Tiger
27. 5	16. 4	F6	C1	Leopard
28. 5	17. 4	F6	D2	Griffon
29. 5	18. 4	F6	E3	Ox
30. 5	19. 4	F6	F4	Bat
31. 5	20. 4	F6	G5	Rat
1. 6	21. 4	F6	H6	Swallow
2. 6	22. 4	F6	J7	Pig
3. 6	23. 4	F6	K8	Porcupine
4. 6	24. 4	F6	A9	Wolf
5. 6	25. 4	F6	B10	Dog
6. 6	26. 4	F6	C11	Pheasant
7. 6	27. 4	F6	D12	Cock
8. 6	28. 4	F6	E1	Crow
9. 6	29. 4	F6	F2	Monkey
10. 6	1. 5	G7	G3	Gibbon
11. 6	2. 5	G7	H4	Tapir
12. 6	3. 5	G7	J5	Sheep
13. 6	4. 5	G7	K6	Deer
14. 6	5. 5	G7	A7	Horse
15. 6	6. 5	G7	B8	Stag
16. 6	7. 5	G7	C9	Serpent
17. 6	8. 5	G7	D10	Earthworm
18. 6	9. 5	G7	E11	Crocodile
19. 6	10. 5	G7	F12	Dragon
20. 6	11. 5	G7	G1	Badger
21. 6	12. 5	G7	H2	Hare
22. 6	13. 5	G7	J3	Fox
23. 6	14. 5	G7	K4	Tiger
24. 6	15. 5	G7	A5	Leopard
25. 6	16. 5	G7	B6	Griffon
26. 6	17. 5	G7	C7	Ox
27. 6	18. 5	G7	D8	Bat
28. 6	19. 5	G7	E9	Rat
29. 6	20. 5	G7	F10	Swallow
30. 6	21. 5	G7	G11	Pig
1. 7	22. 5	G7	H12	Porcupine
2. 7	23. 5	G7	J1	Wolf
3. 7	24. 5	G7	K2	Dog
4. 7	25. 5	G7	A3	Pheasant
5. 7	26. 5	G7	B4	Cock
6. 7	27. 5	G7	C5	Crow
7. 7	28. 5	G7	D6	Monkey
8. 7	29. 5	G7	E7	Gibbon
9. 7	1. 6	H8	F8	Tapir
10. 7	2. 6	H8	G9	Sheep
11. 7	3. 6	H8	H10	Deer
12. 7	4. 6	H8	J11	Horse
13. 7	5. 6	H8	K12	Stag
14. 7	6. 6	H8	A1	Serpent
15. 7	7. 6	H8	B2	Earthworm
16. 7	8. 6	H8	C3	Crocodile
17. 7	9. 6	H8	D4	Dragon
18. 7	10. 6	H8	E5	Badger
19. 7	11. 6	H8	F6	Hare
20. 7	12. 6	H8	G7	Fox
21. 7	13. 6	H8	H8	Tiger
22. 7	14. 6	H8	J9	Leopard
23. 7	15. 6	H8	K10	Griffon
24. 7	16. 6	H8	A11	Ox
25. 7	17. 6	H8	B12	Bat
26. 7	18. 6	H8	C1	Rat
27. 7	19. 6	H8	D2	Swallow
28. 7	20. 6	H8	E3	Pig
29. 7	21. 6	H8	F4	Porcupine
30. 7	22. 6	H8	G5	Wolf
31. 7	23. 6	H8	H6	Dog
1. 8	24. 6	H8	J7	Pheasant
2. 8	25. 6	H8	K8	Cock
3. 8	26. 6	H8	A9	Crow
4. 8	27. 6	H8	B10	Monkey
5. 8	28. 6	H8	C11	Gibbon
6. 8	29. 6	H8	D12	Tapir
7. 8	30. 6	H8	E1	Sheep
8. 8	1. 7	J9	F2	Deer
9. 8	2. 7	J9	G3	Horse
10. 8	3. 7	J9	H4	Stag
11. 8	4. 7	J9	J5	Serpent
12. 8	5. 7	J9	K6	Earthworm
13. 8	6. 7	J9	A7	Crocodile
14. 8	7. 7	J9	B8	Dragon

Solar date	*Lunar date*	*Month HS/EB*	*Day HS/EB*	*Constellation*
15. 8	8. 7	J9	C9	Badger
16. 8	9. 7	J9	D10	Hare
17. 8	10. 7	J9	E11	Fox
18. 8	11. 7	J9	F12	Tiger
19. 8	12. 7	J9	G1	Leopard
20. 8	13. 7	J9	H2	Griffon
21. 8	14. 7	J9	J3	Ox
22. 8	15. 7	J9	K4	Bat
23. 8	16. 7	J9	A5	Rat
24. 8	17. 7	J9	B6	Swallow
25. 8	18. 7	J9	C7	Pig
26. 8	19. 7	J9	D8	Porcupine
27. 8	20. 7	J9	E9	Wolf
28. 8	21. 7	J9	F10	Dog
29. 8	22. 7	J9	G11	Pheasant
30. 8	23. 7	J9	H12	Cock
31. 8	24. 7	J9	J1	Crow
1. 9	25. 7	J9	K2	Monkey
2. 9	26. 7	J9	A3	Gibbon
3. 9	27. 7	J9	B4	Tapir
4. 9	28. 7	J9	C5	Sheep
5. 9	29. 7	J9	D6	Deer
6. 9	1. 8	K10	E7	Horse
7. 9	2. 8	K10	F8	Stag
8. 9	3. 8	K10	G9	Serpent
9. 9	4. 8	K10	H10	Earthworm
10. 9	5. 8	K10	J11	Crocodile
11. 9	6. 8	K10	K12	Dragon
12. 9	7. 8	K10	A1	Badger
13. 9	8. 8	K10	B2	Hare
14. 9	9. 8	K10	C3	Fox
15. 9	10. 8	K10	D4	Tiger
16. 9	11. 8	K10	E5	Leopard
17. 9	12. 8	K10	F6	Griffon
18. 9	13. 8	K10	G7	Ox
19. 9	14. 8	K10	H8	Bat
20. 9	15. 8	K10	J9	Rat
21. 9	16. 8	K10	K10	Swallow
22. 9	17. 8	K10	A11	Pig
23. 9	18. 8	K10	B12	Porcupine
24. 9	19. 8	K10	C1	Wolf
25. 9	20. 8	K10	D2	Dog
26. 9	21. 8	K10	E3	Pheasant
27. 9	22. 8	K10	F4	Cock
28. 9	23. 8	K10	G5	Crow
29. 9	24. 8	K10	H6	Monkey
30. 9	25. 8	K10	J7	Gibbon
1.10	26. 8	K10	K8	Tapir
2.10	27. 8	K10	A9	Sheep
3.10	28. 8	K10	B10	Deer
4.10	29. 8	K10	C11	Horse
5.10	30. 8	K10	D12	Stag
6.10	1. 9	A11	E1	Serpent
7.10	2. 9	A11	F2	Earthworm
8.10	3. 9	A11	G3	Crocodile
9.10	4. 9	A11	H4	Dragon
10.10	5. 9	A11	J5	Badger
11.10	6. 9	A11	K6	Hare
12.10	7. 9	A11	A7	Fox
13.10	8. 9	A11	B8	Tiger
14.10	9. 9	A11	C9	Leopard
15.10	10. 9	A11	D10	Griffon
16.10	11. 9	A11	E11	Ox
17.10	12. 9	A11	F12	Bat
18.10	13. 9	A11	G1	Rat
19.10	14. 9	A11	H2	Swallow
20.10	15. 9	A11	J3	Pig
21.10	16. 9	A11	K4	Porcupine
22.10	17. 9	A11	A5	Wolf
23.10	18. 9	A11	B6	Dog
24.10	19. 9	A11	C7	Pheasant
25.10	20. 9	A11	D8	Cock
26.10	21. 9	A11	E9	Crow

Solar date	*Lunar date*	*Month HS/EB*	*Day HS/EB*	*Constellation*
27.10	22. 9	A11	F10	Monkey
28.10	23. 9	A11	G11	Gibbon
29.10	24. 9	A11	H12	Tapir
30.10	25. 9	A11	J1	Sheep
31.10	26. 9	A11	K2	Deer
1.11	27. 9	A11	A3	Horse
2.11	28. 9	A11	B4	Stag
3.11	29. 9	A11	C5	Serpent
4.11	1.10	B12	D6	Earthworm
5.11	2.10	B12	E7	Crocodile
6.11	3.10	B12	F8	Dragon
7.11	4.10	B12	G9	Badger
8.11	5.10	B12	H10	Hare
9.11	6.10	B12	J11	Fox
10.11	7.10	B12	K12	Tiger
11.11	8.10	B12	A1	Leopard
12.11	9.10	B12	B2	Griffon
13.11	10.10	B12	C3	Ox
14.11	11.10	B12	D4	Bat
15.11	12.10	B12	E5	Rat
16.11	13.10	B12	F6	Swallow
17.11	14.10	B12	G7	Pig
18.11	15.10	B12	H8	Porcupine
19.11	16.10	B12	J9	Wolf
20.11	17.10	B12	K10	Dog
21.11	18.10	B12	A11	Pheasant
22.11	19.10	B12	B12	Cock
23.11	20.10	B12	C1	Crow
24.11	21.10	B12	D2	Monkey
25.11	22.10	B12	E3	Gibbon
26.11	23.10	B12	F4	Tapir
27.11	24.10	B12	G5	Sheep
28.11	25.10	B12	H6	Deer
29.11	26.10	B12	J7	Horse
30.11	27.10	B12	K8	Stag
1.12	28.10	B12	A9	Serpent
2.12	29.10	B12	B10	Earthworm
3.12	30.10	B12	C11	Crocodile
4.12	1.11	C1	D12	Dragon
5.12	2.11	C1	E1	Badger
6.12	3.11	C1	F2	Hare
7.12	4.11	C1	G3	Fox
8.12	5.11	C1	H4	Tiger
9.12	6.11	C1	J5	Leopard
10.12	7.11	C1	K6	Griffon
11.12	8.11	C1	A7	Ox
12.12	9.11	C1	B8	Bat
13.12	10.11	C1	C9	Rat
14.12	11.11	C1	D10	Swallow
15.12	12.11	C1	E11	Pig
16.12	13.11	C1	F12	Porcupine
17.12	14.11	C1	G1	Wolf
18.12	15.11	C1	H2	Dog
19.12	16.11	C1	J3	Pheasant
20.12	17.11	C1	K4	Cock
21.12	18.11	C1	A5	Crow
22.12	19.11	C1	B6	Monkey
23.12	20.11	C1	C7	Gibbon
24.12	21.11	C1	D8	Tapir
25.12	22.11	C1	E9	Sheep
26.12	23.11	C1	F10	Deer
27.12	24.11	C1	G11	Horse
28.12	25.11	C1	H12	Stag
29.12	26.11	C1	J1	Serpent
30.12	27.11	C1	K2	Earthworm
31.12	28.11	C1	A3	Crocodile
1965				
1. 1	29.11	C1	B4	Dragon
2. 1	30.11	C1	C5	Badger
3. 1	1.12	D2	D6	Hare
4. 1	2.12	D2	E7	Fox
5. 1	3.12	D2	F8	Tiger

Solar date	*Lunar date*	*Month HS/EB*	*Day HS/EB*	*Constellation*
6. 1	4.12	D2	G9	Leopard
7. 1	5.12	D2	H10	Griffon
8. 1	6.12	D2	J11	Ox
9. 1	7.12	D2	K12	Bat
10. 1	8.12	D2	A1	Rat
11. 1	9.12	D2	B2	Swallow
12. 1	10.12	D2	C3	Pig
13. 1	11.12	D2	D4	Porcupine
14. 1	12.12	D2	E5	Wolf
15. 1	13.12	D2	F6	Dog
16. 1	14.12	D2	G7	Pheasant
17. 1	15.12	D2	H8	Cock
18. 1	16.12	D2	J9	Crow
19. 1	17.12	D2	K10	Monkey
20. 1	18.12	D2	A11	Gibbon
21. 1	19.12	D2	B12	Tapir
22. 1	20.12	D2	C1	Sheep
23. 1	21.12	D2	D2	Deer
24. 1	22.12	D2	E3	Horse
25. 1	23.12	D2	F4	Stag
26. 1	24.12	D2	G5	Serpent
27. 1	25.12	D2	H6	Earthworm
28. 1	26.12	D2	J7	Crocodile
29. 1	27.12	D2	K8	Dragon
30. 1	28.12	D2	A9	Badger
31. 1	29.12	D2	B10	Hare
1. 2	30.12	D2	C11	Fox

YI SZU YEAR

Solar date	*Lunar date*	*Month HS/EB*	*Day HS/EB*	*Constellation*
2. 2	1. 1	E3	D12	Tiger
3. 2	2. 1	E3	E1	Leopard
4. 2	3. 1	E3	F2	Griffon
5. 2	4. 1	E3	G3	Ox
6. 2	5. 1	E3	H4	Bat
7. 2	6. 1	E3	J5	Rat
8. 2	7. 1	E3	K6	Swallow
9. 2	8. 1	E3	A7	Pig
10. 2	9. 1	E3	B8	Porcupine
11. 2	10. 1	E3	C9	Wolf
12. 2	11. 1	E3	D10	Dog
13. 2	12. 1	E3	E11	Pheasant
14. 2	13. 1	E3	F12	Cock
15. 2	14. 1	E3	G1	Crow
16. 2	15. 1	E3	H2	Monkey
17. 2	16. 1	E3	J3	Gibbon
18. 2	17. 1	E3	K4	Tapir
19. 2	18. 1	E3	A5	Sheep
20. 2	19. 1	E3	B6	Deer
21. 2	20. 1	E3	C7	Horse
22. 2	21. 1	E3	D8	Stag
23. 2	22. 1	E3	E9	Serpent
24. 2	23. 1	E3	F10	Earthworm
25. 2	24. 1	E3	G11	Crocodile
26. 2	25. 1	E3	H12	Dragon
27. 2	26. 1	E3	J1	Badger
28. 2	27. 1	E3	K2	Hare
1. 3	28. 1	E3	A3	Fox
2. 3	29. 1	E3	B4	Tiger
3. 3	1. 2	F4	C5	Leopard
4. 3	2. 2	F4	D6	Griffon
5. 3	3. 2	F4	E7	Ox
6. 3	4. 2	F4	F8	Bat
7. 3	5. 2	F4	G9	Rat
8. 3	6. 2	F4	H10	Swallow
9. 3	7. 2	F4	J11	Pig
10. 3	8. 2	F4	K12	Porcupine
11. 3	9. 2	F4	A1	Wolf
12. 3	10. 2	F4	B2	Dog
13. 3	11. 2	F4	C3	Pheasant
14. 3	12. 2	F4	D4	Cock
15. 3	13. 2	F4	E5	Crow
16. 3	14. 2	F4	F6	Monkey
17. 3	15. 2	F4	G7	Gibbon
18. 3	16. 2	F4	H8	Tapir
19. 3	17. 2	F4	J9	Sheep
20. 3	18. 2	F4	K10	Deer
21. 3	19. 2	F4	A11	Horse
22. 3	20. 2	F4	B12	Stag
23. 3	21. 2	F4	C1	Serpent
24. 3	22. 2	F4	D2	Earthworm
25. 3	23. 2	F4	E3	Crocodile
26. 3	24. 2	F4	F4	Dragon
27. 3	25. 2	F4	G5	Badger
28. 3	26. 2	F4	H6	Hare
29. 3	27. 2	F4	J7	Fox
30. 3	28. 2	F4	K8	Tiger
31. 3	29. 2	F4	A9	Leopard
1. 4	30. 2	F4	B10	Griffon
2. 4	1. 3	G5	C11	Ox
3. 4	2. 3	G5	D12	Bat
4. 4	3. 3	G5	E1	Rat
5. 4	4. 3	G5	F2	Swallow
6. 4	5. 3	G5	G3	Pig
7. 4	6. 3	G5	H4	Porcupine
8. 4	7. 3	G5	J5	Wolf
9. 4	8. 3	G5	K6	Dog
10. 4	9. 3	G5	A7	Pheasant
11. 4	10. 3	F5	B8	Cock
12. 4	11. 3	G5	C9	Crow
13. 4	12. 3	G5	D10	Monkey
14. 4	13. 3	G5	E11	Gibbon
15. 4	14. 3	G5	F12	Tapir
16. 4	15. 3	G5	G1	Sheep
17. 4	16. 3	G5	H2	Deer
18. 4	17. 3	G5	J3	Horse
19. 4	18. 3	G5	K4	Stag
20. 4	19. 3	G5	A5	Serpent
21. 4	20. 3	G5	B6	Earthworm
22. 4	21. 3	G5	C7	Crocodile
23. 4	22. 3	G5	D8	Dragon
24. 4	23. 3	G5	E9	Badger
25. 4	24. 3	G5	F10	Hare
26. 4	25. 3	G5	G11	Fox
27. 4	26. 3	G5	H12	Tiger
28. 4	27. 3	G5	J1	Leopard
29. 4	28. 3	G5	K2	Griffon
30. 4	29. 3	G5	A3	Ox
1. 5	1. 4	H6	B4	Bat
2. 5	2. 4	H6	C5	Rat
3. 5	3. 4	H6	D6	Swallow
4. 5	4. 4	H6	E7	Pig
5. 5	5. 4	H6	F8	Porcupine
6. 5	6. 4	H6	G9	Wolf
7. 5	7. 4	H6	H10	Dog
8. 5	8. 4	H6	J11	Pheasant
9. 5	9. 4	H6	K12	Cock
10. 5	10. 4	H6	A1	Crow
11. 5	11. 4	H6	B2	Monkey
12. 5	12. 4	H6	C3	Gibbon
13. 5	13. 4	H6	D4	Tapir
14. 5	14. 4	H6	E5	Sheep
15. 5	15. 4	H6	F6	Deer
16. 5	16. 4	H6	G7	Horse
17. 5	17. 4	H6	H8	Stag
18. 5	18. 4	H6	J9	Serpent
19. 5	19. 4	H6	K10	Earthworm
20. 5	20. 4	H6	A11	Crocodile

Solar date	*Lunar date*	*Month HS/EB*	*Day HS/EB*	*Constellation*
21. 5	21. 4	H6	B12	Dragon
22. 5	22. 4	H6	C1	Badger
23. 5	23. 4	H6	D2	Hare
24. 5	24. 4	H6	E3	Fox
25. 5	25. 4	H6	F4	Tiger
26. 5	26. 4	H6	G5	Leopard
27. 5	27. 4	H6	H6	Griffon
28. 5	28. 4	H6	J7	Ox
29. 5	29. 4	H6	K8	Bat
30. 5	30. 4	H6	A9	Rat
31. 5	1. 5	J7	B10	Swallow
1. 6	2. 5	J7	C11	Pig
2. 6	3. 5	J7	D12	Porcupine
3. 6	4. 5	J7	E1	Wolf
4. 6	5. 5	J7	F2	Dog
5. 6	6. 5	J7	G3	Pheasant
6. 6	7. 5	J7	H4	Cock
7. 6	8. 5	J7	J5	Crow
8. 6	9. 5	J7	K6	Monkey
9. 6	10. 5	J7	A7	Gibbon
10. 6	11. 5	J7	B8	Tapir
11. 6	12. 5	J7	C9	Sheep
12. 6	13. 5	J7	D10	Deer
13. 6	14. 5	J7	E11	Horse
14. 6	15. 5	J7	F12	Stag
15. 6	16. 5	J7	G1	Serpent
16. 6	17. 5	J7	H2	Earthworm
17. 6	18. 5	J7	J3	Crocodile
18. 6	19. 5	J7	K4	Dragon
19. 6	20. 5	J7	A5	Badger
20. 6	21. 5	J7	B6	Hare
21. 6	22. 5	J7	C7	Fox
22. 6	23. 5	J7	D8	Tiger
23. 6	24. 5	J7	E9	Leopard
24. 6	25. 5	J7	F10	Griffon
25. 6	26. 5	J7	G11	Ox
26. 6	27. 5	J7	H12	Bat
27. 6	28. 5	J7	J1	Rat
28. 6	29. 5	J7	K2	Swallow
29. 6	1. 6	K8	A3	Pig
30. 6	2. 6	K8	B4	Porcupine
1. 7	3. 6	K8	C5	Wolf
2. 7	4. 6	K8	D6	Dog
3. 7	5. 6	K8	E7	Pheasant
4. 7	6. 6	K8	F8	Cock
5. 7	7. 6	K8	G9	Crow
6. 7	8. 6	K8	H10	Monkey
7. 7	9. 6	K8	J11	Gibbon
8. 7	10. 6	K8	K12	Tapir
9. 7	11. 6	K8	A1	Sheep
10. 7	12. 6	K8	B2	Deer
11. 7	13. 6	K8	C3	Horse
12. 7	14 6	K8	D4	Stag
13. 7	15. 6	K8	E5	Serpent
14. 7	16. 6	K8	F6	Earthworm
15. 7	17. 6	K8	G7	Crocodile
16. 7	18. 6	K8	H8	Dragon
17. 7	19. 6	K8	J9	Badger
18. 7	20. 6	K8	K10	Hare
19. 7	21. 6	K8	A11	Fox
20. 7	22. 6	K8	B12	Tiger
21. 7	23. 6	K8	C1	Leopard
22. 7	24. 6	K8	D2	Griffon
23. 7	25. 6	K8	E3	Ox
24. 7	26. 6	K8	F4	Bat
25. 7	27. 6	K8	G5	Rat
26. 7	28. 6	K8	H6	Swallow
27. 7	29. 6	K8	J7	Pig
28. 7	1. 7	A9	K8	Porcupine
29. 7	2. 7	A9	A9	Wolf
30. 7	3. 7	A9	B10	Dog
31. 7	4. 7	A9	C11	Pheasant
1. 8	5. 7	A9	D12	Cock
2. 8	6. 7	A9	E1	Crow
3. 8	7. 7	A9	F2	Monkey
4. 8	8. 7	A9	G3	Gibbon
5. 8	9. 7	A9	H4	Tapir
6. 8	10. 7	A9	J5	Sheep
7. 8	11. 7	A9	K6	Deer
8. 8	12. 7	A9	A7	Horse
9. 8	13. 7	A9	B8	Stag
10. 8	14. 7	A9	C9	Serpent
11. 8	15. 7	A9	D10	Earthworm
12. 8	16. 7	A9	E11	Crocodile
13. 8	17. 7	A9	F12	Dragon
14. 8	18. 7	A9	G1	Badger
15. 8	19. 7	A9	H2	Hare
16. 8	20. 7	A9	J3	Fox
17. 8	21. 7	A9	K4	Tiger
18. 8	22. 7	A9	A5	Leopard
19. 8	23. 7	A9	B6	Griffon
20. 8	24. 7	A9	C7	Ox
21. 8	25. 7	A9	D8	Bat
22. 8	26. 7	A9	E9	Rat
23. 8	27. 7	A9	F10	Swallow
24. 8	28. 7	A9	G11	Pig
25. 8	29. 7	A9	H12	Porcupine
26. 8	30. 7	A9	J1	Wolf
27. 8	1. 8	B10	K2	Dog
28. 8	2. 8	B10	A3	Pheasant
29. 8	3. 8	B10	B4	Cock
30. 8	4. 8	B10	C5	Crow
31. 8	5. 8	B10	D6	Monkey
1. 9	6. 8	B10	E7	Gibbon
2. 9	7. 8	B10	F8	Tapir
3. 9	8. 8	B10	G9	Sheep
4. 9	9. 8	B10	H10	Deer
5. 9	10. 8	B10	J11	Horse
6. 9	11. 8	B10	K12	Stag
7. 9	12. 8	B10	A1	Serpent
8. 9	13. 8	B10	B2	Earthworm
9. 9	14. 8	B10	C3	Crocodile
10. 9	15. 8	B10	D4	Dragon
11. 9	16. 8	B10	E5	Badger
12. 9	17. 8	B10	F6	Hare
13. 9	18. 8	B10	G7	Fox
14. 9	19. 8	B10	H8	Tiger
15. 9	20. 8	B10	J9	Leopard
16. 9	21. 8	B10	K10	Griffon
17. 9	22. 8	B10	A11	Ox
18. 9	23. 8	B10	B12	Bat
19. 9	24. 8	B10	C1	Rat
20. 9	25. 8	B10	D2	Swallow
21. 9	26. 8	B10	E3	Pig
22. 9	27. 8	B10	F4	Porcupine
23. 9	28. 8	B10	G5	Wolf
24. 9	29. 8	B10	H6	Dog
25. 9	1 . 9	C11	J7	Pheasant
26. 9	2. 9	C11	K8	Cock
27. 9	3. 9	C11	A9	Crow
28. 9	4. 9	C11	B10	Monkey
29. 9	5. 9	C11	C11	Gibbon
30. 9	6. 9	C11	D12	Tapir
1 10	7. 9	C11	E1	Sheep
2.10	8. 9	C11	F2	Deer
3.10	9. 9	C11	G3	Horse
4.10	10. 9	C11	H4	Stag
5.10	11. 9	C11	J5	Serpent
6.10	12. 9	C11	K6	Earthworm
7.10	13. 9	C11	A7	Crocodile
8.10	14. 9	C11	B8	Dragon
9.10	15. 9	C11	C9	Badger
10.10	16. 9	C11	D10	Hare
11.10	17. 9	C11	E11	Fox
12.10	18. 9	C11	F12	Tiger
13.10	19. 9	C11	G1	Leopard

Solar date	*Lunar date*	*Month HS/EB*	*Day HS/EB*	*Constellation*
14.10	20. 9	C11	H2	Griffon
15.10	21. 9	C11	J3	Ox
16. 0	22. 9	C11	K4	Bat
17. 0	23. 9	C11	A5	Rat
18.10	24. 9	C11	B6	Swallow
19.10	25. 9	C11	C7	Pig
20.10	26. 9	C11	D8	Porcupine
21.10	27. 9	C11	E9	Wolf
22.10	28. 9	C11	F10	Dog
23.10	29. 9	C11	G11	Pheasant
24.10	1.10	D12	H12	Cock
25.10	2.10	D12	J1	Crow
26.10	3.10	D12	K2	Monkey
27.10	4.10	D12	A3	Gibbon
28.10	5.10	D12	B4	Tapir
29.10	6.10	D12	C5	Sheep
30.10	7.10	D12	D6	Deer
31.10	8.10	D12	E7	Horse
1.11	9.10	D12	F8	Stag
2.11	10.10	D12	G9	Serpent
3.11	11.10	D12	H10	Earthworm
4.11	12.10	D12	J11	Crocodile
5.11	13.10	D12	K12	Dragon
6.11	14.10	D12	A1	Badger
7.11	15.10	D12	B2	Hare
8.11	16.10	D12	C3	Fox
9.11	17.10	D12	D4	Tiger
10.11	18.10	D12	E5	Leopard
11.11	19.10	D12	F6	Griffon
12.11	20.10	D12	G7	Ox
13.11	21.10	D12	H8	Bat
14.11	22.10	D12	J9	Rat
15.11	23.10	D12	K10	Swallow
16.11	24.10	D12	A11	Pig
17.11	25.10	D12	B12	Porcupine
18.11	26.10	D12	C1	Wolf
19.11	27.10	D12	D2	Dog
20.11	28.10	D12	E3	Pheasant
21.11	29.10	D12	F4	Cock
22.11	30.10	D12	G5	Crow
23.11	1.11	E1	H6	Monkey
24.11	2.11	E1	J7	Gibbon
25.11	3.11	E1	K8	Tapir
26.11	4.11	E1	A9	Sheep
27.11	5.11	E1	B10	Deer
28.11	6.11	E1	C11	Horse
29.11	7.11	E1	D12	Stag
30.11	8.11	E1	E1	Serpent
1.12	9.11	E1	F2	Earthworm
2.12	10.11	E1	G3	Crocodile
3.12	11.11	E1	H4	Dragon

Solar date	*Lunar date*	*Month HS/EB*	*Day HS/EB*	*Constellation*
4.12	12.11	E1	J5	Badger
5.12	13.11	E1	K6	Hare
6.12	14.11	E1	A7	Fox
7.12	15.11	E1	B8	Tiger
8.12	16.11	E1	C9	Leopard
9.12	17.11	E1	D10	Griffon
10.12	18.11	E1	E11	Ox
11.12	19.11	E1	F12	Bat
12.12	20.11	E1	G1	Rat
13.12	21.11	E1	H2	Swallow
14.12	22.11	E1	J3	Pig
15.11	23.11	E1	K4	Porcupine
16.12	24.11	E1	A5	Wolf
17.12	25.11	E1	B6	Dog
18.11	26.11	E1	C7	Pheasant
19.12	27.11	E1	D8	Cock
20.12	28.11	E1	E9	Crow
21.12	29.11	E1	F10	Monkey
22.12	30.11	E1	G11	Gibbon
23.11	1.12	F2	H12	Tapir
24.12	2.12	F2	J1	Sheep
25.12	3.12	F2	K2	Deer
26.12	4.12	F2	A3	Horse
27.12	5.12	F2	B4	Stag
28.12	6.12	F2	C5	Serpent
29.12	7.12	F2	D6	Earthworm
30.12	8.12	F2	E7	Crocodile
31.12	9.12	F2	F8	Dragon
1966				
1. 1	10.12	F2	G9	Badger
2. 1	11.12	F2	H10	Hare
3. 1	12.12	F2	J11	Fox
4. 1	13.12	F2	K12	Tiger
5. 1	14.12	F2	A1	Leopard
6. 1	15.12	F2	B2	Griffon
7. 1	16.12	F2	C3	Ox
8. 1	17.12	F2	D4	Bat
9. 1	18.12	F2	E5	Rat
10. 1	19.12	F2	F6	Swallow
11. 1	20.12	F2	G7	Pig
12. 1	21.12	F2	H8	Porcupine
13. 1	22.12	F2	J9	Wolf
14. 1	23.12	F2	K10	Dog
15. 1	24.12	F2	A11	Pheasant
16. 1	25.12	F2	B12	Cock
17. 1	26.12	F2	C1	Crow
18. 1	27.12	F2	D2	Monkey
19. 1	28.12	F2	E3	Gibbon
20. 1	29.12	F2	F4	Tapir

PING WU YEAR

21. 1	1. 1	G3	G5	Sheep
22. 1	2. 1	G3	H6	Deer
23. 1	3. 1	G3	J7	Horse
24. 1	4. 1	G3	K8	Stag
25. 1	5. 1	G3	A9	Serpent
26. 1	6. 1	G3	B10	Earthworm
27. 1	7. 1	G3	C11	Crocodile
28. 1	8. 1	G3	D12	Dragon
29. 1	9. 1	G3	E1	Badger
30. 1	10. 1	G3	F2	Hare
31. 1	11. 1	G3	G3	Fox
1. 2	12. 1	G3	H4	Tiger
2. 2	13. 1	G3	J5	Leopard
3. 2	14. 1	G3	K6	Griffon
4. 2	15. 1	G3	A7	Ox
5. 2	16. 1	G3	B8	Bat
6. 2	17. 1	G3	C9	Rat
7. 2	18. 1	G3	D10	Swallow
8. 2	19. 1	G3	E11	Pig
9. 2	20. 1	G3	F12	Porcupine
10. 2	21. 1	G3	G1	Wolf
11. 2	22. 1	G3	H2	Dog
12. 2	23. 1	G3	J3	Pheasant
13. 2	24. 1	G3	K4	Cock
14. 2	25. 1	G3	A5	Crow
15. 2	26. 1	G3	B6	Monkey
16. 2	27. 1	G3	C7	Gibbon
17. 2	28. 1	G3	D8	Tapir
18. 2	29. 1	G3	E9	Sheep
19. 2	30. 1	G3	F10	Deer
20. 2	1. 2	H4	G11	Horse
21. 2	2. 2	H4	H12	Stag
22. 2	3. 2	H4	J1	Serpent
23. 2	4. 2	H4	K2	Earthworm

Solar date	*Lunar date*	*Month HS/EB*	*Day HS/EB*	*Constellation*
24. 2	5. 2	H4	A3	Crocodile
25. 2	6. 2	H4	B4	Dragon
26. 2	7. 2	H4	C5	Badger
27. 2	8. 2	H4	D6	Hare
28. 2	9. 2	H4	E7	Fox
1. 3	10. 2	H4	F8	Tiger
2. 3	11. 2	H4	G9	Leopard
3. 3	12. 2	H4	H10	Griffon
4. 3	13. 2	H4	J11	Ox
5. 3	14. 2	H4	K12	Bat
6. 3	15. 2	H4	A1	Rat
7. 3	16. 2	H4	B2	Swallow
8. 3	17. 2	H4	C3	Pig
9. 3	18. 2	H4	D4	Porcupine
10. 3	19. 2	H4	E5	Wolf
11. 3	20. 2	H4	F6	Dog
12. 3	21. 2	H4	G7	Pheasant
13. 3	22. 2	H4	H8	Cock
14. 3	23. 2	H4	J9	Crow
15. 3	24. 2	H4	K10	Monkey
16. 3	25. 2	H4	A11	Gibbon
17. 3	26. 2	H4	B12	Tapir
18. 3	27. 2	H4	C1	Sheep
19. 3	28. 2	H4	D2	Deer
20. 3	29. 2	H4	E3	Horse
21. 3	30. 2	H4	F4	Stag
22. 3	1. 3	J5	G5	Serpent
23. 3	2. 3	J5	H6	Earthworm
24. 3	3. 3	J5	J7	Crocodile
25. 3	4. 3	J5	K8	Dragon
26. 3	5. 3	J5	A9	Badger
27. 3	6. 3	J5	B10	Hare
28. 3	7. 3	J5	C11	Fox
29. 3	8. 3	J5	D12	Tiger
30. 3	9. 3	J5	E1	Leopard
31. 3	10. 3	J5	F2	Griffon
1. 4	11. 3	J5	G3	Ox
2. 4	12. 3	J5	H4	Bat
3. 4	13. 3	J5	J5	Rat
4. 4	14. 3	J5	K6	Swallow
5. 4	15. 3	J5	A7	Pig
6. 4	16. 3	J5	B8	Porcupine
7. 4	17. 3	J5	C9	Wolf
8. 4	18. 3	J5	D10	Dog
9. 4	19. 3	J5	E11	Pheasant
10. 4	20. 3	J5	F12	Cock
11. 4	21. 3	J5	G1	Crow
12. 4	22. 3	J5	H2	Monkey
13. 4	23. 3	J5	J3	Gibbon
14. 4	24. 3	J5	K4	Tapir
15. 4	25. 3	J5	A5	Sheep
16. 4	26. 3	J5	B6	Deer
17. 4	27. 3	J5	C7	Horse
18. 4	28. 3	J5	D8	Stag
19. 4	29. 3	J5	E9	Serpent
20. 4	30. 3	J5	F10	Earthworm
21. 4	*1. 3*	*J5*	G11	Crocodile
22. 4	*2. 3*	*J5*	H12	Dragon
23. 4	*3. 3*	*J5*	J1	Badger
24. 4	*4. 3*	*J5*	K2	Hare
25. 4	*5. 3*	*J5*	A3	Fox
26. 4	*6. 3*	*J5*	B4	Tiger
27. 4	*7. 3*	*J5*	C5	Leopard
28. 4	*8. 3*	*J5*	D6	Griffon
29. 4	*9. 3*	*J5*	E7	Ox
30. 4	*10. 3*	*J5*	F8	Bat
1. 5	*11. 3*	*J5*	G9	Rat
2. 5	*12. 3*	*J5*	H10	Swallow
3. 5	*13. 3*	*J5*	J11	Pig
4. 5	*14. 3*	*J5*	K12	Porcupine
5. 5	*15. 3*	*J5*	A1	Wolf
6. 5	*16. 3*	*J5*	B2	Dog
7. 5	*17. 3*	*J5*	C3	Pheasant

Solar date	*Lunar date*	*Month HS/EB*	*Day HS/EB*	*Constellation*
8. 5	*18. 3*	*J5*	D4	Cock
9. 5	*19. 3*	*J5*	E5	Crow
10. 5	*20. 3*	*J5*	F6	Monkey
11. 5	*21. 3*	*J5*	G7	Gibbon
12. 5	*22. 3*	*J5*	H8	Tapir
13. 5	*23. 3*	*J5*	J9	Sheep
14. 5	*24. 3*	*J5*	K10	Deer
15. 5	*25. 3*	*J5*	A11	Horse
16. 5	*26. 3*	*J5*	B12	Stag
17. 5	*27. 3*	*J5*	C1	Serpent
18. 5	*28. 3*	*J5*	D2	Earthworm
19. 5	*29. 3*	*J5*	E3	Crocodile
20. 5	1. 4	K6	F4	Dragon
21. 5	2. 4	K6	G5	Badger
22. 5	3. 4	K6	H6	Hare
23. 5	4. 4	K6	J7	Fox
24. 5	5. 4	K6	K8	Tiger
25. 5	6. 4	K6	A9	Leopard
26. 5	7. 4	K6	B10	Griffon
27. 5	8. 4	K6	C11	Ox
28. 5	9. 4	K6	D12	Bat
29. 5	10. 4	K6	E1	Rat
30. 5	11. 4	K6	F2	Swallow
31. 5	12. 4	K6	G3	Pig
1. 6	13. 4	K6	H4	Porcupine
2. 6	14. 4	K6	J5	Wolf
3. 6	15. 4	K6	K6	Dog
4. 6	16. 4	K6	A7	Pheasant
5. 6	17. 4	K6	B8	Cock
6. 6	18. 4	K6	C9	Crow
7. 6	19. 4	K6	D10	Monkey
8. 6	20. 4	K6	E11	Gibbon
9. 6	21. 4	K6	F12	Tapir
10. 6	22. 4	K6	G1	Sheep
11. 6	23. 4	K6	H2	Deer
12. 6	24. 4	K6	J3	Horse
13. 6	25. 4	K6	K4	Stag
14. 6	26. 4	K6	A5	Serpent
15. 6	27. 4	K6	B6	Earthworm
16. 6	28. 4	K6	C7	Crocodile
17. 6	29. 4	K6	D8	Dragon
18. 6	30. 4	K6	E9	Badger
19. 6	1. 5	A7	F10	Hare
20. 6	2. 5	A7	G11	Fox
21. 6	3. 5	A7	H12	Tiger
22. 6	4. 5	A7	J1	Leopard
23. 6	5. 5	A7	K2	Griffon
24. 6	6. 5	A7	A3	Ox
25. 6	7. 5	A7	B4	Bat
26. 6	8. 5	A7	C5	Rat
27. 6	9. 5	A7	D6	Swallow
28. 6	10. 5	A7	E7	Pig
29. 6	11. 5	A7	F8	Porcupine
30. 6	12. 5	A7	G9	Wolf
1. 7	13. 5	A7	H10	Dog
2. 7	14. 5	A7	J11	Pheasant
3. 7	15. 5	A7	K12	Cock
4. 7	16. 5	A7	A1	Crow
5. 7	17. 5	A7	B2	Monkey
6. 7	18. 5	A7	C3	Gibbon
7. 7	19. 5	A7	D4	Tapir
8. 7	20. 5	A7	E5	Sheep
9. 7	21. 5	A7	F6	Deer
10. 7	22. 5	A7	G7	Horse
11. 7	23. 5	A7	H8	Stag
12. 7	24. 5	A7	J9	Serpent
13. 7	25. 5	A7	K10	Earthworm
14. 7	26. 5	A7	A11	Crocodile
15. 7	27. 5	A7	B12	Dragon
16. 7	28. 5	A7	C1	Badger
17. 7	29. 5	A7	D2	Hare
18. 7	1. 6	B8	E3	Fox
19. 7	2. 6	B8	F4	Tiger

Solar date	*Lunar date*	*Month HS/EB*	*Day HS/EB*	*Constellation*
20. 7	3. 6	B8	G5	Leopard
21. 7	4. 6	B8	H6	Griffon
22. 7	5. 6	B8	J7	Ox
23. 7	6. 6	B8	K8	Bat
24. 7	7. 6	B8	A9	Rat
25. 7	8. 6	B8	B10	Swallow
26. 7	9. 6	B8	C11	Pig
27. 7	10. 6	B8	D12	Porcupine
28. 7	11. 6	B8	E1	Wolf
29. 7	12. 6	B8	F2	Dog
30. 7	13. 6	B8	G3	Pheasant
31. 7	14. 6	B8	H4	Cock
1. 8	15. 6	B8	J5	Crow
2. 8	16. 6	B8	K6	Monkey
3. 8	17. 6	B8	A7	Gibbon
4. 8	18. 6	B8	B8	Tapir
5. 8	19. 6	B8	C9	Sheep
6. 8	20. 6	B8	D10	Deer
7. 8	21. 6	B8	E11	Horse
8. 8	22. 6	B8	F12	Stag
9. 8	23. 6	B8	G1	Serpent
10. 8	24. 6	B8	H2	Earthworm
11. 8	25. 6	B8	J3	Crocodile
12. 8	26. 6	B8	K4	Dragon
13. 8	27. 6	B8	A5	Badger
14. 8	28. 6	B8	B6	Hare
15. 8	29. 6	B8	C7	Fox
16. 8	1. 7	C9	D8	Tiger
17. 8	2. 7	C9	E9	Leopard
18. 8	3. 7	C9	F10	Griffon
19. 8	4. 7	C9	G11	Ox
20. 8	5. 7	C9	H12	Bat
21. 8	6. 7	C9	J1	Rat
22. 8	7. 7	C9	K2	Swallow
23. 8	8. 7	C9	A3	Pig
24. 8	9. 7	C9	B4	Porcupine
25. 8	10. 7	C9	C5	Wolf
26. 8	11. 7	C9	D6	Dog
27. 8	12. 7	C9	E7	Pheasant
28. 8	13. 7	C9	F8	Cock
29. 8	14. 7	C9	G9	Crow
30. 8	15. 7	C9	H10	Monkey
31. 8	16. 7	C9	J11	Gibbon
1. 9	17. 7	C9	K12	Tapir
2. 9	18. 7	C9	A1	Sheep
3. 9	19. 7	C9	B2	Deer
4. 9	20. 7	C9	C3	Horse
5. 9	21. 7	C9	D4	Stag
6. 9	22. 7	C9	E5	Serpent
7. 9	23. 7	C9	F6	Earthworm
8. 9	24. 7	C9	G7	Crocodile
9. 9	25. 7	C9	H8	Dragon
10. 9	26. 7	C9	J9	Badger
11. 9	27. 7	C9	K10	Hare
12. 9	28. 7	C9	A11	Fox
13. 9	29. 7	C9	B12	Tiger
14. 9	30. 7	C9	C1	Leopard
15. 9	1. 8	D10	D2	Griffon
16. 9	2. 8	D10	E3	Ox
17. 9	3. 8	D10	F4	Bat
18. 9	4. 8	D10	G5	Rat
19. 9	5. 8	D10	H6	Swallow
20. 9	6. 8	D10	J7	Pig
21. 9	7. 8	D10	K8	Porcupine
22. 9	8. 8	D10	A9	Wolf
23. 9	9. 8	D10	B10	Dog
24. 9	10. 8	D10	C11	Pheasant
25. 9	11. 8	D10	D12	Cock
26. 9	12. 8	D10	E1	Crow
27. 9	13. 8	D10	F2	Monkey
28. 9	14. 8	D10	G3	Gibbon
29. 9	15. 8	D10	H4	Tapir
30. 9	16. 8	D10	J5	Sheep

Solar date	*Lunar date*	*Month HS/EB*	*Day HS/EB*	*Constellation*
1.10	17. 8	D10	K6	Deer
2.10	18. 8	D10	A7	Horse
3.10	19. 8	D10	B8	Stag
4.10	20. 8	D10	C9	Serpent
5.10	21. 8	D10	D10	Earthworm
6.10	22. 8	D10	E11	Crocodile
7.10	23. 8	D10	F12	Dragon
8.10	24. 8	D10	G1	Badger
9.10	25. 8	D10	H2	Hare
10.10	26. 8	D10	J3	Fox
11.10	27. 8	D10	K4	Tiger
12.10	28. 8	D10	A5	Leopard
13.10	29. 8	D10	B6	Griffon
14.10	1. 9	E11	C7	Ox
15.10	2. 9	E11	D8	Bat
16.10	3. 9	E11	E9	Rat
17.10	4. 9	E11	F10	Swallow
18.10	5. 9	E11	G11	Pig
19.10	6. 9	E11	H12	Porcupine
20.10	7. 9	E11	J1	Wolf
21.10	8. 9	E11	K2	Dog
22.10	9. 9	E11	A3	Pheasant
23.10	10. 9	E11	B4	Cock
24.10	11. 9	E11	C5	Crow
25.10	12. 9	E11	D6	Monkey
26.10	13. 9	E11	E7	Gibbon
27.10	14. 9	E11	F8	Tapir
28.10	15. 9	E11	G9	Sheep
29.10	16. 9	E11	H10	Deer
30.10	17. 9	E11	J11	Horse
31.10	18. 9	E11	K12	Stag
1.11	19. 9	E11	A1	Serpent
2.11	20. 9	E11	B2	Earthworm
3.11	21. 9	E11	C3	Crocodile
4.11	22. 9	E11	D4	Dragon
5.11	23. 9	E11	E5	Badger
6.11	24. 9	E11	F6	Hare
7.11	25. 9	E11	G7	Fox
8.11	26. 9	E11	H8	Tiger
9.11	27. 9	E11	J9	Leopard
10.11	28. 9	E11	K10	Griffon
11.11	29. 9	E11	A11	Ox
12.11	1.10	F12	B12	Bat
13.11	2.10	F12	C1	Rat
14.11	3.10	F12	D2	Swallow
15.11	4.10	F12	E3	Pig
16.11	5.10	F12	F4	Porcupine
17.11	6.10	F12	G5	Wolf
18.11	7.10	F12	H6	Dog
19.11	8.10	F12	J7	Pheasant
20.11	9.10	F12	K8	Cock
21.11	10.10	F12	A9	Crow
22.11	11.10	F12	B10	Monkey
23.11	12.10	F12	C11	Gibbon
24.11	13.10	F12	D12	Tapir
25.11	14.10	F12	E1	Sheep
26.11	15.10	F12	F2	Deer
27.11	16.10	F12	G3	Horse
28.11	17.10	F12	H4	Stag
29.11	18.10	F12	J5	Serpent
30.11	19.10	F12	K6	Earthworm
1.12	20.10	F12	A7	Crocodile
2.12	21.10	F12	B8	Dragon
3.12	22.10	F12	C9	Badger
4.12	23.10	F12	D10	Hare
5.12	24.10	F12	E11	Fox
6.12	25.10	F12	F12	Tiger
7.12	26.10	F12	G1	Leopard
8.12	27.10	F12	H2	Griffon
9.12	28.10	F12	J3	Ox
10.12	29.10	F12	K4	Bat
11.12	30.10	F12	A5	Rat
12.12	1.11	G1	B6	Swallow

Solar date	Lunar date	Month HS/EB	Day HS/EB	Constellation
13.12	2.11	G1	C7	Pig
14.12	3.11	G1	D8	Porcupine
15.12	4.11	G1	E9	Wolf
16.12	5.11	G1	F10	Dog
17.12	6.11	G1	G11	Pheasant
18.12	7.11	G1	H12	Cock
19.12	8.11	G1	J1	Crow
20.12	9.11	G1	K2	Monkey
21.12	10.11	G1	A3	Gibbon
22.12	11.11	G1	B4	Tapir
23.12	12.11	G1	C5	Sheep
24.12	13.11	G1	D6	Deer
25.12	14.11	G1	E7	Horse
26.12	15.11	G1	F8	Stag
27.12	16.11	G1	G9	Serpent
28.12	17.11	G1	H10	Earthworm
29.12	18.11	G1	J11	Crocodile
30.12	19.11	G1	K12	Dragon
31.12	20.11	G1	A1	Badger
1967				
1. 1	21.11	G1	B2	Hare
2. 1	22.11	G1	C3	Fox
3. 1	23.11	G1	D4	Tiger
4. 1	24.11	G1	E5	Leopard
5. 1	25.11	G1	F6	Griffon
6. 1	26.11	G1	G7	Ox
7. 1	27.11	G1	H8	Bat
8. 1	28.11	G1	J9	Rat
9. 1	29.11	G1	K10	Swallow
10. 1	30.11	G1	A11	Pig
11. 1	1.12	H2	B12	Porcupine
12. 1	2.12	H2	C1	Wolf
13. 1	3.12	H2	D2	Dog
14. 1	4.12	H2	E3	Pheasant
15. 1	5.12	H2	F4	Cock
16. 1	6.12	H2	G5	Crow
17. 1	7.12	H2	H6	Monkey
18. 1	8.12	H2	J7	Gibbon
19. 1	9.12	H2	K8	Tapir
20. 1	10.12	H2	A9	Sheep
21. 1	11.12	H2	B10	Deer
22. 1	12.12	H2	C11	Horse
23. 1	13.12	H2	D12	Stag
24. 1	14.12	H2	E1	Serpent
25. 1	15.12	H2	F2	Earthworm
26. 1	16.12	H2	G3	Crocodile
27. 1	17.12	H2	H4	Dragon
28. 1	18.12	H2	J5	Badger
29. 1	19.12	H2	K6	Hare
30. 1	20.12	H2	A7	Fox
31. 1	21.12	H2	B8	Tiger
1. 2	22.12	H2	C9	Leopard
2. 2	23.12	H2	D10	Griffon
3. 2	24.12	H2	E11	Ox
4. 2	25.12	H2	F12	Bat
5. 2	26.12	H2	G1	Rat
6. 2	27.12	H2	H2	Swallow
7. 2	28.12	H2	J3	Pig
8. 2	29.12	H2	K4	Porcupine

TING WEI YEAR

9. 2	1. 1	J3	A5	Wolf
10. 2	2. 1	J3	B6	Dog
11. 2	3. 1	J3	C7	Pheasant
12. 2	4. 1	J3	D8	Cock
13. 2	5. 1	J3	E9	Crow
14. 2	6. 1	J3	F10	Monkey
15. 2	7. 1	J3	G11	Gibbon
16. 2	8. 1	J3	H12	Tapir
17. 2	9. 1	J3	J1	Sheep
18. 2	10. 1	J3	K2	Deer
19. 2	11. 1	J3	A3	Horse
20. 2	12. 1	J3	B4	Stag
21. 2	13. 1	J3	C5	Serpent
22. 2	14. 1	J3	D6	Earthworm
23. 2	15. 1	J3	E7	Crocodile
24. 2	16. 1	J3	F8	Dragon
25. 2	17. 1	J3	G9	Badger
26. 2	18. 1	J3	H10	Hare
27. 2	19. 1	J3	J11	Fox
28. 2	20. 1	J3	K12	Tiger
1. 3	21. 1	J3	A1	Leopard
2. 3	22. 1	J3	B2	Griffon
3. 3	23. 1	J3	C3	Ox
4. 3	24. 1	J3	D4	Bat
5. 3	25. 1	J3	E5	Rat
6. 3	26. 1	J3	F6	Swallow
7. 3	27. 1	J3	G7	Pig
8. 3	28. 1	J3	H8	Porcupine
9. 3	29. 1	J3	J9	Wolf
10. 3	30. 1	J3	K10	Dog
11. 3	1. 2	K4	A11	Pheasant
12. 3	2. 2	K4	B12	Cock
13. 3	3. 2	K4	C1	Crow
14. 3	4. 2	K4	D2	Monkey
15. 3	5. 2	K4	E3	Gibbon
16. 3	6. 2	K4	F4	Tapir
17. 3	7. 2	K4	G5	Sheep
18. 3	8. 2	K4	G6	Deer
19. 3	9. 2	K4	J7	Horse
20. 3	10. 2	K4	K8	Stag
21. 3	11. 2	K4	A9	Serpent
22. 3	12. 2	K4	B10	Earthworm
23. 3	13. 2	K4	C11	Crocodile
24. 3	14. 2	K4	D12	Dragon
25. 3	15. 2	K4	E1	Badger
26. 3	16. 2	K4	F2	Hare
27. 3	17. 2	K4	G3	Fox
28. 3	18. 2	K4	H4	Tiger
29. 3	19. 2	K4	J5	Leopard
30. 3	20. 2	K4	K6	Griffon
31. 3	21. 2	K4	A7	Ox
1. 4	22. 2	K4	B8	Bat
2. 4	23. 2	K4	C9	Rat
3. 4	24. 2	K4	D10	Swallow
4. 4	25. 2	K4	E11	Pig
5. 4	26. 2	K4	F12	Porcupine
6. 4	27. 2	K4	G1	Wolf
7. 4	28. 2	K4	H2	Dog
8. 4	29. 2	K4	J3	Pheasant
9. 4	30. 2	K4	K4	Cock
10. 4	1. 3	A5	A5	Crow
11. 4	2. 3	A5	B6	Monkey
12. 4	3. 3	A5	C7	Gibbon
13. 4	4. 3	A5	D8	Tapir
14. 4	5. 3	A5	E9	Sheep
15. 4	6. 3	A5	F10	Deer
16. 4	7. 3	A5	G11	Horse
17. 4	8. 3	A5	H12	Stag
18. 4	9. 3	A5	J1	Serpent
19. 4	10. 3	A5	K2	Earthworm
20. 4	11. 3	A5	A3	Crocodile
21. 4	12. 3	A5	B4	Dragon
22. 4	13. 3	A5	C5	Badger
23. 4	14. 3	A5	D6	Hare
24. 4	15. 3	A5	E7	Fox
25. 4	16. 3	A5	F8	Tiger

Solar date	*Lunar date*	*Month HS/EB*	*Day HS/EB*	*Constellation*
26. 4	17. 3	A5	G9	Leopard
27. 4	18. 3	A5	H10	Griffon
28. 4	19. 3	A5	J11	Ox
29. 4	20. 3	A5	K12	Bat
30. 4	21. 3	A5	A1	Rat
1. 5	22. 3	A5	B2	Swallow
2. 5	23. 3	A5	C3	Pig
3. 5	24. 3	A5	D4	Porcupine
4. 5	25. 3	A5	E5	Wolf
5. 5	26. 3	A5	F6	Dog
6. 5	27. 3	A5	G7	Pheasant
7. 5	28. 3	A5	H8	Cock
8. 5	29. 3	A5	J9	Crow
9. 5	1. 4	B6	K10	Monkey
10. 5	2. 4	B6	A11	Gibbon
11. 5	3. 4	B6	B12	Tapir
12. 5	4. 4	B6	C1	Sheep
13. 5	5. 4	B6	D2	Deer
14. 5	6. 4	B6	E3	Horse
15. 5	7. 4	B6	F4	Stag
16. 5	8. 4	B6	G5	Serpent
17. 5	9. 4	B6	H6	Earthworm
18. 5	10. 4	B6	J7	Crocodile
19. 5	11. 4	B6	K8	Dragon
20. 5	12. 4	B6	A9	Badger
21. 5	13. 4	B6	B10	Hare
22. 5	14. 4	B6	C11	Fox
23. 5	15. 4	B6	D12	Tiger
24. 5	16. 4	B6	F1	Leopard
25. 5	17. 4	B6	F2	Griffon
26. 5	18. 4	B6	G3	Ox
27. 5	19. 4	B6	H4	Bat
28. 5	20. 4	B6	J5	Rat
29. 5	21. 4	B6	K6	Swallow
30. 5	22. 4	B6	A7	Pig
31. 5	23. 4	B6	B8	Porcupine
1. 6	24. 4	B6	C9	Wolf
2. 6	25. 4	B6	D10	Dog
3. 6	26. 4	B6	E11	Pheasant
4. 6	27. 4	B6	F12	Cock
5. 6	28. 4	B6	G1	Crow
6. 6	29. 4	B6	H2	Monkey
7. 6	30. 4	B6	J3	Gibbon
8. 6	1. 5	C7	K4	Tapir
9. 6	2. 5	C7	A5	Sheep
10. 6	3. 5	C7	B6	Deer
11. 6	4. 5	C7	C7	Horse
12. 6	5. 5	C7	D8	Stag
13. 6	6. 5	C7	E9	Serpent
14. 6	7. 5	C7	F10	Earthworm
15. 6	8. 5	C7	G11	Crocodile
16. 6	9. 5	C7	H12	Dragon
17. 6	10. 5	C7	J1	Badger
18. 6	11. 5	C7	K2	Hare
19. 6	12. 5	C7	A3	Fox
20. 6	13. 5	C7	B4	Tiger
21. 6	14. 5	C7	C5	Leopard
22. 6	15. 5	C7	D6	Griffon
12. 6	16. 5	C7	E7	Ox
24. 6	17. 5	C7	F8	Bat
25. 6	18. 5	C7	G9	Rat
26. 6	19. 5	C7	H10	Swallow
27. 6	20. 5	C7	J11	Pig
28. 6	21. 5	C7	K12	Porcupine
29. 6	22. 5	C7	A1	Wolf
30. 6	23. 5	C7	B2	Dog
1. 7	24. 5	C7	C3	Pheasant
2. 7	25. 5	C7	D4	Cock
3. 7	26. 5	C7	E5	Crow
4. 7	27. 5	C7	F6	Monkey
5. 7	28. 5	C7	G7	Gibbon
6. 7	29. 5	C7	H8	Tapir
7. 7	30. 5	C7	J9	Sheep
8. 7	1. 6	D8	K10	Deer
9. 7	2. 6	D8	A11	Horse
10. 7	3. 6	D8	B12	Stag
11. 7	4. 6	D8	C1	Serpent
12. 7	5. 6	D8	D2	Earthworm
13. 7	6. 6	D8	E3	Crocodile
14. 7	7. 6	D8	F4	Dragon
15. 7	8. 6	D8	G5	Badger
16. 7	9. 6	D8	H6	Hare
17. 7	10. 6	D8	J7	Fox
18. 7	11. 6	D8	K8	Tiger
19. 7	12. 6	D8	A9	Leopard
20. 7	13. 6	D8	B10	Griffon
21. 7	14. 6	D8	C11	Ox
22. 7	15. 6	D8	D12	Bat
23. 7	16. 6	D8	E1	Rat
24. 7	17. 6	D8	F2	Swallow
25. 7	18. 6	D8	G3	Pig
26. 7	19. 6	D8	H4	Porcupine
27. 7	20. 6	D8	J5	Wolf
28. 7	21. 6	D8	K6	Dog
29. 7	22. 6	D8	A7	Pheasant
30. 7	23. 6	D8	B8	Cock
31. 7	24. 6	D8	C9	Crow
1. 8	25. 6	D8	D10	Monkey
2. 8	26. 6	D8	E11	Gibbon
3. 8	27. 6	D8	F12	Tapir
4. 8	28. 6	D8	G1	Sheep
5. 8	29. 6	D8	H2	Deer
6. 8	1. 7	E9	J3	Horse
7. 8	2. 7	E9	K4	Stag
8. 8	3. 7	E9	A5	Serpent
9. 8	4. 7	E9	B6	Earthworm
10. 8	5. 7	E9	C7	Crocodile
11. 8	6. 7	E9	D8	Dragon
12. 8	7. 7	E9	E9	Badger
13. 8	8. 7	E9	F10	Hare
14. 8	9. 7	E9	G11	Fox
15. 8	10. 7	E9	H12	Tiger
16. 8	11. 7	E9	J1	Leopard
17. 8	12. 7	E9	K2	Griffon
18. 8	13. 7	E9	A3	Ox
19. 8	14. 7	E9	B4	Bat
20. 8	15. 7	E9	C5	Rat
21. 8	16. 7	E9	D6	Swallow
22. 8	17. 7	E9	E7	Pig
23. 8	18. 7	E9	F8	Porcupine
24. 8	19. 7	E9	G9	Wolf
25. 8	20. 7	E9	H10	Dog
26. 8	21. 7	E9	J11	Pheasant
27. 8	22. 7	E9	K12	Cock
28. 8	23. 7	E9	A1	Crow
29. 8	24. 7	E9	B2	Monkey
30. 8	25. 7	E9	C3	Gibbon
31. 8	26. 7	E9	D4	Tapir
1. 9	27. 7	E9	E5	Sheep
2. 9	28. 7	E9	F6	Deer
3. 9	29. 7	E9	G7	Horse
4. 9	1. 8	F10	H8	Stag
5. 9	2. 8	F10	J9	Serpent
6. 9	3. 8	F10	K10	Earthworm
7. 9	4. 8	F10	A11	Crocodile
8. 9	5. 8	F10	B12	Dragon
9. 9	6. 8	F10	C1	Badger
10. 9	7. 8	F10	D2	Hare
11. 9	8. 8	F10	E3	Fox
12. 9	9. 8	F10	F4	Tiger
13. 9	10. 8	F10	G5	Leopard
14. 9	11. 8	F10	H6	Griffon
15. 9	12. 8	F10	J7	Ox
16. 9	13. 8	F10	K8	Bat
18. 9	15. 8	F10	B10	Swallow
19. 9	16. 8	F10	C11	Pig

Solar date	*Lunar date*	*Month HS/EB*	*Day HS/EB*	*Constellation*
20. 9	17. 8	F10	D12	Porcupine
21. 9	18. 8	F10	E1	Wolf
22. 9	19. 8	F10	F2	Dog
23. 9	20. 8	F10	G3	Pheasant
24. 9	21. 8	F10	H4	Cock
25. 9	22. 8	F10	J5	Crow
26. 9	23. 8	F10	K6	Monkey
27. 9	24. 8	F10	A7	Gibbon
28. 9	25. 8	F10	B8	Tapir
29. 9	26. 8	F10	C9	Sheep
30. 9	27. 8	F10	D10	Deer
1.10	28. 8	F10	E11	Horse
2.10	29. 8	F10	F12	Stag
3.10	30. 8	F10	G1	Serpent
4.10	1. 9	G11	H2	Earthworm
5.10	2. 9	G11	J3	Crocodile
6.10	3. 9	G11	K4	Dragon
7.10	4. 9	G11	A5	Badger
8.10	5. 9	G11	B6	Hare
9.10	6. 9	G11	C7	Fox
10.10	7. 9	G11	D8	Tiger
11.10	8. 9	G11	E9	Leopard
12.10	9. 9	G11	F10	Griffon
13.10	10. 9	G11	G11	Ox
14.10	11. 9	G11	H12	Bat
15.10	12. 9	G11	J1	Rat
16.10	13. 9	G11	K2	Swallow
17.10	14. 9	G11	A3	Pig
18.10	15. 9	G11	B4	Porcupine
19.10	16. 9	G11	C5	Wolf
20.10	17. 9	G11	D6	Dog
21.10	18. 9	G11	E7	Pheasant
22.10	19. 9	G11	F8	Cock
23.10	20. 9	G11	G9	Crow
24.10	21. 9	G11	H10	Monkey
25.10	22. 9	G11	J11	Gibbon
26.10	23. 9	G11	K12	Tapir
27.10	24. 9	G11	A1	Sheep
28.10	25. 9	G11	B2	Deer
29.10	26. 9	G11	C3	Horse
30.10	27. 9	G11	D4	Stag
31.10	28. 9	G11	E5	Serpent
1.11	29. 9	G11	F6	Earthworm
2.11	1.10	H12	G7	Crocodile
3.11	2.10	H12	H8	Dragon
4.11	3.10	H12	J9	Badger
5.11	4.10	H12	K10	Hare
6.11	5.10	H12	A11	Fox
7.11	6.10	H12	B12	Tiger
8.11	7.10	H12	C1	Leopard
9.11	8.10	H12	D2	Griffon
10.11	9.10	H12	E3	Ox
11.11	10.10	H12	F4	Bat
12.11	11.10	H12	G5	Rat
13.11	12.10	H12	H6	Swallow
14.11	13.10	H12	J7	Pig
15.11	14.10	H12	K8	Porcupine
16.11	15.10	H12	A9	Wolf
17.11	16.10	H12	B10	Dog
18.11	17.10	H12	C11	Pheasant
19.11	18.10	H12	D12	Cock
20.11	19.10	H12	E1	Crow
21.11	20.10	H12	F2	Monkey
22.11	21.10	H12	G3	Gibbon
23.11	22.10	H12	H4	Tapir
24.11	23.10	H12	J5	Sheep
25.11	24.10	H12	K6	Deer
26.11	25.10	H12	A7	Horse
27.11	26.10	H12	B8	Stag
28.11	27.10	H12	C9	Serpent
29.11	28.10	H12	D10	Earthworm
30.11	29.10	H12	E11	Crocodile
1.12	30.10	H12	F12	Dragon
2.12	1.11	J1	G1	Badger
3.12	2.11	J1	H2	Hare
4.12	3.11	J1	J3	Fox
5.12	4.11	J1	K4	Tiger
6.12	5.11	J1	A5	Leopard
7.12	6.11	J1	B6	Griffon
8.12	7.11	J1	C7	Ox
9.12	8.11	J1	D8	Bat
10.12	9.11	J1	E9	Rat
11.12	10.11	J1	F10	Swallow
12.12	11.11	J1	G11	Pig
13.12	12.11	J1	H12	Porcupine
14.12	13.11	J1	J1	Wolf
15.12	14.11	J1	K2	Dog
16.12	15.11	J1	A3	Pheasant
17.12	16.11	J1	B4	Cock
18.12	17.11	J1	C5	Crow
19.12	18.11	J1	D6	Monkey
20.12	19.11	J1	E7	Gibbon
21.12	20.11	J1	F8	Tapir
22.12	21.11	J1	G9	Sheep
23.12	22.11	J1	H10	Deer
24.12	23.11	J1	J11	Horse
25.12	24.11	J1	K12	Stag
26.12	25.11	J1	A1	Serpent
27.12	26.11	J1	B2	Earthworm
28.12	27.11	J1	C3	Crocodile
29.12	28.11	J1	D4	Dragon
30.12	29.11	J1	E5	Badger
31.12	1.12	K2	F6	Hare
1968				
1. 1	2.12	K2	G7	Fox
2. 1	3.12	K2	H8	Tiger
3. 1	4.12	K2	J9	Leopard
4. 1	5.12	K2	K10	Griffon
5. 1	6.12	K2	A11	Ox
6. 1	7.12	K2	B12	Bat
7. 1	8.12	K2	C1	Rat
8. 1	9.12	K2	D2	Swallow
9. 1	10.12	K2	E3	Pig
10. 1	11.12	K2	F4	Porcupine
11. 1	12.12	K2	G5	Wolf
12. 1	13.12	K2	H6	Dog
13. 1	14.12	K2	J7	Pheasant
14. 1	15.12	K2	K8	Cock
15. 1	16.12	K2	A9	Crow
16. 1	17.12	K2	B10	Monkey
17. 1	18.12	K2	C11	Gibbon
18. 1	19.12	K2	D12	Tapir
19. 1	20.12	K2	E1	Sheep
20. 1	21.12	K2	F2	Deer
21. 1	22.12	K2	G3	Horse
22. 1	23.12	K2	H4	Stag
23. 1	24.12	K2	J5	Serpent
24. 1	25.12	K2	K6	Earthworm
25. 1	26.12	K2	A7	Crocodile
26. 1	27.12	K2	B8	Dragon
27. 1	28.12	K2	C9	Badger
28. 1	29.12	K2	D10	Hare
29. 1	30.12	K2	E11	Fox

MOU SHEN YEAR

Solar date	*Lunar date*	*Month HS/EB*	*Day HS/EB*	*Constellation*
30. 1	1. 1	A3	F12	Tiger
31. 1	2. 1	A3	G1	Leopard
1. 2	3. 1	A3	H2	Griffon
2. 2	4. 1	A3	J3	Ox
3. 2	5. 1	A3	K4	Bat
4. 2	6. 1	A3	A5	Rat
5. 2	7. 1	A3	B6	Swallow
6. 2	8. 1	A3	C7	Pig
7. 2	9. 1	A3	D8	Porcupine
8. 2	10. 1	A3	E9	Wolf
9. 2	11. 1	A3	F10	Dog
10. 2	12. 1	A3	G11	Pheasant
11. 2	13. 1	A3	H12	Cock
12. 2	14. 1	A3	J1	Crow
13. 2	15. 1	A3	K2	Monkey
14. 2	16. 1	A3	A3	Gibbon
15. 2	17. 1	A3	B4	Tapir
16. 2	18. 1	A3	C5	Sheep
17. 2	19. 1	A3	D6	Deer
18. 2	20. 1	A3	E7	Horse
19. 2	21. 1	A3	F8	Stag
20. 2	22. 1	A3	G9	Serpent
21. 2	23. 1	A3	H10	Earthworm
22. 2	24. 1	A3	J11	Crocodile
23. 2	25. 1	A3	K12	Dragon
24. 2	26. 1	A3	A1	Badger
25. 2	27. 1	A3	B2	Hare
26. 2	28. 1	A3	C3	Fox
27. 2	29. 1	A3	D4	Tiger
28. 2	1. 2	B4	E5	Leopard
29. 2	2. 2	B4	F6	Griffon
1. 3	3. 2	B4	G7	Ox
2. 3	4. 2	B4	H8	Bat
3. 3	5. 2	B4	J9	Rat
4. 3	6. 2	B4	K10	Swallow
5. 3	7. 2	B4	A11	Pig
6. 3	8. 2	B4	B12	Porcupine
7. 3	9. 2	B4	C1	Wolf
8. 3	10. 2	B4	D2	Dog
9. 3	1 . 2	B4	E3	Pheasant
10. 3	12. 2	B4	F4	Cock
11. 3	13. 2	B4	G5	Crow
12. 3	14. 2	B4	H6	Monkey
13. 3	15. 2	B4	J7	Gibbon
14. 3	16. 2	B4	K8	Tapir
15. 3	17. 2	B4	A9	Sheep
16. 3	18. 2	B4	B10	Deer
17. 3	19. 2	B4	C11	Horse
18. 3	20. 2	B4	D12	Stag
19. 3	21. 2	B4	E1	Serpent
20. 3	22. 2	B4	F2	Earthworm
21. 3	23. 2	B4	G3	Crocodile
22. 3	24. 2	B4	H4	Dragon
23. 3	25. 2	B4	J5	Badger
24. 3	26. 2	B4	K6	Hare
25. 3	27. 2	B4	A7	Fox
26. 3	28. 2	B4	B8	Tiger
27. 3	29. 2	B4	C9	Leopard
28. 3	30. 2	B4	D10	Griffon
29. 3	1. 3	C5	E11	Ox
30. 3	2 3	C5	F12	Bat
31. 3	3. 3	C5	G1	Rat
1. 4	4. 3	C5	H2	Swallow
2. 4	5. 3	C5	J3	Pig
3. 4	6. 3	C5	K4	Porcupine
4. 4	7. 3	C5	A5	Wolf
5. 4	8. 3	C5	B6	Dog
6. 4	9. 3	C5	C7	Pheasant
7. 4	10. 3	C5	D8	Cock
8. 4	11. 3	C5	E9	Crow
9. 4	12. 3	C5	F10	Monkey
10. 4	13. 3	C5	G11	Gibbon
11. 4	14. 3	C5	H12	Tapir
12. 4	15. 3	C5	J1	Sheep
13. 4	16. 3	C5	K2	Deer
14. 4	17. 3	C5	A3	Horse
15. 4	18. 3	C5	B4	Stag
16. 4	19. 3	C5	C5	Serpent
17. 4	20. 3	C5	D6	Earthworm
18. 4	21. 3	C5	E7	Crocodile
19. 4	22. 3	C5	F8	Dragon
20. 4	23. 3	C5	G9	Badger
21. 4	24. 3	C5	H10	Hare
22. 4	25. 3	C5	J11	Fox
23. 4	26. 3	C5	K12	Tiger
24. 4	27. 3	C5	A1	Leopard
25. 4	28. 3	C5	B2	Griffon
26. 4	29. 3	C5	C3	Ox
27. 4	1. 4	D6	D4	Bat
28. 4	2. 4	D6	E5	Rat
29. 4	3. 4	D6	F6	Swallow
30. 4	4. 4	D6	G7	Pig
1. 5	5. 4	D6	H8	Porcupine
2. 5	6. 4	D6	J9	Wolf
3. 5	7. 4	D6	K10	Dog
4. 5	8. 4	D6	A11	Pheasant
5. 5	9. 4	D6	B12	Cock
6. 5	10. 4	D6	C1	Crow
7. 5	11. 4	D6	D2	Monkey
8. 5	12. 4	D6	E3	Gibbon
9. 5	13. 4	D6	F4	Tapir
10. 5	14. 4	D6	G5	Sheep
11. 5	15. 4	D6	H6	Deer
12. 5	16. 4	D6	J7	Horse
13. 5	17. 4	D6	K8	Stag
14. 5	18. 4	D6	A9	Serpent
15. 5	19. 4	D6	B10	Earthworm
16. 5	20. 4	D6	C11	Crocodile
17. 5	21. 4	D6	D12	Dragon
18. 5	22. 4	D6	E1	Badger
19. 5	23. 4	D6	F2	Hare
20. 5	24. 4	D6	G3	Fox
21. 5	25. 4	D6	H4	Tiger
22. 5	26. 4	D6	J5	Leopard
23. 5	27. 4	D6	K6	Griffon
24. 5	28. 4	D6	A7	Ox
25. 5	29. 4	D6	B8	Bat
26. 5	30. 4	D6	C9	Rat
27. 5	1. 5	E7	D10	Swallow
28. 5	2. 5	E7	E11	Pig
29. 5	3. 5	E7	F12	Porcupine
30. 5	4. 5	E7	G1	Wolf
31. 5	5. 5	E7	H2	Dog
1. 6	6. 5	E7	J3	Pheasant
2. 6	7. 5	E7	K4	Cock
3. 6	8. 5	E7	A5	Crow
4. 6	9. 5	E7	B6	Monkey
5. 6	10. 5	E7	C7	Gibbon
6. 6	11. 5	E7	D8	Tapir
7. 6	12. 5	E7	E9	Sheep
8. 6	13. 5	E7	F10	Deer
9. 6	14. 5	E7	G11	Horse
10. 6	15. 5	E7	H12	Stag
11. 6	16. 5	E7	J1	Serpent
12. 6	17. 5	E7	K2	Earthworm
13. 6	18. 5	E7	A3	Crocodile
14. 6	19. 5	E7	B4	Dragon
15. 6	20. 5	E7	C5	Badger
16. 6	21. 5	E7	D6	Hare
17. 6	22. 5	E7	E7	Fox
18. 6	23. 5	E7	F8	Tiger
19. 6	24. 5	E7	G9	Leopard

Solar date	*Lunar date*	*Month HS/EB*	*Day HS/EB*	*Constellation*
20. 6	25. 5	E7	H10	Griffon
21. 6	26. 5	E7	J11	Ox
22. 6	27. 5	E7	K12	Bat
23. 6	28. 5	E7	A1	Rat
24. 6	29. 5	E7	B2	Swallow
25. 6	30. 5	E7	C3	Pig
26. 6	1. 6	F8	D4	Porcupine
27. 6	2. 6	F8	E5	Wolf
28. 6	3. 6	F8	F6	Dog
29. 6	4. 6	F8	G7	Pheasant
30. 6	5. 6	F8	H8	Cock
1. 7	6. 6	F8	J9	Crow
2. 7	7. 6	F8	K10	Monkey
3. 7	8. 6	F8	A11	Gibbon
4. 7	9. 6	F8	B12	Tapir
5. 7	10. 6	F8	C1	Sheep
6. 7	11. 6	F8	D2	Deer
7. 7	12. 6	F8	E3	Horse
8. 7	13. 6	F8	F4	Stag
9. 7	14. 6	F8	G5	Serpent
10. 7	15. 6	F8	H6	Earthworm
11. 7	16. 6	F8	J7	Crocodile
12. 7	17. 6	F8	K8	Dragon
13. 7	18. 6	F8	A9	Badger
14. 7	19. 6	F8	B10	Hare
15. 7	20. 6	F8	C11	Fox
16. 7	21. 6	F8	D12	Tiger
17. 7	22. 6	F8	E1	Leopard
18. 7	23. 6	F8	F2	Griffon
19. 7	24. 6	F8	G3	Ox
20. 7	25. 6	F8	H4	Bat
21. 7	26. 6	F8	J5	Rat
22. 7	27. 6	F8	K6	Swallow
23. 7	28. 6	F8	A7	Pig
24. 7	29. 6	F8	B8	Porcupine
25. 7	1. 7	G9	C9	Wolf
26. 7	2. 7	G9	D10	Dog
27. 7	3. 7	G9	E11	Pheasant
28. 7	4. 7	G9	F12	Cock
29. 7	5. 7	G9	G1	Crow
30. 7	6. 7	G9	H2	Monkey
31. 7	7. 7	G9	J3	Gibbon
1. 8	8. 7	G9	K4	Tapir
2. 8	9. 7	G9	A5	Sheep
3. 8	10. 7	G9	B6	Deer
4. 8	11. 7	G9	C7	Horse
5. 8	12. 7	G9	D8	Stag
6. 8	13. 7	G9	E9	Serpent
7. 8	14. 7	G9	F10	Earthworm
8. 8	15. 7	G9	G11	Crocodile
9. 8	16. 7	G9	H12	Dragon
10. 8	17. 7	G9	J1	Badger
11. 8	18. 7	G9	K2	Hare
12. 8	19. 7	G9	A3	Fox
13. 8	20. 7	G9	B4	Tiger
14. 8	21. 7	G9	C5	Leopard
15. 8	22. 7	G9	D6	Griffon
16. 8	23. 7	G9	E7	Ox
18. 8	24. 7	G9	F8	Bat
18. 8	25. 7	G9	G9	Rat
19. 8	26. 7	G9	H10	Swallow
20. 8	27. 7	G9	J11	Pig
21. 8	28. 7	G9	K12	Porcupine
22. 8	29. 7	G9	A1	Wolf
23. 8	30. 7	G9	B2	Dog
24. 8	*1. 7*	*G9*	C3	Pheasant
25. 8	*2. 7*	*G9*	D4	Cock
26. 8	*3. 7*	*G9*	E5	Crow
27. 8	*4. 7*	*G9*	F6	Monkey
28. 8	*5. 7*	*G9*	G7	Gibbon
29. 8	*6. 7*	*G9*	H8	Tapir
30. 8	*7. 7*	*G9*	J9	Sheep
31. 8	*8. 7*	*G9*	K10	Deer
1. 9	*9. 7*	*G9*	A11	Horse
2. 9	*10. 7*	*G9*	B12	Stag
3. 9	*11. 7*	*G9*	C1	Serpent
4. 9	*12. 7*	*G9*	D2	Earthworm
5. 9	*13. 7*	*G9*	E3	Crocodile
6. 9	*14. 7*	*G9*	F4	Dragon
7. 9	*15. 7*	*G9*	G5	Badger
8. 9	*16. 7*	*G9*	H6	Hare
9. 9	*17. 7*	*G9*	J7	Fox
10. 9	*18. 7*	*G9*	K8	Tiger
11. 9	*19. 7*	*G9*	A9	Leopard
12. 9	*20. 7*	*G9*	B10	Griffon
13. 9	*21. 7*	*G9*	C11	Ox
14. 9	*22. 7*	*G9*	D12	Bat
15. 9	*23. 7*	*G9*	E1	Rat
16. 9	*24. 7*	*G9*	F2	Swallow
17. 9	*25. 7*	*G9*	G3	Pig
18. 9	*26. 7*	*G9*	H4	Porcupine
19. 9	*27. 7*	*G9*	J5	Wolf
20. 9	*28. 7*	*G9*	K6	Dog
21. 9	*29. 7*	*G9*	A7	Pheasant
22. 9	1. 8	H10	B8	Cock
23. 9	2. 8	H10	C9	Crow
24. 9	3. 8	H10	D10	Monkey
25. 9	4. 8	H10	E11	Gibbon
26. 9	5. 8	H10	F12	Tapir
27. 9	6. 8	H10	G1	Sheep
28. 9	7. 8	H10	H2	Deer
29. 9	8. 8	H10	J3	Horse
30. 9	9. 8	H10	K4	Stag
1.10	10. 8	H10	A5	Serpent
2.10	11. 8	H10	B6	Earthworm
3.10	12. 8	H10	C7	Crocodile
4.10	13. 8	H10	D8	Dragon
5.10	14. 8	H10	E9	Badger
6.10	15. 8	H10	F10	Hare
7.10	16. 8	H10	G11	Fox
8.10	17. 8	H10	H12	Tiger
9.10	18. 8	H10	J1	Leopard
10.10	19. 8	H10	K2	Griffon
11.10	20. 8	H10	A3	Ox
12.10	21. 8	H10	B4	Bat
13.10	22. 8	H10	C5	Rat
14.10	23. 8	H10	D6	Swallow
15.10	24. 8	H10	E7	Pig
16.10	25. 8	H10	F8	Porcupine
17.10	26. 8	H10	G9	Wolf
18.10	27. 8	H10	H10	Dog
19.10	28. 8	H10	J11	Pheasant
20.10	29. 8	H10	K12	Cock
21.10	30. 8	H10	A1	Crow
22.10	1. 9	J11	B2	Monkey
23.10	2. 9	J11	C3	Gibbon
24.10	3. 9	J11	D4	Tapir
25.10	4. 9	J11	E5	Sheep
26.10	5. 9	J11	F6	Deer
27.10	6. 9	J11	G7	Horse
28.10	7. 9	J11	H8	Stag
29.10	8. 9	J11	J9	Serpent
30.10	9. 9	J11	K10	Earthworm
31.10	10. 9	J11	A11	Crocodile
1.11	11. 9	J11	B12	Dragon
2.11	12. 9	J11	C1	Badger
3.11	13. 9	J11	D2	Hare
4.11	14. 9	J11	E3	Fox
5.11	15. 9	J11	F4	Tiger
6.11	16. 9	J11	G5	Leopard
7.11	17. 9	J11	H6	Griffon
8.11	18. 9	J11	J7	Ox
9.11	19. 9	J11	K8	Bat
10.11	20. 9	J11	A9	Rat
11.11	21. 9	J11	B10	Swallow
12.11	22. 9	J11	C11	Pig

Solar date	Lunar date	Month HS/EB	Day HS/EB	Constellation
13.11	23. 9	J11	D12	Porcupine
14.11	24. 9	J11	E1	Wolf
15.11	25. 9	J11	F2	Dog
16.11	26. 9	J11	G3	Pheasant
17.11	27. 9	J11	H4	Cock
18.11	28. 9	J11	J5	Crow
19.11	29. 9	J11	K6	Monkey
20.11	1.10	K12	A7	Gibbon
21.11	2.10	K12	B8	Tapir
22.11	3.10	K12	C9	Sheep
23.11	4.10	K12	D10	Deer
24.11	5.10	K12	E11	Horse
25.11	6.10	K12	F12	Stag
26.11	7.10	K12	G1	Serpent
27.11	8.10	K12	H2	Earthworm
28.11	9.10	K12	J3	Crocodile
29.11	10.10	K12	K4	Dragon
30.11	11.10	K12	A5	Badger
1.12	12.10	K12	B6	Hare
2.12	13.10	K12	C7	Fox
3.12	14.10	K12	D8	Tiger
4.12	15.10	K12	E9	Leopard
5.12	16.10	K12	F10	Griffon
6.12	17.10	K12	G11	Ox
7.12	18.10	K12	H12	Bat
8.12	19.10	K12	J1	Rat
9.12	20.10	K12	K2	Swallow
10.12	21.10	K12	A3	Pig
11.12	22.10	K12	B4	Porcupine
12.12	23.10	K12	C5	Wolf
13.12	24.10	K12	D6	Dog
14.12	25.10	K12	E7	Pheasant
15.12	26.10	K12	F8	Cock
16.12	27.10	K12	G9	Crow
17.12	28.10	K12	H10	Monkey
18.12	29.10	K12	J11	Gibbon
19.12	30.10	K12	K12	Tapir
20.12	1.11	A1	A1	Sheep
21.12	2.11	A1	B2	Deer
22.12	3.11	A1	C3	Horse
23.12	4.11	A1	D4	Stag
24.12	5.11	A1	E5	Serpent
25.12	6.11	A1	F6	Earthworm
26.12	7.11	A1	G7	Crocodile
27.12	8.11	A1	H8	Dragon
28.12	9.11	A1	J9	Badger
29.12	10.11	A1	K10	Hare
30.12	11.11	A1	A11	Fox
31.12	12.11	A1	B12	Tiger
1969				
1. 1	13.11	A1	C1	Leopard
2. 1	14.11	A1	D2	Griffon
3. 1	15.11	A1	E3	Ox
4. 1	16.11	A1	F4	Bat
5. 1	17.11	A1	G5	Rat
6. 1	18.11	A1	H6	Swallow
7. 1	19.11	A1	J7	Pig
8. 1	20.11	A1	K8	Porcupine
9. 1	21.11	A1	A9	Wolf
10. 1	22.11	A1	B10	Dog
11. 1	23.11	A1	C11	Pheasant
12. 1	24.11	A1	D12	Cock
13. 1	25.11	A1	E1	Crow
14. 1	26.11	A1	F2	Monkey
15. 1	27.11	A1	G3	Gibbon
16. 1	28.11	A1	H4	Tapir
17. 1	29.11	A1	J5	Sheep
18. 1	1.12	B2	K6	Deer
19. 1	2.12	B2	A7	Horse
20. 1	3.12	B2	B8	Stag
21. 1	4.12	B2	C9	Serpent
22. 1	5.12	B2	D10	Earthworm
23. 1	6.12	B2	E11	Crocodile
24. 1	7.12	B2	F12	Dragon
25. 1	8.12	B2	G1	Badger
26. 1	9.12	B2	H2	Hare
27. 1	10.12	B2	J3	Fox
28. 1	11.12	B2	K4	Tiger
29. 1	12.12	B2	A5	Leopard
30. 1	13.12	B2	B6	Griffon
31. 1	14.12	B2	C7	Ox
1. 2	15.12	B2	D8	Bat
2. 2	16.12	B2	E9	Rat
3. 2	17.12	B2	F10	Swallow
4. 2	18.12	B2	G11	Pig
5. 2	19.12	B2	H12	Porcupine
6. 2	20.12	B2	J1	Wolf
7. 2	21.12	B2	K2	Dog
8. 2	22.12	B2	A3	Pheasant
9. 2	23.12	B2	B4	Cock
10. 2	24.12	B2	C5	Crow
11. 2	25.12	B2	D6	Monkey
12. 2	26.12	B2	E7	Gibbon
13. 2	27.12	B2	F8	Tapir
14. 2	28.12	B2	G9	Sheep
15. 2	29.12	B2	H10	Deer
16. 2	30.12	B2	J11	Horse

CHI YU YEAR

17. 2	1. 1	C3	K12	Stag
18. 2	2. 1	C3	A1	Serpent
19. 2	3. 1	C3	B2	Earthworm
20. 2	4. 1	C3	C3	Crocodile
21. 2	5. 1	C3	D4	Dragon
22. 2	6. 1	C3	E5	Badger
23. 2	7. 1	C3	F6	Hare
24. 2	8. 1	C3	G7	Fox
25. 2	9. 1	C3	H8	Tiger
26. 2	10. 1	C3	J9	Leopard
27. 2	11. 1	C3	K10	Griffon
28. 2	12. 1	C3	A11	Ox
1. 3	13. 1	C3	B12	Bat
2. 3	14. 1	C3	C1	Rat
3. 3	15. 1	C3	D2	Swallow
4. 3	16. 1	C3	E3	Pig
5. 3	17. 1	C3	F4	Porcupine
6. 3	18. 1	C3	G5	Wolf
7. 3	19. 1	C3	H6	Dog
8. 3	20. 1	C3	J7	Pheasant
9. 3	21. 1	C3	K8	Cock
10. 3	22. 1	C3	A9	Crow
11. 3	23. 1	C3	B10	Monkey
12. 3	24. 1	C3	C11	Gibbon
13. 3	25. 1	C3	D12	Tapir
14. 3	26. 1	C3	E1	Sheep
15. 3	27. 1	C3	F2	Deer
16. 3	28. 1	C3	G3	Horse
17. 3	29. 1	C3	H4	Stag
18. 3	1. 2	D4	J5	Serpent
19. 3	2. 2	D4	K6	Earthworm
20. 3	3. 2	D4	A7	Crocodile
21. 3	4. 2	D4	B8	Dragon
22. 3	5. 2	D4	C9	Badger
23. 3	6. 2	D4	D10	Hare
24. 3	7. 2	D4	E11	Fox

Solar date	*Lunar date*	*Month HS/EB*	*Day HS/EB*	*Constellation*
25. 3	8. 2	D4	F12	Tiger
26. 3	9. 2	D4	G1	Leopard
27. 3	10. 2	D4	H2	Griffon
28. 3	11. 2	D4	J3	Ox
29. 3	12. 2	D4	K4	Bat
30. 3	13. 2	D4	A5	Rat
31. 3	14. 2	D4	B6	Swallow
1. 4	15. 2	D4	C7	Pig
2. 4	16. 2	D4	D8	Porcupine
3. 4	17. 2	D4	E9	Wolf
4. 4	18. 2	D4	F10	Dog
5. 4	19. 2	D4	G11	Pheasant
6. 4	20. 2	D4	H12	Cock
7. 4	21. 2	D4	J1	Crow
8. 4	22. 2	D4	K2	Monkey
9. 4	23. 2	D4	A3	Gibbon
10. 4	24. 2	D4	B4	Tapir
11. 4	25. 2	D4	C5	Sheep
12. 4	26. 2	D4	D6	Deer
13. 4	27. 2	D4	E7	Horse
14. 4	28. 2	D4	F8	Stag
15. 4	29. 2	D4	G9	Serpent
16. 4	30. 2	D4	H10	Earthworm
17. 4	1. 3	E5	J11	Crocodile
18. 4	2. 3	E5	K12	Dragon
19. 4	3. 3	E5	A1	Badger
20. 4	4. 3	E5	B2	Hare
21. 4	5. 3	E5	C3	Fox
22. 4	6. 3	E5	D4	Tiger
23. 4	7. 3	E5	E5	Leopard
24. 4	8. 3	E5	F6	Griffon
25. 4	9. 3	E5	G7	Ox
26. 4	10. 3	E5	H8	Bat
27. 4	11. 3	E5	J9	Rat
28. 4	12. 3	E5	K10	Swallow
29. 4	13. 3	E5	A11	Pig
30. 4	14. 3	E5	B12	Porcupine
1. 5	15. 3	E5	C1	Wolf
2. 5	16. 3	E5	D2	Dog
3. 5	17. 3	E5	E3	Pheasant
4. 5	18. 3	E5	F4	Cock
5. 5	19. 3	E5	G5	Crow
6. 5	20. 3	E5	H6	Monkey
7. 5	21. 3	E5	J7	Gibbon
8. 5	22. 3	E5	K8	Tapir
9. 5	23. 3	E5	A9	Sheep
10. 5	24. 3	E5	B10	Deer
11. 5	25. 3	E5	C11	Horse
12. 5	26. 3	E5	D12	Stag
13. 5	27. 3	E5	E1	Serpent
14. 5	28. 3	E5	F2	Earthworm
15. 5	29. 3	E5	G3	Crocodile
16. 5	1. 4	F6	H4	Dragon
17. 5	2. 4	F6	J5	Badger
18. 5	3. 4	F6	K6	Hare
19. 5	4. 4	F6	A7	Fox
20. 5	5. 4	F6	B8	Tiger
21. 5	6. 4	F6	C9	Leopard
22. 5	7. 4	F6	D10	Griffon
23. 5	8. 4	F6	E11	Ox
24. 5	9. 4	F6	F12	Bat
25. 5	10. 4	F6	G1	Rat
26. 5	11. 4	F6	H2	Swallow
27. 5	12. 4	F6	J3	Pig
28. 5	13. 4	F6	K4	Porcupine
29. 5	14. 4	F6	A5	Wolf
30. 5	15. 4	F6	B6	Dog
31. 5	16. 4	F6	C7	Pheasant
1. 6	17. 4	F6	D8	Cock
2. 6	18. 4	F6	E9	Crow
3. 6	19. 4	F6	F10	Monkey
4. 6	20. 4	F6	G11	Gibbon
5. 6	21. 4	F6	H12	Tapir

Solar date	*Lunar date*	*Month HS/EB*	*Day HS/EB*	*Constellation*
6. 6	22. 4	F6	J1	Sheep
7. 6	23. 4	F6	K2	Deer
8. 6	24. 4	F6	A3	Horse
9. 6	25. 4	F6	B4	Stag
10. 6	26. 4	F6	C5	Serpent
11. 6	27. 4	F6	D6	Earthworm
12. 6	28. 4	F6	E7	Crocodile
13. 6	29. 4	F6	F8	Dragon
14. 6	30. 4	F6	G9	Badger
15. 6	1. 5	G7	H10	Hare
16. 6	2. 5	G7	J11	Fox
17. 6	3. 5	G7	K12	Tiger
18. 6	4. 5	G7	A1	Leopard
19. 6	5. 5	G7	B2	Griffon
20. 6	6. 5	G7	C3	Ox
21. 6	7. 5	G7	D4	Bat
22. 6	8. 5	G7	E5	Rat
23. 6	9. 5	G7	F6	Swallow
24. 6	10. 5	G7	G7	Pig
25. 6	11. 5	G7	H8	Porcupine
26. 6	12. 5	G7	J9	Wolf
27. 6	13. 5	G7	K10	Dog
28. 6	14. 5	G7	A11	Pheasant
29. 6	15. 5	G7	B12	Cock
30. 6	16. 5	G7	C1	Crow
1. 7	17. 5	G7	D2	Monkey
2. 7	18. 5	G7	E3	Gibbon
3. 7	19. 5	G7	F4	Tapir
4. 7	20. 5	G7	G5	Sheep
5. 7	21. 5	G7	H6	Deer
6. 7	22. 5	G7	J7	Horse
7. 7	23. 5	G7	K8	Stag
8. 7	24. 5	G7	A9	Serpent
9. 7	25. 5	G7	B10	Earthworm
10. 7	26. 5	G7	C11	Crocodile
11. 7	27. 5	G7	D12	Dragon
12. 7	28. 5	G7	E1	Badger
13. 7	29. 5	G7	F2	Hare
14. 7	1. 6	H8	G3	Fox
15. 7	2. 6	H8	H4	Tiger
16. 7	3. 6	H8	J5	Leopard
17. 7	4. 6	H8	K6	Griffon
18. 7	5. 6	H8	A7	Ox
19. 7	6. 6	H8	B8	Bat
20. 7	7. 6	H8	C9	Rat
21. 7	8. 6	H8	D10	Swallow
22. 7	9. 6	H8	E11	Pig
23. 7	10. 6	H8	F12	Porcupine
24. 7	11. 6	H8	G1	Wolf
25. 7	12. 6	H8	H2	Dog
26. 7	13. 6	H8	J3	Pheasant
27. 7	14. 6	H8	K4	Cock
28. 7	15. 6	H8	A5	Crow
29. 7	16. 6	H8	B6	Monkey
30. 7	17. 6	H8	C7	Gibbon
31. 7	18. 6	H8	D8	Tapir
1. 8	19. 6	H8	E9	Sheep
2. 8	20. 6	H8	F10	Deer
3. 8	21. 6	H8	G11	Horse
4. 8	22. 6	H8	H12	Stag
5. 8	23. 6	H8	J1	Serpent
6. 8	24. 6	H8	K2	Earthworm
7. 8	25. 6	H8	A3	Crocodile
8. 8	26. 6	H8	B4	Dragon
9. 8	27. 6	H8	C5	Badger
10. 8	28. 6	H8	D6	Hare
11. 8	29. 6	H8	E7	Fox
12. 8	30. 6	H8	F8	Tiger
13. 8	1. 7	J9	G9	Leopard
14. 8	2. 7	J9	H10	Griffon
15. 8	3. 7	J9	J11	Ox
16. 8	4. 7	J9	K12	Bat
17. 8	5. 7	J9	A1	Rat

Solar date	*Lunar date*	*Month HS/EB*	*Day HS/EB*	*Constellation*
18. 8	6. 7	J9	B2	Swallow
19. 8	7. 7	J9	C3	Pig
20. 8	8. 7	J9	D4	Porcupine
21. 8	9. 7	J9	E5	Wolf
22. 8	10. 7	J9	F6	Dog
23. 8	11. 7	J9	G7	Pheasant
24. 8	12. 7	J9	H8	Cock
25. 8	13. 7	J9	J9	Crow
26. 8	14. 7	J9	K10	Monkey
27. 8	15. 7	J9	A11	Gibbon
28. 8	16. 7	J9	B12	Tapir
29. 8	17. 7	J9	C1	Sheep
30. 8	18. 7	J9	D2	Deer
31. 8	19. 7	J9	E3	Horse
1. 9	20. 7	J9	F4	Stag
2. 9	21. 7	J9	G5	Serpent
3. 9	22. 7	J9	H6	Earthworm
4. 9	23. 7	J9	J7	Crocodile
5. 9	24. 7	J9	K8	Dragon
6. 9	25. 7	J9	A9	Badger
7. 9	26. 7	J9	B10	Hare
8. 9	27. 7	J9	C11	Fox
9. 9	28. 7	J9	D12	Tiger
10. 9	29. 7	J9	E1	Leopard
11. 9	30. 7	J9	F2	Griffon
12. 9	1. 8	K10	G3	Ox
13. 9	2. 8	K10	H4	Bat
14. 9	3. 8	K10	J5	Rat
15. 9	4. 8	K10	K6	Swallow
16. 9	5. 8	K10	A7	Pig
17. 9	6. 8	K10	B8	Porcupine
18. 9	7. 8	K10	C9	Wolf
19. 9	8. 8	K10	D10	Dog
20. 9	9. 8	K10	E11	Pheasant
21. 9	10. 8	K10	F12	Cock
22. 9	11. 8	K10	G1	Crow
23. 9	12. 8	K10	H2	Monkey
24. 9	13. 8	K10	J3	Gibbon
25. 9	14. 8	K10	K4	Tapir
26. 9	15. 8	K10	A5	Sheep
27. 9	16. 8	K10	B6	Deer
28. 9	17. 8	K10	C7	Horse
29. 9	18. 8	K10	D8	Stag
30. 9	19. 8	K10	E9	Serpent
1.10	20. 8	K10	F10	Earthworm
2.10	21. 8	K10	G11	Crocodile
3.10	22. 8	K10	H12	Dragon
4.10	23. 8	K10	J1	Badger
5.10	24. 8	K10	K2	Hare
6.10	25. 8	K10	A3	Fox
7.10	26. 8	K10	B4	Tiger
8.10	27. 8	K10	C5	Leopard
9.10	28. 8	K10	D6	Griffon
10.10	29. 8	K10	E7	Ox
11.10	1. 9	A11	F8	Bat
12.10	2. 9	A11	G9	Rat
13.10	3. 9	A11	H10	Swallow
14.10	4. 9	A11	J11	Pig
15.10	5. 9	A11	K12	Porcupine
16.10	6. 9	A11	A1	Wolf
17.10	7. 9	A11	B2	Dog
18.10	8. 9	A11	C3	Pheasant
19.10	9. 9	A11	D4	Cock
20.10	10. 9	A11	E5	Crow
21.10	11. 9	A11	F6	Monkey
22.10	12. 9	A11	G7	Gibbon
23.10	13. 9	A11	H8	Tapir
24.10	14. 9	A11	J9	Sheep
25.10	15. 9	A11	K10	Deer
26.10	16. 9	A11	A11	Horse
27.10	17. 9	A11	B12	Stag
28.10	18. 9	A11	C1	Serpent
29.10	19. 9	A11	D2	Earthworm

Solar date	*Lunar date*	*Month HS/EB*	*Day HS/EB*	*Constellation*
30.10	20. 9	A11	E3	Crocodile
31.10	21. 9	A11	F4	Dragon
1.11	22. 9	A11	G5	Badger
2.11	23. 9	A11	H6	Hare
3.11	24. 9	A11	J7	Fox
4.11	25. 9	A11	K8	Tiger
5.11	26. 9	A11	A9	Leopard
6.11	27. 9	A11	B10	Griffon
7.11	28. 9	A11	C11	Ox
8.11	29. 9	A11	D12	Bat
9.11	30. 9	A11	E1	Rat
10.11	1.10	B12	F2	Swallow
11.11	2.10	B12	G3	Pig
12.11	2.10	B12	H4	Porcupine
13.11	4.10	B12	J5	Wolf
14.11	5.10	B12	K6	Dog
15.11	6.10	B12	A7	Pheasant
16.11	7.10	B12	B8	Cock
17.11	8.10	B12	C9	Crow
18.11	9.10	B12	D10	Monkey
19.11	10.10	B12	E11	Gibbon
20.11	11.10	B12	F12	Tapir
21.11	12.10	B12	G1	Sheep
22.11	13.10	B12	H2	Deer
23.11	14.10	B12	J3	Horse
24.11	15.10	B12	K4	Stag
25.11	16.10	B12	A5	Serpent
26.11	17.10	B12	B6	Earthworm
27.11	18.10	B12	C7	Crocodile
28.11	19.10	B12	D8	Dragon
29.11	20.10	B12	E9	Badger
30.11	21.10	B12	F10	Hare
1.12	22.10	B12	G11	Fox
2.12	23.10	B12	H12	Tiger
3.12	24.10	B12	J1	Leopard
4.12	25.10	B12	K2	Griffon
5.12	26.10	B12	A3	Ox
6.12	27.10	B12	B4	Bat
7.12	28.10	B12	C5	Rat
8.12	29.10	B12	D6	Swallow
9.12	1.11	C1	E7	Pig
10.12	2.11	C1	F8	Porcupine
11.12	3.11	C1	G9	Wolf
12.12	4.11	C1	H10	Dog
13.12	5.11	C1	J11	Pheasant
14.12	6.11	C1	K12	Cock
15.12	7.11	C1	A1	Crow
16.12	8.11	C1	B2	Monkey
17.12	9.11	C1	C3	Gibbon
18.12	10.11	C1	D4	Tapir
19.12	11.11	C1	E5	Sheep
20.12	12.11	C1	F6	Deer
21.12	13.11	C1	G7	Horse
22.12	14.11	C1	H8	Stag
23.12	15.11	C1	J9	Serpent
24.12	16.11	C1	K10	Earthworm
25.12	17.11	C1	A11	Crocodile
26.12	18.11	C1	B12	Dragon
27.12	19.11	C1	C1	Badger
28.12	20.11	C1	D2	Hare
29.12	21.11	C1	E3	Fox
30.12	22.11	C1	F4	Tiger
31.12	23,11	C1	G5	Leopard
1970				
1. 1	24.11	C1	H6	Griffon
2. 1	25.11	C1	J7	Ox
3. 1	26.11	C1	K8	Bat
4. 1	27.11	C1	A9	Rat
5. 1	28.11	C1	B10	Swallow
6. 1	29.11	C1	C11	Pig
7. 1	30.11	C1	D12	Porcupine
8. 1	1.12	D2	E1	Wolf

Solar date	*Lunar date*	*Month HS/EB*	*Day HS/EB*	*Constellation*
9. 1	2.12	D2	F2	Dog
10. 1	3.12	D2	G3	Pheasant
11. 1	4.12	D2	H4	Cock
12. 1	5.12	D2	J5	Crow
13. 1	6.12	D2	K6	Monkey
14. 1	7.12	D2	A7	Gibbon
15. 1	8.12	D2	B8	Tapir
16. 1	9.12	D2	C9	Sheep
17. 1	10.12	D2	D10	Deer
18. 1	11.12	D2	E11	Horse
19. 1	12.12	D2	F12	Stag
20. 1	13.12	D2	G1	Serpent
21. 1	14.12	D2	H2	Earthworm
22. 1	15.12	D2	J3	Crocodile
23. 1	16.12	D2	K4	Dragon
24. 1	17.12	D2	A5	Badger
25. 1	18.12	D2	B6	Hare
26. 1	19.12	D2	C7	Fox
27. 1	20.12	D2	D8	Tiger
28. 1	21.12	D2	E9	Leopard
29. 1	22.12	D2	F10	Griffon
30. 1	23.12	D2	G11	Ox
31. 1	24.12	D2	H12	Bat
1. 2	25.12	D2	J1	Rat
2. 2	26.12	D2	K2	Swallow
3. 2	27.12	D2	A3	Pig
4. 2	28.12	D2	B4	Porcupine
5. 2	29.12	D2	C5	Wolf

KENG HSÜ YEAR

6. 2	1. 1	E3	D6	Dog
7. 2	2. 1	E3	E7	Pheasant
8. 2	3. 1	E3	F8	Cock
9. 2	4. 1	E3	G9	Crow
10. 1	5. 1	E3	H10	Monkey
11. 2	6. 1	E3	J11	Gibbon
12. 2	7. 1	E3	K12	Tapir
13. 2	8. 1	E3	A1	Sheep
14. 2	9. 1	E3	B2	Deer
15. 2	10. 1	E3	C3	Horse
16. 2	11. 1	E3	D4	Stag
17. 2	12. 1	E3	E5	Serpent
18. 2	13. 1	E3	F6	Earthworm
19. 2	14. 1	E3	G7	Crocodile
20. 2	15. 1	E3	H8	Dragon
21. 2	16. 1	E3	J9	Badger
22. 2	17. 1	E3	K10	Hare
23. 2	18. 1	E3	A11	Fox
24. 2	19. 1	E3	B12	Tiger
25. 2	20. 1	E3	C1	Leopard
26. 2	21. 1	E3	D2	Griffon
27. 2	22. 1	E3	E3	Ox
28. 2	23. 1	E3	F4	Bat
1. 3	24. 1	E3	G5	Rat
2. 3	25. 1	E3	H6	Swallow
3. 3	26. 1	E3	J7	Pig
4. 3	27. 1	E3	K8	Porcupine
5. 3	28. 1	E3	A9	Wolf
6. 3	29. 1	E3	B10	Dog
7. 3	30. 1	E3	C11	Pheasant
8. 3	1. 2	F4	D12	Cock
9. 3	2. 2	F4	E1	Crow
10. 3	3. 2	F4	F2	Monkey
11. 3	4. 2	F4	G3	Gibbon
12. 3	5. 2	F4	H4	Tapir
13. 3	6. 2	F4	J5	Sheep
14. 3	7. 2	F4	K6	Deer
15. 3	8. 2	F4	A7	Horse
16. 3	9. 2	F4	B8	Stag
17. 3	10. 2	F4	C9	Serpent
18. 3	11. 2	F4	D10	Earthworm
19. 3	12. 2	F4	E11	Crocodile
20. 3	13. 2	F4	F12	Dragon
21. 3	14. 2	F4	G1	Badger
22. 3	15. 2	F4	H2	Hare
23. 3	16. 2	F4	J3	Fox
24. 3	17. 2	F4	K4	Tiger
25. 3	18. 2	F4	A5	Leopard
26. 3	19. 2	F4	B6	Griffon
27. 3	20. 2	F4	C7	Ox
28. 3	21. 2	F4	D8	Bat
29. 3	22. 2	F4	E9	Rat
30. 3	23. 2	F4	F10	Swallow
31. 3	24. 2	F4	G11	Pig
1. 4	25. 2	F4	H12	Porcupine
2. 4	26. 2	F4	J1	Wolf
3. 4	27. 2	F4	K2	Dog
4. 4	28. 2	F4	A3	Pheasant
5. 4	29. 2	F4	B4	Cock
6. 4	1. 3	G5	C5	Crow
7. 4	2. 3	G5	D6	Monkey
8. 4	3. 3	G5	E7	Gibbon
9. 4	4. 3	G5	F8	Tapir
10. 4	5. 3	G5	G9	Sheep
11. 4	6. 3	G5	H10	Deer
12. 4	7. 3	G5	J11	Horse
13. 4	8. 3	G5	K12	Stag
14. 4	9. 3	G5	A1	Serpent
15. 4	10. 3	G5	B2	Earthworm
16. 4	11. 3	G5	C3	Crocodile
17. 4	12. 3	G5	D4	Dragon
18. 4	13. 3	G5	E5	Badger
19. 4	14. 3	G5	F6	Hare
20. 4	15. 3	G5	G7	Fox
21. 4	16. 3	G5	H8	Tiger
22. 4	17. 3	G5	J9	Leopard
23. 4	18. 3	G5	K10	Griffon
24. 4	19. 3	G5	A11	Ox
25. 4	20. 3	G5	B12	Bat
26. 4	21. 3	G5	C1	Rat
27. 4	22. 3	G5	D2	Swallow
28. 4	23. 3	G5	E3	Pig
29. 4	24. 3	G5	F4	Porcupine
30. 4	25. 3	G5	G5	Wolf
1. 5	26. 3	G5	H6	Dog
2. 5	27. 3	G5	J7	Pheasant
3. 5	28. 3	G5	K8	Cock
4. 5	29. 3	G5	A9	Crow
5. 5	1. 4	H6	B10	Monkey
6. 5	2. 4	H6	C11	Gibbon
7. 5	3. 4	H6	D12	Tapir
8. 5	4. 4	H6	E1	Sheep
9. 5	5. 4	H6	F2	Deer
10. 5	6. 4	H6	G3	Horse
11. 5	7. 4	H6	H4	Stag
12. 5	8. 4	H6	J5	Serpent
13. 5	9. 4	H6	K6	Earthworm
14. 5	10. 4	H6	A7	Crocodile
15. 5	11. 4	H6	B8	Dragon
16. 5	12. 4	H6	C9	Badger
17. 5	13. 4	H6	D10	Hare
18. 5	14. 4	H6	E11	Fox
19. 5	15. 4	H6	F12	Tiger
20. 5	16. 4	H6	G1	Leopard
21. 5	17. 4	H6	H2	Griffon
22. 5	18. 4	H6	J3	Ox
23. 5	19. 4	H6	K4	Bat
24. 5	20. 4	H6	A5	Rat

Solar date	*Lunar date*	*Month HS/EB*	*Day HS/EB*	*Constellation*
25. 5	21. 4	H6	B6	Swallow
26. 5	22. 4	H6	C7	Pig
27. 5	23. 4	H6	D8	Porcupine
28. 5	24. 4	H6	E9	Wolf
29. 5	25. 4	H6	F10	Dog
30. 5	26. 4	H6	G11	Pheasant
31. 5	27. 4	H6	H12	Cock
1. 6	28. 4	H6	J1	Crow
2. 6	29. 4	H6	K2	Monkey
3. 6	30. 4	H6	A3	Gibbon
4. 6	1. 5	J7	B4	Tapir
5. 6	2. 5	J7	C5	Sheep
6. 6	3. 5	J7	D6	Deer
7. 6	4. 5	J7	E7	Horse
8. 6	5. 5	J7	F8	Stag
9. 6	6. 5	J7	G9	Serpent
10. 6	7. 5	J7	H10	Earthworm
11. 6	8. 5	J7	J11	Crocodile
12. 6	9. 5	J7	K12	Dragon
13. 6	10. 5	J7	A1	Badger
14. 6	11. 5	J7	B2	Hare
15. 6	12. 5	J7	C3	Fox
16. 6	13. 5	J7	D4	Tiger
17. 6	14. 5	J7	E5	Leopard
18. 6	15. 5	J7	F6	Griffon
19. 6	16. 5	J7	G7	Ox
20. 6	17. 5	J7	H8	Bat
21. 6	18. 5	J7	J9	Rat
22. 6	19. 5	J7	K10	Swallow
23. 6	20. 5	J7	A11	Pig
24. 6	21. 5	J7	B12	Porcupine
25. 6	22. 5	J7	C1	Wolf
26. 6	23. 5	J7	D2	Dog
27. 6	24. 5	J7	E3	Pheasant
28. 6	25. 5	J7	F4	Cock
29. 6	26. 5	J7	G5	Crow
30. 6	27. 5	J7	H6	Monkey
1. 7	28. 5	J7	J7	Gibbon
2. 7	29. 5	J7	K8	Tapir
3. 7	1. 6	K8	A9	Sheep
4. 7	2. 6	K8	B10	Deer
5. 7	3. 6	K8	C11	Horse
6. 7	4. 6	K8	D12	Stag
7. 7	5. 6	K8	E1	Serpent
8. 7	6. 6	K8	F2	Earthworm
9. 7	7. 6	K8	G3	Crocodile
10. 7	8. 6	K8	H4	Dragon
11. 7	9. 6	K8	J5	Badger
12. 7	10. 6	K8	K6	Hare
13. 7	11. 6	K8	A7	Fox
14. 7	12. 6	K8	B8	Tiger
15. 7	13. 6	K8	C9	Leopard
16. 7	14. 6	K8	D10	Griffon
17. 7	15. 6	K8	E11	Ox
18. 7	16. 6	K8	F12	Bat
19. 7	17. 6	K8	G1	Rat
20. 7	18. 6	K8	H2	Swallow
21. 7	19. 6	K8	J3	Pig
22. 7	20. 6	K8	K4	Porcupine
23. 7	21. 6	K8	A5	Wolf
24. 7	22. 6	K8	B6	Dog
25. 7	23. 6	K8	C7	Pheasant
26. 7	24. 6	K8	D8	Cock
27. 7	25. 6	K8	E9	Crow
28. 7	26. 6	K8	F10	Monkey
29. 7	27. 6	K8	G11	Gibbon
30. 7	28. 6	K8	H12	Tapir
31. 7	29. 6	K8	J1	Sheep
1. 8	30. 6	K8	K2	Deer
2. 8	1. 7	A9	A3	Horse
3. 8	2. 7	A9	B4	Stag
4. 8	3. 7	A9	C5	Serpent
5. 8	4. 7	A9	D6	Earthworm

Solar date	*Lunar date*	*Month HS/EB*	*Day HS/EB*	*Constellation*
6. 8	5. 7	A9	E7	Crocodile
7. 8	6. 7	A9	F8	Dragon
8. 8	7. 7	A9	G9	Badger
9. 8	8. 7	A9	H10	Hare
10. 8	9. 7	A9	J11	Fox
11. 8	10. 7	A9	K12	Tiger
12. 8	11. 7	A9	A1	Leopard
13. 8	12. 7	A9	B2	Griffon
14. 8	13. 7	A9	C3	Ox
15. 8	14. 7	A9	D4	Bat
16. 8	15. 7	A9	E5	Rat
17. 8	16. 7	A9	F6	Swallow
18. 8	17. 7	A9	G7	Pig
19. 8	18. 7	A9	H8	Porcupine
20. 8	19. 7	A9	J9	Wolf
21. 8	20. 7	A9	K10	Dog
22. 8	21. 7	A9	A11	Pheasant
23. 8	22. 7	A9	B12	Cock
24. 8	23. 7	A9	C1	Crow
25. 8	24. 7	A9	D2	Monkey
26. 8	25. 7	A9	E3	Gibbon
27. 8	26. 7	A9	F4	Tapir
28. 8	27. 7	A9	G5	Sheep
29. 8	28. 7	A9	H6	Deer
30. 8	29. 7	A9	J7	Horse
31. 8	30. 7	A9	K8	Stag
1. 9	1. 8	B10	A9	Serpent
2. 9	2. 8	B10	B10	Earthworm
3. 9	3. 8	B10	C11	Crocodile
4. 9	4. 8	B10	D12	Dragon
5. 9	5. 8	B10	E1	Badger
6. 9	6. 8	B10	F2	Hare
7. 9	7. 8	B10	G3	Fox
8. 9	8. 8	B10	H4	Tiger
9. 9	9. 8	B10	J5	Leopard
10. 9	10. 8	B10	K6	Griffon
11. 9	11. 8	B10	A7	Ox
12. 9	12. 8	B10	B8	Bat
13. 9	13. 8	B10	C9	Rat
14. 9	14. 8	B10	D10	Swallow
15. 9	15. 8	B10	E11	Pig
16. 9	16. 8	B10	F12	Porcupine
17. 9	17. 8	B10	G1	Wolf
18. 9	18. 8	B10	H2	Dog
19. 9	19. 8	B10	J3	Pheasant
20. 9	20. 8	B10	K4	Cock
21. 9	21. 8	B10	A5	Crow
22. 9	22. 8	B10	B6	Monkey
23. 9	23. 8	B10	C7	Gibbon
24. 9	24. 8	B10	D8	Tapir
25. 9	25. 8	B10	E9	Sheep
26. 9	26. 8	B10	F10	Deer
27. 9	27. 8	B10	G11	Horse
28. 9	28. 8	B10	H12	Stag
29. 9	29. 8	B10	J1	Serpent
30. 9	1. 9	C11	K2	Earthworm
1.10	2. 9	C11	A3	Crocodile
2.10	3. 9	C11	B4	Dragon
3.10	4. 9	C11	C5	Badger
4.10	5. 9	C11	D6	Hare
5.10	6. 9	C11	E7	Fox
6.10	7. 9	C11	F8	Tiger
7.10	8. 9	C11	G9	Leopard
8.10	9. 9	C11	H10	Griffon
9.10	10. 9	C11	J11	Ox
10.10	11. 9	C11	K12	Bat
11.10	12. 9	C11	A1	Rat
12.10	13. 9	C11	B2	Swallow
13.10	14. 9	C11	C3	Pig
14.10	15. 9	C11	D4	Porcupine
15.10	16. 9	C11	E5	Wolf
16.10	17. 9	C11	F6	Dog
17.10	18. 9	C11	G7	Pheasant

Solar date	*Lunar date*	*Month HS/EB*	*Day HS/EB*	*Constellation*
18.10	19. 9	C11	H8	Cock
19.10	20. 9	C11	J9	Crow
20.10	21. 9	C11	K10	Monkey
21.10	22. 9	C11	A11	Gibbon
22.10	23. 9	C11	B12	Tapir
23.10	24. 9	C11	C1	Sheep
24.10	25. 9	C11	D2	Deer
25.10	26. 9	C11	E3	Horse
26.10	27. 9	C11	F4	Stag
27.10	28. 9	C11	G5	Serpent
28.10	29. 9	C11	H6	Earthworm
29.10	30. 9	C11	J7	Crocodile
30.10	1.10	D12	K8	Dragon
31.10	2.10	D12	A9	Badger
1.11	3.10	D12	B10	Hare
2.11	4.10	D12	C11	Fox
3.11	5.10	D12	D12	Tiger
4.11	6.10	D12	E1	Leopard
5.11	7.10	D12	F2	Griffon
6.11	8.10	D12	G3	Ox
7.11	9.10	D12	H4	Bat
8.11	10.10	D12	J5	Rat
9.11	11.10	D12	K6	Swallow
10.11	12.10	D12	A7	Pig
11.11	13.10	D12	B8	Porcupine
12.11	14.10	D12	C9	Wolf
13.11	15.10	D12	D10	Dog
14.11	16.10	D12	E11	Pheasant
15.11	17.10	D12	F12	Cock
16.11	18.10	D12	G1	Crow
17.11	19.10	D12	H2	Monkey
18.11	20.10	D12	J3	Gibbon
19.11	21.10	D12	K4	Tapir
20.11	22.10	D12	A5	Sheep
21.11	23.10	D12	B6	Deer
22.11	24.10	D12	C7	Horse
23.11	25.10	D12	D8	Stag
24.11	26.10	D12	E9	Serpent
25.11	27.10	D12	F10	Earthworm
26.11	28.10	D12	G11	Crocodile
27.11	29.10	D12	H12	Dragon
28.11	30.10	D12	J1	Badger
29.11	1.11	E1	K2	Hare
30.11	2.11	E1	A3	Fox
1.12	3.11	E1	B4	Tiger
2.12	4.11	E1	C5	Leopard
3.12	5.11	E1	D6	Griffon
4.12	6.11	E1	E7	Ox
5.12	7.11	E1	F8	Bat
6.12	8.11	E1	G9	Rat
7.12	9.11	E1	H10	Swallow
8.10	10.11	E1	J11	Pig

Solar date	*Lunar date*	*Month HS/EB*	*Day HS/EB*	*Constellation*
9.12	11.11	E1	K12	Porcupine
10.12	12.11	E1	A1	Wolf
11.12	13.11	E1	B2	Dog
12.12	14.11	E1	C3	Pheasant
13.12	15.11	E1	D4	Cock
14.12	16.11	E1	E5	Crow
15.12	17.11	E1	F6	Monkey
16.12	18.11	E1	G7	Gibbon
17.12	19.11	E1	H8	Tapir
18.12	20.11	E1	J9	Sheep
19.12	21.11	E1	K10	Deer
20.12	22.11	E1	A11	Horse
21.12	23.11	E1	B12	Stag
22.12	24.11	E1	C1	Serpent
23.12	25.11	E1	D2	Earthworm
24.12	26.11	E1	E3	Crocodile
25.12	27.11	E1	F4	Dragon
26.12	28.11	E1	G5	Badger
27.12	29.11	E1	H6	Hare
28.12	1.12	F2	J7	Fox
29.12	2.12	F2	K8	Tiger
30.12	3.12	F2	A9	Leopard
31.12	4.12	F2	B10	Griffon

1971

Solar date	*Lunar date*	*Month HS/EB*	*Day HS/EB*	*Constellation*
1. 1	5.12	F2	C11	Ox
2. 1	6.12	F2	D12	Bat
3. 1	7.12	F2	E1	Rat
4. 1	8.12	F2	F2	Swallow
5. 1	9.12	F2	G3	Pig
6. 1	10.12	F2	H4	Porcupine
7. 1	11.12	F2	J5	Wolf
8. 1	12.12	F2	K6	Dog
9. 1	13.12	F2	A7	Pheasant
10. 1	14.12	F2	B8	Cock
11. 1	15.12	F2	C9	Crow
12. 1	16.12	F2	D10	Monkey
13. 1	17.12	F2	E11	Gibbon
14. 1	18.12	F2	F12	Tapir
15. 1	19.12	F2	G1	Sheep
16. 1	20.12	F2	H2	Deer
17. 1	21.12	F2	J3	Horse
18. 1	22.12	F2	K4	Stag
19. 1	23.12	F2	A5	Serpent
20. 1	24.12	F2	B6	Earthworm
21. 1	25.12	F2	C7	Crocodile
22. 1	26.12	F2	D8	Dragon
23. 1	27.12	F2	E9	Badger
24. 1	28.12	F2	F10	Hare
25. 1	29.12	F2	G11	Fox
26. 1	30.12	F2	H12	Tiger

HSIN HAI YEAR

27. 1	1. 1	G3	J1	Leopard
28. 1	2. 1	G3	K2	Griffon
29. 1	3. 1	G3	A3	Ox
30. 1	4. 1	G3	B4	Bat
31. 1	5. 1	G3	C5	Rat
1. 2	6. 1	G3	D6	Swallow
2. 2	7. 1	G3	E7	Pig
3. 2	8. 1	G3	F8	Porcupine
4. 2	9. 1	G3	G9	Wolf
5. 2	10. 1	G3	H10	Dog
6. 2	11. 1	G3	J11	Pheasant
7. 2	12. 1	G3	K12	Cock
8. 2	13. 1	G3	A1	Crow
9. 2	14. 1	G3	B2	Monkey
10. 2	15. 1	G3	C3	Gibbon
11. 2	16. 1	G3	D4	Tapir
12. 2	17. 1	G3	E5	Sheep
13. 2	18. 1	G3	F6	Deer
14. 2	19. 1	G3	G7	Horse
15. 2	20. 1	G3	H8	Stag
16. 2	21. 1	G3	J9	Serpent
17. 2	22. 1	G3	K10	Earthworm
18. 2	23. 1	G3	A11	Crocodile
19. 2	24. 1	G3	B12	Dragon
20. 2	25. 1	G3	C1	Badger
21. 2	26. 1	G3	D2	Hare
22. 2	27. 1	G3	E3	Fox
23. 2	28. 1	G3	F4	Tiger
24. 2	29. 1	G3	G5	Leopard
25. 2	1. 2	H4	H6	Griffon
26. 2	2. 2	H4	J7	Ox
27. 2	3. 2	H4	K8	Bat

Solar date	*Lunar date*	*Month HS/EB*	*Day HS/EB*	*Constellation*
28. 2	4. 2	H4	A9	Rat
1. 3	5. 2	H4	B10	Swallow
2. 3	6. 2	H4	C11	Pig
3. 3	7. 2	H4	D12	Porcupine
4. 3	8. 2	H4	E1	Wolf
5. 3	9. 2	H4	F2	Dog
6. 3	10. 2	H4	G3	Pheasant
7. 3	11. 2	H4	H4	Cock
8. 3	12. 2	H4	J5	Crow
9. 3	13. 2	H4	K6	Monkey
10. 3	14. 2	H4	A7	Gibbon
11. 3	15. 2	H4	B8	Tapir
12. 3	16. 2	H4	C9	Sheep
13. 3	17. 2	H4	D10	Deer
14. 3	18. 2	H4	E11	Horse
15. 3	19. 2	H4	F12	Stag
16. 3	20. 2	H4	G1	Serpent
17. 3	21. 2	H4	H2	Earthworm
18. 3	22. 2	H4	J3	Crocodile
19. 3	23. 2	H4	K4	Dragon
20. 3	24. 2	H4	A5	Badger
21. 3	25. 2	H4	B6	Hare
22. 3	26. 2	H4	C7	Fox
23. 3	27. 2	H4	D8	Tiger
24. 3	28. 2	H4	E9	Leopard
25. 3	29. 2	H4	F10	Griffon
26. 3	30. 2	H4	G11	Ox
27. 3	1. 3	5	H12	Bat
28. 3	2. 3	J5	J1	Rat
29. 3	3. 3	J5	K2	Swallow
30. 3	4. 3	J5	A3	Pig
31. 3	5. 3	J5	B4	Porcupine
1. 4	6. 3	J5	C5	Wolf
2. 4	7. 3	J5	D6	Dog
3. 4	8. 3	J5	E7	Pheasant
4. 4	9. 3	J5	F8	Cock
5. 4	10. 3	J5	G9	Crow
6. 4	11. 3	J5	H10	Monkey
7. 4	12. 3	J5	J11	Gibbon
8. 4	13. 3	J5	K12	Tapir
9. 4	14. 3	J5	A1	Sheep
10. 4	15. 3	J5	B2	Deer
11. 4	16. 3	J5	C3	Horse
12. 4	17. 3	J5	D4	Stag
13. 4	18. 3	J5	E5	Serpent
14. 4	19. 3	J5	F6	Earthworm
15. 4	20. 3	J5	G7	Crocodile
16. 4	21. 3	J5	H8	Dragon
17. 4	22. 3	J5	J9	Badger
18. 4	23. 3	J5	K10	Hare
19. 4	24. 3	J5	A11	Fox
20. 4	25. 3	J5	B12	Tiger
21. 4	26. 3	J5	C1	Leopard
22. 4	27. 3	J5	D2	Griffon
23. 4	28. 3	J5	E3	Ox
24. 4	29. 3	J5	F4	Bat
25. 4	1. 4	K6	G5	Rat
26. 4	2. 4	K6	H6	Swallow
27. 4	3. 4	K6	J7	Pig
28. 4	4. 4	K6	K8	Porcupine
29. 4	5. 4	K6	A9	Wolf
30. 4	6. 4	K6	B10	Dog
1. 5	7. 4	K6	C11	Pheasant
2. 5	8. 4	K6	D12	Cock
3. 5	9. 4	K6	E1	Crow
4. 5	10. 4	K6	F2	Monkey
5. 5	11. 4	K6	G3	Gibbon
6. 5	12. 4	K6	H4	Tapir
7. 5	13. 4	K6	J5	Sheep
8. 5	14. 4	K6	K6	Deer
9. 5	15. 4	K6	A7	Horse
10. 5	16. 4	K6	B8	Stag
11. 5	17. 4	K6	C9	Serpent
12. 5	18. 4	K6	D10	Earthworm
13. 5	19. 4	K6	E11	Crocodile
14. 5	20. 4	K6	F12	Dragon
15. 5	21. 4	K6	G1	Badger
16. 5	22. 4	K6	H2	Hare
17. 5	23. 4	K6	J3	Fox
18. 5	24. 4	K6	K4	Tiger
19. 5	25. 4	K6	A5	Leopard
20. 5	26. 4	K6	B6	Griffon
21. 5	27. 4	K6	C7	Ox
22. 5	28. 4	K6	D8	Bat
23. 5	29. 4	K6	E9	Rat
24. 5	1. 5	A7	F10	Swallow
25. 5	2. 5	A7	G11	Pig
26. 5	3. 5	A7	H12	Porcupine
27. 5	4. 5	A7	J1	Wolf
28. 5	5. 5	A7	K2	Dog
29. 5	6. 5	A7	A3	Pheasant
30. 5	7. 5	A7	B4	Cock
31. 5	8. 5	A7	C5	Crow
1. 6	9. 5	A7	D6	Monkey
2. 6	10. 5	A7	E7	Gibbon
3. 6	11. 5	A7	F8	Tapir
4. 6	12. 5	A7	G9	Sheep
5. 6	13. 5	A7	H10	Deer
6. 6	14. 5	A7	J11	Horse
7. 6	15. 5	A7	K12	Stag
8. 6	16. 5	A7	A1	Serpent
9. 6	17. 5	A7	B2	Earthworm
10. 6	18. 5	A7	C3	Crocodile
11. 6	19. 5	A7	D4	Dragon
12. 6	20. 5	A7	E5	Badger
13. 6	21. 5	A7	F6	Hare
14. 6	22. 5	A7	G7	Fox
15. 6	23. 5	A7	H8	Tiger
16. 6	24. 5	A7	J9	Leopard
17. 6	25. 5	A7	K10	Griffon
18. 6	26. 5	A7	A11	Ox
19. 6	27. 5	A7	B12	Bat
20. 6	28. 5	A7	C1	Rat
21. 6	29. 5	A7	D2	Swallow
22. 6	30. 5	A7	E3	Pig
23. 6	*1. 5*	*A7*	F4	Porcupine
24. 6	*2. 5*	*A7*	G5	Wolf
25. 6	*3. 5*	*A7*	H6	Dog
26. 6	*4. 5*	*A7*	J7	Pheasant
27. 6	*5. 5*	*A7*	K8	Cock
28. 6	*6. 5*	*A7*	A9	Crow
29. 6	*7. 5*	*A7*	B10	Monkey
30. 6	*8. 5*	*A7*	C11	Gibbon
1. 7	*9. 5*	*A7*	D12	Tapir
2. 7	*10. 5*	*A7*	E1	Sheep
3. 7	*11. 5*	*A7*	F2	Deer
4. 7	*12. 5*	*A7*	G3	Horse
5. 7	*13. 5*	*A7*	H4	Stag
6. 7	*14. 5*	*A7*	J5	Serpent
7. 7	*15. 5*	*A7*	K6	Earthworm
8. 7	*16. 5*	*A7*	A7	Crocodile
9. 7	*17. 5*	*A7*	B8	Dragon
10. 7	*18. 5*	*A7*	C9	Badger
11. 7	*19. 5*	*A7*	D10	Hare
12. 7	*20. 5*	*A7*	E11	Fox
13. 7	*21. 5*	*A7*	F12	Tiger
14. 7	*22. 5*	*A7*	G1	Leopard
15. 7	*23. 5*	*A7*	H2	Griffon
16. 7	*24. 5*	*A7*	J3	Ox
17. 7	*25. 5*	*A7*	K4	Bat
18. 7	*26. 5*	*A7*	A5	Rat
19. 7	*27. 5*	*A7*	B6	Swallow
20. 7	*28. 5*	*A7*	C7	Pig
21. 7	*29. 5*	*A7*	D8	Porcupine
22. 7	1. 6	B8	E9	Wolf
23. 7	2. 6	B8	F10	Dog

Solar date	*Lunar date*	*Month HS/EB*	*Day HS/EB*	*Constellation*
24. 7	3. 6	B8	G11	Pheasant
25. 7	4. 6	B8	H12	Cock
26. 7	5. 6	B8	J1	Crow
27. 7	6. 6	B8	K2	Monkey
28. 7	7. 6	B8	A3	Gibbon
29. 7	8. 6	B8	B4	Tapir
30. 7	9. 6	B8	C5	Sheep
31. 7	10. 6	B8	D6	Deer
1. 8	11. 6	B8	E7	Horse
2. 8	12. 6	B8	F8	Stag
3. 8	13. 6	B8	G9	Serpent
4. 8	14. 6	B8	H10	Earthworm
5. 8	15. 6	B8	J11	Crocodile
6. 8	16. 6	B8	K12	Dragon
7. 8	17. 6	B8	A1	Badger
8. 8	18. 6	B8	B2	Hare
9. 8	19. 6	B8	C3	Fox
10. 8	20. 6	B8	D4	Tiger
11. 8	21. 6	B8	E5	Leopard
12. 8	22. 6	B8	F6	Griffon
13. 8	23. 6	B8	G7	Ox
14. 8	24. 6	B8	H8	Bat
15. 8	25. 6	B8	J9	Rat
16. 8	26. 6	B8	K10	Swallow
17. 8	27. 6	B8	A11	Pig
18. 8	28. 6	B8	B12	Porcupine
19. 8	29. 6	B8	C1	Wolf
20. 8	30. 6	B8	D2	Dog
21. 8	1. 7	C9	E3	Pheasant
22. 8	2. 7	C9	F4	Cock
23. 8	3. 7	C9	G5	Crow
24. 8	4. 7	C9	H6	Monkey
25. 8	5. 7	C9	J7	Gibbon
26. 8	6. 7	C9	K8	Tapir
27. 8	7. 7	C9	A9	Sheep
28. 8	8. 7	C9	B10	Deer
29. 8	9. 7	C9	C11	Horse
30. 8	10. 7	C9	D12	Stag
31. 8	11. 7	C9	E1	Serpent
1. 9	12. 7	C9	F2	Earthworm
2. 9	13. 7	C9	G3	Crocodile
3. 9	14. 7	C9	H4	Dragon
4. 9	15. 7	C9	J5	Badger
5. 9	16. 7	C9	K6	Hare
6. 9	17. 7	C9	A7	Fox
7. 9	18. 7	C9	B8	Tiger
8. 9	19. 7	C9	C9	Leopard
9. 9	20. 7	C9	D10	Griffon
10. 9	21. 7	C9	E11	Ox
11. 9	22. 7	C9	F12	Bat
12. 9	23. 7	C9	G1	Rat
13. 9	24. 7	C9	H2	Swallow
14. 9	25. 7	C9	J3	Pig
15. 9	26. 7	C9	K4	Porcupine
16. 9	27. 7	C9	A5	Wolf
17. 9	28. 7	C9	B6	Dog
18. 9	29. 7	C9	C7	Pheasant
19. 9	1. 8	D10	D8	Cock
20. 9	2. 8	D10	E9	Crow
21. 9	3. 8	D10	F10	Monkey
22. 9	4. 8	D10	G11	Gibbon
23. 9	5. 8	D10	H12	Tapir
24. 9	6. 8	D10	J1	Sheep
25. 9	7. 8	D10	K2	Deer
26. 9	8. 8	D10	A3	Horse
27. 9	9. 8	D10	B4	Stag
28. 9	10. 8	D10	C5	Serpent
29. 9	11. 8	D10	D6	Earthworm
30. 9	12. 8	D10	E7	Crocodile
1. 0	13. 8	D10	F8	Dragon
2.10	14. 8	D10	G9	Badger
3.10	15. 8	D10	H10	Hare
4.10	16. 8	D10	J11	Fox
5.10	17. 8	D10	K12	Tiger
6.10	18. 8	D10	A1	Leopard
7.10	19. 8	D10	B2	Griffon
8.10	20. 8	D10	C3	Ox
9.10	21. 8	D10	D4	Bat
10.10	22. 8	D10	E5	Rat
11.10	23. 8	D10	F6	Swallow
12.10	24. 8	D10	G7	Pig
13.10	25. 8	D10	H8	Porcupine
14.10	26. 8	D10	J9	Wolf
15.10	27. 8	D10	K10	Dog
16.10	28. 8	D10	A11	Pheasant
17.10	29. 8	D10	B12	Cock
18.10	30. 8	D10	C1	Crow
19.10	1. 9	E11	D2	Monkey
20.10	2. 9	E11	E3	Gibbon
21.10	3. 9	E11	F4	Tapir
22.10	4. 9	E11	G5	Sheep
23.10	5. 9	E11	H6	Deer
24.10	6. 9	E11	J7	Horse
25.10	7. 9	E11	K8	Stag
26.10	8. 9	E11	A9	Serpent
27.10	9. 9	E11	B10	Earthworm
28.10	10. 9	E11	C11	Crocodile
29.10	11. 9	E11	D12	Dragon
20.10	12. 9	E11	E1	Badger
31.10	13. 9	E11	F2	Hare
1.11	14. 9	E11	G3	Fox
2.11	15. 9	E11	H4	Tiger
3.11	16. 9	E11	J5	Leopard
4.11	17. 9	E11	K6	Griffon
5.11	18. 9	E11	A7	Ox
6.11	19. 9	E11	B8	Bat
7.11	20. 9	E11	C9	Rat
8.11	21. 9	E11	D10	Swallow
9.11	22. 9	E11	E11	Pig
10.11	23. 9	E11	F12	Porcupine
11.11	24. 9	E11	G1	Wolf
12.11	25. 9	E11	H2	Dog
13.11	26. 9	E11	J3	Pheasant
14.11	27. 9	E11	K4	Cock
15.11	28. 9	E11	A5	Crow
16.11	29. 9	E11	B6	Monkey
17.11	30. 9	E11	C7	Gibbon
18.11	1.10	F12	D8	Tapir
19.11	2.10	F12	E9	Sheep
20.11	3.10	F12	F10	Deer
21.11	4.10	F12	G11	Horse
22.11	5.10	F12	H12	Stag
23.11	6.10	F12	J1	Serpent
24.11	7.10	F12	K2	Earthworm
25.11	8.10	F12	A3	Crocodile
26.11	9.10	F12	B4	Dragon
27.11	10.10	F12	C5	Badger
28.11	11.10	F12	D6	Hare
29.11	12.10	F12	E7	Fox
30.11	13.10	F12	F8	Tiger
1.12	14.10	F12	G9	Leopard
2.12	15.10	F12	H10	Griffon
3.12	16.10	F12	J11	Ox
4.12	17.10	F12	K12	Bat
5.12	18.10	F12	A1	Rat
6.12	19.10	F12	B2	Swallow
7.12	20.10	F12	C3	Pig
8.12	21.10	F12	D4	Porcupine
9.12	22.10	F12	E5	Wolf
10.12	23.10	F12	F6	Dog
11.12	24.10	F12	G7	Pheasant
12.12	25.10	F12	H8	Cock
13.12	26.10	F12	J9	Crow
14.12	27.10	F12	K10	Monkey
15.12	28.10	F12	A11	Gibbon
16.12	29.10	F12	B12	Tapir

Solar date	*Lunar date*	*Month HS/EB*	*Day HS/EB*	*Constellation*
17.12	30.10	F12	C1	Sheep
18.12	1.11	G1	D2	Deer
19.12	2.11	G1	E3	Horse
20.12	3.11	G1	F4	Stag
21.12	4.11	G1	G5	Serpent
22.12	5.11	G1	H6	Earthworm
23.12	6.11	G1	J7	Crocodile
24.12	7.11	G1	K8	Dragon
25.12	8.11	G1	A9	Badger
26.12	9.11	G1	B10	Hare
27.12	10.11	G1	C11	Fox
28.12	11.11	G1	D12	Tiger
29.12	12.11	G1	E1	Leopard
30.12	13.11	G1	F2	Griffon
31.12	14.11	G1	G3	Ox
1972				
1. 1	15.11	G1	H4	Bat
2. 1	16.11	G1	J5	Rat
3. 1	17.11	G1	K6	Swallow
4. 1	18.11	G1	A7	Pig
5. 1	19.11	G1	B8	Porcupine
6. 1	20.11	G1	C9	Wolf
7. 1	21.11	G1	D10	Dog
8. 1	22.11	G1	E11	Pheasant
9. 1	23.11	G1	F12	Cock
10. 1	24.11	G1	G1	Crow
11. 1	25.11	G1	H2	Monkey
12. 1	26.11	G1	J3	Gibbon
13. 1	27.11	G1	K4	Tapir
14. 1	28.11	G1	A5	Sheep
15. 1	29.11	G1	B6	Deer
16. 1	1.12	H2	C7	Horse
17. 1	2.12	H2	D8	Stag
18. 1	3.12	H2	E9	Serpent
19. 1	4.12	H2	F10	Earthworm
20. 1	5.12	H2	G11	Crocodile
21. 1	6.12	H2	H12	Dragon
22. 1	7.12	H2	J1	Badger
23. 1	8.12	H2	K2	Hare
24. 1	9.12	H2	A3	Fox
25. 1	10.12	H2	B4	Tiger
26. 1	11.12	H2	C5	Leopard
27. 1	12.12	H2	D6	Griffon
28. 1	13.12	H2	E7	Ox
29. 1	14.12	H2	F8	Bat
30. 1	15.12	H2	G9	Rat
31. 1	16.12	H2	H10	Swallow
1. 2	17.12	H2	J11	Pig
2. 2	18.12	H2	K12	Porcupine
3. 2	19.12	H2	A1	Wolf
4. 2	20.12	H2	B2	Dog
5. 2	21.12	H2	C3	Pheasant
6. 2	22.12	H2	D4	Cock
7. 2	23.12	H2	E5	Crow
8. 2	24.12	H2	F6	Monkey
9. 2	25.12	H2	G7	Gibbon
10. 2	26.12	H2	H8	Tapir
11. 2	27.12	H2	J9	Sheep
12. 2	28.12	H2	K10	Deer
13. 2	29.12	H2	A11	Horse
14. 2	30.12	H2	B12	Stag

JEN TZU YEAR

15. 2	1. 1	J3	C1	Serpent
16. 2	2. 1	J3	D2	Earthworm
17. 2	3. 1	J3	E3	Crocodile
18. 2	4. 1	J3	F4	Dragon
19. 2	5. 1	J3	G5	Badger
20. 2	6. 1	J3	H6	Hare
21. 2	7. 1	J3	J7	Fox
22. 2	8. 1	J3	K8	Tiger
23. 2	9. 1	J3	A9	Leopard
24. 2	10. 1	J3	B10	Griffon
25. 2	11. 1	J3	C11	Ox
26. 2	12. 1	J3	D12	Bat
27. 2	13. 1	J3	E1	Rat
28. 2	14. 1	J3	F2	Swallow
29. 2	15. 1	J3	G3	Pig
1. 3	16. 1	J3	H4	Porcupine
2. 3	17. 1	J3	J5	Wolf
3. 3	18. 1	J3	K6	Dog
4. 3	19. 1	J3	A7	Pheasant
5. 3	20. 1	J3	B8	Cock
6. 3	21. 1	J3	C9	Crow
7. 3	22. 1	J3	D10	Monkey
8. 3	23. 1	J3	E11	Gibbon
9. 3	24. 1	J3	F12	Tapir
10. 3	25. 1	J3	G1	Sheep
11. 3	26. 1	J3	H2	Deer
12. 3	27. 1	J3	J3	Horse
13. 3	28. 1	J3	K4	Stag
14. 3	29. 1	J3	A5	Serpent
15. 3	1. 2	K4	B6	Earthworm
16. 3	2. 2	K4	C7	Crocodile
17. 3	3. 2	K4	D8	Dragon
18. 3	4. 2	K4	E9	Badger
19. 3	5. 2	K4	F10	Hare
20. 3	6. 2	K4	G11	Fox
21. 3	7. 2	K4	H12	Tiger
22. 3	8. 2	K4	J1	Leopard
23. 3	9. 2	K4	K2	Griffon
24. 3	10. 2	K4	A3	Ox
25. 3	11. 2	K4	B4	Bat
26. 3	12. 2	K4	C5	Rat
27. 3	13. 2	K4	D6	Swallow
28. 3	14. 2	K4	E7	Pig
29. 3	15. 2	K4	F8	Porcupine
30. 3	16. 2	K4	G9	Wolf
31. 3	17. 2	K4	H10	Dog
1. 4	18. 2	K4	J11	Pheasant
2. 4	19. 2	K4	K12	Cock
3. 2	20. 2	K4	A1	Crow
4. 4	21. 2	K4	B2	Monkey
5. 4	22. 2	K4	C3	Gibbon
6. 4	23. 2	K4	D4	Tapir
7. 4	24. 2	K4	E5	Sheep
8. 4	25. 2	K4	F6	Deer
9. 4	26. 2	K4	G7	Horse
10. 4	27. 2	K4	H8	Stag
11. 4	28. 2	K4	J9	Serpent
12. 4	29. 2	K4	K10	Earthworm
13. 4	30. 2	K4	A11	Crocodile
14. 4	1. 3	A5	B12	Dragon
15. 4	2. 3	A5	C1	Badger
16. 4	3. 3	A5	D2	Hare
17. 4	4. 3	A5	E3	Fox
18. 4	5. 3	A5	F4	Tiger
19. 4	6. 3	A5	G5	Leopard
20. 4	7. 3	A5	H6	Griffon
21. 4	8. 3	A5	J7	Ox
22. 4	9. 3	A5	K8	Bat
23. 4	10. 3	A5	A9	Rat
24. 4	11. 3	A5	B10	Swallow
25. 4	12. 3	A5	C11	Pig
26. 4	13. 3	A5	D12	Porcupine
27. 4	14. 3	A5	E1	Wolf
28. 4	15. 3	A5	F2	Dog

Solar date	*Lunar date*	*Month HS/EB*	*Day HS/EB*	*Constellation*	*Solar date*	*Lunar date*	*Month HS/EB*	*Day HS/EB*	*Constellation*
29. 4	16. 3	A5	G3	Pheasant	11. 7	1. 6	D8	K4	Tiger
30. 4	17. 3	A5	H4	Cock	12. 7	2. 6	D8	A5	Leopard
1. 5	18. 3	A5	J5	Crow	13. 7	3. 6	D8	B6	Griffon
2. 5	19. 3	A5	K6	Monkey	14. 7	4. 6	D8	C7	Ox
3. 5	20. 3	A5	A7	Gibbon	15. 7	5. 6	D8	D8	Bat
4. 5	21. 3	A5	B8	Tapir	16. 7	6. 6	D8	E9	Rat
5. 5	22. 3	A5	C9	Sheep	17. 7	7. 6	D8	F10	Swallow
6. 5	23. 3	A5	D10	Deer	18. 7	8. 6	D8	G11	Pig
7. 5	24. 3	A5	E11	Horse	19. 7	9. 6	D8	H12	Porcupine
8. 5	25. 3	A5	F12	Stag	20. 7	10. 6	D8	J1	Wolf
9. 5	26. 3	A5	G1	Serpent	21. 7	11. 6	D8	K2	Dog
10. 5	27. 3	A5	H2	Earthworm	22. 7	12. 6	D8	A3	Pheasant
11. 5	28. 3	A5	J3	Crocodile	23. 7	13. 6	D8	B4	Cock
12. 5	29. 3	A5	K4	Dragon	24. 7	14. 6	D8	C5	Crow
13. 5	1. 4	B6	A5	Badger	25. 7	15. 6	D8	D6	Monkey
14. 5	2. 4	B6	B6	Hare	26. 7	16. 6	D8	E7	Gibbon
15. 5	3. 4	B6	C7	Fox	27. 7	17. 6	D8	F8	Tapir
16. 5	4. 4	B6	D8	Tiger	28. 7	18. 6	D8	G9	Sheep
17. 5	5. 4	B6	E9	Leopard	29. 7	19. 6	D8	H10	Deer
18. 5	6. 4	B6	F10	Griffon	30. 7	20. 6	D8	J11	Horse
19. 5	7. 4	B6	G11	Ox	31. 7	21. 6	D8	K12	Stag
20. 5	8. 4	B6	H12	Bat	1. 8	22. 6	D8	A1	Serpent
21. 5	9. 4	B6	J1	Rat	2. 8	23. 6	D8	B2	Earthworm
22. 5	10. 4	B6	K2	Swallow	3. 8	24. 6	D8	C3	Crocodile
23. 5	11. 4	B6	A3	Pig	4. 8	25. 6	D8	D4	Dragon
24. 5	12. 4	B6	B4	Porcupine	5. 8	26. 6	D8	E5	Badger
25. 5	13. 4	B6	C5	Wolf	6. 8	27. 6	D8	F6	Hare
26. 5	14. 4	B6	D6	Dog	7. 8	28. 6	D8	G7	Fox
27. 5	15. 4	B6	E7	Pheasant	8. 8	29. 6	D8	H8	Tiger
28. 5	16. 4	B6	F8	Cock	9. 8	1. 7	E9	J9	Leopard
29. 5	17. 4	B6	G9	Crow	10. 8	2. 7	E9	K10	Griffon
30. 5	18. 4	B6	H10	Monkey	11. 8	3. 7	E9	A11	Ox
31. 5	19. 4	B6	J11	Gibbon	12. 8	4. 7	E9	B12	Bat
1. 6	20. 4	B6	K12	Tapir	13. 8	5. 7	E9	C1	Rat
2. 6	21. 4	B6	A1	Sheep	14. 8	6. 7	E9	D2	Swallow
3. 6	22. 4	B6	B2	Deer	15. 8	7. 7	E9	E3	Pig
4. 6	23. 4	B6	C3	Horse	16. 8	8. 7	E9	F4	Porcupine
5. 6	24. 4	B6	D4	Stag	17. 8	9. 7	E9	G5	Wolf
6. 6	25. 4	B6	E5	Serpent	18. 8	10. 7	E9	H6	Dog
7. 6	26. 4	B6	F6	Earthworm	19. 8	11. 7	E9	J7	Pheasant
8. 6	27. 4	B6	G7	Crocodile	20. 8	12. 7	E9	K8	Cock
9. 6	28. 4	B6	H8	Dragon	21. 8	13. 7	E9	A9	Crow
10. 6	29. 4	B6	J9	Badger	22. 8	14. 7	E9	B10	Monkey
11. 6	1. 5	C7	K10	Hare	23. 8	15. 7	E9	C11	Gibbon
12. 6	2. 5	C7	A11	Fox	24. 8	16. 7	E9	D12	Tapir
13. 6	3. 5	C7	B12	Tiger	25. 8	17. 7	E9	E1	Sheep
14. 6	4. 5	C7	C1	Leopard	26. 8	18. 7	E9	F2	Deer
15. 6	5. 5	C7	D2	Griffon	27. 8	19. 7	E9	G3	Horse
16. 6	6. 5	C7	E3	Ox	28. 8	20. 7	E9	H4	Stag
17. 6	7. 5	C7	F4	Bat	29. 8	21. 7	E9	J5	Serpent
18. 6	8. 5	C7	G5	Rat	30. 8	22. 7	E9	K6	Earthworm
19. 6	9. 5	C7	H6	Swallow	31. 8	23. 7	E9	A7	Crocodile
20. 6	10. 5	C7	J7	Pig	1. 9	24. 7	E9	B8	Dragon
21. 6	11. 5	C7	K8	Porcupine	2. 9	25. 7	E9	C9	Badger
22. 6	12. 5	C7	A9	Wolf	3. 9	26. 7	E9	D10	Hare
23. 6	13. 5	C7	B10	Dog	4. 9	27. 7	E9	E11	Fox
24. 6	14. 5	C7	C11	Pheasant	5. 9	28. 7	E9	F12	Tiger
25. 6	15. 5	C7	D12	Cock	6. 9	29. 7	E9	G1	Leopard
26. 6	16. 5	C7	E1	Crow	7. 9	30. 7	E9	H2	Griffon
27. 6	17. 5	C7	F2	Monkey	8. 9	1. 8	F10	J3	Ox
28. 6	18. 5	C7	G3	Gibbon	9. 9	2. 8	F10	K4	Bat
29. 6	19. 5	C7	H4	Tapir	10. 9	3. 8	F10	A5	Rat
30. 6	20. 5	C7	J5	Sheep	11. 9	4. 8	F10	B6	Swallow
1. 7	21. 5	C7	K6	Deer	12. 9	5. 8	F10	C7	Pig
2. 7	22. 5	C7	A7	Horse	13. 9	6. 8	F10	D8	Porcupine
3. 7	23. 5	C7	B8	Stag	14. 9	7. 8	F10	E9	Wolf
4. 7	24. 5	C7	C9	Serpent	15. 9	8. 8	F10	F10	Dog
5. 7	25. 5	C7	D10	Earthworm	16. 9	9. 8	F10	G11	Pheasant
6. 7	26. 5	C7	E11	Crocodile	17. 9	10. 8	F10	H12	Cock
7. 7	27. 5	C7	F12	Dragon	18. 9	11. 8	F10	J1	Crow
8. 7	28. 5	C7	G1	Badger	19. 9	12. 8	F10	K2	Monkey
9. 7	29. 5	C7	H2	Hare	20. 9	13. 8	F10	A3	Gibbon
10. 7	30. 5	C7	J3	Fox	21. 9	14. 8	F10	B4	Tapir

Solar date	*Lunar date*	*Month HS/EB*	*Day HS/EB*	*Constellation*
22. 9	15. 8	F10	C5	Sheep
23. 9	16. 8	F10	D6	Deer
24. 9	17. 8	F10	E7	Horse
25. 9	18. 8	F10	F8	Stag
26. 9	19. 8	F10	G9	Serpent
27. 9	20. 8	F10	H10	Earthworm
28. 9	21. 8	F10	J11	Crocodile
29. 9	22. 8	F10	K12	Dragon
30. 9	23. 8	F10	A1	Badger
1.10	24. 8	F10	B2	Hare
2.10	25. 8	F10	C3	Fox
3.10	26. 8	F10	D4	Tiger
4.10	27. 8	F10	E5	Leopard
5.10	28. 8	F10	F6	Griffon
6.10	29. 8	F10	G7	Ox
7.10	1. 9	G11	H8	Bat
8.10	2. 9	G11	J9	Rat
9.10	3. 9	G11	K10	Swallow
10.10	4. 9	G11	A11	Pig
11.10	5. 9	G11	B12	Porcupine
12.10	6. 9	G11	C1	Wolf
13.10	7. 9	G11	D2	Dog
14.10	8. 9	G11	E3	Pheasant
15.10	9. 9	G11	F4	Cock
16.10	10. 9	G11	G5	Crow
17.10	11. 9	G11	H6	Monkey
18.10	12. 9	G11	J7	Gibbon
19.10	13. 9	G11	K8	Tapir
20.10	14. 9	G11	A9	Sheep
21.10	15. 9	G11	B10	Deer
22.10	16. 9	G11	C11	Horse
23.10	17. 9	G11	D12	Stag
24.10	18. 9	G11	E1	Serpent
25.10	19. 9	G11	F2	Earthworm
26.10	20. 9	G11	G3	Crocodile
27.10	21. 9	G11	H4	Dragon
28.10	22. 9	G11	J5	Badger
29.10	23. 9	G11	K6	Hare
30.10	24. 9	G11	A7	Fox
31.10	25. 9	G11	B8	Tiger
1.11	26. 9	G11	C9	Leopard
2.11	27. 9	G11	D10	Griffon
3.11	28. 9	G11	E1	Ox
4.11	29. 9	G11	F12	Bat
5.11	30. 9	G11	G1	Rat
6.11	1.10	H12	H2	Swallow
7.11	2.10	H12	J3	Pig
8.11	3.10	H12	K4	Porcupine
9.11	4.10	H12	A5	Wolf
10.11	5.10	H12	B6	Dog
11.11	6.10	H12	C7	Pheasant
12.11	7.10	H12	D8	Cock
13.11	8.10	H12	E9	Crow
14.11	9.10	H12	F10	Monkey
15.11	10.10	H12	G11	Gibbon
16.11	11.10	H12	H12	Tapir
17.11	12.10	H12	J1	Sheep
18.11	13.10	H12	K2	Deer
19.11	14.10	H12	A3	Horse
20.11	15.10	H12	B4	Stag
21.11	16.10	H12	C5	Serpent
22.11	17.10	H12	D6	Earthworm
23.11	18.10	H12	E7	Crocodile
24.11	19.10	H12	F8	Dragon
25.11	20.10	H12	G9	Badger
26.11	21.10	H12	H10	Hare
27.11	22.10	H12	J11	Fox
28.11	23.10	H12	K12	Tiger
29.11	24.10	H12	A1	Leopard
30.11	25.10	H12	B2	Griffon
1.12	26.10	H12	C3	Ox
2.12	27.10	H12	D4	Bat
3.12	28.10	H12	E5	Rat
4.12	29.10	H12	F6	Swallow
5.12	30.10	H12	G7	Pig
6.12	1.11	J1	H8	Porcupine
7.12	2.11	J1	J9	Wolf
8.12	3.11	J1	K10	Dog
9.12	4.11	J1	A11	Pheasant
10.12	5.11	J1	B12	Cock
11.12	6.11	J1	C1	Crow
12.12	7.11	J1	D2	Monkey
13.12	8.11	J1	E3	Gibbon
14.12	9.11	J1	F4	Tapir
15.12	10.11	J1	G5	Sheep
16.12	11.11	J1	H6	Deer
17.12	12.11	J1	J7	Horse
18.12	13.11	J1	K8	Stag
19.12	14.11	J1	A9	Serpent
20.12	15.11	J1	B10	Earthworm
21.12	16.11	J1	C11	Crocodile
22.12	17.11	J1	D12	Dragon
23.12	18.11	J1	E1	Badger
24.12	19.11	J1	F2	Hare
25.12	20.11	J1	G3	Fox
26.12	21.11	J1	H4	Tiger
27.12	22.11	J1	J5	Leopard
28.12	23.11	J1	K6	Griffon
29.12	24.11	J1	A7	Ox
30.12	25.11	J1	B8	Bat
31.12	26.11	J1	C9	Rat
1973				
1. 1	27.11	J1	D10	Swallow
2. 1	28.11	J1	E11	Pig
3. 1	29.11	J1	F12	Porcupine
4. 1	1.12	K2	G1	Wolf
5. 1	2.12	K2	H2	Dog
6. 1	3.12	K2	J3	Pheasant
7. 1	4.12	K2	K4	Cock
8. 1	5.12	K2	A5	Crow
9. 1	6.12	K2	B6	Monkey
10. 1	7.12	K2	C7	Gibbon
11. 1	8.12	K2	D8	Tapir
12. 1	9.12	K2	E9	Sheep
13. 1	10.12	K2	F10	Deer
14. 1	11.12	K2	G11	Horse
15. 1	12.12	K2	H12	Stag
16. 1	13.12	K2	J1	Serpent
17. 1	14.12	K2	K2	Earthworm
18. 1	15.12	K2	A3	Crocodile
19. 1	16.12	K2	B4	Dragon
20. 1	17.12	K2	C5	Badger
21. 1	18.12	K2	D6	Hare
22. 1	19.12	K2	E7	Fox
23. 1	20.12	K2	F8	Tiger
24. 1	21.12	K2	G9	Leopard
25. 1	22.12	K2	H10	Griffon
26. 1	23.12	K2	J11	Ox
27. 1	24.12	K2	K12	Bat
28. 1	25.12	K2	A1	Rat
29. 1	26.12	K2	B2	Swallow
30. 1	27.12	K2	C3	Pig
31. 1	28.12	K2	D4	Porcupine
1. 2	29.12	K2	E5	Wolf
2. 2	30.12	K2	F6	Dog

KUEI CH'OU YEAR

Solar date	Lunar date	Month HS/EB	Day HS/EB	Constellation
3. 2	1. 1	A3	G7	Pheasant
4. 2	2. 1	A3	H8	Cock
5. 2	3. 1	A3	J9	Crow
6. 2	4. 1	A3	K10	Monkey
7. 2	5. 1	A3	A11	Gibbon
8. 2	6. 1	A3	B12	Tapir
9. 2	7. 1	A3	C1	Sheep
10. 2	8. 1	A3	D2	Deer
11. 2	9. 1	A3	E3	Horse
12. 2	10. 1	A3	F4	Stag
13. 2	11. 1	A3	G5	Serpent
14. 2	12. 1	A3	H6	Earthworm
15. 2	13. 1	A3	J7	Crocodile
16. 2	14. 1	A3	K8	Dragon
17. 2	15. 1	A3	A9	Badger
18. 2	16. 1	A3	B10	Hare
19. 2	17. 1	A3	C11	Fox
20. 2	18. 1	A3	D12	Tiger
21. 2	19. 1	A3	E1	Leopard
22. 2	20. 1	A3	F2	Griffon
23. 2	21. 1	A3	G3	Ox
24. 2	22. 1	A3	H4	Bat
25. 2	23. 1	A3	J5	Rat
26. 2	24. 1	A3	K6	Swallow
27. 2	25. 1	A3	A7	Pig
28. 2	26. 1	A3	B8	Porcupine
1. 3	27. 1	A3	C9	Wolf
2. 3	28. 1	A3	D10	Dog
3. 3	29. 1	A3	E11	Pheasant
4. 3	30. 1	A3	F12	Cock
5. 3	1. 2	B4	G1	Crow
6. 3	2. 2	B4	H2	Monkey
7. 3	3. 2	B4	J3	Gibbon
8. 3	4. 2	B4	K4	Tapir
9. 3	5. 2	B4	A5	Sheep
10. 3	6. 2	B4	B6	Deer
11. 3	7. 2	B4	C7	Horse
12. 3	8. 2	B4	D8	Stag
13. 3	9. 2	B4	E9	Serpent
14. 3	10. 2	B4	F10	Earthworm
15. 3	11. 2	B4	G11	Crocodile
16. 3	12. 2	B4	H12	Dragon
17. 3	13. 2	B4	J1	Badger
18. 3	14. 2	B4	K2	Hare
19. 3	15. 2	B4	A3	Fox
20. 3	16. 2	B4	B4	Tiger
21. 3	17. 2	B4	C5	Leopard
22. 3	18. 2	B4	D6	Griffon
23. 3	19. 2	B4	E7	Ox
24. 3	20. 2	B4	F8	Bat
25. 3	21. 2	B4	G9	Rat
26. 3	22. 2	B4	H10	Swallow
27. 3	23. 2	B4	J11	Pig
28. 3	24. 2	B4	K12	Porcupine
29. 3	25. 2	B4	A1	Wolf
30. 3	26. 2	B4	B2	Dog
31. 3	27. 2	B4	C3	Pheasant
1. 4	28. 2	B4	D4	Cock
2. 4	29. 2	B4	E5	Crow
3. 4	1. 3	C5	F6	Monkey
4. 4	2. 3	C5	G7	Gibbon
5. 4	3. 3	C5	H8	Tapir
6. 4	4. 3	C5	J9	Sheep
7. 4	5. 3	C5	K10	Deer
8. 4	6. 3	C5	A11	Horse
9. 4	7. 3	C5	B12	Stag
10. 4	8. 3	C5	C1	Serpent
11. 4	9. 3	C5	D2	Earthworm
12. 4	10. 3	C5	E3	Crocodile
13. 4	11. 3	C5	F4	Dragon
14. 4	12. 3	C5	G5	Badger
15. 4	13. 3	C5	H6	Hare
16. 4	14. 3	C5	J7	Fox
17. 4	15. 3	C5	K8	Tiger
18. 4	16. 3	C5	A9	Leopard
19. 4	17. 3	C5	B10	Griffon
20. 4	18. 3	C5	C11	Ox
21. 4	19. 3	C5	D12	Bat
22. 4	20. 3	C5	E1	Rat
23. 4	21. 3	C5	F2	Swallow
24. 4	22. 3	C5	G3	Pig
25. 4	23. 3	C5	H4	Porcupine
26. 4	24. 3	C5	J5	Wolf
27. 4	25. 3	C5	K6	Dog
28. 4	26. 3	C5	A7	Pheasant
29. 4	27. 3	C5	B8	Cock
30. 4	28. 3	C5	C9	Crow
1. 5	29. 3	C5	D10	Monkey
2. 5	30. 3	C5	E11	Gibbon
3. 5	1. 4	D6	F12	Tapir
4. 5	2. 4	D6	G1	Sheep
5. 5	3. 4	D6	H2	Deer
6. 5	4. 4	D6	J3	Horse
7. 5	5. 4	D6	K4	Stag
8. 5	6. 4	D6	A5	Serpent
9. 5	7. 4	D6	B6	Earthworm
10. 5	8. 4	D6	C7	Crocodile
11. 5	9. 4	D6	D8	Dragon
12. 5	10. 4	D6	E9	Badger
13. 5	11. 4	D6	F10	Hare
14. 5	12. 4	D6	G11	Fox
15. 5	13. 4	D6	H12	Tiger
16. 5	14. 4	D6	J1	Leopard
17. 5	15. 4	D6	K2	Griffon
18. 5	16. 4	D6	A3	Ox
19. 5	17. 4	D6	B4	Bat
20. 5	18. 4	D6	C5	Rat
21. 5	19. 4	D6	D6	Swallow
22. 5	20. 4	D6	E7	Pig
23. 5	21. 4	D6	F8	Porcupine
24. 5	22. 4	D6	G9	Wolf
25. 5	23. 4	D6	H10	Dog
26. 5	24. 4	D6	J11	Pheasant
27. 5	25. 4	D6	K12	Cock
28. 5	26. 4	D6	A1	Crow
29. 5	27. 4	D6	B2	Monkey
30. 5	28. 4	D4	C3	Gibbon
31. 5	29. 4	D6	D4	Tapir
1. 6	1. 5	E7	E5	Sheep
2. 6	2. 5	E7	F6	Deer
3. 6	3. 5	E7	G7	Horse
4. 6	4. 5	E7	H8	Stag
5. 6	5. 5	E7	J9	Serpent
6. 6	6. 5	E7	K10	Earthworm
7. 6	7. 5	E7	A11	Crocodile
8. 6	8. 5	E7	B12	Dragon
9. 6	9. 5	E7	C1	Badger
10. 6	10. 5	E7	D2	Hare
11. 6	11. 5	E7	E3	Fox
12. 6	12. 5	E7	F4	Tiger
13. 6	13. 5	E7	G5	Leopard
14. 6	14. 5	E7	H6	Griffon
15. 6	15. 5	E7	J7	Ox
16. 6	16. 5	E7	K8	Bat
17. 6	17. 5	E7	A9	Rat
18. 6	18. 5	E7	B10	Swallow
19. 6	19. 5	E7	C11	Pig
20. 6	20. 5	E7	D12	Porcupine
21. 6	21. 5	E7	E1	Wolf
22. 6	22. 5	E7	F2	Dog
23. 6	23. 5	E7	G3	Pheasant
24. 6	24. 5	E7	H4	Cock

Solar date	*Lunar date*	*Month HS/EB*	*Day HS/EB*	*Constellation*
25. 6	25. 5	E7	J5	Crow
26. 6	26. 5	E7	K6	Monkey
27. 6	27. 5	E7	A7	Gibbon
28. 6	28. 5	E7	B8	Tapir
29. 6	29. 5	E7	C9	Sheep
30. 6	1. 6	F8	D10	Deer
1. 7	2. 6	F8	E11	Horse
2. 7	3. 6	F8	F12	Stag
3. 7	4. 6	F8	G1	Serpent
4. 7	5. 6	F8	H2	Earthworm
5. 7	6. 6	F8	J3	Crocodile
6. 7	7. 6	F8	K4	Dragon
7. 7	8. 6	F8	A5	Badger
8. 7	9. 6	F8	B6	Hare
9. 7	10. 6	F8	C7	Fox
10. 7	11. 6	F8	D8	Tiger
11. 7	12. 6	F8	E9	Leopard
12. 7	13. 6	F8	F10	Griffon
13. 7	14. 6	F8	G11	Ox
14. 7	15. 6	F8	H12	Bat
15. 7	16. 6	F8	J1	Rat
16. 7	17. 6	F8	K2	Swallow
17. 7	18. 6	F8	A3	Pig
18. 7	19. 6	F8	B4	Porcupine
19. 7	20. 6	F8	C5	Wolf
20. 7	21. 6	F8	D6	Dog
21. 7	22. 6	F8	E7	Pheasant
22. 7	23. 6	F8	F8	Cock
23. 7	24. 6	F8	G9	Crow
24. 7	25. 6	F8	H10	Monkey
25. 7	26. 6	F8	J11	Gibbon
26. 7	27. 6	F8	K12	Tapir
27. 7	28. 6	F8	A1	Sheep
28. 7	29. 6	F8	B2	Deer
29. 7	30. 6	F8	C3	Horse
30. 7	1. 7	G9	D4	Stag
31. 7	2. 7	G9	E5	Serpent
1. 8	3. 7	G9	F6	Earthworm
2. 8	4. 7	G9	G7	Crocodile
3. 8	5. 7	G9	H8	Dragon
4. 8	6. 7	G9	J9	Badger
5. 8	7. 7	G9	K10	Hare
6. 8	8. 7	G9	A11	Fox
7. 8	9. 7	G9	B12	Tiger
8. 8	10. 7	G9	C1	Leopard
9. 8	11. 7	G9	D2	Griffon
10. 8	12. 7	G9	E3	Ox
11. 8	13. 7	G9	F4	Bat
12. 8	14. 7	G9	G5	Rat
13. 8	15. 7	G9	H6	Swallow
14. 8	16. 7	G9	J7	Pig
15. 8	17. 7	G9	K8	Porcupine
16. 8	18. 7	G9	A9	Wolf
17. 8	19. 7	G9	B10	Dog
18. 8	20. 7	G9	C11	Pheasant
19. 8	21. 7	G9	D12	Cock
20. 8	22. 7	G9	E1	Crow
21. 8	23. 7	G9	F2	Monkey
22. 8	24. 7	G9	G3	Gibbon
23. 8	25. 7	G9	H4	Tapir
24. 8	26. 7	G9	J5	Sheep
25. 8	27. 7	G9	K6	Deer
26. 8	28. 7	G9	A7	Horse
27. 8	29. 7	G9	B8	Stag
28. 8	1. 8	H10	C9	Serpent
29. 8	2. 8	H10	D10	Earthworm
30. 8	3. 8	H10	E11	Crocodile
31. 8	4. 8	H10	F12	Dragon
1. 9	5. 8	H10	G1	Badger
2. 9	6. 8	H10	H2	Hare
3. 9	7. 8	H10	J3	Fox
4. 9	8. 8	H10	K4	Tiger
5. 9	9. 8	H10	A5	Leopard
6. 9	10. 8	H10	B6	Griffon
7. 9	11. 8	H10	C7	Ox
8. 9	12. 8	H10	D8	Bat
9. 9	13. 8	H10	E9	Rat
10. 9	14. 8	H10	F10	Swallow
11. 9	15. 8	H10	G11	Pig
12. 9	16. 8	H10	H12	Porcupine
13. 9	17. 8	H10	J1	Wolf
14. 9	18. 8	H10	K2	Dog
15. 9	19. 8	H10	A3	Pheasant
16. 9	20. 8	H10	B4	Cock
17. 9	21. 8	H10	C5	Crow
18. 9	22. 8	H10	D6	Monkey
19. 9	23. 8	H10	E7	Gibbon
20. 9	24. 8	H10	F8	Tapir
21. 9	25. 8	H10	G9	Sheep
22. 9	26. 8	H10	H10	Deer
23. 9	27. 8	H10	J11	Horse
24. 9	28. 8	H10	K12	Stag
25. 9	29. 8	H10	A1	Serpent
26. 9	1. 9	J11	B2	Earthworm
27. 9	2. 9	J11	C3	Crocodile
28. 9	3. 9	J11	D4	Dragon
29. 9	4. 9	J11	E5	Badger
30. 9	5. 9	J11	F6	Hare
1.10	6. 9	J11	G7	Fox
2.10	7. 9	J11	H8	Tiger
3.10	8. 9	J11	J9	Leopard
4.10	9. 9	J11	K10	Griffon
5.10	10. 9	J11	A11	Ox
6.10	11. 9	J11	B12	Bat
7.10	12. 9	J11	C1	Rat
8.10	13. 9	J11	D2	Swallow
9.10	14. 9	J11	E3	Pig
10.10	15. 9	J11	F4	Porcupine
11. 0	16. 9	J11	G5	Wolf
12.10	17. 9	J11	H6	Dog
13.10	18. 9	J11	J7	Pheasant
14.10	19. 9	J11	K8	Cock
15.10	20. 9	J11	A9	Crow
16.10	21. 9	J11	B10	Monkey
17.10	22. 9	J11	C11	Gibbon
18.10	23. 9	J11	D12	Tapir
19.10	24. 9	J11	E1	Sheep
20.10	25. 9	J11	F2	Deer
21.10	26. 9	J11	G3	Horse
22.10	27. 9	J11	H4	Stag
23.10	28. 9	J11	J5	Serpent
24.10	29. 9	J11	K6	Earthworm
25.10	30. 9	J11	A7	Crocodile
26.10	1.10	K12	B8	Dragon
27.10	2.10	K12	C9	Badger
28.10	3.10	K12	D10	Hare
29.10	4.10	K12	E11	Fox
30.10	5.10	K12	F12	Tiger
31.10	6.10	K12	G1	Leopard
1.11	7.10	K12	H2	Griffon
2.11	8.10	K12	J3	Ox
3.11	9.10	K12	K4	Bat
4.11	10.10	K12	A5	Rat
5.11	11.10	K12	B6	Swallow
6.11	12.10	K12	C7	Pig
7.11	13.10	K12	D8	Porcupine
8.11	14.10	K12	E9	Wolf
9.11	15.10	K12	F10	Dog
10.11	16.10	K12	G11	Pheasant
11.11	17.10	K12	H12	Cock
12.11	18.10	K12	J1	Crow
13.11	19.10	K12	K2	Monkey
14.11	20.10	K12	A3	Gibbon
15.11	21.10	K12	B4	Tapir
16.11	22.10	K12	C5	Sheep
17.11	23.10	K12	D6	Deer

Solar date	*Lunar date*	*Month HS/EB*	*Day HS/EB*	*Constellation*
18.11	24.10	K12	E7	Horse
19.11	25.10	K12	F8	Stag
20.11	26.10	K12	G9	Serpent
21.11	27.10	K12	H10	Earthworm
22.11	28.10	K12	J11	Crocodile
23.11	29.10	K12	K12	Dragon
24.11	30.10	K12	A1	Badger
25.11	1.11	A1	B2	Hare
26.11	2.11	A1	C3	Fox
27.11	3.11	A1	D4	Tiger
28.11	4.11	A1	E5	Leopard
29.11	5.11	A1	F6	Griffon
30.11	6.11	A1	G7	Ox
1.12	7.11	A1	H8	Bat
2.12	8.11	A1	J9	Rat
3.12	9.11	A1	K10	Swallow
4.12	10.11	A1	A11	Pig
5.12	11.11	A1	B12	Porcupine
6.12	12.11	A1	C1	Wolf
7.12	13.11	A1	D2	Dog
8.12	14.11	A1	E3	Pheasant
9.12	15.11	A1	F4	Cock
10.12	16.11	A1	G5	Crow
11.12	17.11	A1	H6	Monkey
12.12	18.11	A1	J7	Gibbon
13.12	19.11	A1	K8	Tapir
14.12	20.11	A1	A9	Sheep
15.12	21.11	A1	B10	Deer
16.12	22.11	A1	C11	Horse
17.12	23.11	A1	D12	Stag
18.12	24.11	A1	E1	Serpent
19.12	25.11	A1	F2	Earthworm
20.12	26.11	A1	G3	Crocodile
21.12	27.11	A1	H4	Dragon
22.12	28.11	A1	J5	Badger
23.12	29.11	A1	K6	Hare
24.12	1.12	B2	A7	Fox
25.12	2.12	B2	B8	Tiger
26.12	3.12	B2	C9	Leopard
27.12	4.12	B2	D10	Griffon
28.12	5.12	B2	E11	Ox
29.12	6.12	B2	F12	Bat
30.12	7.12	B2	G1	Rat
31.12	8.12	B2	H2	Swallow
1974				
1. 1	9.12	B2	J3	Pig
2. 1	10.12	B2	K4	Porcupine
3. 1	11.12	B2	A5	Wolf
4. 1	12.12	B2	B6	Dog
5. 1	13.12	B2	C7	Pheasant
6. 1	14.12	B2	D8	Cock
7. 1	15.12	B2	E9	Crow
8. 1	16.12	B2	F10	Monkey
9. 1	17.12	B2	G11	Gibbon
10. 1	18.12	B2	H12	Tapir
11. 1	19.12	B2	J1	Sheep
12. 1	20.12	B2	K2	Deer
13. 1	21.12	B2	A3	Horse
14. 1	22.12	B2	B4	Stag
15. 1	23.12	B2	C5	Serpent
16. 1	24.12	B2	D6	Earthworm
17. 1	25.12	B2	E7	Crocodile
18. 1	26.12	B2	F8	Dragon
19. 1	27.12	B2	G9	Badger
20. 1	28.12	B2	H10	Hare
21. 1	29.12	B2	J11	Fox
22. 1	30.12	B2	K12	Tiger

CHIA YIN YEAR

23. 1	1. 1	C3	A1	Leopard
24. 1	2. 1	C3	B2	Griffon
25. 1	3. 1	C3	C3	Ox
26. 1	4. 1	C3	D4	Bat
27. 1	5. 1	C3	E5	Rat
28. 1	6. 1	C3	F6	Swallow
29. 1	7. 1	C3	G7	Pig
30. 1	8. 1	C3	H8	Porcupine
31. 1	9. 1	C3	J9	Wolf
1. 2	10. 1	C3	K10	Dog
2. 2	11. 1	C3	A11	Pheasant
3. 2	12. 1	C3	B12	Cock
4. 2	13. 1	C3	C1	Crow
5. 2	14. 1	C3	D2	Monkey
6. 2	15. 1	C3	E3	Gibbon
7. 2	16. 1	C3	F4	Tapir
8. 2	17. 1	C3	G5	Sheep
9. 2	18. 1	C3	H6	Deer
10. 2	19. 1	C3	J7	Horse
11. 2	20. 1	C3	K8	Stag
12. 2	21. 1	C3	A9	Serpent
13. 2	22. 1	C3	B10	Earthworm
14. 2	23. 1	C3	C11	Crocodile
15. 2	24. 1	C3	D12	Dragon
16. 2	25. 1	C3	E1	Badger
17. 2	26. 1	C3	F2	Hare
18. 2	27. 1	C3	G3	Fox
19. 2	28. 1	C3	H4	Tiger
20. 2	29. 1	C3	J5	Leopard
21. 2	30. 1	C3	K6	Griffon
22. 2	1. 2	D4	A7	Ox
23. 2	2. 2	D4	B8	Bat
24. 2	3. 2	D4	C9	Rat
25. 2	4. 2	D4	D10	Swallow
26. 2	5. 2	D4	E11	Pig
27. 2	6. 2	D4	F12	Porcupine
28. 2	7. 2	D4	G1	Wolf
1. 3	8. 2	D4	H2	Dog
2. 3	9. 2	D4	J3	Pheasant
3. 3	10. 2	D4	K4	Cock
4. 3	11. 2	D4	A5	Crow
5. 3	12. 2	D4	B6	Monkey
6. 3	13. 2	D4	C7	Gibbon
7. 3	14. 2	D4	D8	Tapir
8. 3	15. 2	D4	E9	Sheep
9. 3	16. 2	D4	F10	Deer
10. 3	17. 2	D4	G11	Horse
11. 3	18. 2	D4	H12	Stag
12. 3	19. 2	D4	J1	Serpent
13. 3	20. 2	D4	K2	Earthworm
14. 3	21. 2	D4	A3	Crocodile
15. 3	22. 2	D4	B4	Dragon
16. 3	23. 2	D4	C5	Badger
17. 3	24. 2	D4	D6	Hare
18, 3	25. 2	D4	E7	Fox
19. 3	26. 2	D4	F8	Tiger
20. 3	27. 2	D4	G9	Leopard
21. 3	28. 2	D4	H10	Griffon
22. 3	29. 2	D4	J11	Ox
23. 3	30. 2	D4	K12	Bat
24. 3	1. 3	E5	A1	Rat
25. 3	2. 3	E5	B2	Swallow
26. 3	3. 3	E5	C3	Pig
27. 3	4. 3	E5	D4	Porcupine
28. 3	5. 3	E5	E5	Wolf
29. 3	6. 3	E5	F6	Dog
30. 3	7. 3	E5	G7	Pheasant
31. 3	8. 3	E5	H8	Cock

Solar date	*Lunar date*	*Month HS/EB*	*Day HS/EB*	*Constellation*
1. 4	9. 3	E5	J9	Crow
2. 4	10. 3	E5	K10	Monkey
3. 4	11. 3	E5	A11	Gibbon
4. 4	12. 3	E5	B12	Tapir
5. 4	13. 3	E5	C1	Sheep
6. 4	14. 3	E5	D2	Deer
7. 4	15. 3	E5	E3	Horse
8. 4	16. 3	E5	F4	Stag
9. 4	17. 3	E5	G5	Sterpent
10. 4	18. 3	E5	H6	Earthworm
11. 4	19. 3	E5	J7	Crocodile
12. 4	20. 3	E5	K8	Dragon
13. 4	21. 3	E5	A9	Badger
14. 4	22. 3	E5	B10	Hare
15. 4	23. 3	E5	C11	Fox
16. 4	24. 3	E5	D12	Tiger
17. 4	25. 3	E5	E1	Leopard
18. 4	26. 3	E5	F2	Griffon
19. 4	27. 3	E5	G3	Ox
20. 4	28. 3	E5	H4	Bat
21. 4	29. 3	E5	J5	Rat
22. 4	1. 4	F6	K6	Swallow
23. 4	2. 4	F6	A7	Pig
24. 4	3. 4	F6	B8	Porcupine
25. 4	4. 4	F6	C9	Wolf
26. 4	5. 4	F6	D10	Dog
27. 4	6. 4	F6	E11	Pheasant
28. 4	7. 4	F6	F12	Cock
29. 4	8. 4	F6	G1	Crow
30. 4	9. 4	F6	H2	Monkey
1. 5	10. 4	F6	J3	Gibbon
2. 5	11. 4	F6	K4	Tapir
3. 5	12. 4	F6	A5	Sheep
4. 5	13. 4	F6	B6	Deer
5. 5	14. 4	F6	C7	Horse
6. 5	15. 4	F6	D8	Stag
7. 5	16. 4	F6	E9	Serpent
8. 5	17. 4	F6	F10	Earthworm
9. 5	18. 4	F6	G11	Crocodile
10. 5	19. 4	F6	H12	Dragon
11. 5	20. 4	F6	J1	Badger
12. 5	21. 4	F6	K2	Hare
13. 5	22. 4	F6	A3	Fox
14. 5	23. 4	F6	B4	Tiger
15. 5	24. 4	F6	C5	Leopard
16. 5	25. 4	F6	D6	Griffon
17. 5	26. 4	F6	E7	Ox
18. 5	27. 4	F6	F8	Bat
19. 5	28. 4	F6	G9	Rat
20. 5	29. 4	F6	H10	Swallow
21. 5	30. 4	F6	J11	Pig
22. 5	*1. 4*	*F6*	K12	Porcupine
23. 5	*2. 4*	*F6*	A1	Wolf
24. 5	*3. 4*	*F6*	B2	Dog
25. 5	*4. 4*	*F6*	C3	Pheasant
26. 5	*5. 4*	*F6*	D4	Cock
27. 5	*6. 4*	*F6*	E5	Crow
28. 5	*7. 4*	*F6*	F6	Monkey
29. 5	*8. 4*	*F6*	G7	Gibbon
30. 5	*9. 4*	*F6*	H8	Tapir
31. 5	*10. 4*	*F6*	J9	Sheep
1. 6	*11. 4*	*F6*	K10	Deer
2. 6	*12. 4*	*F6*	A11	Horse
3. 6	*13. 4*	*F6*	B12	Stag
4. 6	*14. 4*	*F6*	C1	Serpent
5. 6	*15. 4*	*F6*	D2	Earthworm
6. 6	*16. 4*	*F6*	E3	Crocodile
7. 6	*17. 4*	*F6*	F4	Dragon
8. 6	*18. 4*	*F6*	G5	Badger
9. 6	*19. 4*	*F6*	H6	Hare
10. 6	*20. 4*	*F6*	J7	Fox
11. 6	*21. 4*	*F6*	K8	Tiger
12. 6	*22. 4*	*F6*	A9	Leopard

Solar date	*Lunar date*	*Month HS/EB*	*Day HS/EB*	*Constellation*
13. 6	*23. 4*	*F6*	B10	Griffon
14. 6	*24. 4*	*F6*	C11	Ox
15. 6	*25. 4*	*F6*	D12	Bat
16. 6	*26. 4*	*F6*	E1	Rat
17. 6	*27. 4*	*F6*	F2	Swallow
18. 6	*28. 4*	*F6*	G3	Pig
19. 6	*29. 4*	*F6*	H4	Porcupine
20. 6	1. 5	G7	J5	Wolf
21. 6	2. 5	G7	K6	Dog
22. 6	3. 5	G7	A7	Pheasant
23. 6	4. 5	G7	B8	Cock
24. 6	5. 5	G7	C9	Crow
25. 6	6. 5	G7	D10	Monkey
26. 6	7. 5	G7	E11	Gibbon
27. 6	8. 5	G7	F12	Tapir
28. 6	9. 5	G7	G1	Sheep
29. 6	10. 5	G7	H2	Deer
30. 6	11. 5	G7	J3	Horse
1. 7	12. 5	G7	K4	Stag
2. 7	13. 5	G7	A5	Serpent
3. 7	14. 5	G7	B6	Earthworm
4. 7	15. 5	G7	C7	Crocodile
5. 7	16. 5	G7	D8	Dragon
6. 7	17. 5	G7	E9	Badger
7. 7	18. 5	G7	F10	Hare
8. 7	19. 5	G7	G11	Fox
9. 7	20. 5	G7	H12	Tiger
10. 7	21. 5	G7	J1	Leopard
11. 7	22. 5	G7	K2	Griffon
12. 7	23. 5	G7	A3	Ox
13. 7	24. 5	G7	B4	Bat
14. 7	25. 5	G7	C5	Rat
15. 7	26. 5	G7	D6	Swallow
16. 7	27. 5	G7	E7	Pig
17. 7	28. 5	G7	F8	Porcupine
18. 7	29. 5	G7	G9	Wolf
19. 7	1. 6	H8	H10	Dog
20. 7	2. 6	H8	J11	Pheasant
21. 7	3. 6	H8	K12	Cock
22. 7	4. 6	H8	A1	Crow
23. 7	5. 6	H8	B2	Monkey
24. 7	6. 6	H8	C3	Gibbon
25. 7	7. 6	H8	D4	Tapir
26. 7	8. 6	H8	E5	Sheep
27. 7	9. 6	H8	F6	Deer
28. 7	10. 6	H8	F7	Horse
29. 7	11. 6	H8	H8	Stag
30. 7	12. 6	H8	J9	Serpent
31. 7	13. 6	H8	K10	Earthworm
1. 8	14. 6	H8	A11	Crocodile
2. 8	15. 6	H8	B12	Dragon
3. 8	16. 6	H8	C1	Badger
4. 8	17. 6	H8	D2	Hare
5. 8	18. 6	H8	E3	Fox
6. 8	19. 6	H8	F4	Tiger
7. 8	20. 6	H8	G5	Leopard
8. 8	21. 6	H8	H6	Griffon
9. 8	22. 6	H8	J7	Ox
10. 8	23. 6	H8	K8	Bat
11. 8	24. 6	H8	A9	Rat
12. 8	25. 6	H8	B10	Swallow
13. 8	26. 6	H8	C11	Pig
14. 8	27. 6	H8	D12	Porcupine
15. 8	28. 6	H8	E1	Wolf
16. 8	29. 6	H8	F2	Dog
17. 8	30. 6	H8	G3	Pheasant
18. 8	1. 7	J9	H4	Cock
19. 8	2. 7	J9	J5	Crow
20. 8	3. 7	J9	K6	Monkey
21. 8	4. 7	J9	A7	Gibbon
22. 8	5. 7	J9	B8	Tapir
23. 8	6. 7	J9	C9	Sheep
24. 8	7. 7	J9	D10	Deer

Solar date	*Lunar date*	*Month HS/EB*	*Day HS/EB*	*Constellation*
25. 8	8. 7	J9	E11	Horse
26. 8	9. 7	J9	F12	Stag
27. 8	10. 7	J9	G1	Serpent
28. 8	11. 7	J9	H2	Earthworm
29. 8	12. 7	J9	J3	Crocodile
30. 8	13. 7	J9	K4	Dragon
31. 8	14. 7	J9	A5	Badger
1. 9	15. 7	J9	B6	Hare
2. 9	16. 7	J9	C7	Fox
3. 9	17. 7	J9	D8	Tiger
4. 9	18. 7	J9	E9	Leopard
5. 9	19. 7	J9	F10	Griffon
6. 9	20. 7	J9	G11	Ox
7. 9	21. 7	J9	H12	Bat
8. 9	22. 7	J9	J1	Rat
9. 9	23. 7	J9	K2	Swallow
10. 9	24. 7	J9	A3	Pig
11. 9	25. 7	J9	B4	Porcupine
12. 9	26. 7	J9	C5	Wolf
13. 9	27. 7	J9	D6	Dog
14. 9	28. 7	J9	E7	Pheasant
15. 9	29. 7	J9	F8	Cock
16. 9	1. 8	K10	G9	Crow
17. 9	2. 8	K10	H10	Monkey
18. 9	3. 8	K10	J11	Gibbon
19. 9	4. 8	K10	K12	Tapir
20. 9	5. 8	K10	A1	Sheep
21. 9	6. 8	K10	B2	Deer
22. 9	7. 8	K10	C3	Horse
23. 9	8. 8	K10	D4	Stag
24. 9	9. 8	K10	E5	Serpent
25. 9	10. 8	K10	F6	Earthworm
26. 9	11. 8	K10	G7	Crocodile
27. 9	12. 8	K10	H8	Dragon
28. 9	13. 8	K10	J9	Badger
29. 9	14. 8	K10	K10	Hare
30. 9	15. 8	K10	A11	Fox
1.10	16. 8	K10	B12	Tiger
2.10	17. 8	K10	C1	Leopard
3.10	18. 8	K10	D2	Griffon
4.10	19. 8	K10	E3	Ox
5.10	20. 8	K10	F4	Bat
6.10	21. 8	K10	G5	Rat
7.10	22. 8	K10	H6	Swallow
8.10	23. 8	K10	J7	Pig
9.10	24. 8	K10	K8	Porcupine
10.10	25. 8	K10	A9	Wolf
11.10	26. 8	K10	B10	Dog
12.10	27. 8	K10	C11	Pheasant
13.10	28. 8	K10	D12	Cock
14.10	29. 8	K10	E1	Crow
15.10	1. 9	A11	F2	Monkey
16.10	2. 9	A11	G3	Gibbon
17.10	3. 9	A11	H4	Tapir
18.10	4. 9	A11	J5	Sheep
19.10	5. 9	A11	K6	Deer
20.10	6. 9	A11	A7	Horse
21.10	7. 9	A11	B8	Stag
22.10	8. 9	A11	C9	Serpent
23.10	9. 9	A11	D10	Earthworm
24.10	10. 9	A11	E11	Crocodile
25.10	11. 9	A11	F12	Dragon
26.10	12. 9	A11	G1	Badger
27.10	13. 9	A11	H2	Hare
28.10	14. 9	A11	J3	Fox
29.10	15. 9	A11	K4	Tiger
30.10	16. 9	A11	A5	Leopard
31.10	17. 9	A11	B6	Griffon
1.11	18. 9	A11	C7	Ox
2.11	19. 9	A11	D8	Bat
3.11	20. 9	A11	E9	Rat
4.11	21. 9	A11	F10	Swallow
5.11	22. 9	A11	G11	Pig

Solar date	*Lunar date*	*Month HS/EB*	*Day HS/EB*	*Constellation*
6.11	23. 9	A11	H12	Porcupine
7.11	24. 9	A11	J1	Wolf
8.11	25. 9	A11	K2	Dog
9.11	26. 9	A11	A3	Pheasant
10.11	27. 9	A11	B4	Cock
11.11	28. 9	A11	C5	Crow
12.11	29. 9	A11	D6	Monkey
13.11	30. 9	A11	E7	Gibbon
14.11	1.10	B12	F8	Tapir
15.11	2.10	B12	G9	Sheep
16.11	3.10	B12	H10	Deer
17.11	4.10	B12	J11	Horse
18.11	5.10	B12	K12	Stag
19.11	6.10	B12	A1	Serpent
20.11	7.10	B12	B2	Earthworm
21.11	8.10	B12	C3	Crocodile
22.11	9.10	B12	D4	Dragon
23.11	10.10	B12	E5	Badger
24.11	11.10	B12	F6	Hare
25.11	12.10	B12	G7	Fox
26.11	13.10	B12	H8	Tiger
27.11	14.10	B12	J9	Leopard
28.11	15.10	B12	K10	Griffon
29.11	16.10	B12	A11	Ox
30.11	17.10	B12	B12	Bat
1.12	18.10	B12	C1	Rat
2.12	19.10	B12	D2	Swallow
3.12	20.10	B12	E3	Pig
4.12	21.10	B12	F4	Porcupine
5.12	22.10	B12	G5	Wolf
6.12	23.10	B12	H6	Dog
7.12	24.10	B12	J7	Pheasant
8.12	25.10	B12	K8	Cock
9.12	26.10	B12	A9	Crow
10.12	27.10	B12	B10	Monkey
11.12	28.10	B12	C11	Gibbon
12.12	29.10	B12	D12	Tapir
13.12	30.10	B12	E1	Sheep
14.12	1.11	C1	F2	Deer
15.12	2.11	C1	G3	Horse
16.12	3.11	C1	H4	Stag
17.12	4.11	C1	J5	Serpent
18.12	5.11	C1	K6	Earthworm
19.12	6.11	C1	A7	Crocodile
20.12	7.11	C1	B8	Dragon
21.12	8.11	C1	C9	Badger
22.12	9.11	C1	D10	Hare
23.12	10.11	C1	E11	Fox
24.12	11.11	C1	F12	Tiger
25.12	12.11	C1	G1	Leopard
26.12	13.11	C1	H2	Griffon
27.12	14.11	C1	J3	Ox
28.12	15.11	C1	K4	Bat
29.12	16.11	C1	A5	Rat
30.12	17.11	C1	B6	Swallow
31.12	18.11	C1	C7	Pig
1975				
1. 1	19.11	C1	D8	Porcupine
2. 1	20.11	C1	E9	Wolf
3. 1	21.11	C1	F10	Dog
4. 1	22.11	C1	G11	Pheasant
5. 1	23.11	C1	H12	Cock
6. 1	24.11	C1	J1	Crow
7. 1	25.11	C1	K2	Monkey
8. 1	26.11	C1	A3	Gibbon
9. 1	27.11	C1	B4	Tapir
10. 1	28.11	C1	C5	Sheep
11. 1	29.11	C1	D6	Deer
12. 2	1.12	D2	E7	Horse
13. 1	2.12	D2	F8	Stag
14. 1	3.12	D2	G9	Serpent
15. 1	4.12	D2	H10	Earthworm

Solar date	*Lunar date*	*Month HS/EB*	*Day HS/EB*	*Constellation*
16. 1	5.12	D2	J11	Crocodile
17. 1	6.12	D2	K12	Dragon
18. 1	7.12	D2	A1	Badger
19. 1	8.12	D2	B2	Hare
20. 1	9.12	D2	C3	Fox
21. 1	10.12	D2	D4	Tiger
22. 1	11.12	D2	E5	Leopard
23. 1	12.12	D2	F6	Griffon
24. 1	13.12	D2	G7	Ox
25. 1	14.12	D2	H8	Bat
26. 1	15.12	D2	J9	Rat
27. 1	16.12	D2	K10	Swallow
28. 1	17.12	D2	A11	Pig
29. 1	18.12	D2	B12	Porcupine
30. 1	19.12	D2	C1	Wolf
31. 1	20.12	D2	D2	Dog
1. 2	21.12	D2	E3	Pheasant
2. 2	22.12	D2	F4	Cock
3. 2	23.12	D2	G5	Crow
4. 2	24.12	D2	H6	Monkey
5. 2	25.12	D2	J7	Gibbon
6. 2	26.12	D2	K8	Tapir
7. 2	27.12	D2	A9	Sheep
8. 2	28.12	D2	B10	Deer
9. 2	29.12	D2	C11	Horse
10. 2	30.12	D2	D12	Stag

YI MAO YEAR

Solar date	*Lunar date*	*Month HS/EB*	*Day HS/EB*	*Constellation*
11. 2	1. 1	E3	E1	Serpent
12. 2	2. 1	E3	F2	Earthworm
13. 2	3. 1	E3	G3	Crocodile
14. 2	4. 1	E3	H4	Dragon
15. 2	5. 1	E3	J5	Badger
16. 2	6. 1	E3	K6	Hare
17. 2	7. 1	E3	A7	Fox
18. 2	8. 1	E3	B8	Tiger
19. 2	9. 1	E3	C9	Leopard
20. 2	10. 1	E3	D10	Griffon
21. 2	11. 1	E3	E11	Ox
22. 2	12. 1	E3	F12	Bat
23. 2	13. 1	E3	G1	Rat
24. 2	14. 1	E3	H2	Swallow
25. 2	15. 1	E3	J3	Pig
26. 2	16. 1	E3	K4	Porcupine
27. 2	17. 1	E3	A5	Wolf
28. 2	18. 1	E3	B6	Dog
1. 3	19. 1	E3	C7	Pheasant
2. 3	20. 1	E3	D8	Cock
3. 3	21. 1	E3	E9	Crow
4. 3	22. 1	E3	F10	Monkey
5. 3	23. 1	E3	G11	Gibbon
6. 3	24. 1	E3	H12	Tapir
7. 3	25. 1	E3	J1	Sheep
8. 3	26. 1	E3	K2	Deer
9. 3	27. 1	E3	A3	Horse
10. 3	28. 1	E3	B4	Stag
11. 3	29. 1	E3	C5	Serpent
12. 3	30. 1	E3	D6	Earthworm
13. 3	1. 2	F4	E7	Crocodile
14. 3	2. 2	F4	F8	Dragon
15. 3	3. 2	F4	G9	Badger
16. 3	4. 2	F4	H10	Hare
17. 3	5. 2	F4	J11	Fox
18. 3	6. 2	F4	K12	Tiger
19. 3	7. 2	F4	A1	Leopard
20. 3	8. 2	F4	B2	Griffon
21. 3	9. 2	F4	C3	Ox
22. 3	10. 2	F4	D4	Bat
23. 3	11. 2	F4	E5	Rat
24. 3	12. 2	F4	F6	Swallow
25. 3	13. 2	F4	G7	Pig
26. 3	14. 2	F4	H8	Porcupine
27. 3	15. 2	F4	J9	Wolf
28. 3	16. 2	F4	K10	Dog
29. 3	17. 2	F4	A11	Pheasant
30. 3	18. 2	F4	B12	Cock
31. 3	19. 2	F4	C1	Crow
1. 4	20. 2	F4	D2	Monkey
2. 4	21. 2	F4	E3	Gibbon
3. 4	22. 2	F4	F4	Tapir
4. 4	23. 2	F4	G5	Sheep
5. 4	24. 2	F4	H6	Deer
6. 4	25. 2	F4	J7	Horse
7. 4	26. 2	F4	K8	Stag
8. 4	27. 2	F4	A9	Serpent
9. 4	28. 2	F4	B10	Earthworm
10. 4	29. 2	F4	C11	Crocodile
11. 4	30. 2	F4	D12	Dragon
12. 4	1. 3	G5	E1	Badger
13. 4	2. 3	G5	F2	Hare
14. 4	3. 3	G5	G3	Fox
15. 4	4. 3	G5	H4	Tiger
16. 4	5. 3	G5	J5	Leopard
17. 4	6. 3	G5	K6	Griffon
18. 4	7. 3	G5	A7	Ox
19. 4	8. 3	G5	B8	Bat
20. 4	9. 3	G5	C9	Rat
21. 4	10. 3	G5	D10	Swallow
22. 4	11. 3	G5	E11	Pig
23. 4	12. 3	G5	F12	Porcupine
24. 4	13. 3	G5	G1	Wolf
25. 4	14. 3	G5	H2	Dog
26. 4	15. 3	G5	J3	Pheasant
27. 4	16. 3	G5	K4	Cock
28. 4	17. 3	G5	A5	Crow
29. 4	18. 3	G5	B6	Monkey
30. 4	19. 3	G5	C7	Gibbon
1. 5	20. 3	G5	D8	Tapir
2. 5	21. 3	G5	E9	Sheep
3. 5	22. 3	G5	F10	Deer
4. 5	23. 3	G5	G11	Horse
5. 5	24. 3	G5	H12	Stag
6. 5	25. 3	G5	J1	Serpent
7. 5	26. 3	G5	K2	Earthworm
8. 5	27. 3	G5	A3	Crocodile
9. 5	28. 3	G5	B4	Dragon
10. 5	29. 3	G5	C5	Badger
11. 5	1. 4	H6	D6	Hare
12. 5	2. 4	H6	E7	Fox
13. 5	3. 4	H6	F8	Tiger
14. 5	4. 4	H6	G9	Leopard
15. 5	5. 4	H6	H10	Griffon
16. 5	6. 4	H6	J11	Ox
17. 5	7. 4	H6	K12	Bat
18. 5	8. 4	H6	A1	Rat
19. 5	9. 4	H6	B2	Swallow
20. 5	10. 4	H6	C3	Pig
21. 5	11. 4	H6	D4	Porcupine
22. 5	12. 4	H6	E5	Wolf
23. 5	13. 4	H6	F6	Dog
24. 5	14. 4	H6	G7	Pheasant
25. 5	15. 4	H6	H8	Cock
26. 5	16. 4	H6	J9	Crow
27. 5	17. 4	H6	K10	Monkey
28. 5	18. 4	H6	A11	Gibbon
29. 5	19. 4	H6	B12	Tapir
30. 5	20. 4	H6	C1	Sheep
31. 5	21. 4	H6	D2	Deer

Solar date	*Lunar date*	*Month HS/EB*	*Day HS/EB*	*Constellation*
1. 6	22. 4	H6	E3	Horse
2. 6	23. 4	H6	F4	Stag
3. 6	24. 4	H6	G5	Serpent
4. 6	25. 4	H6	H6	Earthworm
5. 6	26. 4	H6	J7	Crocodile
6. 6	27. 4	H6	K8	Dragon
7. 6	28. 4	H6	A9	Badger
8. 6	29. 4	H6	B10	Hare
9. 6	30. 4	H6	C11	Fox
10. 6	1. 5	J7	D12	Tiger
11. 6	2. 5	J7	E1	Leopard
12. 6	3. 5	J7	F2	Griffon
13. 6	4. 5	J7	G3	Ox
14. 6	5. 5	J7	H4	Bat
15. 6	6. 5	J7	J5	Rat
16. 6	7. 5	J7	K6	Swallow
17. 6	8. 5	J7	A7	Pig
18. 6	9. 5	J7	B8	Porcupine
19. 6	10. 5	J7	C9	Wolf
20. 6	11. 5	J7	D10	Dog
21. 6	12. 5	J7	E11	Pheasant
22. 6	13. 5	J7	F12	Cock
23. 6	14. 5	J7	G1	Crow
24. 6	15. 5	J7	H2	Monkey
25. 6	16. 5	J7	J3	Gibbon
26. 6	17. 5	J7	K4	Tapir
27. 6	18. 5	J7	A5	Sheep
28. 6	19. 5	J7	B6	Deer
29. 6	20. 5	J7	C7	Horse
30. 6	21. 5	J7	D8	Stag
1. 7	22. 5	J7	E9	Serpent
2. 7	23. 5	J7	F10	Earthworm
3. 7	24. 5	J7	G11	Crocodile
4. 7	25. 5	J7	H12	Dragon
5. 7	26. 5	J7	J1	Badger
6. 7	27. 5	J7	K2	Hare
7. 7	28. 5	J7	A3	Fox
8. 7	29. 5	J7	B4	Tiger
9. 7	1. 6	K8	C5	Leopard
10. 7	2. 6	K8	D6	Griffon
11. 7	3. 6	K8	E7	Ox
12. 7	4. 6	K8	F8	Bat
13. 7	5. 6	K8	G9	Rat
14. 7	6. 6	K8	H10	Swallow
15. 7	7. 6	K8	J11	Pig
16. 7	8. 6	K8	K12	Porcupine
17. 7	9. 6	K8	A1	Wolf
18. 7	10. 6	K8	B2	Dog
19. 7	11. 6	K8	C3	Pheasant
20. 7	12. 6	K8	D4	Cock
21. 7	13. 6	K8	E5	Crow
22. 7	14. 6	K8	F6	Monkey
23. 7	15. 6	K8	G7	Gibbon
24. 7	16. 6	K8	H8	Tapir
25. 7	17. 6	K8	J9	Sheep
26. 7	18. 6	K8	K10	Deer
27. 7	19. 6	K8	A11	Horse
28. 7	20. 6	K8	B12	Stag
29. 7	21. 6	K8	C1	Serpent
30. 7	22. 6	K8	D2	Earthworm
31. 7	23. 6	K8	E3	Crocodile
1. 8	24. 6	K8	F4	Dragon
2. 8	25. 6	K8	G5	Badger
3. 8	26. 6	K8	H6	Hare
4. 8	27. 6	K8	J7	Fox
5. 8	28. 6	K8	K8	Tiger
6. 8	29. 6	K8	A9	Leopard
7. 8	1. 7	A9	B10	Griffon
8. 8	2. 7	A9	C11	Ox
9. 8	3. 7	A9	D12	Bat
10. 8	4. 7	A9	E1	Rat
11. 8	5. 7	A9	F2	Swallow
12. 8	6. 7	A9	G3	Pig
13. 8	7. 7	A9	H4	Porcupine
14. 8	8. 7	A9	J5	Wolf
15. 8	9. 7	A9	K6	Dog
16. 8	10. 7	A9	A7	Pheasant
17. 8	11. 7	A9	B8	Cock
18. 8	12. 7	A9	C9	Crow
19. 8	13. 7	A9	D10	Monkey
20. 8	14. 7	A9	E11	Gibbon
21. 8	15. 7	A9	F12	Tapir
22. 8	16. 7	A9	G1	Sheep
23. 8	17. 7	A9	H2	Deer
24. 8	18. 7	A9	J3	Horse
25. 8	19. 7	A9	K4	Stag
26. 8	20. 7	A9	A5	Serpent
27. 8	21. 7	A9	B6	Earthworm
28. 8	22. 7	A9	C7	Crocodile
29. 8	23. 7	A9	D8	Dragon
30. 8	24. 7	A9	E9	Badger
31. 8	25. 7	A9	F10	Hare
1. 9	26. 7	A9	G11	Fox
2. 9	27. 7	A9	H12	Tiger
3. 9	28. 7	A9	J1	Leopard
4. 9	29. 7	A9	K2	Griffon
5. 9	30. 7	A9	A3	Ox
6. 9	1. 8	B10	B4	Bat
7. 9	2. 8	B10	C5	Rat
8. 9	3. 8	B10	D6	Swallow
9. 9	4. 8	B10	E7	Pig
10. 9	5. 8	B10	F8	Porcupine
11. 9	6. 8	B10	G9	Wolf
12. 9	7. 8	B10	H10	Dog
13. 9	8. 8	B10	J11	Pheasant
14. 9	9. 8	B10	K12	Cock
15. 9	10. 8	B10	A1	Crow
16. 9	11. 8	B10	B2	Monkey
17. 9	12. 8	B10	C3	Gibbon
18. 9	13. 8	B10	D4	Tapir
19. 9	14. 8	B10	E5	Sheep
20. 9	15. 8	B10	F6	Deer
21. 9	16. 8	B10	G7	Horse
22. 9	17. 8	B10	H8	Stag
23. 9	18.18	B10	J9	Serpent
24. 9	19. 8	B10	K10	Earthworm
25. 9	20. 8	B10	A11	Crocodile
26. 9	21. 8	B10	B12	Dragon
27. 9	22. 8	B10	C1	Badger
28. 9	23. 8	B10	D2	Hare
29. 9	24. 8	B10	E3	Fox
30. 9	25. 8	B10	F4	Tiger
1.10	26. 8	B10	G5	Leopard
2.10	27. 8	B10	H6	Griffon
3.10	28. 8	B10	J7	Ox
4.10	29. 8	B10	K8	Bat
5.10	1. 9	C11	A9	Rat
6.10	2. 9	C11	B10	Swallow
7.10	3. 9	C11	C11	Pig
8.10	4. 9	C11	D12	Porcupine
9.10	5. 9	C11	E1	Wolf
10.10	6. 9	C11	F2	Dog
11.10	7. 9	C11	G3	Pheasant
12.10	8. 9	C11	H4	Cock
13.10	9. 9	C11	J5	Crow
14.10	10. 9	C11	K6	Monkey
15.10	11. 9	C11	A7	Gibbon
16.10	12. 9	C11	B8	Tapir
17.10	13. 9	C11	C9	Sheep
18.10	14. 9	C11	D10	Deer
19.10	15. 9	C11	E11	Horse
20.10	16. 9	C11	F12	Stag
21.10	17. 9	C11	G1	Serpent
22.10	18. 9	C11	H2	Earthworm
23.10	19. 9	C11	J3	Crocodile
24.10	20. 9	C11	K4	Dragon

Solar date	*Lunar date*	*Month HS/EB*	*Day HS/EB*	*Constellation*
25.10	21. 9	C11	A5	Badger
26.10	22. 9	C11	B6	Hare
27.10	23. 9	C11	C7	Fox
28.10	24. 9	C11	D8	Tiger
29.10	25. 9	C11	E9	Leopard
30.10	26. 9	C11	F10	Griffon
31.10	27. 9	C11	G11	Ox
1.11	28. 9	C11	H12	Bat
2.11	29. 9	C11	J1	Rat
3.11	1.10	D12	K2	Swallow
4.11	2.10	D12	A3	Pig
5.11	3.10	D12	B4	Porcupine
6.11	4.10	D12	C5	Wolf
7.11	5.10	D12	D6	Dog
8.11	6.10	D12	E7	Pheasant
9.11	7.10	D12	F8	Cock
10.11	8.10	D12	G9	Crow
11.11	9.10	D12	H10	Monkey
12.11	10.10	D12	J11	Gibbon
13.11	11.10	D12	K12	Tapir
14.11	12.10	D12	A1	Sheep
15.11	13.10	D12	B2	Deer
16.11	14.10	D12	C3	Horse
17.11	15.10	D12	D4	Stag
18.11	16.10	D12	E5	Serpent
19.11	17.10	D12	F6	Earthworm
20.11	18.10	D12	G7	Crocodile
21.11	19.10	D12	H8	Dragon
22.11	20.10	D12	J9	Badger
23.11	21.10	D12	K10	Hare
24.11	22.10	D12	A11	Fox
25.11	23.10	D12	B12	Tiger
26.11	24.10	D12	C1	Leopard
27.11	25.10	D12	D2	Griffon
28.11	26.10	D12	E3	Ox
29.11	27.10	D12	F4	Bat
30.11	28.10	D12	G5	Rat
1.12	29.10	D12	H6	Swallow
2.12	20.10	D12	J7	Pig
3.12	1.11	E1	K8	Porcupine
4.12	2.11	E1	A9	Wolf
5.12	3.11	E1	B10	Dog
6.12	4.11	E1	C11	Pheasant
7.12	5.11	E1	D12	Cock
8.12	6.11	E1	E1	Crow
9.12	7.11	E1	F2	Monkey
10.12	8.11	E1	G3	Gibbon
11.12	9.11	E1	H4	Tapir
12.12	10.11	E1	J5	Sheep
13.12	11.11	E1	K6	Deer

Solar date	*Lunar date*	*Month HS/EB*	*Day HS/EB*	*Constellation*
14.12	12.11	E1	A7	Horse
15.12	13.11	E1	B8	Stag
16.12	14.11	E1	C9	Serpent
17.12	15.11	E1	D10	Earthworm
18.12	16.11	E1	E11	Crocodile
19.12	17.11	E1	F12	Dragon
20.12	18.11	E1	G1	Badger
21.12	19.11	E1	H2	Hare
22.12	20.11	E1	J3	Fox
23.12	21.11	E1	K4	Tiger
24.12	22.11	E1	A5	Leopard
25.12	23.11	E1	B6	Griffon
26.12	24.11	E1	C7	Ox
27.12	25.11	E1	D8	Bat
28.12	26.11	E1	E9	Rat
29.12	27.11	E1	F10	Swallow
30.12	28.11	E1	G11	Pig
31.12	29.11	E1	H12	Porcupine
1976				
1. 1	1.12	F2	J1	Wolf
2. 1	2.12	F2	K2	Dog
3. 1	3.12	F2	A3	Pheasant
4. 1	4.12	F2	B4	Cock
5. 1	5.12	F2	C5	Crow
6. 1	6.12	F2	D6	Monkey
7. 1	7.12	F2	E7	Gibbon
8. 1	8.12	F2	F8	Tapir
9. 1	9.12	F2	G9	Sheep
10. 1	10.12	F2	H10	Deer
11. 1	11.12	F2	J11	Horse
12. 1	12.12	F2	K12	Stag
13. 1	13.12	F2	A1	Serpent
14. 1	14.12	F2	B2	Earthworm
15. 1	15.12	F2	C3	Crocodile
16. 1	16.12	F2	D4	Dragon
17. 1	17.12	F2	E5	Badger
18. 1	18.12	F2	F6	Hare
19. 1	19.12	F2	G7	Fox
20. 1	20.12	F2	H8	Tiger
21. 1	21.12	F2	J9	Leopard
22. 1	22.12	F2	K10	Griffon
23. 1	23.12	F2	A11	Ox
24. 1	24.12	F2	B12	Bat
25. 1	25.12	F2	C1	Rat
26. 1	26.12	F2	D2	Swallow
27. 1	27.12	F2	E3	Pig
28. 1	28.12	F2	F4	Porcupine
29. 1	29.12	F2	G5	Wolf
30. 1	30.12	F2	H6	Dog

PING CH'EN YEAR

31. 1	1. 1	G3	J7	Pheasant
1. 2	2. 1	G3	K8	Cock
2. 2	3. 1	G3	A9	Crow
3. 2	4. 1	G3	B10	Monkey
4. 2	5. 1	G3	C11	Gibbon
5. 2	6. 1	G3	D12	Tapir
6. 2	7. 1	G3	E1	Sheep
7. 2	8. 1	G3	F2	Deer
8. 2	9. 1	G3	G3	Horse
9. 2	10. 1	G3	H4	Stag
10. 2	11. 1	G3	J5	Serpent
11. 2	12. 1	G3	K6	Earthworm
12. 2	13. 1	G3	A7	Crocodile
13. 2	14. 1	G3	B8	Dragon
14. 2	15. 1	G3	C9	Badger
15. 2	16. 1	G3	D10	Hare
16. 2	17. 1	G3	E11	Fox
17. 2	18. 1	G3	F12	Tiger

18. 2	19. 1	G3	G1	Leopard
19. 2	20. 1	G3	H2	Griffon
20. 2	21. 1	G3	J3	Ox
21. 2	22. 1	G3	K4	Bat
22. 2	23. 1	G3	A5	Rat
23. 2	24. 1	G3	B6	Swallow
24. 2	25. 1	G3	C7	Pig
25. 2	26. 1	G3	D8	Porcupine
26. 2	27. 1	G3	E9	Wolf
27. 2	28. 1	G3	F10	Dog
28. 2	29. 1	G3	G11	Pheasant
29. 2	30. 1	G3	H12	Cock
1. 3	1. 2	H4	J1	Crow
2. 3	2. 2	H4	K2	Monkey
3. 3	3. 2	H4	A3	Gibbon
4. 3	4. 2	H4	B4	Tapir
5. 3	5. 2	H4	C5	Sheep
6. 3	6. 2	H4	D6	Deer

Solar date	*Lunar date*	*Month HS/EB*	*Day HS/EB*	*Constellation*
7. 3	7. 2	H4	E7	Horse
8. 3	8. 2	H4	F8	Stag
9. 3	9. 2	H4	G9	Serpent
10. 3	10. 2	H4	H10	Earthworm
11. 3	11. 2	H4	J11	Crocodile
12. 3	12. 2	H4	K12	Dragon
13. 3	13. 2	H4	A1	Badger
14. 3	14. 2	H4	B2	Hare
15. 3	15. 2	H4	C3	Fox
16. 3	16. 2	H4	D4	Tiger
17. 3	17. 2	H4	E5	Leopard
18. 3	18. 2	H4	F6	Griffon
19. 3	19. 2	H4	G7	Ox
20. 3	20. 2	H4	H8	Bat
21. 3	21. 2	H4	J9	Rat
22. 3	22. 2	H4	K10	Swallow
23. 3	23. 2	H4	A11	Pig
24. 3	24. 2	H4	B12	Porcupine
25. 3	25. 2	H4	C1	Wolf
26. 3	26. 2	H4	D2	Dog
27. 3	27. 2	H4	E3	Pheasant
28. 3	28. 2	H4	F4	Cock
29. 3	29. 2	H4	G5	Crow
30. 3	30. 2	H4	H6	Monkey
31. 3	1. 3	J5	J7	Gibbon
1. 4	2. 3	J5	K8	Tapir
2. 4	3. 3	J5	A9	Sheep
3. 4	4. 3	J5	B10	Deer
4. 4	5. 3	J5	C11	Horse
5. 4	6. 3	J5	D12	Stag
6. 4	7. 3	J5	E1	Serpent
7. 4	8. 3	J5	F2	Earthworm
8. 4	9. 3	J5	G3	Crocodile
9. 4	10. 3	J5	H4	Dragon
10. 4	11. 3	J5	J5	Badger
11. 4	12. 3	J5	K6	Hare
12. 4	13. 3	J5	A7	Fox
13. 4	14. 3	J5	B8	Tiger
14. 4	15. 3	J5	C9	Leopard
15. 4	16. 3	J5	D10	Griffon
16. 4	17. 3	J5	E11	Ox
17. 4	18. 3	J5	F12	Bat
18. 4	19. 3	J5	G1	Rat
19. 4	20. 3	J5	H2	Swallow
20. 4	21. 3	J5	J3	Pig
21. 4	22. 3	J5	K4	Porcupine
22. 4	23. 3	J5	A5	Wolf
23. 4	24. 3	J5	B6	Dog
24. 4	25. 3	J5	C7	Pheasant
25. 4	26. 3	J5	D8	Cock
26. 4	27. 3	J5	E9	Crow
27. 4	28. 3	J5	F10	Monkey
28. 4	29. 3	J5	G11	Gibbon
29. 4	1. 4	K6	H12	Tapir
30. 4	2. 4	K6	J1	Sheep
1. 5	3. 4	K6	K2	Deer
2. 5	4. 4	K6	A3	Horse
3. 5	5. 4	K6	B4	Stag
4. 5	6. 4	K6	C5	Serpent
5. 5	7. 4	K6	D6	Earthworm
6. 5	8. 4	K6	E7	Crocodile
7. 5	9. 4	K6	F8	Dragon
8. 5	10. 4	K6	G9	Badger
9. 5	11. 4	K6	H10	Hare
10. 5	12. 4	K6	J11	Fox
11. 5	13. 4	K6	K12	Tiger
12. 5	14. 4	K6	A1	Leopard
13. 5	15. 4	K6	B2	Griffon
14. 5	16. 4	K6	C3	Ox
15. 5	17. 4	K6	D4	Bat
16. 5	18. 4	K6	E5	Rat
17. 5	19. 4	K6	F6	Swallow
18. 5	20. 4	K6	G7	Pig
19. 5	21. 4	K6	H8	Porcupine
20. 5	22. 4	K6	J9	Wolf
21. 5	23. 4	K6	K10	Dog
22. 5	24. 4	K6	A11	Pheasant
23. 5	25. 4	K6	B12	Cock
24. 5	26. 4	K6	C1	Crow
25. 5	27. 4	K6	D2	Monkey
26. 5	28. 4	K6	E3	Gibbon
27. 5	29. 4	K6	F4	Tapir
28. 5	30. 4	K6	G5	Sheep
29. 5	1. 5	A7	H6	Deer
30. 5	2. 5	A7	J7	Horse
31. 5	3. 5	A7	K8	Stag
1. 6	4. 5	A7	A9	Serpent
2. 6	5. 5	A7	B10	Earthworm
3. 6	6. 5	A7	C11	Crocodile
4. 6	7. 5	A7	D12	Dragon
5. 6	8. 5	A7	E1	Badger
6. 6	9. 5	A7	F2	Hare
7. 6	10. 5	A7	G3	Fox
8. 6	11. 5	A7	H4	Tiger
9. 6	12. 5	A7	J5	Leopard
10. 6	13. 5	A7	K6	Griffon
11. 6	14. 5	A7	A7	Ox
12. 6	15. 5	A7	B8	Bat
13. 6	16. 5	A7	C9	Rat
14. 6	17. 5	A7	D10	Swallow
15. 6	18. 5	A7	E11	Pig
16. 6	19. 5	A7	F12	Porcupine
17. 6	20. 5	A7	G1	Wolf
18. 6	21. 5	A7	H2	Dog
19. 6	22. 5	A7	J3	Pheasant
20. 6	23. 5	A7	K4	Cock
21. 6	24. 5	A7	A5	Crow
22. 6	25. 5	A7	B6	Monkey
23. 6	26. 5	A7	C7	Gibbon
24. 6	27. 5	A7	D8	Tapir
25. 6	28. 5	A7	E9	Sheep
26. 6	29. 5	A7	F10	Deer
27. 6	1. 6	B8	G11	Horse
28. 6	2. 6	B8	H12	Stag
29. 6	3. 6	B8	J1	Serpent
30. 6	4. 6	B8	K2	Earthworm
1. 7	5. 6	B8	A3	Crocodile
2. 7	6. 6	B8	B4	Dragon
3. 7	7. 6	B8	C5	Badger
4. 7	8. 6	B8	D6	Hare
5. 7	9. 6	B8	E7	Fox
6. 7	10. 6	B8	F8	Tiger
7. 7	11. 6	B8	G9	Leopard
8. 7	12. 6	B8	H10	Griffon
9. 7	13. 6	B8	J11	Ox
10. 7	14. 6	B8	K12	Bat
11. 7	15. 6	B8	A1	Rat
12. 7	16. 6	B8	B2	Swallow
13. 7	17. 6	B8	C3	Pig
14. 7	18. 6	B8	D4	Porcupine
15. 7	19. 6	B8	E5	Wolf
16. 7	20. 6	B8	F6	Dog
17. 7	21. 6	B8	G7	Pheasant
18. 7	22. 6	B8	H8	Cock
19. 7	23. 6	B8	J9	Crow
20. 7	24. 6	B8	K10	Monkey
21. 7	25. 6	B8	A11	Gibbon
22. 7	26. 6	B8	B12	Tapir
23. 7	27. 6	B8	C1	Sheep
24. 7	28. 6	B8	D2	Deer
25. 7	29. 6	B8	E3	Horse
26. 7	30. 6	B8	F4	Stag
27. 7	1. 7	C9	G5	Serpent
28. 7	2. 7	C9	H6	Earthworm
29. 7	3. 7	C9	J7	Crocodile
30. 7	4. 7	C9	K8	Dragon

Solar date	*Lunar date*	*Month HS/EB*	*Day HS/EB*	*Constellation*
31. 7	5. 7	C9	A9	Badger
1. 8	6. 7	C9	B10	Hare
2. 8	7. 7	C9	C11	Fox
3. 8	8. 7	C9	D12	Tiger
4. 8	9. 7	C9	E1	Leopard
5. 8	10. 7	C9	F2	Griffon
6. 8	11. 7	C9	G3	Ox
7. 8	12. 7	C9	H4	Bat
8. 8	13. 7	C9	J5	Rat
9. 8	14. 7	C9	K6	Swallow
10. 8	15. 7	C9	A7	Pig
11. 8	16. 7	C9	B8	Porcupine
12. 8	17. 7	C9	C9	Wolf
13. 8	18. 7	C9	D10	Dog
14. 8	19. 7	C9	E11	Pheasant
15. 8	20. 7	C9	F12	Cock
16. 8	21. 7	C9	G1	Crow
17. 8	22. 7	C9	H2	Monkey
18. 8	23. 7	C9	J3	Gibbon
19. 8	24. 7	C9	K4	Tapir
20. 8	25. 7	C9	A5	Sheep
21. 8	26. 7	C9	B6	Deer
22. 8	27. 7	C9	C7	Horse
23. 8	28. 7	C9	D8	Stag
24. 8	29. 7	C9	E9	Serpent
25. 8	1. 8	D10	E10	Earthworm
26. 8	2. 8	D10	G11	Crocodile
27. 8	3. 8	D10	H12	Dragon
28. 8	4. 8	D10	J1	Badger
29. 8	5. 8	D10	K2	Hare
30. 8	6. 8	D10	A3	Fox
31. 8	7. 8	D10	B4	Tiger
1. 9	8. 8	D10	C5	Leopard
2. 9	9. 8	D10	D6	Griffon
3. 9	10. 8	D10	E7	Ox
4. 9	11. 8	D10	F8	Bat
5. 9	12. 8	D10	G9	Rat
6. 9	13. 8	D10	H10	Swallow
7. 9	14. 8	D10	J11	Pig
8. 9	15. 8	D10	K12	Porcupine
9. 9	16. 8	D10	A1	Wolf
10. 9	17. 8	D10	B2	Dog
11. 9	18. 8	D10	C3	Pheasant
12. 9	19. 8	D10	D4	Cock
13. 9	20. 8	D10	E5	Crow
14. 9	21. 8	D10	F6	Monkey
15. 9	22. 8	D10	G7	Gibbon
16. 9	23. 8	D10	H8	Tapir
17. 9	24. 8	D10	J9	Sheep
18. 9	25.-8	D10	K10	Deer
19. 9	26. 8	D10	A11	Horse
20. 9	27. 8	D10	B12	Stag
21. 9	28. 8	D10	C1	Serpent
22. 9	29. 8	D10	D2	Earthworm
23. 9	30. 8	D10	E3	Crocodile
24. 9	*1. 8*	*D10*	F4	Dragon
25. 9	*2. 8*	*D10*	G5	Badger
26. 9	*3. 8*	*D10*	H6	Hare
27. 9	*4. 8*	*D10*	J7	Fox
28. 9	*5. 8*	*D10*	K8	Tiger
29. 9	*6. 8*	*D10*	A9	Leopard
30. 9	*7. 8*	*D10*	B10	Griffon
1. 0	*8. 8*	*D10*	C11	Ox
2.10	*9. 8*	*D10*	D12	Bat
3.10	*10. 8*	*D10*	E1	Rat
4.10	*11. 8*	*D10*	F2	Swallow
5.10	*12. 8*	*D10*	G3	Pig
6.10	*13. 8*	*D10*	H4	Porcupine
7.10	*14. 8*	*D10*	J5	Wolf
8.10	*15. 8*	*D10*	K6	Dog
9.10	*16. 8*	*D10*	A7	Pheasant
10.10	*17. 8*	*D10*	B8	Cock
11.10	*18. 8*	*D10*	C9	Crow

Solar date	*Lunar date*	*Month HS/EB*	*Day HS/EB*	*Constellation*
12.10	*19. 8*	*D10*	D10	Monkey
13.10	*20. 8*	*D10*	E11	Gibbon
14.10	*21. 8*	*D10*	F12	Tapir
15.10	*22. 8*	*D10*	G1	Sheep
16. 0	*23. 8*	*D10*	H2	Deer
17. 0	*24. 8*	*D10*	J3	Horse
18.10	*25. 8*	*D10*	K4	Stag
19.10	*26. 8*	*D10*	A5	Serpent
20.10	*27. 8*	*D10*	B6	Earthworm
21.10	*28. 8*	*D10*	C7	Crocodile
22.10	*29. 8*	*D10*	D8	Dragon
23.10	1. 9	E11	E9	Badger
24.10	2. 9	E11	F10	Hare
25.10	3. 9	E11	G11	Fox
26.10	4. 9	E11	H12	Tiger
27.10	5. 9	E11	J1	Leopard
28.10	6. 9	E11	K2	Griffon
29.10	7. 9	E11	A3	Ox
30.10	8. 9	E11	B4	Bat
31.10	9. 9	E11	C5	Rat
1.11	10. 9	E11	D6	Swallow
2.11	11. 9	E11	E7	Pig
3.11	12. 9	E11	F8	Porcupine
4.11	13. 9	E11	G9	Wolf
5.11	14. 9	E11	H10	Dog
6.11	15. 9	E11	J11	Pheasant
7.11	16. 9	E11	K12	Cock
8.11	17. 9	E11	A1	Crow
9.11	18. 9	E11	B2	Monkey
10.11	19. 9	E11	C3	Gibbon
11.11	20. 9	E11	D4	Tapir
12.11	21. 9	E11	E5	Sheep
13.11	22. 9	E11	F6	Deer
14.11	23. 9	E11	G7	Horse
15.11	24. 9	E11	H8	Stag
16.11	25. 9	E11	J9	Serpent
17.11	26. 9	E11	K10	Earthworm
18.11	27. 9	E11	A11	Crocodile
19.11	28. 9	E11	B12	Dragon
20.11	29. 9	E11	C1	Badger
21.11	1.10	F12	D2	Hare
22.11	2.10	F12	E3	Fox
23.11	3.10	F12	F4	Tiger
24.11	4.10	F12	G5	Leopard
25.11	5.10	F12	H6	Griffon
26.11	6.10	F12	J7	Ox
27.11	7.10	F12	K8	Bat
28.11	8.10	F12	A9	Rat
29.11	9.10	F12	B10	Swallow
30.11	10.10	F12	C11	Pig
1.12	11.10	F12	D12	Porcupine
2.12	12.10	F12	E1	Wolf
3.12	13.10	F12	F2	Dog
4.12	14.10	F12	G3	Pheasant
5.12	15.10	F12	H4	Cock
6.12	16.10	F12	J5	Crow
7.12	17.10	F12	K6	Monkey
8.12	18.10	F12	A7	Gibbon
9.12	19.10	F12	B8	Tapir
10.12	20.10	F12	C9	Sheep
11.12	21.10	F12	D10	Deer
12.12	22.10	F12	E11	Horse
13.12	23.10	F12	F12	Stag
14.12	24.10	F12	G1	Serpent
15.12	25.10	F12	H2	Earthworm
16.12	26.10	F12	J3	Crocodile
17.12	27.10	F12	K4	Dragon
18.12	28.10	F12	A5	Badger
19.12	29.10	F12	B6	Hare
20.12	30.10	F12	C7	Fox
21.12	1.11	G1	D8	Tiger
22.12	2.11	G1	E9	Leopard
23.12	3.11	G1	F10	Griffon

Solar date	*Lunar date*	*Month HS/EB*	*Day HS/EB*	*Constellation*
24.12	4.11	G1	G11	Ox
25.12	5.11	G1	H12	Bat
26.12	6.11	G1	J1	Rat
27.12	7.11	G1	K2	Swallow
28.12	8.11	G1	A3	Pig
29.12	9.11	G1	B4	Porcupine
30.12	10.11	G1	C5	Wolf
21.12	11.11	G1	D6	Dog
1977				
1. 1	12.11	G1	E7	Pheasant
2. 1	13.11	G1	F8	Cock
3. 1	14.11	G1	G9	Crow
4. 1	15.11	G1	H10	Monkey
5. 1	16.11	G1	J11	Gibbon
6. 1	17.11	G1	K12	Tapir
7. 1	18.11	G1	A1	Sheep
8. 1	19.11	G1	B2	Deer
9. 1	20.11	G1	C3	Horse
10. 1	21.11	G1	D4	Stag
11. 1	22.11	G1	E5	Serpent
12. 1	23.11	G1	F6	Earthworm
13. 1	24.11	G1	G7	Crocodile
14. 1	25.11	G1	H8	Dragon
15. 1	26.11	G1	J9	Badger
16. 1	27.11	G1	K10	Hare
17. 1	28.11	G1	A11	Fox
18. 1	29.11	G1	B12	Tiger
19. 1	1.12	H2	C1	Leopard

Solar date	*Lunar date*	*Month HS/EB*	*Day HS/EB*	*Constellation*
20. 1	2.12	H2	D2	Griffon
21. 1	3.12	H2	E3	Ox
22. 1	4.12	H2	F4	Bat
23. 1	5.12	H2	G5	Rat
24. 1	6.12	H2	H6	Swallow
25. 1	7.12	H2	J7	Pig
26. 1	8.12	H2	K8	Porcupine
27. 1	9.12	H2	A9	Wolf
28. 1	10.12	H2	B10	Dog
29. 1	11.12	H2	C11	Pheasant
30. 1	12.12	H2	D12	Cock
31. 1	13.12	H2	E1	Crow
1. 2	14.12	H2	F2	Monkey
2. 2	15.12	H2	G3	Gibbon
3. 2	16.12	H2	H4	Tapir
4. 2	17.12	H2	J5	Sheep
5. 2	18.12	H2	K6	Deer
6. 2	19.12	H2	A7	Horse
7. 2	10.12	H2	B8	Stag
8. 2	21.12	H2	C9	Serpent
9. 2	22.12	H2	D10	Earthworm
10. 2	23.12	H2	E11	Crocodile
11. 2	24.12	H2	F12	Dragon
12. 2	25.12	H2	G1	Badger
13. 2	26.12	H2	H2	Hare
14. 2	27.12	H2	J3	Fox
15. 2	28.12	H2	K4	Tiger
16. 2	29.12	H2	A5	Leopard
17. 2	30.12	H2	B6	Griffon

TING SZU YEAR

18. 2	1. 1	J3	C7	Ox
19. 2	2. 1	J3	D8	Bat
20. 2	3. 1	J3	E9	Rat
21. 2	4. 1	J3	F10	Swallow
22. 2	5. 1	J3	G11	Pig
23. 2	6. 1	J3	H12	Porcupine
24. 2	7. 1	J3	J1	Wolf
25. 2	8. 1	J3	K2	Dog
26. 2	9. 1	J3	A3	Pheasant
27. 2	10. 1	J3	B4	Cock
28. 2	11. 1	J3	C5	Crow
1. 3	12. 1	J3	D6	Monkey
2. 3	13. 1	J3	E7	Gibbon
3. 3	14. 1	J3	F8	Tapir
4. 3	15. 1	J3	G9	Sheep
5. 3	16. 1	J3	H10	Deer
6. 3	17. 1	J3	J11	Horse
7. 3	18. 1	J3	K12	Stag
8. 3	19. 1	J3	A1	Serpent
9. 3	20. 1	J3	B2	Earthworm
10. 3	21. 1	J3	C3	Crocodile
11. 3	22. 1	J3	D4	Dragon
12. 3	23. 1	J3	E5	Badger
13. 3	24. 1	J3	F6	Hare
14. 3	25. 1	J3	G7	Fox
15. 3	26. 1	J3	H8	Tiger
16. 3	27. 1	J3	J9	Leopard
17. 3	28. 1	J3	K10	Griffon
18. 3	29. 1	J3	A11	Ox
19. 3	30. 1	J3	B12	Bat
20. 3	1. 2	K4	C1	Rat
21. 3	2. 2	K4	D2	Swallow
22. 3	3. 2	K4	E3	Pig
23. 3	4. 2	K4	F4	Porcupine
24. 3	5. 2	K4	G5	Wolf
25. 3	6. 2	K4	H6	Dog
26. 3	7. 2	K4	J7	Pheasant
27. 3	8. 2	K4	K8	Cock
28. 3	9. 2	K4	A9	Crow

29. 3	10. 2	K4	B10	Monkey
30. 3	11. 2	K4	C11	Gibbon
31. 3	12. 2	K4	D12	Tapir
1. 4	13. 2	K4	E1	Sheep
2. 4	14. 2	K4	F2	Deer
3. 4	15. 2	K4	G3	Horse
4. 4	16. 2	K4	H4	Stag
5. 4	17. 2	K4	J5	Serpent
6. 4	18. 2	K4	K6	Earthworm
7. 4	19. 2	K4	A7	Crocodile
8. 4	20. 2	K4	B8	Dragon
9. 4	21. 2	K4	C9	Badger
10. 4	22. 2	K4	D10	Hare
11. 4	23. 2	K4	E11	Fox
12. 4	24. 2	K4	F12	Tiger
13. 4	25. 2	K4	G1	Leopard
14. 4	26. 2	K4	H2	Griffon
15. 4	27. 2	K4	J3	Ox
16. 4	28. 2	K4	K4	Bat
17. 4	29. 2	K4	A5	Rat
18. 4	1. 3	A5	B6	Swallow
19. 4	2. 3	A5	C7	Pig
20. 4	3. 3	A5	D8	Porcupine
21. 4	4. 3	A5	E9	Wolf
22. 4	5. 3	A5	F10	Dog
23. 4	6. 3	A5	G11	Pheasant
24. 4	7. 3	A5	H12	Cock
25. 4	8. 3	A5	J1	Crow
26. 4	9. 3	A5	K2	Monkey
27. 4	10. 3	A5	A3	Gibbon
28. 4	11. 3	A5	B4	Tapir
29. 4	12. 3	A5	C5	Sheep
30. 4	13. 3	A5	D6	Deer
1. 5	14. 3	A5	E7	Horse
2. 5	15. 3	A5	F8	Stag
3. 5	16. 3	A5	G9	Serpent
4. 5	17. 3	A5	H10	Earthworm
5. 5	18. 3	A5	J11	Crocodile
6. 5	19. 3	A5	K12	Dragon

Solar date	*Lunar date*	*Month HS/EB*	*Day HS/EB*	*Constellation*
7. 5	20. 3	A5	A1	Badger
8. 5	21. 3	A5	B2	Hare
9. 5	22. 3	A5	C3	Fox
10. 5	23. 3	A5	D4	Tiger
11. 5	24. 3	A5	E5	Leopard
12. 5	25. 3	A5	F6	Griffon
13. 5	26. 3	A5	G7	Ox
14. 5	27. 3	A5	H8	Bat
15. 5	28. 3	A5	J9	Rat
16. 5	29. 3	A5	K10	Swallow
17. 5	30. 3	A5	A11	Pig
18. 5	1. 4	B6	B12	Porcupine
19. 5	2. 4	B6	C1	Wolf
20. 5	3. 4	B6	D2	Dog
21. 5	4. 4	B6	E3	Pheasant
22. 5	5. 4	B6	F4	Cock
23. 5	6. 4	B6	G5	Crow
24. 5	7. 4	B6	H6	Monkey
25. 5	8. 4	B6	J7	Gibbon
26. 5	9. 4	B6	K8	Tapir
27. 5	10. 4	B6	A9	Sheep
28. 5	11. 4	B6	B10	Deer
29. 5	12. 4	B6	C11	Horse
30. 5	13. 4	B6	D12	Stag
31. 5	14. 4	B6	E1	Serpent
1. 6	15. 4	B6	F2	Earthworm
2. 6	16. 4	B6	G3	Crocodile
3. 6	17. 4	B6	H4	Dragon
4. 6	18. 4	B6	J5	Badger
5. 6	19. 4	B6	K6	Hare
6. 6	20. 4	B6	A7	Fox
7. 6	21. 4	B6	B8	Tiger
8. 6	22. 4	B6	C9	Leopard
9. 6	23. 4	B6	D10	Griffon
10. 6	24. 4	B6	E11	Ox
11. 6	25. 4	B6	F12	Bat
12. 6	26. 4	B6	G1	Rat
13. 6	27. 4	B6	H2	Swallow
14. 6	28. 4	B6	J3	Pig
15. 6	29. 4	B6	K4	Porcupine
16. 6	30. 4	B6	A5	Wolf
17. 6	1. 5	C7	B6	Dog
18. 6	2. 5	C7	C7	Pheasant
19. 6	3. 5	C7	D8	Cock
20. 6	4. 5	C7	E9	Crow
21. 6	5. 5	C7	F10	Monkey
22. 6	6. 5	C7	G11	Gibbon
23. 6	7. 5	C7	H12	Tapir
24. 6	8. 5	C7	J1	Sheep
25. 6	9. 5	C7	K2	Deer
26. 6	10. 5	C7	A3	Horse
27. 6	11. 5	C7	B4	Stag
28. 6	12. 5	C7	C5	Serpent
29. 6	13. 5	C7	D6	Earthworm
30. 6	14. 5	C7	E7	Crocodile
1. 7	15. 5	C7	F8	Dragon
2. 7	16. 5	C7	G9	Badger
3. 7	17. 5	C7	H10	Hare
4. 7	18. 5	C7	J11	Fox
5. 7	19. 5	C7	K12	Tiger
6. 7	20. 5	C7	A1	Leopard
7. 7	21. 5	C7	B2	Griffon
8. 7	22. 5	C7	C3	Ox
9. 7	23. 5	C7	D4	Bat
10. 7	24. 5	C7	E5	Rat
11. 7	25. 5	C7	F6	Swallow
12. 7	26. 5	C7	G7	Pig
13. 7	27. 5	C7	H8	Porcupine
14. 7	28. 5	C7	J9	Wolf
15. 7	29. 5	C7	K10	Dog
16. 7	1. 6	D8	A11	Pheasant
17. 7	2. 6	D8	B12	Cock
18. 7	3. 6	D8	C1	Crow

Solar date	*Lunar date*	*Month HS/EB*	*Day HS/EB*	*Constellation*
19. 7	4. 6	D8	D2	Monkey
20. 7	5. 6	D8	E3	Gibbon
21. 7	6. 6	D8	F4	Tapir
22. 7	7. 6	D8	G5	Sheep
23. 7	8. 6	D8	H6	Deer
24. 7	9. 6	D8	J7	Horse
25. 7	10. 6	D8	K8	Stag
26. 7	11. 6	D8	A9	Serpent
27. 7	12. 6	D8	B10	Earthworm
28. 7	13. 6	D8	C11	Crocodile
29. 7	14. 6	D8	D12	Dragon
30. 7	15. 6	D8	E1	Badger
31. 7	16. 6	D8	F2	Hare
1. 8	17. 6	D8	G3	Fox
2. 8	18. 6	D8	H4	Tiger
3. 8	19. 6	D8	J5	Leopard
4. 8	20. 6	D8	K6	Griffon
5. 8	21. 6	D8	A7	Ox
6. 8	22. 6	D8	B8	Bat
7. 8	23. 6	D8	C9	Rat
8. 8	24. 6	D8	D10	Swallow
9. 8	25. 6	D8	E11	Pig
10. 8	26. 6	D8	F12	Porcupine
11. 8	27. 6	D8	G1	Wolf
12. 8	28. 6	D8	H2	Dog
13. 8	29. 6	D8	J3	Pheasant
14. 8	30. 6	D8	K4	Cock
15. 8	1. 7	E9	A5	Crow
16. 8	2. 7	E9	B6	Monkey
17. 8	3. 7	E9	C7	Gibbon
18. 8	4. 7	E9	D8	Tapir
19. 8	5. 7	E9	E9	Sheep
20. 8	6. 7	E9	F10	Deer
21. 8	7. 7	E9	G11	Horse
22. 8	8. 7	E9	H12	Stag
23. 8	9. 7	E9	J1	Serpent
24. 8	10. 7	E9	K2	Earthworm
25. 8	11. 7	E9	A3	Crocodile
26. 8	12. 7	E9	B4	Dragon
27. 8	13. 7	E9	C5	Badger
28. 8	14. 7	E9	D6	Hare
29. 8	15. 7	E9	E7	Fox
30. 8	16. 7	E9	F8	Tiger
31. 8	17. 7	E9	G9	Leopard
1. 9	18. 7	E9	H10	Griffon
2. 9	19. 7	E9	J11	Ox
3. 9	20. 7	E9	K12	Bat
4. 9	21. 7	E9	A1	Rat
5. 9	22. 7	E9	B2	Swallow
6. 9	23. 7	E9	C3	Pig
7. 9	24. 7	E9	D4	Porcupine
8. 9	25. 7	E9	E5	Wolf
9. 9	26. 7	E9	F6	Dog
10. 9	27. 7	E9	G7	Pheasant
11. 9	28. 7	E9	H8	Cock
12. 9	29. 7	E9	J9	Crow
13. 9	1. 8	F10	K10	Monkey
14. 9	2. 8	F10	A11	Gibbon
15. 9	3. 8	F10	B12	Tapir
16. 9	4. 8	F10	C1	Sheep
17. 9	5. 8	F10	D2	Deer
18. 9	6. 8	F10	E3	Horse
19. 9	7. 8	F10	F4	Stag
20. 9	8. 8	F10	G5	Serpent
21. 9	9. 8	F10	H6	Earthworm
22. 9	10. 8	F10	J7	Crocodile
23. 9	11. 8	F10	K8	Dragon
24. 9	12. 8	F10	A9	Badger
25. 9	13. 8	F10	B10	Hare
26. 9	14. 8	F10	C11	Fox
27. 9	15. 8	F10	D12	Tiger
28. 9	16. 8	F10	E1	Leopard
29. 9	17. 8	F10	F2	Griffon

Solar date	*Lunar date*	*Month HS/EB*	*Day HS/EB*	*Constellation*
30. 9	18. 8	F10	G3	Ox
1.10	19. 8	F10	H4	Bat
2.10	20. 8	F10	J5	Rat
3.10	21. 8	F10	K6	Swallow
4.10	22. 8	F10	A7	Pig
5.10	23. 8	F10	B8	Porcupine
6.10	24. 8	F10	C9	Wolf
7.10	25. 8	F10	D10	Dog
8.10	26. 8	F10	E11	Pheasant
9.10	27. 8	F10	F12	Cock
10.10	28. 8	F10	G1	Crow
11.10	29. 8	F10	H2	Monkey
12.10	30. 8	F10	J3	Gibbon
13.10	1. 9	G11	K4	Tapir
14.10	2. 9	G11	A5	Sheep
15.10	3. 9	G11	B6	Deer
16.10	4. 9	G11	C7	Horse
17.10	5. 9	G11	D8	Stag
19.10	6. 9	G11	E9	Serpent
20.10	8. 9	G11	G11	Crocodile
21.10	9. 9	G11	H12	Dragon
22.10	10. 9	G11	J1	Badger
23.10	11. 9	G11	K2	Hare
24.10	12. 9	G11	A3	Fox
25.10	13. 9	G11	B4	Tiger
26.10	14. 9	G11	C5	Leopard
27.10	15. 9	G11	D6	Griffon
28.10	16. 9	G11	E7	Ox
29.10	17. 9	G11	F8	Bat
30.10	18. 9	G11	G9	Rat
31.10	19. 9	G11	H10	Swallow
1.11	20. 9	G11	J11	Pig
2.11	21. 9	G11	K12	Porcupine
3.11	22. 9	G11	A1	Wolf
4.11	23. 9	G11	B2	Dog
5.11	24. 9	G11	C3	Pheasant
6.11	25. 9	G11	D4	Cock
7.11	26. 9	G11	E5	Crow
8.11	27. 9	G11	F6	Monkey
9.11	28. 9	G11	G7	Gibbon
10.11	29. 9	G11	H8	Tapir
11.11	1.10	H12	J9	Sheep
12.11	2.10	H12	K10	Deer
13.11	3.10	H12	A11	Horse
14.11	4.10	H12	B12	Stag
15.11	5.10	H12	C1	Serpent
16.11	6.10	H12	D2	Earthworm
17.11	7.10	H12	E3	Crocodile
18.11	8.10	H12	F4	Dragon
19.11	9.10	H12	G5	Badger
20.11	10.10	H12	H6	Hare
21.11	11.10	H12	J7	Fox
22.11	12.10	H12	K8	Tiger
23.11	13.10	H12	A9	Leopard
24.11	14.10	H12	H10	Griffon
25.11	15.10	H12	C11	Ox
26.11	16.10	H12	D12	Bat
27.11	17.10	H12	E1	Rat
28.11	18.10	H12	F2	Swallow
29.11	19.10	H12	G3	Pig
30.11	20.10	H12	H4	Porcupine
1.12	21.10	H12	J5	Wolf
2.12	22.10	H12	K6	Dog
3.12	23.10	H12	A7	Pheasant
4.12	24.10	H12	B8	Cock
5.12	25.10	H12	C9	Crow

Solar date	*Lunar date*	*Month HS/EB*	*Day HS/EB*	*Constellation*
6.12	26.10	H12	D10	Monkey
7.12	27.10	H12	E11	Gibbon
8.12	28.10	H12	F12	Tapir
9.12	29.10	H12	G1	Sheep
10.12	30.10	H12	H2	Deer
11.12	1.11	J1	J3	Horse
12.12	2.11	J1	K4	Stag
13.12	3.11	J1	A5	Serpent
14.12	4.11	J1	B6	Earthworm
15.12	5.11	J1	C7	Crocodile
16.12	6.11	J1	D8	Dragon
17.12	7.11	J1	E9	Badger
18.12	8.11	J1	F10	Hare
19.12	9.11	J1	G11	Fox
20.12	10.11	J1	H12	Tiger
21.12	11.11	J1	J1	Leopard
22.12	12.11	J1	K2	Griffon
23.12	13.11	J1	A3	Ox
24.12	14.11	J1	B4	Bat
25.12	15.11	J1	C5	Rat
26.12	16.11	J1	D6	Swallow
27.12	17.11	J1	E7	Pig
28.12	18.11	J1	F8	Porcupine
29.12	19.11	J1	G9	Wolf
30.12	20.11	J1	H10	Dog
31.12	21.11	J1	J11	Pheasant

1978

Solar date	*Lunar date*	*Month HS/EB*	*Day HS/EB*	*Constellation*
1. 1	22.11	J1	K12	Cock
2. 1	23.11	J1	A1	Crow
3. 1	24.11	J1	B2	Monkey
4. 1	25.11	J1	C3	Gibbon
5. 1	26.11	J1	D4	Tapir
6. 1	27.11	J1	E5	Sheep
7. 1	28.11	J1	F6	Deer
8. 1	29.11	J1	G7	Horse
9. 1	1.12	K2	H8	Stag
10. 1	2.12	K2	J9	Serpent
11. 1	3.12	K2	K10	Earthworm
12. 1	4.12	K2	A11	Crocodile
13. 1	5.12	K2	B12	Dragon
14. 1	6.12	K2	C1	Badger
15. 1	7.12	K2	D2	Hare
16. 1	8.12	K2	E3	Fox
17. 1	9.12	K2	F4	Tiger
18. 1	10.12	K2	G5	Leopard
19. 1	11.12	K2	H6	Griffon
20. 1	12.12	K2	J7	Ox
21. 1	13.12	K2	K8	Bat
22. 1	14.12	K2	A9	Rat
23. 1	15.12	K2	B10	Swallow
24. 1	16.12	K2	C11	Pig
25. 1	17.12	K2	D12	Porcupine
26. 1	18.12	K2	E1	Wolf
27. 1	19.12	K2	F2	Dog
28. 1	20.12	K2	G3	Pheasant
29. 1	21.12	K2	H4	Cock
30. 1	22.12	K2	J5	Crow
31. 1	23.12	K2	K6	Monkey
1. 2	24.12	K2	A7	Gibbon
2. 2	25.12	K2	B8	Tapir
3. 2	26.12	K2	C9	Sheep
4. 2	27.12	K2	D10	Deer
5. 2	28.12	K2	E11	Horse
6. 2	29.12	K2	F12	Stag

MOU WU YEAR

Solar date	*Lunar date*	*Month HS/EB*	*Day HS/EB*	*Constellation*
7. 2	1. 1	A3	G1	Serpent
8. 2	2. 1	A3	H2	Earthworm
9. 2	3. 1	A3	J3	Crocodile
10. 2	4. 1	A3	K4	Dragon
11. 2	5. 1	A3	A5	Badger
12. 2	6. 1	A3	B6	Hare
13. 2	7. 1	A3	C7	Fox
14. 2	8. 1	A3	D8	Tiger
15. 2	9. 1	A3	E9	Leopard
16. 2	10. 1	A3	F10	Griffon
17. 2	11. 1	A3	G11	Ox
18. 2	12. 1	A3	H12	Bat
19. 2	13. 1	A3	J1	Rat
20. 2	14. 1	A3	K2	Swallow
21. 2	14. 1	A3	A3	Pig
22. 2	16. 1	A3	B4	Porcupine
23. 2	17. 1	A3	C5	Wolf
24. 2	18. 1	A3	D6	Dog
25. 2	19. 1	A3	E7	Pheasant
26. 2	20. 1	A3	F8	Cock
27. 2	21. 1	A3	G9	Crow
28. 2	22. 1	A3	H10	Monkey
1. 3	23. 1	A3	J11	Gibbon
2. 3	24. 1	A3	K12	Tapir
3. 3	25. 1	A3	A1	Sheep
4. 3	26. 1	A3	B2	Deer
5. 3	27. 1	A3	C3	Horse
6. 3	28. 1	A3	D4	Stag
7. 3	29. 1	A3	E5	Serpent
8. 3	30. 1	A3	F6	Earthworm
9. 3	1. 2	B4	G7	Crocodile
10. 3	2. 2	B4	H8	Dragon
11. 3	3. 2	B4	J9	Badger
12. 3	4. 2	B4	K10	Hare
13. 3	5. 2	B4	A11	Fox
14. 3	6. 2	B4	B12	Tiger
15. 3	7. 2	B4	C1	Leopard
16. 3	8. 2	B4	D2	Griffon
17. 3	9. 2	B4	E3	Ox
18. 3	10. 2	B4	F4	Bat
19. 3	11. 2	B4	G5	Rat
20. 3	12. 2	B4	H6	Swallow
21. 3	13. 2	B4	J7	Pig
22. 3	14. 2	B4	K8	Porcupine
23. 3	15. 2	B4	A9	Wolf
24. 3	16. 2	B4	B10	Dog
25. 3	17. 2	B4	C11	Pheasant
26. 3	18. 2	B4	D12	Cock
27. 3	19. 2	B4	E1	Crow
28. 3	20. 2	B4	F2	Monkey
29. 3	21. 2	B4	G3	Gibbon
30. 3	22. 2	B4	H4	Tapir
31. 3	23. 2	B4	J5	Sheep
1. 4	24. 2	B4	K6	Deer
2. 4	25. 2	B4	A7	Horse
3. 4	26. 2	B4	B8	Stag
4. 4	27. 2	B4	C9	Serpent
5. 4	28. 2	B4	D10	Earthworm
6. 4	29. 2	B4	E11	Crocodile
7. 4	1. 3	C5	F12	Dragon
8. 4	2. 3	C5	G1	Badger
9. 4	3. 3	C5	H2	Hare
10. 4	4. 3	C5	J3	Fox
11. 4	5. 3	C5	K4	Tiger
12. 4	6. 3	C5	A5	Leopard
13. 4	7. 3	C5	B6	Griffon
14. 4	8. 3	C5	C7	Ox
15. 4	9. 3	C5	D8	Bat
16. 4	10. 3	C5	E9	Rat
17. 4	11. 3	C5	F10	Swallow
18. 4	12. 3	C5	G11	Pig
19. 4	13. 3	C5	H12	Porcupine
20. 4	14. 3	C5	J1	Wolf
21. 4	15. 3	C5	K2	Dog
22. 4	16. 3	C5	A3	Pheasant
23. 4	17. 3	C5	B4	Cock
24. 4	18. 3	C5	C5	Crow
25. 4	19. 3	C5	D6	Monkey
26. 4	20. 3	C5	E7	Gibbon
27. 4	21. 3	C5	F8	Tapir
28. 4	22. 3	C5	G9	Sheep
29. 4	23. 3	C5	H10	Deer
30. 4	24. 3	C5	J11	Horse
1. 5	25. 3	C5	K12	Stag
2. 5	26. 3	C5	A1	Serpent
3. 5	27. 3	C5	B2	Earthworm
4. 5	28. 3	C5	C3	Crocodile
5. 5	29. 3	C5	D4	Dragon
6. 5	30. 3	C5	E5	Badger
7. 5	1. 4	D6	F6	Hare
8. 5	2. 4	D6	G7	Fox
9. 5	3. 4	D6	H8	Tiger
10. 5	4. 4	D6	J9	Leopard
11. 5	5. 4	D6	K10	Griffon
12. 5	6. 4	D6	A11	Ox
13. 5	7. 4	D6	B12	Bat
14. 5	8. 4	D6	C1	Rat
15. 5	9. 4	D6	D2	Swallow
16. 5	10. 4	D6	E3	Pig
17. 5	11. 4	D6	F4	Porcupine
18. 5	12. 4	D6	G5	Wolf
19. 5	13. 4	D6	H6	Dog
20. 5	14. 4	D6	J7	Pheasant
21. 5	15. 4	D6	K8	Cock
22. 5	16. 4	D6	A9	Crow
23. 5	17. 4	D6	B10	Monkey
24. 5	18. 4	D6	C11	Gibbon
25. 5	19. 4	D6	D12	Tapir
26. 5	20. 4	D6	E1	Sheep
27. 5	21. 4	D6	F2	Deer
28. 5	22. 4	D6	G3	Horse
29. 5	23. 4	D6	H4	Stag
30. 5	24. 4	D6	J5	Serpent
31. 5	25. 4	D6	K6	Earthworm
1. 6	26. 4	D6	A7	Crocodile
2. 6	27. 4	D6	B8	Dragon
3. 6	28. 4	D6	C9	Badger
4. 6	29. 4	D6	D10	Hare
5. 6	30. 4	D6	E11	Fox
6. 6	1. 5	E7	F12	Tiger
7. 6	2. 5	E7	G1	Leopard
8. 6	3. 5	E7	H2	Griffon
9. 6	4. 5	E7	J3	Ox
10. 6	5. 5	E7	K4	Bat
11. 6	6. 5	E7	A5	Rat
12. 6	7. 5	E7	B6	Swallow
13. 6	8. 5	E7	C7	Pig
14. 6	9. 5	E7	D8	Porcupine
15. 6	10. 5	E7	E9	Wolf
16. 6	11. 5	E7	F10	Dog
17. 6	12. 5	E7	G11	Pheasant
18. 6	13. 5	E7	H12	Cock
19. 6	14. 5	E7	J1	Crow
20. 6	15. 5	E7	K2	Monkey
21. 6	16. 5	E7	A3	Gibbon
22. 6	17. 5	E7	B4	Tapir
23. 6	18. 5	E7	C5	Sheep
24. 6	19. 5	E7	D6	Deer
25. 6	20. 5	E7	E7	Horse
26. 6	21. 5	E7	F8	Stag
27. 6	22. 5	E7	G9	Serpent
28. 6	23. 5	E7	H10	Earthworm

Solar date	*Lunar date*	*Month HS/EB*	*Day HS/EB*	*Constellation*
29. 6	24. 5	E7	J11	Crocodile
30. 6	25. 5	E7	K12	Dragon
1. 7	26. 5	E7	A1	Badger
2. 7	27. 5	E7	B2	Hare
3. 7	28. 5	E7	C3	Fox
4. 7	29. 5	E7	D4	Tiger
5. 7	1. 6	F8	E5	Leopard
6. 7	2. 6	F8	F6	Griffon
7. 7	3. 6	F8	G7	Ox
8. 7	4. 6	F8	H8	Bat
9. 7	5. 6	F8	J9	Rat
10. 7	6. 6	F8	K10	Swallow
11. 7	7. 6	F8	A11	Pig
12. 7	8. 6	F8	B12	Porcupine
13. 7	9. 6	F8	C1	Wolf
14. 7	10. 6	F8	D2	Dog
15. 7	11. 6	F8	E3	Pheasant
16. 7	12. 6	F8	F4	Cock
17. 7	13. 6	F8	G5	Crow
18. 7	14. 6	F8	H6	Monkey
19. 7	15. 6	F8	J7	Gibbon
20. 7	16. 6	F8	K8	Tapir
21. 7	17. 6	F8	A9	Sheep
22. 7	18. 6	F8	B10	Deer
23. 7	19. 6	F8	C11	Horse
24. 7	20. 6	F8	D12	Stag
25. 7	21. 6	F8	E1	Serpent
26. 7	22. 6	F8	F2	Earthworm
27. 7	23. 6	F8	G3	Crocodile
28. 7	24. 6	F8	H4	Dragon
29. 7	25. 6	F8	J5	Badger
30. 7	26. 6	F8	K6	Hare
31. 7	27. 6	F8	A7	Fox
1. 8	28. 6	F8	B8	Tiger
2. 8	29. 6	F8	C9	Leopard
3. 8	30. 6	F8	D10	Griffon
4. 8	1. 7	G9	E11	Ox
5. 8	2. 7	G9	F12	Bat
6. 8	3. 7	G9	G1	Rat
7. 8	4. 7	G9	H2	Swallow
8. 8	5. 7	G9	J3	Pig
9. 8	6. 7	G9	K4	Porcupine
10. 8	7. 7	G9	A5	Wolf
11. 8	8. 7	G9	B6	Dog
12. 8	9. 7	G9	C7	Pheasant
13. 8	10. 7	G9	D8	Cock
14. 8	11. 7	G9	E9	Crow
15. 8	12. 7	G9	F10	Monkey
16. 8	13. 7	G9	G11	Gibbon
17. 8	14. 7	G9	H12	Tapir
18. 8	15. 7	G9	J1	Sheep
19. 8	16. 7	G9	K2	Deer
20. 8	17. 7	G9	A3	Horse
21. 8	18. 7	G9	B4	Stag
22. 8	19. 7	G9	C5	Serpent
23. 8	20. 7	G9	D6	Earthworm
24. 8	21. 7	G9	E7	Crocodile
25. 8	22. 7	G9	F8	Dragon
26. 8	23. 7	G9	G9	Badger
27. 8	24. 7	G9	H10	Hare
28. 8	25. 7	G9	J11	Fox
29. 8	26. 7	G9	K12	Tiger
30. 8	27. 7	G9	A1	Leopard
31. 8	28. 7	G9	B2	Griffon
1. 9	29. 7	G8	C3	Ox
2. 9	30. 7	G9	D4	Bat
3. 9	1. 8	H10	E5	Rat
4. 9	2. 8	H10	F6	Swallow
5. 9	3. 8	H10	G7	Pig
6. 9	4. 8	H10	H8	Porcupine
7. 9	5. 8	H10	J9	Wolf
8. 9	6. 8	H10	K10	Dog
9. 9	7. 8	H10	A11	Pheasant
10. 9	8. 8	H10	B12	Cock
11. 9	9. 8	H10	C1	Crow
12. 9	10. 8	H10	D2	Monkey
13. 9	11. 8	H10	E3	Gibbon
14. 9	12. 8	H10	F4	Tapir
15. 9	13. 8	H10	G5	Sheep
16. 9	14. 8	H10	H6	Deer
17. 9	15. 8	H10	J7	Horse
18. 9	16. 8	H10	K8	Stag
19. 9	17. 8	H10	A9	Serpent
20. 9	18. 8	H10	B10	Earthworm
21. 9	19. 8	H10	C11	Crocodile
22. 9	20. 8	H10	D12	Dragon
23. 9	21. 8	H10	E1	Badger
24. 9	22. 8	H10	F2	Hare
25. 9	23. 8	H10	G3	Fox
26. 9	24. 8	H10	H4	Tiger
27. 9	25. 8	H10	J5	Leopard
28. 9	26. 8	H10	K6	Griffon
29. 9	27. 8	H10	A7	Ox
30. 9	28. 8	H10	B8	Bat
1.10	29. 8	H10	C9	Rat
2.10	1. 9	J11	D10	Swallow
3.10	2. 9	J11	E11	Pig
4.10	3. 9	J11	F12	Porcupine
5.10	4. 9	J11	G1	Wolf
6.10	5. 9	J11	H2	Dog
7.10	6. 9	J11	J3	Pheasant
8.10	7. 9	J11	K4	Cock
9.10	8. 9	J11	A5	Crow
10.10	9. 9	J11	B6	Monkey
11.10	10. 9	J11	C7	Gibbon
12.10	11. 9	J11	D8	Tapir
13.10	12. 9	J11	E9	Sheep
14.10	13. 9	J11	F10	Deer
15.10	14. 9	J11	G11	Horse
16.10	15. 9	J11	H12	Stag
17.10	16. 9	J11	J1	Serpent
18.10	17. 9	J11	K2	Earthworm
19.10	18. 9	J11	A3	Crocodile
20.10	19. 9	J11	B4	Dragon
21.10	20. 9	J11	C5	Badger
22.10	21. 9	J11	D6	Hare
23.10	22. 9	J11	E7	Fox
24.10	23. 9	J11	F8	Tiger
25.10	24. 9	J11	G9	Leopard
26.10	25. 9	J11	H10	Griffon
27.10	26. 9	J11	J11	Ox
28.10	27. 9	J11	K12	Bat
29.10	28. 9	J11	A1	Rat
30.10	29. 9	J11	B2	Swallow
31.10	30. 9	J11	C3	Pig
1.11	1.10	K12	D4	Porcupine
2.11	2.10	K12	E5	Wolf
3.11	3.10	K12	F6	Dog
4.11	4 10	K12	G7	Pheasant
5.11	5.10	K12	H8	Cock
6.11	6.10	K12	J9	Crow
7.11	7.10	K12	K10	Monkey
8.11	8.10	K12	A11	Gibbon
9.11	9.10	K12	B12	Tapir
10.11	10.10	K12	C1	Sheep
11.11	11.10	K12	D2	Deer
12.11	12.10	K12	E3	Horse
13.11	13.10	K12	F4	Stag
14.11	14.10	K12	G5	Serpent
15.11	15.10	K12	H6	Earthworm
16.11	16.10	K12	J7	Crocodile
17.11	17.10	K12	K8	Dragon
18.11	18.10	K12	A9	Badger
19.11	19.10	K12	B10	Hare
20.11	20.10	K12	C11	Fox
21.11	21.10	K12	D12	Tiger

Solar date	Lunar date	Month HS/EB	Day HS/EB	Constellation
22.11	22.10	K12	E1	Leopard
23.11	23.10	K12	F2	Griffon
24.11	24.10	K12	G3	Ox
25.11	25.10	K12	H4	Bat
26.11	26.10	K12	J5	Rat
27.11	27.10	K12	K6	Swallow
28.11	28.10	K12	A7	Pig
29.11	29.10	K12	B8	Porcupine
30.11	1.11	A1	C9	Wolf
1.12	2.11	A1	D10	Dog
2.12	3.11	A1	E11	Pheasant
3.12	4.11	A1	F12	Cock
4.12	5.11	A1	G1	Crow
5.12	6.11	A1	H2	Monkey
6.12	7.11	A1	J3	Gibbon
7.12	8.11	A1	K4	Tapir
8.12	9.11	A1	A5	Sheep
9.12	10.11	A1	B6	Deer
10.12	11.11	A1	C7	Horse
11.12	12.11	A1	D8	Stag
12.12	13.11	A1	E9	Serpent
13.12	14.11	A1	F10	Earthworm
14.12	15.11	A1	G11	Crocodile
15.12	16.11	A1	H12	Dragon
16.12	17.11	A1	J1	Badger
17.12	18.11	A1	K2	Hare
18.12	19.11	A1	A3	Fox
19.12	20.11	A1	B4	Tiger
20.12	21.11	A1	C5	Leopard
21.12	22.11	A1	D6	Griffon
22.12	23.11	A1	E7	Ox
23.12	24.11	A1	F8	Bat
24.12	25.11	A1	G9	Rat
25.12	26.11	A1	H10	Swallow
26.12	27.11	A1	J11	Pig
27.12	28.11	A1	K12	Porcupine
28.12	29.11	A1	A1	Wolf
29.12	30.11	A1	B2	Dog
30.12	1.12	B2	C3	Pheasant
31.12	2.12	B2	D4	Cock
1979				
1. 1	3.12	B2	E5	Crow
2. 1	4.12	B2	F6	Monkey
3. 1	5.12	B2	G7	Gibbon
4. 1	6.12	B2	H8	Tapir
5. 1	7.12	B2	J9	Sheep
6. 1	8.12	B2	K10	Deer
7. 1	9.12	B2	A11	Horse
8. 1	10.12	B2	B12	Stag
9. 1	11.12	B2	C1	Serpent
10. 1	12.12	B2	D2	Earthworm
11. 1	13.12	B2	E3	Crocodile
12. 1	14.12	B2	F4	Dragon
13. 1	15.12	B2	G5	Badger
14. 1	16.12	B2	H6	Hare
15. 1	17.12	B2	J7	Fox
16. 1	18.12	B2	K8	Tiger
17. 1	19.12	B2	A9	Leopard
18. 1	20.12	B2	B10	Griffon
19. 1	21.12	B2	C11	Ox
20. 1	22.12	B2	D12	Bat
21. 1	23.12	B2	E1	Rat
22. 1	24.12	B2	F2	Swallow
23 1	25.12	B2	G3	Pig
24. 1	26.12	B2	H4	Porcupine
25. 1	27.12	B2	J5	Wolf
26. 1	28.12	B2	K6	Dog
27. 1	29.12	B2	A7	Pheasant

CHI WEI YEAR

28. 1	1. 1	C3	B8	Cock
29. 1	2. 1	C3	C9	Crow
30. 1	3. 1	C3	D10	Monkey
31. 1	4. 1	C3	E11	Gibbon
1. 2	5. 1	C3	F12	Tapir
2. 2	6. 1	C3	G1	Sheep
3. 2	7. 1	C3	H2	Deer
4. 2	8. 1	C3	J3	Horse
5. 2	9. 1	C3	K4	Stag
6. 2	10. 1	C3	A5	Serpent
7. 2	11. 1	C3	B6	Earthworm
8. 2	12. 1	C3	C7	Crocodile
9. 2	13. 1	C3	D8	Dragon
10. 2	14. 1	C3	E9	Badger
11. 2	15. 1	C3	F10	Hare
12. 2	16. 1	C3	G11	Fox
13. 2	17. 1	C3	H12	Tiger
14. 2	18. 1	C3	J1	Leopard
15. 2	19. 9	C3	K2	Griffon
16. 2	20. 1	C3	A3	Ox
17. 2	21. 1	C3	B4	Bat
18. 2	22. 1	C3	C5	Rat
19. 2	23. 1	C3	D6	Swallow
20. 2	24. 1	C3	E7	Pig
21. 2	25. 1	C3	F8	Porcupine
22. 2	26. 1	C3	G9	Wolf
23. 2	27. 1	C3	H10	Dog
24. 2	28. 1	C3	J11	Pheasant
25. 2	29. 1	C3	K12	Cock
26. 2	30. 1	C3	A1	Crow
27. 2	1. 2	D4	B2	Monkey
28. 2	2. 2	D4	C3	Gibbon
1. 3	3. 2	D4	D4	Tapir
2. 3	4. 2	D4	E5	Sheep
3. 3	5. 2	D4	F6	Deer
4. 3	6. 2	D4	G7	Horse
5. 3	7. 2	D4	H8	Stag
6. 3	8. 2	D4	J9	Serpent
7. 3	9. 2	D4	K10	Earthworm
8. 3	10. 2	D4	A11	Crocodile
9. 3	11. 2	D4	B12	Dragon
10. 3	12. 2	D4	C1	Badger
11. 3	13. 2	D4	D2	Hare
12. 3	14. 2	D4	E3	Fox
13. 3	15. 2	D4	F4	Tiger
14. 3	16. 2	D4	G5	Leopard
15. 3	17. 2	D4	H6	Griffon
16. 3	18. 2	D4	J7	Ox
17. 3	19. 2	D4	K8	Bat
18. 3	20. 2	D4	A9	Rat
19. 3	21. 2	D4	B10	Swallow
20. 3	22. 2	D4	C11	Pig
21. 3	23. 2	D4	D12	Porcupine
22. 3	24. 2	D4	E1	Wolf
23. 3	25. 2	D4	F2	Dog
24. 3	26. 2	D4	G3	Pheasant
25. 3	27. 2	D4	H4	Cock
26. 3	28. 2	D4	J5	Crow
27. 3	29. 2	D4	K6	Monkey
28. 3	1. 3	E5	A7	Gibbon
29. 3	2. 3	E5	B8	Tapir
30. 3	3. 3	E5	C9	Sheep
31. 3	4. 3	E5	D10	Deer
1. 4	5. 3	E5	E11	Horse
2. 4	6. 3	E5	F12	Stag
3. 4	7. 3	E5	G1	Serpent

Solar date	*Lunar date*	*Month HS/EB*	*Day HS/EB*	*Constellation*
4. 4	8. 3	E5	H2	Earthworm
5. 4	9. 3	E5	J3	Crocodile
6. 4	10. 3	E5	K4	Dragon
7. 4	11. 3	E5	A5	Badger
8. 4	12. 3	E5	B6	Hare
9. 4	13. 3	E5	C7	Fox
10. 4	14. 3	E5	D8	Tiger
11. 4	15. 3	E5	E9	Leopard
12. 4	16. 3	E5	F10	Griffon
13. 4	17. 3	E5	G11	Ox
14. 4	18. 3	E5	H12	Bat
15. 4	19. 3	E5	J1	Rat
16. 4	20. 3	E5	K2	Swallow
17. 4	21. 3	E5	A3	Pig
18. 4	22. 3	E5	B4	Porcupine
19. 4	23. 3	E5	C5	Wolf
20. 4	24. 3	E5	D6	Dog
21. 4	25. 3	E5	E7	Pheasant
22. 4	26. 3	E5	F8	Cock
23. 4	27. 3	E5	G9	Crow
24. 4	28. 3	E5	H10	Monkey
25. 4	29. 3	E5	J11	Gibbon
26. 4	1. 4	F6	K12	Tapir
27. 4	2. 4	F6	A1	Sheep
28. 4	3. 4	F6	B2	Deer
29. 4	4. 4	F6	C3	Horse
30. 4	5. 4	F6	D4	Stag
1. 5	6. 4	F6	E5	Serpent
2. 5	7. 4	F6	F6	Earthworm
3. 5	8. 4	F6	G7	Crocodile
4. 5	9. 4	F6	H8	Dragon
5. 5	10. 4	F6	J9	Badger
6. 5	11. 4	F6	K10	Hare
7. 5	12. 4	F6	A11	Fox
8. 5	13. 4	F6	B12	Tiger
9. 5	14. 4	F6	C1	Leopard
10. 5	15. 4	F6	D2	Griffon
11. 5	16. 4	F6	E3	Ox
12. 5	17. 4	F6	F4	Bat
13. 5	18. 4	F6	G5	Rat
14. 5	19. 4	F6	H6	Swallow
15. 5	20. 4	F6	J7	Pig
16. 5	21. 4	F6	K8	Porcupine
17. 5	22. 4	F6	A9	Wolf
18. 5	23. 4	F6	B10	Dog
19. 5	24. 4	F6	C11	Pheasant
20. 5	25. 4	F6	D12	Cock
21. 5	26. 4	F6	E1	Crow
22. 5	27. 4	F6	F2	Monkey
23. 5	28. 4	F6	G3	Gibbon
24. 5	29. 4	F6	H4	Tapir
25. 5	30. 4	F6	J5	Sheep
26. 5	1. 5	G7	K6	Deer
27. 5	2. 5	G7	A7	Horse
28. 5	3. 5	G7	B8	Stag
29. 5	4. 5	G7	C9	Serpent
30. 5	5. 5	G7	D10	Earthworm
31. 5	6. 5	G7	E11	Crocodile
1. 6	7. 5	G7	F12	Dragon
2. 6	8. 5	G7	G1	Badger
3. 6	9. 5	G7	H2	Hare
4. 6	10. 5	G7	J3	Fox
5. 5	11. 5	G7	K4	Tiger
6. 5	12. 5	G7	A5	Leopard
7. 5	13. 5	G7	B6	Griffon
8. 5	14. 5	G7	C7	Ox
9. 5	15. 5	G7	D8	Bat
10. 5	16. 5	G7	E9	Rat
11. 6	17. 5	G7	F10	Swallow
12. 6	18. 5	G7	G11	Pig
13. 6	19. 5	G7	H12	Porcupine
14. 6	20. 5	G7	J1	Wolf
15. 6	21. 5	G7	K2	Dog
16. 6	22. 5	G7	A3	Pheasant
17. 6	23. 5	G7	B4	Cock
18. 6	24. 5	G7	C5	Crow
19. 6	25. 5	G7	D6	Monkey
20. 6	26. 5	G7	E7	Gibbon
21. 6	27. 5	G7	F8	Tapir
22. 6	28. 5	G7	G9	Sheep
23. 6	29. 5	G7	H10	Deer
24. 6	1. 6	H8	J11	Horse
25. 6	2. 6	H8	K12	Stag
26. 6	3. 6	H8	A1	Serpent
27. 6	4. 6	H8	B2	Earthworm
28. 6	5. 6	H8	C3	Crocodile
29. 6	6. 6	H8	D4	Dragon
30. 6	7. 6	H8	E5	Badger
1. 7	8. 6	H8	F6	Hare
2. 7	9. 6	H8	G7	Fox
3. 7	10. 6	H8	H8	Tiger
4. 7	11. 6	H8	J9	Leopard
5. 7	12. 6	H8	K10	Griffon
6. 7	13. 6	H8	A11	Ox
7. 7	14. 6	H8	B12	Bat
8. 7	15. 6	H8	C1	Rat
9. 7	16. 6	H8	D2	Swallow
10. 7	17. 6	H8	E3	Pig
11. 7	18. 6	H8	F4	Porcupine
12. 7	19. 6	H8	G5	Wolf
13. 7	20. 6	H8	H6	Dog
14. 7	21. 6	H8	J7	Pheasant
15. 7	22. 6	H8	K8	Cock
16. 7	23. 6	H8	A9	Crow
17. 7	24. 6	H8	B10	Monkey
18. 7	25. 6	H8	C11	Gibbon
19. 7	26. 6	H8	D12	Tapir
20. 7	27. 6	H8	E1	Sheep
21. 7	28. 6	H8	F2	Deer
22. 7	29. 6	H8	G3	Horse
23. 7	30. 6	H8	H4	Stag
24. 7	*1. 6*	*H8*	J5	Serpent
25. 7	*2. 6*	*H8*	K6	Earthworm
26. 7	*3. 6*	*H8*	A7	Crocodile
27. 7	*4. 6*	*H8*	B8	Dragon
28. 7	*5. 6*	*H8*	C9	Badger
29. 7	*6. 6*	*H8*	D10	Hare
30. 7	*7. 6*	*H8*	E11	Fox
31. 7	*8. 6*	*H8*	F12	Tiger
1. 8	*9. 6*	*H8*	G1	Leopard
2. 8	*10. 6*	*H8*	H2	Griffon
3. 8	*11. 6*	*H8*	J3	Ox
4. 8	*12. 6*	*H8*	K4	Bat
5. 8	*13. 6*	*H8*	A5	Rat
6. 8	*14. 6*	*H8*	B6	Swallow
7. 8	*15. 6*	*H8*	C7	Pig
8. 8	*16. 6*	*H8*	D8	Porcupine
9. 8	*17. 6*	*H8*	E9	Wolf
10. 8	*18. 6*	*H8*	F10	Dog
11. 8	*19. 6*	*H8*	G11	Pheasant
12. 8	*20. 6*	*H8*	H12	Cock
13. 8	*21. 6*	*H8*	J1	Crow
14. 8	*22. 6*	*H8*	K2	Monkey
15. 8	*23. 6*	*H8*	A3	Gibbon
16. 8	*24. 6*	*H8*	B4	Tapir
17. 8	*25. 6*	*H8*	C5	Sheep
18. 8	*26. 6*	*H8*	D6	Deer
19. 8	*27. 6*	*H8*	E7	Horse
20. 8	*28. 6*	*H8*	F8	Stag
21. 8	*29. 6*	*H8*	G9	Serpent
22. 8	*30. 6*	*H8*	H10	Earthworm
23. 8	1. 7	J9	J11	Crocodile
24. 8	2. 7	J9	K12	Dragon
25. 8	3. 7	J9	A1	Badger
26. 8	4. 7	J9	B2	Hare
27. 8	5. 7	J9	C3	Fox

Solar date	*Lunar date*	*Month HS/EB*	*Day HS/EB*	*Constellation*
28. 8	6. 7	J9	D4	Tiger
29. 8	7. 7	J9	E5	Leopard
30. 8	8. 7	J9	F6	Griffon
31. 8	9. 7	J9	G7	Ox
1. 9	10. 7	J9	H8	Bat
2. 9	11. 7	J9	J9	Rat
3. 9	12. 7	J9	K10	Swallow
4. 9	13. 7	J9	A11	Pig
5. 9	14. 7	J9	B12	Porcupine
6. 9	15. 7	J9	C1	Wolf
7. 9	16. 7	J9	D2	Dog
8. 9	17. 7	J9	E3	Pheasant
9. 9	18. 7	J9	F4	Cock
10. 9	19. 7	J9	G5	Crow
11. 9	20. 7	J9	H6	Monkey
12. 9	21. 7	J9	J7	Gibbon
13. 9	22. 7	J9	K8	Tapir
14. 9	23. 7	J9	A9	Sheep
15. 9	24. 7	J9	B10	Deer
16. 9	25. 7	J9	C11	Horse
17. 9	26. 7	J9	D12	Stag
18. 9	27. 7	J9	E1	Serpent
19. 9	28. 7	J9	F2	Earthworm
20. 9	29. 7	J9	G3	Crocodile
21. 9	1. 8	K10	H4	Dragon
22. 9	2. 8	K10	J5	Badger
23. 9	3. 8	K10	K6	Hare
24. 9	4. 8	K10	A7	Fox
25. 9	5. 8	K10	B8	Tiger
26. 9	6. 8	K10	C9	Leopard
27. 9	7. 8	K10	D10	Griffon
28. 9	8. 8	K10	E11	Ox
29. 9	9. 8	K10	F12	Bat
30. 9	10. 8	K10	G1	Rat
1.10	11. 8	K10	H2	Swallow
2.10	12. 8	K10	J3	Pig
3.10	13. 8	K10	K4	Porcupine
4.10	14. 8	K10	A5	Wolf
5.10	15. 8	K10	B6	Dog
6.10	16. 8	K10	C7	Pheasant
7.10	17. 8	K10	D8	Cock
8.10	18. 8	K10	E9	Crow
9.10	19. 8	K10	F10	Monkey
10.10	20. 8	K10	G11	Gibbon
11.10	21. 8	K10	H12	Tapir
12.10	22. 8	K10	J1	Sheep
13.10	23. 8	K10	K2	Deer
14.10	24. 8	K10	A3	Horse
15.10	25. 8	K10	B4	Stag
16.10	26. 8	K10	C5	Serpent
17.10	27. 8	K10	D6	Earthworm
18.10	28. 8	K10	E7	Crocodile
19.10	29. 8	K10	F8	Dragon
20.10	30. 8	K10	G9	Badger
21.10	1. 9	A11	H10	Hare
22.10	2. 9	A11	J11	Fox
23.10	3. 9	A11	K12	Tiger
24.10	4. 9	A11	A1	Leopard
25.10	5. 9	A11	B2	Griffon
26.10	6. 9	A11	C3	Ox
27.10	7. 9	A11	D4	Bat
28.10	8. 9	A11	E5	Rat
29.10	9. 9	A11	F6	Swallow
30.10	10. 9	A11	G7	Pig
31.10	11. 9	A11	H8	Porcupine
1.11	12. 9	A11	J9	Wolf
2.11	13. 9	A11	K10	Dog
3.11	14. 9	A11	A11	Pheasant
4.11	15. 9	A11	B12	Cock
5.11	16. 9	A11	C1	Crow
6.11	17. 9	A11	D2	Monkey
7.11	18. 9	A11	E3	Gibbon
8.11	19. 9	A11	F4	Tapir

Solar date	*Lunar date*	*Month HS/EB*	*Day HS/EB*	*Constellation*
9.11	20. 9	A11	G5	Sheep
10.11	21. 9	A11	H6	Deer
11.11	22. 9	A11	J7	Horse
12.11	23. 9	A11	K8	Stag
13.11	24. 9	A11	A9	Serpent
14.11	25. 9	A11	B10	Earthworm
15.11	26. 9	A11	C11	Crocodile
16.11	27. 9	A11	D12	Dragon
17.11	28. 9	A11	E1	Badger
18.11	29. 9	A11	F2	Hare
19.11	30. 9	A11	G3	Fox
20.11	1.10	B12	H4	Tiger
21.11	2.10	B12	J5	Leopard
22.11	3.10	B12	K6	Griffon
23.11	4.10	B12	A7	Ox
24.11	5.10	B12	B8	Bat
25.11	6.10	B12	C9	Rat
26.11	7.10	B12	D10	Swallow
27.11	8.10	B12	E11	Pig
28.11	9.10	B12	F12	Porcupine
29.11	10.10	B12	G1	Wolf
30.11	11.10	B12	H2	Dog
1.12	12.10	B12	J3	Pheasant
2.12	13.10	B12	K4	Cock
3.12	14.10	B12	A5	Crow
4.12	15.10	B12	B6	Monkey
5.12	16.10	B12	C7	Gibbon
6.12	17.10	B12	D8	Tapir
7.12	18.10	B12	E9	Sheep
8.12	19.10	B12	F10	Deer
9.12	20.10	B12	G11	Horse
10.12	21.10	B12	H12	Stag
11.12	22.10	B12	J1	Serpent
12.12	23.10	B12	K2	Earthworm
13.12	24.10	B12	A3	Crocodile
14.12	25.10	B12	B4	Dragon
15.12	26.10	B12	C5	Badger
16.12	27.10	B12	D6	Hare
17.12	28.10	B12	E7	Fox
18.12	29.10	B12	F8	Tiger
19.12	1.11	C1	G9	Leopard
20.12	2.11	C1	H10	Griffon
21.12	3.11	C1	J11	Ox
22.12	4.11	C1	K12	Bat
23.12	5.11	C1	A1	Rat
24.12	6.11	C1	B2	Swallow
25.12	7.11	C1	C3	Pig
26.12	8.11	C1	D4	Porcupine
27.12	9.11	C1	E5	Wolf
28.12	10.11	C1	F6	Dog
29.12	11.11	C1	G7	Pheasant
30.12	12.11	C1	H8	Cock
31.12	13.11	C1	J9	Crow

1980

Solar date	*Lunar date*	*Month HS/EB*	*Day HS/EB*	*Constellation*
1. 1	14.11	C1	K10	Monkey
2. 1	15.11	C1	A11	Gibbon
3. 1	16.11	C1	B12	Tapir
4. 1	17.11	C1	C1	Sheep
5. 1	18.11	C1	D2	Deer
6. 1	19.11	C1	E3	Horse
7. 1	20.11	C1	F4	Stag
8. 1	21.11	C1	G5	Serpent
9. 1	22.11	C1	H6	Earthworm
10. 1	23.11	C1	J7	Crocodile
11. 1	24.11	C1	K8	Dragon
12. 1	25.11	C1	A9	Badger
13. 1	26.11	C1	B10	Hare
14. 1	27.11	C1	C11	Fox
15. 1	28.11	C1	D12	Tiger
16. 1	29.11	C1	E1	Leopard
17. 1	30.11	C1	F2	Griffon
18. 1	1.12	D2	G3	Ox

Solar date	Lunar date	Month HS/EB	Day HS/EB	Constellation
19. 1	2.12	D2	H4	Bat
20. 1	3.12	D2	J5	Rat
21. 1	4.12	D2	K6	Swallow
22. 1	5.12	D2	A7	Pig
23. 1	6.12	D2	B8	Porcupine
24. 1	7.12	D2	C9	Wolf
25. 1	8.12	D2	D10	Dog
26. 1	9.12	D2	E11	Pheasant
27. 1	10.12	D2	F12	Cock
28. 1	11.12	D2	G1	Crow
29. 1	12.12	D2	H2	Monkey
30. 1	13.12	D2	J3	Gibbon
31. 1	14.12	D2	K4	Tapir
1. 2	15.12	D2	A5	Sheep
2. 2	16.12	D2	B6	Deer
3. 2	17.12	D2	C7	Horse
4. 2	18.12	D2	D8	Stag
5. 2	19.12	D2	E9	Serpent
6. 2	20.12	D2	F10	Earthworm
7. 2	21.12	D2	G11	Crocodile
8. 2	22.12	D2	H12	Dragon
9. 2	23.12	D2	J1	Badger
10. 2	24.12	D2	K2	Hare
11. 2	25.12	D2	A3	Fox
12. 2	26.12	D2	B4	Tiger
13. 2	27.12	D2	C5	Leopard
14. 2	28.12	D2	D6	Griffon
15. 2	29.12	D2	E7	Ox

KENG SHEN YEAR

Solar date	Lunar date	Month HS/EB	Day HS/EB	Constellation
16. 2	1. 1	E3	F8	Bat
17. 2	2. 1	E3	G9	Rat
18. 2	3. 1	E3	H10	Swallow
19. 2	4. 1	E3	J11	Pig
20. 2	5. 1	E3	K12	Porcupine
21. 2	6. 1	E3	A1	Wolf
22. 2	7. 1	E3	B2	Dog
23. 2	8. 1	E3	C3	Pheasant
24. 2	9. 1	E3	D4	Cock
25. 2	10. 1	E3	E5	Crow
26. 2	11. 1	E3	F6	Monkey
27. 2	12. 1	E3	G7	Gibbon
28. 2	13. 1	E3	H8	Tapir
29. 2	14. 1	E3	J9	Sheep
1. 3	15. 1	E3	K10	Deer
2. 3	16. 1	E3	A11	Horse
3. 3	17. 1	E3	B12	Stag
4. 3	18. 1	E3	C1	Serpent
5. 3	19. 1	E3	D2	Earthworm
6. 3	20. 1	E3	E3	Crocodile
7. 3	21. 1	E3	F4	Dragon
8. 3	22. 1	E3	G5	Badger
9. 3	23. 1	E3	H6	Hare
10. 3	24. 1	E3	J7	Fox
11. 3	25. 1	E3	K8	Tiger
12. 3	26. 1	E3	A9	Leopard
13. 3	27. 1	E3	B10	Griffon
14. 3	28. 1	E3	C11	Ox
15. 3	29. 1	E3	D12	Bat
16. 3	30. 1	E3	E1	Rat
17. 3	1. 2	F4	F2	Swallow
18. 3	2. 2	F4	G3	Pig
19. 3	3. 2	F4	H4	Porcupine
20. 3	4. 2	F4	J5	Wolf
21. 3	5. 2	F4	K6	Dog
22. 3	6. 2	F4	A7	Pheasant
23. 3	7. 2	F4	B8	Cock
24. 3	8. 2	F4	C9	Crow
25. 3	9. 2	F4	D10	Monkey
26. 3	10. 2	F4	E11	Gibbon
27. 3	11. 2	F4	F12	Tapir
28. 3	12. 2	F4	G1	Sheep
29. 3	13. 2	F4	H2	Deer
30. 3	14. 2	F4	J3	Horse
31. 3	15. 2	F4	K4	Stag
1. 4	16. 2	F4	A5	Serpent
2. 4	17. 2	F4	B6	Earthworm
3. 4	18. 2	F4	C7	Crocodile
4. 4	19. 2	F4	D8	Dragon
5. 4	20. 2	F4	E9	Badger
6. 4	21. 2	F4	F10	Hare
7. 4	22. 2	F4	G11	Fox
8. 4	23. 2	F4	H12	Tiger
9. 4	24. 2	F4	J1	Leopard
10. 4	25. 2	F4	K2	Griffon
11. 4	26. 2	F4	A3	Ox
12. 4	27. 2	F4	B4	Bat
13. 4	28. 2	F4	C5	Rat
14. 4	29. 2	F4	D6	Swallow
15. 4	1. 3	G5	E7	Pig
16. 4	2. 3	G5	F8	Porcupine
17. 4	3. 3	G5	G9	Wolf
18. 4	4. 3	G5	H10	Dog
19. 4	5. 3	G5	J11	Pheasant
20. 4	6. 3	G5	K12	Cock
21. 4	7. 3	G5	A1	Crow
22. 4	8. 3	G5	B2	Monkey
23. 4	9. 3	G5	C3	Gibbon
24. 4	10. 3	G5	D4	Tapir
25. 4	11. 3	G5	E5	Sheep
26. 4	12. 3	G5	F6	Deer
27. 4	13. 3	G5	G7	Horse
28. 4	14. 3	G5	H8	Stag
29. 4	15. 3	G5	J9	Serpent
30. 4	16. 3	G5	K10	Earthworm
1. 5	17. 3	G5	A11	Crocodile
2. 5	18. 3	G5	B12	Dragon
3. 5	19. 3	G5	C1	Badger
4. 5	20. 3	G5	D2	Hare
5. 5	21. 3	G5	E3	Fox
6. 5	22. 3	G5	F4	Tiger
7. 5	23. 3	G5	G5	Leopard
8. 5	24. 3	G5	H6	Griffon
9. 5	25. 3	G5	J7	Ox
10. 5	26. 3	G5	K8	Bat
11. 5	27. 3	G5	A9	Rat
12. 5	28. 3	G5	B10	Swallow
13. 5	29. 3	G5	C11	Pig
14. 5	1. 4	H6	D12	Porcupine
15. 5	2. 4	H6	E1	Wolf
16. 5	3. 4	H6	F2	Dog
17. 5	4. 4	H6	G3	Pheasant
18. 5	5. 4	H6	H4	Cock
19. 5	6. 4	H6	J5	Crow
20. 5	7. 4	H6	K6	Monkey
21. 5	8. 4	H6	A7	Gibbon
22. 5	9. 4	H6	B8	Tapir
23. 5	10. 4	H6	C9	Sheep
24. 5	11. 4	H6	D10	Deer
25. 5	12. 4	H6	E11	Horse
26. 5	13. 4	H6	F12	Stag
27. 5	14. 4	H6	G1	Serpent
28. 5	15. 4	H6	H2	Earthworm
29. 5	16. 4	H6	J3	Crocodile
30. 5	17. 4	H6	K4	Dragon
31. 5	18. 4	H6	A5	Badger
1. 6	19. 4	H6	B6	Hare
2. 6	20. 4	H6	C7	Fox

Solar date	*Lunar date*	*Month HS/EB*	*Day HS/EB*	*Constellation*
3. 6	21. 4	H6	D8	Tiger
4. 6	22. 4	H6	E9	Leopard
5. 6	23. 4	H6	F10	Griffon
6. 6	24. 4	H6	G11	Ox
7. 6	25. 4	H6	H12	Bat
8. 6	26. 4	H6	J1	Rat
9. 6	27. 4	H6	K2	Swallow
10. 6	28. 4	H6	A3	Pig
11. 6	29. 4	H6	B4	Porcupine
12. 6	30. 4	H6	C5	Wolf
13. 6	1. 5	J7	D6	Dog
14. 6	2. 5	J7	E7	Pheasant
15. 6	3. 5	J7	F8	Cock
16. 6	4. 5	J7	G9	Crow
17. 6	5. 5	J7	H10	Monkey
18. 6	6. 5	J7	J11	Gibbon
19. 6	7. 5	J7	K12	Tapir
20. 6	8. 5	J7	A1	Sheep
21. 6	9. 5	J7	B2	Deer
22. 6	10. 5	J7	C3	Horse
23. 6	11. 5	J7	D4	Stag
24. 6	12. 5	J7	E5	Serpent
25. 6	13. 5	J7	F6	Earthworm
26. 6	14. 5	J7	G7	Crocodile
27. 6	15. 5	J7	H8	Dragon
28. 6	16. 5	J7	J9	Badger
29. 6	17. 5	J7	K10	Hare
30. 6	18. 5	J7	A11	Fox
1. 7	19. 5	J7	B12	Tiger
2. 7	20. 5	J7	C1	Leopard
3. 7	21. 5	J7	D2	Griffon
4. 7	22. 5	J7	E3	Ox
5. 7	23. 5	J7	F4	Bat
6. 7	24. 5	J7	G5	Rat
7. 7	25. 5	J7	H6	Swallow
8. 7	26. 5	J7	J7	Pig
9. 7	27. 5	J7	K8	Porcupine
10. 7	28. 5	J7	A9	Wolf
11. 7	29. 5	J7	B10	Dog
12. 7	1. 6	K8	C11	Pheasant
13. 7	2. 6	K8	D12	Cock
14. 7	3. 6	K8	E1	Crow
15. 7	4. 6	K8	F2	Monkey
16. 7	5. 6	K8	G3	Gibbon
17. 7	6. 6	K8	H4	Tapir
18. 7	7. 6	K8	J5	Sheep
19. 7	8. 6	K8	K6	Deer
20. 7	9. 6	K8	A7	Horse
21. 7	10. 6	K8	B8	Stag
22. 7	11. 6	K8	C9	Serpent
23. 7	12. 6	K8	D10	Earthworm
24. 7	13. 6	K8	E11	Crocodile
25. 7	14. 6	K8	F12	Dragon
26. 7	15. 6	K8	G1	Badger
27. 7	16. 6	K8	H2	Hare
28. 7	17. 6	K8	J3	Fox
29. 7	18. 6	K8	K4	Tiger
30. 7	19. 6	K8	A5	Leopard
31. 7	20. 6	K8	B6	Griffon
1. 8	21. 6	K8	C7	Ox
2. 8	22. 6	K8	D8	Bat
3. 8	23. 6	K8	E9	Rat
4. 8	24. 6	K8	F10	Swallow
5. 8	25. 6	K8	G11	Pig
6. 8	26. 6	K8	H12	Porcupine
7. 8	27. 6	K8	J1	Wolf
8. 8	28. 6	K8	K2	Dog
9. 8	29. 6	K8	A3	Pheasant
10. 8	30. 6	K8	B4	Cock
11. 8	1. 7	A9	C5	Crow
12. 8	2. 7	A9	D6	Monkey
13. 8	3. 7	A9	E7	Gibbon
14. 8	4. 7	A9	F8	Tapir
15. 8	5. 7	A9	G9	Sheep
16. 8	6. 7	A9	H10	Deer
17. 8	7. 7	A9	J11	Horse
18. 8	8. 7	A9	K12	Stag
19. 8	9. 7	A9	A1	Serpent
20. 8	10. 7	A9	B2	Earthworm
21. 8	11. 7	A9	C3	Crocodile
22. 8	12. 7	A9	D4	Dragon
23. 8	13. 7	A9	E5	Badger
24. 8	14. 7	A9	F6	Hare
25. 8	15. 7	A9	G7	Fox
26. 8	16. 7	A9	H8	Tiger
27. 8	17. 7	A9	J9	Leopard
28. 8	18. 7	A9	K10	Griffon
29. 8	19. 7	A9	A11	Ox
30. 8	20. 7	A9	B12	Bat
31. 8	21. 7	A9	C1	Rat
1. 9	22. 7	A9	D2	Swallow
2. 9	23. 7	A9	E3	Pig
3. 9	24. 7	A9	F4	Porcupine
4. 9	25. 7	A9	G5	Wolf
5. 9	26. 7	A9	H6	Dog
6. 9	27. 7	A9	J7	Pheasant
7. 9	28. 7	A9	K8	Cock
8. 9	29. 7	A9	A9	Crow
9. 9	1. 8	B10	B10	Monkey
10. 9	2. 8	B10	C11	Gibbon
11. 9	3. 8	B10	D12	Tapir
12. 9	4. 8	B10	E1	Sheep
13. 9	5. 8	B10	F2	Deer
14. 9	6. 8	B10	G3	Horse
15. 9	7. 8	B10	H4	Stag
16. 9	8. 8	B10	J5	Serpent
17. 9	9. 8	B10	K6	Earthworm
18. 9	10. 8	B10	A7	Crocodile
19. 9	11. 8	B10	B8	Dragon
20. 9	12. 8	B10	C9	Badger
21. 9	13. 8	B10	D10	Hare
22. 9	14. 8	B10	E11	Fox
23. 9	15. 8	B10	F12	Tiger
24. 9	16. 8	B10	G1	Leopard
25. 9	17. 8	B10	H2	Griffon
26. 9	18. 8	B10	J3	Ox
27. 9	19. 8	B10	K4	Bat
28. 9	20. 8	B10	A5	Rat
29. 9	21. 8	B10	B6	Swallow
30. 9	22. 8	B10	C7	Pig
1.10	23. 8	B10	D8	Porcupine
2.10	24. 8	B10	E9	Wolf
3.10	25. 8	B10	F10	Dog
4.10	26. 8	B10	G11	Pheasant
5.10	27. 8	B10	H12	Cock
6.10	28. 8	B10	J1	Crow
7.10	29. 8	B10	K2	Monkey
8.10	30. 8	B10	A3	Gibbon
9.10	1. 9	C11	B4	Tapir
10.10	2. 9	C11	C5	Sheep
11.10	3. 9	C11	D6	Deer
12.10	4. 9	C11	E7	Horse
13.10	5. 9	C11	F8	Stag
14.10	6. 9	C11	G9	Serpent
15.10	7. 9	C11	H10	Earthworm
16.10	8. 9	C11	J11	Crocodile
17.10	9. 9	C11	K12	Dragon
18.10	10. 9	C11	A1	Badger
19.10	11. 9	C11	B2	Hare
20.10	12. 9	C11	C3	Fox
21.10	13. 9	C11	D4	Tiger
22.10	14. 9	C11	E5	Leopard
23.10	15. 9	C11	F6	Griffon
24.10	16. 9	C11	G7	Ox
25.10	17. 9	C11	H8	Bat
26.10	18. 9	C11	J9	Rat

Solar date	Lunar date	Month HS/EB	Day HS/EB	Constellation
27.10	19. 9	C11	K10	Swallow
28.10	20. 9	C11	A11	Pig
29.10	21. 9	C11	B12	Porcupine
30.10	22. 9	C11	C1	Wolf
31.10	23. 9	C11	D2	Dog
1.11	24. 9	C11	E3	Pheasant
2.11	25. 9	C11	F4	Cock
3.11	26. 9	C11	G5	Crow
4.11	27. 9	C11	H6	Monkey
5.11	28. 9	C11	J7	Gibbon
6.11	29. 9	C11	K8	Tapir
7.11	30. 9	C11	A9	Sheep
8.11	1.10	D12	B10	Deer
9.11	2.10	D12	C11	Horse
10.11	3.10	D12	D12	Stag
11.11	4.10	D12	E1	Serpent
12.11	5.10	D12	F2	Earthworm
13.11	6.10	D12	G3	Crocodile
14.11	7.10	D12	H4	Dragon
15.11	8.10	D12	J5	Badger
16.11	9.10	D12	K6	Hare
17.11	10.10	D12	A7	Fox
18.11	11.10	D12	B8	Tiger
19.11	12.10	D12	C9	Leopard
20.11	13.10	D12	D10	Griffon
21.11	14.10	D12	E11	Ox
22.11	15.10	D12	F12	Bat
23.11	16.10	D12	G1	Rat
24.11	17.10	D12	H2	Swallow
25.11	18.10	D12	J3	Pig
26.11	19.10	D12	K4	Porcupine
27.11	20.10	D12	A5	Wolf
28.11	21.10	D12	B6	Dog
29.11	22.10	D12	C7	Pheasant
30.11	23.10	D12	D8	Cock
1.12	24.10	D12	E9	Crow
2.12	25.10	D12	F10	Monkey
3.12	26.10	D12	G11	Gibbon
4.12	27.10	D12	H12	Tapir
5.12	28.10	D12	J1	Sheep
6.12	29.10	D12	K2	Deer
7.12	1.11	E1	A3	Horse
8.12	2.11	E1	B4	Stag
9.12	3.11	E1	C5	Serpent
10.12	4.11	E1	D6	Earthworm
11.12	5.11	E1	E7	Crocodile
12.12	6.11	E1	F8	Dragon
13.12	7.11	E1	G9	Badger
14.12	8.11	E1	H10	Hare
15.12	9.11	E1	J11	Fox
16.12	10.11	E1	K12	Tiger
17.12	11.11	E1	A1	Leopard

Solar date	Lunar date	Month HS/EB	Day HS/EB	Constellation
18.12	12.11	E1	B2	Griffon
19.12	13.11	E1	C3	Ox
20.12	14.11	E1	D4	Bat
21.12	15.11	E1	E5	Rat
22.12	16.11	E1	F6	Swallow
23.12	17.11	E1	G7	Pig
24.12	18.11	E1	H8	Porcupine
25.12	19.11	E1	J9	Wolf
26.12	20.11	E1	K10	Dog
27.12	21.11	E1	A11	Pheasant
28.12	22.11	E1	B12	Cock
29.12	23.11	E1	C1	Crow
30.12	24.11	E1	D2	Monkey
31.12	25.11	E1	E3	Gibbon
1981				
1. 1	26.11	E1	F4	Tapir
2. 1	27.11	E1	G5	Sheep
3. 1	28.11	E1	H6	Deer
4. 1	29.11	E1	J7	Horse
5. 1	30.11	E1	K8	Stag
6. 1	1.12	F2	A9	Serpent
7. 1	2.12	F2	B10	Earthworm
8. 1	3.12	F2	C11	Crocodile
9. 1	4.12	F2	D12	Dragon
10. 1	5.12	F2	E1	Badger
11. 1	6.12	F2	F2	Hare
12. 1	7.12	F2	G3	Fox
13. 1	8.12	F2	H4	Tiger
14. 1	9.12	F2	J5	Leopard
15. 1	10.12	F2	K6	Griffon
16. 1	11.12	F2	A7	Ox
17. 1	12.12	F2	B8	Bat
18. 1	13.12	F2	C9	Rat
19. 1	14.12	F2	D10	Swallow
20. 1	15.12	F2	E11	Pig
21. 1	16.12	F2	F12	Porcupine
22. 1	17.12	F2	G1	Wolf
23. 1	18.12	F2	H2	Dog
24. 1	19.12	F2	J3	Pheasant
25. 1	20.12	F2	K4	Cock
26. 1	21.12	F2	A5	Crow
27. 1	22.12	F2	B6	Monkey
28. 1	23.12	F2	C7	Gibbon
29. 1	24.12	F2	D8	Tapir
30. 1	25.12	F2	E9	Sheep
31. 1	26.12	F2	F10	Deer
1. 2	27.12	F2	G11	Horse
2. 2	28.12	F2	H12	Stag
3. 2	29.12	F2	J1	Serpent
4. 2	30.12	F2	K2	Earthworm

HSIN YU YEAR

Solar date	Lunar date	Month HS/EB	Day HS/EB	Constellation
5. 2	1. 1	G3	A3	Crocodile
6. 2	2. 1	G3	B4	Dragon
7. 2	3. 1	G3	C5	Badger
8. 2	4. 1	G3	D6	Hare
9. 2	5. 1	G3	E7	Fox
10. 2	6. 1	G3	F8	Tiger
11. 2	7. 1	G3	G9	Leopard
12. 2	8. 1	G3	H10	Griffon
13. 2	9. 1	G3	J11	Ox
14. 2	10. 1	G3	K12	Bat
15. 2	11. 1	G3	A1	Rat
16. 2	12. 1	G3	B2	Swallow
17. 2	13. 1	G3	C3	Pig
18. 2	14. 1	G3	D4	Porcupine
19. 2	15. 1	G3	E5	Wolf
20. 2	16. 1	G3	F6	Dog
21. 2	17. 1	G3	G7	Pheasant
22. 2	18. 1	G3	H8	Cock
23. 2	19. 1	G3	J9	Crow
24. 2	20. 1	G3	K10	Monkey
25. 2	21. 1	G3	A11	Gibbon
26. 2	22. 1	G3	B12	Tapir
27. 2	23. 1	G3	C1	Sheep
28. 2	24. 1	G3	D2	Deer
1. 3	25. 1	G3	E3	Horse
2. 3	26. 1	G3	F4	Stag
3. 3	27. 1	G3	G5	Serpent
4. 3	28. 1	G3	H6	Earthworm
5. 3	29. 1	G3	J7	Crocodile
6. 3	1. 2	H4	K8	Dragon
7. 3	2. 2	H4	A9	Badger
8. 3	3. 2	H4	B10	Hare

Solar date	*Lunar date*	*Month HS/EB*	*Day HS/EB*	*Constellation*
9. 3	4. 2	H4	C11	Fox
10. 3	5. 2	H4	D12	Tiger
11. 3	6. 2	H4	E1	Leopard
12. 3	7. 2	H4	F2	Griffon
13. 3	8. 2	H4	G3	Ox
14. 3	9. 2	H4	H4	Bat
15. 3	10. 2	H4	J5	Rat
16. 3	11. 2	H4	K6	Swallow
17. 3	12. 2	H4	A7	Pig
18. 3	13. 2	H4	B8	Porcupine
19. 3	14. 2	H4	C9	Wolf
20. 3	15. 2	H4	D10	Dog
21. 3	16. 2	H4	E11	Pheasant
22. 3	17. 2	H4	F12	Cock
23. 3	18. 2	H4	G1	Crow
24. 3	19. 2	H4	H2	Monkey
25. 3	20. 2	H4	J3	Gibbon
26. 3	21. 2	H4	K4	Tapir
27. 3	22. 2	H4	A5	Sheep
28. 3	23. 2	H4	B6	Deer
29. 3	24. 2	H4	C7	Horse
30. 3	25. 2	H4	D8	Stag
31. 3	26. 2	H4	E9	Serpent
1. 4	27. 2	H4	F10	Earthworm
2. 4	28. 2	H4	G11	Crocodile
3. 4	29. 2	H4	H12	Dragon
4. 4	30. 2	H4	J1	Badger
5. 4	1. 3	J5	K2	Hare
6. 4	2. 3	J5	A3	Fox
7. 4	3. 3	J5	B4	Tiger
8. 4	4. 3	J5	C5	Leopard
9. 4	5. 3	J5	D6	Griffon
10. 4	6. 3	J5	E7	Ox
11. 4	7. 3	J5	F8	Bat
12. 4	8. 3	J5	G9	Rat
13. 4	9. 3	J5	H10	Swallow
14. 4	10. 3	J5	J11	Pig
15. 4	11. 3	J5	K12	Porcupine
16. 4	12. 3	J5	A1	Wolf
17. 4	13. 3	J5	B2	Dog
18. 4	14. 3	J5	C3	Pheasant
19. 4	15. 3	J5	D4	Cock
20. 4	16. 3	J5	E5	Crow
21. 4	17. 3	J5	F6	Monkey
22. 4	18. 3	J5	G7	Gibbon
23. 4	19. 3	J5	H8	Tapir
24. 4	20. 3	J5	J9	Sheep
25. 4	21. 3	J5	K10	Deer
26. 4	22. 3	J5	A11	Horse
27. 4	23. 3	J5	B12	Stag
28. 4	24. 3	J5	C1	Serpent
29. 4	25. 3	J5	D2	Earthworm
30. 4	26. 3	J5	E3	Crocodile
1. 5	27. 3	J5	F4	Dragon
2. 5	28. 3	J5	G5	Badger
3. 5	29. 3	J5	H6	Hare
4. 5	1. 4	K6	J7	Fox
5. 5	2. 4	K6	K8	Tiger
6. 5	3. 4	K6	A9	Leopard
7. 5	4. 4	K6	B10	Griffon
8. 5	5. 4	K6	C11	Ox
9. 5	6. 4	K6	D12	Bat
10. 5	7. 4	K6	E1	Rat
11. 5	8. 4	K6	F2	Swallow
12. 5	9. 4	K6	G3	Pig
13. 5	10. 4	K6	H4	Porcupine
14. 5	11. 4	K6	J5	Wolf
15. 5	12. 4	K6	K6	Dog
16. 5	13. 4	K6	A7	Pheasant
17. 5	14. 4	K6	B8	Cock
18. 5	15. 4	K6	C9	Crow
19. 5	16. 4	K6	D10	Monkey
20. 5	17. 4	K6	E11	Gibbon
21. 5	18. 4	K6	F12	Tapir
22. 5	19. 4	K6	G1	Sheep
23. 5	20. 4	K6	H2	Deer
24. 5	21. 4	K6	J3	Horse
25. 5	22. 4	K6	K4	Stag
26. 5	23. 4	K6	A5	Serpent
27. 5	24. 4	K6	B6	Earthworm
28. 5	25. 4	K6	C7	Crocodile
29. 5	26. 4	K6	D8	Dragon
30. 5	27. 4	K6	E9	Badger
31. 5	28. 4	K6	F10	Hare
1. 6	29. 4	K6	G11	Fox
2. 6	1. 4	A7	H12	Tiger
3. 6	2. 4	A7	J1	Leopard
4. 6	3. 4	A7	K2	Griffon
5. 6	4. 4	A7	A3	Ox
6. 6	5. 4	A7	B4	Bat
7. 6	6. 4	A7	C5	Rat
8. 6	7. 4	A7	D6	Swallow
9. 6	8. 4	A7	E7	Pig
10. 6	9. 4	A7	F8	Porcupine
11. 6	10. 4	A7	G9	Wolf
12. 6	11. 4	A7	H10	Dog
13. 6	12. 4	A7	J11	Pheasant
14. 6	13. 4	A7	K12	Cock
15. 6	14. 4	A7	A1	Crow
16. 6	15. 5	A7	B2	Monkey
17. 6	16. 5	A7	C3	Gibbon
18. 6	17. 5	A7	D4	Tapir
19. 6	18. 5	A7	E5	Sheep
20. 6	19. 5	A7	F6	Deer
21. 6	20. 5	A7	G7	Horse
22. 6	21. 5	A7	H8	Stag
23. 6	22. 5	A7	J9	Serpent
24. 6	23. 5	A7	K10	Earthworm
25. 6	24. 5	A7	A11	Crocodile
26. 6	25. 5	A7	B12	Dragon
27. 6	26. 5	A7	C1	Badger
28. 6	27. 5	A7	D2	Hare
29. 6	28. 5	A7	E3	Fox
30. 6	29. 5	A7	D4	Tiger
1. 7	30. 5	A7	G5	Leopard
2. 7	1. 6	B8	H6	Griffon
3. 7	2. 6	B8	J7	Ox
4. 7	3. 6	B8	K8	Bat
5. 7	4. 6	B8	A9	Rat
6. 7	5. 6	B8	B10	Swallow
7. 7	6. 6	B8	C11	Pig
8. 7	7. 6	B8	D12	Porcupine
9. 7	8. 6	B8	E1	Wolf
10. 7	9. 6	B8	F2	Dog
11. 7	10. 6	B8	G3	Pheasant
12. 7	11. 6	B8	H4	Cock
13. 7	12. 6	B8	J5	Crow
14. 7	13. 6	B8	K6	Monkey
15. 7	14. 6	B8	A7	Gibbon
16. 7	15. 6	B8	B8	Tapir
17. 7	16. 6	B8	C9	Sheep
18. 7	17. 6	B8	D10	Deer
19. 7	18. 6	B8	E11	Horse
20. 7	19. 6	B8	F12	Stag
21. 7	20. 6	B8	G1	Serpent
22. 7	21. 6	B8	H2	Earthworm
23. 7	22. 6	B8	J3	Crocodile
24. 7	23. 6	B8	K4	Dragon
25. 7	24. 6	B8	A5	Badger
26. 7	25. 6	B8	B6	Hare
27. 7	26. 6	B8	C7	Fox
28. 7	27. 6	B8	D8	Tiger
29. 7	28. 6	B8	E9	Leopard
30. 7	29. 6	B8	F10	Griffon
31. 7	1. 7	C9	G11	Ox
1. 8	2. 7	C9	H12	Bat

Solar date	*Lunar date*	*Month HS/EB*	*Day HS/EB*	*Constellation*
2. 8	3. 7	C9	J1	Rat
3. 8	4. 7	C9	K2	Swallow
4. 8	5. 7	C9	A3	Pig
5. 8	6. 7	C9	B4	Porcupine
6. 8	7. 7	C9	C5	Wolf
7. 8	8. 7	C9	D6	Dog
8. 8	9. 7	C9	E7	Pheasant
9. 8	10. 7	C9	F8	Cock
10. 8	11. 7	C9	G9	Crow
11. 8	12. 7	C9	H10	Monkey
12. 8	13. 7	C9	J11	Gibbon
13. 8	14. 7	C9	K12	Tapir
14. 8	15. 7	C9	A1	Sheep
15. 8	16. 7	C9	B2	Deer
16. 8	17. 7	C9	C3	Horse
17. 8	18. 7	C9	D4	Stag
18. 8	19. 7	C9	E5	Serpent
19. 8	20. 7	C9	F6	Earthworm
20. 8	21. 7	C9	G7	Crocodile
21. 8	22. 7	C9	H8	Dragon
22. 8	23. 7	C9	J9	Badger
23. 8	24. 7	C9	K10	Hare
24. 8	25. 7	C9	A11	Fox
25. 8	26. 7	C9	B12	Tiger
26. 8	27. 7	C9	C1	Leopard
27. 8	28. 7	C9	D2	Griffon
28. 8	29. 7	C9	E3	Ox
29. 8	1. 8	D10	F4	Bat
30. 8	2. 8	D10	G5	Rat
31. 8	3. 8	D10	H6	Swallow
1. 9	4. 8	D10	J7	Pig
2. 9	5. 8	D10	K8	Porcupine
3. 9	6. 8	D10	A9	Wolf
4. 9	7. 8	D10	B10	Dog
5. 9	8. 8	D10	C11	Pheasant
6. 9	9. 8	D10	D12	Cock
7. 9	10. 8	D10	E1	Crow
8. 9	11. 8	D10	F2	Monkey
9. 9	12. 8	D10	G3	Gibbon
10. 9	13. 8	D10	H4	Tapir
11. 9	14. 8	D10	J5	Sheep
12. 9	15. 8	D10	K6	Deer
13. 9	16. 8	D10	A7	Horse
14. 9	17. 8	D10	B8	Stag
15. 9	18. 8	D10	C9	Serpent
16. 9	19. 8	D10	D10	Earthworm
17. 9	20. 8	D10	E11	Crocodile
18. 9	21. 8	D10	F12	Dragon
19. 9	22. 8	D10	G1	Badger
20. 9	23. 8	D10	H2	Hare
21. 9	24. 8	D10	J3	Fox
22. 9	25. 8	D10	K4	Tiger
23. 9	26. 8	D10	A5	Leopard
24. 9	27. 8	D10	B6	Griffon
25. 9	28. 8	D10	C7	Ox
26. 9	29. 8	D10	D8	Bat
27. 9	30. 8	D10	E9	Rat
28. 9	1. 9	E11	F10	Swallow
29. 9	2. 9	E11	G11	Pig
30. 9	3. 9	E11	H12	Porcupine
1.10	4. 9	E11	J1	Wolf
2.10	5. 9	E11	K2	Dog
3.10	6. 9	E11	A3	Pheasant
4. 0	7. 9	E11	B4	Cock
5.10	8. 9	E11	C5	Crow
6.10	9. 9	E11	D6	Monkey
7.10	10. 9	E11	E7	Gibbon
8.10	11. 9	E11	F8	Tapir
9.10	12. 9	E11	G9	Sheep
10.10	13. 9	E11	H10	Deer
11.10	14. 9	E11	J11	Horse
12.10	15. 9	E11	K12	Stag
13.10	16. 9	E11	A1	Serpent
14.10	17. 9	E11	B2	Earthworm
15.10	18. 9	E11	C3	Crocodile
16.10	19. 9	E11	D4	Dragon
17.10	20. 9	E11	E5	Badger
18.10	21. 9	E11	F6	Hare
19.10	22. 9	E11	G7	Fox
20.10	23. 9	E11	H8	Tiger
21.10	24. 9	E11	J9	Leopard
22.10	25. 9	E11	K10	Griffon
23.10	26. 9	E11	A11	Ox
24.10	27. 9	E11	B12	Bat
25.10	28. 9	E11	C1	Rat
26.10	29. 9	E11	D2	Swallow
27.10	30. 9	E11	E3	Pig
28.10	1.10	F12	F4	Porcupine
29.10	2.10	F12	G5	Wolf
30.10	3.10	F12	H6	Dog
31.10	4.10	F12	J7	Pheasant
1.11	5.10	F12	K8	Cock
2.11	6.10	F12	A9	Crow
3.11	7.10	F12	B10	Monkey
4.11	8.10	F12	C11	Gibbon
5.11	9.10	F12	D12	Tapir
6.11	10.10	F12	E1	Sheep
7.11	11.10	F12	F2	Deer
8.11	12.10	F12	G3	Horse
9.11	13.10	F12	H4	Stag
10.11	14.10	F12	J5	Serpent
11.11	15.10	F12	K6	Earthworm
12.11	16.10	F12	A7	Crocodile
13.11	17.10	F12	B8	Dragon
14.11	18.10	F12	C9	Badger
15.11	19.10	F12	D10	Hare
16.11	20.10	F12	E11	Fox
17.11	21.10	F12	F12	Tiger
18.11	22.10	F12	G1	Leopard
19.11	23.10	F12	H2	Griffon
20.11	24.10	F12	J3	Ox
21.11	25.10	F12	K4	Bat
22.11	26.10	F12	A5	Rat
23.11	27.10	F12	B6	Swallow
24.11	28.10	F12	C7	Pig
25.11	29.10	F12	D8	Porcupine
26.11	1.11	G1	E9	Wolf
27.11	2.11	G1	F10	Dog
28.11	3.11	G1	G11	Pheasant
29.11	4.11	G1	H12	Cock
30.11	5.11	G1	J1	Crow
1.12	6.11	G1	K2	Monkey
2.12	7.11	G1	A3	Gibbon
3.12	8.11	G1	B4	Tapir
4.12	9.11	G1	C5	Sheep
5.12	10.11	G1	D6	Deer
6.12	11.11	G1	E7	Horse
7.12	12.11	G1	F8	Stag
8.12	13.11	G1	G9	Serpent
9.12	14.11	G1	H10	Earthworm
10.12	15.11	G1	J11	Crocodile
11.12	16.11	G1	K12	Dragon
12.12	17.11	G1	A1	Badger
13.12	18.11	G1	B2	Hare
14.12	19.11	G1	C3	Fox
15.12	20.11	G1	D4	Tiger
16.12	21.11	G1	E5	Leopard
17.12	22.11	G1	F6	Griffon
18.12	23.11	G1	G7	Ox
19.12	24.11	G1	H8	Bat
20.12	25.11	G1	J9	Rat
21.12	26.11	G1	K10	Swallow
22.12	27.11	G1	A11	Pig
23.12	28.11	G1	B12	Porcupine
24.12	29.11	G1	C1	Wolf
25.12	30.11	G1	D2	Dog

Solar date	*Lunar date*	*Month HS/EB*	*Day HS/EB*	*Constellation*
26.12	1.12	H2	E3	Pheasant
27.12	2.12	H2	F4	Cock
28.12	3.12	H2	G5	Crow
29.12	4.12	H2	H6	Monkey
30.12	5.12	H2	J7	Gibbon
31.12	6.12	H2	K8	Tapir
1982				
1. 1	7.12	H2	A9	Sheep
2. 1	8.12	H2	B10	Deer
3. 1	9.12	H2	C11	Horse
4. 1	10.12	H2	D12	Stag
5. 1	11.12	H2	E1	Serpent
6. 1	12.12	H2	F2	Earthworm
7. 1	13.12	H2	G3	Crocodile
8. 1	14.12	H2	H4	Dragon
9. 1	15.12	H2	J5	Badger
10. 1	16.12	H2	K6	Hare
11. 1	17.12	H2	A7	Fox
12. 1	18.12	H2	B8	Tiger
13. 1	19.12	H2	C9	Leopard
14. 1	20.12	H2	D10	Griffon
15. 1	21.12	H2	E11	Ox
16. 1	22.12	H2	F12	Bat
17. 1	23.12	H2	G1	Rat
18. 1	24.12	H2	H2	Swallow
19. 1	25.12	H2	J3	Pig
20. 1	26.12	H2	K4	Porcupine
21. 1	27.12	H2	A5	Wolf
22. 1	28.12	H2	B6	Dog
23. 1	29.12	H2	C7	Pheasant
24. 1	30.12	H2	D8	Cock

JEN HSÜ YEAR

25. 1	1. 1	J3	E9	Crow
26. 1	2. 1	J3	F10	Monkey
27. 1	3. 1	J3	G11	Gibbon
28. 1	4. 1	J3	H12	Tapir
29. 1	5. 1	J3	J1	Sheep
30. 1	6. 1	J3	K2	Deer
31. 1	7. 1	J3	A3	Horse
1. 2	8. 1	J3	B4	Stag
2. 2	9. 1	J3	C5	Serpent
3. 2	10. 1	J3	D6	Earthworm
4. 2	11. 1	J3	E7	Crocodile
5. 2	12. 1	J3	F8	Dragon
6. 2	13. 1	J3	G9	Badger
7. 2	14. 1	J3	H10	Hare
8. 2	15. 1	J3	J11	Fox
9. 2	16. 1	J3	K12	Tiger
10. 2	17. 1	J3	A1	Leopard
11. 2	18. 1	J3	B2	Griffon
12. 2	19. 1	J3	C3	Ox
13. 2	20. 1	J3	D4	Bat
14. 2	21. 1	J3	E5	Rat
15. 2	22. 1	J3	F6	Swallow
16. 2	23. 1	J3	G7	Pig
17. 2	24. 1	J3	H8	Porcupine
18. 2	25. 1	J3	J9	Wolf
19. 2	26. 1	J3	K10	Dog
20. 2	27. 1	J3	A11	Pheasant
21. 2	28. 1	J3	B12	Cock
22. 2	29. 1	J3	C1	Crow
23. 2	30. 1	J3	D2	Monkey
24. 2	1. 2	K4	E3	Gibbon
25. 2	2. 2	K4	F4	Tapir
26. 2	3. 2	K4	G5	Sheep
27. 2	4. 2	K4	H6	Deer
28. 2	5. 2	K4	J7	Horse
1. 3	6. 2	K4	K8	Stag
2. 3	7. 2	K4	A9	Serpent
3. 3	8. 2	K4	B10	Earthworm
4. 3	9. 2	K4	C11	Crocodile
5. 3	10. 2	K4	D12	Dragon
6. 3	11. 2	K4	E1	Badger
7. 3	12. 2	K4	F2	Hare
8. 3	13. 2	K4	G3	Fox
9. 3	14. 2	K4	H4	Tiger
10. 3	15. 2	K4	J5	Leopard
11. 3	16. 2	K4	K6	Griffon
12. 3	17. 2	K4	A7	Ox
13. 3	18. 2	K4	B8	Bat
14. 3	19. 2	K4	C9	Rat
15. 3	20. 2	K4	D10	Swallow
16. 3	21. 2	K4	E11	Pig
17. 3	22. 2	K4	F12	Porcupine
18. 3	23. 2	K4	G1	Wolf
19. 3	24. 2	K4	H4	Dog
20. 3	25. 2	K4	J3	Pheasant
21. 3	26. 2	K4	K4	Cock
22. 3	27. 2	K4	A5	Crow
23. 3	28. 2	K4	B6	Monkey
24. 3	29. 2	K4	C7	Gibbon
25. 3	1. 3	A5	D8	Tapir
26. 3	2. 3	A5	E9	Sheep
27. 3	3. 3	A5	F10	Deer
28. 3	4. 3	A5	G11	Horse
29. 3	5. 3	A5	H12	Stag
30. 3	6. 3	A5	J1	Serpent
31. 3	7. 3	A5	K2	Earthworm
1. 4	8. 3	A5	A3	Crocodile
2. 4	9. 3	A5	B4	Dragon
3. 4	10. 3	A5	C5	Badger
4. 4	11. 3	A5	D6	Hare
5. 4	12. 3	A5	E7	Fox
6. 4	13. 3	A5	F8	Tiger
7. 4	14. 3	A5	G9	Leopard
8. 4	15. 3	A5	H10	Griffon
9. 4	16. 3	A5	J11	Ox
10. 4	17. 3	A5	K12	Bat
11. 4	18. 3	A5	A1	Rat
12. 4	19. 3	A5	B2	Swallow
13. 4	20. 3	A5	C3	Pig
14. 4	21. 3	A5	D4	Porcupine
15. 4	22. 3	A5	E5	Wolf
16. 4	23. 3	A5	F6	Dog
17. 4	24. 3	A5	G7	Pheasant
18. 4	25. 3	A5	H8	Cock
19. 4	26. 3	A5	J9	Crow
20. 4	27. 3	A5	K10	Monkey
21. 4	28. 3	A5	A11	Gibbon
22. 4	29. 3	A5	B12	Tapir
23. 4	30. 3	A5	C1	Sheep
24. 4	1. 4	B6	D2	Deer
25. 4	2. 4	B6	E3	Horse
26. 4	3. 4	B6	F4	Stag
27. 4	4. 4	B6	G5	Serpent
28. 4	5. 4	B6	H6	Earthworm
29. 4	6. 4	B6	J7	Crocodile
30. 4	7. 4	B6	K8	Dragon
1. 5	8. 4	B6	A9	Badger
2. 5	9. 4	B6	B10	Hare
3. 5	10. 4	B6	C11	Fox
4. 5	11. 4	B6	D12	Tiger
5. 5	12. 4	B6	E1	Leopard
6. 5	13. 4	B6	F2	Griffon
7. 5	14. 4	B6	G3	Ox
8. 5	15. 4	B6	H4	Bat

Solar date	*Lunar date*	*Month HS/EB*	*Day HS/EB*	*Constellation*
9. 5	16. 4	B6	J5	Rat
10. 5	17. 4	B6	K6	Swallow
11. 5	18. 4	B6	A7	Pig
12. 5	19. 4	B6	B8	Porcupine
13. 5	20. 4	B6	C9	Wolf
14. 5	21. 4	B6	D10	Dog
15. 5	22. 4	B6	E11	Pheasant
16. 5	23. 4	B6	F12	Cock
17. 5	24. 4	B6	G1	Crow
18. 5	25. 4	B6	H2	Monkey
19. 5	26. 4	B6	J3	Gibbon
20. 5	27. 4	B6	K4	Tapir
21. 5	28. 4	B6	A5	Sheep
22. 5	29. 4	B6	B6	Deer
23. 5	*1. 5*	*B6*	C7	Horse
24. 5	*2. 4*	*B6*	D8	Stag
25. 5	*3. 4*	*B6*	E9	Serpent
26. 5	*4. 4*	*B6*	F10	Earthworm
27. 5	*5. 4*	*B6*	G11	Crocodile
28. 5	*6. 4*	*B6*	H12	Dragon
29. 5	*7. 4*	*B6*	J1	Badger
30. 5	*8. 4*	*B6*	K2	Hare
31. 5	*9. 4*	*B6*	A3	Fox
1. 6	*10. 4*	*B6*	B4	Tiger
2. 6	*11. 4*	*B6*	C5	Leopard
3. 6	*12. 4*	*B6*	D6	Griffon
4. 6	*13. 4*	*B6*	E7	Ox
5. 6	*14. 4*	*B6*	F8	Bat
6. 6	*15. 4*	*B6*	G9	Rat
7. 6	*16. 4*	*B6*	H10	Swallow
8. 6	*17. 4*	*B6*	J11	Pig
9. 6	*18. 4*	*B6*	K12	Porcupine
10. 6	*19. 4*	*B6*	A1	Wolf
11. 6	*20. 4*	*B6*	B2	Dog
12. 6	*21. 4*	*B6*	C3	Pheasant
13. 6	*22. 4*	*B6*	D4	Cock
14. 6	*23. 4*	*B6*	E5	Crow
15. 6	*24. 4*	*B6*	F6	Monkey
16. 6	*25. 4*	*B6*	G7	Gibbon
17. 6	*26. 4*	*B6*	H8	Tapir
18. 6	*27. 4*	*B6*	J9	Sheep
19. 6	*28. 4*	*B6*	K10	Deer
20. 6	*29. 4*	*B6*	A11	Horse
21. 6	1. 5	C7	B12	Stag
22. 6	2. 5	C7	C1	Serpent
23. 6	3. 5	C7	D2	Earthworm
24. 6	4. 5	C7	E3	Crocodile
25. 6	5. 5	C7	F4	Dragon
26. 6	6. 5	C7	G5	Badger
27. 6	7. 5	C7	H6	Hare
28. 6	8. 5	C7	J7	Fox
29. 6	9. 5	C7	K8	Tiger
30. 6	10. 5	C7	A9	Leopard
1. 7	11. 5	C7	B10	Griffon
2. 7	12. 5	C7	C11	Ox
3. 7	13. 5	C7	D12	Bat
4. 7	14. 5	C7	E1	Rat
5. 7	15. 5	C7	F2	Swallow
6. 7	16. 5	C7	G3	Pig
7. 7	17. 5	C7	H4	Porcupine
8. 7	18. 5	C7	J5	Wolf
9. 7	19. 5	C7	K6	Dog
10. 7	20. 5	C7	A7	Pheasant
11. 7	21. 5	C7	B8	Cock
12. 7	22. 5	C7	C9	Crow
13. 7	23. 5	C7	D10	Monkey
14. 7	24. 5	C7	E11	Gibbon
15. 7	25. 5	C7	F12	Tapir
16. 7	26. 5	C7	G1	Sheep
17. 7	27. 5	C7	H2	Deer
18. 7	28. 5	C7	J3	Horse
19. 7	29. 5	C7	K4	Stag
20. 7	30. 5	C7	A5	Serpent
21. 7	1. 6	D8	B6	Earthworm
22. 7	2. 6	D8	C7	Crocodile
23. 7	3. 6	D8	D8	Dragon
24. 7	4. 6	D8	E9	Badger
25. 7	5. 6	D8	F10	Hare
26. 7	6. 6	D8	G11	Fox
27. 7	7. 6	D8	H12	Tiger
28. 7	8. 6	D8	J1	Leopard
29. 7	9. 6	D8	K2	Griffon
30. 7	10. 6	D8	A3	Ox
31. 7	11. 6	D8	B4	Bat
1. 8	12. 6	D8	C5	Rat
2. 8	13. 6	D8	D6	Swallow
3. 8	14. 6	D8	E7	Pig
4. 8	15. 6	D8	F8	Porcupine
5. 8	16. 6	D8	G9	Wolf
6. 8	17. 6	D8	H10	Dog
7. 8	18. 6	D8	J11	Pheasant
8. 8	19. 6	D8	K12	Cock
9. 8	20. 6	D8	A1	Crow
10. 8	21. 6	D8	B2	Monkey
11. 8	22. 6	D8	C3	Gibbon
12. 8	23. 6	D8	D4	Tapir
13. 8	24. 6	D8	E5	Sheep
14. 8	25. 6	D8	F6	Deer
15. 8	26. 6	D8	G7	Horse
16. 8	27. 6	D8	H8	Stag
17. 8	28. 6	D8	J9	Serpent
18. 8	29. 6	D8	K10	Earthworm
19. 8	1. 7	E9	A11	Crocodile
20. 8	2. 7	E9	B12	Dragon
21. 8	3. 7	E9	C1	Badger
22. 8	4. 7	E9	D2	Hare
23. 8	5. 7	E9	E3	Fox
24. 8	6. 7	E9	F4	Tiger
25. 8	7. 7	E9	G4	Leopard
26. 8	8. 7	E9	H6	Griffon
27. 8	9. 7	E9	J7	Ox
28. 8	10. 7	E9	K8	Bat
29. 8	11. 7	E9	A9	Rat
30. 8	12. 7	E9	B10	Swallow
31. 8	13. 7	E9	C11	Pig
1. 9	14. 7	E9	D12	Porcupine
2. 9	15. 7	E9	E1	Wolf
3. 9	16. 7	E9	F2	Dog
4. 9	17. 7	E9	G3	Pheasant
5. 9	18. 7	E9	H4	Cock
6. 9	19. 7	E9	J5	Crow
7. 9	20. 7	E9	K6	Monkey
8. 9	21. 7	E9	A7	Gibbon
9. 9	22. 7	E9	B8	Tapir
10. 9	23. 7	E9	C9	Sheep
11. 9	24. 7	E9	D10	Deer
12. 9	25. 7	E9	E11	Horse
13. 9	26. 7	E9	F12	Stag
14. 9	27. 7	E9	G1	Serpent
15. 9	28. 7	E9	H2	Earthworm
16. 9	29. 7	E9	J3	Crocodile
17. 9	1. 8	F10	K4	Dragon
18. 9	2. 8	F10	A5	Badger
19. 9	3. 8	F10	B6	Hare
20. 9	4. 8	F10	C7	Fox
21. 9	5. 8	F10	D8	Tiger
22. 9	6. 8	F10	E9	Leopard
23. 9	7. 8	F10	F10	Griffon
24. 9	8. 8	F10	G11	Ox
25. 9	9. 8	F10	H12	Bat
26. 9	10. 8	F10	J1	Rat
27. 9	11. 8	F10	K2	Swallow
28. 9	12. 8	F10	A3	Pig
29. 9	13. 8	F10	B4	Porcupine
30. 9	14. 8	F10	C5	Wolf
1.10	15. 8	F10	D6	Dog

Solar date	Lunar date	Month HS/EB	Day HS/EB	Constellation
2.10	16. 8	F10	E7	Pheasant
3.10	17. 8	F10	F8	Cock
4.10	18. 8	F10	G9	Crow
5.10	19. 8	F10	H10	Monkey
6.10	20. 8	F10	J11	Gibbon
7.10	21. 8	F10	K12	Tapir
8.10	22. 8	F10	A1	Sheep
9.10	23. 8	F10	B2	Deer
10.10	24. 8	F10	C3	Horse
11.10	25. 8	F10	D4	Stag
12.10	26. 8	F10	E5	Serpent
13.10	27. 8	F10	F6	Earthworm
14.10	28. 8	F10	G7	Crocodile
15.10	29. 8	F10	H8	Dragon
16.10	30. 8	F10	J9	Badger
17.10	1. 9	G11	K10	Hare
18.10	2. 9	G11	A11	Fox
19.10	3. 9	G11	B12	Tiger
20.10	4. 9	G11	C1	Leopard
21.10	5. 9	G11	D2	Griffon
22.10	6. 9	G11	E3	Ox
23.10	7. 9	G11	F4	Bat
24.10	8. 9	G11	G5	Rat
25.10	9. 9	G11	H6	Swallow
26.10	10. 9	G11	J7	Pig
27.10	11. 9	G11	K8	Porcupine
28.10	12. 9	G11	A9	Wolf
29.10	13. 9	G11	B10	Dog
30.10	14. 9	G11	C11	Pheasant
31.10	15. 9	G11	D12	Cock
1.11	16. 9	G11	E1	Crow
2.11	17. 9	G11	F2	Monkey
3.11	18. 9	G11	G3	Gibbon
4.11	19. 0	G11	H4	Tapir
5.11	20. 9	G11	J5	Sheep
6.11	21. 9	G11	K6	Deer
7.11	22. 9	G11	A7	Horse
8.11	23. 9	G11	B8	Stag
9.11	24. 9	G11	C9	Serpent
10.11	25. 9	G11	D10	Earthworm
11.11	26. 9	G11	E11	Crocodile
12.11	27. 9	G11	F12	Dragon
13.11	28. 9	G11	G1	Badger
14.11	29. 9	G11	H2	Hare
15.11	1.10	H12	J3	Fox
16.11	2.10	H12	K4	Tiger
17.11	3.10	H12	A5	Leopard
18.11	4.10	H12	B6	Griffon
19.11	5.10	H12	C7	Ox
20.11	6.10	H12	D8	Bat
21.11	7.10	H12	E9	Rat
22.11	8.10	H12	F10	Swallow
23.11	9.10	H12	G11	Pig
24.11	10.10	H12	H12	Porcupine
25.11	11.10	H12	J1	Wolf
26.11	12.10	H12	K2	Dog
27.11	13.10	H12	A3	Pheasant
28.11	14.10	H12	B4	Cock
29.11	15.10	H12	C5	Crow
30.11	16.10	H12	D6	Monkey
1.12	17.10	H12	E7	Gibbon
2.12	18.10	H12	F8	Tapir
3.12	19.10	H12	G9	Sheep
4.12	20.10	H12	H10	Deer
5.12	21.10	H12	J11	Horse
6.12	22.10	H12	K12	Stag
7.12	23.10	H12	A1	Serpent
8.12	24.10	H12	B2	Earthworm

Solar date	Lunar date	Month HS/EB	Day HS/EB	Constellation
9.12	25.10	H12	C3	Crocodile
10.12	26.10	H12	D4	Dragon
11.12	27.10	H12	E5	Badger
12.12	28.10	H12	F6	Hare
13.12	29.10	H12	G7	Fox
14.12	30.10	H12	H8	Tiger
15.12	1.11	J1	J9	Leopard
16.12	2.11	J1	K10	Griffon
17.12	3.11	J1	A11	Ox
18.12	4.11	J1	B12	Bat
19.12	5.11	J1	C1	Rat
20.12	6.11	J1	D2	Swallow
21.12	7.11	J1	E3	Pig
22.12	8.11	J1	F4	Porcupine
23.12	9.11	J1	G5	Wolf
24.12	10.11	J1	H6	Dog
25.12	11.11	J1	J7	Pheasant
26.12	12.11	J1	K8	Cock
27.12	13.11	J1	A9	Crow
28.12	14.11	J1	B10	Monkey
29.12	15.11	J1	C11	Gibbon
30.12	16.11	J1	D12	Tapir
31.12	17.11	J1	E1	Sheep
1983				
1. 1	18.11	J1	F2	Deer
2. 1	19.11	J1	G3	Horse
3. 1	20.11	J1	H4	Stag
4. 1	21.11	J1	J5	Serpent
5. 1	22.11	J1	K6	Earthworm
6. 1	23.11	J1	A7	Crocodile
7. 1	24.11	J1	B8	Dragon
8. 1	25.11	J1	C9	Badger
9. 1	26.11	J1	D10	Hare
10. 1	27.11	J1	E11	Fox
11. 1	28.11	J1	F12	Tiger
12. 1	29.11	J1	G1	Leopard
13. 1	30.11	J1	H2	Griffon
14. 1	1.12	K2	J3	Ox
15. 1	2.12	K2	K4	Bat
16. 1	3.12	K2	A5	Rat
17. 1	4.12	K2	B6	Swallow
18. 1	5.12	K2	C7	Pig
19. 1	6.12	K2	D8	Porcupine
20. 1	7.12	K2	E9	Wolf
21. 1	8.12	K2	F10	Dog
22. 1	9.12	K2	G11	Pheasant
23. 1	10.12	K2	H12	Cock
24. 1	11.12	K2	J1	Crow
25. 1	12.12	K2	K2	Monkey
26. 1	13.12	K2	A3	Gibbon
27. 1	14.12	K2	B4	Tapir
28. 1	15.12	K2	C5	Sheep
29. 1	16.12	K2	D6	Deer
30. 1	17.12	K2	E7	Horse
31. 1	18.12	K2	F8	Stag
1. 2	19.12	K2	G9	Serpent
2. 2	20.12	K2	H10	Earthworm
3. 2	21.12	K2	J11	Crocodile
4. 2	22.12	K2	K12	Dragon
5. 2	23.12	K2	A1	Badger
6. 2	24.12	K2	B2	Hare
7. 2	25.12	K2	C3	Fox
8. 2	26.12	K2	D4	Tiger
9. 2	27.12	K2	E5	Laopard
10. 2	28.12	K2	F6	Griffon
11. 2	29.12	K2	G7	Ox
12. 2	30.12	K2	H8	Bat

KUEI HAI YEAR

Solar date	*Lunar date*	*Month HS/EB*	*Day HS/EB*	*Constellation*
13. 2	1. 1	A3	J9	Rat
14. 2	2. 1	A3	K10	Swallow
15. 2	3. 1	A3	A11	Pig
16. 2	4. 1	A3	B12	Porcupine
17. 2	5. 1	A3	C1	Wolf
18. 2	6. 1	A3	D2	Dog
19. 2	7. 1	A3	E3	Pheasant
20. 2	8. 1	A3	F4	Cock
21. 2	9. 1	A3	G5	Crow
22. 2	10. 1	A3	H6	Monkey
23. 2	11. 1	A3	J7	Gibbon
24. 2	12. 1	A3	K8	Tapir
25. 2	13. 1	A3	A9	Sheep
26. 2	14. 1	A3	B10	Deer
27. 2	15. 1	A3	C11	Horse
28. 2	16. 1	A3	D12	Stag
1. 3	17. 1	A3	E1	Serpent
2. 3	18. 1	A3	F2	Earthworm
3. 3	19. 1	A3	G3	Crocodile
4. 3	20. 1	A3	H4	Dragon
5. 3	21. 1	A3	J5	Badger
6. 3	22. 1	A3	K6	Hare
7. 3	23. 1	A3	A7	Fox
8. 3	24. 1	A3	B8	Tiger
9. 3	25. 1	A3	C9	Leopard
10. 3	26. 1	A3	D10	Griffon
11. 3	27. 1	A3	E11	Ox
12. 3	28. 1	A3	F12	Bat
13. 3	29. 1	A3	G1	Rat
14. 3	30. 1	A3	H2	Swallow
15. 3	1. 2	B4	J3	Pig
16. 3	2. 2	B4	K4	Porcupine
17. 3	3. 2	B4	A5	Wolf
18. 3	4. 2	B4	B6	Dog
19. 3	5. 2	B4	C7	Pheasant
20. 3	6. 2	B4	D8	Cock
21. 3	7. 2	B4	E9	Crow
22. 3	8. 2	B4	F10	Monkey
23. 3	9. 2	B4	G11	Gibbon
24. 3	10. 2	B4	H12	Tapir
25. 3	11. 2	B4	J1	Sheep
26. 3	12. 2	B4	K2	Deer
27. 3	13. 2	B4	A3	Horse
28. 3	14. 2	B4	B4	Stag
29. 3	15. 2	B4	C5	Serpent
30. 3	16. 2	B4	D6	Earthworm
31. 3	17. 2	B4	E7	Crocodile
1. 4	18. 2	B4	F8	Dragon
2. 4	19. 2	B4	G9	Badger
3. 4	20. 2	B4	H10	Hare
4. 4	21. 2	B4	J11	Fox
5. 4	22. 2	B4	K12	Tiger
6. 4	23. 2	B4	A1	Leopard
7. 4	24. 2	B4	B2	Griffon
8. 4	25. 2	B4	C3	Ox
9. 4	26. 2	B4	D4	Bat
10. 4	27. 2	B4	E5	Rat
11. 4	28. 2	B4	F6	Swallow
12. 4	29. 2	B4	G7	Pig
13. 4	1. 3	C5	H8	Porcupine
14. 4	2. 3	C5	J9	Wolf
15. 4	3. 3	C5	K10	Dog
16. 4	4. 3	C5	A11	Pheasant
17. 4	5. 3	C5	B12	Cock
18. 4	6. 3	C5	C1	Crow
19. 4	7. 3	C5	D2	Monkey
20. 4	8. 3	C5	E3	Gibbon
21. 4	9. 3	C5	F4	Tapir
22. 4	10. 3	C5	G5	Sheep
23. 4	11. 3	C5	H6	Deer
24. 4	12. 3	C5	J7	Horse
25. 4	13. 3	C5	K8	Stag
26. 4	14. 3	C5	A9	Serpent
27. 4	15. 3	C5	B10	Earthworm
28. 4	16. 3	C5	C11	Crocodile
29. 4	17. 3	C5	D12	Dragon
30. 4	18. 3	C5	E1	Badger
1. 5	19. 3	C5	F2	Hare
2. 5	20. 3	C5	G3	Fox
3. 5	21. 3	C5	H4	Tiger
4. 5	22. 3	C5	J5	Leopard
5. 5	23. 3	C5	K6	Griffon
6. 5	24. 3	C5	A7	Ox
7. 5	25. 3	C5	B8	Bat
8. 5	26. 3	C5	C9	Rat
9. 5	27. 3	C5	D10	Swallow
10. 5	28. 3	C5	E11	Pig
11. 5	29. 3	C5	F12	Porcupine
12. 5	30. 3	C5	G1	Wolf
13. 5	1. 4	D6	H2	Dog
14. 5	2. 4	D6	J3	Pheasant
15. 5	3. 4	D6	K4	Cock
16. 5	4. 4	D6	A5	Crow
17. 5	5. 4	D6	B6	Monkey
18. 5	6. 4	D6	C7	Gibbon
19. 5	7. 4	D6	D8	Tapir
20. 5	8. 4	D6	E9	Sheep
21. 5	9. 4	D6	F10	Deer
22. 5	10. 4	D6	G11	Horse
23. 5	11. 4	D6	H12	Stag
24. 5	12. 4	D6	J1	Serpent
25. 5	13. 4	D6	K2	Earthworm
26. 5	14. 4	D6	A3	Crocodile
27. 5	15. 4	D6	B4	Dragon
28. 5	16. 4	D6	C5	Badger
29. 5	17. 4	D6	D6	Hare
30. 5	18. 4	D6	E7	Fox
31. 5	19. 4	D6	F8	Tiger
1. 6	20. 4	D6	G9	Leopard
2. 6	21. 4	D6	H10	Griffon
3. 6	22. 4	D6	J11	Ox
4. 6	23. 4	D6	K12	Bat
5. 6	24. 4	D6	A1	Rat
6. 6	25. 4	D6	B2	Swallow
7. 6	26. 4	D6	C3	Pig
8. 6	27. 4	D6	D4	Porcupine
9. 6	28. 4	D6	E5	Wolf
10. 6	29. 4	D6	F6	Dog
11. 6	1. 5	E7	G7	Pheasant
12. 6	2. 5	E7	H8	Cock
13. 6	3. 5	E7	J9	Crow
14. 6	4. 5	E7	K10	Monkey
15. 6	5. 5	E7	A11	Gibbon
16. 6	6. 5	E7	B12	Tapir
17. 6	7. 5	E7	C1	Sheep
18. 6	8. 5	E7	D2	Deer
19. 6	9. 5	E7	E3	Horse
20. 6	10. 5	E7	F4	Stag
21. 6	11. 5	E7	G5	Serpent
22. 6	12. 5	E7	H6	Earthworm
23. 6	13. 5	E7	J7	Crocodile
24. 6	14. 5	E7	K8	Dragon
25. 6	15. 5	E7	A9	Badger
26. 6	16. 5	E7	B10	Hare
27. 6	17. 5	E7	C11	Fox
28. 6	18. 5	E7	D12	Tiger
29. 6	19. 5	E7	E1	Leopard
30. 6	20. 5	E7	F2	Griffon
1. 7	21. 5	E7	G3	Ox
2. 7	22. 5	E7	H4	Bat
3. 7	23. 5	E7	J5	Rat
4. 7	24. 5	E7	K6	Swallow

Solar date	*Lunar date*	*Month HS/EB*	*Day HS/EB*	*Constellation*
5. 7	25. 5	E7	H7	Pig
6. 7	26. 5	E7	B8	Porcupine
7. 7	27. 5	E7	C9	Wolf
8. 7	28. 5	E7	D10	Dog
9. 7	29. 5	E7	E11	Pheasant
10. 7	1. 6	F8	F12	Cock
11. 7	2. 6	F8	G1	Crow
12. 7	3. 6	F8	H2	Monkey
13. 7	4. 6	F8	J3	Gibbon
14. 7	5. 6	F8	K4	Tapir
15. 7	6. 6	F8	A5	Sheep
16. 7	7. 6	F8	B6	Deer
17. 7	8. 6	F8	C7	Horse
18. 7	9. 6	F8	D8	Stag
19. 7	10. 6	F8	E9	Serpent
20. 7	11. 6	F8	F10	Earthworm
21. 7	12. 6	F8	G11	Crocodile
22. 7	13. 6	F8	H12	Dragon
23. 7	14. 6	F8	J1	Badger
24. 7	15. 6	F8	K2	Hare
25. 7	16. 6	F8	A3	Fox
26. 7	17. 6	F8	B4	Tiger
27. 7	18. 6	F8	C5	Leopard
28. 7	19. 6	F8	D6	Griffon
29. 7	20. 6	F8	E7	Ox
30. 7	21. 6	F8	F8	Bat
31. 7	22. 6	F8	G9	Rat
1. 8	23. 6	F8	H10	Swallow
2. 8	24. 6	F8	J11	Pig
3. 8	25. 6	F8	K12	Porcupine
4. 8	26. 6	F8	A1	Wolf
5. 8	27. 6	F8	B2	Dog
6. 8	28. 6	F8	C3	Pheasant
7. 8	29. 6	F8	D4	Cock
8. 8	30. 6	F8	E5	Crow
9. 8	1. 7	G9	F6	Monkey
10. 8	2. 7	G9	G7	Gibbon
11. 8	3. 7	G9	H8	Tapir
12. 8	4. 7	G9	J9	Sheep
13. 8	5. 7	G9	K10	Deer
14. 8	6. 7	G9	A11	Horse
15. 8	7. 7	G9	B12	Stag
16. 8	8. 7	G9	C1	Serpent
17. 8	9. 7	G9	D2	Earthworm
18. 8	10. 7	G9	E3	Crocodile
19. 8	11. 7	G9	F4	Dragon
20. 8	12. 7	G9	G5	Badger
21. 8	13. 7	G9	H6	Hare
22. 8	14. 7	G9	J7	Fox
23. 8	15. 7	G9	K8	Tiger
24. 8	16. 7	G9	A9	Leopard
25. 8	17. 7	G9	B10	Griffon
26. 8	18. 7	G9	C11	Ox
27. 8	19. 7	G9	D12	Bat
28. 8	20. 7	G9	E1	Rat
29. 8	21. 7	G9	F2	Swallow
30. 8	22. 7	G9	G3	Pig
31. 8	23. 7	G9	H4	Porcupine
1. 9	24. 7	G9	J5	Wolf
2. 9	25. 7	G9	K6	Dog
3. 9	26. 7	G9	A7	Pheasant
4. 9	27. 7	G9	B8	Cock
5. 9	28. 7	G9	C9	Crow
6. 9	29. 7	G9	D10	Monkey
7. 9	1. 8	H10	E11	Gibbon
8. 9	2. 8	H10	F12	Tapir
9. 9	3. 8	H10	G1	Sheep
10. 9	4. 8	H10	H2	Deer
11. 9	5. 8	H10	J3	Horse
12. 9	6. 8	H10	K4	Stag
13. 9	7. 8	H10	A5	Serpent
14. 9	8. 8	H10	B6	Earthworm
15. 9	9. 8	H10	C7	Crocodile
16. 9	10. 8	H10	D8	Dragon
17. 9	11. 8	H10	E9	Badger
18. 9	12. 8	H10	F10	Hare
19. 9	13. 8	H10	G11	Fox
20. 9	14. 8	H10	H12	Tiger
21. 9	15. 8	H10	J1	Leopard
22. 9	16. 8	H10	K2	Griffon
23. 9	17. 8	H10	A3	Ox
24. 9	18. 8	H10	B4	Bat
25. 9	19. 8	H10	C5	Rat
26. 9	20. 8	H10	D6	Swallow
27. 9	21. 8	H10	E7	Pig
28. 9	22. 8	H10	F8	Porcupine
29. 9	23. 8	H10	G9	Wolf
30. 9	24. 8	H10	H10	Dog
1.10	25. 8	H10	J11	Pheasant
2.10	26. 8	H10	K12	Cock
3.10	27. 8	H10	A1	Crow
4.10	28. 8	H10	B2	Monkey
5.10	29. 8	H10	C3	Gibbon
6.10	1. 9	J11	D4	Tapir
7.10	2. 9	J11	E5	Sheep
8.10	3. 9	J11	F6	Deer
9.10	4. 9	J11	G7	Horse
10.10	5. 9	J11	H8	Stag
11.10	6. 9	J11	J9	Serpent
12.10	7. 9	J11	K10	Earthworm
13.10	8. 9	J11	A11	Crocodile
14.10	9. 9	J11	B12	Dragon
15.10	10. 9	J11	C1	Badger
16.10	11. 9	J11	D2	Hare
17.10	12. 9	J11	E3	Fox
18.10	13. 9	J11	F4	Tiger
19.10	14. 9	J11	G5	Leopard
20.10	15. 9	J11	H6	Griffon
21.10	16. 9	J11	J7	Ox
22.10	17. 9	J11	K8	Bat
23.10	18. 9	J11	A9	Rat
24.10	19. 9	J11	B10	Swallow
25.10	20. 9	J11	C11	Pig
26.10	21. 9	J11	D12	Porcupine
27.10	22. 9	J11	E1	Wolf
28.10	23. 9	J11	F2	Dog
29.10	24. 9	J11	G3	Pheasant
30.10	25. 9	J11	H4	Cock
31.10	26. 9	J11	J5	Crow
1.11	27. 9	J11	K6	Monkey
2.11	28. 9	J11	A7	Gibbon
3.11	29. 9	J11	B8	Tapir
4.11	30. 9	J11	C9	Sheep
5.11	1.10	K12	D10	Deer
6.11	2.10	K12	E11	Horse
7.11	3.10	K12	F12	Stag
8.11	4.10	K12	G1	Serpent
9.11	5.10	K12	H2	Earthworm
10.11	6.10	K12	J3	Crocodile
11.11	7.10	K12	K4	Dragon
12.11	8.10	K12	A5	Badger
13.11	9.10	K12	B6	Hare
14.11	10.10	K12	C7	Fox
15.11	11.10	K12	D8	Tiger
16.11	12.10	K12	E9	Leopard
17.11	13.10	K12	F10	Griffon
18.11	14.10	K12	G11	Ox
19.11	15.10	K12	H12	Bat
20.11	16.10	K12	J1	Rat
21.11	17.10	K12	K2	Swallow
22.11	18.10	K12	A3	Pig
23.11	19.10	K12	B4	Porcupine
24.11	20.10	K12	C5	Wolf
25.11	21.10	K12	D6	Dog
26.11	22.10	K12	E7	Pheasant
27.11	23.10	K12	F8	Cock

Solar date	*Lunar date*	*Month HS/EB*	*Day HS/EB*	*Constellation*
28.11	24.10	K12	G9	Crow
29.11	25.10	K12	H10	Monkey
30.11	26.10	K12	J11	Gibbon
1.12	27.10	K12	K12	Tapir
2.12	28.10	K12	A1	Sheep
3.12	29.10	K12	B2	Deer
4.12	1.11	A1	C3	Horse
5.12	2.11	A1	D4	Stag
6.12	3.11	A1	E5	Serpent
7.12	4.11	A1	F6	Earthworm
8.12	5.11	A1	G7	Crocodile
9.12	6.11	A1	H8	Dragon
10.12	7.11	A1	J9	Badger
11.12	8.11	A1	K10	Hare
12.12	9.11	A1	A11	Fox
13.12	10.11	A1	B12	Tiger
14.12	11.11	A1	C1	Leopard
15.12	12.11	A1	D2	Griffon
16.12	13.11	A1	E3	Ox
17.12	14.11	A1	F4	Bat
18.12	15.11	A1	G5	Rat
19.12	16.11	A1	H6	Swallow
20.12	17.11	A1	J7	Pig
21.12	18.11	A1	K8	Porcupine
22.12	19.11	A1	A9	Wolf
23.12	20.11	A1	B10	Dog
24.12	21.11	A1	C11	Pheasant
25.12	22.11	A1	D12	Cock
26.12	23.11	A1	E1	Crow
27.12	24.11	A1	F2	Monkey
28.12	25.11	A1	G3	Gibbon
29.12	26.11	A1	H4	Tapir
30.12	27.11	A1	J5	Sheep
31.12	28.11	A1	K6	Deer

Solar date	*Lunar date*	*Month HS/EB*	*Day HS/EB*	*Constellation*
1984				
1. 1	29.11	A1	A7	Horse
2. 1	30.11	A1	B8	Stag
3. 1	1.12	B2	C9	Serpent
4. 1	2.12	B2	D10	Earthworm
5. 1	3.12	B2	E11	Crocodile
6. 1	4.12	B2	F12	Dragon
7. 1	5.12	B2	G1	Badger
8. 1	6.12	B2	H2	Hare
9. 1	7.12	B2	J3	Fox
10. 1	8.12	B2	K4	Tiger
11. 1	9.12	B2	A5	Leopard
12. 2	10.12	B2	B6	Griffon
13. 1	11.12	B2	C7	Ox
14. 1	12.12	B2	D8	Bat
15. 1	13.12	B2	E9	Rat
16. 1	14.12	B2	F10	Swallow
17. 1	15.12	B2	G11	Pig
18. 1	16.12	B2	H12	Porcupine
19. 1	17.12	B2	J1	Wolf
20. 1	18.12	B2	K2	Dog
21. 1	19.12	B2	A3	Pheasant
22. 1	20.12	B2	B4	Cock
23. 1	21.12	B2	C5	Crow
24. 1	22.12	B2	D6	Monkey
25. 1	23.12	B2	E7	Gibbon
26. 1	24.12	B2	F8	Tapir
27. 1	25.12	B2	G9	Sheep
28. 1	26.12	B2	H10	Deer
29. 1	27.12	B2	J11	Horse
30. 1	28.12	B2	K12	Stag
31. 1	29.12	B2	A1	Serpent
1. 2	30.12	B2	B2	Earthworm

CHIA TZU YEAR

2. 2	1.12	C3	C3	Crocodile
3. 2	2.12	C3	D4	Dragon
4. 2	3.12	C3	E5	Badger
5. 2	4.12	C3	F6	Hare
6. 2	5.12	C3	G7	Fox
7. 2	6.12	C3	H8	Tiger
8. 2	7.12	C3	J9	Leopard
9. 2	8.12	C3	K10	Griffon
10. 2	9.12	C3	A11	Ox
11. 2	10.12	C3	B12	Bat
12. 2	11.12	C3	C1	Rat
13. 2	12.12	C3	D2	Swallow
14. 2	13.12	C3	E3	Pig
15. 2	14. 1	C3	F4	Porcupine
16. 2	15. 1	C3	G5	Wolf
17. 2	16. 1	C3	H6	Dog
18. 2	17. 1	C3	J7	Pheasant
19. 2	18. 1	C3	K8	Cock
20. 2	19. 1	C3	A9	Crow
21. 2	20. 1	C3	B10	Monkey
22. 2	21. 1	C3	C11	Gibbon
23. 2	22. 1	C3	D12	Tapir
24. 2	23. 1	C3	E1	Sheep
25. 2	24. 1	C3	F2	Deer
26. 2	25. 1	C3	G3	Horse
27. 2	26. 1	C3	H4	Stag
28. 2	27. 1	C3	J5	Serpent
29. 2	28. 1	C3	K6	Earthworm
1. 3	29. 1	C3	A7	Crocodile
2. 3	30. 1	C3	B8	Dragon
3. 3	1. 1	D4	C9	Badger
4. 3	2. 1	D4	D10	Hare
5. 3	3. 1	D4	E11	Fox
6. 3	4. 1	D4	F12	Tiger

7. 3	5. 1	D4	G1	Leopard
8. 3	6. 1	D4	H2	Griffon
9. 3	7. 1	D4	J3	Ox
10. 3	8. 1	D4	K4	Bat
11. 3	9. 1	D4	A5	Rat
12. 3	10. 1	D4	B6	Swallow
13. 3	11. 1	D4	C7	Pig
14. 3	12. 1	D4	D8	Porcupine
15. 3	13. 1	D4	E9	Wolf
16. 3	14. 2	D4	F10	Dog
17. 3	15. 2	D4	G11	Pheasant
18. 3	16. 2	D4	H12	Cock
19. 3	17. 2	D4	J1	Crow
20. 3	18. 2	D4	K2	Monkey
21. 3	19. 2	D4	A3	Gibbon
22. 3	20. 2	D4	B4	Tapir
23. 3	21. 2	D4	C5	Sheep
24. 3	22. 2	D4	D6	Deer
25. 3	23. 2	D4	E7	Horse
26. 3	24. 2	D4	F8	Stag
27. 3	25. 2	D4	G9	Serpent
28. 3	26. 2	D4	H10	Earthworm
29. 3	27. 2	D4	J11	Crocodile
30. 3	28. 2	D4	K12	Dragon
31. 3	29. 2	D4	A1	Badger
1. 4	1. 2	E5	B2	Hare
2. 4	2. 2	E5	C3	Fox
3. 4	3. 2	E5	D4	Tiger
4. 4	4. 2	E5	E5	Leopard
5. 4	5. 2	E5	F6	Griffon
6. 4	6. 2	E5	G7	Ox
7. 4	7. 2	E5	H8	Bat
8. 4	8. 2	E5	J9	Rat
9. 4	9. 2	E5	K10	Swallow

Solar date	*Lunar date*	*Month HS/EB*	*Day HS/EB*	*Constellation*
10. 4	10. 2	E5	A11	Pig
11. 4	11. 2	E5	B12	Porcupine
12. 4	12. 2	E5	C1	Wolf
13. 4	13. 2	E5	D2	Dog
14. 4	14. 3	E5	E3	Pheasant
15. 4	15. 3	E5	F4	Cock
16. 4	16. 3	E5	G5	Crow
17. 4	17. 3	E5	H6	Monkey
18. 4	18. 3	E5	J7	Gibbon
19. 4	19. 3	E5	K8	Tapir
20. 4	20. 3	E5	A9	Sheep
21. 4	21. 3	E5	B10	Deer
22. 4	22. 3	E5	C11	Horse
23. 4	23. 3	E5	D12	Stag
24. 4	24. 3	E5	E1	Serpent
25. 4	25. 3	E5	F2	Earthworm
26. 4	26. 3	E5	G3	Crocodile
27. 4	27. 3	E5	H4	Dragon
28. 4	28. 3	E5	J5	Badger
29. 4	29. 3	E5	K6	Hare
30. 4	30. 3	E5	A7	Fox
1. 5	1. 4	F6	B8	Tiger
2. 5	2. 4	F6	C9	Leopard
3. 5	3. 4	F6	D10	Griffon
4 5	4. 4	F6	E11	Ox
5. 5	5. 4	F6	F12	Bat
6. 5	6. 4	F6	G1	Rat
7. 5	7. 4	F6	H2	Swallow
8. 5	8. 4	F6	J3	Pig
9. 5	9. 4	F6	K4	Porcupine
10. 5	10. 4	F6	A5	Wolf
11. 5	11. 4	F6	B6	Dog
12. 5	12. 4	F6	C7	Pheasant
13. 5	13. 4	F6	D8	Cock
14. 5	14. 4	F6	E9	Crow
15. 5	15. 4	F6	F10	Monkey
16. 5	16. 4	F6	G11	Gibbon
17. 5	17. 4	F6	H12	Tapir
18. 5	18. 4	F6	J1	Sheep
19. 5	19. 4	F6	K2	Deer
20. 5	20. 4	F6	A3	Horse
21. 5	21. 4	F6	B4	Stag
22. 5	22. 4	F6	C5	Serpent
23. 5	23. 4	F6	D6	Earthworm
24. 5	24. 4	F6	E7	Crocodile
25. 5	25. 4	F6	F8	Dragon
26. 5	26. 4	F6	G9	Badger
27. 5	27. 4	F6	H10	Hare
28. 5	28. 4	F6	J11	Fox
29. 5	29. 4	F6	K12	Tiger
30. 5	30. 4	F6	A1	Leopard
31. 5	1. 5	G7	B2	Griffon
1. 6	2. 5	G7	C3	Ox
2. 6	3. 5	G7	D4	Rat
3. 6	4. 5	G7	E5	Rat
4. 6	5. 5	G7	F6	Swallow
5. 6	6. 5	G7	G7	Pig
6. 6	7. 5	G7	H8	Porcupine
7. 6	8. 5	G7	J9	Wolf
8. 6	9. 5	G7	K10	Dog
9. 6	10. 5	G7	A11	Pheasant
10. 6	11. 5	G7	B12	Cock
11. 6	12. 5	G7	C1	Crow
12. 6	13. 5	G7	D2	Monkey
13. 6	14. 5	G7	E3	Gibbon
14. 6	15. 5	G7	F4	Tapir
15. 6	16. 5	G7	G5	Sheep
16. 6	17. 5	G7	H6	Deer
17. 6	18. 5	G7	J7	Horse
18. 6	19. 5	G7	K8	Stag
19. 6	20. 5	G7	A9	Serpent
20. 6	21. 5	G7	B10	Earthworm
21. 6	22. 5	G7	C11	Crocodile

Solar date	*Lunar date*	*Month HS/EB*	*Day HS/EB*	*Constellation*
22. 6	23. 5	G7	D12	Dragon
23. 6	24. 5	G7	E1	Badger
24. 6	25. 5	G7	F2	Hare
25. 6	26. 5	G7	G3	Fox
26. 6	27. 5	G7	H4	Tiger
27. 6	28. 5	G7	J5	Leopard
28. 6	29. 5	G7	K6	Griffon
29. 6	1. 6	H8	A7	Ox
30. 6	2. 6	H8	B8	Bat
1. 7	3. 6	H8	C9	Rat
2. 7	4. 6	H8	D10	Swallow
3. 7	5. 6	H8	E11	Pig
4. 7	6. 6	H8	F12	Porcupine
5. 7	7. 6	H8	G1	Wolf
6. 7	8. 6	H8	H2	Dog
7. 7	9. 6	H8	J3	Pheasant
8. 7	10. 6	H8	K4	Cock
9. 7	11. 6	H8	A5	Crow
10. 7	12. 6	H8	B6	Monkey
11. 7	13. 6	H8	C7	Gibbon
12. 7	14. 6	H8	D8	Tapir
13. 7	15. 6	H8	E9	Sheep
14. 7	16. 6	H8	F10	Deer
15. 7	17. 6	H8	G11	Horse
16. 7	18. 6	H8	H12	Stag
17. 7	19. 6	H8	J1	Serpent
18. 7	20. 6	H8	K2	Earthworm
19. 7	21. 6	H8	A3	Crocodile
20. 7	22. 6	H8	B4	Dragon
21. 7	23. 6	H8	C5	Badger
22. 7	24. 6	H8	D6	Hare
23. 7	25. 6	H8	E7	Fox
24. 7	26. 6	H8	F8	Tiger
25. 7	27. 6	H8	G9	Leopard
26. 7	28. 6	H8	H10	Griffon
27. 7	29. 6	H8	J11	Ox
28. 7	1. 7	J9	K12	Bat
29. 7	2. 7	J9	A1	Rat
30. 7	3. 7	J9	B2	Swallow
31. 7	4. 7	J9	C3	Pig
1. 8	5. 7	J9	D4	Porcupine
2. 8	6. 7	J9	E5	Wolf
3. 8	7. 7	J9	F6	Dog
4. 8	8. 7	J9	G7	Pheasant
5. 8	9. 7	J9	H8	Cock
6. 8	10. 7	J9	J9	Crow
7. 8	11. 7	J9	K10	Monkey
8. 8	12. 7	J9	A11	Gibbon
9. 8	13. 7	J9	B12	Tapir
10. 8	14. 7	J9	C1	Sheep
11. 8	15. 7	J9	D2	Deer
12. 8	16. 7	J9	E3	Horse
13. 8	17. 7	J9	F4	Stag
14. 8	18. 7	J9	G5	Serpent
15. 8	19. 7	J9	H6	Earthworm
16. 8	20. 7	J9	J7	Crocodile
17. 8	21. 7	J9	K8	Dragon
18. 8	22. 7	J9	A9	Badger
19. 8	23. 7	J9	B10	Hare
20. 8	24. 7	J9	C11	Fox
21. 8	25. 7	J9	D12	Tiger
22. 8	26. 7	J9	E1	Leopard
23. 8	27. 7	J9	F2	Griffon
24. 8	28. 7	J9	G3	Ox
25. 8	29. 7	J9	H4	Bat
26. 8	30. 7	J9	J5	Rat
27. 8	1. 8	K10	K6	Swallow
28. 8	2. 8	K10	A7	Pig
29. 8	3. 8	K10	B8	Porcupine
30. 8	4. 8	K10	C9	Wolf
31. 8	5. 8	K10	D10	Dog
1. 9	6. 8	K10	E11	Pheasant
2. 9	7. 8	K10	F12	Cock

Solar date	*Lunar date*	*Month HS/EB*	*Day HS/EB*	*Constellation*
3. 9	8. 8	K10	G1	Crow
4. 9	9. 8	K10	H2	Monkey
5. 9	10. 8	K10	J3	Gibbon
6. 9	11. 8	K10	K4	Tapir
7. 9	12. 8	K10	A5	Sheep
8. 9	13. 8	K10	B6	Deer
9. 9	14. 8	K10	C7	Horse
10. 9	15. 8	K10	D8	Stag
11. 9	16. 8	K10	E9	Serpent
12. 9	17. 8	K10	F10	Earthworm
13. 9	18. 8	K10	G11	Crocodile
14. 9	19. 8	K10	H12	Dragon
15. 9	20. 8	K10	J1	Badger
16. 9	21. 8	K10	K2	Hare
17. 9	22. 8	K10	A3	Fox
18. 9	23. 8	K10	B4	Tiger
19. 9	24. 8	K10	C5	Leopard
20. 9	25. 8	K10	D6	Griffon
21. 9	26. 8	K10	E7	Ox
22. 9	27. 8	K10	F8	Bat
23. 9	28. 8	K10	G9	Rat
24. 9	29. 8	K10	H10	Swallow
25. 9	1. 9	A11	J11	Pig
26. 9	2. 9	A11	K12	Porcupine
27. 9	3. 9	A11	A1	Wolf
28. 9	4. 9	A11	B2	Dog
29. 9	5. 9	A11	C3	Pheasant
30. 9	6. 9	A11	D4	Cock
1.10	7. 9	A11	E5	Crow
2.10	8. 9	A11	F6	Monkey
3.10	9. 9	A11	G7	Gibbon
4.10	10. 9	A11	H8	Tapir
5.10	11. 9	A11	J9	Sheep
6.10	12. 9	A11	K10	Deer
7.10	13. 9	A11	A11	Horse
8.10	14. 9	A11	B12	Stag
9.10	15. 9	A11	C1	Serpent
10.10	16. 9	A11	D2	Earthworm
11.10	17. 9	A11	E3	Crocodile
12.10	18. 9	A11	F4	Dragon
13.10	19. 9	A11	G5	Badger
14.10	20. 9	A11	H6	Hare
15.10	21. 9	A11	J7	Fox
16.10	22. 9	A11	K8	Tiger
17.10	23. 9	A11	A9	Leopard
18.10	24. 9	A11	B10	Griffon
19.10	25. 9	A11	C11	Ox
20.10	26. 9	A11	D12	Bat
21.10	27. 9	A11	E1	Rat
22.10	28. 9	A11	F2	Swallow
23.10	29. 9	A11	G3	Pig
24.10	1.10	B12	H4	Porcupine
25.10	2.10	B12	J5	Wolf
26.10	3.10	B12	K6	Dog
27.10	4.10	B12	A7	Pheasant
28.10	5.10	B12	B8	Cock
29.10	6.10	B12	C9	Crow
30.10	7.10	B12	D10	Monkey
31.10	8.10	B12	E11	Gibbon
1.11	9.10	B12	F12	Tapir
2.11	10.10	B12	G1	Sheep
3.11	11.10	B12	H2	Deer
4.11	12.10	B12	J3	Horse
5.11	13.10	B12	K4	Stag
6.11	14.10	B12	A5	Serpent
7.11	15.10	B12	B6	Earthworm
8.11	16.10	B12	C7	Crocodile
9.11	17.10	B12	D8	Dragon
10.11	18.10	B12	E9	Badger
11.11	19.10	B12	F10	Hare
12.11	20.10	B12	G11	Fox
13.11	21.10	B12	H12	Tiger
14.11	22.10	B12	J1	Leopard

Solar date	*Lunar date*	*Month HS/EB*	*Day HS/EB*	*Constellation*
15.11	23.10	B12	K2	Griffon
16.11	24.10	B12	A3	Ox
17.11	25.10	B12	B4	Bat
18.11	26.10	B12	C5	Rat
19.11	27.10	B12	D6	Swallow
20.11	28.10	B12	E7	Pig
21.11	29.10	B12	F8	Porcupine
22.11	30.10	B12	G9	Wolf
23.11	*1.10*	*B12*	H10	Dog
24.11	*2.10*	*B12*	J11	Pheasant
25.11	*3.10*	*B12*	K12	Cock
26.11	*4.10*	*B12*	A1	Crow
27.11	*5.10*	*B12*	B2	Monkey
28.11	*6.10*	*B12*	C3	Gibbon
29.11	*7.10*	*B12*	D4	Tapir
30.11	*8.10*	*B12*	E5	Sheep
1.12	*9.10*	*B12*	F6	Deer
2.12	*10.10*	*B12*	G7	Horse
3.12	*11.10*	*B12*	H8	Stag
4.12	*12.10*	*B12*	J9	Serpent
5.12	*13.10*	*B12*	K10	Earthworm
6.12	*14.10*	*B12*	A11	Crocodile
7.12	*15.10*	*B12*	B12	Dragon
8.12	*16.10*	*B12*	C1	Badger
9.12	*17.10*	*B12*	D2	Hare
10.12	*18.10*	*B12*	E3	Fox
11.12	*19.10*	*B12*	F4	Tiger
12.12	*20.10*	*B12*	G5	Leopard
13.12	*21.10*	*B12*	H6	Griffon
14.12	*22.10*	*B12*	J7	Ox
15.12	*23.10*	*B12*	K8	Bat
16.12	*24.10*	*B12*	A9	Rat
17.12	*25.10*	*B12*	B10	Swallow
18.12	*26.10*	*B12*	C11	Pig
19.12	*27.10*	*B12*	D12	Porcupine
20.12	*28.10*	*B12*	E1	Wolf
21.12	*29.10*	*B12*	F2	Dog
22.12	1.11	C1	G3	Pheasant
23.12	2.11	C1	H4	Cock
24.12	3.11	C1	J5	Crow
25.12	4.11	C1	K6	Monkey
26.12	5.11	C1	A7	Gibbon
27.12	6.11	C1	B8	Tapir
28.12	7.11	C1	C9	Sheep
29.12	8.11	C1	D10	Deer
30.12	9.11	C1	E11	Horse
31.12	10.11	C1	F12	Stag
1985				
1. 1	11.11	C1	G1	Serpent
2. 1	12.11	C1	H2	Earthworm
3. 1	13.11	C1	J3	Crocodile
4. 1	14.11	C1	K4	Dragon
5. 1	15.11	C1	A5	Badger
6. 1	16.11	C1	B6	Hare
7. 1	17.11	C1	C7	Fox
8. 1	18.11	C1	D8	Tiger
9. 1	19.11	C1	E9	Leopard
10. 1	20.11	C1	F10	Griffon
11. 1	21.11	C1	G11	Ox
12. 1	22.11	C1	H12	Bat
13. 1	23.11	C1	J1	Rat
14. 1	24.11	C1	K2	Swallow
15. 1	25.11	C1	A3	Pig
16. 1	26.11	C1	B4	Porcupine
17. 1	27.11	C1	C5	Wolf
18. 1	28.11	C1	D6	Dog
19. 1	29.11	C1	E7	Pheasant
20. 1	30.11	C1	F8	Cock
21. 1	1.12	D2	G9	Crow
22. 1	2.12	D2	H10	Monkey
23. 1	3.12	D2	J11	Gibbon
24. 1	4.12	D2	K12	Tapir

Solar date	*Lunar date*	*Month HS/EB*	*Day HS/EB*	*Constellation*
25. 1	5.12	D2	A1	Sheep
26. 1	6.12	D2	B2	Deer
27. 1	7.12	D2	C3	Horse
28. 1	8.12	D2	D4	Stag
29. 1	9.12	D2	E5	Serpent
30. 1	10.12	D2	F6	Earthworm
31. 1	11.12	D2	G7	Crocodile
1. 2	12.12	D2	H8	Dragon
2. 2	13.12	D2	J9	Badger
3. 2	14.12	D2	K10	Hare
4. 2	15.12	D2	A11	Fox
5. 2	16.12	D2	B12	Tiger
6. 2	17.12	D2	C1	Leopard
7. 2	18.12	D2	D2	Griffon
8. 2	19.12	D2	E3	Ox
9. 2	20.12	D2	F4	Bat
10. 2	21.12	D2	G5	Rat
11. 2	22.12	D2	H6	Swallow
12. 2	23.12	D2	J7	Pig
13. 2	24.12	D2	K8	Porcupine
14. 2	25.12	D2	A9	Wolf
15. 2	26.12	D2	B10	Dog
16. 2	27.12	D2	C11	Pheasant
17. 2	28.12	D2	D12	Cock
18. 2	29.12	D2	E1	Crow
19. 2	30.12	D2	F2	Monkey

YI CH'OU YEAR

Solar date	*Lunar date*	*Month HS/EB*	*Day HS/EB*	*Constellation*
20. 2	1. 1	E3	G3	Gibbon
21. 2	2. 1	E3	H4	Tapir
22. 2	3. 1	E3	J5	Sheep
23. 2	4. 1	E3	K6	Deer
24. 2	5. 1	E3	A7	Horse
25. 2	6. 1	E3	B8	Stag
26. 2	7. 1	E3	C9	Serpent
27. 2	8. 1	E3	D10	Earthworm
28. 2	9. 1	E3	E11	Crocodile
1. 3	10. 1	E3	F12	Dragon
2. 3	11. 1	E3	G1	Badger
3. 3	12. 1	E3	H2	Hare
4. 3	13. 1	E3	J3	Fox
5. 3	14. 1	E3	K4	Tiger
6. 3	15. 1	E3	A5	Leopard
7. 3	16. 1	E3	B6	Griffon
8. 3	17. 1	E3	C7	Ox
9. 3	18. 1	E3	D8	Bat
10. 3	19. 1	E3	E9	Rat
11. 3	20. 1	E3	F10	Swallow
12. 3	21. 1	E3	G11	Pig
13. 3	22. 1	E3	H12	Porcupine
14. 3	23. 1	E3	J1	Wolf
15. 3	24. 1	E3	K2	Dog
16. 3	25. 1	E3	A3	Pheasant
17. 3	26. 1	E3	B4	Cock
18. 3	27. 1	E3	C5	Crow
19. 3	28. 1	E3	D6	Monkey
20. 3	29. 1	E3	E7	Gibbon
21. 3	1. 2	F4	F8	Tapir
22. 3	2. 2	F4	G9	Sheep
23. 3	3. 2	F4	H10	Deer
24. 3	4. 2	F4	J11	Horse
25. 3	5. 2	F4	K12	Stag
26. 3	6. 2	F4	A1	Serpent
27. 3	7. 2	F4	B2	Earthworm
28. 3	8. 2	F4	C3	Crocodile
29. 3	9. 2	F4	D4	Dragon
30. 3	10. 2	F4	E5	Badger
31. 3	11. 2	F4	F6	Hare
1. 4	12. 2	F4	G7	Fox
2. 4	13. 2	F4	H8	Tiger
3. 4	14. 2	F4	J9	Leopard
4. 4	15. 2	F4	K10	Griffon
5. 4	16. 2	F4	A11	Ox
6. 4	17. 2	F4	B12	Bat
7. 4	18. 2	F4	C1	Rat
8. 4	19. 2	F4	D2	Swallow
9. 4	20. 2	F4	E3	Pig
10. 4	21. 2	F4	F4	Porcupine
11. 4	22. 2	F4	G5	Wolf
12. 4	23. 2	F4	H6	Dog
13. 4	24. 2	F4	J7	Pheasant
14. 4	25. 2	F4	K8	Cock
15. 4	26. 2	F4	A9	Crow
16. 4	27. 2	F4	B10	Monkey
17. 4	28. 2	F4	C11	Gibbon
18. 4	29. 2	F4	D12	Tapir
19. 4	30. 2	F4	E1	Sheep
20. 4	1. 3	G5	F2	Deer
21. 4	2. 3	G5	G3	Horse
22. 4	3. 3	G5	H4	Stag
23. 4	4. 3	G5	J5	Serpent
24. 4	5. 3	G5	K6	Earthworm
25. 4	6. 3	G5	A7	Crocodile
26. 4	7. 3	G5	B8	Dragon
27. 4	8. 3	G5	C9	Badger
28. 4	9. 3	G5	D10	Hare
29. 4	10. 3	G5	E11	Fox
30. 4	11. 3	G5	F12	Tiger
1. 5	12. 3	G5	G1	Leopard
2. 5	13. 3	G5	H2	Griffon
3. 5	14. 3	G5	J3	Ox
4. 5	15. 3	G5	K4	Bat
5. 5	16. 3	G5	A5	Rat
6. 5	17. 3	G5	B6	Swallow
7. 5	18. 3	G5	C7	Pig
8. 5	19. 3	G5	D8	Porcupine
9. 5	20. 3	G5	E9	Wolf
10. 5	21. 3	G5	F10	Dog
11. 5	22. 3	G5	G11	Pheasant
12. 5	23. 3	G5	H12	Cock
13. 5	24. 3	G5	J1	Crow
14. 5	25. 3	G5	K2	Monkey
15. 5	26. 3	G5	A3	Gibbon
16. 5	27. 3	G5	B4	Tapir
17. 5	28. 3	G5	C5	Sheep
18. 5	29. 3	G5	D6	Deer
19. 5	30. 3	G5	E7	Horse
20. 5	1. 4	H6	F8	Stag
21. 5	2. 4	H6	G9	Serpent
22. 5	3. 4	H6	H10	Earthworm
23. 5	4. 4	H6	J11	Crocodile
24. 5	5. 4	H6	K12	Dragon
25. 5	6. 4	H6	A1	Badger
26. 5	7. 4	H6	B2	Hare
27. 5	8. 4	H6	C3	Fox
28. 5	9. 4	H6	D4	Tiger
29. 5	10. 4	H6	E5	Leopard
30. 5	11. 4	H6	F6	Griffon
31. 5	12. 4	H6	G7	Ox
1. 6	13. 4	H6	H8	Bat
2. 6	14. 4	H6	J9	Rat
3. 6	15. 4	H6	K10	Swallow
4. 6	16. 4	H6	A11	Pig
5. 6	17. 4	H6	B12	Porcupine
6. 6	18. 4	H6	C1	Wolf
7. 6	19. 4	H6	D2	Dog
8. 6	20. 4	H6	E3	Pheasant
9. 6	21. 4	H6	F4	Cock

Solar date	*Lunar date*	*Month HS/EB*	*Day HS/EB*	*Constellation*
10. 6	22. 4	H6	G5	Crow
11. 6	23. 4	H6	H6	Monkey
12. 6	24. 4	H6	J7	Gibbon
13. 6	25. 4	H6	K8	Tapir
14. 6	26. 4	H6	A9	Sheep
15. 6	27. 4	H6	B10	Deer
16. 6	28. 4	H6	C11	Horse
17. 6	29. 4	H6	D12	Stag
18. 6	1. 5	J7	E1	Serpent
19. 6	2. 5	J7	F2	Earthworm
20. 6	3. 5	J7	G3	Crocodile
21. 6	4. 5	J7	H4	Dragon
22. 6	5. 5	J7	J5	Badger
23. 6	6. 5	J7	K6	Hare
24. 6	7. 5	J7	A7	Fox
25. 6	8. 5	J7	B8	Tiger
26. 6	9. 5	J7	C9	Leopard
27. 6	10. 5	J7	D10	Griffon
28. 6	11. 5	J7	E11	Ox
29. 6	12. 5	J7	F12	Bat
30. 6	13. 5	J7	G1	Rat
1. 7	14. 5	J7	H2	Swallow
2. 7	15. 5	J7	J3	Pig
3. 7	16. 5	J7	K4	Porcupine
4. 7	17. 5	J7	A5	Wolf
5. 7	18. 5	J7	B6	Dog
6. 7	19. 5	J7	C7	Pheasant
7. 7	20. 5	J7	D8	Cock
8. 7	21. 5	J7	E9	Crow
9. 7	22. 5	J7	F10	Monkey
10. 7	23. 5	J7	G11	Gibbon
11. 7	24. 5	J7	H12	Tapir
12. 7	25. 5	J7	J1	Sheep
13. 7	26. 5	J7	K2	Deer
14. 7	27. 5	J7	A3	Horse
15. 7	28. 5	J7	B4	Stag
16. 7	29. 5	J7	C5	Serpent
17. 7	30. 5	J7	D6	Earthworm
18. 7	1. 6	K8	E7	Crocodile
19. 7	2. 6	K8	F8	Dragon
20. 7	3. 6	K8	G9	Badger
21. 7	4. 6	K8	H10	Hare
22. 7	5. 6	K8	J11	Fox
23. 7	6. 6	K8	K12	Tiger
24. 7	7. 6	K8	A1	Leopard
25. 7	8. 6	K8	B2	Griffon
26. 7	9. 6	K8	C3	Ox
27. 7	10. 6	K8	D4	Bat
28. 7	11. 6	K8	E5	Rat
29. 7	12. 6	K8	F6	Swallow
30. 7	13. 6	K8	G7	Pig
31. 7	14. 6	K8	H8	Porcupine
1. 8	15. 6	K8	J9	Wolf
2. 8	16. 6	K8	K10	Dog
3. 8	17. 6	K8	A11	Pheasant
4. 8	18. 6	K8	B12	Cock
5. 8	19. 6	K8	C1	Crow
6. 8	20. 6	K8	D2	Monkey
7. 8	21. 6	K8	E3	Gibbon
8. 8	22. 6	K8	F4	Tapir
9. 8	23. 6	K8	G5	Sheep
10. 8	24. 6	K8	H6	Deer
11. 8	25. 6	K8	J7	Horse
12. 8	26. 6	K8	K8	Stag
13. 8	27. 6	K8	A9	Serpent
14. 8	28. 6	K8	B10	Earthworm
15. 8	29. 6	K8	C11	Crocodile
16. 8	1. 7	A9	D12	Dragon
17. 8	2. 7	A9	E1	Badger
18. 8	3. 7	A9	F2	Hare
19. 8	4. 7	A9	G3	Fox
20. 8	5. 7	A9	H4	Tiger
21. 8	6. 7	A9	J5	Leopard

Solar date	*Lunar date*	*Month HS/EB*	*Day HS/EB*	*Constellation*
22. 8	7. 7	A9	K6	Griffon
23. 8	8. 7	A9	A7	Ox
24. 8	9. 7	A9	B8	Bat
25. 8	10. 7	A9	C9	Rat
26. 8	11. 7	A9	D10	Swallow
27. 8	12. 7	A9	E11	Pig
28. 8	13. 7	A9	F12	Porcupine
29. 8	14. 7	A9	G1	Wolf
30. 8	15. 7	A9	H2	Dog
31. 8	16. 7	A9	J3	Pheasant
1. 9	17. 7	A9	K4	Cock
2. 9	18. 7	A9	A5	Crow
3. 9	19. 7	A9	B6	Monkey
4. 9	20. 7	A9	C7	Gibbon
5. 9	21. 7	A9	D8	Tapir
6. 9	22. 7	A9	E9	Sheep
7. 9	23. 7	A9	F10	Deer
8. 9	24. 7	A9	G11	Horse
9. 9	25. 7	A9	H12	Stag
10. 9	26. 7	A9	J1	Serpent
11. 9	27. 7	A9	K2	Earthworm
12. 9	28. 7	A9	A3	Crocodile
13. 9	29. 7	A9	B4	Dragon
14. 9	30. 7	A9	C5	Badger
15. 9	1. 8	B10	D6	Hare
16. 9	2. 8	B10	E7	Fox
17. 9	3. 8	B10	F8	Tiger
18. 9	4. 8	B10	G9	Leopard
19. 9	5. 8	B10	H10	Griffon
20. 9	6. 8	B10	J11	Ox
21. 9	7. 8	B10	K12	Bat
22. 9	8. 8	B10	A1	Rat
23. 9	9. 8	B10	B2	Swallow
24. 9	10. 8	B10	C3	Pig
25. 9	11. 8	B10	D4	Porcupine
26. 9	12. 8	B10	E5	Wolf
27. 9	13. 8	B10	F6	Dog
28. 9	14. 8	B10	G7	Pheasant
29. 9	15. 8	B10	H8	Cock
30. 9	16. 8	B10	J9	Crow
1.10	17. 8	B10	K10	Monkey
2.10	18. 8	B10	A11	Gibbon
3.10	19. 8	B10	B12	Tapir
4.10	20. 8	B10	C1	Sheep
5.10	21. 8	B10	D2	Deer
6.10	22. 8	B10	E3	Horse
7.10	23. 8	B10	F4	Stag
8.10	24. 8	B10	G5	Serpent
9.10	25. 8	B10	H6	Earthworm
10.10	26. 8	B10	J7	Crocodile
11.10	27. 8	B10	K8	Dragon
12.10	28. 8	B10	A9	Badger
13.10	29. 8	B10	B10	Hare
14.10	1. 9	C11	C11	Fox
15.10	2. 9	C11	D12	Tiger
16.10	3. 9	C11	E1	Leopard
17.10	4. 9	C11	F2	Griffon
18.10	5. 9	C11	G3	Ox
19.10	6. 9	C11	H4	Bat
20.10	7. 9	C11	J5	Rat
21.10	8. 9	C11	K6	Swallow
22.10	9. 9	C11	A7	Pig
23.10	10. 9	C11	B8	Porcupine
24.10	11. 9	C11	C9	Wolf
25.10	12. 9	C11	D10	Dog
26.10	13. 9	C11	E11	Pheasant
27.10	14. 9	C11	F12	Cock
28.10	15. 9	C11	G1	Crow
29.10	16. 9	C11	H2	Monkey
30.10	17. 9	C11	J3	Gibbon
31.10	18. 9	C11	K4	Tapir
1.11	19. 9	C11	A5	Sheep
2.11	20. 9	C11	B6	Deer

Solar date	*Lunar date*	*Month HS/EB*	*Day HS/EB*	*Constellation*
3.11	21. 9	C11	C7	Horse
4.11	22. 9	C11	D8	Stag
5.11	23. 9	C11	E9	Serpent
6.11	24. 9	C11	F10	Earthworm
7.11	25. 9	C11	G11	Crocodile
8.11	26. 9	C11	H12	Dragon
9.11	27. 9	C11	J1	Badger
10.11	28. 9	C11	K2	Hare
11.11	29. 9	C11	A3	Fox
12.11	1.10	D12	B4	Tiger
13.11	2.10	D12	C5	Leopard
14.11	3.10	D12	D6	Griffon
15.11	4.10	D12	E7	Ox
16.11	5.10	D12	F8	Bat
17.11	6.10	D12	G9	Rat
18.11	7.10	D12	H10	Swallow
19.11	8.10	D12	J11	Pig
20.11	9.10	D12	K12	Porcupine
21.11	10.10	D12	A1	Wolf
22.11	11.10	D12	B2	Dog
23.11	12.10	D12	C3	Pheasant
24.11	13.10	D12	D4	Cock
25.11	14.10	D12	E5	Crow
26.11	15.10	D12	F6	Monkey
27.11	16.10	D12	G7	Gibbon
28.11	17.10	D12	H8	Tapir
29.11	18.10	D12	J9	Sheep
30.11	19.10	D12	K10	Deer
1.12	20.10	D12	A11	Horse
2.12	21.10	D12	B12	Stag
3.12	22.10	D12	C1	Serpent
4.12	23.10	D12	D2	Earthworm
5.12	24.10	D12	E3	Crocodile
6.12	25.10	D12	F4	Dragon
7.12	26.10	D12	G5	Badger
8.12	27.10	D12	H6	Hare
9.12	28.10	D12	J7	Fox
10.12	29.10	D12	K8	Tiger
11.12	30.10	D12	A9	Leopard
12.12	1.11	E1	B10	Griffon
13.12	2.11	E1	C11	Ox
14.12	3.11	E1	D12	Bat
15.12	4.11	E1	E1	Rat
16.12	5.11	E1	F2	Swallow
17.12	6.11	E1	G3	Pig
18.12	7.11	E1	H4	Porcupine
19.12	8.11	E1	J5	Wolf
20.12	9.11	E1	K6	Dog
21.12	10.11	E1	A7	Pheasant
22.12	11.11	E1	B8	Cock

Solar date	*Lunar date*	*Month HS/EB*	*Day HS/EB*	*Constellation*
23.12	12.11	E1	C9	Crow
24.12	13.11	E1	D10	Monkey
25.12	14.11	E1	E11	Gibbon
26.12	15.11	E1	F12	Tapir
27.12	16.11	E1	G1	Sheep
28.12	17.11	E1	H2	Deer
29.12	18.11	E1	J3	Horse
30.12	19.11	E1	K4	Stag
31.12	20.11	E1	A5	Serpent
1986				
1. 1	21.11	E1	B6	Earthworm
2. 1	22.11	E1	C7	Crocodile
3. 1	23.11	E1	D8	Dragon
4. 1	24.11	E1	E9	Badger
5. 1	25.11	E1	F10	Hare
6. 1	26.11	E1	G11	Fox
7. 1	27.11	E1	H12	Tiger
8. 1	28.11	E1	J1	Leopard
9. 1	29.11	E1	K2	Griffon
10. 1	1.12	F2	A3	Ox
11. 1	2.12	F2	B4	Bat
12. 1	3.12	F2	C5	Rat
13. 1	4.12	F2	D6	Swallow
14. 1	5.12	F2	E7	Pig
15. 1	6.12	F2	F8	Porcupine
16. 1	7.12	F2	G9	Wolf
17. 1	8.12	F2	H10	Dog
18. 1	9.12	F2	J11	Pheasant
19. 1	10.12	F2	K12	Cock
20. 1	11.12	F2	A1	Crow
21. 1	12.12	F2	B2	Monkey
22. 1	13.12	F2	C3	Gibbon
23. 1	14.12	F2	D4	Tapir
24. 1	15.12	F2	E5	Sheep
25. 1	16.12	F2	F6	Deer
26. 1	17.12	F2	G7	Horse
27. 1	18.12	F2	H8	Stag
28. 1	19.12	F2	J9	Serpent
29. 1	20.12	F2	K10	Earthworm
30. 1	21.12	F2	A11	Crocodile
31. 1	22.12	F2	B12	Dragon
1. 2	23.12	F2	C1	Badger
2. 2	24.12	F2	D2	Hare
3. 2	25.12	F2	E3	Fox
4. 2	26.12	F2	F4	Tiger
5. 2	27.12	F2	G5	Leopard
6. 2	28.12	F2	H6	Griffon
7. 2	29.12	F2	J7	Ox
8. 2	30.12	F2	K8	Bat

PING YIN YEAR

9. 2	1. 1	G3	A9	Rat
10. 2	2. 1	G3	B10	Swallow
11. 2	3. 1	G3	C1	Pig
12. 2	4. 1	G3	D12	Porcupine
13. 2	5. 1	G3	E1	Wolf
14. 2	6. 1	G3	F2	Dog
15. 2	7. 1	G3	G3	Pheasant
16. 2	8. 1	G3	H4	Cock
17. 2	9. 1	G3	J5	Crow
18. 2	10. 1	G3	K6	Monkey
19. 2	11. 1	G3	A7	Gibbon
20. 2	12. 1	G3	B8	Tapir
21. 2	13. 1	G3	C9	Sheep
22. 2	14. 1	G3	D10	Deer
23. 2	15. 1	G3	E11	Horse
24. 2	16. 1	G3	F12	Stag
25. 2	17. 1	G3	G1	Serpent

26. 2	18. 1	G3	H2	Earthworm
27. 2	19. 1	G3	J3	Crocodile
28. 2	20. 1	G3	K4	Dragon
1. 3	21. 1	G3	A5	Badger
2. 3	22. 1	G3	B6	Hare
3. 3	23. 1	G3	C7	Fox
4. 3	24. 1	G3	D8	Tiger
5. 3	25. 1	G3	E9	Leopard
6. 3	26. 1	G3	F10	Griffon
7. 3	27. 1	G3	G11	Ox
8. 3	28. 1	G3	H12	Bat
9. 3	29. 1	G3	J1	Rat
10. 3	1. 2	H4	K2	Swallow
11. 3	2. 2	H4	A3	Pig
12. 3	3. 2	H4	B4	Porcupine
13. 3	4. 2	H4	C5	Wolf
14. 3	5. 2	H4	D6	Dog

Solar date	*Lunar date*	*Month HS/EB*	*Day HS/EB*	*Constellation*
15. 3	6. 2	H4	E7	Pheasant
16. 3	7. 2	H4	F8	Cock
17. 3	8. 2	H4	G9	Crow
18. 3	9. 2	H4	H10	Monkey
19. 3	10. 2	H4	J11	Gibbon
20. 3	11. 2	H4	K12	Tapir
21. 3	12. 2	H4	A1	Sheep
22. 3	13. 2	H4	B2	Deer
23. 3	14. 2	H4	C3	Horse
24. 3	15. 2	H4	D4	Stag
25. 3	16. 2	H4	E5	Serpent
26. 3	17. 2	H4	F6	Earthworm
27. 3	18. 2	H4	G7	Crocodile
28. 3	19. 2	H4	H8	Dragon
29. 3	20. 2	H4	J9	Badger
30. 3	21. 2	H4	K10	Hare
31. 3	22. 2	H4	A11	Fox
1. 4	23. 2	H4	B12	Tiger
2. 4	24. 2	H4	C1	Leopard
3. 4	25. 2	H4	D2	Griffon
4. 4	26. 2	H4	E3	Ox
5. 4	27. 2	H4	F4	Bat
6. 4	28. 2	H4	G5	Rat
7. 4	29. 2	H4	H6	Swallow
8. 4	30. 2	H4	J7	Pig
9. 4	1. 3	J5	K8	Porcupine
10. 4	2. 3	J5	A9	Wolf
11. 4	3. 3	J5	B10	Dog
12. 4	4. 3	J5	C11	Pheasant
13. 4	5. 3	J5	D12	Cock
14. 4	6. 3	J5	E1	Crow
15. 4	7. 3	J5	F2	Monkey
16. 4	8. 3	J5	G3	Gibbon
17. 4	9. 3	J5	H4	Tapir
18. 4	10. 3	J5	J5	Sheep
19. 4	11. 3	J5	K6	Deer
20. 4	12. 3	J5	A7	Horse
21. 4	13. 3	J5	B8	Stag
22. 4	14. 3	J5	C9	Serpent
23. 4	15. 3	J5	D10	Earthworm
24. 4	16. 3	J5	E11	Crocodile
25. 4	17. 3	J5	F12	Dragon
26. 4	18. 3	J5	G1	Badger
27. 4	19. 3	J5	H2	Hare
28. 4	20. 3	J5	J3	Fox
29. 4	21. 3	J5	K4	Tiger
30. 4	22. 3	J5	A5	Leopard
1. 5	23. 3	J5	B6	Griffon
2. 5	24. 3	J5	C7	Ox
3. 5	25. 3	J5	D8	Bat
4. 5	26. 3	J5	E9	Rat
5. 5	27. 3	J5	F10	Swallow
6. 5	28. 3	J5	G11	Pig
7. 5	29. 3	J5	H12	Porcupine
8. 5	30. 3	J5	J1	Wolf
9. 5	1. 4	K6	K2	Dog
10. 5	2. 4	K6	A3	Pheasant
11. 5	3. 4	K6	B4	Cock
12. 5	4. 4	K6	C5	Crow
13. 5	5. 4	K6	D6	Monkey
14. 5	6. 4	K6	E7	Gibbon
15. 5	7. 4	K6	F8	Tapir
16. 5	8. 4	K6	G9	Sheep
17. 5	9. 4	K6	H10	Deer
18. 5	10. 4	K6	J11	Horse
19. 5	11. 4	K6	K12	Stag
20. 5	12. 4	K6	A1	Serpent
21. 5	13. 4	K6	B2	Earthworm
22. 5	14. 4	K6	C3	Crocodile
23. 5	15. 4	K6	D4	Dragon
24. 5	16. 4	K6	E5	Badger
25. 5	17. 4	K6	F6	Hare
26. 5	18. 4	K6	G7	Fox
27. 5	19. 4	K6	H8	Tiger
28. 5	20. 4	K6	J9	Leopard
29. 5	21. 4	K6	K10	Griffon
30. 5	22. 4	K6	A11	Ox
31. 5	23. 4	K6	B12	Bat
1. 6	24. 4	K6	C1	Rat
2. 6	25. 4	K6	D2	Swallow
3. 6	26. 4	K6	E3	Pig
4. 6	27. 4	K6	F4	Porcupine
5. 6	28. 4	K6	G5	Wolf
6. 6	29. 4	K6	H6	Dog
7. 6	1. 5	A7	J7	Pheasant
8. 6	2. 5	A7	K8	Cock
9. 6	3. 5	A7	A9	Crow
10. 6	4. 5	A7	B10	Monkey
11. 6	5. 5	A7	C11	Gibbon
12. 6	6. 5	A7	D12	Tapir
13. 6	7. 5	A7	E1	Sheep
14. 6	8. 5	A7	F2	Deer
15. 6	9. 5	A7	G3	Horse
16. 6	10. 5	A7	H4	Stag
17. 6	11. 5	A7	J5	Serpent
18. 6	12. 5	A7	K6	Earthworm
19. 6	13. 5	A7	A7	Crocodile
20. 6	14. 5	A7	B8	Dragon
21. 6	15. 5	A7	C9	Badger
22. 6	16. 5	A7	D10	Hare
23. 6	17. 5	A7	E11	Fox
24. 6	18. 5	A7	F12	Tiger
25. 6	19. 5	A7	G1	Leopard
26. 6	20. 5	A7	H2	Griffon
27. 6	21. 5	A7	J3	Ox
28. 6	22. 5	A7	K4	Bat
29. 6	23. 5	A7	A5	Rat
30. 6	24. 5	A7	B6	Swallow
1. 7	25. 5	A7	C7	Pig
2. 7	26. 5	A7	D8	Porcupine
3. 7	27. 5	A7	E9	Wolf
4. 7	28. 5	A7	F10	Dog
5. 7	29. 5	A7	G11	Pheasant
6. 7	30. 5	A7	H12	Cock
7. 7	1. 6	B8	J1	Crow
8. 7	2. 6	B8	K2	Monkey
9. 7	3. 6	B8	A3	Gibbon
10. 7	4. 6	B8	B4	Tapir
11. 7	5. 6	B8	C5	Sheep
12. 7	6. 6	B8	D6	Deer
13. 7	7. 6	B8	E7	Horse
14. 7	8. 6	B8	F8	Stag
15. 7	9. 6	B8	G9	Serpent
16. 7	10. 6	B8	H10	Earthworm
17. 7	11. 6	B8	J11	Crocodile
18. 7	12. 6	B8	K12	Dragon
19. 7	13. 6	B8	A1	Badger
20. 7	14. 6	B8	B2	Hare
21. 7	15. 6	B8	C3	Fox
22. 7	16. 6	B8	D4	Tiger
23. 7	17. 6	B8	E5	Leopard
24. 7	18. 6	B8	F6	Griffon
25. 7	19. 6	B8	G7	Ox
26. 7	20. 6	B8	H8	Bat
27. 7	21. 6	B8	J9	Rat
28. 7	22. 6	B8	K10	Swallow
29. 7	23. 6	B8	A11	Pig
30. 7	24. 6	B8	B12	Porcupine
31. 7	25. 6	B8	C1	Wolf
1. 8	26. 6	B8	D2	Dog
2. 8	27. 6	B8	E3	Pheasant
3. 8	28. 6	B8	F4	Cock
4. 8	29. 6	B8	G5	Crow
5. 8	30. 6	B8	H6	Monkey
6. 8	1. 7	C9	J7	Gibbon
7. 8	2. 7	C9	K8	Tapir

Solar date	*Lunar date*	*Month HS/EB*	*Day HS/EB*	*Constellation*
8. 8	3. 7	C9	A9	Sheep
9. 8	4. 7	C9	B10	Deer
10. 8	5. 7	C9	C11	Horse
11. 8	6. 7	C9	D12	Stag
12. 8	7. 7	C9	E1	Serpent
13. 8	8. 7	C9	F2	Earthworm
14. 8	9. 7	C9	G3	Crocodile
15. 8	10. 7	C9	H4	Dragon
16. 8	11. 7	C9	J5	Badger
17. 8	12. 7	C9	K6	Hare
18. 8	13. 7	C9	A7	Fox
19. 8	14. 7	C9	B8	Tiger
20. 8	15. 7	C9	C9	Leopard
21. 8	16. 7	C9	D10	Griffon
22. 8	17. 7	C9	E11	Ox
23. 8	18. 7	C9	F12	Bat
24. 8	19. 7	C9	G1	Rat
25. 8	20. 7	C9	H2	Swallow
26. 8	21. 7	C9	J3	Pig
27. 8	22. 7	C9	K4	Porcupine
28. 8	23. 7	C9	A5	Wolf
29. 8	24. 7	C9	B6	Dog
30. 8	25. 7	C9	C7	Pheasant
31. 8	26. 7	C9	D8	Cock
1. 9	27. 7	C9	E9	Crow
2. 9	28. 7	C9	F10	Monkey
3. 9	29. 7	C9	G11	Gibbon
4. 9	1. 8	D10	H12	Tapir
5. 9	2. 8	D10	J1	Sheep
6. 9	3. 8	D10	K2	Deer
7. 9	4. 8	D10	A3	Horse
8. 9	5. 8	D10	B4	Stag
9. 9	6. 8	D10	C5	Serpent
10. 9	7. 8	D10	D6	Earthworm
11. 9	8. 8	D10	E7	Crocodile
12. 9	9. 8	D10	F8	Dragon
13. 9	10. 8	D10	G9	Badger
14. 9	11. 8	D10	H10	Hare
15. 9	12. 8	D10	J11	Fox
16. 9	13. 8	D10	K12	Tiger
17. 9	14. 8	D10	A1	Leopard
18. 9	15. 8	D10	B2	Griffon
19. 9	16. 8	D10	C3	Ox
20. 9	17. 8	D10	D4	Bat
21. 9	18. 8	D10	E5	Rat
22. 9	19. 8	D10	F6	Swallow
23. 9	20. 8	D10	G7	Pig
24. 9	21. 8	D10	H8	Porcupine
25. 9	22. 8	D10	J9	Wolf
26. 9	23. 8	D10	K10	Dog
27. 9	24. 8	D10	A11	Pheasant
28. 9	25. 8	D10	B12	Cock
29. 9	26. 8	D10	C1	Crow
30. 9	27. 8	D10	D2	Monkey
1.10	28. 8	D10	E3	Gibbon
2.10	29. 8	D10	F4	Tapir
3.10	30. 8	D10	G5	Sheep
4.10	1. 9	E11	H6	Deer
5.10	2. 9	E11	J7	Horse
6.10	3. 9	E11	K8	Stag
7.10	4. 9	E11	A9	Serpent
8.10	5. 9	E11	B10	Earthworm
9.10	6. 9	E11	C11	Crocodile
10.10	7. 9	E11	D12	Dragon
11.10	8. 9	E11	E1	Badger
12.10	9. 9	E11	F2	Hare
13.10	10. 9	E11	G3	Fox
14.10	11. 9	E11	H4	Tiger
15.10	12. 9	E11	J5	Leopard
16.10	13. 9	E11	K6	Griffon
17.10	14. 9	E11	A7	Ox
18.10	15. 9	E11	B8	Bat
19.10	16. 9	E11	C9	Rat
20.10	17. 9	E11	D10	Swallow
21.10	18. 9	E11	E11	Pig
22.10	19. 9	E11	F12	Porcupine
23.10	20. 9	E11	G1	Wolf
24.10	21. 9	E11	H2	Dog
25.10	22. 9	E11	J3	Pheasant
26.10	23. 9	E11	K4	Cock
27.10	24. 9	E11	A5	Crow
28.10	25. 9	E11	B6	Monkey
29.10	26. 9	E11	C7	Gibbon
30.10	27. 9	E11	D8	Tapir
31.10	28. 9	E11	E9	Sheep
1.11	29. 9	E11	F10	Deer
2.11	1.10	F12	G11	Horse
3.11	2.10	F12	H12	Stag
4.11	3.10	F12	J1	Serpent
5.11	4.10	F12	K2	Earthworm
6.11	5.10	F12	A3	Crocodile
7.11	6.10	F12	B4	Dragon
8.11	7.10	F12	C5	Badger
9.11	8.10	F12	D6	Hare
10.11	9.10	F12	E7	Fox
11.11	10.10	F12	F8	Tiger
12.11	11.10	F12	G9	Leopard
13.11	12.10	F12	H10	Griffon
14.11	13.10	F12	J11	Ox
15.11	14.10	F12	K12	Bat
16.11	15.10	F12	A1	Rat
17.11	16.10	F12	B2	Swallow
18.11	17.10	F12	C3	Pig
19.11	18.10	F12	D4	Porcupine
20.11	19.10	F12	E5	Wolf
21.11	20.10	F12	F6	Dog
22.11	21.10	F12	G7	Pheasant
23.11	22.10	F12	H8	Cock
24.11	23.10	F12	J9	Crow
25.11	24.10	F12	K10	Monkey
26.11	25.10	F12	A11	Gibbon
27.11	26.10	F12	B12	Tapir
28.11	27.10	F12	C1	Sheep
29.11	28.10	F12	D2	Deer
30.11	29.10	F12	E3	Horse
1.12	30.10	F12	F4	Stag
2.12	1.11	G1	G5	Serpent
3.12	2.11	G1	H6	Earthworm
4.12	3.11	G1	J7	Crocodile
5.12	4.11	G1	K8	Dragon
6.12	5.11	G1	A9	Badger
7.12	6.11	G1	B10	Hare
8.12	7.11	G1	C11	Fox
9.12	8.11	G1	D12	Tiger
10.12	9.11	G1	E1	Leopard
11.12	10.11	G1	F2	Griffon
12.12	11.11	G1	G3	Ox
13.12	12.11	G1	H4	Bat
14.12	13.11	G1	J5	Rat
15.12	14.11	G1	K6	Swallow
16.12	15.11	G1	A7	Pig
17.12	16.11	G1	B8	Porcupine
18.12	17.11	G1	C9	Wolf
19.12	18.11	G1	D10	Dog
20.12	19.11	G1	E11	Pheasant
21.12	20.11	G1	F12	Cock
22.12	21.11	G1	G1	Crow
23.12	22.11	G1	H2	Monkey
24.12	23.11	G1	J3	Gibbon
25.12	24.11	G1	K4	Tapir
26.12	25.11	G1	A5	Sheep
27.12	26.11	G1	B6	Deer
28.12	27.11	G1	C7	Horse
29.12	28.11	G1	D8	Stag
30.12	29.11	G1	E9	Serpent
31.12	1.12	H2	F10	Earthworm

Solar date	*Lunar date*	*Month HS/EB*	*Day HS/EB*	*Constellation*
1987				
1. 1	2.12	H2	G11	Crocodile
2. 1	3.12	H2	H12	Dragon
3. 1	4.12	H2	J1	Badger
4. 1	5.12	H2	K2	Hare
5. 1	6.12	H2	A3	Fox
6. 1	7.12	H2	B4	Tiger
7. 1	8.12	H2	C5	Leopard
8. 1	9.12	H2	D6	Griffon
9. 1	10.12	H2	E7	Ox
10. 1	11.12	H2	F8	Bat
11. 1	12.12	H2	G9	Rat
12. 1	13.12	H2	H10	Swallow
13. 1	14.12	H2	J11	Pig
14. 1	15.12	H2	K12	Porcupine
15. 1	16.12	H2	A1	Wolf
16. 1	17.12	H2	B2	Dog
17. 1	18.12	H2	C3	Pheasant
18. 1	19.12	H2	D4	Cock
19. 1	20.12	H2	E5	Crow
20. 1	21.12	H2	F6	Monkey
21. 1	22.12	H2	G7	Gibbon
22. 1	23.12	H2	H8	Tapir
23. 1	24.12	H2	J9	Sheep
24. 1	25.12	H2	K10	Deer
25. 1	26.12	H2	A11	Horse
26. 1	27.12	H2	B12	Stag
27. 1	28.12	H2	C1	Serpent
28. 1	29.12	H2	D2	Earthworm

TING MAO YEAR

29. 1	1. 1	J3	E3	Crocodile
30. 1	2. 1	J3	F4	Dragon
31. 1	3. 1	J3	G5	Badger
1. 2	4. 1	J3	H6	Hare
2. 2	5. 1	J3	J7	Fox
3. 2	6. 1	J3	K8	Tiger
4. 2	7. 1	J3	A9	Leopard
5. 2	8. 1	J3	B10	Griffon
6. 2	9. 1	J3	C11	Ox
7. 2	10. 1	J3	D12	Bat
8. 2	11. 1	J3	E1	Rat
9. 2	12. 1	J3	F2	Swallow
10. 2	13. 1	J3	G3	Pig
11. 2	14. 1	J3	H4	Porcupine
12. 2	15. 1	J3	J5	Wolf
13. 2	16. 1	J3	K6	Dog
14. 2	17. 1	J3	A7	Pheasant
15. 2	18. 1	J3	B8	Cock
16. 2	19. 1	J3	C9	Crow
17. 2	20. 1	J3	D10	Monkey
18. 2	21. 1	J3	E11	Gibbon
19. 2	22. 1	J3	F12	Tapir
20. 2	23. 1	J3	G1	Sheep
21. 2	24. 1	J3	H2	Deer
22. 2	25. 1	J3	J3	Horse
23. 2	26. 1	J3	K4	Stag
24. 2	27. 1	J3	A5	Serpent
25. 2	28. 1	J3	B6	Earthworm
26. 2	29. 1	J3	C7	Crocodile
27. 2	30. 1	J3	D8	Dragon
28. 2	1. 2	K4	E9	Badger
1. 3	2. 2	K4	F10	Hare
2. 3	3. 2	K4	G11	Fox
3. 3	4. 2	K4	H12	Tiger
4. 3	5. 2	K4	J1	Leopard
5. 3	6. 2	K4	K2	Griffon
6. 3	7. 2	K4	A3	Ox
7. 3	8. 2	K4	B4	Bat
8. 3	9. 2	K4	C5	Rat
9. 3	10. 2	K4	D6	Swallow
10. 3	11. 2	K4	E7	Pig
11. 3	12. 2	K4	F8	Porcupine
12. 3	13. 2	K4	G9	Wolf
13. 3	14. 2	K4	H10	Dog
14. 3	15. 2	K4	J11	Pheasant
15. 3	16. 2	K4	K12	Cock
16. 3	17. 2	K4	A1	Crow
17. 3	18. 2	K4	B2	Monkey
18. 3	19. 2	K4	C3	Gibbon
19. 3	20. 2	K4	D4	Tapir
20. 3	21. 2	K4	E5	Sheep
21. 3	22. 2	K4	F6	Deer
22. 3	23. 2	K4	G7	Horse
23. 3	24. 2	K4	H8	Stag
24. 3	25. 2	K4	J9	Serpent
25. 3	26. 2	K4	K10	Earthworm
26. 3	27. 2	K4	A11	Crocodile
27. 3	28. 2	K4	B12	Dragon
28. 3	29. 2	K4	C1	Badger
29. 3	1. 3	A5	D2	Hare
30. 3	2. 3	A5	E3	Fox
31. 3	3. 3	A5	F4	Tiger
1. 4	4. 3	A5	G5	Leopard
2. 4	5. 3	A5	H6	Griffon
3. 4	6. 3	A5	J7	Ox
4. 4	7. 3	A5	K8	Bat
5. 4	8. 3	A5	A9	Rat
6. 4	9. 3	A5	B10	Swallow
7. 4	10. 3	A5	C11	Pig
8. 4	11. 3	A5	D12	Porcupine
9. 4	12. 3	A5	E1	Wolf
10. 4	13. 3	A5	F2	Dog
11. 4	14. 3	A5	G3	Pheasant
12. 4	15. 3	A5	H4	Cock
13. 4	16. 3	A5	J5	Crow
14. 4	17. 3	A5	K6	Monkey
15. 4	18. 3	A5	A7	Gibbon
16. 4	19. 3	A5	B8	Tapir
17. 4	20. 3	A5	C9	Sheep
18. 4	21. 3	A5	D10	Deer
19. 4	22. 3	A5	E11	Horse
20. 4	23. 3	A5	F12	Stag
21. 4	24. 3	A5	G1	Serpent
22. 4	25. 3	A5	H2	Earthworm
23. 4	26. 3	A5	J3	Crocodile
24. 4	27. 3	A5	K4	Dragon
25. 4	28. 3	A5	A5	Badger
26. 4	29. 3	A5	B6	Hare
27. 4	30. 3	A5	C7	Fox
28. 4	1. 4	B6	D8	Tiger
29. 4	2. 4	B6	E9	Leopard
30. 4	3. 4	B6	F10	Griffon
1. 5	4. 4	B6	G11	Ox
2. 5	5. 4	B6	H12	Bat
3. 5	6. 4	B6	J1	Rat
4. 5	7. 4	B6	K2	Swallow
5. 5	8. 4	B6	A3	Pig
6. 5	9. 4	B6	B4	Porcupine
7. 5	10. 4	B6	C5	Wolf
8. 5	11. 4	B6	D6	Dog
9. 5	12. 4	B6	E7	Pheasant
10. 5	13. 4	B6	F8	Cock
11. 5	14. 4	B6	G9	Crow
12. 5	15. 4	B6	H10	Monkey
13. 5	16. 4	B6	J11	Gibbon
14. 5	17. 4	B6	K12	Tapir

Solar date	Lunar date	Month HS/EB	Day HS/EB	Constellation
15. 5	18. 4	B6	A1	Sheep
16. 5	19. 4	B6	B2	Deer
17. 5	20. 4	B6	C3	Horse
18. 5	21. 4	B6	D4	Stag
19. 5	22. 4	B6	E5	Serpent
20. 5	23. 4	B6	F6	Earthworm
21. 5	24. 4	B6	G7	Crocodile
22. 5	25. 4	B6	H8	Dragon
23. 5	26. 4	B6	J9	Badger
24. 5	27. 4	B6	K10	Hare
25. 5	28. 4	B6	A11	Fox
26. 5	29. 4	B6	B12	Tiger
27. 5	1. 5	C7	C1	Leopard
28. 5	2. 5	C7	D2	Griffon
29. 5	3. 5	C7	E3	Ox
30. 5	4. 5	C7	F4	Bat
31. 5	5. 5	C7	G5	Rat
1. 6	6. 5	C7	H6	Swallow
2. 6	7. 5	C7	J7	Pig
3. 6	8. 5	C7	K8	Porcupine
4. 6	9. 5	C7	A9	Wolf
5. 6	10. 5	C7	B10	Dog
6. 6	11. 5	C7	C11	Pheasant
7. 6	12. 5	C7	D12	Cock
8. 6	13. 5	C7	E1	Crow
9. 6	14. 5	C7	F2	Monkey
10. 6	15. 5	C7	G3	Gibbon
11. 6	16. 5	C7	H4	Tapir
12. 6	17. 5	C7	J5	Sheep
13. 6	18. 5	C7	K6	Deer
14. 6	19. 5	C7	A7	Horse
15. 6	20. 5	C7	B8	Stag
16. 6	21. 5	C7	C9	Serpent
17. 6	22. 5	C7	D10	Earthworm
18. 6	23. 5	C7	E11	Crocodile
19. 6	24 5	C7	F12	Dragon
20. 6	25. 5	C7	G1	Badger
21. 6	26. 5	C7	H2	Hare
22. 6	27. 5	C7	J3	Fox
23. 6	28. 5	C7	K4	Tiger
24. 6	29. 5	C7	A5	Leopard
25. 6	30. 5	C7	B6	Griffon
26. 6	1. 6	D8	C7	Ox
27. 6	2. 6	D8	D8	Bat
28. 6	3. 6	D8	E9	Rat
29. 6	4. 6	D8	F10	Swallow
30. 6	5. 6	D8	G11	Pig
1. 7	6. 6	D8	H12	Porcupine
2. 7	7. 6	D8	J1	Wolf
3. 7	8. 6	D8	K2	Dog
4. 7	9. 6	D8	A3	Pheasant
5. 7	10. 6	D8	B4	Cock
6. 7	11. 6	D8	C5	Crow
7. 7	12. 6	D8	D6	Monkey
8. 7	13. 6	D8	E7	Gibbon
9. 7	14. 6	D8	F8	Tapir
10. 7	15. 6	D8	G9	Sheep
11. 7	16. 6	D8	H10	Deer
12. 7	17. 6	D8	J11	Horse
13. 7	18. 6	D8	K12	Stag
14. 7	19. 6	D8	A1	Serpent
15. 7	20. 6	D8	B2	Earthworm
16. 7	21. 6	D8	C3	Crocodile
17. 7	22. 6	D8	D4	Dragon
18. 7	23. 6	D8	E5	Badger
19. 7	24. 6	D8	F6	Hare
20. 7	25. 6	D8	G7	Fox
21. 7	26. 6	D8	H8	Tiger
22. 7	27. 6	D8	J9	Leopard
23. 7	28. 6	D8	K10	Griffon
24. 7	29. 6	D8	A11	Ox
25. 7	30. 6	D8	B12	Bat
26. 7	*1. 6*	*D8*	C1	Rat

Solar date	Lunar date	Month HS/EB	Day HS/EB	Constellation
27. 7	*2. 6*	*D8*	D2	Swallow
28. 7	*3. 6*	*D8*	E3	Pig
29. 7	*4. 6*	*D8*	F4	Porcupine
30. 7	*5. 6*	*D8*	G5	Wolf
31. 7	*6. 6*	*D8*	H6	Dog
1. 8	*7. 6*	*D8*	J7	Pheasant
2. 8	*8. 6*	*D8*	K8	Cock
3. 8	*9. 6*	*D8*	A9	Crow
4. 8	*10. 6*	*D8*	B10	Monkey
5. 8	*11. 6*	*D8*	C11	Gibbon
6. 8	*12. 6*	*D8*	D12	Tapir
7. 8	*13. 6*	*D8*	E1	Sheep
8. 8	*14. 6*	*D8*	F2	Deer
9. 8	*15. 6*	*D8*	G3	Horse
10. 8	*16. 6*	*D8*	H4	Stag
11. 8	*17. 6*	*D8*	J5	Serpent
12. 8	*18. 6*	*D8*	K6	Earthworm
13. 8	*19. 6*	*D8*	A7	Crocodile
14. 8	*20. 6*	*D8*	B8	Dragon
15. 8	*21. 6*	*D8*	C9	Badger
16. 8	*22. 6*	*D8*	D10	Hare
17. 8	*23. 6*	*D8*	E11	Fox
18. 8	*24. 6*	*D8*	F12	Tiger
19. 8	*25. 6*	*D8*	G1	Leopard
20. 8	*26. 6*	*D8*	H2	Griffon
21. 8	*27. 6*	*D8*	J3	Ox
22. 8	*28. 6*	*D8*	K4	Bat
23. 8	*29. 6*	*D8*	A5	Rat
24. 8	1. 7	E9	B6	Swallow
25. 8	2. 7	E9	C7	Pig
26. 8	3. 7	E9	D8	Porcupine
27. 8	4. 7	E9	E9	Wolf
28. 8	5. 7	E9	F10	Dog
29. 8	6. 7	E9	G11	Pheasant
30. 8	7. 7	E9	H12	Cock
31. 8	8. 7	E9	J1	Crow
1. 9	9. 7	E9	K2	Monkey
2. 9	10. 7	E9	A3	Gibbon
3. 9	11. 7	E9	B4	Tapir
4. 9	12. 7	E9	C5	Sheep
5. 9	13. 7	E9	D6	Deer
6. 9	14. 7	E9	E7	Horse
7. 9	15. 7	E9	F8	Stag
8. 9	16. 7	E9	G9	Serpent
9. 9	17. 7	E9	H10	Earthworm
10. 9	18. 7	E9	J11	Crocodile
11. 9	19. 7	E9	K12	Dragon
12. 9	20. 7	E9	A1	Badger
13. 9	21. 7	E9	B2	Hare
14. 9	22. 7	E9	C3	Fox
15. 9	23. 7	E9	D4	Tiger
16. 9	24. 7	E9	E5	Leopard
17. 9	25. 7	E9	F6	Griffon
18. 9	26. 7	E9	G7	Ox
19. 9	27. 7	E9	H8	Bat
20. 9	28. 7	E9	J9	Rat
21. 9	29. 7	E9	K10	Swallow
22. 9	30. 7	E9	A11	Pig
23. 9	1. 8	F10	B12	Porcupine
24. 9	2. 8	F10	C1	Wolf
25. 9	3. 8	F10	D2	Dog
26. 9	4. 8	F10	E3	Pheasant
27. 9	5. 8	F10	F4	Cock
28. 9	6. 8	F10	G5	Crow
29. 9	7. 8	F10	H6	Monkey
30. 9	8. 8	F10	J7	Gibbon
1.10	9. 8	F10	K8	Tapir
2.10	10 8	F10	A9	Sheep
3.10	11. 8	F10	B10	Deer
4.10	12. 8	F10	C11	Horse
5.10	13. 8	F10	D12	Stag
6.10	14. 8	F10	E1	Serpent
7.10	15. 8	F10	F2	Earthworm

Solar date	*Lunar date*	*Month HS/EB*	*Day HS/EB*	*Constellation*
8.10	16. 8	F10	G3	Crocodile
9.10	17. 8	F10	H4	Dragon
10.10	18. 8	F10	J5	Badger
11.10	19. 8	F10	K6	Hare
12.10	20. 8	F10	A7	Fox
13.10	21. 8	F10	B8	Tiger
14.10	22. 8	F10	C9	Leopard
15.10	23. 8	F10	D10	Griffon
16.10	24. 8	F10	E11	Ox
17.10	25. 8	F10	F12	Bat
18.10	26. 8	F10	G1	Rat
19.10	27. 8	F10	H2	Swallow
20.10	28. 8	F10	J3	Pig
21.10	29. 8	F10	K4	Porcupine
22.10	30. 8	F10	A5	Wolf
23.10	1. 9	G11	B6	Dog
24.10	2. 9	G11	C7	Pheasant
25.10	3. 9	G11	D8	Cock
26.10	4. 9	G11	E9	Crow
27.10	5. 9	G11	F10	Monkey
28.10	6. 9	G11	G11	Gibbon
29.10	7. 9	G11	H12	Tapir
30.10	8. 9	G11	J1	Sheep
31.10	9. 9	G11	K2	Deer
1.11	10. 9	G11	A3	Horse
2.11	11. 9	G11	B4	Stag
3.11	12. 9	G11	C5	Serpent
4.11	13. 9	G11	D6	Earthworm
5.11	14. 9	G11	E7	Crocodile
6.11	15. 9	G11	F8	Dragon
7.11	16. 9	G11	G9	Badger
8.11	17. 9	G11	H10	Hare
9.11	18. 9	G11	J11	Fox
10.11	19. 9	G11	K12	Tiger
11.11	20. 9	G11	A1	Leopard
12.11	21. 9	G11	B2	Griffon
13.11	22. 9	G11	C3	Ox
14.11	23. 9	G11	D4	Bat
15.11	24. 9	G11	E5	Rat
16.11	25. 9	G11	F6	Swallow
17.11	26. 9	G11	G7	Pig
18.11	27. 9	G11	H8	Porcupine
19.11	28. 9	G11	J9	Wolf
20.11	29. 9	G11	K10	Dog
21.11	1.10	H12	A11	Pheasant
22.11	2.10	H12	B12	Cock
23.11	3.10	H12	C1	Crow
24.11	4.10	H12	D2	Monkey
25.11	5.10	H12	E3	Gibbon
26.11	6.10	H12	F4	Tapir
27.11	7.10	H12	G5	Sheep
28.11	8.10	H12	H6	Deer
29.11	9.10	H12	J7	Horse
30.11	10.10	H12	K8	Stag
1.12	11.10	H12	A9	Serpent
2.12	12.10	H12	B10	Earthworm
3.12	13.10	H12	C11	Crocodile
4.12	14.10	H12	D12	Dragon
5.12	15.10	H12	E1	Badger
6.12	16.10	H12	F2	Hare
7.12	17.10	H12	G3	Fox
8.12	18.10	H12	H4	Tiger
9.12	19.10	H12	J5	Leopard
10.12	20.10	H12	K6	Griffon
11.12	21.10	H12	A7	Ox
12.12	22.10	H12	B8	Bat
13.12	23.10	H12	C9	Rat

Solar date	*Lunar date*	*Month HS/EB*	*Day HS/EB*	*Constellation*
14.12	24.10	H12	D10	Swallow
15.12	25.10	H12	E11	Pig
16.12	26.10	H12	F12	Porcupine
17.12	27.10	H12	G1	Wolf
18.12	28.10	H12	H2	Dog
19.12	29.10	H12	J3	Pheasant
20.12	30.10	H12	K4	Cock
21.12	1.11	J1	A5	Crow
22.12	2.11	J1	B6	Monkey
23.12	3.11	J1	C7	Gibbon
24.12	4.11	J1	D8	Tapir
25.12	5.11	J1	E9	Sheep
26.12	6.11	J1	F10	Deer
27.12	7.11	J1	G11	Horse
28.12	8.11	J1	H12	Stag
29.12	9.11	J1	J1	Serpent
30.12	10.11	J1	K2	Earthworm
31.12	11.11	J1	A3	Crocodile
1988				
1. 1	12.11	J1	B4	Dragon
2. 1	13.11	J1	C5	Badger
3. 1	14.11	J1	D6	Hare
4. 1	15.11	J1	E7	Fox
5. 1	16.11	J1	F8	Tiger
6. 1	17.11	J1	G9	Leopard
7. 1	18.11	J1	H10	Griffon
8. 1	19.11	J1	J11	Ox
9. 1	20.11	J1	K12	Bat
10. 1	21.11	J1	A1	Rat
11. 1	22.11	J1	B2	Swallow
12. 1	23.11	J1	C3	Pig
13. 1	24.11	J1	D4	Porcupine
14. 1	25.11	J1	E5	Wolf
15. 1	26.11	J1	F6	Dog
16. 1	27.11	J1	G7	Pheasant
17. 1	28.11	J1	H8	Cock
18. 1	29.11	J1	J9	Crow
19. 1	1.12	K2	K10	Monkey
20. 1	2.12	K2	A11	Gibbon
21. 1	3.12	K2	B12	Tapir
22. 1	4.12	K2	C1	Sheep
23. 1	5.12	K2	D2	Deer
24. 1	6.12	K2	E3	Horse
25. 1	7.12	K2	F4	Stag
26. 1	8.12	K2	G5	Serpent
27. 1	9.12	K2	H6	Earthworm
28. 1	10.12	K2	J7	Crocodile
29. 1	11.12	K2	K8	Dragon
30. 1	12.12	K2	A9	Badger
31. 1	13.12	K2	B10	Hare
1. 2	14.12	K2	C11	Fox
2. 2	15.12	K2	D12	Tiger
3. 2	16.12	K2	E1	Leopard
4. 2	17.12	K2	F2	Griffon
5. 2	18.12	K2	G3	Ox
6. 2	19.12	K2	H4	Bat
7. 2	20.12	K2	J5	Rat
8. 2	21.12	K2	K6	Swallow
9. 2	22.12	K2	A7	Pig
10. 2	23.12	K2	B8	Porcupine
11. 2	24.12	K2	C9	Wolf
12. 2	25.12	K2	D10	Dog
13. 2	26.12	K2	E11	Pheasant
14. 2	27.12	K2	F12	Cock
15. 2	28.12	K2	G1	Crow
16. 2	29.12	K2	H2	Monkey

MOU CH'EN YEAR

Solar date	*Lunar date*	*Month HS/EB*	*Day HS/EB*	*Constellation*
17. 2	1. 1	A3	J3	Gibbon
18. 2	2. 1	A3	K4	Tapir
19. 2	3. 1	A3	A5	Sheep
20. 2	4. 1	A3	B6	Deer
21. 2	5. 1	A3	C7	Horse
22. 2	6. 1	A3	D8	Stag
23. 2	7. 1	A3	E9	Serpent
24. 2	8. 1	A3	F10	Earthworm
25. 2	9. 1	A3	G11	Crocodile
26. 2	10. 1	A3	H12	Dragon
27. 2	11. 1	A3	J1	Badger
28. 2	12. 1	A3	K2	Hare
29. 2	13. 1	A3	A3	Fox
1. 3	14. 1	A3	B4	Tiger
2. 3	15. 1	A3	C5	Leopard
3. 3	16. 1	A3	D6	Griffon
4. 3	17. 1	A3	E7	Ox
5. 3	18. 1	A3	F8	Bat
6. 3	19. 1	A3	G9	Rat
7. 3	20. 1	A3	H10	Swallow
8. 3	21. 1	A3	J11	Pig
9. 3	22. 1	A3	K12	Porcupine
10. 3	23. 1	A3	A1	Wolf
11. 3	24. 1	A3	B2	Dog
12. 3	25. 1	A3	C3	Pheasant
13. 3	26. 1	A3	D4	Cock
14. 3	27. 1	A3	E5	Crow
15. 3	28. 1	A3	F6	Monkey
16. 3	29. 1	A3	G7	Gibbon
17. 3	30. 1	A3	H8	Tapir
18. 3	1. 2	B4	J9	Sheep
19. 3	2. 2	B4	K10	Deer
20. 3	3. 2	B4	A11	Horse
21. 3	4. 2	B4	B12	Stag
22. 3	5. 2	B4	C1	Serpent
23. 3	6. 2	B4	D2	Earthworm
24. 3	7. 2	B4	E3	Crocodile
25. 3	8. 2	B4	F4	Dragon
26. 3	9. 2	B4	G5	Badger
27. 3	10. 2	B4	H6	Hare
28. 3	11. 2	B4	J7	Fox
29. 3	12. 2	B4	K8	Tiger
30. 3	13. 2	B4	A9	Leopard
31. 3	14. 2	B4	B10	Griffon
1. 4	15. 2	B4	C11	Ox
2. 4	16. 2	B4	D12	Bat
3. 4	17. 2	B4	E1	Rat
4. 4	18. 2	B4	F2	Swallow
5. 4	19. 2	B4	G3	Pig
6. 4	20. 2	B4	H4	Porcupine
7. 4	21. 2	B4	J5	Wolf
8. 4	22. 2	B4	K6	Dog
9. 4	23. 2	B4	A7	Pheasant
10. 4	24. 2	B4	B8	Cock
11. 4	25. 2	B4	C9	Crow
12. 4	26. 2	B4	D10	Monkey
13. 4	27. 2	B4	E11	Gibbon
14. 4	28. 2	B4	F12	Tapir
15. 4	29. 2	B4	G1	Sheep
16. 4	1. 3	C5	H2	Deer
17. 4	2. 3	C5	J3	Horse
18. 4	3. 3	C5	K4	Stag
19. 4	4. 3	C5	A5	Serpent
20. 4	5. 3	C5	B6	Earthworm
21. 4	6. 3	C5	C7	Crocodile
22. 4	7. 3	C5	D8	Dragon
23. 4	8. 3	C5	E9	Badger
24. 4	9. 3	C5	F10	Hare
25. 4	10. 3	C5	G11	Fox
26. 4	11. 3	C5	H12	Tiger
27. 4	12. 3	C5	J1	Leopard
28. 4	13. 3	C5	K2	Griffon
29. 4	14. 3	C5	A3	Ox
30. 4	15. 3	C5	B4	Bat
1. 5	16. 3	C5	C5	Rat
2. 5	17. 3	C5	D6	Swallow
3. 5	18. 3	C5	E7	Pig
4. 5	19. 3	C5	F8	Porcupine
5. 5	20. 3	C5	G9	Wolf
6. 5	21. 3	C5	H10	Dog
7. 5	22. 3	C5	J11	Pheasant
8. 5	23. 3	C5	K12	Cock
9. 5	24. 3	C5	A1	Crow
10. 5	25. 3	C5	B2	Monkey
11. 5	26. 3	C5	C3	Gibbon
12. 5	27. 3	C5	D4	Tapir
13. 5	28. 3	C5	E5	Sheep
14. 5	29. 3	C5	F6	Deer
15. 5	30. 3	C5	G7	Horse
16. 5	1. 4	D6	H8	Stag
17. 5	2. 4	D6	J9	Serpent
18. 5	3. 4	D6	K10	Earthworm
19. 5	4. 4	D6	A11	Crocodile
20. 5	5. 4	D6	B12	Dragon
21. 5	6. 4	D6	C1	Badger
22. 5	7. 4	D6	D2	Hare
23. 5	8. 4	D6	E3	Fox
24. 5	9. 4	D6	F4	Tiger
25. 5	10. 4	D6	G5	Leopard
26. 5	11. 4	D6	H6	Griffon
27. 5	12. 4	D6	J7	Ox
28. 5	13. 4	D6	K8	Bat
29. 5	14. 4	D6	A9	Rat
30. 5	15. 4	D6	B10	Swallow
31. 5	16. 4	D6	C11	Pig
1. 6	17. 4	D6	D12	Porcupine
2. 6	18. 4	D6	E1	Wolf
3. 6	19. 4	D6	F2	Dog
4. 6	20. 4	D6	G3	Pheasant
5. 6	21. 4	D6	H4	Cock
6. 6	22. 4	D6	J5	Crow
7. 6	23. 4	D6	K6	Monkey
8. 6	24. 4	D6	A7	Gibbon
9. 6	25. 4	D6	B8	Tapir
10. 6	26. 4	D6	C9	Sheep
11. 6	27. 4	D6	D10	Deer
12. 6	28. 4	D6	E11	Horse
13. 6	29. 4	D6	F12	Stag
14. 6	1. 5	E7	G1	Serpent
15. 6	2. 5	E7	H2	Earthworm
16. 6	3. 5	E7	J3	Crocodile
17. 6	4. 5	E7	K4	Dragon
18. 6	5. 5	E7	A5	Badger
19. 6	6. 5	E7	B6	Hare
20. 6	7. 5	E7	C7	Fox
21. 6	8. 5	E7	D8	Tiger
22. 6	9. 5	E7	E9	Leopard
23. 6	10. 5	E7	F10	Griffon
24. 6	11. 5	E7	G11	Ox
25. 6	12. 5	E7	H12	Bat
26. 6	13. 5	E7	J1	Rat
27. 6	14. 5	E7	K2	Swallow
28. 6	15. 5	E7	A3	Pig
29. 6	16. 5	E7	B4	Porcupine
30. 6	17. 5	E7	C5	Wolf
1. 7	18. 5	E7	D6	Dog
2. 7	19. 5	E7	E7	Pheasant
3. 7	20. 5	E7	F8	Cock
4. 7	21. 5	E7	G9	Crow
5. 7	22. 5	E7	H10	Monkey
6. 7	23. 5	E7	J11	Gibbon
7. 7	24. 5	E7	K12	Tapir

Solar date	Lunar date	Month HS/EB	Day HS/EB	Constellation
8. 7	25. 5	E7	A1	Sheep
9. 7	26. 5	E7	B2	Deer
10. 7	27. 5	E7	C3	Horse
11. 7	28. 5	E7	D4	Stag
12. 7	29. 5	E7	E5	Serpent
13. 7	30. 5	E7	F6	Earthworm
14. 7	1. 6	F8	G7	Crocodile
15. 7	2. 6	F8	H8	Dragon
16. 7	3. 6	F8	J9	Badger
17. 7	4. 6	F8	K10	Hare
18. 7	5. 6	F8	A11	Fox
19. 7	6. 6	F8	B12	Tiger
20. 7	7. 6	F8	C1	Leopard
21. 7	8. 6	F8	D2	Griffon
22. 7	9. 6	F8	E3	Ox
23. 7	10. 6	F8	F4	Bat
24. 7	11. 6	F8	G5	Rat
25. 7	12. 6	F8	H6	Swallow
26. 7	13. 6	F8	J7	Pig
27. 7	14. 6	F8	K8	Porcupine
28. 7	15. 6	F8	A9	Wolf
29. 7	16. 6	F8	B10	Dog
30. 7	17. 6	F8	C11	Pheasant
31. 7	18. 6	F8	D12	Cock
1. 8	19. 6	F8	E1	Crow
2. 8	20. 6	F8	F2	Monkey
3. 8	21. 6	F8	G3	Gibbon
4. 8	22. 6	F8	H4	Tapir
5. 8	23. 6	F8	J5	Sheep
6. 8	24. 6	F8	K6	Deer
7. 8	25. 6	F8	A7	Horse
8. 8	26. 6	F8	B8	Stag
9. 8	27. 6	F8	C9	Serpent
10. 8	28. 6	F8	D10	Earthworm
11. 8	29. 6	F8	E11	Crocodile
12. 8	1. 7	G9	F12	Dragon
13. 8	2. 7	G9	G1	Badger
14. 8	3. 7	G9	H2	Hare
15. 8	4. 7	G9	J3	Fox
16. 8	5. 7	G9	K4	Tiger
17. 8	6. 7	G9	A5	Leopard
18. 8	7. 7	G9	B6	Griffon
19. 8	8. 7	G9	C7	Ox
20. 8	9. 7	G9	D8	Bat
21. 8	10. 7	G9	E9	Rat
22. 8	11. 7	G9	F10	Swallow
23. 8	12. 7	G9	G11	Pig
24. 8	13. 7	G9	H12	Porcupine
25. 8	14. 7	G9	J1	Wolf
26. 8	15. 7	G9	K2	Dog
27. 8	16. 7	G9	A3	Pheasant
28. 8	17. 7	G9	B4	Cock
29. 8	18. 7	G9	C5	Crow
30. 8	19. 7	G9	D6	Monkey
31. 8	20. 7	G9	E7	Gibbon
1. 9	21. 7	G9	F8	Tapir
2. 9	22. 7	G9	G9	Sheep
3. 9	23. 7	G9	H10	Deer
4. 9	24. 7	G9	J11	Horse
5. 9	25. 7	G9	K12	Stag
6. 9	26. 7	G9	A1	Serpent
7. 9	27. 7	G9	B2	Earthworm
8. 9	28. 7	G9	C3	Crocodile
9. 9	29. 7	G9	D4	Dragon
10. 9	30. 7	G9	E5	Badger
11. 9	1. 8	H10	F6	Hare
12. 9	2. 8	H10	G7	Fox
13. 9	3. 8	H10	H8	Tiger
14. 9	4. 8	H10	J9	Leopard
15. 9	5. 8	H10	K10	Griffon
16. 9	6. 8	H10	A11	Ox
17. 9	7. 8	H10	B12	Bat
18. 9	8. 8	H10	C1	Rat
19. 9	9. 8	H10	D2	Swallow
20. 9	10. 8	H10	E3	Pig
21. 9	11. 8	H10	F4	Porcupine
22. 9	12. 8	H10	G5	Wolf
23. 9	13. 8	H10	H6	Dog
24. 9	14. 8	H10	J7	Pheasant
25. 9	15. 8	H10	K8	Cock
26. 9	16. 8	H10	A9	Crow
27. 9	17. 8	H10	B10	Monkey
28. 9	18.18	H10	C11	Gibbon
29. 9	19. 8	H10	D12	Tapir
30. 9	20. 8	H10	E1	Sheep
1.10	21. 8	H10	F2	Deer
2.10	22. 8	H10	G3	Horse
3.10	23. 8	H10	H4	Stag
4.10	24. 8	H10	J5	Serpent
5.10	25. 8	H10	K6	Earthworm
6.10	26. 8	H10	A7	Crocodile
7.10	27. 8	H10	B8	Dragon
8.10	28. 8	H10	C9	Badger
9.10	29. 8	H10	D10	Hare
10.10	30. 8	H10	E11	Fox
11.10	1. 9	J11	F12	Tiger
12.10	2. 9	J11	G1	Leopard
13.10	3. 9	J11	H2	Griffon
14.10	4. 9	J11	J3	Ox
15.10	5. 9	J11	K4	Bat
16.10	6. 9	J11	A5	Rat
17.10	7. 9	J11	B6	Swallow
18.10	8. 9	J11	C7	Pig
19.10	9. 9	J11	D8	Porcupine
20.10	10. 9	J11	E9	Wolf
21.10	11. 9	J11	F10	Dog
22.10	12. 9	J11	G11	Pheasant
23.10	13. 9	J11	H12	Cock
24.10	14. 9	J11	J1	Crow
25.10	15. 9	J11	K2	Monkey
26.10	16. 9	J11	A3	Gibbon
27.10	17. 9	J11	B4	Tapir
28.10	18. 9	J11	C5	Sheep
29.10	19. 9	J11	D6	Deer
30.10	20. 9	J11	E7	Horse
31.10	21. 9	J11	F8	Stag
1.11	22. 9	J11	G9	Serpent
2.11	23. 9	J11	H10	Earthworm
3.11	24. 9	J11	J11	Crocodile
4.11	25. 9	J11	K12	Dragon
5.11	26. 9	J11	A1	Badger
6.11	27. 9	J11	B2	Hare
7.11	28. 9	J11	C3	Fox
8.11	29. 9	J11	D4	Tiger
9.11	1.10	K12	E5	Leopard
10.11	2.10	K12	F6	Griffon
11.11	3.10	K12	G7	Ox
12.11	4.10	K12	H8	Bat
13.11	5.10	K12	J9	Rat
14.11	6.10	K12	K10	Swallow
15.11	7.10	K12	A11	Pig
16.11	8.10	K12	B12	Porcupine
17.11	9.10	K12	C1	Wolf
18.11	10.10	K12	D2	Dog
19.11	11.10	K12	E3	Pheasant
20.11	12.10	K12	F4	Cock
21.11	13.10	K12	G5	Crow
22.11	14.10	K12	H6	Monkey
23.11	15.10	K12	J7	Gibbon
24.11	16.10	K12	K8	Tapir
25.11	17.10	K12	A9	Sheep
26.11	18.10	K12	B10	Deer
27.11	19.10	K12	C11	Horse
28.11	20.10	K12	D12	Stag
29.11	21.10	K12	E1	Serpent
30.11	22.10	K12	F2	Earthworm

Solar date	*Lunar date*	*Month HS/EB*	*Day HS/EB*	*Constellation*
1.12	23.10	K12	G3	Crocodile
2.12	24.10	K12	H4	Dragon
3.12	25.10	K12	J5	Badger
4.12	26.10	K12	K6	Hare
5.12	27.10	K12	A7	Fox
6.12	28.10	K12	B8	Tiger
7.12	29.10	K12	C9	Leopard
8.12	30.10	K12	D10	Griffon
9.12	1.11	A1	E11	Ox
10.12	2.11	A1	F12	Bat
11.12	3.11	A1	G1	Rat
12.12	4.11	A1	H2	Swallow
13.12	5.11	A1	J3	Pig
14.12	6.11	A1	K4	Porcupine
15.12	7.11	A1	A5	Wolf
16.12	8.11	A1	B6	Dog
17.12	9.11	A1	C7	Pheasant
18.12	10.11	A1	D8	Cock
19.12	11.11	A1	E9	Crow
20.12	12.11	A1	F10	Monkey
21.12	13.11	A1	G11	Gibbon
22.12	14.11	A1	H12	Tapir
23.12	15.11	A1	J1	Sheep
24.12	16.11	A1	K2	Deer
25.12	17.11	A1	A3	Horse
26.12	18.11	A1	B4	Stag
27.12	19.11	A1	C5	Serpent
28.12	20.11	A1	D6	Earthworm
29.12	21.11	A1	E7	Crocodile
30.12	22.11	A1	F8	Dragon
31.12	23.11	A1	G9	Badger
1989				
1. 1	24.11	A1	H10	Hare
2. 1	25.11	A1	J11	Fox
3. 1	26.11	A1	K12	Tiger
4. 1	27.11	A1	A1	Leopard
5. 1	28.11	A1	B2	Griffon
6. 1	29.11	A1	C3	Ox
7. 1	30.11	A1	D4	Bat
8. 1	1.12	B2	E5	Rat
9. 1	2.12	B2	F6	Swallow
10. 1	3.12	B2	G7	Pig
11. 1	4.12	B2	H8	Porcupine
12. 1	5.12	B2	J9	Wolf
13. 1	6.12	B2	K10	Dog
14. 1	7.12	B2	A11	Pheasant
15. 1	8.12	B2	B12	Cock
16. 1	9.12	B2	C1	Crow
18. 1	10.12	B2	D2	Monkey
18. 1	11.12	B2	E3	Gibbon
19. 1	12.12	B2	F4	Tapir
20. 1	13.12	B2	G5	Sheep
21. 1	14.12	B2	H6	Deer
22. 1	15.12	B2	J7	Horse
23. 1	16.12	B2	K8	Stag
24. 1	17.12	B2	A9	Serpent
25. 1	18.12	B2	B10	Earthworm
26. 1	19.12	B2	C11	Crocodile
27. 1	20.12	B2	D12	Dragon
28. 1	21.12	B2	E1	Badger
29. 1	22.12	B2	F2	Hare
30. 1	23.12	B2	G3	Fox
31. 1	24.12	B2	H4	Tiger
1. 2	25.12	B2	J5	Leopard
2. 2	26.12	B2	K6	Griffon
3. 2	27.12	B2	A7	Ox
4. 2	28.12	B2	B8	Bat
5. 2	29.12	B2	C9	Rat

CHI SZU YEAR

6. 2	1. 1	C3	D10	Swallow
7. 2	2. 1	C3	E11	Pig
8. 2	3. 1	C3	F12	Porcupine
9. 2	4. 1	C3	G1	Wolf
10. 2	5. 1	C3	H2	Dog
11. 2	6. 1	C3	J3	Pheasant
12. 2	7. 1	C3	K4	Cock
13. 2	8. 1	C3	A5	Crow
14. 2	9. 1	C3	B6	Monkey
15. 2	10. 1	C3	C7	Gibbon
16. 2	11. 1	C3	D8	Tapir
17. 2	12. 1	C3	E9	Sheep
18. 2	13. 1	C3	F10	Deer
19. 2	14. 1	C3	G11	Horse
20. 2	15. 1	C3	H12	Stag
21. 2	16. 1	C3	J1	Serpent
22. 2	17. 1	C3	K2	Earthworm
23. 2	18. 1	C3	A3	Crocodile
24. 2	19. 1	C3	B4	Dragon
25. 2	20. 1	C3	C5	Badger
26. 2	21. 1	C3	D6	Hare
27. 2	22. 1	C3	E7	Fox
28. 2	23. 1	C3	F8	Tiger
1. 3	24. 1	C3	G9	Leopard
2. 3	25. 1	C3	H10	Griffon
3. 3	26. 1	C3	J11	Ox
4. 3	27. 1	C3	K12	Bat
5. 3	28. 1	C3	A1	Rat
6. 3	29. 1	C3	B2	Swallow
7. 3	30. 1	C3	C3	Pig
8. 3	1. 2	D4	D4	Porcupine
9. 3	2. 2	D4	E5	Wolf
10. 3	3. 2	D4	F6	Dog
11. 3	4. 2	D4	G7	Pheasant
12. 3	5. 2	D4	H8	Cock
13. 3	6. 2	D4	J9	Crow
14. 3	7. 2	D4	K10	Monkey
15. 3	8. 2	D4	A11	Gibbon
16. 3	9. 2	D4	B12	Tapir
17. 3	10. 2	D4	C1	Sheep
18. 3	11. 2	D4	D2	Deer
19. 3	12. 2	D4	E3	Horse
20. 3	13. 2	D4	F4	Stag
21. 3	14. 2	D4	G5	Serpent
22. 3	15. 2	D4	H6	Earthworm
23. 3	16. 2	D4	J7	Crocodile
24. 3	17. 2	D4	K8	Dragon
25. 3	18. 2	D4	A9	Badger
26. 3	19. 2	D4	B10	Hare
27. 3	20. 2	D4	C11	Fox
28. 3	21. 2	D4	D12	Tiger
29. 3	22. 2	D4	E1	Leopard
30. 3	23. 2	D4	F2	Griffon
31. 3	24. 2	D4	G3	Ox
1. 4	25. 2	D4	H4	Bat
2. 4	26. 2	D4	J5	Rat
3. 4	27. 2	D4	K6	Swallow
4. 4	28. 2	D4	A7	Pig
5. 4	29. 2	D4	B8	Porcupine
6. 4	1. 3	E5	C9	Wolf
7. 4	2. 3	E5	D10	Dog
8. 4	3. 3	E5	E11	Pheasant
9. 4	4. 3	E5	F12	Cock
10. 4	5. 3	E5	G1	Crow
11. 4	6. 3	E5	H2	Monkey
12. 4	7. 3	E5	J3	Gibbon

Solar date	Lunar date	Month HS/EB	Day HS/EB	Constellation
13. 4	8. 3	E5	K4	Tapir
14. 4	9. 3	E5	A5	Sheep
15. 4	10. 3	E5	B6	Deer
16. 4	11. 3	E5	C7	Horse
17. 4	12. 3	E5	D8	Stag
18. 4	13. 3	E5	E9	Serpent
19. 4	14. 3	E5	F10	Earthworm
20. 4	15. 3	E5	G11	Crocodile
21. 4	16. 3	E5	H12	Dragon
22. 4	17. 3	E5	J1	Badger
23. 4	18. 3	E5	K2	Hare
24. 4	19. 3	E5	A3	Fox
25. 4	20. 3	E5	B4	Tiger
26. 4	21. 3	E5	C5	Leopard
27. 4	22. 3	E5	D6	Griffon
28. 4	23. 3	E5	E7	Ox
29. 4	24. 3	E5	F8	Bat
30. 4	25. 3	E5	G9	Rat
1. 5	26. 3	E5	H10	Swallow
2. 5	27. 3	E5	J11	Pig
3. 5	28. 3	E5	K12	Porcupine
4. 5	29. 3	E5	A1	Wolf
5. 5	1. 4	F6	B2	Dog
6. 5	2. 4	F6	C3	Pheasant
7. 5	3. 4	F6	D4	Cock
8. 5	4. 4	F6	E5	Crow
9. 5	5. 4	F6	F6	Monkey
10. 5	6. 4	F6	G7	Gibbon
11. 5	7. 4	F6	H8	Tapir
12. 5	8. 4	F6	J9	Sheep
13. 5	9. 4	F6	K10	Deer
14. 5	10. 4	F6	A11	Horse
15. 5	11. 4	F6	B12	Stag
16. 5	12. 4	F6	C1	Serpent
17. 5	13. 4	F6	D2	Earthworm
18. 5	14. 4	F6	E3	Crocodile
19. 5	15. 4	F6	F4	Dragon
20. 5	16. 4	F6	G5	Badger
21. 5	17. 4	F6	H6	Hare
22. 5	18. 4	F6	J7	Fox
23. 5	19. 4	F6	K8	Tiger
24. 5	20. 4	F6	A9	Leopard
25. 5	21. 4	F6	B10	Griffon
26. 5	22. 4	F6	C11	Ox
27. 5	23. 4	F6	D12	Bat
28. 5	24. 4	F6	E1	Rat
29. 5	25. 4	F6	F2	Swallow
30. 5	26. 4	F6	G3	Pig
31. 5	27. 4	F6	H4	Porcupine
1. 6	28. 4	F6	J5	Wolf
2. 6	29. 4	F6	K6	Dog
3. 6	30. 4	F6	A7	Pheasant
4. 6	1. 5	G7	B8	Cock
5. 6	2. 5	G7	C9	Crow
6. 6	3. 5	G7	D10	Monkey
7. 6	4. 5	G7	E11	Gibbon
8. 6	5. 5	G7	F12	Tapir
9. 6	6. 5	G7	G1	Sheep
10. 6	7. 5	G7	H2	Deer
11. 6	8. 5	G7	J3	Horse
12. 6	9. 5	G7	K4	Stag
13. 6	10. 5	G7	A5	Serpent
14. 6	11. 5	G7	B6	Earthworm
15. 6	12. 5	G7	C7	Crocodile
16. 6	13. 5	G7	D8	Dragon
17. 6	14. 5	G7	E9	Badger
18. 6	15. 5	G7	F10	Hare
19. 6	16. 5	G7	G11	Fox
20. 6	17. 5	G7	H12	Tiger
21. 6	18. 5	G7	J1	Leopard
22. 6	19. 5	G7	K2	Griffon
23. 6	20. 5	G7	A3	Ox
24. 6	21. 5	G7	B4	Bat
25. 6	22. 5	G7	C5	Rat
26. 6	23. 5	G7	D6	Swallow
27. 6	24. 5	G7	E7	Pig
28. 6	25. 5	G7	F8	Porcupine
29. 6	26. 5	G7	G9	Wolf
30. 6	27. 5	G7	H10	Dog
1. 7	28. 5	G7	J11	Pheasant
2. 7	29. 5	G7	K12	Cock
3. 7	1. 6	H8	A1	Crow
4. 7	2. 6	H8	B2	Monkey
5. 7	3. 6	H8	C3	Gibbon
6. 7	4. 6	H8	D4	Tapir
7. 7	5. 6	H8	E5	Sheep
8. 7	6. 6	H8	F6	Deer
9. 7	7. 6	H8	G7	Horse
10. 7	8. 6	H8	H8	Stag
11. 7	9. 6	H8	J9	Serpent
12. 7	10. 6	H8	K10	Earthworm
13. 7	11. 6	H8	A11	Crocodile
14. 7	12. 6	H8	B12	Dragon
15. 7	13. 6	H8	C1	Badger
16. 7	14. 6	H8	D2	Hare
17. 7	15. 6	H8	E3	Fox
18. 7	16. 6	H8	F4	Tiger
19. 7	17. 6	H8	G5	Leopard
20. 7	18. 6	H8	H6	Griffon
21. 7	19. 6	H8	J7	Ox
22. 7	20. 6	H8	K8	Bat
23. 7	21. 6	H8	A9	Rat
24. 7	22. 6	H8	B10	Swallow
25. 7	23. 6	H8	C11	Pig
26. 7	24. 6	H8	D12	Porcupine
27. 7	25. 6	H8	E1	Wolf
28. 7	26. 6	H8	F2	Dog
29. 7	27. 6	H8	G3	Pheasant
30. 7	28. 6	H8	H4	Cock
31. 7	29. 6	H8	J5	Crow
1. 8	1. 7	J9	K6	Monkey
2. 8	2. 7	J9	A7	Gibbon
3. 8	3. 7	J9	B8	Tapir
4. 8	4. 7	J9	C9	Sheep
5. 8	5. 7	J9	D10	Deer
6. 8	6. 7	J9	E11	Horse
7. 8	7. 7	J9	F12	Stag
8. 8	8. 7	J9	G1	Serpent
9. 8	9. 7	J9	H2	Earthworm
10. 8	10. 7	J9	J3	Crocodile
11. 8	11. 7	J9	K4	Dragon
12. 8	12. 7	J9	A5	Badger
13. 8	13. 7	J9	B6	Hare
14. 8	14. 7	J9	C7	Fox
15. 8	15. 7	J9	D8	Tiger
16. 8	16. 7	J9	E9	Leopard
17. 8	17. 7	J9	F10	Griffon
18. 8	18. 7	J9	G11	Ox
20. 8	19. 7	J9	H12	Bat
19. 8	20. 7	J9	J1	Rat
20. 8	21. 7	J9	K2	Swallow
21. 8	22. 7	J9	A3	Pig
22. 8	23. 7	J9	B4	Porcupine
23. 8	24. 7	J9	C5	Wolf
24. 8	25. 7	J9	D6	Dog
25. 8	26. 7	J9	E7	Pheasant
26. 8	27. 7	J9	F8	Cock
27. 8	28. 7	J9	G9	Crow
29. 8	29. 7	J9	H10	Monkey
30. 8	30. 7	J9	J11	Gibbon
31. 8	1. 8	K10	K12	Tapir
1. 9	2. 8	K10	A1	Sheep
2. 9	3. 8	K10	B2	Deer
3. 9	4. 8	K10	C3	Horse
4. 9	5. 8	K10	D4	Stag
5. 9	6. 8	K10	E5	Serpent

Solar date	*Lunar date*	*Month HS/EB*	*Day HS/EB*	*Constellation*
6. 9	7. 8	K10	F6	Earthworm
7. 9	8. 8	K10	G7	Crocodile
8. 9	9. 8	K10	H8	Dragon
9. 9	10. 8	K10	J9	Badger
10. 9	11. 8	K10	K10	Hare
11. 9	12. 8	K10	A11	Fox
12. 9	13. 8	K10	B12	Tiger
13. 9	14. 8	K10	C1	Leopard
14. 9	15. 8	K10	D2	Griffon
15. 9	16. 8	K10	E3	Ox
16. 9	17. 8	K10	F4	Bat
17. 9	18. 8	K10	G5	Rat
18. 9	19. 8	K10	H6	Swallow
19. 9	20. 8	K10	J7	Pig
20. 9	21. 8	K10	K8	Porcupine
21. 9	22. 8	K10	A9	Wolf
22. 9	23. 8	K10	B10	Dog
23. 9	24. 8	K10	C11	Pheasant
24. 9	25. 8	K10	D12	Cock
25. 9	26. 8	K10	E1	Crow
26. 9	27. 8	K10	F2	Monkey
27. 9	28. 8	K10	G3	Gibbon
28. 9	29. 8	K10	H4	Tapir
29. 9	30. 8	K10	J5	Sheep
30. 9	1. 9	A11	K6	Deer
1.10	2. 9	A11	A7	Horse
2.10	3. 9	A11	B8	Stag
3.10	4. 9	A11	C9	Serpent
4.10	5. 9	A11	D10	Earthworm
5.10	6. 9	A11	E11	Crocodile
6.10	7. 9	A11	F12	Dragon
7.10	8. 9	A11	G1	Badger
8.10	9. 9	A11	H2	Hare
9.10	10. 9	A11	J3	Fox
10.10	11. 9	A11	K4	Tiger
11.10	12. 9	A11	A5	Leopard
12.10	13. 9	A11	B6	Griffon
13.10	14. 9	A11	C7	Ox
14.10	15. 9	A11	D8	Bat
15.10	16. 9	A11	E9	Rat
16.10	17. 9	A11	F10	Swallow
17.10	18. 9	A11	G11	Pig
18.10	19. 9	A11	H12	Porcupine
19.10	20. 9	A11	J1	Wolf
20.10	21. 9	A11	K2	Dog
21.10	22. 9	A11	A3	Pheasant
22.10	23. 9	A11	B4	Cock
23.10	24. 9	A11	C5	Crow
24.10	25. 9	A11	D6	Monkey
25.10	26. 9	A11	E7	Gibbon
26.10	27. 9	A11	F8	Tapir
27.10	28. 9	A11	G9	Sheep
28.10	29. 9	A11	H10	Deer
29.10	1.10	B12	J11	Horse
30.10	2.10	B12	K12	Stag
31.10	3.10	B12	A1	Serpent
1.11	4.10	B12	B2	Earthworm
2.11	5.10	B12	C3	Crocodile
3.11	6.10	B12	D4	Dragon
4.11	7.10	B12	E5	Badger
5.11	8.10	B12	F6	Hare
6.11	9.10	B12	G7	Fox
7.11	10.10	B12	H8	Tiger
8.11	11.10	B12	J9	Leopard
9.11	12.10	B12	K10	Griffon
10.11	13.10	B12	A11	Ox
11.11	14.10	B12	B12	Bat
12.11	15.10	B12	C1	Rat
13.11	16.10	B12	D2	Swallow
14.11	17.10	B12	E3	Pig
15.11	18.10	B12	F4	Porcupine
16.11	19.10	B12	G5	Wolf
17.11	20.10	B12	H6	Dog

Solar date	*Lunar date*	*Month HS/EB*	*Day HS/EB*	*Constellation*
18.11	21.10	B12	J7	Pheasant
19.11	22.10	B12	K8	Cock
20.11	23.10	B12	A9	Crow
21.11	24.10	B12	B10	Monkey
22.11	25.10	B12	C11	Gibbon
23.11	26.10	B12	D12	Tapir
24.11	27.10	B12	E1	Sheep
25.11	28.10	B12	F2	Deer
26.11	29.10	B12	G3	Horse
27.11	30.10	B12	H4	Stag
28.11	1.11	C1	J5	Serpent
29.11	2.11	C1	K6	Earthworm
30.11	3.11	C1	A7	Crocodile
1.12	4.11	C1	B8	Dragon
2.12	5.11	C1	C9	Badger
3.12	6.11	C1	D10	Hare
4.12	7.11	C1	E11	Fox
5.12	8.11	C1	F12	Tiger
6.12	9.11	C1	G1	Leopard
7.12	10.11	C1	H2	Griffon
8.12	11.11	C1	J3	Ox
9.12	12.11	C1	K4	Bat
10.12	13.11	C1	A5	Rat
11.12	14.11	C1	B6	Swallow
12.12	15.11	C1	C7	Pig
13.12	16.11	C1	D8	Porcupine
14.12	17.11	C1	E9	Wolf
15.12	18.11	C1	F10	Dog
16.12	19.11	C1	G11	Pheasant
17.12	20.11	C1	H12	Cock
18.12	21.11	C1	J1	Crow
19.12	22.11	C1	K2	Monkey
20.12	23.11	C1	A3	Gibbon
21.12	24.11	C1	B4	Tapir
22.12	25.11	C1	C5	Sheep
23.12	26.11	C1	D6	Deer
24.12	27.11	C1	E7	Horse
25.12	28.11	C1	F8	Stag
26.12	29.11	C1	G9	Serpent
27.12	30.11	C1	H10	Earthworm
28.12	1.12	D2	J11	Crocodile
29.12	2.12	D2	K12	Dragon
30.12	3.12	D2	A1	Badger
31.12	4.12	D2	B2	Hare
1990				
1. 1	5.12	D2	C3	Fox
2. 1	6.12	D2	D4	Tiger
3. 1	7.12	D2	E5	Leopard
4. 1	8.12	D2	F6	Griffon
5. 1	9.12	D2	G7	Ox
6. 1	10.12	D2	H8	Bat
7. 1	11.12	D2	J9	Rat
8. 1	12.12	D2	K10	Swallow
9. 1	13.12	D2	A11	Pig
10. 1	14.12	D2	B12	Porcupine
11. 1	15.12	D2	C1	Wolf
12. 1	16.12	D2	D2	Dog
13. 1	17.12	D2	E3	Pheasant
14. 1	18.12	D2	F4	Cock
15. 1	19.12	D2	G5	Crow
16. 1	20.12	D2	H6	Monkey
17. 1	21.12	D2	J7	Gibbon
18. 1	22.12	D2	K8	Tapir
19. 1	23.12	D2	A9	Sheep
20. 1	24.12	D2	B10	Deer
21. 1	25.12	D2	C11	Horse
22. 1	26.12	D2	D12	Stag
23. 1	27.12	D2	E1	Serpent
24. 1	28.12	D2	F2	Earthworm
25. 1	29.12	D2	G3	Crocodile
26. 1	30.12	D2	H4	Dragon

KENG WU YEAR

Solar date	*Lunar date*	*Month HS/EB*	*Day HS/EB*	*Constellation*
27. 1	1. 1	E3	J5	Badger
28. 1	2. 1	E3	K6	Hare
29. 1	3. 1	E3	A7	Fox
30. 1	4. 1	E3	B8	Tiger
31. 1	5. 1	E3	C9	Leopard
1. 2	6. 1	E3	D10	Griffon
2. 2	7. 1	E3	D11	Ox
3. 2	8. 1	E3	F12	Bat
4. 2	9. 1	E3	G1	Rat
5. 2	10. 1	E3	H2	Swallow
6. 2	11. 1	E3	J3	Pig
7. 2	12. 1	E3	K4	Porcupine
8. 2	13. 1	E3	A5	Wolf
9. 2	14. 1	E3	B6	Dog
10. 2	15. 1	E3	C7	Pheasant
11. 2	16. 1	E3	D8	Cock
12. 2	17. 1	E3	E9	Crow
13. 2	18. 1	E3	F10	Monkey
14. 2	19. 1	E3	G11	Gibbon
15. 2	20. 1	E3	H12	Tapir
16. 2	21. 1	E3	J1	Sheep
17. 2	22. 1	E3	K2	Deer
18. 2	23. 1	E3	A3	Horse
19. 2	24. 1	E3	B4	Stag
20. 2	25. 1	E3	C5	Serpent
21. 2	26. 1	E3	D6	Earthworm
22. 2	27. 1	E3	E7	Crocodile
23. 2	28. 1	E3	F8	Dragon
24. 2	29. 1	E3	G9	Badger
25. 2	1. 2	F4	H10	Hare
26. 2	2. 2	F4	J11	Fox
27. 2	3. 2	F4	K12	Tiger
28. 2	4. 2	F4	A1	Leopard
1. 3	5. 2	F4	B2	Griffon
2. 3	6. 2	F4	C3	Ox
3. 3	7. 2	F4	D4	Bat
4. 3	8. 2	F4	E5	Rat
5. 3	9. 2	F4	F6	Swallow
6. 3	10. 2	F4	G7	Pig
7. 3	11. 2	F4	H8	Porcupine
8. 3	12. 2	F4	J9	Wolf
9. 3	13. 2	F4	K10	Dog
10. 3	14. 2	F4	A11	Pheasant
11. 3	15. 2	F4	B12	Cock
12. 3	16. 2	F4	C1	Crow
13. 3	17. 2	F4	D2	Monkey
14. 3	18. 2	F4	E3	Gibbon
15. 3	19. 2	F4	F4	Tapir
16. 3	20. 2	F4	G5	Sheep
17. 3	21. 2	F4	H6	Deer
18. 3	22. 2	F4	J7	Horse
19. 3	23. 2	F4	K8	Stag
20. 3	24. 2	F4	A9	Serpent
21. 3	25. 2	F4	B10	Earthworm
22. 3	26. 2	F4	C11	Crocodile
23. 3	27. 2	F4	D12	Dragon
24. 3	28. 2	F4	E1	Badger
25. 3	29. 2	F4	F2	Hare
26. 3	30. 2	F4	G3	Fox
27. 3	1. 3	G5	H4	Tiger
28. 3	2. 3	G5	J5	Leopard
29. 3	3. 3	G5	K6	Griffon
30. 3	4. 3	G5	A7	Ox
31. 3	5. 3	G5	B8	Bat
1. 4	6. 3	G5	C9	Rat
2. 4	7. 3	G5	D10	Swallow
3. 4	8. 3	G5	E11	Pig
4. 4	9. 3	G5	F12	Porcupine
5. 4	10. 3	G5	G1	Wolf
6. 4	11. 3	G5	H2	Dog
7. 4	12. 3	G5	J3	Pheasant
8. 4	13. 3	G5	K4	Cock
9. 4	14. 3	G5	A5	Crow
10. 4	15. 3	G5	B6	Monkey
11. 4	16. 3	G5	C7	Gibbon
12. 4	17. 3	G5	D8	Tapir
13. 4	18. 3	G5	E9	Sheep
14. 4	19. 3	G5	F10	Deer
15. 4	20. 3	G5	G11	Horse
16. 4	21. 3	G5	H12	Stag
17. 4	22. 3	G5	J1	Serpent
18. 4	23. 3	G5	K2	Earthworm
19. 4	24. 3	G5	A3	Crocodile
20. 4	25. 3	G5	B4	Dragon
21. 4	26. 3	G5	C5	Badger
22. 4	27. 3	G5	D6	Hare
23. 4	28. 3	G5	E7	Fox
24. 4	29. 3	G5	F8	Tiger
25. 4	1. 4	H6	G9	Leopard
26. 4	2. 4	H6	H10	Griffon
27. 4	3. 4	H6	J11	Ox
28. 4	4. 4	H6	K12	Bat
29. 4	5. 4	H6	A1	Rat
30. 4	6. 4	H6	B2	Swallow
1. 5	7. 4	H6	C3	Pig
2. 5	8. 4	H6	D4	Porcupine
3. 5	9. 4	H6	E5	Wolf
4. 5	10. 4	H6	F6	Dog
5. 5	11. 4	H6	G7	Pheasant
6. 5	12. 4	H6	H8	Cock
7. 5	13. 4	H6	J9	Crow
8. 5	14. 4	H6	K10	Monkey
9. 5	15. 4	H6	A11	Gibbon
10. 5	16. 4	H6	B12	Tapir
11. 5	17. 4	H6	C1	Sheep
12. 5	18. 4	H6	D2	Deer
13. 5	19. 4	H6	E3	Horse
14. 5	20. 4	H6	F4	Stag
15. 5	21. 4	H6	G5	Serpent
16. 5	22. 4	H6	H6	Earthworm
17. 5	23. 4	H6	J7	Crocodile
18. 5	24. 4	H6	K8	Dragon
19. 5	25. 4	H6	A9	Badger
20. 5	26. 4	H6	B10	Hare
21. 5	27. 4	H6	C11	Fox
22. 5	28. 4	H6	D12	Tiger
23. 5	29. 4	H6	E1	Leopard
24. 5	1. 5	J7	F2	Griffon
25. 5	2. 5	J7	G3	Ox
26. 5	3. 5	J7	H4	Bat
27. 5	4. 5	J7	J5	Rat
28. 5	5. 5	J7	K6	Swallow
29. 5	6. 5	J7	A7	Pig
30. 5	7. 5	J7	B8	Porcupine
31. 5	8. 5	J7	C9	Wolf
1. 6	9. 5	J7	D10	Dog
2. 6	10. 5	J7	E11	Pheasant
3. 6	11. 5	J7	F12	Cock
4. 6	12. 5	J7	G1	Crow
5. 6	13. 5	J7	H2	Monkey
6. 6	14. 5	J7	J3	Gibbon
7. 6	15. 5	J7	K4	Tapir
8. 6	16. 5	J7	A5	Sheep
9. 6	7. 5	J7	B6	Deer
10. 6	18. 5	J7	C7	Horse
11. 6	19. 5	J7	D8	Stag
12.16	20. 5	J7	E9	Serpent
13. 6	21. 5	J7	F10	Earthworm
14. 6	22. 5	J7	G11	Crocodile
15. 6	23. 5	J7	H12	Dragon
16. 6	24. 5	J7	J1	Badger
17. 6	25. 5	J7	K2	Hare

Solar date	*Lunar date*	*Month HS/EB*	*Day HS/EB*	*Constellation*
18. 6	26. 5	J7	A3	Fox
19. 6	27. 5	J7	B4	Tiger
20. 6	28. 5	J7	C5	Leopard
21. 6	29. 5	J7	D6	Griffon
22. 6	30. 5	J7	E7	Ox
23. 6	*1. 5*	*J7*	F8	Bat
24. 6	*2. 5*	*J7*	G9	Rat
25. 6	*3. 5*	*J7*	H10	Swallow
26. 6	*4. 5*	*J7*	J11	Pig
27. 6	*5. 5*	*J7*	K12	Porcupine
28. 6	*6. 5*	*J7*	A1	Wolf
29. 6	*7. 5*	*J7*	B2	Dog
30. 6	*8. 5*	*J7*	C3	Pheasant
1. 7	*9. 5*	*J7*	D4	Cock
2. 7	*10. 5*	*J7*	E5	Crow
3. 7	*11. 5*	*J7*	F6	Monkey
4. 7	*12. 5*	*J7*	G7	Gibbon
5. 7	*13. 5*	*J7*	H8	Tapir
6. 7	*14. 5*	*J7*	J9	Sheep
7. 7	*15. 5*	*J7*	K10	Deer
8. 7	*16. 5*	*J7*	A11	Horse
9. 7	*17. 5*	*J7*	B12	Stag
10. 7	*18. 5*	*J7*	C1	Serpent
11. 7	*19. 5*	*J7*	D2	Earthworm
12. 7	*20. 5*	*J7*	E3	Crocodile
13. 7	*21. 5*	*J7*	F4	Dragon
14. 7	*22. 5*	*J7*	G5	Badger
15. 7	*23. 5*	*J7*	H6	Hare
16. 7	*24. 5*	*J7*	J7	Fox
17. 7	*25. 5*	*J7*	K8	Tiger
18. 7	*26. 5*	*J7*	A9	Leopard
19. 7	*27. 5*	*J7*	B10	Griffon
20. 7	*28. 5*	*J7*	C11	Ox
21. 7	*29. 5*	*J7*	D12	Bat
22. 7	1. 6	K8	E1	Rat
23. 7	2. 6	K8	F2	Swallow
24. 7	3. 6	K8	G3	Pig
25. 7	4. 6	K8	H4	Porcupine
26. 7	5. 6	K8	J5	Wolf
27. 7	6. 6	K8	K6	Dog
28. 7	7. 6	K8	A7	Pheasant
29. 7	8. 6	K8	B8	Cock
30. 7	9. 6	K8	C9	Crow
31. 7	10. 6	K8	D10	Monkey
1. 8	11. 6	K8	E11	Gibbon
2. 8	12. 6	K8	F12	Tapir
3. 8	13. 6	K8	G1	Sheep
4. 8	14. 6	K8	H2	Deer
5. 8	15. 6	K8	J3	Horse
6. 8	16. 6	K8	K4	Stag
7. 8	17. 6	K8	A5	Serpent
8. 8	18. 6	K8	B6	Earthworm
9. 8	19. 6	K8	C7	Crocodile
10. 8	20. 6	K8	D8	Dragon
11. 8	21. 6	K8	E9	Badger
12. 8	22. 6	K8	F10	Hare
13. 8	23. 6	K8	G11	Fox
14. 8	24. 6	K8	H12	Tiger
15. 8	25. 6	K8	J1	Leopard
16. 8	26. 6	K8	K2	Griffon
17. 8	27. 6	K8	A3	Ox
18. 8	28. 6	K8	B4	Bat
19. 8	29. 6	K8	C5	Rat
20. 8	1. 7	A9	D6	Swallow
21. 8	2. 7	A9	E7	Pig
22. 8	3. 7	A9	F8	Porcupine
23. 8	4. 7	A9	G9	Wolf
24. 8	5. 7	A9	H10	Dog
25. 8	6. 7	A9	J11	Pheasant
26. 8	7. 7	A9	K12	Cock
27. 8	8. 7	A9	A1	Crow
28. 8	9. 7	A9	B2	Monkey
29. 8	10. 7	A9	C3	Gibbon
30. 8	11. 7	A9	D4	Tapir
31. 8	12. 7	A9	E5	Sheep
1. 9	13. 7	A9	F6	Deer
2. 9	14. 7	A9	G7	Horse
3. 9	15. 7	A9	H8	Stag
4. 9	16. 7	A9	J9	Serpent
5. 9	17. 7	A9	K10	Earthworm
6. 9	18. 7	A9	A11	Crocodile
7. 9	19. 7	A9	B12	Dragon
8. 9	20. 7	A9	C1	Badger
9. 9	21. 7	A9	D2	Hare
10. 9	22. 7	A9	E3	Fox
11. 9	23. 7	A9	F4	Tiger
12. 9	24. 7	A9	G5	Leopard
13. 9	25. 7	A9	H6	Griffon
14. 9	26. 7	A9	J7	Ox
15. 9	27. 7	A9	K8	Bat
16. 9	28. 7	A9	A9	Rat
17. 9	29. 7	A9	B10	Swallow
18. 9	30. 7	A9	C11	Pig
19. 9	1. 8	B10	D12	Porcupine
20. 9	2. 8	B10	E1	Wolf
21. 9	3. 8	B10	F2	Dog
22. 9	4. 8	B10	G3	Pheasant
23. 9	5. 8	B10	H4	Cock
24. 9	6. 8	B10	J5	Crow
25. 9	7. 8	B10	K6	Monkey
26. 9	8. 8	B10	A7	Gibbon
27. 9	9. 8	B10	B8	Tapir
28. 9	10. 8	B10	C9	Sheep
29. 9	11. 8	B10	D10	Deer
30. 9	12. 8	B10	E11	Horse
1.10	13. 8	B10	F12	Stag
2.10	14. 8	B10	G1	Serpent
3.10	15. 8	B10	H2	Earthworm
4.10	16. 8	B10	J3	Crocodile
5.10	17. 8	B10	K4	Dragon
6.10	18. 8	B10	A5	Badger
7.10	19. 8	B10	B6	Hare
8.10	20. 8	B10	C7	Fox
9.10	21. 8	B10	D8	Tiger
10.10	22. 8	B10	E9	Leopard
11.10	23. 8	B10	F10	Griffon
12.10	24. 8	B10	G11	Ox
13.10	25. 8	B10	H12	Bat
14.10	26. 8	B10	J1	Rat
15.10	27. 8	B10	K2	Swallow
16.10	28. 8	B10	A3	Pig
17.10	29. 8	B10	B4	Porcupine
18.10	1. 9	C11	C5	Wolf
19.10	2. 9	C11	D6	Dog
20.10	3. 9	C11	E7	Pheasant
21.10	4. 9	C11	F8	Cock
22.10	5. 9	C11	G9	Crow
23.10	6. 9	C11	H10	Monkey
24.10	7. 9	C11	J11	Gibbon
25.10	8. 9	C11	K12	Tapir
26.10	9. 9	C11	A1	Sheep
27.10	10. 9	C11	B2	Deer
28.10	11. 9	C11	C3	Horse
29.10	12. 9	C11	D4	Stag
30.10	13. 9	C11	E5	Serpent
31.10	14. 9	C11	F6	Earthworm
1.11	15. 9	C11	G7	Crocodile
2.11	16. 9	C11	H8	Dragon
3.11	17. 9	C11	J9	Badger
4.11	18. 9	C11	K10	Hare
5.11	19. 9	C11	A11	Fox
6.11	20. 9	C11	B12	Tiger
7.11	21. 9	C11	C1	Leopard
8.11	22. 9	C11	D2	Griffon
9.11	23. 9	C11	E3	Ox
10.11	24. 9	C11	F4	Bat

Solar date	*Lunar date*	*Month HS/EB*	*Day HS/EB*	*Constellation*
11.11	25. 9	C11	G5	Rat
12.11	26. 9	C11	H6	Swallow
13.11	27. 9	C11	J7	Pig
14.11	28. 9	C11	K8	Porcupine
15.11	29. 9	C11	A9	Wolf
16.11	30. 9	C11	B10	Dog
17.11	1.10	D12	C11	Pheasant
18.11	2.10	D12	D12	Cock
19.11	3.10	D12	E1	Crow
20.11	4.10	D12	F2	Monkey
21.11	5.10	D12	G3	Gibbon
22.11	6.10	D12	H4	Tapir
23.11	7.10	D12	J5	Sheep
24.11	8.10	D12	K6	Deer
25.11	9.10	D12	A7	Horse
26.11	10.10	D12	B8	Stag
27.11	11.10	D12	C9	Serpent
28.11	12.10	D12	D10	Earthworm
29.11	13.10	D12	E11	Crocodile
30.11	14.10	D12	F12	Dragon
1.12	15.10	D12	G1	Badger
2.12	16.10	D12	H2	Hare
3.12	17.10	D12	J3	Fox
4.12	18.10	D12	K4	Tiger
5.12	19.10	D12	A5	Leopard
6.12	20.10	D12	B6	Griffon
7.12	21.10	D12	C7	Ox
8.12	22.10	D12	D8	Bat
9.12	23.10	D12	E9	Rat
10.12	24.10	D12	F10	Swallow
11.12	25.10	D12	G11	Pig
12.12	26.10	D12	H12	Porcupine
13.12	27.10	D12	J1	Wolf
14.12	28.10	D12	K2	Dog
15.12	29.10	D12	A3	Pheasant
16.12	30.10	D12	B4	Cock
17.12	1.11	E1	C5	Crow
18.12	2.11	E1	D6	Monkey
19.12	3.11	E1	E7	Gibbon
20.12	4.11	E1	F8	Tapir
21.12	5.11	E1	G9	Sheep
22.12	6.11	E1	H10	Deer
23.12	7.11	E1	J11	Horse
24.12	8.11	E1	K12	Stag
25.12	9.11	E1	A1	Serpent
26.12	10.11	E1	B2	Earthworm
27.12	11.11	E1	C3	Crocodile
28.12	12.11	E1	D4	Dragon
29.12	13.11	E1	E5	Badger
30.12	14.11	E1	F6	Hare
31.12	15.11	E1	G7	Fox
1991				
1. 1	16.11	E1	H8	Tiger
2. 1	17.11	E1	J9	Leopard
3. 1	18.11	E1	K10	Griffon
4. 1	19.11	E1	A11	Ox
5. 1	20.11	E1	B12	Bat
6. 1	21.11	E1	C1	Rat
7. 1	22.11	E1	D2	Swallow
8. 1	23.11	E1	E3	Pig
9. 1	24.11	E1	F4	Porcupine
10. 1	25.11	E1	G5	Wolf
11. 1	26.11	E1	H6	Dog
12. 1	27.11	E1	J7	Pheasant
13. 1	28.11	E1	K8	Cock
14. 1	29.11	E1	A9	Crow
15. 1	30.11	E1	B10	Monkey
16. 1	1.12	F2	C11	Gibbon
17. 1	2.12	F2	D12	Tapir
18. 1	3.12	F2	E1	Sheep
19. 1	4.12	F2	F2	Deer
20. 1	5.12	F2	G3	Horse
21. 1	6.12	F2	H4	Stag
22. 1	7.12	F2	J5	Serpent
23. 1	8.12	F2	K6	Earthworm
24. 1	9.12	F2	A7	Crocodile
25. 1	10.12	F2	B8	Dragon
26. 1	11.12	F2	C9	Badger
27. 1	12.12	F2	D10	Hare
28. 1	13.12	F2	E11	Fox
29. 1	14.12	F2	F12	Tiger
30. 1	15.12	F2	G1	Leopard
31. 1	16.12	F2	H2	Griffon
1. 2	17.12	F2	J3	Ox
2. 2	18.12	F2	K4	Bat
3. 2	19.12	F2	A5	Rat
4. 2	20.12	F2	B6	Swallow
5. 2	21.12	F2	C7	Pig
6. 2	22.12	F2	D8	Porcupine
7. 2	23.12	F2	E9	Wolf
8. 2	24.12	F2	F10	Dog
9. 2	25.12	F2	G11	Pheasant
10. 2	26.12	F2	H12	Cock
11. 2	27.12	F2	J1	Crow
12. 2	28.12	F2	K2	Monkey
13. 2	29.12	F2	A3	Gibbon
14. 2	30.12	F2	B4	Tapir

HSIN WEI YEAR

15. 2	1. 1	G3	C5	Sheep
16. 2	2. 1	G3	D6	Deer
17. 2	3. 1	G3	E7	Horse
18. 2	4. 1	G3	F8	Stag
19. 2	5. 1	G3	G9	Serpent
20. 2	6. 1	G3	H10	Earthworm
21. 2	7. 1	G3	J11	Crocodile
22. 2	8. 1	G3	K12	Dragon
23. 2	9. 1	G3	A1	Badger
24. 2	10. 1	G3	B2	Hare
25. 2	11. 1	G3	C3	Fox
26. 2	12. 1	G3	D4	Tiger
27. 2	13. 1	G3	E5	Leopard
28. 2	14. 1	G3	F6	Griffon
1. 3	15. 1	G3	G7	Ox
2. 3	16. 1	G3	H8	Bat
3. 3	17. 1	G3	J9	Rat
4. 3	18. 1	G3	K10	Swallow
5. 3	19. 1	G3	A11	Pig
6. 3	20. 1	G3	B12	Porcupine
7. 3	21. 1	G3	C1	Wolf
8. 3	22. 1	G3	D2	Dog
9. 3	23. 1	G3	E3	Pheasant
10. 3	24. 1	G3	F4	Cock
11. 3	25. 1	G3	G5	Crow
12. 3	26. 1	G3	H6	Monkey
13. 3	27. 1	G3	J7	Gibbon
14. 3	28. 1	G3	K8	Tapir
15. 3	29. 1	G3	A9	Sheep
16. 3	1. 2	H4	B10	Deer
17. 3	2. 2	H4	C11	Horse
18. 3	3. 2	H4	D12	Stag
19. 3	4. 2	H4	E1	Serpent
20. 3	5. 2	H4	F2	Earthworm
21. 3	6. 2	H4	G3	Crocodile
22. 3	7. 2	H4	H4	Dragon
23. 3	8. 2	H4	J5	Badger
24. 3	9. 2	H4	K6	Hare

Solar date	*Lunar date*	*Month HS/EB*	*Day HS/EB*	*Constellation*
25. 3	10. 2	H4	A7	Fox
26. 3	11. 2	H4	B8	Tiger
27. 3	12. 2	H4	C9	Leopard
28. 3	13. 2	H4	D10	Griffon
29. 3	14. 2	H4	E11	Ox
30. 3	15. 2	H4	F12	Bat
31. 3	16. 2	H4	G1	Rat
1. 4	17. 2	H4	H2	Swallow
2. 4	18. 2	H4	J3	Pig
3. 4	19. 2	H4	K4	Porcupine
4. 4	20. 2	H4	A5	Wolf
5. 4	21. 2	H4	B6	Dog
6. 4	22. 2	H4	C7	Pheasant
7. 4	23. 2	H4	D8	Cock
8. 4	24. 2	H4	E9	Crow
9. 4	25. 2	H4	F10	Monkey
10. 4	26. 2	H4	G11	Gibbon
11. 4	27. 2	H4	H12	Tapir
12. 4	28. 2	H4	J1	Sheep
13. 4	29. 2	H4	K2	Deer
14. 4	30. 2	H4	A3	Horse
15. 4	1. 3	J5	B4	Stag
16. 4	2. 3	J5	C5	Serpent
17. 4	3. 3	J5	D6	Earthworm
18. 4	4. 3	J5	E7	Crocodile
19. 4	5. 3	J5	F8	Dragon
20. 4	6. 3	J5	G9	Badger
21. 4	7. 3	J5	H10	Hare
22. 4	8. 3	J5	J11	Fox
23. 4	9. 3	J5	K12	Tiger
24. 4	10. 3	J5	A1	Leopard
25. 4	11. 3	J5	B2	Griffon
26. 4	12. 3	J5	C3	Ox
27. 4	13. 3	J5	D4	Bat
28. 4	14. 3	J5	E5	Rat
29. 4	15. 3	J5	F6	Swallow
30. 4	16. 3	J5	G7	Pig
1. 5	17. 3	J5	H8	Porcupine
2. 5	18. 3	J5	J9	Wolf
3. 5	19. 3	J5	K10	Dog
4. 5	20. 3	J5	A11	Pheasant
5. 5	21. 3	J5	B12	Cock
6. 5	22. 3	J5	C1	Crow
7. 5	23. 3	J5	D2	Monkey
8. 5	24. 3	J5	E3	Gibbon
9. 5	25. 3	J5	F4	Tapir
10. 5	26. 3	J5	G5	Sheep
11. 5	27. 3	J5	H6	Deer
12. 5	28. 3	J5	J7	Horse
13. 5	29. 3	J5	K8	Stag
14. 5	1. 4	K6	A9	Serpent
15. 5	2. 4	K6	B10	Earthworm
16. 5	3. 4	K6	C11	Crocodile
17. 5	4. 4	K6	D12	Dragon
18. 5	5. 4	K6	E1	Badger
19. 5	6. 4	K6	F2	Hare
20. 5	7. 4	K6	G3	Fox
21. 5	8. 4	K6	H4	Tiger
22. 5	9. 4	K6	J5	Leopard
23. 5	10. 4	K6	K6	Griffon
24. 5	11. 4	K6	A7	Ox
25. 5	12. 4	K6	B8	Bat
26. 5	13. 4	K6	C9	Rat
27. 5	14. 4	K6	D10	Swallow
28. 5	15. 4	K6	E11	Pig
29. 5	16. 4	K6	F12	Porcupine
30. 5	17. 4	K6	G1	Wolf
31. 5	18. 4	K6	H2	Dog
1. 6	19. 4	K6	J3	Pheasant
2. 6	20. 4	K6	K4	Cock
3. 6	21. 4	K6	A5	Crow
4. 6	22. 4	K6	B6	Monkey
5. 6	23. 4	K6	C7	Gibbon
6. 6	24. 4	K6	D8	Tapir
7. 6	25. 4	K6	E9	Sheep
8. 6	26. 4	K6	F10	Deer
9. 6	27. 4	K6	G11	Horse
10. 6	28. 4	K6	H12	Stag
11. 6	29. 4	K6	J1	Serpent
12. 6	1. 5	A7	K2	Earthworm
13. 6	2. 5	A7	A3	Crocodile
14. 6	3. 5	A7	B4	Dragon
15. 6	4. 5	A7	C5	Badger
16. 6	5. 5	A7	D6	Hare
17. 6	6. 5	A7	E7	Fox
18. 6	7. 5	A7	F8	Tiger
19. 6	8. 5	A7	G9	Leopard
20. 6	9. 5	A7	H10	Griffon
21. 6	10. 5	A7	J11	Ox
22. 6	11. 5	A7	K12	Bat
23. 6	12. 5	A7	A1	Rat
24. 6	13. 5	A7	B2	Swallow
25. 6	14. 5	A7	C3	Pig
26. 6	15. 5	A7	D4	Porcupine
27. 6	16. 5	A7	E5	Wolf
28. 6	17. 5	A7	F6	Dog
29. 6	18. 5	A7	G7	Pheasant
30. 6	19. 5	A7	H8	Cock
1. 7	20. 5	A7	J9	Crow
2. 7	21. 5	A7	K10	Monkey
3. 7	22. 5	A7	A11	Gibbon
4. 7	23. 5	A7	B12	Tapir
5. 7	24. 5	A7	C1	Sheep
6. 7	25. 5	A7	D2	Deer
7. 7	26. 5	A7	E3	Horse
8. 7	27. 5	A7	F4	Stag
9. 7	28. 5	A7	G5	Serpent
10. 7	29. 5	A7	H6	Earthworm
11. 7	30. 5	A7	J7	Crocodile
12. 7	1. 6	B8	K8	Dragon
13. 7	2. 6	B8	A9	Badger
14. 7	3. 6	B8	B10	Hare
15. 7	4. 6	B8	C11	Fox
16. 7	5. 6	B8	D12	Tiger
17. 7	6. 6	B8	E1	Leopard
18. 7	7. 6	B8	F2	Griffon
19. 7	8. 6	B8	G3	Ox
20. 7	9. 6	B8	H4	Bat
21. 7	10. 6	B8	J5	Rat
22. 7	11. 6	B8	K6	Swallow
23. 7	12. 6	B8	A7	Pig
24. 7	13. 6	B8	B8	Porcupine
25. 7	14. 6	B8	C9	Wolf
26. 7	15. 6	B8	D10	Dog
27. 7	16. 6	B8	E11	Pheasant
28. 7	17. 6	B8	F12	Cock
29. 7	18. 6	B8	G1	Crow
30. 7	19. 6	B8	H2	Monkey
31. 7	20. 6	B8	J3	Gibbon
1. 8	21. 6	B8	K4	Tapir
2. 8	22. 6	B8	A5	Sheep
3. 8	23. 6	B8	B6	Deer
4. 8	24. 6	B8	C7	Horse
5. 8	25. 6	B8	D8	Stag
6. 8	26. 6	B8	E9	Serpent
7. 8	27. 6	B8	F10	Earthworm
8. 8	28. 6	B8	G11	Crocodile
9. 8	29. 6	B8	H12	Dragon
10. 8	1. 7	C9	J1	Badger
11. 8	2. 7	C9	K2	Hare
12. 8	3. 7	C9	A3	Fox
13. 8	4. 7	C9	B4	Tiger
14. 8	5. 7	C9	C5	Leopard
15. 8	6. 7	C9	D6	Griffon
16. 8	7. 7	C9	E7	Ox
17. 8	8. 7	C9	F8	Bat

Solar date	*Lunar date*	*Month HS/EB*	*Day HS/EB*	*Constellation*
18. 8	9. 7	C9	G9	Rat
19. 8	10. 7	C9	H10	Swallow
20. 8	11. 7	C9	J11	Pig
21. 8	12. 7	C9	K12	Porcupine
22. 8	13. 7	C9	A1	Wolf
23. 8	14. 7	C9	B2	Dog
24. 8	15. 7	C9	C3	Pheasant
25. 8	16. 7	C9	D4	Cock
26. 8	17. 7	C9	E5	Crow
27. 8	18. 7	C9	F6	Monkey
28. 8	19. 7	C9	G7	Gibbon
29. 8	20. 7	C9	H8	Tapir
30. 8	21. 7	C9	J9	Sheep
31. 8	22. 7	C9	K10	Deer
1. 9	23. 7	C9	A11	Horse
2. 9	24. 7	C9	B12	Stag
3. 9	25. 7	C9	C1	Serpent
4. 9	26. 7	C9	D2	Earthworm
5. 9	27. 7	C9	E3	Crocodile
6. 9	28. 7	C9	F4	Dragon
7. 9	29. 7	C9	G5	Badger
8. 9	1. 8	D10	H6	Hare
9. 9	2. 8	D10	J7	Fox
10. 9	3. 8	D10	K8	Tiger
11. 9	4. 8	D10	A9	Leopard
12. 9	5. 8	D10	B10	Griffon
13. 9	6. 8	D10	C11	Ox
14. 9	7. 8	D10	D12	Bat
15. 9	8. 8	D10	E1	Rat
16. 9	9. 8	D10	F2	Swallow
17. 9	10. 8	D10	G3	Pig
18. 9	11. 8	D10	H4	Porcupine
19. 9	12. 8	D10	J5	Wolf
20. 9	13. 8	D10	K6	Dog
21. 9	14. 8	D10	A7	Pheasant
22. 9	15. 8	D10	B8	Cock
23. 9	16. 8	D10	C9	Crow
24. 9	17. 8	D10	D10	Monkey
25. 9	18. 8	D10	E11	Gibbon
26. 9	19. 8	D10	F12	Tapir
27. 9	20. 8	D10	G1	Sheep
28. 9	21. 8	D10	H2	Deer
29. 9	22. 8	D10	J3	Horse
30. 9	23. 8	D10	K4	Stag
1.10	24. 8	D10	A5	Serpent
2.10	25. 8	D10	B6	Earthworm
3.10	26. 8	D10	C7	Crocodile
4.10	27. 8	D10	D8	Dragon
5.10	28. 8	D10	E9	Badger
6.10	29. 8	D10	F10	Hare
7.10	30. 8	D10	G11	Fox
8.10	1. 9	E11	H12	Tiger
9.10	2. 9	E11	J1	Leopard
10.10	3. 9	E11	K2	Griffon
11.10	4. 9	E11	A3	Ox
12.10	5. 9	E11	B4	Bat
13.10	6. 9	E11	C5	Rat
14.10	7. 9	E11	D6	Swallow
15.10	8. 9	E11	E7	Pig
16.10	9. 9	E11	F8	Porcupine
17.10	10. 9	E11	G9	Wolf
18.10	11. 9	E11	H10	Dog
19.10	12. 9	E11	J11	Pheasant
20.10	13. 9	E11	K12	Cock
21.10	14. 9	E11	A1	Crow
22.10	15. 9	E11	B2	Monkey
23.10	16. 9	E11	C3	Gibbon
24.10	17. 9	E11	D4	Tapir
25.10	18. 9	E11	E5	Sheep
26.10	19. 9	E11	F6	Deer
27.10	20. 9	E11	G7	Horse
28.10	21. 9	E11	H8	Stag
29.10	22. 9	E11	J9	Serpent
30.10	23. 9	E11	K10	Earthworm
31.10	24. 9	E11	A11	Crocodile
1.11	25. 9	E11	B12	Dragon
2.11	26. 9	E11	C1	Badger
3.11	27. 9	E11	D2	Hare
4.11	28. 9	E11	E3	Fox
5.11	29. 9	E11	F4	Tiger
6.11	1.10	F12	G5	Leopard
7.11	2.10	F12	H6	Griffon
8.11	3.10	F12	J7	Ox
9.11	4.10	F12	K8	Bat
10.11	5.10	F12	A9	Rat
11.11	6.10	F12	B10	Swallow
12.11	7.10	F12	C11	Pig
13.11	8. 9	F12	D12	Porcupine
14.11	9. 9	F12	E1	Wolf
15.11	10. 9	F12	F2	Dog
16.11	11. 9	F12	G3	Pheasant
17.11	12. 9	F12	H4	Cock
18.11	13. 9	F12	J5	Crow
19.11	14. 9	F12	K6	Monkey
20.11	15.10	F12	A7	Gibbon
21.11	16.10	F12	B8	Tapir
22.11	17.10	F12	C9	Sheep
23.11	18.10	F12	D10	Deer
24.11	19.10	F12	E11	Horse
25.11	20.10	F12	F12	Stag
26.11	21.10	F12	G1	Serpent
27.11	22.10	F12	H2	Earthworm
28.11	23.10	F12	J3	Crocodile
29.11	24.10	F12	K4	Dragon
30.11	25.10	F12	A5	Badger
1.12	26.10	F12	B6	Hare
2.12	27.10	F12	C7	Fox
3.12	28.10	F12	D8	Tiger
4.12	29.10	F12	E9	Leopard
5.12	30.10	F12	F10	Griffon
6.12	1.10	G1	G11	Ox
7.12	2.10	G1	H12	Bat
8.12	3.10	G1	J1	Rat
9.12	4.10	G1	K2	Swallow
10.12	5.10	G1	A3	Pig
11.12	6.10	G1	B4	Porcupine
12.12	7.10	G1	C5	Wolf
13.12	8.10	G1	D6	Dog
14.12	9.10	G1	E7	Pheasant
15.12	10.10	G1	F8	Cock
16.12	11.10	G1	G9	Crow
17.12	12.10	G1	H10	Monkey
18.12	13.10	G1	J11	Gibbon
19.12	14.10	G1	K12	Tapir
20.12	15.11	G1	A1	Sheep
21.12	16.11	G1	B2	Deer
22.12	17.11	G1	C3	Horse
23.12	18.11	G1	D4	Stag
24.12	19.11	G1	E5	Serpent
25.12	20.11	G1	F6	Earthworm
26.12	21.11	G1	G7	Crocodile
27.12	22.11	G1	H8	Dragon
28.12	23.11	G1	J9	Badger
29.12	24.11	G1	K10	Hare
30.12	25.11	G1	A11	Fox
31.12	26.11	G1	B12	Tiger
1992				
1. 1	27.11	G1	C1	Leopard
2. 1	28.11	G1	D2	Griffon
3. 1	29.11	G1	E3	Ox
4. 1	30.11	G1	F4	Bat
5. 1	1.11	H2	G5	Rat
6. 1	2.11	H2	H6	Swallow
7. 1	3.11	H2	J7	Pig
8. 1	4.11	H2	K8	Porcupine

Solar date	*Lunar date*	*Month HS/EB*	*Day HS/EB*	*Constellation*
9. 1	5.11	H2	A9	Wolf
10. 1	6.11	H2	B10	Dog
11. 1	7.11	H2	C11	Pheasant
12. 1	8.11	H2	D12	Cock
13. 1	9.11	H2	E1	Crow
14. 1	10.11	H2	F2	Monkey
15. 1	11.11	H2	G3	Gibbon
16. 1	12.11	H2	H4	Tapir
17. 1	13.11	H2	J5	Sheep
18. 1	14.12	H2	K6	Deer
19. 1	15.12	H2	A7	Horse
20. 1	16.12	H2	B8	Stag
21. 1	17.12	H2	C9	Serpent
22. 1	18.12	H2	D10	Earthworm
23. 1	19.12	H2	E11	Crocodile
24. 1	20.12	H2	F12	Dragon
25. 1	21.12	H2	G1	Badger
26. 1	22.12	H2	H2	Hare
27. 1	23.12	H2	J3	Fox
28. 1	24.12	H2	K4	Tiger
29. 1	25.12	H2	A5	Leopard
30. 1	26.12	H2	B6	Griffon
31. 1	27.12	H2	C7	Ox
1. 2	28.12	H2	D8	Bat
2. 2	29.12	H2	E9	Rat
3. 2	30.12	H2	F10	Swallow

JEN SHEN YEAR

4. 2	1. 1	J3	G11	Pig
5. 2	2. 1	J3	H12	Porcupine
6. 2	3. 1	J3	J1	Wolf
7. 2	4. 1	J3	K2	Dog
8. 2	5. 1	J3	A3	Pheasant
9. 2	6. 1	J3	B4	Cock
10. 2	7. 1	J3	C5	Crow
11. 2	8. 1	J3	D6	Monkey
12. 2	9. 1	J3	E7	Gibbon
13. 2	10. 1	J3	F8	Tapir
14. 2	11. 1	J3	G9	Sheep
15. 2	12. 1	J3	H10	Deer
16. 2	13. 1	J3	J11	Horse
17. 2	14. 1	J3	K12	Stag
18. 2	15. 1	J3	A1	Serpent
19. 2	16. 1	J3	B2	Earthworm
20. 2	17. 1	J3	C3	Crocodile
21. 2	18. 1	J3	D4	Dragon
22. 2	19. 1	J3	E5	Badger
23. 2	20. 1	J3	F6	Hare
24. 2	21. 1	J3	G7	Fox
25. 2	22. 1	J3	H8	Tiger
26. 2	23. 1	J3	J9	Leopard
27. 2	24. 1	J3	K10	Griffon
28. 2	25. 1	J3	A11	Ox
29. 2	26. 1	J3	B12	Bat
1. 3	27. 1	J3	C1	Rat
2. 3	28. 1	J3	D2	Swallow
3. 3	29. 1	J3	E3	Pig
4. 3	1. 2	K4	F4	Porcupine
5. 3	2. 2	K4	G5	Wolf
6. 3	3. 2	K4	H6	Dog
7. 3	4. 2	K4	J7	Pheasant
8. 3	5. 2	K4	K8	Cock
9. 3	6. 2	K4	A9	Crow
10. 3	7. 2	K4	B10	Monkey
11. 3	8. 2	K4	C11	Gibbon
12. 3	9. 2	K4	D12	Tapir
13. 3	10. 2	K4	E1	Sheep
14. 3	11. 2	K4	F2	Deer
15. 3	12. 2	K4	G3	Horse
16. 3	13. 2	K4	H4	Stag
17. 3	14. 2	K4	J5	Serpent
18. 3	15. 2	K4	K6	Earthworm
19. 3	16. 2	K4	A7	Crocodile
20. 3	17. 2	K4	B8	Dragon
21. 3	18. 2	K4	C9	Badger
22. 3	19. 2	K4	D10	Hare
23. 3	20. 2	K4	E11	Fox
24. 3	21. 2	K4	F12	Tiger
25. 3	22. 2	K4	G1	Leopard
26. 3	23. 2	K4	H2	Griffon
27. 3	24. 2	K4	J3	Ox
28. 3	25. 2	K4	K4	Bat
29. 3	26. 2	K4	A5	Rat
30. 3	27. 2	K4	B6	Swallow
31. 3	28. 2	K4	C7	Pig
1. 4	29. 2	K4	D8	Porcupine
2. 4	30. 2	K4	E9	Wolf
3. 2	1. 3	A5	F10	Dog
4. 4	2. 3	A5	G11	Pheasant
5. 4	3. 3	A5	H12	Cock
6. 4	4. 3	A5	J1	Crow
7. 4	5. 3	A5	K2	Monkey
8. 4	6. 3	A5	A3	Gibbon
9. 4	7. 3	A5	B4	Tapir
10. 4	8. 3	A5	C5	Sheep
11. 4	9. 3	A5	D6	Deer
12. 4	10. 3	A5	E7	Horse
13. 4	11. 3	A5	F8	Stag
14. 4	12. 3	A5	G9	Serpent
15. 4	13. 3	A5	H10	Earthworm
16. 4	14. 3	A5	J11	Crocodile
17. 4	15. 3	A5	K12	Dragon
18. 4	16. 3	A5	A1	Badger
19. 4	17. 3	A5	B2	Hare
20. 4	18. 3	A5	C3	Fox
21. 4	19. 3	A5	D4	Tiger
22. 4	20. 3	A5	E5	Leopard
23. 4	21. 3	A5	F6	Griffon
24. 4	22. 3	A5	G7	Ox
25. 4	23. 3	A5	H8	Bat
26. 4	24. 3	A5	J9	Rat
27. 4	25. 3	A5	K10	Swallow
28. 4	26. 3	A5	A11	Pig
29. 4	27. 3	A5	B12	Porcupine
30. 4	28. 3	A5	C1	Wolf
1. 5	29. 3	A5	D2	Dog
2. 5	30. 3	A5	E3	Pheasant
3. 5	1. 4	B6	F4	Cock
4. 5	2. 4	B6	G5	Crow
5. 5	3. 4	B6	H6	Monkey
6. 5	4. 4	B6	J7	Gibbon
7. 5	5. 4	B6	K8	Tapir
8. 5	6. 4	B6	A9	Sheep
9. 5	7. 4	B6	B10	Deer
10. 5	8. 4	B6	C11	Horse
11. 5	9. 4	B6	D12	Stag
12. 5	10. 4	B6	E1	Serpent
13. 5	11. 4	B6	F2	Earthworm
14. 5	12. 4	B6	G3	Crocodile
15. 5	13. 4	B6	H4	Dragon
16. 5	14. 4	B6	J5	Badger
17. 5	15. 4	B6	K6	Hare
18. 5	16. 4	B6	A7	Fox
19. 5	17. 4	B6	B8	Tiger
20. 5	18. 4	B6	C9	Leopard
21. 5	19. 4	B6	D10	Griffon
22. 5	20. 4	B6	E11	Ox
23. 5	21. 4	B6	F12	Bat

Solar date	*Lunar date*	*Month HS/EB*	*Day HS/EB*	*Constellation*
24. 5	22. 4	B6	G1	Rat
25. 5	23. 4	B6	H2	Swallow
26. 5	24. 4	B6	J3	Pig
27. 5	25. 4	B6	K4	Porcupine
28. 5	26. 4	B6	A5	Wolf
29. 5	27. 4	B6	B6	Dog
30. 5	28. 4	B6	C7	Pheasant
31. 5	29. 4	B6	D8	Cock
1. 6	1. 5	C7	E9	Crow
2. 6	2. 5	C7	F10	Monkey
3. 6	3. 5	C7	G11	Gibbon
4. 6	4. 5	C7	H12	Tapir
5. 6	5. 5	C7	J1	Sheep
6. 6	6. 5	C7	K2	Deer
7. 6	7. 5	C7	A3	Horse
8. 6	8. 5	C7	B4	Stage
9. 6	9. 5	C7	C5	Serpent
10. 6	10. 5	C7	D6	Earthworm
11. 6	11. 5	C7	E7	Crocodile
12. 6	12. 5	C7	F8	Dragon
13. 6	13. 5	C7	G9	Badger
14. 6	14. 5	C7	H10	Hare
15. 6	15. 5	C7	J11	Fox
16. 6	16. 5	C7	K12	Tiger
17. 6	17. 5	C7	A1	Leopard
18. 6	18. 5	C7	B2	Griffon
19. 6	19. 5	C7	C3	Ox
20. 6	20. 5	C7	D4	Bat
21. 6	21. 5	C7	E5	Rat
22. 6	22. 5	C7	F6	Swallow
23. 6	23. 5	C7	G7	Pig
24. 6	24. 5	C7	H8	Porcupine
25. 6	25. 5	C7	J9	Wolf
26. 6	26. 5	C7	K10	Dog
27. 6	27. 5	C7	A11	Pheasant
28. 6	28. 5	C7	B12	Cock
29. 6	29. 5	C7	C1	Crow
30. 6	1. 6	D8	D2	Monkey
1. 7	2. 6	D8	E3	Gibbon
2. 7	3. 6	D8	F4	Tapir
3. 7	4. 6	D8	G5	Sheep
4. 7	5. 6	D8	H6	Deer
5. 7	6. 6	D8	J7	Horse
6. 7	7. 6	D8	K8	Stag
7. 7	8. 6	D8	A9	Serpent
8. 7	9. 6	D8	B10	Earthworm
9. 7	10. 6	D8	C11	Crocodile
10. 7	11. 6	D8	D12	Dragon
11. 7	12. 6	D8	E1	Badger
12. 7	13. 6	D8	F2	Hare
13. 7	14. 6	D8	G3	Fox
14. 7	15. 6	D8	H4	Tiger
15. 7	16. 6	D8	J5	Leopard
16. 7	17. 6	D8	K6	Griffon
17. 7	18. 6	D8	A7	Ox
18. 7	19. 6	D8	B8	Bat
19. 7	20. 6	D8	C9	Rat
20. 7	21. 6	D8	D10	Swallow
21. 7	22. 6	D8	E11	Pig
22. 7	23. 6	D8	F12	Porcupine
23. 7	24. 6	D8	G1	Wolf
24. 7	25. 6	D8	H2	Dog
25. 7	26. 6	D8	J3	Pheasant
26. 7	27. 6	D8	K4	Cock
27. 7	28. 6	D8	A5	Crow
28. 7	29. 6	D8	B6	Monkey
29. 7	30. 6	D8	C7	Gibbon
30. 7	1. 7	E9	D8	Tapir
31. 7	2. 7	E9	E9	Sheep
1. 8	3. 7	E9	F10	Deer
2. 8	4. 7	E9	G11	Horse
3. 8	5. 7	E9	H12	Stag
4. 8	6. 7	E9	J1	Serpent
5. 8	7. 7	E9	K2	Earthworm
6. 8	8. 7	E9	A3	Crocodile
7. 8	9. 7	E9	B4	Dragon
8. 8	10. 7	E9	C5	Badger
9. 8	11. 7	E9	D6	Hare
10. 8	12. 7	E9	E7	Fox
11. 8	13. 7	E9	F8	Tiger
12. 8	14. 7	E9	G9	Leopard
13. 8	15. 7	E9	H10	Griffon
14. 8	16. 7	E9	J11	Ox
15. 8	17. 7	E9	K12	Bat
16. 8	18. 7	E9	A1	Rat
17. 8	19. 7	E9	B2	Swallow
18. 8	20. 7	E9	C3	Pig
19. 8	21. 7	E9	D4	Porcupine
20. 8	22. 7	E9	E5	Wolf
21. 8	23. 7	E9	F6	Dog
22. 8	24. 7	E9	G7	Pheasant
23. 8	25. 7	E9	H8	Cock
24. 8	26. 7	E9	J9	Crow
25. 8	27. 7	E9	K10	Monkey
26. 8	28. 7	E9	A11	Gibbon
27. 8	29. 7	E9	B12	Tapir
28. 8	1. 8	F10	C1	Sheep
29. 8	2. 8	F10	D2	Deer
30. 8	3. 8	F10	E3	Horse
31. 8	4. 8	F10	F4	Stag
1. 9	5. 8	F10	G5	Serpent
2. 9	6. 8	F10	H6	Earthworm
3. 9	7. 8	F10	J7	Crocodile
4. 9	8. 8	F10	K8	Dragon
5. 9	9. 8	F10	A9	Badger
6. 9	10. 8	F10	B10	Hare
7. 9	11. 8	F10	C11	Fox
8. 9	12. 8	F10	D12	Tiger
9. 9	13. 8	F10	E1	Leopard
10. 9	14. 8	F10	F2	Griffon
11. 9	15. 8	F10	G3	Ox
12. 9	16. 8	F10	H4	Bat
13. 9	17. 8	F10	J5	Rat
14. 9	18. 8	F10	K6	Swallow
15. 9	19. 8	F10	A7	Pig
16. 9	20. 8	F10	B8	Porcupine
17. 9	21. 8	F10	C9	Wolf
18. 9	22. 8	F10	D10	Dog
19. 9	23. 8	F10	E11	Pheasant
20. 9	24. 8	F10	F12	Cock
21. 9	25. 8	F10	G1	Crow
22. 9	26. 8	F10	H2	Monkey
23. 9	27. 8	F10	J3	Gibbon
24. 9	28. 8	F10	K4	Tapir
25. 9	29. 8	F10	A5	Sheep
26. 9	1. 9	G11	B6	Deer
27. 9	2. 9	G11	C7	Horse
28. 9	3. 9	G11	D8	Stag
29. 9	4. 9	G11	E9	Serpent
30. 9	5. 9	G11	F10	Earthworm
1.10	6. 9	G11	G11	Crocodile
2.10	7. 9	G11	H12	Dragon
3.10	8. 9	G11	J1	Badger
4.10	9. 9	G11	K2	Hare
5.10	10. 9	G11	A3	Fox
6.10	11. 9	G11	B4	Tiger
7.10	12. 9	G11	C5	Leopard
8.10	13. 9	G11	D6	Griffon
9.10	14. 9	G11	E7	Ox
10.10	15. 9	G11	F8	Bat
11.10	16. 9	G11	G9	Rat
12.10	17. 9	G11	H10	Swallow
13.10	18. 9	G11	J11	Pig
14.10	19. 9	G11	K12	Porcupine
15.10	20. 9	G11	A1	Wolf
16.10	21. 9	G11	B2	Dog

Solar date	Lunar date	Month HS/EB	Day HS/EB	Constellation
17.10	22. 9	G11	C3	Pheasant
18.10	23. 9	G11	D4	Cock
19.10	24. 9	G11	E5	Crow
20.10	25. 9	G11	F6	Monkey
21.10	26. 9	G11	G7	Gibbon
22.10	27. 9	G11	H8	Tapir
23.10	28. 9	G11	J9	Sheep
24.10	29. 9	G11	K10	Deer
25.10	30. 9	G11	A11	Horse
26.10	1.10	H12	B12	Stag
27.10	2.10	H12	C1	Serpent
28.10	3.10	H12	D2	Earthworm
29.10	4.10	H12	E3	Crocodile
30.10	5.10	H12	F4	Dragon
31.10	6.10	H12	G5	Badger
1.11	7.10	H12	H6	Hare
2.11	8.10	H12	J7	Fox
3.11	9.10	H12	K8	Tiger
4.11	10.10	H12	A9	Leopard
5.11	11.10	H12	B10	Griffon
6.11	12.10	H12	C11	Ox
7.11	13.10	H12	D12	Bat
8.11	14.10	H12	E1	Rat
9.11	15.10	H12	F2	Swallow
10.11	16.10	H12	G3	Pig
11.11	17.10	H12	H4	Porcupine
12.11	18.10	H12	J5	Wolf
13.11	19.10	H12	K6	Dog
14.11	20.10	H12	A7	Pheasant
15.11	21.10	H12	B8	Cock
16.11	22.10	H12	C9	Crow
17.11	23.10	H12	D10	Monkey
18.11	24.10	H12	E11	Gibbon
19.11	25.10	H12	F12	Tapir
20.11	26.10	H12	G1	Sheep
21.11	27.10	H12	H2	Deer
22.11	28.10	H12	J3	Horse
23.11	29.10	H12	K4	Stag
24.11	1.11	J1	A5	Serpent
25.11	2.11	J1	B6	Earthworm
26.11	3.11	J1	C7	Crocodile
27.11	4.11	J1	D8	Dragon
28.11	5.11	J1	E9	Badger
29.11	6.11	J1	F10	Hare
30.11	7.11	J1	G11	Fox
1.12	8.11	J1	H12	Tiger
2.12	9.11	J1	J1	Leopard
3.12	10.11	J1	K2	Griffon
4.12	11.11	J1	A3	Ox
5.12	12.11	J1	B4	Bat
6.12	13.11	J1	C5	Rat
7.12	14.11	J1	D6	Swallow
8.12	15.11	J1	E7	Pig
9.12	16.11	J1	F8	Porcupine
10.12	17.11	J1	G9	Wolf
11.12	18.11	J1	H10	Dog
12.12	19.11	J1	J11	Pheasant
13.12	20.11	J1	K12	Cock
14.12	21.11	J1	A1	Crow
15.12	22.11	J1	B2	Monkey
16.12	23.11	J1	C3	Gibbon
17.12	24.11	J1	D4	Tapir
18.12	25.11	J1	E5	Sheep
19.12	26.11	J1	F6	Deer
20.12	27.11	J1	G7	Horse
21.12	28.11	J1	H8	Stag
22.12	29.11	J1	J9	Serpent
23.12	30.11	J1	K10	Earthworm
24.12	1.12	K2	A1	Crocodile
25.12	2.12	K2	B12	Dragon
26.12	3.12	K2	C1	Badger
27.12	4.12	K2	D2	Hare
28.12	5.12	K2	E3	Fox
29.12	6.12	K2	F4	Tiger
30.12	7.12	K2	G5	Leopard
31.12	8.12	K2	H6	Griffon
1993				
1. 1	9.12	K2	J7	Ox
2. 1	10.12	K2	K8	Bat
3. 1	11.12	K2	A9	Rat
4. 1	12.12	K2	B10	Swallow
5. 1	13.12	K2	C11	Pig
6. 1	14.12	K2	D12	Porcupine
7. 1	15.12	K2	E1	Wolf
8. 1	16.12	K2	F2	Dog
9. 1	17.12	K2	G3	Pheasant
10. 1	18.12	K2	H4	Cock
11. 1	19.12	K2	J5	Crow
12. 1	20.12	K2	K6	Monkey
13. 1	21.12	K2	A7	Gibbon
14. 1	22.12	K2	B8	Tapir
15. 1	23.12	K2	C9	Sheep
16. 1	24.12	K2	D10	Deer
17. 1	25.12	K2	E11	Horse
18. 1	26.12	K2	F12	Stag
19. 1	27.12	K2	G1	Serpent
20. 1	28.12	K2	H2	Earthworm
21. 1	29.12	K2	J3	Crocodile
22. 1	30.12	K2	K4	Dragon

KUEI YU YEAR

23. 1	1. 1	A3	A5	Badger
24. 1	2. 1	A3	B6	Hare
25. 1	3. 1	A3	C7	Fox
26. 1	4. 1	A3	D8	Tiger
27. 1	5. 1	A3	E9	Leopard
28. 1	6. 1	A3	F10	Griffon
29. 1	7. 1	A3	G11	Ox
30. 1	8. 1	A3	H12	Bat
31. 1	9. 1	A3	J1	Rat
1. 2	10. 1	A3	K2	Swallow
2. 2	11. 1	A3	A3	Pig
3. 2	12. 1	A3	B4	Porcupine
4. 2	13. 1	A3	C5	Wolf
5. 2	14. 1	A3	D6	Dog
6. 2	15. 1	A3	E7	Pheasant
7. 2	16. 1	A3	F8	Cock
8. 2	17. 1	A3	G9	Crow
9. 2	18. 1	A3	H10	Monkey
10. 2	19. 1	A3	J11	Gibbon
11. 2	20. 1	A3	K12	Tapir
12. 2	21. 1	A3	A1	Sheep
13. 2	22. 1	A3	B2	Deer
14. 2	23. 1	A3	C3	Horse
15. 2	24. 1	A3	D4	Stag
16. 2	25. 1	A3	E5	Serpent
17. 2	26. 1	A3	F6	Earthworm
18. 2	27. 1	A3	G7	Crocodile
19. 2	28. 1	A3	H8	Dragon
20. 2	29. 1	A3	J9	Badger
21. 2	1. 2	B4	K10	Hare
22. 2	2. 2	B4	A11	Fox
23. 2	3. 2	B4	B12	Tiger
24. 2	4. 2	B4	C1	Leopard
25. 2	5. 2	B4	D2	Griffon
26. 2	6. 2	B4	E3	Ox
27. 2	7. 2	B4	F4	Bat

Solar date	Lunar date	Month HS/EB	Day HS/EB	Constellation
28. 2	8. 2	B4	G5	Rat
1. 3	9. 2	B4	H6	Swallow
2. 3	10. 2	B4	J7	Pig
3. 3	11. 2	B4	K8	Porcupine
4. 3	12. 2	B4	A9	Wolf
5. 3	13. 2	B4	B10	Dog
6. 3	14. 2	B4	C11	Pheasant
7. 3	15. 2	B4	D12	Cock
8. 3	16. 2	B4	E1	Crow
9. 3	17. 2	B4	F2	Monkey
10. 3	18. 2	B4	G3	Gibbon
11. 3	19. 2	B4	H4	Tapir
12. 3	20. 2	B4	J5	Sheep
13. 3	21. 2	B4	K6	Deer
14. 3	22. 2	B4	A7	Horse
15. 3	23. 2	B4	B8	Stag
16. 3	24. 2	B4	C9	Serpent
17. 3	25. 2	B4	D10	Earthworm
18. 3	26. 2	B4	E11	Crocodile
19. 3	27. 2	B4	F12	Dragon
20. 3	28. 2	B4	G1	Badger
21. 3	29. 2	B4	H2	Hare
22. 3	30. 2	B4	J3	Fox
23. 3	1. 3	C5	K4	Tiger
24. 3	2. 3	C5	A5	Leopard
25. 3	3. 3	C5	B6	Griffon
26. 3	4. 3	C5	C7	Ox
27. 3	5. 3	C5	D8	Bat
28. 3	6. 3	C5	E9	Rat
29. 3	7. 3	C5	F10	Swallow
30. 3	8. 3	C5	G11	Pig
31. 3	9. 3	C5	H12	Porcupine
1. 4	10. 3	C5	J1	Wolf
2. 4	11. 3	C5	K2	Dog
3. 4	12. 3	C5	A3	Pheasant
4. 4	13. 3	C5	B4	Cock
5. 4	14. 3	C5	C5	Crow
6. 4	15. 3	C5	D6	Monkey
7. 4	16. 3	C5	E7	Gibbon
8. 4	17. 3	C5	F8	Tapir
9. 4	18. 3	C5	G9	Sheep
10. 4	19. 3	C5	H10	Deer
11. 4	20. 3	C5	J11	Horse
12. 4	21. 3	C5	K12	Stag
13. 4	22. 3	C5	A1	Serpent
14. 4	23. 3	C5	B2	Earthworm
15. 4	24. 3	C5	C3	Crocodile
16. 4	25. 3	C5	D4	Dragon
17. 4	26. 3	C5	E5	Badger
18. 4	27. 3	C5	F6	Hare
19. 4	28. 3	C5	G7	Fox
20. 4	29. 3	C5	H8	Tiger
21. 4	30. 3	C5	J9	Leopard
22. 4	*1. 3*	*C5*	K10	Griffon
23. 4	*2. 3*	*C5*	A11	Ox
24. 4	*3. 3*	*C5*	B12	Bat
25. 4	*4. 3*	*C5*	C1	Rat
26. 4	*5. 3*	*C5*	D2	Swallow
27. 4	*6. 3*	*C5*	E3	Pig
28. 4	*7. 3*	*C5*	F4	Porcupine
29. 4	*8. 3*	*C5*	G5	Wolf
30. 4	*9. 3*	*C5*	H6	Dog
1. 5	*10. 3*	*C5*	J7	Pheasant
2. 5	*11. 3*	*C5*	K8	Cock
3. 5	*12. 3*	*C5*	A9	Crow
4. 5	*13. 3*	*C5*	B10	Monkey
5. 5	*14. 3*	*C5*	C11	Gibbon
6. 5	*15. 3*	*C5*	D12	Tapir
7. 5	*16. 3*	*C5*	E1	Sheep
8. 5	*17. 3*	*C5*	F2	Deer
9. 5	*18. 3*	*C5*	G3	Horse
10. 5	*19. 3*	*C5*	H4	Stag
11. 5	*20. 3*	*C5*	J5	Serpent
12. 5	*21. 3*	*C5*	K6	Earthworm
13. 5	*22. 3*	*C5*	A7	Crocodile
14. 5	*23. 3*	*C5*	B8	Dragon
15. 5	*24. 3*	*C5*	C9	Badger
16. 5	*25. 3*	*C5*	D10	Hare
17. 5	*26. 3*	*C5*	E11	Fox
18. 5	*27. 3*	*C5*	F12	Tiger
19. 5	*28. 3*	*C5*	G1	Leopard
20. 5	*29. 3*	*C5*	H2	Griffon
21. 5	1. 4	D6	J3	Ox
22. 5	2. 4	D6	K4	Bat
23. 5	3. 4	D6	A5	Rat
24. 5	4. 4	D6	B6	Swallow
25. 5	5. 4	D6	C7	Pig
26. 5	6. 4	D6	D8	Porcupine
27. 5	7. 4	D6	E9	Wolf
28. 5	8. 4	D6	F10	Dog
29. 5	9. 4	D6	G11	Pheasant
30. 5	10. 4	D6	H12	Cock
31. 5	11. 4	D6	J1	Crow
1. 6	12. 4	D6	K2	Monkey
2. 6	13. 4	D6	A3	Gibbon
3. 6	14. 4	D6	B4	Tapir
4. 6	15. 4	D6	C5	Sheep
5. 6	16. 4	D6	D6	Deer
6. 6	17. 4	D6	E7	Horse
7. 6	18. 4	D6	F8	Stag
8. 6	19. 4	D6	G9	Serpent
9. 6	20. 4	D6	H10	Earthworm
10. 6	21. 4	D6	J11	Crocodile
11. 6	22. 4	D6	K12	Dragon
12. 6	23. 4	D6	A1	Badger
13. 6	24. 4	D6	B2	Hare
14. 6	25. 4	D6	C3	Fox
15. 6	26. 4	D6	D4	Tiger
16. 6	27. 4	D6	E5	Leopard
17. 6	28. 4	D6	F6	Griffon
18. 6	29. 4	D6	G7	Ox
19. 6	30. 4	D6	H8	Bat
20. 6	1. 5	E7	J9	Rat
21. 6	2. 5	E7	K10	Swallow
22. 6	3. 5	E7	A11	Pig
23. 6	4. 5	E7	B12	Porcupine
24. 6	5. 5	E7	C1	Wolf
25. 6	6. 5	E7	D2	Dog
26. 6	7. 5	E7	E3	Pheasant
27. 6	8. 5	E7	F4	Cock
28. 6	9. 5	E7	G5	Crow
29. 6	10. 5	E7	H6	Monkey
30. 6	11. 5	E7	J7	Gibbon
1. 7	12. 5	E7	K8	Tapir
2. 7	13. 5	E7	A9	Sheep
3. 7	14. 5	E7	B10	Deer
4. 7	15. 5	E7	C11	Horse
5. 7	16. 5	E7	D12	Stag
6. 7	17. 5	E7	E1	Serpent
7. 7	18. 5	E7	F2	Earthworm
8. 7	19. 5	E7	G3	Crocodile
9. 7	20. 5	E7	H4	Dragon
10. 7	21. 5	E7	J5	Badger
11. 7	22. 5	E7	K6	Hare
12. 7	23. 5	E7	A7	Fox
13. 7	24. 5	E7	B8	Tiger
14. 7	25. 5	E7	C9	Leopard
15. 7	26. 5	E7	D10	Griffon
16. 7	27. 5	E7	E11	Ox
17. 7	28. 5	E7	F12	Bat
18. 7	29. 5	E7	G1	Rat
19. 7	1. 6	F8	H2	Swallow
20. 7	2. 6	F8	J3	Pig
21. 7	3. 6	F8	K4	Porcupine
22. 7	4. 6	F8	A5	Wolf
23. 7	5. 6	F8	B6	Dog

Solar date	*Lunar date*	*Month HS/EB*	*Day HS/EB*	*Constellation*
24. 7	6. 6	F8	C7	Pheasant
25. 7	7. 6	F8	D8	Cock
26. 7	8. 6	F8	E9	Crow
27. 7	9. 6	F8	F10	Monkey
28. 7	10. 6	F8	G11	Gibbon
29. 7	11. 6	F8	H12	Tapir
30. 7	12. 6	F8	J1	Sheep
31. 7	13. 6	F8	K2	Deer
1. 8	14. 6	F8	A3	Horse
2. 8	15. 6	F8	B4	Stag
3. 8	16. 6	F8	C5	Serpent
4. 8	17. 6	F8	D6	Earthworm
5. 8	18. 6	F8	E7	Crocodile
6. 8	19. 6	F8	F8	Dragon
7. 8	20. 6	F8	G9	Badger
8. 8	21. 6	F8	H10	Hare
9. 8	22. 6	F8	J11	Fox
10. 8	23. 6	F8	K12	Tiger
11. 8	24. 6	F8	A1	Leopard
12. 8	25. 6	F8	B2	Griffon
13. 8	26. 6	F8	C3	Ox
14. 8	27. 6	F8	D4	Bat
15. 8	28. 6	F8	E5	Rat
16. 8	29. 6	F8	F6	Swallow
17. 8	30. 6	F8	G7	Pig
18. 8	1. 7	G9	H8	Porcupine
19. 8	2. 7	G9	J9	Wolf
20. 8	3. 7	G9	K10	Dog
21. 8	4. 7	G9	A11	Pheasant
22. 8	5. 7	G9	B12	Cock
23. 8	6. 7	G9	C1	Crow
24. 8	7. 7	G9	D2	Monkey
25. 8	8. 7	G9	E3	Gibbon
26. 8	9. 7	G9	F4	Tapir
27. 8	10. 7	G9	G5	Sheep
28. 8	11. 7	G9	H6	Deer
29. 8	12. 7	G9	J7	Horse
30. 8	13. 7	G9	K8	Stag
31. 8	14. 7	G9	A9	Serpent
1. 9	15. 7	G9	B10	Earthworm
2. 9	16. 7	G9	C11	Crocodile
3. 9	17. 7	G9	D12	Dragon
4. 9	18. 7	G9	E1	Badger
5. 9	19. 7	G9	F2	Hare
6. 9	20. 7	G9	G3	Fox
7. 9	21. 7	G9	H4	Tiger
8. 9	22. 7	G9	J5	Leopard
9. 9	23. 7	G9	K6	Griffon
10. 9	24. 7	G9	A7	Ox
11. 9	25. 7	G9	B8	Bat
12. 9	26. 7	G9	C9	Rat
13. 9	27. 7	G9	D10	Swallow
14. 9	28. 7	G9	E11	Pig
15. 9	29. 7	G9	F12	Porcupine
16. 9	1. 8	H10	G1	Wolf
17. 9	2. 8	H10	H2	Dog
18. 9	3. 8	H10	J3	Pheasant
19. 9	4. 8	H10	K4	Cock
20. 9	5. 8	H10	A5	Crow
21. 9	6. 8	H10	B6	Monkey
22. 9	7. 8	H10	C7	Gibbon
23. 9	8. 8	H10	D8	Tapir
24. 9	9. 8	H10	E9	Sheep
25. 9	10. 8	H10	F10	Deer
26. 9	11. 8	H10	G11	Horse
27. 9	12. 8	H10	H12	Stag
28. 9	13. 8	H10	J1	Serpent
29. 9	14. 8	H10	K2	Earthworm
30. 9	15. 8	H10	A3	Crocodile
1.10	16. 8	H10	B4	Dragon
2.10	17. 8	H10	C5	Badger
3.10	18. 8	H10	D6	Hare
4.10	19. 8	H10	E7	Fox

Solar date	*Lunar date*	*Month HS/EB*	*Day HS/EB*	*Constellation*
5.10	20. 8	H10	F8	Tiger
6.10	21. 8	H10	G9	Leopard
7.10	22. 8	H10	H10	Griffon
8.10	23. 8	H10	J11	Ox
9.10	24. 8	H10	K12	Bat
10.10	25. 8	H10	A1	Rat
11.10	26. 8	H10	B2	Swallow
12.10	27. 8	H10	C3	Pig
13.10	28. 8	H10	D4	Porcupine
14.10	29. 8	H10	E5	Wolf
15.10	1. 9	J11	F6	Dog
16.10	2. 9	J11	G7	Pheasant
17.10	3. 9	J11	H8	Cock
18.10	4. 9	J11	J9	Crow
19.10	5. 9	J11	K10	Monkey
20.10	6. 9	J11	A11	Gibbon
21.10	7. 9	J11	B12	Tapir
22.10	8. 9	J11	C1	Sheep
23.10	9. 9	J11	D2	Deer
24.10	10. 9	J11	E3	Horse
25.10	11. 9	J11	F4	Stag
26.10	12. 9	J11	G5	Serpent
27.10	13. 9	J11	H6	Earthworm
28.10	14. 9	J11	J7	Crocodile
29.10	15. 9	J11	K8	Dragon
30.10	16. 9	J11	A9	Badger
31.10	17. 9	J11	B10	Hare
1.11	18. 9	J11	C11	Fox
2.11	19. 9	J11	D12	Tiger
3.11	20. 9	J11	E1	Leopard
4.11	21. 9	J11	F2	Griffon
5.11	22. 9	J11	G3	Ox
6.11	23. 9	J11	H4	Bat
7.11	24. 9	J11	J5	Rat
8.11	25. 9	J11	K6	Swallow
9.11	26. 9	J11	A7	Pig
10.11	27. 9	J11	B8	Porcupine
11.11	28. 9	J11	C9	Wolf
12.11	29. 9	J11	D10	Dog
13.11	30. 9	J11	E11	Pheasant
14.11	1.10	K12	F12	Cock
15.11	2.10	K12	G1	Crow
16.11	3.10	K12	H2	Monkey
17.11	4.10	K12	J3	Gibbon
18.11	5.10	K12	K4	Tapir
19.11	6.10	K12	A5	Sheep
20.11	7.10	K12	B6	Deer
21.11	8.10	K12	C7	Horse
22.11	9.10	K12	D8	Stag
23.11	10.10	K12	E9	Serpent
24.11	11.10	K12	F10	Earthworm
25.11	12.10	K12	G11	Crocodile
26.11	13.10	K12	H12	Dragon
27.11	14.10	K12	J1	Badger
28.11	15.10	K12	K2	Hare
29.11	16.10	K12	A3	Fox
30.11	17.10	K12	B4	Tiger
1.12	18.10	K12	C5	Leopard
2.12	19.10	K12	D6	Griffon
3.12	20.10	K12	E7	Ox
4.12	21.10	K12	F8	Bat
5.12	22.10	K12	G9	Rat
6.12	23.10	K12	H10	Swallow
7.12	24.10	K12	J11	Pig
8.12	25.10	K12	K12	Porcupine
9.12	26.10	K12	A1	Wolf
10.12	27.10	K12	B2	Dog
11.12	28.10	K12	C3	Pheasant
12.12	29.10	K12	D4	Cock
13.12	1.11	A1	E5	Crow
14.12	2.11	A1	F6	Monkey
15.12	3.11	A1	G7	Gibbon
16.12	4.11	A1	H8	Tapir

Solar date	*Lunar date*	*Month HS/EB*	*Day HS/EB*	*Constellation*
17.12	5.11	A1	J9	Sheep
18.12	6.11	A1	K10	Deer
19.12	7.11	A1	A11	Horse
20.12	8.11	A1	B12	Stag
21.12	9.11	A1	C1	Serpent
22.12	10.11	A1	D2	Earthworm
23.12	11.11	A1	E3	Crocodile
24.12	12.11	A1	F4	Dragon
25.12	13.11	A1	G5	Badger
26.12	14.11	A1	H6	Hare
27.12	15.11	A1	J7	Fox
28.12	16.11	A1	K8	Tiger
29.12	17.11	A1	A9	Leopard
30.12	18.11	A1	B10	Griffon
31.12	19.11	A1	C11	Ox
1994				
1. 1	20.11	A1	D12	Bat
2. 1	21.11	A1	E1	Rat
3. 1	22.11	A1	F2	Swallow
4. 1	23.11	A1	G3	Pig
5. 1	24.11	A1	H4	Porcupine
6. 1	25.11	A1	J5	Wolf
7. 1	26.11	A1	K6	Dog
8. 1	27.11	A1	A7	Pheasant
9. 1	28.11	A1	B8	Cock
10. 1	29.11	A1	C9	Crow
11. 1	30.11	A1	D10	Monkey

Solar date	*Lunar date*	*Month HS/EB*	*Day HS/EB*	*Constellation*
12. 1	1.12	B2	E11	Gibbon
13. 1	2.12	B2	F12	Tapir
14. 1	3.12	B2	G1	Sheep
15. 1	4.12	B2	H2	Deer
16. 1	5.12	B2	J3	Horse
17. 1	6.12	B2	K4	Stag
18. 1	7.12	B2	A5	Serpent
19. 1	8.12	B2	B6	Earthworm
20. 1	9.12	B2	C7	Crocodile
21. 1	10.12	B2	D8	Dragon
22. 1	11.12	B2	E9	Badger
23. 1	12.12	B2	F10	Hare
24. 1	13.12	B2	G11	Fox
25. 1	14.12	B2	H12	Tiger
26. 1	15.12	B2	J1	Leopard
27. 1	16.12	B2	K2	Griffon
28. 1	17.12	B2	A3	Ox
29. 1	18.12	B2	B4	Bat
30. 1	19.12	B2	C5	Rat
31. 1	20.12	B2	D6	Swallow
1. 2	21.12	B2	E7	Pig
2. 2	22.12	B2	F8	Porcupine
3. 2	23.12	B2	G9	Wolf
4. 2	24.12	B2	H10	Dog
5. 2	25.12	B2	J11	Pheasant
6. 2	26.12	B2	K12	Cock
7. 2	27.12	B2	A1	Crow
8. 2	28.12	B2	B2	Monkey
9. 2	29.12	B2	C3	Gibbon

CHIA HSÜ YEAR

10. 2	1. 1	C3	D4	Tapir
11. 2	2. 1	C3	E5	Sheep
12. 2	3. 1	C3	F6	Deer
13. 2	4. 1	C3	G7	Horse
14. 2	5. 1	C3	H8	Stag
15. 2	6. 1	C3	J9	Serpent
16. 2	7. 1	C3	K10	Earthworm
17. 2	8. 1	C3	A11	Crocodile
18. 2	9. 1	C3	B12	Dragon
19. 2	10. 1	C3	C1	Badger
20. 2	11. 1	C3	D2	Hare
21. 2	12. 1	C3	E3	Fox
22. 2	13. 1	C3	F4	Tiger
23. 2	14. 1	C3	G5	Leopard
24. 2	15. 1	C3	H6	Griffon
25. 2	16. 1	C3	J7	Ox
26. 2	17. 1	C3	K8	Bat
27. 2	18. 1	C3	A9	Rat
28. 2	19. 1	C3	B10	Swallow
1. 3	20. 1	C3	C11	Pig
2. 3	21. 1	C3	D12	Porcupine
3. 3	22. 1	C3	E1	Wolf
4. 3	23. 1	C3	F2	Dog
5. 3	24. 1	C3	G3	Pheasant
6. 3	25. 1	C3	H4	Cock
7. 3	26. 1	C3	J5	Crow
8. 3	27. 1	C3	K6	Monkey
9. 3	28. 1	C3	A7	Gibbon
10. 3	29. 1	C3	B8	Tapir
11. 3	30. 1	C3	C9	Sheep
12. 3	1. 2	D4	D10	Deer
13. 3	2. 2	D4	E11	Horse
14. 3	3. 2	D4	F12	Stag
15. 3	4. 2	D4	G1	Serpent
16. 3	5. 2	D4	H2	Earthworm
17. 3	6. 2	D4	J3	Crocodile
18. 3	7. 2	D4	K4	Dragon
19. 3	8. 2	D4	A5	Badger
20. 3	9. 2	D4	B6	Hare

21. 3	10. 2	D4	C7	Fox
22. 3	11. 2	D4	D8	Tiger
23. 3	12. 2	D4	E9	Leopard
24. 3	13. 2	D4	F10	Griffon
25. 3	14. 2	D4	G11	Ox
26. 3	15. 2	D4	H12	Bat
27. 3	16. 2	D4	J1	Rat
28. 3	17. 2	D4	K2	Swallow
29. 3	18. 2	D4	A3	Pig
30. 3	19. 2	D4	B4	Porcupine
31. 3	20. 2	D4	C5	Wolf
1. 4	21. 2	D4	D6	Dog
2. 4	22. 2	D4	E7	Pheasant
3. 4	23. 2	D4	F8	Cock
4. 4	24. 2	D4	G9	Crow
5. 4	25. 2	D4	H10	Monkey
6. 4	26. 2	D4	J11	Gibbon
7. 4	27. 2	D4	K12	Tapir
8. 4	28. 2	D4	A1	Sheep
9. 4	29. 2	D4	B2	Deer
10. 4	30. 2	D4	C3	Horse
11. 4	1. 3	E5	D4	Stag
12. 4	2. 3	E5	E5	Serpent
13. 4	3. 3	E5	F6	Earthworm
14. 4	4. 3	E5	G7	Crocodile
15. 4	5. 3	E5	H8	Dragon
16. 4	6. 3	E5	J9	Badger
17. 4	7. 3	E5	K10	Hare
18. 4	8. 3	E5	A11	Fox
19. 4	9. 3	E5	B12	Tiger
20. 4	10. 3	E5	C1	Leopard
21. 4	11. 3	E5	D2	Griffon
22. 4	12. 3	E5	E3	Ox
23. 4	13. 3	E5	F4	Bat
24. 4	14. 3	E5	G5	Rat
25. 4	15. 3	E5	H6	Swallow
26. 4	16. 3	E5	J7	Pig
27. 4	17. 3	E5	K8	Porcupine
28. 4	18. 3	E5	A9	Wolf

Solar date	*Lunar date*	*Month HS/EB*	*Day HS/EB*	*Constellation*
29. 4	19. 3	E5	B10	Dog
30. 4	20. 3	E5	C11	Pheasant
1. 5	21. 3	E5	D12	Cock
2. 5	22. 3	E5	E1	Crow
3. 5	23. 3	E5	F2	Monkey
4. 5	24. 3	E5	G3	Gibbon
5. 5	25. 3	E5	H4	Tapir
6. 5	26. 3	E5	J5	Sheep
7. 5	27. 3	E5	K6	Deer
8. 5	28. 3	E5	A7	Horse
9. 5	29. 3	E5	B8	Stag
10. 5	30. 3	E5	C9	Serpent
11. 5	1. 4	F6	D10	Earthworm
12. 5	2. 4	F6	E11	Crocodile
13. 5	3. 4	F6	F12	Dragon
14. 5	4. 4	F6	G1	Badger
15. 5	5. 4	F6	H2	Hare
16. 5	6. 4	F6	J3	Fox
17. 5	7. 4	F6	K4	Tiger
18. 5	8. 4	F6	A5	Leopard
19. 5	9. 4	F6	B6	Griffon
20. 5	10. 4	F6	C7	Ox
21. 5	11. 4	F6	D8	Bat
22. 5	12. 4	F6	E9	Rat
23. 5	13. 4	F6	F10	Swallow
24. 5	14. 4	F6	G11	Pig
25. 5	15. 4	F6	H12	Porcupine
26. 5	16. 4	F6	J1	Wolf
27. 5	17. 4	F6	K2	Dog
28. 5	18. 4	F6	A3	Pheasant
29. 5	19. 4	F6	B4	Cock
30. 5	20. 4	F6	C5	Crow
31. 5	21. 4	F6	D6	Monkey
1. 6	22. 4	F6	E7	Gibbon
2. 6	23. 4	F6	F8	Tapir
3. 6	24. 4	F6	G9	Sheep
4. 6	25. 4	F6	H10	Deer
5. 6	26. 4	F6	J11	Horse
6. 6	27. 4	F6	K12	Stag
7. 6	28. 4	F6	A1	Serpent
8. 6	29. 4	F6	B2	Earthworm
9. 6	1. 5	G7	C3	Crocodile
10. 6	2. 5	G7	D4	Dragon
11. 6	3. 5	G7	E5	Badger
12. 6	4. 5	G7	F6	Hare
13. 6	5. 5	G7	G7	Fox
14. 6	6. 5	G7	H8	Tiger
15. 6	7. 5	G7	J9	Leopard
16. 6	8. 5	G7	K10	Griffon
17. 6	9. 5	G7	A11	Ox
18. 6	10. 5	G7	B12	Bat
19. 6	11. 5	G7	C1	Rat
20. 6	12. 5	G7	D2	Swallow
21. 6	13. 5	G7	E3	Pig
22. 6	14. 5	G7	F4	Porcupine
23. 6	15. 5	G7	G5	Wolf
24. 6	16. 5	G7	H6	Dog
25. 6	17. 5	G7	J7	Pheasant
26. 6	18. 5	G7	K8	Cock
27. 6	19. 5	G7	A9	Crow
28. 6	20. 5	G7	B10	Monkey
29. 6	21. 5	G7	C11	Gibbon
30. 6	22. 5	G7	D12	Tapir
1. 7	23. 5	G7	E1	Sheep
2. 7	24. 5	G7	F2	Deer
3. 7	25. 5	G7	G3	Horse
4. 7	26. 5	G7	H4	Stag
5. 7	27. 5	G7	J5	Serpent
6. 7	28. 5	G7	K6	Earthworm
7. 7	29. 5	G7	A7	Crocodile
8. 7	30. 5	G7	B8	Dragon
9. 7	1. 6	H8	C9	Badger
10. 7	2. 6	H8	D10	Hare

Solar date	*Lunar date*	*Month HS/EB*	*Day HS/EB*	*Constellation*
11. 7	3. 6	H8	E11	Fox
12. 7	4. 6	H8	F12	Tiger
13. 7	5. 6	H8	G1	Leopard
14. 7	6. 6	H8	H2	Griffon
15. 7	7. 6	H8	J3	Ox
16. 7	8. 6	H8	K4	Bat
17. 7	9. 6	H8	A5	Rat
18. 7	10. 6	H8	B6	Swallow
19. 7	11. 6	H8	C7	Pig
20. 7	12. 6	H8	D8	Porcupine
21. 7	13. 6	H8	E9	Wolf
22. 7	14. 6	H8	F10	Dog
23. 7	15. 6	H8	G11	Pheasant
24. 7	16. 6	H8	H12	Cock
25. 7	17. 6	H8	J1	Crow
26. 7	18. 6	H8	K2	Monkey
27. 7	19. 6	H8	A3	Gibbon
28. 7	20. 6	H8	B4	Tapir
29. 7	21. 6	H8	C5	Sheep
30. 7	22. 6	H8	D6	Deer
31. 7	23. 6	H8	E7	Horse
1. 8	24. 6	H8	F8	Stag
2. 8	25. 6	H8	G9	Serpent
3. 8	26. 6	H8	H10	Earthworm
4. 8	27. 6	H8	J11	Crocodile
5. 8	28. 6	H8	K12	Dragon
6. 8	29. 6	H8	A1	Badger
7. 8	1. 7	J9	B2	Hare
8. 8	2. 7	J9	C3	Fox
9. 8	3. 7	J9	D4	Tiger
10. 8	4. 7	J9	E5	Leopard
11. 8	5. 7	J9	F6	Griffon
12. 8	6. 7	J9	G7	Ox
13. 8	7. 7	J9	H8	Bat
14. 8	8. 7	J9	J9	Rat
15. 8	9. 7	J9	K10	Swallow
16. 8	10. 7	J9	A11	Pig
17. 8	11. 7	J9	B12	Porcupine
18. 8	12. 7	J9	C1	Wolf
19. 8	13. 7	J9	D2	Dog
20. 8	14. 7	J9	E3	Pheasant
21. 8	15. 7	J9	F4	Cock
22. 8	16. 7	J9	G5	Crow
23. 8	17. 7	J9	H6	Monkey
24. 8	18. 7	J9	J7	Gibbon
25. 8	19. 7	J9	K8	Tapir
26. 8	20. 7	J9	A9	Sheep
27. 8	21. 7	J9	B10	Deer
28. 8	22. 7	J9	C11	Horse
29. 8	23. 7	J9	D12	Stag
30. 8	24. 7	J9	E1	Serpent
31. 8	25. 7	J9	F2	Earthworm
1. 9	26. 7	J9	G3	Crocodile
2. 9	27. 7	J9	H4	Dragon
3. 9	28. 7	J9	J5	Badger
4. 9	29. 7	J9	K6	Hare
5. 9	30. 7	J9	A7	Fox
6. 9	1. 8	K10	B8	Tiger
7. 9	2. 8	K10	C9	Leopard
8. 9	3. 8	K10	D10	Griffon
9. 9	4. 8	K10	E11	Ox
10. 9	5. 8	K10	F12	Bat
11. 9	6. 8	K10	G1	Rat
12. 9	7. 8	K10	H2	Swallow
13. 9	8. 8	K10	J3	Pig
14. 9	9. 8	K10	K4	Porcupine
15. 9	10. 8	K10	A5	Wolf
16. 9	11. 8	K10	B6	Dog
17. 9	12. 8	K10	C7	Pheasant
18. 9	13. 8	K10	D8	Cock
19. 9	14. 8	K10	E9	Crow
20. 9	15. 8	K10	F10	Monkey
21. 9	16. 8	K10	G11	Gibbon

Solar date	*Lunar date*	*Month HS/EB*	*Day HS/EB*	*Constellation*
22. 9	17. 8	K10	H12	Tapir
23. 9	18. 8	K10	J1	Sheep
24. 9	19. 8	K10	K2	Deer
25. 9	20. 8	K10	A3	Horse
26. 9	21. 8	K10	B4	Stag
27. 9	22. 8	K10	C5	Serpent
28. 9	23. 8	K10	D6	Earthworm
29. 9	24. 8	K10	E7	Crocodile
30. 9	25. 8	K10	F8	Dragon
1.10	26. 8	K10	G9	Badger
2.10	27. 8	K10	H10	Hare
3.10	28. 8	K10	J11	Fox
4.10	29. 8	K10	K12	Tiger
5.10	1. 9	A11	A1	Leopard
6.10	2. 9	A11	B2	Griffon
7.10	3. 9	A11	C3	Ox
8.10	4. 9	A11	D4	Bat
9.10	5. 9	A11	E5	Rat
10.10	6. 9	A11	F6	Swallow
11.10	7. 9	A11	G7	Pig
12.10	8. 9	A11	H8	Porcupine
13.10	9. 9	A11	J9	Wolf
14.10	10. 9	A11	K10	Dog
15.10	11. 9	A11	A11	Pheasant
16.10	12. 9	A11	B12	Cock
17.10	13. 9	A11	C1	Crow
18.10	14. 9	A11	D2	Monkey
19.10	15. 9	A11	E3	Gibbon
20.10	16. 9	A11	F4	Tapir
21.10	17. 9	A11	G5	Sheep
22.10	18. 9	A11	H6	Deer
23.10	19. 9	A11	J7	Horse
24.10	20. 9	A11	K8	Stag
25.10	21. 9	A11	A9	Serpent
26.10	22. 9	A11	B10	Earthworm
27.10	23. 9	A11	C11	Crocodile
28.10	24. 9	A11	D12	Dragon
29.10	25. 9	A11	E1	Badger
30.10	26. 9	A11	F2	Hare
31.10	27. 9	A11	G3	Fox
1.11	28. 9	A11	H4	Tiger
2.11	29. 9	A11	J5	Leopard
3.11	1.10	B12	K6	Griffon
4.11	2.10	B12	A7	Ox
5.11	3.10	B12	B8	Bat
6.11	4.10	B12	C9	Rat
7.11	5.10	B12	D10	Swallow
8.11	6.10	B12	E11	Pig
9.11	7.10	B12	F12	Porcupine
10.11	8.10	B12	G1	Wolf
11.11	9.10	B12	H2	Dog
12.11	10.10	B12	J3	Pheasant
13.11	11.10	B12	K4	Cock
14.11	12.10	B12	A5	Crow
15.11	13.10	B12	B6	Monkey
16.11	14.10	B12	C7	Gibbon
17.11	15.10	B12	D8	Tapir
18.11	16.10	B12	E9	Sheep
19.11	17.10	B12	F10	Deer
20.11	18.10	B12	G11	Horse
21.11	19.10	B12	H12	Stag
22.11	20.10	B12	J1	Serpent
23.11	21.10	B12	K2	Earthworm
24.11	22.10	B12	A3	Crocodile
25.11	23.10	B12	B4	Dragon
26.11	24.10	B12	C5	Badger
27.11	25.10	B12	D6	Hare

Solar date	*Lunar date*	*Month HS/EB*	*Day HS/EB*	*Constellation*
28.11	26.10	B12	E7	Fox
29.11	27.10	B12	F8	Tiger
30.11	28.10	B12	G9	Leopard
1.12	29.10	B12	H10	Griffon
2.12	30.10	B12	J11	Ox
3.12	1.11	C1	K12	Bat
4.12	2.11	C1	A1	Rat
5.12	3.11	C1	B2	Swallow
6.12	4.11	C1	C3	Pig
7.12	5.11	C1	D4	Porcupine
8.12	6.11	C1	E5	Wolf
9.12	7.11	C1	F6	Dog
10.12	8.11	C1	G7	Pheasant
11.12	9.11	C1	H8	Cock
12.12	10.11	C1	J9	Crow
13.12	11.11	C1	K10	Monkey
14.12	12.11.	C1	A11	Gibbon
15.12	13.11	C1	B12	Tapir
16.12	14.11	C1	C1	Sheep
17.12	15.11	C1	D2	Deer
18.12	16.11	C1	E3	Horse
19.12	17.11	C1	F4	Stag
20.12	18.11	C1	G5	Serpent
21.12	19.11	C1	H6	Earthworm
22.12	20.11	C1	J7	Crocodile
23.12	21.11	C1	K8	Dragon
24.12	22.11	C1	A9	Badger
25.12	23.11	C1	B10	Hare
26.12	24.11	C1	C11	Fox
27.12	25.11	C1	D12	Tiger
28.12	26.11	C1	E1	Leopard
29.12	27.11	C1	F2	Griffon
30.12	28.11	C1	G3	Ox
31.12	29.11	C1	H4	Bat

1995

Solar date	*Lunar date*	*Month HS/EB*	*Day HS/EB*	*Constellation*
1. 1	1.12	D2	J5	Rat
2. 1	2.12	D2	K6	Swallow
3. 1	3.12	D2	A7	Pig
4. 1	4.12	D2	B8	Porcupine
5. 1	5.12	D2	C9	Wolf
6. 1	6.12	D2	D10	Dog
7. 1	7.12	D2	E11	Pheasant
8. 1	8.12	D2	F12	Cock
9. 1	9.12	D2	G1	Crow
10. 1	10.12	D2	H2	Monkey
11. 1	11.12	D2	J3	Gibbon
12. 1	12.12	D2	K4	Tapir
13. 1	13.12	D2	A5	Sheep
14. 1	14.12	D2	B6	Deer
15. 1	15.12	D2	C7	Horse
16. 1	16.12	D2	D8	Stag
17. 1	17.12	D2	E9	Serpent
18. 1	18.12	D2	F10	Earthworm
19. 1	19.12	D2	G11	Crocodile
20. 1	20.12	D2	H12	Dragon
21. 1	21.12	D2	J1	Badger
22. 1	22.12	D2	K2	Hare
23. 1	23.12	D2	A3	Fox
24. 1	24.12	D2	B4	Tiger
25. 1	25.12	D2	C5	Leopard
26. 1	26.12	D2	D6	Griffon
27. 1	27.12	D2	E7	Ox
28. 1	28.12	D2	F8	Bat
29. 1	29.12	D2	G9	Rat
30. 1	30.12	D2	H10	Swallow

YI HAI YEAR

Solar date	*Lunar date*	*Month HS/EB*	*Day HS/EB*	*Constellation*
31. 1	1. 1	E3	J11	Pig
1. 2	2. 1	E3	K12	Porcupine
2. 2	3. 1	E3	A1	Wolf
3. 2	4. 1	E3	B2	Dog
4. 2	5. 1	E3	C3	Pheasant
5. 2	6. 1	E3	D4	Cock
6. 2	7. 1	E3	E5	Crow
7. 2	8. 1	E3	F6	Monkey
8. 2	9. 1	E3	G7	Gibbon
9. 2	10. 1	E3	H8	Tapir
10. 2	11. 1	E3	J9	Sheep
11. 2	12. 1	E3	K10	Deer
12. 2	13. 1	E3	A11	Horse
13. 2	14. 1	E3	B12	Stag
14. 2	15. 1	E3	C1	Serpent
15. 2	16. 1	E3	D2	Earthworm
16. 2	17. 1	E3	E3	Crocodile
17. 2	18. 1	E3	F4	Dragon
18. 2	19. 1	E3	G5	Badger
19. 2	20. 1	E3	H6	Hare
20. 2	21. 1	E3	J7	Fox
21. 2	22. 1	E3	K8	Tiger
22. 2	23. 1	E3	A9	Leopard
23. 2	24. 1	E3	B10	Griffon
24. 2	25. 1	E3	C11	Ox
25. 2	26. 1	E3	D12	Bat
26. 2	27. 1	E3	E1	Rat
27. 2	28. 1	E3	F2	Swallow
28. 2	29. 1	E3	G3	Pig
1. 3	1. 2	F4	H4	Porcupine
2. 3	2. 2	F4	J5	Wolf
3. 3	3. 2	F4	K6	Dog
4. 3	4. 2	F4	A7	Pheasant
5. 3	5. 2	F4	B8	Cock
6. 3	6. 2	F4	C9	Crow
7. 3	7. 2	F4	D10	Monkey
8. 3	8. 2	F4	E11	Gibbon
9. 3	9. 2	F4	F12	Tapir
10. 3	10. 2	F4	G1	Sheep
11. 3	11. 2	F4	H2	Deer
12. 3	12. 2	F4	J3	Horse
13. 3	13. 2	F4	K4	Stag
14. 3	14. 2	F4	A5	Serpent
15. 3	15. 2	F4	B6	Earthworm
16. 3	16. 2	F4	C7	Crocodile
17. 3	17. 2	F4	D8	Dragon
18. 3	18. 2	F4	E9	Badger
19. 3	19. 2	F4	F10	Hare
20. 3	20. 2	F4	G11	Fox
21. 3	21. 2	F4	H12	Tiger
22. 3	22. 2	F4	J1	Leopard
23. 3	23. 2	F4	K2	Griffon
24. 3	24. 2	F4	A3	Ox
25. 3	25. 2	F4	B4	Bat
26. 3	26. 2	F4	C5	Rat
27. 3	27. 2	F4	D6	Swallow
28. 3	29. 2	F4	E7	Pig
29. 3	29. 2	F4	F8	Porcupine
30. 3	30. 2	F4	G9	Wolf
31. 3	1. 3	G5	H10	Dog
1. 4	2. 3	G5	J11	Pheasant
2. 4	3. 3	G5	K12	Cock
3. 4	4. 3	G5	A1	Crow
4. 4	5. 3	G5	B2	Monkey
5. 4	6. 3	G5	C3	Gibbon
6. 4	7. 3	G5	D4	Tapir
7. 4	8. 3	G5	E5	Sheep
8. 4	9. 3	G5	F6	Deer
9. 4	10. 3	G5	G7	Horse
10. 4	11. 3	G5	H8	Stag
11. 4	12. 3	G5	J9	Serpent

Solar date	*Lunar date*	*Month HS/EB*	*Day HS/EB*	*Constellation*
12. 4	13. 3	G5	K10	Earthworm
13. 4	14. 3	G5	A11	Crocodile
14. 4	15. 3	G5	B12	Dragon
15. 4	16. 3	G5	C1	Badger
16. 4	17. 3	G5	D2	Hare
17. 4	18. 3	G5	E3	Fox
18. 4	19. 3	G5	F4	Tiger
19. 4	20. 3	G5	G5	Leopard
20. 4	21. 3	G5	H6	Griffon
21. 4	22. 3	G5	J7	Ox
22. 4	23. 3	G5	K8	Bat
23. 4	24. 3	G5	A9	Rat
24. 4	25. 3	G5	B10	Swallow
25. 4	26. 3	G5	C11	Pig
26. 4	27. 3	G5	D12	Porcupine
27. 4	28. 3	G5	E1	Wolf
28. 4	29. 3	G5	F2	Dog
29. 4	30. 3	G5	G3	Pheasant
30. 4	1. 4	H6	H4	Cock
1. 5	2. 4	H6	J5	Crow
2. 5	3. 4	H6	K6	Monkey
3. 5	4. 4	H6	A7	Gibbon
4. 5	5. 4	H6	B8	Tapir
5. 5	6. 4	H6	C9	Sheep
6. 5	7. 4	H6	D10	Deer
7. 5	8. 4	H6	E11	Horse
8. 5	9. 4	H6	F12	Stag
9. 5	10. 4	H6	G1	Serpent
10. 5	11. 4	H6	H2	Earthworm
11. 5	12. 4	H6	J3	Crocodile
12. 5	13. 4	H6	K4	Dragon
13. 5	14. 4	H6	A5	Badger
14. 5	15. 4	H6	B6	Hare
15. 5	16. 4	H6	C7	Fox
16. 5	17. 4	H6	D8	Tiger
17. 5	18. 4	H6	E9	Leopard
18. 5	19. 4	H6	F10	Griffon
19. 5	20. 4	H6	G11	Ox
20. 5	21. 4	H6	H12	Bat
21. 5	22. 4	H6	J1	Rat
22. 5	23. 4	H6	K2	Swallow
23. 5	24. 4	H6	A3	Pig
24. 5	25. 4	H6	B4	Porcupine
25. 5	26. 4	H6	C5	Wolf
26. 5	27. 4	H6	D6	Dog
27. 5	28. 4	H6	E7	Pheasant
28. 5	29. 4	H6	F8	Cock
29. 5	1. 5	J7	G9	Cock
30. 5	2. 5	J7	H10	Monkey
31. 5	3. 5	J7	J11	Gibbon
1. 6	4. 5	J7	K12	Tapir
2. 6	5. 5	J7	A1	Sheep
3. 6	6. 5	J7	B2	Deer
4. 6	7. 5	J7	C3	Horse
5. 6	8. 5	J7	D4	Stag
6. 6	9. 5	J7	E5	Serpent
7. 6	10. 5	J7	F6	Earthworm
8. 6	11. 5	J7	G7	Crocodile
9. 6	12. 5	J7	H8	Dragon
10. 6	13. 5	J7	J9	Badger
11. 6	14. 5	J7	K10	Hare
12. 6	15. 5	J7	A11	Fox
13. 6	16. 5	J7	B12	Tiger
14. 6	17. 5	J7	C1	Leopard
15. 6	18. 5	J7	D2	Griffon
16. 6	19. 5	J7	E3	Ox
17. 6	20. 5	J7	F4	Bat
18. 6	21. 5	J7	G5	Rat
19. 6	22. 5	J7	H6	Swallow
20. 6	23. 5	J7	J7	Pig
21. 6	24. 5	J7	K8	Porcupine

Solar date	*Lunar date*	*Month HS/EB*	*Day HS/EB*	*Constellation*
22. 6	25. 5	J7	A9	Wolf
23. 6	26. 5	J7	B10	Dog
24. 6	27. 5	J7	C11	Pheasant
25. 6	28. 5	J7	D12	Cock
26. 6	29. 5	J7	E1	Crow
27. 6	30. 5	J7	F2	Monkey
28. 6	1. 6	K8	G3	Gibbon
29. 6	2. 6	K8	H4	Tapir
30. 6	3. 6	K8	J5	Sheep
1. 7	4. 6	K8	K6	Deer
2. 7	5. 6	K8	A7	Horse
3. 7	6. 6	K8	B8	Stag
4. 7	7. 6	K8	C9	Serpent
5. 7	8. 6	K8	D10	Earthworm
6. 7	9. 6	K8	E11	Crocodile
7. 7	10. 6	K8	F12	Dragon
8. 7	11. 6	K8	G1	Badger
9. 7	12. 6	K8	H2	Hare
10. 7	13. 6	K8	J3	Fox
11. 7	14. 6	K8	K4	Tiger
12. 7	15. 6	K8	A5	Leopard
13. 7	16. 6	K8	B6	Griffon
14. 7	17. 6	K8	C7	Ox
15. 7	18. 6	K8	D8	Bat
16. 7	19. 6	K8	E9	Rat
17. 7	20. 6	K8	E10	Swallow
18. 7	21. 6	K8	G11	Pig
19. 7	22. 6	K8	H12	Porcupine
20. 7	23. 6	K8	J1	Wolf
21. 7	24. 6	K8	K2	Dog
22. 7	25. 6	K8	A3	Pheasant
23. 7	26. 6	K8	B4	Cock
24. 7	27. 6	K8	C5	Crow
25. 7	28. 6	K8	D6	Monkey
26. 7	29. 6	K8	E7	Gibbon
27. 7	1. 7	A9	F8	Tapir
28. 7	2. 7	A9	G9	Sheep
29. 7	3. 7	A9	H10	Deer
30. 7	4. 7	A9	J11	Horse
31. 7	5. 7	A9	K12	Stag
1. 8	6. 7	A9	A1	Serpent
2. 8	7. 7	A9	B2	Earthworm
3. 8	8. 7	A9	C3	Crocodile
4. 8	9. 7	A9	D4	Dragon
5. 8	10. 7	A9	E5	Badger
6. 8	11. 7	A9	F6	Hare
7. 8	12. 7	A9	G7	Fox
8. 8	13. 7	A9	H8	Tiger
9. 8	14. 7	A9	J9	Leopard
10. 8	15. 7	A9	K10	Griffon
11. 8	16. 7	A9	A11	Ox
12. 8	17. 7	A9	B12	Bat
13. 8	18. 7	A9	C1	Rat
14. 8	19. 7	A9	D2	Swallow
15. 8	20. 7	A9	E3	Pig
16. 8	21. 7	A9	F4	Porcupine
17. 8	22. 7	A9	G5	Wolf
18. 8	23. 7	A9	H6	Dog
19. 8	24. 7	A9	J7	Pheasant
20. 8	25. 7	A9	K8	Cock
21. 8	26. 7	A9	A9	Crow
22. 8	27. 7	A9	B10	Monkey
23. 8	28. 7	A9	C11	Gibbon
24. 8	29. 7	A9	D12	Tapir
25. 8	30. 7	A9	E1	Sheep
26. 8	1. 8	B10	F2	Deer
27. 8	2. 8	B10	G3	Horse
28. 8	3. 8	B10	H4	Stag
29. 8	4. 8	B10	J5	Serpent
30. 8	5. 8	B10	K6	Earthworm
31. 8	6. 8	B10	A7	Crocodile
1. 9	7. 8	B10	B8	Dragon
2. 9	8. 8	B10	C9	Badger
3. 9	9. 8	B10	D10	Hare
4. 9	10. 8	B10	E11	Fox
5. 9	11. 8	B10	F12	Tiger
6. 9	12. 8	B10	G1	Leopard
7. 9	13. 8	B10	H2	Griffon
8. 9	14. 8	B10	J3	Ox
9. 9	15. 8	B10	K4	Bat
10. 9	16. 8	B10	A5	Rat
11. 9	17. 8	B10	B6	Swallow
12. 9	18. 8	B10	C7	Pig
13. 9	19. 8	B10	D8	Porcupine
14. 9	20. 8	B10	E9	Wolf
15. 9	21. 8	B10	F10	Dog
16. 9	22. 8	B10	G11	Pheasant
17. 9	23. 8	B10	H12	Cock
18. 9	24. 8	B10	J1	Crow
19. 9	25. 8	B10	K2	Monkey
20. 9	26. 8	B10	A3	Gibbon
21. 9	27. 8	B10	B4	Tapir
22. 9	28. 8	B10	C5	Sheep
23. 9	29. 8	B10	D6	Deer
24. 9	30. 8	B10	E7	Horse
25. 9	*1. 8*	*B10*	F8	Stag
26. 9	*2. 8*	*B10*	G9	Serpent
27. 9	*3. 8*	*B10*	H10	Earthworm
28. 9	*4. 8*	*B10*	J11	Crocodile
29. 9	*5. 8*	*B10*	K12	Dragon
30. 9	*6. 8*	*B10*	A1	Badger
1.10	*7. 8*	*B10*	B2	Hare
2.10	*8. 8*	*B10*	C3	Fox
3.10	*9. 8*	*B10*	D4	Tiger
4.10	*10. 9*	*B10*	E5	Leopard
5.10	*11. 8*	*B10*	F6	Griffon
6.10	*12. 8*	*B10*	G7	Ox
7.10	*13. 8*	*B10*	H8	Bat
8.10	*14. 8*	*B10*	J9	Rat
9.10	*15. 8*	*B10*	K10	Swallow
10.10	*16. 8*	*B10*	A11	Pig
11.10	*17. 8*	*B10*	B12	Porcupine
12.10	*18. 8*	*B10*	C1	Wolf
13.10	*19. 8*	*B10*	D2	Dog
14.10	*20. 8*	*B10*	E3	Pheasant
15.10	*21. 8*	*B10*	F4	Cock
16.10	*22. 8*	*B10*	G5	Crow
17.10	*23. 8*	*B10*	H6	Monkey
18.10	*24. 8*	*B10*	J7	Gibbon
19.10	*25. 8*	*B10*	K8	Tapir
20.10	*26. 8*	*B10*	A9	Sheep
21.10	*27. 8*	*B10*	B10	Deer
22.10	*28. 8*	*B10*	C11	Horse
23.10	*29. 8*	*B10*	D12	Stag
24.10	1. 9	C11	E1	Serpent
25.10	2. 9	C11	F2	Earthworm
26.10	3. 9	C11	G3	Crocodile
27.10	4. 9	C1	H4	Dragon
28.10	5. 9	C11	J5	Badger
29.10	6. 9	C11	K6	Hare
30.10	7. 9	C11	A7	Fox
31.10	8. 9	C11	B8	Tiger
1.11	9. 9	C11	C9	Leopard
2.11	10. 9	C11	D10	Griffon
3.11	11. 9	C11	E11	Ox
4.11	12. 9	C11	F12	Bat
5.11	13. 9	C11	G1	Rat
6.11	14. 9	C11	H2	Swallow
7.11	15. 9	C11	J3	Pig
8.11	16. 9	C11	K4	Porcupine
9.11	17. 9	C11	A5	Wolf
10.11	18. 9	C11	B6	Dog
11.11	19. 9	C11	C7	Pheasant
12.11	20. 9	C11	D8	Cock
13.11	21. 9	C11	E9	Crow
14.11	22. 9	C11	F10	Monkey

Solar date	*Lunar date*	*Month HS/EB*	*Day HS/EB*	*Constellation*
15.11	23. 9	C11	G11	Gibbon
16.11	24. 9	C11	H12	Tapir
17.11	25. 9	C11	J1	Sheep
18.11	26. 9	C11	K2	Deer
19.11	27. 9	C11	A3	Horse
20.11	28. 9	C11	B4	Stag
21.11	29. 9	C11	C5	Serpent
22.11	1.10	D12	D6	Earthworm
23.11	2.10	D12	E7	Crocodile
24.11	3.10	D12	F8	Dragon
25.11	4.10	D12	G9	Badger
26.11	5.10	D12	H10	Hare
27.11	6.10	D12	J11	Fox
28.11	7.10	D12	K12	Tiger
29.11	8.10	D12	A1	Leopard
30.11	9.10	D12	B2	Griffon
1.12	10.10	D12	C3	Ox
2.12	11.10	D12	D4	Bat
3.12	12.10	D12	E5	Rat
4.12	13.10	D12	F6	Swallow
5.12	14.10	D12	G7	Pig
6.12	15.10	D12	H8	Porcupine
7.12	16.10	D12	J9	Wolf
8.12	17.10	D12	K10	Dog
9.12	18.10	D12	A11	Pheasant
10.12	19.10	D12	B12	Cock
11.12	20.10	D12	C1	Crow
12.12	21.10	D12	D2	Monkey
13.12	22.10	D12	E3	Gibbon
14.12	23.10	D12	F4	Tapir
15.12	24.10	D12	G5	Sheep
16.12	25.10	D12	H6	Deer
17.12	26.10	D12	J7	Horse
18.12	27.10	D12	K8	Stag
19.12	28.10	D12	A9	Serpent
20.12	29.10	D12	B10	Earthworm
21.12	30.10	D12	C11	Crocodile
22.12	1.11	E1	D12	Dragon
23.12	2.11	E1	E1	Badger
24.12	3.11	E1	F2	Hare
25.12	4.11	E1	G3	Fox
26.12	5.11	E1	H4	Tiger
27.12	6.11	E1	J5	Leopard
28.12	7.11	E1	K6	Griffon
29.12	8.11	E1	A7	Ox
30.12	9.11	E1	B8	Bat
31.12	10.11	E1	C9	Rat
1996				
1. 1	11.11	E1	D10	Swallow

Solar date	*Lunar date*	*Month HS/EB*	*Day HS/EB*	*Constellation*
2. 1	12.11	E1	E11	Pig
3. 1	13.11	E1	F12	Porcupine
4. 1	14.11	E1	G1	Wolf
5. 1	15.11	E1	H2	Dog
6. 1	16.11	E1	J3	Pheasant
7. 1	17.11	E1	K4	Cock
8. 1	18.11	E1	A5	Crow
9. 1	19.11	E1	B6	Monkey
10. 1	20.11	E1	C7	Gibbon
11. 1	21.11	E1	D8	Tapir
12. 1	22.11	E1	E9	Sheep
13. 1	23.11	E1	F10	Deer
14. 1	24.11	E1	G11	Horse
15. 1	25.11	E1	H12	Stag
16. 1	26.11	E1	J1	Serpent
17. 1	27.11	E1	K2	Earthworm
18. 1	28.11	E1	A3	Crocodile
19. 1	29.11	E1	B4	Dragon
20. 1	1.12	F2	C5	Badger
21. 1	2.12	F2	D6	Hare
22. 1	3.12	F2	E7	Fox
23. 1	4.12	F2	F8	Tiger
24. 1	5.12	F2	G9	Leopard
25. 1	6.12	F2	H10	Griffon
26. 1	7.12	F2	J11	Ox
27. 1	8.12	F2	K12	Bat
28. 1	9.12	F2	A1	Rat
29. 1	10.12	F2	B2	Swallow
30. 1	11.12	F2	C3	Pig
31. 1	12.12	F2	D4	Porcupine
1. 2	13.12	F2	E5	Wolf
2. 2	14.12	F2	F6	Dog
3. 2	25.12	F2	G7	Pheasant
4. 2	16.12	f2	H8	Cock
5. 2	17.12	F2	J9	Crow
6. 2	18.12	F2	K10	Monkey
7. 2	19.12	F2	A11	Gibbon
8. 2	20.12	F2	B12	Tapir
9. 2	21.12	F2	C1	Sheep
10. 2	22.12	F2	D2	Deer
11. 2	23.12	F2	E3	Horse
12. 2	24.12	F2	F4	Stag
13. 2	25.12	F2	G5	Serpent
14. 2	26.12	F2	H6	Earthworm
15. 2	27.12	F2	J7	Crocodile
16. 2	28.12	F2	K8	Dragon
17. 2	29.12	F2	A9	Badger
18. 2	30.12	F2	B10	Hare

PING TZU YEAR

19. 2	1. 1	G3	C11	Fox
20. 2	2. 1	G3	D12	Tiger
21. 2	3. 1	G3	E1	Leopard
22. 2	4. 1	G3	F2	Griffon
23. 2	5. 1	G3	G3	Ox
24. 2	6. 1	G3	H4	Bat
25. 2	7. 1	G3	J5	Rat
26. 2	8. 1	G3	K6	Swallow
27. 2	9. 1	G3	A7	Pig
28. 2	10. 1	G3	B8	Porcupine
29. 2	11. 1	G3	C9	Wolf
1. 3	12. 1	G3	D10	Dog
2. 3	13. 1	G3	E11	Pheasant
3. 3	14. 1	G3	F12	Cock
4. 3	15. 1	G3	G1	Crow
5. 3	16. 1	G3	H2	Monkey
6. 3	17. 1	G3	J3	Gibbon
7. 3	18. 1	G3	K4	Tapir
8. 3	19. 1	G3	A5	Sheep
9. 3	20. 1	G3	B6	Deer
10. 3	21. 1	G3	C7	Horse
11. 3	22. 1	G3	D8	Stag
12. 3	23. 1	G3	E9	Serpent
13. 3	24. 1	G3	F10	Earthworm
14. 3	25. 1	G3	G11	Crocodile
15. 3	26. 1	G3	H12	Dragon
16. 3	27. 1	G3	J1	Badger
17. 3	28. 1	G3	K2	Hare
18. 3	29. 1	G3	A3	Fox
19. 3	1. 2	H4	B4	Tiger
20. 3	2. 2	H4	C5	Leopard
21. 3	3. 2	H4	D6	Griffon
22. 3	4. 2	H4	E7	Ox
23. 3	5. 2	H4	F8	Bat
24. 3	6. 2	H4	G9	Rat
25. 3	7. 2	H4	H10	Swallow

Solar date	*Lunar date*	*Month HS/EB*	*Day HS/EB*	*Constellation*
26. 3	8. 2	H4	J11	Pig
27. 3	9. 2	H4	K12	Porcupine
28. 3	10. 2	H4	A1	Wolf
29. 3	11. 2	H4	B2	Dog
30. 3	12. 2	H4	C3	Pheasant
31. 3	13. 2	H4	D4	Cock
1. 4	14. 2	H4	E5	Crow
2. 4	15. 2	H4	F6	Monkey
3. 4	16. 2	H4	G7	Gibbon
4. 4	17. 2	H4	H8	Tapir
5. 2	18. 2	H4	J9	Sheep
6. 4	19. 2	H4	K10	Deer
7. 4	21. 2	H4	A11	Horse
8. 4	21. 2	H4	B12	Stag
9. 4	22. 2	H4	C1	Serpent
10. 4	23. 2	H4	D2	Earthworm
11. 4	24. 2	H4	E3	Crocodile
12. 4	25. 2	H4	F4	Dragon
13. 4	26. 2	H4	G5	Badger
14. 4	27. 2	H4	H6	Hare
15. 4	28. 2	H4	J7	Fox
16. 4	29. 2	H4	K8	Tiger
17. 4	30. 2	H4	A9	Leopard
18. 4	1. 3	J5	B10	Griffon
19. 4	2. 3	J5	C11	Ox
20. 4	3. 3	J5	D12	Bat
21. 4	4. 3	J5	E1	Rat
22. 4	5. 3	J5	F2	Swallow
23. 4	6. 3	J5	G3	Pig
24. 4	7. 3	J5	H4	Porcupine
25. 4	8. 3	J5	J5	Wolf
26. 4	9. 3	J5	K6	Dog
27. 4	10. 3	J5	A7	Pheasant
28. 4	11. 3	J5	B8	Cock
29. 4	12. 3	J5	C9	Crow
30. 4	13. 3	J5	D10	Monkey
1. 5	14. 3	J5	E11	Gibbon
2. 5	15. 3	J5	F12	Tapir
3. 5	16. 3	J5	G1	Sheep
4. 5	17. 3	J5	H2	Deer
5. 5	18. 3	J5	J3	Horse
6. 5	19. 3	J5	K4	Stag
7. 5	20. 3	J5	A5	Serpent
8. 5	21. 3	J5	B6	Earthworm
9. 5	22. 3	J5	C7	Crocodile
10. 5	23. 3	J5	D8	Dragon
11. 5	24. 3	J5	E9	Badger
12. 5	25. 3	J5	F10	Hare
13. 5	26. 3	J5	G11	Fox
14. 5	27. 3	J5	H12	Tiger
15. 5	28. 3	J5	J1	Leopard
16. 5	29. 3	J5	K2	Griffon
17. 5	1. 4	K6	A3	Ox
18. 5	2. 4	K6	B4	Bat
19. 5	3. 4	K6	C5	Rat
20. 5	4. 4	K6	D6	Swallow
21. 5	5. 4	K6	E7	Pig
22. 5	6. 4	K6	F8	Porcupine
23. 5	7. 4	K6	G9	Wolf
24. 5	8. 4	K6	H10	Dog
25. 5	9. 4	K6	J11	Pheasant
26. 5	10. 4	K6	K12	Cock
27. 5	11. 4	K6	A1	Crow
28. 5	12. 4	K6	B2	Monkey
29. 5	13. 4	K6	C3	Gibbon
30. 5	14. 4	K6	D4	Tapir
31. 5	15. 4	K6	E5	Sheep
1. 6	16. 4	K6	F6	Deer
2. 6	17. 4	K6	G7	Horse
3. 6	18. 4	K6	H8	Stag
4. 6	19. 4	K6	J9	Serpent
5. 6	20. 4	K6	K10	Earthworm
6. 6	21. 4	K6	A11	Crocodile

Solar date	*Lunar date*	*Month HS/EB*	*Day HS/EB*	*Constellation*
7. 6	22. 4	K6	B12	Dragon
8. 6	23. 4	K6	C1	Badger
9. 6	24. 4	K6	D2	Hare
10. 6	25. 4	K6	E3	Fox
11. 6	26. 4	K6	F4	Tiger
12. 6	27. 4	K6	G5	Leopard
13. 6	28. 4	K6	H6	Griffon
14. 6	29. 4	K6	J7	Ox
15. 6	30. 4	K6	K8	Bat
16. 6	1. 5	A7	A9	Rat
17. 6	2. 5	A7	B10	Swallow
18. 6	3. 5	A7	C11	Pig
19. 6	4. 5	A7	D12	Porcupine
20. 6	5. 5	A7	E1	Wolf
21. 6	6. 5	A7	F2	Dog
22. 6	7. 5	A7	G3	Pheasant
23. 6	8. 5	A7	H4	Cock
24. 6	9. 5	A7	J5	Crow
25. 6	10. 5	A7	K6	Monkey
26. 6	11. 5	A7	A7	Gibbon
27. 6	12. 5	A7	B8	Tapir
28. 6	13. 5	A7	C9	Sheep
29. 6	14. 5	A7	D10	Deer
30. 6	15. 5	A7	E11	Horse
1. 7	16; 5	A7	F12	Stag
2. 7	17. 5	A7	G1	Serpent
3. 7	18. 5	A7	H2	Earthworm
4. 7	19. 5	A7	J3	Crocodile
5. 7	20. 5	A7	K4	Dragon
6. 7	21. 5	A7	A5	Badger
7. 7	22. 5	A7	B6	Hare
8. 7	23. 5	A7	C7	Fox
9. 7	24. 5	A7	D8	Tiger
10. 7	25. 5	A7	E9	Leopard
11. 7	26. 5	A7	F10	Griffon
12. 7	27. 5	A7	G11	Ox
13. 7	28. 5	A7	H12	Bat
14. 7	29. 5	A7	J1	Rat
15. 7	30. 5	A7	K2	Swallow
16. 7	1. 6	B8	A3	Pig
17. 7	2. 6	B8	B4	Porcupine
18. 7	3. 6	B8	C5	Wolf
19. 7	4. 6	B8	D6	Dog
20. 7	5. 6	B8	E7	Pheasant
21. 7	6. 6	B8	F8	Cock
22. 7	7. 6	B8	G9	Crow
23. 7	8. 6	B8	H10	Monkey
24. 7	9. 6	B8	J11	Gibbon
25. 7	10. 6	B8	K12	Tapir
26. 7	11. 6	B8	A1	Sheep
27. 7	12. 6	B8	B2	Deer
28. 7	13. 6	B8	C3	Horse
29. 7	14. 6	B8	D4	Stag
30. 7	15. 6	B8	E5	Serpent
31. 7	16. 6	B8	F6	Earthworm
1. 8	17. 6	B8	G7	Crocodile
2. 8	18. 6	B8	H8	Dragon
3. 8	19. 6	B8	J9	Badger
4. 8	20. 6	B8	K10	Hare
5. 8	21. 6	B8	A11	Fox
6. 8	22. 6	B8	B12	Tiger
7. 8	23. 6	B8	C1	Leopard
8. 8	24. 6	B8	D2	Griffon
9. 8	25. 6	B8	E3	Ox
10. 8	26. 6	B8	F4	Bat
11. 8	27. 6	B8	G5	Rat
12. 8	28. 6	B8	H6	Swallow
13. 8	29. 6	B8	J7	Pig
14. 8	1. 7	C9	K8	Porcupine
15. 8	2. 7	C9	A9	Wolf
16. 8	3. 7	C9	B10	Dog
17. 8	4. 7	C9	C11	Pheasant
18. 8	5. 7	C9	D12	Cock

Solar date	*Lunar date*	*Month HS/EB*	*Day HS/EB*	*Constellation*
19. 8	6. 7	C9	E1	Crow
20. 8	7. 7	C9	F2	Monkey
21. 8	8. 7	C9	G3	Gibbon
22. 8	9. 7	C9	H4	Tapir
23. 8	10. 7	C9	J5	Sheep
24. 8	11. 7	C9	K6	Deer
25. 8	12. 7	C9	A7	Horse
26. 8	13. 7	C9	B8	Stag
27. 8	14. 7	C9	C9	Serpent
28. 8	15. 7	C9	D10	Earthworm
29. 8	16. 7	C9	E11	Crocodile
30. 8	17. 7	C9	F12	Dragon
31. 8	18. 7	C9	G1	Badger
1. 9	19. 7	C9	H2	Hare
2. 9	20. 7	C9	J3	Fox
3. 9	21. 7	C9	K4	Tiger
4. 9	22. 7	C9	A5	Leopard
5. 9	23. 7	C9	B6	Griffon
6. 9	24. 7	C9	C7	Ox
7. 9	25. 7	C9	D8	Bat
8. 9	26. 7	C9	E9	Rat
9. 9	27. 7	C9	F10	Swallow
10. 9	28. 7	C9	G11	Pig
11. 9	29. 7	C9	H12	Porcupine
12. 9	30. 7	C9	J1	Wolf
13. 9	1. 8	D10	K2	Dog
14. 9	2. 8	D10	A3	Pheasant
15. 9	3. 8	D10	B4	Cock
16. 9	4. 8	D10	C5	Crow
17. 9	5. 8	D10	D6	Monkey
18. 9	6. 8	D10	E7	Gibbon
19. 9	7. 8	D10	F8	Tapir
20. 9	8. 8	D10	G9	Sheep
21. 9	9. 8	D10	H10	Deer
22. 9	10. 8	D10	J11	Horse
23. 9	11. 8	D10	K12	Stag
24. 9	12. 8	D10	A1	Serpent
25. 9	13. 8	D10	B2	Earthworm
26. 9	14. 8	D10	C3	Crocodile
27. 9	15. 8	D10	D4	Dragon
28. 9	16. 8	D10	E5	Badger
29. 9	17. 8	D10	F6	Hare
30. 9	18. 8	D10	G7	Fox
1.10	19. 8	D10	H8	Tiger
2.10	20. 8	D10	J9	Leopard
3.10	21. 8	D10	K10	Griffon
4.10	22. 8	D10	A11	Ox
5.10	23. 8	D10	B12	Bat
6.10	24. 8	D10	C1	Rat
7.10	25. 8	D10	D2	Swallow
8.10	26. 8	D10	E3	Pig
9.10	27. 8	D10	F4	Porcupine
10.10	28. 8	D10	G5	Wolf
11. 0	29. 8	D10	H6	Dog
12.10	1. 9	E11	J7	Pheasant
13.10	2. 9	E11	K8	Cock
14.10	3. 9	E11	A9	Crow
15.10	4. 9	E11	B10	Monkey
16.10	5. 9	E11	C11	Gibbon
17.10	6. 9	E11	D12	Tapir
18.10	7. 9	E11	E1	Sheep
19.10	8. 9	E11	F2	Deer
20.10	9. 9	E11	G3	Horse
21.10	10. 9	E11	H4	Stag
22.10	11. 9	E11	J5	Serpent
23.10	12. 9	E11	K6	Earthworm
24.10	13. 9	E11	A7	Crocodile
25.10	14. 9	E11	B8	Dragon
26.10	15. 9	E11	C9	Badger
27.10	16. 9	E11	D10	Hare
28.10	17. 9	E11	E11	Fox
29.10	18. 9	E11	F12	Tiger
30.10	19. 9	E11	G1	Leopard

Solar date	*Lunar date*	*Month HS/EB*	*Day HS/EB*	*Constellation*
31.10	20. 9	E11	H2	Griffon
1.11	21. 9	E11	J3	Ox
2.11	22. 9	E11	K4	Bat
3.11	23. 9	E11	A5	Rat
4.11	24. 9	E11	B6	Swallow
5.11	25. 9	E11	C7	Pig
6.11	26. 9	E11	D8	Porcupine
7.11	27. 9	E11	E9	Wolf
8.11	28. 9	E11	F10	Dog
9.11	29. 9	E11	G11	Pheasant
10.11	30. 9	E11	H12	Cock
11.11	1.10	F12	J1	Crow
12.11	2.10	F12	K2	Monkey
13.11	3.10	F12	A3	Gibbon
14.11	4.10	F12	B4	Tapir
15.11	5.10	F12	C5	Sheep
16.11	6.10	F12	D6	Deer
17.11	7.10	F12	E7	Horse
18.11	8.10	F12	F8	Stag
19.11	9.10	F12	G9	Serpent
20.11	10.10	F12	H10	Earthworm
21.11	11.10	F12	J11	Crocodile
22.11	12.10	F12	K12	Dragon
23.11	13.10	F12	A1	Badger
24.11	14.10	F12	B2	Hare
25.11	15.10	F12	C3	Fox
26.11	16.10	F12	D4	Tiger
27.11	17.10	F12	E5	Leopard
28.11	18.10	F12	F6	Griffon
29.11	19.10	F12	G7	Ox
30.11	20.10	F12	H8	Bat
1.12	21.10	F12	J9	Rat
2.12	22.10	F12	K10	Swallow
3.12	23.10	F12	A11	Pig
4.12	24.10	F12	B12	Porcupine
5.12	25.10	F12	C1	Wolf
6.12	26.10	F12	D2	Dog
7.12	27.10	F12	E3	Pheasant
8.12	28.10	F12	F4	Cock
9.12	29.10	F12	G5	Crow
10.12	30.10	F12	H6	Monkey
11.12	1.11	G1	J7	Gibbon
12.12	2.11	G1	K8	Tapir
13.12	3.11	G1	A9	Sheep
14.12	4.11	G1	B10	Deer
15.12	5.11	G1	C11	Horse
16.12	6.11	G1	D12	Stag
17.12	7.11	G1	E1	Serpent
18.12	8.11	G1	F2	Earthworm
19.12	9.11	G1	G3	Crocodile
20.12	10.11	G1	H4	Dragon
21.12	11.11	G1	J5	Badger
22.12	12.11	G1	K6	Hare
23.12	13.11	G1	A7	Fox
24.12	14.11	G1	B8	Tiger
25.12	15.11	G1	C9	Leopard
26.12	16.11	G1	D10	Griffon
27.12	17.11	G1	E11	Ox
28.12	18.11	G1	F12	Bat
29.12	19.11	G1	G1	Rat
30.12	20.11	G1	H2	Swallow
31.12	21.11	G1	J3	Pig
1997				
1. 1	22.11	G1	K4	Porcupine
2. 1	23.11	G1	A5	Wolf
3. 1	24.11	G1	B6	Dog
4. 1	25.11	G1	C7	Pheasant
5. 1	26.11	G1	D8	Cock
6. 1	27.11	G1	E9	Crow
7. 1	28.11	G1	F10	Monkey
8. 1	29.11	G1	G11	Gibbon
9. 1	1.12	H2	H12	Tapir

Solar date	Lunar date	Month HS/EB	Day HS/EB	Constellation
10. 1	2.12	H2	J1	Sheep
11. 1	3.12	H2	K2	Deer
12. 1	4.12	H2	A3	Horse
13. 1	5.12	H2	B4	Stag
14. 1	6.12	H2	C5	Serpent
15. 1	7.12	H2	D6	Earthworm
16. 1	8.12	H2	E7	Crocodile
17. 1	9.12	H2	F8	Dragon
18. 1	10.12	H2	G9	Badger
19. 1	11.12	H2	H10	Hare
20. 1	12.12	H2	J11	Fox
21. 1	13.12	H2	K12	Tiger
22. 1	14.12	H2	A1	Leopard
23. 1	15.12	H2	B2	Griffon
24. 1	16.12	H2	C3	Ox
25. 1	17.12	H2	D4	Bat
26. 1	18.12	H2	E5	Rat
27. 1	19.12	H2	F6	Swallow
28. 1	10.12	H2	G7	Pig
29. 1	21.12	H2	H8	Porcupine
30. 1	22.12	H2	J9	Wolf
31. 1	23.12	H2	K10	Dog
1. 2	24.12	H2	A11	Pheasant
2. 2	25.12	H2	B12	Cock
3. 2	26.12	H2	C1	Crow
4. 2	27.12	H2	D2	Monkey
5. 2	28.12	H2	E3	Gibbon
6. 2	29.12	H2	F4	Tapir

TING CH'OU YEAR

Solar date	Lunar date	Month HS/EB	Day HS/EB	Constellation
7. 2	1. 1	J3	G5	Sheep
8. 2	2. 1	J3	H6	Deer
9. 2	3. 1	J3	J7	Horse
10. 2	4. 1	J3	K8	Stag
11. 2	5. 1	J3	A9	Serpent
12. 2	6. 1	J3	B10	Earthworm
13. 2	7. 1	J3	C11	Crocodile
14. 2	8. 1	J3	D12	Dragon
15. 2	9. 1	J3	E1	Badger
16. 2	10. 1	J3	F2	Hare
17. 2	11. 1	J3	G3	Fox
18. 2	12. 1	J3	H4	Tiger
19. 2	13. 1	J3	J5	Leopard
20. 2	14. 1	J3	K6	Griffon
21. 2	15. 1	J3	A7	Ox
22. 2	16. 1	J3	B8	Bat
23. 2	17. 1	J3	C9	Rat
24. 2	18. 1	J3	D10	Swallow
25. 2	19. 1	J3	E11	Pig
26. 2	20. 1	J3	F12	Porcupine
27. 2	21. 1	J3	G1	Wolf
28. 2	22. 1	J3	H2	Dog
1. 3	23. 1	J3	J3	Pheasant
2. 3	24. 1	J3	K4	Cock
3. 3	25. 1	J3	A5	Crow
4. 3	26. 1	J3	B6	Monkey
5. 3	27. 1	J3	C7	Gibbon
6. 3	28. 1	J3	D8	Tapir
7. 3	29. 1	J3	E9	Sheep
8. 3	30. 1	J3	F10	Deer
9. 3	1. 2	K4	G11	Horse
10. 3	2. 2	K4	H12	Stag
11. 3	3. 2	K4	J1	Serpent
12. 3	4. 2	K4	K2	Earthworm
13. 3	5. 2	K4	A3	Crocodile
14. 3	6. 2	K4	B4	Dragon
15. 3	7. 2	K4	C5	Badger
16. 3	8. 2	K4	D6	Hare
17. 3	9. 2	K4	E7	Fox
18. 3	10. 2	K4	F8	Tiger
19. 3	11. 2	K4	G9	Leopard
20. 3	12. 2	K4	H10	Griffon
21. 3	13. 2	K4	J11	Ox
22. 3	14. 2	K4	K12	Bat
23. 3	15. 2	K4	A1	Rat
24. 3	16. 2	K4	B2	Swallow
25. 3	17. 2	K4	C3	Pig
26. 3	18. 2	K4	D4	Porcupine
27. 3	19. 2	K4	E5	Wolf
28. 3	20. 2	K4	F6	Dog
29. 3	21. 2	K4	G7	Pheasant
30. 3	22. 2	K4	H8	Cock
31. 3	23. 2	K4	J9	Crow
1. 4	24. 2	K4	K10	Monkey
2. 4	25. 2	K4	A11	Gibbon
3. 4	26. 2	K4	B12	Tapir
4. 4	27. 2	K4	C1	Sheep
5. 4	28. 2	K4	D2	Deer
6. 4	29. 2	K4	E3	Horse
7. 4	1. 3	A5	F4	Stag
8. 4	2. 3	A5	G5	Serpent
9. 4	3. 3	A5	H6	Earthworm
10. 4	4. 3	A5	J7	Crocodile
11. 4	5. 3	A5	K8	Dragon
12. 4	6. 3	A5	A9	Badger
13. 4	7. 3	A5	B10	Hare
14. 4	8. 3	A5	C11	Fox
15. 4	9. 3	A5	D12	Tiger
16. 4	10. 3	A5	E1	Leopard
17. 4	11. 3	A5	F2	Griffon
18. 4	12. 3	A5	G3	Ox
19. 4	13. 3	A5	H4	Bat
20. 4	14. 3	A5	J5	Rat
21. 4	15. 3	A5	K6	Swallow
22. 4	16. 3	A5	A7	Pig
23. 4	17. 3	A5	B8	Porcupine
24. 4	18. 3	A5	C9	Wolf
25. 4	19. 3	A5	D10	Dog
26. 4	20. 3	A5	E11	Pheasant
27. 4	21. 3	A5	F12	Cock
28. 4	22. 3	A5	G1	Crow
29. 4	23. 3	A5	H2	Monkey
30. 4	24. 3	A5	J3	Gibbon
1. 5	25. 3	A5	K4	Tapir
2. 5	26. 3	A5	A5	Sheep
3. 5	27. 3	A5	B6	Deer
4. 5	28. 3	A5	C7	Horse
5. 5	29. 3	A5	D8	Stag
6. 5	30. 3	A5	E9	Serpent
7. 5	1. 4	B6	F10	Earthworm
8. 5	2. 4	B6	G11	Crocodile
9. 5	3. 4	B6	H12	Dragon
10. 5	4. 4	B6	J1	Badger
11. 5	5. 4	B6	K2	Hare
12. 5	6. 4	B6	A3	Fox
13. 5	7. 4	B6	B4	Tiger
14. 5	8. 4	B6	C5	Leopard
15. 5	9. 4	B6	D6	Griffon
16. 5	10. 4	B6	E7	Ox
17. 5	11. 4	B6	F8	Bat
18. 5	12. 4	B6	G9	Rat
19. 5	13. 4	B6	H10	Swallow
20. 5	14. 4	B6	J11	Pig
21. 5	15. 4	B6	K12	Porcupine
22. 5	16. 4	B6	A1	Wolf
23. 5	17. 4	B6	B2	Dog
24. 5	18. 4	B6	C3	Pheasant
25. 5	19. 4	B6	D4	Cock

Solar date	*Lunar date*	*Month HS/EB*	*Day HS/EB*	*Constellation*
26. 5	20. 4	B6	E5	Crow
27. 5	21. 4	B6	F6	Monkey
28. 5	22. 4	B6	G7	Gibbon
29. 5	23. 4	B6	H8	Tapir
30. 5	24. 4	B6	J9	Sheep
31. 5	25. 4	B6	K10	Deer
1. 6	26. 4	B6	A11	Horse
2. 6	27. 4	B6	B12	Stag
3. 6	28. 4	B6	C1	Serpent
4. 6	29. 4	B6	D2	Earthworm
5. 6	1. 5	C7	E3	Crocodile
6. 6	2. 5	C7	F4	Dragon
7. 6	3. 5	C7	G5	Badger
8. 6	4. 5	C7	H6	Hare
9. 6	5. 5	C7	J7	Fox
10. 6	6. 5	C7	K8	Tiger
11. 6	7. 5	C7	A9	Leopard
12. 6	8. 5	C7	B10	Griffon
13. 6	9. 5	C7	C11	Ox
14. 6	10. 5	C7	D12	Bat
15. 6	11. 5	C7	E1	Rat
16. 6	12. 5	C7	F2	Swallow
17. 6	13. 5	C7	G3	Pig
18. 6	14. 5	C7	H4	Porcupine
19. 6	15. 5	C7	J5	Wolf
20. 6	16. 5	C7	K6	Dog
21. 6	17. 5	C7	A7	Pheasant
22. 6	18. 5	C7	B8	Cock
23. 6	19. 5	C7	C9	Crow
24. 6	20. 5	C7	D10	Monkey
25. 6	21. 5	C7	E11	Gibbon
26. 6	22. 5	C7	F12	Tapir
27. 6	23. 5	C7	G1	Sheep
28. 6	24. 5	C7	H2	Deer
29. 6	25. 5	C7	J3	Horse
30. 6	26. 5	C7	K4	Stag
1. 7	27. 5	C7	A5	Serpent
2. 7	28. 5	C7	B6	Earthworm
3. 7	29. 5	C7	C7	Crocodile
4. 7	30. 5	C7	D8	Dragon
5. 7	1. 6	D8	E9	Badger
6. 7	2. 6	D8	F10	Hare
7. 7	3. 6	D8	G11	Fox
8. 7	4. 6	D8	H12	Tiger
9. 7	5. 6	D8	J1	Leopard
10. 7	6. 6	D8	K2	Griffon
11. 7	7. 6	D8	A3	Ox
12. 7	8. 6	D8	B4	Bat
13. 7	9. 6	D8	C5	Rat
14. 7	10. 6	D8	D6	Swallow
15. 7	11. 6	D8	E7	Pig
16. 7	12. 6	D8	F8	Porcupine
17. 7	13. 6	D8	G9	Wolf
18. 7	14. 6	D8	H10	Dog
19. 7	15. 6	D8	J11	Pheasant
20. 7	16. 6	D8	K12	Cock
21. 7	17. 6	D8	A1	Crow
22. 7	18. 6	D8	B2	Monkey
23. 7	19. 6	D8	C3	Gibbon
24. 7	20. 6	D8	D4	Tapir
25. 7	21. 6	D8	E5	Sheep
26. 7	22. 6	D8	F6	Deer
27. 7	23. 6	D8	G7	Horse
28. 7	24. 6	D8	H8	Stag
29. 7	25. 6	D8	J9	Serpent
30. 7	26. 6	D8	K10	Earthworm
31. 7	27. 6	D8	A11	Crocodile
1. 8	28. 6	D8	B12	Dragon
2. 8	29. 6	D8	C1	Badger
3. 8	1. 7	E9	D2	Hare
4. 8	2. 7	E9	E3	Fox
5. 8	3. 7	E9	F4	Tiger
6. 8	4. 7	E9	G5	Leopard

Solar date	*Lunar date*	*Month HS/EB*	*Day HS/EB*	*Constellation*
7. 8	5. 7	E9	H6	Griffon
8. 8	6. 7	E9	J7	Ox
9. 8	7. 7	E9	K8	Bat
10. 8	8. 7	E9	A9	Rat
11. 8	9. 7	E9	B10	Swallow
12. 8	10. 7	E9	C11	Pig
13. 8	11. 7	E9	D12	Porcupine
14. 8	12. 7	E9	E1	Wolf
15. 8	13. 7	E9	F2	Dog
16. 8	14. 7	E9	G3	Pheasant
17. 8	15. 7	E9	H4	Cock
18. 8	16. 7	E9	J5	Crow
19. 8	17. 7	E9	K6	Monkey
20. 8	18. 7	E9	A7	Gibbon
21. 8	19. 7	E9	B8	Tapir
22. 8	20. 7	E9	C9	Sheep
23. 8	21. 7	E9	D10	Deer
24. 8	22. 7	E9	E11	Horse
25. 8	23. 7	E9	F12	Stag
26. 8	24. 7	E9	G1	Serpent
27. 8	25. 7	E9	H2	Earthworm
28. 8	26. 7	E9	J3	Crocodile
29. 8	27. 7	E9	K4	Dragon
30. 8	28. 7	E9	A5	Badger
31. 8	29. 7	E9	B6	Hare
1. 9	30. 7	E9	C7	Fox
2. 9	1. 8	F10	D8	Tiger
3. 9	2. 8	F10	E9	Leopard
4. 9	3. 8	F10	F10	Griffon
5. 9	4. 8	F10	G11	Ox
6. 9	5. 8	F10	H12	Bat
7. 9	6. 8	F10	J1	Rat
8. 9	7. 8	F10	K2	Swallow
9. 9	8. 8	F10	A3	Pig
10. 9	9. 8	F10	B4	Porcupine
11. 9	10. 8	F10	C5	Wolf
12. 9	11. 8	F10	D6	Dog
13. 9	12. 8	F10	E7	Pheasant
14. 9	13. 8	F10	F8	Cock
15. 9	14. 8	F10	G9	Crow
16. 9	15. 8	F10	H10	Monkey
17. 9	16. 8	F10	J11	Gibbon
18. 9	17. 8	F10	K12	Tapir
19. 9	18. 8	F10	A1	Sheep
20. 9	19. 8	F10	B2	Deer
21. 9	20. 8	F10	C3	Horse
22. 9	21. 8	F10	D4	Stag
23. 9	22. 8	F10	E5	Serpent
24. 9	23. 8	F10	F6	Earthworm
25. 9	24. 8	F10	G7	Crocodile
26. 9	25. 8	F10	H8	Dragon
27. 9	26. 8	F10	J9	Badger
28. 9	27. 8	F10	K10	Hare
29. 9	28. 8	F10	A11	Fox
30. 9	29. 8	F10	B12	Tiger
1.10	30. 8	F10	C1	Leopard
2.10	1. 9	G11	D2	Griffon
3.10	2. 9	G11	E3	Ox
4.10	3. 9	G11	F4	Bat
5.10	4. 9	G11	G5	Rat
6.10	5. 9	G11	H6	Swallow
7.10	6. 9	G11	J7	Pig
8.10	7. 9	G11	K8	Porcupine
9.10	8. 9	G11	A9	Wolf
10.10	9. 9	G11	B10	Dog
11.10	10. 9	G11	C11	Pheasant
12.10	11. 9	G11	D12	Cock
13.10	12. 9	G11	E1	Crow
14.10	13. 9	G11	F2	Monkey
15.10	14. 9	G11	G3	Gibbon
16.10	15. 9	G11	H4	Tapir
17.10	16. 9	G11	J5	Sheep
18.10	17. 9	G11	K6	Deer

Solar date	*Lunar date*	*Month HS/EB*	*Day HS/EB*	*Constellation*
19.10	18. 9	G11	A7	Horse
20.10	19. 9	G11	B8	Stag
21.10	20. 9	G11	C9	Serpent
22.10	21. 9	G11	D10	Earthworm
23.10	22. 9	G11	E11	Crocodile
24.10	23. 9	G11	F12	Dragon
25.10	24. 9	G11	G1	Badger
26.10	25. 9	G11	H2	Hare
27.10	26. 9	G11	J3	Fox
28.10	27. 9	G11	K4	Tiger
29.10	28. 9	G11	A5	Leopard
30.10	29. 9	G11	B6	Griffon
31.10	1.10	H12	C7	Ox
1.11	2.10	H12	D8	Bat
2.11	3.10	H12	E9	Rat
3.11	4.10	H12	F10	Swallow
4.11	5.10	H12	G11	Pig
5.11	6.10	H12	H12	Porcupine
6.11	7.10	H12	J1	Wolf
7.11	8.10	H12	K2	Dog
8.11	9.10	H12	A3	Pheasant
9.11	10.10	H12	B4	Cock
10.11	11.10	H12	C5	Crow
11.11	12.10	H12	D6	Monkey
12.11	13.10	H12	E7	Gibbon
13.11	14.10	H12	F8	Tapir
14.11	15.10	H12	G9	Sheep
15.11	16.10	H12	H10	Deer
16.11	17.10	H12	J11	Horse
17.11	18.10	H12	K12	Stag
18.11	19.10	H12	A1	Serpent
19.11	20.10	H12	B2	Earthworm
20.11	21.10	H12	C3	Crocodile
21.11	22.10	H12	D4	Dragon
22.11	23.10	H12	E5	Badger
23.11	24.10	H12	F6	Hare
24.11	25.10	H12	G7	Fox
25.11	26.10	H12	H8	Tiger
26.11	27.10	H12	J9	Leopard
27.11	28.10	H12	K10	Griffon
28.11	29.10	H12	A11	Ox
29.11	30.10	H12	B12	Bat
30.11	1.11	J1	C1	Rat
1.12	2.11	J1	D2	Swallow
2.12	3.11	J1	E3	Pig
3.12	4.11	J1	F4	Porcupine
4.12	5.11	J1	G5	Wolf
5.12	6.11	J1	H6	Dog
6.12	7.11	J1	J7	Pheasant
7.12	8.11	J1	K8	Cock
8.12	9.11	J1	A9	Crow
9.12	10.11	J1	B10	Monkey
10.12	11.11	J1	C11	Gibbon
11.12	12.11	J1	D12	Tapir
12.12	13.11	J1	E1	Sheep
13.12	14.11	J1	F2	Deer
14.12	15.11	J1	G3	Horse
15.12	16.11	J1	H4	Stag
16.12	17.11	J1	J5	Serpent
17.12	18.11	J1	K6	Earthworm
18.12	19.11	J1	A7	Crocodile
19.12	20.11	J1	B8	Dragon
20.12	21.11	J1	C9	Badger
21.12	22.11	J1	D10	Hare
22.12	23.11	J1	E11	Fox
23.12	24.11	J1	F12	Tiger
24.12	25.11	J1	G1	Leopard
25.12	26.11	J1	H2	Griffon
26.12	27.11	J1	J3	Ox
27.12	28.11	J1	K4	Bat
28.12	29.11	J1	A5	Rat
29.12	30.11	J1	B6	Swallow
30.12	1.12	K2	C7	Pig
31.12	2.12	K2	D8	Porcupine
1998				
1. 1	3.12	K2	E9	Wolf
2. 1	4.12	K2	F10	Dog
3. 1	5.12	K2	G11	Pheasant
4. 1	6.12	K2	H12	Cock
5. 1	7.12	K2	J1	Crow
6. 1	8.12	K2	K2	Monkey
7. 1	9.12	K2	A3	Gibbon
8. 1	10.12	K2	B4	Tapir
9. 1	11.12	K2	C5	Sheep
10. 1	12.12	K2	D6	Deer
11. 1	13.12	K2	E7	Horse
12. 1	14.12	K2	F8	Stag
13. 1	15.12	K2	G9	Serpent
14. 1	16.12	K2	H10	Earthworm
15. 1	17.12	K2	J11	Crocodile
16. 1	18.12	K2	K12	Dragon
17. 1	19.12	K2	A1	Badger
18. 1	20.12	K2	B2	Hare
19. 1	21.12	K2	C3	Fox
20. 1	22.12	K2	D4	Tiger
21. 1	23.12	K2	E5	Leopard
22. 1	24.12	K2	F6	Griffon
23. 1	25.12	K2	G7	Ox
24. 1	26.12	K2	H8	Bat
25. 1	27.12	K2	J9	Rat
26. 1	28.12	K2	K10	Swallow
27. 1	29.12	K2	A11	Pig

MOU YIN YEAR

28. 1	1. 1	A3	B12	Porcupine
29. 1	2. 1	A3	C1	Wolf
30. 1	3. 1	A3	D2	Dog
31. 1	4. 1	A3	E3	Pheasant
1. 2	5. 1	A3	F4	Cock
2. 2	6. 1	A3	G5	Crow
3. 2	7. 1	A3	H6	Monkey
4. 2	8. 1	A3	J7	Gibbon
5. 2	9. 1	A3	K8	Tapir
6. 2	10. 1	A3	A9	Sheep
7. 2	11. 1	A3	B10	Deer
8. 2	12. 1	A3	C11	Horse
9. 2	13. 1	A3	D12	Stag
10. 2	14. 1	A3	E1	Serpent
11. 2	15. 1	A3	F2	Earthworm
12. 2	16. 1	A3	G3	Crocodile
13. 2	17. 1	A3	H4	Dragon
14. 2	18. 1	A3	J5	Badger
15. 2	19. 1	A3	K6	Hare
16. 2	20. 1	A3	A7	Fox
17. 2	21. 1	A3	B8	Tiger
18. 2	22. 1	A3	C9	Leopard
19. 2	23. 1	A3	D10	Griffon
20. 2	24. 1	A3	E11	Ox
21. 2	25. 1	A3	F12	Bat
22. 2	26. 1	A3	G1	Rat
23. 2	27. 1	A3	H2	Swallow
24. 2	28. 1	A3	J3	Pig
25. 2	29. 1	A3	K4	Porcupine
26. 2	30. 1	A3	A5	Wolf
27. 2	1. 2	B4	B6	Dog
28. 2	2. 2	B4	C7	Pheasant

Solar date	*Lunar date*	*Month HS/EB*	*Day HS/EB*	*Constellation*
1. 3	3. 2	B4	D8	Cock
2. 3	4. 2	B4	E9	Crow
3. 3	5. 2	B4	F10	Monkey
4. 3	6. 2	B4	G11	Gibbon
5. 3	7. 2	B4	H12	Tapir
6. 3	8. 2	B4	J1	Sheep
7. 3	9. 2	B4	K2	Deer
8. 3	10. 2	B4	A3	Horse
9. 3	11. 2	B4	B4	Stag
10. 3	12. 2	B4	C5	Serpent
11. 3	13. 2	B4	D6	Earthworm
12. 3	14. 2	B4	E7	Crocodile
13. 3	15. 2	B4	F8	Dragon
14. 3	16. 2	B4	G9	Badger
15. 3	17. 2	B4	H10	Hare
16. 3	18. 2	B4	J11	Fox
17. 3	19. 2	B4	K12	Tiger
18. 3	20. 2	B4	A1	Leopard
19. 3	21. 2	B4	B2	Griffon
20. 3	22. 2	B4	C3	Ox
21. 3	23. 2	B4	D4	Bat
22. 3	24. 2	B4	E5	Rat
23. 3	25. 2	B4	F6	Swallow
24. 3	26. 2	B4	G7	Pig
25. 3	27. 2	B4	H8	Porcupine
26. 3	28. 2	B4	J9	Wolf
27. 3	29. 2	B4	K10	Dog
28. 3	1. 3	C5	A11	Pheasant
29. 3	2. 3	C5	B12	Cock
30. 3	3. 3	C5	C1	Crow
31. 3	4. 3	C5	D2	Monkey
1. 4	5. 3	C5	E3	Gibbon
2. 4	6. 3	C5	F4	Tapir
3. 4	7. 3	C5	G5	Sheep
4. 4	8. 3	C5	H6	Deer
5. 4	9. 3	C5	J7	Horse
6. 4	10. 3	C5	K8	Stag
7. 4	11. 3	C5	A9	Serpent
8. 4	12. 3	C5	B10	Earthworm
9. 4	13. 3	C5	C11	Crocodile
10. 4	14. 3	C5	D12	Dragon
11. 4	15. 3	C5	E1	Badger
12. 4	16. 3	C5	F2	Hare
13. 4	17. 3	C5	G3	Fox
14. 4	18. 3	C5	H4	Tiger
15. 4	19. 3	C5	J5	Leopard
16. 4	20. 3	C5	K6	Griffon
17. 4	21. 3	C5	A7	Ox
18. 4	22. 3	C5	B8	Bat
19. 4	23. 3	C5	C9	Rat
20. 4	24. 3	C5	D10	Swallow
21. 4	25. 3	C5	E11	Pig
22. 4	26. 3	C5	F12	Porcupine
23. 4	27. 3	C5	G1	Wolf
24. 4	28. 3	C5	H2	Dog
25. 4	29. 3	C5	J3	Pheasant
26. 4	1. 4	D6	K4	Cock
27. 4	2. 4	D6	A5	Crow
28. 4	3. 4	D6	B6	Monkey
29. 4	4. 4	D6	C7	Gibbon
30. 4	5. 4	D6	D8	Tapir
1. 5	6. 4	D6	E9	Sheep
2. 5	7. 4	D6	F10	Deer
3. 5	8. 4	D6	G11	Horse
4. 5	9. 4	D6	H12	Stag
5. 5	10. 4	D6	J1	Serpent
6. 5	11. 4	D6	K2	Earthworm
7. 5	12. 4	D6	A3	Crocodile
8. 5	13. 4	D6	B4	Dragon
9. 5	14. 4	D6	C5	Badger
10. 5	15. 4	D6	D6	Hare
11. 5	16. 4	D6	E7	Fox
12. 5	17. 4	D6	F8	Tiger
13. 5	18. 4	D6	G9	Leopard
14. 5	19. 4	D6	H10	Griffon
15. 5	20. 4	D6	J11	Ox
16. 5	21. 4	D6	K12	Bat
17. 5	22. 4	D6	A1	Rat
18. 5	23. 4	D6	B2	Swallow
19. 5	24. 4	D6	C3	Pig
20. 5	25. 4	D6	D4	Porcupine
21. 5	26. 4	D6	E5	Wolf
22. 5	27. 4	D6	F6	Dog
23. 5	28. 4	D6	G7	Pheasant
24. 5	29. 4	D6	H8	Cock
25. 5	30. 4	D6	J9	Crow
26. 5	1. 5	E7	K10	Monkey
27. 5	2. 5	E7	A11	Gibbon
28. 5	3. 5	E7	B12	Tapir
29. 5	4. 5	E7	C1	Sheep
30. 5	5. 5	E7	D2	Deer
31. 5	6. 5	E7	E3	Horse
1. 6	7. 5	E7	F4	Stag
2. 6	8. 5	E7	G5	Serpent
3. 6	9. 5	E7	H6	Earthworm
4. 6	10. 5	E7	J7	Crocodile
5. 6	11. 5	E7	K8	Dragon
6. 6	12. 5	E7	A9	Badger
7. 6	13. 5	E7	B10	Hare
8. 6	14. 5	E7	C11	Fox
9. 6	15. 5	E7	D12	Tiger
10. 6	16. 5	E7	E1	Leopard
11. 6	17. 5	E7	F2	Griffon
12. 6	18. 5	E7	G3	Ox
13. 6	19. 5	E7	H4	Bat
14. 6	20. 5	E7	J5	Rat
15. 6	21. 5	E7	K6	Swallow
16. 6	22. 5	E7	A7	Pig
17. 6	23. 5	E7	B8	Porcupine
18. 6	24. 5	E7	C9	Wolf
19. 6	25. 5	E7	D10	Dog
20. 6	26. 5	E7	E11	Pheasant
21. 6	27. 5	E7	F12	Cock
22. 6	28. 5	E7	G1	Crow
23. 6	29. 5	E7	H2	Monkey
24. 6	*1. 5*	*E7*	J3	Gibbon
25. 6	*2. 5*	*E7*	K4	Tapir
26. 6	*3. 5*	*E7*	A5	Sheep
27. 6	*4. 5*	*E7*	B6	Deer
28. 6	*5. 5*	*E7*	C7	Horse
29. 6	*6. 5*	*E7*	D8	Stag
30. 6	*7. 5*	*E7*	E9	Serpent
1. 7	*8. 5*	*E7*	F10	Earthworm
2. 7	*9. 5*	*E7*	G11	Crocodile
3. 7	*10. 5*	*E7*	H12	Dragon
4. 7	*11. 5*	*E7*	J1	Badger
5. 7	*12. 5*	*E7*	K2	Hare
6. 7	*13. 5*	*E7*	A3	Fox
7. 7	*14. 5*	*E7*	B4	Tiger
8. 7	*15. 5*	*E7*	C5	Leopard
9. 7	*16. 5*	*E7*	D6	Griffon
10. 7	*17. 5*	*E7*	E7	Ox
11. 7	*18. 5*	*E7*	F8	Bat
12. 7	*19. 5*	*E7*	G9	Rat
13. 7	*20. 5*	*E7*	H10	Swallow
14. 7	*21. 5*	*E7*	J11	Pig
15. 7	*22. 5*	*E7*	K12	Porcupine
16. 7	*23. 5*	*E7*	A1	Wolf
17. 7	*24. 5*	*E7*	B2	Dog
18. 7	*25. 5*	*E7*	C3	Pheasant
19. 7	*26. 5*	*E7*	D4	Cock
20. 7	*27. 5*	*E7*	E5	Crow
21. 7	*28. 5*	*E7*	F6	Monkey
22. 7	*29. 5*	*E7*	G7	Gibbon
23. 7	1. 6	F8	H8	Tapir
24. 7	2. 6	F8	J9	Sheep

Solar date	*Lunar date*	*Month HS/EB*	*Day HS/EB*	*Constellation*
25. 7	3. 6	F8	K10	Deer
26. 7	4. 6	F8	A11	Horse
27. 7	5. 6	F8	B12	STag
28. 7	6. 6	F8	C1	Serpent
29. 7	7. 6	F8	D2	Earthworm
30. 7	8. 6	F8	E3	Crocodile
31. 7	9. 6	F8	F4	Dragon
1. 8	10. 6	F8	G5	Badger
2. 8	11 6	F8	H6	Hare
3. 8	12. 6	F8	J7	Fox
4. 8	13. 6	F8	K8	Tiger
5. 8	14. 6	F8	A9	Leopard
6. 8	15. 6	F8	B10	Griffon
7. 8	16. 6	F8	C11	Ox
8. 8	17. 6	F8	D12	Bat
9. 8	18. 6	F8	E1	Rat
10. 8	19. 6	F8	F2	Swallow
11. 8	20. 6	F8	G3	Pig
12. 8	21. 6	F8	H4	Porcupine
13. 8	22. 6	F8	J5	Wolf
14. 8	23. 6	F8	K6	Dog
15. 8	24. 6	F8	A7	Pheasant
16. 8	25. 6	F8	B8	Cock
17. 8	26. 6	F8	C9	Crow
18. 8	27. 6	F8	D10	Monkey
19. 8	28. 6	F8	E11	Gibbon
20. 8	29. 6	F8	F12	Tapir
21. 8	30. 6	F8	G1	Sheep
22. 8	1. 7	G9	H2	Deer
23. 8	2. 7	G9	J3	Horse
24. 8	3. 7	G9	K4	Stag
25. 8	4. 7	G9	A5	Serpent
26. 8	5. 7	G9	B6	Earthworm
27. 8	6. 7	G9	C7	Crocodile
28. 8	7. 7	G9	D8	Dragon
29. 8	8. 7	G9	E9	Badger
30. 8	9. 7	G9	F10	Hare
31. 8	10. 7	G9	G11	Fox
1. 9	11. 7	G9	H12	Tiger
2. 9	12. 7	G9	J1	Leopard
3. 9	13. 7	G9	K2	Griffon
4. 9	14. 7	G9	A3	Ox
5. 9	15. 7	G9	B4	Bat
6. 9	16. 7	G9	C5	Rat
7. 9	17. 7	G0	D6	Swallow
8. 9	18. 7	G9	E7	Pig
9. 9	19. 7	G9	F8	Porcupine
10. 9	20. 7	G9	G9	Wolf
11. 9	21. 7	G9	H10	Dog
12. 9	22. 7	G9	J11	Pheasant
13. 9	23. 7	G9	K12	Cock
14. 9	24. 7	G9	A1	Crow
15. 9	25. 7	G9	B2	Monkey
16. 9	26. 7	G9	C3	Gibbon
17. 9	27. 7	G9	D4	Tapir
18. 9	28. 7	G9	E5	Sheep
19. 9	29. 7	G9	F6	Deer
20. 9	30. 7	G9	G7	Horse
21. 9	1. 8	H10	H8	Stag
22. 9	2. 8	H10	J9	Serpent
23. 9	3. 8	H10	K10	Earthworm
24. 9	4. 8	H10	A11	Crocodile
25. 9	5. 8	H10	B12	Dragon
26. 9	6. 8	H10	C1	Badger
27. 9	7. 8	H10	D2	Hare
28. 9	8. 8	H10	E3	Fox
29. 9	9. 8	H10	F4	Tiger
30. 9	10. 8	H10	G5	Leopard
1.10	11. 8	H10	H6	Griffon
2.10	12. 8	H10	J7	Ox
3.10	13. 8	H10	K8	Bat
4.10	14. 8	H10	A9	Rat
5.10	15. 8	H10	B10	Swallow
6.10	16. 8	H10	C11	Pig
7.10	17. 8	H10	D12	Porcupine
8.10	18. 8	H10	E1	Wolf
9.10	19. 8	H10	F2	Dog
10.10	20. 8	H10	G3	Pheasant
11.10	21. 8	H10	H4	Cock
12.10	22. 8	H10	J5	Crow
13.10	23. 8	H10	K6	Monkey
14.10	24. 8	H10	A7	Gibbon
15.10	25. 8	H10	B8	Tapir
16.10	26. 8	H10	C9	Sheep
17.10	27. 8	H10	D10	Deer
18.10	28. 8	H10	E11	Horse
19.10	29. 8	H10	F12	Stag
20.10	1. 9	J11	G1	Serpent
21.10	2. 9	J11	H2	Earthworm
22.10	3. 9	J11	J3	Crocodile
23.10	4. 9	J11	K4	Dragon
24.10	5. 9	J11	A5	Badger
25.10	6. 9	J11	B6	Hare
26.10	7. 9	J11	C7	Fox
27.10	8. 9	J11	D8	Tiger
28.10	9. 9	J11	E9	Leopard
29.10	10. 9	J11	F10	Griffon
30.10	11. 9	J11	G11	Ox
31.10	12. 9	J11	H12	Bat
1.11	13. 9	J11	J1	Rat
2.11	14. 9	J11	K2	Swallow
3.11	15. 9	J11	A3	Pig
4.11	16. 9	J11	B4	Porcupine
5.11	17. 9	J11	C5	Wolf
6.11	18. 9	J11	D6	Dog
7.11	19. 9	J11	E7	Pheasant
8.11	20. 9	J11	F8	Cock
9.11	21. 9	J11	G9	Crow
10.11	22. 9	J11	H10	Monkey
11.11	23. 9	J11	J11	Gibbon
12.11	24. 9	J11	K12	Tapir
13.11	25. 9	J11	A1	Sheep
14.11	26. 9	J11	B2	Deer
15.11	27. 9	J11	C3	Horse
16.11	28. 9	J11	D4	Stag
17.11	29. 9	J11	E5	Serpent
18.11	30. 9	J11	F6	Earthworm
19.11	1.10	K12	G7	Crocodile
20.11	2.10	K12	H8	Dragon
21.11	3.10	K12	J9	Badger
22.11	4.10	K12	K10	Hare
23.11	5.10	K12	A11	Fox
24.11	6.10	K12	B12	Tiger
25.11	7.10	K12	C1	Leopard
26.11	8.10	K12	D2	Griffon
27.11	9.10	K12	E3	Ox
28.11	10.10	K12	F4	Bat
29.11	11.10	K12	G5	Rat
20.11	12.10	K12	H6	Swallow
1.12	13.10	K12	J7	Pig
2.12	14.10	K12	K8	Porcupine
3.12	15.10	K12	A9	Wolf
4.12	16.10	K12	B10	Dog
5.12	17.10	K12	C11	Pheasant
6.12	18.10	K12	D12	Cock
7.12	19.10	K12	E1	Crow
8.12	20.10	K12	F2	Monkey
9.12	21.10	K12	G3	Gibbon
10.12	22.10	K12	H4	Tapir
11.12	23.10	K12	J5	Sheep
12.12	24.10	K12	K6	Deer
13.12	25.10	K12	A7	Horse
14.12	26.10	K12	B8	Stag
15.12	27.10	K12	C9	Serpent
16.12	28.10	K12	D10	Earthworm
17.12	29.10	K12	E11	Crocodile

Solar date	*Lunar date*	*Month HS/EB*	*Day HS/EB*	*Constellation*
18.12	30.10	K12	F12	Dragon
19.12	1.11	A1	G1	Badger
20.12	2.11	A1	H2	Hare
21.12	3.11	A1	J3	Fox
22.12	4.11	A1	K4	Tiger
23.12	5.11	A1	A5	Leopard
24.12	6.11	A1	B6	Griffon
25.12	7.11	A1	C7	Ox
26.12	8.11	A1	D8	Bat
27.12	9.11	A1	E9	Rat
28.12	10.11	A1	F10	Swallow
29.12	11.11	A1	G11	Pig
30.12	12.11	A1	H12	Porcupine
31.12	13.11	A1	J1	Wolf
1999				
1. 1	14.11	A1	K2	Dog
2. 1	15.11	A1	A3	Pheasant
3. 1	16.11	A1	B4	Cock
4. 1	17.11	A1	C5	Crow
5. 1	18.11	A1	D6	Monkey
6. 1	19.11	A1	E7	Gibbon
7. 1	20.11	A1	F8	Tapir
8. 1	21.11	A1	G9	Sheep
9. 1	22.11	A1	H10	Deer
10. 1	23.11	A1	J11	Horse
11. 1	24.11	A1	K12	Stag
12. 1	25.11	A1	A1	Serpent
13. 1	26.11	A1	B2	Earthworm
14. 1	27.11	A1	C3	Crocodile
15. 1	28.11	A1	D4	Dragon
16. 1	29.11	A1	E5	Badger
17. 1	1.12	B2	F6	Hare
18. 1	2.12	B2	G7	Fox
19. 1	3.12	B2	H8	Tiger
20. 1	4.12	B2	J9	Leopard
21. 1	5.12	B2	K10	Griffon
22. 1	6.12	B2	A11	Ox
23. 1	7.12	B2	B12	Bat
24. 1	8.12	B2	C1	Rat
25. 1	9.12	B2	D2	Swallow
26. 1	10.12	B2	E3	Pig
27. 1	11.12	B2	F4	Porcupine
28. 1	12.12	B2	G5	Wolf
29. 1	13.12	B2	H6	Dog
30. 1	14.12	B2	J7	Pheasant
31. 1	15.12	B2	K8	Cock
1. 2	16.12	B2	A9	Crow
2. 2	17.12	B2	B10	Monkey
3. 2	18.12	B2	C11	Gibbon
4. 2	19.12	B2	D12	Tapir
5. 2	20.12	B2	E1	Sheep
6. 2	21.12	B2	F2	Deer
7. 2	22.12	B2	G3	Horse
8. 2	23.12	B2	H4	Stag
9. 2	24.12	B2	J5	Serpent
10. 2	25.12	B2	K6	Earthworm
11. 2	26.12	B2	A7	Crocodile
12. 2	27.12	B2	B8	Dragon
13. 2	28.12	B2	C9	Badger
14. 2	29.12	B2	D10	Hare
15. 2	30.12	B2	E11	Fox

CHI MAO YEAR

16. 2	1. 1	C3	F12	Tiger
17. 2	2. 1	C3	G1	Leopard
18. 2	3. 1	C3	H2	Griffon
19. 2	4. 1	C3	J3	Ox
20. 2	5. 1	C3	K4	Bat
21. 2	6. 1	C3	A5	Rat
22. 2	7. 1	C3	B6	Swallow
23. 2	8. 1	C3	C7	Pig
24. 2	9. 1	C3	D8	Porcupine
25. 2	10. 1	C3	E9	Wolf
26. 2	11. 1	C3	F10	Dog
27. 2	12. 1	C3	G11	Pheasant
28. 2	13. 1	C3	H12	Cock
1. 3	14. 1	C3	J1	Crow
2. 3	15. 1	C3	K2	Monkey
3. 3	16. 1	C3	A3	Gibbon
4. 3	17. 1	C3	B4	Tapir
5. 3	18. 1	C3	C5	Sheep
6. 3	19. 1	C3	D6	Deer
7. 3	20. 1	C3	E7	Horse
8. 3	21. 1	C3	F8	Stag
9. 3	22. 1	C3	G9	Serpent
10. 3	23. 1	C3	H10	Earthworm
11. 3	24. 1	C3	J11	Crocodile
12. 3	25. 1	C3	K12	Dragon
13. 3	26. 1	C3	A1	Badger
14. 3	27. 1	C3	B2	Hare
15. 3	28. 1	C3	C3	Fox
16. 3	29. 1	C3	D4	Tiger
17. 3	30. 1	C3	E5	Leopard
18. 3	1. 2	D4	F6	Griffon
19. 3	2. 2	D4	G7	Ox
20. 3	3. 2	D4	H8	Bat
21. 3	4. 2	D4	J9	Rat
22. 3	5. 2	D4	K10	Swallow
23. 3	6. 2	D4	A11	Pig
24. 3	7. 2	D4	B12	Porcupine
25. 3	8. 2	D4	C1	Wolf
26. 3	9. 2	D4	D2	Dog
27. 3	10. 2	D4	E3	Pheasant
28. 3	11. 2	D4	F4	Cock
29. 3	12. 2	D4	G5	Crow
30. 3	13. 2	D4	H6	Monkey
31. 3	14. 2	D4	J7	Gibbon
1. 4	15. 2	D4	K8	Tapir
2. 4	16. 2	D4	A9	Sheep
3. 4	17. 2	D4	B10	Deer
4. 4	18. 2	D4	C11	Horse
5. 4	19. 2	D4	D12	Stag
6. 4	20. 2	D4	E1	Serpent
7. 4	21. 2	D4	F2	Earthworm
8. 4	22. 2	D4	G3	Crocodile
9. 4	23. 2	D4	H4	Dragon
10. 4	24. 2	D4	J5	Badger
11. 4	25. 2	D4	K6	Hare
12. 4	26. 2	D4	A7	Fox
13. 4	27. 2	D4	B8	Tiger
14. 4	28. 2	D4	C9	Leopard
15. 4	29. 2	D4	D10	Griffon
16. 4	1. 3	E5	E11	Ox
17. 4	2. 3	E5	F12	Bat
18. 4	3. 3	E5	G1	Rat
19. 4	4. 3	E5	H2	Swallow
20. 4	5. 3	E5	J3	Pig
21. 4	6. 3	E5	K4	Porcupine
22. 4	7. 3	E5	A5	Wolf
23. 4	8. 3	E5	B6	Dog
24. 4	9. 3	E5	C7	Pheasant
25. 4	10. 3	E5	D8	Cock
26. 4	11. 3	E5	E9	Crow
27. 4	12. 3	E5	F10	Monkey
28. 4	13. 3	E5	G11	Gibbon
29. 4	14. 3	E5	H12	Tapir
30. 4	15. 3	E5	J1	Sheep

Solar date	*Lunar date*	*Month HS/EB*	*Day HS/EB*	*Constellation*
1. 5	16. 3	E5	K2	Deer
2. 5	17. 3	E5	A3	Horse
3. 5	18. 3	E5	B4	Stag
4. 5	19. 3	E5	C5	Serpent
5. 5	20. 3	E5	D6	Earthworm
6. 5	21. 3	E5	E7	Crocodile
7. 5	22. 3	E5	F8	Dragon
8. 5	23. 3	E5	G9	Badger
9. 5	24. 3	E5	H10	Hare
10. 5	25. 3	E5	J11	Fox
11. 5	26. 3	E5	K12	Tiger
12. 5	27. 3	E5	A1	Leopard
13. 5	28. 3	E5	B2	Griffon
14. 5	29. 3	E5	C3	Ox
15. 5	1. 4	F6	D4	Bat
16. 5	2. 4	F6	E5	Rat
17. 5	3. 4	F6	F6	Swallow
18. 5	4. 4	F6	G7	Pig
19. 5	5. 4	F6	H8	Porcupine
20. 5	6. 4	F6	J9	Wolf
21. 5	7. 4	F6	K10	Dog
22. 5	8. 4	F6	A11	Pheasant
23. 5	9. 4	F6	B12	Cock
24. 5	10. 4	F6	C1	Crow
25. 5	11. 4	F6	D2	Monkey
26. 5	12. 4	F6	E3	Gibbon
27. 5	13. 4	F6	F4	Tapir
28. 5	14. 4	F6	G5	Sheep
29. 5	15. 4	F6	H6	Deer
30. 5	16. 4	F6	J7	Horse
31. 5	17. 4	F6	K8	Stag
1. 6	18. 4	F6	A9	Serpent
2. 6	19. 4	F6	B10	Earthworm
3. 6	20. 4	F6	C11	Crocodile
4. 6	21. 4	F6	D12	Dragon
5. 6	22. 4	F6	E1	Badger
6. 6	23. 4	F6	F2	Hare
7. 6	24. 4	F6	G3	Fox
8. 6	25. 4	F6	H4	Tiger
9. 6	26. 4	F6	J5	Leopard
10. 6	27. 4	F6	K6	Griffon
11. 6	28. 4	F6	A7	Ox
12. 6	29. 4	F6	B8	Bat
13. 6	30. 4	F6	C9	Rat
14. 6	1. 5	G7	D10	Swallow
15. 6	2. 5	G7	E11	Pig
16. 6	3. 5	G7	F12	Porcupine
17. 6	4. 5	G7	G1	Wolf
18. 6	5. 5	G7	H2	Dog
19. 6	6. 5	G7	J3	Pheasant
20. 6	7. 5	G7	K4	Cock
21. 6	8. 5	G7	A5	Crow
22. 6	9. 5	G7	B6	Monkey
23. 6	10. 5	G7	C7	Gibbon
24. 6	11. 5	G7	D8	Tapir
25. 6	12. 5	G7	E9	Sheep
26. 6	13. 5	G7	F10	Deer
27. 6	14. 5	G7	G11	Horse
28. 6	15. 5	G7	H12	Stag
29. 6	16. 5	G7	J1	Serpent
30. 6	17. 5	G7	K2	Earthworm
1. 7	18. 5	G7	A3	Crocodile
2. 7	19. 5	G7	B4	Dragon
3. 7	20. 5	G7	C5	Badger
4. 7	21. 5	G7	D6	Hare
5. 7	22. 5	G7	E7	Fox
6. 7	23. 5	G7	F8	Tiger
7. 7	24. 5	G7	G9	Leopard
8. 7	25. 5	G7	H10	Griffon
9. 7	26. 5	G7	J11	Ox
10. 7	27. 5	G7	K12	Bat
11. 7	28. 5	G7	A1	Rat
12. 7	29. 5	G7	B2	Swallow

Solar date	*Lunar date*	*Month HS/EB*	*Day HS/EB*	*Constellation*
13. 7	1. 6	H8	C3	Pig
14. 7	2. 6	H8	D4	Porcupine
15. 7	3. 6	H8	E5	Wolf
16. 7	4. 6	H8	F6	Dog
17. 7	5. 6	H8	G7	Pheasant
18. 7	6. 6	H8	H8	Cock
19. 7	7. 6	H8	J9	Crow
20. 7	8. 6	H8	K10	Monkey
21. 7	9. 6	H8	A11	Gibbon
22. 7	10. 6	H8	B12	Tapir
23. 7	11. 6	H8	C1	Sheep
24. 7	12. 6	H8	D2	Deer
25. 7	13. 6	H8	E3	Horse
26. 7	14. 6	H8	F4	Stag
27. 7	15. 6	H8	G5	Serpent
28. 7	16. 6	H8	H6	Earthworm
29. 7	17. 6	H8	J7	Crocodile
30. 7	18. 6	H8	K8	Dragon
31. 7	19. 6	H8	A9	Badger
1. 8	20. 6	H8	B10	Hare
2. 8	21. 6	H8	C11	Fox
3. 8	22. 6	H8	D12	Tiger
4. 8	23. 6	H8	E1	Leopard
5. 8	24. 6	H8	F2	Griffon
6. 8	25. 6	H8	G3	Ox
7. 8	26. 6	H8	H4	Bat
8. 8	27. 6	H8	J5	Rat
9. 8	28. 6	H8	K6	Swallow
10. 8	29. 6	H8	A7	Pig
11. 8	1. 7	J9	B8	Porcupine
12. 8	2. 7	J9	C9	Wolf
13. 8	3. 7	J9	D10	Dog
14. 8	4. 7	J9	E11	Pheasant
15. 8	5. 7	J9	F12	Cock
16. 8	6. 7	J9	G1	Crow
17. 8	7. 7	J9	H2	Monkey
18. 8	8. 7	J9	J3	Gibbon
19. 8	9. 7	J9	K4	Tapir
20. 8	10. 7	J9	A5	Sheep
21. 8	11. 7	J9	B6	Deer
22. 8	12. 7	J9	C7	Horse
23. 8	13. 7	J9	D8	Stag
24. 8	14. 7	J9	E9	Serpent
25. 8	15. 7	J9	F10	Earthworm
26. 8	16. 7	J9	G11	Crocodile
27. 8	17. 7	J9	H12	Dragon
28. 8	18. 7	J9	J1	Badger
29. 8	19. 7	J9	K2	Hare
30. 8	20. 7	J9	A3	Fox
31. 8	21. 7	J9	B4	Tiger
1. 9	22. 7	J9	C5	Leopard
2. 9	23. 7	J9	D6	Griffon
3. 9	24. 7	J9	E7	Ox
4. 9	25. 7	J9	F8	Bat
5. 9	26. 7	J9	G9	Rat
6. 9	27. 7	J9	H10	Swallow
7. 9	28. 7	J9	J11	Pig
8. 9	29. 7	J9	K12	Porcupine
9. 9	30. 7	J9	A1	Wolf
10. 9	1. 8	K10	B2	Dog
11. 9	2. 8	K10	C3	Pheasant
12. 9	3. 8	K10	D4	Cock
13. 9	4. 8	K10	E5	Crow
14. 9	5. 8	K10	F6	Monkey
15. 9	6. 8	K10	G7	Gibbon
16. 9	7. 8	K10	H8	Tapir
17. 9	8. 8	K10	J9	Sheep
18. 9	9. 8	K10	K10	Deer
19. 9	10. 8	K10	A11	Horse
20. 9	11. 8	K10	B12	Stag
21. 9	12. 8	K10	C1	Serpent
22. 9	13. 8	K10	D2	Earthworm
23. 9	14. 8	K10	E3	Crocodile

Solar date	*Lunar date*	*Month HS/EB*	*Day HS/EB*	*Constellation*
24. 9	15. 8	K10	F4	Dragon
25. 9	16. 8	K10	G5	Badger
26. 9	17. 8	K10	H6	Hare
27. 9	18. 8	K10	J7	Fox
28. 9	19. 8	K10	K8	Tiger
29. 9	20. 8	K10	A9	Leopard
30. 9	21. 8	K10	B10	Griffon
1.10	22. 8	K10	C11	Ox
2.10	23. 8	K10	D12	Bat
3.10	24. 8	K10	E1	Rat
4.10	25. 8	K10	F2	Swallow
5.10	26. 8	K10	G3	Pig
6.10	27. 8	K10	H4	Porcupine
7.10	28. 8	K10	J5	Wolf
8.10	29. 8	K10	K6	Dog
9.10	1. 9	A11	A7	Pheasant
10.10	2. 9	A11	B8	Cock
11.10	3. 9	A11	C9	Crow
12.10	4. 9	A11	D10	Monkey
13.10	5. 9	A11	E11	Gibbon
14.10	6. 9	A11	F12	Tapir
15.10	7. 9	A11	G1	Sheep
16.10	8. 9	A11	H2	Deer
17.10	9. 9	A11	J3	Horse
18.10	10. 9	A11	K4	Stag
19.10	11. 9	A11	A5	Serpent
20.10	12. 9	A11	B6	Earthworm
21.10	13. 9	A11	C7	Crocodile
22.10	14. 9	A11	D8	Dragon
23.10	15. 9	A11	E9	Badger
24.10	16. 9	A11	F10	Hare
25.10	17. 9	A11	G11	Fox
26.10	18. 9	A11	H12	Tiger
27.10	19. 9	A11	J1	Leopard
28.10	20. 9	A11	K2	Griffon
29.10	21. 9	A11	A3	Ox
30.10	22. 9	A11	B4	Bat
31.10	23. 9	A11	C5	Rat
1.11	24. 9	A11	D6	Swallow
2.11	25. 9	A11	E7	Pig
3.11	26. 9	A11	F8	Porcupine
4.11	27. 9	A11	G9	Wolf
5.11	28. 9	A11	H10	Dog
6.11	29. 9	A11	J11	Pheasant
7.11	30. 9	A11	K12	Cock
8.11	1.10	B12	A1	Crow
9.11	2.10	B12	B2	Monkey
10.11	3.10	B12	C3	Gibbon
11.11	4.10	B12	D4	Tapir
12.11	5.10	B12	E5	Sheep
13.11	6.10	B12	F6	Deer
14.11	7.10	B12	G7	Horse
15.11	8.10	B12	H8	Stag
16.11	9.10	B12	J9	Serpent
17.11	10.10	B12	K10	Earthworm
18.11	11.10	B12	A11	Crocodile
19.11	12.10	B12	B12	Dragon
20.11	13.10	B12	C1	Badger
21.11	14.10	B12	D2	Hare
22.11	15.10	B12	E3	Fox
23.11	16.10	B12	F4	Tiger
24.11	17.10	B12	G5	Leopard
25.11	18.10	B12	H6	Griffon
26.11	19.10	B12	J7	Ox
27.11	20.10	B12	K8	Bat
28.11	21.10	B12	A9	Rat
29.11	22.10	B12	B10	Swallow
30.11	23.10	B12	C11	Pig

Solar date	*Lunar date*	*Month HS/EB*	*Day HS/EB*	*Constellation*
1.12	24.10	B12	D12	Porcupine
2.12	25.10	B12	E1	Wolf
3.12	26.10	B12	F2	Dog
4.12	27.10	B12	G3	Pheasant
5.12	28.10	B12	H4	Cock
6.12	29.10	B12	J5	Crow
7.12	30.10	B12	K6	Monkey
8.12	1.11	C1	A7	Gibbon
9.12	2.11	C1	B8	Tapir
10.12	3.11	C1	C9	Sheep
11.12	4.11	C1	E10	Deer
12.12	5.11	C1	E11	Horse
13.12	6.11	C1	F12	Stag
14.12	7.11	C1	G1	Serpent
15.12	8.11	C1	H2	Earthworm
16.12	9.11	C1	J3	Crocodile
17.12	10.11	C1	K4	Dragon
18.12	11.11	C1	A5	Badger
19.12	12.11	C1	B6	Hare
20.12	13.11	C1	C7	Fox
21.12	14.11	C1	D8	Tiger
22.12	15.11	C1	E9	Leopard
23.12	16.11	C1	F10	Griffon
24.12	17.11	C1	G11	Ox
25.12	18.11	C1	H12	Bat
26.12	19.11	C1	J1	Rat
27.12	20.11	C1	K2	Swallow
28.12	21.11	C1	A3	Pig
29.12	22.11	C1	B4	Porcupine
30.12	23.11	C1	C5	Wolf
31.12	24.11	C1	D6	Dog
2000				
1. 1	25.11	C1	E7	Pheasant
2. 1	26.11	C1	F8	Cock
3. 1	27.11	C1	G9	Crow
4. 1	28.11	C1	H10	Monkey
5. 1	29.11	C1	J11	Gibbon
6. 1	30.11	C1	K12	Tapir
7. 1	1.12	D2	A1	Sheep
8. 1	2.12	D2	B2	Deer
9. 1	3.12	D2	C3	Horse
10. 1	4.12	D2	D4	Stag
11. 1	5.12	D2	E5	Serpent
12. 1	6.12	D2	F6	Earthworm
13. 1	7.12	D2	G7	Crocodile
14. 1	8.12	D2	H8	Dragon
15. 1	9.12	D2	J9	Badger
16. 1	10.12	D2	K10	Hare
17. 1	11.12	D2	A11	Fox
18. 1	12.12	D2	B12	Tiger
19. 1	13.12	D2	C1	Leopard
20. 1	14.12	D2	D2	Griffon
21. 1	15.12	D2	E3	Ox
22. 1	16.12	D2	F4	Bat
23. 1	17.12	D2	G5	Rat
24. 1	18.12	D2	H6	Swallow
25. 1	19.12	D2	J7	Pig
26. 1	20.12	D2	K8	Porcupine
27. 1	21.12	D2	A9	Wolf
28. 1	22.12	D2	B10	Dog
29. 1	23.12	D2	C11	Pheasant
30. 1	24.12	D2	D12	Cock
31. 1	25.12	D2	E1	Crow
1. 2	26.12	D2	F2	Monkey
2. 2	27.12	D2	G3	Gibbon
3. 2	28.12	D2	H4	Tapir
4. 2	29.12	D2	J5	Sheep

KENG CH'EN YEAR

Solar date	*Lunar date*	*Month HS/EB*	*Day HS/EB*	*Constellation*
5. 2	1. 1	E3	K6	Deer
6. 2	2. 1	E3	A7	Horse
7. 2	3. 1	E3	B8	Stag
8. 2	4. 1	E3	C9	Serpent
9. 2	5. 1	E3	D10	Earthworm
10. 2	6. 1	E3	E11	Crocodile
11. 2	7. 1	E3	F12	Dragon
12. 2	8. 1	E3	G1	Badger
13. 2	9. 1	E3	H2	Hare
14. 2	10. 1	E3	J3	Fox
15. 2	11. 1	E3	K4	Tiger
16. 2	12. 1	E3	A5	Leopard
17. 2	13. 1	E3	B6	Griffon
18. 2	14. 1	E3	C7	Ox
19. 2	15. 1	E3	D8	Bat
20. 2	16. 1	E3	E9	Rat
21. 2	17. 1	E3	F10	Swallow
22. 2	18. 1	E3	G11	Pig
23. 2	19. 1	E3	H12	Porcupine
24. 2	20. 1	E3	J1	Wolf
25. 2	21. 1	E3	K2	Dog
26. 2	22. 1	E3	A3	Pheasant
27. 2	23. 1	E3	B4	Cock
28. 2	24. 1	E3	C5	Crow
29. 2	25. 1	E3	D6	Monkey
1. 3	26. 1	E3	E7	Gibbon
2. 3	27. 1	E3	F8	Tapir
3. 3	28. 1	E3	G9	Sheep
4. 3	29. 1	E3	H10	Deer
5. 3	30. 1	E3	J11	Horse
6. 3	1. 2	F4	K12	Stag
7. 3	2. 2	F4	A1	Serpent
8. 3	3. 2	F4	B2	Earthworm
9. 3	4. 2	F4	C3	Crocodile
10. 3	5. 2	F4	D4	Dragon
11. 3	6. 2	F4	E5	Badger
12. 3	7. 2	F4	F6	Hare
13. 3	8. 2	F4	G7	Fox
14. 3	9. 2	F4	H8	Tiger
15. 3	10. 2	F4	J9	Leopard
16. 3	11. 2	F4	K10	Griffon
17. 3	12. 2	F4	A11	Ox
18. 3	13. 2	F4	B12	Bat
19. 3	14. 2	F4	C1	Rat
20. 3	15. 2	F4	D2	Swallow
21. 3	16. 2	F4	E3	Pig
22. 3	17. 2	F4	F4	Porcupine
23. 3	18. 2	F4	G5	Wolf
24. 3	19. 2	F4	H6	Dog
25. 3	20. 2	F4	J7	Pheasant
26. 3	21. 2	F4	K8	Cock
27. 3	22. 2	F4	A9	Crow
28. 3	23. 2	F4	B10	Monkey
29. 3	24. 2	F4	C11	Gibbon
30. 3	25. 2	F4	D12	Tapir
31. 3	26. 2	F4	E1	Sheep
1. 4	27. 2	F4	F2	Deer
2. 4	28. 2	F4	G3	Horse
3. 4	29. 2	F4	H4	Stag
4. 4	30. 2	F4	J5	Serpent
5. 4	1. 3	G5	K6	Earthworm
6. 4	2. 3	G5	A7	Crocodile
7. 4	3. 3	G5	B8	Dragon
8. 4	4. 3	G5	C9	Badger
9. 4	5. 3	G5	D10	Hare
10. 4	6. 3	G5	E11	Fox
11. 4	7. 3	G5	F12	Tiger
12. 4	8. 3	G5	G1	Leopard
13. 4	9. 3	G5	H2	Griffon
14. 4	10. 3	G5	J3	Ox
15. 4	11. 3	G5	K4	Bat
16. 4	12. 3	G5	A5	Rat
17. 4	13. 3	G5	B6	Swallow
18. 4	14. 3	G5	C7	Pig
19. 4	15. 3	G5	D8	Porcupine
20. 4	16. 3	G5	E9	Wolf
21. 4	17. 3	G5	F10	Dog
22. 4	18. 3	G5	G11	Pheasant
23. 4	19. 3	G5	H12	Cock
24. 4	20. 3	G5	J1	Crow
25. 4	21. 3	G5	K2	Monkey
26. 4	22. 3	G5	A3	Gibbon
27. 4	23. 3	G5	B4	Tapir
28. 4	24. 3	G5	C5	Sheep
29. 4	25. 3	G5	D6	Deer
30. 4	26. 3	G5	E7	Horse
1. 5	27. 3	G5	F8	Stag
2. 5	28. 3	G5	G9	Serpent
3. 5	29. 3	G5	H10	Earthworm
4. 5	1. 4	H6	J11	Crocodile
5. 5	2. 4	H6	K12	Dragon
6. 5	3. 4	H6	A1	Badger
7. 5	4. 4	H6	B2	Hare
8. 5	5. 4	H6	C3	Fox
9. 5	6. 4	H6	D4	Tiger
10. 5	7. 4	H6	E5	Leopard
11. 5	8. 4	H6	F6	Griffon
12. 5	9. 4	H6	G7	Ox
13. 5	10. 4	H6	H8	Bat
14. 5	11. 4	H6	J9	Rat
15. 5	12. 4	H6	K10	Swallow
16. 5	13. 4	H6	A11	Pig
17. 5	14. 4	H6	B12	Porcupine
18. 5	15. 4	H6	C1	Wolf
19. 5	16. 4	H6	D2	Dog
20. 5	17. 4	H6	E3	Pheasant
21. 5	18. 4	H6	F4	Cock
22. 5	19. 4	H6	G5	Crow
23. 5	20. 4	H6	H6	Monkey
24. 5	21. 4	H6	J7	Gibbon
25. 5	22. 4	H6	K8	Tapir
26. 5	23. 4	H6	A9	Sheep
27. 5	24. 4	H6	B10	Deer
28. 5	25. 4	H6	C11	Horse
29. 5	26. 4	H6	D12	Stag
30. 5	27. 4	H6	E1	Serpent
31. 5	28. 4	H6	F2	Earthworm
1. 6	29. 4	H6	G3	Crocodile
2. 6	1. 5	J7	H4	Dragon
3. 6	2. 5	J7	J5	Badger
4. 6	3. 5	J7	K6	Hare
5. 6	4. 5	J7	A7	Fox
6. 6	5. 5	J7	B8	Tiger
7. 6	6. 5	J7	C9	Leopard
8. 6	7. 5	J7	D10	Griffon
9. 6	8. 5	J7	E11	Ox
10. 6	9. 5	J7	F12	Bat
11. 6	10. 5	J7	G1	Rat
12. 6	11. 5	J7	H2	Swallow
13. 6	12. 5	J7	J3	Pig
14. 6	13. 5	J7	K4	Porcupine
15. 6	14. 5	J7	A5	Wolf
16. 6	15. 5	J7	B6	Dog
17. 6	16. 5	J7	C7	Pheasant
18. 6	17. 5	J7	D8	Cock
19. 6	18. 5	J7	E9	Crow
20. 6	19. 5	J7	F10	Monkey
21. 6	20. 5	J7	G11	Gibbon
22. 6	21. 5	J7	H12	Tapir
23. 6	22. 5	J7	J1	Sheep
24. 6	23. 5	J7	K2	Deer
25. 6	24. 5	J7	A3	Horse

Solar date	*Lunar date*	*Month HS/EB*	*Day HS/EB*	*Constellation*
26. 6	25. 5	J7	B4	Stag
27. 6	26. 5	J7	C5	Serpent
28. 6	27. 5	J7	D6	Earthworm
29. 6	28. 5	J7	E7	Crocodile
30. 6	29. 5	J7	F8	Dragon
1. 7	30. 5	J7	G9	Badger
2. 7	1. 6	K8	H10	Hare
3. 7	2. 6	K8	J11	Fox
4. 7	3. 6	K8	K12	Tiger
5. 7	4. 6	K8	A1	Leopard
6. 7	5. 6	K8	B2	Griffon
7. 7	6. 6	K8	C3	Ox
8. 7	7. 6	K8	D4	Bat
9. 7	8. 6	K8	E5	Rat
10. 7	9. 6	K8	F6	Swallow
11. 7	10. 6	K8	G7	Pig
12. 7	11. 6	K8	H8	Porcupine
13. 7	12. 6	K8	J9	Wolf
14. 7	13. 6	K8	K10	Dog
15. 7	14. 6	K8	A11	Pheasant
16. 7	15. 6	K8	B12	Cock
17. 7	16. 6	K8	C1	Crow
18. 7	17. 6	K8	D2	Monkey
19. 7	18. 6	K8	E3	Gibbon
20. 7	19. 6	K8	F4	Tapir
21. 7	20. 6	K8	G5	Sheep
22. 7	21. 6	K8	H6	Deer
23. 7	22. 6	K8	J7	Horse
24. 7	23. 6	K8	K8	Stag
25. 7	24. 6	K8	A9	Serpent
26. 7	25. 6	K8	B10	Earthworm
27. 7	26. 6	K8	C11	Crocodile
28. 7	27. 6	K8	D12	Dragon
29. 7	28. 6	K8	E1	Badger
30. 7	29. 6	K8	F2	Hare
31. 7	1. 7	A9	G3	Fox
1. 8	2. 7	A9	H4	Tiger
2. 8	3. 7	A9	J5	Leopard
3. 8	4. 7	A9	K6	Griffon
4. 8	5. 7	A9	A7	Ox
5. 8	6. 7	A9	B8	Bat
6. 8	7. 7	A9	C9	Rat
7. 8	8. 7	A9	D10	Swallow
8. 8	9. 7	A9	E11	Pig
9. 8	10. 7	A9	F12	Porcupine
10. 8	11. 7	A9	G1	Wolf
11. 8	12. 7	A9	H2	Dog
12. 8	13. 7	A9	J3	Pheasant
13. 8	14. 7	A9	K4	Cock
14. 8	15. 7	A9	A5	Crow
15. 8	16. 7	A9	B6	Monkey
16. 8	17. 7	A9	C7	Gibbon
17. 8	18. 7	A9	D8	Tapir
18. 8	19. 7	A9	E9	Sheep
19. 8	20. 7	A9	F10	Deer
20. 8	21. 7	A9	G11	Horse
21. 8	22. 7	A9	H12	Stag
22. 8	23. 7	A9	J1	Serpent
23. 8	24. 7	A9	K2	Earthworm
24. 8	25. 7	A9	A3	Crocodile
25. 8	26. 7	A9	B4	Dragon
26. 8	27. 7	A9	C5	Badger
27. 8	28. 7	A9	D6	Hare
28. 8	29. 7	A9	E7	Fox
29. 8	1. 8	B10	F8	Tiger
30. 8	2. 8	B10	G9	Leopard
31. 8	3. 8	B10	H10	Griffon
1. 9	4. 8	B10	J11	Ox
2. 9	5. 8	B10	K12	Bat
3. 9	6. 8	B10	A1	Rat
4. 9	7. 8	B10	B2	Swallow
5. 9	8. 8	B10	C3	Pig
6. 9	9. 8	B10	D4	Porcupine
7. 9	10. 8	B10	E5	Wolf
8. 9	11. 8	B10	F6	Dog
9. 9	12. 8	B10	G7	Pheasant
10. 9	13. 8	B10	H8	Cock
11. 9	14. 8	B10	J9	Crow
12. 9	15. 8	B10	K10	Monkey
13. 9	16. 8	B10	A11	Gibbon
14. 9	17. 8	B10	B12	Tapir
15. 9	18. 8	B10	C1	Sheep
16. 9	19. 8	B10	D2	Deer
17. 9	20. 8	B10	E3	Horse
18. 9	21. 8	B10	F4	Stag
19. 9	22. 8	B10	G5	Serpent
20. 9	23. 8	B10	H6	Earthworm
21. 9	24. 8	B10	J7	Crocodile
22. 9	25. 8	B10	K8	Dragon
23. 9	26. 8	B10	A9	Badger
24. 9	27. 8	B10	B10	Hare
25. 9	28. 8	B10	C11	Fox
26. 9	29. 8	B10	D12	Tiger
27. 9	30. 8	B10	E1	Leopard
28. 9	1. 9	C11	F2	Griffon
29. 9	2. 9	C11	G3	Ox
30. 9	3. 9	C11	H4	Bat
1.10	4. 9	C11	J5	Rat
2.10	5. 9	C11	K6	Swallow
3.10	6. 9	C11	A7	Pig
4.10	7. 9	C11	B8	Porcupine
5.10	8. 9	C11	C9	Wolf
6.10	9. 9	C11	D10	Dog
7.10	10. 9	C11	E11	Pheasant
8.10	11. 9	C11	F12	Cock
9.10	12. 9	C11	G1	Crow
10.10	13. 9	C11	H2	Monkey
11.10	14. 9	C11	J3	Gibbon
12.10	15. 9	C11	K4	Tapir
13.10	16. 9	C11	A5	Sheep
14.10	17. 9	C11	B6	Deer
15.10	18. 9	C11	C7	Horse
16.10	19. 9	C11	D8	Stag
17.10	20. 9	C11	E9	Serpent
18.10	21. 9	C11	F10	Earthworm
19.10	22. 9	C11	G11	Crocodile
20.10	23. 9	C11	H12	Dragon
21.10	24. 9	C11	J1	Badger
22.10	25. 9	C11	K2	Hare
23.10	26. 9	C11	A3	Fox
24.10	27. 9	C11	B4	Tiger
25.10	28. 9	C11	C5	Leopard
26.10	29. 9	C11	D6	Griffon
27.10	1.10	D12	E7	Ox
28.10	2.10	D12	F8	Bat
29.10	3.10	D12	G9	Rat
30.10	4.10	D12	H10	Swallow
31.10	5.10	D12	J11	Pig
1.11	6.10	D12	K12	Porcupine
2.11	7.10	D12	A1	Wolf
3.11	8.10	D12	B2	Dog
4.11	9.10	D12	C3	Pheasant
5.11	10.10	D12	D4	Cock
6.11	11.10	D12	E5	Crow
7.11	12.10	D12	F6	Monkey
8.11	13.10	D12	G7	Gibbon
9.11	14.10	D12	H8	Tapir
10.11	15.10	D12	J9	Sheep
11.11	16.10	D12	K10	Deer
12.11	17.10	D12	A11	Horse
13.11	18.10	D12	B12	Stag
14.11	19.10	D12	C1	Serpent
15.11	20.10	D12	D2	Earthworm
16.11	21.10	D12	E3	Crocodile
17.11	22.10	D12	F4	Dragon
18.11	23.10	D12	G5	Badger

Solar date	*Lunar date*	*Month HS/EB*	*Day HS/EB*	*Constellation*
19.11	24.10	D12	H6	Hare
20.11	25.10	D12	J7	Fox
21.11	26.10	D12	K8	Tiger
22.11	27.10	D12	A9	Leopard
23.11	28.10	D12	B10	Griffon
24.11	29.10	D12	C11	Ox
25.11	30.10	D12	D12	Bat
26.11	1.11	E1	E1	Rat
27.11	2.11	E1	F2	Swallow
28.11	3.11	E1	G3	Pig
29.11	4.11	E1	H4	Porcupine
30.11	5.11	E1	J5	Wolf
1.12	6.11	E1	K6	Dog
2.12	7.11	E1	A7	Pheasant
3.12	8.11	E1	B8	Cock
4.12	9.11	E1	C9	Crow
5.12	10.11	E1	D10	Monkey
6.12	11.11	E1	E11	Gibbon
7.12	12.11	E1	F12	Tapir
8.12	13.11	E1	G1	Sheep
9.12	14.11	E1	H2	Deer
10.12	15.11	E1	J3	Horse
11.12	16.11	E1	K4	Stag
12.12	17.11	E1	A5	Serpent
13.12	18.11	E1	B6	Earthworm
14.12	19.11	E1	C7	Crocodile
15.12	20.11	E1	D8	Dragon
16.12	21.11	E1	E9	Badger
17.12	22.11	E1	F10	Hare
18.12	23.11	E1	G11	Fox
19.12	24.11	E1	H12	Tiger
20.12	25.11	E1	J1	Leopard
21.12	26.11	E1	K2	Griffon
22.12	27.11	E1	A3	Ox
23.12	28.11	E1	B4	Bat
24.12	29.11	E1	C5	Rat
25.12	30.11	E1	D6	Swallow
26.12	1.12	F2	E7	Pig
27.12	2.12	F2	F8	Porcupine
28.12	3.12	F2	G9	Wolf
29.12	4.12	F2	H10	Dog
30.12	5.12	F2	J11	Pheasant
31.12	6.12	F2	K12	Cock
2001				
1. 1	7.12	F2	A1	Crow
2. 1	8.12	F2	B2	Monkey
3. 1	9.12	F2	C3	Gibbon
4. 1	10.12	F2	D4	Tapir
5. 1	11.12	F2	E5	Sheep
6. 1	12.12	F2	F6	Deer
7. 1	13.12	F2	G7	Horse
8. 1	14.12	F2	H8	Stag
9. 1	15.12	F2	J9	Serpent
10. 1	16.12	F2	K10	Earthworm
11. 1	17.12	F2	A11	Crocodile
12. 1	18.12	F2	B12	Dragon
13. 1	19.12	F2	C1	Badger
14. 1	20.12	F2	D2	Hare
15. 1	21.12	F2	E3	Fox
16. 1	22.12	F2	F4	Tiger
17. 1	23.12	F2	G5	Leopard
18. 1	24.12	F2	H6	Griffon
19. 1	25.12	F2	J7	Ox
20. 1	26.12	F2	K8	Bat
21. 1	27.12	F2	A9	Rat
22. 1	28.12	F2	B10	Swallow
23. 1	29.12	F2	C11	Pig

TABLE OF YEARS WHICH CORRESPOND TO THE CHINESE SIGNS

31/1/1900 - 18/2/1901	RAT	05/2/1924 - 24/1/1925	RAT
19/2/1901 - 07/2/1902	OX	25/1/1925 - 12/2/1926	OX
08/2/1902 - 28/1/1903	TIGER	13/2/1926 - 01/2/1927	TIGER
29/1/1903 - 15/2/1904	RABBIT	02/2/1927 - 22/1/1928	RABBIT
16/2/1904 - 03/2/1905	DRAGON	23/1/1928 - 09/2/1929	DRAGON
04/2/1905 - 24/1/1906	SNAKE	10/2/1929 - 29/1/1930	SNAKE
25/1/1906 - 12/2/1907	HORSE	30/1/1930 - 16/2/1931	HORSE
13/2/1907 - 01/2/1908	RAM	17/2/1931 - 05/2/1932	RAM
02/2/1908 - 21/1/1909	MONKEY	06/2/1932 - 25/1/1933	MONKEY
22/1/1909 - 09/2/1910	COCK	26/1/1933 - 13/2/1934	COCK
10/2/1910 - 29/1/1911	DOG	14/2/1934 - 03/2/1935	DOG
30/1/1911 - 17/2/1912	PIG	04/2/1935 - 23/1/1936	PIG
18/2/1912 - 05/2/1913	RAT	24/1/1936 - 10/2/1937	RAT
06/2/1913 - 25/1/1914	OX	11/2/1937 - 30/1/1938	OX
26/1/1914 - 13/2/1915	TIGER	31/1/1938 - 18/2/1939	TIGER
14/2/1915 - 02/2/1916	RABBIT	19/2/1939 - 07/2/1940	RABBIT
03/2/1916 - 22/1/1917	DRAGON	08/2/1940 - 26/1/1941	DRAGON
23/1/1917 - 10/2/1918	SNAKE	27/1/1941 - 14/2/1942	SNAKE
11/2/1918 - 31/1/1919	HORSE	15/2/1942 - 04/2/1943	HORSE
01/2/1919 - 19/2/1920	RAM	05/2/1943 - 24/1/1944	RAM
20/2/1920 - 07/2/1921	MONKEY	25/1/1944 - 12/2/1945	MONKEY
08/2/1921 - 27/1/1922	COCK	13/2/1945 - 01/2/1946	COCK
28/1/1922 - 15/2/1923	DOG	02/2/1946 - 21/1/1947	DOG
16/2/1923 - 04/2/1924	PIG	22/1/1947 - 09/2/1948	PIG

The dates shown indicate the *FIRST* and *LAST* day of the year of the sign

10/2/1948 - 28/1/1949	RAT	15/2/1972 - 02/2/1973	RAT
29/1/1949 - 16/2/1950	OX	03/2/1973 - 22/1/1974	OX
17/2/1950 - 05/2/1951	TIGER	23/1/1974 - 10/2/1975	TIGER
09/2/1951 - 26/1/1952	RABBIT	11/2/1975 - 30/1/1976	RABBIT
27/1/1952 - 13/2/1953	DRAGON	31/1/1976 - 17/2/1977	DRAGON
14/2/1953 - 02/2/1954	SNAKE	18/2/1977 - 06/2/1978	SNAKE
03/2/1954 - 23/1/1955	HORSE	07/2/1978 - 27/1/1979	HORSE
24/1/1955 - 11/2/1956	RAM	28/1/1979 - 15/2/1980	RAM
12/2/1956 - 30/1/1957	MONKEY	16/2/1980 - 04/2/1981	MONKEY
31/1/1957 - 15/2/1958	COCK	05/2/1981 - 24/1/1982	COCK
16/2/1958 - 07/2/1959	DOG	25/1/1982 - 12/2/1983	DOG
08/2/1959 - 27/1/1960	PIG	13/2/1983 - 01/2/1984	PIG
28/1/1960 - 14/2/1961	RAT	02/2/1984 - 19/2/1985	RAT
15/2/1961 - 04/2/1962	OX	20/2/1985 - 08/2/1986	OX
05/2/1962 - 24/1/1963	TIGER	09/2/1986 - 28/1/1987	TIGER
25/1/1963 - 12/2/1964	RABBIT	29/1/1987 - 16/2/1988	RABBIT
13/2/1964 - 01/2/1965	DRAGON	17/2/1988 - 05/2/1989	DRAGON
02/2/1965 - 20/1/1966	SNAKE	06/2/1989 - 26/1/1990	SNAKE
21/1/1966 - 08/2/1967	HORSE	27/1/1990 - 14/2/1991	HORSE
09/2/1967 - 28/1/1968	RAM	15/2/1991 - 03/2/1992	RAM
20/1/1968 - 16/2/1969	MONKEY	04/2/1992 - 22/1/1993	MONKEY
17/2/1969 - 07/2/1970	COCK	23/1/1993 - 09/2/1994	COCK
06/2/1970 - 26/1/1971	DOG	10/2/1994 - 30/1/1995	DOG
27/1/1971 - 14/2/1972	PIG	31/1/1995 - 18/2/1996	PIG